Twentieth-Century
Literary Criticism

Guide to Gale Literary Criticism Series

When you need to review criticism of literary works, these are the Gale series to use:

If the author's death date is: **You should turn to:**

After Dec. 31, 1959
(or author is still living)

CONTEMPORARY LITERARY CRITICISM

for example: Jorge Luis Borges, William Faulkner,
Ernest Hemingway, Iris Murdoch

1900 through 1959

TWENTIETH-CENTURY LITERARY CRITICISM

for example: Willa Cather, F. Scott Fitzgerald,
Henry James, Mark Twain, Virginia Woolf

1800 through 1899

NINETEENTH-CENTURY LITERATURE CRITICISM

for example: Fyodor Dostoevsky, Nathaniel Hawthorne,
George Sand, William Wordsworth

1400 through 1799

LITERATURE CRITICISM FROM 1400 TO 1800
(excluding Shakespeare)

for example: Anne Bradstreet, Daniel Defoe,
Alexander Pope, François Rabelais,
Jonathan Swift, Phillis Wheatley

SHAKESPEAREAN CRITICISM

Shakespeare's plays and poetry

Antiquity through 1399   *CLASSICAL AND MEDIEVAL LITERATURE CRITICISM*

for example: Dante, Homer, Plato, Sophocles, Vergil

Gale also publishes related criticism series:

BLACK LITERATURE CRITICISM

Covers the most significant black authors of the past 200 years

CHILDREN'S LITERATURE REVIEW

Covers authors of all eras who have written for the preschool
through high school audience

SHORT STORY CRITICISM

Covers the major short fiction writers of all nationalities and
periods of literary history

POETRY CRITICISM

Covers poets of all nationalities and periods of literary history

DRAMA CRITICISM

Covers dramatists of all nationalities and periods of literary
history

ISSN 0276-8178

Volume 45

Twentieth-Century Literary Criticism

**Excerpts from Criticism of the
Works of Novelists, Poets, Playwrights,
Short Story Writers, and Other Creative Writers
Who Lived between 1900 and 1960,
from the First Published Critical
Appraisals to Current Evaluations**

**Laurie DiMauro
Editor**

**Elizabeth Henry
Marie Lazzari
Thomas Ligotti
David Segal
Thomas Votteler
Janet M. Witalec
Associate Editors**

 Gale Research Inc. · DETROIT · LONDON

STAFF

Laurie DiMauro, *Editor*

Elizabeth Henry, Marie Lazzari, Thomas Ligotti, David Segal, Thomas Votteler, Janet M. Witalec, *Associate Editors*

Ian A. Goodhall, Kyung-Sun Lim, Brigham Narins, Kristin Palm, Johannah Rodgers, *Assistant Editors*

Jeanne A. Gough, *Permissions & Production Manager*

Linda M. Pugliese, *Production Supervisor*
Paul Lewon, Maureen Puhl, Camille Robinson,
Jennifer VanSickle, *Editorial Associates*
Donna Craft, Rosita D'Souza, Sheila Walencewicz, *Editorial Assistants*

Victoria B. Cariappa, *Research Manager*
Maureen Richards, *Research Supervisor*
Mary Beth McElmeel, Tamara C. Nott, *Editorial Associates*
Andrea B. Ghorai, Daniel J. Jankowski, Julie K. Karmazin, Robert S. Lazich, Julie Synkonis, *Editorial Assistants*

Sandra C. Davis, *Permissions Supervisor (Text)*
Maria L. Franklin, Josephine M. Keene, Denise M. Singleton, Kimberly F. Smilay, *Permissions Associates*
Brandy C. Johnson, Michele Lonoconus, Shelly Rakoczy, Shalice Shah, *Permissions Assistants*

Margaret A. Chamberlain, *Permissions Supervisor (Pictures)*
Pamela A. Hayes, *Permissions Associate*
Amy Lynn Emrich, Karla Kulkis, Nancy Rattenbury, Keith Reed, *Permissions Assistants*

Mary Beth Trimper, *Production Manager*
Mary Winterhalter, *Production Assistant*

Arthur Chartow, *Art Director*
Nicholas Jakubiak, C. J. Jonik, *Keyliners*

Contents

Preface   vii

Acknowledgments   xi

Preface

Since its inception more than ten years ago, *Twentieth-Century Literary Criticism* has been purchased and used by nearly 10,000 school, public, and college or university libraries. *TCLC* has covered more than 500 authors, representing 58 nationalities, and over 25,000 titles. No other reference source has surveyed the critical response to twentieth-century authors and literature as thoroughly as *TCLC*. In the words of one reviewer, "there is nothing comparable available." *TCLC* "is a gold mine of information—dates, pseudonyms, biographical information, and criticism from books and periodicals—which many libraries would have difficulty assembling on their own."

Scope of the Series

TCLC is designed to serve as an introduction to authors who died between 1900 and 1960 and to the most significant interpretations of these authors' works. The great poets, novelists, short story writers, playwrights, and philosophers of this period are frequently studied in high school and college literature courses. In organizing and excerpting the vast amount of critical material written on these authors, *TCLC* helps students develop valuable insight into literary history, promotes a better understanding of the texts, and sparks ideas for papers and assignments. Each entry in *TCLC* presents a comprehensive survey of an author's career or an individual work of literature and provides the user with a multiplicity of interpretations and assessments. Such variety allows students to pursue their own interests; furthermore, it fosters an awareness that literature is dynamic and responsive to many different opinions.

Every fourth volume of *TCLC* is devoted to literary topics that cannot be covered under the author approach used in the rest of the series. Such topics include literary movements, prominent themes in twentieth-century literature, literary reaction to political and historical events, significant eras in literary history, prominent literary anniversaries, and the literatures of cultures that are often overlooked by English-speaking readers.

TCLC is designed as a companion series to Gale's *Contemporary Literary Criticism,* which reprints commentary on authors now living or who have died since 1960. Because of the different periods under consideration, there is no duplication of material between *CLC* and *TCLC*. For additional information about *CLC* and Gale's other criticism titles, users should consult the Guide to Gale Literary Criticism Series preceding the title page in this volume.

Coverage

Each volume of *TCLC* is carefully compiled to present:

- criticism of authors, or literary topics, representing a variety of genres and nationalities

- both major and lesser-known writers and literary works of the period

- 10-15 authors or 4-6 topics per volume

- individual entries that survey critical response to each author's work or each topic in literary history, including early criticism to reflect initial reactions; later criticism to represent any rise or decline in reputation; and current retrospective analyses.

Organization of This Book

An author entry consists of the following elements: author heading, biographical and critical introduction, list of principal works, excerpts of criticism (each preceded by an annotation and followed by a bibliographic citation), and a bibliography of further reading.

- The **author heading** consists of the name under which the author most commonly wrote, followed by birth and death dates. If an author wrote consistently under a pseudonym, the pseudonym will be listed in the author heading and the real name given in parentheses on the first line of the biographical and critical introduction. Also located at the beginning of the introduction to the author entry are any name variations under which an author wrote, including transliterated forms for authors whose languages use nonroman alphabets.

• The **biographical and critical introduction** outlines the author's life and career, as well as the critical issues surrounding his or her work. References to past volumes of *TCLC* are provided at the beginning of the introduction. Additional sources of information in other biographical and critical reference series published by Gale, including *Short Story Criticism, Children's Literature Review, Contemporary Authors, Dictionary of Literary Biography,* and *Something about the Author,* are listed in a box at the end of the entry.

• Most *TCLC* entries include **portraits** of the author. Many entries also contain reproductions of materials pertinent to an author's career, including manuscript pages, title pages, dust jackets, letters, and drawings, as well as photographs of important people, places, and events in an author's life.

• The **list of principal works** is chronological by date of first book publication and identifies the genre of each work. In the case of foreign authors with both foreign-language publications and English translations, the title and date of the first English-language edition are given in brackets. Unless otherwise indicated, dramas are dated by first performance, not first publication.

• **Criticism** is arranged chronologically in each author entry to provide a perspective on changes in critical evaluation over the years. All titles of works by the author featured in the entry are printed in boldface type to enable the user to easily locate discussion of particular works. Also for purposes of easier identification, the critic's name and the publication date of the essay are given at the beginning of each piece of criticism. Unsigned criticism is preceded by the title of the journal in which it appeared. Some of the excerpts in *TCLC* also contain translated material. Unless otherwise noted, translations in brackets are by the editors; translations in parentheses or continuous with the text are by the critic. Publication information (such as publisher names and book prices) and parenthetical numerical references (such as footnotes or page and line references to specific editions of works) have been deleted at the editors' discretion to provide smoother reading of the text.

• Critical excerpts are prefaced by **annotations** providing the reader with information about both the critic and the criticism that follows. Included are the critic's reputation, individual approach to literary criticism, and particular expertise in an author's works. Also noted are the relative importance of a work of criticism, the scope of the excerpt, and the growth of critical controversy or changes in critical trends regarding an author. In some cases, these annotations cross-reference excerpts by critics who discuss each other's commentary.

• A complete **bibliographic citation** designed to facilitate location of the original essay or book follows each piece of criticism.

• An annotated list of **further reading** appearing at the end of each author entry suggests secondary sources on the author. In some cases it includes essays for which the editors could not obtain reprint rights.

Cumulative Indexes

• Each volume of *TCLC* contains a cumulative **author index** listing all authors who have appeared in Gale's Literary Criticism Series, along with cross-references to such biographical series as *Contemporary Authors* and *Dictionary of Literary Biography.* For readers' convenience, a complete list of Gale titles included appears on the first page of the author index. Useful for locating authors within the various series, this index is particularly valuable for those authors who are identified by a certain period but who, because of their death dates, are placed in another, or for those authors whose careers span two periods. For example, F. Scott Fitzgerald is found in *TCLC,* yet a writer often associated with him, Ernest Hemingway, is found in *CLC.*

• Each *TCLC* volume includes a cumulative **nationality index** which lists all authors who have appeared in *TCLC* volumes, arranged alphabetically under their respective nationalities, as well as Topics volume entries devoted to particular national literatures.

• Each new volume in Gale's Literary Criticism Series includes a cumulative **topic index,** which lists all literary topics treated in *NCLC, TCLC, LC 1400-1800,* and the *CLC* Yearbook.

• Each new volume of *TCLC,* with the exception of the Topics volumes, contains a **title index** listing the titles of all literary works discussed in the volume. In response to numerous suggestions from librarians, Gale has also produced a **special paperbound edition** of the *TCLC* title index. This annual cumulation lists all titles discussed in the series since its inception and is issued with the first volume of *TCLC* published each year. Additional copies of the index are available on request. Librarians and patrons will welcome this separate index: it saves shelf space, is easy to use, and is disposable upon receipt of the following year's cumulation. Titles discussed in the Topics volume entries are not included in the *TCLC* cumulative index.

A Note to the Reader

When writing papers, students who quote directly from any volume in Gale's Literary Criticism Series may use the following general forms to footnote reprinted criticism. The first example pertains to material drawn from periodicals, the second to material reprinted from books.

[1] T. S. Eliot, "John Donne," *The Nation and the Athenaeum,* 33 (9 June 1923), 321-32; excerpted and reprinted in *Literature Criticism from 1400 to 1800,* Vol. 10, ed. James E. Person, Jr. (Detroit: Gale Research, 1989), pp. 28-9.

[2] Clara G. Stillman, *Samuel Butler: A Mid-Victorian Modern* (Viking Press, 1932); excerpted and reprinted in *Twentieth-Century Literary Criticism,* Vol. 33, ed. Paula Kepos (Detroit: Gale Research, 1989), pp. 43-5.

Suggestions Are Welcome

In response to suggestions, several features have been added to *TCLC* since the series began, including annotations to excerpted criticism, a cumulative index to authors in all Gale literary criticism series, entries devoted to criticism on a single work by a major author, more extensive illustrations, and a title index listing all literary works discussed in the series since its inception.

Readers who wish to suggest authors or topics to appear in future volumes, or who have other suggestions, are cordially invited to write the editors.

Acknowledgments

The editors wish to thank the copyright holders of the excerpted criticism included in this volume, the permissions managers of many book and magazine publishing companies for assisting us in securing reprint rights, and Anthony Bogucki for assistance with copyright research. We are also grateful to the staffs of the Detroit Public Library, Wayne State University Purdy/Kresge Library Complex, and the University of Michigan Libraries for making their resources available to us. Following is a list of the copyright holders who have granted us permission to reprint material in this volume of *TCLC*. Every effort has been made to trace copyright, but if omissions have been made, please let us know.

COPYRIGHTED EXCERPTS IN *TCLC*, VOLUME 45, WERE REPRINTED FROM THE FOLLOWING PERIODICALS:

German Life & Letters, v. XXXII, January, 1979; v. XXXVIII, April, 1985; v. XL, January, 1987. All reprinted by permission of the publisher.—*Journal of American Studies,* v. 23, August, 1989 for "Ralph Adams Cram and the Americanization of the Middle Ages" by Michael D. Clark. (c) Cambridge University Press 1989. Reprinted with the permission of Cambridge University Press and the author.—*Kentucky Foreign Language Quarterly,* v. XIII, 1966. © University of Kentucky. Reprinted by permission of the publisher.—*London Magazine,* v. 10, June, 1970. © *London Magazine* 1970. Reprinted by permission of the publisher.—*The Massachusetts Review,* v. XIX, Spring, 1978. © 1978. Reprinted from *The Massachusetts Review,* The Massachusetts Review, Inc. by permission.—*Modern Austrian Literature,* v. 6, 1973. © copyright International Arthur Schnitzler Association 1973. Reprinted by permission of the publisher.—*Modern Drama,* v. VII, May, 1964. Copyright 1964 *Modern Drama,* University of Toronto. Reprinted by permission of the publisher.—*The Modern Language Review,* v. 80, October, 1985 for "Raabe's Poems" by William Hanson. © Modern Humanities Research Association 1985. Reprinted by permission of the publisher and the author.—*Monatshefte,* v. LIX, Spring, 1967. Copyright © 1967 by the Board of Regents of the University of Wisconsin System. Reprinted by permission of The University of Wisconsin Press.—*New German Studies,* v. 3, Summer, 1975. Copyright © 1975 by The Editors, *New German Studies.* Reprinted by permission of the publisher.—*New Orleans Review,* v. 11, Spring, 1984 for "Wallace Stevens" by Fredric Jameson. © 1984 by Loyola University, New Orleans. Reprinted by permission of the author.—*The New York Times Book Review,* September 19, 1937; March 12, 1967. Copyright 1937, © 1967 by The New York Times Company. Both reprinted by permission of the publisher.—*Oxford German Studies,* v. 14, August, 1983 for "Ödön von Horváth: The Strategies of Audience Enticement" by David Midgley. Reprinted by permission of the author.—*Poetry,* v. 83, January, 1954 for "The Poetry of Dylan Thomas" by Elder Olson. Copyright 1954, renewed 1982 by the Modern Poetry Association. Reprinted by permission of the Editor of *Poetry* and the author.—*The Sewanee Review,* v. LIII, Autumn, 1945. Copyright 1945, renewed 1973 by The University of the South. Reprinted with the permission of the editor of *The Sewanee Review.*—*University of Toronto Quarterly,* v. LV, Summer, 1986. © University of Toronto Press 1986. Reprinted by permission of University of Toronto Press.—*The Wallace Stevens Journal,* v. XII, Fall, 1988. Reprinted by permission of the publisher.—*Western Humanities Review,* v. XXIV, Summer, 1970. Copyright, 1970, University of Utah. Reprinted by permission of the publisher.—*yale/theatre,* v. 7, 1975 for "The Volksstücke Revival: Ödön von Horváth" by Dragan Klaic. Copyright © *Theatre,* formerly *yale/theatre* 1975. Reprinted by permission of the publisher and the author.

COPYRIGHTED EXCERPTS IN *TCLC*, VOLUME 45, WERE REPRINTED FROM THE FOLLOWING BOOKS:

Ackerman, John. From *A Dylan Thomas Companion: Life, Poetry and Prose.* The Macmillan Press Ltd., 1991. © John Ackerman 1991. All rights reserved. Reprinted by permission of Macmillan, London and Basingstoke.— Bentley, Eric. From *Bernard Shaw.* Limelight Editions, 1985. Copyright 1947 by New Directions Publishing Corporation. Renewed 1975 by Eric Bentley. Reprinted by permission of Limelight Editions.—Berst, Charles A. From *Bernard Shaw and the Art of Drama.* University of Illinois Press, 1973. © 1973 by the Board of Trustees of the University of Illinois. Reprinted by permission of the publisher and the author.—Bertolini, John A. From *The Playwrighting Self of Bernard Shaw.* Southern Illinois University Press, 1991. Copyright © 1991 by the Board of Trustees, Southern Illinois University. All rights reserved. Reprinted by permission of the publisher.—Cambon, Glauco. From "Giovanni Pascoli (1855-1912): 'Ultimo sogno'," in *The Poem Itself.* Edited by Stanley Burnshaw. Holt, Rinehart and Winston, 1960. Copyright © 1960, renewed 1988 by Stanley Burnshaw. All rights reserved. Reprinted

Ralph Adams Cram

1863-1942

American architect, essayist, journalist, short story writer, and autobiographer.

INTRODUCTION

Cram was the foremost figure in the Gothic Revival in American architecture during the late nineteenth and early twentieth centuries. He was also a cultural commentator who advocated the social, religious, and artistic ideals of the Middle Ages and condemned all aspects of modern life. In addition to his writings on architecture and society, Cram wrote a volume of horror stories, *Black Spirits and White,* several of which continue to be reprinted in anthologies of supernatural fiction.

Cram was born in Hampton Falls, a rural village in New Hampshire. As a teenager his interest in both art and architecture was fostered by his parents, who presented him with C. J. Richardson's *House Building;* this book, together with John Ruskin's *The Seven Lamps of Architecture* (1849) and *The Stones of Venice* (1851-60), inspired Cram to pursue architecture as a career. In 1881, at the age of seventeen, he was apprenticed to the newly formed architectural firm of Arthur Rotch and George Tilden in Boston. His five years there formed the whole of his professional training.

While in apprenticeship with Rotch and Tilden, Cram submitted many letters to the *Boston Transcript* on art and architectural matters, and in 1886 E. H. Clement, the newspaper's editor, offered him the position of art critic. Somewhat disillusioned by his failure to win an architectural competition, Cram accepted and spent several years as a journalist with the *Transcript,* although he continued to enter competitions and to submit plans for proposed building projects. During this time he was affiliated with several informal clubs and associations, including the "Pewter Mugs," the "Visionists," and the "Procrastinatorium," whose members at various times included the poets Bliss Carman, Louise Imogen Guiney, and Richard Hovey; humorists Gelett Burgess and Finley Peter Dunne; painters George Hallowell, Tom Meteyard, and Dawson Watson; and architect Bertram Grosvenor Goodhue. In 1889 a second-place cash prize from another architectural competition enabled Cram and Charles Francis Wentworth to establish their own firm, which Goodhue joined in 1891. Seeking an area of specialization, Cram identified church building as a promising option and eventually became renowned for ecclesiastical architecture, particularly in the Gothic mode.

In 1914 Cram was appointed chairperson of Boston's newly established City Planning Board, one of the first

such attempts on the part of a municipal government to address urban blight and ensure orderly city growth. He held the post until 1922. Also in 1914 he was made head of the department of architecture at Massachusetts Institute of Technology, remaining there until 1921. Cram left both positions in part because funding became widely available for architectural commissions when World War I ended. Throughout the 1920s Cram designed numerous buildings, in a range of architectural styles that included Byzantine, Mexican-Spanish Renaissance, colonial, and Italian Renaissance, as well as his trademark Gothic. By the 1930s the work of Cram's architectural firm was handled primarily by associates, while Cram himself devoted an increasing amount of time to lecturing and writing. Cram died in 1942.

Throughout his life Cram spoke and published extensively on social, political, and religious as well as architectural matters. Theorizing that history runs in approximately 500-year cycles, he maintained that the years between 1000 and 1500 were the most nearly perfect period of Western history, assessing the Middle Ages as a cultural millennium. Cram condemned most modern American art and architecture, as well as contemporary social and political forms and processes, as decadent, vulgar, and corrupt. Attributing this decadence to the decreased importance of religion and community to most Americans, Cram advocated a feudal way of life that included a rigidly stratified patriarchal social order centered on a sacramental church. For example, in *Walled Towns* Cram propounded a return to the closed, insular communities of the Middle Ages. *Convictions and Controversies* and *The End of Democracy* contain some of Cram's most searing indictments of modern society. In *The End of Democracy* Cram presented a negative assessment of the democratic government of the United States and maintained that the Constitution's framers intended to establish a type of constitutional monarchy. In accordance with this theory Cram proposed restricting presidential voting to the members of an elite governing body and suggested that the Presidency should be a lifetime appointment, carrying the title of "Regent" or even "King." *Convictions and Controversies* includes the 1932 polemic "Why We Do Not Behave Like Human Beings," in which Cram challenged the theory of progressive evolution and seriously advanced the notion that the mass of humankind is in fact not strictly human. Reserving that designation for such exemplary figures as Plato, Confucius, Charlemagne, Shakespeare, and Joan of Arc, Cram called for a clear line of demarcation between the "glorified and triumphant human being and the Neolithic mass which was, is now and ever shall be." His volumes on architecture, which include *The Gothic Quest, The Substance of Gothic, Church Building,* and *Impressions of Japanese Architecture and the Allied Arts,* generally provide a mingling of social and architectural theory.

Cram's few works of fiction are atypical of the rest of his writings. He came to regard his first work, *The Decadent,* a derivative novel owing much to seminal works of French and English literary Decadence, as an "early indiscretion," which he regretted because of his opposition to decadence in the arts. The six stories that make up *Black Spirits and White* exploit such traditional literary Gothicisms as haunted castles and incidents of supernatural retribution, thus, according to Robert Muccigrosso, evincing "a committed Gothic imagination." These stories are highly regarded by genre enthusiasts but little known outside of specialized circles.

Because of Cram's prominence as one of the country's foremost architects, his opinions received respectful attention during his lifetime, and his volumes of social, religious, and political theory were widely discussed in the popular and scholarly presses. Commentators have concluded, however, that because of the obscure and highly specialized nature of Cram's polemics, his actual impact as an agitator for social change was slight. He is chiefly remembered as the preeminent advocate of Gothic architecture and a motive force behind the Gothic Revival in late nineteenth- and early twentieth-century American architecture. His iconoclastic cultural theories, though all but forgotten, remain a fascinating page in the history of conservative cultural thought.

PRINCIPAL WORKS

The Decadent: Being the Gospel of Inaction (novel) 1893
Black Spirits and White (short stories) 1895
Church Building: A Study of the Principles of Architecture in Their Relation to the Church (nonfiction) 1901; revised edition, 1924
Impressions of Japanese Architecture and the Allied Arts (essays) 1905; revised edition, 1930
The Gothic Quest (essays) 1907; revised edition, 1915
The Ministry of Art (essays and lectures) 1914
Six Lectures on Architecture [with Thomas Hastings and Claude Bragdon] (lectures) 1917
The Substance of Gothic: Six Lectures on the Development of Architecture from Charlemagne to Henry the VIII (lectures) 1917
The Great Thousand Years (nonfiction) 1918
Gold, Frankincense and Myrrh (essays) 1919
The Nemesis of Mediocrity (essay) 1919
The Sins of the Fathers (essays) 1919
Walled Towns (nonfiction) 1919
Towards the Great Peace (essays) 1922
The Catholic Church and Art (essays) 1930
Convictions and Controversies (essays) 1935
My Life in Architecture (autobiography) 1936
The End of Democracy (essays) 1937

Bertram Grosvenor Goodhue (essay date 1896)

[*Goodhue was an American architect and a partner of Cram from 1891 through 1913. In the following excerpt, he discusses Cram's journalism, poetry, short stories, and novel* The Decadent, *maintaining that the stories in* Black Spirits and White *demonstrate Cram's narrative skill and development as a prose stylist.*]

Not infrequently now-a-days the New England parent finds himself in the trying position of the hen who hatched out a duckling. Indeed, this probably occurs much more frequently than anyone suspects—except possibly the ducklings themselves.

Do not mistake the motive of this opening sentence. I mean only that the reverend parent of the author of **Black Spirits and White** has doubtless smiled with satisfaction many times in the past to observe his offspring glide safely to shore after a short and seemingly hazardous course over the troubled, not to say muddy, waters of the world. It speaks well for the "bringing up" of most New Englanders that they so rarely come to grief, though the mystery of their taking so kindly to water is unexplained.

Every village of our rock-bound East is able to boast at least two or three bitterly opposed and opposing sects. Mr. Cram, senior, was one of the pastors of a small town in southern New Hampshire. Here the subject of this paper was born, perhaps thirty years ago. Mr. Cram was exceptionally fortunate in his choice of parents, since both, besides being of simple tastes and God-fearing habits, are literary, or at least literary-minded, keeping *au courant* with all that is best in contemporaneous letters, native or foreign. Thanks to them, Mr. Cram's early youth was kept free from dime novels and toy-pistols, and later from the Maud Müllers of the vicinage and the works of the Albert Rosses and Laura Jean Libbeys of the period. At last Mr. Cram was sent away to one of the leading inland academies, from which he was graduated in due course of time. (pp. 455-56)

After a short period spent in an architect's office, during which he practiced journalism in a gentle way, and always over his own name, we hear of him as having taken passage on a steamer bound for England, with the intention of making a tour of the effete countries of the old world. It is worthy of mention that the funds for this came out of a prize which he won in the Boston Court House competition. Before his departure, however, the *Boston Transcript* was fortunate enough to arrange with him for a series of letters, dealing, for the most part, with matters artistic. These letters are practically, and for our purpose, Mr. Cram's first published work, although he had already printed a number of clever satirical and poetical verses, as well as art criticisms, in the *Transcript,* and it behooves us to consider them somewhat carefully. Here we find the first hints of the man and his style. Ruskinism is their dominant note, but a Ruskinism so turgid, and with such a barbaric wealth of adjective, as might cause even that much discussed master to lift his lids. Everything is here set down which may have chanced to impress the author during his foreign sojourn; and whether he is critically discussing the pictures of the English prae-Raphaelites, or rhapsodising over some opaline Italian landscape, it is always in the same luxuriant and Persian manner, which bespeaks strange modes of thought in one reared in such simple fashion.

However, these *Transcript* letters were but "by-the-ways" with Mr. Cram, for his prime motive in going abroad was the study of architecture, a motive never lost sight of, which has since stood him in good stead. (pp. 456-58)

On careful investigation it will be found that nearly every author, branded as new or unknown, has written considerably before the success of this or the other of his books sets his name on the lips of the multitude. This is particularly true of Mr. Cram. Even in the *Transcript* letters it is evident that no 'prentice pen is at work; and, as a matter of fact, one discovers, in the verses which began to appear at intervals thereafter, an easy familiarity with rhyme-forms and metrical effects which argues long and careful practice.

It is a number of years now since Mr. Cram wrote the *Transcript* letters, and during this time he has put forth, in a desultory way, stories, pastels, and verses. It is in verse that his best known and appreciated work has been done: yet even this lies now in the limbo of such dead and gone periodicals as the *Knight Errant* and the *Mahogany Tree.* I cannot help hoping that some fine day certain of these contributions may be reprinted in more accessible form, notably the **"Roy René,"** which seems to me one of the best attempts in the essentially Gallic pastel form ever made in English.

Of Mr. Cram's verses it is almost indiscreet to speak, since they are so far from being what is known as magazine poetry as, for the most part, to have escaped publication. Suffice it to say that his lyre is no tetrachord instrument, and though its twang is but too frequently voluptuously Lydian, still on it he can wander at will from the basses of the most ambitious dramatic work to the high piping trebles of amorous trivialities. Fortunately I am permitted to quote from one or two which have been circulated among his friends after the manner of the pugillaria of the Roman authors, and which will serve to show the general character of his verse. Of course the reader will readily catch echoes of Rossetti or Tennyson, and even of Swinburne— Swinburne, so easy to ape, so difficult to approach.

One of the earliest of his sonnets is called **"Last Night,"** and carries in its very title a suggestion of the great prae-Raphaelite, while the figures all hint of him; yet I am sure that, when all is said and done, there will remain the overtone of Mr. Cram's own personal note, less self-conscious than Rossetti's, and naturally enough less perfectly beautiful.

Last Night

As when, aweary with the dying day,
    The traveller stands silent on the height
So hardly won, and, wistful, sees the night
Grow in the east along the road that lay
Dawn-lit, long hours before, now fading gray
    Through wreathing, rising mists: Lo, full in
        sight
    Lie the broad fields, hills, forests, rivers white,
That vanished as he passed them on his way:—

So on time's wind-swept summit, when at last
    The farthest height is reached, and the great
        sea
Lies round the sun of life; the mist-wreathed
        Past
    Glows in the sunset fire of memory:
Forbid forever, and the night sweeps fast
    Across the ocean of Eternity.

Surely it matters little whether this be imitation or no, the sextette could not easily be bettered and remain what it is. **"Last Night"** is, it must be confessed, one of the simplest of Mr. Cram's verses. From it to **"The Boat of Love,"** a masque for music, is a far cry both in the matter of sentiment and the manner of expression. Into the masque are introduced choruses—

First, of Merchants, who sing:

And out of the dubious ways
    Of the uttermost, ultimate land,
Slow caravans crawl in the haze
    Of a desert of shimmering sand.

 . . . . .

With the limitless power of Kings
    I will buy me an Emperor's nod:
With the treasure my galleon brings
    I will buy me the power of God.

And then the Warriors:

Swords were made for men to use;
    Soldiers only crave

Now to win, if then to lose,
Now to love, if then to choose
Fame, or shallow grave.

In progression follow Monks, Crusaders, Friars, and finally the Narrator:

Silence: save a sound of grieving
    While the looming moon of brass
Lifts above the ocean, heaving
    Hungrily. As in a glass
        Dusky shadows stagger by,
        Waving wings along the sky,
Where the tangled winds are weaving
Webs of tempest as they pass.

Ambitious enough, in truth, as is the long blank verse rhapsody, **"Cor Cordium"**:

I built a mighty castle for my heart,
A refuge from the tumult of the End,
A house of memory—and forgetfulness;
A house of dreams and visions, and I said:
"O ye who love me and who have my love,
Forsake the warfare of the crumbling world,
Forsake the bitter sunlight, and the dead
Drear tempest of the coming day of wrath.
The sun is burning to a pestilent ball,
Hopeless, malefic, and the evil stars
Are closing in their courses round the world;
The night is coming: in the crowding dusk
Dream in my castle gardens, and forget."

In a more robust vein runs the ballad of **"The White Ladye,"** of which the burthen is:

Flame and rain and wind go by,
Lightning shatters the shrinking sky:
Ill hap to the dead to-night that die:
        By our Ladye.

And **"Nottingham Hunt,"** with its dashing equestrian lilt:

Oh, the dawn is all about us, and the dew is in
        our faces,
    Dashed from off the rushing branches as we
    ride and
            riding sing:
"Yoicks, the hunt is up, the hounds are out, the
    beaters
            in their places;
'T is a gallant day for hunting in the name of
Charles the
            King!"

I have said that the *Transcript* letters were overburdened with adjective, and that by far the greater part of his verse which has fallen into my hands is too tropically luxuriant of figures-of-speech and bric-à-brac generally. The same tendency is not confined to Mr. Cram's work; it may be found as easily in the writings of a dozen or so New Englanders. It is not necessary to give the names of all of them, but read Miss Gertrude Hall's "Garden Deadly," or Mr. Russell Sullivan's "Lost Rembrandt," and you will find the style in its perfection,—a perfection which suggests rather than catalogues.

Not so long ago, less long than Mr. Cram likes to think, I fancy, there appeared a very limited and generally hand-made edition of a book entitled *The Decadent,* etc.,—the sub-title is far too long to be quoted here. In this book, if you can obtain it, which is unlikely, may be found some of the most poetical prose ever writen in America. Since Mr. Cram himself regards this book as something of a mistake, an indiscretion of youth, as it were, it is, without doubt, equally indiscreet to quote any portion of it here; but since it is perhaps the most characteristic example of his style, I have prepared myself to brave his objurgations. Cast in romance form, it is in reality an anti-socialistic tract, and would be a powerful argument for the winning side, were it not for the odor of drugs and faded flowers with which it is permeated. The *mise* of the book is an imaginary country house in some equally imaginary hollow of the New England hills. To visit its youthful lord comes one Malcolm McCann, a gentleman in a way, but a socialist agitator of the red-whiskered and unshaven sort. Listen to the description of the approach to the house. McCann has left his train at the station of a frightfully typical manufacturing town, and is being driven out across the country to his friend's manor:—

> The sun dropped down and lay on the edge of the world: from the farther side of the valley it poured a suave, golden glory of molten light down over the purple, serrated hills, that lay in the valley like amber wine. Smooth fields of ripening grain and velvet meadow-land chequered the valley irregularly, slim elms and dark, heavy oaks rising among them. In the midst, curling like level smoke, wound a narrow river, with black poplars and golden chestnut trees leaning above. In all the valley was no sign of a dwelling, save far away at the distant end, where, from the midst of thick foliage, rose dark roofs and towers and chimneys as of some château on the Loire.
>
> McCann caught his breath. "Is that the place?" he said quickly.
>
> "Suh, that is Vita Nuova," answered the footman.

But we are still in the open air; it is within this château that Mr. Cram finds himself more at home. The love of beauty and beautiful things which has come to us from none knows where or how, and which can certainly be no heritage of our God-fearing and pleasure-hating ancestry, here reaches its extreme limit. It is a dangerous taste, though, and needs the sure hand and steady eye which are rarely its accompaniment. Hawthorne possessed both it and the power of repressing it. Poe had a connoisseur's appreciation of it, though he frequently sipped too deeply. Theodore Winthrop, writing before the civil war, knew the value of such artistic properties as damaskeened armor and Venetian glass. I have mentioned Miss Gertrude Hall and Mr. Russell Sullivan as of the cult, but in Mr. Cram its finds it most unbridled expression. Within the portals of "Vita Nuova" all is shadowy, exotic. Beautiful as the descriptions are, they are too opium-saturated to be altogether agreeable. It is, nevertheless, pleasant to read of the "violet flames of a drift-wood fire." "Vast and precious missals, gorgeous with scarlet and gold and purple illumination, open, on a carved oak lectern." "The golden gloom of a Giovanni Bellini reft from its home in Venice, and as yet unransomed." "The red splendor of old lacquer, and the green mystery of wrought jade." Yet everywhere is the "warm, sick odor of tobacco and opium," nor does it greatly matter that with this strives the "perfume of sandalwood and roses."

But, after all, it is unfair to quote, in this random fashion, from an immature work. Much that is palling in style here disappears in his last book, while enough of the Persian manner remains to add an interest to the plots of the stories in *Black Spirits and White.* These, in a simple afterword, are frankly acknowledged to be common to all lands, and the mine from which all writers of ghost stories must needs obtain their ore. Furthermore, here Mr. Cram shows himself in a new and somewhat unexpected light, that of a keen, clear narrator; when he wishes for the sake of contrasting effect to introduce a bit of description, we find all the old charm of word-painting, but never at the crucial moment does he wander in this way from the subject.

Out-and-out ghost stories are the first four in *Black Spirits and White;* and the last two, if not ghost stories, are at least grewsome enough to deserve a place in the volume. Personally, as a story, I prefer **"In Kropfsberg Keep."** The scene wherein this is laid precludes any elaboration of the elemental plot, while the vision in the ghostly ball-room, with its dancing rout of spectres, some of them the dead of many years ago, and others the dead of yesterday (or, worse than all the rest, the dead of the day before yesterday), is one of the strongest pieces of work of the sort we can remember to have ever read.

It is interesting to compare **"The White Villa"** in Mr. Cram's volume with "The Graven Image," one of the stories in William Sharp's *Gypsy Christ and Other Tales.* Both authors have evidently worked from the same original, and have ended in precisely the same fashion. Mr. Sharp's ability is well known, and his treatment of this plot is as characteristic in its way as is Mr. Cram's. The one lays the scene in London, and the other in a deserted villa in the neighborhood of Paestum. But why should I set myself to show at length the similarities and differences which exist here? They are but those which are bound to be in the work of two authors, writing simultaneously, with the sea between them. If Mr. Sharp's name is now more familiar than Mr. Cram's, it is partly because he has published vastly more.

Black Spirits and White is something more, then, than a book of capital tales which are bound to be read and enjoyed by many: it is a high fulfillment of the hopes of its author's friends, and, besides this, shows a degree of power in him which was hardly suspected even by the most sanguine. (pp. 459-66)

> *Bertram Grosvenor Goodhue, "The Written Work of Ralph Adams Cram," in* The Chap-Book, *Vol. IV, No. 10, April 1, 1896, pp. 455-66.*

Current Opinion   (essay date 1921)

[*In the following excerpt, the critic discusses Cram's pro-* *motion of a Gothic revival in American art and architecture.*]

The distinguished Boston architect, Ralph Adams Cram, has entered the lists against American ugliness. In an address delivered before the Harvard Chapter of the Phi Beta Kappa, he calls us all, with the fervor of a prophet, to a new enthusiasm in behalf of beauty. He is thinking of spiritual, as well as artistic, beauty. His faith is staked on what he calls the Gothic Revival. "It is no less than Christian civilization," he says, "that we have to restore, and we may find one road to our goal by the way of a Christianized art."

Dr. Cram has preached a similar gospel for many years, and he feels his conviction strengthened by the war and its aftermath. There is nothing small about his thinking. He reckons time not in years, nor in decades, but in centuries. His theory is that cycles of history have to run themselves out before a change for the better is possible.

According to his view, the world at large—not only America—has been going down-hill, esthetically speaking, for upward of four hundred years. The present situation he describes as follows:

> In both the material and the psychological spheres ugliness rules. The city of industrialism, the decadent and vulgarized village, the metropolis of commerce and finance; the means of locomotion and transportation, the music and drama and literature and architecture of the multitude, the newspapers and the advertizing, the very clothes and customs of society are conceived not only without reference to beauty, but in terms that are its antithesis and its destruction. From the greater part of the multifarious religions and philosophies of the day beauty has long since departed; government knows it not, but functions in drab selfishness and venality at the worst, while industrialism, with the trade and finance that are its concomitants, has so utterly destroyed the beauty that inheres in human relationship that at last overt warfare has taken the place of the hundred years' sullen but covert enmity, in the hopeless effort to solve problems that on this plane are unsolvable.

The medieval era, it seems, is the one from which we have all so grievously fallen. Dr. Cram insists on "the fundamental differentiation between the art of the world as it was from the Christian era to the year 1500, and as it has been since that ominous year." He would call us back to "that communal, instinctive, universal art of which the magical years 1000 A.D. to 1500 A.D. give the fullest and most perfect expression." There is something definite, he says, on which one can put one's finger as the greatest synthesis of beauty ever made operative through art, and he tells us what it is:

> It was a Gothic cathedral of the 13th century during a Pontifical High Mass, and somewhere about the middle of the 14th century in England, or the 15th century in France. Every art raised to its highest point was here brought into play in one place and associated in absolute union with the greatest beauty of thought, emotion and action that have ever been the possession of fall-

en man. Painting, sculpture, and a score of exquisite minor arts, as those of glass, needlework and enamel, with the crafts of the goldsmith, the wood-carver and the bell-founder, were here coordinated through the supreme power of the master art of architecture in a unity that was almost divine in its perfection. To this unity entered other arts that they might breathe into it the breath of life: music first of all, and poetry and the drama through the sublime liturgies and ceremonial that had grown up through a thousand years of striving and aspiration and the revelations that are their boon and reward. And all were for the exposition and realization of the supreme beauty of spiritual things; the durable love of God for His children through the Sacrifice of Calvary, eternally renewed upon the altar, and the veritable presence of His Spirit through the miracle of the Mass.

Truly here was all the beauty man may ever know on earth, knit up into perfect unity, and all the art man can achieve used to its highest end and with a poignancy that may never be excelled. Beauty has become life, life beauty, and art the common possession, the common expression, of all the people, and a divine force incomparable.

This is the standard. To this or to something like it we must return. Dr. Cram pays his tribute to Pusey, Pugin, Turner, Ruskin, Arnold, Morris and others of the nineteenth-century leaders of the Gothic Revival. Then he says:

As the sense of inadequacy, if not of failure, in Modernism has worked itself more and more into our consciousness, we have come to know something of what the word "Gothic" implies, and to desire it again because of its significance and not by reason of its outward and historical forms. Something is, of course, preserved of the outer forms, for in the first place it is necessary through these to restore the broken sense of continuity, and to stimulate that "elder memory" which answers to these visible agencies; and in the second place because the power went out of us, when it went out of our society, to create a vital art as did our less highly-trained and highly-civilized forbears. Through these forms spirit is showing itself, and very slowly new forms are being evolved.

The Gothic impulse in architecture, Dr. Cram asserts, is not a fad of archeological fancy galvanized by the sheer nervousness of a jaded fashion impulse, like the flair for "mission" furniture or crinoline. "It is the result of a spirit working hiddenly in men and in society." He continues:

Gothic is not a passing phase of the building art already completed and dead; it is the voicing of an eternal spirit in man, that may now and then withdraw into silence, but must reappear with power when, after long disuse, the energy emerges again. Gothic is the fully developed expression of Christianity, but it is even more the manifestation of Christianity applied to life, that is to say, Christian civilization.

We are not to forget that the word means more

than a dogmatic theology and a form of religious faith: it means a philosophy, a social organism, a polity, an industrial system and a way of life. When it means this it is crescent and compelling, when it means less it is decadent and not in accordance with the will of God.

Dr. Cram speaks of "the return to medievalism," manifested in religion, philosophy and the arts, especially architecture, as the most significant happening of modern times and a reliable prophecy of the future. "It is," he assures us, "the Counter-Renaissance in simple fact, the first stirrings of what will have ultimate issue in the rejection of the new paganism and a restoration of the Christian polity." He adds:

As a result of recent revelations, we know both the need and the significance of a thing that once seemed whimsical and episodic, and again we take up the smoking torch, cast down in weariness and failure. It is no less than Christian civilization we have to restore, and we may find one road to our goal by the way of a Christianized art that leads us to beauty, that in its turn serves as one of the channels of the grace of God.

So there is no unreason in our effort to build Gothic churches to-day, for this particular art we try to recover is the title-deed to our inheritance. Every stone that we cut and lay, however clumsily and by inadequate modern methods, is so much added to the new fabric of a restored civilization. It is not the pandering to an ephemeral fashion, but the proclamation of a creed, "I believe"; no longer the "I deny" of a doubtful faith.

All of which has led to spirited discussion in the Boston *Transcript,* the Brooklyn *Eagle,* the New York *Tribune,* and other papers. The last-named paper thinks that, in spite of despairing critics, "there never was a time when it would be possible to demonstrate the beauty of so many lives"; while the Brooklyn *Eagle* quotes against Dr. Cram an article lately contributed to the *Atlantic Monthly* by William Archer. It is Mr. Archer's view that "New York is by far the most magnificent and marvelous city in the whole world—a wonder to the eye and an incomparable stimulus to the imagination." He says: "Business has put off its grime and has housed itself in the blue spaces of the sky. And we make it our foolish pride that we are earthbound, and boast of our determined propinquity to the gutter. The American elevator exhilaratingly elevates; the British lift laboriously lifts"; and again: "They (the American elevators) are to the crawling, doddering British lift as a race-horse to a pack-mule." He continues:

In every type of building America leads the world. The finest railway stations in Europe, Frankfort, Cologne and the Paris Gare d'Orléans, are paltry in comparison with those vast palaces of marble and of travertin, the Pennsylvania and the Grand Central termini. . . . The Library of Congress and the public libraries of New York and Boston are stately and splendid beyond comparison. . . . In domestic architecture, again, America easily holds first place.

This and the judgments of other foreign critics is "the judgment of posterity," the *Eagle* says. If America has no Middle-Age cathedrals, the same paper comments, it is because she never had any Middle Ages. But "she is not ignoring beauty in architecture. . . . " (pp. 204-06)

The Boston *Transcript,* in a more sympathetic critique of Dr. Cram's address, finds the meat of his argument in his protest against "the failure of the ordinary thing to be beautiful—the sin of the many against the light of beauty that is held up to them by a few." (p. 206)

> *"Dr. Cram Preaches a 'Gothic Revival' in America," in* Current Opinion, *Vol. LXXI, No. 2, August, 1921, pp. 204-06.*

Cram on the influence of Venice:

Venice really settled the matter so far as an architectural career was concerned. . . . *The Stones of Venice* started it all, of course, as far back, perhaps, as the year 1876; but there was also a most engaging essay by W. D. Howells in, I think, *Harper's Magazine,* that gave added incentive. It began, if I remember correctly, "When you are ready to leave Venice, call for your bill, pay it—and stay." In so far as possible I have always followed this advice since.

Frequently, in later years, when architectural students have asked me where they should go and what they should do, I have told them that if they travelled widely, saw the old work clearly, and sketched incessantly, it did not much matter—so long as they ended up with a long stay in Venice. This was not because they would find there what they could use in a "practical" way in future, but because every architect must, and as early in life as possible, immerse himself in beauty. Without this quality there can be no valid art of any kind. I think, perhaps, that if every protagonist of "modernistic" art, from the devotees of Bantu and Congo carving to the kindergarten scribblings of *sur-realiste* painting and the prodigies of *architecture vivante,* could have been exiled (or rather repatriated) in Venice for six months, society would have been spared much, though something would have been lost to its sense of humour.

> *Cram, in his* My Life in Architecture, *Little, Brown, and Co., 1936.*

John Cournos   (essay date 1937)

[*In the following review of* The End of Democracy, *Cournos outlines Cram's proposed American constitutional monarchy and notes some deficiencies in Cram's assessment of the current form of democratic government in the United States.*]

The eminent architect, Ralph Adams Cram, has arrived in his latest book [**The End of Democracy**] at conclusions sufficiently startling to make even the 50 per cent American rub his eyes. For here, in cold print, is the deliberate and reasoned suggestion that this country would be better off under a government approximating a constitutional monarchy. Not that Mr. Cram entertains any real hope of such a felicitous state of affairs coming to pass during his

lifetime, or even later. But having read Ortega y Gasset, Berdyaev, Jay Nock, Agar, Madariaga, Belloc, Chesterton, and in particular Spengler, and done a bit of thinking for himself, he has assumed the role of a modern Quixote tilting at the rickety windmill of democracy. And, there being no nonsense about him, he thinks it about time some one has pronounced the funeral oration for our pet governmental theory. And certainly, if democracy is in the bad way he says it is, then, of course.

> There's something to be said
> For being dead,

to use Edward Bentley's happy phrase.

Democracy being as good as dead, he turns this way and that, in the desperate effort to find a system of government which would answer to this country's needs. Communism is obnoxious, Nazism is vile and, though there are a few desirable things in fascism, yet he falters irresolutely. For, at bottom, perhaps, he still has more than a sneaking fondness for democracy. At any rate, there are for him two kinds of democracy—"high" democracy, which prevailed during the Middle Ages, and still in some measure prevails in England today; and "low" democracy, which afflicts this country. The first, the desirable kind, comes from the top, springing from the aristocratic rule of men of culture and breeding. The second proceeds from below, from the many who have the franchise and don't know how to use it, who don't know what's good for them, who can be persuaded to go the right way but more often go the wrong way, owing chiefly to unscrupulous politicians who use Demos for their own ends. In general, the tendency of the so-called "proletariat" and of the stupid uncouth rich with whom they are in conflict, both really of the same stuff, is to pull every one and everything down to their own level.

Mr. Cram contends that the state of affairs reached today is wholly contrary to the spirit of the aristocratic framers of the American Constitution, which after the Twelfth Amendment has assumed an alien character. The passage and ratification of the Seventeenth Amendment he considers in particular "a vicious piece of legislation, quite expressive of the 'triumphant democracy' period in recent history."

> Like so many other things, the original idea was right, not only in the light of eighteenth-century conditions, but right today. To elect the Senators by popular vote not only vitiates the whole bicameral principle, but it transforms the upper house into a second legislative chamber differing in no respect from the first except in tenure of office. In the eyes of the framers, the Senate was seen to be rather a close replica of the British House of Lords, only non-hereditary. It was urged that members should hold office for life, and serve without pay. . . . What they wanted and we need is a body of men of high character, notable intelligence and wide vision; men of mature judgment, of scholarly attainments and of knowledge of the world.

Moreover, he contends, both the Senate and the Chief Executive should be above party and not be subjected to the abominable custom of campaigning for election or re-election, which takes from the dignity of office and some-times impels even the best of men to stoop to offensive practices.

Nor is Mr. Cram happy about the manner of choosing a President by popular vote, though he admits that occa-sionally voters do the right thing, as they have in the last election. He suggests that if the Senate were the kind of body of men it ought to be, "then it might do to give the power of election into the hands of the House of Represen-tatives, each Senator being potentially a candidate." And he would make the tenure of the Chief Executive for life. Personally he would not mind his having the title of "King," but, allowing for "old animosities and inherited prejudices" which the word awakens, he would be content to see him called "Regent." "As a matter of fact," he adds, "the President of the United States *does* 'reign' even now."

The Supreme Court does not escape Mr. Cram's attack. He seizes in particular upon the recent five-to-four deci-sions to demonstrate the fallibility of the Nine Old Men. "If four eminent jurists think one way, and four of equal prominence think the other, it does not make sense for this odd man to settle what is perhaps a major question that affects a great body of citizens or even the welfare of soci-ety." And he would not even yield to the suggestion of Professor Eliot of Harvard "that where the Supreme Court decides against the constitutionality of an act it should be by a majority of at least two-thirds of the court." Nothing short of unanimity would content Mr. Cram, who seems an all-or-nothing sort of man.

We know that Mr. Cram sets great store by culture and beauty; and, according to his theory, "low" democracy is poor in such things. Yet the Third French Republic, which he particularly reviles, has produced more culture and beauty than any other country during the same peri-od. The books from which he copiously quotes are curi-ously of one type, or nearly one type; he strangely ignores those writers who have of late years written in defense of democracy and liberalism. And there is by far too much of Spengler's *Hour of Decision,* a very questionable docu-ment in any fair discussion of democracy. That there is an-other side to the picture is evident from Wickham Steed's article on the peril of a European war in *New York Times* of July 4, which concludes thus: "Another unknown fac-tor is the degree of open-eyed albeit tacit solidarity be-tween the principal democracies of the world. I verily be-lieve they hold it in their power to forestall a catastrophe by an unyielding albeit unaggressive fidelity to the liberal outlook and the principles of individual human freedom." Democracy, after all, should be judged by things left out of Mr. Cram's book as by those which are included.

John Cournos, "A King for America," in The New York Times Book Review, *September 19, 1937, p. 19.*

Douglass Shand Tucci (essay date 1975)

[*In the following excerpt, Tucci assesses the cultural im-pact of Cram's architectural designs and social theories.*]

Fundamentally, I think that his posterity—laymen and scholars alike—more or less instinctively concluded that Cram did too much. Indeed, it is perhaps the case that he wrote so much, built so much and influenced his time so variously and so improbably, that his posterity having in-herited what amounted to a legend not unnaturally mis-took it for a myth and promptly discounted it. (p. 3)

[Cram's] work will be found in almost every state in the union and abroad as well; whose church work alone (and many of the great churches of America are Cram's) amounts to over seventy cathedrals and churches in thir-ty-five states and two Canadian provinces; built by him not as is often thought just for Episcopalians (only forty of these seventy are Anglican) but also for Swedenbor-gians, Presbyterians, Unitarians, Baptists, Roman Catho-lics, Methodists, Orthodox, Lutherans and Congregation-alists; and not just in gothic, but in every variety of it from Norman to Spanish, and in Byzantine, Lombard and Georgian as well. Nor can one overlook his houses or his office buildings or his libraries. And one certainly can't ig-nore his collegiate work, which includes important build-ings at Wheaton, Richmond, Sweet Briar, University of Southern California, University of the South, Rollins, Notre Dame, Bryn Mawr, Williams, Rice Institute, Princeton and West Point—the last four of which he dom-inated—and in another dimension, a long tenure as Pro-fessor of the Philosophy of Architecture and head of the School of Architecture at the Massachusetts Institute of Technology. Furthermore, through his designs and through his writings, he led and virtually created the last phase of the American Gothic Revival. He was unargu-ably the foremost 20th century American Gothic polemi-cist. He inspired a wide-ranging new school of design and of decorative arts, and in the end he revolutionized the vi-sual image of American Christianity in his time.

Not surprisingly, therefore, his correspondence abounds with letters of the sort written to Cram in 1938 by Joseph Hudnut, then Dean of the Graduate School of Design at Harvard, in which Hudnut allowed that "like all archi-

One of about forty pencil sketches made by Cram during the initial design process for the Cathedral of St. John the Divine in New York City.

tects of my generation, I have been deeply influenced by your designs and writings." But Cram's architecture, and his influence on the national architecture, can only be the beginning of any discussion of his work. For his two dozen books and hundreds of scholarly and polemical articles and as many lectures, ranging in topic from British abbeys to Japanese temples, as often as not went far beyond the arts: one of his last and most widely read books, published in 1937, was entitled *The End of Democracy,* and Cram was by then so much a "household word" that neither in the book nor on the dust jacket did his publishers find it necessary to include any "about the author." Architect, theologian, liturgist, philosopher, medievalist, historian, social theorist, Cram founded or edited (often both) five journals, wrote for all the leading journals, including *The American Mercury* and the *Atlantic Monthly,* was a founder of the Medieval Academy of America, and though not Roman Catholic, was the foremost Catholic polemicist in this country. In sum, he exercised a wider influence on diverse and important aspects of the national culture than any other architect in our history. It is thus scarcely surprising that most scholars, amazed enough by the extent and diversity of his architecture, back away at once from the larger Cram, who is an astonishingly interdisciplinary figure. Even if the "causes" appeal, the enormousness of Cram's achievement is scarcely credible and suggests at once that he cannot have done many or even any of these things well enough to warrant serious inquiry. But if this was the case he successfully deluded quite a large number of people.

Many Anglicans, predictably, thought Cram not only the great religious architect of the world but the foremost ecclesiologist of the Anglican Communion. But what is more surprising is that American Roman Catholic intellectuals, and the hierarchy as well, nearly always puzzled and sometimes defensive about High Church Anglicans like Cram, accepted Cram's leadership enthusiastically. A dean of the Catholic University of America, for example, once admitted in a letter to Cram that though he was an Episcopalian, no one had ever presented Catholic sacramental philosophy "so clearly and so cogently" as did Cram in a paper he gave on the subject. Bishop Ryan, the Rector of Catholic University of America, once allowed Cram's publishers to print a letter of his about one of Cram's books [*Convictions and Controversies*] in a promotional brochure. Even in England, Chesterton and Belloc were glad enough of Cram's support, and Cram's *The Catholic Church and Art* (with both *Imprimatur* and *Nihil Obstat,* though Cram scarcely obscured his Anglicanism in his text) followed Chesterton's *The Catholic Church and Conversion* in 1930 in Belloc's Calvert Series. [In an introduction] Belloc called Cram's book a "powerful essay"—"more definite and critical than I can remember to have seen elsewhere." The *San Francisco Monitor,* the official organ of the Roman Catholic Archdiocese, to cite another instance, after lamenting that Cram was not a Roman Catholic—when he would convert (he never did) exercised as many people in this country as did the same question with respect to Chesterton (who did) in England—nevertheless insisted that Cram was "one of the great men of our time; a leader, almost a prophet," whose **"Ordeal By Beauty"** in *Convictions and Controversies* in-

cluded some "of the most remarkable passages in all literature"! Astonishingly, no Roman Catholic in America ever exerted Cram's influence over the American Catholic Church. . . . (pp. 4-5)

Nor was Cram less well received in more strictly scholarly circles. A seminar on his writings was held in his lifetime at Holy Cross College. And the author of *Impressions of Japanese Architecture,* who succeeded to a degree, incidentally, in carrying out the difficult commission of designing a convincing but not imitative Japanese garden court for the Museum of Fine Arts in Boston, was regularly appointed by the Museum trustees to the Visiting Committee of the Museum's Department of Asiatic Art. The author of *Ruined Abbeys of Great Britain* was invited as well to give the annual address in 1907 to the Royal Society of British Architects: Cram always enjoyed a transatlantic reputation. There were, of course, honorary doctorates, from Yale, Princeton, Williams, Rollins and Notre Dame. Cram was also honorary Phi Beta Kappa at Harvard, where he gave the oration in 1921. And during his lifetime he was elected a fellow of a score of learned societies—including the Royal Society of Arts and the American Academy of Arts and Sciences—in the case of the last at the same time, interestingly, as Edna St. Vincent Millay and Carl Sandburg. He was a member, of course, of a great many more. It was Cram who wrote the article on "American Architecture" in the twelfth edition of the *Encyclopaedia Britannica.* He was also Henry Adams' literary heir in the matter of *Mont St. Michel and Chartres,* the copyright of which he presented to the American Institute of Architects. He wrote the preface to Adams' book, and gave the first of the Institute's Henry Adams Lectures at City Art Museum in St. Louis in 1934. Nor was his appointment to head the School of Architecture at M.I.T. in any sense an honorary affair: the president of "Tech" made it plain that he looked to Cram "to guide the school into a position of greater prestige and power." . . . But Cram's standing as a philosopher—he was often called "the Savant of Sudbury"—seems also to have been secure enough. Dr. Herman Radin, writing in *The Medical Pickwick* (one never knows where Cram will turn up), called Cram "the leading 'humanist' in America" in 1918. Perhaps even more surprisingly, Professor Albert Jay Nock, whose field was American History and Politics, though he was perhaps best known for his translations and commentaries (with C. R. Wilson) on Rabelais, as well as for his numerous articles in the *Atlantic* and *The New Republic,* once wrote to Cram:

> . . . my debt to you is greater than I owe to any other man or school. I have been five years trying to undermine the positions you took in your essay in man's place in Nature; with no success. They appear to be impregnable; and a study of their correlations and implications has given me a philosophical position from which I have been able to account satisfactorily for all the phenomena of the subject which I had found completely puzzling. . . . You may judge from this how profound is the sense of obligation I have for you. Your professional reputation is so great that I believe it has overshadowed your claims as a philosopher. In a book I am preparing to

write . . . I shall set forth your views at full length, if I live to finish the work, and be *ad hoc* your exposition. I re-read your autobiography, your **Convictions** and your **End of Democracy** twice a year, with ever-growing admiration for their quality.

Insofar as his social theory verged on the political, as it often did, Cram's "notices" were naturally more mixed. When one of his most earnest causes was taken up by Franklin Roosevelt in the land subsistence homestead program this involved Cram in vigorous public argument. But even in this area he did not lack accolades: an official of the program in Minnesota wrote him in 1934 that a recent article Cram had written on the homestead plan was "the best that has been done on the subject." Others of Cram's causes were more controversial. He labored strenuously to get this country into the First World War on the Allied side, and his stand earned public rebukes that ranged from "disgusting" to "jackass". He also supported Al Smith strenuously—even to serving as Chairman of the Calvert Association Against Racial and Religious Bigotry that sponsored the series of controversial seminars on the subject at Harvard and at Columbia, one effect of which was Cram's inclusion in the "Who's Who" Issue of *The American Hebrew* as a friend of the Jewish people. Finally, of course, Cram caused something of a sensation by later supporting Franklin Roosevelt. Under the heading "Pro-Cram" and "Anti-Cram," the *Boston Herald* printed five columns of letters in response to Cram's announcement. Elsewhere, R. M. Washburn remarked acidly that Cram had "now broken out in a new rash: He will vote for Franklin. Even worse than all this, Ralph is proud of it, and openly." Cram, of course, thrived on it all. No doubt he thought it a compliment when one academic protested that a paper of his was "terrifically strong medicine" and admitted that "personally I could not have administered this dose." And it certainly was a compliment when one of his editors, T. R. Shields of *The Educational Review,* allowed that he had not been so "stimulated" in years as by one of Cram's articles: "it is good for all of us," he wrote Cram, "to be made to think." Only once did Cram show annoyance: when he had been interpreted as supporting Sir Arthur Conan Doyle's stand on Spiritualism in the preface Cram wrote for a British book, Frederick Bligh Bond's *Hill of Vision.* "On the contrary," retorted Cram, "I tried to controvert it. . . . Evidently, I don't express myself very well!"

Usually, however, no one found any difficulty in discovering Cram's views. And whether pro or con, both his writings and lectures were taken very seriously. Their sheer quantity, of course, is astounding. His commencement addresses alone—which ranged from Yale (twice) to State University of Nebraska and Rice Institute in Texas—would make a good-sized book. In the six years between 1930 and 1936, for instance, he wrote (in addition to four books) at least twenty-six articles, nine for professional journals, four for religious journals, six appeared in *American Mercury,* four in *American Review,* two in the *Atlantic Monthly* and one in *Time.* Even more startlingly, he wrote eight of his books in the nine years between 1914 and 1922—nearly one a year. Nor was he only to be found midst friends: that he should have corresponded with

H. L. Mencken and been published so frequently by Paul Palmer in *American Mercury* is significant. His publishers, moreover, included Scribners, Macmillan, McGraw-Hill and Little Brown, and several of his books lasted through three or more editions.

It was difficult then (as it is now) to separate his popular, scholarly and more nearly polemical writings. But one book, particularly, which could fall under any of these rubrics, **Heart of Europe,** prompted a British critic to [write in the *Times Literary Supplement:* . . . "Those who have never fallen under the spell of Gothic, or have enjoyed it only romantically, may think that (Cram) talks romantic nonsense. But he does not enjoy Gothic romantically or talk romantic nonsense about it. He hears its living music, and it is to him not past but eternal."] The matter of Cram as a stylist, incidentally, also came up in this review, and no critic, I think, was ever more discerning than the *Times* critic when he described Cram's prose as "poured out in a headlong but often moving eloquence." Here is an example having to do with Germany in the First World War, and more particularly of the bombardment of Rheims.

> . . . And now a thing calling itself the highest civilization in Europe, with the name of God in its mouth, again sweeps the already well-swept land. In defiance of Peace Palaces and Conferences: . . . the old arena of Europe flames as at Armageddon, while those things too sacred for pillage and destruction by the armies and the commanders of five centuries are given over to annihilation in order that the peril of the Slav may not menace the treasured civilization of the West, whose vestiges even now are blazing pyres, or cinders and ashes!

In the same work, though, and the *Times* critic quoted this, Cram's creative erudition sparkles in his analysis of early Gothic building. He thought it was characterized by "cohesion, economy and character."

> The first means the synthetic knitting of everything together, and the giving it dynamic power to develop from within outward; it means making structure absolutely central and comprehensive; but also beautiful; ornament, decoration, remaining something added to it, something of the *bene esse* though not of the *esse;* deriving from it in every instance, but not necessary to its perfection. The second is the reducing of mass to its logical and structural (and also optical) minimum, bringing into play the forces of accommodation, balance, and active, as opposed to passive, resistance. The third is the hardest to describe or determine, and probably can only be perceived through comparison. It is the differentiation in quality, the determination of personality, and it is hardly to be defined, though it is instantly perceived. In the Abbaye aux Hommes, or Cérisy, or St. Georges de Bocherville, we find great majesty and beauty, many elements that are distinctive of true Gothic work and persist through its entire course, but none of these buildings is actually Gothic. In St. Germer de Fly, however, and in Sens and Noyan, while there seems at first little differentiation from the others, the Gothic spirit has found itself and is

already working rapidly toward its consummation.

When he was not theologian, philosopher, humanist, medievalist, historian, polemicist or social theorist—and in each both theorist and practitioner—Cram was still more things, though less importantly. The first Chairman of the Boston City Planning board, his proposals ranged from the fantastic (and beautiful) idea of an island in the Charles River to further enlarge the riverfront recreation areas and to provide for a new opera house (an idea revived in some measure by the Boston Arts Center plan of a few years ago) to completely obliterating all the "three-decker" districts in the city in favor of small single-family cottages of the sort he had seen and much liked around Tucson. (He went as often to the Southwest, which he loved, interestingly, as to Europe.) He was too, in his spare time, though indifferently, a poet, dramatist and lyricist. And even in these avocations, at the extreme periphery of his life, he earned attentions many might covet. Fred Bullard once did Cram's best-known song—**"Nottingham Hunt"**—at one of Bullard's Symphony Hall concerts, and in her younger years Rose Standish Nichols delighted in Cram's and Bullard's music at her famous Mt. Vernon Street "evenings." . . . The reader will perhaps now understand why even his eulogists found Cram an incredible figure, who they concluded could hardly have spent too much time at his drafting board, and why it is to some ex-

tent an unenviable task for me now to have to assert as well that he was a very hardworking and even a great architect. George H. Allen may have been right to conclude, in an article in 1931 for *Architectural Record*: "Ralph Adams Cram is a phenomenon." (pp. 5-11)

> *Douglass Shand Tucci, in his* Ralph Adams Cram: American Medievalist, *Boston Public Library, 1975, 49 p.*

Robert Muccigrosso   (essay date 1980)

[*In the following excerpt, Muccigrosso surveys the works of poetry and prose that reflect Cram's involvement with late nineteenth-century literary Aestheticism and Decadence.*]

Three diverse yet interrelated cultural events which took place in Boston during the 1880's first brought Cram into . . . contact with the Aesthetic Movement: the first performance of Wagner's operas, given at Mechanics Hall; the first production of Gilbert and Sullivan's *Patience,* offered at the Boston Museum; and the first public exhibition of Pre-Raphaelite art, displayed at the Art Museum in Copley Square. (pp. 30-1)

More than these events, it was meeting like-minded persons which was most responsible for Cram's wholehearted immersion in the Aesthetic Movement. In the 1880's and 1890's he befriended a number of talented young men (and at least one woman) who shared his artistic sensibilities. Almost all of them, Cram included, became fanatic converts to the Decadent movement, particularly as it was manifesting itself in England. (p. 31)

For many years during the late nineteenth century this coterie of Boston Aesthetes informally met . . . to discuss their work as well as the work of other artists. As painters, architects, musicians, and writers, they were forever organizing social and artistic clubs: the Pewter Mugs, the Visionists, the Procrastinatorium. From all accounts, the conversation and lectures at their meetings were never disappointing. Although most in the group never rose above minor status, a few, such as Cram and his partner in architecture, Bertram Grosvenor Goodhue, were to achieve real fame. Two poets from the group, the Canadian-born Bliss Carman and, more especially, Richard Hovey, also won a certain renown. Another promising artist, Frederick Field Bullard, the musician who was most famed for his "Stein Song," died at a relatively early age (forty), while Louise Imogen Guiney, though fairly well known as a poet, never received, according to Cram, who considered her the most vital member of the group, the just recognition merited by her talents. (pp. 31-2)

In his autobiography Cram recalled this *fin de siècle* milieu with nostalgia, as well as with a certain degree of self-mockery:

> Of course it was quite the thing, at this time, to proclaim the era as one of decadence. . . . This did not disturb us in the least or blur our optimism. Instead we rather gloated over the fact. If the world was indeed decadent, so much louder was the call for crusading. Besides, it was rather fun to envisage a crumbling society in which we

---

An excerpt from "Why We Do Not Behave Like Human Beings"

However repulsive and degrading the general condition of any period in the past, there never has been a time when out of the darkness did not flame into light bright figures of men and women, who in character and capacity were a glory to the human race. . . . Between them and the basic mass there was a difference greater than that which separates, shall we say, the obscene mob of the November Revolution in Russia and the anthropoid apes. They fall into two absolutely different categories, the which is precisely the point I wish to make.

We do not behave like human beings because most of us do not fall within that classification as we have determined it for ourselves, since we do not measure up to standard. . . .

What kinship is there between St. Francis and John Calvin, the Earl of Strafford and Thomas Cromwell, Robert Lee and Trotsky, Edison and Capone? None except their human form. They of the great list behave like our ideal of the human being; they of the ignominious substratum do not, because they are not. In other words, the just line of demarcation should be drawn, not between Neolithic Man and the anthropoid ape, but between the glorified and triumphant human being and the Neolithic mass which was, is now and ever shall be.

> *Cram, in his "Why We Do Not Behave Like Human Beings," The American Mercury, Vol. XXVII, No. 105, September 1932.*

could look on ourselves as superior beings. We rather revelled in Oscar Wilde and the brilliant and epicene drawings of Aubrey Beardsley. We accented our optimism with the vivacious but really most mistaken idea that we were quite wicked. . . . We savoured the varied flowers of the cultural menu with relish, and altogether thought of ourselves as monstrously clever fellows—a conception notably lacking in validity. [*My Life in Architecture*]

It was only in retrospect, however, that he made light of his years as an Aesthete. At the time, both he and his friends were quite in earnest with their endeavors, most of which were of a literary bent. (pp. 32-3)

[Cram's] fiction is stylized and manneristic; the poetry, mawkish and pretentious. From a purely aesthetic point of view, one would do well to pass over these efforts hastily and without fanfare. From the larger perspective, however, one must pause, for the general themes, spirit, and point of view conveyed did not pass with the waning of the century. On the contrary, they became foci for more serious thought. An integral part of his immersion in the Aesthetic Movement, they formed a *point d'appui* for his later attempts to reconstruct society.

In a lighter vein, Cram wrote **Black Spirits and White,** a series of six ghost stories which were published in 1895. The inspiration for the stories seems to have come from his European trip on which he met T. Henry Randall. Indeed, he included Randall in these tales by fictionalizing him as "Tom Rendel," the narrator's traveling companion. Haunted houses and castles, heinous crimes, the terrors of the supernatural—in short, the whole psychopathology of the Middle Ages fairly leaps from the pages at the reader. In one story, an eerie French house, aptly called "La Bouche d'Enfer" ("The Mouth of Hell"), ultimately burns. The fictitious Kropfsberg Castle, scene for another macabre narrative, proves to be the former residence of a mad and debauched Count Albert, who had burned part of the castle with a group of friends trapped inside and then hanged himself after putting on his great-great grandfather's suit of armour. Medieval churches provided other settings. One fairly innocuous recital, for example, is set in a Breton church; a more lurid one takes place in a Sicilian convent in which the narrator and his wide-eyed companion (Rendel) are shown the body of a young girl who, like Poe's victim in "The Cask of Amontillado," was immured while yet alive. Positively reveling in ghostly and ghastly lore, Cram, as narrator, jumps to Sweden for his final offering. Once there, he travels with great difficulty through a dense white fog in what was cheerfully called the Dead Valley, and for his efforts is rewarded with the sight of a skeleton tree, decorated with the heads of humans and animals. Horrified, our narrator hears piercing cries in the distance as the tale ends. What concerns us most about these ghost stories is not so much whether Walpole, Lewis or Mrs. Radcliffe would have been writhing in literary envy, nor what Freud might have said about the man who authored them. The point is simply that, whatever else might be said, they evidence a committed Gothic imagination.

Cram's literary medievalism, fortunately, was not con-

fined to Gothic ghost stories. Throughout the 1880's and 1890's he dabbled in verse dealing with chivalry, romance, and occasionally, the more prosaic aspects of medieval life. As an illustration of how seriously the poetic muse had affected him, one might consider a letter which he wrote to an editor of *The Century* in early 1895. In this letter, he: (1) thanked the editor for having published **"The Nottingham Hunt"** in the magazine's February edition and for his kind words concerning **"The White Ladye,"** a poem which had been rejected; (2) informed him that he was currently writing **"The Wave Song"** as part of a "long series of songs written for music"; (3) expressed his anticipation of having **"The Angelus,"** a one-act play written in blank verse, performed in prose verse; and (4) promised to send him future poems.

Sometimes Cram and his friend Bullard joined forces respectively as lyricist and composer. Their **"Royalist Songs"** (which included **"The Nottingham Hunt"**) were quite popular, at least as Cram tells it, but paled in quality before their secular cantata, **The Boat of Love.** Although the cantata itself was never produced, two years before his death Cram published its lyrics, subtitling them, *A Masque for Music.* An ambitious work, this intensely romantic poem contained a variety of rhyme schemes and a motley cast of medieval characters, including a merchant, a monk, several crusaders, four warriors, a spate of sea-spirits, a girl, a lover, a narrator and a chorus of friars. The following brief selection is fairly representative of the poem as a whole:

> Wavering, wandering waves,
> We who hold in our hands
> The Crystal sphere,
> Alpha, Omega,
> Secret of timeless time:
> Out of the swallowing sea, out of Eternity,
> We call the Wonder of Life.
> Unto the silent deep, into its infinite sleep,
> We yield the Wonder of Death.

One wonders what his poet friends must have said. (pp. 34-6)

The single work, however, which best expresses Cram's commitment to the Aesthetic Movement was **The Decadent,** a work written in 1893 which, along with **Black Spirits and White,** he later characterized as "early indiscretions." A derivative work, it owes a great deal for its central character and general tone to Huysmans' masterpiece, *À rebours,* sometimes called "the breviary of the Decadents." For all its flaws—stylistic, structural, and substantive—this didactic composition of less than fifty pages remains more than a period piece, Cram's self-criticism notwithstanding. Unremarkable as fiction, **The Decadent** contains some genuinely serious reflections.

As the narrative begins, Malcolm McCann, a dour socialist, is en route to visit Aurelian Blake in order to ascertain the reason for the latter's apostasy from socialism. Having passed through a squalid industrial town, he finally reaches Blake's home and is stupefied at its sumptuousness. Vita Nuova, its name conjuring up associations with Dante, scarcely seems a fitting abode for one who had strong socialist sympathies. But as McCann soon will see, the story's protagonist had indeed assumed a "new life."

Aurelian Blake's very name suggests a certain dissatisfaction with modern life and a penchant for the past: Marcus Aurelius, the heroic Stoic exemplar; William Blake, the eighteenth-century mystic in artistic rebellion against society. Or perhaps "Blake" more properly alludes to Cram's grandfather, the "Squire," who was also, in a sense, in revolt against his society. In any case, McCann's initial shock quickly turns to consternation and disgust when he enters Vita Nuova only to find Blake and a few friends freely indulging in drugs and alcohol. Like Des Esseintes, the decadent hero of Huysmans' *À rebours,* Blake has clearly yielded to self-indulgence and the seductions of *la dolce far niente.* Our puritanical socialist, who has rejected his host's offer of some hashish in favor of his own briar bull dog tobacco, is further startled by the arrival of a beautiful Japanese servant "with flesh like firelight on ivory, clad in translucent silk of a dusky purple that made no sound as she came," and who was called "the Honourable White Dew." The subsequent entrance of a black male servant wearing a red fez convinces McCann that the rumors of his friend's renunciation of socialism had been well-founded.

The appalled McCann, described by Cram as a "red-bearded agitator," pleads in vain with his erstwhile disciple to repent his folly. Blake, who has already praised philistinism for having brought forth Decadence, however, claims to despise materialism—this, in the midst of his palatial residence—and desires "only absolute individuality and the triumph of idealism." Inferentially, socialism is neither sufficiently individualistic nor idealistic to suit him. Besides, it was too late for revolution, and even if it were not, to what avail would it be? The French Revolution had led only to capitalism and the Third Republic. Revolution—any revolution—is only part of a larger, cyclical historical pattern and, as such, yields successively to tyranny, chaos, counterrevolution, and finally, still another revolution. As for the present world, the great artists—Turner, Rossetti, and Wagner—are dead; those remaining—Arnold, Pater, Burne-Jones—will die soon enough. Blake, in a phrase Cram often was to use, informs the dejected McCann that "art is a result, not an accident," and that for him, both art and chivalry were dead, leaving the field of battle to materialism and degeneration. Speaking frankly, hashish notwithstanding, he confesses to being numbed with "that despair which kills all effort."

It is, then, a sober aesthete who discloses to McCann that he has been forced reluctantly to turn to decadence out of utter revulsion against modernism. Democracy, freedom of the press, and public opinion—"the idolatrous tritheism of a corrupt generation"—has alienated our hero. "The whole world," he complains, "kneels before them, confessing their dominion. So long as this is so, so long will reform be impossible." Meanwhile, supported by a well-meaning but foolish populace, we have a system "which is the government of the best, by the worst, for the few." Add to this the decline of religion and the ascendency of an irresponsible press which supplies us with our demagogues and destroys canons of beauty and truth, and

you have a composite picture of late nineteenth-century Western European and American ills. As a result, Blake has decided to isolate and insulate himself at Vita Nuova, "the world of the past and the future," and literally and figuratively look down upon the pitiful industrial town through which McCann had passed. Ultimately, he has resigned himself to a hermetic life, "for the night has come when man may no longer work." If Cram (as Blake) seems unduly pessimistic, one must remember that he, too, was faced with what one student of the period has called, "the stunting social shock" of the 1890's. In his own way, he, like the outstanding literary figures of that decade—James, Howells, Twain, Garland, Crane, Norris, and others—was trying "to habituate America to the fact that internal divisiveness was more than geographical, that a civilization which pursued commerce and technology constructed for itself a morality drawn from commerce and technology. . . . "

Two further elements need mentioning to complete the portrait of Cram as Aesthete: his socialism and his monarchism. As to the former, it was scarcely of the virulent variety. Not only did he not consider himself a communist, he had never, and doubted whether his friends had ever, read anything by Karl Marx. Nor could he be considered a Fabian or even municipal socialist. Speaking for himself and his like-minded associates, he confessed: "We were socialists because we were young enough to have generous impulses. We were William Morris enough to hate industrialism, and were rebellious enough to want to attach ourselves to something new and not as yet accorded that popular favour that was so soon to follow in more fashionable circles" [*My Life in Architecture*]. In other words, his socialism was part sentimental, part *pour épater les bourgeois.* He later described socialism as merely "a rather insecure and blundering revolt against the whole economic theory and practice of the last epoch of history" [*The Ministry of Art*]. Nevertheless, the scathing diatribes against capitalism and some of the suggested panaceas of his mature years do mark him as a socialist in spirit, if not name.

In the closing years of the nineteenth century few people this side of mental asylums thought of socialism and monarchism as anything but mutually exclusive terms. Cram, however, saw no ideological incompatibility in the juxtaposition of the two. Neither, apparently, did some of his friends, who joined with him in 1896 to form the Order of the White Rose, an organization long in existence in England and dedicated to that grand old cause of Jacobinism. As Cram describes it, the Order (or at least its Boston version) held "services of mourning and expiation on the Feast of Charles the Martyr and on other Loyalist days, drank our seditious toasts, sang our Jacobite songs, and even indulged in complimentary (but limited) correspondence with Queen Mary of Bavaria, the 'legitimist' King of Spain, and other deposed monarchs" [*My Life in Architecture*].

Three years later, having been elected Prior of this North American Cycle of the Order of the White Rose, Cram issued an encyclical in which he emphasized the necessity of enhancing the organization's membership, even to the point of including women. Not content with memorializing the regicide of Charles I or celebrating St. George's Day, he further recommended that the Order be "Americanized." He confessed to his brethren that although he firmly believed in the divine right of monarchy and deplored "the heresy of popular sovereignty," he realized that the nation was not about to opt for monarchy. "The revolution of 1775," he avowed, "whether or no we may hold it to be unavoidable, is yet an accomplished fact." While the United States might not be ready for salvation by monarchy, however, it might be amenable to a healthy transfusion of Hamiltonianism. For Cram, Alexander Hamilton was "perhaps the greatest man this continent has ever known." The nation, he argued, must reject the "democratic follies" of Jefferson and accept Hamilton's proposed but inoperative constitution. If this were done, the people could at last receive the benefits of a wise and honest government. They could, in sum, enjoy the substance of constitutional monarchy. Having blindly chosen Jefferson rather than Hamilton for their political guide, Americans now must be emancipated from the "dark ages of the eighteenth century." (pp. 37-41)

For Cram, involvement in the [Aesthetic Movement] had brought the joys of human relationships, the memories of which remained vivid throughout his life. Equally as important, involvement presaged more mature attitudes and convictions. Virtually every element which was to form his future intellectual baggage—Christianity, Gothicism, monarchism, socialism (or at least anti-capitalism), craftsmanship, and detestation of modern democracy—found its early expression during his participation in the Aesthetic Movement. Though seemingly inchoate, these elements were soon to solidify from an attitude of discontent to a credo of neo-medievalism. (pp. 41-2)

> *Robert Muccigrosso, in his* American Gothic: The Mind and Art of Ralph Adams Cram, *University Press of America, 1980, 294 p.*

T. J. Jackson Lears   (essay date 1981)

[*In the following excerpt, Lears surveys salient points of Cram's antimodernist, Anglo-Catholic, and medievalist social and religious thought.*]

Ralph Adams Cram was one of the most prolific American architects of the last hundred years; he was also an ardent Anglo-Catholic and medievalist who left dozens of Gothic monuments throughout the United States. The Graduate Center at Princeton; the Post Headquarters at West Point; the Westhampton campus at the University of Richmond; the chapel of St. George's School in Newport, Rhode Island; the cathedrals of St. Alban's in Washington, D.C., and St. John the Divine in New York City—these were only a few of Cram's many designs. He also left a score of books, nearly all filled with firebreathing polemics against modern culture. Since Cram's death in 1942, historians have dismissed him as an elitist crank, a reactionary in art and politics. In doing so, they have oversimplified Cram's lifelong work and overlooked its connections with the wider antimodern response to the crisis of cultural authority. (p. 203)

Cram's essay ["**On the Restoration of Idealism,**" first pub-

lished in 1893], set forth ideas he repeated and elaborated the rest of his life. During the Middle Ages, he assumed, a superior art had been rooted in a vital religious community; the modern decay of art resulted from the double destruction of religion and communal life. Though "the change from the spirit of the fourteenth to that of the sixteenth century came soft and unnoticed," its consequences were incalculable. By the nineteenth century, the West had fallen prey to "a riot of individualism" in artistic as well as intellectual and economic life. Yet Cram insisted that a "restoration of idealism" was underway. Pointing to Wagner, the English medievalists, and the Anglo-Catholic revival, he argued that the restoration would gather strength and power, "until at last, when that chaos has come which is the *reductio ad absurdum* of current individualism, the restored system of idealism shall quietly take its place, to build on the wide ruins of a mistaken civilization a new life more in harmony with law and justice."

Like other antimodernists, Cram found alternatives to modern fragmentation in traditional Japan as well as medieval Europe. He visited Japan in 1900 and celebrated its culture in *Impressions of Japanese Architecture and the Allied Arts* (1905). Japanese art, in Cram's view, reflected the same communal religious feeling embodied in the Gothic cathedral. But Westernizing influences, by pulling up the roots of Japanese culture, were destroying the sources of art. Beauty was disappearing from modernizing Japan. "In three centuries we have sold our birthright for a mess of pottage," Cram wrote. "Japan bartered hers in less than forty years."

Even if Japanese art had been flourishing, it was still too remote from Western Christianity to represent a directly inspiriting example. Instead, Cram declared, antimodern idealists must turn to the Middle Ages. In scores of polemics published between the turn of the century and World War I, Cram presented medieval Europe as an aesthetic, religious, and social paradise lost where all men were artists, all women revered, and all social classes bound in an "organic," deferential social order.

Ironically, Cram's medievalist fantasies animated an increasingly successful architectural career. During the early years of the twentieth century, his firm steadily built a national reputation, winning contracts with West Point, Princeton, and the Episcopal Diocese of New York. His assaults on modern culture continued. His Gothic architectural designs allowed him to join his polemical concerns with his professional role. Seeking his father's vocation through aesthetic achievement, Cram proclaimed "the ministry of art" and spiritualized his work in Platonic terms as an effort to achieve absolute Beauty. Like republican and Ruskinian moralists before him, Cram held that aesthetics and morality were inseparable. In general, "the unbeautiful or the ugly thing is the thing of the wrong or evil shape, whether in art or religion, philosophy, government, or the social fabric."

Cram's aesthetic emphasis betrayed a new relation between art and morality. He departed from the conventional insistence that art must justify itself as uplift. In his view, one did not proceed from absolute moral principles to an evaluation of art. Instead one reversed the procedure: aesthetic judgments preceded and shaped moral judgments. Beauty was an infallible gauge of moral worth.

Cram's developing outlook undergirded aestheticism, Ruskinian moralism, and Platonic idealism with Anglo-Catholic theology. He embraced Anglo-Catholicism because he believed its liturgy embodied the mysterious essence of faith and the hopeful possibility of mediation. In all, he felt, Anglo-Catholicism preserved the emotional legacy of the medieval church. Cram declared that "nothing could be less formal and less abstract" than the creed of the medieval cathedral builders. "It was ardent love for Christ, passionate affection for Our Lady or for some special one of the thousands of Saints under whose personal protection the Church or town or guild had been placed, that determined the quality and beauty of each church," he wrote in 1918. His insistence on the nonrational nature of belief shaped his definition of "the first desideratum of a church"; it was "that, so far as man is concerned, . . . he shall be filled with the righteous sense of awe and mystery and devotion." His religious attitudes allied him with intuitionalist thinkers of the late nineteenth century. He admired William James, and considered Bergson "the greatest philosopher, perhaps, since Thomas Aquinas."

The yoking of Bergson and Aquinas would have perplexed theologians and Bergsonians alike; it suggested that Cram's sacramentalism contained contradictory tendencies. On the one hand he insisted that the Gothic architect, like the priest performing sacred ritual, was engaged in an effort to communicate the incommunicable. On the other hand his exaltation of intuition, shadow, and mystery was bounded by a determination to live and build in accord with Thomistic Natural Law. If the Gothic cathedral's decorations reflected popular emotion, its structural integrity embodied scholastic logic. In his writings, Cram paid frequent homage to the "system of exact thought" devised by Aquinas; in his buildings, he mobilized every available technical resource in an effort to re-create "the most physically complicated style" in Gothic structures like St. John the Divine. Cram's sacramental syntheses joined intuition and rationality, primitivism and professionalism.

Ignoring intellectual inconsistencies, Cram claimed a sacramental purpose for his architectural work. He rejected the arguments of Louis Sullivan and Frank Lloyd Wright for a "national style" because they implied the unified civilization which America lacked. Yet he assaulted uninformed eclecticism for producing "a riot of aesthetic debauchery." Formalism, whether modernist or eclectic, was "an ingenius [sic] but insignificant game." Instead, Cram advocated what might be called a sacramental eclecticism. Admitting that Gothic was out of harmony with modern institutions, he opposed its use for banks, railway stations, office buildings, even (at times) nonliturgical churches. But for ritualized religion and traditional education—both "blazing anachronisms"—Gothic could serve as a "visible protest . . . against their eternal enemy, the new paganism." By replacing meeting houses with cathedrals, by symbolizing the continuing resistance of medieval scholastic traditions against professionalizing tendencies in education, Cram hoped to preserve the seeds of a

"Gothic restoration." He liked to think he stood "a vigil at arms," awaiting the collapse of the modern world.

The coming of World War I spurred Cram's polemical zeal and sharpened his political concerns. From the beginning, his writing had shown incipient parallels with the developing European critique of mass society. Like Emile Durkheim and Ferdinand Tönnies, Cram looked hopefully toward intermediate social groups as mediators between the individual and the state—a political parallel to his religious faith in sacramental mediation between man and God. Cram's wartime essays expressed his hopes for social mediation in more proscriptive, programmatic form. He began to exalt medieval society because it seemed to embody his ideal of decentralized communalism. "The Middle Ages had nothing of imperialism about them; Cecil Rhodes or J. P. Morgan or Kaiser Wilhelm would have perished of inaction," Cram wrote in 1918. Antedating Renaissance absolutism, Cram's Middle Ages were marked by the vitality of parish, family, and guild. Individuals were subordinated to "small groups of human scale." Medieval art reflected medieval society. Its originality derived not from idiosyncratic license but from "liberty made real and secure by obedience." Cram's social views, like those of Arts and Crafts leaders, reflected both communitarian ideals and class anxieties about social mobility in a mass democracy.

Drawing on Morris, Kropotkin, and the English distributist Arthur Penty, Cram presented his blueprint for social salvation in *Walled Towns* (1919). Need was urgent, for the war had "brought modernism to an end." Cram claimed he was trying to imagine a preindustrial New England village with a warmer, lovelier religion. His walled town was founded on the patriarchal family and an established sacramental church. He proposed the barring of "incompetents" from government, education, medicine, and the arts; the restoration of a guild system geared to "production for use" rather than profit; the abolition of usury and the "unearned increment" on land; the revival of sumptuary laws; and (somehow) "the elimination of artificial desires which tend to turn much human energy to futile ends." The key to regeneration, Cram stressed, was not the shuffling of economic arrangements but a "new spiritual energy" released by sacramentalism. By insisting on a sacramental justification for beauty, Cram allayed the scruples he felt toward luxury and artifice. Using a new sacramentalist vocabulary, his utopian writings bespoke traditional republican fears of overcivilization.

Walled Towns was not Cram's final statement. Toward the end of his life, he flirted with fascism, denouncing democracy in Seward Collins's *American Review*, filling his arguments with Spenglerian contrasts between premodern "culture" and modern "civilization." Yet Cram remained a decentralist. He applauded the New Deal's Resettlement Administration and other "back to the land" movements of the 1930s; he claimed intellectual kinship with Lewis Mumford, the Nashville Agrarians, and other critics of industrial society. Still a prolific designer, he remained hopeful that his buildings not only symbolized a dissent from modernity, but also heralded a post-modern spiritual revival.

In the 1930s as in the 1890s, Cram's antimodernism was a response to cultural dilemmas which had first surfaced during the late nineteenth century. Rising to sacramental heights, his polemics were rooted in traditional republican fears of luxury. From his earliest essays, he assaulted modern culture for its deification of "purely material and enervating bodily comfort." He hoped that the First World War might purify an overcivilized Western world, and in **Walled Towns** he warned that "the suffocating qualities of gross luxuriance are sometimes more fatal than the desperate sensations of danger, adversity, and shame." The vision of a flaccid "mass man," morally enervated and glutted with convenience, haunted Cram throughout his career.

Scarred by elitism, Cram's dissent nevertheless articulated widespread and still unresolved dissatisfactions. His faith in sacramental mediation spoke to widespread feelings of moral and spiritual impotence. For the politically impotent, he had less to offer. In formulating his decentralist alternatives, he revealed a concern for salvaging personal morality and an indifference to lower-class powerlessness—qualities shared by many European critics of mass society. The growth of giant organizations, Cram charged, had reduced the individual to "a negligible point in a vast and abstract proposition where all personal relationship, personal duty, personal obligation are impossible." He urged the renovation of the "small, manageable, and personal group," not to empower people rendered politically helpless, but to restore in them a sense of individual moral responsibility. Like the post-World War II sociologists for whom the "community" and the "voluntary association" became panaceas, Cram remained insensitive to class domination in capitalist societies. Yet his political aims, though narrow, were not trivial.

Cram's sacramental eclecticism embodied an equally important purpose: the regeneration of traditional Christian symbols amid a corrosive eclecticism. The late-Victorian concern with archaeological correctness represented a general reaction against the devaluation of symbols, but Cram fought that process more explicitly by insisting that Gothic be used only for appropriate institutions. Like Jung, Cram understood the importance of inherited cultural symbols. "Without these, men cannot live, nor can society endure," he wrote in 1918. His polemical efforts involved far more than a crusade for "good taste"; they were a protest against the symbolic impoverishment of a secularizing culture. And, unlike Jung, Cram knew that the revaluation of Christian symbols was not enough. Christian belief had to undergird them. Cram's Anglo-Catholic commitments reinforced and completed his antimodern dissent.

An irony remained. Cram's sacramental rationale for his professional role concealed entangling alliances with modernity. Against the background of his busy firm, his primitivist pretensions sometimes seemed a little hollow. When he designed the chapel at Whitehall, his country estate, in 1910, he claimed that "the guiding idea was to think and work as would pious but quite ignorant peasants who knew nothing about architecture. . . ." The affectation was apparent. Cram knew a great deal about architecture—both as an art and as a business. Though he sought to emulate the medieval artist's service to God, he often resembled the Renaissance artist, whom he stigmatized as a "mouthpiece and servant" of wealth. Indeed, Cram sustained an exceptionally warm relationship with the patronage establishment. He refused to recognize that his patrons may have preferred Gothic for reasons different from his own, refused to acknowledge that he often designed premodern buildings to house modern institutions. Clinging to his sacramental self-justification, Cram overlooked the indissoluble links between "Gothic" institutions and the commercial society he professed to despise.

However entangled with bourgeois institutions, Cram's Anglo-Catholic medievalism nevertheless generated a thoroughgoing corporatist critique of centrifugal liberalism. (pp. 201-09)

> *T. J. Jackson Lears, "The Religion of Beauty: Catholic Forms and American Consciousness," in his* No Place of Grace: Antimodernism and the Transformation of American Culture, 1880-1920, *Pantheon Books, 1981, pp. 183-215.*

Michael D. Clark   (essay date 1989)

[*In the excerpt below, Clark discusses Cram's aspiration to integrate Gothic and medieval values into twentieth-century American life.*]

"The true democracy of St. Louis, Edward I and Washington is forgotten," lamented the American architect Ralph Adams Cram in 1917 [in his **The Nemesis of Mediocrity**], "and a false democracy has taken its place. . . ." The assertion was no aberration of wartime hysteria, and was less eccentric in the early twentieth century than it would have been before or since. It gave pointed expression to a set of attitudes which had strong appeal to a significant number of Cram's countrymen, and which casts light on the perennial efforts of Americans to define their place in history and to balance the competing claims of tradition and innovation.

Most directly, Cram's comment reflects the vogue for the Middle Ages which flourished on both sides of the Atlantic during the half century and more preceding World War I, drawing on late Romantic sentiment, serious historical interest, and no doubt a need to deny or ennoble an often squalid and troubling industrial civilization. Among its manifestations were the emulation of chivalric values, the rediscovery or even brazen invention of medieval "traditions," and in architecture, the Gothic Revival.

Celebration of the Middle Ages was natural enough in Europe, but in some ways seems anomalous in the United States. Some American historians tirelessly traced their country's Old World roots, but Frederick Jackson Turner's "frontier thesis" more effectively captured the national imagination by lending scholarly support to the myth of America as a new beginning in the world. To be physically removed from the site of medieval civilization and its surviving monuments made it easy to feel historical experience sharply truncated, and for many the Middle

Ages stood for all of the cultural baggage that American immigrants had happily left behind.

Yet many others wholeheartedly succumbed to the appeal of the past. In 1908, indeed, Van Wyck Brooks wondered sardonically if anyone in the world felt the sentiment of tradition more keenly than the American. If much of this sentiment centred on the Middle Ages, one well-understood reason is that of cultural colonialism. Americans imitated Europeans who imitated the Gothic; they followed European architectural authorities like Augustus Charles Pugin, John Ruskin, and Eugène Emmanuel Viol-let-le-Duc, and they designed college quadrangles in imitation of Oxford and Cambridge. Among those most susceptible to the charms of the Gothic were members of old northeastern families who viewed the upstart millionaires and immigrant masses of the post-Civil War period with equal distaste as threats to their position and values. Such "alienated patricians" were wont to complain bitterly of the shallowness and vulgarity of modern American life, and apt to locate in the Middle Ages the standards of faith and beauty by which they reproached the present [Van Wyck Brooks, *The Wine of the Puritans: A Study of Present-Day America*].

Another, less noticed, aspect of American neo-medievalism was evinced by certain writers, particularly historians and critics of Gothic architecture, who identified

St. Thomas's Church, New York City.

certain phases of medieval life directly with American values. Those who felt this affinity were certainly not removed from European influences, and usually not lacking in the impulse to beat modern America with the stick of history, but they went farther by finding in the Middle Ages a special foreshadowing of the American experience, the embodiment, even, of America's truest self.

In the country's best-known champion of the Middle Ages, Henry Adams, this Americanizing tendency was an undercurrent. Adams, of course, compared the thirteenth century to the twentieth with sharply opposed abstractions and symbols: unity and diversity, the Virgin and the Dynamo. Yet the qualities which Adams exalted in the Middle Ages were not those most alien to his own time; they were ones which Anglo-American Edwardians, if they did not possess them, might at least yearn to embrace. The Middle Ages were not, in Adams' rendition, gloomy, monkish, otherworldly, or oppressed by the weight of tradition; they were rather a time of youth, passion and dynamism. In some ways, despite Adams' anti-modern stance, they were strikingly modern: "the nineteenth century moved fast and furious, so that one who moved in it felt sometimes giddy, watching it spin;" he noted, "but the eleventh moved faster and more furiously still" [Henry Adams, *Mont-Saint-Michel and Chartres*].

The comment was characteristic hyperbole, but Adams portrayal of the Middle Ages contained themes which were already mainstays of American commentary: (1) an insistence on the radically innovative, untraditionalist character of the High Middle Ages, as suggested by Adams' description of the twelfth century "greed for novelty"; (2) a vision of the period as one of liberation, represented by Adams in the spiritual or psychological release offered by the Virgin Mary for "the whole unutterable fury of human nature beating itself against the walls of its prison house," but capable of more mundane interpretations; and (3) a motif of popular enthusiasm and participation, demonstrated especially by the townspeople who took part in the building of the Gothic cathedrals. (pp. 195-97)

The most complex expression of such views . . . was probably that of Ralph Adams Cram (1863-1942). Like Henry Adams, whose *Mont-Saint-Michel and Chartres* he called a "revelation" in his preface to the work, Cram could make sense of history only by tracing a six-hundred year declension from medieval glories, and he lived to append to Adams's sad tale another generation of war and depression. Yet the younger man was far more hopeful that the medieval spirit could be rekindled. It was after all, he thought, simply an older and deeper Americanism.

This credo followed with some logic from Cram's leadership in the later phases of the Gothic Revival in the United States. Entering his profession during a period he considered architecturally worse than the Dark Ages, he discerned rays of hope in a few structures like H. H. Richardson's Trinity Church in Boston. Trinity, he recalled, "somehow linked us up with tradition and the great world of the past, giving us a new basis on which we could work." John Ruskin's advocacy of an honest architecture in the service of God and the Pre-Raphaelite revival of religious art gave further encouragement, though Cram later taxed the Pre-Raphaelites with artificiality [in his *My Life in Architecture*]. Ironically, it was his fate to fall under similar stricture. Although he claimed to eschew an "archaeological" revival of the Gothic, and sought to recover the tradition in order to build upon it creatively and in synthesis with the contemporary spirit, it is precisely the sin of archaeology of which many modern critics have found him guilty. Yet Cram is widely conceded an impressive achievement within the bounds which he set for himself; a recent study, for instance, credits him and his followers with giving the Gothic "a stature it had not enjoyed since the Middle Ages."

Cram felt keenly the need to justify the revival of the Gothic in the modern United States, however. This was not merely an aesthetic problem. Cram was temperamentally and intellectually the partisan of what he conceived to be medieval values against those of modernity; at the same time he shared wholeheartedly in the American patriotism natural to one of his genteel New England upbringing. His task was to join medieval to American tradition while dissociating both from the ills of modern America.

Despite the inherent difficulties of this project, Cram's philosophical position changed little over the course of his career. At bottom, his was the familiar quest of the true Tory for a third way between the terrible disorders of capitalism and the even worse disorders of the various radical alternatives. In his youth he espoused both monarchism and Christian socialism, and belonged for a time to a Jacobite society. Although such enthusiasms eventually drained off into less quixotic channels, their religious impulse remained. He found post-Tridentine Roman Catholicism incompletely acceptable theologically, but as an Episcopalian convert (from his minister-father's Unitarianism) he considered himself an Anglo-Catholic, in league with Rome against the Protestants. Reformation joined Renaissance and Revolution in the litany of infamy with which he attempted to account for the failure of western civilization.

The First World War, while it did not fundamentally alter Cram's point of view, necessarily appeared to him as the confirmation of his worst fears: how shocking for the catastrophist to find out that he is right! Like so many others, he hoped that the war would accomplish a great purging that would make possible a restoration of true Christian civilization, but to the architect the image of Reims Cathedral, "the noblest church in Christendom," damaged by German gunfire was enough to chasten optimism [*Heart of Europe*]. It did nothing to lessen his intellectual and emotional engagement, however; on the contrary, the war was the catalyst for his most impassioned efforts to wrest meaning from history.

This search for meaning began with a respect for tradition which coloured all of Cram's judgements, aesthetic or political. It contributed notably, for example, to his enthusiasm for the architecture of Japan, where the visitor could see how a particular style had evolved over the span of twelve hundred years [*Impressions of Japanese Architecture and the Allied Arts*]. Conversely, although he pro-

fessed to welcome modernist "eclecticism and opportunism" as a possible seedbed for a more stable future, he charged the modern artist with denying "beauty in any sense that permits of definition and maintains through the ages continuity and substantial identity." In the Empire State Building he could still discern a strand of "the cord of continuity that reached unbroken from the art of 3000 B.C."; Radio City, on the other hand, struck him as an "apotheosis of megalomania" which defied all precedent and tradition. As in art, so in society at large. Cram endorsed the Burkean principle that those who would not look back to their ancestors would not look forward to their posterity. Good government was government which followed custom and the common law, preserving continuity and tradition [*The Catholic Church and Art*].

Yet the idea of *unbroken* tradition was ultimately unsatisfactory to Cram—not only for its failure to explain the actual course of history, one infers, but because of its uncomfortable resemblance to what he called the nineteenth century dogma of "evolutionary progress." Continuous process, whether viewed as slowly changing tradition or as gradual progress, seemed to reduce history to determinism and to preclude the intervention of the transcendent—for Cram a most important possibility.

Cram accordingly and markedly qualified his traditionalism by emphasizing the sudden emergence of Gothic architecture in the Middle Ages. He described the style in 1904 as "utterly unlike anything that had gone before, confessing in its ancestry far less kinship with the Norman, Romanesque, and Lombard it had discomfited and destroyed, than was so easily traceable between Greek and Egyptian, Byzantine and Roman, for example." The Gothic, "when it had fully found itself, was utterly without psychological or structural antecedents," he concluded. Although he later tacitly modified this judgement, Cram continued to regard the Gothic as a sudden, almost miraculous mutation from previous styles. This interpretation served as much a didactic as a descriptive purpose. Gothic was for him not merely a style of architecture but "the trumpet blast of an awakening world," signifying the triumph of Christianity and human self-knowledge—an "utter emancipation" from the paganism, heresy, and darkness of the Dark Ages [*The Gothic Quest,* rev. ed.]. The kind of liberation that Americans had been wont to associate with the Pilgrims or the Patriots of 1776 was thus pushed back five or six hundred years.

Generalizing from the rapid emergence of the Gothic, and struck too by the "baffling fact" that the earliest human civilization seemed suddenly to have emerged as a completely articulated society rather than as a result of steady development [*Convictions and Controversies*], Cram arrived at a cyclical theory of history. Evolution was balanced in the "cosmic process" by devolution, he hypothesized. But the cycle moved unevenly; its "upward drive" was swift, for each era of civilization began with a great burst of energy. The downside was more languid. Probably because of his central concern with the easily bisected millennium of the Middle Ages, Cram thought that he described a law of history in a five-hundred-year cycle from one upswing to the next. In company with the Adams brothers and others, he viewed the events of the early twentieth century as marking the exhaustion of one wave of creative energy and the gathering of the forces of the next [*Towards the Great Peace*].

The cyclical scheme allowed Cram to realize a kind of compromise between the continuity of tradition and the discontinuity of creative vigor. It was a natural solution for a Gothic Revivalist who as an American was also heir to an anti-traditionalist tradition which insisted upon the virtue of the fresh start. It accorded as well with Cram's conviction of the timeless, transcendent beauty of the Gothic by making this beauty perennially accessible. That which is timeless can have, in the literal sense, no antecedents, and of course can never be outdated. If the energy of one wave of history miscarried, one could recover its object on the next. Although the Gothic had succumbed to the Renaissance and Reformation, it was not truly dead. In Cram's own figure it only slumbered at Avalon with King Arthur, and the architect believed that the moment of awakening was at hand [*Gothic Quest*].

Cram was sufficiently imbued with a nineteenth-century historicism and sense of evolution to doubt that medieval Gothic could simply be duplicated in the modern world, however. He did not view the style as a set of static forms; half its significance was its dynamism, and its expressions were accordingly manifold. Once regained, he acknowledged, the Gothic tradition could only be followed self-consciously until such time as it might burst "forth of its own impulse." We should return to the Gothic, he emphasized, only "for the sake of getting a fresh start." A living Gothic would adapt to at least the more congenial aspects of the contemporary world, and, he speculated, become as different from the fifteenth century style as the fifteenth was from the thirteenth.

Further, if the Gothic spirit was to take new root, it must have congenial soil. Cram believed that art, in the loose terminology of his day, was "racial"; that is, it expressed the "soul" of a people or nation. If the medieval and American souls resembled each other, so legitimately might their art; if they were mutually alien, the implication was, all Cram's work as a Gothic Revivalist was wasted effort. Clearly both would have to be very nicely defined.

The question, as Cram put it in 1905, was whether Americans were the spiritual successors of the Borgias and Medici, "or do we hark back to the mighty glories of Church and State in the thirteenth century in Italy, France, Germany, and England?" Cram's answer boldly spliced American to medieval tradition, while rooting the modern desecrations of both in the time of the Renaissance and Reformation.

For a scheme embracing medieval communes as well as modern democracies, a theory of the people was most basic. Cram developed in effect two theories, without bothering clearly to choose between them or to reconcile their mutual inconsistencies. One expressed an undisguised and vitriolic disgust with modern "mass-man"—a figure loosely influenced by José Ortega y Gasset. The crucial distinction, Cram wrote in *The American Mercury* in

1932, is "not between Neolithic Man and the anthropoid ape, but between the glorified and triumphant human being and the Neolithic mass which was, is now and ever shall be." "Neolithic Man" supplies "an endless flood of basic raw material," which flows on without change century after century, he argued. From this mass "fountains" those fine and exceptional personalities to whom Cram, in this mood, would have limited the claim to full humanity. If nothing else, this formulation enabled him to give scattershot vent to peeves and prejudices: "from the Australian 'blackfellow,' the writer of popular songs or the publisher of a tabloid newspaper to Akhnaton, Leonardo da Vinci, or Pope Leo XIII is a space that almost needs to be measured in astronomical terms," he mused.

While affording polemical satisfaction, this thesis of the exceptional man was too narrow to sustain Cram's rosy view of both medieval and traditional American society. His more considered solution postulated a vaguely defined medieval population of rural and urban "producers" as a healthy social base. "Mass-man," in this version, was not an historical constant but the result of the subversion of this society of producers. With the Renaissance, Cram wrote, power had become the chief object of life, and "a type of man emancipated from the restraints of religion, tradition and the sense of ethical and social responsibility" had consequently arisen. The "human scale" of the Middle Ages was supplanted by "Imperial Modernism," which from the fifteenth century on worked to eliminate essential distinctions among human beings and break the ties of their traditional relationships, so that it could group and order them mechanically [*End of Democracy, The Great Thousand Years; Great Peace*].

"Mass-man" embraced both the highest and lowest orders of society, it is to be noted. "Imperial Modernism" had fostered two new classes: an aggressive bourgeoisie sub-

---

An excerpt from *My Life in Architecture*

When I began my study of architecture with Rotch and Tilden in 1881, . . . its operating methods were primitive in the extreme. There were no blueprints, no typewriters, no telephones. Every drawing had to be traced by hand, sometimes repeatedly; all letters and specifications were written long-hand, and laboriously copied on flimsy paper by the use of water, blotting paper, and a hand press. The office boy ground the India ink in soapstone dishes, and the product was used until the natural process of decomposition resulted in so revolting a condition of things that a new supply was necessary. . . .

Of course, there was no heat in winter, or at best a putative and diminutive coal stove in one corner, while the floor was covered with layers of straw which, in cold weather, became clogged with snow and slush, thereby augmenting rather than decreasing the general discomfort.

Cram, in his My Life in Architecture, *Little, Brown, and Co., 1936.*

sisting on trade, usury, and management, and a sub-merged proletariat—both "non-producers" according to Cram's rather arbitrary definition. Modern "financial-technological civilization" remained similarly bifurcated: "the nether millstone is that of organized, proletarian labour, the upper is that of organized financial, industrial and commercial power."

Ground between was the "Forgotten Class." (If Cram was indebted to William Graham Sumner's "Forgotten Man" for the term, he did not acknowledge it.) Cram regarded this as essentially a middle class, but his definition of it was uncommonly broad, leaving one to wonder how such a large agglomeration could ever be forgotten. It included farmers, small businessmen, professionals, intellectuals, "small rentiers," even skilled and unskilled manual laborers, if non-union. The class descended from the medieval "producers," but it served in its modern context as simply a benign representation of "the people," shorn of such disagreeable, "adventitious adjuncts" as organized labor and powerful capitalists. In this country it stood, Cram summarized, for "the old, original Americanism" [*End of Democracy*].

With a basic social continuity established, Cram could present the Middle Ages as modern America's better self. Had twentieth century life become "a riot of individualism," threatened by its antithesis of collectivism? The High Middle Ages had managed to foster the growth of true individuality within a spirit of "real communism": "never before or since was personality developed so completely, nor the community of human interests so largely realized." Had industrial-technological civilization become a "Frankenstein Monster" spreading death and devastation? The Middle Ages, Cram pointed out, had had their own less menacing industrial economy. Did modern labour unions array the masses of workers against the power of capital? The medieval guild combined the interests of capital and labour without exploitation, maintained high standards of craftsmanship, and promoted fellowship and mutual aid. Even feminism, Cram seconded Henry Adams, had had its better medieval counterpart. While men of the Middle Ages flaunted the "glitter and show" of power, women often retained its substance. The result was "a certain feminine dominance," based on nothing so mundane as the suffrage but on superior spiritual qualities. [*Heart of Europe*].

It was a familiar game of social criticism: the past shamed the present; Eleanor of Aquitaine trumped Susan B. Anthony. Where Cram went most conspicuously beyond others of this bent was in his extraordinary, sustained claim for medieval democracy. True, historians of the school of Herbert Baxter Adams had traced the roots of liberty and democracy through the Middle Ages to the German forests. Of this "germ theory" of democratic contagion Cram barely took note, however, and when he did it was to argue that "the roots of liberty and free democratic government . . . are to be found far deeper in the old parish of the Medieval Church than in Parliament or folk-thing or shiremote." And Cram was far beyond looking for "roots" or "germs"; it was true democracy, he held, which had flourished in the Middle Ages, and what went by the name

in the twentieth century was at best a shabby counterfeit [*The Substance of the Gothic: Six Lectures on the Development of Architecture from Charlemagne to Henry VIII; End of Democracy*].

Those who have labelled Cram an antidemocrat have understandably not taken this interpretation very seriously, but clearly he valued his own conception of democracy highly to enshrine it in his favorite period of history. Making his case historically was another matter. His most plausible gambit was to identify democracy with decentralization of power, in contradistinction to the massive aggregates of "imperial modernism." "The essence of democracy is differentiation, local autonomy, and a building up of authority from primary units," he explained. More subtly, he associated democracy with art; naturally enough for an architect, his was at bottom more an aesthetic than an historical vision. Amid all the modern concern over the "rights of man," he thought, it was well to remember "the right to beauty in life and thought and environment," a right denied in the nineteenth and twentieth centuries. He was struck by the "curious fact" that the year 1828 in America had marked not only "the moment when the last traces of real beauty disappeared from architecture and the other arts and the fifty years' interlude of excruciating ugliness began," but also the election to the presidency of Andrew Jackson, avatar of the new and false democracy. By counter-association, Chartres and Reims became temples of the authentic democratic faith [*The Sins of the Fathers; Heart of Europe; Convictions and Controversies*].

Fundamentally, Cram contended that democracy consisted in substance rather than procedure—"not in miscellaneous machinery and vicissitudinous panaceas, but in certain ends of right and justice" [*The Substance of Gothic*]. Given this vague formulation, supported by equally vague historical evidence, Cram could argue summarily that the "feudalism" of the High Middle Ages

> came nearer a real democracy than any other of the manifold optimistic experiments of man, for it more nearly abolished privilege, established equal opportunity and utilized ability, while it fixed the means of production in the hands of the people, guaranteed a fairly even distribution of wealth, and organized workmen and craftsmen and artists on a just and equable basis of labour and compensation. . . . [*The Substance of Gothic*]

Cram acknowledged the existence of a traditional aristocracy and a servile class, but in between were his urban and rural producers, no "Forgotten Class" in the Middle Ages but "the proudest product of Christian civilization." There was even scope for the self-made man: "as through the Church, the schools and the cloister there was room for the son of a peasant to achieve the Papacy," he pointed out, "so through the guilds, chivalry, war and the court, the layman, if he possessed ability, might from an humble beginning travel far [*Great Peace*].

If this was an idealized picture of the Middle Ages, it was as much an idealized picture of the American past projected onto the earlier period. Cram believed both societies to have been based on cooperation and self-sufficiency, production for use rather than profit, and life in a "human scale" of small economic and social units. Personal and family experience suggested the association. In recalling "the unity of place and character" at his grandfather's rural New York home, Cram felt that he had glimpsed "a lingering episode out of the eighteenth century," which in turn followed much older patterns of life. In memory and nostalgia, indeed, the ancestral hearth became a "last phase of . . . feudalism" [*Convictions and Controversies*].

To explain the connection historically, however, Cram had to rescue the American Founding Fathers, post-medieval men as they so clearly were, from the taint of the intervening centuries. As the political absolutism born of the Renaissance had grown intolerable, he supposed, the ideals of medieval freedom had appeared in a new guise in the eighteenth and early nineteenth centuries. The Declaration of Independence, the Tennis Court Oath which committed members of the National Assembly to the initial and more moderate phase of the French Revolution, and the British parliamentary reform laws held brief sway as expressions of true democracy. Like its medieval counterpart, this was a democracy underpinned by gentlemanly leadership and based on contract. (The same contractual principle operated, Cram believed, in the modern constitutional covenants as in the relationship of lord and vassal, king and people, even seigneur and serf.) Most fundamental of all was the quality of "spiritual liberty" which Cram ascribed to medieval political theory, issuing in the principle that "all men are free and equal before God and the Law" [*Nemesis of Mediocrity; End of Democracy; Great Peace*].

With the loss of this sense of spiritual liberty, Cram thought, society had become enslaved to the "quantitative," materialistic standards of "mass-man," who like Herbert Marcuse's later "one-dimensional man," was so in thrall as to be even "unconscious of his own enslavement." A false democracy, pinning its hopes on universal suffrage and majority rule as the means of human perfectability in this world, naturally followed. Occasionally, especially in the period of the First World War, Cram muddied his analysis with a racial argument, evincing the usual anxiety for the fate of "pure blood" where democratization let down "the just and normal barriers of race. . . ." Racial amalgamation combined with capitalism, proletarianization, egalitarianism, and the loss of spiritual qualities to produce—Cram's indictment of modernity ended in a cliché of twentieth century social criticism—"the reign of mediocrity."

Crabbed and desperate as he sometimes sounded, Cram was never without hope. With World War I he was more than ever convinced that an epoch was ending and an "entirely new world" in the offing. It was a new world which he dared hope would be built on the restoration of an old tradition. He professed to see signs of a "startling and anomalous return to Medievalism," for which his "Gothic Quest" offered a starting point. The Gothic was no less than "the title-deed to our inheritance," and with its recovery a new architecture, proclaiming a new society,

would become possible [*Substance of Gothic; Convictions and Controversies; The Ministry of Art*].

While Cram's model for art was the Gothic cathedral, his model for society was the monastery. By monasticism he meant simply the freely associated community, self-sufficient and cooperative, separated from "the world," and centred on a religious ideal. A modern monasticism, he believed, would be based on associations of families rather than communities of celibates. Families would combine in "Walled Towns," a term which he used for its historical and metaphorical values rather than as a literal description. Entering "into a communal but not by any means 'communistic' life," the inhabitants of the Walled Towns would create islands of simple and joyful living in the midst of the larger world. There were to be none of the excesses of Fourier, Owen, Henry George, or the Shakers, he emphasized; the preservation of individuality, private property and of course the family itself would be fundamental to the scheme [*Great Thousand Years; Walled Towns*].

"Communal life conceived in the human scale" is a recurring dream in western history, of course, and one of countless permutations. In his own time Cram found kindred spirits in such writers as Nicholas Berdyaeff and Salvador de Madariaga, in the English Distributists G. K. Chesterton and Hilaire Belloc, and in the Southern Agrarians of his own country. His difficulty in finding a practical embodiment for the "Walled Town" confirmed the elusiveness of *Gemeinschaft* in the twentieth century, however. He had hopes during the 1930s that the New Deal's "subsistence homestead" programme or the corporate state of Italian Fascism would take up the "Mediaeval Sequence." (He rejected Bolshevism and National Socialism as having cut themselves off from the "living current of history") [*Great Thousand Years; Convictions and Controversies; Ministry of Art; My Life; End of Democracy*]. Needless to say, all such hopes went unfulfilled.

The "Mediaeval Sequence" was far from an inevitable choice for American traditionalists, but as interpreted by Ralph Adams Cram, at least, it met several basic requirements. First, in what seems a distinctly American approach, Cram invoked medieval tradition not as something predetermined or prescribed, but as freely chosen. Despite his cyclical theory of history, he was no determinist, and even amidst the shock and horror of World War I held the shape of the future to lie within the compass of human will. He seems to have understood tradition not so much in its Burkean sense as a continuous series of adjustments to experience, but as an array of options to be selected from the warehouse of history, as one of his professional clients might have chosen a Colonial, Tudor, or Gothic Revival style of house. The American's very paucity of native tradition could equip him better to choose that which suited him.

Second, tradition had to be usable. As dubious as his understanding of history often was, Cram never proposed to recover the Middle Ages, but only a medieval tradition which he was convinced could be as instrumental in serving contemporary needs as one of his neo-Gothic churches was in housing Christian worship. Tradition so conceived represented certainly not the dead weight of the past; there was in it a pragmatic and even, despite Cram's distrust of the term, a progressive element. But to be usable in the United States, medieval tradition had to be Americanized, and so Cram stretched history to show the Middle Ages as liberating, innovative, and democratic.

Finally, for Cram, tradition was not an end in itself, but the bearer of transcendence. A pure traditionalism yields no final or timeless answers; its authority is that of past experience and it looks only to future experience as a corrective. But Americans (not uniquely) appear most comfortable in invoking past experience when they can associate it with universal or transcendent principles: Christians defining the one true tradition of the church, distressed agrarians or classical liberals invoking a golden age when timeless economic laws prevailed, Thomas Jefferson (influenced by Blackstone and others) identifying Anglo-Saxon allodial land tenure with natural law. Cram valued medieval tradition because he believed that it led to an aesthetic and spiritual revelation of universal import, best expressed in the Gothic cathedral. The "sacramental philosophy" of the Middle Ages truly made matter the vehicle of the spirit, he argued [*Convictions and Controversies; Sins of the Fathers; Gold, Frankincense and Myrrh*]; thus a monument of stone and glass could transcend the work of generations of masons and glaziers. The Gothic cathedral was the product of centuries of architectural experience, yet it was unlike anything that had gone before. Continuity made possible the moment of discontinuity which escaped all limitations of time and place. (pp. 200-13)

Michael D. Clark, "Ralph Adams Cram and the Americanization of the Middle Ages," in Journal of American Studies, *Vol. 23, No. 2, August, 1989, pp. 195-213.*

FURTHER READING

Bibliography

Frank, Frederick S. "Gothic Authors and Works." In his *Through the Pale Door: A Guide to and through the American Gothic,* pp. 1-265. New York: Greenwood Press, 1990.
   Selective bibliography of American Gothic literature that includes an entry on *Black Spirits and White,* listing the original and reprint editions. Frank characterizes several of the stories in the volume as "traditionally Gothic in their use of horrible interiors" and compares "The Dead Valley" favorably with stories by Edgar Allan Poe that utilize the theme of fatal allurement.

Biography

Maginnis, Charles D. "Ralph Adams Cram: An Appreciation by an Old Friend." *The Commonweal* XXXVII, No. 7 (4 December 1942): 162-64.
   Obituary tribute.

Williams, Michael. "Views and Reviews." *The Commonweal* XXXVI, No. 25 (9 October 1942): 592-93.

Reminiscence commending Cram's character.

Criticism

Allen, George H. "Cram—The Yankee Mediaevalist." *The Architectural Forum* LV, No. 1 (July 1931): 79-80.
   Enthusiastic, appreciative assessment of Cram's work and character.

Byrne, Barry. "Tangled Thinkers of Today." *The Commonweal* XIV, No. 5 (3 June 1931): 131-32.
   Response to "The Tangled Towers of Today" (cited below), suggesting that Cram's religious and social ideas are inappropriate in discussions of architecture.

"The Tangled Towers of Today." *The Commonweal* XIII, No. 25 (22 April 1931): 673-74.
   Discusses Cram's assessments of modern architecture, in particular, the skyscraper, noting Cram's insistence that architecture must serve social and religious purposes and that Gothic architecture does so best.

Lovecraft, H. P. "The Weird Tradition in America." In his *Supernatural Horror in Literature,* pp. 60-75. 1945. Reprint. New York: Dover Publications, 1973.
   Mentions that "in 'The Dead Valley,' the eminent architect and mediaevalist Ralph Adams Cram achieves a memorably potent degree of vague regional horror through subtleties of atmosphere and description."

Review of *The Nemesis of Mediocrity,* by Ralph Adams Cram. *North American Review* CCVII, No. 750 (May 1918): 771-73.
   Commends the force and directness with which Cram questions the aims and methods of modern democratic processes in *The Nemesis of Mediocrity.*

Rusk, W. S. Review of *The Ministry of Art,* by Ralph Adams Cram. *The Sewanee Review* XXIV, No. 2 (April 1916): 261-63.
   Notes that the collected essays and addresses of *The Ministry of Art* both document and advance the neo-Gothic movement in art and architecture.

Spitz, David. "The Incompetence of Democracy and of the Average Man." In his *Patterns of Anti-Democratic Thought: An Analysis and a Criticism, with Special Reference to the American Political Mind in Recent Times,* pp. 95-129. New York: Macmillan Co., 1949.
   Summarizes Cram's anti-democratic thought.

Stone, Geoffrey. "*The End of Democracy:* Ralph Adams Cram's Plea for a New Order." *American Review* 9, No. 3 (September 1932): 365-79.
   Examines Cram's theory that the American democratic system represents the decadence of a historical epoch, and considers his assessment of the Middle Ages "as the period most nearly perfect in form, and therefore a fit model for the age which will succeed the present one."

Tallmadge, Thomas E. "Mr. Cram's Brilliant but Unconvincing Scammon Lectures." *The Architectural Record* XLII, No. 11 (August 1917): 189-91.
   Reviews *Six Lectures on Architecture,* characterizing Cram's idiosyncratic pronouncements on Gothic architecture as eloquent but unconvincing.

———. "Eclecticism—1893-1917." In his *The Story of Architecture in America,* pp. 234-89. New York: W. W. Norton & Co., 1927.

Comments on Cram's influence as an architect and notes the controversial nature of his social theories, writing that "if the learned doctor could have his way he would have us living in walled towns, vassals of some baron or bishop, and we would be dragging the stones to the rising cathedral, yoked to wooden carts, chanting the *Dies Irae.*"

Tucci, Douglass Shand. "Ralph Adams Cram and Boston Gothic." In his *Built in Boston, City and Suburb: 1800-1950,* pp. 155-81. Boston: New York Graphic Society, 1978.

Includes discussion of Cram's role as a prominent Medievalist and mentions his literary works in an assessment of his principal Gothic structures in the Boston area.

White, James F. "Theology and Architecture in America: A Study of Three Leaders." In *A Miscellany of American Christianity: Essays in Honor of H. Shelton Smith,* edited by Stuart C. Henry, pp. 362-90. Durham, N.C.: Duke University Press, 1963.

Asserts that Cram's career represents the culmination of the Gothic Revival and survey's Cram's architectural and historical theories. White pronounces Cram instrumental in helping to develop "the demand for good art and architecture on the part of all sections of American Christianity" during the 1920s.

Williams, Michael. "Highly Provocative." *The Commonweal* XXVI, No. 17 (20 August 1937): 406-07.

Assesses Cram's theories of modern democracy in *The End of Democracy* as "a revival of traditional American beliefs" and commends the volume "as a significant document testifying to the fundamental character of our social crisis."

John Galsworthy

1867-1933

(Also wrote under the pseudonym John Sinjohn) English novelist, dramatist, short story writer, poet, and essayist.

For further information on Galsworthy's career, see *TCLC,* Volume 1.

INTRODUCTION

An important literary figure of the early twentieth century, Galsworthy is best known as the author of *The Forsyte Saga,* a collection of novels and short stories that meticulously depicts upper-middle-class English life. *The Forsyte Saga* centers on the character of Soames Forsyte, a wealthy solicitor who values money and property above all else. Acknowledged as one of the most complex and intriguing figures in English literature, Soames is considered Galsworthy's most memorable creation.

Born on a family estate in Kingston Hill, Surrey, near London, Galsworthy was the second child of a wealthy family. His father was a successful solicitor who had financial interests in mining companies in Canada and Russia, and who later served as the model for Old Jolyon Forsyte in *The Forsyte Saga.* At the age of nine Galsworthy was sent to Saugeen Preparatory, a boarding school in Bournemouth. Five years later he entered the prestigious Harrow School in London, where he excelled in athletics. In 1886 he went to Oxford to study law, graduating with second degree honors in 1889. The following year he was admitted to the bar and began writing legal briefs for his father's firm. Galsworthy, however, had little interest in law. In 1891 his father sent him on an extended inspection tour of his mining interests in Canada, and during the next few years he traveled widely. While on a two-month voyage aboard the *Torrens* in 1893, he formed a close friendship with the first mate of the ship, Joseph Conrad, who was then at work on his first novel and who later encouraged and guided Galsworthy's own literary efforts. Between 1897 and 1901 Galsworthy published two novels and two volumes of short stories under the pseudonym John Sinjohn. The last of these works, *A Man of Devon,* contains the first short story dealing with the Forsytes.

After his father's death in 1904 Galsworthy began publishing under his own name. In 1906 the first "Forsyte" novel, *The Man of Property,* appeared, and a production of his play *The Silver Box* was favorably reviewed by critics. Throughout the early part of the century, his works continued to garner attention from critics and the public, and Galsworthy received several awards and honors. In 1917 he was offered a knighthood, which he declined; he later accepted the Order of Merit for his literary achievements. For twelve years he served as the first president of PEN, the international writers' organization. In 1932,

shortly before his death, Galsworthy was awarded the Nobel Prize in literature.

Galsworthy first achieved prominence as a dramatist. His most esteemed plays are noted for their realistic technique and insightful social criticism. While working for his father, Galsworthy collected rents from the tenants of London slum properties, and several of his plays examine the contrast between the rights of the privileged upper classes and the poor. In *The Silver Box,* for example, the son of a wealthy member of Parliament steals a purse from a prostitute. Later, the husband of one of the family's servants steals a cigarette box from the purse. While the wealthy young man is released, the servant's husband is convicted and sent to prison. *Justice* examines the practice of solitary confinement in prisons and has been credited with prompting Prime Minister Winston Churchill to introduce legislation for prison reforms. Although a few critics consider Galsworthy's social plays his most important works, most maintain that *The Forsyte Saga* is his most accomplished literary achievement.

Three novels and two short stories comprise *The Forsyte Saga. The Man of Property, In Chancery,* and *To Let* are linked by the short stories "Indian Summer of a Forsyte" and "Awakening." In *The Man of Property,* Soames Forsyte is introduced as a successful solicitor and investor who regards his wife, Irene, as one of his most cherished properties. Irene despises her husband and begins an affair with Philip Bosinney, an architect who has been commissioned to build a mansion for the Forsytes. After discovering his wife's infidelity, Soames takes revenge by ruining Bosinney financially and raping Irene. The architect later dies in a mysterious accident. In the next volume, *In Chancery,* Irene leaves Soames and marries Young Jolyon, with whom she has a son, Jon. Desperate for a male heir, Soames also remarries but has a daughter, Fleur. *To Let* focuses on the romance between Jon and Fleur. While Soames is agreeable to their relationship, Irene is still bitter about the past and persuades Jon to break off his engagement with Fleur. Jon complies and Fleur marries another man. The two stories that complete *The Forsyte Saga,* "Indian Summer of a Forsyte" and "Awakening," continue the story of Irene and Jon, respectively. With the wide critical and financial success of *The Forsyte Saga,* Galsworthy continued the story of the Forsytes in *A Modern Comedy,* another collection of novels and short fiction. While not as popular as *The Forsyte Saga,* the work nonetheless attracted a loyal following. Commentators have noted that while Galsworthy satirized the wealthy in his early works, he presented a more sympathetic view of the Forsytes in his later works, especially those collected in *A Modern Comedy.* Collectively the volume of short stories *On Forsyte 'Change, The Forsyte Saga* and *A Modern Comedy* have been referred to as "The Forsyte Chronicles."

After completing "The Forsyte Chronicles," Galsworthy began work on a novel trilogy, which was published posthumously as *End of the Chapter.* His other works include several volumes of short stories, essays, and poetry. Although Galsworthy's dramas and novels were highly regarded during his lifetime, their critical and popular repute declined abruptly after his death. In 1967 the British Broadcasting Corporation aired a twenty-six–hour serial adaptation of *The Forsyte Saga* for television. Repeated the following year and syndicated in more than forty countries, this adaptation is credited with renewing interest in Galsworthy's novels. Contemporary critics now recognize Galsworthy as an important chronicler of English life, with Sanford Sternlicht praising "The Forsyte Chronicles" as "the finest written portrait of the passing from power of England's upper middle class."

PRINCIPAL WORKS

From the Four Winds [as John Sinjohn] (short stories) 1897
Jocelyn [as John Sinjohn] (novel) 1898
Villa Rubein [as John Sinjohn] (novel) 1900
A Man of Devon [as John Sinjohn] (short stories) 1901
The Island Pharisees (novel) 1904
*The Man of Property (novel) 1906
The Silver Box (drama) 1906
The Country House (novel) 1907
Joy (drama) 1907
A Commentary (essays) 1908

Fraternity (novel) 1909
Strife (drama) 1909
Justice (drama) 1910
A Motley (essays) 1910
The Little Dream (drama) 1911
The Patrician (novel) 1911
The Eldest Son (drama) 1912
The Inn of Tranquillity: Studies and Essays (essays) 1912
Moods, Songs & Doggerels (poetry) 1912
The Pigeon (drama) 1912
The Dark Flower (novel) 1913
The Fugitive (drama) 1913
The Mob (drama) 1914
The Freelands (novel) 1915
The Little Man, and Other Satires (essays) 1915
A Sheaf (essays) 1916
Beyond (novel) 1917
Five Tales (short stories) 1918
Addresses in America (essays) 1919
Another Sheaf (essays) 1919
The Burning Spear (essays) 1919
Saint's Progress (novel) 1919
*Awakening (short story) 1920
*In Chancery (novel) 1920
The Skin Game (drama) 1920
Tatterdemalion (short stories) 1920
The Bells of Peace (poetry) 1921
*To Let (novel) 1921
The Forsyte Saga (novels and short stories) 1922
Loyalties (drama) 1922
Captures (short stories) 1923
The Works of John Galsworthy. 30 vols. (novels, dramas, essays, poetry, and short stories) 1923-36
Abracadabra, and Other Satires (essays) 1924
Old English (drama) 1924
†The White Monkey (novel) 1924
Caravan: The Assembled Tales of John Galsworthy (short stories) 1925
Escape (drama) 1926
†The Silver Spoon (novel) 1926
Verses New and Old (poetry) 1926
Castles in Spain (essays) 1927
†Two Forsyte Interludes: A Silent Wooing; Passers By (short stories) 1927
†Swan Song (novel) 1928
A Modern Comedy (novels and short stories) 1929
On Forsyte 'Change (short stories) 1930
‡Maid in Waiting (novel) 1931
Candelabra: Selected Essays and Addresses (essays) 1932
‡Flowering Wilderness (novel) 1932
‡Over the River (novel) 1933; also published as *One More River,* 1933
The Collected Poems of John Galsworthy (poetry) 1934
End of the Chapter (novels) 1934
Forsytes, Pendyces, and Others (short stories) 1935

---

*These works and the short story "Indian Summer of a Forsyte" from *Five Tales* (1918) were published as *The Forsyte Saga* in 1922.

†These works were published as *A Modern Comedy* in 1929.

‡These works were published as *End of the Chapter* in 1934.

Joseph Conrad   (essay date 1906)

[*A contemporary and friend of Galsworthy, Conrad is best known for* Lord Jim, Nostromo, *and* Heart of Darkness, *novels that examine the ambiguous nature of good and evil. In the following excerpt originally published in the London* Outlook *in 1906, he praises Galsworthy's perceptive observations about the middle-class English family.*]

When in the family's assembly at Timothy Forsyte's house there arose a discussion of Francie Forsyte's verses, Aunt Hester expressed her preference for the poetry of Shelley, Byron and Wordsworth, on the ground that, after reading the works of these poets, "one felt that one had read a book." And the reader of Mr. Galsworthy's latest volume of fiction, whether in accord or in difference with the author's view of his subject, would feel that he had read a book.

Beyond that impression one perceives how difficult it is to get critical hold of Mr. Galsworthy's work. He gives you no opening. Defending no obvious thesis, setting up no theory, offering no cheap panacea, appealing to no naked sentiment, the author of **The Man of Property** disdains also the effective device of attacking insidiously the actors of his own drama, or rather of his dramatic comedy. This is because he does not write for effect, though his writing will be found effective enough for all that. This book is of a disconcerting honesty, backed by a discouraging skill. There is not a single phrase in it written for the sake of its cleverness. Not one. Light of touch, though weighty in feeling, it gives the impression of verbal austerity, of a *willed* moderation of thought. The passages of high literary merit, so uniformly sustained as to escape the notice of the reader, expose the natural and logical development of the story with a purposeful progression which is primarily satisfying to the intelligence, and ends by stirring the emotions. In the essentials of matter and treatment it is a book of to-day. Its critical spirit and its impartial method are meant for a humanity which has outgrown the stage of fairy tales, realistic, romantic or even epic.

For the fairy tale, be it not ungratefully said, has walked the earth in many unchallenged disguises, and lingers amongst us to this day wearing, sometimes, amazingly heavy clothes. It lingers; and even it lingers with some assurance. Mankind has come of age, but the successive generations still demand artlessly to be amazed, moved and amused. Certain forms of innocent fun will never grow old, I suppose. But the secret of the long life of the fairy tale consists mainly in this, I suspect: that it is amusing to the writer thereof. Whatever public wants it supplies, it ministers first of all to his vanity in an intimate and delightful way. The pride of fanciful invention; the pride of that invention which soars (on goose's wings) into the empty blue is like the intoxication of an elixir sent by the gods above. And whether it is that the gods are unduly generous, or simply because the sight of human folly

amuses their idle malice, that sort of felicity is easier attained pen in hand than the sober pride, always mingled with misgivings, of a single-minded observer and conscientious interpreter of reality. This is why the fairy tale, in its various disguises of optimism, pessimism, romanticism, naturalism and what not, will always be with us. And, indeed, that is very comprehensible; the seduction of irresponsible freedom is very great; and to be tied to the earth (even as the hewers of wood and drawers of water are tied to the earth) in the exercise of one's imagination, by every scruple of conscience and honour, may be considered a lot hard enough not to be lightly embraced. This is why novelists are comparatively rare. But we must not exaggerate. This world, even if one is tied fast to its earthy foundations by the subtle and tyrannical bonds of artistic conviction, is not such a bad place to write fiction in. At any rate, we can know of no other; an excellent reason for us to try to think as well as possible of the world we do know.

In this world, whose realities are discovered, interpreted, commented on, criticized and exposed in works of fiction, Mr. Galsworthy selects for the subject-matter of his book the Family, an institution which has been with us as long, I should think, as the oldest and the least venerable pattern of fairy tale. As Mr. Galsworthy, however, is no theorist but an observer, it is a definite kind of family that falls under his observation. It is the middle-class family; and even with more precision, as we are warned in the subtitle, an upper middle-class family anywhere at large in space and time, but a family, if not exactly of to-day, then of only last evening, so to say. Thus at the outset we are far removed from the vagueness of the traditional "once upon a time in a far country there was a king," which somehow always manages to peep through the solemn disguises of fairy tales masquerading as novels with and without purpose. The Forsytes walk the pavement of London and own some of London's houses. They wish to own more; they wish to own them all. And maybe they will. Time is on their side. The Forsytes never die—so Mr. Galsworthy tells us, while we watch them assembling in old Jolyon Forsyte's drawing room on the occasion of June Forsyte's engagement to Mr. Bosinney, incidentally an architect and an artist, but, by the only definition that matters, a man of no property whatever.

A family is not at first sight an alarming phenomenon. But Mr. Galsworthy looks at the Forsytes with the individual vision of a novelist seeking his inspiration amongst the realities of this earth. He points out to us this family's formidable character as a unit of society, as a reproduction in miniature of society itself. It is made formidable, he says, by the cohesion of its members (between whom there need not exist either affection or even sympathy) upon a concrete point, the possession of property.

The solidity of the foundation laid by Mr. Galsworthy for his fine piece of imaginative work becomes at once apparent. For whichever came first, family or property, in the beginnings of social organization, or whether they came together and were indeed at first scarcely distinguishable from each other, it is clear that in the close alliance of these two institutions society has found the way of its development and nurses the hope of its security. In their sense of property the Forsytes establish the consciousness of their right and the promise of their duration. It is an instinct, a primitive instinct. The practical faculty of the Forsytes has erected it into a principle; their idealism has expanded it into a sort of religion which has shaped their notions of happiness and decency, their prejudices, their piety, such thoughts as they happen to have and the very course of their passions. Life as a whole has come to be perceptible to them exclusively in terms of property. Preservation, acquisition—acquisition, preservation. Their laws, their morality, their art and their science appear to them, justifiably enough, consecrated to that double and unique end. It is the formula of their virtue.

In this world of Forsytes (who never die) organized in view of acquiring and preserving property, Mr. Galsworthy (who is no inventor of didactic fairy tales) places with the sure instinct of a novelist a man and a woman who are no Forsytes, it is true, but whom he presents as in no sense the declared adversaries of the great principle of property. They only happen to disregard it. And this is a crime. They are simply two people to whom life speaks imperatively in terms of love. And this is enough to establish their irreconcilable antagonism and to precipitate their unavoidable fate. Deprived naturally and suddenly of the support of laws and morality, of all human countenance, and even, in a manner of speaking, of the consolations of religion, they find themselves miserably crushed, both the woman and the man. And the principle of property is vindicated. The woman being the weaker, it is in her case vindicated with consummate cruelty. For a peculiar cowardice is one of the characteristics of this great and living principle. Strong in the worship of so many thousands and in the possession of so many millions, it starts with affright at the slightest challenge, it trembles before mere indifference, it directs its heaviest blows at the disinherited who should appear weakest in its sight. Irene's fate is made unspeakably atrocious, no less—but nothing more. Mr. Galsworthy's instinct and observation serve him well here. In Soames Forsyte's town house, whose front door stands wide open for half an hour or so on a certain foggy night, there is no room for tragedy. It is one of the temples of property, of a sort of unholy religion whose fundamental dogma, public ceremonies and awful secret rites, forming the subject matter of this remarkable novel, take no account of human dignity. Irene, as last seen crushed and alive within the hopeless portals, remains for us a poignantly pitiful figure and nothing more.

This then, roughly and summarily, is the book in its general suggestion. Going on to particulars which make up the intrinsic value of a work of art, it rests upon the subtle and interdependent relation of Mr. Galsworthy's intellect and feelings which form his temperament, and reveals Mr. Galsworthy's very considerable talent as a writer—a talent so considerable that it commands at once our respectful attention. The foundation of this talent, it seems to me, lies in a remarkable power of ironic insight combined with an extremely keen and faithful eye for all the phenomena on the surface of the life he observes. These are the purveyors of his imagination, whose servant is a style clear, direct, sane, illumined by a perfectly unaffected sincerity. It is the style of a man whose sympathy with mankind is too genuine to allow him the smallest gratification of his vanity at the cost of his fellow creatures. In its moderation it is a style sufficiently pointed to carry deep his remorseless irony and grave enough to be the dignified vehicle of his profound compassion. Its sustained harmony is never interrupted by those bursts of cymbals and fifes which some deaf people acclaim for brilliance. Before all, it is a style well under control, and therefore it never betrays this tender and ironic writer into an odious cynicism of laughter or tears. For there are two kinds of cynicism, the cynicism of the hyena and the cynicism of the crocodile, which last, by the way, commands all sorts of respects from the inhabitants of these Isles. Mr. Galsworthy remains always a man, whether he is amused or moved.

I am afraid that my unavowed intention in writing about this book (of which I have talked so much and said so little) has been discovered by now. Therefore I confess. Confession—public, I mean—is good for one's conscience. Such is my intention. And it would be easier to carry out if I only knew exactly the motives which prompt people to read novels. But I do not know them all. Some of us, I understand, take up a novel to gratify a natural malevolence, the author being supposed to hold the mirror up to the odiously ridiculous nature of our next-door neighbour. From laboriously collected information I am, however, led to believe that most people read novels for amusement. This is as it should be. But, whatever be their motives, I entertain towards all novel-readers (for reasons which must remain concealed from the readers of this paper) the feelings of warm and respectful affection. I would not try to deceive them for worlds. Never! This being understood, I go on to declare, in the peace of my heart and the serenity of my conscience, that if they want amusement they will find it between the covers of this book. They will find plenty of it in this episode in the history of the Forsytes, where the reconciliation of a father and son, the dramatic and poignant comedy of Soames Forsyte's marital relations, and the tragedy of Bosinney's failure are exposed to our gaze with the remorseless yet sympathetic irony of Mr. Galsworthy's art, in the light of the unquenchable fire burning on the altar of property. They will find amusement, and perhaps also something more lasting—if they care for it. I say this with all the reserves and qualifications which strict truth requires around every statement of opinion. Mr. Galsworthy may possibly be found disappointing by some, but he will never be found futile by any one, and never uninteresting by the most exacting. I myself, for instance, am not so sure of Bosinney's tragedy. But this hesitation of my mind, for which the author may not be wholly responsible after all, need only be mentioned and no more, in the face of his considerable achievement. (pp. 125-31)

> *Joseph Conrad, "John Galsworthy," in his* Last Essays, *Doubleday, Page, & Company, 1926, pp. 125-31.*

John Galsworthy   (essay date 1909)

[*In the following essay, written in 1909 and originally published in* The Inn of Tranquillity *(1919), Galsworthy describes the elements that constitute "a good play."*]

A drama must be shaped so as to have a spire of meaning. Every grouping of life and character has its inherent moral; and the business of the dramatist is so to pose the group as to bring that moral poignantly to the light of day. Such is the moral that exhales from plays like *Lear, Hamlet,* and *Macbeth.* But such is not the moral to be found in the great bulk of contemporary Drama. The moral of the average play is now, and probably has always been, the triumph at all costs of a supposed immediate ethical good over a supposed immediate ethical evil.

The vice of drawing these distorted morals has permeated the Drama to its spine; discoloured its art, humanity, and significance; infected its creators, actors, audience, critics; too often turned it from a picture into a caricature. A Drama which lives under the shadow of the distorted moral forgets how to be free, fair, and fine—forgets so completely that it often prides itself on having forgotten.

Now, in writing plays, there are, in this matter of the moral, three courses open to the serious dramatist. The first is: To definitely set before the public that which it wishes to have set before it, the views and codes of life by which the public lives and in which it believes. This way is the most common, successful, and popular. It makes the dramatist's position sure, and not too obviously authoritative.

The second course is: To definitely set before the public those views and codes of life by which the dramatist himself lives, those theories in which he himself believes, the more effectively if they are the opposite of what the public wishes to have placed before it, presenting them so that the audience may swallow them like powder in a spoonful of jam.

There is a third course: To set before the public no cut-and-dried codes, but the phenomena of life and character, selected and combined, *but not distorted,* by the dramatist's outlook, set down without fear, favour, or prejudice, leaving the public to draw such poor moral as nature may afford. This third method requires a certain detachment; it requires a sympathy with, a love of, and a curiosity as to, things for their own sake; it requires a far view, together with patient industry, for no immediately practical result.

It was once said of Shakespeare that he had never done any good to any one, and never would. This, unfortunately, could not, in the sense in which the word "good" was then meant, be said of most modern dramatists. In truth, the good that Shakespeare did to humanity was of a remote, and, shall we say, eternal nature; something of the good that men get from having the sky and the sea to look at. And this partly because he was, in his greater plays at all events, free from the habit of drawing a distorted moral. Now, the playwright who supplies to the public the facts of life distorted by the moral which it expects, does so that he may do the public what he considers an immediate good, by fortifying its prejudices; and the dramatist who supplies to the public facts distorted by his own advanced morality, does so because he considers that he will at once benefit the public by substituting for its worn-out

ethics, his own. In both cases the advantage the dramatist hopes to confer on the public is immediate and practical.

But matters change, and morals change; men remain—and to set men, and the facts about them, down faithfully, so that they draw for us the moral of their natural actions, may also possibly be of benefit to the community. It is, at all events, harder than to set men and facts down, as they ought, or ought not to be. This, however, is not to say that a dramatist should, or indeed can, keep himself and his temperamental philosophy out of his work. As a man lives and thinks, so will he write. But it is certain, that to the making of good drama, as to the practice of every other art, there must be brought an almost passionate love of discipline, a white-heat of self-respect, a desire to make the truest, fairest, best thing in one's power; and that to these must be added an eye that does not flinch. Such qualities alone will bring to a drama the selfless character which soaks it with inevitability.

The word "pessimist" is frequently applied to the few dramatists who have been content to work in this way. It has been applied, among others, to Euripides, to Shakespeare, to Ibsen; it will be applied to many in the future. Nothing, however, is more dubious than the way in which these two words "pessimist" and "optimist" are used; for the optimist appears to be he who cannot bear the world as it is, and is forced by his nature to picture it as it ought to be, and the pessimist one who cannot only bear the world as it is, but loves it well enough to draw it faithfully. The true lover of the human race is surely he who can put up with it in all its forms, in vice as well as in virtue, in defeat no less than in victory; the true seer he who sees not only joy but sorrow, the true painter of human life one who blinks nothing. It may be that he is also, incidentally, its true benefactor.

In the whole range of the social fabric there are only two impartial persons, the scientist and the artist, and under the latter heading such dramatists as desire to write not only for to-day, but for to-morrow, must strive to come.

But dramatists being as they are made—past remedy—it is perhaps more profitable to examine the various points at which their qualities and defects are shown.

The plot! A good plot is that sure edifice which slowly rises out of the interplay of circumstance on temperament, and temperament on circumstance, within the enclosing atmosphere of an idea. A human being is the best plot there is; it may be impossible to see why he is a good plot, because the idea within which he was brought forth cannot be fully grasped; but it is plain that *he is a good plot.* He is organic. And so it must be with a good play. Reason alone produces no good plots; they come by original sin, sure conception, and instinctive after-power of selecting what benefits the germ. A bad plot, on the other hand, is simply a row of stakes, with a character impaled on each—characters who would have liked to live, but came to untimely grief; who started bravely, but fell on these stakes, placed beforehand in a row, and were transfixed one by one, while their ghosts stride on, squeaking and gibbering, through the play. Whether these stakes are made of facts or of ideas, according to the nature of the dramatist who planted them, their effect on the unfortunate characters is the same; the creatures were begotten to be staked, and staked they are! The demand for a good plot, not unfrequently heard, commonly signifies: "Tickle my sensations by stuffing the play with arbitrary adventures, so that I need not be troubled to take the characters seriously. Set the persons of the play to action, regardless of time, sequence, atmosphere, and probability!"

Now, true dramatic action is what characters do, at once contrary, as it were, to expectation, and yet because they have already done other things. No dramatist should let his audience know what is coming; but neither should he suffer his characters to act without making his audience feel that those actions are in harmony with temperament, and arise from previous known actions, together with the temperaments and previous known actions of the other characters in the play. The dramatist who hangs his characters to his plot, instead of hanging his plot to his characters, is guilty of cardinal sin.

The dialogue! Good dialogue again is character, marshalled so as continually to stimulate interest or excitement. The reason good dialogue is seldom found in plays is merely that it is hard to write, for it requires not only a knowledge of what interests or excites, but such a feeling for character as brings misery to the dramatist's heart when his creations speak as they should not speak—ashes to his mouth when they say things for the sake of saying them—disgust when they are "smart."

The art of writing true dramatic dialogue is an austere art, denying itself all license, grudging every sentence devoted to the mere machinery of the play, suppressing all jokes and epigrams severed from character, relying for fun and pathos on the fun and tears of life. From start to finish good dialogue is hand-made, like good lace; clear, of fine texture, furthering with each thread the harmony and strength of a design to which all must be subordinated.

But good dialogue is also spiritual action. In so far as the dramatist divorces his dialogue from spiritual action—that is to say, from progress of events, or toward events which are significant of character—he is stultifying το δραμα the thing done; he may make pleasing disquisitions, he is not making drama. And in so far as he twists character to suit his moral or his plot, he is neglecting a first principle, that truth to Nature which alone invests art with hand-made quality.

The dramatist's license, in fact, ends with his design. In conception alone he is free. He may take what character or group of characters he chooses, see them with what eyes, knit them with what idea, within the limits of his temperament; but once taken, seen, and knitted, he is bound to treat them like a gentleman, with the tenderest consideration of their mainsprings. Take care of character; action and dialogue will take care of themselves! The true dramatist gives full rein to his temperament in the scope and nature of his subject; having once selected subject and characters, he is just, gentle, restrained, neither gratifying his lust for praise at the expense of his offspring, nor using them as puppets to flout his audience. Being himself the nature that brought them forth, he guides them in the

course predestined at their conception. So only have they a chance of defying Time, which is always lying in wait to destroy the false, topical, or fashionable, all—in a word—that is not based on the permanent elements of human nature. The perfect dramatist rounds up his characters and facts within the ring-fence of a dominant idea which fulfils the craving of his spirit; having got them there, he suffers them to live their own lives.

Plot, action, character, dialogue! But there is yet another subject for a platitude. Flavour! An impalpable quality, less easily captured than the scent of a flower, the peculiar and most essential attribute of any work of art! It is the thin, poignant spirit which hovers up out of a play, and is as much its differentiating essence as is caffeine of coffee. Flavour, in fine, is the spirit of the dramatist projected into his work in a state of volatility, so that no one can exactly lay hands on it, here, there, or anywhere. This distinctive essence of a play, marking its brand, is the one thing at which the dramatist cannot work, for it is outside his consciousness. A man may have many moods, he has but one spirit; and this spirit he communicates in some subtle, unconscious way to all his work. It waxes and wanes with the currents of his vitality, but no more alters than a chestnut changes into an oak.

For, in truth, dramas are very like unto trees, springing from seedlings, shaping themselves inevitably in accordance with the laws fast hidden within themselves, drinking sustenance from the earth and air, and in conflict with the natural forces round them. So they slowly come to full growth, until warped, stunted, or risen to fair and gracious height, they stand open to all the winds. And the trees that spring from each dramatist are of different race; he is the spirit of his own sacred grove, into which no stray tree can by any chance enter.

One more platitude. It is not unfashionable to pit one form of drama against another—holding up the naturalistic to the disadvantage of the epic; the epic to the belittlement of the fantastic; the fantastic to the detriment of the naturalistic. Little purpose is thus served. The essential meaning, truth, beauty, and irony of things may be revealed under all these forms. Vision over life and human nature can be as keen and just, the revelation as true, inspiring, delight-giving, and thought-provoking, whatever fashion be employed—it is simply a question of doing it well enough to uncover the kernel of the nut. Whether the violet come from Russia, from Parma, or from England, matters little. Close by the Greek temples at Pæstum there are violets that seem redder, and sweeter, than any ever seen—as though they have sprung up out of the footprints of some old pagan goddess; but under the April sun, in a Devonshire lane, the little blue scentless violets capture every bit as much of the spring. And so it is with drama—no matter what its form—it need only be the "real thing," need only have caught some of the precious fluids, revelation, or delight, and imprisoned them within a chalice to which we may put our lips and continually drink.

And yet, starting from this last platitude, one may perhaps be suffered to speculate as to the particular forms that our renascent drama is likely to assume. For our drama is renascent, and nothing will stop its growth. It is not renascent because this or that man is writing, but because of a new spirit. A spirit that is no doubt in part the gradual outcome of the impact on our home-grown art, of Russian, French, and Scandinavian influences, but which in the main rises from an awakened humanity in the conscience of our time.

What, then, are to be the main channels down which the renascent English drama will float in the coming years? It is more than possible that these main channels will come to be two in number and situate far apart.

The one will be the broad and clear-cut channel of naturalism, down which will course a drama poignantly shaped, and inspired with high intention, but faithful to the seething and multiple life around us, drama such as some are inclined to term photographic, deceived by a seeming simplicity into forgetfulness of the old proverb, "Ars est celare artem," and oblivious of the fact that, to be vital, to grip, such drama is in every respect as dependent on imagination, construction, selection, and elimination—the main laws of artistry—as ever was the romantic or rhapsodic play. The question of naturalistic technique will bear, indeed, much more study than has yet been given to it. The aim of the dramatist employing it is obviously to create such an illusion of actual life passing on the stage as to compel the spectator to pass through an experience of his own, to think, and talk, and move with the people he sees thinking, talking, and moving in front of him. A false phrase, a single word out of tune or time, will destroy that illusion and spoil the surface as surely as a stone heaved into a still pool shatters the image seen there. But this is only the beginning of the reason why the naturalistic is the most exacting and difficult of all techniques. It is easy enough to *reproduce* the exact conversation and movement of persons in a room; it is desperately hard to *produce* the perfectly natural conversation and movements of those persons, when each natural phrase spoken and each natural movement made has not only to contribute toward the growth and perfection of a drama's soul, but also to be a revelation, phrase by phrase, movement by movement, of essential traits of character. To put it another way, naturalistic art, when alive, indeed to be alive at all, is simply the art of manipulating a procession of most delicate symbols. Its service is the swaying and focussing of men's feelings and thoughts in the various departments of human life. It will be like a steady lamp, held up from time to time, in whose light things will be seen for a space clearly and in due proportion, freed from the mists of prejudice and partisanship.

And the other of these two main channels will, I think, be a twisting and delicious stream, which will bear on its breast new barques of poetry, shaped, it may be, like prose, but a prose incarnating through its fantasy and symbolism all the deeper aspirations, yearning, doubts, and mysterious stirrings of the human spirit; a poetic prose-drama, emotionalising us by its diversity and purity of form and invention, and whose province will be to disclose the elemental soul of man and the forces of Nature, not perhaps as the old tragedies disclosed them, not necessarily in the epic mood, but always with beauty and in the spirit of discovery.

Such will, I think, be the two vital forms of our drama in the coming generation. And between these two forms there must be no crude unions; they are too far apart, the cross is too violent. For, where there is a seeming blend of lyricism and naturalism, it will on examination be found, I think, to exist only in plays whose subjects or settings—as in Synge's *Playboy of the Western World,* or in Mr. Masefield's *Nan*—are so removed from our ken that we cannot really tell and therefore do not care, whether an absolute illusion is maintained. The poetry which may and should exist in naturalistic drama, can only be that of perfect rightness of proportion, rhythm, shape—the poetry, in fact, that lies in all vital things. It is the ill-mating of forms that has killed a thousand plays. We want no more bastard drama; no more attempts to dress out the simple dignity of everyday life in the peacock's feathers of false lyricism; no more straw-stuffed heroes or heroines; no more rabbits and goldfish from the conjurer's pockets, nor any limelight. Let us have starlight, moonlight, sunlight, and the light of our own self-respects. (pp. 189-202)

John Galsworthy, "Some Platitudes Concerning Drama," in his The Inn of Tranquillity, *Charles Scribner's Sons, 1912, pp. 189-202.*

Ashley Dukes   (essay date 1911)

[*Dukes was an English drama critic. In the following excerpt, he examines Galsworthy's depiction of the common man in* Strife, Justice, *and* The Silver Box.]

Mr. Galsworthy has reaffirmed the existence of the common man; an individual long ignored upon the English stage. The West End society drama had no place for him. The man in the drawing-room is not upon speaking terms with the man in the street. Epigrammatic comedy gave him no part, for the common man does not deal in epigrams. The music halls burlesqued him, figuring him only with a battered silk hat, a red nose and a pair of particoloured trousers. Even melodrama failed to represent him fairly, for the common man is not addicted to crime. Bernard Shaw, engaged in bombarding the very civilisation in which the common man believes, burlesqued him as completely as the music hall, stuffed him with persiflage to bursting point, and hurled him at the social order as a new weapon of offence.

At this point Mr. Galsworthy arrived. To all appearance he might never have read a line of Shaw, but he had just as little in common with Sir Arthur Pinero. The Court Theatre opened its doors and Mr. Galsworthy walked in. He proceeded at once to set up his pair of scales upon the stage and to test the social values. In the one pan a Liberal member of Parliament and his son; in the other Mrs. Jones, the charwoman, and her husband. As a makeweight the silver box. Here we see at once that interpenetration of classes which distinguishes Mr. Galsworthy. As in the novel **Fraternity,** and the plays **Strife** and **Justice,** he refuses to accept the class divisions which separate ordinary West End drama from life as a whole. He takes up the floor of the drawing-room and shows us the kitchen. He examines the psychology of the butler as minutely as that of the member of Parliament. He follows the charwoman home to her tenement dwelling. He gives us the history of her husband in search of work. He introduces the solicitor, the detective, the prostitute. He accompanies the police-court missionary upon his rounds. He sits upon the bench with the magistrate. Each of these persons moves upon a separate daily round, a separate social plane; but he brings them all together and makes drama of their lives. Briefly, his case is this. No one can live his own life merely by virtue of possessing a thousand a year. No class can seal itself hermetically from others. Mrs. Jones' children will come and cling to the railings of the are, and even through the closed window their crying can be heard. One day there arises a petty complication, a workmen's strike, a moment of folly or crime, and the sky-scraper civilisation collapses. We are all on the ground floor together, scrambling. The graduated coinage of society is in the melting-pot. Interest fights interest upon common ground.

Upon that common ground stands Mr. Galsworthy with his pair of scales. He is scrupulously fair. Even in a drama of the vices no virtue escapes his notice. No individual is altogether a blackguard. *The Silver Box,* in some respects the most one-sided of his plays, shows this discrimination clearly. The Liberal member of Parliament means well. If he does not understand Jones' unemployment, at least he is always prepared to "ask a question in the House." His wife is unscrupulous, but only in defence of her son. The son himself, although a vicious type, is amiable enough. He has a rudimentary notion of playing the game. Jones did not steal the silver box; he "took it" half-contemptuously while he was in liquor. The magistrate is kindly. The police-court trial is as fair as it can humanly be considering the balance of interests. Jones is sent to prison, it is true, in order to prevent a newspaper scandal. But "one law for the rich and another for the poor" is not merely a propagandist cry; it is a platitude. The trial scene is as mechanically inevitable as all the forces which move Mr. Galsworthy's characters. The limitations of free will are narrow. In a social crisis the common man is helpless. He must accept his fate for good or evil. *The Silver Box* is an indictment of society, although not one of its characters would accept it as such. It is more than an indict-ment—a complete trial, in which Mr. Galsworthy appears both for the prosecution and the defence.

In *Joy* he failed because the subject did not suit him. Still the balance of pleading is honourably adjusted. On the one hand the mother of middle age with a lover; on the other the daughter who cannot comprehend until she, too, discovers romance. In *Strife* he returned to social drama on the larger scale. Here class meets class once more. A strike of quarrymen brings them together. The conflict appears at first sight individual, for two figures, the chairman of the employing firm and the leader of the strikers, stand out clearly from the rest. Actually neither drives. Both are driven. *Strife,* like *Justice* and *The Silver Box,* is an inter-play of forces rather than of persons. The collective will to resist concentrates upon either hand in the strongest in-dividuality. In the quarrymen's leader it is active; in the old employer obstinate and passive. The lesser characters propose compromise, offer sympathy, attempt reconcilia-tion; but the forces are too strong for them. The play ends with a settlement which might have been made at the be-ginning. The balance remains steady.

In *Justice* the scales are loaded. Mr. Galsworthy is as fair as ever to individuals, but he attacks deliberately a part of the social system that they have created. In the first act we learn that William Falder, a clerk in a lawyer's office, has stolen eighty-one pounds for the purpose of carrying off the woman whom he loves and rescuing her from a brutal husband. He is found out, arrested and sentenced to three years' penal servitude at the following assizes. The third act shows him in solitary confinement, and in the fourth, returning to the world after two years on ticket-of-leave, he finds conditions against him, is arrested again for forg-ing testimonials, and commits suicide. That is, baldly stat-ed, the history of William Falder. He is no heroic figure pursued by Fate; nothing but a pitiful creature who is not wanted, an unsolved problem in a world too busy with its own affairs to study him. It is his life that is pitiful; his death brings nothing but a feeling of intense relief.

Mr. Galsworthy has named this play a tragedy. Just as Mr. Barker has created a new type in the hero-raisonneur, so he has created a new form in the tragedy without a hero. There is not a single person in *Justice* whose remov-al could be a loss to the world in any but a limited personal sense; no one (with the possible exception of the counsel for the defence) who could conceivably entertain a univer-sally valuable idea; no one with the individual power and passion which alone can give inspiration to drama. Law-yers and clerks, judge, jury and officers of the court; gover-nor, warders and chaplain of the prison—they all exist by the thousand, and they could all be replaced a hundred times a day. They go about their work as slaves of inexora-ble law. Their human feelings, their kindliness and sympa-thy, are the emotions of people who, in the midst of a world unknown, and therefore presumably hostile, find two friendly camps of men and women like-minded to themselves—the family and the office—and cling to both as instinctively as sheep huddle beneath a hedge for shelter from the drifting snow. There is no colour, no mystery, no surprise about them. We can see not only their part in the passing incidents of the play, but the whole round of their lives. They may be interesting or uninteresting personally, but their chief business in life is to be a part of the social machinery. William Falder is one of them. He becomes en-tangled in the machinery, and it crushes him. The process is as mechanical as an execution. One feels that it is inhu-man, barbaric, detestable; but never that it is tragic. It arouses anger and pity, not inspiration. And inspiration is the test of tragedy. In the conflict of gods and men the sense of the tragic depends upon the greatness of the pro-tagonists. He who fights well cannot but die nobly. Mr. Galsworthy's Falder does not fight at all, and he dies like a rat in a trap.

It should be the tritest commonplace to say that no play-wright can make great drama out of little people. The nat-uralistic drama has had opportunities enough in Europe during the past thirty years, and it has justified itself only in proportion as it has created exceptional figures and splashed the grey background of actuality with living col-ours; in proportion, that is to say, as it has become unnaturalistic. Its naturalism is then only external. Mr. Galsworthy's is internal. The characters of *Justice* are grey at heart. The play has many extraordinarily moving passages. It is a fine destructive attack upon solitary confinement as a part of the prison system, but it is not a tragedy, and it is not great drama. Mr. Galsworthy has a place of his own upon the modern stage. Every play of his has a strongly marked individual atmosphere; his characters are distinctive without being distinguished. He understands the limitations of the theatre as well as its advantages, and he has never sacrificed drama to dialectics. At the beginning of the newer movement the English theatre was out of touch alike with art, with ideas and with actual life. The latter two are only accessories—but let that pass. Bernard Shaw and Mr. Barker brought the ideas; in a measure, too, the art. Mr. Galsworthy's preoccupation is with actuality. A gulf still remains. (pp. 141-50)

> Ashley Dukes, "England: John Galsworthy," in his Modern Dramatists, *Charles H. Sergel, 1911, pp. 141-50.*

Sheila Kaye-Smith   (essay date 1916)

[*Kaye-Smith was an English novelist, short story writer, and critic best known for her portrayals of the land, people, and history of Sussex, England. In the following excerpt, from an essay originally published in 1916, she analyzes Galsworthy's poetry, short stories, and essays.*]

Villa Rubein and four short stories under the title of *A Man of Devon* were published anonymously. All early efforts, they are not on a line with Galsworthy's later work, but they have about them a certain beauty and individuality which makes them worth considering. Perhaps their chief characteristic is delicacy: they are water-colours, in many ways exquisitely conceived and shaded, but perhaps a trifle pale and washed out, a trifle—it must be owned—uninteresting.

Villa Rubein, describing with much sensitive charm the life of a half-Austrian household, is full of tenderness, but lacking somehow in grip. The characters are more attractive than most of Galsworthy's—in fact, in no work of his do we meet such a uniformly charming group of people. They are sketched, even the less pleasing, with an entire absence of bitterness, and the heroine, Christian, and her little half-German sister are delightful in their freshness and grave sweetness. Miss Naylor and old Nic Treffry are also drawn with a loving and convincing hand. The book seems to have been written in a mellow mood which passed with it. Yet we pay for any absence of bitterness, propaganda or pessimism, by a corresponding lack of force. It must be confessed that Galsworthy is most effective when he is most gloomy, most penetrating when he is most bitter, most humorous when he is most satirical.

The short stories call for no special comment except "The Salvation of a Forsyte," where we meet for the first time Swithin Forsyte, later to figure in *The Man of Property.* We are introduced to an early adventure of his, which is treated with some technical skill and an impressive irony. The tale has grip, and is not far off French excellence of craft. The other stories are too long for their themes,

which, if not actually thin in themselves, are dragged out in the telling.

Of very different stuff are the four volumes of sketches—*A Commentary, A Motley, The Inn of Tranquillity,* and *The Little Man.* In these, except, perhaps, in the last, we have some of Galsworthy's best work, much of it equal, in its different way, to the finest of the plays and novels.

A Commentary deals chiefly with the life of the very poor, showing the intimacy of the author's knowledge, and the depths of his sympathy. Some of the sketches are indictments of the social order which favours those who have money and tramples those who have none. *Justice,* for instance, is a fresh exposure of the oft-exposed inequality of the divorce laws where rich and poor are concerned. "A Mother" is a piteous revelation of those depths of horror and humiliation which form the daily life of many. Continually, in the plays and in the novels, Galsworthy reveals the utter brutishness of some of these submerged ones. He never attempts to enforce his social ethics by glorification of those he champions. Such men as Hughes, in *Fraternity,* or the husband, in "A Mother," are absolutely of the lowest stuff and, it would seem, unworthy of a hand to help them out of the mud in which they roll. But here lies the subtlety of the reproach—it is the social system with its cruelties and stupidities which is responsible for this. There is something more forceful than all the sufferings of the deserving in this grim picture of utter degradation, the depths of bestialism into which mismanaged civilisation can grind divine souls.

In other of the sketches we are shown the opposite side of the picture—the selfishness of the prosperous, their lack of ideals and imagination. Now Galsworthy becomes bitter; with a steely hardness he describes the comfortable life of the upper middle classes, of the fashionable and wealthy. The bias of *A Commentary* is obvious throughout, and throughout propaganda takes the first place. The fragments are held together by the central idea, which is the exposure—ironic, indignant, embittered, infinitely pitying—of the inequalities between the poor and the rich. True, there is atmosphere, style, a sense of character; but in *A Commentary* the artist takes second place.

A Motley is, as the title implies, a collection linked up by no central view-point. Character sketches, episodes of the streets and of the fields, reflections on life, art, manners, anything, and all widely different in style and length, crowd together between the covers, without any definite scheme. They show extraordinary powers of observation and intuition, and at the same time a certain lack of grip, which is always the first of Galsworthy's weaknesses to come to light in a failing situation. Some of the sketches are too slight, over-fined. On the other hand, some have true poetry and true pathos in their conception. The style is more polished, the pleading less special, the knowledge less embittered than in *A Commentary.* Particularly successful is "A Fisher of Men," in which Galsworthy is at his best, giving us a sympathetic and tragic picture of a type with which we know he has little sympathy—there is no bitterness here, just pathos. "Once More" is a study of lower-class life slightly recalling "A Mother," but here again is far more tenderness, due partly, no doubt, to the wistfulness of youth that creeps into the story. Then there are sketches of life and the furtive love of the London parks; no one has realised more poignantly than Galsworthy all the tragedy of hidden meetings and hidden partings with which our public places are filled.

The Inn of Tranquillity is also a mixed collection, and in it we see far more of Galsworthy the poet and the artist than of Galsworthy the social reformer. There are in the book fragments of sheer beauty which would be hard to beat anywhere in modern prose. Take, for instance, the painting of dawn in **"Wind in the Rocks"**:

> That god came slowly, stalking across far over our heads from top to top; then, of a sudden, his flame-white form was seen standing in a gap of the valley walls; the trees flung themselves along the ground before him, and censers of pine gum began swinging in the dark aisles, releasing their perfumed steam. Throughout these happy ravines where no man lives, he shows himself naked and unashamed, the colour of pale honey; on his golden hair such shining as one has not elsewhere seen; his eyes like old wine on fire. And already he had swept his hand across the invisible strings, for there had arisen the music of uncurling leaves and flitting things.

Take also just this sentence from **"A Novelist's Allegory"**: "those pallid gleams . . . remain suspended like a handful of daffodils held up against the black stuffs of secrecy."

Galsworthy allows himself to play with words, blend them, contrast them, savour their sweet sound and the roll and suck of them under the tongue . . . he becomes a poet in prose. But it is not only words that make his poetry. He seizes aspects of beauty and gives them to us palpitating, fresh from their capture, a poet's prey. Such is **"Riding in Mist,"** a consummate study of the misty moor, damp, sweet, and dangerous. There is, too, a wonderful sense of locality in **"That Old-Time Place"**—it throbs with atmosphere.

But we have many studies besides of words and place. There is **"Memories,"** in which Galsworthy uses his real understanding of dog-nature, faithful and true. There is **"The Grand Jury,"** in which he shows the fullness of his sympathy for the human dog, the bottom dog, so generally and necessarily ignored by laws which are inevitably made for the upper layer of humanity. We have, too, some illuminating comments on the world of letters. In **"About Censorship"** there is fine irony, and in **"Some Platitudes Concerning the Drama"** plenty of illumination. Indeed, in this article we are given a plain enough statement of the rules which evidently govern Galsworthy's own work. For instance: "A good plot is that sure edifice which slowly rises out of the interplay of circumstance on temperament and temperament on circumstance, within the enclosing atmosphere of an idea." There could be no clearer definition of the plan governing *Strife* and *The Silver Box*. The pronouncement on dramatic dialogue, too, applies admirably to much of Galsworthy's own achievement:

> The art of writing true dramatic dialogue is an austere art, denying itself all license, grudging every sentence devoted to the mere machinery of

the play, suppressing all jokes and epigrams severed from character, relying for fun and pathos on the fun and tears of life. From start to finish good dialogue is hand-made, like good lace; clear, of fine texture, furthering with each thread the harmony and strength of a design to which all must be subordinated.

In his last book of sketches—*The Little Man and Other Satires*—Galsworthy has made a deliberate sacrifice of beauty. He has left the luminous Italian backgrounds of *The Inn of Tranquillity,* the rustling English twilights of *A Motley,* for the midnight lamp on his study table. This is why, perhaps, *The Little Man* depresses me. Galsworthy has not stood the test—he has grown bitter. His satire is more akin to that of Swift than Samuel Butler, but without Swift's redeeming largeness, his tumbling restlessness. Galsworthy's bitterness is the well-bred bitterness of the pessimist at afternoon tea; Swift is the pessimist in the tavern, raging round and breaking pots.

However, an author's point of view is not a fair subject for criticism, any more than the shape of his head; he probably cannot help it. But it may be deplored.

The most striking thing about the book itself is the subdivision titled **"Studies in Extravagance."** Here we have some remorseless, if only partial, truth—the fierce glow of the searchlight, more concentrated though more limited than the wide shining of the sun. We have **"The Writer,"** **"The Housewife,"** **"The Plain Man,"** etc., all pierced through to their most startling worst. Galsworthy will make no concessions—he will not show us a single motherly redeeming virtue in that woman of schemes and covert horribleness whom he presents as a possible variety of British matron. So too with his Writer—those flickers of amiable naivety which occasionally humanise the writers most of us know are shut out from this portrait of an ape playing with the ABC. It is clever, fierce, vindictive, and partly true.

There are some gentler sketches in the book—for instance, the name-piece, in which we have a really witty and typical picture of an American, with his God's own gift of admiring good deeds he will not do himself. There is also *Abracadabra,* in which the satire is fundamentally tender, and with little significant bitterness—though in time one comes to resent Galsworthy's inalienable idea that every woman is ill-used in marriage. There is also such genuine wit, terseness, and point in **"Hall Marked"** that one can afford to skip the humours of the parson's trousers. **"Ultima Thule"** is more in *The Motley* and *Commentary* vein. We are glad to meet the old man who could tame cats and bullfinches. But why sigh over him so much? He was happy and to be envied, even though he lived in a back room on a few farthings. This misplaced pity is becoming irritating in Galsworthy. His earlier works—*Strife, The Man of Property*—are innocent of it, but lately it has grown to be a habit with him. He cannot resist the temptation to weep over everyone whose clothes are not quite as good as his own.

It is scarcely surprising that a writer with Galsworthy's sense of words and atmosphere should have written a book of verse—the only surprise is that his solitary experiment in poetry should not have been more successful. When we remember the exquisite prose of his plays, novels and sketches, the admirable description, the sense of atmosphere, not forgetting also the genuine poetry of much of **The Little Dream,** we are surprised not to find in **Moods, Songs and Doggerels,** anything of permanent quality, or worthy to stand beside his other work. There are some delightful songs of the country, of Devon, one or two little fragrant snatches, like puffs of breeze. But the more ambitious pieces, the **Moods,** are for the most part wanting in inspiration. They are just prose, and not nearly such fine prose as we have a right to expect from Galsworthy. One or two stand out as poetry, and these are mostly studies in atmosphere, such as **"Street Lamps":**

> Lamps, lamps! Lamps ev'rywhere!
> You wistful, gay, and burning eyes,
> You stars low-driven from the skies
> Down on the rainy air.
>
> You merchant eyes, that never tire
> Of spying out our little ways;
> Of summing up our little days
> In ledgerings of fire—
>
> Inscrutable your nightly glance,
> Your lighting and your snuffing out,
> Your flicker through the windy rout,
> Guiding this mazy dance.
>
> O watchful, troubled gaze of gold,
> Protecting us upon our beats—
> You piteous glamour of the streets,
> Youthless, and never old!

(pp. 86-99)

Sheila Kaye-Smith, in her John Galsworthy, *H. Holt and Company, 1916, 128 p.*

R. H. Coats   (essay date 1926)

[*In the following excerpt, Coats examines the traits that characterize Galsworthy's plays: sincerity, sympathy, impartiality, irony, pity, and indignation.*]

In the drama of to-day Galsworthy occupies an important and a distinctive place. He has his affinities, it is true, with other eminent playwrights of the past and of the present. His naturalism is akin to that of Ibsen; he shares the moral earnestness of Shaw; in his preoccupation with the sores and diseases of society he resembles Brieux. Yet the essential qualities of his art are not borrowed. When we see his plays upon the stage, or read them in the quietness of the study, we are impressed by a psychological insight, a social passion, an artistic economy and restraint, which are manifestly the author's own. The plays of Galsworthy bear a close resemblance to his novels, and it would be a fascinating subject of enquiry to trace correspondences between the two. But the nineteen dramas—apart from one-act plays—which he has published since 1906, present us with a world which is sufficiently diversified and absorbing to call for investigation on its own account. (pp. 1-2)

The first thing we notice in reading the plays of Galsworthy is the evident *sincerity* of the writer, his desire to maintain artistic integrity of soul. The dramatist of to-day, he

tells us, may pursue one of three aims. He may give the public those views or codes of life in which it already believes, or desires to believe. He may give them the views or codes of life in which he himself believes. "There is a third course: To set before the public no cut-and-dried codes, but the phenomena of life and character, selected and combined, *but not distorted,* by the dramatist's outlook, set down without fear, favour, or prejudice, leaving the public to draw such poor moral as nature may afford. This third method requires a certain detachment; it requires a sympathy with, a love of, and a curiosity as to, things for their own sake; it requires a far view, together with patient industry, for no immediately practical result" [**"Some Platitudes Concerning Drama,"** in **The Inn of Tranquillity**].

These words clearly and admirably express Galsworthy's aim throughout. He is resolved, like a good golfer, to keep his eye firmly fixed on the object that is before him. He will see life steadily and see it whole, avoiding all artifice, sentimentality, and straining after effect. With due allowance made for personal temperament, he will be faithful and conscientious in representing reality, whether what he writes be to the taste of his audience or no. All thought of the box-office or the business manager, of the dramatic critic or the limelight operator, of the occupant of the gallery or of the stalls, must be dismissed from the mind of the dramatist when he begins to write. There must be included in his work "nothing because it pays, nothing because it will make a sensation, no situations faked, no characters falsified, no fireworks, only something imagined and put down in a passion of sincerity" [**Another Sheaf**].

The author who writes in this fashion is evidently in the full tide of reaction against Victorianism. It was a generally accepted convention in the nineteenth century to draw a sentimental veil over the disreputable and the unpleasant. In literature and in life the glamour of illusion, respectability, romance, was preferred to unshrinking veracity in facing unpalatable facts. The moderns, on the other hand, are all for plain speaking and the smiting of cant and shams. We live in a scientific age, an age resolved to know and to face the truth and give it honest expression in terms of art. Galsworthy's sincerity admirably illustrates this general tendency as it affects drama.

Another marked characteristic of Galsworthy the dramatist is *sympathy*. "It is not the artist's business to preach," he writes. "His business is to portray, but portray truly he cannot if he is devoid of the insight which comes from instinctive sympathy. . . . The sincere artist is bound to be curious and perceptive, with an instinctive craving to identify himself with the experience of others. This is his value, whether he express it in comedy, epic, satire, or tragedy" [**Another Sheaf**].

This capacity "to identify himself with the experience of others" is conspicuous in all Galsworthy's writings. Every student of these must have noticed how keen, for example, is his sympathy with animals, especially such as are harshly treated. "If a sparrow comes before my window," wrote Keats, "I take part in its existence and pick about the gravel." Of Galsworthy it may be said that he "takes part in the existence" of not only the sparrow perched outside a window, but also of the lark imprisoned inside a cage, the dog stretched on a dissecting-table, the pony drooping in the darkness of a mine, the wounded pheasant creeping away to die a lingering death. The cruelty we inflict upon these harmless creatures arises, he thinks, from nothing but *lack* of sympathy, the sluggish laziness of unimaginative minds, our inability to put ourselves in the place of those we torture.

This imaginative sympathy in Galsworthy, so keenly felt for all suffering animals, naturally extends in a much greater degree to the toiling, oppressed classes of humanity. Galsworthy is a typical representative of modern humanitarianism. (pp. 2-6)

A third characteristic of Galsworthy the dramatist is his *impartiality*. This is the mental correlative of sympathy. Impartiality is sympathy expressed in the form of an intellectual or moral judgment. If the objects of one's sympathies range themselves into two opposing camps, impartiality steps in to do equal justice to the claims of each. This quality of impartiality is particularly required in a dramatist, who has to deal in his plays with mutually opposed and perhaps violently conflicting forces. If he shows undue partiality to the one or to the other, so that the case for either of them is understated, the dramatic interest of the play is bound to suffer. His merit as a dramatist is to hold the balance even as long as possible, and so maintain suspense in the reader's mind.

In that respect this author is unusually successful, no doubt because of his training as a barrister. Galsworthy knows that "there are two sides to every coin," as one of his characters puts it. Take, for example, the struggle for precedence between a cultured, aristocratic, conservative landowner of the old school on the one hand, and a vulgar, upstart, newly-rich manufacturer on the other. One might be disposed to think that all one's sympathies should go

Galsworthy with his wife at Bury, Sussex.

out to the former. Galsworthy shows that this would not be fair. There is a very great deal to be said for the latter's point of view, and it ought to be honestly and impartially set forth. It is the same with the struggle between Labour and Capital, between the Individual and the Community. Even where Galsworthy's own sympathies are obvious, he is scrupulously careful to put the case for the other side so fairly that its own advocates will recognize it as a true exposition of their views. Anything else would be a burlesque or a caricature.

Galsworthy carries dramatic impartiality to the point of aspiring after perfect impersonality of feeling. "Let me try to eliminate any bias," he writes, "and see the whole thing as should an umpire—one of those pure beings in white coats, purged of all the prejudices, passions, and predilections of mankind. Let me have no temperament for the time being. . . . Only from an impersonal point of view, if there be such a thing, am I going to get even approximately at the truth" [*Another Sheaf*].

One disadvantage of complete impartiality is that it is apt to make a play seem inconclusive. If something is to be said for everything, then no special importance is to be attached to anything. There is no finality, no clear solution. Here again Galsworthy differs widely from Shaw. There is never any doubt regarding *his* remedy for the ills which he deplores. Shaw is like a doctor called to the bedside of a patient, who at once prescribes a cure with dogmatic self-assurance and damns all other medicines as worthless. Galsworthy, similarly consulted, resembles one who provides an exceedingly careful diagnosis of the disease, but fails to suggest a remedy. To anyone complaining of this unsatisfactory result he might reply that his function as an artist goes no further. All that a dramatist is called upon to do is to reveal a given situation in terms of art, and then retire. His proper sphere is not to advocate or even to suggest reforms, but simply to arouse the emotions that shall demand them.

Once more, there is in the plays of Galsworthy a prevailing *irony*. He constantly reminds us that, even after the spirit of fairness and impartiality has been exercised to the utmost, there is a disconcerting twist in things which cannot be wholly accounted for or eliminated. Two modern writers are pre-eminent for their treatment of this aspect of human life. Hardy deals mainly with the irony of external circumstances, the baffling and inscrutable element of fate which appears sometimes almost gleefully to intervene in order to upset all human contrivings. Such are "Time's Laughing-Stocks" and "Life's Little Ironies." Galsworthy on the whole eschews these ultimate problems of metaphysics and confines himself rather to the thwartings and frustrations which arise out of human fallibility and folly.

The Law, for example, devises an elaborately contrived machine for the purpose of dispensing justice; and lo! its product is marked injustice. Again, when social unfortunates find themselves in the mire, would-be deliverers bestir themselves to help; but alas! the professional reformers lack humanity, and the genial humanists lack system, so that the last case of the patient is worse than the first. Once more, two mighty forces, Capital and Labour, come into collision, with a resultant shock which causes infinite suffering and wastage to all concerned; when both parties are thoroughly exhausted a compromise is reached which proves to be exactly the same as that originally proposed before the strife began. "That's where the fun comes in," remarks one of the characters at this conclusion, and indeed the remark has more truth in it than might appear. Only on an ironic view of life are its woes endurable. Says Ferrand in *The Pigeon,* "There is nothing that gives more courage than to see the irony of things."

In the plays of Galsworthy, moreover, there is an all pervading feeling of *pity and indignation.* This spirit of compassion combined with hot anger may be termed the most important of Galsworthy's characteristics, though it is the least obtrusive. Some think him cold, aloof, indifferent, analytical, severely logical and judicial. Such an interpretation of his attitude to life would be quite mistaken. Galsworthy's manner may be quiet and his face impassive, but his firmly set lips are meanwhile quivering with feeling, and we must never forget that it is his supreme aim as a dramatist to convey *emotion* to his audience. The impartiality above spoken of is more or less a mask. Galsworthy may be impartial as between one character and another, but he is not impartial when faced by the human short-sightedness and folly which make these characters what they are. The plays are really a tremendous indictment of the whole fabric of modern civilization, and at the same time a passionate appeal for understanding sympathy with the innocent victims of a social system for which all of us are responsible. Galsworthy is no mere spinner of pleasant tales and fantasies. He is "a Daniel come to judgment."

Perhaps this is the chief reason why he can hardly be regarded as a popular dramatist. He is too serious, too weighty, too great a disturber of complacency, to be a favourite with those who frequent the theatre in order to escape boredom, digest a good dinner, or exchange the world of realities for a world of dreams. Shaw, indeed, never fails to give us a good scolding, but he does it so entertainingly that we quite enjoy the experience; and in his case it is always possible to still the risings of conscience by concluding quite comfortably that Shaw is only a buffoon or a mountebank after all, and that he has his tongue in his cheek all the time. With Galsworthy this is impossible. Where Shaw tickles, Galsworthy is apt to prick or even stab. His wholesome pills have very little coating of sweet sugar. Shaw diverts the mind by the most brilliant paradoxes and amazing somersaults. Galsworthy goes straight for the conscience and leaves it horribly raw and wounded. Instead of laughing we feel inclined to weep. The worst of it is that, as has been well pointed out, Galsworthy puts no villain upon the stage on whom we can vent our spleen. The villain, we find, is in the audience itself, and especially in the seat where we happen to be sitting. It is hardly surprising that in these circumstances the light-hearted playgoer returns no more. He feels like one who has paid for soporifics and has been given qualms.

We may close this chapter by adding a few observations on Galsworthy's *artistry.* There are those who contend that themes of the kind above described have no proper place in art. Drama, we are told by an engaging modern writer whose excess of emphasis is one of his chief attractions, should make provision only for our gayer moments and our lighter moods. The temple of the arts, in other words, ought to be reserved for festive occasions and entered only in the holiday spirit of relaxation.

> The theatre is not always . . . a kind of church with a low pulpit; and it is not a place for too much talk. It is magic ground, and it is neutral ground. . . . If politics, if the sciences, if religions, if trade must be painful, must be handled with becoming fear, caution, and solemnity, with angular precision by the water-drinkers, why cannot they recognize that the arts are just the opposite of such things, and need quite another way of approach and touch? With ease, and with happiness, in the holiday spirit . . . not as propaganda—which is a notion utterly puerile and wasteful—but to give delight, to relax the stiff poker minds and persons among us [E. Gordon Craig, *Books and Theatres*].

Such a view of art, however, would unduly restrict its scope. To Galsworthy, at least, the true intent of art is not only for delight, but also for enlightenment and edification. Its chief function is moral. "A drama must be shaped so as to have a spire of meaning. Every grouping of life and character has its inherent moral; and the business of the dramatist is so to pose the group as to bring that moral poignantly to the light of day" ["**Some Platitudes Concerning Drama,**" in *The Inn of Tranquillity*]. The temple of the arts, that is to say, should have an altar. But an altar is something different from a pulpit. Anything in the shape of didacticism or preaching should be excluded. The moral should exhale from the work of art as a whole, and not proceed from any one part of it; and it should be strictly subordinated to the first requirement of a work of art, that it should give imaginative pleasure.

Galsworthy's plays, with one or two possible exceptions, conform to these conditions. In those of Shaw the preaching is loud, emphatic, and unashamed. *Major Barbara,* for example, is obviously written for the sole purpose of proclaiming the gospel of Andrew Undershaft, a gospel which spills over from the play itself and fills the large vessel of the preface which precedes it. But Galsworthy is not primarily a missionary dramatist. He has indeed a message to deliver, but he takes care that it shall be artistically embodied in the drama as a whole, and not didactically enforced by the long propagandist speeches of one outstanding character. The moral of a good play, like that of a good story, should be held in solution and not obtruded. It is true that, in Galsworthy, the interpretation of the play's significance is occasionally assigned to a particular person in it; but he is generally a butler or some such minor character, and the value of his comment is apt to be correspondingly overlooked. Everywhere there is becoming reticence and restraint in these matters. Galsworthy is too skilled a dramatist to let his moral indignation get the better of his imagination. Only very rarely does he allow the artist in him to be handcuffed by the pamphleteer. (pp. 9-19)

R. H. Coats, in his John Galsworthy as a Dramatic Artist, *Charles Scribner's Sons, 1926, 240 p.*

D. H. Lawrence (essay date 1928)

[*Lawrence was an English novelist, poet, and essayist noted for introducing themes of modern psychology to English fiction. In his lifetime he was a controversial figure, both for the explicit sexuality he portrayed in such novels as* Lady Chatterley's Lover *(1928) and for his unconventional personal life. In the following excerpt, he criticizes Galsworthy's work as "messy," sentimental, and lacking in sensual qualities.*]

Literary criticism can be no more than a reasoned account of the feeling produced upon the critic by the book he is criticising. Criticism can never be a science: it is, in the first place, much too personal, and in the second, it is concerned with values that science ignores. The touchstone is emotion, not reason. We judge a work of art by its effect on our sincere and vital emotion, and nothing else. All the critical twiddle-twaddle about style and form, all this pseudo-scientific classifying and analysing of books in an imitation-botanical fashion, is mere impertinence and mostly dull jargon.

A critic must be able to *feel* the impact of a work of art in all its complexity and its force. To do so, he must be a man of force and complexity himself, which few critics are. A man with a paltry, impudent nature will never write anything but paltry, impudent criticism. And a man who is *emotionally* educated is rare as a phœnix. The more scholastically educated a man is generally, the more he is an emotional boor.

More than this, even an artistically and emotionally educated man must be a man of good faith. He must have the courage to admit what he feels, as well as the flexibility to *know* what he feels. So Sainte Beuve remains, to me, a great critic. And a man like Macaulay, brilliant as he is, is unsatisfactory, because he is not honest. He is emotionally very alive, but he juggles his feelings. He prefers a fine effect to the sincere statement of his æsthetic and emotional reaction. He is quite intellectually capable of giving us a true account of what he feels. But not morally. A critic must be emotionally alive in every fibre, intellectually capable and skilful in essential logic, and then morally very honest.

Then it seems to me a good critic should give his reader a few standards to go by. He can change the standards for every new critical attempt, so long as he keeps good faith. But it is just as well to say: This and this is the standard we judge by.

Sainte Beuve, on the whole, set up the standard of the "good man." He sincerely believed that the great man was essentially the good man in the widest range of human sympathy. This remained his universal standard. Pater's standard was the lonely philosopher of pure thought and pure æsthetic truth. Macaulay's standard was tainted by a political or democratic bias, he must be on the side of the weak. Gibbon tried a purely moral standard, individual morality.

Reading Galsworthy again—or most of him, for all is too much—one feels oneself in need of a standard, some conception of a real man and a real woman, by which to judge all these Forsytes and their contemporaries. One cannot judge them by the standard of the good man, nor of the man of pure thought, nor of the treasured humble nor the moral individual. One would like to judge them by the standard of the human being, but what, after all, is that? This is the trouble with the Forsytes. They are human enough, since anything in humanity is human, just as anything in nature is natural. Yet not one of them seems to be a really vivid human being. They are social beings. And what do we mean by that?

It remains to define, just for the purpose of this criticism, what we mean by a social being as distinct from a human being. The necessity arises from the sense of dissatisfaction which these Forsytes give us. Why can't we admit them as human beings? Why can't we have them in the same category as Sairey Gamp for example, who is satirically conceived, or of Jane Austen's people, who are social enough? We can accept Mrs Gamp or Jane Austen's characters or even George Meredith's Egoist as human beings in the same category as ourselves. Whence arises this repulsion from the Forsytes, this refusal, this emotional refusal, to have them identified with our common humanity? Why do we feel so instinctively that they are inferiors?

It is because they seem to us to have lost caste as human beings, and to have sunk to the level of the social being, that peculiar creature that takes the place in our civilisation of the slave in the old civilisations. The human individual is a queer animal, always changing. But the fatal change to-day is the collapse from the psychology of the free human individual into the psychology of the social being, just as the fatal change in the past was a collapse from the freeman's psyche to the psyche of the slave. The free moral and the slave moral, the human moral and the social moral: these are the abiding antitheses.

While a man remains a man, a true human individual, there is at the core of him a certain innocence or *naïveté* which defies all analysis, and which you cannot bargain with, you can only deal with it in good faith from your own corresponding innocence or *naïveté*. This does not mean that the human being is nothing but naïve or innocent. He is Mr Worldly Wiseman also to his own degree. But in his essential core he is naïve, and money does not touch him. Money, of course, with every man living goes a long way. With the alive human being it may go as far as his penultimate feeling. But in the last naked him it does not enter.

With the social being it goes right through the centre and is the controlling principle no matter how much he may pretend, nor how much bluff he may put up. He may give away all he has to the poor and still reveal himself as a social being swayed finally and helplessly by the money-sway, and by the social moral, which is inhuman.

It seems to me that when the human being becomes too much divided between his subjective and objective consciousness, at last something splits in him and he becomes a social being. When he becomes too much aware of objective reality, and of his own isolation in the face of a universe of objective reality, the core of his identity splits, his nucleus collapses, his innocence or his *naïveté* perishes, and he becomes only a subjective-objective reality, a divided thing hinged together but not strictly individual.

While a man remains a man, before he falls and becomes a social individual, he innocently feels himself altogether within the great continuum of the universe. He is not divided nor cut off. Men may be against him, the tide of affairs may be rising to sweep him away. But he is one with the living continuum of the universe. From this he cannot be swept away. Hamlet and Lear feel it, as does Œdipus or Phædra. It is the last and deepest feeling that is in a man while he remains a man. It is there the same in a deist like Voltaire or a scientist like Darwin: it is there, imperishable, in every great man: in Napoleon the same, till material things piled too much on him and he lost it and was doomed. It is the essential innocence and *naïveté* of the human being, the sense of being at one with the great universe-continuum of space-time-life, which is vivid in a great man, and a pure nuclear spark in every man who is still free.

But if man loses his mysterious naïve assurance, which is his innocence; if he gives *too* much importance to the external objective reality and so collapses in his natural innocent pride, then he becomes obsessed with the idea of objectives or material assurance; he wants to *insure* himself, and perhaps everybody else: universal insurance. The impulse rests on fear. Once the individual loses his naïve at-oneness with the living universe he falls into a state of fear and tries to insure himself with wealth. If he is an altruist he wants to insure everybody, and feels it is the tragedy of tragedies if this can't be done. But the whole necessity for thus materially insuring oneself with wealth, money, arises from the state of fear into which a man falls who has lost his at-oneness with the living universe, lost his peculiar nuclear innocence and fallen into fragmentariness. Money, material salvation is the only salvation. What is salvation is God. Hence money is God. The social being may rebel even against this god, as do many of Galsworthy's characters. But that does not give them back their innocence. They are only anti-materialists instead of positive materialists. And the anti-materialist is a social being just the same as the materialist, neither more nor less. He is castrated just the same, made a neuter by having lost his innocence, the bright little individual spark of his at-oneness.

When one reads Mr Galsworthy's books it seems as if there were not on earth one single human individual. They are all these social beings, positive and negative. There is not a free soul among them, not even Pendyce, or June Forsyte. If money does not actively determine their being, it does negatively. Money, or property, which is the same thing. Mrs Pendyce, lovable as she is, is utterly circumscribed by property. Ultimately, she is not lovable at all, she is part of the fraud, she is prostituted to property. And there is nobody else. Old Jolyon is merely a sentimental materialist. Only for one moment do we see a man, and that is the road-sweeper in *Fraternity* after he comes out of prison and covers his face. But even *his* manhood has

to be explained away by a wound in the head: an abnormality.

Now it looks as if Mr Galsworthy set out to make that very point: to show that the Forsytes were not full human individuals, but social beings fallen to a lower level of life. They have lost that bit of free manhood and free womanhood which makes men and women. ***The Man of Property*** has the elements of a very great novel, a very great satire. It sets out to reveal the social being in all his strength and inferiority. But the author has not the courage to carry it through. The greatness of the book rests in its new and sincere and amazingly profound satire. It is the ultimate satire on modern humanity, and done from the inside, with really consummate skill and sincere creative passion, something quite new. It seems to be a real effort to show up the social being in all his weirdness. And then it fizzles out.

Then, in the love affair of Irene and Bosinney, and in the sentimentalising of old Jolyon Forsyte, the thing is fatally blemished. Galsworthy had not quite enough of the superb courage of his satire. He faltered, and gave in to the Forsytes. It is a thousand pities. He might have been the surgeon the modern soul needs so badly, to cut away the proud flesh of our Forsytes from the living body of men who are fully alive. Instead, he put down the knife and laid on a soft, sentimental poultice, and helped to make the corruption worse.

Satire exists for the very purpose of killing the social being, showing him what an inferior he is and, with all his parade of social honesty, how subtly and corruptly debased. Dishonest to life, dishonest to the living universe on which he is parasitic as a louse. By ridiculing the social being, the satirist helps the true individual, the real human being, to rise to his feet again and go on with the battle. For it is always a battle, and always will be.

Not that the majority are necessarily social beings. But the majority is only *conscious* socially: humanly, mankind is helpless and unconscious, unaware even of the thing most precious to any human being, that core of manhood or womanhood, naïve, innocent at-oneness with the living universe-continuum, which alone makes a man individual and, as an individual, essentially happy, even if he be driven mad like Lear. Lear was *essentially* happy, even in his greatest misery. A happiness from which Goneril and Regan were excluded as lice and bugs are excluded from happiness, being social beings, and, as such, parasites, fallen from true freedom and independence.

But the tragedy to-day is that men are only materially and socially conscious. They are unconscious of their own manhood, and so they let it be destroyed. Out of free men we produce social beings by the thousand every week.

The Forsytes are all parasites, and Mr Galsworthy set out, in a really magnificent attempt, to let us see it. They are parasites upon the thought, the feelings, the whole body of life of really living individuals who have gone before them and who exist alongside with them. All they can do, having no individual life of their own, is out of fear to rake together property, and to feed upon the life that has been given by living men to mankind. They have no life, and so they live forever, in perpetual fear of death, accumulating property to ward off death. They can keep up conventions, but they cannot carry on a tradition. There is a tremendous difference between the two things. To carry on a tradition you must add something to the tradition. But to keep up a convention needs only the monotonous persistency of a parasite, the endless endurance of the craven, those who fear life because they are not alive, and who cannot die because they cannot live—the social beings.

As far as I can see, there is nothing but Forsyte in Galsworthy's books: Forsyte positive or Forsyte negative, Forsyte successful or Forsyte *manqué*. That is, every single character is determined by money: either the getting it, or the having it, or the wanting it, or the utter lacking it. Getting it are the Forsytes as such; having it are the Pendyces and patricians and Hilarys and Biancas and all that lot; wanting it are the Irenes and Bosinneys and young Jolyons; and utterly lacking it are all the charwomen and squalid poor who form the background—the shadows of the "having" ones, as old Mr Stone says. This is the whole Galsworthy gamut, all absolutely determined by money, and not an individual soul among them. They are all fallen, all social beings, a castrated lot.

Perhaps the overwhelming numerousness of the Forsytes frightened Mr Galsworthy from utterly damning them. Or perhaps it was something else, something more serious in him. Perhaps it was his utter failure to see what you were when you *weren't* a Forsyte. What was there *besides* Forsytes in all the wide human world? Mr Galsworthy looked, and found nothing. Strictly and truly, after his frightened search, he had found nothing. But he came back with Irene and Bosinney, and offered us that. Here! he seems to say. Here is the anti-Forsyte! Here! Here you have it! Love! Pa-assion! PASSION.

We look at this love, this PASSION, and we see nothing but a doggish amorousness and a sort of anti-Forsytism. They are the *anti* half of the show. Runaway dogs of these Forsytes, running in the back garden and furtively and ignominiously copulating—this is the effect, on me, of Mr Galsworthy's grand love affairs, Dark Flowers or Bosinneys, or Apple Trees or George Pendyce—whatever they be. About every one of them something ignominious and doggish, like dogs copulating in the street, and looking round to see if the Forsytes are watching.

Alas! this is the Forsyte trying to be freely sensual. He can't do it; he's lost it. He can only be doggishly messy. Bosinney is not only a Forsyte, but an anti-Forsyte, with a vast grudge against property. And the thing a man has a vast grudge against is the man's determinant. Bosinney is a property hound, but he has run away from the kennels, or been born outside the kennels, so he is a rebel. So he goes sniffing round the property bitches, to get even with the successful property hounds that way. One cannot help preferring Soames Forsyte, in a choice of evils.

Just as one prefers June or any of the old aunts to Irene. Irene seems to me a sneaking, creeping, spiteful sort of bitch, an anti-Forsyte, absolutely living off the Forsytes—yes, to the very end; absolutely living off their money and trying to do them dirt. She is like Bosinney, a property

mongrel doing dirt in the property kennels. But she is a real property prostitute, like the little model in *Fraternity.* Only she is *anti*! It is a type recurring again and again in Galsworthy: the parasite upon the parasites, "Big fleas have little fleas, etc." And Bosinney and Irene, as well as the vagabond in *Island Pharisees,* are among the little fleas. And as a tramp loves his own vermin, so the Forsytes and the Hilarys love these, their own particular body parasites, their *antis*.

It is when he comes to sex that Mr Galsworthy collapses finally. He becomes nastily sentimental. He wants to make sex important, and he only makes it repulsive. Sentimentalism is the working off on yourself of feelings you haven't really got. We all *want* to have certain feelings: feelings of love, of passionate sex, of kindliness, and so forth. Very few people really feel love, or sex passion, or kindliness, or anything else that goes at all deep. So the mass just fake these feelings inside themselves. Faked feelings! The world is all gummy with them. They are better than real feelings, because you can spit them out when you brush your teeth; and then to-morrow you can fake them afresh.

Shelton, in *The Island Pharisees,* is the first of Mr Galsworthy's lovers, and he might as well be the last. He is almost comical. All we know of his passion for Antonia is that he feels at the beginning a "hunger" for her, as if she were a beefsteak. And towards the end he once kisses her, and expects her, no doubt, to fall instantly at his feet overwhelmed. He never for a second feels a moment of gentle sympathy with her. She is class-bound, but she doesn't seem to have been inhuman. The inhuman one was the lover. He can gloat over her in the distance, as if she were a dish of pig's trotters, *pieds truffés:* she can be an angelic *vision* to him a little way off, but when the poor thing has to be just a rather ordinary middle-class girl to him, quite near, he hates her with a comical, rancorous hate. It is most queer. He is helplessly *anti*. He hates her for even existing as a woman of her own class, for even having her own existence. Apparently she should just be a floating female sex-organ, hovering round to satisfy his little "hungers," and then *basta*. Anything of the real meaning of sex, which involves the whole of a human being, never occurs to him. It is a function, and the female is a sort of sexual appliance, no more.

And so we have it again and again, on this low and bastard level, all the human correspondence lacking. The sexual level is extraordinarily low, like dogs. The Galsworthy heroes are all weirdly in love with themselves, when we know them better, afflicted with chronic narcissism. They know just three types of women: the Pendyce mother, prostitute to property; the Irene, the essential *anti* prostitute, the floating, flaunting female organ; and the social woman, the mere lady. All three are loved and hated in turn by the recurrent heroes. But it is all on the debased level of property, positive or *anti*. It is all a doggy form of prostitution. Be quick and have done.

One of the funniest stories is **"The Apple Tree"**. The young man finds, at a lonely Devon farm, a little Welsh farm-girl who, being a Celt and not a Saxon, at once falls for the Galsworthian hero. This young gentleman, in the throes of narcissistic love for his marvellous self, falls for the maid because she has fallen so utterly and abjectly for him. She doesn't call him "My King," not being Wellsian; she only says: "I can't live away from you. Do what you like with me. Only let me come with you!" The proper prostitutional announcement!

For this, of course, a narcissistic young gentleman just down from Oxford falls at once. Ensues a grand pa-assion. He goes to buy her a proper frock to be carried away in, meets a college friend with a young lady sister, has jam for tea and stays the night, and the grand pa-assion has died a natural death by the time he spreads the marmalade on his bread. He has returned to his own class, and nothing else exists. He marries the young lady, true to his class. But to fill the cup of his vanity, the maid drowns herself. It is funny that maids only seem to do it for these narcissistic young gentlemen who, looking in the pool for their own image, desire the added satisfaction of seeing the face of drowned Ophelia there as well; saving them the necessity of taking the narcissus plunge in person. We have gone one better than the myth. Narcissus in Mr Galsworthy doesn't drown himself. He asks Ophelia, or Megan, kindly to drown herself instead. And in this fiction she actually does. And he feels so *wonderful* about it!

Mr Galsworthy's treatment of passion is really rather shameful. The whole thing is doggy to a degree. The man has a temporary "hunger"; he is "on the heat" as they say of dogs. The heat passes. It's done. Trot away, if you're not tangled. Trot off, looking shamefacedly over your shoulder. People have been watching! Damn them! But never mind, it'll blow over. Thank God, the bitch is trotting in the other direction. She'll soon have another trail of dogs after her. That'll wipe out my traces. Good for that! Next time I'll get properly married and do my doggishness in my own house.

With the fall of the individual, sex falls into a dog's heat. Oh, if only Mr Galsworthy had had the strength to satirise this too, instead of pouring a sauce of sentimental savouriness over it. Of course, if he had done so he would never have been a popular writer, but he would have been a great one.

However, he chose to sentimentalise and glorify the most doggy sort of sex. Setting out to satirise the Forsytes, he glorifies the *anti,* who is one worse. While the individual remains real and unfallen, sex remains a vital and supremely important thing. But once you have the fall into social beings, sex becomes disgusting, like dogs on the heat. Dogs are social beings, with no true canine individuality. Wolves and foxes don't copulate on the pavement. Their sex is wild and in act utterly private. Howls you may hear, but you will never see anything. But the dog is tame—and he makes excrement and he copulates on the pavement, as if to spite you. He is the Forsyte *anti.*

The same with human beings. Once they become tame they become, in a measure, exhibitionists, as if to spite everything. They have no real feelings of their own. Unless somebody "catches them at it" they don't really feel they've felt anything at all. And this is how the mob is today. It is Forsyte *anti.* It is the social being spiting society.

Oh, if only Mr Galsworthy had satirised *this* side of Forsy-

tism, the anti-Forsyte posturing of the "rebel," the narcissus and the exhibitionist, the dogs copulating on the pavement! Instead of that, he glorified it, to the eternal shame of English literature.

The satire, which in *The Man of Property* really had a certain noble touch, soon fizzles out, and we get that series of Galsworthian "rebels" who are, like all the rest of the modern middle-class rebels, not in rebellion at all. They are merely social beings behaving in an anti-social manner. They worship their own class, but they pretend to go one better and sneer at it. They are Forsyte *antis,* feeling snobbish about snobbery. Nevertheless, they want to attract attention and make money. That's why they are *anti.* It is the vicious circle of Forsytism. Money means more to them than it does to a Soames Forsyte, so they pretend to go one better, and despise it, but they will do anything to have it—things which Soames Forsyte would not have done.

If there is one thing more repulsive than the social being positive, it is the social being negative, the mere *anti.* In the great debacle of decency this gentleman is the most indecent. In a subtle way Bosinney and Irene are more dishonest and more indecent than Soames and Winifred, but they are *anti,* so they are glorified. It is pretty sickening.

The introduction to *Island Pharisees* explains the whole show:

> Each man born into the world is born to go a journey, and for the most part he is born on the high road. . . . As soon as he can toddle, he moves, by the queer instinct we call the love of life, along this road: . . . his fathers went this way before him, they made this road for him to tread, and, when they bred him, passed into his fibre the love of doing things as they themselves had done them. So he walks on and on. . . . Suddenly, one day, without intending to, he notices a path or opening in the hedge, leading to right or left, and he stands looking at the undiscovered. After that he stops at all the openings in the hedge; one day, with a beating heart, he tries one. And this is where the fun begins.

Nine out of ten get back to the broad road again, and sidetrack no more. They snuggle down comfortably in the next inn, and think where they might have been. "But the poor silly tenth is faring on. Nine times out of ten he goes down in a bog; the undiscovered has engulfed him." But the tenth time he gets across, and a new road is opened to mankind.

It is a class-bound consciousness, or at least a hopeless social consciousness which sees life as a high road between two hedges. And the only way out is gaps in the hedge and excursions into naughtiness! These little *anti* excursions, from which the wayfarer slinks back to solid comfort nine times out of ten; an odd one goes down in a bog; and a very rare one finds a way across and opens out a new road.

In Mr Galsworthy's novels we see the nine, the ninety-nine, the nine hundred and ninety-nine slinking back to solid comfort; we see an odd Bosinney go under a 'bus, because he hadn't guts enough to do something else, the poor *anti!* but that rare figure side-tracking into the unknown we do *not* see. Because, as a matter of fact, the whole figure is faulty at that point. If life is a great highway, then it must forge on ahead into the unknown. Side-tracking gets nowhere. That is mere *anti*. The tip of the road is always unfinished, in the wilderness. If it comes to a precipice and a canyon—well, then, there is need for some exploring. But we see Mr Galsworthy, after *The Country House,* very safe on the old highway, very secure in comfort, wealth, and renown. He at least has gone down in no bog, nor lost himself striking new paths. The hedges nowadays are ragged with gaps, anybody who likes strays out on the little trips of "unconventions." But the Forsyte road has not moved on at all. It has only become dishevelled and sordid with excursionists doing the *anti* tricks and being "unconventional," and leaving tin cans behind.

In the three early novels, *Island Pharisees, The Man of Property, Fraternity,* it looked as if Mr Galsworthy might break through the blind end of the highway with the dynamite of satire, and help us out on to a new lap. But the sex ingredient of his dynamite was damp and muzzy, the explosion gradually fizzled off in sentimentality, and we are left in a worse state than before.

The later novels are purely commercial, and, if it had not been for the early novels, of no importance. They are popular, they sell well, and there's the end of them. They contain the explosive powder of the first books in minute quantities, fizzling as silly squibs. When you arrive at *To Let,* and the end, at least the *promised* end, of the Forsytes, what have you? Just money! Money, money, money and a certain snobbish silliness, and many more *anti* tricks and poses. Nothing else. The story is feeble, the characters have no blood and bones, the emotions are faked, faked, faked. It is one great fake. Not necessarily of Mr Galsworthy. The characters fake their own emotions. But that doesn't help us. And if you look closely at the characters, the meanness and low-level vulgarity are very distasteful. You have all the Forsyte meanness, with none of the energy. Jolyon and Irene are meaner and more treacherous to their son than the older Forsytes were to theirs. The young ones are of a limited, mechanical, vulgar egoism far surpassing that of Swithin or James, their ancestors. There is in it all a vulgar sense of being rich, and therefore we do as we like: an utter incapacity for anything like *true* feeling, especially in the women, Fleur, Irene, Annette, June: a glib crassness, a youthful spontaneity which is just impertinence and lack of feeling; and all the time, a creeping, "having" sort of vulgarity of money and self-will, money and self-will, so that we wonder sometimes if Mr Galsworthy is not treating his public in real bad faith, and being cynical and rancorous under his rainbow sentimentalism.

Fleur he destroys in one word: she is "having." It is perfectly true. We don't blame the young Jon for clearing out. Irene he destroys in a phrase out of Fleur's mouth to June: "Didn't she spoil your life too?"—and it is precisely what she did. Sneaking and mean, Irene prevented June from getting her lover. Sneaking and mean, she prevents Fleur. She is the bitch in the manger. She is the sneaking *anti*. Irene, the most beautiful woman on earth! And Mr Galsworthy, with the cynicism of a successful old sentimentalist, turns it off by making June say: "Nobody can spoil a

life, my dear. That's nonsense. Things happen, but we bob up."

This is the final philosophy of it all. "Things happen, but we bob up." Very well, then, write the book in that key, the keynote of a frank old cynic. There's no point in sentimentalising it and being a sneaking old cynic. Why pour out masses of feelings that pretend to be genuine and then turn it all off with: "Things happen, but we bob up"?

It is quite true, things happen, and we bob up. If we are vulgar sentimentalists, we bob up just the same, so nothing has happened and nothing can happen. All is vulgarity. But it pays. There is money in it.

Vulgarity pays, and cheap cynicism smothered in sentimentalism pays better than anything else. Because nothing *can* happen to the degraded social being. So let's pretend it does, and then bob up!

It is time somebody began to spit out the jam of sentimentalism, at least, which smothers the "bobbing-up" philosophy. It is time we turned a straight light on this horde of rats, these younger Forsyte sentimentalists whose name is legion. It is sentimentalism which is stifling us. Let the social beings keep on bobbing up while ever they can. But it is time an effort was made to turn a hosepipe on the sentimentalism they ooze over everything. The world is one sticky mess, in which the little Forsytes indeed may keep on bobbing still, but in which an honest feeling can't breathe.

But if the sticky mess gets much deeper, even the little Forsytes won't be able to bob up any more. They'll be smothered in their own slime along with everything else. Which is a comfort. (pp. 52-72)

D. H. Lawrence, "John Galsworthy," in Scrutinies, *edited by Edgell Rickword, Wishart & Company, 1928, pp. 52-72.*

Hugh Walpole   (essay date 1933)

[Walpole was a popular English novelist whose works focus on the lives of the English upper and middle classes. In the following essay, he praises Galsworthy's technique and style in The Man of Property.*]*

Had John Galsworthy died in 1910, leaving behind him *The Man of Property* and *The Country House* as his principal novels, *The Silver Box* and *Strife* as his two important plays, it is probable that he would appear, to critics of every school to-day, as an artist of fine performance and yet greater promise, untimely cut off.

The savage article by D. H. Lawrence in the first volume of *Scrutinies,* the scorn and derision of the critics of the post-war generation, the half-hearted apologetic articles that appeared after his death, would certainly seem incredibly false and unjust to all the critical schools of 1910 could they encounter them.

It may be also that again in 1960 the literary critics who are interested in the history of the novel and the theatre from 1900 to 1930 (and it will offer many curious and opposite subjects for study) will regard Lawrence, in his critical moods, as hysterically unbalanced and the younger critics of 1930 as too self-conscious to be born. Galsworthy will then receive his just appreciation.

Had he died in 1910 he would seem to us now, I fancy, as possessing something near to genius in his appropriateness, a prophet, who created more wisely and more truly than he knew.

As artist it cannot be questioned that he lived too long, but of how many artists is that not true?—of Tolstoi, of Balzac, of Tennyson and Wordsworth, of Meredith and Anatole France. Nor in the final estimate is this of importance. An artist lives by his finest work—one single work, if it is grand enough, is sufficient. Time sweeps away the débris.

That Galsworthy wrote his best novel—*The Man of Property*—and his best play—*The Silver Box*—early in his career was perhaps his personal misfortune, for every artist wishes to feel that, as the years pass, he moves forward in his art. And it is true that the origin of all the adverse criticism encountered by him in his later years comes from this: that both as man and writer he deliberately shut himself off, as the years passed, from the general action of the outside world.

By this I do not of course mean any physical retirement. He was interested in many things, in the success of the Pen Club which he helped to found, in many public causes, in the adventures of his friends; he lectured in America and Germany and Austria; no writer in England felt more deeply than he the horrors of the War and the suffering that the War brought to the world. His isolation was a spiritual one. Any study of his work brings one to the certainty that, early in his career, he received an impression of injustice and intolerance so deep and moving that he was unable, after it, to step beyond it. It confined him inside its own experience, and everything that later happened to him, however various, received the same shape and colour.

But it was his destiny to live and work through the greatest changes that the world, within so short a space of time, has seen. To those who knew him only casually, to all who knew him only by his photograph or the written word, he appeared a man apart. His portrait with the austere, rather melancholy features, the meticulous neatness of dress, the anxious kindliness, as of a man who wished his fellow men well but feared for their future, had about it something almost inhuman, a reserved nobility.

To his intimates he was very different from this. I have heard his friends—Conrad and Hudson, for example—speak of him with passionate affection, as of someone rare amongst men for unswerving loyalty and integrity and fidelity. But his shyness, his innate modesty, his hatred of interfering in the privacy of others allowed him few intimacies, and it is certain that the real man was little known to the outside world. He scarcely ever replied to criticism, and was moved to protest only by injustice to others, never by injustice to himself. It followed therefore that his work was static. What he thought and felt in 1910 he thought and felt in 1930—the same injustice, the same intolerances moved him always.

The technique of his work also did not change. *The Man of Property* represents him technically assured and accomplished as does the *Flowering Wilderness* of 1932. Behind him, around him, however, between 1910 and 1930 the world of men suffered a complete transformation, not, it may be, in its deeper, more spiritual characteristics—for the impulses of the human soul do not alter—but in all the material visible circumstances; and it is of these that the novelist and dramatist must constantly be aware.

This awareness is the more important in Galsworthy's case because his principal work is a social chronicle, and depends for its essential truth on exactly this perception of social differences, and by "social" I mean something more important than the changing sequence of external manners and customs.

As I have said, had he never published any other novel than *The Man of Property* (it was conceived as a single work, and, when writing it, he intended no sequel) the whole of his art might have been found there. It is a study of social and moral injustice brought about by the greed and possessiveness of man. It appeared at a time when England was at the end of a period of possessive and wealthy domination, when the Forsytes were at the very top of the world and must, themselves, believe that they were there for all time.

Their power was derived from their tenacious adhesiveness, and the melancholy brooding over every page of this book comes, it seems, from Galsworthy's own belief at that time—that this tenacity will never be broken; all rebels against it will be broken by it.

These are the opening paragraphs of *The Man of Property:*

> Those privileged to be present at a family festival of the Forsytes have seen that charming and instructive sight—an upper middle-class family in full plumage. But whosoever of these favoured persons has possessed the gift of psychological analysis (a talent without monetary value and properly ignored by the Forsytes) has witnessed a spectacle, not only delightful in itself, but illustrative of an obscure, human problem. . . . He is like one who, having watched a tree grow from its planting—a paragon of tenacity, insulation, and success, amidst the deaths of a hundred other plants less fibrous, sappy, and persistent—one day will see it flourishing with bland, full foliage, in an almost repugnant prosperity, at the summit of its efflorescence.

In these rather stilted sentences Galsworthy states his terms, not only for this book, but for every other book that he was ever afterwards to write—his scorn of the top-dog who is in possession, his tenderness and pity for the under-dog.

The danger of this theme is at once apparent—unfairness to the top-dog (for whom there is always something to be said) and disgust of the under-dog at being pitied. In *The Man of Property* itself the danger is not so apparent—although it does sufficiently appear—but suppose that time passes and the top-dog changes places with the under-dog—what then? Will the under-dog forgive that tenderness? He will not only deeply resent it but it will seem to him the falsest of sentimentalities.

Nevertheless, *The Man of Property*—whose period is the late 'eighties—is, in itself, true to its time. This is not to say that every man in the England of the 'eighties was a Forsyte—Galsworthy does not pretend that it was so; there *were* sufficient Forsytes, their power and self-confidence and authority were strong and important enough to justify the emphasis. But even there—even in those opening sentences—the emphasis does not seem quite fair. The author's dislike is too strong for justice, and from the very first page we feel that we would like to hear something on the other side. In this city was there not one just man? Yes—old Jolyon Forsyte—he and he alone.

I believe *The Man of Property* to be a very fine novel, an important one in the progress of English literature of the early twentieth century, but I must admit at once to a serious handicap in my estimate of it, namely, that I cannot abide its two suffering under-dogs, the architect Bosinney and Irene, wife of Soames Forsyte. Now this is in all probability a personal defect in myself, but is there not also an irony in the fact that in all the Galsworthy novels and in some of the plays (Mrs. Jones of *The Silver Box* is an under-dog who has all my affection and admiration if she will allow me to say so), it is the upper-dogs rather than the under-dogs who win our sympathy? If the under-dogs *do* win our sympathy it is not because they are ill-treated by the upper-dogs, but because they are ill-treated (in his tenderness and care of them) by Galsworthy.

Consider for a moment Bosinney and Irene Soames. In Galsworthy's behaviour to them are to be found, I think, all the grounds for the charges of falseness and sentimentality brought against him. It is not that Bosinney and Irene are themselves false. Very far from it. The charge that Galsworthy cannot create human beings (a charge brought against him by Lawrence, whose own weakness, as novelist, this especially was) is ludicrously false. He was always creating them, from Soames and Jolyon and Swithin and Bosinney to the heroine of *Flowering Wilderness.* No. The sentimentality comes in, of course, through his personal attitude to them.

Bosinney and Irene are, Galsworthy feels (and makes us feel that he feels), creatures monstrously ill-treated. They are the victims of the Forsyte possessiveness. But are they? Irene (for reasons never sufficiently clear to us) has married a man whom she hates and, in the pages of this novel at least, she never ceases to show that she hates him. Soames may not be the most endearing of men (in the later pages of the Saga, Galsworthy grows fonder and fonder of him), but at least he is ready to do all that he can, save give his wife her freedom. There lies his criminal fault in his creator's eyes. But does Irene, on her side, make the slightest attempt to keep *her* part of the bargain? She hates Soames, and that justifies her, it seems, in playing the part from first to last of a female cad. Her own callous selfishness is to one reader at least infinitely more appalling than Soames's possessiveness. As for Bosinney, he is surely one of the most unattractive men in all fiction! Galsworthy seems to feel that there is something delightful in Bosinney's boorish rudeness to all the Forsytes and something

charming in his dishonourable breaking of his bargains in the matter of the House. He was, it appears, quite irresistible to Irene, but his gifts as a lover are concealed from us, for we are never permitted, in the course of the whole book, to be present at any encounter between the lovers, but, as though we were all Forsytes (which very probably we are), we are kept at a distance, and only with gigantic Swithin or vagabondish George are we allowed to overhear them as in a dream.

Irene's misery and Bosinney's snarling unhappiness are, throughout the book, uninterrupted. Did Irene never know a happy moment? Did she never smile at some organ-grinder's monkey nor delight in a spring flower, nor enjoy, in a self-forgetful moment, a fragment of the excellent meals that Soames provided for her? Did a new dress never give her pleasure nor an evening at the theatre amuse her? If such things occurred (and we fancy that she was a far brighter creature than Galsworthy allows us to believe), we are not told of them.

Having, however, thrown the under-dogs (not only in this book but in all that followed it) to the Forsyte lions, how excellent a story this is!

The English novel in 1910 was struggling out of a morass of romanticism, was struggling hard to tell the truth about life, with Henry James acquiring new subtleties, with H. G. Wells and Arnold Bennett new backgrounds, with Conrad new nobilities. Galsworthy, with *The Man of Property,* gave it a new technique. It is a queer fact that the two novelists who influenced him most strongly were Turgenieff and Dickens, two men as opposite as God could make them. His aim was to give the English novel the meticulous self-conscious care of the author of *On the Eve,* and to create, within the beautiful form, a life as vigorous and various as the world of *Martin Chuzzlewit* and *Great Expectations.* An impossible ambition, but the first attempt at a struggle to reconcile self-conscious artistry with spontaneous unself-conscious creation—the principal struggle for the English novelist to-day and for many days to come.

He had, also, in these pre-war novels an advantage that in his post-war novels he, and all his contemporaries, were to lose, namely, a fixed and cohesive background.

The London of the late 'eighties hung behind them like a rich figured tapestry. The room where it was he had in his most sensitive years occupied. He knew every detail of it, the odd little figures slightly out of drawing, the houses and trees, the shadows of purple and rich brown, a wash of gold over it all. So we have it in this first of the famous series. On page 5 of *The Man of Property* there is Swithin:

> Over against the piano a man of bulk and stature was wearing two waistcoats on his wide chest, two waistcoats and a ruby pin, instead of the single satin waistcoat and diamond pin of more usual occasions, and his shaven, square, old face, the colour of pale leather, with pale eyes, had its most dignified look, above his satin stock.

"The colour of pale leather"—is that not this artist's sign, the butterfly in the corner of the page? We shall meet it often again.

And what do they have for dinner at Swithin's—"a Tewkesbury ham, together with the least touch of West India"—that "least touch," the touch of the connoisseur, how often we shall encounter it as the Forsytes go down the ages!

They live, not only the Forsytes, but all the characters in all the Galsworthy novels, in a world composed of Russian leather, emeralds, cherry-coloured moons, azaleas, spring buds, spanking horses, gold-mounted Malacca canes, water-colours, Tewkesbury hams "with the least touch of West India," dogs, and a number of delicate and almost imperceptible scents. The characters who do not share this world of the connoisseur are the under-dogs who spend very much of their time hanging about in the rain at street corners.

Every novelist of character has his idiosyncrasies and a world furnished over and over again with the same furniture, but with Galsworthy (as with Balzac in a greater instance) these details are so significant that it may be that the cut of an emerald or the scent of a cigar is of more importance than a human being. They are used, these details, with the utmost adroitness, to heighten the drama, to express the pathos, to rub in the contrast, and the only possible criticism of them is that sometimes we see Galsworthy arranging them as a stage-hand places the table, the vase, and the bookcase before the curtain rises. There is a striking example of this in the last chapter of *The Man of Property,* when Soames desperately walks the streets. "Along the garden rails a half-starved cat came rubbing her way towards him." And later: "Something soft touched his legs, the cat was rubbing herself against them." We are forced to ask ourselves—what would Galsworthy have done had the cat been plump and well fed!

Nevertheless, what technical triumphs this book contains. The chapter entitled "Drive with Swithin" is possibly the finest thing he ever wrote, and should be given, as an example of perfect technical and emotional mastery, to any young student of the novel.

As the novel develops you can feel the Forsytes pressing like a slowly invading wall upon the prisoners, June, Bosinney, and Irene. The hum of gossip from the old maids, the solemn despotism of Forsytes at a business meeting, Forsytes slumbering in their clubs, Forsytes driving "a pair of spanking bays," Forsytes puckering brows over the evaluation of a piece of silver or a Bonnington or a pearl necklace, Forsytes holding in mid-air a bottle of "crusted Port," Forsytes going to bed and rising again, Forsytes in the bath and at breakfast, making love to their wives or their mistresses, all these symbolic figures crowd the London air, scatter gold-dust, and eagerly bend to gather it again while the Oppressed, the Undervalued, the true citizens of Galsworthy's ultimate spiritual Battersea Dogs' Home, struggle to survive for Galsworthy's sake if not for their own!

But, in this first volume of the Forsyte Saga, it is the true, deep and experienced passion, behind every page, implicit in every line, that gives the book its especial power. Because the background is so firmly dated that it is dateless, because the emotion from which the book sprang is so real

and true, because of the freshness and originality of the technique, because so many real people live in its pages, therefore *The Man of Property* is one of the important books in the history of the English novel.

The Saga follows it. It was not, as I have said, originally intended, and it has all the formlessness of a work that grows without knowing the reasons of its growth. There *were* no reasons except the one excellent one that "people wanted to hear some more about those Forsytes."

Now this is a reason at which every superior critic will scoff. So self-conscious has the Higher Criticism of the novel now become that all simple joys are denied it. A novel must not have readers, at most only a *very* few. Readers must not enjoy themselves. Novelists must be ashamed, rather than proud, if they are happy.

It is one of the finest things about Galsworthy that, self-conscious artist as he was, he never lost the simple but, for a novelist, profoundly important love of story-telling. He says that he always found writing very difficult, that he had to struggle and wrestle before he could achieve a good ordinary page of simple narrative. But when, forgetting himself as artist, he was carried away into the world of spontaneous creation he was, like Fielding and Thackeray and Dickens before him, lost in the company of his characters. It is this that gives its value to the Forsyte Saga, not its social commentary which is often forced, not the philosophy of Forsyte possessiveness which is often monotonous, not its tenderness which is often sentimental, but its sheer creative zest. The characters in the Saga must often have felt that they could give a better account of themselves than Galsworthy has given (have not the characters of a novelist always a just and reasonable complaint against their interpreter?), but on the whole they permit him his discoveries, and sometimes, as with Swithin, old Jolyon, Soames himself, and his French wife (a wonderful sketch this last), they take hold of him, carry him away with them and exist, as every great character in fiction does, independently of their author. It is notorious that Soames took charge of him in this way—he has himself acknowledged it—and in Soames he does what every true novelist longs to do—adds a universal figure to the small company of immortals. Soames Forsyte, although he may be small in stature and tight about the nose, belongs to the company that includes Uncle Toby, Sophia Western, Dandie Dinmont, Mr. Bennett, Mr. Micawber, Beatrix, John Silver, the Reddle Man, and Uncle Ponderovo.

Of the novels outside the Forsyte Saga two were successful—*The Country House* and *Fraternity*—and there were some unhappy failures. *The Country House* is Galsworthy's best novel after *The Man of Property,* and Mrs. Pendyce, after Soames and old Jolyon, his most successful creation.

These novels all reveal Galsworthy's virtues and failings—the charm and delicacy of detached scenes (Galsworthy paints always in water-colour), a narrative gift expended sometimes on incredible themes like the Moslem incident in *Flowering Wilderness,* unceasing pity for the oppressed who so often move restlessly under his tenderness, an Englishness that is sometimes fine poetry, sometimes sheer parochialism, irony but no humour (he is at his worst when he is playful—recall if you dare the old lady with the nostrums in *The Freelands*), a passion (almost as though he were a Forsyte collector) for furniture, jewellery, clothes, and food, and the eternally recurrent theme of unhappy and restless physical love. There is no spiritual life in any of his characters, no mysticism, no religious faith. When his people are dead they are *dead.*

One change there is in the later novels, both in the second half of the Saga and in the books that are un-Forsyte. He is no longer sure of his background. This uncertainty is revealed especially in the dialogue and, most notably of all, in the slangy talk of the younger and more sporting generation of Forsytes.

But who *can* be certain of this post-war background? It is one of the problems of the new novelist that he must disregard the changing tumult and hunt for the permanencies. The Vicar of Wakefield, Quixote, Prince Andrew are of no time nor country nor fashion, or rather they are of *all* times, countries, and fashions! It is just this imperviousness to fashion that, I think, Galsworthy lacks in his later novels.

He tries to catch the accents, the tone, the snarl of the current traffic. He is distressed by a world that seems to him vulgar, cruel, and selfish. But no period, no stage in man's history can be stated in terms as simple as that. Man at any time and seen in any light asks deeper questions than those that concern his immediate safety or unhappiness. It is not enough to say that he is unjustly treated, because so many men will always rise magnificently beyond their own personal misfortune. This is what Galsworthy has but rarely shown us, and then in the plays rather than the novels—Mrs. Jones of *The Silver Box,* the antagonists of *Strife,* the proletarian in *The Skin Game,* the Jew in *Loyalties*—these are almost heroic figures. Old Jolyon is the only hero in the whole of the Forsyte Saga, and as it grows, the figures in it, except Soames himself, dwindle and dwindle until at last they vanish in the smoke of Soames's conflagration.

So, looking back, we greet that austere, lonely, dignified figure, apart save for a few intimates, generous, unselfish, courageous, distressed by the distresses of others. Through all his life he never did a mean nor disloyal act. He lived, immaculately, up to his own severe set standards, and his heart was as warm as his acts of generosity were secret. As artist he suffered because it was his fate to live through two violently opposed states of society to only one of which he really belonged. But *that*—his own individual possession—he seized, and preserved. The new world—the world of Joyce and Lawrence, of Epstein and Schönberg, of Stalin and Hitler—was not his, and could never have been his. It seemed to him to break all his rules of order, restraint, and courtesy. But that other world, that other England of the spanking bays, the club windows set with faces politely interested (but not too eagerly) in the passing crowd, the polite but tyrannous Board Meetings, the tyranny of class, a world built up out of the past, shining with gold, aromatic with delicate odours, sanctified by caste, this, as he himself said, he embalmed in amber; he was too modest to add—for posterity.

No one will ever be born again who has known that world at first hand; it is gone never to return; and Galsworthy is, and will always be, the most authentic of its painters. (pp. 175-85)

> *Hugh Walpole, "John Galsworthy," in* The Post Victorians, *edited by Rev. W. R. Inge, Ivor Nicholson & Watson, Ltd., 1933, pp. 175-85.*

Edward Wagenknecht   (essay date 1954)

[*Wagenknecht is an American biographer best known for his profiles of such nineteenth-century writers as Nathaniel Hawthorne, Washington Irving, William Dean Howells, and Harriet Beecher Stowe. In the following excerpt, he surveys* The Forsyte Saga, A Modern Comedy, *and* End of the Chapter *and discusses literary influences on Galsworthy's work.*]

1. *March to Mastery*

When John Galsworthy killed his most famous character, at least one London paper headlined the event

DEATH OF SOAMES FORSYTE

as if a man of flesh and blood had passed. At the writer's own death in 1933 he was generally regarded as the most distinguished of British novelists. It had not always been so. Paging through the publishers' advertisements in old *Harpers* and *Atlantics,* one can still find a new novel "by John Galsworthy"—*Fraternity* or maybe *The Patrician*—modestly listed in small type among the "also rans," while the bold face at the top of the page proudly proclaims another piece of trash by some already forgotten writer. This was the period when a distinguished British ecclesiastic, visiting the University of Chicago, picked up a book from the desk of the president's secretary, and mumbled, "Galsworthy? Galsworthy? And is he, then, one of your rising young American writers?" As late as 1916, in the first critical study of Galsworthy's books ever to be graced with the dignity of boards, Sheila Kaye-Smith permitted herself one of the worst prophecies on record: "Galsworthy will never be widely read. . . ."

Galsworthy had almost deliberately made haste slowly. He was born in Surrey, August 14, 1867; his father, a prosperous attorney, descended from Devonshire yeoman stock, his mother from a line of provincial squires, gentlemen farmers, and men of commerce. He was not a remarkable student either at Harrow or at Oxford, where his literary passions were *Ruff's Guide* and the novels of Whyte-Melville; and he finally became a barrister not because he loved the law but because it was considered a genteel profession for a dandified young sportsman with no particular ambition in life. Foreign travel may have helped destroy his insular outlook, but the really determinative influence was that of his cousin, Ada Galsworthy. "Why don't you write?" she had asked him in 1894, when she was still the wife of his cousin Arthur. "You're just the person." Through the difficult years up to their marriage in 1905, Galsworthy played Young Jolyon to her Irene; thus he attained his spiritual maturity. An elegant young trifler died; a serious artist was born. It is not too much to say that John Galsworthy experienced a non-religious conversion.

The first-fruits were two volumes of short stories—*From the Four Winds* (1897) and *A Man of Devon* (1901)—and two novels—*Jocelyn* (1898) and *Villa Rubein* (1900). These books are interesting as prefiguring the work that an important writer was to do rather than as positive achievements. No doubt the same might be said of *The Island Pharisees* (1904), but if this book is only a prologue it is a remarkable one; every motif later employed in Galsworthy's work is already sounded in it.

Complete maturity came suddenly in 1906 with *The Man of Property,* at about the same time that *The Silver Box* marked its author's arrival as a dramatist. But not until the complete *Forsyte Saga* appeared in 1922 did Galsworthy become a world figure. He refused knighthood in 1918 but accepted the Order of Merit in 1929 and the Nobel Prize in 1932. His death occurred January 31, 1933.

2. *The Forsytes*

Though *The Forsyte Saga* was the title he first had in mind for *The Man of Property,* Galsworthy did not then see that novel as one of a series. In the terrible last chapter, Irene, utterly defeated by the death of her lover, returns to her husband's house; and as late as 1911 Galsworthy was still telling questioners that he did not know what they did afterwards. In **"Indian Summer of a Forsyte,"** written in 1917, Irene is described as having left Soames again that same night, but it was not until one Sunday in the summer of 1918 that the idea of the complete *Saga* came into Galsworthy's mind.

The Forsytes are rich London bourgeoisie, "the very people," as Wilbur Cross has remarked, "who entered largely into the novels of Dickens and Thackeray." Dickens hated them; Thackeray was impressed principally by their snobbery. There is considerable sensitiveness in the Jolyon branch of the family, but there is less in Soames's line, for though Soames is a noted connoisseur, he is never able to forget the monetary value of his pictures. We are told that "In my father's house are many mansions" is one of Aunt Juley's favorite texts; it comforts her "with its suggestion of house property." The tragedy of it is that a Forsyte cannot stop with regarding houses as property. Everything is property. Wives are property. Soames regards Irene as property, and the climax of their history is a legalized rape—a "supreme act of property"—which poisons the lives of the Forsytes through two generations.

The Man of Property, which opens with a gathering of the clan on June 15, 1886, and which ends in 1888, is the most "packed" of all the Forsyte novels, and the most discursive as to method. All ten of the old Forsytes are still alive at the beginning of this book—(Soames himself, James's son, "the man of property," belongs to the younger generation)—and after the author gets through the tedious "charactery" of his opening chapters, he is very successful in welding diverse materials together. The material is presented from many different points of view, but never from that of Irene or her lover, Bosinney. Irene is a "concretion of disturbing Beauty impinging on a possessive world"; we see her only as she is reflected in the minds of others; Bo-

sinney we can hardly be said to see at all. In the first draft Galsworthy actually had Bosinney commit suicide after Soames's crime on Irene, and it took all Edward Garnett's persuasive powers to convince him that this would not do. The accidental death of the published text is a skillful evasion.

In Chancery (1920) opens in 1899 and ends with the famous description of Queen Victoria's funeral. After an abortive attempt to rewin Irene, which only succeeds in driving her into the arms of Young Jolyon, Soames finally frees himself of the past, and marries the French girl, Annette, in the hope that she may bear him a son. *In Chancery* is lighter and far less complicated than *The Man of Property,* and though it has its own merits, many readers think of it as preparing the way for the moving love-affair between Fleur, daughter of Soames and Annette, and Jon, Irene's son by Young Jolyon.

Skipping the First World War, *To Let* (1921) opens May 12, 1920. Galsworthy's epigraph deliberately challenges the comparison with *Romeo and Juliet:*

> From out [*sic*] the fatal loins of these two foes
> A pair of star-crossed lovers take their life.

Ignorant of the bitter past, the children meet and love. When the revelation comes, Fleur would go on, but Jon draws back. Juliet does not kill herself with Romeo's dagger, for the day of old heroic passions has gone by; instead she marries Michael Mont, who is much too good for her. But one may bleed to death internally without a dagger.

The Man of Property left us speculating about the future of Soames and Irene. In the same way, *To Let* leaves us wondering about Fleur and Jon and Michael. So Galsworthy gave us his second Forsyte trilogy, *A Modern Comedy.*

In the first novel of this series, *The White Monkey* (1924), the first test of Fleur's marriage comes when Wilfrid Desert, a typical representative of the "lost generation," conceives a passion for her. Fleur is reckless enough to give Michael a pretty bad time temporarily, but in the end she sends Wilfrid on his way. In *The Silver Spoon* (1926) modern "morality" goes on trial in a society scandal which involves Fleur and Marjorie Ferrars. If this seems a flimsy theme for a serious novel, we must remember that the drifting aimlessness of post-war lives is precisely what Galsworthy is writing about. *Swan Song* (1928) rises to a much higher emotional level with its tragic revival of Fleur's passion for Jon and the fatal consequences of that affair for Soames.

Critics generally feel that the *Comedy* does not reach the level of the *Saga,* and they have been very busy trying to figure out why. Galsworthy's sympathies are not with the period covered, they tell us. Or, it is impossible to achieve "completeness . . . in the portrayal of a generation whose destiny . . . [is] still obscure." Sometimes it is even suggested that Galsworthy has now become the professional novelist, "carried forward more by the momentum already acquired than by any powerful creative impulse; each book follows immediately on the year in which the action is placed, as if the author were somewhat hastily and perfunctorily keeping his chronicle up to date."

Certainly there can be no question as to the contemporaneousness of the *Comedy*. Practically every fad and foible of the twenties enters somewhere—jazz, cubism, dadaism, futurism, osteopathy, birth-control, mental healing, psychoanalysis. Couéism, and what-have-you. *Swan Song* opens on a hostile picture of the General Strike of 1926; in *The Silver Spoon* Michael identifies himself with "Foggartism," a scheme for the economic salvation of England which includes, among other things, the emigration of large numbers of English children. The business background of *The White Monkey* is dark and murky, and the lower-class story of Bicket and Victorine is not closely enough connected with the main plot to be judged other than an extraneous element.

But if the *Comedy* has not quite the force of the *Saga,* it has gained in humanity. This is due largely to the fact that Soames is much more attractive as an old man than he was in middle age—to that and to Fleur. Fleur is the Beatrix Esmond of post-war fiction. She has Beatrix's limitations of character, Beatrix's clear-sighted realization of her own shortcomings, and Beatrix's incapacity to do anything about them. She has too—and here she is unlike Beatrix—an endearing childlikeness, which crops out, despite her sophistication, in every crisis, and which disarms the reader as completely as it disarms her husband. Doubtless our kindliness toward her, despite all her faults, is largely a tribute to the skill and fine humanity with which Galsworthy has portrayed her. By the time we get through the *Comedy,* we have suffered with her through her terribly young heartbreak over Jon; we have stood by her side through the agonies of motherhood; we have trembled for her soul when she flings her cap over the windmill; and we have tasted the salt tears of her bitter remorse when her father is killed. There are not many women in English fiction whom we know so well.

Her brief reappearances in *End of the Chapter* are not wholly satisfactory. In *Maid in Waiting* she has nothing to do save motor Dinny and her friends around the country! But Galsworthy leaves us in no doubt that she has kept the promise she made her dying father when she said, "Yes, Dad; I will be good!" Only her own soul knows what it has cost her. Something vivid, something lovable has gone from the willful girl we used to know. To achieve such self-mastery a woman must either become a saint or else she must partly kill herself.

I have got over now into another trilogy, *End of the Chapter,* which is a kind of addendum to the story of the Forsytes, its heroine, Dinny Charwell, being a connection of Fleur's on her husband's side. These books may be dismissed quickly; here if anywhere Galsworthy transgressed his own advice to Ralph Mottram never to write anything unless he must. The first, *Maid in Waiting* (1931), is the worst; it scatters; its pictures of contemporary society lack vividness and pass too rapidly before our eyes; the staccato dialogue is all on the surface. In *Flowering Wilderness* (1932), Wilfrid Desert returns to England much less a rotter than one might have expected after *The White Monkey,* but his genuine romance with Dinny is wrecked by

the fact that public opinion will not condone his having abjured Christianity at the point of an Arab's pistol. *Over the River* (American title: *One More River*) (1933) has value merely as one more illustration of Galsworthy's ability to write breathless courtroom scenes.

3. *The Others*

The non-Forsyte novels divide themselves into two groups: four novels of social criticism and three novels of passion. The first group comprises *The Country House* (1907); *Fraternity* (1909); *The Patrician* (1911); and *The Freelands* (1915). The second group consists of *The Dark Flower* (1913); *Beyond* (1917); and *Saint's Progress* (1919).

Galsworthy himself was inclined to regard *The Country House* as the best of his non-Forsyte books. Among the wealthy landed gentry, "Pendycitis" replaces Forsyteism; "Pendycitis" is indeed as close to Forsyteism as a class can come which cherishes tradition and refuses to place a strictly commercial valuation upon the experience of living. As so often in Galsworthy, *The Country House* uses social scandal to test a society. George Pendyce is in love with Mrs. Bellew, who resembles Irene as an extraneous element in her lover's world, but who differs from her in being a thoroughly bad woman. His father would disinherit George on principle, but Mrs. Pendyce stands by him—and even risks a break with her husband to do so—not because she thinks him right, but because she loves him, and love is higher than law. In the end, George recovers, and Mrs. Pendyce returns to her husband. Nothing has "happened," but a way of life has been critically examined.

Fraternity, a study in frustration, is Galsworthy's most hopeless book, and technically it is probably the most perfect. Nearly every one of the upper middle-class intelligentsia who occupy the foreground has his "shadow" among the submerged; but despite the best intentions in the world the gulf between the classes cannot be bridged. If you try, the most elementary facts of life defeat you; Hilary's marriage-vow does not keep him from running off with the Little Model, but "the scent of stale violet powder . . . warmed by her humanity," when she throws her arms round his neck and kisses him on the mouth, can and does. So the girl drops into the underworld presumably, and the man's last chance to escape utter sterility has passed him by. Fraternity exists only in the interminable pages of old Mr. Stone's crazy book, which he goes on writing and writing in that hopeless household where no human being ever meets another on common ground.

In *The Patrician,* which goes over into the world of the aristocracy, the conflict is between Lord Miltoun's love for Audrey Lees Noel, whose clergyman-husband refuses to divorce her, and his career. The man cannot take his love in secret, for he will not be a hypocrite. At one time he decides to relinquish his career, but Lord Dennis convinces him that this would be unfair to Mrs. Noel. In the end she solves her lover's problem by going away.

Miltoun's young sister, Barbara, the most splendid of all Galsworthy's girls, is wiser. Barbara loves Courtier, a radical democrat, and she would have taken him, too, if circumstances had not defeated her. In the end she makes a sensible, suitable, and eminently fitting marriage with a fine young man whom she does not love.

The Freelands is Galsworthy's most unappreciated novel and one of his best. This, as Leon Schalit has remarked, is a rural *Fraternity;* the problem of the poor is now presented in a country setting. The Preface expounds the moral, which is "that England will never be sound and safe till the land is again what it once was, the very backbone and blood of our race." There is surprising variety in the Freeland clan, and much fine characterization.

It seems strange that Galsworthy, who handled passion so movingly in the Fleur-Jon romance and in the greatest of his shorter pieces, **"The Apple Tree,"** should have failed when he tried to make passion the theme of a whole novel. Perhaps *Beyond* is not really a novel of passion. Gyp gives her worthless first husband, Fiorsen, an embodiment of the "artistic temperament" at its worst, "everything except her heart"; the reader finds it nearly as difficult as her father does to explain why she married him. *Beyond* is a "woman's novel"; it reminds me of Margaret Ayer Barnes, though it is far below the best of that author's work. In *Saint's Progress,* which is the story of a clergyman's daughter and her "war baby," Galsworthy fails for a different reason. He had often used social scandal to test society; here he seems to be using it for its own sake, and this proves much less interesting. He is handicapped also by his failure to understand mystical experience; because the author is quite unable to describe Edward Pierson's religious life, it must seem to the reader that he has none. Indeed *Saint's Progress* has little value save as a social document depicting life in England during the First World War, and as an expression of Galsworthy's own humane and civilized refusal to surrender to a savage wartime mood.

Galsworthy would not have objected to anything I have said about these two books; he set little store by either of them. On the other hand, he regarded *The Dark Flower* highly, and this is a view which I cannot share. This book presents three detached episodes in the love life of Mark Lennan. As a young man, he spurns the middle-aged professor's wife who has conceived a passion for him; in his maturity, he finds the grand passion, only to have it snatched from him by death; growing old, he is pursued by a young girl, whom he rejects at last out of consideration for his wife. Mark's passion is considerably more real than he is, which is likely the inevitable result of omitting everything in his life that does not bear upon the erotic experience. Galsworthy's tendency to shift his point of view continually does not help this story either; very likely we might find Part I more palatable if we saw Anna only through Mark's eyes.

4. *Literary Ideals and Practice*

Galsworthy regarded Tolstoy's *War and Peace* as the greatest modern novel, but he claimed to have learned less from Tolstoy than he learned from Turgenev and de Maupassant. There has been much discussion as to just how these literary idols affected him. Sheila Kaye-Smith derives his pity from Russia, his irony from France. But, she

adds, his Russian pity is "shorn of its mysticism," his French irony of its gaiety. Frank Swinnerton, who calls him the first English novelist "to turn for what may be called technical inspiration to Russia," points out that while French realism is objective, Russian realism "was always tinged with philosophy (that is to say, with ethics and metaphysics) and with politics." Ford Madox Ford thought that Turgenev was responsible for transforming Galsworthy from the Trollope he might otherwise have been to the novelist of pity he became.

Personally I do not take any of this too seriously. As for Ford, the dates plainly contradict his assumption that *Villa Rubein,* which he liked, was free of Turgenev's influence, and that this entered first in *The Island Pharisees* and *The Man of Property,* which he did not like. In general, I believe that Galsworthy wrote sympathetically because he was Galsworthy. He did not learn pity out of anybody's book. And if he needed an example there were plenty before him in nineteenth-century England.

Except in the play, *Justice* (1910), which did produce changes in English prison administration, Galsworthy did not actually work for reform in the good old fashion of Charles Dickens and Charles Reade. Again and again he insists that he is not trying to reform anything; he is simply expressing his view of life, describing the world as it appears to him in the light of his particular temperament. He thought of art as "the one form of human energy in the whole world, which really works for union, and destroys the barriers between man and man." To his way of thinking, the artist could only see life as in a state of flux; for him no questions were closed questions; he could have no desire to impose his temperament upon another.

Galsworthy might possibly have been more strongly tempted to use his art for propaganda purposes had he possessed a more hopeful nature. Wells and Shaw are great crusaders because they are great believers in human perfectibility. To be sure, everything is wrong now, but everything might so easily be made right if only we would listen to them! Galsworthy had no such faith. For him the roots of human maladjustments lay deep in the stuff of human nature itself. Palliation might be possible, but there could never be a cure.

Naturally none of this obviates the necessity for pity, and it was along this line that Galsworthy was sometimes reproached for his "sentimentality." "The sight of a butterfly," remarks Philip Guedalla, "makes him think of wheels." I am not surprised to learn through Mr. H. V. Marrot that Galsworthy greatly admired the work of Robert Nathan, for some of his references to animals are curiously like Nathan's. But on the whole I think Galsworthy's "sentimentality" very nicely balanced by his love of irony, by the under-expression to which he and his characters alike (nearly all modern cultivated Englishmen) are so notoriously given, and by his preference for what he himself calls "the negative method." He did not admire Jane Austen, but he might have said with her that "pictures of perfection" made him "sick and wicked." What he did say was that angelic conceptions are for poetry, not prose. A novelist must not "look up" to his characters.

As for the influence of de Maupassant and Turgenev on Galsworthy's form specifically, this is made difficult to determine by the fact that in the novel, as distinguished from the medium-length story of the *Five Tales,* he never considered form of any particular importance. Yet he is "arty" (for want of a better word) as few of his English predecessors before Meredith had been. He lacks the companionable quality of Dickens and Thackeray; not for him is the novel a long conversation between author and reader. No, he holds himself in reserve; he carves his statue with far more regard than they showed for purity and clarity of line; he is fastidious; he must load every rift with ore. This aristocratic reserve was, no doubt, largely a matter of temperament, but was it not this fastidiousness in his temperament that caused him to turn to continental models, and must it not have been immensely encouraged by them? So it comes about that Galsworthy is emphatically one of the novelists that need to be savored. His pages are full of delicate perceptions and lovely but quite unpretentious turns of expression, and this is a large part of the charm he has for his devotees.

The profoundest of Galsworthy's critics, André Chevrillon, has paid warm tribute to his use of indirect speech. He has also tried to justify Galsworthy's frequent shifts in point of view:

> The idea that governs his art is that the inner life of a man is seen only in flashes, that we never get a direct view of it—therefore that no direct description of it can be true—and further, that a character is part of an ever-moving group, where no single figure appears for a moment in the foreground without being eclipsed by others—therefore that it should not be kept too long before the footlights, and studied separately.

But this tendency is not universally praised. Professor Joseph Warren Beach, for example, goes so far as to connect Galsworthy's "paleness" with "his inability to regard any person, place, or object steadily for any length of time." It would be difficult to deny that this "paleness" does exist at times in all save his very finest work. He himself recognized variations even within the same book; he knew that he had failed with Bosinney, for example. It is interesting that he did not always succeed with the characters he liked best. In *The Patrician* he admires Mrs. Noel and dislikes Miltoun, but Miltoun is the one he makes real.

5. *Criticism of Life*

As a critic of life, Galsworthy is sometimes judged nihilistic. He believed that life is a mess and that we should be kind; and this, say the authoritarians, is not enough. Religiously speaking, he rejected all the distinctive Christian doctrines; to him a creed was only the expression of a temperament, and he attributed the decline of the church in modern times to its vain attempt to cling to an outgrown conception of religious authority.

Yet he had a vague metaphysic of his own, and here and there we find traces of a Meredith-like nature-mysticism. Now and again, his characters discuss their religious problems. In *The Freelands,* Cuthcott finds belief in God inevitable, "some kind of instinct toward perfection," "some kind of honor forbidding one to let go and give up." A

conversation between Young Jolyon and Jolly in *In Chancery* comes closer to orthodox Christianity than Galsworthy gets anywhere else. Young Jolyon proclaims his faith in "the Unknowable Creative Principle" and also in "the Sum of altruism in man"; it remains for Jolly to point out that these two ideas have been joined in Christ.

As Galsworthy himself draws nearer the Mystery, his interest in religion seems to be increasing, though his orthodoxy clearly is not. In *Maid in Waiting,* God is defined as "perpetual motion in perpetual quiet," but not as a God of mercy in the ordinary sense, or as "of much immediate use to mortals." Hilary, the good parson, who admits that he would be unfrocked if his real beliefs were known, reads to a dying child not from the Bible but from *Alice in Wonderland!*

Galsworthy has commented on the difference between himself and Dickens in this matter of faith, and it troubled him, for he wished to preserve the Christian ethic, and he was intelligent enough to know that this is difficult to do without Christian sanctions. In *Maid in Waiting* there is a long didactic passage from Hubert's diary, arguing against the view that with religious values gone, "There's nothing for it but to enjoy ourselves as best we can." Hubert argues that "You can't . . . disbelieve in consideration for others without making an idiot of yourself and spoiling your own chances of a good time." Galsworthy had no faith in sacrifice as a virtue in and for itself, but even Fleur must learn in the end that sacrifice is a necessary prerequisite to conquest. This is the subject of Michael's meditation during the terrible hours when Fleur writhes in childbirth: "To have a creed that nothing mattered—and then run into it like this! Something born at such a cost, must matter, should matter. One must see to that!"

It was not hard for Michael to learn that, for Michael was, as it were, a "natural" Christian. It is harder for Soames and for Fleur. Wisdom comes to him through his love for his daughter, the first selfless, unpropertied love he has ever known. He learns the truth perhaps more completely than she ever does, but he learns it later in life than it comes to her. And in the end he dies for her, as the only way he can pass his knowledge on. Very nearly the last words Fleur speaks in *Over the River* make the point inescapable:

> Of course I know what you've been through [she tells Dinny], but the past buries its dead. It is so, I've been through it, too. It's the present and the future that matter, and we're the present, and our children are the future.

So, in the last analysis, the comparison between Fleur and Beatrix Esmond becomes a contrast. Beatrix's last years are a degradation redeemed only by her vitality; Fleur, like Gwendolen Harleth, though quite unemotionally, in her hard little post-war way, is saved, "as by fire."

But all this comes about through man, not God, for it is only in human life that justice can be found, and so humanism comes to seem increasingly the only possible faith for a modern man. Perhaps "being in love with life" is enough; it is Soames's great criticism of Fleur's contemporaries that they have no interest in being alive. And it is Galsworthy himself who tells us that "life for those who still have vital instinct in them is good enough in itself even if it lead to nothing, and we have only ourselves to blame if we, alone among animals, so live that we lose the love of life for itself."

This passionate humanism is the key to his inmost spirit; he disliked metaphysics as he disliked institutionalism because he was not ready to sacrifice his direct experience of human reality to either. On the same ground he hated "systems" of morality, hated "water-tight compartments" and glib assumptions of superiority; he was always against the rule and for the exception.

This leads him at times to dispose somewhat cavalierly of the great conflict between freedom and authority, between mercy and justice which lies at the root of so much great art; if there is any true sentimentality in Galsworthy, here is where it is to be encountered. There is nothing gross about John Galsworthy, but theoretically he goes the whole way in his demand for freedom. If a departure from established codes can justify itself pragmatically no other questions need be asked. It is interesting that this disillusioned intellectualist should be at one with the medieval romancers in his feeling that love is irresistible. He was one of the first to state frankly in English fiction that a man cannot live celibate without suffering psychic injury, and sexual antagonism—a theme never treated as such by Victorian novelists—is the very mainspring of the vast *Saga.* His best heroines are never vulgar in their attitude toward sex, but they do not feel that celibacy in itself is very important; from the men who love them, they demand devotion first of all. Galsworthy has been accused of evasion because he calls Irene, Beauty, instead of frankly calling her Sex; the criticism quite misses the point that for him Sex is Beauty, and there can be no Beauty without it. In Sex is the fundamental manifestation of the creative impulse in human nature, the thing which stands opposed to the lust to possess and to destroy.

6. *Vale*

All this cuts sharply across many sacred beliefs and even more sacred prejudices; the reader's response must be determined by many things. Nor has the time come yet to pass the final esthetic judgment upon John Galsworthy, to assign him his "place" in the development of the novel. At the present time, few critics would claim for him either the massive solidity of Hardy or the puckish vitality of Meredith. Yet perhaps no other novelist builds a book more artfully, joining various elements, pulling threads together, looking backwards and forwards, yet never forcing the note, never over-analyzing and wearying the reader. And perhaps none other makes us feel that we are more steadily in the presence of a fastidious intelligence.

Fastidiousness, to be sure, has its own dangers in art, and it would be too much to say that Galsworthy has escaped them all. There are artificialities even in the Forsyte chronicles; the transmission and transmutation of Soames's hapless passion for Irene into Fleur's passion for Irene's son, and the magnificently theatrical death of Soames (Greek proverb-wise) through her he has loved

most—all these things are impressive, but they can hardly be said to have been achieved with complete spontaneity.

Similar reservations must be made with regard to his penchant for characterization by types and his use of symbolism. The charge that his characters are types has often been made insensitively, and he did well to resent it; modern men, he points out, "are part of the warp and woof of a complicated society"; they cannot "exactly be depicted isolated by the sea, or standing out against the sky." Yet it is a far cry from this admission to the allegory of the scene in *The Country House* in which Horace Pendyce, Hussel Barter, Edmund Paramor, and Gregory Vigil discuss George's affairs from the point of view of the Church, the State, the Law, and philanthropy.

At its best, Galsworthy's symbolism is wonderfully effective. Hilary's dog in *Fraternity,* who can only find his perfect mate in a manufactured article—"The latest—sterilised cloth—see white label underneath: 4s. 3d"—is a perfect commentary on Hilary's sterility and that of his class. Nor could there be a better image of the post-war futilitarians than the picture of the White Monkey who has sucked the orange dry and still feels dissatisfied as he looks about helplessly for—what? On the other hand, the symbolical hornet in *The Patrician* is treated almost as cruelly by Galsworthy as by Lady Casterley; and when the Forsytes themselves go in for symbolism, and find Bosinney's whole personality in his very unsuitable soft, gray hat, which Aunt Hester tries to shoo off the chair in the dark hall, "taking it for a strange, disreputable cat," it is time to realize that even in symbolism one may have too much of a good thing.

No doubt it was unfortunate for Galsworthy's immediate reputation that his last three novels should have fallen so far below the level of his best work. Here he seemed to have abandoned the thing for which he had always been honored most—his fulfillment of Goethe's adjuration to pass judgment upon his own class. The "Service-classes" are the acknowledged heroes of these novels, and the books are not quite free of smugness. In *Flowering Wilderness,* society is not on trial; society is trying a man. Wilfrid had no religious faith. None of his critics have any religious faith. Yet they feel he ought to have permitted the Arab fanatic to blow him to bits rather than make his recantation because, forsooth, he showed the white feather, he let England down!

Ernest Sutherland Bates may have the correct explanation of this when he sees Galsworthy reverting to a narrower, more nationalistic standpoint with the bitter post-war conviction that England will never again hold her old place in the sun. Or he may be running true to form in championing the under-dog; in *The Silver Box* the poor man found it impossible to get justice in the courts, but now judges are trying so hard to be fair that they lean over backwards, and the upperclassman must hesitate to bring a suit, no matter how just his cause! Whatever the final explanation, the matter will not, at long last, prove very important, for every novelist has a right to ask that he be judged by his best work. That granted him, Galsworthy's place may not be with the greatest, but it must always, I think, be a high and honorable one. (pp. 477-93)

Edward Wagenknecht, "Pity, Irony, and John Galsworthy," in his Cavalcade of the English Novel: From Elizabeth to George VI, *Henry Holt and Company, 1954, pp. 477-93.*

Gary J. Scrimgeour (essay date 1964)

[*Scrimgeour is a New Zealand-born novelist and educator. In the following excerpt, he examines the realistic nature of Galsworthy's dramas.*]

Fifty years ago naturalism was the great new movement in the English theater, and John Galsworthy was its dignified prophet. But yesterday's masterpieces have become today's museum-pieces, and Galsworthy's voice is stilled. If he had been a bad dramatist, there would be no critical problem, but his plays have the virtues—serious content, clear structure, interesting characters, brilliant individual scenes—that usually guarantee long life in the theater; some of his scenes, such as that of Falder's isolation in *Justice,* are as good now as they ever were. As a whole, however, his work has not worn well, and what astonished its first audiences now often seems pallid or melodramatic or naive. My purpose is to suggest that this lack of durability is the fault not of Galsworthy's incompetence but of his strict adherence to naturalist theory.

Unlike many of his contemporaries, Galsworthy was not so adept in literary techniques that he could choose whichever he felt best. Where the careers of most dramatists of the period show a gradual move away from realism, Galsworthy was from the beginning to the end true to his original ideas, and his sole attempt at another mode (*The Little Dream,* 1911) is a self-confessed failure. By temperament, by instinct, he was a realist: "My dramatic invasion and the form of it, was dictated rather by revolt at the artificial nature of the English play of the period, and by a resolute intention to present real life on the stage" [*The Life and Letters of John Galsworthy*]. As late as 1925, close to the end of his dramatic career, he said: "With plays it is only a question of the 'fourth wall'; if you have a subject of sufficient dramatic interest, and visualize it powerfully enough, perfectly naturally, as if you were the fourth wall, you will be able to present it to others in the form of a good play." The "others" agreed. Galsworthy made his name as a realist even with his first play, *The Silver Box,* which opened in 1906 as part of the famous Court Theatre seasons. As he himself wrote years later: "I think I can claim that *The Silver Box* was something really new on the English stage. It was certainly taken as such." The public acclaimed *Strife* in 1909, and in 1910 *Justice* had such a sensational closeness to real life and to problems of immediate interest to its audience that it produced changes in the regulations governing the solitary confinement of prisoners.

In the next decade, Galsworthy, with Shaw and Granville-Barker, led the Renaissance of the New Drama. Ashley Dukes' comment (made in 1911) shows how they were regarded: "Bernard Shaw and Mr. Barker brought the ideas; in a measure, too, the art. Mr. Galsworthy's preoccupation is with actuality." In 1913 one critic [A. R. Skemp, "The Plays of Mr. Galsworthy" in *Essays and Studies of The English Association,* IV] listed Galsworthy's leading

characteristics as "concentration on the graver common aspects of contemporary life, strong emphasis on incidents as the outcome of forces stronger than the individual, and austere fidelity to actual fact." In 1918 another wrote of his work that it was "strong, realistic, and, above all, it has no taint of the theatre. No faintest suspicion of stagey effect clings to a single one of his plays. They are, to use his own epithet, 'photographic' drama" [Harold Williams, in *Modern English Writers*]. After the war, Galsworthy repeated his prewar successes in the repertory theaters by becoming commercially profitable with *The Skin Game* (1920) and *Loyalties* (1922), and before his death in 1933 he had received both the Order of Merit and the Nobel Prize.

Real life, uncontaminated by the theater—dramatist and critics agreed. The old gods seemed totally thrown down, and Galsworthy's claims for naturalism seemed genuinely modest:

> My own method was the outcome of the trained habit (which I was already employing in my novels) of naturalistic dialogue guided, informed, and selected by a controlling idea, together with an intense visualisation of types and scenes. I just wrote down the result of these two, having always in my mind's eye not the stage, but the room or space where in real life the action would pass. This is the method I have always adopted and continue to adopt.

> I think I may say (without exaggeration) that I came into theatre-land quite free from the influence of any dramatist or any kind of stage-writing.

This is a breath-taking claim. In fact, Galsworthy was subject not only to the usual influences from his reading and from the physical form of the theater but also to more individual forces. He had taken part in amateur theatricals from childhood, and he went so frequently to the theater that as early as 1905 he could seriously consider becoming a drama critic. His theatrical career found its strength in revolt, and it is clear to the aloof eyes of today that, like all revolutionaries, he owed more than he knew to what he scorned.

For instance, his statement about the nature of plot promises a completely new development: "A good plot is that sure edifice which slowly rises out of the interplay of circumstance on temperament, and temperament on circumstance, within the enclosing atmosphere of an idea. A human being is the best plot there is. . . . The dramatist who hangs his characters to his plot, instead of hanging his plot to his characters, is guilty of cardinal sin" [**"Some Platitudes Concerning Drama"** in *The Inn of Tranquility*]. (So much for the well-made play!) But his practice scarcely lives up to his creed. The heavily plotted play had triumphed in the nineteenth century. Audiences apparently demanded that all the non-spectacular forms of theater be based on an elaborate sequence of events designed to arouse emotion and directed to moral ends, so that even the lowliest of melodramas share a tendency which in the higher forms, such as the well-made play, becomes an end in itself. Galsworthy's plays belong to the same tradition, and their taut, clear structure produces exactly similar experiences of suspense, irony, and catharsis. *The Silver Box* is typical of his favorite method, wherein both plot and meaning depend on the fortuitous parallelism between the actions of the two leading characters.

Usually Galsworthy will couple a contrast in concept between the privileged and the underprivileged with a chance conjunction of events in the plot—pregnancy, for example, in *The Eldest Son,* or theft in *The Silver Box*— to create an artificial parallelism out of which the meaning and the events of his play arise. In *Strife* the structure is very clear both in the simultaneous overthrow of Anthony and Roberts and in the use of the classic device of the well-timed death (of Annie Roberts) to bring about the dénouement. Ironic contrast, again usually fortuitous, is a favorite trick, sometimes made crudely obvious (as in *The Silver Box*), sometimes slight but pungent (as in *The Pigeon,* when the two social theorists show their forgetfulness of the individual by tumbling over the object of their charity), sometimes irritatingly obtrusive (as in the Christian pretensions of the gossipy villagers in *A Bit o' Love*). Again, the gradual revelation of a secret, one of the hoariest techniques of the old drama, forms the basic plot of *The Skin Game, A Bit o' Love,* and *Loyalties.* On occasion the machinery emits loud creaking noises; Galsworthy did not altogether subdue his liking for "strong" curtains, for instance, or for using the chance entrance of a character as the mainspring of the action. There at least two cases (*The Family Man* and *The Pigeon*) where the action of a play receives its impetus from the ancient device of the accidental eavesdropper. While the endings of his plays are not often so neatly arranged as those of the well-made plays, they all nevertheless bring a series of events to a definite close beyond which life does not in any sense continue. The dénouement of *The Mob,* in which Stephen More is accidentally knifed, is the most blatant example of a manipulated ending based on poetic, rather than blindfold, justice. This evidence does not suggest that his plots depend wholly on character.

Technique controls idea, and the way Galsworthy arranged the events of his plots amalgamated with the way he saw life—as a battle between the individual and society—to produce many of the characteristics of the melodramatic formula typical of the nineteenth century theater, that is, the conflict between Good and Bad. Galsworthy, to be sure, abandoned the noble heroes and dark-browned villains of the popular theater; Falder is no more a hero than his judge or his employers are villains. But in their place we have a dehumanized villain, Society (sometimes with such human embodiments as the police), against which all humans battle with varying degrees of skill, knowledge, and success. In the five plays which end with the death of the leading figure (*Justice, The Fugitive, The Mob, Loyalties, Old English*) we can see the closeness to melodrama. Each of the central characters is a basically good person who, because of events outside his control, is brought into jeopardy. Unable to defend himself, unable to speak forth and proclaim his position with any strength, he grows increasingly isolated as his enemies turn on him and his friends prove powerless. As a result of this carefully arranged isolation of characters who remain basically good throughout, their deaths result not from simple accident perhaps, but certainly from accidental and untypical behavior.

The same inarticulate isolation, the inability even to decry one's fate or welcome it, means that the final conflict is between neither ideas nor characters but emotional attitudes; instead of coming to focus in the death scenes, the previous suggestions about character and idea are simply abandoned. (In Ibsen's plays, for example, the final scenes are the most complex; in Galsworthy's the most stark.) These are all characteristics familiar both in the reputable plays of Augier or Dumas *fils* and also in melodrama. Many nineteenth century plays end disastrously for the poor but honest victim of the Establishment's villainy or callousness; the final happy curtain of *Black-Ey'd* Susan is famous, for example, but it is not so well-known that exactly one year later Jerrold deliberately wrote another melodrama of almost identical pattern except that here the noose closes around the hero's neck (*The Mutiny at the Nore,* 1830). The emotionality of Galsworthy's final scenes was deliberate. Like his predecessors, he arranged his plots to produce any of a range of emotions from shock or horror to humor and whimsical irony. We have his own testimony as to his intentions. Concerning the use of the child's cry at the end of Act Two of *The Silver Box* he wrote: "You know my theory (founded on personal experience) that the physical emotional thrill is all that really counts in a play." Or again "The artist takes life as he finds it, observes, connotes and stores with all his feelers, then out of his store constructs (creates according to his temperament) with the *primary* object of stirring the emotional nerves of his audience, and thereby, *actively giving pleasure.*" And finally: "To quicken the pulse in one way or another is to me the only purpose, or, to be accurate, by far the chief purpose of dramatic art" [*The Life and Letters of John Galsworthy*]. Of course audiences like their joy and tears, but these are strong, strange statements to come from an avowed naturalist.

A similar problem arises with Galsworthy's characters, who owe a great deal more to his predecessors and to his audience than to his desire to reflect reality. When his plays first appeared, he was praised for bringing back to the stage a wide range of social classes—one of the standard measurements of realism. One critic [Ashley Dukes in *Modern Dramatists*] wrote at the time: "Mr. Galsworthy has reaffirmed the existence of the common man; an individual long ignored upon the English stage." Unfortunately, Galsworthy's common men have a higher proportion of titles and country homes than we might today think fit. He made valiant efforts to meet and understand the "underprivileged classes," touring slums and prisons, talking to his cabmen and servants, but he always remained a visitor—in his life and his work—from the upper middle-class of which he was personally so shining an example. His low-life characters are seen socially and morally from that viewpoint. They have, for example, many fewer lines than his socially acceptable people, usually because they are in the position of servants or others who speak only when spoken to. He rarely allows them to occupy the stage alone, and when he does the effect is often unfortunate, as in Act Two, scene two of *A Bit o' Love* or Act Two, scene one of *The Silver Box.* We can see that he is attempting to create dramatic interest from such people, but when he succeeds it is usually by means of a traditional type, such as the low-life philosopher, Mr. Bly, in **Windows.** One perceptive critic of the time pointed out that many of his characters go back to old stage types and that even his great hero of the common man, Falder, "is haunted by that ghost of English melodrama, the desire to do the right thing, which in this connection is nearly always the sentimental, stupid and wrong thing" [Edward Storer, "Dramatists of Today," *British Review,* 1913]. Galsworthy's characters are, in fact, part of the long process of the humanization of basic stage types which Shaw noted as typical of the theater of the eighteen-sixties and described as "a discovery of saying sympathetic qualities in personages hitherto deemed beyond redemption" [*Our Theatre in the Nineties*].

There is no doubt that Galsworthy's restriction of real understanding to what Masefield called his "gallery of country-house people" strongly lessens the realistic effect of his plays today. Try as he might, it was impossible for him to escape entirely from the class and kind of character that his audiences accepted as legitimate for dramatic study. He took the characters given to him by Jones, Pinero, and Grundy and stretched them as far as he could. He himself saw very well the problem that he faced in producing low-life characters: "It might be said of Shaw's plays that he creates characters who express feelings which they have not got. It might be said of mine, that I create characters who have feelings which they cannot express. And—so far as my plays are concerned—I think this comes from the sort of subject and the range of character which I temperamentally select; and still more from the severely naturalistic medium to which I am predisposed" [*The Works of John Galsworthy*]. Three of his best plays show one of his successful methods of compromise, where he solved the problem of communicating grand principles and high ideals in the naturalistic medium by placing the central statements in the mouths of people whose job it is to be naturally impassioned and eloquent. In **Strife** we have the great oratory of Roberts' speech to the strikers, and in **Justice** and **The Silver Box** the fine courtroom speeches by the lawyers, which combine the verbal fervor of the older rhetorical theater that Galsworthy scorned with the lifelike situation and muted setting demanded by realism.

The point to be emphasized about Galsworthy's characters, and about his plots, is not that his method is necessarily wrong or inferior to another method. Quite obviously his practice is different from that of his immediate predecessors and usually has a more worthy, or more serious, aim. It may well be good drama, but—we must not call it realism. The desire to mirror real life on the stage is a perilous ambition, for the conventions of the theater die hard; but they do die, and the more dead they become, the more recognizable they are. In Galsworthy's case, the conventions of the older theater remove the sense of actuality, so that "theater-land" triumphs again.

Let us assume for the moment that Galsworthy could have escaped the influence of the theater and successfully captured his own view of real life. A second force—his temperament—acts with equal subtlety and greater inevi-

tability to bring about his present neglect. As is apparent from both his life and his work, Galsworthy was that rare being, a consistent moralist. It is therefore doubly unfortunate that he chose the techniques of realism in which to express himself, because the dictates of moralism and the dogma of realism are in direct conflict, and in his work they so successfully undermined each other that his morality was cheapened and his scientific impartiality destroyed. We may feel today that the ideal of impartiality in literature is naive and that one of the great flaws in the theory of naturalist drama is its stubborn underestimation of the irreconcilability of "science" and the individual artist. It is extraordinarily difficult to provide both an accurate reflection of contemporary life and a play that is meaningful and bearable. The individual point of view always distorts, and unedited transcripts are only spasmodically appealing. It is certainly true that Galsworthy's temperament was so strongly and naturally moral that by itself it undermined the actuality of his plays.

Before we discuss this problem, however, let us distinguish his moralism carefully from the propagandism of which he is frequently accused. If we compare him with an avowed propagandist playwright (such as his contemporary Eugène Brieux) we see at once that Galsworthy's work rarely contains either the fervor or the particularity of the platform-speaker, and rarely sacrifices dramatic integrity for the sake of proving a point or arguing an issue. Galsworthy only incidentally deals with problems which he believes to be soluble. He is interested not so much in their removal as in recognition of their sources in human nature, and any minor problem in his work is at once related to a concept, to something which is not "soluble" but "comprehensible." His own defense against charges of propagandism is the best:

> The sociological character of my plays arises from the fact that I do not divorce creation from life; that, living and moving, feeling and seeing amongst real life, I find myself moved now and then—not deliberately and consciously—to present to myself the types, and ideas, and juxtapositions of life that impinge on my consciousness, and clarify it all out in the form of a picture. . . .

> What does the work point to? It appears to me, of course, that the work as a whole is an indictment of harshness, intolerance and brutality. . . . The message is a plea for humanity, for more sympathy and love; conveyed *almost* absolutely negatively by attack on the opposites of those things. [*The Life and Letters of John Galsworthy*]

These are certainly more ambitious attitudes than those of the writers of problem plays and should be distinguished from them. When he is specific about which idea each play "incarnates" he achieves grandness of concept which goes beyond the temporary or the remediable. Like Shaw, Galsworthy had the potential for a greater permanence than the problem playwrights because his moralism ran so deep that he could not see the world in other than moralistic terms and had a totally consistent view of the events of real life.

Why then did this permanence remain potential? He himself gives us the clue in his formulation of the basic concept of his realist theory. The dramatist's best course was, he wrote, "To set before the public no cut-and-dried codes, but the phenomena of life and character, selected and combined, *but not distorted,* by the dramatist's outlook, set down without fear, favour, or prejudice, leaving the public to draw such poor moral as nature may afford." This method alone, he thought, would bring to a play "the selfless character which soaks it with inevitability" ["**Some Platitudes Concerning Drama**" in *The Inn of Tranquillity*]. He felt that this was the method of Euripides, Shakespeare, and Ibsen and that it justified some hope for the permanence of his work. Apparently what he did not see was the difficulty of reconciling the force of moralism with the desire to translate contemporary life impartially onto the stage. Naturalism seeks to make its points, as Galsworthy said, by particular and impartial observation (the fourth-wall convention); the reflection of real life becomes an end in itself. But if drama wishes to rise above the merely entertaining and to reveal meaning in any way, it must immediately become moralistic in that it expresses an organized and consistent point of view. In this sense, Shaw and Strindberg, Chekov and Ibsen, are all moralistic (though they differ widely in their use of realistic techniques). The realism of their plays is only a means to an end. A doctrinaire realist, on the other hand, if he wishes to go beyond the "slice-of-life" and have any point at all, has twice as much trouble as the non-realist. Like the non-realist, he must select his material, but unlike the non-realist he must order it *with the pretense* that he is not selecting or ordering at all. He is simply presenting the naked truth. Unfortunately, as soon as the pretense is discovered, the logical structure of his plays collapses—disprovable by the very particularity in which he sought his strength. But this is not the truth, we say, nor anything like the truth!

There is no doubt that the pretense in Galsworthy's work is apparent. His ordering is obvious in the fact that every natural act or real person in his plays stands in a clear relationship to his moral theme—there is nothing here, as in life, of the random or the irrelevant. For example, the conversations of the minor characters must bear doggedly on the theme (as in the opening scene of *The Fugitive*), and no activity can be simply incidental (as in the use of *Caste* in *The Eldest Son*). The effect of this purposefulness is to reveal that the world of his plays is not just controlled but created by a particular set of principles. It is such tightness of structure that has doubtless led to the charges of propagandism, since in failing to provide an atmosphere in which either characters or actions are in any way independent of his moral argument, Galsworthy destroyed the vitality, the complexity, and hence the realism of his plays.

Reciprocally, as soon as the moralism of his world undermines its effect of reality, the theory of realism undermines the morality, because, if this is not real life that they see, then the audience can escape (quite fairly) the force of its moral argument. Dedicated to realistic theory, Galsworthy could not deal with Justice (though his title shows that he wanted to) but with one act of justice, not with society's domination by money but with the domination of a group of people in a particular society by a particular incident involving money, not with the duty of man to be true to the best in himself, but with one special individual facing a specific choice. The usual artistic method of avoiding the appearance of thus arguing from the specific to the general is symbolism, the course taken by Chekov and Ibsen, for example. But though Galsworthy always saw the symbolic nature of his dramatic action (or the general relevance of his ideas), he was unable to use symbolic theory. Instead he compromised, trying to give symbolic value to a single element in naturalistic surroundings, and of course the result is unfortunate. In *A Bit o' Love,* for instance, the feather which floats down from the moon is entirely inadequate to symbolize the vast concept of Christian compassion that it foreshadows. In *Windows,* if one tries to follow the intended symbolism of the windows in the text to their appearances in performance, the result is bathos, the product of a ludicrous dissimilarity between two things seriously compared.

In essence all drama is symbolic; every act and every actor is a refinement of life off-stage, and no object or setting can receive attention from the audience without gaining symbolic value. This offers great freedom to the moralist playwright, who can thereby avoid the fallacy of the specific by creating a general conceptual structure in which his audience can roam freely. Realism, on the other hand, relies for its force on immediacy and particularity—it carries itself to the life of the audience rather than waiting for the audience to make use of it. To use realism to carry a weighty moral argument is thus to bring both into danger. The audience which saw Galsworthy's plays as intensely realistic *was* right, in that it shared his way of looking at life. But we too are right, who see them at best as presenting a special point of view and at worst as unreal, biased, and propagandistic.

In Galsworthy then we may have the case of a potentially great artist who saw the real world and the moral world as coextensive and who neither destroyed his art to make a point (like the propagandists) nor falsified life to suit his audiences' tastes (like the melodramatists). But he was ruined by his desire for realism, reduced to impermanence by the strength of his desire to communicate his great truths with both vivid passion and complete immediacy. There is a strong element of irony in the lasting success of his greatest single scene, that of Falder's isolation in *Justice,* which is the only scene he wrote for a definite propagandist purpose and which was thought to have produced its astonishing effect because it was so intensely realistic. Perhaps the truth is that it made its first impression, and continues to be moving, not because it is a detailed picture of contemporary life. As a burning metaphor of any man in any confinement in any era, it brought the strength of a universal symbol to bear on a contemporary issue.

In both the theater for which he wrote and in his own temperament Galsworthy found elements which would vitiate his aims. In the audiences before which it plays, realistic drama finds a more inevitable difficulty. Even if it should successfully avoid irritating the members of its first audience, convincing them of its *trueness* to life, those very

John Bennett and Nyree Dawn Porter as Philip Bosinney and Irene Forsyte in the BBC production of The Forsyte Saga.

characteristics which produced its verisimilitude will later, with subsequent audiences, convict it of falsehood. It was apparent even at the time of their first performances that Galsworthy's plays rely heavily on the interests of their audiences. At its original performance in America (New Theatre, New York, 1909) *Strife* changed its locale to Ohio. *Justice* had to wait until 1916 for its first professional American performance when, after having been refused by seven managers, it was finally accepted by John D. Williams after a newspaper uproar over the management of Sing Sing. To illustrate the effect that the passage of time has had on the immediacy of his plays, we can take the two elements which were most highly praised for their naturalness, the settings and the dialogue. The effect of both today is to mark his plays as period-pieces.

The response of a present-day audience to, say, Jones' room in *The Silver Box* or Roberts' house in *Strife* is quite naturally to accept them as accurate pictures of such places about 1910, and subsequently to accept his characters and ideas as being those of 1910. The immediacy desired by realistic drama at once vanishes. Perhaps the reason that Galsworthy's plays are more read than performed today is that a reader can either dismiss or conveniently alter the settings, or the elaborate and meaningful manners, or the significant differences of costume of which Galsworthy is so fond, whereas an audience must do battle with them. (And it should be said that there is more than one over-literary American with the strangest ideas of

contemporary England gained from writers like Galsworthy.) In dialogue even the readers are at a disadvantage. Is it fair to ask them to suspend their disbelief so far as to accept as realistic dialogue such as this: "I say, Freda, your father missed a wigging this morning when they drew a blank at Warnham's spinney"? Or, from the lips of a rakish male, "Of course I'm awfully sorry. I've had such a beastly headache all day." The very words which struck home originally as natural speech now stand out as the slangy mannerisms of a particular class and period, and consequently the plays are about as lifelike as high-class waxworks.

Such surface matters could of course be changed by meticulous rewriting and restaging; but this would be another play. Alternatively, once the surface of the play is well-worn, it can still be played as a costume-drama so that audiences can accept and ignore the surface and concentrate on the meaning; this is the course usually chosen with plays as realistic as *The Cherry Orchard* or *Ghosts*. But something in the very nature of Galsworthy's naturalism has made it less likely that his work will be thus treated. At least part of the survival-rate of non-realistic plays is due to their vagueness. Dealing in general terms with "imaginative" or "inner" truth, they allow the audience to reinterpret them almost at will. (Hence, perhaps, their popularity with both critics and directors.) Audiences will accept almost anything as imaginative truth—without understanding it, or deliberately ignoring it, or politely cutting it to their own measure—but they will accept almost nothing for long as factual truth, for what pretends to be factual will stimulate their critical faculties and, quite properly, their disagreement. Even if they accept an idea as perfectly right, future audiences may feel that its place in the scheme of things has been incorrectly emphasized. This is clearly what has happened to the moral realizations of Galsworthy's plays, all of which are in abstract reasonably acceptable. It would take a courageous (and probably Shavian) individual to argue that a man should *not* live up to his principles, or practise personal charity, or resent the extreme rigor of the law, and we do not have to worry lest an audience consist entirely of such courageous individuals. But Galsworthy's applications of these ideas seem to us today to be examples of special pleading and to lack the subtlety which we bring to their study.

Such a loss of belief is deadly to Galsworthy because it undercuts the concept underlying all his plays, and in fact most naturalistic plays, that of environmental determinism. Galsworthy states his own view vigorously:

> To deal austerely and naturalistically with the life of one's day is to find the human being so involved in environment that he cannot be dissociated. . . . [My characters] are part of the warp and woof of a complicated society, in which the individual is as much netted-in by encircling fates as ever were the creations of Greek dramatists. . . . I do not know if it is a discovery of mine that Society stands to the modern individual as the gods and other elemental forces stood to the individual Greek; but one has seen it hinted at so often that one inclines to think it must be. In any case it can be understood how a dramatist, strongly and pitifully impressed by the encircling pressure of modern environments, predisposed to the naturalistic method, and with something in him of the satirist, will neither create characters seven or even six feet high, nor write plays detached from the movements and problems of his times. [*The Works of John Galsworthy*]

The intervening years have increased our understanding of the importance of environment to such an extent that we now take it for granted, so that it is almost the donnée of our approach to literature and we expect much more than "that old stuff" from our writers. The philosophy of naturalism has won a Pyrrhic victory; environment to us is a determining factor of the human situation, but not the whole secret. It is this change of attitude on the part of the audience that makes it impossible to discuss Galsworthy's plays seriously as tragedy. To Galsworthy, Society had replaced God or at least the gods as arbiter of our fate. As the Greeks explored the superhuman, and the Elizabethans the human, as the causes of tragedy, so the naturalists explored the inhuman, and if all the current debates about the death of tragedy do nothing else, they prove that we have compared the three explanations and found the inhuman inadequate. As soon as environment has been put in its place, Galsworthy's explanations of the human condition seem very pallid indeed, and all that remains of them are isolated moments such as Falder's imprisonment

or the defeat of Anthony, which picture rather than explain that condition.

The desire to reflect contemporary life on the stage, then, defeated Galsworthy's prospects for permanence. Owing too much to his predecessors and uneasy with the symbolism of his contemporaries that could have carried his message to further generations, led by the necessities of his medium and his method to a compactness that relied heavily on common signals no longer received by the audience, impeded by a drama enmeshed in staginess and a philosophy trapped in dubious theory, he failed to win any enduring audience for his plays. His fate is typical of the naturalist movement, and indicative of the problems that confront any playwright who counts over-largely on the surface of things to bear the weight of his message. This does not mean, of course, that realistic drama is worthless. Comedy lives under a different dispensation. Realism, of one sort or another, treated with the respect due to a technique rather than with the adoration suited to a theory, is essential to the great majority of enduring plays. The danger of a purely non-realistic drama is that it tends towards a vagueness which requires a theatrical sophistication belonging only to coterie audiences, and that it easily degenerates into arrant nonsense. Some current plays might suggest that the last hundred years have brought us full circle so that we are now back to a pretentious theatricality without meaning or depth, that where the eighteen-sixties offered violence and piety, perhaps we offer only violence and despair. But the serious dramatist who wishes to make use of the peculiar virtues of realist theory—to find and to stir up a wide contemporary audience, to present in precise, comprehensible, and forceful terms the guise which the old problems have taken in his own generation—may well have to accept the penalty of the ephemeral and be content that his audience will soon be confined to historians of the drama. (pp. 65-78)

> *Gary J. Scrimgeour, "Naturalist Drama and Galsworthy," in* Modern Drama, *Vol. VII, No. 1, May, 1964, pp. 65-78.*

Pamela Hansford Johnson   (essay date 1967)

[Johnson was an English novelist and critic. In the following review, she praises the social and psychological insight of The Forsyte Saga.*]*

It looks as though, in the case of most writers of stature, it is necessary for the grain to die before the new harvest grows. When the writer himself dies, almost at once his reputation suffers an eclipse. "Never be too proud to be present" is an excellent maxim, especially for committee meetings and academic rumpuses; but presence, where death is concerned, is not a matter for personal option.

After the slump there may, with any luck, be a sharp revival within any period between 10 and 30 years. Sometimes, despite the efforts of devotees, there is no revival at all—this seems to have happened with Gissing and with Meredith, the latter seriously considered by Bloomsbury in the early years of this century to be not only one of the best writers who ever lived, but the best.

In England, the reputation of Galsworthy fell like a shot bird and is only now, in the centenary year of his birth, rocketing up again: owing chiefly to a TV presentation in 26 episodes of "The Forsyte Saga," both paperback and hardcover editions are selling like hot cakes. But in the U.S.S.R. it never slumped at all; he has always been read avidly there, in enormous editions, and it is hard for some Russians to understand why we refuse to rank him on a par with Tolstoy.

Now this is a very curious business indeed. The reason most commonly given in England, when the question arose as to why Galsworthy was so sadly in eclipse, was that he represented *fin de siècle* snobbery at its worst. To the best of my belief, the Russians never took this view, regarding his work as analytic social satire, which, basically, it is. There is a very fine piece of irony at the end of the Saga, when, by Fleur's marriage to Michael Mont, the heir to a baronetcy, the Forsytes are dragged screaming (if one can imagine a Forsyte screaming) out of their bourgeois bastion and dumped down upon the dangerous borders of the upper classes. It is not for nothing that Michael apologizes facetiously to Soames for being "the son of a baronight."

To imagine that the Russians enjoy Galsworthy only because they think he exposes the hollowness of English society would be naive. They feel, instinctively, that he is a superb social analyst, almost Marxian in his historical method, though within a very narrow framework; I have tried to persuade them to regard Proust in this light, but since the first four volumes of *Remembrance of Things Past* appeared in the nineteen-twenties, with a preface by Lunacharsky, they have not shown many signs of wanting more of him. (It is, of course not the social side of Proust which worries them, or they would be worried by Tolstoy: it is the aspect of Proust's so-called "degeneracy" with which they are not yet ready to come to terms.)

For English-speaking readers the real stumbling-block, where Galsworthy is concerned, seems to me a different one. There is not a single character in the entire Saga with whom self-identification is easily possible, unless it is with the unfortunate Soames. When we feel that all the dice are loaded against us, that we are integrally unlovable, that maybe our breath smells, it is then that Soames appears to us much in the comforting light of an antihero. And the truth is, that when we study the work as a whole, Irene emerges quite unmistakably in the light of a Female Cad.

Galsworthy did not intend this. Since she is never seen "from within," she must stand or fall as an ideal of earthly beauty, beauty to which all things must be forgiven. In **The Man of Property**, by far the finest volume in the series and the only one, I believe, that is going to be taken quite seriously while our literature lasts, her behavior is at least explicable, though it is difficult not to feel that it is mean.

She has married Soames, under heavy pressure, for the security he can give her, has done so without promise of love and has exacted from him an agreement that if ever she would want to be free, he will let her go without fuss or commotion. She now finds she has towards him an unconquerable aversion; certainly she does not make the at-tempt, which any prostitute must by necessity have done, to conquer it. She barely speaks to him, except when she can't help it; she denies him children; she steals June's lover, the ill-conceived, and to my mind crooked, architect, Bosinney, and she flaunts him in Soames's face until the wretched man, feeling himself something of a dog at long last, "exerts his rights as a husband." That is, he rapes her. Well, this is, of course, a serious outrage, and to Irene, who seems to me as cold as a fish can be, it would be worse than for some people.

Yet consider her as time goes on. She leaves Soames, and it is 12 years before he asks her for a divorce. She has lived in chastity, mourning her dead lover. Meanwhile, she will not even shake the poor chap's hand. (*Was* he physically malodorous? Sometimes one wonders.)

She then marries Jolyon, by whom she has a son: to this child she presents herself, from his infancy up, as the Venus Anadyomene. Soames marries nasty Annette and has a daughter by her. One mustn't forget at this point that, when there seems to be a question of deciding whether wife or child shall be saved in childbirth, he shocks the doctors by opting for the child. In the event, both come through safely.

When they grow up, young Jo and Fleur fall passionately in love, but are denied fulfilment by furious pressures on both sides—but the most furious are from Irene who, while pretending to give her son his head, is insidiously presenting Fleur in an ugly light. "You are a giver, she is a taker." (From Irene, what impudence!) It is in this light that Galsworthy, ambiguously, himself seems to present Fleur. Yet is it a true one? It is she who is brokenhearted at the end, while young Jo appears to find sufficient consolation in Mummy, with her hair *couleur de feuille morte*. Two young lives have been wrecked by a savagely bitter quarrel among their elders which has nothing to do with them whatsoever, and the prime mover in the wrecking operation is the enigmatic Irene.

A long time ago I undertook, in a lecture to the National Book League, to put her case. I convinced nobody. Worse, I did not convince myself. It was the most hypocritical lecture I have ever given in my life.

Could my view of this key-figure by any stretch of the imagination be Galsworthy's own? Almost certainly not. It is Irene who betrays her creator. Figures symbolizing "perfect beauty," the Dream of Fair Women, are simply not enough. I am inclined to think that **The Man of Property** derives very closely from *Anna Karenina*. Karenin: Soames, Anna: Irene. Vronsky: Bosinney. June: Kitty Levin. Anna-Irene steals June's-Kitty's young man. Anna-Irene feels an insuperable physical aversion towards Karenin-Soames. Might it conceivably be that the Russians admire Galsworthy so much *because* of the Tolstoyan overtones?

Yet with Anna Karenina we can sympathize, can identify, as we cannot with Irene, because Anna not only suffers, as Irene is said to do, *but is seen to suffer*. Also, where Karenin is concerned, she tries repeatedly to be kind, to do her best—and if she has failed, well, anyway, she did try.

In *The Forsyte Saga,* a work of profound social insight and patchy psychological insight, there is a deadness at the core. It is this, I think, that prevents it from being a major novel. Galsworthy, a tenderhearted, even a sentimental writer (**"Indian Summer of a Forsyte"** is very spongy at heart), was always trying to appear a tough one. It is his treatment of parents and children, especially of mother and son, that gives the game away. Irene's beauty is thrust down our necks, and so is her son's receptiveness to it; but her inordinate selfishness comes out persistently, despite Galsworthy's attempts to smother it. I suppose it is much to be said for him that he was capable of creating a character powerful enough—and she is powerful—to get completely out of hand.

As for poor Fleur, with all the cards stacked against her, she too gets out of hand. Read the last part of the novel carefully. *Is* she a "taker"? In the case of young Jo, what on earth is there to take? One might have expected the mercenary daughter of a Soho shopkeeper to delight in the prospect of one day becoming Lady Mont, but on her wedding-day she cries her eyes out in June's lap. Certainly she is subtle, even devious, but her deviousness is directed towards the goal of her desire, and this goal is the mother-ridden young man who lets her down with quite distressing gutlessness.

Another marked failure of characterization is the "buccaneer," Philip Bosinney. He comes out as nothing more than a Bohemian fake, an Angry Young Man of an earlier day. We are, in our own times, inclined to reject the importance of behavior as against stated intention: what a man says he is doing is one thing, but what he actually does is quite another. And I do not like what Bosinney does.

Must it mark Soames out so determinedly from the run of connoisseurs (for he is one) that he knows the value of what he buys? Was Bosinney really justified in upping his expenses for that horrible-sounding house, Robin Hill, till Soames was forced to sue him? He seems to me consistently rude, and as consistently dishonest. I take, with some solidity, the old-fashioned view that it is preferable to be pleasant to a man while picking his pocket than to insult him in the process. Bosinney is to my mind just the thin creature who would have attracted a thin-souled Irene: all gas and gaiters.

Yet I do not know another novel which can be read so entirely against the spirit of the writer's intention, and by doing so still make psychological sense. Is this, in a bizarre way, some sort of achievement? Because *The Forsyte Saga* is, in fits and starts, a forceful work, the clear social apprehensions taking grip upon the reader's mind just at those points where the same reader may be regarding the characters with a dubious eye.

Like Proust, Galsworthy has created a world into which one can step, as over the frame of a picture, into painted distances; yet, with Proust, how glittering that world is, an Earthly Paradise, however debased in some of its aspects it may deliberately have been made to seem! With Galsworthy, we button our gloves and take up our umbrella like a swordstick, before we dare to enter that area

of majestic gossip, majestic chill, which nevertheless gives us a panoramic view of England as it was, as it will never be again: as, paradoxically, much of it still is. (pp. 2, 36)

Pamela Hansford Johnson, "Speaking of Books: 'The Forsyte Saga'," in The New York Times Book Review, *March 12, 1967, pp. 2, 36.*

Peter Marchant   (essay date 1970)

[*In the following essay, Marchant reconsiders* The Forsyte Saga, *stating that although rife with "flabby" prose and "absurd" imagery, it is nevertheless a work of "enduring vitality."*]

One has only to glance through the relevant sections of the *Times Index* and the *PMLA* bibliography for the past few years to see that these days neither in England or America do literary critics take *The Forsyte Saga* seriously. The fact that the work was reprinted in England in 1967 . . . to become a best seller again is attributed by Maurice Richardson to the BBC TV serial that was produced that year, and which has been shown in this country on N.E.T. No doubt Mr. Richardson is partly right. After all, "Peyton Place" has been popular in the U.S. for a decade, but no doctoral candidate in his senses would offer a dissertation on Grace Metalious.

The comparison isn't facetious. *The Forsyte Saga* has some of the same ingredients that make "Peyton Place" a money-making TV serial—sex, money, dramatic situations and dialogue. Galsworthy was not a successful playwright for nothing. But these qualities are also the qualities of the soap operas and who takes them seriously?

"Galsworthy!" Paul West exclaimed in 1966, "He's unreadable! Who cares about *The Forsyte Saga* nowadays? It's trash!"

Mr. West was wrong about the unreadability (as Galsworthy's publishers would no doubt corroborate); but it's easy to support his view that the work is trash. Galsworthy's literary offenses are flagrant. His prose is often flabby, his imagery absurd. He writes, for instance, that June Forsyte has "a heart as warm as the colour of her hair."

He writes of Soames that his

> acquisition of the real Goya rather beautifully illustrated the cobweb of vested interests and passions which mesh the bright winged fly of human life.

And there is this description of spring:

> The Earth gave forth a fainting warmth, stealing up through the chilly garment in which winter had wrapped her. It was her long caress of invitation, to draw men down to lie within her arms, to roll their bodies on her, and put their lips to her breast.

Then there is clumsy exposition, for example, the encounter of Soames and Fleur Forsyte with Irene and Jon Forsyte, in June Forsyte's art gallery, which is almost as funny as Thurber's parody of it.

There is pathos, melodrama and soap opera characterization. Bosinney, the Byronic, antibourgeois architect, whose death is the climax of *A Man of Property,* jilts June Forsyte for her best friend, Soames' wife, Irene, without a qualm; but so distraught is he when Irene tells him of Soames' attempt to assert his marital rights, that he either kills himself or gets himself killed in a London fog (Galsworthy was argued out of a definite suicide into a degree of ambiguity, by Edward Garnett). Since Irene has already become Bosinney's mistress, and since she's only too anxious to leave Soames for him anyway, it is unacceptable that a grown man should be driven into so untimely an end merely by Soames' desperate last stand.

Then there is Galsworthy's insistence that his hero Young Jolyon is ironic. For example, here is Young Jolyon at the age of 50, in Paris after two marriages (both unsuccessful) and a lifetime of being an artist:

> He spoke French well, had some friends, knew places where pleasant dishes could be met with, queer types observed. He felt philosophic in Paris, the edge of irony sharpened; life took on a subtle, purposeless meaning, became a bunch of flavours tasted, a darkness shot with shifting gleams of light.

The effect is to make Young Jolyon sound like an undergraduate. Galsworthy himself must have felt that he had not shown Young Jolyon's ironic perception sufficiently for he keeps on referring to it—which makes it not one jot more convincing.

Galsworthy repeats himself about Young Jolyon's irony, and his sensitivity; he repeats his sermon against the Forsyte "sense of property"; and he repeats himself in insisting that

> The figure of Irene, never, as the reader may possibly have noticed, present, except through the senses of other characters, is a concretion of disturbing Beauty impinging on a possessive world.

Keats made his comment on Beauty, as Somerset Maugham noted, only once. As for Galsworthy, once would have been too often.

There is plenty to laugh at in *The Forsyte Saga*—it's far easier to argue that it's trash than to defend it. But there is an interesting and important literary problem. First, *The Saga* has had a curious longevity—47 years of popular success as an omnibus, and 63 from the publication of the first book, *The Man of Property.* We can't dismiss lightly Doctor Johnson's well-known concurrence with the common reader:

> . . . for by the common sense of readers, uncorrupted by literary prejudices, after all the refinements of subtilty and the dogmatism of learning, must be generally decided all claim to poetical honors.

Second, when *The Forsyte Saga* was first published, it was by and large a major critical success. *The Nation* said of it:

> A noble volume. Nowhere else in the entire range of English fiction has the propertied class

of the Islands been given with such knowledge, accuracy, and distinction.

W. L. Phelps wrote in *The New York Times:*

> It is a positive and permanent contribution to the social history and to the literature of England.

R. D. Thompson wrote in *Outlook:*

> This is a magnum opus in both senses, physical magnitude and breadth of artistic achievement.

"Oeuvre d'un poète!" Conrad exclaimed, and he wrote to Galsworthy:

> For the last two days I have been reading the *Saga,* which makes a wonderful volume. The consistency of inspiration, the unfailing mastery of execution, the variety of shades and episodes have impressed me tremendously. It's a great art achievement, in which every part is worthy of the whole in a great creative unity of purpose.

Siegfried Sassoon wrote:

> I take off my hat to him and all his Forsytes; that the family is becoming a part of the national consciousness, I am surer than ever.

The evidence in 1970 is that Sassoon was right. Soames Forsyte and his relatives are as familiar in England as Mrs. Proudie, Squeers, and Becky Sharp. They are certainly more familiar than Ernest Pontifex, Leopold Bloom, and Mrs. Dalloway.

Against *The Forsyte Saga* then, are the weight of contemporary literary critics as well as critics like Virginia Woolf and D. H. Lawrence. In favor of it, are a majority of the reviewers of 1922 and '23, and almost half a century of common readers. Can such a strange mixture of failure and success, condemnation and praise, be explained?

"How are we to know trash when we see it?" asks Mr. J. Mitchell Morse in *The Hudson Review,* "and why do so many people who might be expected to know it not know it?" It's a good question, and so is its converse, "How do we know that which isn't trash when we see it?"

Mr. Morse's answer is essentially formalist:

> Just as in the flattest expository writing a failure of language is a failure of thought, so in fiction a failure of technique is a failure of insight. . . . In a novel technical banality is total banality.

Now technique, or the lack of it, is easy to analyse and judge, but Mr. Morse himself agrees that technique isn't everything.

> The skill of a few contemporary technicians so dazzles us that we don't see either their emptiness or the more considerable excellencies of less dazzling writers.

If technique, then, is not the only quality of good writing, is it the *sine qua non*? One thinks of Hardy's bad sentences in *The Mayor of Casterbridge;* one thinks of *Crime and Punishment* in Constance Garnett's translation; one thinks of *Pamela* and *Clarissa.* Don't all these works survive in spite of all sorts of technical banality? Don't they survive, not only as literary history, but as works with a genuine life of their own? Isn't a work like Sidney's *Arcadia* utterly dead?—what Orwell called "bad good literature"—that which is technical accomplishment without vitality.

Works like *The Mayor of Casterbridge* and *Crime and Punishment* in translation are indisputably great, and so is *Clarissa,* and the technical flaws of their language are minor and irrelevant. *Pamela* and **The Forsyte Saga,** on the other hand, might be described in Orwell's terms as "good bad literature," the existence of which, he remarks

> —the fact that one can be amused or excited or even moved by a book that one's intellect simply refuses to take seriously—is a reminder that art is not the same thing as cerebration. . . . What is necessary for a book to survive is some sort of indefinable literary vitamin that makes some music-hall songs . . . better poems than three quarters of the anthologies. . . . And by the same token, I would back *Uncle Tom's Cabin* to outlive the complete works of Virginia Woolf or George Moore, though I know of no strictly literary test which would show where the superiority lies.

If George Orwell is right, then, failures of technique, even when they are major, do not necessarily limit the longevity of a work. What counts is the "indefinable literary vitamin." But we can't leave the matter at that; we must attempt to determine the nature of the vitamin, or literary critic and common reader will never make sense of one another.

Part of the vitality of **The Forsyte Saga** is obviously sexual. This shows itself in the awful personifications of spring that I've quoted. It shows itself in the attention paid to women's clothes, their breasts, lips, eyes, scent—"the scent of festivity, the odour of flowers, and hair, of essence that women love. . . ." It shows itself in the way in which Irene's lovers observe her swaying walk, the curve of her neck, her erotic softness and vulnerability.

> [Soames] longed to cry: 'Take your hated body, that I love, out of my house! Take away that pitiful white face, so cruel and soft—before I crush it. Get out of my sight; never let me see you again!'

Then there is sensual gusto in Galsworthy's descriptions of the Forsytes' property—their furniture, their horses and carriages, their houses and gardens, their food and drink. Just as Young Jolyon, the anti-Forsyte hero of **The Saga,** condemns The Sense of Property again and again, but can't help relishing his own considerable portion of it, so Galsworthy, apparently, rejoices in what he intends to attack. "This is the whole Forsyte gamut," wrote D. H. Lawrence, "all absolutely determined by money, and not an individual soul among them."

But Galsworthy's essential enjoyment of money is shared by many of his readers, common and not so common. If the attack fails because of the sensual gusto of the details, it is nonetheless enjoyable to read. Also, the reader is spared any sense of guilt, because most of the Forsytes are

not people but types—we can condemn them for our own vices without having to identify with any of them.

". . . the rum thing to me," Gilbert Murray remarked, "is that after reading it all and admiring it and loving it, I don't feel I know in the least what a Forsyte is like, and I'm not conscious of having seen one."

As effective satire, **The Forsyte Saga** is a flop (hence the tedious and unconvincing sermons that Galsworthy and Young Jolyon repeat); but it is fortunate for its publishers that the weak satire and repetitious didacticism (cf. *Pamela*) are not enough to spoil the sensual pleasure they attempt to condemn.

Galsworthy, like Young Jolyon, was conscious of this aspect of his ambivalence. He was also aware of his ambiguous relationship to Young Jolyon and Soames, hero and villain. Dudley Barker in his biography of Galsworthy quotes his letter to Edward Garnett in which he says that the novels were "simply the criticism of one half of myself by the other."

Soames is "He who would bind to himself a joy," seeking to possess Irene as he possesses his houses and paintings. Irene, helpless in his clutches, has "a strange resemblance to a captive owl, bunched in its soft feathers against the wires of a cage." Soames "does the winged life destroy."

Young Jolyon, in contrast, can "kiss the joy as it flies." He is detached, purged of possessiveness and lust. Whereas Soames' passion for Irene is overtly physical, Young Jolyon's is muted, controlled, repressed into an abstract worship of Beauty that is all but asexual.

The patterns revealed by the lustful Soames and Young Jolyon, purged of lust, are significant. They are repeated in **The Saga** in several ways, until they become the concealed but dominant theme.

Young Jolyon really falls in love for the first time at the age of fifty, after two unsuccessful marriages, with Irene (who is the love object of no less than five men). But Irene apart, Young Jolyon doesn't like women. His mother and first wife are barely mentioned. His second wife, for whom he left his first, cutting himself off from his own daughter and father (whom he adores), has a very small place in his heart—he feels for her only "a half-amused, half-ironic affection." He never understands her. When Old Jolyon, after ostracising his son because of his marriage to her for fourteen years, finally visits them, she breaks down—not, one would say, surprisingly.

> Her shoulders were shaking with sobs. This passion of hers for suffering was mysterious to him. He had been through a hundred of these moods; How he had survived them he never knew, for he could never believe they *were* moods, and that the last hour of his partnership had not struck. In the night she would throw her arms round his neck and say: 'O! Jo, how I make you suffer!' as she had done a hundred times before.
>
> He reached out his hand, and, unseen, slipped his razor case into his pocket.
>
> 'I can't stay here,' he thought, 'I must go down.' Without a word he left the room.

Young Jolyon is also "half-amused, half-ironic" in his affection for his daughter June. He doesn't credit her with either business sense, or artistic perception. Her friends and protégés are merely "lame ducks." Most revealing of all, when June is heart-broken by Bosinney's jilting of her, it is the jilter Bosinney, almost a total stranger to him, for whom Young Jolyon feels real pity.

Young Jolyon outstrips his father in emotional development by 37 years. Old Jolyon falls in love for the first time with Irene, too, at the age of 87, when he is so clearly *hors de combat* that he is as pure as Father Zossima. For him, Irene is "an intimate incarnation of the disturbance of Beauty" as holy as the Virgin Mary. To her he can confide:

> I never told a woman that I loved her when I didn't. In fact I don't know when I've told a woman I admired her, except in the old days; and wives are funny. . . . She used to expect me to say it more often than I felt.

Old Jolyon and Young Jolyon are rewarded for their remarkable temperance by the willingness of Beauty to dwell with them. Soames, on the other hand, is guilty of physical lust and its inevitable concomitant, possessiveness, and he is punished for it. Like the Jolyons, Young and Old, he is truly in love but once, and he is doomed to lose his love, and find a substitute, the hard, calculating Annette, who gives him her body whenever he requires it (which is not too often), and who, at other times, indulges herself with lovers *à la carte*.

Young Jolyon's son, Jon, also falls in love physically with Soames' daughter, Fleur. Like Soames, he is punished by having to give up physical love for Beauty spiritualized—his wretched mother, Irene.

The colors the women wear also suggest the battle between lust and love. Irene, Beauty incarnated, is always in muted clothes—violet, grey, black, dull gold, creme, fawn. Soames' wife Annette and his daughter Fleur, who are sexy, and naughty and selfish as a consequence, one feels, are dressed in vivid, sensual colours.

The lovers of women are part of a Puritan psychomache in which the main issue is the forms of sexuality that are acceptable and those that are not. Like a whole progress of English lovers—Spenser's Sir Mordant, Richardson's Lovelace, Lawrence's Paul Morel—the sexual lovers of *The Forsyte Saga,* Soames, Bosinney and Jon, are punished with either death or the deprivation of their beloved. The lovers who transform sexual passion into the worship of aesthetic Beauty are rewarded.

But Galsworthy is ambivalent in his treatment of Irene, Beauty Incarnate. First, she marries Soames only out of moral weakness and economic necessity. She never loves him, and never feels even a twinge of compassion for him. She has no sympathy for him, or understanding of his physical passion, which merely disgusts her. Thirty years later she still doesn't understand her son Jon's physical passion for Fleur. She tells him:

> "You are fearfully young, my darling, and fear-

fully loving. Do you think you can possibly be happy with this girl?"

Staring at her dark eyes, darker now from pain, Jon answered:

"Yes; oh yes—if you could be."

Irene smiled.

"Admiration of beauty and longing for possession are not love. If yours were another case like mine, Jon—where the deepest things are stifled; the flesh joined, and the spirit at war!"

"Why should it, Mother? You think she must be like her father, but she's not. I've seen him."

Again the smile came on Irene's lips, and in Jon something wavered; there was such irony and experience in that smile.

"You are a giver, Jon; she is a taker."

That unworthy doubt, that haunting uncertainty again! He said, with vehemence:

"She isn't—she isn't. It's only because I can't bear to make you unhappy, Mother, now that father——" He thrust his fists against his forehead.

So Jon gives up Fleur and leaves England, which has become "choky," for British Columbia, where Mother promises to join him as soon as he feels he wants her. Now it is Fleur, marrying Michael Mont on the rebound, who is compared to a caged bird. Irene has had her revenge.

In contrast to her is Soames, who moves from the ruthless self-love of *The Man of Property* to a generous willingness to humiliate himself before Irene for his daughter's sake. In *To Let,* he brings himself to visit Irene to ask her to let the past be forgotten and let her son and his daughter marry. He tells her:

> I consider my daughter crazy, but I've got into the habit of indulging her; that's why I'm here. . . . So far as I'm concerned . . . you may make your mind easy. I desire to see neither you nor your son if this marriage comes about. Young people in these days are—are unaccountable. But I can't bear to see my daughter unhappy.

Soames, for all Galsworthy's insistence that he's unlovable, is capable of loving others—not only Fleur, the apple of his eye, but his father, for whom he shows great tenderness; his sister Winifred; his absurd aunts and uncles—even Timothy Forsyte, whose excessive care for his own health allows him to preserve himself so long that everyone else but Soames forgets him.

What Galsworthy calls Soames' "supreme act of property"—his attempt to force himself on Irene when she's in love with Bosinney, seems nowadays more pathetic than evil. Like all the other male lovers in *The Saga,* Old Jolyon, Young Jolyon, Bosinney, Val Dartie and Jon, Soames is sexually immature. His clumsy efforts to force Irene to love him are the result of ignorance and desperation. But whereas by the end of *The Saga* he has learned to put his daughter's wishes before his own, Irene indulges her own egocentric possessiveness without the smallest sense of guilt, without the faintest of doubts entering her mind that she might be wrong in condemning Fleur.

Galsworthy does his gentlemanly best to absolve her from blame. "Where she seems hard and cruel," he writes in the Preface, "she is but wisely realistic."

Again, to all appearances, it isn't Irene who blackmails Jon into giving up Fleur for his mother's sake, but Young Jolyon, in his last letter to him. Irene's judgment on Fleur that she is "a taker," not "a giver," is echoed twice by Jon's half-sisters, and is reinforced by his brother-in-law, Val. But after all, what does such a judgment mean? It is Mrs. Morel's judgment on Miriam in *Sons and Lovers,* where it amounts to the same thing: "the taker" is the predatory female who wants the love the son gives to his mother.

This is the crux of *The Forsyte Saga,* the battle of and between the sexes. Like the Wife of Bath's Jankyn and Clarissa's Lovelace, Soames (who is the namesake of the first suitor Clarissa rejects) tries desperately to assert his masculine power over the sex which is supposed to be the weaker.

> The gods had given Irene dark brown eyes and golden hair, that strange combination, provocative of men's glances, which is said to be the mark of a weak character.

Irene's weakness, passiveness, and vulnerability are part of her allure, because, like The Wife of Bath and Clarissa, she lives in a society in which intelligent and aggressive women are unwomanly and wicked like Annette, or, merely absurd like June. But like The Wife of Bath, Clarissa Harlowe, and Annette Forsyte, Irene gains *sovraynitee* in the end, and takes away from men unworthy of it their patriarchal power.

Like Jankyn and Lovelace, Soames feels that if he can't dominate his woman he will lose his identity and be destroyed; and like Jankyn and Lovelace, in the end Soames and Young Jolyon yield to the weaker sex.

The Forsyte Saga moves from a norm of patriarchy to rejection of it. Old Jolyon, Young Jolyon and Jon all become as small boys with Irene; Val is as a small boy with his wife, Holly (Young Jolyon's daughter); Soames becomes a small boy with Annette. They become Worshippers, all, at the shrine of the Woman Triumphant.

But matriarchy, in spite of The Wife of Bath's convincing argument and exemplum, is no better for women than patriarchy for men. "All power corrupts, absolute power corrupts absolutely." If Soames as a patriarch and sexual tyrant is ugly, Irene as a matriarchal tyrant is no less ugly in deviously exerting her power over Soames and Jon. Soames, the beast, gives up his *sovraynitee* and learns compassion and humility; Irene, Beauty Incarnate, learns how to dominate her men and becomes a Beast. The corollary of this is that women may love their tyrant men, but they hate them; and men may think they love their tyrant woman, but they hate them, too.

The "literary vitamin" of *The Forsyte Saga,* as I've said, is its sexual energy; its interest lies in the metaphor it

creates of the battle of the sexes that is an intrinsic part of English culture. What the metaphor suggests about men and women, lust and love, pursuit and rejection goes far deeper than the surface world of the Forsytes, their manners and mores, which is what Galsworthy and many of his critics thought the work was about.

The treatment of this battle reveals meanings and ambiguities that are like those of *The Canterbury Tales, Pamela, Clarissa,* and *Sons and Lovers.* Not that Galsworthy has the power and technical virtuosity of Chaucer and Lawrence—of course, he doesn't approach them. He is technically (with Richardson) a literary journeyman. Had he been a more able writer, that is to say more perceptive of the ambiguities of his vision, he would probably have censored them, for after all the book is intended as a compliment to his wife, to whom it is dedicated.

Dudley Barker in his biography of Galsworthy tells of a nephew that once beat Mrs. Galsworthy at billiards.

"You must understand, my dear old man," his uncle said to him, "that in this house Auntie always wins."

That's what John Galsworthy, the English gentleman, thought he wanted to say. What he succeeded in saying was that such winners, male or female, are detestable.

The enduring vitality of *The Forsyte Saga,* seems to me, lies, just as it does with *Pamela,* in the ultimate validity of its unconscious meaning. In this way, Conrad was surely right when he described it as "oeuvre d'un poète," even though the formalist critics are also right that the work is technically mediocre. Although it is a splendid example of what Mr. Morse calls "technical banality," it is not a total banality. Like Richardson, Galsworthy lacked a sense of irony. Like Richardson, what he says is profoundly ironic because of his very inability to perceive that it is. As Orwell said, "Art is not the same thing as cerebration." (pp. 221-29)

> Peter Marchant, " 'The Forsyte Saga' Reconsidered: The Case of the Common Reader Versus Literary Criticism," in Western Humanities Review, *Vol. XXIV, No. 3, Summer, 1970, pp. 221-29.*

Alec Fréchet (essay date 1979)

[*In the following excerpt from a study originally published in French in 1979, Fréchet evaluates Galsworthy as a literary artist, focusing on Galsworthy's use of imagery, dialogue, and satire.*]

When Galsworthy was writing his novels, he had to maintain the sense of restraint and balance which his mentor, Edward Garnett, rightly saw as one of his most outstanding and characteristic qualities. Given all that is to be found in his prose fiction and absent from his drama, the plays may be seen as black and white, and the novels in colour. Of course, the plays do have their own complexity and divergences. An extreme subjectivity still pervades them. But they are less multidimensional than the novels. They are overstated, in contrast with the novels, where an instinctive, and at the same time deliberate, sense of restraint prevails, intended precisely to harmonise and blend his different inspirations. The difficulty of this task, and the lesser complexity of the plays, are illustrated by information that is available on the time he needed for each: writing a play required a few weeks, while a novel could take more than a year. His romanticism, his cult of beauty, particularly natural beauty, his observance of a liberal, considered and rigorous morality, his humour, his use of well-tried techniques are what gives his prose its plasticity and 'fluidity', its delicacy, and veiled lyrical or sensuous reverberations, conferring a fullness and sureness of touch not to be found in the plays, which, although bold, hazardous attempts that sometimes come off, do not possess the unity of his novels. There is a gulf between his achievements in both these forms. Herman Ould, a man of the theatre, and a friend of Galsworthy who knew his complete dramatic works, puts the same idea in his own expressive terms:

> The reformer in Galsworthy is as evident in the plays as in the novels, but in little else do these two sides of his genius meet. There are a few passages in the novels which might, without alteration, be incorporated in some unwritten play—little scenes whose effectiveness on the stage can be visualised, pages of dialogue, particularly in the later novels, which only a dramatist could have written. From such indications his capacity for writing a play might have been deduced if he had never written one. But his novels could not be justly described, as Bernard Shaw's might have been, as a playwright's novels, nor his plays, as George Moore's might have been, as a novelist's plays. In both forms he wrote as to the manner born; the integrity of each art is perfectly preserved. [*John Galsworthy,* 1934].

Before examining the component features of his art as a novelist, it is worth looking at the overall effect obtained. In 1911, Galsworthy became impatient about the slowness of his breakthrough, and in a letter of complaint about his publisher's lack of vigour, he wrote: 'My own writing has this distinction . . . from the work, say, of James, Meredith, or Conrad—that it is absolutely clear in style, and not in the least exotic, and can be read by the average person without straining the intellect'.

Earlier comments about the novel plots make it impossible to accept fully these claims to clarity. There are different ways of reading Galsworthy, and it is quite possible that some people read him without 'straining their intellect'. But how much of the meaning do they apprehend?

It is clear what Galsworthy means, however, and how it is justified. In opening himself to Meredith's influence, he was careful not to borrow his style. The argument of clarity is perhaps even more valid today than at the time. There is a marked contrast with the obscurity of some of his contemporaries, or of some present-day writers. His renewed popularity, in fact, may arise partly from the fact that his narratives are comprehensible, and form a coherent story. His novels are easier to read than Joyce's or Meredith's, or even Virginia Woolf's or Aldous Huxley's, and equivalent in difficulty to those of Lawrence or Forster.

One cause of difficulty or obscurity is, of course, the inter-

mittent nature of the narrative thread. The main plot is usually flanked by one or more subplots. This multiple structure, which may owe something to Tolstoy's influence, is no guarantee of success, being found even in a mediocre work like *The White Monkey.* Galsworthy offers slices of narration. Retrospection and anticipation are neither frequent nor lengthy, and cause no more complication than in Conrad. However, they do mean that the story has to be pieced together like a jigsaw puzzle.

Even when there is hardly any subplot, the narrative is not continuous, for Galsworthy, influenced without admitting it by Henry James, usually adopts the multiple-viewpoint technique. There is no single narrator. In fact, it might even be said that there are no narrators, for observers such as Young Jolyon, Felix Freeland and Courtier provide very little genuine narration. They are merely witnesses on their own account.

The point of view changes from one chapter to the next, sometimes within the same chapter. Events are related from the point of view of one character, then of another. Each of the main characters can almost be said to have his own chapter or chapters. The self-contained nature of the chapter is sometimes so perfect that it could be likened to a short story, although an extremely brief one. Galsworthy leaves it to the reader to situate the components of the narrative in relation to one another, and link them together. As has already been said, indications of time also make for greater textual difficulty, while increasing interest by their precision. They are often given after the event, irrationally and have to be interpreted.

On the other hand, Galsworthy sometimes makes the reader's task easier by providing an all-embracing view of his subject, right at the beginning of the novel. This is how *The Man of Property* begins. The Forsyte family tree is described and the Forsyte character set forth. *Maid in Waiting* also offers an initial overall view, although it is less expansive. Like the Forsytes, the Charwell family is shown gathered together. The opening lines of *The Country House* contain an especially dense, skilful and lively exposition of circumstances, period, time, place, essential character of the action (the word 'feudal' is used), and an indirect presentation of the main character (through the description of one of his servants):

> The year was 1891, the month October, the day Monday. In the dark outside the railway-station at Worsted Skeynes Mr Horace Pendyce's omnibus, his brougham, his luggage-cart, monopolised space. The face of Mr Horace Pendyce's coachman monopolised the light of the solitary station lantern. Rosy-gilled, with fat close-clipped whiskers and inscrutably pursed lips, it presided high up in the easterly air like an emblem of the feudal system.

These panoramic introductions are brief, never as much as a page. An equally traditional technique is used for individual portraits, which are also limited in length. Galsworthy provides a physical and psychological portrait of each character, usually on his first appearance. They may be extremely short, fewer than six lines, sometimes longer and accompanied by a résumé of the character's past, but even these passages hardly go beyond two pages. They are always written from the omniscient author's point of view. The second part of *Swan Song* begins thus:

> Whether or not the character of Englishmen in general is based on chalk, it is undeniably present in the systems of our jockeys and trainers. Living for the most part on Downs, drinking a good deal of water, and concerned with the joints of horses, they are almost professionally calcareous, and at times distinguished by bony noses and chins.
>
> The chin of Greenwater, the retired jockey in charge of Val Dartie's stable, projected, as if in years of race-riding it had been bent on prolonging the efforts of his mounts and catching the judge's eye. His thin, commanding nose dominated a mask of brown skin and bone, his narrow brown eyes glowed slightly, his dark hair was smooth and brushed back; he was five feet seven inches in height, and long seasons, during which he had been afraid to eat, had laid a look of austerity over such natural liveliness, as may be observed in—say—a water-wagtail. A married man with two children, he was endeared to his family by the taciturnity of one who had been intimate with horses for thirty-five years. In his leisure hours he played the piccolo. No one in England was more reliable.

The best portraits are not the most factual ones, but those which, like the one just quoted, create a solid and simple bond between physical and psychological. The portrait of Soames is very soberly executed, with no colouring whatsoever. But it provides a perfect evocation of the man of property. The American critic W. L. Myers perspicaciously points out the sureness, vigour and rapidity with which Galsworthy selects the one trait that will individualise a character: Soames' scornful sniff, Swithin's broad chest, James' rounded shoulders, June and her flaming hair, Cramier's animal-like neck. His skill as a dramatist sometimes emboldens him to add a few expressions to these visual details: James' 'Nobody tells me anything', or Aunt Juley's inevitable gaffes. They add the final touch that brings the character to life. As Myers says, Galsworthy observes traditional methods, while making them evolve: he equals and even surpasses George Eliot in the art of the literary portrait, and shows greater skill than either Wells or Bennett.

However, not all his portraits are so successful. There are some brief physical descriptions that have little point to them. One reason for their weakness is that, even when he wants to make fun of a character, Galsworthy never caricatures him. He cannot bring himself to give someone an uncomely body, deformities or even over-accentuated features. This lack of realism arises from his own feeling of repulsion for ugliness. It reduces his evocative power, and makes it impossible for him to sketch characters with the same ferocious force as Dickens.

Certain psychological portraits confined to a one-line or even one-word definition are also unsatisfactory. At the beginning of *Saint's Progress,* for instance, Nollie is described as 'a darling, but rather a desperate character', while Hilary, the hero of *Fraternity,* is defined in the abstract as 'an intellectual'. Such superficial comments, undramatic presentation and arbitrary statements, to be taken or left, betray occasional flaws in his art as a portraitist.

But what a contrast there is between these moments of stiffness and the portrait of Margery Pendyce, a model of delicacy, a kind of pastel portrait that, in its elegance and clarity, recalls the French 18th century. Another originality is that it forms an integral part of the narrative, and is found, not at the beginning, but towards the end of the novel:

> The first morning song ceased, and at the silence the sun smiled out in golden irony, and everything was shot with colour. A wan glow fell on Mrs Pendyce's spirit, that for so many hours had been heavy and grey in lonely resolution. For to her gentle soul, unused to action, shrinking from violence, whose strength was the gift of the ages, passed into it against her very nature, the resolution she had formed was full of pain. Yet painful, even terrible in its demand for action, it did not waver, but shone like a star behind the dark and heavy clouds. In Margery Pendyce (who had been a Totteridge) there was no irascible and acrid 'people's blood', no fierce misgivings, no ill-digested beer and cider—it was pure claret in her veins—she had nothing thick and angry in her soul to help her; that which she had resolved she must carry out, by virtue of a thin, fine flame, breathing far down in her—so far that nothing could extinguish it, so far that it had little warmth. It was not 'I will not be overridden' that her spirit felt, but 'I must not be overridden, for if I am overridden, I, and in me something beyond me, more important than myself, is all undone.' And though she was far from knowing this, that *something* was her country's civilisation, its very soul, the meaning of its all-gentleness, balance.

Although sometimes subject to criticism in itself, the brevity of his portraits is one of the most general features of his art as a novelist. They could never be taxed with cumbersomeness. It was Henry James, in 1914, who defined this selective skill, putting Galsworthy together with Maurice Hewlett and Edith Wharton among the partisans of choice and intention, and setting this method against the saturation treatment of Bennett and Wells—who indeed do retain far more of the Victorian heaviness.

The lightness and variety of Galsworthy's style can perhaps best be illustrated by examining in detail a passage from *The Man of Property,* in which numbers have been inserted to indicate the different techniques he uses, and how he switches or moves from one to another:

> (1) James wiped his napkin all over his mouth.
>
> 'You don't know the value of money,' he said, avoiding her eye.
>
> 'No! And I hope I never shall!' and, biting her lip with inexpressible mortification, poor June was silent.
>
> (2) Why were her own relations so rich, and Phil never knew where the money was coming from

for to-morrow's tobacco. Why couldn't they do something for him? But they were so selfish. Why couldn't they build country houses? (3) She had all that naïve dogmatism which is so pathetic, and sometimes achieves such great results. (4) Bosinney, to whom she turned in her discomfiture, was talking to Irene, and a chill fell on June's spirit. Her eyes grew steady with anger, like old Jolyon's when his will was crossed.

(5) James, too, was much disturbed. He felt as though someone had threatened his right to invest his money at five per cent. Jolyon had spoiled her. None of *his* girls would have said such a thing. James had always been exceedingly liberal to his children, and the consciousness of this made him feel it all the more deeply. (6) He trifled moodily with his strawberries, then, deluging them with cream, he ate them quickly; (7) they, at all events, should not escape him.

(8) No wonder he was upset. Engaged for fifty-four years (he had been admitted a solicitor on the earliest day sanctioned by the law) in arranging mortgages, preserving investments at a dead level of high and safe interest, conducting negotiations on the principle of securing the utmost possible out of other people compatible with safety to his clients and himself, in calculations as to the exact pecuniary possibilities of all the relations of life, he had come at last to think purely in terms of money. Money was now his light, his medium for seeing, that without which he was really unable to see, really not cognisant of phenomena; (9) and to have this thing, 'I hope I never shall know the value of money!' said to his face, saddened and exasperated him. He knew it to be nonsense, or it would have frightened him. What was the world coming to? Suddenly recollecting the story of young Jolyon, however, he felt a little comforted, for what could you expect with a father like that! This turned his thoughts into a channel still less pleasant. What was all this talk about Soames and Irene?

(1) Scenic, with a mixture of description and dialogue.

(2) An interior monologue by June, in which the dramatic element dominates.

(3) Panoramic: a comment by the author on June, followed by a more general opinion.

(4) Scenic: a conversation is indicated, but not quoted; June's mood is defined, and a slight change in her physical appearance described.

(5) An interior monologue by James, but which tends to turn into a panoramic analysis of his flow of consciousness.

(6) Scenic, describing James' action.

(7) Eight words of interior monologue, expressing a pure state of mind.

(8) Entirely panoramic: the author's eye embraces nearly the whole of James' life and describes it, using this knowledge to explain his present state, then penetrating more

deeply, and finally returning to the present, but this time with a general explanation of his mentality.

(9) A gradual transformation of the panoramic view into an interior monologue: these lines repeat the fragment of conversation and give James' reaction to it, then a series of questions that assail his mind, all giving a dramatic character to the interior monologue, which ends with a twinge of his greatest anxiety, as Soames' father.

A single page contains eight modifications of literary technique. Dialogue is confined to two half-lines, which go on echoing throughout the passage. The dramatic tension they express persists and even increases. Visible action is minimal: June is silent, and only her eyes betray her anger; James does not even notice this, engrossed as he is in his own worries. Yet the whole passage, with all its gradations of style, is predominantly dramatic, with the symptomatic reverberations of June's exclamation in James' mind. Everything goes to intensify the crescendo leading to the climax, which is also internal. The dramatic interior monologue is the most significant form of expression, alternating with all the other forms, which contribute to its effect.

This technique is used to greatest effect in passages where Soames is present, often alone. They can cover four or five pages, without ever becoming tiresome. Michael Mont, who also thinks silently on occasion in ***Swan Song,*** realises how difficult the situation with regard to Fleur is, for both him and Soames: they have chosen the 'hardest of all courses because least active'. To remain silent, take no action, whatever happens: that is what makes the interior monologue dramatic, particularly since the temptation to act has to be surmounted at any moment.

This indirect narration has its psychological justifications. By its continuity, lack of exclamations and hyperbole of any kind, it reflects the thoughtful, reserved, solitary and uneasy character of the protagonists. In particular, it comes very naturally to people who talk little. Galsworthy's heroes are not loquacious. This was typical of the period when they lived, in the class to which they belonged. But it is especially marked in them, as it was in Galsworthy himself. It distinguishes them from Meredith's characters. There are very few chatterboxes, apart from Aunt Juley and Michael Mont.

What could be more vivid than the kind of mute dialogue established between Old Jolyon and his butler, when the butler comes into the dining-room to serve the meal, and finds him apparently asleep? The thoughts of each one about the other are described. The butler's reflections occupy only a few lines. When he felt it suitable, Galsworthy could move into the mind of a minor character, even one who makes only a fleeting appearance. After Soames' death, the thoughts of his faithful employee, old Gradman, are reported in the same way.

The influence of the interior monologue may explain quite a common practice of Galsworthy's: dialogue reported indirectly in the past tense: 'The future—according to Annette—was dark. Were skirts to be longer or shorter by the autumn? If shorter, she herself would pay no attention; it might be all very well for Fleur, but she had reached the limit herself—at her age she would *not* go above the knee.'

Galsworthy may have taken the idea of the interior monologue from Samuel Butler. However, despite the frequency and skill with which he uses it, and the number of characters revealed through his form of expression, not all of them main characters, it does seem that, unless certain conditions exist, Galsworthy does not use it. Is it his violent hostility to Squire Pendyce that explains its absence from *The Country House,* the feeling that no stream of consciousness could be attributed to a man so bereft of ideas, or merely the wish to achieve the greatest possible concision? It is not known. But although the narrative is of a high artistic level, there are a few awkwardnesses of detail in the style, precisely whenever the interior monologue is being avoided.

It is sparingly used in *The Patrician,* and very little in *Fraternity.* Some familiarity seems to be needed between the author and his character (not necessarily sympathy) to make the use of this form of expression possible.

It is not only in the opening pages or in portraits that Galsworthy takes a panoramic view of his subject. He adopts the method whenever he feels like it: hardly surprising on the part of a writer who, while abstaining from any preaching, yet claims to be a philosopher and moralist, and proposes his vision of the world. This is why he sometimes steps back from the character in whom he best managed to express himself. In a startlingly brief and dense sentence, he interrupts Soames' meditations, during a visit to the area his family had sprung from, shortly before his death: 'For a moment he seemed to understand even himself.'

His opinions are expounded with less restraint in *Fraternity.* But even there, he is careful not to over-expatiate:

> Like flies caught among the impalpable and smoky threads of cobwebs, so men struggle in the webs of their own natures, giving here a start, there a pitiful small jerking, long sustained, and failing into stillness. Enmeshed they were born, enmeshed they die, fighting according to their strength to the end; to fight in the hope of freedom, their joy; to die, not knowing they are beaten, their reward. Nothing, too, is more to be remarked than the manner in which Life devises for each man the particular dilemmas most suited to his nature; that which to the man of gross, decided, or fanatic turn of mind appears a simple sum, to the man of delicate and speculative temper seems to have no answer.

> So it was with Hilary. . . . Inclination, and the circumstances of a life which had never forced him to grips with either men or women, had detached him from the necessity for giving or taking orders. He had almost lost the faculty.

The variety of his talents is further illustrated in the last page of the chapter in *The Country House* entitled 'Mrs Bellew Squares her Accounts', already mentioned for its concision. It shows Galsworthy excelling in a purely scenic, narrative style, without the least personal intrusion:

> Mrs Bellew walked fast down a street till, turning a corner, she came suddenly on a small garden with three poplar trees in a row. She opened its green gate without pausing, went down a path, and stopped at the first of three green doors. A young man with a beard, resembling an artist, who was standing behind the last of the three doors, watched her with a knowing smile on his face. She took out a latch-key, put it in the lock, opened the door, and passed in.

> The sight of her face seemed to have given the artist an idea. Propping his door open, he brought an easel and canvas, and setting them so that he could see the corner where she had gone in, began to sketch. . . .

> Mrs Bellew came out soon after he was gone. She closed the door behind her, and stood still. Taking from her pocket the bulky envelope, she slipped it into the letter-box; then bending down, picked up a twig, and placed it in the slit, to prevent the lid falling with a rattle. Having done this, she swept her hands down her face and breasts as though to brush something from her, and walked away. Beyond the outer gate she turned to the left, and took the same street back to the river. She walked slowly, luxuriously, looking about her. Once or twice she stopped, and drew a deep breath, as though she could not have enough of the air. She went as far as the Embankment, and stood leaning her elbows on the parapet. Between the finger and thumb of one hand she held a small object on which the sun was shining. It was a key. Slowly, luxuriously, she stretched her hand out over the water, parted her thumb and finger, and let it fall.

Long private discussions are rare. They hardly ever touch on personal problems, but involve exchanges of ideas on subjects of general interest. They are held between the moralist, when there is one, and other characters. Such moralists and observers include Gregory Vigil, Martin Stone, Courtier, Felix Freeland, George Laird and Young Jolyon. Their remarks are sometimes less interesting than other parts of the narrative, for lack of direct connection with the plot. And it is not only in such discussions that the intellectual substance of the novels is to be found.

It is significant that the only long passages of dialogue occur in courtroom scenes. The characters speak under constraint or in the performance of their functions. The following passage from *Over the River* illustrates this kind of dialogue. Scenic comments are reduced to four words, and Clare's responses to her husband's counsel are extremely laconic. The scene could be taken from one of his plays, except that it has nothing tragic about it:

> 'You saw your husband alone on that occasion?'

> 'Yes.'

> 'How did you receive him?'

> 'Coldly,'

> 'Having just parted from the co-respondent?'

> 'That had nothing to do with it.'

> 'Did your husband ask you to go back to him?'

> 'Yes.'

'And you refused?'

'Yes.'

'And that had nothing to do with the co-respondent?'

'No.'

'Do you seriously tell the jury, Lady Corven, that your relations with the co-respondent, or if you like it better, your feelings for the co-respondent, played no part in your refusal to go back to your husband?'

'None.'

'I'll put it at your own valuation: You had spent three weeks in the close company of this young man. You had allowed him to kiss you, and felt better for it. You had just parted from him. You knew of his feelings for you. And you tell the jury that he counted for nothing in the equation?'

Clare bowed her head.

'Answer please.'

'I don't think he did.'

'Not very human, was it?'

'I don't know what you mean by that.'

'I mean, Lady Corven, that it's going to be a little difficult for the jury to believe you.'

'I can't help what they believe, I can only speak the truth.'

'Very well! When did you next see the co-respondent?'

'On the following evening, and the evening after that he came to the furnished rooms I was going into and helped me to distemper the walls.'

'Oh! A little unusual, wasn't it?'

'Perhaps. I had no money to spare, and he had done his own bungalow in Ceylon.'

'I see. Just a friendly office on his part. And during the hours he spent with you there no passages took place between you?'

'No passages have ever taken place between us.'

'At what time did he leave?'

'We left together both evenings about nine o'clock and went and had some food.'

'And after that?'

Galsworthy, though less brilliant and witty than several of his contemporaries, could handle dialogue most impressively. Professor Gilbert Murray told me that, without ever having been comparable to Shaw as a conversationalist, Galsworthy could write more natural and realistic conversation than anything to be found in *Plays Pleasant and Unpleasant.* But he never misused his gift.

In studying Galsworthy's descriptive style, a distinction needs to be made between indoor and outdoor scenes. His outdoor scenes are immeasurably more important than the indoor ones. The novels contain descriptions of interior decoration, furniture, costumes, hair-styles and jewellery. But they are far from being as meticulous and extensive as Robert Liddell claims in *A Treatise on the Novel,* where he quotes Galsworthy's style as an example of what not to do in this respect. Arnold Kettle shows Liddell's misapprehension, and rightly points out how Galsworthy enriches his characterisation of the Forsytes by describing their furniture and their favourite dish, saddle of mutton.

But he does not properly discuss the actual technique of description. Galsworthy's settings are evoked far more than described. That was enough for his contemporary readers. Nowadays, the illustrations of Anthony Gross for *The Forsyte Saga* or, even better, Donald Wilson's television film are needed to recreate the world of the novels. To grasp the full richness of the text without such aids requires imagination and thorough knowledge of the period.

Here is the description of the drawing-room when the Forsytes meet. Old Jolyon enters:

> He found the front drawing-room full. It was full enough at the best of times—without visitors—without any one in it—for Timothy and his sisters, following the tradition of their generation, considered that a room was not quite 'nice' unless it was 'properly' furnished. It held, therefore, eleven chairs, a sofa, three tables, two cabinets, innumerable knicknacks, and part of a large grand piano.

It would hardly be possible to write more deftly. Far from becoming bogged down in details, Galsworthy sketches in the characteristic overburdening of Victorian decoration.

The same lightness of touch is to be found in outdoor descriptions; and no visual aids are needed to perceive all their shades and detail. One needs only to share Galsworthy's vivid feeling for nature, and his sense of the poetic. The setting nearly always plays an important role. Even *Fraternity,* the most urban of the novels, evokes nature, greenery, spring, with its glimpses of Hilary's garden and the London parks. Perhaps because of the rage that fills it, *The Island Pharisees* contains fewest factual or poetic elements of this kind. Galsworthy was temporarily blinded to what informed his love of nature. The bitterness and satire of *The Burning Spear* have the same effect. All the other novels reflect these feelings. They are most intense in novels like *The Dark Flower, The Patrician* and *The Freelands.*

Another distinction has to be made: what Galsworthy loves and describes is nature rather than the countryside. And those familiar with the London skies and its river, who stroll in its parks and appreciate the nocturnal spectacle of the city, know that nature is continually present. Galsworthy was such a person.

There are limitations on his vision of the rural or urban landscape, however. He describes the seasons, in which he sees the forces of nature revealed, except for winter, which he did not like. He normally left England before the bad weather, and did not return until the spring. He was not fond of the sea either, and there are little more than occasional glimpses of it in the background of a novel. Despite the importance he attached to farming, and his work in the fields at harvest time, his vision of the country is not entirely realistic. He sees it from the point of view of a rambler and poet, not as a farmer, even a gentleman farmer. Only gardeners were ever under his orders, and he never ran an estate. He talks very little of the soil, not saying whether it is good or bad, heavy or light, never notices weeds, nettles, thistles or briars. Farms, villages, country houses seldom appear in his narratives. (The house built by Bosinney at Robin Hill is the only one to be described in detail.) But he often describes wild or cultivated flowers, gardens, meadows, streams, heathland, shrubberies, orchards, and above all the great trees that add such majesty to English woodland scenery. Like Turgenev, he loved woods, and described them wonderfully. He was also aware of hills.

His landscapes are inhabited by domestic animals, dogs and horses, and cattle, and by wild animals, mainly birds. There are also bees, and sometimes moths.

The dominant component of his descriptions is light, rather than colour. He likes to follow its constantly shifting play and effects, as sun, moon and stars come and go. Night holds a fascination for him. The scents and smells that are so redolent in moments of great passion enrich the perception of the world. Noises are less appreciated, and he often makes an almost religious silence reign.

The Galsworthian landscape is not a fixed composition; it is a changing vision rather than a picture. Its outlines are shifting, its appearance ephemeral. It is usually evoked in ten to twenty lines, seldom more than a page. Only the great scene in the second part of *The Dark Flower,* immediately before the death of Olive, consists of a succession of admirable images and episodes.

The vision has lyrical and dramatic, rather than plastic, unity, for it is never a mere setting, a décor. It blends with a state of mind, a situation, although it is never possible to say whether it is man who loses himself in nature, or nature which reflects human thought. Without there being firm evidence, this probably shows the influence of Hardy. Like the plot, the landscape is full of mystery. Nature is in turn indifferent, cruel, smiling, divine, feminine, in voluptuous collusion with the scene. But it always offers a spectacle of extraordinary beauty—thereby distinguishing Galsworthy from Hardy.

A few passages will illustrate the great charm of his descriptions and the components that contribute to it:

> A misty radiance clung over the grass as the sun dried the heavy dew; the thrushes hopped and ran and hid themselves, the rooks cawed peacefully in the old elms. . . .

> George lagged behind, his hands deep in his pockets, drinking in the joy of the tranquil day, the soft bird sounds, so clear and friendly, that chorus of wild life. The scent of the coverts stole to him, and he thought:

> 'What a ripping day for shooting!'

> The Squire, wearing a hat carefully coloured so that no bird should see him, leather leggings, and a cloth helmet of his own devising, ventilated by many little holes, came up to his son; and the spaniel John, who had a passion for the collection of birds almost equal to his master's, came up too.

> 'You're end gun, George,' he said; 'you'll get a nice high bird!'

> George felt the ground with his feet, and blew a speck of dust off his barrels, and the smell of the oil sent a delicious tremor darting through him. Everything, even Helen Bellew, was forgotten. Then in the silence rose a far-off clamour; a cock pheasant, skimming low, his plumage silken in the sun, dived out of the green and golden spinney, curled to the right, and was lost in undergrowth. Some pigeons passed over at a great height. The tap-tap of sticks beating against trees began; then with a fitful rushing noise a pheasant came straight out. George threw up his gun and pulled. The bird stopped in mid-air, jerked forward, and fell headlong into the grass sods with a thud. In the sunlight the dead bird lay, and a smirk of triumph played on George's lips. He was feeling the joy of life.

After this passage from *The Country House* comes another from *The Forsyte Saga:*

> It was that famous summer when extravagance was fashionable, when the very earth was extravagant, chestnut-trees spread with blossom, and flowers drenched in perfume, as they had never been before; when roses blew in every garden; and for the swarming stars the nights had hardly space; when every day and all day long the sun, in full armour, swung his brazen shield above the Park, and people did strange things, lunching and dining in the open air. Unprecedented was the tale of cabs and carriages that streamed across the bridges of the shining river, bearing the upper-middle class in thousands to the green glories of Bushey, Richmond, Kew, and Hampton Court. Almost every family with any pretensions to be of the carriage-class paid one visit that year to the horse-chestnuts at Bushey, or took one drive amongst the Spanish chestnuts of Richmond Park. Bowling smoothly, if dustily, along, in a cloud of their own creation, they would stare fashionably at the antlered heads which the great slow deer raised out of a forest of bracken that promised to autumn lovers such cover as was never seen before. And now and again, as the amorous perfume of chestnut flowers and fern was drifted too near, one would say to the other: 'My dear! What a peculiar scent!'

The other two passages are more purely descriptive, although they fit into the narrative, particularly the second. First, here is the end of a day's shooting spent by Squire Pendyce's guests, showing an apparently Keatsian influence:

> The sun had fallen well behind the home wood when the guns stood waiting for the last drive of the day. From the keeper's cottage in the hollow, where late threads of crimson clung in the brown

network of Virginia creeper, rose a mist of wood smoke, dispersed upon the breeze. Sound there was none, only that faint stir—the far, far callings of men and beasts and birds—that never quite dies of a country evening. . . . But a gleam of sunlight stole down the side of the covert and laid a burnish on the turned leaves till the whole wood seemed quivering with magic. [*The Country House*]

Finally, there is another evocation of night-fall, as Mark Lennan awaits Olive, the whole of nature seeming also to be hushed and waiting:

All wind had failed, and the day was fallen into a wonderful still evening. Gnats were dancing in the sparse strips of sunlight that slanted across the dark water, now that the sun was low. From the fields, bereft of workers, came the scent of hay and the heavy scent of meadow-sweet; the musky odour of the backwater was confused with them into one brooding perfume. No one passed. And sounds were few and far to that wistful listener, for birds did not sing just there. How still and warm was the air, yet seemed to vibrate against his cheeks as though about to break into flame. That fancy came to him vividly while he stood waiting—a vision of heat simmering in little pale red flames. [*The Dark Flower*]

The flames that pass through Mark's imagination fuse two elements in the novelist's art, description and poetry. By its descriptiveness and poetic inspiration, *The Dark Flower* is predominantly a lyrical novel. It is regrettable that the American critic Ralph Freedman omitted to mention it in his remarkable study of the *genre;* whereas the poet and novelist Richard Church was more penetrating when he wrote [in his *The Growth of the English Novel*]:

Galsworthy . . . was an artist of sombre, almost feline sensuousness beneath his austere stoicism. His prose is like warm burgundy, poured into a glass of irony that instantly clouds at the contact. His *Dark Flower* (1913) is a novel written in a romantic intensity comparable to the poetic fervour which inspired Edith Wharton's *Ethan Frome* and Compton Mackenzie's *Guy and Pauline*. Here are three novels permanent in our literature, as single as perfect lyrics.

The Dark Flower is Galsworthy's longest prose poem, and one of his finest, but there are shorter ones that are even more purely lyrical. These are brief sketches in which narrative tends to disappear. It is a pity that they were not included in the collection entitled **Caravan,** and can be found only in old editions inaccessible to the general public. Galsworthy was wrong to abandon them to their fate. They are among the most delightful, original and modern texts he ever wrote, and would serve well as a counterweight to over-simplified opinions of his art or lack of it.

Symbolism is important. The flames seen and felt by Mark are the symbol of his destructive love for Olive. The tree he climbs with Sylvia, and where they spend some idyllic moments, is symbolic of their union and future happiness. The silver spoon that makes Fleur such a privileged child symbolises the ancient fortune of England, which is being dissipated, despite the country's reluctance to admit it. As

Myers points out, Robin Hill is also a symbol, offering a dozen different interpretations, which combine in the word 'beauty'. Certain aspects of nature become symbols, to be found throughout Galsworthy's writings, thus becoming a kind of language, creating an atmosphere. Woods and orchards in bloom lend their own magic to the love scenes that take place there.

Symbols lose their artistic force when they are overexplicit, and become tiresomely over-simplified allegories. This is the case of the spaniel John in **The Country House.** Every appearance of the creature illustrates faithfulness to his master. The storms that accompany or presage unhappy events are also overdone.

It is not in accordance with the conventional image of Galsworthy to recognise an element of the supernatural in his work. It exists, particularly in some of the sketches already mentioned, describing trance-like states. Such effects are sometimes found in the novels. Soames' mind is haunted for some time by the face of his dead rival Bosinney. Irene returns to Robin Hill, probably to seek a mystic contact with her lover's shade. However, Galsworthy rightly shows circumspection in introducing such elements into his long narratives. In all the descriptive and poetic passages, in fact, he shows the restraint and deftness that pervade all his work. Despite his great admiration for the work of W. H. Hudson, he does not adopt his descriptive style. *Green Mansions* is continuously or at least consistently descriptive; this is quite unlike Galsworthy's method. It is Hudson's vivid feeling for nature that influences him, however different the landscapes described by the two writers.

Finally, there is the comic aspect of Galsworthy's art. The very existence of such a vein is contested by Swinnerton, while Ould devotes only a few pages to it. It is being considered here as something that is not of major importance. Analysis of the novels has shown that the plots are by no means comic. Comedy seems marginal and almost paradoxical, in view of Galsworthy's own disquiet and the tensions that prevail in his narratives. It does exist, however, and systematic investigation reveals many examples. It is one of the hidden aspects of this strange and Protean writer. Here too, there is a great contrast between plays and novels, which offer far more comic shades of meaning. None of the twenty-seven plays is an outright comedy, despite the Wildean and Shavian influences apparent in them.

His commonest forms of comedy are devoid of any gaiety. They involve satire and dramatic irony. Satire plays a negligible or slight role in the first two novels, but appears in its most virulent forms in the following ones: **The Island Pharisees, The Man of Property** and **The Country House.** It is found again in **In Chancery,** but from **To Let** on, it becomes steadily milder. Its role is reduced, though still significant, in the five 'lyrical' novels. It predominates in **The Burning Spear.**

This satire is itself complex. Humour is combined with it in varying proportions. The portraits of heroes, as has been seen, all contain something autobiographical. When he is speaking of himself in this way, Galsworthy is humorous, and keeps his emotions in check. This is particularly noticeable in Young Jolyon, Felix Freeland, then Michael Mont, who display a gentle, kindly irony, inspired by their creator's own sense of restraint and measure. Soames is not the object of the fiercest satire. Even in **The Man of Property,** he is not systematically blackened. In contrast, Squire Pendyce and the Reverend Barter, his friend and ally, are treated ferociously, though Galsworthy never becomes peevish in his condemnation. Here is the Squire's creed, which some might well regard as blasphemous:

> I believe in my father, and his father, and his father's father, the makers and keepers of my estate; and I believe in myself and my son and my son's son. And I believe that we have made the country, and shall keep the country what it is. And I believe in the Public Schools, and especially the Public School that I was at. And I believe in my social equals and the country house, and in things as they are, for ever and ever. Amen. [**The Country House**]

The mediocrity of the Reverend Barter's oratorical gifts and intellectual faculties is more cruelly depicted:

> God—he said—wished men to be fruitful, intended them to be fruitful, commanded them to be fruitful. God—he said—made men, and made the earth; He made man to be fruitful in the earth; He made man neither to question nor answer nor argue; He made him to be fruitful and possess the land. . . . God had set bounds, the bounds of marriage, within which man should multiply, and that exceedingly—even as Abraham multiplied. In these days dangers, pitfalls, snares, were rife; in these days men went about and openly, unashamedly advocated shameful doctrines. Let them beware. It would be his sacred duty to exclude such men from within the precincts of that parish entrusted to his care by God. . . . They were not brought into this world to follow sinful inclination, to obey their mortal reason. God demanded sacrifices of men. Patriotism demanded sacrifices of men, it demanded that they should curb their inclinations and desires. It demanded of them their first duty as men and Christians, the duty of being fruitful and multiplying, in order that they might till this fruitful earth, not selfishly, not for themselves alone. It demanded of them the duty of multiplying in order that they and their children might be equipped to smite the enemies of their Queen and country, and uphold the name of England in whatever quarrel, against all who rashly sought to drag her flag in the dust. [**The Country House**]

Although satire is less violent in **The Forsyte Saga,** it appears there in more varied, concrete and numerous forms. It contains an unparalleled number of comic characters: Aunt Juley, James and (except at the beginning) June, with their fads and oddities; George, a wag and buffoon; Montague Dartie, a gay Lothario always short of the ready; Timothy, who keeps out of sight to avoid infection; and Swithin, the least cultivated of the Forsytes.

The most comic work after the Saga is **A Modern Comedy,** but the inspiration is different. The endless chatter of Michael Mont and his father, Sir Lawrence, who are more sophisticated than the Forsytes, more aristocratically dashing, gives it lightness and joviality. But only the second novel, **The Silver Spoon,** justifies calling the whole trilogy 'a modern comedy'. The theme of the novel is not comic, particularly when the image of the silver spoon, which Fleur is assumed to have been born with, is widened to apply to the whole English nation, unaware that its age of supremacy is gone, and that it is living beyond its means. The threats are not imminent, however, and in the meantime people enjoy themselves to the full. The quarrel between Fleur and Marjorie, Soames' intervention, the libel suit, the squabble between Michael and Sir Alexander MacGowan, are all related in a facetious tone, unusual for Galsworthy. Marjorie, her uncle the Marquess of Shropshire, and the theoretician Sir James Foggart are presented largely in a humorous way. But before the end of the novel it is learnt that a fresh crisis in Fleur's life is gathering, and the tone changes. **The Silver Spoon** is a long interlude between two more sombre narratives.

Finally, the main inspiration of **The Burning Spear** is satirical. But its humour is so weighed down with bitterness that it becomes absurd.

Galsworthy uses the device of dramatic irony in his satirical passages. Under the influence of Greek drama, he likes to show the vanity of men's efforts. In trying to regain possession of Irene, Soames pushes her into Jolyon's arms. He spends huge amounts to have her shadowed, only to be taken for her lover himself, because of the way he keeps following her. Finally, having sacrificed everything to have a son, he is presented with a daughter.

Galsworthy is also fond of parody, particularly to mock the press, lawyers and politicians. Word play and wit are less common. He possesses a certain gift for describing a comic situation, such as the collision between Swithin's phaeton and a costermonger's cart, Soames' conversation with a hitch-hiker, the mosquito hunt in **The Dark Flower,** and the sight of Fiorsen falling into a trap in **Beyond.** Occasionally, Galsworthy is quite ready to indulge in action comedy.

Restraint, delicacy, lightness, variety and lyricism are Galsworthy's essential qualities as a novelist, and contribute to the mellowness and soft charm of his novels. They were not accidental, but were deliberately cultivated by him. So it is not surprising to find a description by him of the novel *genre* containing not the slightest trace of the 'materialism' Virginia Woolf so bitterly attacked in him: 'The novel is the most pliant and far-reaching medium of communication between minds. . . . The novel supplies revelation in, I think, the most secret, thorough, and subtle form.'

The most striking, and certainly the most penetrating of Galsworthy's verdicts on his own writing was entered in his diary on Christmas Day 1910:

> [**The Patrician**] discloses me . . . as an impressionist working with a realistic or naturalistic technique, whereas Wells is a realist with an impressionistic technique, Bennett a realist with a

realistic technique, Conrad an impressionist with a semi-impressionistic, semi-naturalistic technique, and Forster an impressionist with a realistically impressionistic technique.

His use of the word 'naturalistic' could lead to misapprehension of the extent of French influence, which I have been at pains not to exaggerate. Realism also has its limits, which have been pointed out in various areas. But it does exist, particularly if one admits, as Galsworthy here himself does, that it is a *means*. The word 'impressionism' can, of course, be criticised when it is used in the context of literature. However, in this case, it is accurate. It reflects his constant quest for beauty, and the highly personal character of his works, a 'spiritual examination', an immediate vision, even where the most general and objective problems are involved.

But however accurate, it is inadequate as a definition of Galsworthy's complex art, which blends traditionalism with a modernism that is only beginning to be appreciated. It is an imperfect but original combination. In his symbolism, he is perhaps closer to the Pre-Raphaelites than to the Impressionists. However, the pervading sense of restraint in his narratives is somehow reconciled with their romanticism. This rules out any exaggeration, the extravagances of Lawrence's vitalism, Virginia Woolf's creative but vacillating subjectivism, or James Joyce's abstruseness. (pp. 152-74)

> *Alec Fréchet, in his* John Galsworthy: A Reassessment, *translated by Denis Mahaffey, Barnes & Noble Books, 1982, 229 p.*

FURTHER READING

Bibliography

Stevens, Earl E., and Stevens, H. Ray. *John Galsworthy: An Annotated Bibliography of Writings about Him.* De Kalb: Northern Illinois University Press, 1980, 484 p.
    Comprehensive bibliography of primary and secondary sources.

Biography

Gindin, James. *John Galsworthy's Life and Art: An Alien's Fortress.* London: Macmillan Press, 1987, 616 p.
    Biography of Galsworthy, focusing on the events and people that shaped his life and work.

Holloway, David. *John Galsworthy.* International Profiles, edited by Edward Storer. London: Morgan-Grampian, 1968, 92 p.
    Brief introductory biography of Galsworthy. Includes photographs from productions of Galsworthy's plays and the 1967 BBC adaptation of *The Forsyte Saga.*

Marrot, H. V. *The Life and Letters of John Galsworthy.* New York: Charles Scribner's Sons, 1936, 819 p.
    Official biography of Galsworthy.

Sauter, Rudolf. *Galsworthy the Man: An Intimate Portrait.* London: Peter Owen, 1967, 176 p.
    Appreciative biography by Galsworthy's nephew.

Criticism

Review of *A Man of Property,* by John Galsworthy. *The Academy* 70, No. 1769 (31 March 1906): 309-10.
    Reviews *A Man of Property,* noting of the work: "The book is remarkable: it has strength without the least taint of sensation; and is written with a finish which is both rare and delightful."

Dooley, D. J. "Character and Credibility in *The Forsyte Saga.*" *The Dalhousie Review* 50 (Autumn 1970): 373-77.
    Praises the BBC adaptation of *The Forsyte Saga,* concluding: "*The Forsyte Saga* could have been one of the most expensive blunders in the history of television; instead it was one of the most conspicuous triumphs."

Edgar, Pelham. "John Galsworthy." In his *The Art of the Novel: From 1700 to the Present Time,* pp. 206-16. New York: Macmillan Co., 1933.
    Surveys the novels that make up *The Forsyte Saga* and *A Modern Comedy.*

Fisher, John. *The World of the Forsytes.* London: Martin Secker & Warburg, 1976, 224 p.
    Discusses England's social and political climate from 1886 to 1926, a period that Fisher calls the "Forsyte Era." The critic provides photographs and illustrations from that era and comments on various passages from *The Forsyte Saga.*

Frazer, June M. "Galsworthy's Narrative Technique in *The Man of Property.*" *English Literature in Transition* 19, No. 1 (1976): 15-24.
    Examines *The Man of Property* as both a moral and psychological novel.

Goldman, Emma. "John Galsworthy." In her *The Social Significance of the Modern Drama,* pp. 196-225. Boston: The Gorham Press, 1914.
    Praises Galsworthy for presenting realistic characters and situations in *Strife, Justice,* and *The Pigeon.*

Hart, John E. "Ritual and Spectacle in *The Man of Property.*" *Research Studies of the State College of Washington* 40, No. 1 (March 1972): 34-43.
    Examines ritual (family celebrations) and spectacle (tribal ceremonies) in *The Man of Property.*

Higdon, David Leon. "John Galsworthy's *The Man of Property:* 'now in the natural course of things'." *English Literature in Transition* 21, No. 3 (1978): 149-57.
    Studies time in *The Man of Property.*

Lewisohn, Ludwig. "The Foundations of the Modern Drama." In his *The Modern Drama: An Essay in Interpretation,* pp. 207-18. New York: B. W. Huebsch, 1915.
    Evaluates Galsworthy as a dramatist, concluding: "The special note of Galsworthy's art is its restraint. His vision is wonderfully keen and clear and sober."

McQuitty, Peter. "The Forsyte Chronicles: A Nineteenth-Century Liberal View of English History." *English Literature in Transition* 23, No. 2 (1980): 99-114.
    Argues that Galsworthy did not attack Victorian modes of behavior—specifically, the acquisition of property—

in "The Forsyte Chronicles" but that he justified and embraced its ideals.

Reilly, Joseph J. "John Galsworthy: An Appraisal." *The Bookman* LXXIV, No. 5 (January-February 1932): 488-93.
Appraises Galsworthy as a novelist, focusing on *The Forsyte Saga* and *A Modern Comedy.*

Smit, J. Henry. *The Short Stories of John Galsworthy.* New York: Haskell House, 1966, 157 p.
Examines Galsworthy's short stories, including *From the Four Winds, The Inn of Tranquillity, A Sheaf,* and *Forsytes, Pendyces and Others,* and discusses plot, characterization, and setting.

Sternlicht, Sanford. "*The Forsyte Saga.*" In his *John Galsworthy,* pp. 48-60. Boston: Twayne, 1987.

Discusses the works that are included in *The Forsyte Saga.*

Stevens, Earl E. "John Galsworthy." In *British Winners of the Nobel Literary Prize,* edited by Walter E. Kidd, pp. 130-67. Norman: University of Oklahoma Press, 1973.
Explores Galsworthy's contribution to English literature. Includes a brief biography and survey of the author's works.

Wilson, Angus. "Galsworthy's *Forsyte Saga.*" In *Diversity and Depth in Fiction,* edited by Kerry McSweeney, pp. 149-52. New York: The Viking Press, 1984.
Negatively reviews *The Forsyte Saga,* faulting Galsworthy for poor characterization, weak plot, and "heavy" writing.

Ödön von Horváth

1901-1938

Hungarian dramatist, novelist, and short story writer.

INTRODUCTION

Horváth's astute social criticism, keen psychological insights, and distinctive dialogue earned him a reputation as one of the most respected German-language dramatists of his time. His focus on the plight of the lower-class and his staunch opposition to fascism prompted comparisons to such highly regarded political dramatists as Bertolt Brecht and Friedrich Dürrenmatt, as well as to satirists Johann Nestroy and Karl Kraus. Horváth's *Volksstücke,* a series of "folk-plays" conveying intolerance of what he perceived as a materialistic, patriarchal society, have been acclaimed by critics as his most important works.

Horváth was born in Fiume (now Rijeka, Croatia) but spent little time in his native land. The family relocated often due to his father's position as a diplomat. Horváth received his early schooling in Budapest and Vienna. He began to study German at the age of fourteen, and it soon became his primary language. In 1919 Horváth entered Ludwig-Maximilian University in Munich as a student of philosophy and German philology. After four semesters he withdrew from the university and moved with his parents to Murnau, Germany, a mountain village near Munich. There he concentrated on his writing, having already created a pantomime commissioned by the composer Siegfried Kallenberg. Soon after the family moved to Murnau, three Austrian workers died in an accident nearby during the construction of a mountain railway. Surviving workers blamed the railroad management for the accident, and the police were eventually called in to settle a confrontation between the two groups. This sequence of events provided the basis for Horváth's drama *Revolte auf Côte 3018,* the first of his *Volksstücke* which was later retitled *Die Bergbahn.*

As Nazi influence grew during the 1930s, Horváth's plays and novels were banned from German stages and publishing houses, and his work was publicly condemned. Rainer Schlösser, a prominent Nazi apologist, commented in 1931, "Horváth [has] nothing to say to Germans, absolutely nothing." Denunciation of Horváth's works increased after Adolf Hitler gained power, and in 1933 a Berlin theater canceled the premiere of *Glaube Liebe Hoffnung* (*Faith, Hope, and Charity*), the last in Horváth's series of *Volksstücke.* Shortly thereafter, Horváth went into self-imposed exile in Vienna. He continued to write plays, experimenting with many different dramatic forms, but none met with as much success as the *Volksstücke.* Of these later works, *Die Unbekannte aus der Seine, Der jüngste Tag, Hin und Her,* and *Don Juan kommt aus dem Krieg* (*Don Juan Comes Back from the War*) are the most

notable. While these dramas include social commentary, the presence of mystical, fantastic, and comic elements precludes their being classified as *Volksstücke.* Because of Horváth's controversial reputation, most producers were deterred from financing these works and, as a result, the plays reached limited audiences during his lifetime. In contrast, two of his novels garnered significant attention. *Jugend ohne Gott* (*Youth without God*) and *Ein Kind unserer Zeit* (*A Child of Our Time*) were both published in Holland in 1938 and translated widely. These works were Horváth's last; he died in a freak accident in 1938 while en route to Switzerland, where he had planned to settle.

Horvath's most important works reflect the political turmoil and economic hardship that marked the period he spent in Murnau and later in Berlin. His *Volksstücke,* especially, dramatize the greed and oppression of an increasingly fascist Central European society. *Die Bergbahn, Italienische Nacht, Geschichten aus dem Wiener Wald* (*Tales from the Vienna Woods*), *Kasimir und Karoline,* and *Faith, Hope, and Charity* all utilize satire, exaggerated dialects, and a generally negative portrayal of working and middle-class citizens to convey disapproval of Central European culture following World War I. The *Volksstück* was a traditional dramatic form, but Horváth sought to shatter previous notions of what the genre entailed. He reclassified the *Volk,* or common folk, for the industrial age, identifying the *Volksstück*'s new subjects as the *Kleinbürger,* or members of the lower-middle-class. Horváth focused on the *Kleinbürger* because he believed this sector constituted the majority of society and that they were highly susceptible to fascist rhetoric. Horváth's innovative dialogue drew the most critical attention. In an attempt to fuse realism and irony, he shunned traditional dialects and insisted that his characters speak in *Bildungsjargon,* a hodgepodge of vernaculars specific to people in such educated or high-profile professions as academia, business, law, entertainment, and politics. The sterility of the resulting dialogue reflected the spiritual impoverishment Horváth believed typified the era. Horváth shifted his focus to economic hardship in the latter three *Volksstücke,* setting them in the Great Depression. In all of these plays, Horváth's sympathies lie with the two groups that he saw as the most oppressed: women, who suffered under male dominance, and the lower-class, who were victims of capitalist greed.

Horváth's novels reflect the same balance of individual and social consciousness as his plays. An early novel, *Der ewige Spießer,* utilizes humor and tragedy to tell the story of two typical *Kleinbürger* and a prostitute with whom they become involved. *Youth without God* and *A Child of Our Time* decry the evils of fascism while highlighting personal development and failure. The characters in these novels speak *Parteijargon,* the conformist mode of speech adopted by the fascists. Written in the first person, the novels exhibit Horváth's shift in focus from mass ideology to individual consciousness as well as his heightened interest in Christianity. In 1938, shortly after Horváth's death, *A Child of Our Time* appeared on a Nazi blacklist. Nonetheless, like *Youth without God* the novel received international acclaim.

The pinnacle of Horváth's brief career came with his acceptance of the coveted Kleist Prize for drama in 1931. Horváth's popularity waned during the 1930s and 1940s due to Nazi censorship, but his works took on added significance after World War II as Europeans began to assess the reasons behind Hitler's rise to power. Only following the publication of his collected writings in the early 1970s, however, was Horváth's importance fully recognized as the growing political consciousness of the era fostered an audience receptive of such polemical work. Krishna Winston noted: "Horváth's plays summon us to ponder the causes of human beastliness, to rethink the present social order. Far from being dated, the plays are just coming into their own." Horváth's political themes, inventive dialogue, and psychological insights continue to inspire contemporary dramatists. Alan Best observed: "Horváth's contribution to modern drama, a resurgence of interest in the *Volksstück* as a form of contemporary social criticism, bore fruit in the generation of young writers who came to the fore in the 1960s. Wolfgang Bauer, Franz Xaver Kroetz and Martin Sperr, sharing Horváth's experience of the Austro-Bavarian region, owe their predecessor a considerable debt."

PRINCIPAL WORKS

Revolte auf Côte 3018   (drama)   1927; also performed as
   Die Bergbahn [revised version], 1929

Rund um den Kongreß   (drama)   1929

**Sladek der schwarze Reichswehrmann*   (drama)   1929

Der ewige Spießer   (novel)   1930

Geschichten aus dem Wiener Wald   (drama)   1931
   [*Tales from the Vienna Woods,* 1977]

Italienische Nacht   (drama)   1931

Kasimir und Karoline   (drama)   1932

Hin und Her   (drama)   1934

Glaube Liebe Hoffnung   (drama)   1936
   [*Faith, Hope, and Charity,* 1989]

Figaro läßt sich scheiden   (drama)   1937

Der jüngste Tag   (drama)   1937

Jugend ohne Gott   (novel)   1938
   [*Youth without God* published in *A Child of Our Time:
   Being "Youth without God" and "A Child of Our Time,"*
   1938; also published as *The Age of the Fish,* 1939]

Ein Kind unserer Zeit   (novel)   1938
   [*A Child of Our Time* published in *A Child of Our Time:
   Being "Youth without God" and "A Child of Our Time,"*
   1938]

†*Die Unbekannte aus der Seine*   (drama)   1949

†*Don Juan kommt aus dem Krieg*   (drama)   1952
   [*Don Juan Comes Back from the War,* 1978]

‡*Pompeji, Komedie eines Erdbebens*   (drama)   1959

Gesammelte Werke. 4 vols.   (dramas, novels, short stories, lectures, essays)   1970-71

*This work is a revision of *Sladek, oder die schwarze Armee,* an unpublished drama.

†These works were written in 1933 and 1935 respectively.

‡This work is a revision of *Ein Sklavenball,* an unpublished drama
written in 1937.

Philip Rahv   (essay date 1939)

[A Russian-born American critic, Rahv was a prominent and influential member of the Marxist movement in American literary criticism. For thirty-five years he served as coeditor of Partisan Review, *the prestigious literary journal that T. S. Eliot once called "America's leading literary magazine." Rahv's criticism usually focused on the intellectual, social, and cultural milieu influencing a work of art. His approach was intellectually eclectic and nonideological. In the following excerpt,*

Rahv examines Horváth's political commentary in The
Age of the Fish.]

Horvath found a simple and inevitable image for what has
happened in the Third Reich. His novel, **The Age of the
Fish,** is hardly anything more than a brief, compact sermon built around this image and illustrated by a few dramatic episodes in the life of a schoolmaster and his numb
little pupils. The schoolmaster intrudes upon the sphere
"ruled by the radio" when one day he reproaches a boy
for writing in his composition that "all niggers are dirty,
cunning, and contemptible." Having touched one of the
tentacles of the Moloch-state, the hapless man will never
again sleep in peace. But the schoolboys hate not only the
"niggers" but one another; and as one of them commits
a murder for the sake of the mite of warmth the sensation
provides, the teacher, now deeply compromised, takes a
hand in discovering the culprit, only to be deprived of his
position for his pains. And in the end that beehive of culture called Europe is caught in a final beam of irony as we
sigh with relief watching the schoolmaster—nicknamed
"the Nigger"—depart for Africa to teach in a missionary
school. Expelled from civilization for believing that all
men are human, it is to the jungle that this refractory individual exports his obsolescent reveries.

But at bottom he is no warrior against fascism, this scurry-
ing little man with a conscience, this searcher for tokens
of divinity. Every time his ideas get twisted, a supernatural
power reaches out to enlighten him. The author, one feels,
is on much too familiar terms with God, whose intervention resolves the conflicts outlined in the narrative. The
problem it raises is primarily one of understanding the
process of dehumanization, and this shifting of the burden
to God, though it may have helped Horvath to finish his
story, in no way helps the reader to complete the experience he has been offered. Nor is it a question of objecting
to the author's faith on ideological grounds. It really is a
matter of observing how through the license of mysticism
he evades the responsibilities of his medium. To drop, as
he does, a concrete human situation—which at its start is
presented with high integrity and a beautiful economy of
means—into the lap of the infinite is to convert religion
into a literary man's ruse.

Odon von Horvath was a gifted young playwright and
novelist who was accidentally killed in Paris last year. His
prose, quite apart from any of its specific themes, strikes
an ominous note, a note that during the last few decades
we have come to recognize and to expect from the troubled writers of Central Europe. It can be described as a
kind of portentous buzz of the psyche. In different keys we
have heard this grave sound in the work of the Expression-
ists, in the poems of Rilke, in the fictions of Kafka, in the
pseudo-Dostoyevskyean novels of Wassermann; and people of the type of Franz Werfel repeat it on a conventional
level. It is a tone of foreboding, peculiar to the air of cities
like Prague, Vienna, and Berlin, on the one hand related
to religion and on the other to pathology. Of course, the
literature of most countries has for many years now been
stirred by sinister rumors. But the Central European note
has a certain timbre of its own—the modulation of a state
of anxiety at once reflective and intuitive. (pp. 106-07)

Philip Rahv, "A Variety of Fiction," in Partisan Review, *Vol. VI, No. 3, Spring, 1939, pp.
106-13.*

Alfred Kazin   (essay date 1939)

[*A highly respected American literary critic, Kazin is
best known for his essay collections* On Native Grounds
(1942), The Inmost Leaf *(1955), and* Contemporaries
(1962). Below, Kazin reviews A Child of Our Time.]

When Odon Von Horvath's brilliant little novel, **The Age
of the Fish,** was published recently, the gloomy record of
fiction written by the exiles from Hitler was suddenly
brightened. For Von Horvath, whose tragic death in Paris
gave his wry and original talent a peculiar vividness, had
turned his back on the mournful realism of the emigres,
with their passion for easy caricature and their desire for
revenge. He had realized with extraordinary acuteness
that to meet the horror of reality with a horror literature
was no longer possible or useful; that the reality of Fascism was in fact so overwhelming and catastrophic that
no realism, particularly the agonized naturalism of the
twentieth century, could do it justice.

What Odon Von Horvath discovered, in short, was what
Kafka and Rilke had absorbed even before Hitler: that if
literature is to survive in our day it must return to symbolism, turn a flank on the postwar and perennially pre-war
world, and find the literary equivalent of terror. The most
distinguished literature of our time, in fact, has ever since
T. S. Eliot's *The Waste Land* understood that irony must
become the supreme style. We are beaten by too many
bludgeons to use our minds as bludgeons; we have exhausted too many disillusionments to be surprised by disillusion. A sensitive writer today lives by compromise, even
by permission; and to write at all he must wind his way
like a worm over the boots of the storm troopers and
across the thousand callous fronts that block literature,
the search for literature, and the need of expression.

Von Horvath's subject, in **A Child of Our Time,** as in **The
Age of the Fish,** is totalitarianism as an idea. His books
are little dramatic fantasies in which dolls in uniform jerk
out their grisly roles on a dark stage. The atmosphere
through which they move is so elemental that the very na-
ivete of the action seems to equate sensation with despair.
Von Horvath's achievement, in short, was to make the
wildest horror seem possible; by reducing his scale, by giving his work a severely personal simplicity, he indicated
the epic disasters of Fascism in the figure of one man.

In truth, there is only one character in **A Child of Our
Time.** He is not any German boy raised through the block-
ade and inflation and succumbing out of sheer hunger to
the blandishments of Hitler; he is one juvenile storm
trooper, completely realized, whose story is so suggestive
at all points that it seems to combine the experiences of
millions. More, it is always his story, his personal history;
he tells it to you quietly and confidently, he boasts of being
a "volunteer" in Spain, he despises his poor old liberal father, he adores his captain. The maniacal lies of Hitlerism,
as this boy repeats them, are thus not headline reports one

distrusts by instinct; they have the intensity of alchemy, and are morbidly real.

"If a man doesn't suit the times he lives in," the boy writes in one passage, "we should do more than merely cut him off from us. Let him hang high on the gallows of his free will till the crows get him!" And one knows why he believes that. Hunger gave him an appetite; joblessness made him lonely; when the S. S. drew him in, he found not only bread but a name. Henceforth he was not merely an individual but a soldier with a purpose. Nothing is so burningly real in this little novel as the slow development of that idea, his new-found communal sense, the feeling that he belonged. Thus, the man who gave him a cot, a uniform, a philosophy, gave him protection and a fictitious sense of security. His father, a shambling old waiter beggaring tips, could offer only the forlorn mockery of liberalism.

German Fascism, says Von Horvath, captivated the youth because it offered them spiritual security. As a member of the Nazi party, one belonged to the caste, the elite, the Nordic world; one was no longer lonely. For the one thing the derelicts of German society had feared was loneliness: the utter isolation and shame of joblessness that was as bad as its deprivations. By declaring that the individual no longer counted, each recruit felt at last that he counted; by surrendering his personal aspirations, taste and personality to the Fascist military mass, he felt for the first time the importance and weight of his personal contribution. Fascism, then, has exploited the leavings of liberal capitalism: it boasts of its scorn for the individual; and paradoxically gives him a chance to believe that he is an individual again.

But what happens when the Fascist mass turns on its own members? Like any army, Fascism supports its own; but it will crush dissidents or those who have become useless to it. It is along these lines that Von Horvath narrates the boy's growing disillusion. The falsity of the *ersatz* state can be experienced only by those who have believed in its illusions. When the boy returns from Spain to look for the girl he loves he learns that she has been discarded by her employer. Why? The girl is ill; she is no longer useful. But what of her, the boy asks. How can a human being be thrown aside? Is she not an individual? If you prick her, will she not bleed? The employer answers him: the individual no longer counts. The Fascist state, always a despot, is benevolent only when benevolence pays. That is the pinch of Fascism. And that is what the young storm trooper comes to know.

> Alfred Kazin, "Novels of Youth and Art," in
> New York Herald Tribune Books, *November
> 5, 1939, p. 12.*

Ian C. Loram   (essay date 1967)

[In the excerpt below, Loram provides a chronological survey of Horváth's work.]

The majority of Horváth's early plays are primarily concerned with various aspects of political and social justice and decency, but it soon becomes clear that the decisive element for him is not things, but people, not institutions, but human beings. With his biting, often inconsiderate tone, he held a mirror up to his time, and the audiences did not like the reflection. He was perfectly well aware of this. "Der Widerwille eines Teiles des Publikums gegen meine Stücke beruht wohl darauff, daß dieser Teil sich in den Personen auf der Bühne selbst erkennt. Und es gibt natürlich Menschen, die über sich selbst nicht lachen können, und besonders nicht über ihr mehr oder minder bewußtes, höchst privates Triebleben." One writer has claimed, perhaps justifiably, that the public resented Horváth's way of treating many of his characters as toys with which he is playing, as a child will play—cruelly, imaginatively, and sometimes with an innocent and naive lack of concern about their fate.

Die Bergbahn, as we have seen, depicts the struggle between capital and labor; *Sladek der schwarze Reichwehrsmann* tries to prove that the individual is little more than a small part of the mass. *Rund um den Kongreß,* which has never been performed, points up the senselessness of expecting organizations or institutions to "humanize" mankind or to improve the lot of the individual. More interesting than the play itself, which revolves around the "internationaler Kongreß zum internationalen Kampf des internationalen Mädchenhandels," is Horváth's transfer of characters from one play to another; for instance, we meet again the pacifist and idealist Schminke from *Sladek* as well as the hotel manager from *Zur schönen Aussicht.* Here too we find another device reminiscent of the modern grotesque theater, or even of the comedy of romanticism. Schminke is executed by a firing squad in the course of the play, but remains alive, because he is an "idea," and as such cannot be destroyed. Unfortunately, as an "idea" he cannot become "reality," and Horváth seems to be saying that Schminke is therefore incapable of helping Sladek—or anyone else, for that matter. Again, a member of the public attending the congress forces a happy ending on the play because it was announced as a farce, and he does not wish to see "ein tragisches Klamauk." The most important of the early plays is *Italienische Nacht.* The action derives in part from an actual brawl in Murnau between Nazis and those with whom Horváth's political sympathies lay at the time—"Links-liberal-Sozialdemokraten," as Zuckmayer described them. Horváth was actually present at the riot, but he was no stranger to such excitement. "Wird gerauft," he once told Csokor, "muß man vor allem die Lampe einschlagen und den Tisch umstürzen, ehe man durchs Fenster hinausspringt." From the vantage point of hindsight we can today see only too clearly how Horváth was trying to warn of the dangers of Nazism, as it took root in the middle class, in the *Spießer,* and as it manifested itself in the confused and illogical thought and action of that class. . . . Horváth's admonitions went unheeded. Audiences laughed when they should have shuddered.

In 1930 Horváth published his first novel, *Der ewige Spießer.* This "Kleinbüger" is a type which we have met before, which developed and then predominated as a social group between the wars, and helped sign the death warrant of democracy in Germany. For Horváth this new petty bourgeoisie was the ruling class, marked by stupidity, indifference, cruelty, mental and spiritual laziness, selfishness, and a tendency toward falsehood. "Ich habe nur zwei Dinge, gegen die ich schreibe," he once wrote, "das ist die Dummheit und die Lüge." Add to these "Egoismus," and we have the sources of most human problems as far as Horváth is concerned. He sees them as a convenient refuge, quite *consciously* sought after, from everyday difficulties and awkward situations, involving a deliberate closing of the eyes and pretending that they aren't there. Martin Esslin, writing about Alfred Jarry's play *Ubu Roi,* which was first performed in Paris in 1896, says: "Mit der Intuition eines großen Dichters hatte Jarry in den Zügen des respektablen Bürgers, in seinem Egoismus und seiner Dummheit bereits die Keime des kulturellen und sozialen Zusammenbruchs der Zukunft erkannt." This could just as easily have been said of Horváth in the early thirties. "Der Spießer," says Horváth in the foreword, "ist bekanntlich ein hypochondrischer Egoist, und so trachtet er danach, sich überall feige anzupassen, und jede neue Formulierung der Idee zu verfälschen, indem er sie sich aneignet."

The characters in the novel carry on long and senseless conversations which are frequently monologues, because neither partner is listening to the other, or if he is, does not make the effort to understand. What they say consists of a series of clichés or platitudes, sometimes pathetic, sometimes stupid, sometimes cruel, but rarely sincere or selfless. Theirs is a world, as Csokor described it, "darin sich eine aus Klischee verhaftete Romantik gleichwohl mit einem brutalen Wirklichkeitssinn zu koppeln versteht, wenn es sie zur Machtergreifung drängt. . . .Es handelt sich also in diesem Roman um den Befund einer menschlichen Eiszeit, die nur ein Nebeneinander kennt und nie ein Miteinander; die Trägheit des Herzens wird festgestellt."

The atmosphere of the works mentioned so far, with their pimps and prostitutes, their con-men and Philistines, their neophyte SA and SS men, points toward a play which, in November of 1931, under the direction of Heinz Hilpert, was to be a sensation in Berlin, and with *Geschichten aus dem Wiener Wald* Horváth reached a new stage of his development. During this period he also wrote *Kasimir und Karoline, Glaube Liebe Hoffnung,* and *Die Unbekannte aus der Seine.* Professor Weisstein sees *Geschichten aus dem Wiener Wald* as a political play, but while Horváth does take the opportunity to ridicule the Nazis, social and human elements outweigh the political aspect. The motto of the play reads: "Nichts gibt so sehr das Gefühl der Unendlichkeit als die Dummheit." It might also have been another of Horváth's aphorisms: "Jeder Mensch begeht täglich durchschnittlich zehn Schweinereien. Zumindest als Gedankensünde." What the play depicts is the awful loneliness and hopelessness of a society which is made up almost solely of stupid and selfish individuals, who help destroy one another emotionally and spiritually. Here Horváth goes about what he calls "die Demaskierung des Bewußtseins," removing the patina of sentimentality, "Kitsch," bathos and pathos to expose what Emrich describes as "der gegenseitige Selbstbetrug." The waltz of the title is heard all through the play, ironically underlining the dialogue. Alfred, the would-be lover, has a hand in killing Marianne's love, but is no less guilty than her fi-

ancé Oskar the butcher, who, in his smug and brutal self-righteousness has already succeeded in stifling it. The audience heard the cynicism and the harshness rather than the "Weichheit" that they had expected from the title, and, finding it hard to believe that this mixture of empty commonplaces and uninhibited feeling could mean anything, reacted vigorously. The "bestialische Dummheit," as Horváth called it, is further illustrated in the person of a budding Nazi, a heel-clicking law student and a distant relative of Knuzius in *Der fröhliche Weinberg,* although he is far more dangerous. *Geschichten aus dem Wiener Wald* is almost the perfect illustration for Horváth's statement: "Für mich ist die Komik etwas Tragisches. Ich schreibe Tragödien, die nur durch ihre 'Menschlichkeit' komisch sind."

In *Kasimir und Karoline,* the Bavarians were equally horrified and indignant at what they assumed was Horváth's portrait of themselves. With the ironic motto: "Und die Liebe höret nimmer auf," he shows love among the "Kleinbürger" to be simply a kind of animal-like instinctive reaction that comes and goes, like pain or weariness or thirst. The scene of the play is the *Oktoberfest,* and, as is fitting in this fairground atmosphere, among the freaks and oddities that Horváth knew so well, life—and love—turn out to be numbers on a wheel of fortune. The love of Kasimir and Karoline is destroyed by the emptiness in which they live and from which they cannot escape. The unhappy part of it is that these people do not recognize this void, because their thought processes are, as it were, too primitive and underdeveloped to enable them to form a picture of it. Krischke has said (and this underscores Horváth's remark about "bestialische Dummheit"): "Horváth's Menschen haben alle etwas erschreckend Animalisches. Sie fürchten sich wie Tiere—und beißen um nicht selbst gebissen zu werden. Sie zerstören—und stehen verwundert vor den Trümmern und wollen nicht glauben, daß sie selbst die Ursache dieser Zerstörung und dieser Verwundung waren." This goes as far back as Sladek, who says repeatedly: "In der Natur wird ermordet, das ändert sich nicht," and so allows himself to be party to murder. It is discouraging that Horváth nowhere indicates that there is a way out of this depressing situation. On the one hand, he claims that new human relationships are the only escape from the dilemma, on the other, he can almost never bring himself to show us that such relationships are actually possible. With the exception of *Italienische Nacht,* where the issues are fairly clear-cut, none of these plays ends with the hope that things will change for the better. This is surely one reason why the public, for the most part, rejected him, and why Bernard Diebold, in his review of *Kasimir und Karoline* in 1932, asked whether Horváth disliked his characters so much that he could bequeath them only selfishness and hardness of heart.

In *Glaube Liebe Hoffnung,* which has the possibilities of a real tragedy, Horváth just misses the mark because of the tendency, which Zuckmayer had noted earlier, toward the anecdotal, and the only partial development and exploitation of a dramatic situation. Again, an actual episode was the germ of the play, but Horváth seems to have forgotten that the episode must be transformed in order to come alive. He subtitled it "ein kleiner Totentanz," and his original intention was to write a play "gegen die bürokratisch-verantwortungslose Anwendung kleiner Paragraphen . . . mit [der Hoffnung], daß man jene kleinen Paragraphen vielleicht (verzeihen Sie bitte das harte Wort) humaner machen könnte." But the play became more than simply a piece of social criticism, more than a plea for flexibility within the law. In the figure of the poor girl who is fined because she works without proper papers, because she has not been able to work to earn the money to procure the papers, and has then borrowed money under false pretenses to pay the fine, we have a cousin of Friedrich Voigt, "der Hauptmann von Köpenick." Horváth again displays his uncanny ability to unmask people, as he depicts for us the young policeman with whom the girl falls in love, but who thinks more of his job and promotion than he does of her. Here again the individual is defeated by "bestialische Dummheit" and self-centeredness. (One might also add self-pity.) All the policeman can say when he looks at his Elizabeth, who has drowned herself, is "Ich hab kein Glück. Ich hab kein Glück."

In *Die Unbekannte aus der Seine* Horváth presents a possible explanation for the suicide of a girl whose death mask with its enigmatic smile has been reproduced hundreds of times, hangs in hundreds of living rooms, and about whom no one knows anything, not even her name. One would like to think that here a note of hope is sounded, in that the unknown girl, the only person who knows the identity of a murderer, dies voluntarily out of love for him so that her secret will never be revealed, that this self-sacrifice, for such it surely is, indicates a change in Horváth's bitter belief that people have time only for their own petty desires. But Horváth still cannot quite convince himself of this. There is, however, the first indication of an element which was to appear again in Horváth's plays: the supernatural. We have to assume, without Horváth's ever saying so, that the unknown girl comes from a world beyond ours.

In the later plays we can detect a maturer, even perhaps a more optimistic Horváth. *Hin und Her,* the bittersweet story of a man expelled from one country and refused admission to the next, so that he has to spend his time on the bridge over the river which marks the border, is a political satire with a happy ending. *Himmelwärts,* a play about a pact with the devil, pokes fun in a good-natured and satirical manner at the problem of good and evil. Even the devil is "kleinbürgerlich," and heaven and hell resemble, as one writer said, "eine Art österreichischer Amtskanzeleien." *Dorf ohne Männer* is a farcical adaptation with satirical overtones of a Hungarian novel. "Ich stehe zu Satire absolut positiv. Ich kann gar nicht anders," Horváth once wrote. "Die Parodie lehne ich als dramatische Form ab. Parodie hat meines Erachtens mit Dichtung nichts zu tun, und ist ein ganz billiges Unterhaltungsmittel." Here he departs from the Nestroy tradition, but there is still some justification for seeing, both in the language of these plays and in the half-joking, half-admonishing tone, characteristics of the older Viennese "Volksstück." More important, however, is the tendency now, even in these more light-hearted plays, to have the characters approach decisions, to accept responsibility, to illuminate more brightly the difference between good and evil, action and inertia.

In the important works of the last period Horváth emphasizes two things: the irrational and the political. In *Der jüngste Tag,* a stationmaster, accused of causing a railroad accident, is absolved of responsibility through the testimony of the girl who, with him, is at fault. The spirit of the engineer killed in the wreck attempts to persuade him to commit suicide by way of penance, but the shade of the girl, whom the stationmaster has meantime murdered, thereby making himself truly guilty, convinces him that he should give himself up. The stationmaster then is able to persuade himself that he should stand responsible before an earthly judge. Here, for the first time, Horváth openly accepts and emphasizes the awakening of morality and conscience, and points to the workings of a higher power. Here the decision is finally reached, thrusting aside the vacillation and reluctance to decide of so much of the early work.

Figaro läßt sich scheiden, says Weisstein, is Horváth's first real attempt to advocate a kind of political tolerance, but again it seems to me that for Horváth personal human relationships are more important than politics. Figaro, the former revolutionary, who flees the revolution with Graf Almaviva and then decides to settle down to barbering, almost becoming a *Spießer* in the process, must have his eyes opened, both as a political animal and as a human being. From the Figaro who claims: "Wir leben in Zeitläuften, wo die Läufte wichtiger sind als die Menschen," to the man who can say at the end: "Jetzt erst hat die Revolution gesiegt, indem sie es nicht mehr nötig hat, Menschen in den Keller zu sperren, die nichts dafür tun können, ihre Feinde zu sein," there is a clear-cut development. In a short preface to the first version of the play, Horváth wrote: "In der *Hochzeit des Figaro* wetterleuchtet die nahe Revolution, in *Figaro läßt sich scheiden* wird zwar voraussichtlich nichts wetterleuchten, denn die Menschlichkeit wird von keinen Gewittern begleitet, sie ist nur ein schwaches Licht in der Finsternis. Wollen wir immerhin hoffen, daß kein noch so starker Sturm es auslöschen kann."

Horváth's second venture into drama focussed on a character from world literature does not come off quite so well. In *Don Juan kommt aus dem Krieg* he sees his hero as a tragic figure, a man searching for the absolute, something that he thought he had found in the woman he once loved and then deserted. But he keeps blinding himself to that which he is seeking. In a note to the play Horváth said: "Die tragische Schuld Don Juans ist, daß er seine Sehnsucht immer wieder vergißt oder gar verhöhnt, und so wird er zum zynischen Opfer seiner Wirkung, aber nicht ohne Trauer." We are, however, still left with the question: Is his death the result of tragic guilt, or is it merely pathetic? Horváth has not given us the answer, perhaps because he attempts to make out of his hero a type rather than an individual.

Both *Figaro* and *Don Juan* were completed in 1937, and before the year was out he had reworked *Ein Sklavenball* (1936) and called it *Pompeji, Komödie eines Erdbebens.* . . . A slave named Toxilus and a hetaera, Lemniselenis, fall in love. Social conventions decree that they shall die, but the sudden eruption of Vesuvius, while destroying the city, saves them, because they have been imprisoned in the catacombs to await being thrown to the wild beasts. During this imprisonment Toxilus hears from another slave about the beliefs of a mysterious religious sect. Curiously enough, in a nearby room of the catacombs there is a man who is extremely busy writing. "Er schreibt Briefe," Lemniselenis is told, "so gleich an ganze Städte, zum Beispiel, die Korinther." The destruction of Pompeii heralds therefore the death of the old Roman beliefs and the birth of a new humanity with the beginnings of Christianity. Each character in the play is at one time or another confronted with the new faith, and their reactions to it are what interest Horváth. The tragic and the comic are here so used as almost to force us to conclude that the play is *really* a comedy. This technique, the sudden and unexpected change from the tragic to the comic, enables the reader in most cases, if he is careful, to view the problems from more than one level, but if he does not realize what Horváth is doing, he will think that the author is contradicting himself, or at least accuse him of inconsistency.

Some time in 1937 Horváth must have come to feel that there was a higher power capable of exerting its influence on mankind. In his novel *Jugend ohne Gott* he writes: "Gott ist die Wahrheit." Not a terribly original thought perhaps, but for Horváth it apparently amounted to a revelation. At the moment there seems to be no other way of explaining this breakthrough. Franz Werfel was sure that Horváth had come to some sudden insight into the problem of good and evil, into the meaning of conscience, of responsibility, or morality. "Hätte Horváth . . . aus seiner Talentfülle das Niedrige, die Niedertracht, als Norm betrachtet und mit beinahe unschuldiger Verspieltheit gestaltet, so tritt nun mit blitzhaftem Schreck Erkenntnis auf und Leiden. Die Niedertracht ist nicht mehr selbstverständlich . . . Die Idee der Schuld erscheint." Csokor put it this way: "In dem Augenblick nämlich . . . wo [der Künstler] merkt, daß die Frage nach Schuld und Bekenntnis gestellt werden muß, und zwar an sich selbst—wo er sozusagen zum Schreibtisch seines Gewissens wird—in diesem Augenblick öffnet er sich . . . der Anerkennung Gottes." *Jugend ohne Gott* is generally thought of as a warning against the pernicious corruption of youth by the Nazis, but more important for Horváth and his development is the gradual awakening in a young teacher of moral and religious forces. If, in the earlier works, much of Horváth's energy was directed against stupidity, here he also attacks the lie.

In *Ein Kind unserer Zeit,* a soldier who commits murder, not out of passion, not out of curiosity, but for no reason at all, dies (rather like Don Juan) on a park bench in the cold and the snow and the night, because he comes to realize what he has done and that he must atone for it.

After all this, what kind of a writer *is* Ödön von Horváth? Or should one ask what kind of writer he might have been? Both questions seem to me to be valid. In 1931 Alfred Kerr said of him: "Eine stärkste Kraft unter den Jungen . . . Köstliches strömt und quillt. Nicht im Bau steckt sein Vorzug, sondern in der Füllung." Csokor has said that perhaps since the death of Büchner no more promising talent has been cut off so abruptly. Ulrich Becher wrote: "Müßige Spekulation oder nicht: für mich besteht kein Zweifel, daß er, hätte er überlebt, neben Brecht der größte zeitgenössische Bühnendichter deutscher Sprache geworden wäre." Becher exaggerates, I think, but there is no doubt, as Herbert Ihering realized too, that Horváth had an extraordinary talent, although he might have established himself as a novelist rather than as a playwright. One difficulty (as Zuckmayer noted) was that he was too often in a hurry. A scribbled note headed "Vorwort" (we do not know to what; possibly *Ein Kind unserer Zeit*), reads as follows: "Ich muß dies Buch rasch schreiben. Ich habe keine Zeit, dicke Bücher zu lesen, denn ich bin arm und muß arbeiten, um Geld zu verdienen, um essen zu können, zu schlafen. Auch ich bin nur ein Kind meiner Zeit. Ich will nicht leugnen, ich möchte gut leben. Aber es kommt nicht darauf an, wieviel Bücher man las, denn es dreht sich immer um den *Menschen,* und es sei hier vom Standpunkt des einfachen Menschen aus geschrieben, des einfachen Bürgers." One difficulty is that we cannot pigeonhole him, convenient though it might be, and this is a reason why he has not received the attention that he deserves. Although he wrote "Volksstücke," he is not traditional; he was never really under the spell of Expressionism because he is too realistic, too satirical, too "schnoddrig." He does not fit into "Neue Sachlichkeit" or the absurd theater. Apparently the mixture of the serious with the trivial, poetry with satire, reality with fantasy, does not strike a sympathetic note, although in all fairness one must say that his plays have been appearing frequently in Austria in recent years, on television as well as the stage. His plays are frequently cabaret-like, sometimes almost farcical—a combination of seriousness and lightheartedness. Even his use of language is disconcerting. He uses a kind of dialect, as we have seen, but his characters lapse into linguistic anachronisms, and there are scenes in which *Hochdeutsch* and dialect are spoken indiscriminately by the same figure, and where even foreigners speak "Weanerisch." But one cannot claim that the dialogues are naturalistic. As a note to his first play, Horváth had written: "Dialekt ist mehr als ein philologisches, ein psychologisches Problem. Verfasser befolgte im Folgenden weder philologische Gesetze, noch hat er einen Dialekt . . . schematisch stilisiert, sondern er versucht Dialekt als Charaktereigenschaft der Umwelt, des Individuums, oder auch nur einer Situation, zu gestalten." The clichés which so many characters indulge in are not a sign of weakness on the playwright's part, but are intended to convey the emptiness and lack of substance which these people assume to be a way of life. Like most moralists, he provokes and annoys. If much of his work concerns itself with disappointment, inconsiderateness, stupidity, lying, and despair, if Horváth has been regarded as a misanthrope because he strips his characters of their illusions with bitter satire and irony and allows them unwittingly to expose their inner fears, he remains nevertheless a protagonist of mankind, one who chastises that which he loves. One is perhaps too inclined to remember the despair of Marianne in *Geschichten aus dem Wiener Wald* when she asks: "Wenn es einen lieben Gott gibt—was hast du mit mir vor, lieber Gott?—Lieber Gott, ich bin im achten Bezirk geboren und hab die Bürgerschul besucht, ich bin kein schlechter Mensch—hörst du mich?—Was hast du mit mir vor, lieber Gott?" But on the other hand we must not forget the outburst of a Fanchette, who defies Figaro: "Du wirst mir nicht alles Menschliche zerstören, du nicht!" And above all we can remember how Horváth expressed his belief in humanity and man's ability to overcome his own stupidity and indifference. Some unpublished lines in the archive read as follows:

> Und die Leute werden sagen,
> In fernen blauen Tagen
> Wird es einmal recht,
> Was falsch ist und was echt.
> Was falsch ist, wird verkommen,
> Auch wenn es heut regiert.
> Was echt ist, das soll kommen,
> Auch wenn es heut krepiert.

(pp. 23-32)

Ian C. Loram, "Ödön von Horváth: An Appraisal," in Monatshefte Vol. LIX, No. 1, Spring, 1967, pp. 19-34.

Vincent R. Kling   (essay date 1973)

[*In the following essay, Kling contends that Horváth's early dramas openly criticize the social, political, and economic institutions of the time while his later works are less comprehensive, focusing instead on the individual.*]

If one can speak of cliches in reference to a renaissance of interest so recent as that centering in Ödön von Horváth, then the most worn of all is the persistent observation that this author's works underwent a radical transformation in content and theme during 1933 in reaction to the bewildering shock of forced emigration following Hitler's assumption of power. Horváth's *Volksstücke,* all written between 1929 and 1933, are set in exactly contemporary times and places and are quite overtly critical of then-existing social, political and economic institutions. By contrast, the plays written after 1933 are usually set in remote times or places and concentrate mostly on the individual who derives human stature only from his inner dimensions. This neat division suggests a split of Horváth's creative life into two distinct periods of pre- and post-emigration works, providing critics with a rationale for extolling the works of one period to the detriment of those from the other. While exponents of Marxian criticism and literary sociology admire the *Volksstücke* as documents of social analysis, other critics favor the later works for their metaphysical and religious orientation.

A closer look causes this clear dividing line to blur, and justly so, for it is an arbitrary boundary drawn in by the cartographer and not a natural feature of the landscape. *Geschichten aus dem Wiener Wald,* for instance, a work continually interpreted solely as a documentation of the lower middle-class mind, has a pronounced metaphysical strain going beyond the famous scene of Marianne in St. Stephen's Cathedral, while *Ein Dorf ohne Männer,* set in fifteenth-century Hungary and construed as only a light farce with contrasting lyrical moments, provides a devastating commentary on political leaders of the 1930's and

their followers. Instead of a decided break with his previous concerns, then, we find in Horváth a gradual and subtle series of modulations, a slight shift in view from work to work. The change occurred in many short steps, not in one large leap, and these steps can be traced in a chronological consideration of some of the works.

The traces are nowhere easier to follow than in the field of politics, which fascinated Horváth for most of his life. As a young man, he believed in and accepted the proposition that political institutions could effect definite social and economic progress toward an ideal millennium of peace and prosperity. Later disillusioning experiences, however, brought about in Horváth first skepticism, then bitter criticism, and finally rejection of this proposition, and he came to see all political parties and institutions, as well as other established organizations, as destroyers, *a priori,* of the humanity of their adherents.

As an adolescent in Budapest, Horváth became interested in the revolutionary writings of the Hungarian author Endre Ady, and in 1918, he sympathized strongly with the Galilei Circle, a radical revolutionary youth organization in Budapest. His orientation at the time was toward a fairly orthodox brand of Marxism, an orientation mirrored in the first of his plays to be performed, *Revolte auf Côte 3018* (1926). Pitted against each other are the cruel, exploiting, capitalistic employers and the long-suffering, oppressed, abused workers. But even at this early date, Horváth created his characters as fully rounded persons with their own psychological motivations, and not as flat, intellectualized *raisonneurs* of social and economic viewpoints. For the première of this play in 1927, Horváth wrote a short autobiographical note. A comment in it about his Budapest years suggests that he already felt a disparity between eros and politics, that is, between the individual's need for lone self-discovery in his private emotional life and the collective demands of the organization. It is as if the two could not exist together, at least not on an equal footing. "Bei einer ungefähren Höhe von 1, 52 erwachte in mir der Eros, aber vorerst ohne mir irgendwelche besonderen Scherereien zu bereiten—(meine Liebe zur Politik war damals bereits ziemlich vorhanden)."

In the years right after World War I in Bavaria, Horváth had become acquainted with the illegal paramilitary organizations of the extreme right. The title character of *Sladek oder die schwarze Armee* (1928) is a pathetic, stupid recruit in such an organization, into which deep feelings of inferiority and inadequacy have driven him. His failure as a human being is shown in his relationship with Anna, an older woman who has kept him for years and is more mother than mistress to him. Sladek is incapable of sustaining a mature love relationship based on equality and feels only panic and revulsion at Anna's physical overtures. He cannot admit these unpleasant truths to himself; rather, he leaves Anna, dreaming of the strong, conquering personality he will acquire as a member of the *schwarze Reichswehr.* This is Horváth's first indictment of collective or institutional thinking as such, for the other members of the organization, tough and brutal as they seem, are just as weak and insecure as Sladek, but greater experience has given them more skill in hiding that fact.

Sladek's motif, "Ich kann nämlich selbständig denken," is doubly ironic, not only because it is not true, but also because it is not desired by his comrades or superiors. These other members of the illegal army had hoped to find strength in numbers, like Sladek, but instead they have inevitably found multiplication by zero. The situation is truly hopeless for Sladek, for things are not better on the legal side of society. He becomes involved with the police for relieving himself against the back wall of a flea circus, which offense is taken momentarily by the law with greater seriousness than his membership in the illegal army and his participation in murder. Later, Sladek is free to emigrate to Nicaragua. Absorbed in acute self-pity, Sladek thinks of a new start and a bright future, foredoomed, of course, by the puniness of his own character.

It is perhaps natural to expect such an indictment of the extreme right from a leftist sympathizer like Horváth, but he began looking at left-wing slogans and attitudes in a skeptical light soon after this. The naive fool in **Rund um den Kongress** (1928-1929) turns out to be Schminke, a socialist-minded journalist who considers prostitution a product of capitalism and therefore capable of elimination by a change in the economic structure. A different view is taken by the secretary-general of the *Internationaler Kongress für internationale Bekämpfung der internationalen Prostitution,* who explains that "die Prostitution ist bekanntlich unausrottbar . . . man möchte fast sagen: die käufliche Liebe ist ein wesentlicher Bestandteil des Menschlichen schlechthin." The principle underlying this utterance, amusing as it is, was to become more and more clear to Horváth, namely that evil and vice are not external, but inherent in the human soul, so that no political institution would ever be able to lead humanity to a utopian tomorrow. The human condition is unchanging; basic experiences are not linked to time or place, and so progress toward a better world through collective action, the kernel of all political programs, is absolutely a sham. Politics fosters only the negative qualities of men by permitting them to pool their personal failures in an anonymous whole. The delegates to the congress, for instance, most of whom had begun as sincere reformers, end by consulting about the most convenient routes for the white slave traffic.

Skepticism turns to full-fledged criticism in *Italienische Nacht* (1931), a play prompted in part by a beer hall fight in which Horváth accidentally became involved. An even stronger impetus was provided by the results of the elections of September, 1930, in which the National Socialist party received 6.4 million votes and became the second strongest group in parliament, while the left-oriented parties remained silent through cowardice and complacency. Democracy was being officially ignored anyway, since Brüning and his cabinet were governing without reference to parliamentary decisions. Small wonder, then, that in *Italienische Nacht,* Horváth criticizes the various leftist groups with the same rigor and disapproval he applies to the right. The *Stadtrat,* Ammetsberger, is a study in unconscious ironies. His actions are the opposite of his words, but, too stupid to see a discrepancy, he talks on, making a greater and greater fool of himself. He exemplifies well the method of unconscious self-revelation that Horváth called "Demaskierung des Bewusstseins." He

fancies himself a champion of Marx's economic principles, but he is proud to be a property owner. He prides himself on his political integrity and *savoir-faire,* but he readily resorts to smear techniques and attempted intimidation. A dedicated egalitarian and humanitarian in theory, he is brutal and autocratic to his wife in practice.

Horváth's severest criticism, however, is directed against Martin and his companions, who comprise the younger and more radical, Communistic group. Like Ammetsberger, whom he scorns as a weak old man, Martin is fond of big talk and empty phrases. He pretends modesty while actually dreaming of unlimited power and he talks of forceful, armed action against the Fascists but is too cowardly to act when the possibility of a confrontation presents itself. He lets a courageous woman rout the rightwing faction for him, but this does not prevent him from taking full credit. His presumable internationalism as a true Marxist is in ludicrous contrast to his distrust of a comrade because he speaks in Prussian dialect. He treats his friend Anna with condescension, stressing his gallant generosity in rescuing her from prostitution, but he is willing to use her as a small-time Mata Hari, demanding that she lead the Fascists on sexually to discover their plans. Eros, again representing the whole emotional, inner life, has become perverted in Martin, who sends Anna into a new and colder kind of prostitution, but with the best of intentions, of course. Needless to say, Anna's feelings must simply be subjugated to the cause. Such abuses of one's fellow men, such utter callousness, such "Kälte als Schuld," as Franz Werfel called it, was to become a dominant theme of Horváth's later work, but this coldness is already fully present in Martin. None of the other characters recognizes the immoral calculation in Martin's behavior except the erotically healthy and basically antipolitical Karl, who says to Anna, "Wenn er nämlich sowas von dir verlangt, er schickt dich doch gewissermassen auf den politischen Strich," and then, after a significant pause, "—ob er dabei innere Kämpfe hat?"

Another episode from this play sums up in one speech the opposition of eros and politics. Drunk and complaining of the endless political harangues he is forced to hear every day, the owner of the tavern in which the last scene is set reminisces:

> Ich denk jetzt an meinen Abort. Siehst, früher da waren nur so erotische Sprüch an der Wand dringestanden, hernach im Krieg lauter patriotische und jetzt lauter politische—glaubs mir: solangs nicht wieder erotisch werden, solang wird das deutsche Volk nicht wieder gesunden—

After this play, with its unmasking of the posturings and empty rhetoric of all politics, Horváth turned away from directly political themes to deeper analysis of the kind of character who can always find an excuse to justify his every failure. *Geschichten aus dem Wiener Wald, Kasimir und Karoline,* and *Glaube Liebe Hoffnung* show the demoralizing effects of unemployment, ignorance, inflation and social turmoil, but they also show how the characters find it all too convenient to evade recognition of their inadequacies by blaming everything on the unsettled times. Erna from *Kasimir und Karoline* is typical when she says,

" . . . die Menschen wären doch garnicht schlecht, wenn es ihnen nicht schlecht gehen tät."

The outright conflict between eros and politics returns in *Figaro lässt sich scheiden* (1936). Figaro has lost the dash and verve so characteristic of him in Beaumarchais, Mozart and Rossini, and he is now a stodgy, boring conformist, contemptibly eager to fit in. While he has permitted the revolution to work on his fears and make a weakling of him, Susanne has retained her sparkle and sprightly wisdom. Figaro rates advantage over love and leaves Susanne for a lucrative job as manager of Almaviva's castle; but he begins to miss her, and this erotic lack forms the basis of Figaro's growth into or return to human sympathy. His yearning causes him to see the guilt of his behavior. He is a representative figure of the later Horváth, able to recognize his errors and repent by taking a more positive direction. In answer to Almaviva's question whether the revolution is over, Figaro answers, "Im Gegenteil, Herr Graf. Jetzt erst hat die Revolution gesiegt, indem sie es nicht mehr nötig hat, Menschen in den Keller zu sperren, die nichts dafür können, ihre Feinde zu sein". Figaro's transformation is a reflection of a whole society which can combine *Realpolitik* with humane tolerance. Since political conditions almost everywhere were so far the opposite of such a situation in 1936, this play could be construed as Horváth's indulgence in a fond dream, which would explain his choice of an already established fictional character as his hero.

Ein Dorf ohne Männer (1937), a brilliant comic masterpiece, uses one of Hungary's national heroes, King Mathias Hunyadi I (1440-1490), to express doubt about the legitimacy of hero-worship. The yearning for great men of decisive leadership had already produced Mussolini, Franco, and Hitler on the right. In reaction, writers defending the left wing and democratic politics in general began looking for their own great men, forceful cultural and political leaders whose dealings were marked by justice, honesty, fairness and tolerance. For example, Heinrich Mann turned to the figure of Henry IV of France, while Thomas Mann modeled many of the humane traits of his Joseph on his beloved Franklin D. Roosevelt. Mathias, called "der Gerechte" by his adoring subjects, fights off the Turks, eradicates corruption, hamstrings the bureaucrats, keeps peace, and rules with both justice and mercy. Yet he can achieve these goals only by deceit, lies, threats, and underhand behavior. He is not immoral, but he is the ultimate pragmatist. Horváth, having rejected the political right, left and center by this time, creates a character of great goodness who governs, at least externally, by the same methods as the Fascist dictators of the 1930's, but who achieves totally different results because he recognizes the strength of his virtuous character and acts on it. To the right, Horváth reveals thereby the inner rottenness of its leaders; to the left, he issues a warning not to be deceived by slogans and glib images.

Pompeji, Komödie eines Erdbebens (1937) was part of a projected but never completed *Komödie des Menschen*, a series of plays that was to dramatize the turning points of human history. In this play, we see inhumanity and brutality pass from an old social and political structure to a new one. At first, the play appears to condemn the degeneracy of Roman institutions, and the eruption of Vesuvius seems a just fate for Pompeii, a city soon to be forgotten as the fresh, idealistic values of Christianity replace jaded decadence. The slaves Lemniselensis and Toxilus have fallen in love and become Christians, so they flee to the catacombs during the uproar, where they seem to find peace and freedom. But a man enters, unpleasant, cold, stifling, peremptorily demanding silence and acting like a polite but repressive dictator. Who is he? To quote one of the characters, "Ich weiss nicht, wie er heisst . . . Ich weiss nur, dass er Briefe schreibt . . . so gleich an ganze Städte. Zum Beispiel, an die Korinther—". Indicatively, he interrupts whenever Lemniselensis and Toxilus are trying to declare their love. As soon as they become fervent and passionate, politics enters to stifle eros. There is little doubt that Paul is depicted here as a consummate politician, a brilliant and ruthless organizer exercising power to forge a durable institution. What Horváth suggests here is that the Church failed as soon as it lost its spontaneous appeal and borrowed the power mechanisms of the old establishment, taking over the administrative and political functions of the empire.

Since *Pompeji* is Horváth's last play, it would appear that he ended his career as a dramatist in deep pessimism, rejecting all established institutions as stultifying but without naming alternatives. Actually, Horváth seems to have been on the verge of new recognitions, to be incorporated into new works, at the moment of his grotesque and accidental death. One sign of this is the increasingly positive note that crept into the plans for the *Komödie des Menschen*. At any rate, Horváth's view of man, although merciless in its accuracy, never descended to wholesale scorn or rejection of the race. Although he repudiated politics and organized activity in general, he seems never to have abandoned hope in the human heart's making its way back to decency, as the verse found in his pocket after his death attests:

> Und die Leute werden sagen
> In den fernen blauen Tagen
> Wird es einmal recht,
> Was falsch ist und was echt.
>
> Was falsch ist, wird verkommen
> Obwohl es heut regiert.
> Was echt ist, das soll kommen—
> Obwohl es heut krepiert.

(pp. 182-89)

Vincent R. Kling, "The Conflict of Eros and Politics in Some Dramas of Ödön von Horváth," in Modern Austrian Literature, *Vol. 6, Nos. 3 & 4, 1973, pp. 182-90.*

K. Stuart Parkes   (essay date 1975)

[*Parkes is an English educator and critic. In the essay below, he provides a survey of Horváth's fiction.*]

Recent years have seen a great revival of interest in the works of Ödön von Horváth. While this has largely been confined to his plays, there is considerable evidence that in Horváth's own time it was the three novels that attracted particular attention. Whereas, especially in the dark days of emigration, when the number of German-speaking theatres outside the control of the Nazis was constantly being reduced, he had great difficulties in having his plays produced, the novels were all published immediately and received wide acclaim. Thomas Mann found *Jugend ohne Gott* the best book of its period, whilst *Ein Kind unserer Zeit* ran to three editions in Chinese. Thus Horváth's own view that the novel was a more suitable genre for a time when production possibilities for plays were so limited proved to be correct. Yet the novels must be regarded as more than the efforts of a frustrated dramatist. It is the aim of this article to show that they have considerable merit in their own right.

Of the three novels, *Jugend ohne Gott* and *Ein Kind unserer Zeit,* written towards the end of Horváth's life and both published in 1938, the year of his death, are connected by the common theme of Fascism, whilst *Der ewige Spießer,* published in 1930, belongs to an earlier stage of its author's literary development. In contrast to the plays of the same period such as *Geschichten aus dem Wiener Wald* and *Kasimir und Karoline,* which generally concentrate on the fate of individuals within the bourgeoisie, *Der ewige Spießer* aims at a much wider picture of this class. The novel form affords the opportunity for a panoramic view of the bourgeoisie in a more generalised way than might be possible in a play. *Der ewige Spießer* is, therefore, a complement to the plays of the same period. If one were to categorize it as a novel, it might well be described as almost picaresque. The main framework is provided by the relation of the journey of a Herr Kobler from his home in Munich to the Barcelona World Exhibition, which Horváth himself visited. This affords the opportunity for a portrayal of the lands and peoples of Europe, something no doubt Horváth's own cosmopolitan background especially equipped him to undertake. Thus Kobler meets a Hungarian democrat, whose behaviour and attitudes are anything but democratic, Austrian Fascists associated with the 'Heimwehr' and also travels the length of Mussolini's Italy. A sad picture emerges, as the novel is written from the left-wing standpoint of most of Horváth's early works. Speaking of Kobler's landlady, he writes:

> Wie alle ihresgleichen haßte sie nicht die uniformierten und zivilen Verbrecher, die sie durch Krieg, Inflation, Deflation und Stabilisierung begaunert hatten, sondern ausschließlich das Proletariat, weil sie ahnte, ohne sich darüber klar werden zu wollen, daß dieser Klasse die Zukunft gehört.

The portrayal of the bourgeoisie, referred to in the title and personified by Herr Kobler, reflects this kind of political standpoint. Kobler significantly obtains the money to visit Spain by selling a dilapidated old car to a gullible provincial Bavarian. As a beneficiary of the system, he naturally approves of the capitalist order which makes such deals possible. Horváth himself apparently sees the whole of capitalism as based on similar swindles, usually on a larger scale. Otherwise, Kobler is not very interested in politics until a disaster befalls him in Spain. The purpose of his journey was to find a rich wife, preferably an Egyptian. In fact, he meets a rich German, who, despite her

preference for Kobler, is to marry an American, because her father's business needs American capital. This misfortune converts Kobler to Pan-Europeanism, a political creed preached at him by his travelling companion from Italy to Spain, the journalist and frustrated poet Schmitz. Although he was always antinationalist, Horváth does not, on the evidence of the novel, appear to embrace this creed, unless it were to include socialism. This seems to be the significance of a brief meeting Kobler has on his return from Spain with a mysterious unnamed figure, who accepts the idea of Pan-Europe only if it entails 'Befreiung des Proletariats'.

Horváth's picture of the bourgeoisie is clearly extremely critical. In his introduction to the novel, he writes:

> Der Spießer ist bekanntlich ein hypochondrischer Egoist, und so trachtet er danach, sich überall feige anzupassen und jede neue Formulierung der Idee zu verfälschen, indem er sie sich aneignet.

This is the type exemplified by Kobler and Schmitz. Whatever merit there may be in a creed like Pan-Europeanism, it is destroyed by such advocates. There is, however, one action in the work which counterbalances the egoism of Kobler and his ilk. In the two short final parts of the novel, which no longer have to do with Kobler, Horváth describes the plight of two unemployed people, a waiter Reithofer and a girl Anna, who is gradually sinking into prostitution. Like a number of Horváth's other female characters, for instance Elisabeth in *Glaube Liebe Hoffnung,* she is being led into moral danger by the society of the depression. Although she treats Reithofer shabbily, he acts selflessly in helping her to find a job. This action, which is entirely unlike anything the self-seeking Kobler undertakes, appears to be regarded by Horváth as exemplary, even if he does present it somewhat oversentimentally.

The above description of the themes of *Der ewige Spießer* shows Horváth as principally concerned with ridiculing a certain type in society. Coupled with this, there is a scarcely-admitted didactic aim: 'Der Verfasser wagt natürlich nicht zu hoffen, daß er durch diese Seiten ein gesetzmäßiges Weltgeschehen beeinflußen könnte, jedoch immerhin.' The narrative technique he chooses for this is marked by its ironic distance. The narrator stands aloof from his characters, whose actions are in this way presented as utterly trivial. There are countless instances of ironic techniques. One favourite device is to take something said in a conversation into the main narrative, as when a friend advises the hapless Bavarian to buy Kobler's card:

> 'Das ist ein Notsitz!' rief er. 'Ein wunderbarer Notsitz! Ein gepolsterter Notsitz! Der absolute Notsitz! Kaufs, du Rindvieh!' Das Rindvieh kaufte es auch gleich.

Equally frequent are unusual contrasts, which serve to stress the incongruities among the characters and the situations described in the novel. Thus it is said that Graf Blanquez, an acquaintance of Kobler's, was educated 'teils von Piaristen, teils von einem homosexuellen Stabsarzt in einem der verzweifelten Kriegsgefangenenlager Sibiriens'.

Elsewhere, Schmitz meditates about Van Gogh, whilst primarily being concerned with loosening his bowels:

> 'Auch van Gogh ist verkannt worden', resign-
> ierte er, 'es versteht bald keiner den anderen
> mehr, es ist halt jeder für sich sehr einsam.' So
> blieb er noch lange sitzen und starrte grübelnd
> auf das Klosettpapier.

This kind of writing is clearly amusing and frequently successful. It is a highly suitable style for revealing the weaknesses of a social group. Equally though, the sovereign stance adopted by the narrator allows him to indulge any whim and include any detail that pleases him. Thus the reader is even told something about the compiler of the Spanish phrase book that Kobler has with him. Over a longer period, the style can only become repetitive and the cuts to the novel made by the original publisher seem to confirm this danger.

It can be argued against this that a novel with a picaresque element will by definition contain many passages that are not strictly 'relevant' and that 'relevance' is a totally false criterion to use. Even so this need not mean that the narrative must lack all tension. What sustains a picaresque novel is the relationship between the hero and the outside world. This is true of the more recent German novels that incorporate elements of the picaresque, for instance Walser's *Halbzeit* and Grass' *Die Blechtrommel.* Kobler, however, is not interesting enough as a person to create any tension; he is as empty as the world that surrounds him. He is not a person against whom the reader can react with any variety of feeling in the way he does to Anselm Kristlein and Oskar Matzerath. *Der ewige Spießer,* interesting as it is as a forerunner of the post-war German novel, cannot, therefore, be said to be entirely successful.

The two later novels are different from their precursor in both style and theme. As already stated, the common factor between them is the theme of Fascism. In *Jugend ohne Gott,* Horváth concentrates on the attitudes of people, including expecially the narrator, who are not committed Fascists, to life in a Fascist state. The atmosphere of such a state is successfully evoked, for instance, by references to the rôle of the mass media and popular celebrations, such as the birthday of the leader, contemptuously called the 'Oberplebejer' in the novel. These references also show that Horváth was able to discern the elements of the Fascist state that differentiated it from its authoritarian forerunners. Only in his descriptions of the life-style of the N family, who, as supporters of official ideology, take exception to what they consider to be the over-liberal views of the schoolmaster narrator, is Horváth less than convincing. The letter of Frau N. to her son, which is intended to reveal her mentality, is too much of a caricature in its mixture of brutality and sentimentality:

> Denk Dir nur, Mandi ist gestern gestorben. Vor-
> gestern hüpfte er noch so froh und munter in
> seinem Käfiglein herum und trilierte uns zur
> Freud. Und heute war er hin . . . Vater läßt
> Dich herzlichst grüßen, Du sollst ihm nur
> immer weiter Bericht erstatten, ob der Lehrer
> nicht wieder solche Äußerungen fallen läßt wie
> über die Neger. Laß nur nicht locker! Vater
> bricht ihm das Genick.

Except for this family Horváth is more concerned with people prepared to compromise with Fascism, the kind of compromise that was surely very much a contributory factor to the tragedy of Nazi Germany. In this, there is a connection with *Der ewige Spießer,* where, as has already been shown, the *Spießer* is presented as one who goes in for cowardly compromise. To this compromising group belong the headmaster, who accepts the prevailing doctrines because he does not wish to jeopardise his pension, the soldier, who is in charge of the boys' military training at camp but is no warmonger, and initially the narrator. Although he is opposed to Fascism, thus being that exceedingly rare figure in German literature, a liberal schoolmaster, he, too, is concerned with keeping a steady job with the prospect of a pension later. The novel is the story of his change of attitude. It begins with his disputed remark about negroes being human, continues whilst he is away at camp with the boys, where one of them is murdered, and is completed during the trial of another pupil for the murder.

The change that takes place in the narrator does not have its roots in a political reawakening but in religious feelings. It stems from a growing awareness of God. At the beginning of the novel, he has lost the religion of his parents. Partly through the influence of the priest of the village near the camp, he becomes confronted more and more with God. The crisis is brought about by the murder. When he feels implicated in the boys' jealousies that apparently lead to the murder, the narrator feels capable of resolving matters without reference to any external force like God: 'ich will ihm einen Strich durch die Rechnung machen. Mit meinem freien Willen.' After the murder, he becomes aware of the folly of trying to influence events against what he now considers to be a superior force. Yet the god he is now aware of is a terrible rather than a benevolent force:

> Die Zeit, in der ich an keinen Gott glaubte, ist
> vorbei. Heute glaube ich an ihn. Aber ich mag
> ihn nicht . . . Er muß stechende, tückische
> Augen haben—kalt sehr kalt. Nein er ist nicht
> gut.

Only at the end of the novel, as he comes to the view that the destruction of evil is good, does the narrator modify his view of God. Yet God remains in this novel very much the God of the Old Testament, vengeful, terrible and intervening in everyday events on earth. If this is Horváth's own God, and his later works are marked by their metaphysical themes, He is very much the traditional personalized God, far removed from the more abstract conceptions of modern theology.

Perhaps surprisingly, religion as an opposing force to Fascism does not entirely replace the social themes of Horváth's earlier works. The village near the camp is shown to be poor because capitalism has caused the local saw mill to be closed down. Poverty in the village has thrown up a gang of juvenile criminals led by a girl, Eva, with whom the schoolboys become involved. The mind of the murderer of the boy N. is shown to be the product of a rich home, where the parents had no time for him. The narrator connects this with the closed saw mill. Thus Horváth includes a mixture of social, religious and psychological themes in the novel. Certainly the movement towards religion does not preclude social concern but gives it a changed basis. This leads to the question of ways to combat Fascism. At the end of the novel, the narrator goes off to a mission school in Africa and is thus withdrawing himself from the struggle. Yet, the tone at the end of the novel is optimistic. The narrator has only become more settled in his mind after he has told the complete truth at the trial. His example has also spurred on a small group of pupils opposed to the system to redouble their secret efforts to combat it. Truth appears then to be the quality needed. The boys opposed to the system only confide in the narrator because he is the only adult they know, 'der die Wahrheit liebt'. Truth, as an ideal, permeates many of Horváth's statements about his art. Here, too, there is a connection with God. At the end of *Jugend ohne Gott,* the narrator brings together truth and his conception of God: 'Denn Gott ist die Wahrheit'. Divinely inspired moral principles are set against the evil of Fascism.

In contrast to *Jugend ohne Gott, Ein Kind unserer Zeit* is narrated by someone who has succumbed to Fascist ideology, although he, too, subsequently undergoes a change of attitude. Initially he is a willing soldier in the Fascist army. After he has been wounded during an attack on another country, he is obliged to leave the army. Especially when he discovers that his former idol, the captain, let himself be killed during the campaign because he was appalled at the cruel way it was conducted, he becomes more and more disenchanted. There is, however, even less of a solution to his problem then there was for the narrator of *Jugend ohne Gott.* Finally, he commits a murder and then allows himself to freeze to death, a similar fate to Horváth's Don Juan in the play *Don Juan kommt aus dem Krieg.* The soldier, too, is confronted with religion when a nurse who is tending his wounds speaks of the power of prayer but he does not achieve anything approaching a clear religious standpoint. He does not go beyond a vague awareness: 'Gott hat mit jedem einzelnen etwas vor, sagte meine dicke Schwester, und ich glaube allmählich, sie hatte recht.'

By making his narrator, at least initially, a committed Fascist, Horváth is able to give a broad view of Fascism with a different perspective from that of *Jugend ohne Gott.* In fact, it appears that he is trying to write as generally as possible. Whereas, in the first versions of the novel, the word 'Führer' is used in the singular, the final version uses it in the plural. Nor is the Fascist attack on the neighbouring country comparable to any that Nazi Germany had undertaken at the time the novel was written. It is against a state that speaks a foreign tongue and whose army offers resistance. The invading soldiers are said to be volunteers helping an internal group. Although they cannot be compared to any one historical campaign, the events described clearly belong to the pattern of the 1930s. Horváth's descriptions are in keeping with the age. In fact, he is much concerned with relating the phenomenon of Fascism to the time of its appearance. To some extent its appeal is seen as the result of the age, the product of the years of chaos that precede it. The attraction of Fascism is credible when the narrator relates:

> Ich bin doch auch ein anständiger Mensch, und es war ja nur die Hoffnungslosigkeit meiner Lage, daß ich so schwenkte wie das Schilf im Winde—sechs trübe Jahre lang. Die Ebene wurde immer schiefer und das Herz immer trauriger. Ja, ich war schon sehr verbittert . . . Heute kenne ich keine Angst mehr, ob ich morgen fressen werde. Und wenn die Stiefel hin sind, werden sie geflickt . . .

This raises the question, so essential to any discussion of Horváth's works, of how far the individual is responsible for his own actions and how much he is the product of external forces. It is certainly more than coincidence that in nearly all his works the main protagonists had not reached maturity by the outbreak of the First World War and are, therefore, permanently marked by the deprivations of the war and post-war period. There is good reason to regard Horváth's works as the testimony of this, his own generation. Thus it is possible to have some sympathy with the narrator of *Ein Kind unserer Zeit,* when the novel concludes with this plea: 'Bedenk es doch; er wußt sich nicht anders zu helfen, er ware eben ein Kind seiner Zeit'. At the same time, the idea of individual responsibility is certainly not omitted. Previously the narrator has stated: 'Für das Gute und für das Böse, da hat sich nur der einzelne zu verantworten und keinerlei Vaterland zwischen Himmel und Hölle'. Although it is impossible to determine exactly how much significance Horváth attaches to either of these two factors, the later works definitely put more stress on individual responsibility as opposed to the collectivism he had praised in earlier writing. The importance of the individual together with the false security offered by the collective of the army is one of the major themes of *Ein Kind unserer Zeit.*

The initial views of the narrator are a reflection of Fascist ideology, as it might be expected to have imprinted itself on the mind of a soldier. The narrator has picked up something of the pseudoscientific laws of nature formulated by the Nazis and intersperses the jargon of their arguments with clichés and more colloquial forms of language:

> Die Generation unserer Väter hat blöden Idealen von Völkerrecht und ewigem Frieden nachgegangen und hat es nicht begriffen, daß sogar in der niedrigen Tierwelt einer den anderen frißt. Es gibt kein Recht ohne Gewalt. Man soll nicht denken, sondern handeln.

As in the plays, Horváth concentrates on the characterization of individuals through their language. Thus the narrator's views on women, too, are a mixture of clichés and expressions like 'und so weiter', which show how incapable he is of using language in an original way:

> Bei dem weiblichen Geschlechte weißt du nie, woran du bist. Da findest du keine Treu und keinen Glauben, immer kommens zu spät, ein Nest voller Lügen und so weiter . . .
>
> Jaja, die Herren Weiber sind ein Kapitel für sich.

Through the soldier narrator Horváth presents a highly credible picture of the Fascist sympathiser as someone semieducated and semiliterate. Only occasionally might he be thought to exaggerate or approach caricature, as in the descriptions of the narrator's reactions to the dogs of the neighbouring country. This reference is, however, only one element in what is otherwise a highly successful reflection of Fascist racial attitudes:

> Ihre Fenster sind niedrig, eng und schmutzig. Sie waschen sich nie und stinken aus dem Mund . . . Selbst ihre Hunde taugen einen Dreck. Raudig und verlaust streunen sie durch die Ruinen. Keiner kann die Pfote geben.

Although the narrator clearly accepts the Fascist view of the world, he is never entirely without doubts. Before he takes part in the invasion, he sees a man to whom he takes an instant dislike. When he realises that such a person is in official eyes his 'Volksgenosse' and that he is supposed to fight on his behalf, he has to stifle this thought: 'Nein, hör auf. Nur nicht denken! Durch das Denken kommt man auf ungesunde Gedanken.' This dichotomy between official ideology and thought is referred to subsequently. It is the factor, coupled with his religious awakening, that leads the narrator to modify his views. Thus it would appear that Horváth is optimistic, in as far as he believes that not even an ordinary soldier can suppress his capacity for thought, something, as has been seen, the Fascist collective demands.

A subject that is considered in more detail in *Ein Kind unserer Zeit* than in *Jugend ohne Gott* is the relationship between Fascism and economic conditions. Initially the narrator is not worried about profits that might be made by supplying arms, provided that delivery is prompt. Later he realises, again apparently without disapproval, that the motive for the invasion is economic. The neighbouring country is rich in raw materials. When he becomes more critical, his attention is focussed more on everyday economic conditions. After he has had to leave the army, he knows that he has little chance of a job. He does not even believe official statistics about a drop in unemployment. He also doubts whether he will benefit from any promised economic prosperity. These references show the continuity of Horváth's concern about social conditions. Here, he does not merely discern a connection between capitalism and Fascism. He also doubts that Fascism brought about much economic progress or even did much about unemployment, something that is generally not denied.

The social and political themes of *Jugend ohne Gott* and *Ein Kind unserer Zeit* raise the question of how far Horváth had didactic aims comparable to those hinted at in connection with *Der ewige Spießer.* Of the two novels, *Jugend ohne Gott* does have the more obvious didactic elements, for instance the plea for truth, whilst the title itself contains clear implications. The different narrative situation of *Ein Kind unserer Zeit,* the narrator being less capable of forming coherent thoughts, makes a direct statement of the author's opinions less possible. Yet, here, too, there is the implied idea of a socially conscious Christianity. What is certainly lacking in both novels is any call to direct political action, such as that implied by Thomas Mann's story *Mario und der Zauberer.* This does not necessarily mean that Horváth believed that the position of the writer faced with totalitarian societies was hopeless. The evidence of his letters written at the time of the two

later novels suggests that he thought that writing was always purposeful. A letter to the Austrian writer Franz Theodor Csokor significantly connects writing with the ideal of truth:

> Die Hauptsache, leiber guter Freund, ist: Arbeiten! Und nochmals: Arbeiten! Und wieder: Arbeiten! Unser Leben ist Arbeit—ohne sie haben wir kein Leben mehr. Es ist gleichgültig, ob wir den Sieg oder auch nur die Beachtung unserer Arbeit erfahren,—es ist völlig gleichgültig, solange unsere Arbeit der Wahrheit und der Gerechtigkeit geweiht bleibt.

The tone here is not optimistic. It is one of defiance, of hope against hope, in contrast to the tone of the introduction of *Der ewige Spießer,* which does not suggest great concern about the possible lack of influence of the work.

If Horváth's two later novels are marked by new themes, there is also a considerable change of style, which goes beyond replacing the previous omniscient narrator by a first-person narrative. The indulgent style of *Der ewige Spießer* is replaced by a much more controlled, taut prose. The following passage from *Jugend ohne Gott* is a good example of this style:

> Das Pfarrhaus liegt neben der Kirche. Die Kirche ist ein strenger Bau, das Pfarrhaus liegt gemächlich da. Um die Kirche herum liegt der Friedhof, um das Pfarrhaus herum ein Garten. Im Kirchturm läuten die Glocken, aus dem Rauchfang des Pfarrhauses steigt blauer Dunst. Im Garten des Todes blühen die weißen Blumen, im Garten des Pfarrers wächst das Gemüse. Dort stehen Kreuze, hier steht ein Gartenwerg. Ein ruhendes Reh. Und ein Pilz.

Although many of the things described here belong to the world of 'Kitsch', the overall effect is not trite. What is immediately noticeable is the shortness of the sentences, some of which do not contain a verb, and the complete absence of subordinate clauses. Equally clear are the contrasts within almost every sentence, for example, between 'streng' and 'gemächlich' and between 'Friedhof' and 'Garten'. The picture of the church and adjoining manse is built up on a series of contrasting, almost conflicting impressions: there is no broad description, which might be a verbal equivalent to landscape art. Such a style appears rather to reflect the uncertainties and contradictions of the world the novel describes. The individual has to come to terms with brief contradictory impressions. The overall atmosphere created by this kind of writing is, therefore, one of tension, matching the tensions in the individual's life. Indeed, this might be the best word to characterize Horváth's prose style in the two later novels. Its aptness is reinforced by the countless short paragraphs, some of them consisting of only three or four word sentences, whose frequency is immediately visible from the briefest of glances at the printed page. There is also the choice of the present tense for major sections of the narrative. Indeed, the present and past tenses are interchanged very freely, as in this passage from *Ein Kind unserer Zeit,* where the narrator describes his visit to the dead captain's widow:

> Den Rock legte ich über einen Stuhl, aber dann zog ich ihn wieder an, denn die Nacht wurde bit-

terkalt. Es ist natürlich ein Sturm gekommen,
und die Vorhänge bewegen sich . . .

This kind of change of narrative perspective, which means that the exact point of time when the narrator is relating the events is left unclear, cannot create any sense of objective distance. Again the feeling is one of a mass of impressions flashing before the narrator's consciousness. Even the lapidary titles given to the chapters, for example 'Der Hund' and 'Der Köder' in *Jugend ohne Gott,* add to this feeling.

The overall effect of this style is not, however, confusion. Horváth holds the narrative together in a variety of ways. The tautness of individual passages is complemented by a general tautness of construction. In the case of *Jugend ohne Gott,* there is much that is reminiscent of the *Novelle.* The murder provides an 'unerhörte Begebenheit', around which the narrative is constructed, whilst the narrator's decision to speak the whole truth in court is the turning point that leads to the dénouement. More significant though are the use of repeated motifs and the reflection of earlier scenes and incidents at a later stage of the narrative. One such motif is that of the fish. The phrase 'Zeitalter der Fische' is coined by a retired teacher, whom the narrator meets, to describe the coldness of the age. The murderer T. is later described as having eyes like fish; his horrible deed is thus connected with the ethos of the time. An episode that is seemingly unimportant for the main narrative, the death of another pupil after an illness, also assumes significance in relation to T. and the fish motif. At the funeral, the narrator noticed T. staring at him, the first time he had been aware of his fish-like eyes. Eyes, too, are a major motif in the novel. When he tells the truth at the trial, the narrator feels comforting eyes on him. He takes them to be those of the girl Eva, who is a witness. Later he connects them with God, whose eyes, as mentioned above, he had once regarded as terrible.

The major motif of *Ein Kind unserer Zeit* is, as the title implies, that of the time. The narrator realises that the captain with his chivalrous ideas does not fit into the age and also, as his opinions change, comes to realise that he no longer does either. This point is reinforced by the way he is continually being confronted with events and attitudes from the past when he accepted the ideology of the state. When he seeks out a girl he once knew, he learns that she has lost her job on becoming pregnant, because profitability was more important than the individual. This painfully reminds him of the time when he, too, considered the individual as such worthless. An ironic balance to the change of attitude by the narrator is provided by the way his father becomes more militaristic as he loses his enthusiasm for the state's policies. Thus *Ein Kind unserer Zeit* is also held together by the interrelation of themes and incidents.

Horváth's style ranges from the vitriolic, when the ladies of polite society who attend the court hearing in *Jugend ohne Gott* are described as 'geil auf Katastrophen,' to the lyrical, when, in the same novel, the narrator reflects on Eva, who, as benefits her name, comes to be connected with nature:

    . . . ich denke an ihre Augen. Und an die stillen

Seen in den Wäldern meiner Heimat. Sie liegt im
Spital. Und auch jetzt ziehen die Wolken über
sie hin, die Wolken mit den silbernen Rändern.

In the later novels, Horváth certainly masters an individual style which in turn provides a suitable medium for the themes he chooses.

There remains the question, especially appropriate to *Jugend ohne Gott* and *Ein Kind unserer Zeit,* of whether the use of the novel form for the subjects chosen adds a different dimension which could not have been provided in a play. It is useful, therefore, to compare the two later novels with the type of play Horváth wrote, without attempting to formulate any general theory of what is possible in the novel and the play. If one takes *Geschichten aus dem Wiener Wald,* generally regarded as the major play, it becomes clear that Horváth is trying to show the reality of the bourgeois mind and of bourgeois life beneath the surface of what appears to the characters and possibly to the audience, too, a harmless mode of existence. This is the 'Demaskierung des Bewußtseins' he speaks of. Since the characters themselves are not capable of reflection, this has to be done by showing their relationships and their reactions to external events. It goes without saying that the play is a suitable genre for portraying personal relations of this kind. By contrast, in the novels, Horváth shows the relationship of an individual with a world dominated by a given political or social order that will be known to the reader. He concentrates on the individual's self-analysis, the changes that take place in his mind. The action is inter-

---

Horváth on stages of his life:

I was born on 9th December 1901, and it was in Fiume on the Adriatic, at 4.45 in the afternoon (4.30 according to another report). When I weighed twenty-two pounds I left Fiume and loafed about partly in Venice and partly in the Balkans, and experienced all sorts of things, among others the murder of H. M. King Alexander of Serbia along with his better half. When I was four foot tall I moved to Budapest and lived there for half an inch. There I was a keen visitor to numerous children's playgrounds and was conspicuous in a rather disagreeable way because of my dreamy and mischievous personality. At a height of about 5′0½″ Eros awoke in me, but initially without causing me any bother— (my love of politics was already quite apparent at that time). My interest in art, especially in the classics of literature, stirred relatively late (at a height of about 5′7½″) but it only became an urge from 5′11½″, not, it is true an irresistible one, but there all the same. When the first World War broke out I was already 5′6″, and when it ended I was 6′ (I shot up very quickly during the war). At 5′7″ I had my first proper sexual experience—and today, now that I have long since stopped growing (6′1″). I think back with tender nostalgia to those portentous days.

Now I only grow outwards it is true—but I can't tell you any more about that, because I'm still too close to myself.

Ödön von Horváth in his Gesammelte Werke, *Suhrkamp, 1970-1971. Translated by Ian Huish in* Horváth: A Study, 1980.

nal with external events like the invasion in **Ein Kind un-serer Zeit** only important in the effect they have on the protagonists' consciousness. Thus, there is not the same interplay among different people that there is in the plays. This element, the concentration on an individual rather than a group, requires a different form. Horváth uses the novel for a more analytical psychological approach, which probes deeper into the characters' minds. To this extent the novels make a major contribution to Horváth's work. (pp. 81-96)

> *K. Stuart Parkes, "The Novels of Ödön von Horváth," in* New German Studies, *Vol. 3, No. 2, Summer, 1975, pp. 81-97.*

Dragan Klaić   (essay date 1975)

[*In the following excerpt, Klaić discusses the contempo-rary revival of Horváth's* Volksstücke, *or "folk-plays," all written before 1938.*]

A student of contemporary West German theater must be impressed by the variety of its repertory. For more than two centuries, German theater has been a prestigious ar-tistic, educational and ideological institution. Heavy sub-sidies to the municipal and regional repertory theaters, the good will of publishers and, of course, a large and curious audience stimulate the great number of plays that appear each year. German dramaturgs, obviously, do not share the anxieties of their European and American colleagues who have trouble filling the repertory with new and ap-pealing domestic works.

Given such an atmosphere, one might expect a neglect of older playwrights. And yet, the plays of Ödön von Hor-váth, all written before 1938, have become a standard if not a dominant feature of contemporary German theater. It is almost impossible to find a German theater that has not produced at least one play by von Horváth in the last ten years. The avalanche of von Horváth productions has been accompanied by a great number of essays, doctoral dissertations and critical and biographical studies on this author. It is, thus, a further proof of the parochialism of the English-speaking theater that thirty-seven years after von Horváth's death and at the height of his popularity in Germany, his plays, which could be translated into En-glish without too many difficulties, still remain unknown, untranslated, and unproduced in the Anglo-Saxon world. (p. 106)

The current rediscovery of von Horváth coincides with the arrival of a new generation of German playwrights who were born during World War II. The first works of such dramatists as Franz Xaver Kroetz, Martin Sperr and Wolfgang Bauer were published and produced at the end of the nineteen sixties and at the beginning of the seven-ties. It is difficult to establish whether these new plays have stimulated the revival of interest in von Horváth or recent productions of this author facilitated the breakthrough of Kroetz and his fellow writers. However, these young play-wrights are indebted to the genre of *Volksstück,* to the "folk-plays" which von Horváth, Marieluise Fleisser and Carl Zuckmayer wrote during the Weimar Republic.

But von Horváth, Fleisser, and Zuckmayer looked back to an even older tradition. They renewed rather than initi-ated the *Volksstück.* This dramatic genre is defined by its concern with the lives of the common people. It uses a dia-lect or colloquial language to reconstruct a specified social milieu. Such plays usually combine entertainment with moralizing. The *Volksstück* flourished in Vienna where it was introduced with the Hanswurst plays of Josef Anton Stranitzky (1676-1726), and reached its height in the works of the nineteenth-century Austrian writers Johann Nestroy and Ferdinand Raimund. Their stages were locat-ed in the outskirts of Vienna, in Josefstadt and Leopold-stadt, since the *Innerstadt* was dominated by the Burgthe-ater and the Opera, state institutions under Court patron-age.

The *Volksstücke* of von Horvath observe the basic features of the genre. Von Horváth always chooses a particular so-cial environment and models his protagonists on the *Kleinbürger.* The best translation of this term is, perhaps, petty bourgeoisie, but this is only an approximate term which applies to various concepts in English. The *Klein-bürger* does not have an equivalent in American society where the middle class and its blended culture dominate. In Europe, however, the *Kleinbürger* form a distinct social class, between the wealth of the big business and the pro-fessions on the one hand, and the urban poor on the other. The main concerns of a *Kleinbürger* are social and eco-nomic stability, since any radical move or upheaval might, he fears, endanger his status and force him into the lower social strata. The cultural consumption of a *Kleinbürger* is limited chiefly to a commercial schlock, dime-novels, gossipy magazines, melodramatic movies and sentimental songs.

The *Kleinbürger* of von Horváth include (besides the members of the lower middle class and the proletariat) even the peasantry, or at least those villagers who do not work in agriculture, but are merchants, innkeepers, or po-licemen. His characters are mainly low clerks, artisans, owners of small shops, house-maids, petty hustlers, and, in general, people from the poorer sections of the city or from small provincial towns. In their world of daily rou-tine and quiet neighborhoods, everyone knows what his neighbors are having for dinner and small secrets are com-mon knowledge within one hour. The beer-gardens, cards, Sunday walks at the town square and occasional popular festivals, such as the "Italian Night" in von Horváth's play with the same title (**Italienische Nacht**) provide the only entertainment.

Rare celebrations, such as family outings, county fairs and Fall carnivals sometimes modify the otherwise stable so-cial roles and transform the patterns of life for a while. In von Horváth's plays, at such times, communal standards of morality and authority are temporarily suspended, or at least loosened. For a day or two, the distinct notions of propriety and decency fade away. A society segmented into classes is infused with a feeling of community.

The setting of von Horváth's play **Kasimir und Karoline** is the October Festival in Munich, a contemporary form of Medieval carnivals. This ancient celebration of the har-vest, new wine and nature's cycle of seasons has become today a vulgar amusement for all classes. Only within the framework of frenetic drinking, fights, and silly attractions of the Festival, can von Horváth's characters mix with the members of other classes: Schürzinger drinks with his boss, and Karoline, a poor employee, socializes with the businessmen and government officials, who temporarily lose their respectability.

But even before the festival's conclusion, the festive spirit collapses under the impact of other emotions: loneliness and a sense of failure overwhelm Kasimir, the unemployed chauffeur in *Kasimir und Karoline,* and the small-town folk in *Italienische Nacht.* The *Kleinbürger* of von Horváth recognizes the differences in personality that isolate him from his community and the class distinctions which separate him from the higher social strata. The "other world" of affluence, power and extravagance is hardly known to him. He noticed it on his trips to and from the factory or the office, and on his rare excursions to the glamorous downtown of the metropolis. The festival gives the *Kleinbürger* access to this other world or, at least, stimulates his dreams about it, but also forces him to recognize the painful limits of his own existence. He sees the gap between his life and the life he seeks but cannot have.

Such experiences bring some individuals to despair and induce other von Horváth characters to seek refuge in pretension and empty boasting. If the "other" life cannot be reached, it can be approached through imitation, day dreaming, and make-believe. The *Kleinbürger* turns to social mimicry to convince himself and others that he is what he is not. He tries to act and talk as he thinks members of the richer and better-educated classes do. This is the behavior of Valerie, a tobacco-shop owner, and Alfred, a would-be playboy, in von Horváth's *Geschichten aus dem Wiener Wald (Tales from Vienna Woods).* They disseminate knowledge, sophistication and sensibility which they do not possess and, consequently, end up as pathetic figures and sentimental fools. Although they try to be members of the elite, their language never fails to give them away.

The presence of regional dialects and highly colloquial language in von Horváth's plays serves a specific purpose. The use of the vernacular made the *Volksstücke* of the eighteenth and nineteenth century a "low" dramatic genre, as distinguished from the plays written in *Hochdeutsch.* At the same time, this feature gave the *Volksstücke* an air of social authenticity which the *Hochdeutsch* plays could hardly claim. Similarly, von Horváth's *Volksstücke* can be contrasted to most contemporary German plays, which are written in *Hochdeutsch.* Since *Hochdeutsch* is an artificial or, at least, an academic language (which Franz Xaver Kroetz says, perhaps hyperbolically, ninety-five per cent of all Germans do not speak), von Horváth's plays seem closer to the folk than most other plays of his era.

Some of von Horváth's characters try to avoid the vernacular since it obstructs their personal ambitions and their hunger for status. They contaminate their original language with the language they, in fact, do not possess; however, they absorb only bits and pieces, clichés and empty phrases from the jargon of learning, poetic discourse and "high" culture. Such characters use "sophisticated" language in order to perpetuate their private fantasy-life or to try to become what they want to be. Language here serves as a substitute for the nonexistent social mobility, but fails to bring the expected results. Valerie and Alfred cannot improve their status, and Marianne, who broke her engagement with an honest butcher, actually worsens hers.

This borrowed language of pretense cannot help von Horváth's characters become someone else; in fact, the abandonment of vernacular and the incorrect use of the "other" language curb their ability to react adequately to the events in their own environment. It becomes almost impossible for such characters to express emotions sincerely and to communicate effectively. For example, the small-town leftists in *Italienische Nacht* are so obsessed with their political jargon, that they do not even try to prevent the rise of Nazi power. The Zauberkönig (literally: King of Magic), a toy-shop owner from the *Geschichten aus dem Wiener Wald,* scorns his daughter Marianne in highly moralistic terms. His fondness for dogmatic language prevents him from understanding the tragic circumstances in which Marianne lives. She, in turn, is the victim of her lover Alfred, who had tricked her with his "elegant" charm and fake eloquence.

In some of von Horváth's plays, the pretense cannot resist the onslaught of reality. The political jargon of the Alderman in *Italienische Nacht* cannot hide his real language: that of a rude domestic tyrant. In the same play, Karl uses radical political rhetoric until the moment when his fiancée Leni promises to bring him a dowry of four thousand marks, which will enable them to open a grocery store.

Von Horvath creates comic effects by switching from the language of pretense to the vernacular, and because of his use of this device, von Horváth was sometimes considered a satirist. It was often assumed that the *Geschichten aus dem Wiener Wald* satirized the Viennese folk, that *Kasimir und Karoline* laughed at the October Festival in Munich, and that small-town politicking is the target of the *Italienische Nacht.* Von Horváth resented being called a satirist, however, probably because he disliked the detachment which the position of a satirist implies. Although he abandoned the moral didacticism of the traditional *Volksstück,* von Horváth preserved a sense of personal involvement in the world of his characters. His critical stance did not preclude empathy with the ambitions and illusions of these people.

The language of von Horváth's *Volksstücke* serves as an authenticating convention, but also as an expression of comic and tragic emotion. This last aspect—the language of tragedy—secures von Horváth's place in the repertories of German theaters, even more than his irony, the authenticity of his characters, and the recognizability of their milieu.

One of the major difficulties of modern drama has been the construction of a language that can express tragic emotion. German dramatists often have tried to reach this goal by the use of verse, in hope that dialogue in verse will, by the virtue of its artificiality, provide the detachment necessary to perceive a dramatic action as a tragic one. More recently, some German playwrights, such as Peter Weiss and Heinar Kipphardt, have turned to the language of documents, news-reports and court proceedings; they thought that the "raw" facts from the real human experience, such as those on Nazi cruelties or on colonialism, could provoke tragic feelings more effectively than any myth or invented action. Plays in verse are still quite common in German theater, while the documentary drama has lost its impetus during the last few years.

German playwrights, such as Kroetz, Sperr, and Bauer, follow the path of von Horváth; he found a potential for tragedy in the language of the common folk of Vienna, Munich, and Bavarian provinces that was previously used only for dramatic caricatures and didactic comedies. This metaphysical quality within *Geschichten aus dem Wiener Wald* and *Kasimir und Karoline,* together with their sociological postulates, stimulates contemporary German playwrights to perpetuate the tradition of the *Volksstück.* (pp. 107-12)

> *Dragan Klaić, "The Volksstücke Revival: Ödön von Horváth," in yale/theatre, Vol. 7, 1975, pp. 105-13.*

Krishna Winston   (essay date 1978)

[*Winston is an American educator, translator, and critic. In the following excerpt, she examines Horvath's contemporary significance, theorizing that the translation of his plays into English would add a new dimension to American theater.*]

[Horváth] slips into the skin of an unemployed hairdresser, a policeman, a tobacco shop proprietor, a secretary, a waitress, a travelling salesman, and out comes the pretentious verbiage that the characters use in their attempts to sound urbane and sophisticated. The jargon of pseudo-cultivation (*Bildungsjargon*) is a hybrid language consisting of usually secondhand borrowings from the specialized vocabularies of business, law, entertainment, politics, science, and so on. Horváth's characters derive their phrases and speech mannerisms from newspapers and radio, from movie dialogue, from advertising, from political speeches, from almanachs, from sermons, and (the women especially) from the kitschy novels serialized in newspapers and magazines.

Horváth was not alone in recognizing the phenomenon of *Bildungsjargon.* Karl Kraus spent the better part of a lifetime denouncing abuse of the German language by the press and those who read it. His drama *The Last Days of Mankind* is a monstrous collage of *Bildungsjargon,* most of which he had actually heard or read during the war (the play appeared in 1921). Kurt Tucholsky and Erich Kästner likewise recognized *Bildungsjargon* as characteristic of much contemporary speech. But Horváth was unique in developing an entire style based on *Bildungsjargon,* a style he used ironically in his prose and even in letters and conversation. By entering into his characters' speech, he succeeded in at least partially understanding how their minds worked, and this insight made him compassionate in a

way that Kraus, who thoroughly dissociated himself from those he attacked, could never be.

When they open their mouths, Horváth's characters exemplify the curse of the age of mass media, the curse of semi-literacy. Their speech makes them simultaneously despicable, laughable and pitiable. The unintentional stylistic break forms one of the key features of this speech. For the "jargon" is always mixed with grammatical and lexical holdovers from dialect, meaningless fad words and fillers, invective and obscenity, and the awkward syntactical structures of persons trying to reproduce a style with which they are not wholly at ease. The stylistic contradictions in Horváth's characters' speech reflect a world in disorder. Concepts from the old morality like "the humane," "duty," "true love," or "the good Lord" have a hollow ring but are still used for impression-making, for no one dares point out that they have become meaningless.

Horváth puts his characters on the stage and lets them talk. The plots of most of his plays are simple, the events the stuff of everyday life. The dialogue is punctuated with frequent silences. They occur when characters are embarrassed or at a loss for words, or when they suddenly realize the implications of something just said. During these pauses the previous lines echo in our ears. Bad faith, spurious logic, pathetic delusions become audible. Seemingly casual, the dialogue is actually very dense, a concentrate of characteristic elements Horváth selected from the speech he heard all around him. The attentive listener catches the involuntary puns and Freudian slips that betray unconscious preoccupations or associations. Unintentional repetition of words or sounds shows that a character is talking without listening to himself. Some words are mispronounced or misused, evidence that the speaker is not as educated as he wishes to appear. And it becomes clear that phrases apparently borrowed from an inappropriate sphere often have a profound appropriateness in another sense. The man who uses business jargon in a discussion with a woman who loves him unconsciously reveals that economic considerations determine the course of all his relationships.

The characters unmask themselves through their words and actions, often through the discrepancies between the two. Their language enables us to identify the source of their woes. When trying to sound worldly-wise and cultured, they emulate any speech they consider fancy, dignified, superior, in short, anything they associate with the ruling classes. They are fixated on values that do not correspond to their own situation, and the gap between their awareness and that situation causes constant slippage, leading to psychic dislocation. Their expectations, their standard interpretations of the world, fail to explain the things that happen to them. In the face of economic crisis—unemployment, inflation, depression, overwhelming competition—Horváth's petty bourgeois remain stubbornly individualistic. They thus strengthen a system that depends on their lack of unified resistance. From the repeated humiliations they suffer, and from having to cope daily with others who are equally insecure, they become suspicious, calculating or parasitic. Aggression, intolerance, xenophobia, misogyny, sentimentality and self-pity are some of their responses to the experience of being help-less.

Horváth never decided on one explanation or one remedy for the sickness of the modern European petty bourgeoisie. In his younger years he was very sympathetic to the Marxian view that economic exploitation and alienation suppress man's natural goodness. Yet he was as merciless toward the jargon of Marxism as toward the invective of Nazism. Later he leaned more toward a religious construction, suggesting that man, though naturally wicked, could achieve ethical stature and human dignity by struggling against his harmful impulses. Horváth was a pessimist who paradoxically always hoped that things would improve. He did more than hope; he wrote his plays—to help his audiences understand their predicament better and, by understanding it, rise above it. Mixed with the savagery in his portrayal of his contemporaries are generous portions of humor and sympathy. He realized, long before Hannah Arendt put it into words, that evil can be incarnated in an unobtrusive little man with a scraggly neck. In his plays he presents many such individuals, at once conveying the ugliness and the poignancy of each ruined life and letting us glimpse the terrible things that might result if all that frustration were contained and channelled.

Horváth wrote eighteen plays in all. Why have they not been translated into English? Surely they have as much to say to America today as to the Federal Republic of Germany. In place of Horváth's "full-fledged or frustrated petty bourgeois" we have Nixon's "great silent majority" and Wallace's "great middle class." We have a jargon of pseudo-cultivation that may be spoken by anyone from a garage mechanic to a presidential adviser. Thanks to television, our expression and our thoughts are increasingly dominated by advertising catchphrases, news clichés, technical jargon, political slogans, sports terminology, and other elements of prefabricated speech. People assume an air of expertise when discussing matters they have heard explained for all of three minutes, with a commercial interruption, on radio or television. They misuse words and unconsciously adopt the latest official euphemisms like "inoperative" and "at this point in time."

Horváth's plays would indeed enrich the American theatre. But there exists an obstacle to their being translated directly into English and put on the stage. Although we are familiar with the general history of Europe in the twenties and thirties and with the stereotyped images of Munich, Vienna and Berlin, to appreciate Horváth's plays we must also be able to place the speech patterns and the cultural clichés. Humor and social criticism depend for their effectiveness on the audience's recognizing specific allusions. Most of Horváth's plays would have to be adapted, so as to make the references as instantly recognizable as those in "All in the Family," a series which, by the way, shares numerous techniques with Horváth's *Volksstücke.* American equivalents or interpretive translations would have to be found, not only for the verbal clichés, proverbs and other ready-made phrases, but for many of the situations and even some of the imagery.

And even if an inspired adapter were found, there would remain the question of audience. In Germany today the petty bourgeois who are lured into the theatre by the popular-sounding titles of Horváth's plays and by the description *Volksstück* quickly come to the conclusion that they are being attacked and mocked. They react as the characters in the play do, defensively. Those who enjoy Horváth's work are educated liberal or leftist members of the intellectual elite, secure in the sense of their own superiority. Laughing at the petty-bourgeois jargon, they usually fail to notice that they, too, often fall into mannered and inauthentic speech. Do the Archie Bunkers of this country react indignantly to Norman Lear's portrait of them? Do better educated members of the audience derive pleasurable feelings of satisfaction from recognizing Archie's mistakes in phrases like "prostate from the heat" or "infectuous hepatitis"?

Perhaps those are questions for sociologists and psychologists to grapple with. The fact remains that Horváth found the petty bourgeois mentality at all levels of his society, among barons and baronesses as among chauffeurs and waitresses. *Italian Night* even gives us a petty-bourgeois Marxist. Horváth's plays summon us to ponder the causes of human beastliness, to rethink the present social order. Far from being dated, the plays are just coming into their own. (pp. 177-80)

> *Krishna Winston, "Ödön von Horváth: A Man for This Season," in* The Massachusetts Review, *Vol. XIX, No. 1, Spring, 1978, pp. 169-80.*

P. M. Potter   (essay date 1979)

[*In the essay below, Potter examines Horváth's use of the themes of death and guilt.*]

Ödön von Horváth was killed by a falling tree in the Champs Élysées on 1st June, 1938. Such bizarre circumstances seem almost unreal and indeed strangely in accord with the way in which some of Horváth's own characters met their deaths. Although the topic has been mentioned in general terms the fate of the characters in his works will repay more detailed study.

Few of Horváth's characters die in their beds. There are some, however, whose deaths may at first sight be ascribed to 'natural causes'. Those characters whose deaths occur in or around the year 1918 form a clearly identifiable group. The cause of death may be specified (e.g. Agnes Pollinger's mother and grandmother in *Geschichten vom Fräulein Pollinger*) or simply assumed to be the result of unfavourable economic conditions, as was the case with Christine's mother in *Zur schönen Aussicht.* It is significant that both Agnes and Christine lose their mothers in this way, for it is clear that these deaths are directly attributable to material factors and as such are little different from the deaths during the war of their respective fathers. The fact that Horváth uses identical devices to account for the deaths of both sets of parents illustrates his desire to show that the circumstances of the two young women are to be regarded as typical of their age. The changes, whether political, social or material, which took place after 1918 are also portrayed as being responsible for the deaths of Agnes' grandmother and of Franz Xaver Loibl, the protagonist of *Der Tod aus Tradition.* The role played by contemporary material circumstances in causing the death of a character is strongly emphasised in *Glaube Liebe Hoffnung* where Elisabeth states categorically to the lover who had deserted her, 'Bild dir doch nicht ein, dass ich wegen dir ins Wasser bin, du mit deiner grossen Zukunft! Ich bin doch nur ins Wasser, weil ich nichts mehr zum Fressen hab—'. This interpretation of Elisabeth's suicide is summed up in the title of the play's French translation, *Cent Cinquante Marks ou la Foi, l'Espérance, la Charité,* which refers to the sum needed to obtain a work permit.

In this play, however, the cause of death is not simply ascribed to external circumstances but also to certain pressures within society which have been working against her. Hence such features as greed and hypocrisy, represented in the policeman and other characters of the play, are clearly guilty of causing Elisabeth's death. Ultimately it is therefore contemporary society which kills her and the play must be seen as a protest against it. The element of social criticism in Horváth's work has been widely commented on, and an examination of the portrayal of death in his works will provide further examples. One case in point is Horváth's first play, *Revolte auf Côte 3018* where the engineer's death occurs during a fight with some workers, the result of hostility arising from the engineer's unfeeling treatment of them. What is significant about this death, however, is the fact that an earlier scene reveals to the audience that the engineer's attitudes are not held from conviction but are forced on him by the company directors. The deaths of several workers in this play are ascribed to the harsh conditions in which they were working and in particular to the lack of concern for their safety by the directors of the company. These deaths are therefore in effect caused by those responsible for the social and economic circumstances of the time and as such the play is a condemnation of the capitalist system, in a more specific manner than the generalised comments concerning the deaths of the parents of Agnes Pollinger and Christine.

Social criticism is also the most striking feature in what is most probably the best known of the deaths in Horváth, that of 'der kleine Leopold' in *Geschichten aus dem Wiener Wald.* This time the victim is a baby who is placed near an open window by his great-grandmother. Leopold was sent to her at the insistence of Alfred, his father, 'Wir können doch nicht drei Seelen hoch in diesem Loch vegetieren! Das Kind muß weg!'. The material aspect is underlined in Alfred's conversation with der Hierlinger Ferdinand: 'Weisst du aber auch, was meine Grenzen total übersteigt? Sich in der heutigen Krise auch noch ein Kind anzuschaffen—', to which Alfred can only agree and he puts the blame on Marianne. Later it is the great-grandmother who gives the phrase 'Das Kind muss weg' more sinister overtones: 'Mutterl im Zuchthaus und Vaterl ein Hallodri! Für manche wärs schon besser, wenns hin wären!'. This reasoning is pure self-deception, bearing no relation to Marianne's feelings. What the great-grandmother does suppose, and with a certain degree of accuracy, behind her generalised excuses, is that the baby ties Alfred to Marianne, whom she considers worthless. The situation, according to her, can only be changed by the child's death, so that Alfred's consequent freedom will

Bernd Spitzer as Sladek in a 1967 Viennese production of Sladek, oder die schwarze Armee.

improve his chances of success in the world. Since Alfred owes her money, as she constantly reminds him, it is also possible that she desires an improvement in Alfred's fortunes from purely selfish motives. To follow this reading to its logical conclusion, the child is therefore sacrificed for financial gain, just as were the workers in *Revolte auf Côte 3018.*

Her reasoning is, however, based on a false premise. After the estrangement of Marianne and Alfred it was true that the baby stood in the way of a reconciliation between Marianne and her father and former fiancé. This is stated specifically in Oskar's wishful thinking, 'Ich hab sie noch immer lieb—vielleicht stirbt das Kind . . . ', but the scene immediately preceding that in which the baby's death is announced is one of general reconciliation. The baby's death does not therefore contribute to any essential change in the relationships that had existed between the characters at the end of the previous scene. It becomes instead a grotesque piece of irony, with which Oskar's summing up of the situation, 'Nachdem sich alles so eingerenkt hat' is quite in keeping.

The baby is, like its mother, a victim of selfishness in society which seeks to remove any obstacle in the path of its more powerful members, without questioning the necessity or rightness of such an act. Also attacked is society's ability to justify events by appealing to its own ideas of respectability, which is shown for instance when the great-grandmother contrasts her own family circumstances with those of Leopold, as well as in Oskar's hypocritical moralising in the final scene.

The characters so far considered are therefore victims of

their environment, in particular that which existed after 1918. The cause of death is not material circumstances alone, however, but also the pressures which the attitudes of society put on the individual, thus possibly robbing him of the will to live. Perhaps the most bizarre example of these pressures are those to which the waiter called Suppe in *Geschichten vom Fräulein Pollinger* succumbs. His name resulted in his being the butt of innumerable jokes and, as a consequence of being moved to violence by them, he was sent to prison 'und ist dann dort an Verzweiflung gestorben.' The fact that coincidences made the attempt to change his name unsuccessful appears to indicate that, once an individual is marked out as a victim of society, there is no escape.

This inevitability is also illustrated elsewhere. It may be observed in the time factor inherent in several instances, that is, where one is led to expect the death of a character because of threats or premonitions, for example in *Sladek der schwarze Reichswehrmann, Die Unbekannte aus der Seine* and *Jugend ohne Gott*. The fact that certain deaths are at the same time shown to be avoidable increases the awareness of their inevitability when they take place in spite of the efforts and precautions of others. There is one expected death which does not occur, that of the great-grandmother in *Geschichten aus dem Wiener Wald*. The possibility of her death is mentioned by Alfred and his mother as well as by the great-grandmother herself, 'Dir tät es ja schon lange passen, wenn ich schon unter der Erden war—nicht? Aber ich geh halt noch nicht, ich geh noch nicht . . . '. Here the unexpected has not happened because, as her last sentence shows, she possesses a strong will to live. Instead it is the youngest and most helpless who has died. Even this is not unexpected, as the words of Alfred and his grandmother have shown, and it is also unconsciously wished for by Oskar. At one point it is also wished for by the 'Zauberkönig', who says to Marianne 'So wirf dich doch vor den Zug! . . . Samt deiner Brut!!'. Finally this use of the word 'Zug' turns out to be a gruesome pun on the part of the playwright, another instance of the fact that, once society had unconsciously decreed the death of the child, its end, like that of Sladek's Anna, is inevitable in spite of subsequent changes of situation or opinion.

Attention has been drawn to the role played by natural phenomena as a cause of death in Horváth's work. The deaths of Don Juan and the soldier of *Ein Kind unserer Zeit* are a type of involuntary suicide and thus the motif of death by exposure can be interpreted as the characters' wish to surrender themselves, having failed to assert their individual personalities, to an all-embracing nature, symbolised here by the mantle of snow which covers them. In the motif of death by drowning a more positive action is implied since Elisabeth at least is more clearly a victim of social and economic pressures. This intervention by nature has the effect of emphasising the victim element in the characters concerned and according to Urs Jenny, these are situations 'wo die Natur eins ihrer Geschöpfe, das sich ohne Hoffnung verirrt hat, in sich zurücknimmt'. This statement does not, however, fully explain those cases where the forces of nature cause a character's death. Many of the deaths in Horváth's work are merely futile. It is per-

haps more true to say that the characters have not 'sich verirrt' but that their deaths are a result of the inhospitable environment that society offers to the individual and which is reflected by various inhospitable manifestations in nature.

The images aroused by a character dying in a snowstorm are ones which contrast with the stark realism found elsewhere in Horváth, and this motif has thus been compared to the world of dreams. Hartmut Reinhardt, although he does not specifically refer to these two deaths, points out that 'Die Verwendung von Märchenmotiven bleibt fortan ein charakteristisches Mittel, um den Kontrast menschlicher Wunschwelt zu vorgegebenen Zwängen zu maskieren'. In the case of Don Juan and the soldier, the immediate cause of their deaths forms a cloak, like the snow itself, over the actual factors which brought about their deaths. This dreamlike or fairy-tale covering is, however, immediately recognisable as such and its contrast with the preceding events of the works is only too obvious. Here we are dealing with an instance of 'Demaskierung', a term which has been widely discussed in Horváth criticism. There is the difference in that here it is Horváth who both creates and applies the mask instead of exposing what he sees as the reality beneath the conventionally acceptable. By their very artificiality the final scenes of these two works create the same effect of 'Demaskierung' that is elsewhere achieved by his use of a realism based on close observation. This artificiality is also implied in the contrast between the participation of the forces of nature in these deaths and the fact that such cases are generally termed 'unnatural'. It is not possible to say, however, that it is nature itself, or indeed an image of nature based on 'Kitsch' that is here 'demaskiert'.

With the exception of *Geschichten aus dem Wiener Wald,* all the works in which death by exposure occurs belong to the period of exile after 1933. A definite change has been noted in Horváth's work in this period, and Kurt Kahl has pointed out that it is towards a more personal concept of responsibility. The examination of the 'feines Geflecht von Schuld' in *Jugend ohne Gott* is not apparent in the episode of W's death. The emphasis is on the helplessness of the victim, 'es fiel mir ein, dass er der Kleinste der Klasse war', and a sentimental note is introduced by the figure of the goalkeeper, whose presence at the boy's deathbed gives this scene an air of unreality reminiscent of the two incidences of death in a snowstorm. If the portrayal of death in these works is not used to expose failings of society or of nature, that which is 'demaskiert' must be sought elsewhere. In all three instances, death marks the end of the individual's pretensions: Don Juan's attempts to find stability in relationships with women; the soldier's identification with the state and its militaristic spirit; and W's wish to resemble his footballer heroes. The futility of these pretensions is now revealed, exposed by the unreal circumstances surrounding the deaths. Hence the portrayal of death in these later works affords an example of the manner in which Horváth's concern has moved from the guilt borne by society to a more critical examination of the individual.

In the portrayal of death in Horváth's works one notices

a tendency to repeat motifs and to use identical means to bring about the deaths of characters in different works. This is in keeping with Horváth's liking for self-quotation and transfer of incidents from one work to another. More specifically such a technique is indicative of a tendency to see the world from fixed viewpoints: one which repeatedly condemns a society which is directly or indirectly responsible for the deaths of individual members, but one which changes later to see them less as victims but as individuals who, in death, come to terms with forces greater than contemporary society. (pp. 148-52)

> P. M. Potter, "Death and Guilt in the Works of Ödön von Horváth," in German Life & Letters, *Vol. XXXII, No. 2, January, 1979, pp. 148-52.*

Ian Huish   (essay date 1980)

[*In the following excerpt from his* Horváth: A Study, *Huish examines stupidity, hypocrisy, and self-deception in Horváth's characters as well as the dramatist's use of* Bildungsjargon *and other linguistic techniques to emphasize class divisions.*]

As must be apparent to any student of Horváth's plays, characters are more often than not generously endowed with [stupidity, hypocrisy, and self-deception]. Indeed their conversation would in many cases become nonexistent without them. In *Sladek* it is firstly the violent language of racial hatred that strikes the audience— 'Judenknecht' (Jew-server), 'Syphilitische Neger' (syphilitic niggers), 'jüdisch-jesuitische Fetzen von Weimar' (Jewish-Jesuitical tatters from Weimar); in *Italienische Nacht* it is the self-satisfied utterances on the strength of the Weimar Republic and the weakness of the Fascists. The political slogan-mongering that Horváth so roundly condemned is illustrated on page after page in both plays.

On another level there are 'intellectual' discussions: between Sladek and Schminke, Betz and Martin. In these the characters are seen playing with half-digested ideas. In the case of Sladek and Schminke it is the role of the individual in society. Sladek is so indoctrinated with the ideals of Fascism that he is even able to answer the question

>   Was verstehst du unter Vaterland?

with

>   Zu guter Letzt mich.

>   What do you mean by fatherland? When it comes down to it—myself,

adding a few lines later that he can think for himself! His 'thoughts' run along these lines:

>   Soon everything will be one town, the whole German Reich. We need our colonies again, Asia, Africa—there are really too many of us. Pity that the war's over!

('Why we need colonies' was later to become the title for a Geography essay in *Jugend ohne Gott.*) In *Italienische Nacht* the discussion on Freud leads to this delightful conclusion:

I can tell you that our aggressive urges play a predominant role in the realization of Socialism. I fear that in this respect you are being a political ostrich.

The underlying truth of Betz's assertion is made comic not only by Martin's obscene rejoinders but also by his own pomposity in presenting the argument and his undigested regurgitation of it.

The third and most prevalent form of stupidity lies in the ordinary conversation of the characters. When Sladek is found by Anna (just after he has paid a barmaid to strip for him) he tries to convince her of his desire to return to her; in fact he is preparing the ground for her murder:

> SLADEK. Anna—. I wanted to come back to you.
>
> ANNA. (*Looking at him in horror*) That's not true!
>
> SLADEK. Yes it is.
>
> ANNA. (*Looking round anxiously*) Where were you?
>
> SLADEK. With the soldiers. I've thought it all over.
>
> ANNA. What do you want from me? What are you thinking now?
>
> SLADEK. That everything'll be all right.
>
> ANNA. That's impossible.
>
> SLADEK. I'm fond of you.
>
> ANNA. No, No.
>
> SLADEK. I'm not lying.
>
> ANNA. This very evening you could've killed me.
>
> SLADEK. I've never hated you.

Sladek, the 'independent' thinker is merely repeating in colourless fashion what Knorke has told him to say. The irony in this absurd piece of hypocrisy is that Anna, the one person in the play who has genuine emotions and shows them, finally makes Sladek realize that he *did* care for her, but only when it is too late.

Horváth was a master at portraying the inconsequential leaps that occur in everyday conversations, especially where characters are trying to impress one another. In this he leaves behind the drama of carefully constructed, logical development in dialogue and anticipates the postwar dramatists who have taken the absurdities of speech to its extremes. Horváth's writing is no parody and the inconsequentialities, however comic they may be, always remain credible; each character follows his train of thought, drops his cliché or *bon mot* into the ring and—just occasionally—says what he is really thinking:

> COUNCILLOR. When you go to a woman, don't forget the whip.
>
> BETZ. That's Nietzsche.
>
> COUNCILLOR. And damn all I care! She obeys

me to the letter. This is a glorious spot here! These age-old tree trunks and the air filled with ozone—(*He takes a deep breath.*)

BETZ. Those are the wonders of nature.

COUNCILLOR. The wonders of creation—there's nothing more glorious. I can judge that better than you because I was born on a farm. When you look up into the sky, you seem so tiny in comparison—those eternal stars! What are we next to them?

BETZ. Nothing.

COUNCILLOR. Nothing. God really has got good taste.

BETZ. Everything's relative of course.
(*Silence*)

COUNCILLOR. You know what, Betz, I've bought myself a piece of land.

A conversation between Karl and Leni shows how self-deception leads to an absurd inflation of language and, as in *Zur schönen Aussicht,* heart-strings and purse-strings are plucked simultaneously: nothing is so sure to quicken the emotions as the mention of cash! Once again God is the starting point, but Leni and Karl are not really talking of religion any more than they are talking of love. Karl's self-pitying defeatism is treated with tenderness and understanding by Leni (who makes some of the most pertinent comments in the play), but she too succumbs here to an illusion:

LENI. Do you believe in God? (*Karl is silent.*) There is a God and there is a salvation too.

KARL. If only I knew who had put a curse on me.

LENI. Let me be your salvation.

KARL. You? My salvation?

LENI. I have four thousand Marks and we'll set up a grocery shop—

KARL. We?

LENI. Out at my uncle's.

KARL. We?

LENI. Me and you.
(*Silence*)

KARL. In cash?

LENI. Yes.
(*Silence*)

KARL. What are you thinking now? Are you thinking of a business marriage? No, you're too good for that!

LENI. Don't be so hard-hearted! I know you through and through already although I've only known you for a short while. (*She throws her arms around his neck—big kissing scene.*)

KARL. I've always dreamed of salvation coming through a woman, but I've never been able to be-

lieve it possible—I'm very embittered, you know.

LENI. (*Giving him a kiss on the forehead*) Yes, the world is full of envy.

Language—and especially the language of 'Bildungsjargon' . . .—is a cover, a mask that conceals true feelings. More often than not it is in the silences that the real thoughts of the characters are revealed, while their words merely serve to give a semblance of continuity and of communication in relationships where none exists. (pp. 33-8)

Just as music and silence play an essential part in unmasking what lies beneath the surface [of Horváth's dramas] so too do the clichés and received ideas that pour out of the characters' mouths. In his **'Gebrauchsanweisung'** Horváth clearly indicated the way in which the dialogue should be spoken:

Not a word of dialect is to be spoken! Every word must be spoken in correct German, though admittedly as if by people who normally only speak dialect and who are now straining themselves to speak correct German. This is very important! Since it is in this way that every word is imbued with the synthesis of realism and irony.

Elsewhere in the same text Horváth explains that what has replaced dialect is 'Bildungsjargon'—an acquired language or artificial jargon—and this is what must be spoken by his characters. Apart from the obvious use of foreign words and phrases, proverbs, quotations (and a misquotation from Goethe's poem *Selige Sehnsucht* when Oskar recites the last verse in part III scene 3) and clichés, the ideas and conversation are shot through with 'Bildungsjargon'. The Zauberkönig's speech at the engagement party is an excellent example of the form at its best:

Just a minute, I shan't be much longer, and now we've all gathered here, that's to say, I've invited you all here, to celebrate simply but with dignity, in a small but select circle, a very important moment in the lives of these two, now in the flower of their youth. My only deep regret today is that Almighty God has not spared Marianne's dear precious mother, God rest her soul, my unforgettable wife, to share this day of joy with her only daughter. But I'm sure of one thing, she's somewhere up there now in Heaven, standing behind a star and looking down on us . . .

From the first word here in Latin, through the polite pomposities and hypocrisies, Horváth shows mastery of the speechmaker's jargon. The Zauberkönig says all the right things, the formula is correct, and indeed he feels it his duty to speak in such a way. What he thinks and does subsequently show not only how 'unvergeßlich' his wife is (as he flirts with Valerie and tells what he really thought of his wife) but also how select the circle of friends is and how much this is a 'Freudentag' (for Marianne in particular as she throws the engagement ring at Oskar's face). Seriousness and irony are truly fused in this speech.

The meeting between Alfred and Marianne and their declaration of love shows 'Bildungsjargon' in a less formalized setting. From Alfred's first statement that he knew Marianne would come out of the river at this place (how could he know it?), the tone is fake and the emotions are cobbled together with borrowed phrases and spurious moral sentiments:

> ALFRED. We've turned our real natures into a strait-jacket. Nobody's allowed to do what they want to do.
>
> MARIANNE. And nobody wants to do what they're allowed to do.
> (*Silence*)
>
> ALFRED. And nobody's allowed to do what they're able to do.
>
> MARIANNE. And nobody's able to do what they ought to do.
> (*Alfred embraces her dramatically and she makes no move to resist him. A long kiss.*)
>
> MARIANNE. (*Gets her breath*) I knew it, I knew it—

Once again the idea of some destiny is implied in Marianne's last words and, tragically, she at least really believes it when she takes the love-scene cliché one step further:

> I don't care if they find us. Stay with me, you've been sent down from Heaven, you're my guardian angel—

(pp. 43-5)

Ian Huish, in his Horváth: A Study, *Heinemann, 1980, 105 p.*

Horváth on reaction to his plays:

They say I'm too crude, too disgusting, too weird, too cynical . . . and they just don't see that my only aim is to show the world as it really is. . . . I annoy people because they recognize themselves in the characters on stage—and of course some people just cannot laugh at themselves, especially when what they are shown are their own highly personal instincts, of which they are often only half-aware themselves.

Ödön von Horváth, in his Gesammelte Werke, *Suhrkamp, 1971.*

Stuart Parkes (essay date 1982)

[*In the essay below, Parkes discusses the political statements made in Horváth's novels and dramas.*]

[It] seems appropriate to begin an appraisal of Horváth's writing with those works that have received universal acclaim, the folk-plays that were written before he left Germany. The term 'folk-play' or *Volksstück* is taken from an Austrian theatrical tradition, that had been perfected in the comedies of Nestroy in the nineteenth century. What Horváth sought to do was not to revive this old theatrical genre but to adapt it to a changed world. Furthermore, de-

spite what the term seems to imply, he was not seeking to portray the people in the plays in any kind of idealized way. The following brief outlines will show how far removed his plays are from earlier forms of the folk-play.

There are five folk-plays, the first of which exists in two versions. ***Revolte auf Côte 3018 (Revolt on Slope 3018;*** first performed in 1927) or ***Die Bergbahn (The Mountain Railway***), as the second version is entitled, is a minor early work. It portrays the hardships of workers building a mountain railway as they are pressed to make faster progress before the onset of winter. Besides showing the exploitation of the workers—the company director in the play is a caricature of a 'wicked capitalist'—the action also concentrates on the engineer, who takes up a position between capital and labour. The technologist's devotion to the completion of his task is presented as a kind of professional fanaticism, a portrayal that is reminiscent of Expressionism.

Italienische Nacht (Italian Night), first performed in 1931, has a clear political theme. It shows how provincial politicians react, or more exactly, fail to react to the Nazi threat, something Horváth saw for himself in the year of the play's publication, when he witnessed a brawl provoked by National Socialists at a political meeting in Bavaria. In the play, the republicans of a small town are intent on holding their Italian celebration, regardless of the presence of Nazis in the town. When the Nazis break up the gathering, the humiliation of the republicans is only prevented by the actions of a group of left-wing activists, who had previously been expelled because they had objected to their elders' political blindness. The play implies that concerted action will be necessary if Nazism is to be defeated; it does not, however, portray any political group in an uncritical way.

That Horváth by no means idealizes the people he portrays is underlined by the title of the third folk-play ***Geschichten aus dem Wiener Wald (Tales from the Vienna Woods:*** first performed 1931). Instead of the light-hearted atmosphere of a Strauss operetta, the audience is confronted with a series of sordid events. The play centres around a girl, Marianne, who seeks to escape the stifling atmosphere of her home and petty bourgeois environment by breaking her engagement to a neighbour and going to live with the ne'er-do-well Alfred, who has previously lived off older women and various gambling enterprises. The liaison results in a child, which then dies because of Alfred's grandmother, who deliberately exposes it to cold draughts. The death occurs out of town—Alfred's mother and grandmother are the custodians of a historic tower in a beautiful setting—an indication that Horváth does not regard the country as an idyllic alternative to life in the city.

Another city, Munich, is the setting for ***Kasimir und Karoline*** (first performed 1932). This play shows the breakup of a relationship against the background of the city's famous Oktoberfest. The recently redundant Kasimir is in no mood to enjoy the event's various attractions. Because of this, Karoline becomes so incensed that she leaves him for another, whilst he turns to Erna, the former girlfriend of a small-time crook, who is arrested during the play.

Otherwise there is hardly any plot in the play, whose 117 brief scenes concentrate rather on the characters' personalities and their interaction.

A court case which Horváth heard about from a Munich journalist provided the background to the last of the folk-plays *Glaube Liebe Hoffnung (Faith, Hope, and Charity;* written 1932, first performed 1936). As a preface by Horváth makes clear, it consists partly of a plea for a more humane application of statutes relating to petty offences. Elisabeth has been fined for selling ladies' underwear without a licence. She eventually manages to borrow the money to pay the fine by saying it is for a licence to get a job selling. When her deceit comes to light she is given a 14-day prison sentence. This criminal record also destroys her relationship with a policeman, who puts his career before everything. In despair, Elisabeth drowns herself.

These brief plot summaries show that the folk-plays have many similarities. In fact, a study of Horváth's draft versions reveals that more than one of the plays are developed from the same initial conception. The world of the Great Depression provides the social and political background in nearly every case, whilst the predicaments of the characters, especially the young female ones, are often similar. Even the settings of the scenes do not vary much; cheap furnished rooms and quiet streets regularly recur as favourite locations.

Together with the misery of the Depression of the late twenties and early thirties, Horváth portrays the ominous rise of National Socialism. Although *Italienische Nacht* is the only work with an obvious political dimension, the political events of the day provide an unhappy background to most of the other works. Even *Geschichten aus dem Wiener Wald* with its Austrian setting contains one character, a German law student, with openly fascist views. In *Kasimir und Karoline,* there is a nationalistic doctor, who complains whilst treating the victims of drunken brawls that these are all Germans who have been fighting one another. The policeman in *Glaube Liebe Hoffnung* has been on duty at political demonstrations, which are frequently referred to in the play. The political turbulence of the age is an essential part of the world of Horváth's folk-plays. Even more stressed than the political background are the effects of the Depression, most particularly in *Kasimir und Karoline* and *Glaube Liebe Hoffnung.* Kasimir's anger at being unemployed is evident throughout the play. It expresses itself in bitter condemnation of the prevailing economic conditions and it will not be diverted by the sight of a Zeppelin, which other onlookers admire as a marvel of technology: 'Up there 20 captains of industry are flying around and down here below 20 million are starving. I couldn't give a bugger about the Zeppelin, I know their bloody tricks and I've formed my own opinions'. Elisabeth too, in *Glaube Liebe Hoffnung,* is faced with a constant struggle for physical survival. In the first scene, she is enquiring whether it is possible to sell her body 'in advance' for medical research so that she might raise the money she desperately needs to pay her fine. After her imprisonment she is one of the many who wait in front of the Welfare Office hoping for some kind of assistance.

Although the importance of political and social themes in Horváth's folk-plays cannot be overlooked, it is not easy to determine the exact nature of his political views and to answer the related question of whether he is to be regarded principally as a politically committed writer or not. As already indicated, his characters do express political views. In *Kasimir und Karoline,* it is not only Kasimir who is critical of the existing state of affairs; the man Karoline meets at the *Oktoberfest,* Schürzinger, tells her: 'Human beings are neither good nor evil. Of course they are forced by our present economic system to be more egotistic than they otherwise would be, as after all they have to scrape a living'. At the beginning of *Italienische Nacht* the left-winger, Martin, who finally saves the Republicans from the National Socialists, complains: 'the proletariat pays the taxes and the gentlemen of business fiddle the republic'. It does not necessarily follow from such statements that the characters are expressing Horváth's own views. In the case of Schürzinger's comment, both the pompous language and the context rob it of any substance it might have as a political statement. He ends by asking Karoline if she understands what he is trying to say: 'D' you understand me?' only to receive the blunt answer: 'No'. The credibility of Martin's political views and actions is lessened by the way he treats his girl. He unfeelingly asks her to consort with one of the fascists to gain more information about their plans. When she returns bruised, it is this personal factor as much as wider political considerations that make him go into action to aid the republicans. Kasimir expresses his political opinions in extremely crude terms, as the passage quoted above shows. In view of all these factors, it seems somewhat simplistic to regard the views of any of the characters as in any way Horváth's own.

Despite these reservations, it is clear that, at least at the time of the folk-plays, Horváth had left-wing sympathies. Even if one disregards biographical factors like his association with the German League for Human Rights, a play like *Italienische Nacht* is clearly anti-fascist to the extent that the portrayal of the Nazis themselves scarcely rises above caricature. One Nazi wears an ex-colonial uniform, whilst another is an adolescent seeking to escape from his mother's influence. One of the clearest statements of Horváth's opinions at this time is contained in the novel *Der ewige Spießer (The Eternal Bourgeois:* published 1930), in which it is said of one middle-class character: 'Like all her kind she did not hate the uniformed and civilian criminals, who had conned her through war, inflation, deflation and stabilization, but exclusively the proletariat, because she suspected, without wishing to get it clear in her mind, that the future belonged to this class'. In as far as the novel is narrated in the third person by an omniscient narrator, it is tempting to assume that this passage reflects Horváth's own views.

What the plays do not suggest, however, unlike those of Brecht, is any means by which prevailing injustices might be put right. Besides there being no mouthpiece of Horváth himself in the plays, there are no dramatic techniques or external statements that suggest a solution to the political and social problems portrayed. Furthermore, what he does say often suggests that he is not certain whether such solutions exist. *Geschichten aus dem Wiener Wald* is prefaced with the comment: 'Nothing gives so much the feeling of infinity as stupidity', which implies that the events of the play are caused not solely by social factors but also by perennial human weaknesses. The preface to *Glaube Liebe Hoffnung* accepts that there will always be statutes of the kind the play deals with and that conflicts between the individual and society are incapable of solution.

To point out that Horváth does not present easy solutions to social and political questions is not necessarily to criticize him. It is merely to state that he cannot be regarded simply as a sociopolitical writer. His interest lies equally in the analysis of human character and human relations, neither of which are seen in purely social terms. In general, it is possible to say that the 'folk' of the folk-plays do not appear in a favourable light, irrespective of their social class. The workers of *Die Bergbahn* include the brutish Moser, who savagely beats up a new colleague who has made advances to his girl, whilst the two upper middle-class characters of *Kasimir und Karoline,* the businessman Rauch and the lawyer Speer can only be described as drunken lechers. After having praised the Oktoberfest as an example of democracy, because all social classes mix there, Rauch shows his true nature by ordering away his employee Schürzinger so that he can pursue his designs on Karoline. It is, however, on the lower middle-classes, the Kleinbürger, that Horváth concentrates. He regards this class as the major grouping within society, claiming that, at least as far as mentality is concerned, the majority of society can be labelled Kleinbürger. In almost all cases, the portrayal of the Kleinbürger is negative. The young male members of the class are nearly always heartlessly ambitious, like Schürzinger, who is willing to hand over Karoline to Rauch if this will further his career, or the policeman of *Glaube Liebe Hoffnung,* who abandons Elisabeth for similar reasons when he learns of her 'criminal' past. His ambition is compounded with an unfeeling sense of duty and with self-pity, which, on Elisabeth's death, soon replaces any sense of sorrow about her fate. He repeats: 'I never have any luck!', when she dies in his presence. The most telling portrait of an older Kleinbürger is the Zauberkönig (magician) in *Geschichten aus dem Wiener Wald,* described by another character as a typical Viennese of the old sort. He is first seen bullying his daughter Marianne about some clothes which have been mislaid— by him, in fact, and not by her as he claims. This incident reflects his whole attitude to women, a mixture of contempt and lasciviousness. Whilst he regards financial independence as a step on the road towards Bolshevism, he takes great interest in female underclothing during a bathing trip to celebrate Marianne's engagement. When his daughter is in desperate straits after the birth of her illegitimate child, he shows no mercy, thinking only of himself: 'Oh you filthy slut, what are you trying to do to me in my old age . . . It's one disgrace after another—I'm just a poor old man, what have I done to deserve this?!'. It is bitterly ironical that when he is willing to be reconciled with Marianne and her child, the baby is already dead. The structure of *Geschichten aus dem Wiener Wald*—the repeated use of the same settings and the frequent repetitions—underlines the unchanging nature of the world of the Kleinbürger. It seems that nothing will improve in the

next generation either. When Marianne is accused a second time of having mislaid some clothes, it is her lover Alfred who makes the accusation in much the same way as her father.

Horváth's view of human character, which, as has been pointed out, does not regard people solely as the product of their social environment, appears to owe something to the ideas of Freudian psychology. There is one character in *Italienische Nacht,* Betz, who has half digested some of these ideas. He tells Martin, for example: 'I think you are overlooking something very important in your judgements of the world's political situation, and that's love-life in nature. I've been studying the works of Professor Freud recently, I can tell you'. There is, however, no reason to believe that this statement is any more a reflection of Horváth's own views than any other in his plays. At the same time, his own use of such terms as 'consciousness', the 'sub-conscious', 'urges' in his theoretical writings indicates the influence of psychoanalysis. Any discussion of Horváth's conception of man raises the question of whether his plays reflect a contemptuous, aristocratic scorn of his fellow creatures. The presentation of some of the characters, as described above, might seem to suggest this, as do the reminiscences of acquaintances, who refer to his frequent use of the adjective 'tierisch' (bestial) to describe people. In this connection, it can be pointed out that his characters are at their worst when they are supposed to be enjoying themselves, be it at the Oktoberfest or in a Viennese night-club. Critics, too, have accused him of such an attitude, something he was at pains to defend himself against in his own lifetime, saying that he only sought to portray the world as it was.

It would be an oversimplification to describe Horváth as a writer who regards his fellow men without pity as totally stupid and incapable of any decent act. There is one group of characters in the folk-plays that are consistently presented with sympathy as to a large extent the victims of the world around them, namely the young women. This is not to say that they are entirely blameless. Marianne's attempt in *Geschichten aus dem Wiener Wald* to break away from her own environment, which arises from her thwarted interest in rhythmic gymnastics and her unwise love for Alfred, is clearly the result of great delusions. Yet her expression of her predicament in the cathedral when she goes to confession manages to be at the same time almost a parody of the cathedral scene in Goethe's *Faust,* and in its helplessness a sympathetic reflection of a real crisis: 'If there is a God . . . what's to become of me, God? Dear God, I was born in Vienna 8 and went to the local secondary school, I'm not a bad person . . . are you listening? What's to become of me, God?'. Towards the end of the play she finds bitter words to express her fate, as she acquiesces in a reconciliation with her father and her former fiancé Oskar: 'I just want to say one thing. When it really comes down to it, I don't give a shit. What I'm doing, I'm doing for Leopold, because none of this is his fault'. Similarly, Karoline comes to realize her true situation, after she has let herself be humiliated by Rauch because she felt he might further her social ambitions: 'Often you simply have a sort of longing in you—but then you come back down to earth again with broken wings and life goes on as if you'd never been part of it'. Elisabeth, too, before she dies, is able to express her contempt for her former lover, telling him that her suicide is not because of him but because she has nothing to eat. In these moments, the characters achieve a clarity, a lack of self-delusion that contrasts positively with the world around them. This makes them sympathetic, even if their insights do little to improve their material position. In fact, it is only rarely that individual action helps to achieve something good in Horváth's plays. One occasion not surprisingly involves a female character; in *Italienische Nacht,* the wife of the city councillor, despite the callous way her husband treats her, stoutly defends him in the face of the Nazis. Her action, together with the intervention of Martin and his comrades, helps to put them to flight. To find another example of a 'good deed' in a work by Horváth of this period, one has to look to the novel *Der ewige Spießer,* where surprisingly it is a man who does good by finding a job for a girl in danger of becoming a prostitute. The narrative speaks of the importance of such small acts, possibly another indication that Horváth does not see universal political solutions to the problems of the world he portrays.

As has been suggested the portrayal of the Kleinbürger is a major element in Horváth's folk-plays. He is showing the class that, at the time, through its acceptance of Fascist ideology played a decisive role in the history of Germany. It is not surprising that the contemporary dramatist Franz Xaver Kroetz regards Horváth's characters as providing a convincing explanation of why Hitler could come to power. Such cold careerists as Schürzinger and the policeman in *Glaube Liebe Hoffnung* would make excellent National Socialist functionaries.

The merit of Horváth's folk-plays is not simply that they are written about an important social group, it also lies in the nature of its portrayal. Immediately striking in this respect is his presentation of the language of the Kleinbürger. In his few theoretical statements Horváth is conspicuously at pains to explain the nature of his characters' language. He defines it as *Bildungsjargon* (jargon of education), that is to say a linguistic code that has been assimilated by them during the universal educational process but which is external to their real selves. He adds that no dialect should be spoken in his plays, but the standard language as acquired must be spoken as if the character were naturally a dialect speaker. Critics have discussed Horváth's pronouncements at considerable length in view of their somewhat confusing terminology. What he seems to be meaning is a similar distinction to that made in English between accent and dialect. His characters no longer speak a regional language but its influence remains as they attempt to cope with the standard language.

The exact nature of *Bildungsjargon* can be seen from the plays; it is characterized by clichés, a mixture of linguistic levels and occasional solecisms. These are not merely a source of amusement for the audience; their language is a part of the characters' overall predicament. When Marianne in *Geschichten aus dem Wiener Wald* complains about the way she was treated by the police—her desperation has led her at one point to steal—the only response is: 'You can't expect the police to wear kid gloves', an im-

personal generalization that allows no sympathy for her previous distress. One of the best examples of a mixture of linguistic levels, again involving generalization, occurs not in a folk-play but in another play of the pre-emigration period, *Sladek, der schwarze Reichswehrmann* (*Sladek, the Soldier of the Black Army;* first performed in 1929). Sladek makes what appears to be a lofty pronouncement on the role of first love in a person's life, saying 'first love plays a momentous part in life'. He then adds 'so I've heard', in this way revealing the received nature of the original statement and reducing it to banality. As Horváth's characters speak largely in clichés, they are incapable of any real communication. They become the victims of a language that constrains all aspects of their life. This explains why Horváth's work arouses such interest in the contemporary writer, Peter Handke, who in his play *Kaspar* presents the socialization process as a series of manipulations by fixed linguistic patterns that force the ideology of society on to the individual.

In the case of Horváth's Kleinbürger, there is of course no awareness of the role of language in their life. It is one of his major tasks as a dramatist to reveal to his audience, which might itself in certain circumstances be carried along on the wave of clichés, what the real significance of the characters' language is. In the case of Sladek's statement on love, the character himself expresses some doubt as to the validity of the statement he has made. Elsewhere, an interlocutor may express what seem to be similar doubts. For example, the Councillor's high-flown phrase in *Italienische Nacht:* 'Our unshakeable desire for peace will repel all the bayonets of international reaction' is greeted by the comment: 'Waffle, you apostle of humanitarianism', by one of the left-wingers. Such objections to others' clichés do not mean that the person making them provides the model of an ideal use of language. In this particular case, Martin's left-wing followers only seem capable of derogatory chants such as 'A fine Marxist', repeated four times as a chant aimed at the Councillor, and a little later: 'Crap! Crap! Crap!' In this context, therefore, criticism of others' clichés is itself a kind of cliché.

One major method through which Horváth reveals the relationship between the characters and the language they use is interrupting its flow with pauses. The stage direction *Stille* (Silence) occurs frequently and Horváth insists that it should not be overlooked. In his theoretical statement '*Gebrauchsanweisung*' (*Instructions for Use*), he says of these silences that they show the struggle between the characters' consciousness and their sub-conscious. This is probably something of an erudite oversimplification, as a close study of the play shows that the stage direction *Stille* is used in a variety of differing contexts. In general, it provides a moment of understanding for the audience, in which it can step back and consider the flow of words at a distance. Thus the silence that follows the line 'then life is a joke', during the singing at the Oktoberfest in *Kasimir und Karoline,* suggests that the opposite is true. Generally, the silences occur within a dialogue. In the 83rd scene of *Kasimir und Karoline,* for example, which takes place when Karoline appears to be about to accept Rauch's advances, there are four silences in less than ten lines of dialogue. One occurs when Rauch asks her how much she earns. Her eventual answer is the simple and presumably truthful one that she earns 55 marks a month. The silence helps to underline to the audience that Rauch is exploiting his financial position; if Karoline herself does not realise this, the delay in her answer is psychologically explicable in terms of her misplaced social ambitions. It is hard for her to admit her lowly financial position. In this way, the silence fulfils a function for the audience, whilst representing the kind of internal conflict Horváth refers to. Elsewhere a silence may simply indicate a breakdown in communication. When Marianne tells Alfred the date, the ensuing silence followed by his question: 'So what?', shows that he is unaware of any significance the date may have. Since it is actually the date on which they first saw each other a year earlier, the exchange underlines how the relationship has lost its meaning, at least for Alfred. Thus, in a variety of ways, the silences underline what the language of the folk-plays already shows, the helplessness of the Kleinbürger when they seek to communicate.

In that they without exception fail to provide a linguistic or any other kind of model, Horváth's characters cannot be a vehicle for his critical intentions. Before any discussion of the dramatic techniques he employs for this purpose, it is necessary to consider more closely what these intentions are, beyond the social and political ones already discussed in connection with individual plays. It has been argued above that Horváth's main interest lies in the presentation of character. In this connection he describes his aim as 'unmasking of consciousness'. This is another expression that has aroused controversy among critics, some of whom have claimed, for instance, that the term is meaningless, as Horváth's shallow characters have no consciousness to unmask. However, the term is probably better understood as a statement of general critical intent, the desire to reveal to the audience the true nature of his characters, which is nearly always different from the way they see themselves. To do this, Horváth must alienate their self-presentation. His intentions are therefore similar to those of Brecht, namely to prevent the audience from identifying with the events on the stage. The use of silences has already been discussed as an example of a dramatic technique used for this purpose. As such, it differs from many techniques used by Brecht in that the silences are not an external device but a credible part of the events taking place on the stage. Occasionally music is used as an external background to the events on the stage; so for example, in *Geschichten aus dem Wiener Wald,* some of the interpolated waltz tunes provide an ironic contrast to the sordid happenings in the play. Elsewhere music and songs are part of the dramatic context, although they usually have a particular significance. The jolly songs sung at the Oktoberfest in *Kasimir und Karoline* underline the empty futility of the characters' search for enjoyment. An alienation effect is achieved here without recourse to external devices. Even if Horváth does not use the techniques of Brecht's 'epic theatre', it would be wrong to regard him as in any way a naturalist dramatist attempting solely to hold up a mirror to reality. There is, for example, conscious use of symbols in his plays; the white asters in the room where Elisabeth and the policeman temporarily enjoy happiness are a sign that things will not end happily. Furthermore, Horváth is very forceful in demanding that his plays be produced in a stylized way. He sees this kind of presentation as essential if he is to achieve his aim of revealing truth through a synthesis of seriousness and irony.

The combination of factors discussed above gives Horváth's folk-plays their unique quality. Perceptive observations of people in a specific historical situation, together with a technique that allows the audience to be amused, concerned and unsettled at more or less the same time, make up a major dramatic achievement. Finally, the economy of construction of Horváth's plays should not be overlooked. He needs only a few apparently insignificant figures, generally short scenes and almost no interpolated external events to fashion successful plays out of situations of which even the word trivial might seem an exaggerated description.

To dwell at such length on the folk-plays does not mean that Horváth's other plays are of no interest or merit. He wrote far more comedies than folk-plays, concentrating especially on this *genre* after his emigration from Germany. Of the two comedies written at approximately the same time as the folk-plays, *Zur schönen Aussicht (The Fine Prospect:* written 1926) and *Rund um den Kongress (Round about the Congress:* written 1929), it is fair to say that they suffer in comparison, because they lack subtlety and precision. The humour tends to be crude in places, often akin to the most primitive forms of farce. This is especially true of *Rund um den Kongress,* which is a satire on an international congress convened to fight international prostitution. The members of the congress are more interested in living well than attending to the matter in hand. When a girl about to be sold into prostitution appears before them, they show more sympathy towards the unscrupulous trader who is selling her. This criticism of officialdom is balanced by the portrayal of the crusading journalist Schminke—the name means grease paint—whose opposition to prostitution exists only in the realm of theory, and not at the level of individual cases. The play fails because Horváth never gives the impression that he is treating a subject that needs to be taken seriously; on a technical level, it seems a dubious theatrical trick that a representative of the audience has to intervene as a kind of *deus ex machina* before a happy ending can be engineered. Even if one takes into account that the play is called a *Posse* (farce) by its author, it lacks substance.

Zur schönen Aussicht (the title is the name of the hotel where the action takes place) is altogether a more convincing work. It is akin to the folk-plays in that Christine, the main character, is a girl who has suffered and suffers during the play at the hands of unfeeling men. The difference is that she has come into money. This factor alone finally changes the way she is treated; even if it is impossible to speak of a happy end to the play, there is a different atmosphere from the folk-plays where, even if the events do not lead to death as in *Glaube Liebe Hoffnung,* any resolution of the conflicts presented appears temporary and contrived. The sociopolitical background of the play is also sharply focused. The effect on the characters of the depression becomes clear when they hear about Christine's money. They come to refer to it as 'the good Lord', an indication of the values of the age. One of them, Müller, reflects the political mood of the age in that he combines his belief in male superiority with extreme nationalistic views. Above all, the play is funny, even if it contains elements that are somewhat stereotyped: for instance, the setting in a rundown hotel and the character of the rich but ugly old woman, whose wealth alone allows her to hold sway.

The later comedies lack the focus of *Zur schönen Aussicht.* It seems that in emigration Horváth was intending, or given the nature of his potential audience, was forced to write in a more generalized way. The result of this is a certain degree of confusion. This is the case with *Figaro läßt sich scheiden (Figaro Gets Divorced;* first performed 1937), whose title shows in itself an attempt to adapt a known literary subject rather than rely solely on personal observation. The play takes up the story of Figaro after the count has emigrated during the French Revolution. Horváth is obviously using the figures of Figaro and the count to write about 'emigration' as such, and the presentation of the boredom and frustration experienced is almost entirely convincing. What this kind of conception ignores, however, is the great difference between the situations of exiles from the French Revolution and those from the Third Reich. Given the nature of Figaro in Beaumarchais' plays, it is also difficult to believe that Figaro would not be on the side of the revolution; despite references to the influence of Susanne, this point is never satisfactorily resolved by Horváth. Eventually Figaro does return to France but he has no sympathy for the direction the Revolution has taken, and when the count returns, he rejects any idea of imprisoning him with the pronouncement: 'Only now is the Revolution victorious by no longer feeling it necessary to lock people up, who cannot help being its enemies'. This generalization, in aesthetic terms a rather contrived ending to the play, seems to be a reflection of Horváth's own views at this period and, as such, represents a considerable change in attitude.

The direction Horváth's views took during emigration, in particular the influence of Christianity, is very clearly illustrated by his last comedy *Ein Sklavenball or Pompeji (A Slaves' Ball;* second version *Pompeii;* written 1937). The setting is the Roman Empire at the time of the coming of Christianity, with the second version making specific reference to the Pompeii earthquake. Christianity is seen as a liberating force for the slaves in the play, especially in the first version, but the conversion of their Punic master, the financier K. R. Thago, in the second version suggests that it is not seen solely as a movement on behalf of the oppressed. It is difficult to make any connections between the plays and Horváth's own times; the envy many Romans show towards Thago is, however, reminiscent of anti-Semitism. This is somewhat unfortunate in the first version, as Thago drowns and this is presented as a great day for his slaves. What these later plays show is that Horváth has not lost his concern for social questions; the major change is that he sees a possibility of their resolution more through the application of Christian ideas than through socialistic ones.

The criticisms already made of *Rund um den Kongress* can also be levelled at some of the later comedies. Two, *Him-*

melwärts (Heavenwards; written 1934) and *Mit dem Kopf durch die Wand (Tilting at Windmills;* first performed 1934), are little more than light satires aimed at the world of actors and showing the desire for fame, the problems of launching a new project and so on. There is one play, however, where Horváth's use of farce does seem entirely appropriate. This is *Hin und Her (To and Fro;* first performed 1934), which shows the fate of an individual without a country, something akin to Horváth's own position at the time. The main character, Havlicek, has been expelled from the country where he has lived for many years because he has become unemployed. The country of his birth will not accept him back because he has been away for so long. The action of the play takes place on the frontier bridge between the two countries where the poor man is marooned because of bureaucratic intransigence. This is a situation that is truly farcical, yet at the same time serious, as not only Horváth's own experiences but those of millions of refugees and displaced people both in his day and subsequently show. He also uses the play to satirize the irrational feelings of hostility that often exist between people of neighbouring countries. Even if all Havlicek's problems are resolved in a somewhat contrived way—not only does he help in the capture of some smugglers and thus gain a reward, he is also mistaken for the prime minister of one of the countries by his opposite number, who has come for border talks and is subsequently so embarrassed that he grants him entry—this does not matter, since the play is about a state of affairs that is essentially grotesque. Horváth exploits this to the full to excellent comic effect.

A small number of Horváth's plays do not fit into either the category of folk-play or comedy. These include the Sladek plays, already referred to (first version: *Sladek, oder Die schwarze Armee; Sladek, or The Black Army;* written 1928). Sladek is a young man who is recruited into one of the illegal right-wing armies that flourished in the early years of the Weimar Republic. The first version consists of a series of loosely connected scenes which make up a chronicle of the time. In the second version, the events are more compressed. Instead of being imprisoned and finally allowed to emigrate, Sladek is killed during an attack on the private army by regular soldiers. Because of this, the play becomes less of a realistic chronicle. The nature of justice in the Weimar Republic is, for instance, no longer a theme. When Sladek is tried in the first version, it is for the murder of his landlady, which is treated as a 'normal' murder and not as the politically motivated one it was. The court is unwilling to accept that there were any private armies, because the people who were behind them, members of the same social class as the judiciary, no longer wish to be reminded of their existence. They now prefer to undermine the Weimar system from within. These antidemocratic forces are heavily criticized by Horváth; it is, however, problematical that the leader of the private army, whose extreme nationalistic ideas make him reject any kind of compromise with the Weimar state, assumes by contrast an heroic stature, because his principles prevent him from entering into the shabby deals of his former backers. Along with Sladek, he becomes a major figure in the plays, more credible than the left-wing journalist Franz, or Schminke as he is called in the second version.

He has many of the characteristics of his namesake in *Rund um den Kongress,* putting abstract principle before practical help. Sladek himself is portrayed as the confused victim of the age. He is the archetype of many of Horváth's characters, who, born like their creator at the beginning of the century, have had their life and development strongly influenced by the war and its aftermath. He is a weak person, masquerading as a strong one behind the clichés of extreme right-wing ideology, and as such a victim of events beyond his control. Two plays written almost ten years after *Sladek, Der jüngste Tag (Judgement Day;* first performed 1937) and *Don Juan kommt aus dem Krieg (Don Juan Comes Home;* written 1936) underline further the differences between Horváth's earlier and later work. *Der jüngste Tag* is close to being a traditional tragedy. A fatal rail crash occurs because of the negligence of an official, who at the same time cannot be entirely blamed because his attention was distracted by the actions of a young woman. The play becomes an examination of the nature of guilt, a guilt the official finally accepts. The setting of the play is vaguely central European and there is no reference to specific historical events. This is not true of *Don Juan kommt aus dem Krieg,* where a literary figure is put in a certain context, the period of inflation after the First World War. The figure of Don Juan is a permanent human type, as are the various women Don Juan encounters. The play aims at a generalized portrayal of the theme of love. Don Juan searches for love in vain, defeated by his own lack of feeling; that he should finally freeze to death is a sign of his coldness, a negative symbol that recurs in Horváth's later novels. These two later plays have an abstract, almost metaphysical quality entirely missing from earlier works.

That in the last two years of his life Horváth should write two novels is often seen as a remarkable change of direction, brought about by the decreasing number of theatres in which uncensored German plays could be performed. Whatever the truth of this, it must be remembered that Horváth wrote a considerable amount of prose before this time, most particularly the novel *Der ewige Spießer* at the time of the folk-plays. This in turn was preceded by an interesting prose work *Sportmärchen (Sport Fairy-tales;* published 1924), in which sport is seen not as a means of self-fulfilment but as a social phenomenon. In his stories, Horváth satirizes society's exaggerated interest in sport. He is equally satirical in his first novel. This work seeks to show the unchanging nature of a certain type within the bourgeoisie, it again being noteworthy that in his introduction to the novel he speaks of the 'biology' of this type, another sign that he sees his subjects not solely in sociopolitical terms.

The novel itself consists of three parts, with the events of the first part, the most substantial one, being only loosely connected with those of the other two. In view of Horváth's conception of his subject, the loose construction of the novel is not surprising. He describes the *Spießer* as a type of person who appropriates an idea only to distort and falsify it. The novel becomes a series of potentially endless illustrations of this thesis.

The first part, on which it is proposed to concentrate here, describes how a Herr Kobler becomes a supporter of Pan-Europeanism. There is nowhere any indication of Horváth's own attitude to this political idea, which was a forerunner of the later attempts to achieve a united Europe. The reason for Kobler's conversion to this cause is that the girl whom he meets during a trip to the World Exhibition in Barcelona and with whom he hopes to conclude an advantageous marriage is in fact to marry an American, because her father's firm needs more capital. Kobler has obtained the money for the trip by selling at an excessive price the old car of an ageing female friend and deceiving her about the exact amount of money he has received. The first part of the novel describes the journey to Barcelona and back and the people Kobler meets. As this outline shows, its main character is very much akin to some of the types found in the folk-plays. As the young man who lives by his wits and, if possible, off other people, Kobler is comparable to Alfred in *Geschichten aus dem Wiener Wald.* The other characters, too, would not be out of place in the plays. Kobler's companion on the journey to Barcelona is a journalist, who propounds his idea of Paneuropa between bouts of drinking, a visit to a brothel in Marseilles and coping with his digestive problems. The language the characters use is also that of the folk-plays. An hotelier twice tells Kobler his political credo: 'In these economically depressive times a German should not take his honestly earned money abroad', whilst Schmitz, the journalist, speaks pure *Bildungsjargon,* as when his explanation of the economic role of colonies is interspersed with colloquialisms: 'Believe you me, if the poor old negroes wasn't so shamelessly exploited, that would be the case, because then after all every product from the colonies would be impossibly dear, because then the plantation owners would simply want to earn a thousand times more right away'. The novel as a genre provides Horváth with endless opportunities to pursue his satirical aims. There are, however, dangers in this. Without the constraints that the dramatic form imposes, the narrative becomes somewhat self-indulgent, as when the history of the family of the editor of a pocket dictionary is related in excessive detail. The language of the narrative, too, is problematical, often being hardly different from the jargon of the characters. A description of the sea is one example of this:

> Outside was the sea, our maternal source. It is supposed, you see, to have been the sea in which many hundreds of million years ago life originated, in order to crawl out later on to the land, on which it evolves higher and higher in that wonderfully complicated way, because it is forced to adapt in order not to come to a halt.

As a statement of the narrator rather than a reflection of the thoughts of a character, such a jargon-riddled passage serves little purpose. The result of this unrestrained kind of writing, together with Horváth's conception of the *Spießer* as an unchanging type, is that the novel, although amusing in parts, becomes repetitive, almost a series of anecdotes around the given theme.

Horváth's two later novels are very different from their predecessor. Both attracted considerable attention at the time of their publication and the second one, *Ein Kind unserer Zeit (A Child of our Time;* published 1937), was even translated into Chinese. Its forerunner, *Jugend ohne Gott* (*Youth without God;* published 1937), has as its narrator a teacher in a fascist state, whose attitude changes from one of passive dislike of the régime, resulting from his wish not to lose the security of his job, to a hostility that finally leads him to emigrate. The plot of the novel has many aspects that are reminiscent of a *novella*. The central incident is a murder that takes place in a schoolboy paramilitary camp; the rest of the work shows how the truth about this incident comes to light. The narrator feels implicated in the events because he delays acting to resolve a quarrel between two boys, one of whom is the victim of the murder. He sees this projected action at the time as a way of thwarting God. After the murder he comes to realize the true power of God and is willing to submit himself to His will. This is another aspect of his development: from indifference towards religion to awareness of God. The God that he learns to respect is presented as a terrible, almighty force with little compassion. The significance Horváth attaches to religion is already visible in the novel's title, in itself an indication of the growing importance of metaphysical themes in his later works.

The title also raises the question of Horváth's attitude towards the young people in the novel, the implication being that their lack of religion has a detrimental effect on their character. This is confirmed by the narrator's portrayal, which is largely negative. They are seen in general as all too willing followers of fascist ideology. This presentation has been criticized as implying that Horváth is blaming the children for the horrors of the fascist state, when the fascist state should be blamed for the nature of the children. Against this, it can be pointed out that there is one group of children in the novel who have formed a club which is opposed to the present state and dedicated to truth. Nor are the children's parents presented in any better light. The teacher has long fallen foul of the parents of the boy who is eventually murdered, because he has had the temerity to suggest that negroes are human. A letter from the boy's mother to her son at camp contains a revealing mixture of sentimentality and brutality:

> Just think, Mandy died yesterday. The day before he was still hopping about his little cage so happily and cheerfully and was chirping for our delight . . . Father sends you his love. You should just report it to him every time the teacher makes remarks like that about the negroes. Father will break his neck.

Such a passage suggests that parental influence has been a factor in making the boys what they are. Furthermore, it would be wrong to assume an exact affinity between the narrator and Horváth. There is, for instance, an implied rebuke for the narrator when he is reminded of the dreadful fate of the murdered boy, something he admits to have forgotten in his search for the murderer.

Whatever doubts there may be about the nature of Horváth's diagnosis of the ills of fascism, *Jugend ohne Gott* is a gripping story. It is written in a terse style, divided into short chapters and sentences. It does not, however, seek to recount the events that take place in a strictly realistic way. The narrator's interpretation of these events, which is influenced by the changes in his attitudes, provides a

major dimension of the narrative, which comes to acquire a symbolic level. The most effective symbol is that of 'coldness', the coldness of the murderer coming to symbolize the coldness of the age. At times, the symbolic elements are less effective; one wonders why Eva, a local girl the boys meet at camp, apparently comes to symbolize both womanhood and nature for the narrator. In general though, the symbolic style contributes to the power of a novel which had few equals at the time of its writing.

Horváth's second novel of the period, *Ein Kind unserer Zeit,* also traces a change of attitude by an individual in a fascist society. This time, the narrator is a soldier, who at the beginning of the novel fully identifies with the ideology of the state. His disillusionment begins after he is wounded during an attack on a neighbouring country and he is eventually forced to leave the army. He finally freezes to death in a park after he has murdered the bookkeeper, who was responsible for dismissing a girl he once loved. This girl is now in prison for having an illegal abortion. The change that takes place in the narrator's mind is not solely the result of his being injured; he too experiences a religious awakening thanks to the influence of a nurse who cares for him after his accident. This religious experience is not, however, very deep; nor indeed is his general change of attitude. Although he has reversed some of his opinions, he still expresses himself like the soldier of the fascist state he once was. For example, after regarding the individual initially as worthless, he comes to stress his importance. He adds: 'And whoever says anything different deserves to be exterminated, fully and utterly'. This is still the language of a fascist. The limited extent of the change is entirely convincing; the nature of the soldier's death is equally appropriate. Once again, Horváth is using coldness to symbolize the condition of a person corrupted by the influence of an uncaring society.

In view of the nature of the narrator, there is no danger of identifying him with Horváth himself. Only in the last sentences, when he is allowed to speak after his death, does it seem that it is really Horváth speaking. The plea for compassion to the reader 'Do not curse me' is not out of place and belies the view that Horváth is uncaring towards his characters. The final sentence: 'Just bear in mind: he didn't know how to do anything different, he was just a child of his time', is a reflection of the title, which shows that Horváth is still concerned to relate his work to its sociopolitical background. What he does is to give a generalized picture of a fascist dictatorship. The attack on the neighbouring country, for instance, in which the soldier is wounded, cannot be said to be a description of any specific historical event of the 1930s, but it reflects the nature of a fascist state in that it combines aggression and racialism. Equally significant is that the word *Führer* used in the singular in an early version is used in the plural in the final one. It is principally through the attitudes of the soldier that the picture of fascism is built up. His pride in his uniform results from the poverty and unemployment of his earlier life; the security it provides means that he is not concerned about the people who are making big profits out of supplying the army. Such details give a wider view of the nature of fascism than is found in *Jugend ohne*

Gott, where the murder and subsequent events come to dominate the novel.

This is not to say that *Ein Kind unserer Zeit* should be regarded as a contribution to academic discussion on the nature of fascism. Even if there is less emphasis on plot than in the previous novel, it is convincing as a work of art. This is primarily because of the choice of narrative viewpoint. Horváth's use of language makes the soldier come alive as a credible figure of his age. Furthermore, several aspects of the novel are skilfully structured, for example the relationship between the narrator and his father. When he is filled with patriotic fervour, he despises his father for his different political persuasions and for the subservience of his job as a waiter. It does not of course occur to him that he is even more subservient as a soldier. Later when his opinions are changing, his father becomes filled with nationalistic pride at the conquest of the neighbouring country. In general, *Ein Kind unserer Zeit* is less ambitious than *Jugend ohne Gott,* but together they show that Horváth is to be taken seriously as a novelist. Before his untimely death another novel was planned: *Adieu Europa* (*Farewell Europe*), the title indicating his own intention to go to America. This frenzy of activity is explicable in the light of what he wrote to a fellow writer Franz Theodor Csokor at this time:

> The main thing, my dear good friend, is: work! And again: work! And once more: work! Our life is work—without it we have no life any more. It does not matter whether we experience the victory of our work, or even whether it is noticed. It does not matter a jot, as long as our work is dedicated to truth and justice.

At the beginning of this survey a number of points were raised, which have not all been fully dealt with. On the question of Horváth's social and political attitudes, it is clear that a change took place in the 1930s, left-wing sympathies giving way to more Christian ones, although the previous social concern does not disappear. A change of style away from that of the folk-plays, possibly an inevitable result of emigration, accompanies this. The result is that the combination of factors that characterizes the folk-plays is lost and with it their penetrative power as a precise analysis of a social class in a specific social situation. The generally held view that the later plays are of less merit is correct.

A final point that requires an explanation is Horváth's sudden rediscovery in the 1960s. One simple reason might be that the discontinuity in German literature brought about by the Nazi era would inevitably lead to some authors being temporarily forgotten. This is not, however, a satisfactory explanation of the phenomenon. The negative reaction to the rare productions of Horváth's work in Germany in the 50s reflects that time, when the main emphasis was on the material rebuilding of the country and anything that smacked of the unhappy days of the depression and the Third Reich was shunned. By the middle 60s this had changed. A new generation of West German writers like Martin Walser and Siegfried Lenz had already written plays about the Third Reich; their dramatic techniques owed much to the influence of Brecht. People were now willing to confront the past again and to accept the kind

of critical stance evident in most of Horváth's plays. In the late 60s there followed a spate of regional plays, in which the regions were not glorified as examples of an uncorrupted world but whose major aim was critical realism. Since Bavaria is the part of Germany that has the most clearly defined regional culture, it is not surprising that many of these plays were set there. One of the plays in Martin Sperr's Bavarian Trilogy, *Jagdszenen aus Niederbayern* (Hunting Scenes from Lower Bavaria), deals with discrimination against homosexuals. With his Bavarian connections, Horváth was a forerunner of this development, as was his contemporary Marieluise Fleisser, another Bavarian whose plays were revived at much the same time as Horváth's. An era whose art was marked by a realistic and critical portrayal of social and political questions naturally took a great interest in Horváth's work.

Now, almost ten years after the height of this Horváth revival, it is necessary to consider what the lasting merit of his work is and what general interest it has, especially to the nonspecialist in German literature. The folk-plays and novels at least retain their interest as a picture of the age they were written in. At the same time, they are more than historical documents. It is the portrayal of character, particularly in the folk-plays, that gives Horváth's works their significance. A salient feature of many of his characters is their total misunderstanding of their situation; they conceal or seek to conceal this from themselves in many ways but most especially through their language. These attempts to escape the truth often provide the comic elements in Horváth's work. Yet they also reveal the reality of the characters' position, their helplessness in a world where they are the victims of events beyond their control. Because of this, Horváth's work is often marked by a tension between comic and serious elements which gives it its particular power. The contrast between appearance and reality is the source of this tension; it would be a brave or foolish person who would say that the gap between many people's conception of themselves and their real situation was not equally wide today. (pp. 122-37)

> *Stuart Parkes, "Ödön von Horváth," in* Weimar Germany: Writers and Politics, *edited by A. F. Bance, Scottish Academic Press, 1982, pp. 121-37.*

David Midgley   (essay date 1983)

[In the following essay, Midgley explores Horváth's strategies for audience enticement.]

At the end of his early comedy *Rund um den Kongress* Horváth brings a supposed member of the audience onto the stage to protest indignantly that what had been advertised as a 'Posse in fünf Bildern' is turning out to have a tragic ending. This device in itself is not particularly striking in a theatrical tradition which, by the year 1929 when the play was written, had learned to accommodate such manifestations of 'open theatre' as the Masked Man in Wedekind's *Frühlings Erwachen,* the deliberate affront to theatrical illusion at the end of Brecht's *Trommeln in der Nacht,* or indeed the more exactly contemporary arrival of the King's Messenger to contrive a happy ending in the

Dreigroschenoper. An unsympathetic reader of Horváth might even conclude that his particular fusion of theatrical spectacle and ostensible reality merely represents an attempt to overcome tensions in the work which the author could not otherwise resolve. The subject of **Rund um den Kongress** is prostitution, or more specifically some less than determined attempts on behalf of the League of Nations to inquire into the international traffic in saleable young ladies; and while the most obvious satirical edge of the play is directed against the (bourgeois) pretensions of such an international commission, the figure of the (Marxist) journalist Schminke, who is used to expose the fatuousness of the exercise, does not escape ridicule either. In the last 'Bild' especially, Schminke's mechanical insistence on an inexorable social logic—which demands that the story end with the sale of the nameless 'Fräulein' to South America—is defied by the simple humane profession of another character, Ferdinand, that he is ready to re-marry her, renounce his material ambitions, and settle down to a modest existence as the proprietor of a tobacco shop. It might appear, then, that the intrusion of the 'member of the public' is no more than a convenient ploy to cut through the tangled ideological arguments about the nature of prostitution, as well as the sense of indecision which pervades the play as to whether the subject ought to be treated seriously or flippantly.

In the context of Horváth's collected works, however, this appearance of the 'Vertreter des Publikums' takes on the significance of an early indication of the author's concern with audience expectations. The protest on behalf of the audience is raised at the point where Ferdinand's humane solution has met with the combined resistance of the Marxist analyst (who sees it as a falsification of 'wirkliche Verhältnisse'), the General Secretary of the Commission (who sees the 'problem' he is investigating threatening to disappear), the pimp (whose vested interest is self-explanatory) and the Fräulein herself, who simply announces that there can be no going back. The conventional expectation of the man who has paid his money to see a five-act farce is precisely that the Fräulein should finally marry her Ferdinand and live happily ever after. The characters enact this wishful ending, but grudgingly, and it is on a feeble insult to the real audience's intelligence—a resounding boozy belch from the disappointed (female) rival for the Fräulein's affections—that the curtain falls. In this indecorous manner it becomes apparent that the kitschy demands of the popular imagination are as much under attack in this ending as are the stereotyped attitudes of major protagonists. The purpose of this essay is to examine the development of Horváth's theatrical technique beyond this crude affront to conventional expectations, his exploration of strategies which lure the audience more effectively into a recognition of the illusions which it has itself brought to the theatre.

In the course of an interview for Bavarian radio in 1932, occasioned by the award of the Kleist Prize the previous year for his more accomplished comedy *Italienische Nacht,* Horváth indicated his special interest in the audience's imagination as a factor in the theatrical process:

> Das Theater phantasiert für den Zuschauer, und gleichzeitig lässt es ihn auch die Produkte dieser

Phantasie erleben. [. . .] Es ist doch eine sonderbare Tatsache, dass sich Leute einen Platz kaufen und ins Theater gehen und sich schön anziehen und parfümieren, um dann auf der Bühne mehr oder minder ehrenrührigen Dingen zu lauschen oder zuzuschauen, wie einer oder auch zwei umgebracht werden,—und hernach das Theater verlassen und zwar in einer weihevollen Stimmung, ethisch erregt. Was geht da in dem einzelnen Zuschauer vor? Folgendes: seine scheinbare Antipathie gegen die kriminellen Geschehnisse auf der Bühne ist keine wahre Empörung, sondern eigentlich ein Mitmachen, ein Miterleben und, durch dieses Miterleben ausgelöst, Befriedigung asozialer Triebe. Der Zuschauer ist also gewissermassen über sich selbst empört. Man nennt diesen Zustand Erbauung.

The principles formulated here in the tone of casual conversation and with an ironic manipulation of platitudes ('weihevolle Stimmung', 'Erbauung') are elaborated more fully in Horváth's only extant attempt at a coherent statement of policy towards his own plays, the **'Gebrauchsanweisung'**; but the essential points remain consistently the same. Regardless of the specific aims of a work (whether these are primarily aesthetic, didactic or sheer entertainment), the unique potency of the darkened auditorium, in Horváth's view, is the opportunity to excite and gratify the subconscious impulses of individual audience members— and in this respect, only the cinema can exceed the potential of live theatre. But this also enables the playwright surreptitiously to confront the audience with the potential consequences of those impulses. The 'Demaskierung des Bewusstseins', which Horváth proclaims in the **'Gebrauchsanweisung'** and elsewhere to be his prime goal as a writer for the theatre, is directed at the audience itself as much as at the characters mercilessly represented on the stage.

It was Horváth's conscious policy, then, to encourage his audience to 'identify' with the actions of the characters in his plays, but with the purpose of presenting the brutal consequences of those actions the more forcefully. It will be found that certain audience expectations are frequently implied by Horváth's texts, but that these are subtly exploited to entice the audience into a system of carefully prepared pits of realisation—to adapt an image which Horváth himself uses in the **'Gebrauchsanweisung'**, when writing of his own most characteristic work:

> daher kommt es auch, dass Leute meine Stücke oft ekelhaft und abstossend finden, weil sie eben die Schandtaten nicht so miterleben können. Sie werden auf die Schandtaten gestossen—sie fallen ihnen auf und erleben sie nicht mit.

It will be apparent, too, that at the very time when Brecht is enunciating his seeming rejection of audience empathy as the essential premise for theatrical performance (the key element, surely, in his notion of a 'non-Aristotelian' theatre), Horváth is taking the possibly more radical step of turning precisely that capacity for empathy against the audience, with a view to stimulating it to greater self-awareness. This distinction on the theoretical plane should not necessarily be taken to imply a fundamental contrast in theatrical practice, however. On the one hand it is questionable whether Brecht ever really discounted empathy as an effective element in the theatrical experience (how he attempted to manipulate it or override it is another matter). On the other hand, Horváth's directions for the presentation of his own plays share not a few features which can readily be associated with Brechtian precepts. The 'Gebrauchsanweisung' makes several specific demands which are clearly aimed at a stylized and demonstrative mode of presentation: Horváth asks, for example, that the extras in his plays, such as the ice-cream salesman in the opening scenes of **Kasimir und Karoline,** should actually leave the stage at points where their presence might distract attention from the behaviour of the main characters; there should be no attempt to do more than suggest a setting by means of scenery, which should be eye-catching, but not naturalistic; and the dialogue of the main characters themselves, while written with a recognisable Southern German regional colouring, should be delivered, he requests, as 'Hochdeutsch' in order that the frequently banal content of what is said should appear the more remarkable. Horváth emphasizes the psychological aspect of what is being demonstrated in his dialogues in this way, what he calls the struggle between the conscious and the subconscious mind,—but he also makes it clear that the stylization he requires demonstrates, in addition, the representative quality in individual characters and the behaviour modification that these individuals are shown to undergo in interaction with others. When Willi Cronauer, in the Bavarian radio interview, applied the concept of 'epic theatre' to his plays, Horváth immediately concurred that his new form of Volksstück was 'mehr eine schildernde als eine dramatische'. It will be obvious from the discussion of individual plays which follows, that 'Zeigen' is, in practice, quite as much a key dramaturgical concept for Horváth as it is for Brecht.

Taking the plays in chronological order, the only one which Horváth expressly exempts from the policy outlined in the **'Gebrauchsanweisung'** is his earliest completed work, **Die Bergbahn** (an earlier version of the play, which is similar in all essential respects, bears the title **Revolte auf Côte 3018**). The reason for this exemption is obvious. Dealing with the conflicting interests of capital and labour, and with the equivocal position of the intelligentsia as represented by the engineer who has designed the funicular railway in question, the text patently calls for the generation of conventional naturalistic illusion, and a sense of tragic inevitability, culminating in acts of mutual violence between the engineer and the workforce. The only artifice used in the work which does go beyond the requirements of naturalistic imitation can only be construed as lending emphasis to the play's symbolic dimension as a representation of man's earthly destiny, and is of a kind with the famous death rattle at the end of Kaiser's *Von morgens bis mitternachts* which is supposed to sound like the words 'Ecce homo': in Horváth's play it is the intensifying stormwind—which has precipitated the discharge of human tensions among the mountain peaks, heralding as it does the onset of winter and the peremptory interruption of work on the project—that is said to howl the monitory expression 'Kreatur'. But in other works that were written in the years 1927-29, Horváth can already be seen to be developing a highly individual technique for presenting contemporary issues on the stage.

The disruption of theatrical illusion at the end of **Rund um den Kongress** was described above. This play also attempts to throw the ostensible reality of the action into relief with a sequence purporting to represent the anxiety dream of Luise Gift, the character whose resonant curtain line was also invoked earlier. The device of the dream allows for the explicit presentation of associations between characters which otherwise remain only latent in the action, notably the suggestion that the Secretary of the Congress could easily be implicated in the very trade he is appointed to investigate; it is a means of penetrating social façades—even if, like much of the action of the play, it ultimately performs rather a subservient function as vehicle for a series of somewhat obtrusive gags. The title rôle in **Sladek,** however, another play which exists in two broadly similar versions, clearly commands the author's interest both as a problematical personality and as a phenomenon of the times, and for that very reason seems to have called for the development of a more analytical mode of presentation. The closing scene of the original version, for example, uses a form of collage technique to depict Sladek's continued disorientation in the fast-moving world of the late 1920s into which he has been released from prison. It is largely composed of purposefully selected references to accomplishments in technology and the sporting field (understood in the wide sense of including an attempt to fly single-handed over the North Pole), and to the way that the Great War, which has been seen to have profoundly influenced Sladek's attitudes and behaviour earlier in the play, has now receded in the public mind onto the cinema screen and into the popular novel. Another simple device which Horváth uses here to demonstrate the unmoved and unmoving face which the apparatus of state presents towards the events of the play, is to ask for all the key representatives of officialdom—Secretary of State, judge, examining magistrate and policemen—to be played by the same actor. (The satirical element of the play, attenuated to the point of obfuscation in the revised version which reached the Berlin stage in October 1929, is at its clearest in scene VIII of the original which expressly pillories the notoriously reactionary 'Justiz der Wiedererstarkung' by depicting the trial of the journalist for having exposed the existence of the underground 'schwarze Armee' around which the action is centered.)

More indicative still of the direction in which Horváth is moving is the evidence in **Sladek** of studied attention to the structure of the dialogue—not only in the sections of overt political satire where the language of public discourse is marshalled to ironic effect, but also in the delineation of individual personalities. There is a marked tendency to self-characterisation in the dialogue, partly attributable to Sladek's own restless rationalizing of the pathological solipsism into which he has fallen, but extending particularly into the portrayal of Horst, another representative of nationalist youth who boasts of a similar cold-blooded amoralism, and into the rôles of Anna (the 'elder woman' for whose murder Sladek is held responsible), Knorke and the Fräulein at the Weinhaus. The last two instances may be explicable, again, in terms of the stark depiction of political attitudes and atmospheres in the work. But Anna's need to account for herself in express terms is determined much more by her personal relationship with Sladek which is characterised by an unstable fusion of erotic and maternal yearnings. The effect of removing her from her own living quarters (in the revised version of the play) is to make her self-revelation before the egregious figure of Knorke seem much less plausible; on home territory, however, both the self-characterisation and her political defiance appear as an integral part of a forlorn defence against the invasion of her privacy on the one hand, and a competing demand for Sladek's loyalty on the other. Both here and in her subsequent exchange with Sladek, the author isolates significant moments in the shifting relationships between characters by interrupting the dialogue with pregnant pauses denoted by the word 'Stille'. The effect of the first punctuation is to establish the antagonism of interests between Anna and Knorke; there follows her plaintive defence of her emotional needs, revealing a weakness which Knorke is able to exploit; this imbalance of forces is emphasized with a further pause, after which Anna's threat to betray the secret army may be seen to bear the full weight of her private desperation. At the end of the scene, the effect of the pauses is to highlight Sladek's emotional detachment, first by adding resonance to the overt self-contradiction which signals his yielding indifference ('Es ist nicht aus'/'Gut. Es ist aus'), secondly by isolating Anna's observation of his cold-blooded nature ('Du kannst nicht lieben, du kannst nur lieb sein'), and finally by emphasizing her resumption of the conversation with an attempt, which flies in the face of what has been established, to woo him once more sensually. The very stuff of contemporary politics is presented in these scenes, but refracted through the psychological complexities of individual characters in ways which both encourage the audience to sympathize with their personal position and at the same time hold their words and actions up for scrutiny.

Segmentation of the dialogue by pregnant pauses was to become, as it were, the hallmark of Horváth's most distinctive work for the theatre. If it is not altogether a conspicuous feature of *Italienische Nacht,* the play which brought him fame in 1931, that is because the dialogue there is in any case divided by the rhythmic cadences which often characterise successful comedy. An obvious example of the comic cadences of the piece is Martin's deflatory rejoinder—a line which is repeated in identical circumstances at the close, to give the play a sense of cynical completeness—to the Stadtrat's boast that under his chairmanship of the local association the Republic may sleep peacefully in its bed: 'Gute Nacht!'. No stage direction is needed at such a point to remind an actor to pause for laughter; while the obverse case is represented by the emphatic request in the script for 'Totenstille' which precedes the Major's bellowed 'Ruhe!' in the final scene. Elsewhere in the play, the word 'Stille' often denotes little more than a natural hiatus in the public-house banter which dominates the tone of the piece. Nevertheless, the technique is applied to conversations between members of the opposite sex especially, where thoughts are shown to run on in the minds of either party and to resurface abruptly after a pause. The effect is to suggest depth of

character in situations which are essentially manufactured out of stock comic material: the Stadtrat and his downtrodden wife who turns out to have more backbone than he does; the upsurge of sexual jealousy in Martin, the socialist activist who has sent his girlfriend to fraternise with the fascist enemy; the nonsequiturs by which the girlfriend's dissembling conversation with the fascist proceeds; and her rebuke of the hapless fellow-traveller, Karl, for his—unspoken—dirty thoughts. In each instance the comic impact of individual lines is enhanced by the glimpses of hidden motivations made more obvious by the structure of the dialogue.

It was this potential for engaging the audience's attention in the operation of subconscious forces that Horváth developed to the full in his best known Volksstücke. Perhaps the classic instance of it is the exposition of the relationship between Oskar and Marianne in *Geschichten aus dem Wiener Wald,* where the dialogue segments fix for us the image of the bridegroom's latent aggression and craving for affection, both of which he rationalises in a vengeful religiosity:

> OSKAR. Ich bin so glücklich, Mariann. Bald ist das Jahr der Trauer ganz vorbei, und morgen leg ich meinen Flor ab. Und am Sonntag ist offizielle Verlobung und Weihnachten Hochzeit.—Ein Bussi, Mariann, ein Vormittagsbussi—
>
> MARIANNE. (*Gibt ihm einen Kuss, fährt aber plötzlich zurück*) Au! Du sollst nicht immer beissen!
>
> OSKAR. Hab ich denn jetzt?
>
> MARIANNE. Weisst du denn das nicht?
>
> OSKAR. Also ich hätt jetzt geschworen—
>
> MARIANNE. Dass du mir immer weh tun musst. (*Stille*)
>
> OSKAR. Böse?
> (*Stille*)
> Na?
>
> MARIANNE. Manchmal glaub ich schon, dass du es dir herbeisehnst, dass ich ein böser Mensch sein soll—
>
> OSKAR. Marianne! Du weisst, dass ich ein religiöser Mensch bin und dass ich es ernst nehme mit den christlichen Grundsätzen!
>
> MARIANNE. Glaubst du vielleicht, ich glaub nicht an Gott? Ph!
>
> OSKAR. Ich wollte dich nicht beleidigen. Ich weiss, dass du mich verachtest. [. . .] Jetzt möcht ich in deinen Kopf hineinsehn können, ich möcht dir mal die Hirnschale herunter und nachkontrollieren, was du da drinnen denkst—

This exchange, which begins with an invocation of the most conventional patterns of human respect and affection imaginable (mourning, engagement, wedding), abruptly reveals to the audience the oppressive and violent impulses concealed, at a personal level, within those conventions. The double pause which isolates Oskar's inquiry 'Böse?' acts, moreover, as a hinge between the conventional expectations within which he is operating and the sub-conscious perceptions of either character. His question, in context, is plainly aimed at Marianne's superficial displeasure at the overzealous kiss; her reply, however, interprets the word at an altogether more profound level of meaning and provides—unexpectedly, but cogently—a lead into the exposition of Oskar's fundamentally authoritarian personality and of Marianne's apprehension at being sacrificed to his emotional needs. The strategic placing of pauses to such effect is a prominent feature, too, of the section omitted from the above passage; but it can also be found to characterise the mutually mistrustful conversations between Alfred and Valerie in the same play, between Alfred and Marianne, and between Alfred and his mother in the very first scene, where the effect is to emphasize Alfred's evasiveness or the mother's seeing through it. And much the same principle is applied to the presentation of kaleidoscopically shifting sexual relationships in *Kasimir und Karoline,* where the fragmentation of the action into over a hundred short scenes makes for the impression of a form of theatrical vivisection.

A central element in either play is a tendency to romantic escapism on the part of the heroine. Karoline's fantasies of flying, the play having begun with the spectacular appearance of the Zeppelin above the Oktoberfest fairground, will be contrasted with an image of broken wings at the end of the evening, while Marianne rebels against the prospect of an arranged marriage, fashioning a dream image of the footloose Alfred, only to sink within a year into a squalid routine which echoes precisely the life she had led under her authoritarian father. But in both cases, Horváth seeks to enhance the audience's own susceptibility to the kind of self-delusion that is to be unmasked, by evoking an atmosphere that has given rise to one sort of popular legend or another. *Geschichten aus dem Wiener Wald* begins with the Strauss waltz of that name wafting above a set which depicts an idyllic scene commemorated in another popular melody, 'Draussen in der Wachau'. The idyll is immediately disturbed—although we see only indistinct ripples of human mischief at first—by the more or less overt suspicion with which the characters regard each other. A fuller contrast with the banal reality of their lives is effected with the first scene change, which takes us to a row of suburban shops in Vienna VIII, with the title waltz transposed to a neglected piano played as if by an ungifted schoolgirl. Despite this early deflation of audience expectations, musical associations can nevertheless be used again later to evoke unrealistic longings, notably by having an aria from Puccini's *La Bohème* played on a portable gramophone at the engagement party near the banks of an indubitably blue and allegedly velvety (!) Danube, in this case to reinforce the expectation that Marianne will cling to her fanciful image of Alfred. Whether or not any given audience member naively succumbs to the mood suggested by the music, or merely recognizes the mechanics of the device being employed, Horváth's use of popular song serves to indicate an affinity and a tension between the situation of the distraught individual on stage and the collective emotional experience—or folk memory—of the public at large. These examples from *Geschichten* have their counterparts in *Kasimir und Karoline* in familiar jingles of the twenties which reinforce the fair-

ground illusions of the Oktoberfest setting: 'Glow, little Glowworm', the 'Parade of the Tin Soldiers', and 'The Last Rose of Summer'. More pointedly still, we have a raucous chorus of 'Und dennoch hab' ich harter Mann/Die Liebe schon gespürt',—and the waltz 'Bist Du's, Lachendes Glück', which accompanies the emergence of the evening's casualties from the first-aid tent. Horváth's peculiar talent for revealing the potential aggression harboured by conventional delusions becomes apparent in this way also.

In both plays, too, the disillusionment of the audience is carried relentlessly through to the final curtain. The published sketches, drafts and variants for either play are instructive in this regard, showing how the author deliberately worked at forestalling the resolution of conflicts which he appears to have envisaged originally. The early drafts of *Geschichten* show the characters to be generally remarkably articulate about their own problems by comparison with the finished play, and this articulacy extends into a dénouement characterised by conscious renunciation and cordial forgiveness. Such hopeful expectations are the reverse of what is shown in this play as normally performed, where Alfred's unswallowed pride and economic self-interest are all too apparent as he stylizes his return to Valerie as a 'Gang nach Canossa'; where Valerie's pleading with the Zauberkönig owes its success to his fear of an imminent heart-attack and to a large concession to his stereotyped image of Marianne as a 'dummes Weiberl'; and where Oskar is able to continue in his characteristic vein of ominous self-righteous platitudes once the death of Marianne's child has removed the only obstacle he sees to the marriage: 'Ich habe dir mal gesagt, Mariann, due wirst meiner Liebe nicht entgehn.' These closing scenes retain the power to appal even a latter-day audience, surely, because they so patently subvert the traditional expectation of a comic—or Volksstück—dénouement: the pairs are indeed reunited, but ironically the only vestige of a true reconciliation through mutual comprehension is to be found in a display of chummy bonhomie between the former rivals, Oskar and Alfred, who are able to confirm each other in the sense of having been wronged. In a similar way, Horváth can be shown to have rejected and undermined the expectation of a reconciliation between Kasimir and Karoline, leaving us instead, at the end of their story, with an apparently emotionless realignment of detached partners.

In a sense, this outcome of *Kasimir und Karoline* appears simply as the fulfilment of what Kasimir has gloomily predicted from the very beginning. His first substantial speeches, uttered between self-absorbed assaults on the try-your-strength machine, concern the intractability of his socioeconomic circumstances and the inevitability that Karoline will leave him now that he has lost his job—sentiments which are even reinforced immediately by Schürzinger, the rival who then appears on the scene. Dramatic tension is nevertheless sustained, and with it a kind of conventional hope in the audience, by Karoline's initially strong insistence that a 'wertvolles Weib' will do the decent thing and stand by her man. The process by which that hope is gradually undermined on this occasion is embodied in Kasimir's recurring attempts to reassert his macho self-esteem, attempts which invariably reveal his jealousy and sense of insecurity, and degenerate into a sarcasm which reinforces that very estrangement he professes to fear:

> KASIMIR. Wer ist denn das, mit dem du dort sprichst?
>
> KAROLINE. Ein Bekannter von mir.
>
> KASIMIR. Seit wann denn?
>
> KAROLINE. Schon seit lang. Wir haben uns gerade ausnahmsweise getroffen. Glaubst du mir denn das nicht?
>
> KASIMIR. Warum soll ich dir das nicht glauben? (*Stille*)
>
> KAROLINE. Was willst du? (*Stille*)
>
> KASIMIR. Wie hast du das zuvor gemeint, dass wir zwei zu schwer füreinander sind? (*Karoline schweigt boshaft*) Soll das eventuell heissen, dass wir zwei eventuell nicht zueinander passen?
>
> KAROLINE. Eventuell.
>
> KASIMIR. Also das soll dann eventuell heissen, dass wir uns eventuell trennen sollen—und dass du mit solchen Gedanken spielst?
>
> KAROLINE. So frag mich doch jetzt nicht!
>
> KASIMIR. Und warum nicht, wenn man fragen darf?

In the case of **Kasimir und Karoline,** the particular convention which is to be affronted by the conclusion is represented by the Mailied which Erna sings—probably in thin tones and a halting manner—at the final curtain. The melancholy appropriateness of the song, despite the play's October setting, lies in the fact that it contrasts the annual regeneration of the natural world with the single and irretrievable springtime of humankind; it acquires a sardonic quality from the context in which it is placed, as commentary on the desolate image presented in the play of sexual relationships seemingly condemned to a half-life of permanent decay.

Either play, then, can be interpreted as a sustained (and deliberately 'retarded') attempt to disabuse the audience of the artificial hopes it has previously been encouraged to invest in the romantic yearnings of the heroine in particular. But there is another feature emerging from a comparison of these texts with earlier draft versions of them, which still more clearly represents a conscious strategy of audience enticement, and that is that much material formerly made explicit in dialogue form has been retracted into passing allusion or latent motive in the script for performance. In part this may simply reflect the author's growing sense of stagecraft. For instance, the political violence of the times continued to fascinate Horváth, and he considered making the brawl in **Kasimir und Karoline** into the product of overt political animosities—the characters of Rauch and Speer, who represent the professional and managerial classes in the play, are derived from a group of nationalistic students and their fathers, who bore such

'speaking names' as Stunk and Krach. In the finished play this material is almost entirely eliminated from the concentrated presentation of sexual rivalries in the broad context of a major crisis of capitalism; nor is the brawl actually enacted, so that from a purely theatrical point of view a heightened comic impact is given to the first-aid man's long-suffering reconstruction of the incident, in which characters familiar to the audience in somewhat more dignified circumstances are characterised in belittling and dismissive terms. A comparable process in the evolution of **Geschichten aus dem Wiener Wald** is the elimination of the Marxist intellectual Schminke—no isolated case of Horváth's resorting to the same character for different projects—who, in early sketches, had been an obvious vehicle for overt analysis of the circumstances in which the heroine found herself. The final version adopts instead that policy which Horváth stresses in his **'Gebrauchsanweisung',** and which seeks to capture the audience's minds by stealth, preparing pits of realisation into which they may fall. The heroine's quest for economic independence, which had previously been expounded in terms of an abstract principle to be actively pursued, is thus shown to be prompted in large part by Alfred's emphatically self-interested desire to shake off responsibility for her. Nor is Marianne allowed to remain sufficiently self-aware to conceptualise her sense of oppression when appealing to her fiancé not to tyrannise her, nor even to call him a sadist to his face; it is characteristic of the finished text, on the contrary, that the only occasion on which the word 'Sadist' occurs is when Oskar is protesting that he is not one, and that the plea against tyranny has been requisitioned to make the figure of Alfred (whose deceit of Valerie has been but recently exposed) appear the more callow and disingenuous.

The result of these changes to the original drafts is that the audience is encouraged to be more active in the pursuit of insights reflected in the script, rather than being forcibly confronted with those insights. In order to convey that sense of a struggle between vapid consciousness and volatile subconscious which Horváth invokes in the **'Gebrauchsanweisung',** the utterances of characters are made to contrast palpably with what has been shown by their action to be the true state of affairs. The assertion of male domination which Oskar had been allowed to speculate on himself in draft, reappears in the form of advice from the Zauberkönig which contrasts with his evident dependence on his daughter; at the engagement party Oskar is himself admired as a father-figure, although his butcher's gaze has been shown to terrify the girl Ida; and the grandmother's violent threats—and actions—are a telling pointer to her own anxieties in the face of death. Moreover, the dialogue has been stripped of the upper middle class courtesies in which it had initially been couched—the father had at one stage been conceived not as a down-at-heel Zauberkönig, but a Hofrat—and the characters appear instead as people groping for adequate terms to express what they perceive and feel, or grasping at clichés which conceal it. Horváth's own justification for this concentration on the petty bourgeoisie in his plays generally, took roughly the form of arguing that this social category—as the very conceptual imprecision of the term 'Kleinbürger' serves to confirm—most obviously reflected the dynamic social pressures of his day. But dramaturgical considerations, too, seem to have demanded a social setting which would allow for a more effective presentation of the hollowness of conventional sentiments and aspirations. Both Oskar and Alfred (mis)appropriate gilded phrases with which to conceal their embarrassment over past events—and when the artificiality of their words is challenged by Marianne, Oskar retrieves his composure by promptly disowning his little learning, and the very sentiment, altogether:

> ALFRED. Nur wer sich wandelt, bleibt mit mir verwandt.
>
> OSKAR. (*Zu Marianne*)
> Denn so lang du dies nicht hast,
> Dieses 'Stirb und Werde!'
> Bist du noch [sic] ein trüber Gast
> Auf der dunklen Erde!
>
> MARIANNE. (*Grinst*) Gott, seid ihr gebildet—
>
> OSKAR. Das sind doch nur Kalendersprüch!

This artificiality of borrowed sentiments is still more obvious in the more clearly proletarian setting of *Kasimir und Karoline.* One effect of suppressing the depiction of Karoline's family background, explicit in the early drafts, is to make even her self-vindication seem to take place in the form of quotations: 'weil ich keinen *Beamten genommen* hab und nicht *von dir gelassen* hab und immer *deine Partei ergriffen* hab?!' (My emphasis.) The same quality adheres to her mechanical repetition of the advertised flight plan of the Zeppelin, or more distressingly to her haughty and hyper-literate announcement to Kasimir mid-way through the disintegration of their liaison: 'Mein Herz und mein Hirn waren ja umnebelt, weil ich dir hörig war!' Her male counterpart is perhaps more aggressively terse, but no less arbitrary when seizing upon phrases to dramatize his self-pity or his self-satisfaction: 'Und jetzt lass ich dich stehn' 'Du verkennst deine Lage' 'Träume sind Schäume'. Erna, finally, who accepts Kasimir's automatic embrace at the end of the play after watching her brutal previous partner be led away by the police, rebuffs Karoline with the following biblical travesty: 'Sie weiss ja nicht, was sie tut'. Either play provides a rich seam for exploring what Horváth calls the dissolution of authentic dialect speech by 'Bildungsjargon', as has been adequately demonstrated elsewhere. What is especially noteworthy in the context of this essay, is that Horváth's deliberate retraction of *explicit* analysis from the surface of his text allows greater scope for the free play of associations in the audience's mind, encouraged by what remains *implicit* in the dialogue.

The **'Gebrauchsanweisung'** may be seen in large part as a response by the author to what he felt to be errors of direction in the productions of *Geschichten aus dem Wiener Wald* and *Kasimir und Karoline* which were mounted in Berlin in the course of 1932. It is conceivable, therefore, that the more forcefully demonstrative character of the text for his next play, *Glaube Liebe Hoffnung,* which was prevented from being staged in 1933 by political circumstances, owes something to Horváth's determination to leave less to chance or the misguided instincts of theatrical managers. The published drafts for *Glaube Liebe Hoffnung* show that much of the material was originally very close in conception to that of the previous two plays. The heroine-victim even appears under the name Karoline at first, and familiar motifs include the sensational appearance of the Zeppelin overhead and a calculated seduction in a motor car, while the figure also shares with the Marianne of *Geschichten aus dem Wiener Wald* the prospect of being drawn into the employ of a shady gentleman 'gewissermassen aus der Vergnügungsbranche'. Familiar song melodies are used, again, in these early drafts to instil conventional expectations in the audience, and it seems likely that the eventual name of the heroine was decided by one of these: 'Wenn die Elisabeth nicht so schöne Beine hätt'. In the final version, only the Chopin funeral march remains as an ostinato accompaniment, together with a passing allusion to *Aida* which might serve to suggest a contrast between the loyalty of Verdi's Radames and the betrayal which Elisabeth experiences. Indeed, it is in the author's departures from what had become his established routine that the peculiar flavour of this lugubrious little 'Totentanz in fünf Bildern' becomes identifiable.

Whole sequences of expansive characterisation, which survive in seemingly complete draft form, were exercised in the interests of a demonstrative and even clinical precision. The image of Elisabeth's desperation is fixed from the very beginning of the finished play, in her concentrated exchanges with the policeman and the Präparator. The breaks in the dialogue once more emphasize the latent structure in what are only superficially acts of communication. They underscore Elisabeth's satisfaction at having located the place 'wo man halt die Leichen zersägt'; also her impassibility towards the gruesome contents of the Anatomical Institute; and more intricately, they accentuate the precise nature of the transaction in which she is seeking to engage. It is a transaction which is only expressed succinctly—which can only be expressed succinctly if it is not to appear bizarre—at the onset of the third dialogue fragment in scene 4, with the Präparator's words: 'Seine eigene Leiche verkaufen'. The atmosphere of drained emotion established in these opening scenes is maintained subtly in what follows. The second 'Bild', for example, opens with a visual echo of the autopsies previously referred to: here it is tailor's dummies which stand 'in Reih und Glied'. Elisabeth's periodic compulsive laugh also serves in later scenes to remind us of her accumulated dehumanized encounters. But the enormity of her situation has been forcefully presented already in the first 'Bild' by showing her explaining herself to men inured to the ultimate fate of others, the functionaries of an Anatomical Institute which is as much hidebound by the conventional demands of bureaucratic routine as any of the other state institutions Elisabeth is going to have to deal with in the course of the play.

Elisabeth's story was conceived, as the foreword to the play explains, in terms of the struggle of the individual against society, or more specifically against the 'kleine Paragraphen' in which social pressures are codified. The focussing of attention on that struggle led to the omission of material which could have elucidated at length the behaviour of characters who contribute further to Elisabeth's demoralisation. The reversal of the Präparator's attitude from the generosity of the opening to the disillusioned petulance of the second 'Bild' is allowed to rest without elaboration on an apparent misunderstanding, and is subordinated to a demonstrative presentation of the impact of the incident on Elisabeth. It is the revelation that she is 'vorbestraft' that brings the concentrated wrath of collective conventionality upon her; but Horváth makes it no less apparent by what psychological mechanisms such wrath has accumulated. The Präparator, in addition to his probable sexual disappointment, believes Elisabeth to have been claiming for her father a higher social status than is in fact the case. Her employer in this second 'Bild', Irene Prantl, obsequiously colludes in protecting the dignity of the Frau Amtsgerichtsrat (who would have it known that she is only selling underwear 'von wegen persönlicher Zerstreuung und so') while rebuking Elisabeth for coming out with precisely the same excuse which she herself used to extol the performance of her more prestigious apprentice: 'die Leut schlagen einem die Tür vor der Nase zu!' As for the Frau Amtsgerichtsrat herself, who attributes her success as a saleswoman directly to her social connections, she dependably rehearses the courtroom logic she has acquired from her husband:

> ELISABETH. (*Fährt plötzlich los*) Ich bin doch keine Betrügerin!
>
> FRAU AMTSGERICHTSRAT. Darauf kommt es auch nicht an, Fräulein! Sondern ob der Tatbestand des Betruges erfüllt ist, darauf kommt es an!

The constellation of characters, then, appears calculated to illustrate that mesh of disappointed expectations, hierarchical assumptions and confirmed prejudices in which Elisabeth is caught. Her protestation of personal integrity is quite unavailing: in an attempt to avoid being jailed for failure to pay a fine, she has used money willingly given her by the Präparator,—and for this she will be jailed. The relationships established here are so vividly characterised by the social mechanisms which determine them, that when the Frau Amtsgerichtsrat is subsequently allowed a display of personal sympathy towards Elisabeth, this too appears in the suspect light of that 'human nature' which she seeks to defend in the bureaucracy of which her husband is a representative.

The rôle of Elisabeth is itself imbued with a submissive awareness of the representative nature of her case, even if the character herself is once more able to articulate the problems which confront her only in the most lapidary terms: 'weil halt die Menschen keine Menschen sind'. And it is with measured theatricality that the play concludes on a tableau which assembles around Elisabeth, who has been 'saved' from drowning herself, the men who have figured most prominently in her misfortune—men whose socially conditioned responses have denied her that economic independence which alone might have sustained the hope that is emphasized by the unconventional word order of the play's title. The element of stylization in the work, it should be made clear, does not lend itself directly to the presentation of social circumstances as changeable; on the contrary, Elisabeth's dying words contribute to the sense of a closing ellipse of inescapable earthly suffering by echoing her opening question to the Präparator, while

Alfons, the man who abandoned her, is left to revive the self-pity with which he had earlier responded to the news of her 'past'. What Horváth achieves in this play is rather a sense of the implication of upright, honest citizens in the machinery which relentlessly destroys a hapless, if not entirely innocent fellow human being. *Glaube Leibe Hoffnung* must be numbered among Horváth's most striking creations; the crystallization of the play around an unrelentingly laconic conception of Elisabeth's plight, however, leads to a much more direct and consistently demonstrative mode of presentation than we have found to be characteristic of his previous work.

It is difficult to imagine how Horváth might have wished to refocus his talents after the extreme economy of *Glaube Liebe Hoffnung,* but there is in any case a perfunctory quality about some of his output in the years immediately following 1933, something which led the author himself subsequently to speak of having prostituted his talents, and which is no doubt partly attributable to the fact that political circumstances had made Berlin inaccessible and Vienna somewhat unreceptive to his more serious works. He attempted an inventive fusion of the tragic and the comic-grotesque based on the legend of the *Inconnue de la Seine,* and when this was not accepted for performance he incorporated the material into a comedy of illusions and deceits, *Mit dem Kopf durch die Wand* (1935). Both here and in the burlesque 'Märchen' *Himmelwärts* (1934), Horváth's art acquires a distinctly introverted character by dwelling on the world of show business and theatrical careers. And in *Hin und Her* (1934) he had somewhat lamely fashioned a comedy of errors out of that topos of exile, the stateless person. Even here his flair for misplaced idioms gives rise to some engaging play on Austro-Hungarian officialese—'Grenzorgan', 'zuständig', 'ausgeschlossen'—or other self-conscious juxtapositions reminiscent of Nestroy: 'Geschmuggelt wird dann, dass die Fetzen fliegen', 'bis die noch einmal in andere Umständ kommt vor lauter Liebe'. Officialdom finds a natural home in the hell of *Himmelwärts,* while Horváth's characteristic undermining of kitschy expectations is very much in evidence in the vernacular speech and down-to-earth manner of a Saint Peter who watches at the gate of a heaven festooned with violins. Indeed, it is in the manipulation of conventional audience expectations once again, and more especially in the reworking of established legend, that Horváth reasserts his individuality as a playwright in the few years before his accidental death in 1938.

In 1936 he completed a Don Juan play which poignantly treats the case of a mythical figure seeking to escape from his own stereotype but being reconfirmed in it by the various women with whom he comes into contact. By setting his play *Don Juan kommt aus dem Krieg* in the period, roughly, 1918-24 Horváth provides concrete historical pretexts for the title figure's would-be conversion, the potential overthrow of patriarchal assumptions in revolutionary circumstances, and the eventual 'normalisation' of social relations which provides the background for his denunciation, resignation and death. *Figaro lässt sich scheiden,* which was also completed in 1936, depends for its effect much more closely on a previous acquaintance with the characters of its Mozartian model. Horváth pictures the Count and Countess Almaviva on the run from the French Revolution with Figaro and Susanne in attendance, while Cherubino, for example, emerges as the cagey proprietor of an emigré nightclub. This, too, is a re-interpretation which succeeds in illuminating certain aspects of the original by the light of historical hindsight: Figaro progresses through a highly bourgeoisified emancipation from his master—which is precisely what alienates Susanne—before returning as an unabashed opportunist to administer the state Kindergarten which has been set up in the palace in his absence, ousting Pedrillo who has emerged as a doctrinaire but ham-fisted Jacobin. Two lighter-weight pieces which followed in 1937 similarly make much play on popular preconceptions of the Middle Ages and classical antiquity respectively: *Ein Dorf ohne Männer* and *Pompeji* (revised version of *Ein Sklavenball*). And even in the psychological drama *Der Jüngste Tag* (1935-36), which returns to the provincial tone of the earlier Volksstücke, we find Horváth exercising his feel for the way that contemporary human actions are readily encompassed by traditional (religious) concepts and superstitions: a 'God of judgement', the 'light of day', or more fundamental to the mood of the play, 'das grosse Unbekannte'.

Having lost the audiences and the sense of a specific social context which had enabled him to establish himself in Berlin in the closing years of the Weimar Republic, Horváth clearly turned to a more internationally familiar body of cultural traditions, and to more 'universal' themes after 1933. It is nevertheless possible to discern a coherence in his work as a whole which allows it to stand as a model for live theatre alongside, rather than in opposition to that of Brecht. By his evocation of familiar settings, whether idyllic or euphoric, Horváth entices his audience into a mood of relaxed anticipation; by withdrawing explicit analysis from the surface of his text he gives full rein to the audience's imaginative involvement in the action it witnesses; and by the calculated structure of his dialogues he reveals the latent capacity for human aggression and social oppression lurking behind conventional behaviour. Among his other plays, *Glaube Liebe Hoffnung* appears exceptional only in the degree of demonstrative force with which these principles are put into practice. But whether we think primarily of the subverted romanticism of *Geschichten aus dem Wiener Wald* and *Kasimir und Karoline,* or rather of the inventive treatment of traditional literary material in some of the later plays, Horváth may be seen to display a peculiar sensitivity to both the intellectual and the emotional demands which twentieth-century audiences bring to the theatre. The type of theatrical experience which he offers is both dynamic and multifaceted, and derives its energies from the tensions in the audience's perceptions between inherited conceptual patterns and contemporary realities, between conventional stereotypes and the living present. (pp. 125-41)

David Midgley, "Ödön von Horváth: The Strategies of Audience Enticement," in Oxford German Studies, Vol. 14, August, 1983, pp. 125-42.

Alan Bance   (essay date 1985)

[*Bance is an English educator and critic. In the essay below, he examines the relationship between sex and politics in Horváth's dramas.*]

My main concern here is with Horváth as author of the now famous 'Volksstücke' written around the beginning of the 1930s. I shall attempt to point out some of the ways in which the politics of sex in Horváth reflects the politics of the period in general, an aspect of his work which has received little critical attention. My intention is to show that there are parallels between the two spheres, and to indicate some lines of thought which might be productive. In the space available, it is not possible to arrive at any definitive conclusions, but only to suggest some connexions, possibly even a cause-and-effect nexus, relating affairs between men and women to the affairs of state.

The 'Volksstücke' represent a fund of wisdom about the social and political climate of the pre-Nazi years; yet we learn about political reality, as Horváth perceives it, not through the documentary recording of events but through a range of subtle linguistic conflicts and confrontations, the often unconscious projection of one ego asserting itself against another. Very often the egos concerned are a male and a female one respectively, so that politics proper—inevitably a central preoccupation of ordinary Germans at the fateful turn of the decade—is refracted in and through sexual politics: in that sense alone it is difficult to disentangle the two. Furthermore, this is a period in which enlightened Germans are quite conversant with the discussion about a relationship between sexual and political motivation: numerous references by Horváth's characters reflect that awareness, even if sometimes in a distorted form. The playwright's perceptions often appear to correspond to other contemporary analyses of the role of sexuality in relation to mass movements, political ones included.

The 'Volksstücke' are imbued with a political spirit by their very nature and context, and this is reflected in their style and form: most of what is expressed in them can in a wider sense be construed as political. It is because Horváth is dealing with extraordinary times that even what he might see merely as realism inevitably acquires with hindsight a satirical or parodistic note (though his attitude to these modes was mostly negative), as for example in the grotesque presentation, in *Geschichten aus dem Wiener Wald,* of the operetta-style setting of the bucolic Wachau, the drunken and sentimental self-celebration of the Viennese at the 'Heurige', or the bizarre events by the Danube, where the cast attempts to live up to the legend of Golden Vienna, while the audience is carried along with them by the seductive power of Johann Strauss waltzes. In *Kasimir und Karoline,* Karoline and her latest pick-up, Schürzinger, play at courtship at the 'Oktoberfest' freakshow to the sound of the Barcarole from the *Tales of Hoffmann* played by Juanita the Gorilla-Girl on a worn-out piano. And as with the piano in this travesty of romanticism, so with the whole culture, even here at its roots, where one would look for more vigour. There is commonly a sensation of powerlessness against impersonal and overwhelming economic forces. In the opening scene of *Kasimir und Karoline* a national prestige-project, the Zeppelin, mocks by its passage overhead Kasimir's newfound experience of the unemployment scrapheap. Horváth's tone captures a world-weary, cynical view of power relationships, a moral and intellectual defeatism which in itself makes the advance of the Nazis' cult of 'Kraft', dynamism and war seem inevitable. A veneer of frivolity covers an underlying violence close to eruption: so the fairground becomes a battleground in *Kasimir und Karoline.* A façade of 'normality' can be deeply disturbing, as in *Geschichten aus dem Wiener Wald,* where the apparently changeless respectability of the 'stille Straße' in Vienna 8 is made sinister by the prominence of the butcher's shop and much stage-business with knives and cleavers.

Horváth is particularly interested in the concept of 'Uneigentlichkeit des Bewußtseins' or alienated thinking, revealed dramatically by an 'unmasking of consciousness' which occurs when there is an inherent or contextually obvious discrepancy between the actual content of the assumptions that lie behind what is being said, and what Horváth's characters, with their inadequate language, think they are trying publicly to convey. Behind the struggle either to express or conceal feelings lies the incapacity of the characters' thought-processes to form an adequate model of the reality with which they are attempting to come to terms. The effects of this 'Demaskierung des Bewußtseins' are very similar to what G. W. Pabst achieves in his contemporary film *Die Büchse der Pandora,* except that Horváth does through language what Pabst does with images: nothing is fixed, nothing has an essence. The split between 'Bewußtsein' and 'Unterbewußtsein' is often manifested in 'Bildungsjargon' or 'Hochdeutsch' forms that overlay an obsolete and dispossessed dialect. The conflict between the conscious and unconscious mind is also apparent, and takes on its most crass form, in the discrepancy between the high-sounding talk and the abominable behaviour of Horváth's characters, such as the smug and sadistic 'Vereinsmeier', the Social Democrat Stadtrat Ammetsberger in *Italienische Nacht,* who mouths humanitarian slogans and tortures his wife. (That it is a woman who is the victim of his 'Uneigentlichkeit' typifies the manner in which Horváth frequently carries out his 'Demaskierung', and points towards the links between politics and sexual politics which I shall go on to explore.)

Almost all examples of 'Demaskierung' have some political implications—which would be purely depressing if the effect were not so richly comic—for the shape of things to come. The self-delusion of the majority Socialists in *Italienische Nacht* is one source of examples of mental kitsch and dispossession of language. Horváth is acute enough to perceive that there is only a little to choose (and much in common) between them and the Fascists' 'uneigentlich' style of reasoning, which slides from nebulous targets like 'Materialismus' to a specific scapegoat, the Jews. In the later novel, *Ein Kind unserer Zeit,* it takes a personal catastrophe to force a young soldier to see through the transparent dual justification officially put forward to legitimize his country's blitzkrieg invasion of a 'Nachbarland': as well as representing a threat to the Fatherland, it is not viable, 'ein lebensunfähiges Gebilde' too weak to govern itself. To question the compatibility of these two irreconcil-

able assertions is to reject them immediately; but such contradictions are constantly *not* seen through. In the very title of his novel Horváth puts forward this failure of insight implicitly as a paradigm for much contemporary thinking. In *Geschichten aus dem Wiener Wald* the character known as the 'Zauberkönig' casually relays a newspaper item concerning the threat posed by the Czechs and 'the liberties they're taking again'. In fact, of course, the relative status of the new Czech state in size and power compared to its German neighbours makes this propaganda ridiculous, if nothing else does; but it is essential that passive Czechoslovakia be assigned an active role to justify others' aggressive intentions towards her. It is hardly coincidental that, only a few lines before, male-female relationships were presented in similar terms. Oskar the butcher, in whose hands his fiancée, Marianne, is a hapless victim, declares that 'der Mann ist ja nur der scheinbar aktive Teil und das Weib nur der scheinbar passive'. He maintains that men are naive and ripe for exploitation by women ('wir sind halt zu naiv'), and the Fascist in *Italienische Nacht* makes a similar point, by implication, about Germans in their dealings with other groups. Exploited by Jews, they are the naive 'male' in their relations with 'female' political opponents.

Such thinking is all part of the complex of alienation from any logical process of thought itself, and one can perceive a clear link with the psychology of Fascism as plotted by, for example, Horváth's contemporary Wilhelm Reich in his book *The Mass Psychology of Fascism,* first published in 1933. (Whatever lunatic-fringe notions became attached to Reich's name in later years, in the thirties he has some illuminating things to say about Fascism.) In this light, it is no accident that the political and the sexual-political are associated by Horváth. He puts forward almost pure 'Reichian' evidence for sexual disjunction arising out of social conditions, or, to reverse this relationship—because Horváth as a dramatist is not obliged to supply an exhaustive analysis of cause and effect—one could say the social conditions arising out of inadequate sexuality (an insight comparable with Reich's 'sexual-economic' complex). So, for example, the sadism of males towards females, like that of Oskar in *Geschichten aus dem Wiener Wald,* Merkl Franz in *Kasimir und Karoline,* Stadtrat Ammetsberger in *Italienische Nacht,* can be associated with the rise of Fascism as a cult of personality deriving from a fear of impotence, a 'homosexual' politics (according to Peter Nathan) arising out of female emancipation. The weak, whether it be the weaker race, country or sex, are labelled a threat, because a weak target is needed in order to be able to prove one's own undiminished strength. In addition, economic conditions degrade many males (e.g. Kasimir). They pass their degradation on to a weaker party, women, whom Kasimir at one point refers to as 'minderwertige Subjekte' (compare the psychological workings of anti-Semitism, *mutatis mutandis*). Women become the repository of all that men fear in themselves, by the same kind of 'uneigentlich' thought process that led the puritanical Nazi, Frick, to introduce a Reichstag bill in October 1930 demanding castration for homosexuality, 'this peculiarly Jewish pestilence'. Female 'weakness' in Horváth's plays is seen as provocation: the more willingly women comply with male wishes, the more savagely they are handled. But indirectly it is 'the feminine' in themselves that men are attacking, for the males in Horváth's plays are in fact passive, reactive beings, however dynamically they attempt to project themselves. A good example of this kind of false consciousness is the petty criminal Merkl Franz in *Kasimir und Karoline,* a pathetically impotent would-be 'Kraftmensch' who resembles a last, degenerate survivor of Schiller's band of 'Räuber'. Men's active energy is an illusion, served and epitomized, for example, by that 'Hautden-Lukas' in the fairground in *Kasimir und Karoline,* a vent for male aggressions: customers receive an 'Orden' for making the bell ring three times, a travesty of ambition and its 'rewards'. The aggressiveness and self-assertion of men is merely a commuting of their inner weakness and insecurity.

Following another productive line of comparison with contemporary psychopolitical interpretation, the Social Democrats in *Italienische Nacht* show clearly what Wilhelm Reich means when he talks of the tendency of 'Verbürgerlichung' to prepare the way for Fascism. Reich says that the political implications of these aspects of everyday living, such as the adoption by working-class people of evening dress, deserve much more attention. Horváth gives attention to precisely those aspects. Reich writes:

> When the Fascist . . . promised 'abolition of the proletariat' and was successful in such propaganda, his success, in ninety out of a hundred cases, was due not to his economic platform but to the 'evening dress'.

Horváth's language is evening dress in verbal form, the borrowed garb of the dispossessed. The Italian Evening itself is a model illustration of the undermining of the proletarian movement, and the role of women within it, by a kitsch version of bourgeois manners. Young Martin and his followers—the equivalent of later 'Jusos', or the Militant Tendency—are right to condemn it. (But on the other hand, as Reich says, 'the revolutionary mass propaganda in Germany [that of Martin's faction] was restricted almost exclusively to the propaganda "against hunger"', inadequate in itself to win the battle for minds.)

Horváth implies the same misgivings as Reich expresses when the latter writes of the incapacity of the 'masses' for social self-government. There were those in Weimar, Hitler prominent among them, who believed the masses to be stupid and endlessly manipulable. Horváth distances himself from such a point of view by the infinite pains he takes over stupidity, and by his implicit faith in his audience's instincts, shown for example by his forcing or asking them to fill in those famous spaces, the 'Stillen' in his stage-directions which reveal the struggle between conscious and unconscious motivation. Horváth's doubts about intellect (as against instinct) as a force for salvation are conveyed by the fact that his relatively 'enlightened' characters (chiefly males), that is to say those with some pretensions to insight into socioeconomic reality, are particularly suspect because they so conspicuously lack either self-knowledge, on the one hand, or integrity, on the other. We might think of the time-serving social analyst Schürzinger in *Kasimir und Karoline,* or the ambitious Martin in *Italienische Nacht;* or, particularly, Betz in the same play, a

man who has read his Freud and makes his enlightenment an excuse for being a bad socialist. In his own eyes he becomes superior through knowledge, and therefore exempt from the common political struggle. In a lordly way, he writes off Martin's genuine and agitated attempts to resist the SPD leadership's capitulation to 'Verbürgerlichung' as 'Aggressionstriebe'. In doing so he indulges in a typical piece of Horváth 'Bildungsjargon', and at the same time displays the partial insight commonly found among Horváth's characters. (Betz is partly right, because Martin *is* libidinously aggressive: yet Betz fails to see or care that he has good political reason for his aggression.) Fossilized ideologies, reduced to a set of interchangeable formulae such as the Stadtrat mindlessly declaims, do the Fascists' work for them. To the Stadtrat's wife, Adele, it seems that his 'ideals' are the cause of his maltreatment of her, and she puts her finger on the truth when she protests 'Glaubens mir, daß ein Mann, der wo keine solchen öffentlichen Ideale hat, viel netter zu seiner Familie ist', an inversion which, in the Weimar context, is very convincing, and presents a genuine alternative female view of politics. For 'öffentliche Ideale' represent an 'uneigentlich', detached and unapproachable version of male intentionality. It is males who are more prone to the self-deception of employing 'Hochdeutsch' for the sake of acquiring dignity and to give themselves the spurious credentials of autonomous agency (one thinks of the Stadtrat's pride in his empty position of leadership), when in fact they are no more in control of their circumstances than females.

It is this intentionality—the male's response to impotence—that the out-of-work Kasimir is asserting in *Kasimir und Karoline,* rather than his desire for a true relationship with Karoline. Intentionality can ultimately even be reduced to the sort of mindless violent act recommended by Merkl Franz in the same play. Significantly, the only examples of males shedding this intentionality feature characters who have admitted defeat and become 'less than men', like Kasimir at the end of *Kasimir und Karoline.* The patriarchal 'Zauberkönig' in *Geschichten aus dem Wiener Wald* is only able to drop his intentionality and become more human when he is 'gebrochen'; just as the soldier in *Ein Kind unserer Zeit* only begins to question the self-evident nationalistic and masculine values of his beloved Army after he has been invalidated out. The most complete model of intact, dynamic intentionality is Martin in *Italienische Nacht.* Horváth brings out Martin's quality as a model by creating a contrast with the musician Karl, a politically vacillating 'artist' and ladies' man, who takes Martin precisely as an autonomous standard against which to measure himself, with miserable results. It may be that Horváth shares some of Martin's political attitudes, but it is typical of his writing for the theatre that his analysis of an individual psychology prevents a complete identification between the author and his character's attitudes, and equally prevents the audience from wholly identifying with a particular character. In Martin's case, politics and sexual politics are ominously at odds, and the conflict can only undermine an audience's faith in Martin's integrity, or at the very least his ultimate potential as a political force for reform. It is a particularly unpleasant male trick of Martin's to send his girlfriend Anna out as a kind of political prostitute to employ her sex to gather information about the activities of the Fascist enemy. Consciously or not, he is using his patriarchal sex domination, in the name of an antibourgeois ideal, to degrade the woman. A complex of underlying motives suggests that he is simultaneously testing her feelings for himself and thereby boosting his ego, while making an apparent personal demonstration of, and sacrifice to, his Marxist convictions.

The ubiquitous function of women in Horváth is to bolster male egos. Men have need of this support because the negative mirror of male intentionality—which inevitably fails in its aims—is self-pity, often of a selfish and puerile kind ('man ist und bleibt allein') demonstrated by numerous males in Horváth's plays, but rarely by females. The 'Randbemerkung' to *Glaube Liebe Hoffnung* talks of humanity as 'Geil auf Mitleid', but this vice, along with its corollary, 'geltungsbedürftige Bequemlichkeit' (almost a paraphrase for 'intentionality'), is above all a male attribute. It too is suspect from a political point of view, since it leads to the 'gang' mentality as a resource for transcending solitude and obtaining redress for supposed wrongs and lack of recognition as an individual. The relief and the almost mystical fervour with which the soldier in *Ein Kind unserer Zeit* surrenders his individuality to become a part of the destructive military machine is an obvious example.

I might so far seem to have been implying that only males suffer from 'Uneigentlichkeit', which is not the case. But I do want to suggest that there is a qualitative and effective difference between male and female 'Uneigentlichkeit'. The female's alienation from self-determination in thought and deed is often a 'secondary' kind of dispossession, conditioned by that of the male. There is perhaps a faint glimmer of hope for the future here. Certainly, there is evidence in the plays of the idea that women are closer than men to healthy instincts: both Marianne and Alfred's mother share a maternal impulse in *Geschichten aus dem Wiener Wald,* for instance. Admittedly it is a relative matter, but female 'Uneigentlichkeit' is a marginally less depressing spectacle than men's—at least on the conceptual level. In practice, within the plays, women's consciousness usually makes them victims of the male. Masculine kitschthinking or false consciousness (e.g. Oskar's in *Geschichten aus dem Wiener Wald*) equips men to be exploiters of others, while women's is more likely to make them vulnerable to exploitation. Marianne, for example, has a pure and private ideal of freedom, in contrast to Stadtrat Ammetsberger's corrupt, so-called 'public ideals'; but freedom for females in Horváth's late-patriarchal world is no more than availability for exploitation and prostitution. Marianne's lover, who initially represented escape, treats her in the same way that her tyrannical father did, and in the end she is returned as a lamb to the slaughter, into the hands of the sadistic Oskar, keenly sharpening his butcher's knife for a life-long revenge. Almost his last words in *Geschichten aus dem Wiener Wald* are 'du wirst meiner Liebe nicht entgehn'.

The dependent position of women in Horváth's plays makes them mental prisoners too. It is only through Martin that Anna in *Italienische Nacht* sees herself acquiring an 'Inhalt', some content to her life, a borrowed identity (like the borrowed evening dress of the working class) which could not be sustained without him. Conversely, women in Horváth who do not have men to 'fulfil' them, often turn against themselves. Anna relates how ugly, useless and unworthy she was before Martin came into her life. Elisabeth in *Glaube Liebe Hoffnung,* having been brought to the point of death largely by the heartlessness of men in a world of indifferent male 'Instanzen', turns her pain inwards, mentally flagellating herself rather than the male world. A bitter and apparently unmotivated laugh becomes the stage-gesture expression of her suppressed suffering. She enters into what is here a typically female inner opposition, or 'inner emigration', after an initial attempt at resistance. In *Geschichten aus dem Wiener Wald,* when Marianne's suffering finally becomes unbearable, she vents her feelings not upon her lover, Alfred, but upon another woman, the demonic old grandmother in the picturesque Wachau, herself merely a deformed reflection of the male world (she is made to echo the patriarchal condemnation of the priest who refused to give Marianne absolution).

Horváth's females are consigned, and self-consigned, to the private sphere. While to be male is to be a public entity (or feel pressure to be one), with its correlative in 'intentionality', to be female is to be committed to keeping public issues out of account in one's private life, except in so far as male public life is occasionaly welcomed, 'privatised' temporarily by the female: the example of Anna's acquisition of Martin's ideals and aims has already been mentioned. Women are 'realistic' in the sense that, for example, they frequently reject any notion of a 'Zukunft' for themselves; they reserve the word exclusively for males. As their male-defined sex-identity will be forfeit with increasing age and unattractiveness, women, as 'themselves', have no long-term future.

They suffer also other kinds of male-induced 'secondary' deformations of consciousness. Even the rare example of the independent woman, like the widow, Valerie, in *Geschichten aus dem Wiener Wald,* is subject to the law of diminishing returns which governs women's relationships with men. Her money buys her a living (the small 'Tabaktrafik') as it buys her lovers. But with increasing age the price she has to pay for the latter will also increase, not only financially but in terms of their increasingly overt contempt. The process is made apparent in the course of the play. For the most part, however, even such chimerical independence is unavailable to women. For men, power is sex, in the sense that power bestows the ability to acquire sexual dominance; and therefore sexual possession is also equated with power. The woman is kept 'unmündig' by successful men, selling out her self-determination for little consolations, signified by the sweets given alike to Marianne, and to Juanita the Gorilla-Girl in the freakshow in *Kasimir und Karoline.* Or she is used as an ego-boosting punchbag (like the 'Haut-den-Lukas', a trial of male 'strength') by unsuccessful men.

Horváth offers two kinds of strategy for women to use in dealing with this male-dominated world: they can embrace the kitsch about 'romance' produced by the dream-factory of the mass entertainment industry; or, at the other and logical extreme, they can take up a 'sachlich', practical and functional view of the male as their prey. This attitude does not of itself render them independent, of course. On occasion, the decision to become more 'practical' can be a euphemism for entering upon a career of prostitution. At other points, the 'romantic' and the 'practical' undergo combinations and permutations which leave the audience wondering how far the female actually believes in her own romantic convention. An example can be found in the parody of an operetta-style proposal scene in *Italienische Nacht,* where Leni proposes to Karl. In neither case is there the slightest encouragement to the audience to believe that the woman has achieved any genuine autonomy. Karoline in *Kasimir und Karoline* displays the pattern of progress from one pole to another. When 'romantic dreams' have faded under the sobering impact of Kasimir's unemployment, she issues what amounts to a typical Weimar 'Gebrauchsanweisung' for a 'sachlich' age: 'Das Leben ist hart und eine Frau, die wo etwas erreichen will, muß einen einflußreichen Mann immer bei seinem Gefühlsleben packen'.

If women are depicted as greater opportunists than men, this is because they have very little choice in the matter. 'La donn' è mobile': they are allowed a recognised 'false consciousness' as part of their essential sexual-political armoury. The resort to cunning, imposed upon them by the dominant party, inevitably confirms the prejudiced view of them held by that party (and since in this respect they are no different from any other subordinate group subjected to prejudice, the link with the wider political scene is again in evidence). When the old reactionary, Rauch, who has tried to buy Karoline's favours, finally discards her because his health gives out, he dismisses her as a 'Sauweib' who deserves to be 'ausgerottet'. She conforms to the image he has made of her, and descends to the level of the quasi-prostitutes Elli and Maria by hurling coarse invective at Rauch from a safe distance, a juvenile revenge—like a defiant gesture behind a teacher's back. The corollary of this kind of deformation, which deprives females of adult autonomy, is the almost complete absence of solidarity among women where survival itself is at issue. Erna, in *Kasimir und Karoline,* willingly supplies males with ammunition against females in general, in order to curry favour for herself. One could compare Valerie's treachery to, or failure to support, Marianne in *Geschichten aus dem Wiener Wald,* or the combined attack on Elisabeth by 'Die Prantl' and the Frau Amtsgerichtsrat in *Glaube Liebe Hoffnung.*

It is all too understandable that women in Horváth's 'Volksstücke' commonly subscribe to theories of fate, predestination and the influence of the planets, in order to generalise their own lack of self-determination. Popular interest in astrology, palmistry and the occult was a Weimar phenomenon. In the case of males, however, with their lord-of-creation attempts to impose their will on the circumscribed world they inhabit, recourse to explanations involving 'Schicksal' has a satirical rather than a pathetic effect. The dangers inherent in the prevalence of such habits of thought are evident in the Stadtrat's equating of 'fate' with the Fascists in *Italienische Nacht,* and,

worse still, his belief at the end of the play that he has 'overcome' this fate by good luck, whereas in fact his escape was achieved by the muscle of Martin and his followers. When it suits them, men can renounce their masterful role in favour of a passive stance as victims of fate. For women, the result of men's failure to take responsibility for the outcome of their self-chosen domination contains yet another bitter irony. The prime example is that of the 'Zauberkönig' in *Geschichten aus dem Wiener Wald,* who patriarchally banishes his daughter from his door, but is appalled at the consequences: lacking any marketable skills or training, Marianne is forced to make a living by appearing nude in a nightclub revue, portraying 'Die Jagd nach dem Glück' (a Weimar theme, the universal search for success, happiness and orgasm). The irony of the double standard operating here is compounded by poetic justice when the 'Zauberkönig', himself a voyeur, having greeted the cabaret at first with an enthusiastic 'Nackete Weiber, sehr richtig!', then realizes with horror, but with absolute self-righteousness and not a trace of remorse, that it is his own daughter who is thus degrading herself.

The sexual-political and (therefore?) the political failure of the Weimar years is most starkly presented in *Glaube Liebe Hoffnung.* Elisabeth, seeking like Marianne to become independent, is hounded to death by a curious combination of neglect (no-one is 'zuständig' for her in her plight) and overattention, from the law and from the police. Horváth calls the play 'Ein kleiner Totentanz', with the implication that all are involuntarily involved in Elisabeth's dance of death: no *one* intentionality controls the whole. What takes place on the level of sexual politics is indicative of the political outcome of the era in general. The policeman-lover, Alfons, 'does his duty', but in the process he helps to kill Elisabeth. At the end, he dones his white ceremonial gloves as a symbol of his clean hands in the affair. Finally, the sinister 'Vizepräparator' at the Anatomical Institute does become 'zuständig' for her, *after* her death. With all the confidence of a male representative of science licensed to violate bodies, he declares in effect that in Elisabeth's case 'tomorrow will bring all the answers': 'Na wir werden es ja morgen sehen'—in the course of the autopsy. There is an echo here of the brutal Oskar's desire to open up Marianne's cranium (as he is a butcher, it is easy to imagine him performing this gruesome operation) in order to take possession of her elusive and personal thoughts, the only part of her existence over which she retains any rights of ownership. The National Socialist state, too, was to be jealous of the thoughts of its subjects. To own them in body was not enough: they must also be possessed in soul.

The idol of masculinity, like the totalitarian state, demands innocent sacrifices. The 'Schupo' in *Glaube Liebe Hoffnung* calmly reports that during the course of political disturbances an 'Unbeteiligter' has been shot—a parallel to the fate of the innocent and 'unbeteiligt' Elisabeth herself, and a foreshadowing of the fate of many a victim of the institutionalized violence to come. *Glaube Liebe Hoffnung* takes place before a predominantly masculine background of 'latenter Bürgerkrieg', marches, streetfighting, political assassination, a bitterly fought election. In the name of law and order and the preservation of values formerly associated with respectability, bestial impulses are 'enabled' by the state, while society frustrates positive aims, the legitimate desires of the individual and the simple wish for 'Selbständigkeit' that belongs above all (because it is most blatantly denied to them) to females. Sexual-political failure is at the least a symptom and, ultimately, perhaps even a part of the cause of political failure in the widest sense. (pp. 249-58)

Alan Bance, "Ödön von Horváth: Sex, Politics and Sexual Politics," in German Life & Letters, *Vol. XXXVIII, No. 3, April, 1985, pp. 249-59.*

Russell E. Brown   (essay date 1987)

[*In the essay below, Brown uses the example of baby Leopold to analyze the treatment of children in* Tales from the Vienna Woods.]

One of the most disturbing incidents in Ödön von Horváth's **Geschichten aus dem Wiener Wald,** the author's most enduring success, is the death of a baby, Leopold, 'most probably the best known of the deaths in Horváth', [according to P. M. Potter]. Left in the care of its father Alfred's mother and grandmother in the country, the illegitimate infant is allowed to die of pneumonia by its great-grandmother, who first exposes it to the cold night air and then ignores its decline. As the mother, released from pre-

Horváth's self-portrait.

trial custody, and a party of her relatives and friends arrive to welcome the child into their world, the father's grandmother and mother are composing a letter announcing its death. As a consequence the baby's mother, Marianne, is forced into an unwanted marriage, from which her affair with Alfred and especially the existence of the baby had rescued her.

The realistic motivation for the grandmother's horrible deed is twofold. Her strict conventional morality and concern for family respectability do not permit her to accept the baby of her unmarried grandson. She stresses the legitimacy of her own children and herself. Just as important is her desire to maintain strong ties with Alfred, to whom she lends sums of money, and for whom the relation with Marianne and their producing a child are perceived as a threat. Thus the baby is allowed to die from motives of petit-bourgeois family honour and of possessiveness by the zither-playing grandmother, who appears at once senile and demonically calculating. In a macabre touch, the grandmother plays with a toy that has been brought to the dead baby. As well as wanting to be Alfred's partner, she wants to be a baby herself. Sensing her guilt, Marianne tries to beat her with the zither, but is forcibly restrained (strangled) by Oskar.

While the brutal egoism of the grandmother seems shocking, it is actually consistent with the actions of other characters. As she dominates the country (Wachau) setting, so Marianne's father, the 'Zauberkönig', dominates the city setting, the 'stille Straße im achten Bezirk' of Vienna. Both are supernatural figures, at least residually. Having failed to maintain control over his daughter and force her to marry Oskar, the sadistic butcher from the adjoining shop, the 'Zauberkönig' breaks totally with his daughter: 'Ich habe keine Tochter! Ich hab noch nie eine Tochter gehabt!'. Like the paternal grandmother he also disclaims any family relationship to the baby. He is especially angry that it has been named after him:

> Was?! Leopold?! Der Leopold, das bin doch ich! Na, das ist aber der Gipfel! Nennt ihre Schand nach mir! Das auch noch!

Thus while he does not kill the child, his rejection of it is like the grandmother's, from a narrow morality which masks a desire to control and possess *his* one of the two parents. In this sense, the horrible deed of killing the baby is not unique, but typical of local society in general, the mother's side ('stille Straße') as well as the father's side ('Wachau'). The actual element of sadistic violence is embodied more in Marianne's original fiancé and final husband, the butcher Oskar from the same street. As [Peter] Stenberg writes: 'The slaughter of the innocents is not actually carried out by the butchers themselves, but by the society, which is damned to its own slaughter.'

The oppressiveness of the society and its false culture (epitomized by the omnipresent popular music like Strauss waltzes) is epigrammatically captured by [Winfried] Nolting: 'Was Leopold umbringt, ist aber eigentlich die Luft.' But the grandmother does have a special fairy-tale quality which transcends the petty tradesmen of the city street setting. Her grandson calls her a witch five times in a single scene. And indeed she resembles a witch from Grimms' fairy tales, for example from *Hänsel und Gretel*. Like a witch she is an old, unmarried or widowed women who lives far from the city, in nature, by a tower ruin. She is treacherous, ill-humoured, and violent. Like a witch she has a hidden treasure, the fortune from which she doles out loans to hold her grandson. Her letting a baby die is perhaps less diabolical than planning to eat the children, Hänsel and Gretel, but she is still a child-killer like fairy-tale witches, an embodiment of unmotivated evil.

In fairy tales, however, only the witch is an exceptional demonic figure, while all around her are innocent or at worst understandably weak (Hänsel's and Gretel's father). In Horváth's depraved society, her personality is not at all exceptional. As [Helga] Hollmann writes: 'Das Erschreckende an der Tat der Großmutter ist, daß sie ihre Skrupellosigkeit aus der Gewißheit gewinnt, sich im Einklang mit der bürgerlichen Moral zu finden.'

Alfred's mother, for example, shares the guilt of infanticide, having observed that the grandmother left the window open on purpose, but herself failing to close the window on the first occasion, or in the period following until the baby has died of pneumonia. Others, like Oskar, simply wish for the baby's death: 'Vielleicht stirbt das Kind.' Or the 'Zauberkönig' tells his daughter 'So wirf dich doch vor den Zug! . . . Samt deiner Brut!'

The witch quality of the grandmother is reinforced by the fact that she has earlier been a party to another infant's death. The sick Leopold reminds Alfred's mother of another child: '—damals beim armen kleinen Ludwig hats genau so begonnen—' Who Ludwig was is not explained in the play and most critics do not even mention him (Winston assumes he was Alfred's baby brother); yet whether he was such or perhaps another illegitimate child of the promiscuous Alfred, the effect is to invoke a fairy-tale sequence of baby murders, the mechanical repetitions seen in mythological materials. The grandmother is a person in whose proximity babies do not survive, with the exception of Alfred, for whom most of the play's female characters—grandmother, mother, Valerie, and Marianne—compete.

The chief male character on the mother's side, the 'Zauberkönig' or wizard, is like the witch grandmother, in that wizards deal in magic, spells and alchemy; Merlin, and other wizards of medieval tales are the male counterparts to female witches. Mennemeier also sees the 'Zauberkünstler' occupation as an allusion to nineteenth-century Viennese 'Zauberpossen', like Ferdinand Raimund's *Der Alpenkönig und der Menschenfeind* of 1828. (See also Peter Stenberg's 'The Last of the Magicians . . . Horváth's "Zauberkönig" and his Ancestors'.)

In an early draft of the play the grandmother-mother team with whom the baby is left is not related to its father; in his place there is a daughter with whom Alfred flirts when he arrives to visit the baby. When she finds out who he is, she is afraid to tell him of the child's death. Unlike that in the final version, the cause of death seems to be an actual accident: 'Er hat bei der Donau gespielt und ist hineingefallen—'. Even in this early version popular culture is

brought into connection with the child's death; here he is not killed by the music-filled air, but by the river Donau itself which is prominently featured in the music and operetta stereotypes. When other visitors appear the child is still being searched for in the river. Incidentally, in stories of unmarried women's pregnancies (well into the twentieth century) it is usually the expectant mother who ends up by drowning herself in the local river.

While the grandmother in this three-generations female family is not made specifically responsible for the baby's death, for which she has no personal selfish motive, she nevertheless is overjoyed by the accident:

> Wir haben doch das Kind alle so gern gehabt!
> Nur die Großmutter hat das gleich geahnt—die
> war immer dagegen, daß wir ein Kind in Pflege
> nehmen—jetzt triumphiert sie natürlich.

And as in the final play, grandmother condemns the illegitimacy of the baby, considering it altogether proper that the baby should die. One might even suspect she had a hand in the death of this (unrelated) baby as well, especially with the hindsight of knowing the final version. The only element which is different for her is the absence of a family link to the baby, through its father, and the resultant jealousy-possessiveness motive.

In relation to the grandmother-baby theme in the *Geschichten aus dem Wiener Wald* it should be mentioned that Horváth wrote an unpublished, undated short story 'Großmütterleins Tod.' In this story a young married couple lives together with the husband's mother, called 'Großmütterlein' in anticipation of a baby they are expecting. Her possessive and imperious nature drives the pregnant wife away; when the husband takes a train to bring her home, the grandmother who accompanied him to the railway station sits too long in the cold wind there, catches pneumonia, and dies, freeing the reunited couple for a normal marriage and parenthood without opposition. In this parallel story the contest between possessive maternal grandmother and baby is resolved in favour of the baby, with the same cause of death being 'applied'. Potter has classified types of death for Horvath characters; such a death by exposure to the elements is frequent.

In this variation of the motif, undoubtedly produced earlier, the death of the hateful old person appears in a positive light, removing an obstacle to family normalcy, whereas in the dramatic versions the grandmother is raised to a fairy-tale figure characteristic of an evil society in general, which prevents positive regeneration by destroying guiltless new life. The death of the grandmother here is neither horrifying nor poignant since it seems to be deserved; it does not imply a criticism of the whole social milieu with its false and sentimental banalities (as is the case with the baby's death in the play): the story ends laconically 'Man hat ihren Tod nicht betrauert, weil sie alt war.' The story's unfinished state is illustrated by the reference to an already born child ('ihr kleines Kind zurücklassen'), when it is later stated that their first child is not yet born.

To return to *Geschichten aus dem Wiener Wald,* the murder of little Leopold and the reported death of a baby Ludwig are not the only examples of children in the play. The references to other children are made primarily in the stage directions (which play so great a role that Nolting calls the play 'primär ein Lesedrama'). They cast a curious light on the main example of child abuse, the death of Leopold.

As relatives and friends of Oskar and Marianne assemble early in the play for the engagement party in the Vienna woods on the banks of the 'schönen blauen Donau', the list of those present concludes 'und kleine weißgekleidete häßliche Kinder'. The term 'häßliche' seems gratuitous, unless we think of Horváth intending a comic clash with 'weißgekleidete' as Winston suggests, a 'contrast between the sweetness and innocence traditionally represented by white clothing in European culture and the grotesque qualities of its wearers', [observed Franz Norbert Mennemeier]. While Horváth certainly means to portray the adult society of the play as grotesque, as well as hypocritical, selfish, and infantile, it seems premature to apply this quality of grotesqueness to children, who at least in Rousseau's enlightenment terms might be imagined to be still unspoiled noble savages, not yet ruined by popular culture, capitalism, and false ideology.

In any case, the term Horváth actually used, 'häßliche', is strange; while one might imagine one individual child to be ugly, it is unlikely all members of the children's group could fairly be called ugly, especially since the term is never used in the author's stage directions about adults.

It is when we connect the 'häßliche' reference with the other child actually portrayed in the play that a definite pattern is revealed. In the first 'stille Straße' scene a girl emerges from the butcher's shop, followed by the insult of the butcher's assistant Havlitschek, who is angry because she has criticized his blood sausage: 'Dummes Luder, dummes—'. He fantasizes about butchering her like one of his pigs. This judgment is expressed by the character who, with identical words, later denigrates a grown-up servant girl, Emma, as she leaves his shop, just after she agrees to a date with him.

But the preceding stage direction, which stems from Horváth himself of course, reads: 'Ida ein elfjähriges, herziges, mageres, kurzsichtiges Mäderl'. Two of the three terms the author uses to describe Ida are pejorative in the same unnecessary way as 'häßliche' for the collective children above: the plot is not served by Ida being too thin and nearsighted.

When the same girl appears in the engagement scene (she is included in the 'weißgekleidete häßliche Kinder' group), she recites a banal, sentimental poem for the assembled guests. Her stage direction description is repeated unnecessarily, as if Horváth relished the deprecatory adjectives, 'jenes magere, herzige, kurzsichtige Mäderl', to which the author now adds a further negative: 'rezitiert mit einem Sprachfehler'. The feature of a speech impediment is like that of poor eyesight. It is true that the stuttering (or lisping) interferes with and undermines the recital of the bad poem, suggesting an inner resentment of the text, almost a Brechtian alienation effect. But Horváth is loading little Ida with negative features which make of her a defective, almost grotesque character.

As Marianne's baby is attacked by the grandmother and hated by other characters and as Ida is menaced by Havlitschek, so the author himself bullies the children of the play in his tendentious stage instructions. Even the never-seen 'Realschülerin im zweiten Stock' who produces the waltz music constantly heard in the 'Stille Straße' plays 'auf einem ausgeleierten Klavier'. Ida's 'Sprachfehler' in recitation is projected into the out-of-tune piano, whereby Horváth criticizes the girl along with the music.

These consistently pejorative references to children occur in successive scenes early in the play and are not repeated. They may, however, be linked to the scene in an 'äußerst preiswert' 'möbliertes Zimmer im achtzehnten Bezirk' (such rooms are a favourite private setting of Horváth). Marianne used her engagement party excursion to escape from an unwanted marriage with the frightful butcher by plunging into a sudden liaison with Alfred; almost a stranger, she tells him 'Von dir möcht ich ein Kind haben—'. Now she is discovered here in the furnished room, exactly one year later, with the fulfilment of her wish.

While Alfred lies in bed smoking and Marianne brushes her teeth, the baby's presence is indicated by negative objects: 'ein alter Kinderwagen—auf einer Schnur hängen Windeln'. The age of the pram, justified by the couple's poverty, is nevertheless a gratuitous negative descriptive like the hanging nappies, both of which contribute to the disillusionment experienced by the mother—and to the general negative image of children and babies.

Although the baby is invisible and silent during the scene, Marianne fears its crying: 'Nicht so laut! Wenn das Kind aufwacht, dann kenn ich mich wieder nicht aus vor lauter Geschrei.' Leopold is just eight weeks old in this second part of the play; in another month he will be dead. (In this time his mother will be turned away from confession at the 'Stephansdom', have performed naked on a cabaret stage, tried prostitution, and been in jail, accused of theft.)

Crying, nappies, an old pram are the entire group of motifs in this single family scene which characterize the infant Leopold, which the unmarried couple had tried to abort at the insistence of the father. Horváth does not even bother here to suggest contrasting positive features (for Ida 'herziges') in his bitter portrayal of brutal economic necessity and short-lived passion. In other situations he presents a veneer of popular, mendacious stereotypes, like the Viennese waltzes or patriotic songs, which are then stripped away to reveal the naked egoism and deformed personalities of the characters.

Baby Leopold, the only character to die in the course of the play, cannot be described as anything but innocent, so Horváth concentrates on the baby's effect on others, his burdensomeness, while ignoring the many pleasurable aspects of parenthood, such as singing a lullaby, caressing the infant, and the like, which could as easily have been introduced. In short, the portrayal of babies and children in this play stems more from the author's imagination, his consistent selection and invention of negative features, than from a neutral depiction of character and incident.

In a glimpse from another social sphere and era, the 'Rittmeister' recalls a colonel's wife in his old regiment, herself unable to bear children, who readily accepted into her own family an illegitimate child fathered by her husband. Perhaps the petit-bourgeois mentality and the milieu of the characters here can be blamed for their perniciousness. Mennemeier has criticized Horváth's tendency to generalize unfairly the critique of the lower middle-class segment of society he portrays: 'Horváth verallgemeinert seine gesellschaftliche Diagnose zu unbedenklich; diese betrifft . . . nur einen Ausschnitt der Sozietät." But in this case the upper class reacts in a markedly different, more humane manner toward the innocent fruit of an extramarital relationship.

We may finally mention the only customer shown to make a purchase from the shop of the 'Zauberkönig', a mother who on two separate occasions seeks tin soldiers for her son's birthday, 'drei Schachteln Schwerverwundete und zwei Schachteln Fallende', because her son wants to play 'Sanitäter'. The bloodthirsty boy appears to reflect the attitudes of both the sadistic butcher-pair Oskar and Havlitschek and the unregenerate cavalry officer, the 'Rittmeister', as well as to supply a fair prediction of Baby Leopold's probable future personality as a boy and man, had he survived. Schober has gathered additional negative appraisals of schoolchildren, especially in *Jugend ohne Gott* (1937).

Thus Horváth's 'children' appear deformed both physically (Ida) and spiritually (the birthday boy), only in part as a result of their relations with adults in this milieu. The author, who had numerous liaisons but who never had children and married only briefly to supply a friend with a Hungarian passport in the Hitler period, apparently saw no hope in the next generation for a renewal of human society, at least in this play where babies are victims of their families and children are victims of the author's verbal aggression. This contributes to the profound pessimism apparent in his works.

It is in this ambiguous light that we must see the central episode of child portrayal in the play: the brief life (12 weeks) and macabre death of the infant Leopold. The oldest person in the play, its eighty-one-year-old great-grandmother, kills the youngest. What seems a shocking crime in a traditional sense is only a typical event in relations between men and women, between adults and children which are at once predatory and foolish. (Nolting: 'Doch ist Leopold ebensowenig wie sein gleichnamiger Großvater ein Opfer.') The mere absence of negative cultural and economic deformation in Baby Leopold does not make of him a good person in a world of evil persons. Like his mother, Marianne, he is only weaker than others who exploit, destroy, and bury him. (pp. 151-57)

> *Russell E. Brown, "The Death of Baby Leopold: Hostility to Children in Horváth's 'Geschichten aus dem Wiener Wald'," in Ger-*

man Life & Letters, *Vol. XL, No. 2, January, 1987, pp. 151-57.*

FURTHER READING

Best, Alan. "Ödön von Horváth: The *Volksstück* Revived." In *Modern Austrian Writing: Literature and Society after 1945,* edited by Alan Best and Hans Wolfschütz, pp. 108-27. Totowa, N.J.: Barnes & Noble, 1980.

> Discusses the revival of the *Volksstück,* hailing it as "a form of contemporary social criticism." Best credits Horváth for the resurgence of the genre and claims that the dramatist inspired a new generation of politically conscious writers.

Greenville, A. B. J. "The Failure of Constitutional Democracy: The SPD and the Collapse of the Weimar Republic in Ödön von Horváth's *Italienische Nacht." The Modern Language Review,* 82, Part 2 (April 1987): 399-414.

> Explores the historical and political developments surrounding the creation of *Italienische Nacht.* Viewing the play as "the product of the highly-charged political situation of the final years of the Weimar Republic," Greenville focuses especially on the failure of the Prussian social democratic party to effectively counter a Nazi takeover and the ways in which that situation is reflected in the play.

Winston, Krishna. "The Old Lady's Day of Judgment: Notes on a Mysterious Relationship Between Friedrich Dürrenmatt and Ödön von Horváth." *The Germanic Review* LI, No. 4. (November 1976): 312-22.

> Compares Horváth's *Der jüngste Tag* and *Zur schönen Aussicht* with Dürrenmatt's *Der Besuch der alten Dame,* noting structural, thematic, and symbolic similarities as well as the likenesses and differences of two crucial characters: Ada Freifrau von Statten in *Zur schönen Aussicht* and Claire Zachanassian in *Der Besuch der alten Dame.*

———. *Horváth Studies.* Las Vegas: Peter Lang, 1977, 233 p.

> Analyzes six plays: *Revolte auf Côte 3018, Zur schönen Aussicht, Sladek, oder Die schwarze Armee, Rund um den Kongreß, Italienische Nacht,* and *Geschichten aus dem Wiener Wald.*

———. "The Unbuttoned Nightgown of Anna Schramm: Dress and Undress in the Plays of Ödön von Horváth." *Modern Austrian Literature* 11, No. 2 (1978): 53-72.

> Discusses Horváth's use of dress and undress to offer insight into his characters and situations. Noting the importance the dramatist placed on self-presentation, Winston contends: "States of dress or undress give clues as to the characters' economic situation, their pretenses and delusions, their morals and their drives."

> Additional coverage of Horváth's life and career is contained in the following sources published by Gale Research: *Contemporary Authors,* Vol. 118 and *Dictionary of Literary Biography,* Vol. 85.

E. Phillips Oppenheim

1866-1946

(Also wrote under the pseudonym Anthony Partridge)
English novelist, short story writer, and autobiographer.

INTRODUCTION

Oppenheim is chiefly remembered for establishing the spy novel as a well-defined literary genre. The author of a large body of work that includes romances, social melodramas, and mysteries, he combined elements from these and other types of popular fiction to inaugurate a narrative form characterized by political intrigue, the machinations of spies and counterspies, and the internecine struggles of dinner-jacketed power brokers. While Oppenheim has been criticized for his flawed prose style and dated attitudes, his spy novels nevertheless make him the literary forebear of such authors as Ian Fleming, Frederick Forsyth, and John le Carré.

Oppenheim was born in London and grew up in Leicester. He left school at sixteen to work in his father's leather business, and, manifesting what he would later call a "natural instinct" to tell stories, he devoted his free time to writing. Oppenheim's first short story was published when he was eighteen, and two years later, with partial funding from his father, he saw the publication of his first novel, *Expiation.* Over the next nine years Oppenheim wrote three novels and numerous short stories. In 1896 his output increased dramatically: he published five novels that year and continued to write three to five books a year for the rest of his life.

Due to the financial success of his books and the sale of his father's business, Oppenheim became quite wealthy, and the manner in which he lived in many ways reflected the glamorous life-style depicted in his fiction. He resided most of the year in a villa on the French Riviera, was known as a great womanizer, and was a regular presence in the casinos of Monaco. His work habits, as well, were in keeping with the image of a dashing raconteur: he dictated his stories to a secretary who took them down in short hand and later submitted a typed draft for approval. "I . . . found it by far the most effective method of getting my work on paper," he said, adding, "thus only about half my time is devoted to writing or dictating, so that the other half is available for exercise and sport, visits to London, and travel." To readers of the time, part of the appeal of an Oppenheim novel was the suspicion that its author had firsthand experience of the glamorous people, places, and events it described. In 1940 the imminent Nazi invasion of France forced Oppenheim to leave his villa on the Riviera, and he and his wife settled on Guernsey in the Channel Islands. Oppenheim died there early in 1946.

Oppenheim's reputation today is based almost solely on

his contribution to the development of spy fiction. His first spy novel, *Mysterious Mr. Sabin,* in many ways represents Oppenheim's entire body of espionage fiction: it employs elements from various popular genres of the day, particularly novels of adventure, mystery, and romance; draws upon a highly publicized contemporary event for the kernel of its plot; contains clichéd dialogue; and exhibits flaws in style and structure. Another characteristic feature of Oppenheim's spy novels is their obvious valorization of monarchy as a form of government. In *Mysterious Mr. Sabin,* for example, the triumph of the Boulangist forces in their struggle to restore the Bourbons and Bonapartes to monarchic rule in France is depicted as more desirable than the reform and success of the democratic government. However, as many critics point out, Oppenheim was not an ideologue; even when he was writing what have been called "war prophecy" novels—which often focused, as *Sabin* does, on the potential invasion of England by Germany—he did so simply to entertain readers. Oppenheim was more intrigued by the romantic sweep of royalty restored to power and splendor than by arid parliamentary debates on government reform. Thus he offers a story involving a Bourbon princess who regains her throne only to renounce it for the man she loves—who, it is later revealed, is of royal blood. In addition to being a romance and a war prophecy novel dealing in the details of international diplomacy, *Sabin* is also reminiscent of Victorian detective stories in its use of a blackmail scheme as a central plot device. The title character, Mr. Sabin, blackmails a number of people in his steadfast machinations in support of Boulanger. As LeRoy L. Panek notes, it "is a short step from threatening an individual with exposure of his secrets to threatening a nation with exposure of its weaknesses and secrets. Mr. Sabin fills both roles." However, the problem critics find with the novel, aside from dialogue such as: "So you are a lacquey after all, then? . . . a common spy," is that everything that makes it a spy novel is concluded and resolved some eighty pages before the book ends; the rest of the story concerns Sabin's attempt to restore his good name in the eyes of the other major characters. Nonetheless, *Mysterious Mr. Sabin* and Oppenheim's score of similar books, including *The Great Impersonation*—which has served as the basis for three films—are credited as the first true expressions of the spy novel.

PRINCIPAL WORKS

Expiation (novel) 1887
A Daughter of Astrea (novel) 1898
Mysterious Mr. Sabin (novel) 1898
The Man and His Kingdom (novel) 1899
The Traitors (novel) 1902
A Prince of Sinners (novel) 1903
Anna the Adventuress (novel) 1904
A Maker of History (novel) 1905
A Lost Leader (novel) 1906
The Secret (novel) 1907; also published as *The Great Secret,* 1907
Jeanne of the Marshes (novel) 1908
The Golden Web [as Anthony Partridge] (novel) 1910; also published as *The Plunderers,* 1912
The Mischief-Maker (novel) 1912
The Way of These Women (novel) 1913
The Amazing Partnership (short stories) 1914
The Vanished Messenger (novel) 1914
The Double Traitor (novel) 1915
Mr. Grex of Monte Carlo (novel) 1915
The Kingdom of the Blind (novel) 1916
The Pawns Count (novel) 1918
The Zeppelin's Passenger (novel) 1918; also published as *Mr. Lessingham Goes Home,* 1919
The Great Impersonation (novel) 1920
The Great Prince Shan (novel) 1922
My Books and Myself (autobiography) 1922
The Wrath to Come (novel) 1924
Gabriel Samara (novel) 1925; also published as *Gabriel Samara, Peacemaker,* 1925
The Golden Beast (novel) 1926
The Quest For Winter Sunshine (travel essay) 1926

Miss Brown of the X.Y.O. (novel) 1927
Mr. Billingham, The Marquis, and Madelon (short stories) 1927
The Treasure House of Martin Hews (novel) 1929
Up the Ladder of Gold (novel) 1931
The Ostrekoff Jewels (novel) 1932
Murder at Monte Carlo (novel) 1933
The Spy Paramount (novel) 1935
The Dumb Gods Speak (novel) 1937
A Pulpit in the Grill Room (short stories) 1938
The Milan Grill Room: Further Adventures of Louis, the Manager, and Major Lyson, the Raconteur (short stories) 1940
The Pool of Memory: Memoirs (memoirs) 1941
Mr. Mirakel (novel) 1943
The Hour of Reckoning, and the Mayor of Ballydaghan (short stories) 1944

Ward Clark (essay date 1908)

[*In the following review of* The Great Secret, *Clark assesses Oppenheim's work from the competing vantage points of the general reader and the discerning literary critic.*]

Novelists who have envied Mr. Oppenheim his evident possession of the Great Secret may be pardoned for regarding the title of his latest book as a deliberate taunt flung in the faces of his less successful rivals. Of the men who supply the staple product of the fiction market not one has more fully mastered the trick of turning out a perfectly regular and dependable article. The Oppenheim brand is justly esteemed by shrewd buyers. The stories bearing this label always "grade" well, for they contain the best of materials and workmanship. Nothing better for their purpose is manufactured anywhere.

Mr. Oppenheim is actually a manufacturer of a superior kind. No reproach is implied in this. On the contrary, there is no reason why the supplying of the market demand for fiction of a certain class should be put on any other plane, and Mr. Oppenheim deserves applause and thanks for conducting his business in a conscientious manner. I have not read all of his stories, but I have never read one of them without pleasure.

Yet in spite of the most scrupulous care and the utmost impersonality of method, fiction cannot be turned out with quite the uniformity of steel rails. I doubt whether the most zealous admirer of Mr. Oppenheim could name every one of his novels and properly differentiate them; but differences nevertheless exist, and this or that book may stand out from the others with some individuality of outline. It is not likely that ***The Great Secret*** will be distinguished for merit above its fellows; but it may achieve a mild distinction in this country because its author has allowed himself to indulge in gentle sarcasm at the expense of the American woman. Never has he constructed a more remarkable scene than the one which he represents as taking place in a Lenox country house, the seat of a great

American financial magnate. Mrs. Van Reinberg has returned to her native land from Europe, bringing in tow the legitimist heir to the French throne. In her library, after a dinner party, she assembles six millionaires, including her husband, and their wives. These representatives of American finance and American society are addressed by the French heir, who proposes that each of the men shall furnish two million dollars to a fund for the purpose of placing him on the throne. In consideration of this slight assistance the respective wives are to be allowed to take their pick of French titles of nobility and thus realise their social ambitions. The proposal is discussed gravely, but the well-known subserviency of American men to their wives' whims leaves no room for doubt as to the result. The men good-naturedly consent, and the wives proceed to draw lots for the available titles. The incident is described not in a spirit of burlesque, but quite seriously as a link in the chain of international plotting with which the story is concerned.

This, it may be thought, is going it rather steep. Mr. Oppenheim makes partial amends, however, to a country which buys his books in liberal numbers by making his heroine a lovely if somewhat erratic American girl, and he more than evens matters by holding up Germany and her ruler to the scorn and hatred of mankind. If America is ridiculous, Germany is desperately wicked; for the arch villain of this story is no less a personage than the Kaiser himself. The Great Secret, which leaks out bit by bit in the course of the narrative, is a German plot to destroy the English fleet and bring about the downfall of England as a world power. The ingredients in the plot are exactly the same as in all such concoctions, and if they furnish an hour's amusement it is not because of their originality.

Mr. Oppenheim undeniably has the gift of keeping his story moving. It would be cruel, however, to subject it to an analysis which should follow the threads of the plot an inch outside of his pages. This is not one of those mystery stories which offer a real challenge to the reader's analytical faculty. The truth is that Mr. Oppenheim, entertaining as he may sometimes be, is sadly superficial. His story has but two dimensions. Never does he allow himself to follow a motive below the surface. Incident after incident is introduced to keep the plot boiling, the leadings of which are abandoned the instant they have served their immediate purpose. Superficially the thing hangs together after a fashion. But the test of a really good mystery story is that it should sound consistent and plausible on a second reading, with the end plainly in view at every step. This test would work havoc with the plot of *The Great Secret.* Even in retrospect, without reference to the text for the refreshing of the memory, one can recall many a loose end—inconsistencies and gaps, false scents that lead nowhere, motives that do not motivate, promises of explanations that never come. One shudders to think what a careful re-reading might reveal.

And yet this is perhaps the crowning proof of Mr. Oppenheim's cleverness. Doubtless he knows his public better than any one else. There are plenty of novel readers whose memories extend no further back than the page they have

just turned. *The Great Secret* will suit them down to the ground. (pp. 61-2)

Ward Clark, "Mr. Oppenheim's 'The Great Secret'," in The Bookman, *New York, Vol. XXVII, No. 1, March, 1908, pp. 61-2.*

The Bookman, NEW YORK   (essay date 1911)

[*In the following excerpt, the critic favorably reviews one of Oppenheim's short stories, offers an assessment of his value as a writer, and then quotes from a letter in which Oppenheim discusses why and how he writes.*]

A recent magazine short story that we have read with considerable enjoyment is Mr. E. Phillips Oppenheim's **"The Deserter,"** which appears in the January issue of the *Strand,* and which is not in the least obscured by the fact that the magazine contains the first part of another experience of Mr. Sherlock Holmes. **"The Deserter"** is one of those direct little tales which an author needs only to start, for after that the yarn tells itself. It concerns a little London clerk, a kind of Bob Cratchit, seventy years after the conversion of Mr. Scrooge, whose life is soured by the tyranny of a domineering wife and unappreciative children. There is not so much definite hardness, only a very marked contempt for the shabby little husband and father who is the slave of them all. Peter Hayes thinks of all this, as he looks back upon the monotonous years one night just before Christmas as he is struggling homeward burdened with the family parcels. He arrives at his house, lets himself in with his latch key, and is aware of the presence of a visitor. This visitor is a lawyer who has come to announce that, through the death of a sister, Mrs. Hayes has come into a property estimated to be between twenty-five and thirty-five thousand pounds. Unperceived, Peter Hayes listens to the family plan for the disposal of the property, and hears himself derided as a handicap to their social ambitions. Wounded, and yet somewhat elated at the opportunity, he throws off the yoke then and there, leaves his wife and children to the enjoyment of their apparent prosperity, and slips out into the night to begin a new life.

With a beginning like this there is hardly any need to tell what the rest of the story will be. Of course, Peter Hayes enjoys immensely his first hours of freedom, and finds huge delight in the long forbidden cigar and the tankard of ale. Of course, after these mild excesses he emigrates to America with the determination of carving out a career. Of course he succeeds in this, becomes a rich man, and seven years later returns to England expecting to find his family in the enjoyment of prosperity and social position. Of course the legacy has proved to be almost all smoke and the American millionaire arrives just in time to avert the sheriff's sale. It is the old, old device, but it is told with a very genuine freshness and sparkle.

We have no illusions about the literary work of Mr. Oppenheim. He is not a Field Marshal or a General of Division, so to speak, but a very good officer of the line, and when contemplating the books of men like him we are always impressed by how much better the service is than it was seventy-five or a hundred years ago. It is all very well to talk of the brave old days when Scott and Thackeray and Dickens were in their prime, but compare the minor men of that age with the minor men of to-day and you will be forced to a very profound respect for the present time. Of men like Mr. Oppenheim it must be said that they are good workmen. Perhaps there is not so much genius now, but there is plenty of talent and it is conscientiously applied. We print a letter which Mr. Oppenheim recently sent to his American publishers:

There is probably no question which an author has to answer more frequently than the exceedingly hackneyed one of how he came to take up writing, and in a general way there is none more difficult to answer, because he very seldom knows.

I frankly admit that I have no idea why it occurred to me in my younger days to make a nuisance of myself to editors, and to watch the slow absorption of my limited pocket money in postage stamps and manuscript paper. The thing came about, however, and the usual small measure of success which perseverance generally commands, encouraged me in time to take up the profession of story-writing seriously.

I was eighteen years old when my first short story was published, and only twenty when my first novel appeared. I have, therefore, had more than twenty years of story-writing, and the first thing which occurs to me to say about it is that I don't think there can be another profession in the world which maintains its hold upon its disciples to such an extraordinary extent. I spent nearly an hour before starting these few lines, trying to avoid being egotistical. I have now given up the idea. One can't write about one's work without being egotistical. These, therefore, are my personal experiences and feelings.

I don't know how to account for the fact that at forty-four years old I sit down to commence a new story with exactly the same thrill as at twenty. The love of games, of sport, of sea and mountains, the call of strange cities, wonderful pictures and unusual people, however dear they may still remain to one, lose something of their first and vital freshness with the passing of the years. Not so the sight of that blank sheet of paper. The untrodden world of romance, the virgin field into which one is about to plunge, never loses its unspeakable and indescribable fascination. Personally, I can't account for it. I don't try. Sometimes it seems to me that it is because all one's life one hopes for one particular idea which never comes. There is always something elusive about the genesis of an idea of any sort. Perhaps it is the inextinguishable hope that on one of those occasions when one sits and waits, there will come the most wonderful idea that has ever dawned upon the brain of a writer of fiction, something of which dim glimmerings have passed through one's brain when one is half awake and half dreaming. Every writer of fiction knows what those will-o'-the-wisps of the mind are. With the morning their light has gone but they do their good work. They keep hope alive.

The moderate amount of success which my stories have attained enables me to write them in the manner I like best. I live in a cottage upon the east coast, with a view of the North Sea from my windows, excellent golf links within a few yards, and plenty of rough shooting within easy distance. I have no system of work, but, generally speaking, half my time is devoted to actual writing, and the other half is divided between exercise and sport, visits to London, and travel. My work itself is accomplished with the help of a secretary. Many a time, earlier in life, when I used to write my stories with my own hand, I have found my ideas come so much faster than my fingers could work that I have prayed for some more speedy method of transmission. Now I usually dictate my stories as they unfold themselves, to my secretary, who takes them down in shorthand. She then transcribes them roughly by means of a typewriter, and from these sheets I dictate the final effort, subject to the inevitable revision. These things, of course, are all a matter of custom, but whereas many of my fellow-writers have told me that they found it impossible to dictate satisfactorily, I myself, from the very first moment, found it by far the most effective method of getting my work on to paper. This is naturally a matter of individual idiosyncrasy.

I have never, I am sorry to say, been a great traveller. I have visited, in a cursory fashion, most European countries, and I have been to the United States a dozen times, but so far as regards actual influence upon my work, I would be perfectly content to spend the rest of my days in London. It is no gift of mine to impart reality into scenes and events taking place in a country in which I have not lived. Half a dozen thoroughfares and squares in London, a handful of restaurants, the people whom one meets in one single morning, are quite sufficient for the production of more and greater stories than I shall ever write. The real centres of interest to the world seem to me to be the places where human beings are gathered together more closely, because in such places the great struggle for existence, whatever shape it may take, must inevitably develop the whole capacity of man and strip him bare to the looker-on, even to nakedness. My place as a writer, if I might claim one, should be at a corner of the market-place.

(pp. 575-77)

A review of "The Deserter," in The Bookman, *New York, Vol. XXXII, No. 6, February, 1911, pp. 575-78.*

Grant Overton   (essay date 1924)

[*In the following essay, Overton offers a favorable assessment of Oppenheim's novels and a general introduction to the man and his work.*]

The other evening I picked up a novel called **The Lighted Way**, which, although it was published in May, 1912, I hadn't chanced ever to read. The page blurred slightly before my eyes, I think, because in going back over it some of the names and particulars seemed entirely changed. But this, as I took it in first, was the way it ran:

> Mr. E. Phillips Oppenheim, sole proprietor of the firm of E. Phillips Oppenheim & Nobody, wholesale entertainers of London and Europe, paused suddenly on his way from his private office to the street. There was something which until that second had entirely slipped his memory. It was not his title, for that, tastefully chosen, was already under his arm. Nor was it the Plot, for that, together with the first chapter, was sticking out of his overcoat pocket, the shape of which it completely ruined. As a matter of fact, it was more important than either of these—it was a commission from his conscience.
>
> Very slowly he retraced his steps until he stood outside the glass-enclosed cage where twelve of the hardest-worked clerks in London bent over their ledgers and invoicing. With his forefinger—a fat, pudgy forefinger—he tapped upon a pane of glass, and an anxious errand boy bolted through the doorway.
>
> "Tell Mr. Reader to step this way," his employer ordered.
>
> Mr. Reader heard the message and came hurrying out. He was an undersized man, with somewhat prominent eyes concealed by gold-rimmed spectacles. He was possessed of extraordinary zest for the details of the business, and was withal an expert and careful adviser. Hence his hold upon the confidence of his employer.
>
> The latter addressed him with a curious and altogether unusual hesitation in his manner.
>
> "Mr. Reader," he began, "there is a matter—a little matter—upon which I—er—wish to consult you."
>
> "Those American serial rights—"
>
> "Nothing to do with business at all," Mr. Oppenheim interrupted, ruthlessly. "A little private matter."
>
> "Indeed, sir?"

Now as I say, at this point I went back and found to my bewilderment at first, but perfect satisfaction afterward, that Mr. Oppenheim seemed to be Mr. Weatherley, a worthy provisioner; the title, an umbrella; the Plot, a copy of the London Times; and the alarming commission from Mr. Oppenheim's conscience, a possibly no less embarrassing commission from Mr. Weatherley's wife. Thereupon everything went smoothly and excitingly through thirty-seven chapters. But afterward it occurred to me that perhaps, after all, my blunder, visual or mental, was not an unnatural one. Who has not had in his mind's eye a picture of Mr. Oppenheim with a Plot, or Plots, bulging from his pockets, and with as many titles in his mental wardrobe as most men have neckties? And what one of his readers has not felt himself, time and again, personally summoned by the author to the consideration of a matter—a little matter—a quite private matter just then upon the author's conscience. . . .

It is the secret of Mr. Oppenheim's success, not detected as such by his readers, very probably not a trifle of which he himself is consciously aware. This engaging gift of confiding something, this easy air, this informality of his beginnings, disarms us and interests us as could no elaborately staged effort to arrest our attention and intrigue our minds. Even when he commences his story dramatically with such a confrontation as that which opens his *The Wrath to Come,* the air of naturalness is upon the scene. And the source of this effect? It comes from the fact that Mr. Oppenheim is imparting to you all that he himself knows at the given moment. Yes, literally. For our notion of him as a man with plots distending his pockets is entirely a mistaken notion. He has no plots; at least, he has no ready-made plots; he does not, so to say, plot his plots. "Just the first chapter, and an inkling of something to follow," was his answer to some one who asked him how much of his leading character he saw when he began a novel. What other method, when you stop to reflect upon it, would be possible for the author of eighty-six published novels? Certainly no one could map out his tales, even in essentials, and then write them to that number, not if he were to do the plots one by one, as occasion arose. He would be a slave, and the book, as written, would soon come to be lifeless. Nor, by such a method, would thirty-eight years afford time. In thirty-eight years the pace would be lost. Only spontaneity is capable of guaranteeing such a record as stands to Mr. Oppenheim's credit. "Two or three people in a crowded restaurant may arouse my interest, and the atmosphere is compelling. I start weaving a story around them—the circumstances and the people gradually develop as I go on dictating to my secretary the casual thoughts about them that arose in me while I was looking at them and their surroundings. First of all I must have a congenial atmosphere—then the rest is easy." And again:

> Writing for the movies is a ghastly business. I speak from experience. I shall never do it again. The picture people came to me and said, "Next time you have a novel in your head, why not, instead of writing 80,000 words, write a 5,000-word synopsis and let us have it? Then write your novel from the synopsis."
>
> Well, they paid well and I did it. I wrote the synopsis first and then set to work on the novel. I have never had a harder job in my life. Some writers, no doubt, do sketch out their plots beforehand, but I never work that way. When I start a story I never know just how it is going to end. All I have to start with is an idea. As I go along the idea grows and develops. So do the characters. I sort of live with them through the story and work out their salvation as it goes along. It is like a game.
>
> But when you write for the movies you have to reverse the process. In my case, it is fatal. Novels, even the kind that I write—and they are solely for amusement—must have some soul, something that gives them a human quality. This the author puts into the story as he goes along. When, however, he writes a synopsis and then sits down to enlarge and expand it into a novel, the spell is broken. He has a cold and rigid

plan to follow. It nearly killed me to novelize my first scenario.

He dictates his novels, revising the sheets as they come from the typewriter, sometimes re-dictating a passage or chapter. In summer he works outdoors; in winter he may pace up and down his study. "Many a time, earlier in life, when I used to write my stories with my own hand, I have found that my ideas would come so much faster than my fingers could work that I have prayed for some more speedy method of transmission. My present method is not only an immense relief to me, but it enables me to turn out far more work than would have been possible by any other means." Story-writing, he believes, is an original instinct, "just as it is an original instinct with a sporting dog to sniff about in every bush he passes for a rabbit. One writes stories because if one left them in the brain one would be subject to a sort of mental indigestion. As to plots, there are only about a score in the world, and when you have used them all, from A to Z"—which he pronounced "Zed," for this was in an after-dinner speech—"you can turn around and use them from Z to A." A favorite illustration with him is taken from a day's walk in London. "You can take the same walk every day in the year and you will meet a different crowd of people. These people contain the backgrounds of 365 stories a year." One person a day will keep the typewriter in play, for "I create one more or less interesting personality, try to think of some dramatic situation in which he or she might be placed, and use that as the opening of a nebulous chain of events."

What he said of himself at 55 is still, two years later, true without abatement. "Even if, like one of the heroes of fiction, I should make a million dollars out of a ten-cent piece in Wall Street, I should still continue to write stories so long as I can sit in an easy chair and my voice will carry as far as my secretary before a typewriter." Which is reminiscent of Hugh Walpole's remark in conversation the same year, that he was perfectly sure if a beam fell on his head and made him imbecile, he would continue to write novels for the pleasure of writing them.

Mr. Oppenheim was born in 1866 and went from school into his father's leather business at Leicester—but he had started writing stories before that. He began to write them at fifteen, and showed his first to the headmaster of the school, "who, instead of giving me the birching I deserved, wished me luck and encouraged me to persevere." The leather business was successful and was bought up by Blumenthals, a large American and Paris leather firm, who appointed young Oppenheim their director at Leicester. "His experience in that trade," asserts Mr. A. St. John Adcock in his *Gods of Modern Grub Street,*

> has proved immensely useful to him. It has not only helped him to material for his tales, but it was through the American head of Blumenthals that he had his chief incentive to the writing of the type of story that has brought him such success as a novelist. This gentleman introduced him to the proprietor of the Café de Rat Mort, the once famous Montmartre haunt, for Oppenheim was frequently in Paris on the affairs of his leather company, and at the Café he acquired his taste for the mysteries of those international in-

triguings and rascalities that figure so largely in several of his books, for the proprietor used to tell him all manner of thrilling yarns about political and international adventurers, some of whom had been among his customers, and his listener formed a habit of weaving stories around the more striking personalities in the cosmopolitan crowd that he met in the Dead Rat.

He was eighteen years old when his first short story was published, and only twenty when his first novel appeared. Before he was thirty he married Miss Elsie Hopkins, of Chelsea, Massachusetts. Mr. Oppenheim and his wife called their cottage in Sheringham, Norfolk, "Winnisimmet," which was the Indian name of her Massachusetts home town. The house overlooked the North Sea. Perhaps this detail, as much as another, led the author to the construction in the years before the world war of that series of stories in which, as an element of his plots, Mr. Oppenheim kept repeating Germany in the rôle of the villain. Legend has it that during the war itself his name was on the list of Britons to be shot if captured, although lists of that sort are usually myths. "There was one period," he has commented since, "in the autumn of 1918, when a well-directed bomb upon the Ministry of Information might have cleared the way for the younger novelists at the expense of Arnold Bennett, John Buchan, Dion Calthrop, E. Temple Thurston, Hugh Walpole and myself." He visited America in 1911 and again in 1922, when Mrs. Oppenheim came with him. On the latter occasion he made by far the wittiest comment of any visitor in reply to the usual question: what he thought of prohibition. "My only fear," with a smile, "is that it may make me a drunkard." Those who met the victim of this reasonable dread saw a sturdy, broad-shouldered figure developed by air and outdoor exercise; and those who played golf with him respected his handicap of seven strokes only. His large, florid face seemed to kindle into laughter from the constant humorous gleam in his blue eyes. Among his own titles he confessed to a fondness for *A Maker of History, The Double Life of Mr. Alfred Burton, The Great Impersonation* and—perhaps influenced a little by its then impending publication—*The Great Prince Shan.* At this time he was subjected to one of those sets of questions from the answers to which one may construct a totally wrong picture of the person. However, we may note that his idea of happiness was tied up with his work, and that he gave as his notion of unhappiness, "No ideas." His particular aversion, he said, was fog. Fog? Yet he has said: "I would be perfectly content to spend the rest of my days in London. Half a dozen thoroughfares and squares in London, a handful of restaurants, the people whom one meets in a single morning, are quite sufficient for the production of more and greater stories than I shall ever write." He describes himself as no great traveller; he has, though, been in most European countries, and he pretty regularly spends his winters at his villa in Cagnes on the Riviera. He divides his time in England between the house in Norfolk and his rooms in London.

Mr. Oppenheim does not take himself seriously in the rôle of prophet.

Large numbers of people have noted the fact

that in certain of my earlier novels I prophesied wars and world events that actually did come to pass. In *The Mysterious Mr. Sabin,* I pictured the South African Boer war seven years before it occurred. In *The Mischief Maker, The Great Secret,* and *A Maker of History* I based plots upon the German menace and the great war that did actually occur. The romance of secret diplomacy has enthralled me for years. In writing my novels I have had no particular advance knowledge of world affairs. I have reasoned to myself, "This nation is aiming toward this," and "That nation is aiming toward that"; then I have invented my puppets representing these conflicting ambitions and set them in action. It was the story first of all that appealed to me, and not any burning desire to express political convictions and lay bare great conspiracies.

He takes himself seriously only in the rôle of entertainer, of storyteller. "If you tell him you like his books," says Gerald Cumberland, in *Written in Friendship,* "he is frankly pleased; but if you pay him high-flown compliments he will begin to yawn." There need be no paying of compliments in a consideration of Mr. Oppenheim's work, but no analysis of his method could fairly withhold considerable praise. We have spoken of his confidential, easy manner with the reader as a secret of his toward establishing plausibility for the things he is about to tell. But there is more to be noted. Like the best writers of his sort among his countrymen—and like far too few Americans in the same field—he is unhurried. He is never afraid to pause for the amplification of sentiment, the communication of the moment's feeling, a bit of characterization or a passage of pure description. And these are the matters which give an effect of rondure, and not infrequently touches of charm, to a story of whatever sort. At the moment I can think of only one American—Hulbert Footner—who has had the wisdom, or perhaps the temperament, to follow British practice in this by no means negligible affair of workmanship; and it is significant that Mr. Footner, an American, has so far had a better reception in England than in his own country. Apparently we value this certain leisureliness when it comes to us from abroad, for Mr. Footner, re-exported to us, is making distinct headway. What the American writer generally does is to accelerate his action to the pitch of implausibility (if he only knew it). This does very well, and may be indispensable, for all I know, with the readers of a certain type of American magazines; unfortunately the habitual buyers and readers of books demand something more careful.

The other interesting point of excellence in Oppenheim's work derives from his method of spontaneity. He once said: "The lure of creation never loses its hold. Personally I cannot account for the fact. Perhaps it springs from the inextinguishable hope that one day there will be born the most wonderful idea that has ever found its way into the brain of a writer of fiction." For the creator, the superlative never arrives; but certainly for the reader Mr. Oppenheim has materialized more than one wonderful idea. *The Great Impersonation,* deservedly one of his most successful books, is a fairly recent illustration. But I would like to call particularly to attention an earlier story, both for what seems to me to be its astonishing merit and for its

interesting light on the method of spontaneity which is Oppenheim's special technique. This is *The Way of These Women,* now ten years old. That it still sells is evidence that its merit is recognized; that one never hears mention of it in any offhand mention of its author's work shows that the recognition is by no means wide enough.

Sir Jermyn Annerley, a young man of fine taste and high honor, though certainly inclined toward priggishness, is a playwright of the intellectual type. Sybil Cluley, the actress who has aroused London by her performance in Jermyn's drama, comes to Annerley Court as his weekend guest. They are to discuss his new play in which Sybil is to appear. Aynesworth, Marquis of Lakenham and Jermyn's second cousin, chances to pay a visit at the same time. Another distant cousin of Jermyn, Lucille, who has divorced a French nobleman, is Jermyn's hostess. Lucille is in love with Jermyn. During the visit Jermyn surrenders to his love for Sybil; they announce their engagement to the others. Sybil is obviously afraid of Lakenham to a degree not to be accounted for by his reputation for excesses, and after some time Lakenham confirms and shares with Lucille his knowledge of a discreditable episode in Sybil's career before her success on the stage.

Lakenham is murdered at Annerley Court. Suspicion points directly to Sybil, but Lucille has aided Sybil and Jermyn in the removal of very incriminating evidence. As the price for protecting Sybil, Lucille requires Jermyn to marry her within two months.

The story is developed with admirable intervals and suspense. The point of the first quarter of the book is Lakenham's knowledge of something in Sybil's past, and Lucille's determination to fight Sybil for Jermyn. Then Lakenham is killed. Almost half the book lies between the murder and its solution. It is evident that as he wrote Mr. Oppenheim saw (what he may not have grasped at the beginning) that Lucille was his most striking character. As the novel proceeded he became absorbed in the possibilities Lucille offered; if, as may well be the case, he vaguely contemplated solving the murder and bringing Sybil and Jermyn happily together for a quick "curtain," he deliberately abandoned so conventional and easy an ending. Jermyn and Lucille are married under the hateful terms Lucille has imposed as the price of Sybil's safety.

It is this that lifts *The Way of These Women* out of the run of Mr. Oppenheim's work. Did Sybil kill Lakenham? If she did not, who did she think killed him? If Lucille used fraud with Jermyn, why not annul the marriage for fraud and bring down the curtain? (And in putting these questions I decline responsibility for your wrong inferences as to the answers.) In any case, the solution of the murder would seem to end the story. But something larger and more fateful, something of very near universal significance, had by this time lodged in Mr. Oppenheim's mind. The "wonderful idea" had come. The last quarter of *The Way of These Women* is the material, intrinsically, for a very great novel. And Mr. Oppenheim handles it with touches of greatness. He could, of course, by slashing off most he had already written, by adopting some such technical device as W. B. Maxwell used in *The Devil's Garden,* have made it a masterpiece, for his knowledge of his theme and his appreciation of its character are plain to be seen. I do not know whether this novel has ever been dramatized, but it is incredible that it should not have been dramatized; the possibilities of Lucille are greater than those of Camille, for they are less artificial and they are not either sentimental or cheap. Why did Mr. Oppenheim not rework it; why did he let it go as the book is, a mixture? Of several possible extenuations, I think the best is that by leaving it alone he probably was able to take the reader who sought merely to be entertained into a very high place whither that reader could not have been lured directly. And it is an elevation to which the writer of ready-made plots never leads. (pp. 126-38)

> Grant Overton, "A Great Impersonation by E. Phillips Oppenheim," in his Cargoes for Crusoes, D. Appleton & Company, 1924, pp. 126-42.

The Dreyfus Affair and the origins of the spy novel:

The Franco-Prussian War, so argues I. F. Clarke in *Voices Prophesying War,* gave birth to the war prophecy movement, but it also added another event necessary for the start of the spy novel in Oppenheim and [William] LeQueux—the Dreyfus case. In December, 1894 a court martial convicted Alfred Dreyfus of spying against France for the Germans. The international furor over this verdict culminated in Zola's "J'Accuse" early in 1898, as well as the novelist's flight to England. Dreyfus added just what LeQueux and Oppenheim needed to bring them to the spy novel: a hot public issue and a figure of great sentimental potential. The connection of the Dreyfus case and the spy novel was not lost on contemporary reviewers. Thus, in reviews of one of LeQueux's novels we get critics saying that "the subject of international espionage and the possibilities of secret service have been suggested to novelists by the Dreyfus case." and that "the Dreyfus case has probably inspired the author." Responding to this particular issue, therefore, the writers scraped up some material from the Dreyfus case and tossed it together with some old motifs, and with **The Mysterious Mr. Sabin** (1898) and *The Day of Temptation* (1899) they concocted the spy novel—of sorts.

> LeRoy L. Panek, in his The Special Branch: The British Spy Novel, 1890-1980, Bowling Green University Popular Press, 1981.

Reg Gadney (essay date 1970)

[*Gadney is an English novelist, filmmaker, and critic. In the following excerpt, he discusses some of the features that contributed to the popular appeal of Oppenheim's novels in a general assessment of his life and works.*]

The eclipse of E. Phillips Oppenheim is now almost total. I suppose that the post-war generation of thriller readers very rarely switches off the wireless, or anything else, to read any of Oppenheim's 13,000,000 or so written words. Neither, I imagine, do they know or care much about the legend of Oppenheim. But for those who do the search for

facts about his working methods and indeed about his life will be a difficult one. When he died on 3 February 1946, in Guernsey, his diaries, notes and papers were still in his Riviera villa in Roquefort-les-Pins, where they had lain for six years. A year later, in 1947, the bonfire they were thrown on burned for a week. His only daughter died last year. But all she had were some scrap albums, some of the books and one or two photos. Her son, the victim of a monstrous glandular disease, had died a year before. The Oppenheim legend ended finally with Oppenheim's daughter dying in a loneliness which her father's heroes and heroines had never known. They shared with other pre-war fictional adventurers the paternity of Bond and his progenitors.

'The cook is preparing you some luncheon,' the doctor announced, 'which it will do you good to eat. I cannot give you whisky at this moment, but you can have some hock and seltzer with bay leaves' (**The Great Impersonation,** 1920). And a few pages later, still in the middle of 'German Africa' with his old friend His Excellency the Major-General Baron Leopold von Ragastein ('late of Eton—Horrock's House—semi-final in the racquets—Magdalen afterwards number five in the boat') the suave Sir Everard Dominey exclaims, 'By Jove. I hadn't eaten for thirty hours when I rolled up here last night, and drunk nothing but filthy water for days. Tonight fricassée of chicken, white bread, cabinet hock and Napoleon brandy.' Von Ragastein and Dominey looked incredibly alike, so much so that von Ragastein succeeds in poisoning Dominey, assumes the role of the latter and then begins his adventures in London. On the other hand, not quite: because Dominey had foiled the German's plot, so what actually happened was that Dominey—the real Dominey—returned to London, pretending that he was the disguised von Ragastein.

On this device Oppenheim embroidered **The Great Impersonation,** a classic Oppenheim in technique and in sales. The American publishers alone, Little Brown & Co., sold 1,013,047 copies, and according to Robert Standish in his book on Oppenheim *The Prince of Storytellers,* the book was still selling in 1956. It was published in 1920, so he was presumably engaged on writing it when he was interviewed by a reporter from the *Newcastle Sunday Sun.* The interview came out on 6 January, 1919, and Oppenheim is quoted as saying; 'I am a maker of stories while you wait . . . Sex is dropping a little. Crime is coming in again. A good, sound, romantic story is what they want. France wants nothing else but sex. I get less from my translation rights into French than even Jugoslavian. I don't talk sex. I attribute my popularity to having kept away from sex.' But what **The Great Impersonation** did contain were all the Oppenheim hallmarks. He launches straight into his story in the first paragraph, as Everard Dominey blunders into the camp of von Ragastein. The *fantasy* is established with the meal. Oppenheim readers did not want to hear of the jungle's menace. Rather they liked to hear of old Etonians camping in the jungle, dining off chicken fricassée, hock and seltzer and then dragging their 'chairs a little further out into the darkness, smoking cigars and drinking some rather wonderful coffee'. But the story comes first, and like most natural storytellers he clearly derived as much enjoyment from his inventions as did his readers.

There is little sense of struggle in them, they just poured out, as Oppenheim himself admitted: 'I do not know how else to account for the fact that today I sit down to commence a new story with exactly the same thrill as I did at twenty. The love of games and sport, of sea and mountains, the call of strange cities, wonderful pictures and unusual people, however dear they may still remain to one, lose something of their first and vital freshness with the passing of the years. Not so the sight of that blank sheet of paper waiting for the thoughts and pictures which crowd their way into the brain. For every story has about it something new; every slowly unwinding skein of fancy leads along some untrodden paths into virgin fields. The lure of creation never loses its hold'. 'Story writing,' Oppenheim said, 'is an instinct.'

This is what he told the guests at the Little, Brown Centenary Dinner in New York on 31 March 1937. How far the blank 'sheet of paper' itself really set his instinct on fire is debatable, because he dictated the majority of his books to a series of young girl secretaries. And, as his daughter told me, as often as not he left the editing to them as well.

Robert Standish says, rightly, that the speech to the Little, Brown dinner carries 'a ring of truth!' It was at that same dinner that he made his celebrated observations on plot:

> If I were to attempt to work from a synopsis I should be done. My characters would resent it and at once kick over the traces. My readers would at once say 'Pshaw! He has written too much!' and my publishers would hint at the high price of paper and an old-age pension. So I leave the synopsis alone. And as to plots, there are only about a score in the world and when you have used them all from A to Z you can turn around and use them again from Z to A.

On the Riviera the dictation usually took place in the early afternoons, followed by a sleep (with the secretary of the moment according to legend, but 'sleep and labial flirtation' according to his daughter—without improbable admissions from some very old ladies one cannot be sure). The rest of the time was divided between casino visits, golf with a woman friend, left-handed golf, fishing (between 15 June and 6 September 1938 the catches totalled 160 lobsters, 23 crabs, 522 whiting and 638 mackerel, all hauled up onto *Echo II* his 28-ton 62-foot motor yacht), colonic irrigation and luncheon parties, one of which was attended by Sir Hugo and Lady de Bathe (Sir Hugo's distinction was that he had been formerly married to Lily Langtry).

At this time, Oppenheim was seventy-two years old, with another eight years of life left. Some indication of the sources of the legend of his love-making may be gained from a story recorded by Robert Standish. During the first week in June 1938 Oppenheim must have been in London, for he made a complaint to his chemist. The complaint was to do with his supply of contraceptives. The chemist sought to please his loyal customer, provided Oppenheim with a new batch and, best of all, told Oppenheim that if anything went wrong he, the chemist, would adopt the child.

What the facts were about his adventures in love-making it is now virtually impossible to establish, and in any case the task of discovering them is hardly worth while. Oppenheim's fictional females probably bear little resemblance to the army of women who are supposed to have warmed his bed. But, more importantly, they do give an indication of what his readers conjured up in their minds as ideals. When Oppenheim talked to Renée Davis of *La France* in August 1928 he was describing, no doubt, what he tried to present his readers with: 'Je n'aime pas les femmes d'aujourd'hui avec leurs cheveux courts et plaques et leurs figures peinturlurées, leurs sourcils "éminces" et tout le reste . . . j'aime qu'une femme ait l'air d'une femme. J'en connais une . . . dans *The Treasure House of Martin Hews,* mon prochain livre.'

And sure enough, in 1929 in that book the ideal emerges in the form of Beatrice Essiter.

> She had changed her dress, but she was still wearing black—a gown of cunningly devised simplicity, which seemed to fall in one line from her neck to the hem of her skirt. She wore no ornaments, and her strangely coloured hair was arranged in unfashionable and severely simple coils . . . she was an unusually beautiful young woman. Although her voice, her eyes, her changeless poise seemed to bespeak a curious lack of human sensibility, she had the air of living in a world of her own from which she emerged upon necessity with a certain amount of resentment.

Beatrice contrasts with Rachel (in the same book) who is of an altogether different class: 'Her frock was of the sort which had probably come from Shaftesbury Avenue— daring but in its way well fashioned. It disclosed the lines of her exquisite little figure with purposeful artistry. Her silk-clad legs, beautifully shaped, were both extended upon the fender.'

Sex may have been dropping a little in 1919, but by 1929 Oppenheim had caught more than a little of it on the way down: 'Rachel was lying back in the chair, bound with the cruellest of ropes. Her eyes were open, but glazed and set with terror, and every particle of her colour had left her cheeks and lips.' Rachel had been shaved, 'And her bald scalp! She had the appearance of some terrible mummy dragged from its grave by an over-curious civilisation . . . "They've cut my legs too," she cried hysterically. "One man said he was a surgeon" '. This was the fate of a woman who lived too far from Mayfair or the Riviera.

Lady Jane Partington in *Nobody's Man* of 1921 ' . . . had the reputation of living out of doors, winter and summer, [and] had a complexion which, notwithstanding its finest shade of tan, would have passed muster for delicacy and clearness in any Mayfair drawingroom'. And, of course, ' . . . she appeared wholly unconscious of the admiration she excited'.

This was the Oppenheim charm which seduced his readers and on more than one occasion his reviewers as well. 'D.F.G.' wrote in the *Boston Evening Transcript* (1932):

> . . . with just a few words of delicate implication, with what might be described as a literary

sigh, or an emotional aside, he blows the breath of idealism, soft as a literary zephyr, over even the most consummate criminals in his stories. A handsome alluring Oppenheim adventuress, for example, no matter how merciless she may seem at first, has her gentle moments. Sometimes the young diplomat in her clutches reminds her of her first love, or of her last love or of her lost youth. This results in a melting heart, a kind word and perhaps eventually an avenue of escape for the diplomat.

This is the formula in *The Great Impersonation,* somewhat elaborated, and in *The Light Beyond* (1928), where there is the familiar structure of confident hero, mean villain and girl in between hopelessly caught up. The distinctions are sharply drawn, as for example in *Mr Grex of Monte Carlo* (1915), when Richard Lane faces Miss Grex:

> She turned and looked at him almost wonderingly. He was very big and very confident; good to look upon, less because of his actual good looks than because of a certain honesty and tenacity of purpose in his expression; a strength of jaw, modified and rendered even pleasant by the kindness and humour of his clear grey eyes. He returned her gaze without embarrassment and he wondered less than ever at finding himself there. Her complexion in this clear light seemed more beautiful than ever. Her rich golden-brown hair was waved becomingly over her forehead. Her eyebrows were silky and delicately straight, her mouth delightful. Her figure was girlish, but unusually dignified for her years.

The speed of dictation tells; it is really just an inventory of looks, a sort of specification for a waxworks modeller; and when Richard Lane contemplates his own presence there, the passage disintegrates—'he wondered less than ever at finding himself there.'

But such lapses hardly bothered the readers, particularly when they were followed by this kind of vintage Oppenheim: 'You know,' he said suddenly, 'you look to me like one of those beautiful plants you have in the conservatory there, just as though you'd stepped out of your little glass home and blossomed right here. I am almost afraid of you.' These are the words of E. Phillips Oppenheim—seducer of a mass readership. He liked his men to be just a little frightened of these perfumed creatures. And when killings occur, the details are skimped, or at least made palatable. In *Murder at Monte Carlo* (1932) 'His knees crumpled beneath him . . . The electrician found him about a quarter of an hour later, lying like a man who had fallen backwards and broken his neck. There were two small holes in his shirtfront exactly over the heart and his pockets were empty.' Tidy, convenient, no stained carpet and the reader is left to imagine what a man who has fallen backwards and broken his neck looks like.

So, too, is the reader asked to fill in much of the background of the stories. 'D.F.G.' ended his review for the *Boston Evening Transcript* with this, 'It was in Germany that the beautiful book by Baroness von Suttner called *Lay Down Your Arms* first appeared. Germany also knifed Belgium in the back. So let us be prepared for possible events.' Even in 1920 in *The Great Impersonation* Oppenheim was busy with prediction. Seaman, the German lackey, rants at Everard Dominey 'He [the Kaiser] will see himself the knight in shining armour. All Europe will bow down before this self-imagined Caesar, and no one except we who are behind will realise the ass's head. There is no one else in this world whom I have ever met so well fitted to lead our great nation on to the destiny she deserves.' And as a photograph testifies in the Wiener Library Hitler did have himself painted precisely as a knight in shining armour.

But all this was inspired guesswork. Some of Oppenheim's stories written before the First War had hinted at the German threat. Oppenheim himself was not a German, and genuinely loathed Germany. During the First War he held a minor post in the Ministry of Information, writing inadequate propaganda, as well as no less than some 13 books of his own. Perhaps he thought he had unique qualifications to be of use to his country when the Second War broke out, perhaps he thought his intuition might be of use. So he left Guernsey for London and presented himself to the Ministry of Information once again. But he was nearing eighty and shown the door.

Robert Standish tells of Oppenheim's return to the South of France after war had been declared, and he published an anonymous eyewitness's account of Oppenheim's abortive departure with 1,200 others on two filthy coal boats from Cannes. Oppenheim and his wife, Elsie, appeared on the quayside with luncheon hampers and champagne. Oppenheim emerged from his limousine to inspect the boats. He was dressed '. . . in a pearl gray tropical worsted suit, with white buckskin shoes and the solar topee that he always affected in summer, and stood with blank horror and amazement on his face looking at the accommodation, if it can be called such, available for 1,200 people'. Oppenheim returned to his car, and drove off with Elsie, allowing the 1,200, including Somerset Maugham, to get on with it.

They spent the rest of the summer at their villa, and eventually an American consular official arranged for them to travel to Portugal through Spain. They reached England some time during the first few months of 1941. Not until 1945 did the elderly couple persuade a yachtsman to take them to Guernsey, on what Oppenheim probably thought was the first part of his return to the Riviera. But he never continued the journey and died in Guernsey on 3 February 1946.

Between 1887 (*Expiation*) and 1943 (*Mr Mirakel*) he wrote about 115 novels (including those under his pseudonym of Anthony Partridge) but excluding the various pirated versions which appeared in America. He published 39 books of short stories between 1908 (*The Long Arm*) and 1940 (*The Milan Grill Room*); a travel book (*The Quest for Winter Sunshine.* 1927) and his much derided autobiography (*The Pool of Memory.* 1941).

In addition there were newspaper articles and short stories in magazines.

Whether or not his output equals sixteen or seventeen bibles, or whether it amounts to 13 or 14 million words is finally unimportant. What is perhaps of greater interest lies in the appeal of the books: the combination of rambling storytelling, unattainable women, suave, wholesome heroes, conspiratorial villains, and of course the backgrounds of the Riviera, English country estates and the hotels peopled almost always both by the rich, and the efficient and cringing *maîtres d'hôtel*. The snobbery of it all was snobbery for those who believe that snobs do not bitch and are unperturbed by those 'below' them. This may have something to do with why Oppenheim's characters are now so dated. Of course the pre-war Riviera society of Oppenheim has now disappeared and all values of its so-called manners and eccentricities have vanished too.

The recipe of Oppenheim's stories, much like that of his life, was summed up by Robert van Gelder in the *New York Times* of 27 January 1934: 'Incident! Incident! Incident! Surprise! Surprise! Surprise!' But the trouble was, as Charles Williams observed in the *News Chronicle* the following week: '. . . . his language is often too lofty for his story. His characters sometimes descend to dinner jackets; his words always wear white ties.'

Even the distinction, along with the reputation of E. Phillips Oppenheim, is now all but lost. (pp. 19-27)

> Reg Gadney, "Switch Off the Wireless—It's an Oppenheim," in London Magazine, Vol. 10, No. 3, June, 1970, pp. 19-27.

LeRoy L. Panek (essay date 1981)

[*Panek, an American professor of English, has written widely on the history of British detective and spy fiction. In the following excerpt from his* The Special Branch: The British Spy Novel, 1890-1980, *Panek discusses Oppenheim's spy fiction written at the beginning, middle, and end of his career, focusing on* The Mysterious Mr. Sabin, The Pawns Count, *and* Up the Ladder of Gold.]

His publishers called him "The Prince of Storytellers," and John Buchan said that "E. Phillips Oppenheim is the greatest Jewish writer since Isaiah." Buchan, I think, was being ironic, but Oppy's publishers had sales figures to back up their title. He was hot stuff, but Oppenheim was scarcely a great or even a good writer. He wrote lousy plots, wooden characters, cliched dialogue, and bogus description. Any other age would have immediately relegated him to the dusty storerooms of libraries and musty used book shops—our age certainly has. Fortunately for Oppenheim, he began to write at a time when the British reading public expanded and the American reading public thirsted for snobby English novels, when enterprising merchants pushed popular literature by means of commercial lending libraries, and when readers had not yet seen the potential of the action/adventure spy novel. Having the faculties of writing quickly, of joining popular forms together, and of merging fantasy and fact, Oppenheim made enough money to deserve at least the first part of the "Prince of Storytellers" tag.

Oppenheim spread his limited talents to most of the forms of the novel popular in the nineties and afterward. He wrote romances about love, like *A Daughter of Marionis* (1895), which dwell on the various exercises of the pas-

sions. He wrote finance romances, like *The Millionaire of Yesterday* (1900), or *The Lighted Way* (1912), which tells of the trials and glories of having and losing money. He also wrote what reviewers of the period called "novels of social political life" like *A Prince of Sinners* (1903) or *A Lost Leader* (1906). Further, Oppy cranked out mystery novels of every shape: there are action detective stories like *The Black Box* (1915), revenge stories like *The Avenger* (1907), and in the thirties there are puzzle concoctions like *General Besserley's Puzzle Box* (1935), and *General Besserley's Second Puzzle Box* (1939). Most of these mystery stories are pretty transparent and, in fact, exist as containers for Oppenheim's other interests. He wrote some reasonably unadorned adventure yarns like *The Daughter of Astrea* (1898), but most importantly for us, Oppy wrote a whole cartload of spy novels. He is, indeed, one of the first practitioners of the form.

Oppy's spy novels present numerous problems to anyone attempting to survey the history of the form. The primary problem is that they are bad novels, bad technically, stylistically, and bad morally. Reading much Oppenheim tests the resolve of any analyst. About the best thing I can say about them is that they are not quite as bad as LeQueux's. Few people really mind reading a couple of rotten novels for the cause, but Oppenheim, by Hubin's list, wrote one hundred and sixteen novels. That is a lot for the cause. I will begin, therefore, with the admission that I have not read all of Oppenheim's novels: I have, though, read some seventy of them, and this is more than enough to give authority to my discussion. The second problem with Oppenheim is that he wrote over a considerable period—*Expiation* appeared in 1887 and *Mr. Mirakel* came out in 1943. What I am going to do, rather than trying to survey all of the books, is to discuss three representative novels from the beginning, middle and end of Oppenheim's career.

Oppenheim's first spy novel, *The Mysterious Mr. Sabin* (1898), uses the war prophecy formula: it is a prediction of an averted war instead of an actual one, and it thereby takes the predictive war story and channels it into the course which would be expanded by Childers in 1903 and lots of others later on. He is also somewhat in advance of his contemporaries in the selection of England's enemy. In *Voices Prophesying War* Clark notes that France and Russia were England's main antagonists in early fictional contests of the future, but here, five years before *The Riddle of the Sands*, Oppenheim factors Germany into the equation. In spite of these exceptions, *The Mysterious Mr. Sabin* does introduce motifs common to the predictive war story. Oppenheim mentions the weakness of the fleet, the feebleness of England's coastal defenses, the precariousness of defending the Empire, and the devastating effect of secret weapons (Mr. Sabin has invented electric mines in Addison's laboratories in America). Later in *The Great Impersonation* (1920) Oppenheim dedicated a novel to Lord Roberts, the patron of LeQueux's predictive story *The Great War in England in 1897* (1894). He does not in *The Mysterious Mr. Sabin* or any of his other novels make war prophecy motifs into political propaganda, but uses them merely as details of the plot. Instead he bases the plot of *The Mysterious Mr. Sabin* on historical events. Oppy builds this plot on the Boulangist risings in France in 1888-9 (with Boulanger flirting with the Bourbons and the Bonapartes, only to give up his chance for power for Marguerite de Bonnemains) just as he inclines to build his wartime plots on actual events. He adapts the historical material into Mr. Sabin's plot to restore the Princess Helene of Bourbon and Prince Henri of Ortens to the French throne which fails partly because Helene gives up her ambition for the man she loves. This theme of restoring monarchies becomes one of Oppenheim's standards, only he shifted his ground to Russia, predicting the ouster of the communists in favor of a new Czar in *Gabriel Samara Peacemaker* (1925) and *The Dumb Gods Speak* (1937). Indeed, Oppy's bias in government is toward monarchy, and he usually expresses this by centering his spy novels on the one great man who moves, shapes, or prevents events. This continues even in his last novel, *Mr. Mirakel,* which is really the story of a king in mufti.

The projected French revolution in *The Mysterious Mr. Sabin,* though, does not involve revolutionaries: monarchists, being what they are, can have no truck with grimy revolutionaries, and in all of Oppy's fiction the portrait of the revolutionary is one of a wretched reptile. If they cannot use internal rising, the monarchists have to depend upon external force to seat them on the throne of their ancestors. Mr. Sabin markets for a suitable external force in *The Mysterious Mr. Sabin,* but first he must secure payment for other states monkeying with the internal affairs of France, and the payment which he decides on is England. Sabin plans to sell England's liberty to her jealous neighbors. Now, colonial friction rubbed particularly hot in the 1880s and the 1890s. Britain and Russia collided over Afghanistan and Persia, and Oppenheim does show a Russian spy trying to sneak a peek at the plans of England's defense, but, we are assured in the novel, Russia is fairly honorable and will not sell its republican ally, France, down the river regardless of its love for monarchy. Who will? The Germans. Thus the German Ambassador, Baron von Knignstein, gives Sabin this diatribe:

> It is the ties of kindred . . . which breed irritability, not kindliness! I tell you, my friend, that there is a great storm gathering. It is not for nothing that the great hosts of my country are ruled by a war lord! I tell you that we are arming to the teeth, silently, swiftly, and with a purpose. It may seem to you a small thing; but let me tell you this—we are a jealous nation! And we have cause for jealousy. In whatever part of the world we put down our foot, it is trodden on by our ubiquitous cousins! Wherever we turn to colonize, we are too late; England has already secured the finest territory, the most fruitful of the land. We must either take her leavings or go abegging. Wherever we develop, we are held back by the commercial and colonizing genius— it amounts to that of this wonderful country. There is no room for a growing England and a growing Germany! So! one must give way, and Germany is beginning to mutter that it shall not always be her sons who go to the wall. You say that France is our natural enemy. I deny it! France is our historical enemy—nothing else! In military circles today a war with England would

be wildly, hysterically popular; and sooner or later a war with England is as certain to come as the rising of the sun and the waning of the moon: I can tell you even now where the first blow will be struck! It is fixed! It is to come! So!

After a few more exclamation points and cliches we learn that Germany intends to provoke England into war over colonial issues in Africa, and Oppenheim brings the novel to the brink of war between England and Germany: the Kaiser blusters and the Prime Minister reacts coolly. But there is no war. Sabin cannot deliver England up to her foes.

England's danger and deliverance rest on papers. *The Mysterious Mr. Sabin* is a paper chase novel without much chase—perhaps paper possession would be a better term. Oppenheim centers lots of his spy books on papers: take *A Maker of History* (1905) or *Miss Brown of the XYO* (1927) for instance. This motif is not only a way of introducing lady typists, one of Oppy's character types, but more importantly it shows the evolution of the spy novel from the Victorian detective novel. Blackmail forms the basis for many Victorian detective stories—probably because of the fetish for outward propriety. It is a short step from threatening an individual with exposure of his secrets to threatening a nation with exposure of its weaknesses and secrets. Mr. Sabin fills both roles: he blackmails Lady Deringham with her old love letters which expose her momentary weakness, and he steals papers which threaten to expose the strategic and tactical debility of Britain. In *The Mysterious Mr. Sabin* England's safety depends on the scantily guarded work of the half-mad Lord Deringham who is preparing the definitive study of Britain's naval preparedness and defense. Swallowing this, however, is the same as believing the fact that the naval defense plans pilfered in *The Thirty Nine Steps* cannot be remade or altered. It is unlikely that knowledge of flaws in ship design or the orientation of coastal defenses would absolutely insure the victory of an invader, yet these form the base for the political haggling in *The Mysterious Mr. Sabin* and innumerable later spy books by Oppy and his successors.

But this is not simply a novel of international politics, it is a spy book. For Oppenheim there is spying and there is spying. Mr. Sabin does a lot of underhanded things in this novel: he blackmails Lady Deringham, coshes Wolfenden and assorted servants, employs thieves, lies and steals. Yet he refuses to consider himself a spy and the readers are not supposed to do so either. Thus when Felix reveals his mission to Sabin, we get

> "So you are a lacquey after all, then?" he remarked—"a common spy."

Spies do things for money and do not formulate policy. An even baser example of spying is among the Germans. One particular branch of German agents are the "Doomschen," people who

> . . . have committed a crime punishable by death,—that . . . are on parole only so long as . . . [they] remain in the service of the Secret Police.

If you formulate policy and do your work for nothing, though, you are not a spy but a patriot or a diplomatist. This class attracts Oppy's attention and admiration, as it does LeQueux, and there are innumerable examples of the diplomatist-spy in his novels. In fact, Oppenheim distorts the structure of *The Mysterious Mr. Sabin* in order to make the point that his heroes are people of larger being than those limited by political events. Thus the novel shows the salvation of England and the frustration of Sabin's plans fully eighty pages before the end of the book. The last eighty pages show us that Sabin is suave, witty, and courageous; he escapes from nasty Germans and also atones for having been a rake. Look, Oppy says, you may not like this man's politics, but he is as noble as all get out. Further, the stereotype about spies and police agents causes one of the gargantuan flaws in the plot. Sabin does not fail because he does not have the goods or the will to use them. His plot fails because a mysterious representative of an even more mysterious underground organization plummets out of the heavens and tells him that the High Council has decided that he should stop fooling around with the balance of power in the world, and he drops his plans at once. Oppenheim has recourse to this *deus ex machina* because he does not want to sully his young aristocratic romantic lead (Wolfenden) with action. Thus, all that Wolfenden does is get the girl and stand around looking, to eyes conditioned by action heroes, like a ninny.

For Oppenheim, characters are to serve one, settled, unchangeable role. Wolfenden is the romantic lead, Sabin is the Byronic hero (complete with club foot), Helene is the female lead, Blanche Merton is the fallen woman, and Lord Deringham is the mad genius. Each has his or her own cliche. The only development which Oppy allows is with secrets that people hold about themselves but eventually release. Thus, Lady Deringham eventually confesses her indiscretion with Sabin, Helene reveals her real name and her heart after Wolfenden pursues them for a couple of hundred pages, and we find out that Sabin is the Duc de Souspenier, who aspires to be the Richelieu to the new French monarchy. No one surprises or acts out of character. The readers know them, Oppenheim intends them to appeal to specific romantic fantasies, and the readers will meet them again and again in Oppy's later novels.

Mr. Sabin ends up in New England quietly playing golf (one of Oppenheim's passions, many of his heroes are scratch golfers) until an international secret society kidnaps his wife and sets him running again in *The Yellow Ribbon* (1903). Most of Oppenheim's books, moreover, have an American connection, and the reason is obvious. A best selling writer can make a fair living from the British public, but if he aspires to yachts, to fancy motor cars, to the opulent life of his own fictions, then he must sell more books. Where? In the United States. Thus, fairly early in his career Oppenheim looked toward American markets, and his books came out first from Little, Brown and Company in Boston. To appeal to this market Oppenheim combines romance and high life of the Old World (the sloe-eyed woman and the aristocrat's son) with the technology, wealth, and spunk of the New World (the energetic, rich inventor) and evolves a formula where the two

worlds meet. All of this becomes more acute in the books written before America's entry into World War I, where Oppy adds out and out flattery in order to move public opinion in the U.S. toward the camp of the Allies. Thus, in *The Pawns Count* (1918) we find that American women are prettier:

> Pamela was beautiful and unusual. She had the long, slim body of the New York girl, the complexion and eyes of a Southerner, the savoir faire of a French woman. She was extraordinarily cosmopolitan, and yet extraordinarily American.

and Washington D.C., is the new Rome:

> The stateliness of the city, its sedate and quiescent air after the turmoil of New York, impressed him profoundly. Everywhere its diplomatic associations made themselves felt. Congress was in session, and the faces of the men whom he met in the hotels and restaurants seemed to him some index of the world power which flung its far-reaching arms from beneath the Capitol dome.

This transparent flattery of the U.S., though, does not in itself make Oppenheim's war-time spy novels different from his early books (in many ways they are quite similar), but in some ways his books of the second phase do present a slightly different face of diplomacy and espionage.

For one thing, Oppenheim shifts the focus of his heroes. In the early books he generally segregates the romantic hero from the action and adventure: indeed, action and adventure generally get little attention in Oppy's novels from first to last, carrying out the diplomatist-spy distinction. During the war, however, his heroes act more. Francis Newgate runs about to expose German plotting in *The Double Traitor* (1915), Thomson in *The Kingdom of the Blind* (1916) runs about a good bit to discover German spies in London, and John Lutchester is energetically ubiquitous in *The Pawns Count.* Mind you, Oppenheim never gives us the details of the action—we never find out in *The Pawns Count,* for instance, just how Lutchester appears at exactly the right moment to save Pamela from the Japanese agent—but there is plenty of action in these books, almost too much. Instead of being passive heroes like Wolfenden or like Wrayson in *The Avenger* (1907), these men act. Lutchester, for example, works some sort of oriental system of self-defense on Nikasti, the Japanese Secret Service man, and he also bests a Bowery assassin on the streets of New York. But Oppenheim joins this action with romantic suavity, financial genius, and political adroitness. Thus Lutchester shows the virtues of Oppenheim's wartime agents, but he also highlights the writer's difficulty in dealing with a new sort of popular hero. Lutchester is, as I have indicated, active, intelligent, and efficient. He thwarts the secret weapon plot, and unravels the Germany, America, Japan triangle in the novel. He saves the reputation of one woman, wins another for his wife, and makes a bundle on the stock market without even trying. He knows how to dress, how to order dinner, and how to play golf. Further, he is related to the Duke of Worcester: "one of the oldest families in England." Yet Lutchester is not Oppy's ideal hero: he is Oppenheim's attempt to portray the droll sportsman who plays the game with ease and wit. He cops the secret formula without wrinkling his suit, he belittles his accomplishments with Oppenheim reduction, making fun of the melodramatic potential in his acts. This passage comes after rescuing Graham from his captors:

> "I had pictured for myself a dramatic entrance . . . a quiet turning of the key, a soft approach—owing to my shoes . . . a cough, perhaps or a breath . . . discovery, me with a revolver in my hand pointed at the arch villain—'If you stir you're a dead man!' . . . Natural collapse of the villain. With my left hand I slash the bonds holding Graham, with my right I cover the miscreants. One of them, perhaps, might creep behind me, and I hesitate. If I move my revolver the other two will get the drop on me—I think that is the correct expression? A wonderful moment, that, Miss Van Teyl!"

This kind of hero, however, discomfited Oppenheim. His real heroes connect to nineteenth century concepts of style, versus the newer concepts of self-consciousness and action. In *The Pawns Count* Oppenheim's themes, particularly the contrast of the lackadaisical game player opposed to the machine-like troglodytes of Germany, moved him to the new hero who would inhabit the detective and spy novels of the twenties and the thirties. But he never did like this hero, and he switched quickly back to the sober hero, as Dominey in *The Great Impersonation* shows. Oppy did, though, keep the stress on action, which was new in his war time novels.

Another quiver (it is scarcely a movement) resides in Oppenheim's treatment of women. In his earlier books, women's main role lies in defying authority and marrying for love. This happens in *The Mysterious Mr. Sabin* as well as in romances like *Jeanne of the Marshes* (1909): it happens all over the lot. Whether Oppenheim altered his diagnosis of the reading public and its tastes, or whether the activity of American women changed it, or whether women's new roles in war time Britain changed it, Oppenheim's women change during and after the war. In *The Pawns Count* we meet Pamela Van Teyl who runs at a pretty fast pace during the first part of the novel: she participates in dangerous situations, has physical confrontations with evil men (made especially more threatening in that one is a Turk, one a Black, and one a Japanese), and she acts the part of a secret agent for the American government with muscular patriotism. She involves herself in danger, moreover, as she puts it, because "I love adventures." In the middle of the book, however, Lutchester takes over the important action roles and additionally shows that Pamela never really played an essential role in the spy business but was unwitting bait to draw out the enemy. At this she falls into the hero's arms to become his wife and return to England to do some suitably feminine war work. Perhaps the purest statement of this theme comes in *Miss Brown of the XYO* (1927) where Miss Brown tells the Great Man:

> There is nothing I should like so much in the world as to be your secretary, and go on with the work.

This is a real leap for Oppy's women, but hardly a step for womankind.

Oppenheim's novels during the war ostensibly serve as lessons in security consciousness. *The Kingdom of the Blind* overtly teaches that "loose lips sink ships" with sailors blabbing away in front of a German spy and with a young woman prying into her man's war work. *The Pawns Count* likewise begins with a buoyant young engineer recklessly gassing about his new explosive and later being killed as a sort of just desert. The war books get a bit more specific about secret weapons than *The Mysterious Mr. Sabin* does. We find underwater telescopes, trawling nets for subs, new explosives, green rays, etc., but Oppenheim uses these as subsidiary motifs much as he did in the earlier spy books. The war rearranges international conspiracies; they form the basis of the political plots, not because of their nature but because they rest on written documents. In *The Pawns Count,* for instance, Germany offers its aid to Japan if she decides to attack America (an idea repeated in *The Wrath to Come* 1924), and also offers its aid to the United States in case of Japanese attack. And the Germans are stupid enough to put all of this down on papers which they let float around in the States. Likewise, the war simply rearranged Oppy's use of real events as organizers in his spy books. Thus, *The Kingdom of the Blind* culminates in the April, 1915 zeppelin raids on London, and *The Pawns Count* is an apology for the Battle of Jutland.

The use of the Battle of Jutland brings up another theme which increases in volume as we head toward the thirties: the ineptness of British governments. *The Pawns Count* points out that any sane government would have called Jutland a great victory, but that the British government is so limp wristed that its first announcement makes the battle sound like a German victory. Perhaps the peak of Oppy's frankness about governments comes in *Miss Brown of the XYO* where we get this: "This country, since the war, has been governed by a nursery full of nincompoops." When we probe through Oppenheim's rhetoric, though, we find that his political opposition does not rest on any international platform, but that he simply abhors any government which uses an income tax. And if they do not have income taxes he prefers monarchies or dictatorships.

The Pawns Count is in many ways representative of all of Oppy's books in that it intends to appeal to readers on a number of levels. The war does shape some of the concerns in the book, but others remain the same as in Oppenheim's first novels. For one thing, he wants to capture readers through their fascination with wealth and the prospect of getting rich quick. In his finance novels he concentrates on this, superficially showing that money alone will not buy happiness, but really proving that it is pretty good to be rolling in dough. This motive seeps into *The Pawns Count,* too. Here we find that German-Americans use their money to subvert British interests in the States, and Fischer tries to buy a U.S. Senator as well as a wife for himself, but money does not work this way. Instead, we find that Lutchester makes a bundle on the stock market because he has faith in his country, because he needs it to humiliate his German competitor, and because it proves his competence. We will see more of this later. Another popular taste which Oppenheim appeals to is that engendered in the British by Edgar Wallace, the taste for the gangster story. In *The Pawns Count* the main German agent goes to Hell's Kitchen in New York where he not only sees the denizens of a gangster saloon, but he also hires a bruiser to murder Lutchester. In fact Fischer hires all of the gangsters to sabotage American munitions plants. Another fad which we see Oppy exploiting in *The Pawns Count* is that of orientalism. Oppenheim early on appreciated the public's interest in the Orient—shortly after the Russo-Japanese War (1905) he features the Japanese aristocrat, Prince Maiyo, in *The Illustrious Prince* (1910). He continues this in *The Pawns Count* with Prince Nikasti, the agent of Japan who receives the Kaiser's mendacious offer. Ironic in the light of the screaming bigotry expressed toward other non-Europeans (particularly Blacks), Oppenheim lambastes the ignorant racism of the floor valet at the hotel toward Nikasti, and presents him as an admirable exotic, disciplined, anxious to avoid Western mental and moral flab, and awake to delicate beauty (he has a bowl of roses in his room). Other races should have had wars with Russia, as it did alter stereotypes—in Oppenheim at least. Later Oppenheim shifted the same attitudes and roles to Chinese characters, as in *The Dumb Gods Speak.* Also in *The Pawns Count* Oppy carries over his favorite blackmail-spying connection. Fischer, the German agent, lures Pamela's brother into embezzling from his stock broking firm, and then uses this fact as a lever to try to get the secret papers. Finally, in this novel we see Oppy flirting with low-class spying, what with gangsters going around blowing up munitions plants, but the main action of the book concentrates on Fischer and Lutchester, who are not spies but diplomatists, high on the social scale and high in the councils of their governments. This shows best in Oppy's final view of Fischer. He does not treat him as a contemptuous thug but as a patriot, and at the close of *The Pawns Count* Fischer sails for Germany with almost the same mix of pathos and admiration that Oppenheim gives to Mr. Sabin when he departs for the New World.

Up the Ladder of Gold (1931) marks Oppenheim's last phase, the phase of the Great Man. He had been working toward this for a long time, but here we find novels definitely centered on the Great Man's manipulation of history. This last phase shows, indeed magnifies, the defects in Oppy's workmanship. *Up the Ladder of Gold* reeks of dictation: throughout the characters refer to each other by their full names ("do you mean Warren Rand" or "John Glynde can you") as if the author were working from a list of characters while he wove his story. Wove is not, however, a good term, since the plot of *Up the Ladder of Gold* incompetently joins three separate stories. First, Oppy recounts Rand's attempt to coerce the governments of the world into peace. Then he tells the love story of Tellesom and Rand's daughter. Finally he narrates the taming of Stanley Erdish—a woman who aspires to a man's job but then realizes that she cannot cut it. He does not have enough material or imagination to flesh out any of these strands into a full novel, so Oppy joins them together hoping that the German spy, Behrling, will serve as a bridge. He does not. Oppenheim's essential problem here

as elsewhere is that his conception of character is so limited and routine that he cannot find many resources in people to exploit or explore.

The political part of *Up the Ladder of Gold* rests on Warren Rand. Rand is the latest incarnation of the Great Man in Oppenheim's books. Here the Great Man combines several motifs. First he is, like Humberstone in *The Dumb Gods Speak,* rich, but Rand is not just rich, mind you; he is "the world's richest man." Attendant upon this, he possesses the organizational drive, the channeled vision, and the daring enterprise which all of Oppy's rich men have. This part of his personality, the tunnel vision which creates the money-mad usurer, however, Oppenheim uses another way. Rand transfers his financial genius to international diplomacy and tries to force the nations of the world to buy peace as they can be forced to buy arms or oil or enriched uranium. In Oppy's world, though, organizational drive, vision and energy are not enough to make the quintessential millionaire. Rand comes from America and he has the habits and situational morality of elite gangsterism which Oppy and much of Europe half-admired and half-feared. The Great Man has created revolutions where it has suited him, has ordered cement shoes for his enemies, and is not in the least fastidious about shedding blood himself. Indeed, in *Up the Ladder of Gold* he kills a hired thug and blows up two new French warships in order to preserve himself and his plans. Finally, Rand has the other desideratum of the Great Man—he owns the press. Money without influence tinkles like a cymbal, but backed by most of the newspapers in the world it resounds like a bass drum.

In many ways Rand repeats the cliches of Mr. Sabin. His Byronic loneliness, his single-minded vision, his insistence on ends over means all match the first incarnation of the Great Man. Coming also from the 1890s, *Up the Ladder of Gold* is an optimistic picture of the naturalists' and muckrakers' world. Like Frank Norris, Oppenheim shows his hero cornering the world market of a precious commodity—here it is gold and not wheat. Oppy describes the externals of Rand's blackmail, extortion, murder, etc. All this, however, gets laundered by Rand's political intent. By fair means or foul Rand brings the world to disarmament and peace. The other ingredients, the focusing lenses, in the Great Man's character come from Oppenheim's liking for biography. Rand presents a pretty clear version of Lord Northcliffe, the press lord, in his manipulation and forming of public opinion through the press. He is also an updating of Henry Ford and his sponsorship of the "peace ship" *Oscar II* in 1915 to end the European war. Here, though, farce turns into victory.

Although Oppenheim always felt that the British government consisted of a bunch of incompetent bunglers, his conviction grew after the war. In Italy and Germany he saw fascism doing things, and he came to the belief that individuals always represent the will of the nation better than cabinets or parliaments. *Up the Ladder of Gold* is a new version of *l'etat c'est moi.* Warren Rand acts like a government. He corners the gold market and through his financial lever forces states, because of their poverty, to agree to peace. He runs his own secret service which provides better information than the intelligence organs of governments. He praises more lavishly (in money) and blames more scathingly (with bullets) than the weak-kneed governments can or will. Quite the same thing happens in **The Dumb Gods Speak** and by negative implication in **Mr. Mirakel,** where the Great Man gives up on the world and creates his own kingdom aloof from the unreason and untidiness of World War II.

The major sub-plot of **Up the Ladder of Gold** involves Rand's secret service ace, Tellesom, and Sarah Hincks, Rand's daughter, who has taken on her divorced mother's name. Tellesom, for all his chin and chest, does not do a lot in the espionage line—anonymous agents or one-shot characters (like Phillipson who has spent five years spying and sabotaging in the Soviet Union) do the real spying. Further, Rand knows more than his chief security man and protects himself pretty well without Tellesom's aid. Tellesom simply hangs around doing an odd job here and there, like watching the German, British and Italian statesmen who collude to thwart the peace treaty which Rand is boosting. His prowess exists largely on paper and, like Wolfenden in **The Mysterious Mr. Sabin,** his role is mostly that of lover. He fills two species of this genus: he is the man (who exists only in fiction) who has never really thought about women, and he is the older man who cannot believe that a young woman could possibly fall in love with him. His woman, Sarah Hincks, points out for the experienced reader the first irony of the novel. Oppenheim has a persistent prejudice against fast, gay young people. We constantly find his purposeful folks censuring insouciant, witty wastrels. Oppy does not like Noel Coward, or Wimsey, or Campion, or Bertie, or any of their kin. In **Up the Ladder of Gold,** Sarah Hincks travels with fun-seeking young people who spend most of their time dancing, drinking, blathering and otherwise kicking up their heels. She rejects these clotpolls for the serious, reserved Tellesom. So, where is the irony? Oppy dedicated **Up the Ladder of Gold** to P. G. Wodehouse, founder of the Drones, lover of the cross-talk act, and the onlie begettor of Bertie and Jeeves. As much as admitting his failure to integrate Tellesom in the main action, Oppy gives him some very local and limited detective action where he pulls rabbits out of hats to destroy Behrling's plot to frame him for murder.

The other sub-plot in the novel is one of those in which Oppenheim almost makes a reasonable statement but then retreats. Rand is a doctrinaire misogynist who believes that women's places are in the typing pool. Because of her androgynous name, Stanley Erdish, through correspondence, gets the job of being Rand's English press agent. She does an impeccable job of keeping his name out of the papers, and she blackmails Rand into keeping her in the position in spite of her sex. In practice she not only does her own job,

> " . . . but she is the most valuable stenographer I have ever known in my life. She took Madame deRiga's telephone message from Paris—a woman who speaks like a hurricane—without a mistake. She also listened in to the Prime Minister's conversation the last time you were with him and transcribed it faultlessly. We must be

served, Warren Rand. Our work demands the finest service in the world. Miss Stanley Erdish gives it to us."

Well, Stanley Erdish longs for a spot of adventure in her life and she inveigles John Glynde (who has a weakness for her) into sending her on a mission—to abstract a treaty from a swinish Afghan potentate who is bargaining with the Soviets. She does get the treaty, but she also bungles the job and has the police on her trail when Tellesom, who is handy, saves her bacon. After this she hares it back to London, marries John Glynde and sinks into the bliss of being a banker's wife. There is a place for everything and everything in its place.

On the whole, **Up the Ladder of Gold** fits into Oppenheim's general habit of adapting the predictive war book. Indeed, many of his post-war spy books hinge on predictions of the future; **Gabriel Samara, Peacemaker,** for instance, takes place in the 1940s when the Russian people have kicked out the Soviets. **Up the Ladder of Gold** makes the requisite warning, in this case about the ineptness of governments and the impotence of the League of Nations to really do good work. He works in passing reference to the secret weapon (in this case, for once, a grimly accurate prediction of cluster bombs) just as he works ray weapons into **The Dumb Gods Speak.** But Oppy does not really care about any of this: the predictive story or the adventure story is simply something to hang characters on.

Oppy's characters, however, never acquire flesh—none of them ever existed or could exist in life. They are creatures of snobbish sentiment. Snobbish sentiment is the constant burden of all of Oppenheim's novels. They all, for instance, open at some posh spot inhabited by high society people. His heroes all possess high minds and fancy titles. Ordinary people, well, they do not count. Norgate's valet in **The Double Traitor** is incinerated by a German bomb, and the hero barely mentions that his valet died in his stead. The same sort of thing happens in **Up the Ladder of Gold.** Oppy's people are above considerations of regular folks; they want to shape policy. This diplomatic connection robs his heroes of the redeeming quality of being hemen. They are, consequently, a collection of boobs, just as his heroines are a gallery of brainless twits. In terms of theme, Oppenheim does little better. He returns again and again to the virtues of monarchy, the putrid state of government, and to invective against the Soviet Union—usually this boils down to portraying Soviet leaders as dissolute, maniacal deviants. He never deals with the issues of man's aggression as a cause for war in **Up the Ladder of Gold** even though he brings it up, and his only response to the Hitler War takes the beautiful people out of the world's conflict to a perfume-scented bower. As a stylist Oppy ranks near the bottom, and his sense of description is unbalanced and stultifying.

Still, unfortunately, Oppenheim is one of the first important spy writers. He adapted the popular form of the predictive war story and came up with novels which center on secret and clandestine diplomacy. The problem is that he did not create a spy hero. We can probably attribute this failure to Oppy's writing for a mostly female audience. He comes from the sensation novel of the last century and from the love romance to the spy book and he writes it in that direction. For creation of the tradition of British espionage novels (leaving out Childers and Conrad) we have to wait for the materials of the boy's adventure tale to be bent to the service of espionage. We have to wait for the Great War and for John Buchan. (pp. 17-31)

> *LeRoy L. Panek, "E. Phillips Oppenheim," in his* The Special Branch: The British Spy Novel, 1890-1980, *Bowling Green University Popular Press, 1981, pp. 17-31.*

FURTHER READING

Biography

Jenkins, Herbert Franklin. "E. Phillips Oppenheim at Home." *The Independent* LXXIII, No. 3327 (5 September 1912): 548-51.
    Biographical sketch.

Orcutt, William Dana. "Oppenheim the Prophet." In his *From My Library Walls: A Kaleidoscope of Memories,* pp. 142-45. New York: Longmans, Green and Co., 1945.
    Gracious reminiscence with a brief description of Oppenheim's working method.

Standish, Robert. *The Prince of Storytellers: The Life of E. Phillips Oppenheim.* London: Peter Davies, 1957, 253 p.
    Includes a primary bibliography.

Stokes, Sewell. "Mr. Oppenheim of Monte Carlo." *The Listener* LX, No. 1536 (4 September 1958): 344-45.
    Anecdotal sketch stressing the eccentric and self-important aspects of Oppenheim's life.

Criticism

Adcock, A. St. John. "E. Phillips Oppenheim." In his *Gods of Modern Grub Street: Impressions of Contemporary Authors,* pp. 263-70. London: Sampson Low, Marston & Co., 1923.
    Includes biographical material, plus a defense of popular fiction over literature written "neatly for a future that will never read" it.

Cooper, Frederic Taber. "The Taint of Melodrama and Some Recent Books." *The Bookman* XXII, No. 6 (February 1906): 633.

Favorable review of *A Maker of History.*

Cournos, John. Review of *The Pool of Memory,* by E. Phillips Oppenheim. *The New York Times Book Review* (22 February 1942): 5.
    Positive review of Oppenheim's autobiography.

Flower, B. O. Review of *A Prince of Sinners,* by E. Phillips Oppenheim. *The Arena* XXX, No. 4 (October 1903): 437-41.
    Review of one of Oppenheim's early romances; of the novel Flower states that "considered as a clever story of present-day social life in England [it] has few peers in recent fiction," although "its economic theories impress us as being shallow and worse than valueless."

Hovey, Carl. Review of *The Traitors,* by E. Phillips Oppenheim. *The Bookman* XVII, No. 3 (May 1903): 258-59.
    Favorable review of one of Oppenheim's early spy novels.

Lehman, David. "Gilt-Edged Intrigue." *Newsweek* 104 (17 September 1984): 81-2.
    Brief review of reissued editions of the novels *The Wrath to Come, The Great Impersonation, Gabriel Samara, Peacemaker,* and the short story collection *Mr. Billingham, The Marquis, and Madelon,* works which, according to Lehman, "remain irresistibly readable."

Mason, M. M. Review of *Anna the Adventuress,* by E. Phillips Oppenheim. *The Critic* XLV, No. 1 (July 1904): 91-2.
    Brief, generally positive review which, nevertheless, suggests some of Oppenheim's limitations as a writer of fiction.

"A Weaver of Plots." *The Outlook* 130 (22 March 1922): 452-53.
    Writing on the occasion of Oppenheim's lecture tour of the United States, the critic suggests that in the invention of plots, "Mr. Oppenheim, even more than Conan Doyle, shows dexterity and ingenuity."

Review of *The Mysterious Mr. Sabin,* by E. Phillips Oppenheim. *The Spectator* 81, No. 3668 (15 October 1898): 530.
    Favorable review of Oppenheim's first spy novel.

Watson, Colin. "De rigueur at Monte." In his *Snobbery with Violence: Crime Stories and Their Audience,* pp. 53-62. London: Eyre and Spottiswoode, 1971.
    Discussion of the theme of wealth in Oppenheim's novels that includes a brief biographical sketch.

Additional coverage of Oppenheim's life and career is contained in the following sources published by Gale Research: *Contemporary Authors,* Vol. 111; and *Dictionary of Literary Biography,* Vol. 70.

Giovanni Pascoli

1855-1912

Italian poet, critic, dramatist, and essayist

INTRODUCTION

Pascoli is regarded as the progenitor of modernism in Italian poetry. His early works in particular are noted for innovations that represent a departure from traditional subjects and forms. His later poetry focuses on issues associated with the Risorgimento, a nineteenth-century movement that worked toward, and eventually achieved, political unity in Italy.

The fourth of ten children, Pascoli was born in the rural village of San Mauro, Romagna. When Pascoli was twelve his father was murdered; that same year, Pascoli's mother died of heart failure and a sister died of typhus, leaving his older brother, Giacomo, as head of the family. Pascoli attended the University of Bologna but terminated his studies to take care of his younger siblings after Giacomo's death from typhus in 1875. During this time he became involved in radical politics. Biographers have surmised that Pascoli's antigovernment activities were triggered by his anger over his father's murder and the fact that, although the identity of his father's killer was widely known, the police refused to pursue the case. In 1879, after he was arrested at a political demonstration and imprisoned for over three months, Pascoli moderated his political views and began to advocate the goals of the Risorgimento. He returned to the University of Bologna and developed his interest in poetry. Giosuè Carducci, a prominent poet and teacher at the university, greatly influenced Pascoli's artistic and intellectual development. After Pascoli graduated in 1882, he held a series of teaching positions and began to publish his work in various journals. *Myricae,* his first volume of poetry, was issued in 1891. Shortly thereafter, Pascoli received the Hoefft medal for Latin poetry from the Royal Academy of Amsterdam for the poem "Veianius." Pascoli continued to write in Latin as well as Italian and was awarded the Hoefft medal eleven more times during his career. In addition to poetry, Pascoli published three volumes of criticism on the work of Dante. Pascoli's reputation as a poet facilitated his appointment to Carducci's position as chair of Italian literature at the University of Bologna when the elder poet retired in 1904. Pascoli held this post until one month before his death in 1912.

Myricae exemplifies Pascoli's modernist departure from the themes and forms of traditional Italian poetry. Rejecting the lofty subject matter, distanced perspective, and ordered verse structure of earlier Italian poets, Pascoli wrote about everyday subjects using simple, often colloquial language, impassioned descriptions, and fragmented forms. The major topics in *Myricae* are nature, peasant life, and the mystery of death. Pascoli explained the theories behind *Myricae* in "Il fanciullino," a poetic manifesto pub-

lished in 1897 which stressed the notion that all poetry should be written from the viewpoint of a *fanciullino,* or young child. The poetic traits for which Pascoli was most widely recognized—fresh descriptions of nature, a sense of awe regarding the universe, and a focus on the cycle of life—stem from this theory. With his third collection, *Canti di Castelvecchio,* Pascoli departed somewhat from the tenets outlined in "Il fanciullino." Unlike Pascoli's earlier work, the poems in this volume contain autobiographical elements, most notably relating to his father's murder, and exhibit a more complex verse structure. Later volumes such as *Odi e inni* and *Poemi del Risorgimento,* with their overtly political tone, mark a significant change in Pascoli's thematic focus and have received less praise than his earlier verse.

Criticism on Pascoli's poetry can be divided into pre- and post-1950s schools of thought. While initial reviews expressed dismay at the poet's departure from traditional form, Pascoli found supporters in such illustrious contemporaries as Carducci and Gabriele D'Annunzio. Perhaps his most ardent critic was Benedetto Croce, who condemned Pascoli as an anticlassicist. It was not until the 1950s, when Gianfranco Contini published an in-depth analysis of Pascoli's poetic style, that Pascoli's poetry was fully recognized for its powerful language and innovative form.

PRINCIPAL WORKS

Myricae (poetry) 1891
*Poemetti (poetry) 1897
Minerva oscura (criticism) 1898
Sotto il velame (criticism) 1900
La mirabile visione (criticism) 1902
Canti di Castelvecchio (poetry) 1903
Odi e inni (poetry) 1906
Poemi conviviali (poetry) 1911
Poemi italici (poetry) 1911
Poemi del Risorgimento (poetry) 1913
Tradzioni e ridzioni (translations) 1913
Carmina (poetry) 1914
Poems (poetry) 1923
Nell'Anno Mille e schemi di altri drammi (plays) 1924
Poems (poetry) 1927
Selected Poems of Giovanni Pascoli (poetry) 1935

*This volume was divided and published as *Primi poemetti* (1904) and *Nuovi poemetti* (1909).

Gertrude E. T. Slaughter (essay date 1907)

[*In the following excerpt Slaughter provides an overview of themes and techniques in Pascoli's poetry.*]

Pascoli is . . . a man of learning. He is a Dante scholar, a translator of Homer, a literary critic, and the successor of Carducci in the chair of Latin literature at Bologna. As a literary scholar the mantle of Carducci seems to have fallen upon him. He has the same zeal for the enlightenment of his countrymen, the same stern faith in sanity and right reason, the same industry of scholarship. (pp. 504-05)

And yet it was not Carducci's odes that made Pascoli a poet. He would claim attention, apart from schools and movements, for the quality of his lyrics. Our interest in him is enhanced by the fact that he embodies, more than any other living poet, the spirit which Carducci has striven to awaken. But it is because he is so genuine a poet, more than for any other reason, that he is able to carry on the work which Carducci has held out to the youth of Italy.

Italians write poetry with a fatal facility. Their very language is poetry. They have but to say, *'l'immensità del cielo azzurro,'* or *'l'infinito mare,'* and the poetic mood is produced. And what does it matter about the nature of a poet's thought if he can call his thought *il pensiero?* It is small wonder that they are easily contented with *Il verso che suona e non crea.* Against the limitations which such a tendency implies Carducci and his followers have resolutely set themselves. They have striven for a vigorous expression. They have often chosen harsh and rugged sounds as a healthful reaction against the too mellifluous

strains of facile poetizers. To Pascoli verse is but a medium. Its expressiveness is its most important quality. He has made so many innovations in the language of cultivated Italians that in one volume he has felt obliged to add a glossary to the text! He has managed a great variety of meters. The critic, Dino Mantovani, who is much impressed with the combination in Pascoli of the genuine countryman, the rustic, with the artist and the scholar, has said of him:

> This solitary dreamer, who knows all the life of the country, who listens to the conversations of birds, and knows all the sounds that vibrate and sing in the open air, he is also an artist of exquisite perceptions, one who knows the virtues of words and of rhythm, one who is a skilled workman in the subtle industry of style. When he writes he forgets the example of others and writes in his own way. But into that writing is distilled the innumerable precepts of a learned art governed by a delicate taste. Such a genius, united to such a character, produces a poetry that is unique in our times.

This poetry, which is indeed unique, has two qualities which must disturb, one imagines, the Italian reader with his native sense of good form. One of them is an oversimplicity. Led by his desire for reality, the poet has been, at times, too frankly imitative of the sounds of nature. He has reproduced the language of birds with unmistakable success as in the **'Song of March,'** when the birds come chirping back and

> Cinguettano in loro linguaggio
> Ch' è ciò che ci vuole, Si, ciò che ci vuole.

The other quality of his verse which troubles Italian readers is its over-subtlety and occasional obscurity. The poet combines the observation of a scientist with the perceptions of a mystic. He sees a significance in the smallest detail, and he produces a certain indefinable suggestiveness which has its own charm. It leaves in the mind that mingling of clear outlines with indefinite blendings which the contemplation of the actual world produces. But it results often in a degree of lyric vagueness that is a proof of inability to find the fitting medium of expression. It is the kind of lyric vagueness of which Shelley is often guilty. But Shelley had the gift of moulding the subtlest fancy into images as clear cut and definite as Shakespearian metaphor. We are more surprised to find that the vagueness and subtlety of the northern lyrist are paralleled in the Italian Pascoli than that he never quite attains to Shelley's finality of expression. But it will lead us less far afield if we compare the form of Pascoli with that of other Italian poets. And it is safe to assert that, in spite of this fine thread of symbolism, he approaches very near, at times, to the simple dignity and force of a line of Dante.

> L'anima mia tu percuotesti, e il mio
> Corpo di tanto e tal dolor ch'è d'ogni
> Dolcezza assai piu dolce ora l'oblio.

> My soul thou hast tormented and my body
> With such and so great grief that now at last
> Sweeter than any sweetness is oblivion.

The total effect of this poetry is to convey the feeling of

a close intimacy, 'an almost mystical touch between man and nature.' It possesses that modern faculty for truth which is recognized, it has been said, as 'the power of distinguishing and fixing delicate and vanishing detail.' But it does more. The poems are not mere pictures. They do not merely reproduce certain harmonies of the natural world. They are not alone what their author calls them, 'the flutter of wings, the rustling of cypresses, the echo of distant bells.' They are saturated with the meaning and mystery underlying outward manifestations. A somber sense of the inscrutability of man's place in the universe pervades them not unlike the background of fate and death which the Greek poet always felt even when he sang of joy and beauty. Yet Pascoli's temperament is not that of the Greek, of whom he himself writes, who is 'happy if the heavens sing to him and the earth sends up her odors.' He is far too modern to escape from a consciousness of the whole world's weal or woe. And yet he does not seek relief in nature for his own overwrought feelings. He does not personify her and long to 'lie down like a tired child and weep away this life of care' on her bosom. He does not even seek in nature 'that blessed mood in which the burden of the mystery is lightened,' nor does he seek 'escape' into a world of dreams and unrealities. His first desire is for realities. The lark does not, like Meredith's thrush, sing to him of 'the new time and the life ahead.' But he sings of the real life around him; he sings the songs of all forests and all gardens, of all times and seasons, and of the labor of men. Keenly sensitive to the sights and sounds about him, Pascoli is always in the reflective mood. Not even Leopardi had a more constant realization of the insignificance of man in the universe, of his solitude and misery, his chance and ephemeral existence. But Leopardi could have had no abiding love of nature, for he took no joy in her. His nearest approach to joy was when he looked out over the world and said, 'Sweet is shipwreck in such a sea.' Pascoli is free from the personal weariness and satiety of that poet of the *Weltschmerz*. He is one of those who, having early learned that the fruit of life is bitter, cannot fail to see that its flowers are sweet. His mood is one of reconciliation with nature because he has found it possible to 'satisfy his eyes with beauty.'

Approaching the world with the unconscious intimacy of a child and with the contemplative mind of a sage, he finds it, first of all, pervaded with mystery: *'Questo mondo odorato di mistero.'* He says in an early poem:

> Climb high in thought the steep and lonely fast-
> ness
> Where nests the eagle, and the mountain stream,
> And stand remote mid solitude and vastness,
>   O Man of Wisdom!
>
> Send far adown the obscure, unfathomed spaces
> Of the abyss thine eye's most piercing beam.
> Ever more near will draw what thine eye
>   traces—
>   Shadow and mystery!

Sometimes the mood of the sage contemplating the significance of things is quite forgotten in the child's delight, and the poet sings some simple nature song, like the **'Song of April.'**

> A phantom you come
> And a mystery you go.
> Are you near? Are you far?
> For the pear trees are bursting,
> The quince trees are budding
>   Anew.
>
> The bank is resounding
> With tomtits and finches.
> Are you there in the ash trees?
> Is it you in the brushwood?
> A dream or a soul or a shadow—
>   Is't you?

                                                              (pp. 505-08)

Sometimes a bit of scenery or an incident is described with realistic vividness, like the description of the people pouring out of a little church and climbing down the hill in the soft May evening, while the houses of the village stand closed and sleeping, waiting for them in the valley, and up above, among the birch trees, the little church gleams red in the Alpine silence, and the rumble of the songs of praise still vibrates in the air and the odor of incense mingles with the broomflower and the mint.

In the **'Fountain of Castelvecchio'** the water sings to the girls, who come bearing jars on their heads, of its life in the cool and silent woods, before it became a prisoner, and asks them for news of the beautiful world which it can no longer see, and, especially, of the good old woman who used to come for water to the spring in the woods, always chattering to herself, while the spring chattered even faster and filled her vessel, and they talked on together, as a voice in the shady valley talks to its echo.

This little poem is one of many that take the reader into the country of Italy and make him feel that Italian peasant life is as near to the life of flocks and herds, of bees and flowers, as it was in the days of Theocritus or Vergil. The peasants of these poems love the beauty even while they bend under the labor of the country. They are close to the invisible spirits in things. The bells have a thousand messages of hope and fear and joy and grief, while 'white dawn scatters the flocks over the fields' or 'a star leads them clambering home.' The farmer hears the song of the cricket telling him all night long that it is time to sow his seed. It is a country far removed from that land of Arcadia which Tasso and his followers peopled with idle swains piping in perennial sunshine to fair-haired shepherdesses. It is a country of incessant toil. Man and nature are forever at work. But they are not the labor-laden peasants of Millet's paintings. They have the temper of the poet's own sunny Romagna—'*Romagna solatia, dolce paese.*' We seem them at the plow and at their prayers. We hear the sounds of the *festa* coming down the steep mountain side, and the low peal of the Ave Maria which calls them from labor in the fields, or from the dance on the green hilltop, into the quiet church. (pp. 509-10)

The external landscape is Italian, not because of descriptions of definite places, but touches of color and outline, contrasts of warm sunshine and heavy shadows, softened by an atmosphere of harmonious melancholy. One is never taken into rugged, massive regions, into the solitude of enormous forests. One is always near to the life of the people. The orange trees that shine in the sun and the dark poplars that file along the stream are not far away from the narrow street filled with old women at their spinning and children at their play. The sounds of life, the murmuring voices of fishermen, bringing in their boats through the limitless blue of a morning on the Adriatic, or the chatter of the Tuscan women whose wooden shoes rattle on the cobblestones of the marketplace, alternate with the hush of the noon hour or the stillness of night, when the 'slow hours are dropping, dropping down into the eternal silence.' Long roads wind around old castles through immovable fir trees and swaying pines, where a fountain sighs eternally, and over the wall, near the bust of a Roman emperor, climb laurel and rose trees, while yellow broom and blue cornflowers and poppies choke the paths. The grasshoppers are intoxicated with the sun and the lizards creep out to bask at the noon hour. On a green hillside, from which one looks down into the plain and sees a long line of towns and villas lying like a serpent lulled by the ocean, up against the evening sky, like a dark reef in a roseate sea, stands, black and still as a mystery, the donkey and his cart. In some homely barnyard, enclosed by hedges of pomegranates and thickets of tamarisk, with the turkey strutting over the stubble and the duck on the pond, the duck so well described as *'l'anatra irridata,'* and the ponds as *'gli stagni lustreggianti,'* we look on at the yoking and unyoking of the oxen; or we go forth into wide, aërial spaces and watch the interchange of day and night. Nothing could better reproduce the silent hour of dawn than **"Il Transito:"**

A swan sings in the infinite silence of a polar night. Above the level floor of the sea rise mountains of eternal ice. The swan sings and, slowly, a faint green light rises in columns and colors the heavens. Like a harp touched lightly sounds the clear metal of that voice. As the color grows, a great, iridescent arch arises in the dark sky and Aurora opens her mighty portals. The arch glows green and red; arrows of light dart forth and with the sound of the first morning bell the swan spreads his wings and soars into the distance, pure white in the boreal light.

Midway between descriptive poems like this one and those that have a definite significance are others which convey merely a feeling, weird and mysterious, never ghastly and grim, partly by sounds and repetitions, after the manner of Poe, and partly by the picture presented to the imagination. One of them is entitled **'In the Mist.'**

> I looked into the valley. Every form
>   Was lost, immersed in a vast level main,
> Waveless and shoreless, gray and uniform.
>
> No sound emerged from out the misty plain
>   Save wild, thin voices crying on the air
> Of lost birds wand'ring through the world in
>   vain.
>
> In the dim sky above I was aware
>   Of skeletons of trees and shadows drear
> Of hermit solitudes suspended there.
>
> And shades of silent ruins. I could hear
>   A distant bay of hounds, and down below
> A sound of footsteps neither far nor near.

                                     (pp. 510-11)

Another characteristic bit of poetry is **'The Great Aspiration,'** which describes the futile effort of trees struggling away from their roots in the earth toward the radiant liberty of the sun,—*la raggiante libertà del sole.*

> O trees enslaved, you turn and twist like one
> In desperation, spreading across the heavens
> The slow, imprisoned shadow of your limbs.
>
> 'Ah! had we wings instead of branches, feet
> Instead of ignorant, blindly groping roots,'
> Your flowers seem to chant melodiously.
> And man, O trees, man, too, is a strange tree.
> He has, 'tis true, the power to move but naught
> Besides of all his longing. We, too, are slaves.
> Our vain dream is of flowers, yours of words.

Very often the symbolism of these poems is strained. They are too plainly allegorical. A wandering knight arrived at a castle in search of Felicità is told that he pursues a shadow and that by the magic of the castle she cannot be seen when she is there, and only when she is not there can she be seen; and if, at length, he finds a book and reads therein words none have ever told, he shall see her, but on the instant, the castle, which is life, will vanish.

Sometimes the symbolism is of a higher order, being but an expression of the inward meaning of human things which really exists for those who see. **'The Virgin's Dream'** and **'The Sleep of Odysseus,'** which show the poet at his best, are symbolic only in this general sense, and in **'The Blind Bard of Chios,'** the atmosphere and the delicate sympathy with which the persons of the poem are portrayed have so great a charm that one is not tempted to search out further meaning. (pp. 512-13)

But Pascoli is not a poet of objective lyric only. The theme of many of his works is the tragedy of his childhood, and his conception of life and the world is easily traceable to the effect of that experience on his temperament. He sometimes seems to be the solitary poet of his own lines who had learned but one note from the nightingale,—the note which 'fills the heart with memories of things that are no more.' He does not cry out against fate or nature. He identifies his suffering with that of humanity, and the intensity of his grief heightens the contrast between the natural beauty of things which he loves and craves and the misery which the cruelty of man has caused. And because he believes that all mankind has caused this misery, and that all mankind suffers the wrong, he does not hesitate to take his readers into the intimacy of a personal grief. He tells again and again, by many references and recollections, the story of the mysterious murder of his father, a mystery which was never explained and hung like the shadow of a dark Fate over his childhood. He tells of the destitution and friendlessness into which that one moment reduced the family, of how the sense of injustice done the father embittered their already bitter state, of the death of his mother after a year of mourning, followed by the death of four brothers and sisters, to whom he says: 'You have preserved half of your life in me, as I have lost half of mine in you.' His earliest poetic impulse was his desires to make them live on in the world. 'A man,' he says, in one of his notes, 'unknown and unpunished, has willed that an entire family should miserably die. But I will that they shall not die. And if what I have written shall increase in any degree the hatred of cruelty and injustice, then will they even in their tomb, be rendering good for evil.' (pp. 513-14)

Of the four large volumes of Pascoli's verse which have appeared since 1892, when he was thirty-five years of age, there is nothing more powerful and original than the poem entitled '**Il Giorno dei Morti**,' in which the poet visits in imagination, on a dark and stormy day of the dead, the Camposanto, which is the sad dwelling place of his family, and while the wind moans and the wreaths on the crosses drop tears of rain, the family draw together under the cypress tree, as they used to gather about the fire, and utter their lamentations and their prayers. The father speaks to his sons, and tells them of his death, of how in that last instant of life he loved them for a whole eternity, and how he prayed that his sons might not lack bread, begging that God would hear the dying prayer of a murdered father. And he prayed for pardon for his murderer, saying: 'If he has no sons, ah, God! he knows not. And if he has sons, in their name pardon him. Only let my sons not lack bread!' It is a poem in which nature and man, the living and the dead, are mourning a common grief, and the effect is to produce that high mood which is created by all deep harmonies whether of joy or grief.

Gradually, this personal grief becomes universalized, and he writes '**Il Focolare**,' in which he describes a mass of human beings moving through a snowy night past gleams of lamplight until the darkness drowns them, moving on and on, each one lamenting but not hearing the complaints of others, towards a single light that shines from a hut in the desert. And they enter, saying: 'At last I shall rest,'— they who have come from the four winds and know each other not. While the tempest roars outside they gather about the hearth only to find that its fire is spent. But as the poor creatures huddle together and one talks to the others who listen, they find one another out, they hear each other's heart beats, and they seem to find a warmth in the spent fire, for they have found the comfort and sweetness of a common destiny. (pp. 514-15)

It is thus that out of the poet's preoccupation with death and mystery grows a very fair philosophy of life. Out of his sense of injustice in the early days came the belief that the one evil from which we all suffer is a residuum of cruelty left in the race. 'If it must continue thus,' he says, 'Let us open the social cage in which the wild beasts are more ferocious and less able to defend themselves. Or, let us tame the beasts, and then we shall no longer have need of a cage.' Out of the sense of beauty comes the gradual softening of the bitter feeling of injustice into pity. Leopardi knew not whether to laugh at the race of men or pity them. Pascoli has only pity. And he more and more longs to satisfy his eyes with beauty and reveal it to others, because the cure for the evil is simply the recognition of the realities of life. 'I call upon you,' he says, 'to bless life, which is beautiful, all beautiful; or, rather, it would be all beautiful if we did not spoil it for ourselves and others. Beautiful it would be even in sorrow, for our weeping would be as dew beneath clear skies, not as the crashing of a tempest (*la rugiada di sereno non scroscio di tempesta*). Beautiful, even in the last moment, when the eyes, tired with too much gazing, close themselves as if to draw in the vision and shut it within the soul forever. But men have loved darkness rather than light, and the evil of others more than their own good. And for their own voluntary evil they wrongly lay the blame on Nature, *Madre dolcissima,* who, even in extinguishing us, seems to rock us and lull us to sleep. Ah! let us leave it all to her, for she knows what she is doing and she wishes us well.'

In one of his later poems Pascoli represents Homer as describing how his blindness came upon him. He says that before he was blind he plucked the flowers of things, which still breathed their perfume on the dark silence. And when the goddess who had caused his blindness came to him with softened heart and wished to make a blessing out of his misfortune, she granted him the happiness of seeing into the long, immense, inviolate shadow, in the pale light of sunset. And Pascoli would be himself a poet who sees the beauty in the shadow as well as in the sunlight. The tears of things and the flowers of things—these are always near together in his poetry. And the flower is no 'fretful orchid hot-housed from the dew.' It grows in the open air under the low-hanging Italian sky. His conception of beauty is very different from that of D'Annunzio, who represents his heroes as going madly on through life from destruction to destruction, led by the fatal instinct for beauty. And, with a very different view of humanity from D'Annunzio's, who thinks that the most we can do is to offer music and flowers to a dying man, Pascoli, from having always seen 'the dim face of beauty haunting all the world,' comes to see in it the light that lightens the darkness. The spirit of poetry says:

> I am the lamp that burneth tranquilly
> In thy darkest and loneliest hours,
> In the saddest and heaviest shadows.
> The gleam of my pure ray shineth
> Afar on the wanderer treading
> By night with a heart that is weeping
> The pallid pathway of life.
> He stops, and, anon, he beholdeth
> The gleam of my light in the Soul.
> He takes up again his dark journey
> And lo! he is singing.

Pascoli declares that the thought of death is religion, and without it life would be a delirium. He thinks that man has returned by the guidance of science to that sad moment when he first became conscious of his mortality, before he had set up illusions and denied death. And now poetry must join hands with science in the fearless recognition and veneration of our Destiny. It is true that the poet does not quite believe in the religion of Death. For, when he sees a sprout shooting out of an old lichen-covered log, he wonders if perhaps death, too, is not a dream. And when he goes out under the stars and looks up among the myriads of worlds as he does in the very striking poem, '**Il Ciocco**,' he says: 'Because the time will come when I must close my eyelids, the vision will not be therefore ended (*Non però sia la vision finita*).' And when our life, which is but a speck of dust on the wing of a moth that flits about a light which itself is but one of a myriad of lights, when that is scattered and our earth has perished and suns have contended with suns, when, after all the storms of the universe, the slow snows of eternity have destroyed the suns and silence has entered into the sepulchre of dead stars and fossil worlds, even then, he thinks, the Great Spirit will take up new constellations in his hand and fling them anew to be shipwrecked in the sea of ether, to endure ever new death and ever new life. Even then some one searching for truth through the Cosmos may find in the spectrum of a ray the trace of human thought.

Just as he who declares the religion of death believes in life, even so he who strives for realities and would have poetry join hands with science, he is, like all true poets, a believer in dreams. His Hermit says: 'There are two vanities, the shadow of things and the shadow of dreams. And the shadow of things is darkness for him who would see, and the shadow of dreams is grateful shade for the tired soul.' And Alexander the Great, the doer of deeds, when he thinks of the mountains he has climbed and the rivers he has crossed, exclaims:

> O azure-tinted mountains! and you, too,
> O Rivers! blue as skies and seas are blue;
> Better it were to stand by you and dream
> Nor look beyond.
> Dream is the infinite shadow of the true.

'The poetry of earth is never dead,' and if one sometimes grows alarmed at the form it assumes in the mind of a D'Annunzio, one may turn with reassurance to the work of a poet like Pascoli. It would be a serious mistake to suppose that the future of poetry in Italy is in the hands of trivial poetasters whose only aim is to relieve the tediousness of modern life by amorous songs and figments of enchantment. The fatherland is, indeed, no longer the poet's theme. His interest is in humanity. He has become cosmopolitan in spirit even while he remains a native born. In the universality of his spirit Pascoli goes back to Leopardi and bridges the gulf between. And, yet, he is typically modern. Carducci represents a transition. In Pascoli the modern spirit, with its desire of reality and its scorn of illusion and its sentiment of universal pity, is fully awake. Pascoli is a child of nature who longs to 'enclose the turbid universe in lucid words.' But he burns with the ardor of Lucretius to free men from their doubts and their fears and their self-inflicted torments. He yearns toward a new era when poetry shall take up the sceptre of the priest and become the pacifier and purifier of humanity. (pp. 515-18)

> *Gertrude E. T. Slaughter, "Pascoli and Recent Italian Poetry," in* Poet Lore, *Vol. XVIII, No. IV, Winter, 1907, pp. 501-18.*

Ruth Shepard Phelps   (essay date 1924)

[*In the following excerpt, Phelps examines Pascoli's theory that poetry should be written from the viewpoint of* il fanciullino *("the little child").*]

The poet who is said to have died young in all of us is a little child, a *fanciullino,* as Pascoli calls him. And what things interest him? Not romantic love, certainly, nor his own psychology, nor philosophy. It is external objects that attract him, especially the near and the little; and these, according to Pascoli, are the subject-matter of your true poet. Homer, says Pascoli, was such a poet. We are to

think of him as an old blind man whom a little child led by the hand. The child tells him what it sees, and he sings of it. "It is not love," says Pascoli in a long passage in which he describes the *fanciullino,* "it is not women, however fair and goddess-like, that interest little children, but bronze shields and war-chariots and distant journeys and storms at sea. So such things were recounted to Homer by his *fanciullino,* and he made his report in his own infantile speech. He returned from villages perhaps no further distant than the hamlet which lies up nearest the shepherds on the mountainside; but he talked of it to other children who had never been there at all. He talked at length, with enthusiasm, telling the particulars one after another, omitting nothing. For to him everything that he had seen appeared new and beautiful, and it seemed to him must appear to his auditors beautiful and new. He was always engraving upon his discourse a mark to know each thing by. He would say that the ships were black, that they had their prows painted, . . . that the sea was of diverse colours, was always in motion, was salty, was foamy. So as not to be misunderstood, he would repeat the same thought under another form and say: 'very little, by no means much.' . . . He can never be too clear: 'The chicks were eight, nine with the mother, who had made the chicks.' . . . For the blind man's *fanciullino* did not seek to do himself honour, but only to be understood; he never exaggerated, because the facts which he recounted seemed to him wonderful enough just as they were."

His Homeric *fanciullino* had a profound influence upon Pascoli's language. For if one sets out to present as many objects as a child sees, one must have names for them, and Pascoli found Italian poetry still bound under the classical tradition of a "poetic" vocabulary. Specific words, names of things familiar to prose, were excluded. There had been some argument on this before Pascoli. De Amicis had recommended, in a volume on language (*L'idioma gentile*), that young poets study the special vocabularies of the carpenter's shop and the smithy, of the garden and the dairy and the kitchen, and Croce had attacked this theory very bitterly, asking if it were intended that young Italians should become cooks in order to become poets. But few English readers will disagree with Pascoli's desire to extend the vocabulary of poetry. Indeed, one of the great difficulties at first for the English reader of Italian verse (with the bright exception of Dante) is its too generalized vocabulary. Even such personal lyrists as Petrarch and Leopardi, although they analyse themselves minutely, generalize external objects to excess. Once, it is true, Leopardi does specify roses and violets as combined in the nosegay of his village beauty, and Pascoli maliciously inquires whether we are to suppose Leopardi believed them to be in blossom at the same season.

Now Pascoli was not a stranger to anything that bloomed or sang near his study. From his books might be compiled a manual of the flora and fauna of the Lunigiana. As a reviewer said of Madison Cawein, he "wrote with exactness of dittany and the yellow puckworth, of mallow, ironweed, bluet and jewel-weed, the cohosh, oxalis and Indian pipe." To be sure, he overdid his search for the *mot juste;* he ransacked the dialects of all the localities where he lived, borrowed from the queer Americanized Italian of returned emigrants, and invented onomatopoetic vocabularies for the birds and the frogs, for pots and pans and brooms, for the bicycle-bell and the church-bell, and was driven at last to insert glossaries in his volumes of verse. But English readers, since the Romantic Movement banished our own classical canon, are not to be abashed by the homely, and it is hard for us to sympathize with Croce's rather savage criticism of Pascoli's use in poetry of the Bolognese form of his own name Giovanni—Zvanì. It occurs in the poem entitled **"The Voice,"** wherein he tells how his mother's remembered voice at critical moments has recalled him to duty by speaking in his ear his pet-name, "Zvanì." What! says Croce, use a trivial dialect word to represent the stately speech of the dead? He thinks it almost irreverent, certainly in bad taste. Yet Dante does not disdain to repeat fragments of baby-talk in the august circles of the *Inferno;* and if our dead came back to us speaking only the high idiom of heaven, would they not more embarrass us than comfort?

Such, then, is Pascoli's theory of poetry, and at first thought it is a seductive one. The *fanciullino* describes what he sees, describes the beautiful externals of the world and the minute things of the hearthside, and we remember and are glad. But on second thought we recall how many things we are interested in that our *fanciullino* knows nothing of. Love and philosophy interest us; are we to hear nothing of them in our poetry? No, says Pascoli, love is not poetic, but dramatic; and he cites as an example Roland, who in *Orlando innamorato* is merely dramatic, not poetic as he was in the old French epic. Very true. But the difference lies less in the subject-matter than in the manner of presenting it. Thuroldus the minstrel was in earnest, Boiardo in the same degree was not. And we may argue that the analogy with Homer breaks down at the same point. He sang of a world that was new to everybody, to auditors who had not yet seen it reflected in literature. He had the delight of giving things their first literary shape. To name them in poetry for the first time was in some measure to create them. He and his hearers were all young together, as young as the *fanciullino.* But for a modern poet to strive to denude himself of all we have since acquired of sophistication and subtlety, to try consciously to be as naïve as Homer, is to adopt so limited a point of view as to make himself almost a *poseur.* Is this what Croce meant, perhaps, by the breath of insincerity? At any rate, it partly explains that form of insincerity, sentimentality, for whose presence we were prepared. For if we rule out passion and thought from the realm of poetry, we must throw an undue weight of feeling into the more purely idyllic aspects of human life—family affection, childhood, the sweet minutiæ of country life. More emotion will find its way into such things than they will hold. It is clear that if we are to have poetry written exclusively by the *fanciullino,* it must be small in scope. Very beautiful in kind, no doubt; it might have included the "Faerie Queene," "Tiger, tiger, burning bright!", "Snow-Bound," "The Lake Isle of Innisfree"; but the *fanciullino* could never have written "Adonais," or "The Duchess of Malfi," or the "Ode on the Intimations of Immortality." Matthew Arnold, Milton, Austin Dobson, Dryden, to name but these, could hardly have written at all if they had had to listen to their *fanciullino,* for it is much to be doubted

whether they had one. The *fanciullino* could not write dramatic poetry, nor meditative poetry, nor love poetry. He could not even write lyric poetry, because for this it is not enough to be personal, one must be personal about one's emotions; and Pascoli is content to remember incidents without telling, as Petrarch did, how they made him feel. "All recollection," he says in one of his prefaces, "is poetry. Poetry is only recollection." But in such a poem as **"A Memory,"** it is more than recollection, it is "total recall." For the *fanciullino* is no artist; his memory is no more selective than a child's. Even in **"A Memory"** the translator would prefer to suppress certain lines as being too strained, too sentimental. What is an English translator to make of a line of blank verse which runs?:

> No, no! Papa! No, no! Papa! No, no!

Or take this poem, **"The Elder Sister,"** written of Margherita, who died at sixteen:

> She rocked to sleep the baby brother,
> She mended what the rest had torn;
> She knew not, little maiden-mother,
> How we are born.
>
> She'd sit and careful stitches set,
> In her small corner, busy, wise,
> For babies Mother was to get
> From the skies.
>
> But now the sparrows chirp their lay
> Around a little cross near by,
> For well she learned, poor child, one day,
> How we die.

Allowing for the drawbacks of translation, is not this perfect in construction, as well as poetic in feeling? But the *fanciullino* has no instinct for construction, he does not know how much is enough, so he goes on writing until his little poem runs to three times this length.

If, then, the *fanciullino* is too literal to write acceptably of his own life, too young for philosophy or love, what kind of poetry can he write, what kind can be written on Pascoli's theory? The epic, perhaps—though not such epics as *Paradise Lost* and the *Divine Comedy*—but certainly the nature poem and the idyl; for these, the *fanciullino's* eye for little things, his very literalness, are qualities and not defects. And, for these, Pascoli's gifts were of the first order—the fidelity of his memory, his minute powers of observation, more than all, perhaps, his feeling for place. This, we have been told by an English poet, is deeply characteristic of English poets. One of their great accomplishments, according to Mr. Masefield, has been their consecration of place; "they made places interesting simply by mentioning them." This has not been a quality of Italian poets. Their poetry has never had a strongly native hue. They seem not to feel the poetry of Italy as Englishmen feel the poetry of England, or when they do, it is of some part that is a little strange to them; the Piedmontese will thrill to the beauty of Naples, a Central Italian pay a compliment to Venice. But Pascoli has a truly English love for his own corner, his own Romagna, his own village, which he succeeds in communicating. The poetic *carte de tendre* must hereafter have marked upon it San Mauro, Castelvecchio, the church of San Niccolò, the village of San Pietro in Campo. When Pascoli says "half-way between San Mauro and Savignano," he evokes at once that familiar glare of long white road, the procession of small shapely hills to one side with rows of mulberries looped with grapevines stretching away to the other, and far ahead a walled city of rose-tinged grey fitting a hill-top like a coronet.

Pascoli's most delightful and most successful work is to be found in the idyls of the volumes called *Poemetti,* in which he treats his subjects in a manner somewhat more impersonal and objectified than in *Myricæ* and the *Songs of Castelvecchio.* It is the poets in this world who have chiefly taught us our expectations, and if life does not often meet them, we do not therefore bear any grudge against the poets; rather we love to be so deceived, and are grateful to each new one who gives us fresh expectation, who encourages us to feel intensely, to believe that life is to be felt intensely about. The sight of one who seems to find contentment in small, old-fashioned things casts a glamour over our own quiet commonplace, and colours it with romance. This is a thing Pascoli can pre-eminently do for us, above all by idealizing country life; and in this series of pictures of the daily activities of a single family of *contadini,* he found the happiest use for the talents of his *fanciullino.* These poems are a kind of modern Italian "Georgics," evoking under the same skies and against the same landscape the descendants of those who ploughed or kept bees in the Virgilian poems. His family of peasants are hardly more characterized than the speakers of an eclogue, but as we see the little group about their various tasks, Pascoli's exquisite details, delicate and clear as a Japanese print, reveal anew the lost beauty of a patriarchal world, the vivid sense of reality and stability which inheres in a life that must be built up afresh out of its elements every morning—water drawn, fires laid, meals made ready—and the poetry in each one of these activities that minister so directly to living. (pp. 43-51)

It is not impossible that there are poets who can address only our *fanciullino.* Perhaps Pascoli was one of them. We have no quarrel with this, since the idyllic is so beautiful and precious a kind of poetry; what we challenge is his erecting his own limitations into a theory, his saying that such, and such only, is poetry. But if he made the naïve mistake of building a rule and canon out of that kind of poetry which he chanced to be able to write, we may leave it to the historians of criticism to judge his theories while lovers of poetry neglect them for his poems. (p. 54)

> *Ruth Shepard Phelps, "Giovanni Pascoli," in her* Italian Silhouettes, *Alfred A. Knopf, 1924, pp. 33-54.*

Giovanni Cecchetti   (essay date 1951)

[*In the essay below, Cecchetti surveys Pascoli's dramatic work, collected in the volume* Nell'Anno Mille e schemi di altri drammi.]

It is common in modern times that a writer (and especially a poet) does not consider himself full-fledged until he has tried to create a dramatic masterpiece. This seems to be true even of those who are least capable of understanding

a reality which is outside themselves: the lyric poets. Pascoli is one of them. Ever intent on the beating of his own heart, he is perhaps, by the very bent of his nature, most remote from the theater. His emotions may expand beyond the boundaries imposed by his personality only in symbolic form; they cannot be transmuted into action and flesh-and-blood characters. The reason is to be found in the fact that he lived a drama of his own from childhood on so intensely that he was not able to gain perspective on it, separate it from himself, and grant it an autonomous existence. However, for the very reason that he was indissolubly engaged in a tragedy, all his life he cherished the ambition of writing theatrical works. Many he sketched out; one only, and a very brief one, he finished; and he never ceased to believe that one day he would see the others completed.

In 1924, twelve years after the poet's death, the Bologna publisher Zanichelli brought out a book edited by Maria Pascoli, *Nell'Anno Mille e schemi di altri drammi.* This book, ignored by the critics, had at least the effect of casting some light on an aspect of Pascoli's personality hitherto unknown: a yearning for dramatic verse which never became a reality on the stage, but which achieved stature independently as lyric poetry. This is the meaning of the book: it tells us something about the origins of Pascoli's more ambitious works, the finest *Canti di Castelvecchio,* the loftiest of the *Poemi Conviviali* ("Solon") and the most famous of his Latin poems: **"Thallusa."**

Nell' Anno Mille is the first of the dramas planned by Pascoli and the only one he completed. It was revised several times to satisfy the exacting taste of Renzo Bossi, a young composer who wanted to adapt it as an opera.

For years Pascoli entertained the idea of basing a play on the legend of the last night of the year 999 A.D., a legend created by the imagination of Romantic writers, followed by such authors as Sismondi and Michelet, and later taken up and embellished by Carducci. Pascoli's first notes date from 1895, while the last version, newly entitled *Il Ritorno del Giullare,* must be assigned to the year 1910. Evidently he conceived the play at the beginning of his career as a poet.

The first of Carducci's "discorsi", *Dello svolgimento della letteratura nazionale,* must have impressed him as an excellent background for a drama in which the action was to be nothing but a symbol, or rather a succession of symbols culminating in one alone: man's life unfolding on this earth between the poles of joy and pain, of love and death.

The facts propounded by Carducci are central to the theme of ***Nell'Anno Mille;*** they are the atmosphere in which Pascoli's characters move and act. It might prove useful to make a brief comparison between the play and the first "discorso".

In both cases we are at the last night of the first millennium after Christ. In ***Nell'Anno Mille,*** on the stage, we see "a castle tower" near "a village church" and not far from a cloistered cemetery; the crowd assemble and pray. Carducci speaks of "throngs gathered silently in groups about the feudal manors, crouched and sobbing in the dark churches and cloisters." In Pascoli there is a prophet who

The house in San Mauro, where Pascoli was born.

says, quoting from Revelation: "The dragon shall stay in the abyss a thousand years"; and then he repeats: "one thousand, no more." And in Carducci we find: "A thousand and no more, according to tradition Jesus had said: after a thousand years, one could read in the Apocalypse, Satan shall be unchained." Another passage directly based on Carducci is to be found in the finale of Pascoli's play. A song is heard:

> ORIOR. A cry . . .
>
> IL TORRIERE. It's the skylark.
>
> ORIOR. It's . . .
>
> IL TORRIERE. (*Cries out*) Life, happiness.
>
> PEOPLE. (*In a whisper*) The day? The sun?

And Carducci had written: "And what a joyful amazement, what a cry went up to the sky . . . when the sun, eternal fountain of light and life, rose triumphantly on the first morning of the year 1000!"

But if the framework is removed there is nothing else which recalls Carducci. There was too much difference between the two poets. Carducci was a spirit turned outward, and his poetry, even at its most impressive, most powerful, as in "Alle fonti del Clitunno" and in "Miramar," was often tinged by oratory and, one might say, by a certain descriptive quality; moreover, the poet frequently wasted his inward power in polemics. Carducci was a classicist who lived in a romantic era, and his rebellious spirit felt little need to go beyond the expression of the struggle between Classicism and Romanticism. Pascoli, on the other hand, was by nature contemplative, removed from turmoil, ever bent on intensifying an idea or a human emotion; so intent was he, indeed, that his poetry was often weakened by an excess of tension. His purpose of expressing humanity in symbolic form caused him to grasp at any symbol, which he sometimes squeezed to the point of making it say what he wanted it to say; from this exaggeration stem many of the defects that can be found in his poetry. But when Pascoli reaches the necessary balance and fusion between the story and its meaning, he creates his greatest lyrics such as **"Il Libro"** and **"Paulo Ucello."** It follows that the central and profoundly poetic theme of *Nell' Anno Mille* does not and could not trace its origins to Carducci, even if the latter provided the external atmosphere of the play.

In *Nell'Anno Mille* the young Torriere, in love with Orior, cannot believe in death or in the end of the world; he feels that Orior is his, his for eternity. And if he does happen to speak of death, he says that even the angels, seeing them together, will say: "Those are two lives of the world that died . . . they loved for their moment and will love for ever." This is exclaimed by Torriere after Orior has said to him: "Do not think of the sadness of love," and has begged him to kill her because: "I shall die by your hand." This is the theme of love linked with death, which will later become a paean to life.

The theme of death permeates the brief play throughout, in a way far more human than the expectation of the end of the world would imply. We see a young mother who has lost her child. Leaning over the grave she delivers a lullaby in the Pascoli manner, such as we find in *Myricae* or in the *Canti di Castelvecchio*. She awaits death, because afterwards she will be enabled to see the child once more. (This theme will be taken up again by Pascoli and enriched greatly in one of his most memorable creatures: the slave-mother Thallusa, who anticipates seeing her child in heaven, but weeps because she has lost him before he had smiled and fears that when she sees him again he will not be able to smile at her). In *Nell'Anno Mille* the mother is disconcerted when the sun reappears, because death is not vouchsafed to her. At that moment she breaks into a loud lament: "I still live . . . he is still dead." The play closes with these words that balance the final cry of the two lovers ("Life, happiness") and are at one and the same time the tones of death and a song to life; the mother, in her grief, draws close to the cross, embraces it, and thus signifies that she is reconciled to living. So we have the main aspects of human existence: love and death, joy and grief; joy in the "life and happiness" of the lovers, grief in the life and tribulations of the mother who has lost her child.

A balance of the themes is already achieved in the first draft of *Nell'Anno Mille*. Among the other versions the only one which deserves attention is that entitled *Il Ritorno del Giullare*, where the troubadour Gaucelm, who sings fragments of his poems, is substituted for Torriere. The action is faster-paced and the short play is superior because it has been relieved of the prosaic passages that were to be found in the first version. There remain, however, the over-facile and colorless lullaby and the too-catching strophes addressed to the dead by the people.

The other plays drafted by Pascoli are little more than fragments. One of them, *I due cavrioli*, is a rendering of a *Decameron* novella in which Boccaccio tells of a woman nicknamed "la Cavriuola" who finds her two sons stolen from her as infants by corsairs. Pascoli basically reorients the tale by introducing new elements, such as the killing of Giusfredi by Giannotto ("lo Scacciato") with the mother witnessing the scene and recognizing the slain man as her son. In Boccaccio the woman lives her drama, but does not absorb in herself all the elements of the story; in Pascoli's account everything is instead concentrated in her tragedy and what is left serves only as a backdrop. A story previously of great stature and considerable scope is limited to a one-sided interpretation and is turned merely into a new rendition of the scene of the mother embracing the cross in the finale of *Nell'Anno Mille*, that is to say, into

a further development of the concept of the identity of life and tribulation.

Among the other outlines, most of which it will not be possible to consider here, by far the most noteworthy is *Gretchen's Tochter*, which was to be entitled in final form *La figlia di Ghita*. It is written in prose, ready for rendering into verse; that is, it has passed the first two phases or "respiri" as Alfieri would put it. Here Pascoli continues *Faust* in a new and original manner.

The short drama opens with a quotation from Marlowe: "Be I a devil, yet God may pity me." These words, that Marlowe puts on Faustus' lips, are now assigned to Mephistopheles. Indeed the whole work is centered on Mephistopheles, who sheds the devilish nature to which Marlowe and Goethe had relegated him and becomes human. The plot is very simple: a group of students want to see Faust; on the way they meet Marta Schwerdlein, who has raised Margarethe's daughter, Perdita, by now fully adult. Mephistopheles mingles with them. Soon he is left alone with Perdita, who feels a certain apprehensive attraction towards him. Gradually, under the goad of her stepmother's reproaches, she determines to leave her home and follow the stranger, having found in him the pity and the compassion she needs. At the same time an extraordinary event occurs: Mephistopheles has been reverent in his treatment of Perdita, and the angels sing: "His Hell has had a remembrance of heaven. It is Hell no more." The voice of the Lord replies: "Demon he is but he partakes of the angelic. Let him be man!" And Mephistopheles, by virtue of the little good he has done, suddenly is transformed into a man. Now he looks at the world with different eyes and utters a definition of evil that explains many aspects of Pascoli's poetry: "Evil is a discord, a blow to the quiet, solemn, mild, gentle harmony of the universe." Perdita, who comes to meet him, finds him radically altered. He says that God forgives (as he had forgiven the dying Margarethe) and urges her to return to her home. Now that he is a man he must die. Perdita gives this man the name of Love; and he, while speaking of death, defines love: "Death! . . . Love is an impulse of the soul to hold back the fleeing life . . . that makes death non-existent."

In the lyric play (for Pascoli is always lyric) we find a revival of the ancient story of the creation of man, half angel and half devil, and at the same time the everlasting motif of love conjoined with death, a theme that reaches here a happier conclusion than in *Nell' Anno Mille*. It is a time-honored motif, especially popular during the romantic era. Pascoli himself, when he first outlined the plot of this play, either had already taken it up or was about to do so in one of his best poems: **"Solon,"** where the song of love and the song of death coalesce into a single strain for the old lawgiver, who at the end exclaims: "May I learn it and die!"

It may be useful to note how the poet exploited the mythical character of Mephistopheles. In Goethe he is the necessary evil on earth, "the spirit of negation", so much so that Faust must reaffirm again and again his faith in action and in life. In Pascoli's play Mephistopheles becomes an incarnation of that goodness which conquers evil by dint of compassion; hence he is accorded the boon of humanity and of death. Essentially this is in perfect harmony with the goodness of the poet—that goodness which was at times "too good."

These and a few other outlines are Pascoli's dramas. He traced them all between 1894 and 1904 (if the dates of further elaborations are excluded). It was the period of his greatest works: the **Primi Poemetti,** the **Poemi Conviviali,** and the **Canti di Castelvecchio.** Of course, many of the images and ideas that we find in these three volumes of poems are similar to those which appear in the plays. In **Nell'Anno Mille** there are many phrases that recall the most beautiful cosmic lines of **"Il Ciocco,"** as when the sun is spoken of as "dead like a lantern hanging from a branch"; or when one meets with a passage of lyric inspiration, such as the following: *"Orior:* Do you not know that dawn is dead?—*Torriere:* Let us go and seek the dawn among the faded stars"; or like this simile, "The sky closed like a book nevermore to be opened," which recalls a well known symbol of Pascoli's: **"Il Libro."** Of the other numerous similarities I shall quote only one; in **Gretchen's Tochter** we read: "The stars are there . . . eternal, brief vision," which must be contrasted with these lines from **"Le Ciaramelle":** "Now that the stars are yonder, sublime, aware of our brief mystery."

It is apparent that what Pascoli might have expressed in a theatrical work, had he ever produced an important one, was being expressed or had already been said by him in his poems. What we have seen, moreover, tends to confirm the idea with which this paper opened. Pascoli is a lyric poet, too much bound up with his inner world to be able to disengage it from himself and give it an independent existence. The little that has survived of his dramatic works is enough to show that as a playwright he would have failed irretrievably. Reading **Nell'Anno Mille** and the outlines of the other plays, one senses the lack of solid construction, the excessive importance attached to the symbol, and the consequent weakness of the characters, who are indeed pallid and passive, devoid of any appearance of real life. The quality of the verse need not be mentioned here; since we are dealing with unfinished works, the considerable failure in poetic power may be passed over. If Pascoli had completed all his plays, they would be read today perhaps only to discover some few fine images or to find the relationship of certain lines and themes with those of his poems, but no one would regard them as theatrical works. They would be read, that is to say, for the same reason for which it is interesting to read these sketches. (pp. 118-25)

Giovanni Cecchetti, "Giovanni Pascoli as Playwright," in Modern Language Forum, *Vol. XXXVI, Nos. 3 & 4, September & December, 1951, pp. 118-25.*

Glauco Cambon (essay date 1960)

[*Cambon was an Italian-born American educator, translator, and author. In the essay below, he translates and analyzes Pascoli's poem "Ultimo sogno."*]

Ultimo sogno

Da un immoto fragor di carriaggi
ferrei, moventi verso l'infinito
tra schiocchi acuti e fremiti selvaggi . . .
un silenzio improvviso. Ero guarito.

Era spirato il nembo del mio male
in un alito. Un muovere di ciglia;
e vidi la mia madre al capezzale:
io la guardava senza meraviglia.

Libero! . . . inerte sì, forse, quand' io
le mani al petto sciogliere volessi:
ma non volevo. Udivasi un fruscìo
sottile, assiduo, quasi di cipressi;

quasi d'un fiume che cercasse il mare
inesistente, in un immenso piano:
io ne seguiva il vano sussurrare,
sempre lo stesso, sempre piú lontano.

　　　　　　　　　　　　　　(**Myricae.** 1892)

Giovanni Pascoli, like d'Annunzio, had begun his career as a close follower of the fiery classicist Carducci, but his gentler nature led him to a Virgilian pastoral reminiscent of Wordsworth or Frost. He was at his best in poems inspired by Italian country life and by his personal sorrows. He can draw vivid sketches, experimenting with sound, color, and tone in a way that anticipates the Crepuscolari and Montale, but his elegies incline to the sentimental and he indulges in excessive onomatopoeia. These flaws are absent from **"Ultimo sogno,"** a poem worthy of Leopardi in gravity and strength. It is a "last dream," or rather an "ultimate dream," a dream of last things: of death. Not nightmare but liberation. The poet has experienced a recovery from the "illness" and "evil" (*mio male*) of life, a recovery that came as an awakening in the midst of sleep.

(1) *From a motionless roar of wagons* (2) *of iron, moving on towards infinity,* (3) *among sharp crashes and wild vibrations . . .* (4) *a sudden silence. I had recovered (was healed).* (5) *The stormcloud of my illness (evil) had spent itself* (6) *in a soft breath. A movement of my eyelids;* (7) *and I saw my mother at my bedside:* (8) *I was looking at her without amazement.* (9) *Free!. . . powerless, perhaps, had I* (10) *wished to unfold my hands on my breast:* (11) *but I did not wish to. A rustling was heard* (12) *thin, insistent, as though of cypresses;* (13) *as though of a river seeking the sea* (14) *that does not exist, on an enormous plain:* (15) *I followed its vain whispering,* (16) *always the same, always more remote.*

Seeing his dead mother is a confirmation of such a crucial transition, beyond sorrow and wonder itself; the climactic vision emerges from an initial roar of vehicles to be resolved in a ceaseless murmur of trees and water, so that the awe is transfigured into a softer mystery, and the impression of what is heard prevails over that of what is seen. But the visual experience has its turn, for along with the exclamation in which it culminates (9) it constitutes the focus of the poem, the defining element at the center of the indefinite sounds. Such function is neatly clinched by the tense-shift from the dominant mood of unlimited duration in the past (*Ero guarito. . . Era spirato,* 4-5) to that single verb which expresses time-limited action (*e vidi,* 7) and then back to indefinite past continuity (*io la guardava,* 8). This is a passage to a new state, for the verbs before the turning point imply a past within the past, while those following the definite "I saw" suggest contemporaneity in the past. The movement from indefiniteness to definition to a soothing indefiniteness is enhanced by the lack of verbs in the initial clause, for after it the explanatory "I had recovered (and was healed)" (4) begins to give shape to form and perception, and a climax is reached in the verb of focused consciousness *e vidi* ("and I saw," 7), to be transcended in the verbless utterance *Libero!* ("Free!" 9) as a further awareness, almost an ecstasy. One might also notice that the opening word is *da* ("from"), a preposition denoting separation, derivation, or emergence, and that the whole poem comes to rest in the final word *lontano*

An excerpt from 'To Giovanni Pascoli' by Gabriele D'Annunzio

My song, before I depart for my exile,
go along the Serchio, and ascend the hill
to the last son of Virgil, divine
offspring,

the one who understands the language of
the birds, the cry of the falcons, the
plaint of the doves, the one who sings
with a pure heart to the flowers as well as
to the tomb,

the one who dared to look earnestly
in the black and azure eye of the eagle
of Pella, and who heard the song of Sappho the
     beautiful
on the monsoon wind.

The son of Virgil rests silently
under a cypress and waits not for
thee. Fly! Thou art not brought by
the woman of Eresso, but thou cans't go alone;

he will receive thee with his generous
hand; he who perhaps was intent
on the alternation of his woof, or on
the bees, or "the late hour of Barga,"
or on his eternal verse.

And who today should crown the poet,
if not I myself, the poet of solitude?
The ignorant Scita and the masked
Medo are the sycophants of Glory;

and, if barbarity generates new monsters
on the wind, no more shall Febo Apollo
descend against this horror as castigator,
with his silver bow,

because thou, Poet, art the custodian
of the purest forms. With unflagging
pulse thy ancestral gentle blood
lives in all thy images.

Thy thought nourishes and illumines
men, just as the placid olive-tree
produces for man its pallid berry
that is both food and light.

Gabriele D'Annunzio, in his Alcione, *1904.
Excerpt translated by Anne Simon, 1916.*

("far away"). It is as if the dreamer, awakening to death, had arrived at an infinite peace, but kept moving on with that river which still seeks an unreachable sea—recalling Leopardi's image of shipwreck at the close of "L'Infinito" (p. 276).

The rolling wagons (1) vaguely evoke a column of emigrants, a hearse, a military convoy: some ineluctable situation. The balancing contrast between *immoto* ("steady" and "motionless") and *moventi* ("moving")—perhaps more forceful in the Italian—contributes to the ambiguous atmosphere of dream. In itself the unexpected explanation "I had recovered" explains very little, for we know nothing of any previous illness of the dreamer. But he assumes it as a matter of course and thereby intimates that the illness was life itself. In line 5 we find another pregnant expression: *era spirato,* which refers literally to the exhalation of one's last breath. But since this refers to the "stormcloud" of illness and not to the dreamer's own self, death is both suggested and denied: it has destroyed only the anguish of existence. *Spirato, nembo,* and *alito* here are related by the theme of moving air: breath and winds of varying intensities, from softness to violence to a final softness. In line 8, the negative expression "without amazement" deepens the very idea of the wonder it denies. The unquestioning lucidity of dream, or dream-waking, makes for uncanny acceptance. Thus we are introduced to the passive awareness of line 9, with the violent contrast of freedom and paralysis in the juxtaposition of "Free!" and "powerless, perhaps." Here the only exclamation of the poem is a weird gesture of unqualified assertion that gives relief to, but does not break, the dominant tone. This is not the freedom of action, but of a transcendental perception beyond anxiety; and the sibilant sounds of the third and fourth quatrains (*volessi . . . fruscìo . . . assiduo . . . cipressi . . . cercasse . . . sussurrare . . . stesso*) bear this out, superseding as they do the clangorous tumult of the opening. (pp. 288-89)

Glauco Cambon "Giovanni Pascoli (1855-1912): 'Ultimo sogno'," in The Poem Itself, *edited by Stanley Burnshaw, Holt, Rinehart and Winston, 1960, pp. 288-89.*

Michael Ukas   (essay date 1964)

[*In the following essay, Ukas examines nature in Pascoli's poetry. The essay was presented at a foreign language conference in 1964 and published in 1966.*]

Giovanni Pascoli's interpretation of the world around him is directly related to the meaning that he attaches to the word "poetry." He goes to considerable trouble in his treatise **"Il fanciullino"** to explain just what the term means to him and to show that, in his opinion, there is a vital connection between poetry and the various creatures, phenomena, and objects of nature. Poetry, according to his definition, is equated with everything that is pure and beautiful, just as its counterpart, the unpoetic, represents all that is evil and ugly. What is more, poetry is the good that can arise only out of unblemished innocence, and it can be apprehended only by the very young simply because they have not been spoiled by various forms of prejudice. Pascoli makes it quite clear that it is not a question of the age of a person, but of his attitude: to compose a poem, one must be young at heart. This is what he means when he says: "Sappiate che per la poesia la giovinezza non basta: la fanciullezza ci vuole!"

The poet, because he is this *fanciullino* at heart, is endowed with the faculty of being able to see the truth that is found in all things, that is, he can discover the poetry that each thing contains within itself. He does not invent; he perceives and then reveals what has always been there, and what will remain there independent of him or anyone else. One need not go far afield in search of novelty, since there is always something new to discover in the simple things with which one comes into contact every day.

Because it is the poetical that constitutes the good that is inherent in the things and creatures of nature, it follows that poetry itself renders a moral and social service to mankind: " . . . la poesia, in quanto è poesia, la poesia senza aggettivo, ha una suprema utilità morale e sociale." This statement by Pascoli is not to be construed as meaning that he advocates the writing of didactic poetry as such, and he makes this fact clear when he says: "La poesia, per ciò stesso che è poesia, senz, essere poesia morale, civile, patriottica, sociale, giova alla moralità, alla civiltà, alla patria, alla società." It is the *fanciullino* in us that makes it possible for us to distinguish between good and evil, between the beautiful and the ugly, between the useful and the harmful; in short, between the poetic and the unpoetic.

The state to which Pascoli applies the term *"impoetico"* includes all that is chaotic and discordant. It is a condition brought about by men themselves because they have deliberately preferred darkness to light, and have spoiled the natural beauty of existence. In so doing they have lost all sense of direction and wander about aimlessly, no longer knowing whence they have come or whither they are going. They are like so many lost souls groping in the dark of night, caught in the cold blast of death. Some are alone in their self-created predicament, others try to extend a hand to their straying fellows; some turn their eyes heavenward as they lament, while others rage in silence. All have one thing in common—they are hopelessly bewildered and lost. The confusion of the *impoetico* in which mankind finds itself is vividly described in the poem **"Il focolare"**:

> È notte. Un lampo ad or ad or s'effonde,
> e rileva in un gran soffio di neve
> gente che va nè dove sa nè donde.
> . . . .
> Piangono i più. Passano loro grida
> inascoltate: niuno sa ch'è pieno,
> intorno a lui, d'altro dolor che grida.

Concern for mankind in his predicament sometimes leads Pascoli to compositions that tend to be more didactic than poetic. We have an example of this in the poem **"I due farciulli,"** where the poet indulges in some outright sermonizing as he admonishes:

> Uomini, nella truce ora dei lupi,
> pensate all'ombra del destino ignoto
> che ne circonda, e a' silenzi cupi

> che regnano oltre il breve suon del moto
> vostro e il fragore della vostra guerra,
> ronzio d'un'ape dentro il bugno vuoto.

On reading Pascoli's social poems we get the impression that he, too, is bewildered by the political and economic changes taking place in Italy after the conclusion of the *Risorgimento.* The prospect of industrial development and technological advances, instead of attracting him, seems to alarm him. Unable to accept the present or face the future, and not having the historical vision of Carducci, he seeks salvation, perhaps it would be more correct to say consolation, in the world of nature, where he sees, or imagines he sees, an ideal state of existence. The obvious solution, therefore, is to go back to nature and learn from her how to live in the harmony of poetical understanding, and so to break free from the discordant existence of the unpoetic. Pascoli states this view quite categorically, so that there can be no mistaking his meaning:

> La vita bella sarebbe; anche nel pianto che fosse
> però rugiada di sereno, non scroscio di tempesta;
> anche nel momento ultimo, quando gli occhi,
> stanchi di contemplare, si chiudono come a rac-
> cogliere e riporre nell-anima la visione, per sem-
> pre. Ma gli uomini amarono più le tenebre che
> la luce, e più il male altrui che il proprio bene.
> E del male volontario danno a torto biasimo alla
> natura, madre dolcissima, che anche nello
> spegnerci sembra che ci culli e addormenti. Oh!
> lasciamo fare a lei, che sa quello che fa, e ci vuol
> bene.

Having resolved to turn to nature for consolation, Pascoli, quite literally, mingles with all her creatures, both animate and inanimate. The word that he uses to express this concept is *riconfondersi,* suggesting that early in our lives we do have such contact with nature, at the time, that is, when the *fanciullino* still rules our hearts. If one is to be a true poet, he must look around him without prejudice, he must see through the ingenuous eyes of a child who beholds everything with surprise, just as he would if he were seeing this or that thing for the first time. Poetry is there for the asking in even the smallest and humblest things: "Guardate i ragazzi quando si trastullano seri seri. Voi vedete che hanno sempre alle mani cose trovate per terra, nella loro via, che interessano soltanto loro e che perciò sol essi sembrano vedere: chioccioline, ossicciuoli, sassetti. Il poeta fa il medesimo."

Since poetry is not an invention, but the discovery of a quality that is already there in this or that thing, nothing is too small to arouse the writer's interest. The lowly briar, despite its insignificance, is as worthy of his attention as is the majestic chestnut tree or the magnificent great oak. The *fanciullino* can find poetry in a tiny colony of ants under the bark of a piece of firewood as well as in the infinite universe of which we ourselves are an infinitesimal part.

Pascoli examines nature from two quite different points of view. First, there is the world seen from the outside, appraised and described from the point of view of the poet-observer who investigates some particular aspect, draws his conclusions, and then shares his impressions with his readers. Then there is the second method, the one that makes Pascoli's poetry so different from that of any other writer and presents us with a fascinating and even fantastic world, but one that is nevertheless very plausible in the eyes of the *fanciullino,* and which, perhaps, gives the truest representation of the world. Pascoli calls this approach "*(barattare)* le vesti e magari l'anima con altri." Here we not only see this or that creature, but we are told, sometimes by the creature itself, how it feels and what it thinks, and the way that it sees and understands the other beings among which it finds itself. What the poet does is to tell us what the world is like when beheld by, say, a sparrow, an ox, an oak, or any objects of nature other than man himself.

There are notable advantages to such an approach. It provides the poet with an almost unlimited number of subjects, and thus enables him to present an equally large number of viewpoints. Besides, since each object is considered in the context of the surroundings in which it is found, its condition or situation never remains the same. What the *rondine* feels in the spring when it takes care of its young is not what it is likely to feel in the autumn as it prepares to leave its home in search of a warmer climate. Therefore, the large range of subject matter and the constantly changing situation make it possible for the poet, every time that he writes about some aspect of nature, to speak of something new and to use a fresh approach. There is also the important fact that the world that is described also varies, depending on who or what it is that is conscious of it, on the time of day, the season, on the total existing situation, and on other pertinent factors. And, finally, one must also bear in mind the fact that no two mornings, or evenings, or seasons are ever exactly the same.

Pascoli never speaks in general terms about any of the things he describes. When, for example, he writes about a plant, he refers to it by name and presents it in its most characteristic setting. This is just as true of the plants that man cultivates as it is of those growing wild. Similar treatment is accorded by Pascoli to the world of animals. One of the criticisms leveled at Pascoli has been that this attention to detail is excessive, and that some poems lose in effect because of the minuteness of the description. Such criticism is perhaps partly valid since there are few people, for example, who can identify dozens of wildflowers by name. On the other hand, one need not have a direct acquaintance with, say, the foxglove, in order to be able to appreciate the symbolism and the delicate sense of mystery that Pascoli weaves so skilfully around this flower in the poem **"Digitale purpurea."** Needless to say, however, one must be willing to admit that plants do exist and that they are in some way related to us, if one is to appreciate poetry of this sort.

Many instances could be given which would illustrate the way in which Pascoli observes and interprets the outside world through the consciousness of the beings he describes. In the poem **"Il bove,"** for example, we are presented with a view of the landscape as it appears to the ox. It is an immense and mysterious world that it beholds with its naïve eyes. The not-so-large stream assumes the dimensions of a great river, ordinary trees look like giants, the

clouds overhead become fantastic creatures that move slowly in the sky, an enormous sun sets behind towering mountains, and great shadows spread over a huge world. Here are two of the images:

> Al rio sottile, di tra vaghe brume,
> guarda il bove, coi grandi occhi: nel piano
> che fugge, a un mare sempre più lontano
> migrano l'acque d'un ceruleo fiume;
>
> . . . .
>
> il sole immenso, dietro le montagne
> cala, altissime: crescono già, nere,
> l'ombre più grandi d'un più grande mondo.

It is this aspect of Pascoli's poetry that is so intriguing. In his search for new values, he creates what amounts to a mythological world of his own. The poem **"Passeri a sera"** is one of the finest examples of the way that a myth comes into being, as well as of the strange logic of other creatures as they interpret the actions of man. In the eyes of these sparrows, man is god: he is wise, benevolent, and sometimes stern. They completely misconstrue his motives as they sing in praise of his generosity. It is good of him to build a house and set a roof on top of it—all this for no other reason than to provide them with a place where they can take shelter from the cold blasts of winter. How considerate he is when he shakes out the crumbs from his table cloth, giving them food which is of just the right size for their tiny beaks. Nor is this all: when the time comes for the sparrows to start feeding their young in the nests, man scatters seed over the ploughed field, and does this so that sparrows can find food with a minimum of difficulty. It is unfortunate that at times he playfully covers the seed with so much earth that they are unable to find it:

> Vero che a volte ce li nascondi,
> quei chicchi; vero; ma fai per giuoco.
> Ma ecco, a volte son così fondi,
> che noi diremmo, Badaci un poco!

In the long run, however, every act of this great deity called man turns out to be for the best. The seed that was buried too deep for the sparrows to find grows into plants bearing more food. There can be no doubt about the boundless wisdom and goodwill of man:

> Pure il tuo male mai non fa male:
> quelli che copre l'invida zappa,
> poi, col frinire delle cicale,
> mettano un gambo, fanno una rappa:
> che poi ci sgrani . . . Dal male il bene:
> bene che nasce, male che fu.

The worlds described by Pascoli are not always as peaceful and charming as this world of the sparrows. Perhaps this is the mystery of existence, since Pascoli has told us that nature is good and knows what it is doing. In any case, interspersed with the joys there are also occasional tragedies. A storm brings down an oak, and with it the homes of the birds that had nested in it. A log is thrown on the fire and a colony of ants is destroyed in a nightmare of flames. This last-mentioned incident is found in the poem **"Il ciocco,"** and the tragedy is described from the point of view of the ants themselves. As they perish in the flames of the burning log, quite unable to comprehend the reason why such punishment should have been sent down upon them, they are dimly aware of the monstrous world before them, which they do not understand. If these doomed creatures had been able to make out the details in the room more clearly, the glasses of wine held by the gods chatting around the fire would have looked like concave lakes of blood, and the gods like giants, of such dimensions as to defy all imagination:

> Nè pur vedea la gente
> là, che moriva, i mostri dalla ferrea
> voce e le gigantesse filatrici:
> i mostri che reggean concavi laghi
> di sangue ardente, mentre le compagne
> con moto eterno, tra un fischiar di nembi,
> mordean le bigie nuvole del cielo.
> Ma non vedeva il popolo morente
> gli dei seduti intorno alla sua morte,
> fatti di lunga oscurità . . .

Pascoli has said: "La poesia consiste nela visione d'un particolare inavvertito." Certainly he has succeeded in perceiving details that only the true poet can see, but his contribution consists of more than this. He has shown, perhaps better than anyone else, the relationship that exists between all the things in this universe. Plants and animals are linked to inanimate nature, and man is related to them all. This idea, bordering on the pantheistic, is not new with Pascoli, of course. His originality lies in the fact that each thing described by him becomes a conscious being in its own right. As a result, there exists a state of active communication between all of nature's creatures. The more we realize this fact, the better will be our understanding of the universe and of ourselves. Only understanding of the world and all its creatures can lead to the poetical harmony of *fratellanza umana,* so dear to Pascoli's heart. (pp. 51-9)

> *Michael Ukas, "Nature in the Poetry of Giovanni Pascoli," in* Kentucky Foreign Language Quarterly, *Vol. XIII, No. 1, 1966, pp. 51-9.*

P. R. Horne (essay date 1983)

[*In the following excerpt, Horne discusses Pascoli's stylistic innovations.*]

In their own way and within the limits imposed by a conservative temperament, Pascoli's innovations were as significant for the history of Italian poetry as were those of the *Symbolistes* for the development of the lyric in France. This having been said, it should not be thought, however, that the Italian poet intended to start a new movement or that he elaborated, like some of his French contemporaries, radically new theories about poetic language and technique. Echoes of pronouncements on the subject by Mallarmé and Claudel may be found in the writings of d'Annunzio, but not in those of Pascoli. Moreover, in view of the very different poetic traditions and personalities involved, it would be surprising if one were to find in the works of the Italian poet the specific influence of Mallarmé, Verlaine or any of the other poets at work in France whilst Pascoli's style was maturing. Attempts to trace these influences have all been inconclusive, except in the case of the **Poemi conviviali,** which seem to owe something to Parnassian influence. At the same time, one cannot rule out the possibility that Pascoli's poetic methods may have been affected in a general way by an awareness of what his French contemporaries were doing. The more obvious affinities between him and them are: a new feeling for the sensuous and symbolic value of words, as distinct from their logical connotations; a tendency to reject explicit statement in favour of suggestion and implication; the development of a technique of versification aimed at avoiding sonority; the use of a more relaxed diction that is expressive without being elevated, solemn or oratorical.

Pascoli's technical expertise was evident from the outset. D'Annunzio drew attention to it in his review of the 1892 edition of **Myricae** and was to repeat his admiring comments two decades later, after the poet's death: 'Penso che nessun artefice moderno abbia posseduto l'arte sua come Giovanni Pascoli la posseduta . . . Nessuno meglio di lui sapeva e dimostrava come l'arte non sia se non una magia pratica' (*Contemplazione della morte*). This fulsome tribute gains in significance from the fact that in one area of the poet's craft—the choice and handling of metre—the paths followed by the two poets had diverged, d'Annunzio taking up *vers libre* in pursuit of greater freedom and musicality, whilst Pascoli preferred to demonstrate his craftsman's delight in technical problems by staying with and exploring the limitations of closed metrical schemes, avoiding monotony by the use of a wide variety of metres and stanza-forms. A striking example of his originality in this field was his frequent use of the *novenario,* a metre almost wholly ignored by poets in the literary as distinct from the folk tradition, except for the sporadic use of it by some earlier nineteenth-century poets. (pp. 23-4)

Although Pascoli's use of the *novenario* was an interesting innovation in itself, it was less significant from the point of view of subsequent developments in the history of the Italian lyric than his handling of the most traditional and most expressive of all the Italian metres, the *endecasillabo.* Here the full extent of his innovatory technique was more readily apparent to contemporary readers, for there was a centuries-old tradition with which to make comparisons, going back through Foscolo and Leopardi to Dante and Petrarch. The techniques of versification he used were similar to the ones employed in the *novenario,* but the more complex structure of the longer line made it more amenable to manipulation, and in its extreme form his method of versification succeeded in attenuating the potential sonority of the *endecasillabo* to the level of a conversational whisper. (pp. 27-8)

Many of Pascoli's poems were written in long-established forms belonging to the Italian literary tradition: the sonnet and madrigal for short compositions, *endecasillabi sciolti* for long ones. *Terza rima,* traditionally the metre of long poems like the epic or the *capitolo,* is used by Pascoli for short lyrics too. In addition, the waning folk tradition furnished him with other ready-made stanza-forms, his use of the ballad and *strambotto* being more than just a metrical exercise (as it had been for Carducci) and yet not motivated, as with the early Romantics, by an interest in popular poetry for its own sake. His comparative indifference towards the purity of the genre shows itself in the readiness with which he adapted popular forms (as in 'Nevicata'), or created hybrid ones out of a contamination of the popular with the literary tradition ('Lo stornello,' 'Lavandare'). Such procedures may indeed be *alessandrinismo,* but they in no way invalidate Pascoli's method of exploiting the short *schemata* of the popular tradition: even where his adaptations are less than faithful to the spirit of the originals, they are not on that account any the less aesthetically consonant with the style and content of other poems of *Myricae* with a rural setting. It is curious that Pascoli never employed the noblest of all Italian lyric metres in the literary tradition, the *canzone.* Perhaps its complex structure would have been too tight a straitjacket for his purposes, though many of the stanza-forms that he devised for **Canti di Castelvecchio** are extremely intricate. An idea of their complexity can be got from the metrical notes accompanying individual poems in this selection, and no further comment is called for here, except to draw attention to Pascoli's frequent and skilful use of the refrain as a structural or tonal device.

Speculation about the particular source or sources from which Pascoli may have derived his use of refrains does not seem very profitable. It has been strenuously maintained—and equally strongly denied—that he owed it to the theory and practice of Edgar Allan Poe: a plausible enough suggestion considering that Pascoli was acquainted with Poe's works and translated into Italian part of 'The Raven'. On the other hand the device was not the sole prerogative of the American poet, and other near-contemporary models present themselves with equal plausibility, Tennyson being just one. The primary function of the refrain is to mark the divisions of the poem, and in doing this it can (as in **Il sonno di Odisseo'**) undergo modifications that indicate a temporal or other progression. It may simultaneously serve as a tonal device for sustaining a particular mood or atmosphere, as is the case with onomatopoeic refrains like the *uuh . . . uuuh . . . uuuh* of **'Notte di vento'** (*Myricae*) or the *trr trr trr terit tirit* of **'L'uccellino del freddo'** (*Canti di Castelvecchio*). **'La voce'** is another poem with a refrain (*Zvanì*) which performs both functions.

Turning now from metrics to the subject of poetic diction, the first feature deserving of comment is the colloquial syntax which Pascoli deploys over a wide area of his poetic production and which has been regarded as possibly the most noteworthy innovation introduced by him into Italian poetry. . . . There are two ways of looking at the peculiarities of Pascoli's poetic syntax. On the one hand, its fragmentation may be seen as a stylistic device intended to lower the level of the poetic discourse and so prevent the tone from becoming solemn and hieratical. It may also be the case, as [Alfredo] Schiaffini has argued [in his article 'Giovanni Pascoli disintegratore della forma poetica tradizionale'], that the absence of careful syntactical organization is symptomatic of a particular mode of vision and reflects an habitual way of seeing things as an assemblage of discrete particulars rather than as a synthetic whole. Pascoli's discursive prose proceeds in a comparable manner, the argument being developed by a succession of paratactic statements, between which it is sometimes difficult to make a logical connection.

Not surprisingly, in view of the fact that much of his poetry aims at an effect of almost prosaic matter-of-factness, Pascoli was sparing in his use of literary images. To English readers, familiar with the richly figurative language of much English poetry, his diction must appear wanting in this respect, though it is less chaste and 'classical' than, say, Leopardi's. Pascoli's literary images, though relatively scarce, can be striking and highly expressive, as the following examples show. In the first illustration ('La siepe') the image serves to reinforce a sentiment (possessiveness):

> Siepe del mio campetto, utile e pia,
> che al campo sei *come l'anello al dito,*
> che dice mia la donna che fu mia.

A more complex example is the following, which occurs in **'Il lampo'**.

> bianca bianca nel tacito tumulto
> una casa apparí sparí d'un tratto;
> *come un occhio, che, largo, esterrefatto*
> *s'aprí si chiuse, nella notte nera.*

The simile is a graphic one, but its expressiveness is not confined to the visual dimension, and the emotional component is equally important. The image of terror brings to a climax the series of metaphors used earlier in the poem to suggest a landscape convulsed with fear (*terra ansante . . . in sussulto*) under a storm-racked sky (*cielo . . . tragico, disfatto*). The description is not really conceived in naturalistic terms at all, but calls to mind the expressionistic landscapes of Van Gogh, where the distorted and contorted outlines are manifestations of the painter's own feelings of uneasiness. Another noteworthy use of imagery is the *'Albeggia Dio!'* of **'La pecorella smarrita'**, line 11. Here the image, which clothes with sensuous form an abstract idea (the second coming of Christ) is rooted in the metaphorical language of Christian mysticism, and would not have been unworthy of Dante. Finally, one should call attention to Pascoli's use of synaesthetic images, some of which are particularly memorable, like the *pigolío di stelle* in **'Il gelsomino notturno'** (line 16) or the *cader fragile (di foglie)* in **'Novembre'** (line 11).

A second reason for the comparative infrequency of images in Pascoli's poetry is to be found in the nature of his descriptive technique. Depiction of the exterior aspects of reality features prominently in his work, and his chief concern here is with achieving the maximum of immediacy and precision. For this purpose he relies, broadly speaking, on a strictly proper, nonfigurative use of words. He supplements the generic vocabulary of traditional Italian poetry with dialectalisms and with specialized vocabularies appropriate to a rather more technical register, notably in the fields of botany and ornithology. His method is selective and focusses sharply on individual details: 'il passero saputo in cor già gode, / e il tutto spia dai rami irti del moro' (**'Arano'**); the robin 'fa un salto, un frullo, un giro, un volo; / molleggia, piú qui, piú lí' (**'Il compagno dei taglialegno.'**). In the descriptive context metaphors tend to be chosen for their aptness and capacity for graphic representation: the mistletoe berry is a 'pearl' (**'Il vischio'); the flowers of the Persian acacia are 'pink plumes' (**'Romagna'**). English readers may be reminded of the descriptive manner of Tennyson (e.g. 'more crumpled than a poppy from the sheath'), another poet with an eye for the characteristic detail in nature. The proliferation of plant- and bird-names in Pascoli's poetry, so different from the conservatism and sobriety of Leopardi's vocabulary, is regarded by many as a fault, but a comparison of Pascoli's 'landscapes' with those of Leopardi's idylls reveals how different they are in conception and how wrong it is to judge the success of one in terms of the techniques used in the other. A generic vocabulary was entirely appropriate for Leopardi's purpose, for his idylls were concerned with the universal, not with the particular in nature, and the scenes he painted were not ends in themselves, but metaphors of the human condition or correlatives of his own thoughts, feelings and emotions. In contrast to this procedure, Pascoli's 'poetica degli oggetti' requires a vocabulary that can differentiate between blackbirds and bullfinches, myrtles and mulberries, saucepans and stewpots. This entails the use of a precise nomenclature as a way of evoking accurately and succinctly, without circumlocution, the object denoted. The theoretical justification for this is given in [**'Il fanciullino'**] (Section XIV), where Pascoli complains of the generic nature of the Italian literary language and of the difficulty of finding, in Italian, words to denote common objects:

> Il nome loro non è fatto, o non è divulgato, o non
> è commune a tutta la nazione o a tutte le classi
> del popolo. Pensate ai fiori e agli uccelli . . .
> S'ha sempre a dire uccelli, sí di quelli che fanno
> *tottaví* e sí di quelli che fanno *crocro?* Basta dir
> fiori o fioretti, e aggiungere, magari, vermigli e
> gialli, e non far distinzione tra un greppo coperto
> di margherite e un prato gremito di crochi?

The poetic vocabulary envisaged by Pascoli is in danger of failing in its purpose as a means of communication through being unintelligible, and there is a limit beyond which even a sympathetic reader is not prepared to keep reaching for the dictionary. D'Annunzio quite often ignored this limit and became precious, indulging his interest in rare words for their own sake. Pascoli, on the other hand, kept his philological enthusiasm under tighter control, recognizing perhaps that readers cannot be expected to follow the poet too far into the semantic stratosphere, and mindful also that the use of unfamiliar terminology, if it is to be acceptable, must remain a means to an end, not become an end in itself. Similar considerations apply to his use of dialect words, which means to a small extent the dialect of Romagna, but principally those of the Tuscan Maremma and the Garfagnana. These words are justified by their expressive function in providing local colour, but the author knew that a regional vocabulary would be incomprehensible to the wider reading public; he therefore added a glossary to the second edition of *Canti di Castelvecchio.*

Another problem raised by Pascoli's poetic vocabulary concerns his over-frequent use of elementary onomatopoeic effects like the ones in the following quotation from **'The Hammerless Gun'** in *Canti di Castelvecchio:*

> E me segue un *tac tac* di capinere,

> e me segue un *tin tin* di pettirossi,
> un *zisteretetet* di cincie, un *rererere*
> di cardellini.

These onomatopoeic expressions, unlike dialectalisms and technical words, cannot be criticized for incomprehensibility, nor is there any question but that they fulfil their expressive function admirably at the sensory level, but most readers and critics reject them as being too crude or too infantile. It is possible to rationalize the objection in artistic terms by saying that the use of pure onomatopoeia disrupts the linguistic medium of intelligible words, substituting pure sound for the semantic dimension. Consequently they are an intrusive element in the poem analogous in their effect to the sound of real cannon in the *1812 Overture.* (pp. 31-5)

After what has just been said about the exactness and 'particularity' of Pascoli's descriptive technique, it must seem paradoxical . . . [to illustrate Pascoli's] procedures of suggestion and concealment, which work in a diametrically opposite direction. Such, however, is the case with many of Pascoli's most successful and original lyrics. They combine clarity and precision in individual details with a certain vagueness of the overall picture, sometimes with uncertainty about the exact implications of the poem. Indeed, it is in the nature of any poetry which, unlike 'classically' conceived compositions, works through implication and allusion instead of through explicit statement, that it leaves room for individual interpretation. One of the reasons for its appeal is that it acts as a stimulus for imaginings that may never succeed in finding a definite restingplace. It should be stated, however, that unlike some examples of French *Symbolisme,* Pascoli's lyrics, even when their meaning is ambiguous, do not lend themselves to completely open-ended interpretations. Moreover, it is by no means the general rule that his poems imply second meanings over and above their overt signification; in fact the opposite is the norm in his earlier poems. **'Arano',** for example, is typical of the kind of poem which works exclusively at the descriptive level. But a comparison of **'Arano'** with **'Lavandare'** shows how slight an addition is needed to change a descriptive scene into something quite different. Neither the title of the latter poem, nor the descriptive scene into something quite different. Neither the title of the latter poem, nor the descriptive details of the first six lines (a plough standing unattended in a field; the sound of women singing; the splash and thud of clothes being washed in the water of the mill-stream) prepare the reader for the emotive ending in which are heard the words of the *strambotto* that the washerwomen are singing in the distance:

> Il vento soffia e nevica la frasca,
> e tu non torni ancora al tuo paese!
> quando partisti, come son rimasta!
> come l'aratro in mezzo alla maggese.

The words of the song operate retrospectively on the opening lines of the poem, changing them from landscape description into a metaphor of the deserted woman's sense of loss. A similar transformation is brought about in **'Carrettiere'** by the interjection of a single question: 'che mai diceva il querulo aquilone / che muggía nelle forre e fra le grotte?' A simple description of country life is thus turned into a poem about the contrast between the blissful existence of dreams and the harshness of waking reality.

The procedures used in 'Lavandare' and 'Carrettiere' (both published in the *Myricae* of 1894) recur in later poems such as 'L'ora di Barga' (1900), in which the reader is made to realize at the end of the poem (but only then) that the message of the striking clock is more than just a reminder that the evening is advancing and that it is time to go indoors. During the intervening period Pascoli had begun—rather in the manner of Leopardi in *La ginestra*—to use an overtly symbolic metaphor as the starting-point and central organizing principle of a poem. The method is used in 'Il nunzio' (one of the later *Myricae*) and in a number of the *Poemetti* and the *Canti di Castelvecchio* . . . : 'Il libro,' 'Digitale purpurea,' 'La quercia caduta' and 'La poesia.' In all these examples the purport of the symbolic image is defined by the context in which it is used. Not so, however, recurring images like the cypress-tree, the nest, the isolated house or the sound of bells, to which precise meanings are less easily attached. Such images are superficially indistinguishable from the purely descriptive elements that accompany them, but the fact that they occur repeatedly and are highly charged with emotion gives them a privileged status beyond that of 'properties' in a naturalistic description. They are private symbols, which relate not only to the poet's environment, but also and more significantly to his inner world of anxieties, preoccupations and fears. To be more explicit, they connect up with Pascoli's feelings of insecurity, his preoccupation with death and his timidity with respect to personal relationships outside the family circle.

The poem 'Il gelsomino notturno,' written to celebrate a friend's marriage, is a unique example of the technique of allusiveness. . . . [The] poem follows faithfully the tradition of the classical epithalamium in expressing the hope that the marriage will be blessed with children, but there is no open reference to the love-making of the wedding-night, only a description of lights going out in the house as the couple retires to bed, and an allusion to the fertilization of the flower in the garden.

Equally original, considering the date at which they were written and the bold way in which they break with traditional methods of poetic organization, are poems like 'Patria' [and] 'La tessitrice' . . . , which use the device sometimes called *l'inizio a indovinello*. The true subject of the poem, or the precise nature of the situation described, is concealed from the reader at the beginning and is made clear only at the end of the poem, where it may either come as a complete surprise or as the final stage of a progressive revelation.

It would be impossible to conclude this review of Pascoli's technical innovations without considering briefly his use of assonance and alliteration, although here the innovation lies not in the devices as such, but in the extent to which Pascoli uses them, either to enhance the melodic effect, or for a more specific purpose, mimetic, tonal or structural. . . . [Among] the ones most elaborately constructed as regards the sound-stratum are 'Alba festiva,' which uses assonance for imitative and tonal purposes,

and 'L'ora di Barga', which combines assonance with word-repetition and rhythmic effects to produce an atmosphere of torpor. Precisely because of the extent to which these poems rely for effect on the manipulation of sound, they seem a little too contrived for modern tastes, and may be rejected by some readers on that account. 'Alba festiva,' for instance, is constructed on the basis of no fewer than three series of assonances. There is a long sequence associated with the sound of the bell with the voice of gold (ronzano—or—oro—implori—sonoro—Adoro), another long one associated with the bell with the voice of silver (squillano—tintinno—squilla—argentina—Dilla, dilla—tranquilla), and finally a shorter one associated with the idea of the tomb (profonda—rimbomba—risponda—tomba). The effect is anything but subtle, and would hardly warrant further comment were it not for the fact that certain misconceptions about the operation of sound in poetry take a long time to die. It is therefore necessary to stress that, with the exception of genuinely onomatopoeic words like 'crash', 'bang', 'plop', the sound of words is only a *potential* source of expressive effect, and requires the assistance of meaning or context in order to become actually expressive in a specific manner. Thus in 'Alba festiva' the meanings of certain key words have a crucial part to play in actualizing the potential for expressiveness latent in the contrasting vowel-sounds *o* and *i*. If we ascribe a full, resonant sound to the vowel *o* in the first series of assonances, it is because of the meaning of the word *ronzano* and the notions of opulence associated with gold. Likewise the thinner sound ascribed to *i* depends partly on the meaning of *squillano* (often used of shrill sounds), partly on the onomatopoeic *tintinno*, and partly on the less opulent associations of the word for silver. Finally, the effect produced by the third sequence, which is no longer imitative but tonal, depends in part on the onomatopoeic *rimbomba*, in part on the meanings of the words *profonda* and *tomba*. Assonance and alliteration are not always used by Pascoli in such an obvious manner, and their effectiveness seems to increase the more discreetly they are employed. In 'Novembre,' for instance, both devices are used to obtain sensorial effects, but they pass almost unnoticed at a first reading. Other poems in the selection (for example 'Patria' and 'Orfano') use assonance and alliteration with equal success.

In conclusion, the reader should be reminded that this rapid survey of Pascoli's innovations was undertaken with the specific and limited aim of illustrating the features of his work which were important for the subsequent development of Italian poetry. The approach is not intended to imply that technical brilliance is synonymous with poetic excellence. In fact, some of Pascoli's worst failures were occasioned precisely by technical expertise carried to excess in ways that have been adequately discussed by Croce and other critics. . . . D'Annunzio found nothing to criticize in Pascoli's onomatopoeic effects, in his use of bird-names, or in most of the mannerisms which so exasperated Croce. Could it be that Pascoli is essentially a poet's poet? (pp. 35-9)

P. R. Horne, in an introduction to Selected Poems *by Giovanni Pascoli, edited by P. R.*

Horne, Manchester University Press, 1983, pp. 1-40.

FURTHER READING

Biography

Bermann, Sandra. "Giovanni Pascoli." In *European Writers: The Romantic Century, Charles Baudelaire to the Well-Made Play,* Vol. 7, edited by Jacques Barzun and George Stade, pp. 1825-54. New York: Charles Scribner's Sons, 1985.
   Outlines the major events in Pascoli's life, traces the evolution of his various works, and surveys critical response to *Myricae, Il fanciullino,* and the Dante criticism.

Criticism

Giachery, Emerico. "Pascoli Today." In *Italian Books and Periodicals* XXVIII, No. 1-2 (January-December 1985): 5-8.
   Survey of post–World War II criticism of Pascoli's works. Giachery divides this criticism into four categories: socio-political, historical-cultural, psycho-critical, and phenomenological.

Horne, P. R. "Pascoli, Tennyson, and Gabriele Briganti." In *The Modern Language Review* 80, No. 4 (October 1985): 833-44.
   Studies the influence of Tennyson's poetry and Brigan-

ti's tutelage on Pascoli's work, and discusses Pascoli's translation of *Ulysses.*

Montale, Eugenio. "The Fortunes of Pascoli." In *The Second Life of Art: Selected Essays of Eugenio Montale,* edited and translated by Jonathan Galassi, pp. 82-7. New York: Ecco Press, 1982.
   Survey of Pascoli's critical reputation in Italy. Observing that Pascoli's poems exhibit "lapses in tone" and "an absence of great memorable lines," Montale concludes: "Even more than the constant formal and psychological indecision which we find in [Pascoli's] poetry, what perplexes us in the end is that it is only rarely that a lyric of his is a detached 'object' which can live on its own."

Perugi, Maurizio. "Pascoli, Shelley, and Isabella Anderton." In *The Modern Language Review* 84, No. 1 (January 1989): 51-65.
   Discusses the influence of such English poets as Shelley and Wordsworth on Pascoli's verse.

——. "The Pascoli-Anderton Correspondence." In *The Modern Language Review* 85, No. 3 (July 1990): 595-608.
   Details the relationship between Pascoli and Isabella Anderton, who planned to write an article on Pascoli's work, through an examination of their correspondence.

Wilkins, Ernest Hatch. "Pascoli and Other Poets." In his *A History of Italian Literature,* pp. 460-69. Cambridge: Harvard University Press, 1954.
   Highlights Pascoli's major themes and delineates ways in which his poetry represents a departure from the Italian lyrical tradition.

Wilhelm Raabe

1831-1910

(Also wrote under the pseudonym Jakob Corvinus) German novelist, short story writer, and poet.

INTRODUCTION

Raabe is considered one of the most important German novelists of the nineteenth century. Praised for his complex characterizations and innovative narrative techniques, Raabe explored a variety of socially relevant subjects in his works, including industrial progress, materialism, war, and the relationship between the individual and the community. As one of the earliest novelists to exploit such devices as multiple or unreliable narrators and nonlinear narratives, Raabe is also noted as a progenitor of the modern novel.

Raabe was born in Eschershausen, a small German village in lower Saxony. Soon after his birth, the family moved to the larger town of Holzminder, where Raabe spent most of his childhood. His father, a mid-ranking judicial officer, died when Raabe was fourteen, leaving Raabe's mother to care for the family with only a limited income. In 1845 the family moved to Wolfenbüttel, where Raabe attended the local high school but never officially graduated. After spending four years as an apprentice to a bookseller in Magdeburg, reading voraciously and teaching himself English, Raabe moved to Berlin in 1852. He was unable to register at the University of Berlin after he failed the entrance exam, but he audited classes in literature, law, and philosophy. He also began reading the works of Arthur Schopenhauer, whose pessimistic philosophy exerted a lasting influence on Raabe's novels. While at the university, he also wrote his first novel, *Die Chronik der Sperlingsgasse*. Raabe returned home in 1855 after completing this novel, which he had privately printed the following year. Despite the obscurity of its author, *Die Chronik der Sperlingsgasse* received wide critical acclaim and later achieved popular success. Determined to make his living as a writer, Raabe produced four novels in the next five years.

In 1862 Raabe married Berthe Leiste and moved to Stuttgart. There he completed what some critics refer to as his "Stuttgart Trilogy," which comprises the novels *Der Hungerpastor* (*The Hunger Pastor*), *Abu Telfan,* and *Der Schüdderump.* In 1870 he moved to the smaller town of Braunschweig amid the Franco-Prussian War. Biographical information from Raabe's Stuttgart and Braunschweig periods is scant and has been gathered primarily from his terse but frequent journal entries and letters. Averse to personal testimony, as evidenced by his numerous refusals to write his autobiography, Raabe generally referred critics to his novels if they sought information regarding his life. Raabe's opinions concerning a writer's public persona

are perhaps summarized by the character Uhusen, who states in the novel *Im alten Eisen:* "We play our roles well and do not let the mob into our personal affairs of feeling and privacy. We know how to make faces." Although Raabe continued to publish prodigiously during his Braunschweig period, it was not until late in his life that he achieved the public recognition he had sought throughout his career. Raabe published his last complete novel, *Hastenbeck,* in 1899. That same year he began *Alterhausen* but abandoned the unfinished novel in 1901, declaring that he had retired. He died a nationally recognized author in 1910.

Considered by many as the foremost representative of realism in nineteenth-century Germany, Raabe approached the problem of verisimilitude in a manner that differed from such novelists as Charles Dickens and Emile Zola. Like Dickens, Raabe openly criticized the materialism and selfishness that he understood as characteristics of the nineteenth-century bourgeoisie. However, his allegorical novels forego the documentary reportage often associated with realism and represent reality through various literary devices and techniques. For example, *Pfisters Mühle* (*Pfister's Mill*), which depicts the closing of a local mill as a result of industrial pollution, is related as a series of diary entries from a young man's journal that describe events only peripherally related to the closing. Nevertheless, the novel successfully recounts the effects of the closing on those associated with the mill and condemns nascent industrialism in Germany. *Das Odfeld,* one of Raabe's many historical novels, focuses on the Seven Years' War. As in *Pfister's Mill,* Raabe studiously avoided describing the event central to the novel; instead, the narrator of *Das Odfeld* conjures the destruction and violence of the war through literary symbols and glimpses at the psyches of individuals. In a noted instance of this technique, the narrator describes an altercation between two groups of ravens that takes place on a legendary battlefield. Noah Buchius, a school teacher and the protagonist of the novel, cares for the wounded birds and documents his reactions to the bloody incident. Presenting the ravens as polymorphous symbols of the experience of war, Raabe achieved a highly original form of realism that communicated the import of historical and contemporary events.

Raabe's narrative techniques are as relevant as plot or theme in many of his novels. In *Stopfkuchen* (*Tubby Schaumann*), which Raabe once called an allegory of his art, the unreliable and evasive narrator Eduard confronts the reader with the possibility that his description of scenes and characters is incomplete, biased, and self-serving. The multiple perspectives offered by the three narrators of *Die Akten des Vogelsangs* is another example of Raabe's experimentalism, as is the fluid temporal scheme in *Die Chronik der Sperlingsgasse.* In the latter novel, which is related as a memoir of its elderly narrator, the narrative mimics the act of memory by including time lapses, sudden revelations, and forgotten facts. Raabe also called attention to the role of the narrator by alluding to his own novels in his works. For example, in *Alte Nester* the narrator of the novel meets the narrator of Raabe's earlier novel *Die Kinder von Finkenrode* while both are aboard a train destined for the town of Finkenrode.

The length and prolificacy of Raabe's career accounts for the uneven quality of his works in the view of many commentators. Although thematic continuity exists in his oeuvre, critical overviews of his career have not revealed any sense of development. The ideologically tainted reception of his novels augments the difficulty encountered by critics in assessing his career. Early in the century the Raabe Society, which was controlled by proponents of nazism in Germany, asserted the concordance of Raabe's works with fascism and anti-Semitism. Much of their propaganda was based on Raabe's popular novel *The Hunger Pastor,* which presents a caricatured portrait of a Jewish spy. Recent criticism has focused on Raabe's advanced narrative technique and his influence on the modern novel. Several critics have highlighted similarities in the tone and narrative structure of Raabe's later novels and those of Thomas Mann, while others have pointed to parallels between *Alterhausen* and Virginia Woolf's stream-of-consciousness narratives. Although divided on any summation of Raabe's career, critics agree that his novels addressed the mechanics of realist representation in original terms. As Jeffrey L. Sammons wrote: "[The] paradox that the real must be represented in the fictive was constantly

before [Raabe's] eyes. . . . When this realism about realism comes to be more clearly defined, more exactly related to the details of his strategies and struggles, [his] significance among the writers of the international Victorian age will become manifest."

PRINCIPAL WORKS

Die Chronik der Sperlingsgasse [as Jakob Corvinus] (novel) 1856
Ein Frühling (novel) 1857
Die Kinder von Finkenrode (novel) 1859
Die Leute aus dem Walde (novel) 1862-63
Der Hungerpastor (novel) 1863-64
  [*The Hunger Pastor,* 1885]
Else von der Tanne (novella) 1865
  [*Elsa of the Forest,* 1972]
Sankt Thomas (novella) 1866
Abu Telfan (novel) 1867
  [*Abu Telfan,* 1881]
Der Schüdderump (novel) 1869-70
Der Dräumling (novella) 1872
Christoph Pechlin (novel) 1873
Meister Autor (novel) 1873, imprint 1874
Zum wilden Mann (novella) 1874
Horacker (novel) 1876
  [*Horacker,* published in *Novels,* 1983]
Deutscher Adel (novel) 1878-79
Alte Nester (novel) 1879
Krähenfelder Geschichten (short stories) 1879
Das Horn von Wanza (novella) 1880
Prinzessin Fisch (novel) 1882-83
Pfisters Mühle (novella) 1884
  [*Pfister's Mill,* 1956]
Villa Schönow (novel) 1884
Unruhige Gäste (novel) 1885
  [*Restless Guests,* 1885]
Im alten Eisen (novel) 1887
Das Oldfeld (novel) 1888
Stopfkuchen (novel) 1891
  [*Tubby Schaumann,* published in *Novels,* 1983]
Die Akten des Vogelsangs (novel) 1896
Hastenbeck (novel) 1899
Alterhausen (unfinished novel) 1911
Gesammelte Gedichte (poetry) 1922
Sämtliche Werke. 20 vols. (novels, novellas, short stories, poetry, and letters) 1960-

---

The Bookman, NEW YORK (essay date 1901)

[*In the following excerpt, the critic reflects on Raabe's scholarly and popular reception in Germany and abroad and evaluates his stature as a novelist.*]

The festivities, private and public, and the number of magazine and newspaper articles with which the seventieth birthday of Wilhelm Raabe has been celebrated this autumn in Germany came somewhat in the nature of a surprise to many who believed themselves well acquainted with modern literature. Raabe is one of those writers who have become "classics" during their lives. The great mass of readers who crowd the bookshops and the circulating libraries in hurried eagerness for the latest novel, those who devour the popular successes of the day, know absolutely nothing of Raabe. But the thoroughness of the German public-school education limited their ignorance to a lack of knowledge of his work. His name at least was known, and he was put on the mental bookshelves in a line with Schiller, Goethe, Heine and others of whom we speak with reverence, but whom we do not always read. Yet this sort of platonic admiration is a cold and hungry fate for a writer. It is hardly possible to believe that in our present loud-voiced hurrying century a writer can live neglected and almost forgotten, and hardly earning a bare livelihood from his works, whom yet those in literary authority term one of the very greatest names in German literature of the past hundred years—indeed, of the whole history of German literature. Lovers of Raabe's works are indeed lovers with all their hearts. For the superficial reader his novels have no interest. But for those to whom a book is a friend to commune with in a quiet hour, a source of joy that grows with each return of companionship—for such readers German literature, or indeed any literature, has few poets who come with so strong an appeal. His ripe maturity of thought, his exquisite humour, his tender keenness of observation and his easy, unhurried style, which does not feel the need of hastening on the action, but lingers to pluck a flower here, a leaf there, to enjoy a vista, or an outlook wherever they may offer—these are all mingled in an infinite charm, an impression of lasting sweetness and pleasure. Raabe's talent has stood apart from the highroad, and has created gardens of beauty in half-hidden corners, where it is a pleasure to linger.

All this and more was dealt out to Raabe in rich meed of praise on his seventieth birthday, but it could hardly deceive the aging poet as to the cold facts of his past forty years of patient, conscientious work, which was crowned with so little outer show of success. He had never condescended to write down to public taste, and public taste turned away uncomprehending from his works, so much so that few of his novels ran through more than two or three editions, and even those are scattered about among publishers in various German cities. But the efforts of the small but faithful circle of his admirers have apparently been able to secure for Raabe a measure of popularity for the evening of his life, and the sudden interest manifested in his works has called forth a fund to have a complete edition brought out by one house. The Prussian Government has apportioned a considerable sum to have this edition given to all school libraries.

Raabe was a novelist mainly, but was also a master of the short story, and the four volumes of his tales contain gems which must charm even those to whom his somewhat too involved style in the longer narrative appears tiresome. His prose is poetry itself, and the few poems scattered throughout the novels and short stories attest his great poetic gift. The best known of Raabe's works are his first book, **The Chronicle of Sparrow Street** and the novels **The Hunger-pastor** and **Horacker,** both of them works of great charm and lasting value. If the suddenly awakened inter-est in Raabe puts his works on the market again it will be a boon for readers of more serious mind, for whom the average run of modern German novels offers very little of interest. (pp. 220-22)

"Wilhelm Raabe," in The Bookman, *New York, Vol. XIV, November, 1901, pp. 220-22.*

E. O. Eckelman   (essay date 1919)

[*In the following excerpt, Eckelman examines the themes, characters, and "philosophical unity" of Raabe's "Stuttgart Trilogy."*]

Wherein lies the unity of [Raabe's three novels **Der Hungerpastor, Abu Teflan,** and **Der Schüdderump**]? To what extent may they be termed a trilogy? There is no unity of plot, no persistent character, no recurrence of scene or situation and yet Raabe testifies to an inner relation. The last paragraph of his **Schüdderump** reads as follows: "We have come to the close. And it was a long and hard road to travel from the pastorate of the **Hungerpastor** at Grunzenow on the Baltic via Abu Telfan in Tumurkieland under the shadows of the Moon Ridge to the poorhouse at Krodebeck at the base of the old Germanic Zauberberg."

The usual method of procedure in determining such a question would be that of a close analysis of the author's personality and the conditions under which these works were produced, with the end in view of weighing and determining the reflex of the author's personality and experience in the choice of his motifs, the shaping of his plot, the form and growth of his characters, and his distribution of life's destinies. But the difficulties of such a course are at once apparent, when one considers the taciturn nature of the man. His sole means of communication with the outer world, and for him no doubt the only adequate and satisfactory means, lay in his works. And in the brief period of his lifetime (1831-1910) the German nation grew richer by some thirty-eight volumes of stories and novels written by him. Yet although we have so little supplementary information from autobiographical material, a study of the trilogy in the light of Raabe's contemporaries will, I think, be found very illuminating.

In a certain sense, Storm's development is perhaps as typical of a certain phase of nineteenth-century thought and craftsmanship as any that could be adduced. His first serious literary effort, *Immensee,* stamps the youthful author a romanticist, who expresses the fullness of his emotional life in a *Stimmungsnovelle.* His last novel, *Der Schimmelreiter,* depicts a totally different type of hero and points to a totally different outlook upon life. Hauke Haien is a man whose life is a constant struggle against the hostile elements of the North Sea and the inferiority, superstition, meanness, and parsimony of his home community. *Der Schimmelreiter* is a splendid type of the *Konfliktsnovelle; Immensee* treats of the fame and fortune of an individual in its individual aspects.

A further phase of nineteenth-century thought we have represented in Hebbel. He grew to manhood amidst want and poverty; his early life presents a scene of constant conflict. What further development does he show beyond Storm? His most mature works embody the more tragic aspects of life. He brings the message that the wholly innocent and guiltless too often suffer from the tyranny of unwarranted social conditions. The tragedy of the misfit in its various forms and aspects, the hardships accruing to the individual in transition periods, when values and standards are undergoing change—these are the subjects that attract him.

Raabe shows a development similar to that of Storm and Hebbel. This is our thesis. In the three novels above mentioned he deals with the question, What is life? In formulating his first answer, he begins with the *Entwickelungsnovelle* like Storm. His outlook upon life broadens and he gives his second answer to the question in the form of a *Konfliktsnovelle.* This too is inadequate to express the fulness of his observations, and he shapes his third answer like Hebbel in a tragedy of unwarranted social conditions.

All these novels, however, have their meaning. The third answer to the question, What is life? does not make the first or second superfluous. All three present equally valuable aspects of the one great problem. To answer it implied the closest observation and the fullest experience. "We have come to the close," says Raabe in the last of the series, "it was a long and hard road to travel."

The first of the series, ***Der Hungerpastor,*** in which Raabe treats the problem of individuality in its individual aspect, was written in 1863, when the theory of evolution was rapidly gaining ground in German literature, primarily no doubt, through the life-work of Goethe. The opening scene is laid in a German village in the year 1815. It is therefore meant on the whole as a treatment of life and conditions in the present. There are two persistent characters depicted in sharp contrast: the one in his development to ever greater wisdom and usefulness, the other as he sinks into hopeless degradation. What they have in common is *Hunger,* the desire to grow, that force which, in the opinion of the author, is at the basis of all life. Even a superficial examination of the novel will confirm the opinion that its theme is the individual impulse to grow both in its salutary and in its destructive aspect.

Hans Unwirrsch is the son of a poor shoemaker, who plies his needle and drives his pegs under the gleam of an iridescent globe hanging there before him to catch and concentrate the rays of light from a small lamp in his dingy workshop. His life is one of unceasing toil and of golden dreams never to be realized. When death comes his son falls heir to the shoemaker's globe and to his father's longing for knowledge and understanding.

The first step in this direction is the community school for the poor. The scenes described remind us of Dickens. When the master Silberlöffel breathes his last, it is with this sad plaint, "I have been very hungry, hungry for love and thirsty for knowledge; all else was nought."

Hans enters the *Gymnasium.* His mother cannot understand the boy's striving, his groping from the darkness into the light, but with the instinct of love and the sacred memory of her husband's dreams to prompt her, she slaves at her washtub and adds to the meager store of the

paternal inheritance. The shoemaker's globe is the symbol of their lives.

The author stops to philosophize. Man is born with the hunger for eternal things; he feels its prompting in an unselfish longing for something that is yet to come. But when the years of discretion are at hand, its sacred impulse is stifled all too easily in a compromise with the comforts of life and the all-absorbing pursuit of its showy baubles.

Not so with Hans Unwirrsch. Love beckoned him and Love stood at his side. There was the sacred memory of his father to guide him, the daily sacrifice of his mother to spur him onward. To trudge along the hard road of poverty ennobled him, for it pledged him to unselfish duty, and it fortified him to strive on without flinching. So his years at the university hurried on all too quickly and his experiences as a private tutor in the homes of wealth and opulence began. There was a time when there came to his ear much loud laughter—laughter with no ring of joy in it—and for a nature like Hans Unwirrsch's, whose "why" went out to every contradiction of life, this was a dangerous period. But it left him sad, not bitter. The undefined *Hunger* of his youth eventually became a calm, well-poised, everpresent, purpose of life, such as, active in millions of hearts, leads humanity onward in its course and upward.

So we say farewell to Hans, happily married in a modest parish on the bleak coast of the Baltic, devoting himself to a life of service among poor fisher-folk. This is his prayer as he assumes the duties of his charge:

> I have gone the way that thou, Father Unwirrsch, hast directed.
> I have erred much; and often my heart has failed me.
> It is hard to come from the huts of the lowly; *his* heart must be strong midst good and evil.
> He who is born in the depths, shall be the liberator of mankind.
> There is nothing greater in man, than his longing for eternal values.
> Father Unwirrsch, I have followed my pathway and been sore at heart; I have found the truth; I have learned to choose the genuine and despise the trivial.
> I have no fear, for Love stands at my side.

And in his Christmas sermon at Grunzenow, the old retiring pastor Fillenius told of the good tidings that gladdened the hearts of men—how great and splendid was the Roman Empire and yet how desolate and waste this earth; how Christ was born into the hungry world and all mankind raised aloft its arms for the bread of life; how the heavens were opened and there appeared a great light, and men and women knelt and heard the words, "Truth! Freedom! Love!"

Raabe's first answer then to the question, What is life? is an answer in its individual aspect. Life is a striving of the noble soul for eternal values. Like Faust, Hans Unwirrsch is led from obscure aspirations through love, experience, beneficent activity, to a knowledge of the "one true way." Like Faust in his last moments, he devotes his life to the service of love on a bleak and storm-driven coast and builds free and happy homes for the coming generations of men. "Hand on your weapons, Hans Unwirrsch!" is the slogan at the close. It means guidance, control, direction of the inner impulse for self-development and for service.

The contrast figure introduced to bring home this truth is Moses Freudenstein, the son of a down-trodden Jewish peddler and dealer in second-hand goods. Moses is directed to know and to understand, so that he may the more effectually shield himself against oppression and the more surely triumph over his enemies. These are the old Jew's words: "You will grow to be a great man; you need fear no one; and the 'cake' you will have, too. They'll have to give it to you. And I'll help you to get the money." Moses grows in knowledge and in selfishness. His father rejoices, "He will never bend his back in humility." But Moses forgets the love that attaches to the penuriously gained wealth his father is amassing for him and secretly despises the childish old man. What is dark in the boy's soul grows darker and Egoism stretches forth its hundred arms to seize the world. His desires are always gratified—gratified at any cost. His father, his friend, a few trusting women, his own inner approbation, his wife—he sacrifices all for his vain ambitions. In 1852 the convert to Catholicism, Dr. Theophile Stein, the privy counselor and government spy on the movements of suspicious personages in Paris, is feared by many, hated by all, and dead to his fellowmen—dead in the most awful sense of the word.

Though this may be a splendid novel, it is entirely inadequate as an answer to the question, What is life? It is as though at this time Raabe had assumed the viewpoint of the ordinary man of affairs, who has no conception of himself as a historic phenomenon, as a unit of life that has been molded and welded into shape by the forces of the present and the accumulations of the past. It is as though he were still naïvely classifying all phenomena (witness the character of Moses) into the one category of good and evil without relation to the causes that make for good and evil. To him at this time life seems to have been isolated and quite independent of its environment. Let man strive unselfishly for the benefit of others is his gospel.

But what of the darkness that too often obscures the vision? What of the chains and fetters that impede one's movements and to which the wanderer is all but oblivious? And even with worthy ideals steadfastly pursued, is the rock of purpose impervious to the attack of hostile forces—to the drip, drip, drip of falling water? It is perhaps with these thoughts in mind that Raabe once referred to his *Hungerpastor* as *eine Jugendsünde.*

The second novel of the series is his *Abu Telfan* in which he takes up these very problems involving the relation of the individual to his environment. The tragic heroine of this tale is Nicola von Einstein. The parallel figure, serving as a magic mirror of her situation and experiences, is Leonhard Hagebucher. These are the two persistent characters. Both are striving like Hans Unwirrsch for higher things. The Moses Freudenstein of this novel is Herr von Glimmern. Nicola figures as the victim of Herr von Glimmern, who in turn comes to an untimely end as a punishment for his rascality.

As already mentioned Leonhard Hagebucher's experiences serve as a companion piece to those of the heroine. At the opening of the story he makes his appearance with a history that leaves the reader in no doubt about his situation. The study of theology had disagreed with him, he had taken sudden leave, and after many adventures with slave-dealers in Egypt, was himself taken captive on the Upper Nile and held the slave and servant of a big fat beauty, Kulla Gulla, in the land of Abu Telfan under the shadows of the Moon Ridge. Now, at the beginning of events, after eleven years of bondage, with his fetters unclasped, he returns home—penniless but free, free to his native town of Nippenburg, to his parents, to his uncle, and to his Aunt Schnödler.

What is Nippenburg? Like Keller's Seldwyla, the home of the Philistine, Abu Telfan with a vengeance. A community of those dull, narrow-minded souls, whose lives are bounded by the conventional, whose mass-instinct relentlessly crushes the helpless unit that dares to depart from the beaten path of tradition, and then applauds its terrible deed of savagery in complacent self-righteousness. This is the home to which Leonhard Hagebucher returns, the Nippenburg of his golden dreams during eleven years of abject slavery. And the author pauses to remark: "As our acquaintance grew with this splendid fellow we have come to the conclusion that his most varied, astounding, dangerous, and mysterious adventures were not experienced in Egypt, Nubia, Abyssinia, and the Kingdom of Darfur, but here, where by long centuries of established usage the name of Germany appears upon the map." Let it suffice to say that in the relentless conflict, waged for the preservation of his personality and self-respect, Leonhard Hagebucher eventually gains peace of heart and mind and is able to administer to the needs of another more helpless than himself.

This poor unfortunate is Nicola von Einstein, one of his first acquaintances upon his return from slavery. Nicola's father had been a general at a petty German court with never an opportunity to prove his valor. Upon his death the mother and daughter were left destitute and Nicola was educated as befitted her station by the favor of the duchess. She became one of a brilliant court constellation and was betrothed to Victor von Fehlleysen, an officer of her set. A rascally, but carefully masked plot by Herr von Glimmern, the confidant of the prince, destroyed her happiness. Her betrothed left for parts unknown, unable to bear the seeming disgrace of his father's ruin, and Nicola was left to mourn and hope for his return.

She is twenty-seven when she meets Leonhard Hagebucher, the fugitive from Abu Telfan and the slave of Nippenburg. Her misfortunes have cleared her vision. She sees that she, too, is beating her wings helplessly against the bars of her golden cage. What has life to offer her? A dull routine of trivialities from which she cannot escape, a fairy-tale world with but one object of existence: to live up to the standards of her station. To make matters worse, her mother is championing the suit of Herr von Glimmern, who offers her an assured position in society and a varied round of pleasures for her distraction. Thus she maintains the hard struggle to remain true to her better self. But the hopelessness of the future, the constant appeals and admonitions of her mother finally undermine her strength of purpose. She "buries her heart and takes life as it is." She "closes the book of her hopes and her dreams and resigns herself to the inevitable." (A quotation from her letters.)

Nicola succumbs to the drip, drip, drip of falling water and pays the penalty. When the rascality of Herr von Glimmern is revealed to the world, she takes refuge in the solitude of the deserted mill. Silence reigns about her and no wave sweeps to the threshold of her retreat. "If you knew what I know," says Mahomet, "your laughter would cease and your tears would flow." This is the motto upon the title-page.

But Nicola von Einstein lost heart! True, the odds were overwhelmingly against her, but if she had clung to hope like the old woman in the deserted mill she would have suffered no such shipwreck. Raabe's second answer seems to have been: life presents a relentless conflict in the pursuit of eternal values. Life is what the individual makes it in spite of opposition. And compromise spells ruin.

Is this an adequate answer? Not long, for Raabe. What was he to say of many an unfortunate, who had begun life's journey with him in the golden chariot of Hope, as Schiller describes it in his *Ideale*. Did life here fall short of its glorious possibilities because like Nicola they lost heart in the struggle? Though some may have lost heart, is it not equally true that others never wavered? And then the end came and they greeted Death as the great Comforter. This is Raabe's third answer in his ***Schüdderump,*** the death-cart.

The scenes of this story are laid in the little village of Krodebeck near the Harz Mountains. Dietrich Häuszler, the village barber, had served his apprenticeship in Berlin, that great center of wealth, and left it inspired with an ideal—the ideal of having a beautiful daughter, over whose destiny he might lord it at his pleasure. He was married in 1820. His wife died at Krodebeck in 1839, a deserted woman, one year after the departure of her husband from Krodebeck with his ideal realized and "beautiful Mary," as she was called, at his side. In 1850 "beautiful Mary" returned to Krodebeck with her little daughter Antonie. This poor mother returned, lying on a litter of straw in a two-wheeled cart, to die in the poorhouse. In 1861, the scion of the Häuszler family, Antonie's grandfather, was likewise destined to return to Krodebeck, at a time when Marie Häuszler's child, Antonie, had grown to beautiful womanhood. And then the title of the novel was to find its fullest exemplification.

There on her deathbed in the poorhouse at Krodebeck, Marie Häuszler felt no remorse for the life she had led, for they had all been against her. Only when she thought of her child, the anguish of her heart convulsed her frame and she sobbed, "They will make her pay for what I have taken." Jane Warwolf heard it and sighed: "Alas, it has been the way of the world for more than a thousand years."

Marie Häuszler soon passed away and brighter days followed. There in the poorhouse at Krodebeck, Hanne Alt-mann found herself repaid in caring for the little waif during one brief year of unalloyed happiness, for all her seventy-five years of suffering and wretchedness. Then she too passed away.

Upon the estate Lauenhof near by lived a rare man, one of those of whom Jane Warwolf could say: "He lost his way and came from another world into ours and now he is searching for the way home and gives heed to nought else at the wayside that attracts men." He was a retired officer from the Wars of Liberation, a poor refugee, who lived at the Lauenhof dependent upon the good wishes of its energetic mistress, quite unaware that he gave far more than he received. But Frau Adelhaid knew and came to him often for counsel. Sometimes there were tears in her eyes because of the love and charity in his heart.

He was a strange man, too. A man whose life was filled with many misgivings; who strove without interruption by many queer turns and devious routes to probe the mysteries of existence. Ill satisfied merely to become cognizant of evil and to alleviate misery, his heart went out to the suffering and groped about in anguish for the why and the wherefore. A simple man! Not one of those unhappy fortunates whose life is filled with some great purpose ever beyond realization, but a child with the quaint wisdom of years, the inner need to question and the faith that Christ commended.

When little Tonie Häuszler first caught his attention in that miserable two-wheeled cart going to the poorhouse, this knight of Gläubigern did not turn away like Lady Adelaide Klotilde Paula de St. Tronin. On the contrary, he intervened to send the angry mob of Krodebeck citizens about their business and, after the sufferers had been cared for, he returned to the Lauenhof with little appetite for the evening meal and retired somewhat earlier than was his custom to the seclusion of his rooms.

A year later, when Hanne Altmann had passed away and little Tonie had fled in terror from the poorhouse to his arms, he took her to his heart, watched over her, and reared her like his own child. The seed fell upon rich ground. She became the treasure of his heart. "I had grown to be sixty-eight," he confesses, "ever searching for the missing something in my life—until she came to tell me and to tell us all. For they all lived in want of what she brought to Krodebeck, though perhaps they strove less for it and suffered less for want of it."

Now what a beautiful story it would have been, the author reflects, to have pretty Tonie Häuszler, accomplished, the handmaid of all the Graces, duly installed at the Lauenhof as the life-companion of her close friend and playmate, Hennig von Lauen! For there were moments when he thought in all truth that he loved her. But, alas! 1861 was near at hand, when "the serene blue of the etherial skies above was to resound with Olympian laughter."

Dietrich Häuszler, Tonie's grandfather, had been all but forgotten these many years. Picture the consternation at the Lauenhof when the report was spread abroad that Dietrich Häuszler, a wealthy dealer in government supplies and incidentally the willing tool of the unscrupulous, was on his way to Krodebeck in a coach-and-four to claim his long-forgotten granddaughter. He came and pressed her to his heart and none could say him nay, when he kissed her lips again and again and fondly vowed that they should never part. It was in 1861 that this beautiful girl of sixteen summers, her heart filled with golden dreams and rosy hopes of youth, mounted the *Schüdderump,* the death-cart, though to all outward appearances it was her grandfather's coach-and-four. Not that Dietrich Häuszler was to traffic shamelessly with his granddaughter, as he had with his child; he had wealth now and there was no need of offending his good taste with brutalities. But he brought her to Vienna into his world of vice, hypocrisy, and charlatanism, and four long years in this stifling atmosphere sufficed to sap her strength and bring her to an untimely end.

The tale draws to a close. One more view of the feeble, aged knight, hurrying to the side of his helpless child to tear her from the clutches of her foes. But how pitiful his errand! How ineffectual all human aid! Oh, the agony of his helplessness! Grimly the terrible Sphinx of Destiny directed her gaze upon him with those large, cold, unfathomable eyes. His head sank low upon his breast and feebly he groped about in the darkness. "Tonie, Tonie," broke from his lips. But she understood. "We shall be together," she whispered, "no one can do us harm." And he too knew—knew how utterly his last brave dash to the rescue had failed—knew too how completely it had been successful.

To those who are earnestly striving for their hearts' highest ideals, Death appears at the end as the great Comforter. This is Raabe's third answer in his *Schüdderump.* Life's course is not a golden chariot-race. It is what society makes it for the individual in spite of his enduring pursuit of eternal values. For many an unfortunate, because of the criminal disregard or failure of society's sacred duties, it is but a journey to the grave where all is peace. This is not pessimism, with which Raabe has sometimes been charged. It is the unflinching utterance of the close observer. When Böcklin painted his portrait, it was with a quiet, pensive look in his eyes, listening to the dirge that grinning Death is fiddling to him from the background. Yet his hand never deserts his brush and palette. For him Death, like Raabe's *Schüdderump,* is not a specter of terror; it is but a further incentive to make life's work enduring.

Thus Raabe's trilogy is philosophically a unit, though not such in point of form.

We have come to the close—and it was a long and hard road to travel from the ideal of beneficent activity on the part of the individual in the *Hungerpastor* through scenes of struggle and conflict with the inertia of the masses in *Abu Telfan* to the contemplation of the tragedy of unwarranted social conditions enacted in the poorhouse at Krodebeck at the foot of the old Germanic Zauberberg. (pp. 525-35)

In conclusion we summarize as follows: Raabe's "trilogy" is a philosophic unit, representing at successive stages of maturity equally valuable aspects of the one great problem, What is life? *Der Hungerpastor* represents this problem for the individual in its salutary and destructive as-

pects of development; *Abu Telfan,* for those "unhappy fortunates" whose life is filled with some great purpose so often beyond realization, in its stern aspects of struggle and conflict; *Der Schüdderump,* in its tragic aspect, where the wholly innocent and guiltless suffer from the tyranny of unwarranted social conditions. Thus the "poetic realist" Raabe, leaving the Romanticism of his boyhood days behind him, links himself in his treatment of the social problem with the great writers of the post-classical tragedy, Grillparzer and Hebbel. (pp. 540-41)

> *E. O. Eckelman, "Wilhelm Raabe's Trilogy, 'Der Hungerpastor, Abu Telfan, Der Schüdderump'," in* Modern Philology, *Vol. XVI, No. 10, February, 1919, pp. 525-41.*

Barker Fairley   (essay date 1952)

[*Fairley was an English educator and critic who was a seminal figure in the critical reevaluation of Raabe's works that has occurred in the twentieth century. The author of* Wilhelm Raabe: An Introduction to His Novels *(1961) as well as numerous essays on Raabe," he also wrote "The Modernity of Wilhelm Raabe," which is considered a landmark in Raabe scholarship. In the following excerpt from that essay, Fairley analyzes narrative technique in Raabe's novels.*]

'Look out of the window and see what the weather is doing', said the old lady to Dorsten, 'it seems to me to have shifted in the last hour or so'. 'Clouded over and a wind getting up', said Dorsten, pulling the curtain aside. 'I can always count on my rheumatism to tell me', she continued. 'Well, we had a nice run of autumn days and must be grateful, but I am sure it will turn to rain before morning and', addressing her nephew Bernhard, 'what would you be doing in that humid Thüringerwald, why don't you stay here a few days longer?' And so the nephew's visit, on which the tale hangs, is extended and a doubt removed. A slight incident and not an indispensable one, but characteristic of Raabe, who is not content simply to tell his readers the state of the weather, but prefers to communicate it through the minds of his characters—three of them in this case: Dorsten, who peers out into the dark from the lamplit room; the old lady with her aches and pains and her command of the situation; and Bernhard whose plans are immediately altered. All this from an early chapter in *Das Horn von Wanza.*

In *Das Odfeld* Magister Buchius, the old schoolmaster, now left behind in the deserted school at Amelungsborn with a battle impending in the neighbourhood—the date is 1761, and it is the Seven Years War—looks out at the weather in the first glimmer of daylight. 'It was a little lighter', says Raabe, 'though it would be some time till day. The rain had stopped, but a thick fog lay in the Hooptal and all around Amelungsborn, as if the old monastery had pulled its former monk's cap over its ears again to escape the horrors of the world'. And then he let Magister Buchius speak. 'It will hold', said the Magister, meaning the fog. 'If anyone wanted to get out of here and dodge the misery, he might do it to-day—unless a wind comes or there is too much artillery fire', not knowing, though perhaps anticipating, that he is about to be evicted and will have to take his chance. Here not only the apprehensions of Magister Buchius are involved in the weather, but also the history of Amelungsborn, once a monastery, later a school, and now neither.

It is merely an extension of the same way of feeling the story when Raabe, looking over the Odfeld later in the day and observing the battle in progress, finds it impossible to say what was fog clinging to the hillsides or rising out of the hollows and what was the smoke of battle. Or, when in **Hastenbeck** he returns to the theme of the first snow—dear to him, as we know, from earlier books—and lets it fall gently on a battle-scarred countryside and not be above laying its purity on patches of blood, ruins, and corpses—a passage that perhaps only Raabe could have written: Der kam nun herunter in grossen, reinlichen, weissen Flocken und legte sich auf ganz Niedersachsen; er ekelte sich nicht.

There is no need to restrict ourselves to the weather in observing the close connection in Raabe's stories between humanity and the setting in which he shows it. It comes out in his treatment of environment as a whole, whether atmospheric or otherwise. If we return to **Das Horn von Wanza** we find that the little town which Bernhard is visiting is seen at first in tantalizing glimpses only, partly late at night with the help of a lantern, and it is not till he has slept in an attic in his aunt's house that our attention is drawn to the setting as a whole. Bernhard gets up and looks out of his dormer window and sees the little town below him and the hills of the Thüringerwald in the distance and such a scene of beauty spread between that he instinctively realizes why she put him here at the top of the house. It was here, he divines, that she used to come to hide from the ruffian of a husband, now long deceased, that she had told him about the night before, and she had put him here in the hope that he would understand. The setting is introduced in such a way as immediately to enhance the perspicacity of one of the characters and the delicacy of another. (pp. 66-7)

If Raabe's characters cannot be detached from their environment or the environment from the characters, neither can the characters be detached from one another. To an extent not easy to match in other novelists Raabe makes us see his folk as they are seen by one another rather than separately or as seen simply by himself. This comes out in all his books, but it comes out conspicuously in **Der Schüdderump** which by its very plot requires this treatment, depending, as it does, first on a group of characters so closely held together that we cannot think of one without our minds quickly flitting to another; and, secondly, on a single character whom they adopt and who becomes the centre of their lives.

The group is supplied by the household at the Lauenhof in the village of Krodebeck, consisting chiefly of the widowed Adelheid von Lauen and her son Hennig; a German tutor, von Glaubigern; a French governess; and a couple of lowly people with whom they associate, Hanne Altmann, who lives in the poor-house, and Jane the pedlar who comes and goes but finally comes and stays—a strange assortment, though not strange in Raabe who favours just such cross-sections. What strikes us most

about them as a group of figures in a novel is that so little happens to them. There is no serious dissension, no problem arising out of their interrelations. A couple of them die, one early, one late; Hennig goes away to school and returns; but this is all. Apart from this they remain almost static throughout. For knowledge of them we have to rely on what they tell us about themselves and also, since they are not given to introspection, on what they tell us about one another. But in this way we do come to know them, and very intimately, so that when towards the close old von Glaubigern rouses himself for his critical journey to Vienna and is shown in action for the first time, we are not surprised to find him equal to the occasion because we have seen him so long with the eyes of his near associates and know his worth. (p. 69)

From here it is only a step to giving his personages charge or partial charge of the narrative and letting them tell it themselves or, more characteristically, tell it in turn. In **Das Horn von Wanza** the tale as a whole is narrated by the author in the traditional way. Nothing could be triter than the opening sentence—Den Possenturm bei Sondershausen in weiter Ferne vor Augen, wanderte der Student auf der Landstrasse dahin. But it isn't long before we find that he has handed the task over to the people he has introduced us to and made himself, as it were, superfluous. In **Kloster Lugau,** after telling the bulk of the tale himself, though always with the tendency to surrender it to someone else, he suddenly sets four of his characters down to write letters and lets us read them one after another. This, it will be agreed, is not quite the same as writing a whole novel in letters, as the eighteenth century did, nor is it quite the same as the single letter introduced. In **Die Akten des Vogelsangs** the tragic story of Velten Andres is told by his sober and successful friend, Karl Krumhardt, much as in the more elaborate case of *Doktor Faustus* Zeitblom tells the story of Leverkühn. But Krumhardt in his turn keeps entrusting the tale to others who tell it for him. Something of this handing the story round can be discovered in almost everything Raabe wrote. The beginning of it can be detected in his very first book, **Die Chronik der Sperlingsgasse.**

If so many are involved in the narrating why should not the author frankly show his hand too? And, while he is about it, why not involve the reader? It only makes two more. And so we find him beginning that memorable little tale **Die Innerste** as follows: 'This is the story of a river and two mills. And it is true. Everything happened as you will hear. If you think it could have ended differently, tell it differently'. Variations on this *tête-à-tête* with the reader are a not uncommon feature of Raabe's tales, at first sight possibly unwelcome, later not so, when we realize how consistent it is with his whole attitude.

What we arrive at in our exploration of Raabe is an interdependence and an involvement—a richness of cross-reference—far in excess of what we expect in a novelist. The weather, the surroundings, involved in the personages, they in their turn involved in one another, any or all of them involved in the narrating, the author with them and the reader too. Raabe, it would seem, writes habitually in the light of this complexity, in which everything and everybody becomes environmental in turn, not merely the atmosphere and the setting environmentally containing the characters, but the characters also environmentally containing one another, even the line between narrator and narrated being broken down as also that between narrator and listener, since the tale itself is full both of narrators and listeners. The sum total of possibilities implied or released in the act of telling a story seems to lie at the back of Raabe's mind ready to be drawn on at need.

Here, if you like, are the premises for what is psychologically the most richly conceived body of fiction in the German language. This does not mean that it is necessarily the best. It was almost inevitable that a writer with this complexity of approach should run into difficulties and not always overcome them. Committed, as he was, by this complexity to an experimental attitude in which each tale had to develop its own way of telling itself, since it was impossible to apply all the possibilities to any one subject, Raabe felt his way through half-a-century of almost uninterrupted writing and produced the uneven body of fiction that still awaits our considered judgment. In such a mass of writing some sort of canon has to be established, yet it is not too much to say that a beginning has hardly been made. If we list *Stopfkuchen, Horacker, Die Akten des Vogelsangs, Das Horn von Wanza,* and *Hastenbeck* as a first choice, who will agree? And what about *Im alten Eisen* and *Pfisters Mühle?* And do the longer novels, does even *Der Schüdderump,* quite rank with the shorter ones? We need a working answer to these questions and it will probably be some time before we have one. Meanwhile it is easier to reach conclusions about Raabe's technique than about his performance. Technically, as has been suggested, he touches, at one point or another, all the forms that fiction can take, from the traditional straight narrative, as in some of his historical tales, through more shifting forms, in which the characters are drawn into participation, to what we call the psychological form in which the author as nearly as possible effaces himself, as in *Die Akten des Vogelsangs, Pfisters Mühle,* or *Stopfkuchen.*

The difference between Raabe and others who have experimented in fiction is that he does not seem to have come by his innovations theoretically or through any dissatisfaction with tradition but rather out of his general awareness, from the start, of what is involved mentally in the process of narration. This differentiates him somewhat from writers like Joseph Conrad or Virginia Woolf whom he nevertheless anticipates. To the end Raabe is as ready to use the old form as the new. If *Stopfkuchen* and *Die Akten des Vogelsangs* break new ground, *Fabian und Sebastian* and *Hastenbeck* stay mainly on old. This, perhaps, indicates his position in the history of the novel, that of a writer who, being German or perhaps simply being a lone hand—not unlike those 'Originale' that he was able to create half a dozen at a time whenever he wanted—found himself outside the main currents of European fiction and so worked out the whole development for himself in his own time and in his own way. When he stopped writing just about the turn of the century he had as much to teach his European contemporaries as to learn from them.

This is not quite the prevailing view of Raabe, which tends to see him as an old-fashioned and even a somewhat clumsy practitioner. But the prevailing view will have to go. It is true that he is partly to blame, if only for the confused openings that he evidently favours. A study of his first chapters, as he recognizes, would be amusing, to say the least. Thus after writing a page of *Der Lar* he breaks off to say that this is another of those openings of which his aunt, if she were alive, would say: Nein! so was! After writing a page or so of *Meister Autor* Raabe announces that he is going to start again, and does, and yet again doesn't, since he lets the first page stand. But we must not assume that he was unsure of himself. If he chose to begin as he did, was it because he preferred to conceal his cunning rather than to parade it? Or was he possibly like those painters who have to get their canvases in a mess before they can paint at all, the creative process consisting then in pulling the canvas out of the mess? If we examine *Kloster Lugau* we might favour the latter alternative, because Raabe starts by putting a mysterious emphasis on a character who later slips into a second place. And we may note that at the end of Chapter 2 of *Deutscher Adel* he confesses that he is not pleased with the way he has handled the narrative thus far. But on the whole we can satisfy ourselves that Raabe was in command. It is impossible to begin *Horacker* or *Stopfkuchen* without undergoing some initial perplexity as to what it is all about, yet, as the tale develops, what skill in the management of complex narrative, direct in the first place, indirect in the second. The cunning with which in *Horacker* the subplot—that of the pastor's quarrel with his congregation—is solved incidentally in the course of the main plot—that of the escaped Horacker—is hard to beat, while, as for *Stopfkuchen,* what is it but supreme mastery of a situation displaying its supremacy by pretending not to possess it? Schaumann, the teller of the tale within the tale, feigns clumsiness, delays, digresses, confuses to the despair of his listeners, till they finally surrender and recognize that he knows exactly what he is doing.

But it was not by technical standards, we may be sure, that Raabe wished to be judged and it is not by these, or these alone, that we remember him. It cannot have been technical considerations that made him see his tales in such involvement. The problems were too great for any writer willingly to court them. It is truer to the spirit of these tales to say that the involvement was the consequence of his view of life and that the technique was the only way in which he could record it.

If we try to characterize Raabe's view of life by saying, as has been said, that he sees life in depth, we mean not necessarily philosophical depth, though there is a sufficiency of that, but depth in the sense in which Rembrandt has it. If in a Rembrandt canvas the picture surface is lost and a dark space created out of which the subject emerges, so with Raabe the elements of his tale do not deploy themselves in linear succession, as in a Keller or Fontane novel, but come through from behind one another out of a twilight. In *Das Horn von Wanza*—the most straightforward of the better Raabe novels and therefore useful as an approach to him—the story is set in 1869, when Bernhard Grünhage in a summer vacation forgathered in the little town of Wanza an der Wipper with Dorsten, a former Kommersbruder and now Mayor of Wanza; an aunt by marriage, Tante Grünhage, now well on in years; her life-long friend Thekla Overhaus, who is eighty and blind; and the night-watchman, now in his fiftieth year of service. Apart from an incidental waitress or servant-girl or passer-by these five are the only figures that we meet in person. There is no plot. Instead of plot we are given a process of reminiscence, almost an excavation, with Bernhard looking delightedly on, while the other four do the digging. Tante Grünhage leads off with the story of her marriage in 1819; Dorsten takes over and looks up the records; the old watchman and Thekla follow, and between them take us back to the battle of Leipzig and the death of a soldier, Thekla's lover. The depth that is created here is a real depth, not as frequently with Theodor Storm an artificial shift from one generation to another with the help of a newly-discovered manuscript. The time-recession, the sense of travelling back through half a century to reach a point half a century ago, is completely achieved; we feel the passage of time as well as the interval.

Bernhard realizes what is happening. He finds it harder and harder to remember that he is living in 1869 and he drifts back through the years. He speaks for the whole of Raabe, or rather for all the readers of Raabe, when he says that he arrived by the ordinary route, the common highway, expecting to leave the way he came, only to find himself taken on a strange journey backwards. . . . (pp. 72-6)

It would be too much to say that this will serve as a characterization of Raabe's genius, because he is as much at home when he explores the present or the immediate past as when he takes us back to an earlier generation. We have to think of him applying the same powers to the contemporary scene as he applies here to the vanished. In *Gutmanns Reisen* he makes vivid fiction out of a political convention; in *Prinzessin Fisch* he finds it in the growth of an adolescent boy; in *Pfisters Mühle* in the breaking of the business world into the rural, as in Tchehov's *Cherry Orchard*. But in his best work the sense of depth is always there, whether historical or social or psychological. *Das Horn von Wanza* is a simple case. For a complex one we have *Stopfkuchen.* If in *Das Horn von Wanza* we move in a single direction from the plane of the present through parallel planes of the past, in *Stopfkuchen* the planes, as it were, dissolve and the second dimension is wholly merged into the third.

But this calls for explanation. What we are given in *Stopfkuchen* is the unusual experience of finding ourselves established at a focal or central point with the depth, the space, rotating round us. In terms of narrative the focal point is the so-called 'rote Schanze', an old earth-work thrown up in the Seven Years War from which to bombard the town below and now a somewhat sequestered farmhouse owned by Heinrich Schaumann, the Stopfkuchen of the story, so nicknamed in boyhood because of his greedy habits and perhaps his lethargy. But Schaumann is not as lethargic as he seems. Quite early in life he develops a passion, not for a person or a cause or a study, but simply for a place—a place not distant but within easy reach—the 'rote Schanze' itself, half-hidden behind its

ramparts and its thorn hedge, which, as he tells us, had caught his imagination almost before he could walk. He remembers being wheeled in a go-cart on a Sunday afternoon outing with his father and mother and seeing the place and hearing it named for the first time:

Woher stammen im Grunde des Menschen Schicksale, Eduard? he says, and as usual gives the answer:

> Von meinem Kinderwagen her—du weisst Eduard, ich war seit frühester Jugend etwas schwach auf den Beinen—erinnere ich mich noch ganz gut jener Sonntagsnachmittagsspazierfahrtstunde, wo mein Dämon mich zum erstenmal hierauf anwies, in welcher mein Vater sagte: 'Hinter der roten Schanze, Frau, kommen wir gottlob bald in den Schatten. Der Bengel da könnte übrigens auch bald zu Fusse laufen. Meinst du nicht?' 'Er ist so schwach auf den Füssen', seufzte meine selige Mutter, und dieses Wort vergess ich ihr nimmer. Ja, Eduard, ich bin immer etwas schwach, nicht nur von Begriffen, sondern auch auf den Füssen gewesen, und das ist der besagte Punkt. Ich habe mich wahrhaftig nicht weiter in der Welt bringen können, als bis in den Schatten der roten Schanze.

How Schaumann makes his slow way to his goal is a long story, but the next incentive comes from a cannon-ball of the Seven Years War fired at the town by Prince Xaver of Saxony from the 'rote Schanze' and still lodged in the gable of his father's house, and from there his curiosity takes him to the place itself where, having forced an entry, he finds himself held in thrall for life by the household of Andreas Quakatz, a solitary suspected of murder and ostracized by the community, who lives there with his dogs and his neglected daughter, Valentine or Tinchen. The spell of a locality that most of us have experienced in early life on seeing or half-seeing some house or habitation that fascinates us is conveyed here with such finality that it need never be done again:

> Da stieg sie auf im wohlerhaltenen Viereck. Nur durch einen Dammweg über den tiefen Graben mit der übrigen Welt in Verbindung. Mit allem, was sie der Knabenphantasie zu einem Entzücken und Geheimnis gemacht hatte: mit den Kanonen und Mörsern des Prinzen Xaver und mit der undurchdringlichen Dornenhecke, die der böse Bauer Andreas Quakatz auf ihrer Höhe um sich, sein Tinchen, sein Haus, seine Ställe und Scheunen und alles, was sonst sein war, zum Abschluss gegen die schlimme Welt gezogen hatte.

But the miracle here is that Schaumann accepts the challenge, solves the murder mystery—an unforgettable episode beautifully handled—marries the daughter, inherits the farm, yet never loses the spell that first bound him.

This is the tale that Schaumann for the most part tells himself in his inimitable way, seated—or so we usually picture him—on his ramparts and looking out at his native town and the wide landscape enclosing it. It is not a small thing that the book gives us the opportunity to sit there with him and share his mastery of life, which we feel to be complete, though we don't quite know how or why.

Was sagen sie nun zu ihm, says Valentine when he is out of hearing,

> Er erfährt das Wichtigste und Schrecklichste, was Herz und Seele bewegen kann und lässt dabei seine Pfeife nicht ausgehen. Sagt keinen Laut bis es ihm passt!

And even as a boy at school, when Eduard protests a point and says: Du verkennst mich aber riesig, Heinrich, and he answers: Gar nicht, Eduard, ich kenne euch nur. Alle kenne ich euch, in- und auswendig, we have to concede his right to say it. But it is not enough for the book to have a centre, it also has, in the most flexible sense of the term, a circumference, a periphery, towards which we find ourselves travelling in one direction or another as the tale soaks into our minds. One of the first characters we hear about is an old postman who had just died, Störzer, who delivered letters on a rural route for thirty-one years, during which time he is playfully estimated to have walked the equivalent of five times round the globe:

> Also der alte Störzer ist tot . . . hat sich zur Ruhe gesetzt, nachdem er fünfmal die Weglänge um den Erdball zurückgelegt hat.

And again:

> Fünfmal. Rund um den Erdball. Siebenundzwanzigtausendundzweiundachtzig Meilen in vierundfünfzigtausendeinhundertvierundsechzig Berufsgehstunden.

Not only this, but Störzer, we learn, had a passion for geography and used to spend his evenings compensating himself for his monotonous routine by reading travel-books and especially Le Vaillant's account of central Africa: Die Geographie, die Geographie, Eduard—this is the Eduard who years afterwards plays the listener to Schaumann but is now, in a flash-back, a twelve-year old boy keeping the postman company on his rounds—

> Was wäre und wo bliebe unsereiner ohne die Geographie . . . Numm nur mal an, so Tag für Tag, jahrein jahraus die nämlichen Wege. . . . Könntest du das auf Lebenszeit und immer auf denselben Wegen aushalten, Eduard, ohne deine Gedanken und Einbildungskraft und Phantasien und Lektüre, Eduard? Müsste dir das nicht auch auf die Länge langweilig werden ohne die Geographie?

And this leads further, because it was Störzer's musings on geography that infected Eduard and finally took him as a settler to South Africa, from where—as it were, from the ends of the earth—he returns after many days to hear Schaumann tell his tale.

It may be difficult to get the hang of this on a first reading, but Raabe knows what he is doing. As little Eduard says to the postman, his schoolfellow Schaumann doesn't care about geography: Der frägt aber nichts nach Afrika. Dem seine tägliche Sehnsucht ist dort die rote Schanze; na, das weisst du ja. And so at this early stage Raabe begins to extract the values there are to extract from contemplating the man who goes away and the man who stays where he began. Listen to Schaumann again, whose adventures at home have been more surprising than Eduard's abroad and who knows it and says:

> nur nicht zu hastig. Weshalb sollen wir uns nicht Zeit nehmen? Was könnte ich Hinhocker einem Weltwanderer gleich dir Merkwürdiges zu weisen haben, was solch ein rasendes Drauflosstürzen erforderte? Nur mit aller Bequemlichkeit, Freund.

The perspectives multiply. Schaumann, as we have seen delves into his own tormented boyhood, excavates his past like Tante Grünhage and, like her again, writes a piece of local history in doing so. The Seven Years War fascinates him, as it fascinated Raabe, but he prefers not to make too much of this:

> Und den historischen Sinn im Menchen erklären heutzutage ja viele Gelehrte für das Vorzüglichste, was es überhaupt im Menschen gibt . . . Dass ich mich mit ihm, immer dem historischen Sinn, einzig und allein auf die rote Schanze zu beschränken wusste, spricht, meines Erachtens, zuletzt denn doch dafür, dass noch etwas in mir lag, was selbst über den historischen Sinn hinausging.

If he is to go farther into the past he prefers the natural past to the human and in this spirit digs up the soil under his feet and collects fossils, his great find being the skeleton of a giant sloth, a Riesenfaultier, which we are repeatedly invited to regard as a geological portrait of himself. Over his front door Schaumann has a motto painted: Da redete Gott mit Noah und sprach: Gehe aus dem Kasten. Eduard, the traveller, is surprised, but Schaumann puts him right: Weil ihr ein bisschen weiter als ich in die Welt hinein euch die Füsse vertreten habt, meint ihr selbstverständlich, dass ich ganz und gar im Kasten sitzen geblieben sei.

Everything in *Stopfkuchen* works to the same end, building up in our minds the sense of a focus, a hearth, a home, on the one hand, and on the other, of great vistas and radial lines reaching out into them. Basically the form of the book is that of centre and circumference. Consider for a moment how suggestively appropriate it is that the recording of the tale should be made by Eduard while on his way back to South Africa, sitting in his cabin on board the *S.S. Hagebucher*—named after the native who returns from Africa in *Abu Telfan*—en route from Hamburg to Cape Town. He begins his manuscript early in the voyage and, when he finishes, Table Mountain is in sight. We make the voyage with him as we read, and the ship's arc drawn on the earth's surface reinforces the spherical or planetary shape that the book slowly assumes. So, too, the glimpse we are given in the opening pages of the stars—'das Übermass der Sterne', as Raabe calls it in one of his not uncommon references to Goethe. Not the stars of one hemisphere, but of both, since Eduard looking at the northern recalls the southern and so shows us at once the Southern Cross and the Great Bear. It is not till long afterwards that we realize how this astronomical opening locks in with the rest of the tale. We can say of this book what we can say of few, that it doesn't have to speak words of wisdom in order to be wise. So completely is the thought, the meaning, taken up in the form and the situation that there is no need to articulate it separately.

Raabe wrote on the last page of *Der Schüdderump*—years before *Stopfkuchen*—that it had been a long journey from *Der Hungerpastor* to this breathing-place, and the note of finality in his often-quoted words has contributed not a little to the impression that his work was now completed and rounded out. The popularity of *Der Hungerpastor,* a book which does credit to his heart but less credit to his genius, has reinforced the impression and stamped it on the histories of literature. It is nearer the truth to say that he was a young man—thirty-nine in 1870 when he published *Der Schüdderump*—and only now beginning. As a writer he still had twenty or thirty years to go and from *Horacker* (1876) to *Die Akten des Vogelsangs* (1895) and his posthumously published *Altershausen,* written about 1900, was seldom below his best. All that is needed is to shift the emphasis thus, from early to late, and Raabe will cease to be the unread name that he largely is to this day with so many good readers and take his place as a modern novelist, almost a contemporary, of uncanny skill and penetration. (pp. 77-81)

> *Barker Fairley, "The Modernity of Wilhelm Raabe," in* German Studies Presented to Leonard Ashley Willoughby *by Barker Fairley and others, Basil Blackwell, 1952, pp. 66-81.*

Roy Pascal   (essay date 1956)

[*Pascal was an English educator and critic who wrote extensively on German literature, culture, and society. In the following excerpt, he assesses narrative technique and the role of comedy in Raabe's fiction and places his novels in the literary and social context of nineteenth-century Germany.*]

Raabe is one of the most subjective of novelists; his personality obtrudes directly into his works. Some of his novels begin with general comments on the 'moral' of the story he is to tell, others begin with a short explanation of how he came across the story. His personal character—his delight in oddities, his somewhat pedantic facetiousness, his attitude to life—is expressed in all the elements of his style, which emphatically reminds us of the moral and cultural standpoint from which the stories are told. It is the reverse of a 'classical' style, for Raabe seems always to be seeking some direct point of contact with his readers. In his mature work, however, these subjective elements become fused with the whole theme and themselves interpret its essential bearing.

In the early works, Raabe shows sharp observation of the scenes and characters of small-town life, but his composition is faulty. The varied existences in *The Chronicle of Sperling Street* are linked only in the memory of an old man; in *Der Hungerpastor* the hero passes through several milieux, each of which propounds new problems without any corresponding growth on his part. But the characters and incidents of *Abu Telfan* are more tightly disposed round a single moral situation, and more firmly subordinated to the author's purpose. *Der Schüdderump* again is

closely knit, and the only milieux which are fully described are the Manor House and the Poor House, the two poles of the theme. In the mature works there is a still greater simplicity and sobriety of construction, a more austere selection of character and detail. Many of the novels are built round a slight and undramatic incident, and even where a life-story is related, as in *Old Nests, Stopfkuchen* or *The Vogelsang Documents,* events are only lightly touched on and closely related to the moral situation.

Because of this simplification of structure, certain central features of his later tales acquire so intense a meaning that they become symbols. Raabe rarely forces symbols into his works: it might be held that his imagination was not vigorous enough to condense experiences into simple plastic images. He begins *Der Schüdderump* with a description of the old plague-cart that gives a symbolic title to the novel, but this symbol is not adequate to the complex theme and seems rather forced. The macabre battle of the crows over the future battle-field of *Das Odfeld* is a rare example of a striking and poetic symbol of this kind. But at his best, a natural realistic feature of the tale emerges bit by bit with the force of a symbol. The 'Red Redoubt' of *Stopfkuchen* sums up his isolation and security; the death of the old postman expresses the end of Eduard's nostalgic idealisation of the past. The manor house of *Old Nests* sums up the loveliness and the deadness of childhood; the Vogelsang suburb likewise. These symbols are not fixed, they change with time, and their transformation symbolises the conflict of values in the characters, and the nature of their decisions: the stone of the derelict manor house is used in the building of a bridge. The most harrowing and profound of all Raabe's symbols is the idiot in *Altershausen,* the old man with the mentality of a child, the embalmed past.

Even in his historical novels Raabe never shows much narrative skill. The variety of the early novels is provided by profusion of character rather than of incident, and later there is a marked lack of action. Yet there is tension in his works, for the small action there is involves a decision that brings a whole character into play. (pp. 162-63)

We see the characteristic clarification of Raabe's purpose and technique if we compare the historical novels *Unsers Herrgotts Kanzlei* (1862) and *Das Odfeld* (1887). The former, a story of burgher resistance to princely power in the age of the Reformation, describes numerous military engagements with the enemy and civil unrest within the city of Magdeburg. But events and figures are thin, sharply differentiated into good and bad, and there is no moral tension or development. The setting of *Das Odfeld* is also a battle. But it is one of the many indecisive engagements of the Seven Years' War, and the military events are of absolutely no significance. Though the sympathy of the main characters goes entirely to the Prussian allies, we see both armies engaged in purposeless fighting and senseless destruction and pillage. The real story is that of a small group of civilians, thrown out of a plundered homestead, who wander for two days over the battlefield, hiding from both armies. An old schoolmaster, the laughing-stock of the community, comforts them in their anxiety and distress, and guides them back to the devastated farm to take up their labours once again, richer in suffering and sorrow but also in wisdom and inner serenity. What is important is not, who will win, what great deeds will be done, but how the common people can grow wise through experience.

It is characteristic of Raabe that usually, in order to show this inner change, he makes extensive use of conversation. Description often seems a bare preparation for the actual speech of his characters, who suddenly acquire a sharp precision as they begin to speak. Dr. Wimmer, of *The Chronicle,* is a vague person until he begins to talk; in *Der Hungerpastor,* the hero's uncle and aunt really live only when we hear them speaking. The most vivid moments of *Abu Telfan* are those when direct speech is reported: the verdict of the family-council on Hagebucher or the garrulous and rampageous exuberance of Uncle Wassertreter. Nikola von Einstein, who in Raabe's description remains a somewhat nebulous, intangible creature, suddenly springs to life in the reckless gaiety and timid insecurity of her letter of submission. The substance of *Horacker* depends on the actual quality of speech of the old schoolmaster and his wife. The stories of *Villa Schönow* and *Stopfkuchen* are woven round the monological discourse of Schönow and Schaumann. But also in *Pfister's Mill* or *Old Nests* the actual scraps of reported conversation interpret the 'problem' of the story more incisively than the statements of the rather naïve, timid tellers of the tale. It is noticeable that Raabe devotes extremely little attention to the lawsuit and exterior facts in *Pfister's Mill;* the story is poised on, and culminates in, the *words* of Asche and the old miller.

Many of Raabe's works are written in a form which makes them ostensibly the tale of a particular teller, a form which thus carries the use of direct speech to its ultimate conclusion. In *The Chronicle of Sperling Street* and other early works, this device is used as Storm frequently used it, in order to throw the veil of distance over events, to soften their sharpness through a mellow melancholy, and it allows Raabe to sentimentalise and idealise the past. Later it is used in order to intensify and deepen the problematic of events.

There is a certain sameness in the character of these pseudo-narrators. In *Pfister's Mill, Old Nests,* and *The Vogelsang Documents,* they are all men with an academic education, successful in their modest way, contented with what they have achieved and their manner of life. They have all, to some extent, participated in the events they describe, but always without energy and impact, themselves following normal careers and accepting normal standards. But they are all men who are able to understand and sympathise with their energetic or idealistic friends who have protested against the conventions, and they suffer from a deep feeling of insecurity, which often finds naïve, almost unconscious expression. This conflict is expressed in Ebert Pfister through the wry contrast between the sadness of his tale and his present happiness, through his wife's reluctance to let him dwell on his tale, through his own subdued comments. It is expressed in Fritz Langreuter's awareness of the inhibitions within his own crippled char-

acter [in *Old Nests*]; in Eduard's submission to Stopfkuchen's garrulousness; in Krumhardt's irony about his own career [in *The Vogelsang Documents*]. Thus the story-teller provides us not only with a standpoint from which events are focused, but himself is the embodiment of the conflict of values which is the centre of his tale. The apparently incidental delineation of his present position and his character is as important as the tale he has to tell; the story proceeds on two or three planes, which ultimately intersect in the story-teller's own person. Raabe himself seems to be most at ease when he adopts this device of the fictitious story-teller, and it gives his novels a depth that they sometimes lack. It has a further advantage. Raabe's own style is somewhat laboured, clumsy, amorphous; in these reminiscence-novels it appears, however, as the appropriate form of expression of the pseudo-narrators.

Raabe's handling of this technique is always deft; in *Stopfkuchen* it is bold. Eduard writes down the story of his visit as he sits in the liner, on the way home to South Africa; and the whole of the tale breathes his contented anticipation of his return to his farm and family in the new world. From the beginning we feel therefore that the old world of the small town and Spiessbürger has receded, has been overcome by new opportunities; his visit has actually brought him little profit—except the meeting with Stopfkuchen. Then, as Stopfkuchen takes up his own tale, we are in the midst of a real and successful struggle at close quarters with the old world, and Eduard's temporary effacement illustrates the greater severity and worth of Stopfkuchen's struggle. The latter's own words, interrupted only by short pauses when Eduard describes their walk round the 'Redoubt', the meal, the wife, make us feel the uniqueness of Stopfkuchen's life; and as Stopfkuchen, after accompanying Eduard down to the town, takes his leave and returns to his fastness, we feel how lonely has been his struggle. Eduard now turns from his old friends of the 'Stammtisch' with a deeper consciousness of the narrowness of their lives; the funeral of the old postman acquires the symbolic character of the death of an illusion. (pp. 164-66)

[In "The Modernity of Wilhelm Raabe"] Barker Fairley has pointed out how deeply rooted in Raabe's artistic personality are these various aspects of his technique—his groping towards his readers, his lack of dramatic narrative, his use of conversation. Fairley sums up his work as 'the most richly conceived body of fiction in the German language'. He calls Raabe's composition, as opposed to the 'linear' type of narrative, a representation of 'life in depth', and compares it with Rembrandt's. Events and scenes are somewhat blurred, or emerge only slowly from a dark background, because they exist not for themselves, but in relation to the characters; each character itself emerges only in its meaning and reality for others. This is a rich conception of the novel indeed, and as Fairley points out, a very modern conception too. It was not consciously evolved by Raabe, but arose 'out of his general awareness, from the start, of what is involved mentally in the process of narration'. The unity of Raabe's important novels, that is, of the later novels, lies in the mysterious and elusive point of intersection of description and narrative in the minds of the characters. *Stopfkuchen* itself, as

Raabe, second from the right, with his family in Niendorf, a resort on the Baltic coast.

Heinrich Meyer has said [in "Raum und Zeit in Raabe's Erzählkunst," *Deutsche Vierteljahrschrift für Literaturwissenschaft*] is a *non plus ultra* of composition, for the story of Heinrich Schaumann is the point of intersection of the colonial world, the small town, and the 'Red Redoubt'; of the present, childhood, and the remote past unobtrusively recalled by Stopfkuchen's collection of prehistoric remains, which places the whole story in a perspective of infinite time and gives it a depth recalling that of Hardy's great novels.

Raabe is known most popularly as a humorous writer, and it is easy to see his affinity with Sterne and Jean Paul (whom he often quotes), and with Dickens and Thackeray. Like the former, he continually contrasts, to humorous effect, the colourfulness of fantasy with the drabness of reality; like the latter, he delights in the oddities of life, in eccentric characters and incongruous situations. These elements are evident in an undigested form in his early novels; in his later they merge into the general body of his work, in which his humour gains a specific character and philosophic function.

All through his life Raabe kept one form of humour—farce, gay make-believe—as a refuge from an oppressive

world. We have already seen how he wrote ***Christoph Pechlin*** as a piece of fooling at a time when he was bitterly disappointed over the materialistic greed of the years following the foundation of the Reich. Such works are based on accurate observation of characters, but with a conscious exaggeration of oddities, a frankly far-fetched plot, and much stylistic freakishness. They are at best a relaxation; when such a character as Mutter Cruse, the old-iron collector in ***Old Iron,*** is placed in a serious framework, one is a little disconcerted by the determination of the author to avoid serious issues when they threaten to arise. In such situations Raabe's humour may easily become crude and tasteless; it is certainly much overdone in ***Villa Schönow,*** where the misfortunes of a young boy and girl are heavily overlaid with an ostentatious and inescapable humour; there is something of the same crudity in the historical novel, ***Hastenbeck.***

In the first place Raabe's humour interprets a distrust of self, characteristic of the dejection of the patriotic and liberal middle class during the 1850s. In the early works it betrays a wistful consciousness of the contrast between the ideals within men, and the pettiness of their actual circumstances, and the contrast is humorous because it is accompanied by irony and distrust of self. ***The Children of***

Finkenrode displays this sort of humour in a variety of ways. The hero Bösenberg (who is the story-teller) is a smart, modern journalist, who can write of his job, his office, and his colleagues only with irony. His keenly anticipated visit to the scenes of his childhood is damped by the desolate inhospitability of the village where he changes from train to coach. The horses are ready for the knacker, the coach itself breaks down, and our hero enters his native town on foot, in a heavy downpour, unnoticed by anyone (Raabe often gets fun out of the contrast between exalted spirits and bad weather). Bösenberg spends his time in screwing up his courage to avow his love for a childhood friend, but discovers at the end that she is promised to another; but this theme is always humorously treated, for at no time is he a character who takes himself seriously or who asks us to take him seriously. The triviality of Bösenberg's character is emphasised by the ironical bombast and preciosity of his descriptions. A child scratching its head is 'a native disturbing the harmless settlements of little backwoodsmen in the primeval forest of his head'. An umbrella is 'a silken storm-roof'. A chamber-maid is a 'nymph', a pot an 'amphora'. Through this pervasive and irritating facetiousness Bösenberg escapes the responsibility of grappling with the real unsatisfactoriness of his life and profession.

In the later works this forced whimsicality develops into a philosophic humour. Its prevailing theme is the conflict between the humaneness of inner conviction and the cramping effect of actual concerns, but this conflict can be presented humorously because the tensions, though recognised, are left unresolved. Thus, the humour of Hagebucher's encounters [in *Abu Telfan*] with the police in the various states, as he goes from Africa to his home-town, introduces us deftly to the central theme of personal freedom. His father, and the other Spiesser, are both soberly and humorously described, for their mode of life has a value as well as being a challenge. The eccentricity of the former patriotic student, Wassertreter, his liking for a drop, his noisy exuberance, form a commentary on the times, which frustrate and injure the most generous. Similarly the comic treatment of the little professor, with his pipe and domestic comfort, his absent-mindedness, reveals the limitations of his protest against the pressure of society. The irony of Hagebucher is his manner of coming to terms with a reality too strong for him—Nikola tells him that 'he tries to hold his shattered life together through savage irony, and thinks he can rescue himself through the laughter with which he hurls himself into contradictions'. Hagebucher accommodates himself to the burgher world, and it is thus that his struggle appears in humorous form; his humour anticipates his ultimate surrender, and is his revenge for it. The court of the small state is treated without humour, for Raabe does not accept a compromise with it.

This is the mature form of Raabe's humour, and it has many gradations. A man like Krumhardt (*The Vogelsang Documents*) is the reverse of a humorist in the usual sense, for he is a prudent and pedantic lawyer, weighed down by the consciousness of his responsibilities, burdened and puzzled by the story he has to tell. Only an occasional ironical comment, as when he remarks incidentally that he has married into one of the best families, allows us to see that he is conscious of the equivocalness of his career. In *Gutmann's Travels,* the proceedings of the first conference of the 'Nationalverein' are accurately reproduced, while the humour is apparently reserved for the love-affair of the shy young couple. But the intertwining of the two themes, the fretting of young Gutmann through the long speeches, constitutes an essential commentary on the proceedings, which are thus made to appear far less important than the union of the couple; it is a sort of tender farewell to illusions. Raabe himself was later to call it a 'Bismarckiad'! So also the tender humour with which the old-fashioned, impractical old schoolmaster is described in *Das Odfeld* brings out most subtly both the fragility of the humanity he represents, and its deep roots.

More obviously humorous are those characters like Hagebucher who acutely feel a conflict of values within themselves, and express this through a fantastic and often fierce irony. Velten Andres [*The Vogelsang Documents*] is no social reformer, though he sets himself against the world, and his revolt expresses itself in savage irony of the ideal of success. But he writes with the same bitter irony of himself, of his love for Helene and of his plan to become a tailor in order to be able to follow her to America. His mother calls his plan 'a tragic farce', and Krumhardt asks himself at times if Velten's life is serious or farcical. Asche (*Pfister's Mill*), Schönow, Herberger (*Kloster Lugau*), all try to smother their unease with humour; the more they devote themselves to practical business, the more their fancy luxuriates. Schönow and Asche are not just self-opinionated, garrulous, powerful personalities; their expansive humour expresses the tension in capable and enterprising men between their resolute realism and their humane idealism. In less resolute characters, like Ebert Pfister, the humour is expressed more indirectly, through the unconscious apposition of values and circumstances in the shaping of the story. Ebert is not the man to face up to all the reality of his times, and so Raabe subtly shows him at times dwelling on his present happiness and hopes, at other times recalling with wistful idealisation the life of the old mill.

When this basic conflict of values is presented without humour, Raabe often falls into sentimentality, and particularly so when childhood or youth appears as the symbol of humaneness. In his early works childhood is a period of unsullied happiness, and scarcely any of his children suffer. His depiction of childhood has nothing of the power and insight of Dickens', for instance. Even the poorest of his children are sheltered by devoted parents or adopted parents, and his adults remember their childhood as an idyll in the country or rural town. He scarcely touches on the psychological stresses of adolescence. Characters like Hans Unwirrsch and Tonie Häussler grow up without conflict and are innocence personified; even in a later work like *Old Nests,* where past and present are humorously and significantly contrasted, childhood is recalled as an idyll. But also when young people are treated ironically, as in *Gutmann's Travels* or *Horacker* or *Hastenbeck,* Raabe tends to sentimentalise them by exaggerating their helpless innocence in the midst of the big affairs of the world. In the best of his works we can glimpse, as in *The*

Vogelsang Documents, the conflicts of age already present in childhood, and their presence in childhood is all the more poignant since the pseudo-narrator, Krumhardt, himself unconsciously tries to see his childhood as idyllic. *Stopfkuchen* is one of the rare works where (in contrast to Eduard's illusions) childhood itself is represented as full of conflict, embodying the limitations of the society in which the child grew.

The most curious and ambiguous of all the novels, in this respect, is Raabe's last, unfinished work, *Altershausen.* On the face of it, the theme is simple and characteristic. A distinguished medical man, at the end of a career full of honours, visits incognito the small town in which he was born, to recapture himself, the real self that the years have overlaid. Little is changed, and bit by bit he rediscovers this 'better' self of his, which he had left behind at the age of eleven or twelve. He meets again two old school fellows and feels that they have done as well with their small humble lives as he with his. What is startling, however, is that one of these, a lad he and everyone else had much admired, is an idiot, whose mental development had been arrested through an accident at the age of twelve. Here then is the picture of his childhood as it was, preserved in its original form, yet macabre and distressing, and even ludicrous. It is a bleak statement that childhood is good but must be outlived. Yet the distinguished doctor still finds more comfort and substance in the company of this idiot and his companion than in his own career, and if there is grotesque humour in the behaviour of the idiot, the finer irony is kept for the doctor himself.

Raabe's humour is seen at its deepest in *Stopfkuchen;* the humorousness with which Schaumann tells his story defines exactly the measure of his achievement. The very character of his language—he uses the complex literary style of the educated middle class, often with a parodistic relish which reveals that this culture itself has become philistine—reminds us at all moments of what normal people think about his achievement. He puts matters in such a way that momentarily we are led to believe that all he has done is to win the right to be lazy and comfortable; and this is indeed part of the truth. But his humorous concessions to normal views, his refusal to idealise or dramatise his struggle, his almost ostentatious self-depreciation, only strengthen the impression of his moral power. As he imposes his tale and his views on Eduard, we feel he is asserting his personality as against the philistines, and Eduard's half-comic resignation to the role of a listener is his vindication:

> 'Where does a man's fate spring from, at bottom, Eduard?' he first asked, and before I could answer (what could I have answered?) he gave his opinion: 'Usually, if not always, from one point. From my pram-days—you know, Eduard, I've always been a little feeble on my feet—I can very well remember that Sunday afternoon walk on which my Dæmon first directed me up here, when my father said: "Praise be, wife, we shall soon find some shade behind the Red Redoubt. And it's high time this rascal walked on his own feet, what do you think?"—"He's so feeble on his feet", sighed my dear mother, and I'll never forget her for these words. Yes, Eduard, I've al-

ways been a bit feeble, not only in my head, but also on my feet, and that's the point in question. It's absolutely true that I have not managed to get farther in the world than the shade of the Red Redoubt. I really can't help it. That was my weak point, or if you insist, my strong point. This is where fate got hold of me. I struggled, but I had to submit, and I submitted with a sigh. [Your friend] the postman and [the book of] Le Vaillant carried you, Eduard, to burning Africa, and my feeble intellectual powers and still feebler feet held me fast in the cool shade of this farm. Eduard, you see, fate mostly utilises our weak points to make us attentive to what may be serviceable to us.'

> This man was so impudently ungrateful that at this moment, I tell you, he fetched a sigh from the depths of his paunch. Naturally, only to make his contentment seem even more enviable. But I did not fall into the trap. I did not do him the pleasure of sighing too, still deeper and with more justification.

Stopfkuchen's humour, embracing himself as well as the world, puts him in an unassailable position, so that contradiction and agreement both simply confirm his values. His wife, a simple woman, protests that he underrates himself; but his apparent self-irony only shows how secure he is. 'In *Stopfkuchen',* wrote Raabe, 'I felt myself most free and secure above the world.'

Raabe deserves a place among the important novelists of his time, for the sureness with which he grasped the moral dilemma of his world, and the truth with which he portrays it. But his limitations are such that he can only be accounted a minor writer. His works lack intellectual insight and the energy of passion; and their social range is very narrow.

In several of the novels Raabe shows a character destroyed by the times, but the conflict is never passionate or bitter. Tonie Häussler, Velten Andres, even the miller Pfister, succumb without a real effort, inwardly convinced of the unavailingness of struggle. The most conscious of them are ironically aware that they have no right to move the clock back, however much they refuse to seek a place within this new world. Those men who, though torn by misgivings, conform to the new society—Schönow or Asche—overcome their unease by irony. Raabe's contemplative tolerance prevented him from envisaging the process of his time as a dire conflict of energies, and he lacks the exaltation of great effort and feeling; his work as a whole suffers from drabness. The sobriety and truth of his work is much to be esteemed, especially when we compare it with the melodrama and hysteria of many of his German contemporaries. But it not only betrays an emotive narrowness in his temperament, but also a failure fully to grasp the implications of the social changes he observed, the growing social and moral crisis in which the following generation was involved. *The Vogelsang Documents* is an anticipation of Thomas Mann's *Doctor Faustus,* but an innocent, naïve anticipation, for the author has no inkling of the 'diabolical' might of the tensions of which he writes. The loneliness of his heroes is a naïve anticipation of one of the mightiest modern themes.

Closely associated with this emotive and intellectual narrowness is the narrowness of social range. Raabe's favourite setting is the bourgeoisie of the small towns, and the tensions within the main characters arise from their double relationship, appreciative and critical, to this 'Philisterium'. To the small-town background, therefore, there is contrasted in different books the world of the peasantry, that of the nobility, that of the industrial modern town, and that of government and high society. It must be said that, with one or two exceptions, Raabe markedly fails in his presentation of these other worlds, and this is a serious criticism, for his very intention demanded that their moral character, their inner tensions, should be clearly delineated.

He was most successful, in *Der Schüdderump* and elsewhere, in his portrayal of the country nobility, the squirearchy. But the peasantry appears continually as an undifferentiated mass of barbarians, engrossed by material interests and vindictive to the weak. Thus they appear in *Der Schüdderump,* in *Horacker,* in *Restless Guests.* For the village outcasts Raabe has great sympathy, linking their fate with that of those men and women who are at odds with modern society; but this sympathy is based on the assumption of the spiritual superiority of the bourgeoisie, and Schönow's concern for a workman, or Eckerbusch's protection of Horacker, is expressed in bullying tones which border on arrogance.

Court-circles are portrayed in *Abu Telfan* with a petty-bourgeois horror as homes of sophisticated heartlessness and vice. On the whole, Raabe fortunately refrains from the attempt to describe courts and the upper classes, for his sketches of social gatherings do not rise above rather trite satire of conventional elegance (*Old Iron*), and compare most unfavourably with, say, Fontane's. His criticism of high society is most solid when he restricts himself to the delineation of the character of the high official, worn out and morally distressed by social convention and the arid preoccupations of his duties (*Der Hungerpastor, The Vogelsang Documents*). On no occasion does he deal with great political and social issues as they are fought out within ruling circles or political parties.

The industrialist plays a much bigger part in his works as the main agent of social change, and while at first he forms a sinister background to his stories, later he comes right into the foreground as a characteristic and problematical figure of the times. But, while Raabe gives great attention to the relation of the industrialist to the old society he is shattering, it is very noticeable that he scarcely raises the problems arising from his relations with the modern industrial proletariat. And this is most surprising in an age in which Social Democracy became a great social and political force. The only communist that appears in Raabe's pages is a village carpenter in *Restless Guests,* and his 'communism' appears only as sympathy for the village outcasts and for the charitable sister of the parson. None of Raabe's industrialists or officials finds any moral or practical problem arising out of his relationships with his workmen or subordinates. We pay a visit to Asche's factory and Schönow's quarry, but are not made aware that there are workers there.

Raabe knew of course of the existence of social conflict; there is a passing and vague reference in the early novel, *Der Hungerpastor,* to the distress and unrest in a factory. But the theme does not recur in later novels. In the first version of *A Springtide* (1857) there is a prophecy of a coming proletarian revolution, but this was deleted from the second edition of 1870. Raabe, like Dickens, has great sympathy for the poor, for social misfits, for workers in isolated occupations like shepherds, foresters, carters, millers, but he never attempts to describe factory-workers. The modern industrial masses seem to have inspired him with repugnance—in a letter he talks of the modern masses as 'pulp' ('Bevölkerungsbrei'). In his novels he often shows a horror of the great cities, the vast streets and anonymous apartment-houses, though with delightful humour he recognises, in *Pfister's Mill,* that the Berliner may be deeply attached to his flat and suburb, to his 'country' walks through the modern cemetery.

Raabe's imaginative range is, then, very narrow. He is a bourgeois story-teller, and bourgeois too in a limited way. His best work is confined to the 'burghers' of the small town, and the great problem of his times, the transformation of Germany into an industrial power, is grasped only in its relation to this class. The men who grow out of this class and become industrialists, bankers, or high officials, are measured not against new problems but against the old values. And within this class Raabe concentrates with preference on the professional people, those with an academic, usually classical education, the schoolmasters, parsons, officials, who are rooted in the class and yet often at odds with it. They sympathise with more humane personal relationships, they seek to guide, but they do not struggle directly against the world; ironically and humorously they admit that they can at best only modify people's attitudes within a general process which cannot be withstood. Sometimes indeed they are only onlookers, only seeking a modest refuge for themselves and their ideals. Raabe's work in general lacks the sweep and energy of the more impassioned social novelists, like Balzac and Tolstoy; he was utterly at a loss with writers like Zola, Ibsen, and the German naturalists.

While the world narrows in Raabe's imagination to this small burgher setting, there is criticism as well as appreciation of the 'Spiesser'. On the one hand his novels are impregnated with the philistinism of the small town, and his best and most beloved characters are those who love the 'Stammtisch', the familiar streets and faces, the old grooves, the gossip. But on the other hand, the limitations of this philistinism are always firmly grasped, its moral rigidity, its lack of enterprise, the heartlessness within its easy-going good nature. Raabe's own character contained the two elements. He was for nearly three decades the leading spirit of the 'Kleiderseller', a club of Brunswick burghers, mostly professional men with an academic education, who met weekly to drink and talk, to celebrate personal and national festivals with recitations and speeches, at their ease in the typical 'Stammtisch' manner. Yet they felt that they were here upholding themselves against the 'philistines', nourishing a civic patriotism and a moral and aesthetic culture that the practical world around them disregarded. Raabe wrote in 1875 to Paul Heyse: 'I have taken the old romantic battle-cry, "War on the philistines" very seriously', and later he said: 'We are the people who pass freely through the ranks of the philistines.' His friend Hänselmann extravagantly claimed that they were 'a club of inquiring lovers of the naked Adam'. As [Georg] Lukács has well said [in his *Deutsche Realisten des 19 Jahrhunderts*], Raabe lays bare the dilemma of the petty-bourgeoisie, but within the framework of the petty-bourgeoisie, not from outside. Raabe himself was aware of his limitations. He attributed his insight to his 'Dummheit', his thick-headedness, which Heess amends to 'mother-wit' [in his *Wilhelm Raabe*]. His range and insight were limited, but his works show a remarkable harmony between capacity and intention, and a modesty and humour which set the seal on their integrity. (pp. 166-77)

> *Roy Pascal, "Wilhelm Raabe (1831-1910)," in his* The German Novel: Studies, *Manchester University Press, 1956, pp. 143-77.*

James H. Reid   (essay date 1969)

[*In the following excerpt, Reid discusses Raabe's novels as critiques of the sociopolitical order in nineteenth-century Germany.*]

What is important and original in Raabe's writings is that he binds . . . metaphysical problems into a precisely described social and historical milieu. Raabe's heroes are not wrestling with the world in a social vacuum as the heroes of the German novels of the earlier part of the nineteenth century often seem to be; they are on the contrary preoccupied with a vital social problem, which has not lost its actuality since Raabe's day. Viewed from this angle, Raabe's basic theme is the question: How is it possible for the individual to retain his individuality—and therefore his humanity—in the face of ever-increasing industrialisation, standardisation, rationalisation?

Raabe himself denied wishing to write a "Zeitroman". Nevertheless his novels are highly significant depictions of their age. Raabe was remarkably well informed on all that was going on around him and for a time he was committed to a specific political cause. The "Nationalverein" was founded in Frankfurt-am-Main in September 1859 specifically to further the cause of German unity and had at the height of its popularity about 40,000 members. It was frowned on by the authorities, especially in Hanover, and membership in the days of the paternalistic "Kleinstaat" was felt to be incompatible with service of the State. Raabe became a member of the local group in Wolfenbüttel in April 1860 and was present at the first general meeting of the society in Coburg in September of the same year. Thirty years later in the novel *Gutmanns Reisen* (1890-91) Raabe described the assembly from the perspective of a number of individuals from various parts of Germany and Austria. The "Nationalverein" and all it stood for is undoubtedly the most important political factor in Raabe's writings. For only a unified Germany which had overcome the provincialism described in *Abu Telfan* (1865-67) could provide the background of a social community in which the human values for which literature stands have their rightful place. From this standpoint alone is it possi-

ble for us today to understand Raabe's enthusiasm for the Prussian wars of 1866 and 1870-71. He as a North German experienced the former in Stuttgart, where South German particularism favoured France rather than German-speaking Prussia, and he got into trouble over his Prussian sympathies. Raabe's admiration for Bismarck is to be seen in this light also. It is unfortunate that his enthusiasm for the cause of German unity took him so far as what appears in some of his letters as downright jingoism or at best narrow-mindedness. When Sacher-Masoch invited him in 1881 to contribute to his specifically "international" periodical *Auf der Höhe,* Raabe refused:

> Je weniger *heute* das Deutsche Volk sich seinen frühern internationalen Zuvorkommenheiten hingiebt, desto besser!
>
> [The less *today* the German people pander to their former international obsequiousness the better!]

In Raabe's defence it can be pointed out that there was some justification in shunning attempts at superficial international harmony and unity before Germans themselves had been genuinely united, and attention is worth drawing to the passage in *Abu Telfan* which looks forward to a time when "die Vereinigten Staaten von Europa" ["The United States of Europe"] will be "dieser glückselige und wahrhaft normale Zustand" ["this blissful and truly normal condition"]; a letter of 1885 suggests that Germany was not yet worthy of a place in the "United States of the Universe".

In the event Raabe was disappointed in the quality of German unity after 1871. No great spiritual rebirth of the nation took place and Raabe, who had hoped that the Germans would at last have time for his books, was quickly disillusioned. The two novels which deal most directly with the cause of German unity both clearly show this disillusionment. *Der Dräumling* (1870-71) describes a small North German town preparing to celebrate the hundredth anniversary of the birth of Friedrich Schiller, the greatest poet of German national unity. While the schoolmaster is determined to make it a great occasion with a pageant, speeches and the public recital of poems by Schiller and himself, the local ratepayers are much more concerned about how much this will cost them than about the poet himself or anything he stands for. *Der Dräumling* was written during the war which Raabe hoped would fulfil his dreams; that it presents such an ironic view of the people who had to carry the dream into effect suggests that as a novelist he was more clear-sighted than as a private individual. *Gutmanns Reisen* adds an epilogue to the cause of German unity. The convocation of the "Nationalverein" is relativised by reference to the shy love-affair it sparks off between two of the participants; this, Raabe implies, is much more productive of unity than all the enthusiastic speeches.

The reason for Raabe's disillusionment, implied in *Der Dräumling,* is stated specifically in the 1890 preface to the second edition of *Christoph Pechlin* (1871-72):

> Die Wunden der Helden waren noch nicht verharscht, die Tränen der Kinder, der Mütter, der

Gattinnen, der Bräute und Schwestern noch nicht getrocknet, die Gräber der Gefallenen noch nicht übergrünt: aber in Deutschland ging's schon—so früh nach dem furchtbaren Kriege und schweren Siege—recht wunderlich her. Wie während oder nach einer großen Feuersbrunst in der Gasse ein Sirupsfaß platzt, und der Pöbel und die Buben anfangen, zu lecken; so war im deutschen Volke der Geldsack aufgegangen, und die Taler rollten auch in den Gossen, und nur zu viele Hände griffen auch dort danach. Es hatte fast den Anschein, als sollte dieses der größte Gewinn sein, den das geeinigte Vaterland aus seinem großem Erfolge in der Weltgeschichte hervorholen könnte!

[The wounds of the heroes had not yet healed, the tears of the children, the mothers, the wives, the brides and sisters had not yet dried, the graves of the fallen were not yet green; but already in Germany—so soon after the fearful war and arduous victory—things were happening in an odd manner. Just as during or after a great fire a barrel of treacle bursts in the street and the mob and the little boys began to lick; so in the German people the money-bag had opened and the dollars too were rolling about in the gutters and all too many hands clutched out at them too. It almost looked as if this was to be the extent of the profit that the united Fatherland was to gather from its great success in world history!]

Preoccupation with the material benefits of political unification had made the Germans lose sight of spiritual values. Already in *Der Schüdderump,* written between the wars and published in 1870, materialism is seen as the supreme evil and is linked with death itself. The striking image which Raabe uses in this novel is that of the plague-cart, "der Schüdderump", to which the narrator refers again and again. The symbol relates to death, but specifically to material, physical death and can therefore be associated with Dietrich Häußler, the sometime barber of Krodebeck, who makes his fortune in the South and returns to claim his lovely granddaughter, an asset which he wishes to realise by selling her off to an important business connection. *Meister Autor* too deals with the corrupting power of money. Unlike Tonie Häußler, Gertrud Tofote is seduced by her fortune, estranged from her former friends and protectors and lost to materialist, mindless society. Where this novel presents an advance on the previous one is in the figure of the narrator, a Herr von Schmidt, who, far from rescuing Gertrud, himself succumbs to the enticements of society.

The years 1870-1914 laid the foundations of modern Germany. During this time the industrial revolution took place, turning Germany from a predominantly rural into a predominantly urban country—in 1871 only 36 per cent of the population lived in towns of more than 2000 inhabitants; by 1910 it was 60 per cent—and making Germany the largest producer of steel and chemicals in Europe. Raabe was thus writing his best novels in a rapidly changing society. Here we must differ from Barker Fairley, who claims that few of Raabe's novels, despite their exact dating in the course of the narrative, are necessarily connected to a specific time in history, and furthermore that

Raabe never gives us the sense of impending change, of something nearing its end [*Wilhelm Raabe: An Introduction to his Novels*]. *Pfisters Mühle,* which Fairley admits as an exception, describes very poignantly the effects of the industrial revolution on the old Germany with the idyllic mill and its chestnut trees, the students and the open-air restaurant. But this is a theme to be found also in *Meister Autor* with its lament over the demolition of picturesque medieval buildings to facilitate access to the railway station and the destruction of a rococo house and garden to make way for a main road. Great stress is laid at the beginning of *Horacker* on the fact that Eckerbusch is the last holder of his office, the post of "Konrektor" having since been abolished; at the close of the novel this theme is taken up again in the remark by Nagelmann to Neubauer, both representatives of the new order (the latter's name is obviously important):

Alle diese grauköpfigen, muntern Kerle hier herum hängen merkwürdig freundschaftlich miteinander zusammen. Daß wir jetzigen Leute diese heitern, naiven Zustände aufrechterhalten werden, scheint mir lieder unwahrscheinlich.

[All these grey-headed jolly chaps about here hang together in a remarkably friendly way. I'm afraid it's improbable that we people of today will keep up these happy, naive conditions.]

In *Alte Nester* (1877-79) a road now runs through the place where the nut-trees of the protagonists' idyllic childhood stood. *Das Horn von Wanza* (1879-80) takes its title from the horn which the night-watchman is no longer allowed to blow to mark the hours of the night; it has been replaced by a whistle in the cause of "progress". *Prinzessin Fisch* describes the coming of the tourist traffic to the sleepy town of Ilmenthal—satire of modern mass tourism is also to be found in *Unruhige Gäste;* at the same time industrial progress causes the romantic Ilme to be tamed to provide power for a paper works. *Die Akten des Vogelsangs* shows the process of industrialisation and urbanisation which turn the idyllic Vogelsang suburb into a noisy and noisome place dominated by factories and a fairground. Even in *Stopfkuchen,* where time seems mostly to stand still, we can detect impending change. Schaumann complains that the hedges under which he used to lie as a boy are gradually being replaced by walks and fences. Moreover, although he has overcome the world, his triumph is but precarious; he is childless, whereas Eduard, the worldly-wise, returns to his wife and children, and the novel ends with the clamouring of Eduard's children. His is the tradition which will continue.

Raabe is thus keenly aware of the transitional nature of the age he is describing. But he is not simply the "laudator temporis acti", as Lukács describes him [in his *Essays on Thomas Mann*]. On the contrary, he postulates the necessity of development. *Alte Nester* is at least partly about this necessity and the impropriety of trying to cling to the past. This is made clear in the fate of Ewald Sixtus. During his exile Ewald has been planning to restore the past, to marry Irene Everstein and reinstate her in her father's mansion. But the mansion proves to be quite uninhabitable and its only proper use can be in the cause of progress: it is pulled down and used as material for a bridge across the Weser. Sophie Grünhage puts Raabe's standpoint as clearly as anybody in *Das Horn von Wanza,* when, complaining about the abolition of the night-watchman's horn and the German orthographic reform, she says to her nephew:

> Kind, Kind, ich will euch gewiß nicht das Recht nehmen, in den Tagen zu leben, wie sie jetzt sind, und auf sie zu schwören; aber manchmal meine ich doch, ein wenig mehr Rücksicht auf das Alte könntet ihr auch nehmen.

> [Child, child, I certainly don't want to deny your right to live in the present and according to the present; but sometimes I must say you might have a little more consideration for older things.]

For one of Raabe's main aims is to rescue what is valuable from the past into a present which is ever more inclined to forget it.

In this aim we have the real reason for the complicated time structures of Raabe's later novels which have so struck readers from Erwin Rohde in 1877 to the present day. Raabe tends to concentrate the external "action" of his stories into a short space, a few days in *Im alten Eisen* and *Das Horn von Wanza,* a short holiday in *Pfisters Mühle,* a single day in *Horacker, Das Odfeld* and *Stopfkuchen.* At the same time, by various devices he extends this period deep into the past, so that past and present merge into one. In these works, especially the last-named, he is anticipating the "spatial form" of such twentieth-century novels as *Mrs Dalloway* and *Ulysses,* which, in the words of Joseph Frank, "the reader is intended to apprehend . . . in a moment of a time, rather than as a sequence" ["Spatial Form in Modern Literature," in *Criticism: The Foundation of Modern Literary Judgment,* Schorer, Miles, McKenzie, eds., revised ed.]. The internal system of references and cross-references, of symbols and counter-symbols, is in other words more important than the external system of time by the clock. The "nüchterne Muse des Nacheinander" ["sober-minded muse of things in succession"] is replaced by the "Göttin des Durcheinander" ["goddess of things all at once"] (*Der Dräumling*). Thus *Stopfkuchen* is, superficially, the account of the last day of Eduard's visit to his native Germany. But at least five different levels of time can be distinguished in the story: the time of Eduard's writing about his experiences as he voyages back from Hamburg to Cape Town; the time of the day he is describing; the time of the story which his friend Schaumann related to him on that day; the time when the Rote Schanze was built during the Seven Years' War; and finally prehistoric time, the time of the giant sloth whose fossilised remains are in Schaumann's collection. As Schaumann himself is both the giant sloth and Prince Xaver of the Seven Years' War, we can see how complex the system of references can become. Related to this technique of the mingling of time levels is the important use of leitmotivs. In *Stopfkuchen* the motto "Gehe aus dem Kasten" ["Go forth of the ark"] is one such: a quotation from Noah, it might seem to refer to what Eduard has done, namely to emigrate and colonise the earth and at one point Eduard calls his ship an "ark"; but Eduard as little as any of the other philistines has left

the herd and it is stay-at-home Schaumann who has been most true to his maxim. In *Unruhige Gäste* the leitmotivs of light and shadow play an important role, while *Die Akten des Vogelsangs* makes great use of the tree-motiv: the trees of the Vogelsang, which yield to industrial development, the tree from which Helene Trotzendorff is rescued by Velten Andres, the Tree Yggdrasil, the Tree of Life, in which Andres in turn has become inextricably lost. And finally in this connection the quotations which Raabe introduces so generously in all his novels, requiring his readers at times to be encyclopedically well-read, extend the leitmotiv technique on to a universal level. They further relativise the temporal aspects of the story and provide yet another superstructure of references. *Prinzessin Fisch* makes this function clear when Bruseberger tells Theodor:

> Es wiederholt sich alles in der Welt, auch die Geschichte von der Zauberprinzessin in eurem alten Homer, und selbst die gelehrtesten Gymnasiumsprofessoren können noch für einen Moment in die Falle gehen und alle ihre neun Musen aus einem Sumpfe auffischen wollen.

> [Everything repeats itself in the world, even the story of the magic princess in your old Homer, and even the most learned grammar school teachers can still momentarily fall into the trap and try to fish all their nine muses at once out of a marsh.]

Das Odfeld provides the most obvious examples of history repeating itself: the Seven Years' War is merely another version of the Thirty Years' War, of the wars of the Franks against the Saxons and of the Romans against the Cheruskans. In other words, Raabe's stories do not relate an action during which something new takes place, but are about the general human situation as it has always been. He emphatically contradicts the typical nineteenth-century facile belief in progress.

These structures successfully reflect the situation of Raabe's own day. For if industrialisation and urbanisation meant the end of the old Germany with its organic traditions which had grown and developed gradually over a long stretch of time, then they had also in a sense put an end to the whole conception of time as a maturing process. The "Entwicklungsroman" which is so peculiar to German literature of the first two-thirds of the nineteenth-century depends on this conception of time and becomes therefore less and less appropriate as a vehicle of expression. This can be seen in Raabe's own "Entwicklungsroman", *Der Hungerpastor,* which belongs to his early period and is among the works he repudiated later. It is a poor example of the type, much of it derivative, and its ideology was later to be reversed in the maturer novels. Henriette Trublet, the French good-time girl, is damned as a "sinner" and eventually reformed; her counterpart in *Im alten Eisen* is truly humane and Raabe expressly refuses to have her reformed in the end to suit his readers. "Stopfkuchen" was actually intended by his parents to become a "Hungerpastor", but did not and the Faustian ideology of Hans Unwirrsch's "Streben nach oben" ["striving upwards"] is turned upside-down by Schaumann, the "giant sloth". Industrialisation is presented in *Der Hungerpastor* in one short episode and Berlin plays an important—negative—part, but Raabe fails to see the consequences of these developments for his literature. A trite ideology and a trite form go hand in hand. Raabe later abandoned the "Entwicklungsroman" form, which was by this time as doomed as the Vogelsang suburb. *Alte Nester* provides the nearest equivalent in the later works. Just Everstein, the counterpart of Ewald Sixtus, also returns from emigration, but succeeds in restoring the old peasant traditions of his "Steinhof". This search for salvation on the land, however, is fortunately an isolated instance in Raabe; it would otherwise have brought him dangerously close to the "Heimatkünstler" and their followers in the Third Reich.

As we have seen, Raabe is not simply content to keep up with his times. He is also concerned with saving what can be saved from the past. For this purpose his narrative structures serve equally admirably. Concentration of the external "action" goes hand in hand with extension of it into the past; this is as true of *Das Horn von Wanza, Im alten Eisen* and *Stopfkuchen* as it is of *Mrs Dalloway* and the contemporary novels of Heinrich Böll. Memory plays a very important part in Raabe's works and is linked to his attack on contemporary philistine Germans, who, as the already quoted passage from the preface to *Christoph Pechlin* declares, were quick to forget the wounds still bleeding from the 1870-71 war in order to reap the material benefits of victory. Ludolf Amelung in *Villa Schönow* (1882-83) dies ten years after of wounds received in France, and his unhappy fate leaves the community in some embarrassment: on the one hand they are delighted at the opportunity of holding a patriotic demonstration at the funeral, on the other they are unwilling to do anything practical to help Amelung's younger brother, who has now been left completely alone. Apart from the more immediate past, it is the Wars of Liberation at the beginning of the century which stand out most clearly for Raabe's heroes from Wassertreter in *Abu Telfan,* who afterwards participated in the German students' Wartburg convention and was imprisoned in the reaction which followed under Metternich—the "Wartburgfest" is an important point of reference in *Horacker*—via von Glaubigern in *Der Schüdderump* to Marten Marten of *Das Horn von Wanza,* who still limps fifty years after from a wound received in the wars: this limp itself is Raabe's symbol for the way in which the past lives in the present. The Wars of Liberation are important for Raabe as representing a time when the Germans were, however briefly, united. The revolution of 1848 is, as Lukács points out, much less important. Only in *Gutmanns Reisen* do we find a relic of this revolution in the person of Alois von Pärnreuther, an Austrian who had been Willi Gutmann's boyhood hero, but has now turned into a bald, fat and very placid Viennese wine-merchant. In this way Raabe, rightly or wrongly, presents 1848 as something which does *not* live on in the present.

Raabe's diagnosis of his age as one of transition from a rural society of organic traditions into an unhistorical, industrial one is reflected in other ways too. The most important of these relates to his presentation of character. Industrialisation and urbanisation have had two at first sight contradictory effects on humanity. On the one hand the flight from the country into the anonymity of the towns meant that community life was broken up and the individual thrown back on himself. On the other, the loss of any personal relationship between the craftsman and his work brought standardisation and the individual's personal loss of identity. Both of these effects are reflected in Raabe's eccentric heroes. In Raabe's early works community and communication are guaranteed by the restricted locality in which the characters live, the Sperlingsgasse in the first story, the Kröppelstraße in *Der Hungerpastor,* which represents for Hans throughout a haven of wholeness. Raabe's espousal of the cause of German unity may be regarded as his desire to strengthen this sense of community on a national level, a desire which, however, was not fulfilled. The later novels lack the ideal community of the early works and *Die Akten des Vogelsangs* provides a striking counterpart to *Der Hungerpastor* in this respect. The Vogelsang suburb, where all were as one family, is destroyed and the concept of "neighbourhood" lost. Krumhardt reflects:

> Die Nachbarschaft! Ein Wort, das leider Gottes immer mehr Menschen zu einem Begriff wird, in den sie sich nur mühsam und mit Aufbietung von Nachdenken und Überdenken von allerlei behaglicher Lektüre hineinzufinden wissen. Unsereinem, der noch eine Nachbarschaft hatte, geht immer ein Schauder über, wenn er hört oder liest, daß wider eine Stadt im deutschen Volk das erste Hunderttausend ihrer Einwohnerzahl überschritten habe, somit eine Großstadt und aller Ehren und Vorzüge einer solchen teilhaftig geworden sei, um das Nachbarschaftsgefühl dafür hinzugeben.

> [Neighbourhood! A word that alas is for more and more people turning into a concept to which they can give meaning only with difficulty and after much thought and reflection on all kinds of old-fashioned books. We who have known a neighborhood always shudder when we hear or read that the population of yet another German town has passed the first hundred thousand, thereby becoming a city and enjoying all the honors and advantages for the loss of the feeling of neighbourhood.]

The most striking and intense description of urban non-community is to be found in *Im alten Eisen,* in which two young children are left for three days and nights in an enormous Berlin tenement full of people—the description is at times reminiscent of parts of Kafka's *Der Prozeß* —but with only their dead mother for company. The second effect, standardisation, is seen mainly as bureaucracy. Krumhardt's tidy, bureaucratic mind has difficulty in following the eccentricities of his non-conformist friend Velten. The first part of *Unruhige Gäste* hinges on the refusal of Volkmar Fuchs to conform to the demands of bureaucracy and allow his dead wife to be buried in the churchyard by those who had refused to give her a decent life but now insist on giving her a "decent" burial—that Volkmar in the end becomes as much a philistine as the rest is a particularly effective comment on the difficulty of individualism in a society whose motto, according to *Horacker,* is the jingle:

Stramm, stramm, stramm;
Alles über einen Kamm.

Against these conditions Raabe sets his eccentric heroes. Autor Kunemund of *Meister Autor* introduces himself with the words:

Ich verstehe die Welt wohl noch, aber sie versteht mich nicht mehr, und so werden wir wohl nie mehr so zusammenkommen, wie damals, als wir beide noch jünger waren.

[I probably still understand the world, but it no longer understands me, and so we shall probably never again come together as we did in earlier days when we were both younger.]

Eckerbusch and Windwebel of *Horacker* are two schoolmasters whom nobody takes seriously. Sophie Grünhage of *Das Horn von Wanza* is an elderly, solitary widow, her friend Marten Marten likewise does not "belong". Heinrich Schaumann of *Stopfkuchen* is the most obvious "outsider": he has followed his motto "Gehe aus dem Kasten", has abandoned the philistine herd and taken up residence in an old redoubt outside the town, from which he metaphorically bombards the bourgeois as his predecessor had done in the Seven Years' War. In the historical novels too humanity is found only among the social outcasts: Buchius of *Das Odfeld,* who was left behind when his school moved to a safer place, and Frau Wackerhahn of *Hastenbeck,* who, like Stopfkuchen, lives well apart from the villagers in an old tower and enjoys the reputation of a witch. The chief function of these eccentrics is to hold up a mirror to society: true humanity is to be found only outside society. And in this way too Raabe is indirectly reflecting the standardisation and loss of individuality in modern society; those who belong are faceless ghosts.

Here is Raabe's answer to the problem posed earlier. Individuality and humanity can be preserved in an industrial age only in spite of society, by remaining, spiritually at least, outside it. This is, of course, a form of resignation. Raabe has no political solution to offer after the collapse of his hopes in 1871. He ignores the rise of socialism, speaks with scorn of the future "Bebel State", and in a letter to Clara Zetkin writes of having no intention of helping the Social-Democratic vision on its way. In spite of his theme, the industrialisation of Germany, his characters are taken from a very narrow social range, mainly the lower middle-class professions: parsons, teachers, the occasional civil servant, doctor, professor. There are a few craftsmen among his positive characters: a bookbinder in *Prinzessin Fisch,* a carpenter in *Unruhige Gäste.* One or two villainous industrialists and business-people *(Der Hungerpastor, Der Dräumling)* are to be found, but no artisans, no factory-workers, not even in those novels, like *Im alten Eisen,* which are set in proletarian Berlin. This lack in itself is significant as a negative indication of Raabe's view of the standardisation and depersonalisation caused by industry: "individuals" in Raabe's sense can be found only among the intellectuals and archaic craftsmen outside the factories, which are thereby indirectly indicted. Nevertheless, Raabe's reaction to his society can be described as a kind of "innere Emigration" ["emigration into the interior"] not very different from that of the more respectable writers in Hitler's Reich. The "Katzenmühle" to which everybody retreats at the end of *Abu Telfan* is an obviously facile Utopia. More important are the later figures who remain in society while detaching themselves from it mentally. Even Schaumann is a respected, if odd, figure of the "Stammlokal" life of the town; the philistines merely fail to notice that he is laughing at them all the time when he invites them to his wedding or when he tells his story to Eduard with the express intention of letting the barmaid overhear it, so that the news can be spread in the way the philistines appreciate—by rumour. That Raabe was aware of the basic sterility of this attitude is implied, as we have seen, in his insistence on the archaic nature of his heroes. To that extent he is completely honest in his presentation of the conflict between individual and society.

In conclusion we may ask to what extent Raabe is a "modern" writer. His basic theme is as appropriate today as it was then: individuality and mass society are the antinomies with which all modern literature has to wrestle. (pp. 255-65)

> *James H. Reid, "Wilhelm Raabe," in* German Men of Letters: Twelve Literary Essays, Vol. V, *edited by Alex Natan, Oswald Wolff, 1969, pp. 251-71.*

J. P. Stern   (essay date 1971)

[*Stern is a Czechoslovakian educator and critic. In the following excerpt, he compares* Die Chronik der Sperlingsgasse *to Raabe's later novels in terms of their approach to realism, narrative technique, and relationship to nationalist ideologies of the time.*]

Wilhelm Raabe's literary career is a prolonged and somewhat unhappy tussle with the public and critics of Wilhelminian Germany. His first novel, *Die Chronik der Sperlingsgasse,* 1857, achieved a popular success he never quite equalled in the half-century of novel-writing which followed it; and the masterpieces of his last decade were only written when he at last reconciled himself to the insecure position of a literary outsider. Yet throughout his long career the concerns of the German middle-class public remained intimately the concerns of his fiction. Raabe's novels, like those of Theodor Fontane, his senior by twelve years but his exact contemporary as a practising novelist, are created from a fruitful compromise between European realism and the German literary tradition. But whereas in Fontane the compromise is achieved on the European side, as a local variant of European realism, the work of Raabe's maturity lies well to the German side of the continuum of nineteenth-century literary conventions. Is Raabe's then another case of self-impalement through otherworldliness and provincialism? The suspicion is unjustified wherever he takes issue with it, by turning the conflict between the worldly world and German inwardness into a major theme of his fiction. Nor is there anything provincial about the fairly complex narrative techniques of those of his novels where a characteristic self-indulgence and prolixity of style is turned to parodistic and critical account. But the narrative manner is far from consistently critical, and to impose an overall pattern of conscious social criticism would be as misleading as in the case of Dickens. The fact is that neither early popular success nor later academic (and popular) neglect appears to have helped Raabe to cultivate a consistent understanding of his finest literary gifts. His lasting achievement springs neither from conformity nor open conflict with the society of his day and its professed ideals; nor could he create in such radical and occasionally indignant isolation as did Adalbert Stifter. His achievement is to be found where he writes as his society's sympathetic domestic chronicler and critic. This is Raabe's characteristic way of fulfilling one of the conditions, perhaps the most paradoxical, of nineteenth-century realistic prose, whose universal and permanent appeal springs from its creators' utmost immersion in the palpable circumstances of a very specific and particular time and place. The specificity of vision: the immersion in the domestic particular: the rendering of the familiar detail—these are the objects of the realist's Eros, and one of the main sources of his relevance beyond his time and place.

The narrator of **The Chronicle of Sparrow Lane** is that paragon of the cultural aspirations of the German middle class, 'ein Privatgelehrter', taking time off from his labours on an obscure *magnum opus* of great erudition and Schopenhauerian dimensions, to be entitled *De vanitate hominum*. In the garrulously anecdotal and associative style of old age (and, incidentally, of *The Pickwick Papers*), Dr Johannes Wacholder recounts episodes from his life and the lives of a few of his friends and neighbours, all living cheek by jowl in an inconspicuous narrow side-street of old lodging houses and garrets; the locale is one of the poorer districts of Berlin. The artless way in which these reminiscences fill the pages of Dr Wacholder's chronicle is deceptive, for what at first looks like an ill-assorted huddle of tales turns out to be a carefully wrought sequence of contrasting moods. Lyrical evocations of childhood and early sorrow; pictures of the Hessian countryside and of Berlin in all seasons; the hurly-burly of liberal journalism under the Prussian censorship; the plight of proletarian emigrants on their way to America; old age and its moods of happy and melancholy recollection—all this would hardly make one suspect that the author of this *tour de force* was twenty-four years old, a hapless bookseller's assistant lately turned student, who had never written a line of fiction.

The mastery Raabe achieved in the **Chronicle** seems all but lost in the writings that followed it. **Der Hungerpastor** (1864), which became almost as popular as the **Chronicle** though for worse reasons, takes up the structure of the traditional *Bildungsroman* and sentimentalises it into a self-consciously 'German' scheme of values. As to the Novellen and long historical novels of Raabe's middle period, there seems little point in attempting to rescue them from the limbo of literary history. Even **Abu Telfan** (1868), by which Raabe himself set great store, is disfigured by long-windedness and the author's uncertainty—reflected in its lopsided structure—as to what kind of novel he is writing and how seriously he wants us to take the social criticism it contains. Some of the most chauvinistic purple patches of these novels have been singled out for praise by the ide-

Raabe in 1901.

ologists of the 1930s, among them the astonishing Alfred Rosenberg, and academic trimmers like Hermann Pongs. From this kind of advocacy, Raabe's reputation in Germany has not fully recovered to the present day.

It is more rewarding to concentrate on the masterpieces of Raabe's last decade, in which some of the contrasting moods and ideas of the early **Chronicle** reappear. . . . And this task is made all the easier through the work of Barker Fairley, in whom Raabe has found an undogmatic and happily perceptive critic. Fairley particularly excels at retracing the complex yet unemphatic narrative structures of Raabe's best novels. What these structures embody is an outlook which is consistent and yet has nothing of a raw *Weltanschauung* about it: 'It is [Raabe's] sense of life that makes his novels so cherishable, not his ideas about it [*Wilhelm Raabe: An Introduction to his Novels*]. And, having quoted Raabe's praise of 'Treuherzigkeit'— 'Und ist nicht Treuherzigkeit das erste und letzte Zeichen eines wahren Kunstwerks?'—that truthfulness and simplicity of the heart which, in German, is inseparable from a certain cosiness and, in Raabe's German, a certain good-humoured philistinism—Fairley concludes:

> His outlook on life . . . was that of the plain
> man or of common humanity or whatever we

like to call it when an author does not claim to have anything of his own that we could not reach without him, or so he would say. . . . What [Raabe] succeeded in doing was to carry his simple outlook, his 'Treuherzigkeit', to the summit of life, of creative life, and vindicate it there, without abating a jot of it or finessing with it in any slightest degree.

Author and critic, we can see, are bound by a special bond of sympathy.

An old man, articulate to the point of loquacity yet self-effacing at the same time, ponders on the events of his past life, and on the fate of his childhood companions—such was the framework of the early *Chronicle of Sparrow Lane.* The narrators of Raabe's last novels are hardly more than middle-aged, and yet with them too we feel that the emotionally rich days of their lives are over, and that what is left is the routine existence of a settled job and family life. Emphasising their own withdrawal, they often unwittingly betray some good reason for not wishing to stress the part, considerable or otherwise, which they played in the events they are unfolding. Now, by the second half of the nineteenth century, this 'framework narration' has become a fashionable device of German prose, used as a means of securing greater credence or fictional authenticity for inherently improbable events. If proof is needed that for Raabe the framework technique is a good deal more than that, it is to be found in the three great novels of his last phase—*Alte Nester* (1879) *Stopfkuchen* (1890) and *Akten des Vogelsangs* (1895). Here the quiet of a scholar's study, or the cabin of a ship on its voyage to the Cape of Good Hope, provide a natural contrast to the turbulent world in which the recollected stories were enacted (and incidentally the book-lined garret offers an excuse for all those overt or playfully hidden quotations—bookish and a little sententious but never falsely 'literary'—with which Raabe's novels abound). Moreover, Raabe allows the framework to merge with the picture. By making the narrator in his partial withdrawal an integral part of each plot and story, he turns the formal device into a major part of the theme. The contrast between the brown study and 'the world' (or *'Sæculum',* to use a favourite expression of Raabe's) comes to be seen as one example of a contrast and conflict which has many different forms. The security of childhood, counterpointing the turmoil of adult life; village life, or the old house on the edge of the forest, or again the modest little castle above the village, contrasted with the uncertain life of the city; family, friendship and love, contrasted with the ups and downs of professional life; the narrow life of the German provinces, made narrower still in the grand perspective of voyagers returning from Africa or America: these are some of the variations on the theme, which in Raabe's novels becomes a major German theme. Of course, there is nothing original in his choosing such contrasts for his novels; the numerous though questionable company he appears in seems to place him in the blighted region of sentimental patriotic clichés on the borderline of the nationalist ideology.

Is Raabe then a 'Heimatsdichter', a 'Poet of the Homeland' after all? No term in German literary criticism has suffered a worse fate at the hands of the nationalist myth-

mongers and literary chauvinists. Raabe himself, Stifter and the 'Nordic' Theodor Storm, Gustav Freytag and Mörike, the 'dæmonic' Annette von Droste-Hülshoff and even the sober-minded Fontane—they have all been subjected to the 'chthonic' or 'völkisch' treatment. Even Heine was included, by the simple device of calling the author of his most popular poems 'Anon'. They all emerge from this treatment as spokesmen for the 'Germanic'—later 'Aryan'—values of authenticity and honesty, depth of feeling and inwardness and starry-eyed innocence, determinedly facing French worldliness and (later) decadence, English commercialism, Semitic craftiness etc. These rhapsodies of the critics of yesteryear are not, alas, entirely unjustified. In Freytag's *Soll und Haben* (1855), for instance, the German business probity of a Silesian firm of merchant bankers is contrasted with Jewish sharp practice on the one hand and Polish lawlessness and 'Unkultur' on the other; and the difference between the (German) rate of interest up to 7 per cent and the (Jewish) rate of 10 per cent and over is raised to a metaphysical principle. Later German developments make it difficult to read this kind of fiction, to which Richard Wagner too contributed (*Ein Ende in Paris,* 1841), with the necessary scholarly detachment; and the effort to do so fails to be repaid by any literary interest. In *Der Hungerpastor,* it must be confessed, Raabe too exploits these familiar prejudices.

The scheme on which 'Heimatsdichtung' (in this chauvinistic sense) relies is simple enough. It has at all events this much in common with twentieth-century fascist literature, that it is essentially undialectical. It supports a black-and-white evaluation of the conflict and contrast between 'the world' (which is always wicked) and 'the German soul' (which is always pure, often a victim of 'the world's' sinister machinations). The 'conflict' has a foregone conclusion and the author's value judgements are always predictable—that is, clichés—simply because they follow a premeditated (or prefabricated) ideology, which the fiction illustrates and on occasions helps to propagate. 'What shall it profit a man if he shall gain the whole world, and lose his own fatherland'—this, roughly, is the theme; like the bulk of the nationalist ideology, it is derived from secularised and misappropriated Christian ideas. And if we ask why, in the heyday of European realism and after, this ideology hasn't produced a single work of lasting *literary* value (leaving aside the complex question of Wagner's libretti), the answer lies in its undialectical, predictable narratives, in its presumption that nothing of any value is to be discerned on the other side. Where realism refuses to commit itself to anything narrower than a perceptive concern for and an intelligent interest in the contingencies of social life, offering as its questionable 'social message' not advocacy but (if anything) disillusionment with advocacy, the literature of nationalism is unrealistic precisely because it advocates a scheme of values which is said to transcend all realistic considerations. The association of literary realism with a broadly democratic outlook, we can see, is not accidental.

The framework technique fashionable in German fiction has several uses. One of them is to accentuate the nationalistic bias by creating a perspective in which the movement of individual lives, and of the society they compose, is recorded from a point at rest. No more is needed than to make the point at rest safe and cosy, the movement precipitate and dangerous—and a whole set of contrasting loyalties, displaying always the same black-and-white pattern of values, falls into place.

The novels of Raabe's maturity too use the technique and exploit the perspective, but they do so critically. It is their distinction that, while they too are founded in this commonplace contrast, there is nothing black-and-white about the way they present it. Here nothing is prefabricated. The value-judgements his later novels contain are unsentimental, subtle, and implicit: the way judgements are made and apportioned is integral to the development of each narrative. Provincial back-water, countryside or scholar's study are not necessarily a haven of authenticity, the great world is not necessarily Sodom and Gomorrah; the cosiness *can* be stifling, the world a liberation. (pp. 139-45)

> *J. P. Stern, "Wilhelm Raabe: Home and Abroad," in his* Idylls & Realities: Studies in Nineteenth-Century German Literature, *Frederick Ungar Publishing Co., 1971, pp. 139-62.*

Horst S. Daemmrich   (essay date 1981)

[*Daemmrich is a German-born American educator and critic. In the following excerpt, he investigates the manner in which plot, characterization, and narrative technique contribute to the originality of Raabe's representations of the historical past in* Das Oldfeld *and* Hastenbeck.]

Decades of Raabe criticism have produced opinions ranging from the assumption that Raabe's historical novels and tales vividly portray the past to the belief that they capture recurrent, timeless situations of persons exposed to violent changes in their lives. Literary historians tend to observe that these narratives, like those of other writers of the nineteenth century, are rooted in the past. Even those scholars who would not rank Raabe with such popular writers as Felix Dahn, Gustav Freytag, Joseph Victor Scheffel, Ernst Eckstein, Georg Ebers, Adolf Hausrath or Wilhelm Heinrich Riehl convey perhaps unintentionally the impression that, aside from individual artistic merits, his historical novels exhibit certain uniform features: the skillful use of historical detail, a colorful description of setting, manners, and ideas, and their ability to portray the development of communities. We are told that German novelists, as Sir Walter Scott before them, tried to show that bygone ages were filled by living men, not documents, figures, and dates.

A reexamination of Raabe's narratives supports some specific observations made by critics. However, a thorough comparative textual analysis of individual scenes, characterization of figures, and narrative technique shows that the general assessment is inaccurate and that Raabe, in contrast to other novelists of his time, succeeded in questioning a fundamental trend in nineteenth-century historical thinking. He countered certainty with the spirit of uncertainty. In fact, he cast doubt on man's ability to survey history objectively, to discover the course of its development, or to comprehend its meaning fully. (p. 98)

Raabe already evokes a feeling of uncertainty in the historical narratives written between 1860 and 1870. Still, while such action-filled stories as *Die schwarze Galeere* (1860), *Das letzte Recht* (1862), *Else von der Tanne* (1865), and *Sankt Thomas* (1866) indicate doubt about man's ability to comprehend historical processes, they tend toward a dramatic presentation of events and the psychological analysis of characters. They show a definite development in Raabe's thinking and shed light on the philosophical and formal issues Raabe had to resolve before succeeding in expressing his main interest. Initially the stories focus on single events and individuals. They externalize the inner struggle of persons caught in action and conflict. The first vignettes, in which the historical milieu serves as background, are followed by narratives which present human conflict in a clearly identifiable historical period but in a world without recognizable laws. The action shifts toward questions of individual responsibility for events and widens the discussion about human nature. As a result, the figures often appear equally preeminent and simultaneously insignificant. The individual experience appears shattered as persons grope with the wider problems of whether history shapes individuals, whether human nature can be explained within the social framework, whether the individual fits into a design of human destiny, or whether he is responsible for his own action. Raabe addresses these questions directly in *Der Marsch nach Hause, Das Odfeld,* and *Hastenbeck.* In these novels he also develops a narrative technique which enables him to express his central concern. In *Der Marsch nach Hause* (1870), Raabe explores a person's restricted perception of immediate events and tries to fathom the limits of historical knowledge. The novel is organized around the key motif sequence of the wanderer and shelter and traces the odyssey of the Swedish sergeant Sven Knudson Knäckabröd. He is the sole survivor of the Swedish commando patrol which reached the mountains behind Lake Constance in the year 1647, where it was attacked and wiped out by armed women of the villages. One of their leaders, Fortunata Madlener, took pity on the severely wounded Sven and transported him to her inn "The Dove" in Alberschwende. Years have passed. The people have become accustomed to Sven who once even considered proposing to the widow Fortunata. He has helped her raise her now married daughter Aloysia. During the summer he herded the cows and made cheese in the mountain hut. During the summer he herded the cows and made cheese in the mountain hut. During the winter he attended to all the necessary chores in the inn. When he thinks of the past, he is confused and sometimes wonders where he really is. Yet this world, in which he has spent over twenty years, is his home.

When the story opens on August 7, 1674, Sven is celebrating with others the feast of St. Gebhard and sits at one of the tables placed under the trees in Bregenz on Lake Constance. As he drinks, the memories of the past return. He suddenly rises, walks to the lake, jumps into a boat, cuts the rope, and sails toward Lindau. There he meets the former Swedish corporal Rolf Rolfson Kok, who has become the town's harbormaster. When they hear that a Swedish army is preparing to invade Brandenburg, they decide to return to the Swedish flag. They join the Swedish troops and participate in a first skirmish at Rathenow, where General Derfflinger hits Sven across the nose and knocks him into a gully. On June 28, 1675, they are drawn into the battle of Fehrbellin, where the Brandenburgian troops led by the Great Elector rout the Swedish Army. Sven's friend is killed on a Sunday in September 1675. The old man slowly makes his way home. Worried about Fortunata's reaction to his long absence, he cautiously approaches the village. Once recognized in a neighboring town, he runs until he is almost exhausted. When he reaches the inn and sees Fortunata, terror strikes his heart anew and he flees to the mountain hut. As he collapses in exhaustion and once again dreams of the past events, a young farm boy runs down to the inn to announce his return. The laconic Fortunata, who has suffered the unusual emotion of a "powerful heartache," is willing to forgive and believe everything. But she cannot fathom the story he tells her. Indeed, she believes that he fantasizes about a performance of a historical play. In the end, as he reaches for her hand and tells her that homesickness had driven him from the mountain but now he has returned "in old friendship and thankfulness," she welcomes him back: "God greet you at home, you old Swede!"

Chaos, bewilderment, and incomprehension form a distinct pattern in the story. Sven's response is a curious blend of dream and reality, as he struggles to comprehend the events of his life. He dreams of being with his own people, delights when he joins Rolf, and weeps in despair when the Swedish troops are defeated. But instinct drives him back to his true home which he shares with those who have become his family. And there he awakens from a nightmare in which he clutches the blood-spattered Rolf to listen to the stories to be told by Aloysia about the children and all the daily incidents he missed. Eventually, his second participation in a great battle will merge into the first to become the material of his dreams.

The narrative technique which combines the observations and perspective of an omniscient narrator with Sven's immediate vision and recollections enables Raabe to show one individual's shattered experience of his age. Sven's perception of time seems to be fragmented. The world is in flux. Dream and reality intermingle. Initially he sees war as a conflict in which outstanding strategists such as Wrangel or Derfflinger try to outmaneuver the enemy. Once in battle however, he sees only total disorder, flight, destruction, human misery, and momentarily feels that a sausage in the "Dove" is more real than the events around him. From the narrator's point of view, he and his friend become "two drops in a flood . . . hurled toward the Rhine." As an individual participant, Sven loses all control over the events. He is forced to adjust to constantly shifting, unforeseen situations, having only one certainty: death. As his dream reveals, even death is more a feeling than a conscious recognition for Sven. Faced with incomprehension of both history and the immediate events and the necessity of adjusting to every aspect of the ever-changing situation, his only free choice is to commit his life to his friend. As a consequence, Sven appears as a truly

modern figure flung into the world and propelled by forces over which he has no control.

Raabe resolves the issue of order and disorder in history in *Das Odfeld* (1888) by presenting a sequence of events which apparently work at cross purposes. These take place within a twenty-four hour period on November 5, 1761. A battle ensues on Odin's field in Lower Saxony between a Prussian army made up of German, Scottish, and British soldiers under the leadership of Ferdinand von Braunschweig and the Allied troops of French, Austrians, and Germans. Yet, sections of the novel reach back to the legendary beginnings of man, as the central figure Noah Buchius envisions himself successively as a Roman, a Biblical figure, and as the first wanderer looking for shelter in a cave after being expelled from his home. The work also points to the future in projecting a new basis for human action. The circular pattern of the old man's departure from his little room, his journey across the battlefield, his refuge in the cave, and his return provide the overall structure for the novel. As the reader perceives how Noah unrelentingly seeks to comprehend every observation by relating it to his vast knowledge of history, he is persuaded to adopt his viewpoint. He attributes timelessness to Noah's wanderings across the battlefield. But when the reader sees carefully planned action suddenly exposed as incongruous and even wonders with the participants whether manifestations of nature, such as the behavior of the ravens, have meaning, he begins to comprehend the central issue raised: he must participate in the constant process of observing and judging, which is nothing less than the reflection of the mind upon itself. When both levels of the story blend into one, the reader suddenly realizes that he is not asked to observe an event but rather a participant's judgment regarding the event. After reaching the limit of man's capacity to understand history, the story thrusts the human mind against the boundary where the comprehension of reality appears in doubt.

This purpose is already apparent in Noah's foreboding in watching the battle of the ravens on the evening before the armies meet. The birds appear as organized flocks which follow leaders into a battle. All order disappears as the combat progresses. When the raging birds slash at each other, their leaders are "pushed aside." The desire to maim, kill, and survive dominates the scene until the birds separate. Corpses, the dying, and the crippled litter the plain. Neither flock is truly victorious. As Buchius contemplates the scene's meaning, he relates it to man's history. The following day he links his observations of the battle to past historical battles in a continuous process of statement and restatement. By giving the French name, *Chalons sur Marne,* as well as the German, *Katalaunische Felder,* for the same battle, Noah interjects national concerns into the timeless flow of history. He remembers the Roman Aetius and thinks of Charlemagne, Theoderic, and Widukind. He also fuses these historical incidents into a recurrent mythic pattern of primeval conflict in which the gods wage battle. As in the *Edda,* Odin wears many masks. He is supreme god and leader of the wild hunt just as the raven is simultaneously messenger and participant in the struggle. The field of Odin, then, becomes a center at the crossroads of civilization where not only east and west or north and south clash but where also the spirit of the *Muspilli* struggles with the world view of the *Heliand.*

When Noah crosses the battlefield where individuals and groups follow their instincts instead of their leaders' strategies, when he looks at the rage of the meaningless ebb and flow of forces across the field, he again tries to bridge centuries in his mind to bring order into chaos. His imagination is stretched to the limits when he attempts to comprehend the disorder of the battle and the actuality of the incidents. The individual's odyssey, his desire for peace, his search for shelter appear as timeless as the mythical battles, the recurring conflicts, and the personal inhumanity. Order and destiny, disorder and loss of all direction seem to balance each other. In the end, neither ideals nor ideas have ultimate reality. Buchius begins to question his judgment and wonders whether he understands what he perceives. Moments recur in which a perception too vague to be put in words dawns in him. In one instant, the part of his mind believing in order controls his speech. Yet at other moments, Buchius gropes for answers in his dreams or suddenly wonders, "Why should we endlessly worry what the next hour shall bring? It always happens differently than we think in our life's anguish." He experiences the struggle for survival and the inhumanity of the combatants. He sees how the old, the sick, women, and children are maltreated in "the haste of the times." However, he is not a detached observer but an active participant drawn into the thick of danger. At one moment, when he tells the others that he knows a place of safety, he is almost overwhelmed by his importance. Yet, at the next instant his certainty is shattered by the events. Crossing the river with the young people he is trying to save, he calls to Pluto and Neptune to spare them. While looking at a dead raven, he quotes from the Psalms. He is horrified when he and his friends open the knapsacks of fallen soldiers in the cave and suddenly see the loot mixed with blood and bread. To the very end, he wrestles with integrating these impressions.

The attitudes and behavior of the other figures show a far more limited perspective of reality. Yet as their conflicting thoughts rise above the clamor of individual scenes, the reader is again forced to reflect upon man's capacity for synthesizing experiences. The steward of the monastery, a crude egotistical man, reacts in mad rage against the war. Always ready to abuse those under him, he hits blindly at anyone in his incomprehension. The two servants, Heinrich and Wieschen, are unhappy with the steward's treatment and seek an avenue of escape. While Wieschen is undecided which way to turn, Heinrich wants to join the Prussian army. During the battle Heinrich is wounded and becomes resigned to the fact that servants will always suffer at the hand of others.

Thedel von Münchhausen, a former student of Buchius, returns to the monastery to bid farewell to his old teacher and Selinde Fegebanck. Always joyously acclaiming life, he does not reflect upon the past or try to comprehend the future but lives for the moment. To hear Thedel is to witness the hard pitch of the life force which joyously and recklessly asserts itself. Yet his thirst for adventure is tempered by a basic gentleness and kindness which gives his

quest for action a humaneness contrasting sharply with the steward's brutality and Selinde Fegebanck's search for liberation at all costs. Gay and unreflective, Selinde does not care whether a French officer or someone else carries her off on a horse. Consequently, she fails to raise her dream in which a charming French lieutenant fades into Thedel, and both burst forth in an apocalyptic vision, to a conscious level. When they are caught between the armies, she accuses Thedel of being the "fool" and "harlequin." Later she is annoyed by Noah's description of the past, his Latin quotes, his attempts to relate the present to the strife of forgotten ages and tells him to stop his incomprehensible "croaking."

Even the portrait of the sympathetically drawn Duke Ferdinand who pities the plight of his people and seeks to relieve their suffering is tinged by the helplessness with which he looks at the puzzle of history and the incongruity between his actions and their ultimate outcome. He tries to bring peace to his land but can do this only at the cost of a war which devastates everything. He orders the small group of civilians to be guided to safety. But as his order is passed on through the chain of command, it loses all significance until in the end a reluctant sergeant pushes the people aside and points to the general direction of their home. Their collective views in addition to the shouts of Scottish soldiers and the moaning of the dying point to the limitation of individual judgment.

Similarly, the past utterly fails to console Buchius when he finds Thedel killed during the afternoon. He embraces the boy, weeps bitterly, and falls into a brief sleep of exhaustion. Still, as if his mind had not been stretched to the limits, Buchius has to face the ultimate terror. Returning home, he looks dazed at the jumble of desks and benches in the deserted classroom. Reaching his door, he hesitates in utter astonishment. It is locked and amidst the carnage and destruction, his little room seems untouched and safe. But entering he is once again faced with devastation. The raven which he had rescued is mad with hunger and has destroyed everything Noah owned. He has shredded the "Book of Solace," broken a collection of historic pottery, dropped prehistoric bones and arrows from the shelf, and now screeches at Buchius. As he wonders how he can bury Thedel and the other dead, he is struck by a horror which seems to surpass anything he had experienced during that day. Looking at the wild beast, he sees the real gravedigger. In desperation he opens the window to let the bird fly into the night. Noah's certainty is completely shattered by these events.

Raabe's skillful use of distancing effects enables him to offset the intensity of incidents with reflective commentary. This technique sharpens the dialectic of certainty and uncertainty, judgment and doubt. As a result, individual emotions, no matter how sincere at the moment, suddenly receive a new interpretation. When Selinde wrings her hands over the dead Thedel, for example, she is as "inconsolate" as she was previously when the handsome, polite French lieutenant had died. Pangs of hunger seem momentarily more important than the loss of life. Buchius compared to a noble Roman prepared for action because of his daily "joyous occupation with Antiquity" staggers along, "deafened, confused, unable to comprehend." The reader hears that "he remains our hero" but is also told that Noah's adventure not only creates displeasure but may seem boring. The thunder of cannons, the wild shouts and howling first near and then far are interrupted with the question: "What would Professor Gottsched say and do?" The comment "Leipzig did not give an answer" suddenly casts doubt on the whole tradition of literary history. Is this really the age of literary debates concerning the superiority of the French classical tradition, the struggle between sensibility and formal unities for preeminence, the age of fables, idyls, and drinking songs?

Ultimately, the continuous questioning creates an atmosphere in which even the detached narrator is uncertain of the meaning of the events he reports. His perception of good and evil, hero and coward is limited and may be wrong. At a given moment, reality is open to various interpretations. Reflection upon the past itself is not sufficient. Man's recording of 4000 years of history does not guarantee understanding. The spirit of culture appears neither ascending nor declining. Even recurring phenomena raise new questions. The parallel movement in both the ravens' and the armies' battles from order to disorder contradicts the view of an organic development. The continuous confrontation of opposing perceptions of the present with the exploration of the past indicates that the individual must master these counterpositions through a continuous process of inquiry. Only then can he hope to obtain the freedom of mind which no longer needs history as a solace for man's misfortune and misunderstanding. The diverse points of view in the narrative which embrace the contrast between an ordered world and one governed by chance, moral imperatives and amoral processes, perfectly executed maneuvers and involuntary actions, the rational and the completely irrational, ultimately combine to present a view of the individual flung into the world and called upon to establish a set of tenets for life that will enable him to survive. Only after an individual has freely decided to respect life can he increase the freedom of others. His freedom begets freedom in the world. This challenge to establish a basis for self-realization which builds upon a profound reverence for life, rings an almost revolutionary note in **Das Odfeld,** a narrative which not only underscores the timelessness of human suffering but also questions the confidence that nineteenth-century historians had in their judgment of history. What persists is not man's capacity to endure but his ability to ask questions about the world.

The odyssey of the central figures in **Hastenbeck** (1899) is more extended in time and space than in the **Odfeld** and the capacity of the individual to survive the inhumanity of his age is more pronounced. The narrative resembles the **Odfeld** in its continuous questioning of man's judgment of events. It differs in its forceful affirmation of the sheer necessity for individuals to continue living no matter what the human condition may be.

The action is set in the Third Silesian War. After Frederick the Great has marched through Saxony to invade Austria, a strong coalition formed by Maria Theresa, which includes Austria, Russia, Sweden, Saxony, and France,

dispatches its forces to attack Prussia from all sides. After the battle of Hastenbeck, troops invade the Duchy of Brunswick and threaten Hanover. While in 1757 the world around them seems to disintegrate, Bienchen (Immeke), the adopted daughter of Pastor Holtnicker in Boffzen, and Hans Leopold Wille, a painter of fine porcelain, fall in love. Despite their youth and inexperience, they survive several trials including the threat of losing their lives and an exhausting journey in the midst of winter. They endure and find an asylum through the aid of others, notably the soldier Uttenberger who is on his deathbed, and old Mother Wackerhahn. An epilogue set years later concludes with the vista of a possible peaceful existence which is tempered however by the knowledge that man's anguish will never cease.

Within the narrated time, space is primarily devoted to the struggle of various individuals to reach the right decision. For this reason, single episodes, days, and evenings are covered in a broad scenic description. The narrator reports only briefly events of the immediate past that include Leopold's forced induction into the army and his subsequent desertion, Uttenberger's previous behavior in the war, Mother Wackerhahn's story of her life, and the decision of Duke Karl to pay a high sum in order to retain a neutral area in the Duchy of Blanckenburg when threatened by the French army's move into the area. The young couple's actual journey is succinctly narrated. The stations of Immeke's and Leopold's odyssey, such as dangers at home, betrothal, wedding meal, honeymoon of anguish, arrival in the asylum, and return home highlight the strength of those persons who overcome their selfish interest in order to help the young couple.

The characterization of the figures also focuses on their decisions, their need for guidance, and their struggle with accepting responsibility for their actions. The specific conception of two childlike, trusting and helpless figures whose dilemma calls forth the intervention of others enables Raabe to represent human existence between the counterpositions of order and disorder, peace and war, trust and doubt. Essentially the happy ending of the couple's romance is due to the action of others. Thus when Leopold is in imminent danger of being arrested as a deserter, Uttenberger saves him by concealing him in his room. During the journey, the sensitive Leopold who delights in painting lovely scenes on fine china, helplessly sobs, whimpers, and weeps. Were it not for Mother Wackerhahn's aid, he and Immeke would never reach Blanckenberg to ask Duke Karl for protection. Similarly when the strong-willed Mother Holtnicker demands that Immeke should marry Pastor Störenfreden, he rejects the plan because he sees that the girl loves Leopold. Eventually the good pastor overcomes all scruples and marries the pair during their journey. While all these persons try to shape the fleeting moments of their experience, they look to the past for answers. The ensuing dynamic process of inquiry moves from the questions of whether a person submits to undiscernible forces or is guided by a plan in the universe to the consideration of the possibility that man can act freely by attending to the needs of others. By being concerned with the lives of others, the individual overcomes his limitations. He creates a vision of society in his own thought and action. In fact, the narrative projects a growing awareness that each individual defines his own existence through conscious decisions.

Pastor Holtnicker, who reads sermons in Cober's *Der aufrichtige Cabinet-Prediger* (1711) in the evening, is reassured by the strong faith expressed in the vision of God's marvellous chariot moving across the world and taking everyone to his destination. He almost hears and sees the chariot, a symbol of grace which surpasses human understanding. It is this visionary chariot which brought Immeke, a child abandoned in war, to his doorstep, so that he could raise her. The same chariot unloaded Balthazar Uttenberger, an old, tired, and wounded enemy soldier, who tries to recuperate in the pastor's house while reading a copy of Salomon Gessner's writings which is marked by a bullet hole and dried blood on its cover. The old soldier shakes his head and wonders whether the peaceful life portrayed in *Daphnis und Chloe* (1757) by his countryman is at all possible. Though amazed, he begins to believe in the literary revelation of a totally different existence. Eventually a work of art holding forth hope and comfort transforms a soldier who has killed others and has smashed his rifle over the heads of many who pleaded for help. Uttenberger comes to believe that nobility of spirit can exist and acts in accordance with his new ethos. He decides to help Immeke by hiding Leopold. He conveys to the young man his utter astonishment at the fact that after having participated in the slaughter of men, he is permitted to live among the dear, kind people in the parish. He is agitated in deep concern—"Gessner sings, Cober talks, but what shall become of you two?"—and only finds peace when another refugee of the war, Mother Wackerhahn, intervenes on their behalf.

Once a beautiful girl, then widowed by raging poachers, later still a suttlerwoman who traveled with different armies, Wackerhahn has returned to Boffzen where she lives in an old watchtower. Cynical and battlewise, she listens as in a dream to the pastor's reading and to Uttenberger's account of Gessner. She shakes her head, wishes to believe, but is also the first one to take immediate, strong action based on her own judgment. She consciously participates in a miracle greater than the ones the pastor reads about by becoming together with the "old child" Uttenberger a nursemaid to the lovers. Literally taking the young people by the hand and guiding them to safety, the "bloody widow" assumes the role of Immeke's second mother. Against all odds she manages to have the two marry and reach asylum. Only then does she reflect wistfully that probably "Cober was not too far off with his miracle chariot."

When she returns the next summer, she finds the old soldier dead. The first to discover him, she can look at the old man without being disturbed. Was he right? Does art hold forth hope and comfort? She nods. Still, she knows that idyls cannot be found in a pastoral seclusion. They just root in a powerful assertion of the will to act freely for others. The old woman stays in the village and becomes a beloved member of the pastor's family. But even after children are born to Immeke and Leopold she insists on living out her days in the watchtower. She indicates to Immeke that she waded too much in blood to be so close to the "grandchildren." She permits, however, the tower's windows to be widened. A sturdy ladder leads to her room, where she keeps Gessner's book. Although she still cannot read, she has found through her behavior the vision of a peaceful society portrayed by a literary work written during her lifetime but seemingly centuries removed from her.

The focus on Gessner's idyl not only complements the action by creating a ray of hope in a troubled world but also serves as a contrast to situations in which "the earth is red with blood, the heavens red from fire." There is little comfort in literature when the troops leave the countryside. By sustaining such contrasts instead of resolving them, the narrative testifies to the unity of experience without which true growth of self-insight seems impossible.

Similarly, the motif sequence blossom-blood does not function as a simple contrast. It provides the framework for a portrait of the human condition between affirmation and destruction of life. The blossoms reveal the formative powers of nature which sustain life. In the summer they spring forth in the bloody battlefield.

They recur and enable Immeke, the little bee, to buzz among them. They dot the landscape and reach toward light. Leopold captures their appearance on his china. Gessner found in their existence a testimony to a timeless recurrence which enabled him to compose serenely a work of art that praised love in the midst of suffering. As the blossoms blend into artistic creations, they symbolize the creative energy of mankind. The destructive urge in the world caught in recurrent images of blood seems equally prevalent. Pastor Holtnicker fears waking up on a bloody pillow. The army paints in the colors "blue-red, rose-red, bloody-red." During the winter, snow falls in large, clean, white flakes and covers what stinks "to heaven: Blood, burned out areas, forgotten corpses and cadavers . . . ". Starved soldiers in rags drive the cattle together to be butchered. Mother Wackerhahn carries a bullet with teeth marks around, which continually reminds her of a young soldier who died in her lap screaming on the bloody straw for his mother. On the battlefield in "the blood-dripping middle of the eighteenth century" Uttenberger picks up a pastoral song which, though it could not prevent terror, did help some to reflect upon a long cherished dream of mankind. Therefore Uttenberger can refer to the "bloody summer of blossoms" when he sees love spring forth in destruction. The motif sequence expresses the totality of the human condition in the experience of personal potential and restriction, in the timeless and the temporal. Raabe welds together blossoms and blood to show his readers that they coexist, that the ideal and reality are simultaneously present, and that the confidence in the formative powers of the world prevails over the disillusioned mind. They know as well as the fictional characters that the struggle will continue even after the war has ended. They will once more experience fear, anguish, and the loss of direction caused by disruptive forces they cannot fully comprehend. They will look for guidance to God's miracle chariot and to the vision of a peaceful existence in art. Above all, they will remember Mother Wackerhahn and begin to realize that the conscious decision to act carries the responsibility to think of others. Ultimately the narrative's intricate pattern of contrast motifs, copious allusions to literature, and the alternation between direct discourse and reflections of the narrator form a grand design for man's attempt to persevere in his time. In the process of living and becoming, each individual is called upon to project himself outward and reach for another human being. In so doing, he takes the first step toward self-realization and gains the strength to endure. (pp. 101-12)

Raabe offers no simple answers. Instead of acting with certainty gained from the knowledge of the past, the figures in Raabe's narratives are acted upon and their response betrays a changed consciousness. But in these tales of conflict and war a call sounds at times perplexed and wavering, at others clear and firm: The individual must try to comprehend the forces that shape his age. Raabe never states that history is unknowable, never argues against the significance of historical insight for civilized society, never counters history with a one-sided timeless pattern of man's suffering. He questions the false security afforded by views of historical progress, evolutionary development, and the impact of great statesmen. The narratives even offer sufficient evidence for the argument that Raabe felt that the history of civilization was indifferent to values and that a knowledge thereof would not enable man to foretell the future. Yet, as the growth in self-consciousness seemed possible only through interaction with others in a society reflecting the struggles of its age, each person is forced to search for answers in a realm where they may not be forthcoming. Consequently, reflections on the failure and success of the arts and philosophy as civilizing forces in society coupled with thoughts on the horror of war and the individual's failure to understand history shape the fictional world in which physically and spiritually uprooted individuals seek to survive. Their very survival depends on an existential commitment to share their life with others. The act of freely shaping their destiny, however, would require them to reach the insight that eludes them. (p. 112)

> *Horst S. Daemmrich, "Raabe's View of Historical Processes," in* Wilhelm Raabe: Studien zu seinem Leben und Werk, *edited by Leo A. Lensing and Hans-Werner Peter, Braunschweig, 1981, pp. 99-114.*

William Hanson   (essay date 1985)

[In the following excerpt, Hanson offers an overview of Raabe's poetry and considers the relevance of the poems to his novels.]

Raabe's poetic output is relatively small and stems almost wholly from the early phase of his career, indeed from three short periods of activity in 1857, 1859, and 1861, coming during what he called his 'lyrical' period, which he felt he outgrew. . . . Yet although, with one or two important exceptions, he virtually ceased to write poetry once he had returned to Brunswick from Stuttgart in 1870, it is clear from the fiction which he wrote in his final phase that the specifically lyrical response continued to be important to him. . . . (pp. 858-59)

The sixty-nine poems published in the 'Braunschweiger Ausgabe', together with the fragments in the 'Nachträge' and occasional verses in the as yet unpublished *Notizbücher,* are worthy of attention on several counts. They reveal and underline aspects of the Raabe we know from the fiction, but occasionally also they show a surprising and unexpected side of the writer. While in his fiction there is a lack of subjectivity that frequently makes the biographical approach to it misleading and misguided, his poems offer a rare insight into his personality at a crucial period in his development. Moreover, the real tension in some of the poems indicates how precarious was the psychological balance that he was able to present in his best novels. The purpose of this article, however, is not to mount an exaggerated case for the quality of the poems. What I want to argue is rather that the poems are of value for our understanding of Raabe's development. Whilst recognizing that certain individual poems stand in a significant relation to specific prose works, my wider aim will be to outline the categories and themes of the poems, to offer some assessment of their poetic character and their relation to certain traditions (particularly those of late Romanticism), and finally to assess the extent to which he achieves an independent lyric voice.

Raabe's poems range from historical and political ballads in regular metrical forms to personal lyrics in free verse. Some are written for inclusion in specific prose works and clearly belong in that context, while others are quite independent responses, sometimes written as *Gelegenheitsgedichte.* An obvious example of the former type is **'Der Winter ist vergangen'**, a nature poem with a very traditional ring to it (underlined by the repeated 'Jubilate'— twelve times in the three strophes of the poem), where May is greeted and heralds a festival of youth, the *Wanderlied* style ideally fitting the context of the *Student von Wittenberg* in which the poem appears. The same can be said of **'Beruhigung'**, in that it reflects the quietism of *Der Hungerpastor* of which it is a part. Quite independently of the novel, however, it is an important poem which Raabe revised many times; it vividly contrasts former objectives with present realities and indicates the importance of domestic happiness and a spiritual 'Gelassenheit'. In general, the poems fall into four categories: historical, political ballads, and narrative poems; poems about poetry; nature poems; and finally a number of poems which can broadly be described as philosophical.

The poems in the first category show clearly Raabe's political liberalism, his historical sense, his concern (which is also apparent in the fiction) to reflect the great historical moments in specifically local small-town communities, and his patriotism. Probably the most widely known of these poems is **'Zum Schillerfest 1859'**, with its repeated 'Die Zeit ist schwer' taking up again the theme that had dominated his first novel, *Die Chronik der Sperlingsgasse* of 1856, whilst maintaining a degree of hope in the future: 'Schwer ist die Zeit, doch gut sind ihre Zeichen'. Unfortunately this is the kind of poem of high pathos that was used by conservative critics in the 1930s in support of their distorted conception of Raabe's patriotism (reinforced by the motto that Raabe used for *Hastenbeck,* 'Ich habe nur ein Vaterland, das heißt Deutschland!'); in fact the poem reflects a non-chauvinistic view representing the sincere hopes of the liberal in 1859 and is written in the Schillerian spirit of freedom. It is only with hindsight that the hope to be led ('Um *einen* Führer scharen sich die Stämme') becomes hard for the modern reader to take. Similarly, the patriotic call to action in a poem like '**Ans Werk**' has more in common with Goethe's *Faust* than with the 'Blut- und Bodendichtung' of National Socialism. These patriotic songs must be seen in the context of Raabe's political outlook as it was developing in the period when they were written—a time when Raabe joined the 'Nationalverein' (26 May 1860) and attended the Coburg Convention (September 1860). Some are less strident, taking on a balladesque quality in the narration—often vivid and dramatic—of a specific historical event, for example, '**Königseid!**', where a strong ethical point is maintained, and most successfully '**Des Königs Ritt**', a poem which impresses because of the authenticity of its London setting. More parochially the effects of war and political decisions on the small-town community are reflected in poems like '**Belagerte Stadt**' and '**Verlorene Stadt**' which, characteristically, are in themselves contrasting statements, and develop sharp internal contrasts as well. Very early on in his career—these two poems were both written in 1857—Raabe is able to balance convincingly a positive sense of human potential and love against a lament for the hollow victories of war and the frailty of things. In '**Belagerte Stadt**' the lovers exchange kisses amid the siege; there is a contrast between the disturbed world of war and the *Biedermeier* world of the lovers. As the city is saved the hero lies dying in the arms of his beloved. Despite the exaggeratedly heroic tone, the poem works well as an evocation of political upheaval set against a simple love story. '**Verlorene Stadt**' also works by contrast; in this case the brave are defeated and the victory of the Imperial forces is a hollow one. The first stanza has the power of a lament; the second a bitter irony.

Throughout his life Raabe remained concerned with his craft (and frequently reflected that concern in his novels), and though he never succumbed to the obsession with the *malheur d'être poète* of the Romantic generation, there are several poems of his that treat poetry and his view of the role of the poet. The poem '**Über den Marktplatz zu schweifen**', which was published in *Die Kinder von Finkenrode* in 1859, is an aphoristic definition of the 'Dichterberuf' and is a succinct statement of Raabe's priorities, his concern with the everyday and his need to balance positive and negative forces in life:

> Über den Marktplatz zu schweifen,
> Durch die Gassen zu streifen,
> Licht aus Schatten zu greifen,
> Das ist Dichterberuf!—

The poem '**Wunsch und Vorsatz**', written shortly after this and published (also in 1859) in *Halb Mähr, halb mehr,* shows Raabe's growing feeling of independence and his reluctance to turn to the great, the influential, and the intellectuals as a source for his writing. He is concerned with the simple, the common people:

> Aber wollen die Großen
> Nichts von mir hören,

> Will zu den Kleinen
> Schnell ich mich kehren.

Raabe's work is full of figures who have never gone beyond the limited bounds of their town or village and yet have come to know and understand the world.

Like Goethe, who is a dominant influence in many of these poems, Raabe frequently combines a response to nature with an expression of romantic love. His range of mood and emotion is quite impressively wide, from the playfulness and lightness of '**Osterhas**' to the powerful drama of '**Die Nacht, die Nacht ist still und mild**'. '**Osterhas**', a poem that reads like a *Volkslied,* is wholly without irony and describes a love game that might have been played by Ebert and Emmy Pfister. It is spring and this is the love of children; the poem ends succinctly and well:

> Und Dämmerung ward es,
> Eh wir nach Haus kamen.

'**Die Nacht**', however, creates a wholly different mood, revealing the night-time of the soldier at war and in love; it is a poem of real pain and gentleness;

> Die Stirne küßt der Morgenwind,
> Das Herz, das Herz zerbricht!

Probably the largest group of poems that Raabe published are what might be called 'Weltanschauungslyrik', though, with one possible exception, to be discussed later, he did not write genuinely philosophical poetry to compare with Schiller's. Many of the poems nevertheless reflect his developing view of the world and are personal responses to death, war, and the hardship and contradictions of life. One of the fragmentary verses in the *Notizbücher,* written in October 1861, touches the theme of many of these poems:

> In düsterer Zeit
> Die tönende Harfe zu schlagen.

For Raabe the Orphic vision of the poet clearly did not preclude a sense of social commitment in hard times. In at least one poem, '**In schönen Frühlingstagen**', there is a genuine tragic sense as high ideals and heroic life come to nothing:

> Wie war mein Herz so traurig!
> Wie war die Welt so schaurig!
> Die Harfe tu ich schlagen,
> Mein Leid davon zu sagen!

The theme of death—a dominant one in Raabe's fiction—recurs in these verses, frequently with a stylized, even baroque quality, reminiscent of Gryphius, as in, for example, '**Den Tod hab ich gesehen**', where the repetitions and the build-up to the question 'Wem mag es wohl gelingen, / Den grimmen Tod zu zwingen?' create a convincing sense of the ubiquity and inevitability of death. The poem that most impressively treats the theme, however, is '**Die Regennacht**', a sombre narrative poem in which a refrain opening and closing the poem is used to good effect, recording a night spent by a cold and sick man as the life cycle passes before him and he is watched over by an old woman who personifies disease and death:

> Ein armer Mann lag auf seinem Lager

Und horchte, wie der Regen niederrauschte;
Ein altes Weiblein, giftig, gelb und hager,
Krankheit genannt, hielt Wacht,
Und es war Nacht,
War lange, schaurig kalte Regennacht.

There is, however, no 'Todessehnsucht' nor Schopen-hauerian 'Abgrundsstimmung' in these verses. The spirit of resilience and hope which ultimately informs much of Raabe's best fiction is present in the poetry also, but—with one or two exceptions to be discussed later—without the ironic distance, the humorous stance that this same spirit was able to bring to the mature novels. Shortly after writing **'Die Regennacht'** in October 1861 (when he was ill) he wrote **'Sonnenschein'**, by no means a total reversal of the mood in the earlier poem, but a reminder that there is a possibility of personal happiness, however fleeting. Raabe's world view was always based on a sense of contrast and apparent contradiction: 'Denk: Schatten im Sonnenschein!'

These, then, are some of the characteristic themes of Raabe's poems. What can be said of their character and qualities? There are clearly certain poets and particular traditions towards which he is drawn and which are also influential in his writing as a whole; and his work as a poet is clearly more derivative than the highly individual prose he came to write in his later years. Inevitably several poems in the published collection invite comparison—albeit an ultimately unfavourable one—with Goethe or with Schiller, the writers for whom he probably had the deepest respect throughout his creative life. One genuinely philosophical poem, **'Wen ein Gott'**, is concerned with the Goethean mentality. Like Schiller's 'Der Genius', it is written as a contrast between the naive and 'sentimental' genius, the one a child led by God to the heights and a sovereign understanding of life, the other for whom

> Die Schrecken des Todes
> Sind um ihn und in ihm;
> Gestein und Gestrüppe
> Versperrt ihm den Weg.

As lines 12-13 and also the context of *Der Dräumling,* in which this poem first appeared, make clear, Raabe had the figure of Dante specifically in mind here, as a contrast to Goethe; but there is clearly a link intended to Schiller too. The high pathos of some of the political and historical poems, particularly **'Lieder der Völker'**, is reminiscent of Schiller's idealistic and patriotic verses. Some individual nature poems echo Goethean models without being deliberately allusive: for example **'Abschied'** seems to be related to 'Willkommen und Abschied', though Raabe shows little of the ability to render a whole range of emotional responses that characterizes Goethe's ballad. In the nature poem **'Vorüber'**, where with the passing of the storm the sun shines into the very heart of the poet to create a sense of the union of man with nature, there is something of that total absorption that is characteristic of Goethe's best nature lyrics. The influence of Goethe is clear in the language and style of Raabe's poem:

> Wie leuchtet die Sonne
> Mit glänzendem Schein
> Über Berg, über Tal

Ins Herz mir hinein!

Or again **'Stille der Natur'** is close to Goethe's 'Dämmerung senkte sich von oben' in its suggestion of the total harmony between Man and nature, and in its evocation of a sense of change and growth; but unlike Goethe, Raabe is unable as a lyric poet to get beyond expressing this sense in a traditional simile. Where Goethe could produce the consummate and highly individual

> Durch bewegter Schatten Spiele
> Zittert Lunas Zauberschein
> Und durch's Auge schleicht die Kühle
> Sänftigend ins Herz hinein

Raabe has:

> Wie aus dem Nebelkleide
> Der Mond sich glänzend ringt,
> So aus dem Erdenleide
> Aufwärts das Herz sich schwingt.

If Goethe is the single poet who most seems to influence Raabe's lyrics, the tradition that his verse echoes time and again is the Romantic one of Brentano, Eichendorff, and Heine. He writes lullabies and balladesque poems with refrains, and employs some of the stock motifs of popular Romantic tradition, particularly that of the 'verlassenes Mägdlein'. Typically, in **'An der Landstraß im Graben'**, which Susanna sings in *Lorenz Scheibenhart,* the girl is finally left alone when her soldier lover is called back to war:

> Es rief die Trompete, es sank das Gezelt,
> O du weite, weite, weite Welt!
> O du armes verlassenes Kind!

'Mädchen am Ofen' echoes both Brentano's 'Spinnerin Lied' and Goethe's 'Gretchen am Spinnrad' and has some effective linguistic and rhythmic formulations linking the activity of spinning, the girls' isolation, and the poet's dreams:

> Spule surrt—
> Rädchen schnurrt—
> Dämmrungsgedanken!
> Mädchentraum
> Dichtertraum
> Wachsen und ranken.

There is, on the other hand, none of Brentano's sustained musicality here and none of Goethe's intense realism. Raabe can, however, in a lullaby (**'Trauriges Wiegenlied'**), create a real sense of pain and disillusion as the poet watches the child asleep and dreaming:

> Spiel fort deinen Traum,
> Blinzäugelein!
> Schaukelnd und gaukelnd
> Sitz ich und wein.

There is some music in this, as there is in **'Glockenklang'**, which has been called both a 'Gelegenheitsgedicht' and a 'Heimatgedicht' (it was written for his fiancée Bertha Leiste on hearing the bells of the Marienkirche in Wolfenbüttel). The rhythmic variety of the three parts of this poem amply demonstrates that, despite his own protestations to the contrary, Raabe did possess a musical sense: this is shown particularly in the way he reproduces the rhythm of one church bell in the first section, which then mingles in the second with all the church bells in the town. Many of the linguistic and rhythmic formulations are reminiscent of Eichendorff in 'Die zwei Gesellen', though without the skill and subtlety in modulating the central image ('die klingende, singende Welle') that Eichendorff shows in that poem. . . . Eichendorff again is very much the model for 'In wonniger Jugend fuhr ich hinaus', though this poem ends with an image that is Raabe's own:

> Viel besser, im Sturme zugrunde zu gehn,
> Als langsam verkommen, versinken im Sand!

Many of the heroes of Raabe's fiction—most memorably perhaps Knäckabröd in *Der Marsch nach Hause*—are near to sinking in sand or bog. In *Die Chronik der Sperlingsgasse* the narrator Wachholder, likening the chronicle he is writing to a little stream, is aware of the dangers of the sand: '[Das Wässerchen] . . . wird seine eigne Sprache reden in wagehalsigen Sprüngen über Felsen, im listigen Suchen und Finden der Auswege—Gott bewahre es nur vor dem Verlaufen im Sande!' In the poem the high hopes of the traveller will be dashed by the storm at sea, but the poet will dance and not sink in the sand.

Above all, perhaps, it is late Romanticism that is reflected in Raabe's verse; and it is to Heine, the contemporary of his youth, that he is most closely drawn. As he once put it, 'Heine ist stets mein Liebling gewesen'. The poem **'Das ist die Jungfrau im Wald'** shows Raabe clearly influenced by Romantic fantasy, but if it is compared with Heine's superlative 'Dämmernd liegt der Sommerabend', it appears unsubtle and merely derivative; certainly it has none of Heine's delicate eroticism or his sharp irony. Another poem, **'Ich weiß im Wald ein kleines Haus'**, while still using traditional Romantic motifs, strikes a more characteristic note in setting the attractions of a quiet idyll against the independence of the 'Jäger'. The idyll in Raabe's world is both attractive *and* a danger to authentic living. The poem **'Es ist ein eigen Ding'** is a beautiful word-painting, evoking images reminiscent of Spitzweg and giving a clear indication of the attractions of home and hearth: **'Nun ist die Welt dein Haus . . . '**. It is also a very successful sound-poem, every sound being recorded and sensed:

> Und jeder leise Klang
> Ein altes Bild ruft wach.

Raabe, then, writing virtually all his verse in the late 1850s and 1860s, uses many of the conventions of late Romanticism. Indeed, taken as a whole, the degree of derivativeness in many of these poems marks them basically as the work of an epigone. In a small number, however, we hear an authentic independent voice. It is these poems above all that lead one to regret that Raabe did not continue to publish verse in his mature period in Brunswick during the last forty years of his life. His best poems are perhaps most succinctly defined in his own term, as 'Dämmrungsgedanken', where a gentle melancholy is given an edge by a sense of purpose; his modest view of his 'Büchlein' of verse does not conceal a belief in the importance of the 'Dichtersinn' as a corrective force in a philistine world, seeing value where others see none, and maintaining values from the past. These are standards he maintains in his fiction, but the quiet sadness is particularly poignant here:

> Welk Blatt, grün Blatt und Blütenblatt
> Der Wind mir hergetrieben hat . . .

The same quiet melancholy pervades the fine nature poem 'Es hat geschneit die ganze Nacht', where Raabe seems very much in control of his art. As the snow falls, nature is covered in a shroud and the poet bemoans a lost love.

In at least three of the longer narrative poems Raabe shows a marked ability to create a dramatic atmosphere. In **'Türmers Töchterlein'**, another poem on the theme of the 'verlassenes Mägdlein', the impact derives from laconic statement—'Sie neigt sich, sie beugt sich, sie schauet herab'—repeated and modified as the poem progresses and as the girl lives through the execution of her loved one. Emotion is restrained, but intensely present nevertheless. The girl is shocked and numbed by her pain—'Ihr Auge ist starr, ist tränenleer'—and she too will die. It is all understated, but we know the pain of the girl is so great that it will take her to join her loved one in the grave. With a crucial tense change the poem ends, 'Sie fanden im Grabe sich wieder'. This poem is complex; the natural backcloth is contrastingly beautiful and serene, and there is also a contrast between the voices of the girl and of the narrator: the questions are hers, the cool depiction of the execution is his. In a much lighter, humorous vein, in **'Roderich von der Leine'** Raabe recaptures with some irony an actual experience in Linz in 1859: a rainy day is suddenly brightened by the sight of a girl at her window; it rains, but the gods have smiled. By far the most successful of the longer poems is **'Der Kreuzgang'**, a finely-balanced depiction of the religious struggle in the mind of a monk in a scene observed by a disturbed and involved narrator:

> Er schreitet fort, bis Nacht und Tag sich gatten
> Im Morgennebel, der den Kreuzgang füllet,
> Den finstern Wandrer meinem Blick verhüllet.

The poem succeeds in the way Raabe contrasts the wonderful summer night—'Kaum weiß die Blum, ob sie sich schließen soll . . . ', which at every moment seems to indicate a living God—with the distress and anger of the monk in the cloisters, who can no longer believe in God. A lively sense of place in the cloister itself is combined with a deep sense of dread in the monk. Just such a combination of place and mood occurs in the best fiction of Raabe's later phase. Written in 1859, the poem also reflects something of Raabe's own religious doubts at the time.

It is, however, in the shorter poems that Raabe's touch seems most sure, his lyric sense most clearly developing. The following poems at least, all successful poetic statements in their own right, are also of interest both for the indications they give of the development of Raabe's ideals in the 1860s and as pointers to the way the German lyric in general is developing in the mid-nineteenth century; they indicate a move away from Romantic conventions, an emergent realism, and a characteristically 'modern' sense of shifting values and existential contradictions. **'Des Menschen Hand'**, an example of Raabe's 'Weltanschauungslyrik' written in 1861, adds a further dimension to the developing picture of his view of the child and the childlike which is a dominant concern of his fiction. In the four regular strophes of the poem he expresses a typical double-edged view of life which brings together the two aspects—'Komik und Elend' in Thomas Mann's phrase—of his view: 'Und klagen müssen nun, die eben lachten.' Man is subject not only to fate, which treats him capriciously, but also to himself, for he behaves like a child and is destructive:

> Des Menschen Hand ist eine Kinderhand
> Sie greift nur zu, um achtlos zu zerströren.

That which is beautiful and good is destroyed and man must weep—but implicit is the message that the childlike heart, if not the childish manner, can be a positive force. It is this kind of sombre realism, this 'Dämmrungsgedanke', that is reflected time and again in these verses. He expresses a similar world view in lighter vein, however, in the classicizing humour of **'Gute Stunde'**, where human fate is seen in terms of man's having a golden hour of temporary freedom as the gods in Olympus take their meal. This is one of the surprisingly rare traces in the poetry of Raabe the humorist. At this stage he has not broken through to that distinctive form of his writing where the tragic sense is totally balanced by a distanced, controlled humour. Nevertheless there are indications enough in the poetry that this development *is* taking place. (pp. 859-67)

It would be foolhardy, of course, on the evidence of the small number of poems that Raabe wrote, to try to argue that he is a major late-nineteenth-century poet. There is none of the concreteness and symbolist concentration that Meyer, say, achieves in 'Der römische Brunnen'. Only in **'Das Reh'** is there the kind of steady objective focus that might have led to symbolism. Nor is Raabe capable of the sustained *Stimmungslyrik* of such poems as Storm's 'Die Stadt'. Nevertheless there are enough successful verses in the published collection for us to regret that Raabe did not continue to write poetry seriously after he left Stuttgart. He was developing an impressively laconic manner. In a handful of poems he begins to look forward in time, and in some the private man is in evidence. For the biographer of Raabe's inner life the poems are of considerable value. As Wilhelm Brandes puts it, they are 'kein Ab- und Irrweg, sondern ein natürlicher und darum notwendiger Durchgang in seiner Entwicklung' ['Wilhelm Raabes lyrische Zeit', *Eckart*, 1907-08]. A poem like **'Abschied von Stuttgart'** tells us more of Raabe's doubts and prospects as a writer than any amount of speculation based on the Jensen correspondence. (pp. 869-70)

> *William Hanson, "Raabe's Poems," in* The Modern Language Review, *Vol. 80, No. 4, October, 1985, pp. 858-70.*

Jeffrey L. Sammons (essay date 1987)

[*Sammons is an American educator and critic who has written extensively on nineteenth-century German literature. In the following excerpt from his* Wilhelm Raabe: The Fiction of the Alternative Community, *he discusses the characterization of Jews in* The Hunger Pastor *in order to evaluate the extent of Raabe's complicity with proto-Fascist ideologies of his time. Sammons then addresses what many critics have called Raabe's "preternaturally modern" narrative technique by analyzing his use of a multiple perspective narrative and unreliable narrator in several novels.*]

Readers of today, coming to Raabe for the first time and reading him from end to end, would not be likely to conclude that Jewish themes and characters were a major issue in his career. Such readers might be disturbed by one work, *The Hunger Pastor,* but since they would find nothing else in the oeuvre reiterating its troubling features, they might well regard it as an unfortunate aberration. But the reception history, entwined as it is with the catastrophic history of modern Germany, does not permit us to take this offhand approach. *The Hunger Pastor,* once the centerpiece of Raabe's fame, has turned into one of the main hindrances to a just appraisal of him. The problem is not a simple one, and dealing with it even summarily will require, unfortunately, a good deal of detail. That Raabe was not an anti-Semitic writer and that *The Hunger Pastor* is not an anti-Semitic novel in its intention have been so well established in literary scholarship for so long that it would seem redundant to argue the point any more. Nevertheless, legends of reception are often tenacious; for example, in Gordon Craig's widely acclaimed book *The Germans* it is said that Raabe, Gustav Freytag, and Felix Dahn "resorted in their most popular books to the technique of parallelism, placing in contrast the careers of their Christian protagonist, who was always portrayed as being honorable, idealistic and dedicated to the service of others, and his Jewish counterpart, who was self-centered, cowardly, materialistic, and unscrupulous," as though Raabe, or, for that matter, Freytag, had done nothing but write such novels their whole lives long. Therefore it is not superfluous to make the case again; but in reopening it, we will find that the matter is rather more complicated than it is normally made out to be. Neither the anti-Semitic view of Raabe nor its refutation in conventional presentations has exhausted the subject of Raabe and his reputation in regard to Jews and anti-Semites.

The case that Raabe cannot be regarded as an anti-Semitic writer was made long ago. It can only be sketched here; there has not yet been a thorough study on modern principles of Jewish characters and their situations and of Jewish references in Raabe's works, but the point is that positive as well as neutral Jewish figures appear in numerous places. The earliest example is in the second novel, *One Springtime,* in which a Jewish old-clothes dealer, Rosenstein, though portrayed with some stereotypical features, is nevertheless a positive figure amiably regarded by his fellow Gentiles, and his two kindly, well-bred daughters quite clearly belong to Raabe's ideal community of the good and the gentle. *Lilac Blossom,* written during the genesis of *The Hunger Pastor,* is the reminiscence of an elderly doctor who recalls with sorrow how, as a young student, he aroused the feelings of a girl he met in the Jewish Cemetery of Prague, but did not love her, and she dies, like her prefigurative ancestor, the dancer Mahalath, of a symbolically enlarged heart. This does not strike me as one of Raabe's most successful works; it suffers from the sentimentality that plagued his writing in its first phases, and it falls into the pattern commonly met with in nineteenth-century German fiction of regarding the Jew as exotic or "oriental," thus foreign and inaccessible. All the same, despite the stress on the filth and nastiness of the Jewish community and the stereotyping of the girl's pawnbroker father, the novella expresses sympathy and understanding for the plight of the Jews, as well as respect for Jewish dignity in the image of the grave of the great rabbi Judah Löw (which Raabe visited; his diary entry of May 18, 1859, shows a particular interest in the site). In fact, the symbol of the enlarged heart—which inspired the narrator to become an accomplished heart specialist—refers not only or even primarily to obstructed love, but to grief at the sufferings of the Jewish people, who, it has been argued, are portrayed as the suffering servants of the world. It is here as well as anywhere that one can see the two reasons why Raabe could not have been an anti-Semite even had he wanted to: his strong feelings about the integrity and just rights of a people, an extension of his own pronounced nationalism, and his profound gift of sympathy that vibrates through his entire oeuvre with human suffering, despair, and oppression.

Three other works must be mentioned in this connection. One is *Gedelöcke* (1866), a farcical and improbable story, which, like many of the most improbable fictions, is drawn directly from real life, a tale recounted in a book Raabe found in a flea market. The Danish free-thinker Gedelöcke, owing to his friendship with Jews and his interest in learning from them, has put himself into the reputation of having virtually converted to Judaism; while he has not actually done so, the very idea of it drives the community and his wife into hysterics of gossip, bigotry, and superstition. He creates a situation that makes it impossible to bury him either in Christian or in Jewish ground, and so he is buried and dug up and buried again and dug up and finally deposited in the common field. Here we have an expression of Raabe's secular and often aggressively anticlerical outlook; the religious Jews, who expel their cantor from the community for bringing this trouble by associating with Gedelöcke, are no better than the religious Christians, but, on the other hand, the Christians are no better than the Jews, and Gedelöcke's posthumous whipsawing of his fellow men with their own prejudices certainly has the effect of making anti-Semitism one more symptom of a mean and trivial spirit.

Of particular interest is the novella *Madame Salome* (1875), whose title figure is in some ways the most remarkable Jewish character I know of in nineteenth-century German fiction. Not only is she intelligent and energetic; in her competent readiness in a chaotic disaster and as a refuge for the daughter of the half-mad sculptor Querian she is clearly another member of the alternative community of the good, the generous, and the sympathetic. But, even more remarkably, she is the millionaire widow of a Jewish banker, the kind of person who would almost never appear in a positive light in the fiction of the time. That she can exchange urbane repartee about her Jewishness with her Gentile friend, the Judicial Councillor Scholten, merely expresses her and her author's sovereignty over common prejudice. Salome, Scholten, and the girl Eilike

Querian are bound together by the central, original symbol of the novella: the "ichor," the blood of the gods that flows in their veins and sets them apart from vulgar mankind. It has been suggested that, with this image, Raabe wished to join the Jewish and Greek spirits as "opposing forces to the more dangerous and stifling aspects of the German mythical atmosphere." The characterization of Salome not only exhibits Raabe's cross-grained opposition to cliché and convention; I rather suspect that she may have been conceived out of a bad conscience about *The Hunger Pastor.* The novella, incidentally, is full of reminiscences from Heine's *Harz Journey.* There is also the splendid historical novella *Höxter and Corvey* (1875), one of Raabe's several evocations of the bloody misery of the historical past. As is frequently the case in his historical fiction, the blood and misery are the consequence of Catholic-Protestant conflict, but here both factions turn on helpless and harmless Jews, and the protagonists risk life and limb in an attempt to shield an elderly Jewish woman and her granddaughter from murderous ruffians and howling mobs. To these cases may be added the painter Rudolf Haeseler, the spirit of shrewd wit and realism in *The Dräumling Swamp* (1872), whose mother, the daughter of a converted Jew, was "black-haired, corpulent, and aesthetic"; his Gentile father is the money-changer, i.e., banker. It is important to observe here that Haeseler, who has the reddish hair and beard of the anti-Semitic stereotype, is one of the alter egos of Raabe's own personality encountered in various disguises in his works. Parenthetically, it might be noted that Raabe never refers to the people of the Old Testament as Hebrews or Israelites, as an anti-Semite might have done, but always as Jews.

It is true that there are scattered, occasional, disrespectful passages. As an example one may take a quotation from *The People from the Forest,* since it has sometimes been cited by anti-Semitic admirers: "Many a black-haired, hook-nosed businessman kept his sharp Semitic eyes focused on the house in the town." Apart from the fact that, in this case, it is actually the Gentile servants who are systematically robbing the property, an examination of such passages would show that in almost every case they reflect the association of Jews with money and commerce, graspingness and greed, and in spirit they differ in no way from often harsher passages in Heine or Marx. Heine could easily have a written a sentence in the same novel in which party guests are referred to as "Christian bankers with Jewish veneer and Jewish bankers with feudal titles"; along the same line is the remark in *Old Nests* that Count Everstein's property is pledged to a Shylock. Raabe could fall into this vulgar tone in his irritation at his publishers, some of whom were Jewish; he once wrote that his vacation would depend on what the Jews were prepared to pay for *The Rumbledump,* and in his diary on March 19, 1879, he grouches about the newspaper editors who had turned down *Old Nests* as "the Berlin Jewish scoundrels." He irritably referred to R. M. Meyer, who had written dismissively of him in his history of nineteenth-century German literature, as "Richard Moses Meyer" and again as "Moses Meyer."

To say that these were shared commonplaces of discourse is not meant to be an excuse but simply an observation necessary to place the stereotypes in their historical context. Social, class, ethnic, and national typology is virtually universal in nineteenth-century literature, a central feature of its anthropology and, if one will, "realism"; it appears in Raabe in many forms, among which the Jewish types are neither prominent nor striking. One could write another little essay on his images of blacks, but that would lead too far afield here. Furthermore, one must be careful about voice. One must also bear in mind the sarcastic edge of his temperament, most acidly articulated in his social satire. That the Jews have it worse than all the other human types falling under his scourge no one could plausibly claim. There are several instances in which negative characters exhibit anti-Jewish attitudes. In a conversation Raabe is said to have argued against stereotypes by asserting that a Jew can be anything, even a colonizer, and to the familiar prejudice that a Jew could not be truly creative he responded with silence.

As far as his personal life is concerned, his acquaintances and connections included a substantial number of Jews. In his boyhood he seems to have had a Jewish friend named Seckel Falkenstein, who, we are assured, bore no resemblance to Moses Freudenstein of *The Hunger Pastor.* In the diary we find several Jewish names among his social relations in Wolfenbüttel and Stuttgart. Paul Heyse, with whom Raabe had cordial relations, was half Jewish, as was his dear friend Marie Jensen. Wilhelm Jensen was rather

militantly anti-Jewish, though he once commented that the writer Ludwig Fulda was one of the none too common "descendants of the 'old tribe' " who make one realize that anti-Semitic affects are not universally applicable. Raabe's vastly expanding correspondence during his Braunschweig years contains exchanges with a number of Jewish people, from literary figures such as Gustav Karpeles and Karl Emil Franzos to a rabbi in Galicia. It is reported that "at his table Lutherans, Catholics, and Israelites sat peacefully beside one another," while he observed that the Jews were "our oldest nobility . . . their ancestors climbed the stairs to the David Palace in Jerusalem in trailing garments and gold jewelry while the ancestors of our proudest German lords sat clad with skins in primitive huts in the primeval forest and slaughtered human beings at the sacrificial fire." He was curious about the Jews as he was about most things, and at the time of writing *The Hunger Pastor* he read a definitive history of the Jewish people.

With the most prominent German-Jewish writer of his time, Berthold Auerbach, he maintained, by his standards, friendly relations; it has already been mentioned that his only book review is a notice of an anthology edited by Auerbach. In Stuttgart Auerbach was one of his drinking companions, according to the diary. Raabe has Eyring, the amiable eighteenth-century narrator of *The Geese of Bützow* (1866), reading the poems of the Jewish apho-

Raabe's study.

193

rist Ephraim Kuh; this at least suggests an acquaintance with Auerbach's novel *Poet and Merchant* (1840), a fictionalized biography of Kuh. The diary shows that Raabe read other works of Auerbach from time to time. In the texts there are scattered references to Auerbach, for example, in **German Nobility.** Always grateful for recognition, Raabe wrote Auerbach a most cordial letter of thanks for his review of **The Horn of Wanza.** The community of admirers that clustered around Raabe in his late years and became the core of the Raabe Society included people of Jewish origin. . . . There is not one shred of evidence that Raabe's associations with Jewish people differed in the slightest nuance from his habits of personal relations generally.

In the light of all this, **The Hunger Pastor** comes to look like an anomaly in Raabe's career, an eccentricity that we might justifiably put to one side if it were not for the reception history, which made of this episode in his grueling search for his own voice and posture his most famous work, at home and abroad. By the 1950s it had appeared in over sixty editions totalling well over a quarter of a million copies. It is a double-plotted *Bildungsroman* paralleling the development of a model German youth, Hans Unwirrsch, to that of an exact Jewish contemporary, Moses Freudenstein. The poor shoemaker's son Hans, in his hunger for light and truth, passes through a series of discouraging and sobering social experiences, until he finds his vocation as a pastor in a bleak community of fishermen on the remote shores of the Baltic. Moses, in his hunger for power, status, and worldly goods, transforms himself into a Frenchified Catholic intellectual named Théophile Stein, ruining various women along the way, and eventually becoming a social success as well as a political agent of the oppressive German governments but, in the narrator's judgment, "civilly dead *(bürgerlich tot)* in the most terrible sense of the word." His political turn, as an agent of the repressive governments, is the main reason why Moses is not to be identified with Heine, despite Moses's own attempts so to identify himself. There is some reason to suppose that Raabe was thinking of Joel Jacoby, who had become a police spy and government agent in the 1840s. Raabe's amalgamation of the reprehensible Jew with repressive authority rather than with rebellious opposition, as was more common on the right then and later, is a significant indicator of his political position.

It would certainly seem that anyone familiar with mid-nineteenth-century German literature must be struck by the similarity in pattern of this novel to the great best-seller of those times, Gustav Freytag's *Soll und Haben* (*Debit and Credit,* 1855). Though obvious to the Raabe experts of the past, this connection came to be treated gingerly, and, while it seems to be accepted by now, to my knowledge a thorough comparison has never been undertaken. The reason may be that, although Raabe met Freytag personally on his mini-grand tour in 1859, the two writers did not admire one another very much; furthermore, a comparison may have seemed odious to Raabe admirers, for, whatever the failings of **The Hunger Pastor,** as a work of literature it is undoubtedly superior to *Debit and Credit.* But Freytag's novel, too, pairs the exactly contemporaneous careers of an innately good, if in this case

somewhat priggish and occasionally slow-witted bourgeois Gentile, and a crudely ambitious, unethical, and greedy Jewish boy. In both novels the career of the Jew keeps impinging on that of the Gentile, creating nasty complications that require to be repelled and set right. In neither novel is there any pronounced sense of the Jews as a religious community; they are an ethnic foreign body in a German nation struggling for an elusive identity and cohesiveness. Both novels have very much the cast of ideological tracts in the interest of German nationalism and a liberal bourgeois ethos, although the tenets of classical liberalism are much more explicitly articulated by Freytag, whereas Raabe has a scene of a proletarian revolt that the protagonist observes sympathetically. Both novels understand the condition of the Jews to be historically and socially determined but nevertheless pass ethical judgments on them. Freytag was no more of an anti-Semite or racist than Raabe; he was a national and class partisan. But despite nuances in the texts sometimes adduced in defense of both, despite their authors' subsequent embarrassment and implicit disclaimers, the books took on lives of their own and nourished calamitous prejudices.

While this is not the place for a detailed comparison, some differences might be mentioned, apart from the considerable qualitative gap in style and thoughtfulness. In the first place, Freytag was much more extensively concerned than Raabe with the Jews as a social problem. Apart from minor figures, there are six important Jewish characters in *Debit and Credit,* distributed along the ethical spectrum that is a vertical axis of the novel: three negative ones—the antagonist Veitel Itzig, the oily financier Hirsch Ehrenthal, and the *gonif* tavern keeper and fence Löbel Pinkus; and three, in a qualified way, positive ones—the ethically assimilated but physically feeble scholar Bernhard Ehrenthal, the comic and seedy but ultimately Biblically righteous Orthodox peddler Schmeie Tinkeles, and a Jewish innkeeper who represents an outpost of *German* ethics in the even more degenerate environment of the Poles. In **The Hunger Pastor,** Moses Freudenstein is the only important Jewish figure. Otherwise there are Moses's father, who hoped by avarice and labor to win strength and survival for his son, only to earn his son's contempt and to die of horror when he realizes what a monster he has sired, and the Jewish housemaid of the family, who abhors Moses as a renegade (both motifs are prefigured in *Debit and Credit).* In Raabe's overall scheme of things Moses is less a Jewish type than an example of the *canaille* that he found infesting mankind everywhere; there are parallels to his brutal cynicism in other, Gentile figures, such as the obnoxious swindler and loan shark Pinnemann in **Three Pens,** the corrupt Baron von Glimmern in **Abu Telfan,** or the terrifyingly invincible Dietrich Häussler in **The Rumbledump.** As we shall see in another context, there is a non-Jewish parallel to the exotic, mistreated, ultimately vengeful racial outcast in the Wendish piper Kiza in **The Pied Piper of Hamelin.**

On the other hand, however, Moses is a much more serious and impressive antagonist than Veitel Itzig. Freytag's Jew, though he has a pronounced capacity for hard work and self-improvement, remains an unappetizing and inferior character throughout; he has no dialectical relationship to the protagonist Anton Wohlfart, who is never attracted to him, and he represents nothing in the realm of ideas. But Moses is a forceful and elegant personality, with a strong if egocentric imagination, quick in learning and in the acquisition of Epicurean taste and savoir faire, a juggler of Machiavellian and cynical ideas of some penetration. While Itzig's chief intellectual accomplishment is to learn standard German and commercial correspondence, Freudenstein becomes a scholar of Semitic languages and aspires to a professorship. Despite his conversion to Catholicism and change of name, Moses does not hide his Jewishness but employs it, for example, in his seduction of the excessively emancipated Kleophea Götz, when he stresses the heroism and stoicism of the Jewish people. Hans, who has been his protector against anti-Semitic roughhousing in his boyhood (another motif prefigured in *Debit and Credit),* feels an unrequited friendly attachment to him and has some difficulty arriving at a true assessment of his character—an aspect of the novel rather poorly handled by Raabe. In fact it is Hans's envy of Moses's humanistic education and Latin studies that impels him to rebellion against his destiny as a shoemaker. The figure of Moses has absorbed some of the dexterity and mental sharpness of Freytag's other parallel figure, the renegade aristocrat Fink, who despite his need for some instruction in bourgeois ethics, rather overshadows the boring Anton Wohlfart, even in the narrative voice, in attractiveness and ultimate competence. It is Moses who, in the middle of the work, denominates Hans as the "hunger pastor," thus contributing a faint dimension of ironic distance. The suggestion has been ventured that Moses's demonically nihilistic nature and his sarcastic vengefulness represent a fraction of Raabe's own spirit. I find this hard to accept, for Raabe goes to extremes in making him a villain, but his stature and role are certainly more imposing than Itzig's, and there is no doubt that he contributes to Hans's education. Finally, Raabe disposes of him differently. Itzig, while being pursued by Anton, drowns, with more melodramatic than poetic justice, in the same place where he had originally drowned his mentor, the degenerate Gentile Hippus. Raabe had originally planned to have Moses shipwrecked and washed up on the hunger pastor's shore, to die in his arms, but wisely thought the better of it and let him live on, "civilly dead," perhaps, but nevertheless surviving as an image of the endurance of human evil in the world, which continues to balk the supersession of bourgeois values.

As in the case of Freytag, critics have from time to time attempted to mitigate the effect of this portrayal, for example, by pointing to the fact that Moses is a renegade Jew, not a representative one (a tack Raabe himself took in self-defense, as we shall see), or by citing the passages about the mistreatment of Jews, now fortunately in the past, and about Moses Mendelssohn's humiliations, passages clearly showing Raabe to have been a supporter of Jewish emancipation. But the case is not wholly persuasive and readers of the past were easily able to admire the portrayal as healthily anti-Semitic. Repeatedly Moses's characteristics are identified as "Semitic": his intellectual quickness, seen as sophistry and Talmudic quibbling; his unchildlike nature, even as a boy; his tendency to materialism; his vengefulness; the cynicism with which he turns Catholic and be-

comes a government agent, thus in both ways an enemy of the liberal, Protestant, progressive, bourgeois German; his rootless cosmopolitanism. It is a curious fact, however, that all of this diction is on the authorial level of narration; good Hans never employs it, even when he is at last obliged to turn against Moses. In one odd passage, Hans find himself on a train with some Eastern Jews in caftans, who, we are told, do not smell very agreeably, but Hans courteously converses with them in Hebrew. This distinction might give pause to a subtle reader, aware of the complexities of Raabe's narrative technique; nevertheless, the overall effect comports too well with what Mark Gelber has defined as "literary anti-Semitism," as distinct from authorial intention: "the potential or capacity of a text to encourage or positively evaluate anti-Semitic attitudes or behaviors ["Aspects of Literary Anti-Semitism: Charles Dickens' *Oliver Twist* and Gustav Freytag's *Soll und Haben,* "(Diss. Yale University, 1980)]. Undoubtedly, at the center of the portrayal lies Raabe's nationalism. Moses himself has an interesting speech in which he talks of the freedom of Jews, who are Germans only insofar as it pleases them, passengers on the ship of liberalism, cosmopolitan adherents of the idea rather than the nation. But, as strong as the nationalistic affect was in Raabe, elsewhere in his works it does not commonly overrun his deep sympathy with the fragility and sorrowfulness of the human condition, which in fact he expresses, perhaps somewhat uneasily, in the motto to ***The Hunger Pastor,*** from Sophocles's *Antigone,* line 523: "I cannot share in hatred, but in love." How, then, did the literary anti-Semitism of *The Hunger Pastor* come into being?

The answer must lie in Raabe's struggle for acknowledgment by the public. As I imagine it, Raabe read *Debit and Credit* and observed its success, then said to himself quite rightly that if that was the sort of thing the public wanted, he could do it better. I have suggested that Raabe, in his earlier phases, struggled to amalgamate his own voice with the kind of literature that others wrote and the public accepted. but this is the only time, as far as I can see, that he drew direct inspiration from a specific contemporary work. The result shows that it was a compromising mistake, for, perhaps subliminally, he drew into the undertaking some of the prejudices of a public with which, in his deepest instincts, he was out of harmony. The tension continues in the ambivalence of his subsequent estimation of the novel. At times he appeared to repudiate it as immature along with almost all of his earlier writing before he began to find his way to his own voice and form in the later 1860s; at other times, his longing for recognition made him more indulgent of a work that had contributed to his fame and saw thirty-four editions by the end of his life. Walking a tightrope, he fell off into a trap, but that it was a trap was far from evident for a long time.

How enduring the tension remained appeared in an episode in 1903, when Raabe received a letter from a Jewish lady, Philippine Ullmann. She must have been quite elderly, for she begins with reminiscences of Raabe's family during his earliest childhood in Stadtoldendorf. Then she goes on to express her concern about the effect of ***The Hunger Pastor,*** asking whether in his long life he has never met a Jew with character. In this connection there emerges a set of curious parallels and coincidences. For the same thing had happened to Dickens forty years earlier: he received a letter also from a Jewish lady, Eliza Davis, observing that the portrayal of Fagin in *Oliver Twist* "has encouraged a vile prejudice against the despised Hebrew," and rather pertly suggesting that Dickens atone with a charitable donation. The repetition is not without significance, for it is well known that Raabe owed much to Dickens, and in fact he re-read *David Copperfield* while working on **The Hunger Pastor;** furthermore, it has long been established that *Debit and Credit* was structurally modelled on *David Copperfield.* If, as I suppose, **Madame Salome** was meant to be some kind of compensation for **The Hunger Pastor,** this would constitute yet another parallel, to Dickens's creation of the kindly, upright Jew, Mr. Riah, in *Our Mutual Friend* as an antidote to Fagin in *Oliver Twist.* That the correspondence of Mrs. Davis and Dickens is virtually contemporaneous with the publication of **The Hunger Pastor** may be mentioned as a detail.

Dickens replied to Mrs. Davis that if the Jews feel wronged, "they are far less sensible, a far less just, and a far less good-tempered people than I have always supposed them to be." He defended himself on the grounds of realistic typology. But his sense of justice must have been touched all the same, for he revised *Oliver Twist* to remove some of the direct references to Fagin's Jewishness. Raabe, in his response, went even more on the offensive. He thanks Philippine Ullmann for her reminiscences of his boyhood milieu, but then his reply turns testy. He says it is the Jews' fault if they count the renegade Moses as one of their own, and adds that she seems to have an accidental acquaintance with his writings, calling her attention to **Madame Salome** and **Höxter and Corvey.** He denies that he is to be counted among anti-Semites and says that Jews have always been among his best friends and most appreciative readers. Here his irritable obsession with neglect by the public rises to the surface again. He quite evaded the question that had been put to him, but one wonders whether it was completely settled in his own mind. When a rabbi raised it with him in 1902, asking whether Moses was meant to be a representative figure and apparently pointing to the rise of political anti-Semitism and the agitation of the Prussian court preacher Adolf Stöcker, Raabe replied with one of the rudest letters of his life. However, it is also true that he made a spirited reply to a man who solicited an anti-Semitic novella from him in 1883. Here he rejects the anti-Semitic writings and illustrations sent to him, observing that he does not think they will do the Jews much harm and adding that Israel does no harm to the real German people. He is not a partisan writer, and, if he wrote **The Hunger Pastor,** he also wrote **Madame Salome.** He ends by firmly rejecting the request. Perhaps the rise of anti-Semitism induced him to avoid Jewish characterizations altogether in his late works. He had originally intended to make the wise mentor in **Princess Fish** a Jewish bookbinder named Abraham Veigel, but decided to conflate the character with a non-Jewish one. The name of the real-life biologist Ferdinand Cohn is changed to Kühn in **Pfister's Mill,** although the microorganism named for him, Cladothrix Cohn, remains unchanged. The narcissistic aesthete Albin Brokenkorb in

On the Scrap-Iron was originally named Levin Bodenstaub, a name that need not be Jewish but might be. (pp. 73-84)

[The burden placed on Raabe's reputation by the Raabe Society] became especially burdensome when the anti-Semitic potential of the disciples burgeoned in the Nazi period. The Society's president, Franz Hahne, in his younger days had met Raabe, who insisted that he was in no way anti-Semitic, but Hahne would not believe him. Instead, he asked himself why Raabe had never "attacked the Jews" after **The Hunger Pastor** and guessed that the reason might have been his fear of Jewish power. Needless to say, the Jewish members of the Raabe community had no role to play in this phase. Most striking is the case of Heinrich Spiero, a modestly talented but productive literary historian who met Raabe during the seventieth-birthday celebration in 1901 and subsequently devoted a third of a century of service to the cause. He became vice-president of the Raabe Society and was for many years president of the Berlin chapter. Among more than forty publications on Raabe, he wrote the first general biography, composed a lexicon of Raabe's cultural allusions, and edited an elaborate Festschrift for the hundredth anniversary of his birth in 1931. Spiero was completely assimilated—loyal, patriotic, and conservative, perhaps, in his own way, racist: he once wrote of "Austria's sub-Germanic Danubian peoples." In his memoirs, published in 1929, he does not refer to his Jewish origins with a single word, presenting himself as an active liberal Protestant; after World War I he was a member of a committee that tried without success to devise a progressive constitution for the Protestant Church. His cultic loyalty to Raabe yielded to no one's: "to grow up in succession to him is a German task." No matter; he was unceremoniously forced out when the Raabe Society was Aryanized. In 1937 [Wilhelm] Fehse gave him a little kick when he was down by writing dismissively of his pioneering biography. As far as I can see, only one Raabe enthusiast was sufficiently offended to make a gesture: Constantin Bauer, who resigned the editorship of the *Communications.*

Obviously, it has been necessary to rescue Raabe from his own reception history on this front more than any other. The task, however, is not simple. The initial post-war amnesia of his traditional admirers falls far short of meeting the need. But standing his reputation on its head will not serve the purpose, either. For the reception history is not something that just *happened* to Raabe; he himself was involved in it for particular reasons that no one in the modern phase of Raabe scholarship has yet thought worthy of attention.

When Raabe replied to Philippine Ullmann that, like our Lord God, he let his light shine upon the just and the unjust, he was not turning a phrase. For one thing, he was tolerantly curious about the new ideas of his time, without distinguishing those that in retrospect appear ominous and odious to us. He noted in his diary that on April 29, 1893, he attended a lecture on Jews in art and science by a prominent anti-Semitic politician and propagandist, Paul Förster. He showed a polite interest in the race theories of Gobineau, which were pressed on him by his friends. For another, not only were there numerous Jews in his circle of acquaintance; there were also numerous anti-Semites. It will be remembered that the Raabe Society grew out of that circle of acquaintance, the clubby atmosphere of his entourage in Braunschweig. It therefore had some reasonable claim to succession and its members to special privileges as initiates. Both Fehse and Hahne, along with others who participated in the Nazified phase, had been in his circle. The author of the essay on Raabe and Hitler is found among his correspondents in 1907. One surprising character encountered here is Adolf Bartels, the popular, hysterically anti-Semitic literary historian who devoted some two dozen publications to a campaign to destroy Heine's reputation; this is a bit odd, since Rabe's admiration of Heine is now well established. Perhaps one might mention here also Raabe's encouragement of Gustav Frenssen's best-selling novel *Jörn Uhl.* While this novel is a work of some substance that may owe something to Raabe's narrative ingenuity, and especially in its dénouement does not wholly deserve the opprobrium of blood-and-soil literature into which it has fallen, Frenssen did evolve into a Nazi supporter of a particularly fatuous kind, judging from his memoirs. The circumstance is striking because Raabe was normally very chary of interest in and critical approval of the work of his German literary contemporaries.

In the writings of the closest personal friend of his old age and the real founder of the Society, Wilhelm Brandes, I do not find much of an anti-Semitic nature, but there is one passage that shows how the conservative ideological attitude of that class of men in those times had become second nature: while attempting to distinguish Raabe's humor from the liberal succession to Jean Paul, Brandes remarks on "the Jewish wing of Young Germany." What can this possibly mean? None of the Young Germans was Jewish. Brandes mentions Moritz Saphir and Adolf Glassbrenner, but the shallow satirist Saphir had nothing to do with Young Germany, and the populist Glassbrenner, who in any case was not Jewish either, was at most on the periphery of the movement. It is a defamatory transference of the Jewishness of the Young Germans' model figures, Heine and Börne, and a continuation of the influential critic Wolfgang Menzel's strategy in the 1830s of denouncing Young Germany as "Young Palestine." This strikes me as unfaithful to Raabe's origins and foundations. For, apart from his demonstrably positive relationship to Heine and hints that he was also an admirer of Börne, with the sarcastic and bitter tone of the innumerable political observations in his works he seems to me to preserve more of the Young German spirit than any other mid-century writer I know. It is unfortunate that we do not know what he thought of the Dreyfus Case. We can only guess; Zola was the only Naturalist writer Raabe at all admired, and in his diary on February 23, 1898, he noted without comment Zola's sentence of one year in prison. It is in such matters that the taciturnity of the diary becomes most frustrating; he also noted without comment on November 22, 1880, the debate in the Prussian parliament on the petition, signed by a quarter of a million Germans, to abrogate the civil rights of Jews. However, since his political hero Bismarck was deter-

mined to quash the petition and succeeded in doing so, one may assume that Raabe agreed with him in this policy.

If the keepers of Raabe's reputation were guilty of a breach of faith in turning him into an anti-Semite and prophet of Nazism, he was not without complicity in it insofar as he welcomed such people into his fold. But I do not think this indicates a change in him, an accommodation on his part to the Wilhelminian ideological atmosphere. His ideological commitments and social views were formed early in life and thereafter changed some in form and perspective, but not very much in substance to the end of his days. Furthermore, we do not know what Raabe, in his innermost heart, thought of any of these people. The answer must lie again in his need for an audience. He made his light to shine upon the just and the unjust, as long as the just and the unjust were his readers and adherents. He repelled out-and-out anti-Semites who made demands upon him, but otherwise he did not subject his adherents to ideological tests. This tolerance was a product of his personal priorities and helps to account for the combination of pleasant conviviality and mild aloofness in his relations with his friends. This would explain Bartels, for example, who wrote positively of Raabe during the seventieth-birthday revival of 1901. But he not only sought popularity; he also feared it, and in this he was right also. Like many major writers, he was both of his time and out of phase with it. His desire for a public created dangers that I believe he sensed but did not fully grasp. As he did not see the extent to which he had trapped himself in his imitative excursion into the commonplace with **The Hunger Pastor,** so he was in no position to see the risk of imprisoning his reputation by encouraging a band of disciples who were not content to admire and enjoy, but who enhanced their own self-regard as a chosen people by grafting their more petty vision and their parochial preoccupations onto his supple, subtle, and questioning art. It is only just and realistic to recognize that he cannot be separated or isolated from the first phases of his twentieth-century reception, that his involvement in it was rooted in his own ambivalent but intense manner of coping with the threatening isolation and homelessness of the nineteenth-century bourgeois artist. (pp. 84-7)

. . . . .

Wilhelm Raabe was the most ingenious experimenter with narrative perspective in nineteenth-century German literature. He was, one recent scholar has written, "constantly aware of an entire spectrum of different narrative-structural possibilities and chooses at random first one approach, then another. In doing so, he explores his potentials as a writer, discovers his weaknesses, recognizes his strong sides; as a result he establishes the firm foundation in his later highly complex narrative structures."[Erich Weniger, "Wilhelm Raabe und das bürgerliche Leben," in *Raabe in neuer Sicht,* ed. Hermann Helmers]. In this regard no one in his own time can match him. He wrote frame stories like Storm—it has been estimated that about a third of his narrations are of this type—but he did not specialize in them as Storm did, and in Raabe the relationship of frame and story is much more subtle and varied. Of course his contemporaries, such as Keller and Stifter, probed the possibilities of first-person narration, but for Raabe's peers one would have to go back to Goethe's subtly and ironically translucent narration in *Werther* or forward to the stream-of-consciousness experiments of Schnitzler or even to such a modern contemporary as Max Frisch. In demonstrative third-person narration Raabe has no peers at all in his time; for comparisons one would have to look back to the Romantics or even to Wieland's awareness of the stress between authorial sovereignty and authorial limitation, between realism and illusion, and forward to Thomas Mann. Both Raabe and his critics were well aware of his eccentricity in this regard, and almost all the public complaint of him throughout his career is about his authorial, intrusive, subjective, in short, "Jean-Paulian" or, in my view, Thackerayan manner. When in 1894 the influential critic Ferdinand Avenarius, in a generally positive review of *Cloister Lugau,* complained of a confusing opening like a series of hedgerows balking the reader's access to the story and trying his patience, he was reformulating objections that Raabe had been hearing for decades. For the literary establishment of his time was committed to the "objective" narration propagated by the programmatic realists, which meant nothing more profound than silencing the authorial voice as far as possible. Raabe seems to have been aware that this alleged objectivity was a delusion, since it was only technical, and in retrospect we can see clearly that it was a kind of ideological hoax, presenting partial and biased perspectives as universal truth and objective reality. His traditional admirers paid almost no attention to his narrative technique, though for other reasons: they were insistent that he was a wise man rather than an artist, and the harmonious equilibrium they were determined to find in him is highly vulnerable to the irony and polyperspectivism of narrative self-consciousness.

Conversely, the recognition of his exceptional narrative variety has been the main lever that has pried him away from his "friends" and elevated his standing in modern criticism. Much of the best British and American Raabe scholarship has been focused on narrative technique, and there have been an increasing number of German contributions to this topic as well. For it is by this means that Raabe, often thought of in his own time as a stubbornly old-fashioned writer, comes to appear to us as a harbinger of the modern. [In his *The Rhetoric of Fiction*] Wayne Booth has said that "it was not until this century that men began to take seriously the possibility that the power of artifice to keep us at a certain distance from reality could be a virtue rather than simply an inevitable obstacle to full realism. This statement may be a little misleading, in view of the eighteenth-century and Romantic roots of ironic artifice in narration, but it points up the centrality of narrative experimentation and, in its wake, narrative theory, in modernism. In this as in other matters the pioneer was Barker Fairley, who in a now classic essay stressed Raabe's polyperspectivism and observed quite rightly that he "touches, at one point or another, all the forms that fiction can take," and that, though not a theoretician, he had a "general awareness, from the start, of what is involved mentally in the process of narration ["The Modernity of Wilhelm Raabe"].

Thus Raabe has been rescued for us on essentially formalist grounds as a proto-modern. Yet, if we are honest with ourselves, there is something about this procedure that ought to make us a little uneasy. There is first of all the large question whether the modernist reevaluation of a writer often perceived in his own time as a Romantic throwback, in form, at any rate, does not imply a substantial Neo-Romantic component in modernism. More specifically, the critical concentration on narration postulates a high degree of conscious artistry, but Raabe utterly declined to play the Flaubertian role of obsessive artist. He almost entirely avoided all theoretical or aesthetic pronouncements, except for tantalizing, often obscurely aphoristic scraps in his private notebooks. He displayed a pronounced dislike of aestheticism and, except by example, did not so much combat the reigning theory of objective narration as ignore it contemptuously. He admired other writers, such as Goethe, not so much for their artistry as for the example they set in surviving the battle of life. One of his notebook entries of 1880 reads: "For real man the time is perhaps coming when he will no longer seek art, the aesthetic, in the works of authors, in order to achieve peace in the storm of life, but indications of how they found their way in the great struggle."

In the contemporary critical atmosphere it has become bad form to speak of Raabe as a supplier of consolation to the reader and of *Lebenshilfe,* guidance in life. It is therefore frustrating that he explicitly claimed this to be his office from one end of his career to the other. In one of his aphoristic early poems we read: "To grasp light out of shadow, / That is the poet's vocation!" The apostrophe at the end of *The Hunger Pastor* became virtually proverbial: "Pass on *your* weapons, Hans Unwirrsch!"; that is, the reader is to draw sustenance from Hans's experiences and his survival of them. Many years later, Raabe wrote in the first chapter of *The Odin Field:*

> May the consolation that we personally have drawn from the old schoolmaster, from Noah Buchius, be granted to many another. This is our most cordial wish as we arise from the folios, quartos, parchments, and bundles of documents in which we have listened from afar to the uproar, the clangor from Wotan's field, the Odin Field, in the noise of the present, the roar of the day, that tomorrow always lies behind us as though it had been a hundred thousand years ago.

In his embarrassed letter to [the socialist feminist] Clara Zetkin of 1908 he asserted: "For me the main thing is that, through my whole literary life, I have been less an aesthetic author than a good friend, advisor, and consoler of the wretchedly burdened, of those of *all* classes in need of courage to live and to die." These utterances, which could easily be multiplied, cannot be ignored, and indeed there is much evidence that he had in fact such an influence on many of his readers. For this reason there have been justified warnings from scholars of impeccable contemporary credentials against excessively formalist interpretation fixated on narrative technique.

But it is not merely contemporary critical fashion that prevents us from falling back into a view of Raabe as a naive, insouciant storyteller, oblivious to the complexities of narrative perspective and subordinating artistry to message. For as soon as he was taken as such, he rebelled: "In my life work I have always cared more about the *work of art* than the effect. You call me a 'quiet and modest artist.' The noun I accept, the two attributive adjectives by no means." This is not just contrariness on his part; it is merely another facet of his self-understanding, one that he rarely articulated but that is undeniably present in the texts. For him the medium and the message were compounded, and it is for us to try to understand how the message required the narrative ingenuity. We are not dealing here with a set of quirks and mannerisms, but with one of the most insistently self-conscious narrators in European literature after Sterne. One could compose a substantial and satisfactory textbook of narrative technique and point-of-view theory with no other resources than Raabe's body of fiction.

For . . . the variety in the range and intensity of his narrative devices is extraordinary, one more aspect that should deter us from homogenizing him and ignoring his experimental dimension. He shifted back and forth between first- and third-person narration; one novel, *Princess Fish,* was originally drafted in the first person but recast in the third; and in his very last work, the fragmentary *Altershausen,* he experimented for the first time with another variant: a first-person narrator tells of himself in the third person. The degree of authorial intrusiveness can differ considerably from work to work: it can be subdued but persistent; it can be concentrated at the beginning, or at chapter beginnings, or at crucial junctures, or at the conclusion; or it can be pervasively aggressive and mannered, sometimes to the point of self-parody. Traditionally, the display of authorial manipulation has been associated with humorous or, more exactly, ironic narration. It can also generate rhetorical heightening at solemn moments. When, in *Elsa of the Fir,* the narrator pauses to say, in a one-sentence paragraph: "This, however, is the story of the death of the maiden," he reminds us strongly of the famous opening of the second-last chapter of Thomas Mann's *Buddenbrooks,* describing the death of Hanno: "With typhus the course of things is as follows." Furthermore, lest we suspect that his manner is merely a matter of naivety, of not knowing the rules, it must be noted that he intermittently approached omniscient, "objective" narration in cases where his authorial presence is as subdued as one is likely to find in nineteenth-century fiction, and in one of his most mature works, *Restless Guests,* he suppressed the authorial narrator almost entirely. The suggestion made recently that he did so in order to accommodate himself to the normal family-magazine reader is, in my view, to be rejected. . . . *Restless Guests* is one of his most brilliantly executed works, and the suppression of the narrator is quite appropriate to the novel's sober, thoughtful, observant tone and to its psychological realism.

This is not to say that he fully and flawlessly mastered the craft at every point. The price of experimentation is the risk of falling short of the mark; furthermore, the annoyance of his readers at his mannerisms cannot be dismissed as total obtuseness on their part. Even the modern, sympa-

thetic reader will occasionally come to be irritated at what may seem to be authorial affectation, even a relentless nerve-wracking jabbering, as though one were locked in a room with the Ancient Mariner. Even a modern, sympathetic critic has sighed that, in the Stuttgart trilogy, "We cannot say that Raabe's narrators . . . succeed in making themselves interesting at all times"; there are places where "the intrusion is not a valid extension of the narrator's personality but rather an empty posturing" [James Robert Reece, "Narrator and Narrative Levels in Raabe's Stuttgart Novels" (Diss. Univ. of Oregon, 1975)]. One reason is probably that Raabe's formal sense matured much more rapidly than his imaginative mastery of content. Not unreasonably it has been argued that the narrator of the early *One Springtime* tries to force consistency of meaning by authorial rhetoric and that the story does not show what the narrator says it does. In *The Rumbledump,* which shifts between an exceptionally personal authorial opening and relatively omniscient narration, it is hard to get quite clear about the author's view of the characters; he circles around them with voices of public discourse that may need correcting. [Stephen Gould has] said that the strategy "results in a narrator who is unusually authoritarian in his control of the reader's fictional participation," but whether in this case he is as persuasive as he is authoritarian is another question ["Ontology and Ethics: The Rhetorical Role of the Narrator in Wilhelm Raabe's Early Novels" (Diss. University of Nebraska, 1976)]. The novel falls in the Stuttgart period, which one critic has seen as a time of transition, of increasing subjectification of narrative and emphasis on the way the story is told, and a decreasing concern with linear narrative. It is true that his instinctive polyperspectivism, when applied to relatively conventional materials, could make his plot management overcomplicated and obscure. [Laurel Eason] has fairly observed that in *The People from the Forest* Raabe was "trying to be in too many characters' minds and too many places at once" ["Beginning and Conclusion: Structure and Theme in the Early Novels of Wilhelm Raabe" (Diss. Vanderbilt University)]. While his development was not a steady progression, over his career he undoubtedly grew stronger in matching matter to manner, in part by dissolving plot and dissipating suspense.

As a general principle it may be said that the effect of his authorial technique is to stress fictionality, *poiesis* over *mimesis.* His realism is more a realism of the narrative act than of what is narrated. To this end he calls on a wide variety of devices, most of them, to be sure, familiar from the history of literature. There is first of all the collapse of the narrator into the empirical self of the author. Raabe often does this, and we should be wary of applying to him a dogmatic point-of-view theory or a strict insistence on the narrator's fictional second self. The narrating self is not layered but fluid, slipping in and out of roles from a virtually essayistically presented empirical self through various levels of fictionalized narrative selves, deflections, partial and full disguises, to fully fictionalized alter egos of the author's imagined self. A theoretical position that anything within the boundary of a fictional work must be treated as fictional will miss the point of Raabe's protean dynamic.

He begins *The Rumbledump* by telling us under what circumstances he saw a rumbledump: we know this to be a fact, and it does not become a fiction because it is recounted in the novel. He began his teasing on this point early, in the melodramatic story *On Dark Ground* (1861), where the narrator constructs a frame in which he introduces himself in his quotidian life and slides from his storytelling environment into the fictional narration, and at the end of "this touching story" he is exhausted, can't drink his tea, goes to a wine shop to read his newspaper and smoke his cigar. At the end of *The Children of Finkenrode* he inserts himself into the fictive environment under his pseudonym "Corvinus" and appears on his way to the theater to see the tragicomedy of *The Children of Finkenrode*. Much later, in *German Nobility,* he repeats the device: in the "Epilogue" the author and his fictional characters meet. In *The Holy Spring* he tells us how industrious his historical research has been; in *Our Lord God's Chancellory* he discusses the selection process that distinguishes the work from a mere chronicle; at the beginning of Chapter 13 of *The People from the Forest* he puzzles over how to proceed, complains that most people don't realize how hard storytelling is, and assures the reader that he should be happy he does not have to write the book, a conceit that recalls Heine. Later in the novel he tells us that he is a harmless, naive individual, like his characters, and at the end the character Fiebiger recites the motto "that we have prefixed to this book," thus collapsing character and author. Hans and Fränzchen in *The Hunger Pastor* get married on Raabe's birthday. At the beginning of *Abu Telfan* he mounts a self-defense of his career, then slips into the narrative role of limited omniscience. To see both kinds of utterances occurring on the same fictional plane, to deny the shift from the narrator's "first" to his "second" self, would be mere theoretical obstinacy.

The examples of Raabe showing himself being a writer could be multiplied almost endlessly. In *Höxter and Corvey* he tells us that he began it on November 23, 1873, almost exactly two hundred years after the date of the story. This almost pedantic self-consciousness can be observed in his writing habits outside the fictional context as well; from the diary we see that *Fabian and Sebastian* was begun around January 20, 1880—the name day of Saints Fabian and Sebastian. Raabe's aunt, he tells us, would have thought the beginning of *The Lar* disorderly, but she is dead; why should he force himself for the sake of readers who prefer pleasant, light reading to his "lack of discipline" and "jumpy nature," especially as his readers, unlike his aunt, will not leave him a legacy. In that same novel he inserted a personal reminiscence of his old Stuttgart friend Friedrich Notter and similarly memorialized another, Johann Georg Fischer, in *Gutmann's Travels.* The frantic arabesque of *Christoph Pechlin* opens with an uneasy defense of the author's worth:

> The man who submits himself to the heavy and fearfully responsible task of telling stories to his fellow citizens and is continually aware that he writes on the discarded shirts of just these fellow citizens, will seldom deposit on the white, innocent paper something altogether worthless, that is, something harmful to his advantage and earthly comfort or, more briefly, to his good con-

cord with his neighbors. I, the writer of this book, keep myself constantly aware of this and so on my desk I have only with the most sensitive feeling of delicacy made the necessary new folds in the—fine linen of my dear friends in the public, male and female, after its admittedly somewhat weird journey from their body through the sack of the rag-collector. I can certify on my behalf that I have always approached my task very carefully. But today I am telling an *international* story and go to work with heightened anxiety.

This anxiety is justified, as the novel threatens repeatedly to escape the author's control. At one point "we tame our gasping, trembling zeal and narrate calmly and in an orderly fashion," but at another the usually cool narrator's nerves are shattered by a decision made by the characters.

Raabe repeatedly reminds us of the status of the text as *poiesis,* something made. For example, he is not only familiar with the traditional inexpressibility topos, but he exhibits his awareness that it is a topos: "The epic author describes many kinds of feelings by stating that he cannot describe them; Hans's feeling on this occasion were of such a kind" *(The Hunger Pastor).* He was also aware that he often worked with typological characters; when the crude, self-important businessman Knackstert enters the story of *The Dräumling Swamp,* the narrator refrains from describing him, because, as he says, everyone knows what he looks like. After having played with the possibility of conventional openings to *Gutmann's Travels,* he continues: "There is nothing new to tell people. The house, the household, and the family are already present in the imagination of every cultured reader." Chapter 18 of *Abu Telfan* begins with the statement that it is in form and content the middle point of the story, the peak of the pyramid upon which Hagebucher sits. This is indeed, by page count, the middle of the book; Raabe calls our attention to the book as a crafted, even material object, and connects its planned, external disposition with its internal formal shape. When *Old Nests* grows rather talky and immobile toward the end, the narrator admits his repetitiousness, blandly asserting that he can't do anything about it. Whether this is to be categorized as sovereign irony or a self-critical confession is hard to say.

Raabe knew very well that omniscience is also a fiction. Where would we be with our vocation, he asks in *On the Scrap-Iron,* if we could not pass through all doors and go uninvited where we please? This novel, perhaps the most realistic, even naturalistic, of his major works, not surprisingly contains a good deal of reflection on the question of realism, to which the author finds some surprising answers. He begins with half-sardonic reflections on stories that begin well and end badly, or begin badly and come to a desirable end; these are not like real life, which lacks beginnings and endings. But instead of constructing the fiction that *his* story is more like real life, he opts for the traditional conventions of a *story;* this one ends fairly well "by human standards," and therefore, by implication, more like literature than real life. The main thing is for the narrator to breathe freely in his own cause or that of others, and to find the right listener; he then launches into a fairy-tale tone. At the end he gives us five possible endings to choose from, of which only the first and possibly the second happen. The ironic-comic side of the choice of fiction over illusion is the pretense that the story is escaping the author's control. In *Horacker* the narrator complains that the story is getting out of hand; he has too much stuff and has to get rid of some of it, like Dutch merchants burning nutmegs to keep the price up. At the end of the second chapter of *German Nobility* there is another complaint, this time that a narrative method has crept in that cannot please us. Raabe's most fantastic tale, *Of Old Proteus,* opens with a rumination on how best to make it credible to the reader. One beginning, in the manner of mimetic naturalism, is tested and rejected. The narrator starts again in the romance mode of Shakespeare's *Midsummer Night's Dream,* but a voice from the public objects that no one could stand it anymore without Mendelssohn's music. Yet the narrator comes to be encouraged that it can work by hopefully imagining the right kind of reader, by the appearance of the shade of Aristophanes, and by recalling Bottom's frank rejection of illusion in the awareness of fictionality: "If you think I come hither as a lion, it were pity of my life: no, I am no such thing: I am a man as other men are; and there indeed let him name his name, and tell them plainly he is Snug the joiner."

From this and others of my examples it can easily be seen that Raabe's narrative irony comes to be closely involved with his ongoing fencing match with his reader. He alternates between wistfully projecting an ideal reader and imagining, with varying degrees of exasperation, his real readers. The most famous example of the first kind is doubtless the passage in *Horacker* with the image of the story as a new house; only one person in a thousand will ask what will happen in it—this is the reader for whom the narrator writes. In Chapter 12 of *Cloister Lugau* he expresses the hope that in Chapter 6 the reader, with exact attentiveness, has begun to get a notion that the story would make some sense. But more often he jabs irritably at the reader. In *The Good Day* he inserts a dream scene to make the "female reader" aware of "poetic intensification." We have seen in the chapter on Raabe's public that, whether fairly or unfairly, like many others in the literary world, he blamed the female readership for the dead weight of convention. In *Wunnigel* he tells us that he will get the young man Weyland married, though perhaps not in the way that will suit all female readers. In *Hastenbeck* he projects the female reader, "her serene highness," as objecting to digressions and demanding that the narrator get on with the love story. From early on Raabe put himself in the willfully perverse posture of balking the reader's appetite. A notebook entry of 1864 reads: "It is, to be sure, a fine age, in which people still think that the final and happy joining of the lover and his girl is the ultimate and highest thing with which the drama or the novel can occupy itself." Chapter 20 of *The Rumbledump* begins with an image of the well-meaning, tepid Hennig weeping bloody tears and wringing his hands—that is the way it would be if one were to write in a way to gain the sympathy and approval of readers, but it is not the way it was. The author informs us that he has no love story with which to conclude *Fabian and Sebastian,* no fiancé for Konstanze. *The Lar* bears a motto from a private letter from a friend who wanted him to write a story where the boy and girl "get"

one another; Raabe sabotages all suspense about this by writing a preface in which the boy and the girl are shown at the christening of their first child. He repeats the gesture in *Gutmann's Travels,* telling us plainly that the boy will get the girl. In *Cloister Lagau* he hints at a story that he will not tell, a scandal at a petty court, on the ground that it is too trivial. It has been pointed out [by Katherine Kaiser] that the happy ending of *Owls' Pentecost* is "purposefully superficial because conflicts are smoothed over rather than truly resolved" ["Structure and Narrative Technique in Wilhelm Raabe's *Krähenfelder Geschichten*" (Diss. Brown University, 1974)]. In that same work he rejects, less humorously and more irritably than usual, any role of the reader as a participant in the creative process: "We accede to nothing so far as the claims of the reader on the story are concerned. What we have to do, we know, and what we have to say, likewise, and this satisfies us completely." But obviously it did not satisfy him, or he would not have made such an ado about it.

What has been said so far about narrative irony, authorial intrusion, stressed fictionality, and ongoing confrontation of the reader, all the Thackerayan devices, applies, naturally, more obviously to Raabe's third-person narrations. It has long been noticed, however, that the boundary between third-person and first-person narration in Raabe is not sharp, and it appears even less so if we regard the intrusive narrator as a fictional figure. There is a distinction, however, which is illustrated by *Elsa of the Fir,* a text where the two modes tend to converge and which is therefore identifiable as an innovation in Raabe's oeuvre. This is a third-person narration with a perspective very close to the consciousness of the central figure, Pastor Leutenbacher. The point of view, which at first might seem to be tending toward an interiorized free indirect discourse, is not strictly sustained; there is an occasional shift into the omniscient, authorial first-person plural. Formally, therefore, the text is a hybrid. Nevertheless, by Raabe's standards the authorial voice is generally subordinate to the protagonist's reminiscing consciousness. More significantly, the narrative reduplicates certain reticences and inhibitions of Leutenbacher, particularly his erotic attraction to Elsa, which comes to strike the reader more and more forcibly, but which the pastor is unable to articulate explicitly and which he sublimates into idealization and worship. This technique is closely related to some of Raabe's major achievements in first-person narration.

In that department, Raabe is virtually without peer over a long stretch of German literary history. Here, as so often, the *Urtext* is *The Chronicle of Sparrow Alley.* One of the most striking features of this work—that a quite young, novice author, instead of fictionalizing his own personal experience, imagines the consciousness of a quite elderly man—already shows an intact instinct for narrative distancing in a rather daring form. As [Horst] Daemmrich has observed [in his *Wilhelm Raabe*], the memoirist Wachholder's "attitude toward writing is precarious"; while he disclaims any novelistic ambitions, he experiments with the tenses, narrating the past in the present and the present in the past, achieving overall "a genuinely new novelistic technique." The non-linear reminiscence is intended not so much for memory as an exorcism of memory: "I linger in the minute and leap over years; I paint pictures and provide no plot; I break off, without allowing the old tone to die away: I do not want to teach, but I want to forget, I—am writing no novel!" But the most ingenious device is the introduction of an encapsulated second narrator. This is Wachholder's friend Strobel, who criticizes the disorderly narration, its absence of firm images and rambling commentary, like the "concoction of an inexperienced literary light"—an obvious self-irony of the author. Wachholder invites Strobel to participate in the text, and he does make an effort, but falls into impressionistic association, as the same narrative spirit overcomes him. In exasperation he concludes: "the devil take the chronicle of Sparrow Alley!" Here young Raabe appears to be insisting that his unorthodox manner of narration is not arbitrary but necessary.

Over the course of his career Raabe experimented with several varieties of first-person narration. Perhaps the most elementary of these and the one most easily available to the inexperienced writer is the epistolary novel, long familiar from literary tradition. For the first and only time, Raabe experimented with it in *After the Great War.* I do not know why he never returned to it, except to hazard the guess that the artistic failure of that novel deterred him from a second attempt. As *Elsa of the Fir* is a third-person narration on the boundary to first person, so *Celtic Bones* is a first-person narration close to third person: the narrator is unnamed and plays no part in the action, confining himself to highlighting its comic absurdity. *In the Victory Wreath* (1866) brings for the first and only time an elderly, reminiscing, *female* narrator, doubtless because Raabe had heard the story from his mother-in-law, in whose family it had occurred. But his most innovative experiment was undertaken somewhat earlier in the Stuttgart period: the short novel *Three Pens* (1865).

Here Raabe revives and elaborates the polyperspectivism of *The Chronicle of Sparrow Alley.* In his first novel, Wachholder's friend Strobel intervenes in the text and tries to write some of it himself. Variations on this technique appear here and there in subsequent works, for example, the unconsciously comic passages from Aurora Pogge's diary in *The People from the Forest,* of which the narrator observes: "We learn from this that other people view the persons of our story differently than we do ourselves." In *The Horn of Wanza* there is a handed-around narration of first-person reminiscences that undergo an unexpected turn. First the late old soldier Grünhage appears as a brute; then it turns out he has been laughed to death by his wife Sophie and her old friend Thekla when he postures as head of the local militia, which causes us to see him more as a victim; then previously unperceived stresses and resentments emerge between Sophie and Thekla, who turns out ultimately to have been somewhat sympathetic to old Grünhage. The absorption of all these perspectives one after another into the narration gives us something new: an unreliable third-person narrator!

In *Three Pens,* however, polyperspectivism is the structural principle. Here there are six parts by three authors, each appearing twice. This seems never to have been tried before in German literature. The first part, dated 1829, is

a memoir of a young curmudgeon of thirty, August Hahnenberg, whose impoverished, loveless childhood has turned him into a bitter misanthrope, aged before his time. He has loved once, but lost his beloved to Joseph Sonntag, a pleasant but sluggish, stupid, and incompetent friend. The second part, obviously written much later, is a commentary on this document by Mathilde Sonntag, wife of the offspring of that union, the young doctor August Sonntag. Mathilde is pert, confident of her own superiority, extremely conventional, and quite lacking in subtlety or insight. She regards Hahnenberg as an old monster and objects to his tone. The third part is written by August Sonntag, who after his father's bankruptcy became Hahnenberg's ward. Under his care the boy experienced a gloomy, lonely childhood as his mentor attempted to harden him, combat the traces of his father's weakness, and make him emotionally indifferent as he claims himself to be. Nevertheless, in retrospect August is not without gratitude. It soon appears that August is a much more substantial and thoughtful character than his wife's condescending view of him would lead us to believe; we later learn that he has made a significant, acknowledged biological discovery. In the fourth part Mathilde grabs the pen on the grounds that she is the better narrator; she introduces the plot line of the novel, which concerns a slimy conniver named Pinneberg who gains control over and swindles his employer Hahnenberg; he seems rather obviously descended from Dickens's Uriah Heep in *David Copperfield.* The details of this plot need not concern us here; however, it is not uninteresting that the plot line, with its rather conventional, suspenseful, and sentimental elements, is initially narrated by the most conventional and short-sighted of the narrators. August continues the story in the fifth part. Part six is dated 1862 and is a commentary on the whole document by Hahnenberg, who must now be sixty-three. How much he has learned is hard to say. He is still loveless and burdened by the sadness of his life. He has striven to be strong and without sympathy, and he kept August poor and endangered for pedagogical reasons. But he has loved August in his own perverse way and is delighted at the boy's rebellion against him, his emergence as an independent and competent personality.

Raabe worked very hard on this novel; it was written a good deal more slowly and laboriously than usual. To his publisher he wrote: "I am just beginning to master my art and have, I hope, the best years of my life before me," and many years later he spoke of it as his "first independent work." . . . With his polyperspectival narration Raabe gains a dimensional depth that cannot be achieved by straightforward realistic narration of the sort that satisfies a depressingly normal mind like Mathilde's. We see that even so damaged a self as Hahnenberg, an almost Balzacian villain in his constricted, malign egocentricity, can be sympathetically understood with differentiated and patient judgment. One of the ironies of the work is that, although Hahnenberg labored to educate empathy out of August's character, it is just that capacity for empathy that enables him to view his tormentor with comprehension, without hatred, even with forgiveness. Yet as impressive as this experiment in multiple narrative turned out to be, it remained an isolated one, for Raabe never employed the form again. One reason may be that the critical reaction at the time was almost uniformly negative, with the formal innovation once again, maddeningly, deplored as "Jean-Paulizing method." In any case, it was with a different device of first-person narration that Raabe found his most productive line of development.

This device we may, for the sake of brevity, call the "unreliable narrator." There are few literary techniques, apart from outright obscurity, that put such demands on a reader's attention or go so far toward making the reader a partner in the creative process. Thus there are few so likely to lead to misunderstanding and incomprehension in the common reader. Nothing, therefore, better illustrates Raabe's stubbornness as a writer, his commitment to his own artistic vision, than his pursuit of a narrative device of which hardly anyone, as far as I can see, had the faintest comprehension in his own nineteenth-century environment. That it must seem so obvious to us today is a good index of the revolution that has taken place in criticism between his time and our own. (pp. 172-84)

It may be, for all I know, quite difficult to write a story in which the first-person narrator must appear to us as morally dense and reprehensible—classic examples are Ring Lardner's "Haircut" or Henry James's *The Aspern Papers*—but surely it is more difficult to remain in close moral and psychological intimacy with the narrator and still edge him into unreliability. Learning how to do this was one of Raabe's great achievements.

The intimations of this development can be traced in a number of works. One . . . is **The Geese of Bützow,** with its facetious, garrulous, philistine narrator affecting a somewhat heavy-handed tone, whose perspective, nevertheless, is not so much askew as merely limited. But a genuine breakthrough was to occur in the mid-1870s with **Master Author** (published in 1873 with the imprint 1874 but begun in 1872). . . . Its central figure, Kunemund, is an isolated, unpopular author who takes the view that he understands the world, but the world does not understand him. Clearly he incarnates Raabe's own feelings at a time when he felt himself to be at the bottom of his literary fortunes. The rambling, sometimes opaque story concerns Kunemund's effort to care for Gertrud Tofote, orphan of his forester friend. Kunemund loses her to the world of wealth, egotism, and shallow urbanity because she receives an inheritance from Kunemund's brother, an evil-spirited colonial businessman, who leaves her the legacy, out of malice toward his brother, in the expectation that it will corrupt her.

Our concern here, however, is not with these matters, but with the narrator, one Emil von Schmidt. As so often, already the name attracts our attention: the combination of one of the commonest of German surnames with the particle of nobility—presumably a very minor nobility in consequence of some public service in the family past—constitutes a kind of oxymoron that Schmidt himself finds droll. More than that, it indicates an incongruity of the common and the elevated that marks Schmidt's character throughout. A man of independent means, he has abandoned his position as a mining engineer in the civil service to become "an unoccupied amateur of inexpensive aes-

thetic pleasures" and to write "dainty novellas" that no one reads; in that respect he is a comic counterpart to Kunemund. He is a man of reasonably lively mind but rather tepid affects, whose deprecating self-irony is a symptom of weakness rather than sovereignty and who recognizes his pleasure in being alone as "the most sublimated egotism." He likes to recite Schopenhauerian apothegms but in a wholly self-indulgent spirit. Schmidt's character contributes considerably to the opacity of the story, which he does not always seem intensely interested in telling. His claims of friendship with and for Kunemund sometimes seem exaggerated, and it is not clear that Kunemund fully trusts him. Schmidt in fact belongs to that world into which Gertrud is seduced by wealth and apparently innate secularism. He ultimately marries a formidably self-indulgent society lady whom he has initially perceived as a witch; the marriage occurs together with Gertrud's bleakly conventional one in an atmosphere both cynical and banal. (pp. 185-86)

The consequence is that it is hard to know what to think about what Schmidt tells us, particularly in regard to Kunemund. . . . [Schmidt] is not malign like Hahnenberg, but a vaguely well-meaning person, and he is not as complacently comfortable in his social role as he pretends, but is uncomfortable, even neurotic. He is the intellectual, aestheticist version of the *homme moyen sensuel,* and as such, with all his goodwill, he points up the profundity of Kunemund's isolation. He forces us to read through him to the story he purports to tell and makes us worry whether we can do it, for perhaps we are more like him than we are congruent with Kunemund. Here is one of Raabe's most original inventions: the basically sympathetic, intelligent narrator in whom there is nevertheless something lacking, some organ of perception, some ability to get out of his own skin.

He perhaps did not reach his full mastery of the technique here. Hajek has complained that Raabe sometimes collapses himself into his fictive narrator, "suddenly gives up his reserve and begins to give dictation to his chronicler ["Diskussionshorizonte: 'Meister Autor' im Kontext realistischen Erzählens," *Jahrbuch der Raabe-Gesellschaft,* 1981]. I am not sure that I accept this criticism, which is similar to that made of **The Children of Finkenrode.** It may fail to perceive that the characterization of the narrator is not only an assault on the public and the undercompetent reader, but can also be a vehicle of authorial self-analysis and self-irony. Still, the characterization of Schmidt may be shifted a little too much into the pejorative for Raabe's purposes, especially toward the end of the novel. Schmidt begins to resemble the caricatured aesthete Albin Brokenkorb in **On the Scrap-Iron.** Later, in **Old Nests,** Raabe tried another variant: the subdued narrator Fritz Langreuter, crippled in body and somewhat in soul, bereft of laughter and self-confidence. He is not unreliable in *what* he narrates; he is observant and often expresses Raabe's own views, but there is something lacking in him in interpersonal sensibility; he is utterly astonished to learn, when it is many years too late, that Eva Sixtus had liked him. Here Raabe has relieved the excessively pejorative characterization, but has replaced it with too much pathos that draws excessive attention to itself, unbalancing the delicate narrative relationship in another way. The fulfillment . . . was yet to come in the great first-person novels of his last phase: **Stuffcake** and **The Documents of the Birdsong.**

We may now return to our original question: what might the reason be for this complex, persistent experimentation with narrative technique on the part of an author who appeared to disclaim any strictly aesthetic or formalist ambitions? The question does not admit of an easy answer. Is it an unresolved dichotomy? Recently [Jost Schillemeit has] . . . said that Raabe wanted to narrate and also wanted something else "for which traditional literary typology offers no right name, something that is neither philosophy nor edifying tract nor aphorism but has something of all three of these genres and that was obviously often more important to him than carrying his plots forward" ["Ruminationen. Zur Entstehungsweise Raabescher Erzählungen," *Jahrbuch der Raabe-Gesellschaft,* 1981]. Actually, I think many writers want to do something like this; Raabe thought especially hard about how it might be done credibly. What was not credible for him was the alleged objectivity of programmatic realists. As Daemmrich has rightly said: Raabe's "use of devices abandoned by other novelists and the exploration of new possibilities in the reminiscence technique prevent the hidden subjectivism in the impersonal narrator of other Realists." While conventional realists seek mimetic intimacy, Raabe seeks distance, and, as Wayne Booth has said, "distance along one axis is sought for the sake of increasing the reader's involvement on some other axis." The one axis, along which Raabe distances himself, is clearly that of elementary storytelling—"and then . . . and then . . . and then . . . what next?" What is the other axis along which he means to involve us? One might say that it is the ethical, and one would not be wholly wrong. But his ethical "message," as elaborate as it may have been, was not so intricate as to require this vast repertoire of narrative devices. Something more must be at stake here. I think it may have been truth and integrity. Raabe had a strong realistic *motivation;* he really wanted to tell it how it was. But how things are is complicated, elusive, subject to perspective. Furthermore, mimetic conventions, he found, could not tell how things are; they only generated illusion by masking fictionality. To tell how things *really* are required a repudiation of illusion, an acknowledgment of fictionality, and a shift of focus onto the telling. Thus by logic, instinct, and the profoundest artistic probity, not by theory, not by epistemological conundrums, not by some preternatural "modernism," he came to the narrative experimentalism that strikes us as so "modern" and obstinately held to it in the teeth of a chorus of voices insisting that he was wrong, that he should get on with the story and tell the readers what to think so that they might be reassured in their own sense of rightness. (pp. 186-88)

Jeffrey L. Sammons, in his Wilhelm Raabe: The Fiction of the Alternative Community, *Princeton University Press, 1987, 421 p.*

FURTHER READING

Brill, E. V. K. "Raabe's Reception in England." *German Life and Letters* VIII, No. 4 (July 1955): 304-12.
 Examines the reception of *Abu Telfan* and *The Hunger Pastor.*

Bullivant, Keith. "Wilhelm Raabe and the European Novel." *Orbis Litterarum* 31, No. 4 (1976): 263-81.
 Contends that Raabe's representations of the alienated individual, social class, and political movements in his works signified a "crucial turning point" in German literature.

Coenen, F. E. "Wilhelm Raabe's Treatment of the Emigrant." *Studies in Philology* XXXIV, No. 4 (October 1937): 612-26.
 Discusses Raabe's nationalism and analyzes his characterization of German emigrés in several novels and stories.

Daemmrich, Horst S. *Wilhelm Raabe.* Boston: Twayne, 1981, 171 p.
 Offers critical interpretations of "those texts which are representative of Raabe's development as a novelist" and also includes discussion of biographical and historical facts relevant to Raabe's career.

Fairley, Barker. *Wilhelm Raabe: An Introduction to His Novels.* Oxford: Oxford University Press, 1961, 272 p.
 Overview of Raabe's major works and his place in the German literary canon.

———. "A Misinterpretation of Raabe's *Hastenbeck.*" *The Modern Language Review* LVII, No. 4 (October 1962): 575-78.
 Refutes Walter Frölich's interpretation of *Hastenbeck* in his essay "Das Verhältnis der Wackerhahuschen zum Bienchen von Boffzen" (*Mitteilungen der Raabe-Gesellschaft,* 1944) as untenable according to the facts of Raabe's story.

Field, G. Wallis. "Poetic Realists in Prose." In his *A Literary History of Germany: The Nineteenth Century 1830-1890,* pp. 94-130. London: Ernest Been, 1975.
 Examines Raabe's life, writing career, and the critical reception of his works.

Goetz, Marketa. "The Short Stories: A Possible Clue to Wilhelm Raabe." *The Germanic Review* XXXVII, No. 1 (January 1962): 55-67.
 Proposes that Raabe's later stories offer the clearest evidence of his anticipation of themes central to twentieth-century literature.

Hanson, William. "Some Basic Themes in Raabe." *German Life and Letters* XXI (1967-68): 121-30.
 Examines the philosophical and ethical import of Raabe's writings in order to illustrate that Raabe is "not interested in what is temporarily relevant but in what is universally significant."

———. "Raabe's Region." *Seminar* XXII, No. 4 (November 1986): 277-98.
 Contends that the importance of the *Heimat* ("native region") in Raabe's novels and stories has been obfuscated by critical biases toward the political intent of regional literature.

Holub, Robert C. "Raabe's Impartiality: A Reply to Horst Denkler." *The German Quarterly* 60, No. 4 (Fall 1989): 617-22.

Contests several remarks made by Horst Denkler in his essay "Das 'wirkliche Juda' und der 'Renegat' " (*German Quarterly,* 1987) on the subject of Raabe and anti-Semitism, writing that Denkler's essay, rather than objectively assessing Raabe's alleged anti-Semitism, instead conducts us "to the center of a seat of prejudices which even today in Germany refuse to go away."

Kaiser, Nancy A. "Reading Raabe's Realism: *Die Akten des Vogelsangs.*" *The Germanic Review* LIX, No. 1 (Winter 1984): 2-9.

Analyzes the role and persona of the narrator in *Die Akten des Vogelsangs.*

———. "The Elusive Center: Narration as Disorientation." In her *Social Integration and Narrative Structure: Patterns of Realism in Auerbach, Freytag, Fontane, and Raabe,* pp. 133-50. New York: Peter Lang, 1986.

Investigates narrative strategies and the role of the reader in several early and mature novels.

Kleineberger, H. R. "Charles Dickens and Wilhelm Raabe." *Oxford German Studies* 4 (1969): 90-117.

Compares similarities and differences between Charles Dickens's realist novels and those by Wilhelm Raabe and outlines the influence that Dickens's works exerted on Raabe.

Lensing, Leo A. *Narrative Structure and the Reader in Wilhelm Raabe's "Im Alten Eisen."* Bern, Germany: Peter Lang, 1977, 115 p.

Analyzes the "narrator-reader complex" in *Im Alten Eisen* in order to establish the "central importance of formal considerations in Raabe's attitude towards the novel."

———. "Reading Raabe: The Example of Kurt Tucholsky." *Seminar* XIX, No. 2 (May 1983): 122-35.

Contrasts the early twentieth-century critic and satirist Kurt Tucholsky's interest in Raabe with that espoused by the Raabe Society in order to illustrate that Raabe's works appealed to right-wing and liberal readers alike.

———, and Peter, Hans-Werner, eds. *Wilhelm Raabe: Studien zu seinem Leben und Werk.* Braunschweig: Verlag, 1981, 609 p.

Collects essays in English and German that address the themes, style, and relevance of Raabe's works from a number of critical perspectives, including feminist, New Critical, historicist, and formalist.

Pascal, Roy. "The Reminiscence-Technique in Raabe." *The Modern Language Review* XLIX, No. 3 (July 1954): 339-48.

Considers Raabe's use of reported speech, a fictional narrator, and reminiscence technique in order to define the relationship between narrative structure and thematic content in his novels.

Radcliffe, S. "Wilhelm Raabe, the Thirty Years War and the Novelle." *German Life and Letters* XXII (1968-69): 220-29.

Discusses Raabe's treatment of the Thirty Years War in the novella *Else von der Tanne* as an allegory that reflects his understanding of historical progress and the social community.

———. "Wilhelm Raabe and the Railway." *New German Studies* 2, No. 2 (Summer 1974): 131-44.

Examines images of the railway and accounts of train-travel in Raabe's novels and outlines the social significance of the railroad in nineteenth-century Germany.

———. "Gottfried Keller's 'Keltische Knochen' and Wilhelm Raabe's 'Mammoth'." *German Life and Letters* XLI, No. 2 (January 1988): 99-105.

Compares Raabe's and Keller's respective stories based on archaeological discoveries, concluding that there exist "considerable disparities between their two apparently parallel developments."

Sammon, Jeffrey L. "Wilhelm Raabe as Successor to Young Germany." *Monatshefte* 77, No. 4 (Winter 1975): 449-59.

Cites evidence of Raabe's personal acquaintance with such Young German authors as Karl Gutzkow, Ferdinand Freiligrath, and Georg Herwegh and his references to their works in several novels as evidence that Raabe was influenced by and preserved the "Young German Spirit."

———. "Raabe's Ravens." *Michigan Germanic Studies* XI, No. 1 (Spring 1985): 1-15.

Examines the frequent use of the raven as a symbol in Raabe's novels. The raven acts, according to Sammons, not as an allegorical symbol with a single meaning but as a polyvalent symbol "to which several associations accrue."

———. "The Mill on the Sewer." *Orbis Litterarum* 40, No. 1 (1985): 16-32.

Analyzes the style and socially engaged themes of *Pfister's Mill.*

Sander, Volkmar. Introduction to *Novels,* by Wilhelm Raabe, translated by John E. Woods and Barker Fairley and edited by Volkmar Sander, pp. xi-xvii. New York: Continuum, 1983.

Sketch of Raabe's life and works.

Sanford, David. "Wilhelm Raabe's *Der Hungerpastor:* The Quest for the Golden Apples." *The Germanic Review* LXI, No. 2 (Spring 1986): 42-9.

Analyzes allusions to Norse mythology in *The Hunger Pastor* in order to elucidate several characters, symbols, and events, thus establishing "a new level of meaning in a work which, despite its flaws and shortcomings, continues to deserve critical attention."

Silz, Walter. "Freytag's *Soll und Haben* and Raabe's *Der Hungerpastor. Modern Language Notes* XXXIX, No. 1 (January 1924): 10-18.

Highlights similarities between *The Hunger Pastor* and Gustav Freytag's *Soll und Haben,* suggesting that Raabe was influenced by Freytag's popular novel.

———. "Pessimism in Raabe's Stuttgart Triology." *Publications of the Modern Language Association of America* XXXIX, No. 3 (September 1924): 687-704.

Analyzes the major characters and themes in the novels *The Hunger Pastor, Abu Telfan,* and *Der Schüdderump,* contending that each novel progressively develops Raabe's pessimistic worldview.

Stankiewicz, Marketa Goetz. "The Tailor and the Sweeper: A New Look at Wilhelm Raabe." In *Essays on German Literature in Honour of G. Joyce Hallamore,* edited by Michael S.

Batts and Marketa Goetz Stankiewicz, pp. 152-76. Toronto: University of Toronto Press, 1968.

Discusses the moral, ethical, and philosophical issues raised in Raabe's works.

Webster, W. T. "Hesitation and Decision: Wilhelm Raabe's Road to Reality." *Forum for Modern Language Studies* XV, No. 1 (January 1979): 69-85.

Examines Raabe's objectives as a realist and discusses the themes and techniques of *Alte Nester* and the novel fragment *Alterhausen.*

————. "Social Change and Personal Insecurity in the Late Novels of Wilhelm Raabe." In *Formen Realistischer Erzählkunst: Festschrift for Charlotte Jolles,* edited by Jörg Thunecke and Eda Sagarra, pp. 233-43. Nottingham, England: Sherwood Press Agencies, 1979.

Formalist analysis of the images, symbols, and motifs found in the late novels *Unruhige GÄste* and *Die Akten des Vogelsangs,* highlighting Raabe's treatment of existential, artistic, and philosophical issues.

Bernard Shaw

Pygmalion

(Full name George Bernard Shaw; also wrote under the pseudonym Corno di Bassetto) Irish dramatist, essayist, critic, novelist, short story writer, and poet.

The following entry presents criticism of Shaw's drama *Pygmalion: A Romance in Five Acts,* first published and performed (in German) in 1913; first English performance in 1914. For discussion of Shaw's complete career, see *TCLC,* Volumes 3 and 9; for discussion of his drama *Man and Superman: A Comedy and a Philosophy,* see *TCLC,* Volume 21.

INTRODUCTION

Shaw is generally considered the greatest dramatist to write in the English language since William Shakespeare, and *Pygmalion* is one of his most popular and critically esteemed plays. An account of a Cockney flower-seller who is trained, chiefly through phonetics, to pass as a lady in society, *Pygmalion* addresses such economic, social, and educational issues as the inequitable distribution of wealth, the differences between social classes and obstacles to overcoming them, and the value of education.

Beginning in the 1890s Shaw helped effect the intellectual revival of the English theater through his drama reviews, his own plays, and critical works promoting the best European drama. In *The Quintessence of Ibsenism* (1891), for example, he championed the Norwegian dramatist Henrik Ibsen, whose social-problem plays revolutionized late nineteenth-century drama; many commentators have discerned Shaw's own aesthetic principles in his analyses of Ibsen's works. By the time that six of Shaw's early dramas were collected in 1898 as *Plays: Pleasant and Unpleasant,* he was established as one of England's foremost dramatists and most renowned intellectual figures. Always vitally interested in the production of his plays, he worked closely with actors, managers, directors, and producers, forming friendships with many of them, including the acclaimed Mrs. Patrick Campbell. She undertook some of Shaw's most substantial roles, including that of Raina Petkoff in *Arms and the Man* (1894) and Vivie Warren in *Mrs. Warren's Profession* (1902). Shaw wrote in 1897 that he imagined Campbell in the role of "an east end doña in an apron" opposite an aristocratic male lead. Sustaining this conception for more than fifteen years, Shaw would consider no other actress for the role of eighteen-year-old Eliza Doolittle when the first English cast of *Pygmalion* was assembled in 1914, although Campbell was forty-seven at the time. Shaw and Campbell engaged in a romantic affair believed to have been one of Shaw's most serious extramarital involvements, despite the fact that Campbell, then a widow, was contemplating marriage to another man. Shortly before the play opened in 1914 she

abruptly disappeared and returned after missing rehearsal to reveal that she was newly wed. This exacerbated tensions between Shaw, Campbell, and Sir Herbert Beerbohm Tree, who was cast as Henry Higgins. These strong-willed individuals clashed personally and professionally during pre-production, but when the play premiered in England on 11 April 1914, it was enthusiastically received. Drawing record audiences over the course of its initial English run, *Pygmalion* represents a pinnacle in the careers of those involved.

Pygmalion derives its title from a classical myth recorded by Ovid that has inspired numerous works of prose, poetry, and painting: repulsed by the imperfections of human women but craving companionship, the artist Pygmalion sculpts a perfect female figure with which he falls in love. The goddess Venus grants the statue life, and maker and creation are married. Shaw's *Pygmalion* centers on the relationship between Henry Higgins, an overbearing middle-aged professor of phonetics, and Eliza Doolittle, a Cockney flower-seller who wants to master genteel speech in order to become "a lady in a flower shop" instead of a street peddler. Higgins wagers with an associate, Colonel Pickering, that six months of his phonetic training will eradicate all traces of the young woman's origins, enabling her to move freely in the highest levels of society. She agrees to be tutored by Higgins and studies assiduously, while he and Pickering relish her candid responses to elevated social and cultural spheres. In what is regarded as one of the funniest scenes ever written for the English theater, Eliza shocks a group of socialites by reminiscing in her newly mastered perfect English about incidents which she does not realize her listeners consider unspeakably sordid. She caps the episode by uttering, with impeccable diction, the vulgarism "Not bloody likely!" Ultimately Eliza meets with unqualified social success at a garden party, a dinner party, and an ambassadorial reception, where a professional interpreter and phonetician, a rival of Higgins, insists that her elegant speech betokens royal blood.

While the depiction of Eliza's success in high society would have concluded a traditional well-made play, the triumphant scene at the reception was not even included in the original production, but only recapitulated by Higgins and Pickering at the beginning of Act IV. True to the dictates of the Shavian discussion drama or problem play, *Pygmalion* continues for two more acts—a dramatic structure resembling that of Ibsen's *A Doll's House* (1879)—in order to address the question of Eliza Doolittle's future, which is closely tied to the economic, social, and educational issues that underlie the action. Throughout *Pygmalion* various characters display widely disparate attitudes toward money. Eliza, though somewhat parsimonious, is willing to commit a large percentage of her income as a flower-seller to the education that she believes will enable her to rise above her social class. Her father, on the other hand, who describes himself as one of "the undeserving poor," extorts a small amount of money from Higgins but refuses the offer of a larger sum, explaining that substantial wealth would hinder his preferred mode of existence by requiring responsibility. When an unexpected bequest makes him rich, he regrets being forced into a "respectable" way of life. Representing another perspective, Higgins's mother perceives that through her education Eliza has acquired "the manners and habits that disqualify a fine lady from earning her own living without giving her a fine lady's income." Eliza, too, maintains that after living as an upper-class lady, she is equally unfit to return to the streets or to work in a shop. She determines to join Higgins's rival as a speech instructor and to marry and support Freddy Eynsford Hill, a well-meaning but ineffectual and impoverished young man who fell in love with her when she first ventured into society.

This denouement has been one of the most problematic aspects of *Pygmalion* since its first performance, and it remains the most analyzed feature of the play. Convinced that only the implication of romance between the two principals would draw audiences, during the play's English premier Beerbohm Tree sought to imply that Higgins and Eliza would reconcile and eventually marry. He introduced an unscripted bit of stage direction, tossing a bouquet to the departing Eliza between the closing dialogue and the fall of the curtain, and many subsequent directors have adhered to Tree's interpretation of the play as a conventional love story of attraction between opposing personalities. In an attempt to correct the impression created by Tree's performance, in 1915 Shaw wrote and published a prose epilogue detailing Eliza's subsequent career and marriage to Eynsford Hill. Some commentators consider Shaw's the only reasonable conclusion, given the clearly adversarial relationship that has been established and Eliza's hard-won poise and self-sufficiency. Others, however, suggest that a thematically unambiguous play would not need such emphatic explication as Shaw's epilogue; they continue to explore the question of affectionate or erotic ties between Higgins and Eliza. Gabriel Pascal filmed *Pygmalion* in 1938 with Shaw's ending as well as one of his own, in which Eliza comes back to Higgins. Shaw permitted the film's release with Pascal's conclusion. In 1956 Alan Jay Lerner based the musical comedy *My Fair Lady* on *Pygmalion*, retaining much of Shaw's original dialogue but following Pascal's lead in reversing Shaw's denouement; in 1964 the lavish Hollywood film of the musical garnered numerous awards and honors.

A play of great vitality and charm, *Pygmalion* retains enormous appeal for audiences and continues to inspire numerous analyses for Shavian scholars. Commentators have analyzed *Pygmalion* as a comedy, traditional romance, social-problem play, modern retelling of classical myth, and as an indictment of the factors that contribute to class distinctions in a capitalist society. Acknowledging its success, Shaw commented that "there must be something radically wrong with the play if it pleases everybody, but at the moment I cannot find what it is." *Pygmalion* combines characteristic Shavian concerns, including educational and economic issues, with apt characterizations and scintillating dialogue, all drafted by perhaps the surest comic hand in modern dramaturgy.

Desmond MacCarthy (essay date 1914)

[*MacCarthy was one of the foremost English literary and drama critics of the twentieth century, serving for many years on the staff of the* New Statesman *and as editor of* Life and Letters. *In the following excerpt from a review of a 1914 performance of* Pygmalion, *MacCarthy considers the principal ideas presented in the play.*]

Pygmalion? It looked like a misnomer. The story of Mr Shaw's play on the face of it was that of an artist who turns a live girl into a work of art, and then by a considerable effort of self-control refrains from falling in love with her! It is an exhilarating, amusing, and often a deep comedy. . . . Like all good comedies, it is full of criticism of life; in this case criticism of social barriers and distinctions, of the disinterested yet ferocious egotism of artists, of genteel standards, of the disadvantages of respectability, of the contrast between man's sense of values and woman's, and of the complexity and misunderstanding which a difference of sex introduces into human relations, however passionately one of the two may resolve to sink the He and She. During the course of the story, light—and sometimes it is a penetrating ray indeed—is thrown into all these corners of life. I hardly know how to tackle a play which bristles with so many points, especially as I must confess that I am not certain I understood the play as a whole. Has it an idea or does it simply bristle? The merriment of intellectual antics is in it; the wit of penetration: 'the difference between a flower girl and a duchess is not how she behaves but how she is treated'—there is a good deal in that comment upon manners. Mr Doolittle . . . is Mr Shaw's most amusing achievement, in his Dickens vein of exaggeration. Doolittle (if he were a horse he might be described as by High-Spirits out of Social Science) is the philosophy of 'the undeserving poor', incarnate and articulate. He does not exist; but he is sufficiently like a type to make one fancy Nature may have been aiming at him. All the minor characters are well drawn.

Henry Higgins is an extremely interesting study; Eliza is excellent, but she is interesting chiefly from her situation—a flower-girl who after six months' training at the hands of Higgins, the professor of phonetics, can be passed off in society as a lady. That, of course, is the story, the simple circumference of the play; but where does the centre of interest lie? In the relation between Pygmalion-Higgins and Eliza-Galatea? I though so while I was in the theatre, and my feelings at the end of the play were in one sense highly flattering to the dramatist, to his power of entertaining and interesting, for when the curtain fell on the mutual explanations of this pair I was in a fever to see it rise on Acts VI and VII; I wanted to see those two living together; I wanted to get to the *point* which I conceived was still ahead. Afterwards I grasped what I now take to be the idea: there was point in the title **Pygmalion** after all; the statue did become alive; Acts II, III, and IV, during which Eliza was being moulded into a lady, were not the miracle, but merely the chipping of the statue itself from the rough block; but in Act V something happened, she had got a soul, and therefore the play was really over. I felt inclined, however, to credit myself with uncommon penetration when I discovered what had happened to Eliza in the fifth act. Perhaps when I read my fellow critics I shall discover that what I found with effort was quite obvious to them. In that case I retract in advance the criticism that Mr Shaw has huddled up his climax, and failed to arrange the perspective of the dialogue so that the mind is led easily up to the central point. Now the last act is, and is not, a love scene; Pygmalion-Higgins, like other Shavian heroes, is running away from passion. . . . The experiment is over; it has been a triumph for his art as professor of phonetics; Eliza has passed through the stage of talking like a flower girl with a mechanical meticulous pronunciation (Act III); she has become, both in the matter as well as the manner of her conversation, indistinguishable from a born lady; Higgins has won his wager. She has run away from him because she has found intolerable his tyranny and his disregard for her as a human being with feelings (Act IV). All along she has shown a spaniel-like docility and gratitude which he has never thought of recognising. He has fagged her about right and left; she has become useful, almost necessary to him in practical ways; but the more she tries to please and touch him the more harshly impersonal he becomes. But when she runs away he is frantic to get her back. The question is on what terms; he won't offer her anything more than he gave her before and does not understand at first that

she only wants to be treated like a human being. Then she turns on him: threatens to his dismay, to go off to his rival with all the secrets of his art; in short, shakes him off and stands on her own feet as an independent human being. The statue has become alive, during the six months' hard training she had acquired the outward signs of self-respect, but she never had the inward reality till this moment. Henceforward she is a person he can reckon upon, and his fear of her disappears. That I take it is the theme of the play.

Higgins is called a professor of phonetics, but he is really an artist—that is the interesting thing about him, and his character is a study of the creative temperament. We have met him before in an early novel by Mr Shaw; he is Mr Jack the composer in **Love among the Artists.** The gesture with which Higgins flings money at Eliza in the first act after browbeating her, the chivalry and roughness of it, is a repetition of the scene at Paddington when Jack gives all the money he has in his pockets to Gwendolen to whom, by the bye, he also subsequently taught elocution, bullying her into perfection and bitterly disappointing and puzzling her by treating their relation, which had begun so romantically, as a sternly matter-of-fact impersonal one the moment she became his pupil. Jack thought only of the job in hand. If, on the one hand, he treated her as though she were a machine he had to get into order, on the other, when he had made her a fine actress he no more expected gratitude from her than he did from the paper on which he had written a sonata. Higgins behaves in the same way to Eliza. Like Jack he has a total disregard of people's feelings, he is outrageously inconsiderate, and yet he is most human. His impatience is the impatience of the artist who only asks Heaven for peace to devote himself to his work. (pp. 108-11)

Act IV is the most dramatic of the five. The three of them have been out to a fashionable dinner; Eliza has been perfect. She is to all intents and purposes a *lady*. The two men begin talking, Eliza sits apart. They are triumphant and tired. What a grind it has been—oof! it's over *at last,* what a blessing, what a triumph! While they are talking like this in her presence, there she sits, stony, miserable, stunned . . . ; Higgins has not the smallest inkling of what all this drilling and training has cost Eliza herself, or how hard she has tried to learn. It has been hard enough work for him chipping the statue out of the block, but the marble itself has suffered more. (p. 111)

> *Desmond MacCarthy, in his* Shaw, *MacGibbon & Kee, 1951, 217 p.*

Eric Bentley   (essay date 1947)

[*Bentley is considered one of the most erudite and innovative critics of the modern theater. He was responsible for introducing Bertolt Brecht, Luigi Pirandello, and other European dramatists to American audiences through his commentary, translations, and adaptations of their works. In his criticism, Bentley concentrates on the playwright and the dramatic text, rather than on production aspects of the play. In the following excerpt, he assesses the structure of* Pygmalion, *focusing on the function of the final two acts.*]

Pygmalion is a characteristic instance of a personal play. And it is characteristic that many people think of it as very disquisitory. At least it at first seems to conform to Shaw's formula: exposition, complication, discussion. But let us take a closer look.

Pygmalion is the story, in five Acts, of Henry Higgins' attempt to make a duchess out of a flower girl. Act I is really a sort of prologue in which the two main characters encounter each other. The action proper starts in Act II when Higgins decides to make the experiment. In Act III the experiment reaches its first stage when Eliza appears in upper-class company behaving like an imperfectly functioning mechanical doll. Readers of Bergson will understand why this scene gets more laughs than all the others put together, so that to the groundlings the rest of the play seems a prolonged anti-climax. Has not Shaw blundered? What ought to be the climax seems to have been left out: it is between Acts III and IV that Eliza is finally passed off as a duchess at an ambassador's party. Would not Sarcey have called this the *scène à faire?* When the curtain goes up on Act IV all is over; Eliza has triumphed. Higgins is satisfied, bored, and wondering what to do next. The comedy is over. But there are two more acts!

"The play is now virtually over but the characters will discuss it at length for two Acts more." Such is the curtain line of Act I in a later Shaw play. It is one of those Shavian jokes which appear to be against Shaw but are really against the vulgar opinion of Shaw. The two Acts that follow (in *Too True To Be Good*) are *not* a discussion of what happens in Act I. Nor are the last two acts of *Pygmalion* as purely disquisitory as they at first seem.

Certainly, the big event occurs between the Acts, and the last two Acts *are* a "discussion" of the consequences. But the discussion is of the second of the types defined above: it is not so much that the consequences are discussed as that the consequences are worked out and determined by a conflict that is expressed in verbal swordplay. There is no pretence of objectivity. Each character speaks for himself, and speaks, not as a contributor to a debate, but as one whose life is at stake. Eliza is talking to free herself. Higgins is talking to keep his domination over her. The conclusion of conversations of this kind is not the statement of a principle (as in Plato's symposia or even Shaw's *Getting Married*) but the making of a decision. Ibsen's Nora slams the door, his Ellida decides to stay at home. What happens to Eliza? What *can* happen, now that the flower girl is a duchess, the statue a flesh-and-blood Galatea?

In the original romance, so lyrically revived by Shaw's friend William Morris, Pygmalion marries Galatea. Might not something of the kind be possible for Shaw, since Pygmalion is a life-giver, a symbol of vitality, since in Eliza the crime of poverty has been overcome, the sin of ignorance cancelled? Or might not Higgins and Eliza be the "artist man" and "mother woman" discussed in *Man and Superman*? They might—if Shaw actually went to work so allegorically, so abstractly, so idealistically. Actually *Pygmalion: a Romance* stands related to Romance precisely as *The Devil's Disciple* stands to Melodrama or *Candida* to Domestic Drama. It is a serious parody, a

translation into the language of "natural history." The primary inversion is that of Pygmalion's character. The Pygmalion of Romance turns a statue into a human being. The Pygmalion of "natural history" tries to turn a human being into a statue, tries to make of Eliza Doolittle a mechanical doll in the role of a duchess. Or rather he tries to make from one kind of doll—a flower girl who cannot afford the luxury of being human—another kind of doll—a duchess to whom manners are an adequate substitute for morals.

There is a character named Pygmalion in *Back to Methuselah.* He is a sort of Frankenstein or Pavlov. He thinks that you can put together a man by assembling mechanical parts. Henry Higgins also thinks he has made a person—or at least an amenable slave—when he has "assembled" a duchess. But the monster turns against Frankenstein. Forces have been brought into play of which the man-maker knows nothing. And Shaw's Pygmalion has helped into being a creature even more mysterious than a monster: a human being.

If the first stage of Higgins' experiment was reached when Eliza made her *faux pas* before Mrs. Higgins' friends, and the second when she appeared in triumph at the ball, Shaw, who does not believe in endings, sees her through two more stages in the final acts of his play, leaving her still very much in flux at the end. The third stage is rebellion. Eliza's feelings are wounded because, after the reception, Higgins does not treat her kindly, but talks of her as a guinea pig. Eliza has acquired finer feelings.

While some have felt that the play should end with the reception, others have felt that it could end with the suggestion that Eliza has begun to rebel. It seems, indeed, that the creator of the role of Eliza thought this. In her memoirs Mrs. Patrick Campbell wrote:

> The last act of the play did not travel across the footlights with as clear dramatic sequence as the preceding acts—owing entirely to the fault of the author.

The sympathetic analyst of the play will more probably agree with Shaw himself who, Mrs. Campbell says, "declared I might be able to play a tune with one finger, but a full orchestral score was Greek to me." The fifth act of *Pygmalion* is far from superfluous. It is the climax. The arousing of Eliza's resentment in the fourth Act was the birth of a soul. But to be born is not enough. One must also grow up. Growing up is the fourth and last stage of Eliza's evolution. This consummation is reached in the final "discussion" with Higgins—a piece of dialogue that is superb comedy not only because of its wit and content but also because it proceeds from a dramatic situation, perhaps the most dramatic of all dramatic situations: two completely articulate characters engaged in a battle of words on which both their fates depend. It is a Strindbergian battle of wills. But not of sex. Higgins will never marry. He wants to remain in the relation of God the Creator as far as Eliza is concerned. For her part Eliza will marry. But she won't marry Higgins.

The play ends with Higgins' knowingly declaring that Eliza is about to do his shopping for him despite her protestations to the contrary: a statement which actors and critics often take to mean that the pair are a Benedick and Beatrice who will marry in the end. One need not quote Shaw's own sequel to prove the contrary. The whole point of the great culminating scene is that Eliza has now become not only a person but an independent person. The climax is sharp:

> LIZA. If I can't have kindness, I'll have independence.
>
> HIGGINS. Independence? That's middle class blasphemy. We are all dependent on one another, every soul of us on earth.
>
> LIZA. (*rising determinedly*) I'll let you see whether I'm dependent on you. If you can preach, I can teach. I'll go and be a teacher.
>
> HIGGINS. What'll you teach, in heaven's name?
>
> LIZA. What you taught me. I'll teach phonetics.
>
> HIGGINS. Ha! ha! ha!
>
> LIZA. I'll offer myself as an assistant to Professor Nepean.
>
> HIGGINS. (*rising in a fury*) What! That impostor! That humbug! That toadying ignoramus! Teach him *my* methods! *my* discoveries! You take one step in his direction and I'll wring your neck. (*He lays hands on her.*) Do you hear?
>
> LIZA. (*defiantly non-resistant*) Wring away. What do I care? I knew you'd strike me some day. (*He lets her go, stamping with rage. . . .*)

With this cry of victory (it rings in my ears in the intonation of Miss Gertrude Lawrence who succeeded where Mrs. Patrick Campbell seems to have failed) Eliza wins her freedom. Higgins had said: "I can do without anybody. I have my own soul." And now Eliza can say: "Now . . . I'm not afraid of you and can do without you." After this it does not matter whether Eliza does the shopping or not. The situation is clear. Eliza's fate is settled as far as Higgins is concerned. The story of the experiment is over. Otherwise her fate is as unsettled as yours or mine. This is a true naturalistic ending—not an arbitrary break, but a conclusion which is also a beginning.

Pygmalion is a singularly elegant structure. If again we call Act I the prologue, the play falls into two parts of two Acts apiece. Both parts are Pygmalion myths. In the first a duchess is made out of a flower girl. In the second a woman is made out of a duchess. Since these two parts are the main, inner action the omission of the climax of the outer action—the ambassador's reception—will seem particularly discreet, economical, and dramatic. The movie version of *Pygmalion* was not the richer for its inclusion. To include a climax that is no climax only blurs the outline of the play. *Pygmalion* is essentially theatrical in construction. It is built in chunks, two by two. The fluidity of the screen is quite inappropriate to it. On the screen, as in the novel, a development of character naturally occurs gradually and smoothly. Natasha in *War and Peace* passes imperceptibly from girlhood to womanhood; Eliza in *Pygmalion* proceeds in dramatically marked stages—one,

two, three, four, Act by Act. Perhaps we never realized before how utterly "of the theatre" the Shaw movies how utterly "of the theatre" the Shaw plays are.

As we might have learned to expect, *Pygmalion* follows the pattern of earlier Shavian works, not duplicating them but following up another aspect of a similar problem. We have seen how the eponymous character is often the representative of vitality and that he remains constant like a catalyst while producing change in others, especially in the antagonist whom he is educating, disillusioning, or converting. *Pygmalion* diverges from the type in that the life-giver, for all his credentials, and his title of Pygmalion, is suspect. He is not really a life-giver at all. To be sure, Eliza is even more palpably his pupil than Judith was Dick's or Brassbound Lady Cicely's. But the "education of Eliza" in Acts I to III is a caricature of the true process. In the end Eliza turns the tables on Higgins, for she, finally, is the vital one, and he is the prisoner of "system," particularly of his profession.

Ironically parallel with the story of Eliza is the story of her father. Alfred Doolittle is also suddenly lifted out of slumdom by the caprice of Pygmalion-Higgins. He too has to break bread with dukes and duchesses. Unlike his daughter, however, he is not reborn. He is too far gone for that. He is the same rich as he was poor, the same or worse; for riches carry awful responsibilities, and Doolittle commits the cardinal sin on the Shavian scale—he is irresponsible. In the career of the undeserving poor suddenly become undeserving rich Shaw writes his *social* comedy, his Unpleasant Play, while in the career of his deserving daughter he writes his *human* comedy, his Pleasant Play. Those who think that *Pygmalion* is about class society are thinking of Doolittle's comedy rather than Eliza's. The two are carefully related by parallelism and contrast. One might work out an interpretation of the play by comparing their relation to the chief "artificial system" depicted in it—middle-class morality.

In short, the merit of *Pygmalion* cannot be explained by Shaw's own account of the nature of modern drama, much less by popular or academic opinion concerning Problem Plays, Discussion Drama, Drama of Ideas, and the like. It is a good play by perfectly orthodox standards and needs no theory to defend it. It is Shavian, not in being made up of political or philosophic discussions, but in being based on the standard conflict of vitality and system, in working out this conflict through an inversion of romance, in bringing matters to a head in a battle of wills and words, in having an inner psychological action in counterpoint to the outer romantic action, in existing on two contrasted levels of mentality, both of which are related to the main theme, in delighting and surprising us with a constant flow of verbal music and more than verbal wit. (pp. 119-26)

> *Eric Bentley, in his* Bernard Shaw, *New Directions Books, 1947, 242 p.*

Milton Crane (essay date 1951)

[*Crane was an American educator, anthologist, and critic. In the following essay, he analyzes the extent to which*

Pygmalion *adheres to Shaw's critical theories regarding the discussion drama.*]

In the last of his many discussions of the so-called play of ideas, Bernard Shaw remarked, "I was, and still am, the most old-fashioned playwright outside China and Japan" [*Theatre Arts,* August, 1950]. This is one of the few statements that Shaw made about his own work of which we may safely believe every word—always assuming him to be correct about China and Japan. He was, to be sure, merely echoing his earlier confession in the Preface to **Three Plays For Puritans,** in which he had defended **The Devil's Disciple** against a reckless charge of originality: "If it applies to the incidents, plot, construction, and general professional and technical qualities of the play, [it] is nonsense; for the truth is, I am in these matters a very old-fashioned playwright." He elsewhere admonished us: "Remember that my business as a classic writer of comedies is 'to chasten morals with ridicule' . . . " [Preface, *The Complete Plays of Bernard Shaw*]. It is my purpose here to describe and interpret some of the stages through which Shaw passed and some of the attitudes which he assumed in the course of coming to such conclusions.

The revised edition of **The Quintessence of Ibsenism** "now completed to the death of Ibsen" was published in 1913.

It contained two new chapters, one of which, "The Technical Novelty in Ibsen's Plays," remains a crucial statement of Shaw's dramatic theory. It argues that Ibsen effected a revolution in dramaturgy, although the critics characteristically remained unaware of it. "To this day," says Shaw,

> they remain blind to a new technical factor in the art of popular stage-play making which every considerable playwright has been thrusting under their noses night after night for a whole generation. This technical factor in the play is the discussion. Formerly you had in what was called a well made play an exposition in the first act, a situation in the second, and unravelling in the third. Now you have exposition, situation, and discussion; and the discussion is the test of the playwright. The critics protest in vain. They declare that discussions are not dramatic, and that art should not be didactic. Neither the playwrights nor the public take the smallest notice of them. The discussion conquered Europe in Ibsen's *Doll's House;* and now the serious playwright recognizes in the discussion not only the main test of his highest powers, but also the real centre of his play's interest.

But, Shaw goes on to complain, *A Doll's House,* in spite

Mrs. Patrick Campbell, the first English performer to portray Eliza Doolittle, for whom Shaw intended the role.

of its success in driving out the well made play, concentrated the element of discussion in the final scene, so that this epoch-making play, in spite of its supposedly great technical advance, "might be turned into a very ordinary French drama by the excision of a few lines, and the substitution of a sentimental happy ending for the famous last scene." In performance, it had proved only too simple to omit the discussion in the final scene, and, Shaw admits, "The disadvantage of putting the discussion at the end was not only that it came when the audience was fatigued, but that it was necessary to see the play over again, so as to follow the earlier acts in the light of the final discussion, before it became fully intelligible." Consequently, it became necessary not merely to replace the dénouement of the well made play by discussion, but also to disperse the discussion throughout the entire play. "Accordingly," Shaw continues, "we now have plays, including some of my own, which begin with discussion and end with action, and others in which the discussion interpenetrates the action from beginning to end."

Surely the admission that *A Doll's House* requires only "the excision of a few lines" and some manipulation of the final scene to become a well made play is enough to make one wonder whether Ibsen might not, after all, have been writing a well made play. Shaw's tendentious praise of *A Doll's House* required Ibsen to appear in the guise of a technical innovator, but the modern reader is very likely to conclude that Ibsen employed a conventional and very effective dramatic technique for the presentation of novel and startling subject matter. Shaw apparently felt that the success of his polemic against the critics depended upon an exaltation of the peculiar and original character of the achievement of Ibsen both as thinker and artist.

If *A Doll's House* does not afford Shaw a perfectly satisfactory illustration of the discussion play, Ibsen's other plays are scarcely more helpful. Shaw's own analyses of *The Wild Duck* and *Hedda Gabler,* for example, emphasize Ibsen's brilliant craftsmanship, but cannot be used to demonstrate the revolutionary nature of Ibsen's technique. We remember Shaw's significant parenthesis, with reference to the development of the discussion play: "We now have plays, *including some of my own,* which begin with discussion and end with action. . . . " Very well: let us admit that Shaw merely fathered on Ibsen a theory which applied not to Ibsen's plays but to Shaw's own; let us agree with G. K. Chesterton and his many imitators that Shaw's book should have been called *The Quintessence of Shavianism.* But to what extent is Shaw's theory reflected even in Shaw's own work?

Pygmalion, one of Shaw's greatest popular successes, seems an especially appropriate play on which to test the theory. It was written in 1912 and first produced, in Berlin, in 1913—the year of the revised edition of *The Quintessence of Ibsenism.* It is, according to Shaw, an extremely didactic play; the Preface, entitled "A Professor of Phonetics," informs us that *Pygmalion* "is so intensely and deliberately didactic, and its subject esteemed so dry, that I delight in throwing it at the heads of the wiseacres who repeat the parrot cry that art should never be didactic. It goes to prove my contention that art should never be any-

thing else." Doubtless a play with so much to teach could use the discussion form to excellent advantage. Let us briefly analyze *Pygmalion* in terms of Shaw's formula to see how well the play actually follows the pattern.

The five acts of *Pygmalion* dispose themselves as follows. Act I introduces the chief characters—in fact, almost all the characters—of the play, presenting them in significant action and clearly foreshadowing the lines of development of the action. Act II, in which Higgins accepts Liza as a student and makes his bet with Colonel Pickering, and Act III, in which Liza discourses on the weather and other themes in Mrs. Higgins' drawing room, show us the transformation of Liza from a ragamuffin into a talking doll. Acts IV and V, the aftermath of Liza's triumph at the garden party, deal with the transformation of the doll into a woman. [In *Bernard Shaw*] Eric Bentley has with reason praised the "singularly elegant structure" of *Pygmalion,* pointing out that the metamorphosis of Galatea occurs not once but twice. How does this "intensely and deliberately didactic" play employ the all-important element of discussion?

Act I is far too much concerned with exposition to allow any time for contemplation or discussion. Act II has a brief interlude of discussion contributed by that paragon of dustmen, Alfred Doolittle. His theme is "middle class morality," the bugaboo that prevents him from selling Liza to Higgins—hardly a significant element in the play. Doolittle delivers a superb comic monologue and disappears until he is again needed, in Act V, for much the same purpose. Act III has even less discussion than Act II, being chiefly taken up with violent comic action. Acts IV and V, on the other hand, are a discussion but, as Eric Bentley says, in a very special sense of the word: "It is not so much that the consequences [of Liza's success at the garden party] are discussed as that the consequences are worked out and determined by a conflict that is expressed in verbal swordplay." In other words, an important event takes place offstage, altering the relationship of the principal characters. The remainder of the action of the play may be described as the efforts of these characters to define their new relationship. Like all characters in all plays, they are moved to comment at some length on this profoundly interesting subject. If this be discussion, as Shaw understands the term, then the greatest of all discussion plays is obviously *Hamlet.*

Virtually nowhere in *Pygmalion* do the characters discuss phonetics, despite Shaw's specific statement that phonetics is the subject of the play. The discussion in Acts IV and V deals with quite a different matter: the transformation of Liza as a result of Higgins' experiment. Moreover, it comes at the climax of the play, when the principals, far from engaging in any discussion of phonetics, are locked in a violent emotional struggle.

But another possibility suggests itself. Granted that Act I of *Pygmalion* deals with exposition, and that Acts II and III develop a dramatic situation: is it forbidden to think that Act IV offers a catastrophe much like that of the more conventional play, and that Act V carries us to a conclusion of classic comedy?

Here we must briefly reopen an ancient argument. The celebrated—or notorious—ending of *Pygmalion,* with its ambiguity about the future of Liza and Higgins, has of course been explained at length and with vigor by Shaw in his Epilogue to the published play. Liza was to marry Freddy, because psychology and sociology demanded it. She could not possibly marry Higgins; she was too sensible, and he too much attached to his mother. It must be so, since Shaw tells us so. But what then becomes of that important element in the play which is symbolized by the title? Pygmalion creates Galatea, yes; but Pygmalion is also the victim of his own creation. The Higgins who plucked the "squashed cabbage leaf" out of her squalor is a comic protagonist in the classic pattern of satirical comedy. He must do more than merely recognize Liza's independence of him; he must himself become dependent upon her; he must, in short, be brought to the realization that he loves her. Shaw, in his memoir of Sir Herbert Beerbohm Tree as Higgins, expressed his disgust with Tree for tossing a bouquet out of the window to the departing Liza, just before the final curtain. Whatever one may think of Tree's device for symbolizing Higgins' love of Liza, Tree's interpretation of the part of Higgins was not entirely unsound. And Shaw's condemnation of the sentimentality of the audience does not close the question.

If *Pygmalion* offers an almost perfect illustration of one form of classic satirical comedy, the traditionally gratifying story of the biter bit, then the audience's desire to see Higgins at the mercy of Liza does not proceed from the audience's debased and vulgar taste but from the success of Shaw's manipulation of a familiar theme. And it is Shaw himself who has in recent years furnished evidence in support of this contention. Gabriel Pascal's admirable film of *Pygmalion* has a more tenderly romantic conclusion than that which Tree supplied: Higgins is shown walking the streets of London in search of his lost Liza, and returning home to find her waiting before his fire. The fade-out shows them regarding each other with warm affection: Freddy Eynsford-Hill has vanished. If Shaw, who prepared the screen-play for Pascal and actually wrote such fresh material as the scene of the ambassador's reception, was willing to permit the audience to carry away the impression that Higgins and Liza had been more than reconciled, then one must assume either that he changed his mind about the ending of his own play or that his Epilogue was something less than serious.

All in all, the second conclusion appears the more probable. Shaw's pronouncements about his own plays are normally of two kinds: the literal truth and the fantastic untruth. Both show him at his best as an advertising man. When he called *The Devil's Disciple* a melodrama, he was describing it quite accurately. When he called *Pygmalion* a romance, he was equally accurate; but he then turned on his unsuspecting audience and denounced it for expecting the normal conclusion of a comic romance. If that audience had believed Liza's statement in Act V that she was going to marry Freddy, Shaw doubtless had another Epilogue already in type to prove that Liza was in fact going to marry Higgins.

Certainly the play makes every effort to convince us that

Higgins, the arrogant, self-centered genius, is dangerously ignorant both of himself and of Liza. When he and Pickering interview Liza, in Act II, Pickering asks him, "Does it occur to you, Higgins, that the girl has some feelings?" Higgins' reply is: "Oh no, I don't think so. Not any feelings that we need bother about." And, in the same act, the housekeeper Mrs. Pearce warns him: "When you get what you call interested in people's accents, you never think or care what may happen to them or you." The word *you* is clearly important. And what is Higgins' view of himself? When Mrs. Pearce has uttered her warnings, Higgins tells Pickering: "You know, Pickering, that woman has the most extraordinary ideas about me. Here I am, a shy, diffident sort of man. I've never been able to feel really grown-up and tremendous, like other chaps. And yet she's firmly persuaded that I'm an arbitrary overbearing bossing kind of person. I cant account for it." Mrs. Higgins, at her first meeting with Liza, is moved to ask her son and Pickering about "the problem of what is to be done with [Liza] afterwards," but Higgins is confident that no problem exists.

Once Galatea has thrown the slippers and walked out, Pygmalion is forced to begin to see himself as he really is. In other words, the protagonist of the satirical comedy realizes that he has cut a ridiculous figure. When Liza makes her entrance in Act V he becomes so furious as to be speechless—a unique occurrence. He tells his mother: "Let her speak for herself. You will jolly soon see whether she has an idea that I havnt put into her head or a word that I havnt put into her mouth. I tell you I have created this thing out of the squashed cabbage leaves of Covent Garden; and now she pretends to play the fine lady with me." But at last he must humble himself: "I shall miss you, Eliza. I have learnt something from your idiotic notions: I confess that humbly and gratefully. And I have grown accustomed to your voice and appearance. I like them, rather." Finally, when Liza threatens to become the assistant of the humbug Professor Nepean, Higgins so far loses control of himself as to strike her. His confusion is complete. Galatea has subdued Pygmalion; the comedy is ended.

This, then, is what has become of our "intensely and deliberately didactic" play: a satirical comedy in which Shaw, the "classic writer of comedies" that he recognized himself to be, chastens his comic protagonist with ridicule. It may perhaps be argued that *Pygmalion* is Shaw's unique failure to write a discussion play. Not at all. Consider *Man and Superman.* The published play, complete with the prefatory epistle to Arthur Bingham Walkley, the long scene in Hell, and Tanner's "The Revolutionist's Handbook," is a clear enough expression of Shaw's conception of the Superman. But the play in the theatre is quite another matter. As Desmond MacCarthy put it [in *The Court Theatre*], only four years after the play was first presented in 1903, "If the case of Ann and Tanner is taken as an individual case, which it becomes when shorn of preface and appendices on the stage, the general significance which the author attributes to it need not annoy us." Shaw himself writes down the play as "a trumpery story of modern London life, a life in which, as you know, the ordinary man's main business is to get means to keep up the position and habits of a gentleman and the ordinary woman's business is to get married." As is his habit, Shaw is here trying to confuse us with the irony of literal truth. *Man and Superman,* for all that Shaw tells us so, is indeed the "Victorian farce" that Eric Bentley has styled it. How else is one to explain its continuing popularity? Hardly in terms of its alleged message: at Maurice Evans' delightful production of the play, I overheard a member of the audience complain: "I see who the man is, all right; but who is Superman—the woman?"

That other much admired and frequently revived work of Shaw—*The Doctor's Dilemma,* which he considers his major achievement in tragedy—is not merely conventional in structure, but has all the look of a genuine *pièce bien faite.* Its *scène-à-faire* is obviously the highly dramatic death of Louis Dubedat, surrounded by his wife, his admirers, and his murderer. If we look at the play as Shaw looked at the wellmade play in his Preface to *Three Plays by Brieux,* we find that Shaw has invented the dramatic situation of an artist dying under strange circumstances, condemned to death by a man who is in love with the artist's wife. But the murderer must be able to kill with impunity, subject to the conditions imposed by the realistic treatment of contemporary life. Let him, therefore, be a doctor, and let him further be influenced by the fact that he must choose between the morally reprehensible artist and a physician of sterling morality. The rest follows of itself. Thus the medical profession gets into the play almost by accident, although it is the subject of the celebrated Preface. What price Sardoodledom now?

It has been said of Shaw that he is primarily a thinker, who chose for purely rhetorical reasons to cast his ideas in dramatic form; and it has also been said of Shaw that he is a playwright who doggedly insisted on placing his art at the service of more or less dubious ideas. Both statements, of course, miss the mark. Shaw, as he himself has told us at various times, is a playwright who learned much from the popular theatre of his day and from the great drama of former ages. His technique is old-fashioned, not because he was too lazy or uninventive to devise a new one, but because, as a practical dramatist, he recognized the soundness and effectiveness of the technique employed in the best dramatic literature. In his anxiety to exalt Ibsen, Brieux, and himself at the expense of Scribe and Sardou, he laid down a smoke-screen of blather about the technical innovations of the Ibsen-Shaw drama, with the double object of baiting the critics and attracting attention. But the truth about Shaw's technique appears (characteristically shrouded in dark mutterings against the critics) in some of his *obiter dicta,* and most clearly of all in his plays themselves. The conventionality of Shaw's technique follows naturally from his conception of his own art, which he himself summed up for all time [in *Sixteen Self Sketches*]: "Would anyone but a buffleheaded idiot of a university professor, half crazy with correcting examination papers, infer that all my plays were written as economic essays, and not as plays of life, character, and human destiny like those of Shakespear or Euripides?" (pp. 879-85)

Milton Crane, " 'Pygmalion': Bernard Shaw's Dramatic Theory and Practice," in PMLA, *Vol. LXVI, No. 6, December, 1951, pp. 879-85.*

An excerpt from Shaw's "prose sequel" to *Pygmalion*

[Eliza] knows that Higgins does not need her, just as her father did not need her. The very scrupulousness with which he told her that day that he had become used to having her there, and dependent on her for all sorts of little services, and that he should miss her if she went away (it would never have occurred to Freddy or the Colonel to say anything of the sort) deepens her inner certainty that she is "no more to him than them slippers"; yet she has a sense, too, that his indifference is deeper than the infatuation of commoner souls. She is immensely interested in him. She has even secret mischievous moments in which she wishes she could get him alone, on a desert island, away from all ties and with nobody else in the world to consider, and just drag him off his pedestal and see him making love like any common man. We all have private imaginations of that sort. But when it comes to business, to the life that she really leads as distinguished from the life of dreams and fancies, she likes Freddy and she likes the Colonel; and she does not like Higgins and Mr Doolittle. Galatea never does quite like Pygmalion: his relation to her is too godlike to be altogether agreeable.

Shaw, in his **Pygmalion,** *Penguin Books, 1951.*

Louis Kronenberger   (essay date 1952)

[*A dramatist, novelist, and drama critic for* Time *from 1938 to 1961, Kronenberger was a distinguished historian and literary critic esteemed for his expertise in eighteenth-century English history and literature. In the following excerpt, he evaluates* Pygmalion *as a sympathetic comedy concerned with human issues.*]

Pygmalion is one of Shaw's pleasantest plays: it is also, in spite of appearances, one of his most human. Nothing would seem less human, or more peculiarly Shavian, than a play that turned on the science of phonetics; no one would seem a worse hero—or *is* a worse hero in the romantic sense—than Shaw's phonetics professor. As fascinating as Professor Higgins' experiment is, the matter of making a duchess out of a flower girl by teaching her to speak like one, is scientific rather than human, a question of vowels and consonants rather than flesh and blood. Moreover, Shaw refuses to humanize his story by making what begins as something between teacher and pupil wind up as a matter of husband and wife. Pygmalion never marries Galatea.

Shaw actually humanizes his story by *not* having Pygmalion marry Galatea, by not letting a phonetical experiment end up a mere mechanical romance. It is Shaw who brings Galatea to life by realizing that that is precisely what Pygmalion has not done; for to Pygmalion—whom let us from here on call Higgins, and the lady Liza—all this was purely an experiment, was transforming a flower girl into a duchess with no sense that she was also a woman. Shaw is very generally the champion of life, reality, humanity; Shaw is very generally on the side of the non-angels. But he doesn't always make us feel that his people are quite flesh and blood—just to begin with, they are never at a loss for the right word or the wrong opinion. But in Higgins, Shaw offers some one so wholeheartedly scientific and inhuman, so much more enraptured by vowel sounds than the Life Force, that Shaw can emerge not only as one who champions humanity, but even, for the nonce, as one who breathes it.

As a story, this is one of Shaw's prettiest ones—a pure scientific fairy tale. The plot is so immemorial and indestructible as to make us wonder whether Shaw's own contribution isn't, theatrically speaking, immaterial. The public will always watch—whatever the method—drudges being turned into duchesses; nevertheless, Shaw has freshened the story and made it fit for cultivated audiences. His particular merit is his treating a fairy-tale in scientific terms, his creating a duchess by scientific means, and his sense not only of what the undertaking involves but of what the upshot involves—for when one has at last become a lady, life does not end but begins.

Much of the outright fun of the play consists in watching Liza on the way to duchessdom; and the midway scene at Mrs. Higgins' At Home—where Liza has learned to pronounce but not yet to converse, and where her lapses into billingsgate are palmed off as samples of the latest fashionable slang—is usually, in the theater, the show-piece of the evening. But if the fun of the play has to do with Liza's becoming a lady, the point of the play involves her becoming a woman. Always a person of strong feelings, she is now equally a person of sensitive ones. And what was sport for Higgins is a matter of life-and-death for her: having been raised to a world of culture and breeding, shall she now be tossed back into the gutter? Having been brought into her teacher's own house, having lived in the closest contact with him, shall she now be—without even a "thank you"—dismissed? She has, beyond question, the right on her side. Although Higgins' experiment may be finished, Liza's new life has only just begun, and Higgins owes her something. The fact is, however, that Liza's rights have got tangled up with her resentments, that her claim on Higgins for what might be termed social security is mixed up with her demanding of Higgins a great deal of personal attention. Her vanity is everywhere wounded—not just for being a mere experiment in Higgins' life, but equally for *not* being an experience. Thus, so far as Liza resents Higgins as heartless, we must condemn him, but not where she resents him as heartfree.

Hence, it is not just the audience that assumes Higgins must marry Liza: it is almost equally Liza herself. For him not to marry her, for the fairy prince not to claim Cinderella, for Pygmalion not to grant his statue her statutory rights, is to do more than insult the lady: it is to sin against romance. Still, in the moment of her rage Liza isn't in a fury because Higgins hasn't fallen in love with her and suggested marriage—that much she hasn't consciously yet come to expect: she is in a rage because she really doesn't mean anything to him at all. And in a sense she doesn't, which is why he can stand up to her and fight back with solid, reasonable arguments—if his emotions were involved, the arguments might occur to him less promptly. As it is Higgins can suggest that there is no way for him to be properly protective of Liza since she, given any chance, will at once become boldly possessive of him. Higgins is shrewd enough to grasp that with Liza there can be no middle ground; she must constitute for him either an experiment or an experience.

Higgins' fate might for all that have been ultimately John Tanner's—he might have been sealed of Liza Doolittle through passion or propinquity or the Life Force—had it not been for his mother-fixation. Liberated by phonetics, Liza was done in by Freud. The lady Pygmalion brought to life from a statue had no chance against the lady he had set up on a pedestal. Hence we have here not simply a play whose ending is unromantic; we have a hero who from the outset is incapacitated for romance. Pygmalion isn't Pygmalion at all, he is Oedipus.

So Liza—as we are told in Shaw's epilogue—marries Freddy and with help from Higgins and the Colonel makes a fair go of things running a flower shop. In the end, she doesn't become a duchess, after all: But if she doesn't become a duchess, at least she doesn't remain Higgins' mere doll; and if snubbed by romance, she is at any rate not sacrificed to irony or crude realism, not flung back into the gutter.

Mother fixation or not, Higgins is a very good teacher, for the incidental no less than the intended things he has Liza learn. By his manner toward her—even though it was very much his manner toward everyone—she learned that big fact that "the difference between a lady and a flower girl is not how she behaves, but how she is treated." One may question how much she profited from his insisting that

> The great secret, Eliza, is not having bad manners or good manners or any other particular sort of manners, but in having the same manner for all human souls—the question is not whether I treat you rudely, Liza, but whether you ever heard me treat any one else better.

Her answer is at least as good as his defense because it is much more germane to their relationship: "I don't care how you treat me; I don't mind a black eye; but I won't be passed over."

Pygmalion is, I repeat, one of Shaw's most human plays, one where we are more concerned with the psychology of the characters than with their ideas, and with their relationship one to another than to the world at large. It is human, too, in being the most concrete sort of social comedy—a comedy of accents, one might call it; and in England a comedy of accents is in itself a comedy of manners. The play's humanity extends also to Liza's father, Alfred Doolittle, who strikes a very human note, however difficult he may be to swallow as a human being. He is, in fact, a brazen piece of Shavian ingenuity, but a successful and a likable one. His frankness about being a member of the *un*deserving poor is, of course, part of his game, exactly as artful creations like Alfred Doolittle are part of Shaw's. Just who, one must sometimes wonder, *is* the underdog, in a world where things are looked at upside down? (pp. 263-66)

Louis Kronenberger, "Shaw," in his The Thread of Laughter: Chapters on English

Stage Comedy from Jonson to Maugham, *Alfred A. Knopf, 1952, pp. 227-78.*

Myron Matlaw   (essay date 1958)

[*In the following essay, Matlaw assesses whether* Pygmalion *can be considered successful on Shaw's terms since it commonly arouses romantic expectations regarding the denouement that are not fulfilled.*]

Alan Jay Lerner, probably the most successful adapter of Shaw's *Pygmalion,* commented: "Shaw explains how Eliza ends not with Higgins but with Freddy and—Shaw and Heaven forgive me!—I am not certain he is right" [Prefatory Note, *My Fair Lady*]. Many critics would agree with this sentiment. A recent analysis of the play goes so far as to dismiss the Epilogue as a bit of Shavian frivolity and to cite the "happy ending" Shaw himself wrote for Pascal's film as the proper denouement of a play which is persuasively categorized by one critic as a play which follows "the classic pattern of satirical comedy" [Milton Crane, *PMLA,* 1951].

Such an ending has been popular also with audiences and actors ever since the play first appeared in 1913. Shaw chided both Mrs. Patrick Campbell and Beerbohm Tree for their romantic interpretations in the first productions: "I say, Tree, must you be so treacly?" he asked during the rehearsals. Tree's stage business before the curtain fell left no doubts in the minds of audiences that Higgins's marriage to Eliza was imminent. Justifying it, Tree wrote Shaw: "My ending makes money; You ought to be grateful." Shaw replied: "Your ending is damnable: You ought to be shot" [quoted in Hesketh Pearson's *Beerbohm Tree: His Life and Laughter*]. And he continued fulminating against romantic portrayals of an ending which caters to what, in the Epilogue written for *Pygmalion* later, he called "imaginations . . . so enfeebled by their lazy dependence on the ready-mades and reach-me-downs of the rag-shop in which Romance keeps its stock of 'happy endings' to misfit all stories."

Nonetheless, the recurrent arousing of inappropriate audience expectations and the apparent inability of the play to arouse the appropriate expectations (or those which Shaw considered appropriate) raise a question about *Pygmalion's* success on the playwright's terms. Perhaps even more important, they call for a re-examination of these terms; for I think that the ending is significant and dramatically inevitable, and that it is the ending Shaw himself rewrote for the film (thereby confusing the matter further)—rather than his Epilogue—which is frivolous.

What, then, are the terms of *Pygmalion?*

The title of the play underlines the parallel of Shaw's story and the myth of the artist-life-giver. At the same time, however, there are differences between the two, the most obvious one being in the endings. Pygmalion's ardent wish, as is well known, is miraculously granted. The romance, in the erotic sense, is consummated, presumably in the time-worn fashion of the rag shop. It is relevant here only to note that this consummation is anticipated

throughout the myth: Pygmalion ardently yearns for it all along.

A second difference between the play and the myth is perhaps less obvious. While the heroes of both are artists, Higgins, in the framework of Shaw's philosophy, is the greater one. "Artist-philosophers are the only sort of artists I take quite seriously," Shaw remarked in the Epistle Dedicatory to *Man and Superman,* and he frequently voiced his belief that art must be didactic, that in fact art by its very nature *is* didactic and can never be anything else. (Significantly, he makes the point again in the Preface to *Pygmalion.*) Pygmalion's artistry, the creation of a beautiful statue, evokes, in the artist himself, a passion of the senses. Higgins's artistry and passion, on the other hand, are cerebral: didactic and philosophic, phonetics and Milton.

While the comparison of the myth and the play could be pursued further—such matters as the use of a *deus ex machina* and the complete passivity of Galatea, for example, clearly contrast with Shaw's treatment—it is evident that Shaw's title appears to be almost ironic, for, according to his own standards, his plot (didactic and philosophic rather than erotic and sentimental) is artistically superior. In writing *Pygmalion,* however, Shaw was not primarily concerned with demonstrating his superiority as a myth-maker, and the title was not chosen for purposes of irony. He chose the title, I think, because his play and the myth had one basic thing in common which he wished to underline: both are stories of the creation of human life.

That Higgins did not consider Eliza human at first he hardly takes any pains to disguise. His expressions of contempt for her in the first two acts are as shocking to Pickering and Mrs. Pearce as they are amusing to the audience. "This creature with her kerbstone English," he says, "[has] no right to live." He refers to her as a "squashed cabbage leaf," "baggage," "draggletailed guttersnipe"—in short, as he himself says, an object which is "incapable of understanding anything."

Much later in the play he states his beliefs more explicitly if less amusingly. Describing her earlier life and the lives of the poor in general, he emphasizes their non-human, animal-like characteristics: "Work til youre more a brute than a human being; and then cuddle and squabble and drink til you fall asleep. Oh, it's a fine life, the life of the gutter. It's real: it's warm: it's violent: you can feel it through the thickest skin: you can taste it and smell it without any training or any work. Not like Science and Literature and Classical Music and Philosophy and Art."

It is a product of that subhuman environment which Higgins undertakes to transform into a "duchess." The process of the transformation itself, however, does not constitute either the major theme or the major conflict of the play. Indeed, while both the motion picture and Lerner's *My Fair Lady* do, Shaw's play does not contain a single scene which illustrates this process.

What the play portrays is a conflict between Higgins and Eliza which is of a far greater magnitude. At first the antagonists appear unevenly matched. Higgins's verbal fluency and wit reduce Eliza to "crooning like a bilious pigeon," as Higgins puts it. The turning point begins, conventionally enough, at the midpoint of the play, at Mrs. Higgins's At-Home. Eliza by now has undergone considerable training in manners and speech and makes a decided hit. The play reaches a climax at her sensation-causing "not bloody likely" *faux pas,* which made **Pygmalion** such a *succès de scandale.* After this scene, as they become less unevenly matched, the conflict between Eliza and Higgins gains in intensity, although it loses some of its comic effect.

What is the nature of the conflict between them? In spite of the initial unevenness of the match, Eliza fights back in an outrage at Higgins's contempt for her—and is probably attracted to him at the same time. In any case, conforming to the aspirations of the poor, she wants to improve her economic lot. The conflict at this point arises because the two take very different views of the lessons: to Eliza they are a mutually advantageous commercial arrangement wherein Higgins is to get paid by her in order to teach her to talk properly to enable her to open a flower shop; to Higgins, on the other hand, the commercial and economic factors are simply nonexistent. Training her so as to pass her off as a duchess is an inspired folly done for the fun of it, a challenge because, as he says, "she's so deliciously low—so horribly dirty." Yet he meets this challenge in dead earnest, and with devastating consequences to the personality of Eliza. Both in a literal and a figurative sense Higgins and Eliza do not speak the same language.

The difference in their attitudes, particularly in the second act, naturally follows from the differences in their backgrounds and personalities. Eliza has the qualities of character—manifested in the "good ear and a quick tongue" Higgins hopes for when he decides to take her on—which enable her to rise out of her lowly origins. Nonetheless, her origins have left their stamp on her. Joan of Arc too came from modest circumstances, but Shaw's Joan was a genius. Eliza is only very gifted. She personifies the potential of a human being—perhaps any human being—given the proper guidance. But her primary wants are mundane: marriage and the security of an income, or, as she puts it, "Freddy loves me: that makes him king enough for me. . . . I'll go and be a teacher."

The tremendous gulf between her and Higgins, particularly in the last act, is not one of social class. Higgins, as a matter of fact, is throughout the play even less representative of his class than Eliza later is of the class she has left. His preoccupation is with phonetics. He appears, at first glimpse, to be two-dimensional precisely because of this preoccupation, which is juxtaposed with the personality of a spoiled child who lacks even a vestige of manners (as Mrs. Pearce points out in the second act and Mrs. Higgins thereafter) and who (as he cheerfully points out himself) is subject to an infantile mother fixation.

But this childish simplicity is misleading. "Childish" attributes in Shaw's protagonists are too often coupled with, if not the very trademarks of, his true heroes. One immediately thinks of Caesar's propensity to celebrate his birthday when the mood strikes him and to pout when he is reminded of the bald spot on his head, and of Joan's irreverence toward various dignitaries and her apparent naïveté

in theology, politics, and war. So, on further observation, it is with Higgins. Like them, in some ways even like the Ancients in **Back to Methuselah** (who, however, are neither charming nor witty), Higgins is Shaw's ideal hero: "childish," unfeeling (unsentimental), almost devoid of any sense perception, particularly one relating to sex (Higgins comments on his mother fixation as blandly as Joan does on her breach-of-promise suit or Caesar on his age which protects him against Cleopatra's physical charms), witty, and preoccupied with intellectual or philosophical questions put to play in a particular problem usually not understood by the people around him.

For Higgins is another protagonist of the *élan vital,* an ideal of human perfection which Shaw voices in Lilith's speech which concludes **Back to Methuselah,** the lengthiest and perhaps most explicit dramatic expression of Shaw's ideals: "redemption from the flesh, to the vortex freed from matter, to the whirlpool in pure intelligence." Higgins's particular enunciation of this force is manifested in his creation. He transforms an ignorant, filthy, poor flower girl into a lady who can be passed off as a duchess. But this transformation is clearly symbolic of more, just as proper enunciation is symbolic of the higher form of life Higgins has in mind when he calls English "the language of Shakespear and Milton and The Bible."

So—beneath his bad manners, childish pouting, and limitless egotism—he views his actions, and the fact that his comments are amusing makes them no less significant and true than, say, the naïve formulation of Joan's comments. When Cauchon questions Joan about the truth of her vision: "And you, and not The Church, are to be the judge?" and Joan exasperates the court by exclaiming: "What other judgment can I judge by but my own?" she neatly summarizes her own greatness, the more so since she herself is unaware of both the heresy and the genius of the simple remark. Higgins is more sophisticated but equally accurate when he neatly summarizes his creation when Eliza complains that he has made trouble for her by making her a lady: "Would the world ever have been made if its maker had been afraid of making trouble? *Making life means making trouble*" (italics mine).

Higgins has created life itself. Eliza, coming from an environment which, save for its curious speech patterns, is, if at all human, sub-human, is made into a "duchess;" that is, into "a human being with a soul and the divine gift of articulate speech," as Higgins elsewhere describes civilized man.

Thus, while one of the most penetrating and suggestive of the analyses of Shaw's work accepts the original ending of **Pygmalion,** it seems to do so for the wrong reasons. I cannot agree with the assertion in that analysis that "the 'education of Eliza' in Acts I to III is a caricature of the true process." No educative process is in fact represented in the play (although Shaw inserted "a sample" for film production at a later date—a hint which was deftly developed in *My Fair Lady*). But more important, the conclusion that "Eliza turns the tables on Higgins, for she, finally, is the vital one, and he is the prisoner of 'system,' particularly of his profession," seems to me to miss the point [Eric Bentley, *Bernard Shaw, 1856-1950*].

Rather the reverse is true. The magnificent comic subplot underlines the point, for Doolittle was once, like Higgins, outside of class or "system" and had vitality. Both Doolittle and Eliza are brought to join the middle class. What is sharply contrasted, however, is the consequence of the transformation: for Doolittle it is a descent while for Eliza it is an ascent—the transformation makes the previously articulate (vital) father comically impotent while it gives the previously inarticulate ("crooning like a bilious pigeon") daughter human life. In sum, Higgins, the life-giver, will continue his study of phonetics while Eliza will settle for the life her father describes so picturesquely in the last act when all the cards are put on the table. Higgins, that is, will continue to teach proper, *civilized* articulation, a superman attempting to transform subhumans into humans; while Eliza will lead an admirable if circumscribed middle-class existence, having been given humanity—life—by Higgins.

Her ability to undergo successfully such a transformation evidences her superior qualities and often makes her appear as the hero of the play. She is only a Shavian hero *manqué,* however, and she is not the wife for Higgins. She can not even understand him, their values and interests being so different. Higgins genuinely admires Eliza, although he is first shocked and then amused by her values: in a most effective and inevitable denouement, the curtain falls as "he roars with laughter"—at the thought of her marrying Freddy. Admirable as she now is—especially when compared with what she was when he met her—she is not, and never can be, his equal. She is now part and parcel of the system of "middle class morality" which the early Doolittle and Higgins find ludicrous. Higgins and Eliza, then, still do not speak the same language, although this is true now only in the figurative sense. This does not, however, preclude the existence of an affinity between them, perhaps one comparable to the one existing between Caesar and Cleopatra. Nevertheless, marrying Eliza would be preposterous for Higgins, a superman with the vitality of a soul and a "Miltonic mind" (as he himself labels it) who lives on an entirely different plane, a plane where sex and marriage, indeed, are unknown.

What causes audiences to wish for it (as Eliza herself, for that matter, was wishing for it) is the Cinderella guise of the plot—which buttresses audiences' perennial desires, as Shaw rightly said in the Epilogue, for the marriage of the hero and the maiden—and the sentimental part of the myth which the title incidentally also calls to mind. The Cinderella guise, however, is accidental and irrelevant; it is purposely negated by the omission of scenes depicting the process of the transformation and by the omission of the grand ball scene, the highpoint of any Cinderella story. The title specifically and intentionally focuses attention away from the heroine and on Higgins, and on Higgins's life-giving qualities in particular.

It is very appropriate, therefore, that the most recent popular production is called *My Fair Lady,* focusing attention, as the musical itself does, on the Cinderella theme. At the same time, with all the brilliance of this version, even with the dialogue culled from the original play, this one is a very different play throughout. All the non-comic lines I have quoted are omitted, for in *My Fair Lady* Higgins is the conventional romantic hero and not what he surely is in *Pygmalion:* the Shavian hero, standing alone, a superman embodying a life force divorced from human social and sensual drives, but representative of the vitality and creative evolution in which, in Shaw's philosophy, lies the ultimate hope of mankind. (pp. 29-34)

> *Myron Matlaw, "The Denouement of 'Pygmalion'," in* Modern Drama, *Vol. I, No. 1, May, 1958, pp. 29-34.*

Martin Meisel   (essay date 1963)

[*Meisel is an American educator and critic. In the following excerpt, he examines Shaw's use of such traditional fairy-tale motifs as the magical transformation and test of suitability in* Pygmalion.]

Pygmalion and *Cinderella*

The misalliance motif of courtship comedy needs only a slight change of emphasis to become the Cinderella story of romance with its inevitable concomitants, a magical transformation and a fairytale test. When the lover himself prepares the transformation, he enacts the Pygmalion story; and it is therefore Shaw's own title which excused Beerbohm Tree's natural desire to end with a match instead of a mystery. [In a footnote, the critic adds the following quotation from Archibald Henderson's *George Bernard Shaw: Man of the Century:* " . . . for all Shaw's inflexibility as a stage manager, in the end the obstinate and clever Tree succeeded in circumventing the unromantic Irishman. By his insertion of the ingenious business of throwing flowers to Eliza in the very brief interval between the end of the play and the fall of the curtain, he achieved an instantaneous miracle of schizophrenia, transforming the disagreeable curmudgeon into the sympathetic lover."] (p. 168)

Shaw's full title for *Pygmalion* is *Pygmalion: A Romance in Five Acts.* In his postscript Shaw writes, "Now, the history of Eliza Doolittle, though called a romance because the transfiguration it records seems exceedingly improbable, is common enough. Such transfigurations have been achieved by hundreds of resolutely ambitious young women since Nell Gwynne set them the example by playing queens and fascinating kings in the theatre in which she began by selling oranges." The transformation of Eliza, from flower girl to what Higgins calls "my creation of a Duchess Eliza," by learning to speak and to play the part of a lady, is in fact a staple of theatrical romance.

The theatrical antecedents of Shaw's *Pygmalion* are epitomized in Dion Boucicault's *Grimaldi; or The Life of an Actress* (London, 1862). Like Eliza, Violet in Boucicault's play is a Covent Garden flower girl. She is made over into an actress through patient education by Grimaldi, an old Utility, and in the end she becomes a duchess, not only, like Eliza, in metaphor and manner but in fact. Violet has the beginnings of a great triumph on the stage, interrupted by melodramatic machinations. In the last act, however, she appears as the great new sensation of the London theater at an aristocratic garden party, like the Ambassador's party in *Pygmalion.* We hear rumors of her forthcoming marriage to Lord Alfred Shafton and of her presentation to the Queen. The Countess of Beaumaris, Lord Alfred's dragon mother, objects and attempts to buy Violet off, but she is won over at last when Grimaldi, the old actor, turns out to be a duke and a former lover of the Countess in Naples, and Violet, the former flower girl, is adopted as heir to his title.

In a theatrical romance like *Grimaldi,* the more wonderful the transformation the better. It is better in *Grimaldi* that Violet be a flower girl turned duchess than a shopkeeper's daughter turned wholesaler's wife. But in a society where the duchess and the flower girl can be said to belong to two nations, a miraculous transformation is almost a necessary part of a match between the classes. Despite their beauty and their goodness, Cinderella and Galatea in the nineteenth-century romance had to be touched by the magic wand of an education.

A transformation, by education or otherwise, requires a test, a Cinderella's slipper. The candidate must prove her fitness to be the mate of the prince. In Bulwer-Lytton's *Money* (1840), a hidden act of charity finally traced to its true owner permits Arthur Evelyn to take the poor but good-hearted Clara as his bride. In *The Lady of Lyons* (1838), renunciation, heroic service, wealth, and rank in Napoleon's army, and the most honorable self-effacement, enable Claude Melnotte to claim the bride he was presumptuous enough to marry. (pp. 170-72)

The transformation test-scene was an obvious high point in any drama based on the Cinderella-Pygmalion romance, and such a scene was the starting point of Shaw's *Pygmalion.* Its "obligatory scene," he himself declares, "the scene in which Eliza makes her successful début at the Ambassador's party was the root of the play at its inception. But when I got to work I left it to the imagination of the audience, as the theatre could not afford its expense and it made the play too long. Sir James Barrie spotted this at once and remonstrated. So when the play was screened, I added the omitted scene. . . ."

When Higgins is bent on persuading Liza to submit to his experiment, he dangles all sorts of prospects before her, including the fairy tale test:

> HIGGINS. . . . At the end of six months you shall go to Buckingham Palace in a carriage, beautifully dressed. If the King finds out youre not a lady, you will be taken by the police to the Tower of London, where your head will be cut off as a warning to other presumptuous flower girls. If you are not found out, you shall have a present of seven-and-sixpence to start life with as a lady in a shop. If you refuse this offer you will be a most ungrateful wicked girl; and the angels will weep for you.

This makes much more sense to Eliza than Higgins' earlier appeals to high romance ("you shall marry an officer in the Guards, with a beautiful moustache: the son of a marquis, who will disinherit him for marrying you, but will relent when he sees your beauty and goodness"); but she takes Higgins literally about the test, and objects to having her head cut off.

Even in the play-house version Shaw was evidently reluctant to do without a test scene altogether. He therefore introduces an intermediate test scene with inconclusive results. The whole of Act III concerns the trying-out of Eliza in Mrs. Higgins' drawing-room. Eliza passes the test in that she is not recognized by the Eynsford Hills, who had seen her in Covent Garden on the very night Higgins had picked her up (Act I). Eliza indeed makes a conquest of the younger Eynsford Hills; but while her voice, diction, and appearance are dazzlingly perfect, she speaks, with the tongue of angels, the small talk of a flower girl. Her exit line, the notorious "Not bloody likely," was in test-scene terms a catastrophe.

Eliza's real test, the Ambassador's party, was a public debut in "society. . . ." (pp. 172-74)

Shaw helps himself to this test motif in other plays besides *Pygmalion.* In *The Millionairess* Epifania's father, like Portia's, has instituted the test of worthiness. "I was like a princess in a fairy tale offering all men alive my hand and fortune if they could turn my hundred and fifty pound cheque into fifty thousand within six months." On the other hand, the mother of the man she wants as her second husband has instituted a test also: any aspirant to the hand of her son must earn her living alone and unaided for six months, with nothing more than the clothes on her back and two hundred piastres. Of course Shaw uses these tests to make a philosophical and social point: Epifania's first husband passes the test because "ninety per cent of our selfmade millionaires are criminals who have taken a five hundred to one chance and got away with it by pure luck. Well, Alastair was that sort of criminal." On the other hand, Epifania herself goes out into the world with her two hundred piastres and builds a small empire because she is one of those few people with a genius for organization, management, and the making of money.

Grimaldi's transformation of Violet the flower girl into Violet the actress in a spirit of paternal benevolence was designed to provide her with a vocation and a way of life. But in *Pygmalion,* Mrs. Higgins sees the education of Eliza beyond her station or opportunities as "(*unconsciously dating herself by the word*) A problem." It seems incredible to everyone that Higgins should have "created this thing out of the squashed cabbage leaves of Covent Garden" without any motive, either acquisitive or benevolent, that bore upon Eliza as a person; and in the seduction scene of the second act, presented in the pattern of the poor-but-good girl who has been picked up off the streets and tempted with furs and chocolates by the wealthy rake, everyone suspects Higgins' designs. His housekeeper ventures to say, "Mr Higgins: youre tempting the girl. It's not right. She should think of the future." Eliza herself fears the seducer's opiate: "Ive heard of girls being drugged by the like of you." Even Colonel Pickering, Higgins' fellow phonologist, asks "Excuse the straight question, Higgins. Are you a man of good character where women are concerned?" Doolittle comes in a pose of "wounded honor and stern resolution" to "rescue her from a fate worse than death"—or to settle the matter for five pounds. For his interest in a girl so far beneath him, Higgins is [suspect] . . . , though his interest (however perverse in its limitations) is strictly artistic and scientific.

The difference between *Pygmalion* and *Grimaldi* is in Shaw's serious concern with the nature of the barrier between the "two nations" and with the real difference between a lady and a flower girl. The barrier may be largely a technical matter, as Higgins believes; but it is not the real difference, as Shaw points out, in the intermediate test scene, and in the scenes of Eliza's rebellion. Eliza declares that by becoming a lady she has been disqualified from making a living in any way but by selling herself in marriage. Moreover, she credits her transformation not to Higgins and his techniques, but to Colonel Pickering, who treated her like a lady and behaved like a gentleman. But Higgins' defense, that he treats duchess and flower girl alike, that he believes in behaving "as if you were in Heaven, where there are no third-class carriages, and one soul is as good as another," is a radical attack on the very concept of the lady, on the social and economic structure it presupposes, and is the dialectical destination of the play.

For all the passing unconventionalities in his rehandling of the Cinderella-Pygmalion motif, Shaw relies so heavily on its fundamental appeal throughout *Pygmalion* that his refusal to end with a match between Higgins and Eliza was considered mere perversity. Actually Shaw took care to make the ending perfectly ambiguous on the stage, and was provoked into writing the long final note for the reader which now ends the play only by the ingenuity of the actors in finding ways to resolve the ambiguity. [The critic adds in a footnote that: "In his account to his wife of the first performance, Shaw was particularly violent over 'the raving absurdity of Tree's acting,' and full of praise for Mrs. Patrick Campbell. Though he never saw Tree toss flowers at Mrs. Campbell, Shaw's most specific complaint concerned the distortion of the ending. 'I had particularly coached him at the last rehearsal in the concluding lines, making him occupy himself affectionately with his mother, & throw Eliza the commission to buy the ham &c, over his shoulder. The last thing I saw as I left the house was Higgins shoving his mother rudely out of his way and wooing Eliza with appeals to buy a ham for his lonely home like a bereaved Romeo'."] The film version and the musical-comedy version succeed in implying the romantic resolution, though Shaw himself wrote the additions to the script of the film and worked closely with the entire production. In a number of ways the original ambiguity is preferable to the alternative resolutions provided for readers and spectators. The point of the ending is not Eliza's marriage, but her casting loose, her achievement of independence. Almost to the very end Higgins always speaks of having made a duchess of a flower girl; but after her assertion of independence and equality he cries "By George, Eliza, I said I'd make a woman of you; and I have." The deliberately unresolved ending tells much about the art of a play whose social and intellectual heterodoxies flourish in a traditional setting of orthodox popular appeal. (pp. 175-77)

> *Martin Meisel, in his* Shaw and the Nineteenth-Century Theater, *Princeton University Press, 1963, 477 p.*

Louis Crompton   (essay date 1969)

> [*Crompton is a Canadian educator and critic. In the following excerpt, he identifies the antiromantic unsentimentality of* Pygmalion *as the chief distinction of the play.*]

Pygmalion, as all the world knows, is the story of a flower girl who passes as a duchess after taking phonetics lessons. Shaw himself did not rank this adaptation of the Cinderella story very high among his plays, calling it deprecatingly the last of his "pot-boilers." It has, of course, fully achieved the popularity he aimed at. Its sensational triumphs as a drama, as a film, and as a musical comedy, however, have not been without their ironies. The paperback edition of the musical, for instance, claims to recapture "one of the most beautiful love stories the world has ever taken to its heart." The reader who knows Shaw and the ways of Broadway may be amused at this, reflecting that what the world takes to its heart the world is likely to remold after its heart's fancy.

It is perhaps to be expected that producers, actors, and the general public should have delighted in the fairy-tale aspect of Shaw's play, and have steadfastly repudiated the antiromantic side of *Pygmalion* as so much perverse nonsense from a man who always insisted on teasing as well as pleasing. But the joke deepens when we look at scholarly journals and discover that professors of literature are just as prone as advertisers to assume that Shaw should have let Higgins marry Eliza. In reaction one is inclined to recall gently but firmly such amiable sentimentalists to their senses by reminding them that *Pygmalion* is, after all, not a comedy by James M. Barrie, but a serious study of human relationships by the author of *Caesar and Cleopatra* and *Back to Methuselah.* It is, in fact, just this refusal to sentimentalize that gives the play its distinction.

It must be admitted at the start, however, that Shaw's preface is a somewhat misleading guide to the meaning of the play. There Shaw enthusiastically applauds the new scientific approach to language by phoneticians, if only because it raised pronunciation above the intense self-consciousness and class snobbery which had always bedeviled the subject in England. Then he goes on to imply that the main theme of his comedy will be phonetics. But it takes only a little reflection to realize that dialects, in and of themselves, have no intrinsic dramatic or social significance. Our response to them as pure sounds is largely arbitrary: a Brooklynite's pronunciation of "girl" may strike one ear as exquisitely refined (it did Shaw's) and another as comically vulgar. The real basis for our reaction to anyone's dialect is our association of particular kinds of speech with particular classes and particular manners. Here we are much closer to the real stuff of drama, and especially of comedy. Manners have been a central concern of the comic stage from Roman times through Shakespeare and Molière down to our own day. And, for all the shop talk about phonology, it is possible with a little analysis to see that it is really manners and not speech patterns that provide the clue to the character contrasts in *Pygmalion,* accents being, so to speak, merely their outer clothing.

Shaw's opening scene is admirably suited to bring out

these contrasts. It is a brilliant little genre-piece that sets a group of proletarians—some timidly deferential, some sarcastically impolite—over against an impoverished middle-class family with genteel pretensions, a wealthy Anglo-Indian, and the haughtily self-sufficient Professor Higgins, all jostling beneath a church portico. The moment is chosen to show class antagonisms and personal idiosyncrasies at their sharpest. Brute necessity prompts a flower girl to wheedle a few last coins from the opera-goers while they in turn face that acid test of middle-class manners, the scramble for taxis in a sudden squall. The scene highlights two kinds of vulgarity. The first is the comico-pathetic, specifically lower-class vulgarity of the flower girl. Eliza is vulgarly familiar when she tries to coax money out of prospective customers, and vulgarly hysterical when she thinks she is suspected of soliciting as a prostitute, on the theory that, as she belongs to a class that cannot afford lawyers, she had best be loud and vigorous in her protestations of virtue. Later, she is vulgarly keen on lording it—or ladying it—over her neighbors with her windfall of coins. What is interesting, however, is that Shaw by no means regards vulgarity as specifically a class trait. All the time he is treating us to Eliza's plangent diphthongs he is also dissecting the manners of the girl in the middle-class family, Clara Eynsford Hill. Compared to Eliza, Clara comes off the worse. For Clara is also pushing, and, in her dealings with strangers, as vulgarly suspicious and as quick to take offense as the flower girl, her rebuke to Higgins—"Dont dare speak to me"—being less comically naïve than Eliza's "I'm a good girl, I am"—but just as silly. And Eliza's pushiness at least has the excuse of springing from her wholly understandable desire to escape from the squalor of the slums into a bourgeois world which can offer her some kind of independence and self-respect.

The next day in Higgins' laboratory Eliza is first vulgarly determined not to be cheated, and then suspicious of being drugged and seduced, as the impetuous professor bullies and tempts her. Later, *Pygmalion* reaches its climax as a comedy of manners at Mrs. Higgins' at-home, where Eliza, now master of enunciation as a parrot might be master of it, delivers pompous recitations and spicy Lisson Grove gossip with the same impeccable air. The joke lies in the way the old vulgarian peeps out from behind the new façade, as in her theories about her aunt's death. At the same time, Eliza, for all her absurdity, still manages to think and feel naturally behind the veneer. By contrast, Clara is mere bright affectation, a much less vital person. She even outdoes Eliza's parroting when she repeats her slum expletive as the latest thing. Shaw, who disliked hearing the word "bloody" used "by smart or would-be smart ladies as a piece of smartness," was trying to kill its vogue by ridiculing Clara's callowness.

Shaw's attitude toward manners was not a simple one. Obviously, he preferred social poise and considerateness to mere crudity. He seems even to have harbored some limited admiration for the dignified code of manners of the Victorian period, though he found its artificialities cramping. He gives Mrs. Hill, Mrs. Higgins, and the Colonel exquisite manners to contrast with the girls' lack of them. Yet Shaw is clearly no latter-day Castiglione here or else-

where. His hero is, after all, the creative rebel, not the courtier. He preferred Beethoven to Liszt, and the rough-tongued Joan of Arc to Ninon de Lenclos. He would have been the first to remind us that on the score of mere gentlemanliness, Charles I would carry the day over Cromwell, and Czar Nicholas II over Lenin. And in *Back to Methuselah*, Shaw's Superrace cannot even imagine what the word "manners" could have meant.

Professor Higgins, Shaw's Prometheus of phonetics, is equally without manners. Consider the Olympian tirade he visits on Eliza's head while she sits snivelling in Covent Garden:

> A woman who utters such depressing and disgusting sounds has no right to be anywhere—no right to live. Remember that you are a human being with a soul and the divine gift of articulate speech: that your native language is the language of Shakespear and Milton and The Bible; and dont sit there crooning like a bilious pigeon.

Clearly, the man who can vent such splendid wrath upon a street vendor is neither a snob nor a vulgarian, but neither is he a gentleman, and he just as certainly has no more manners than the petulant daughter or the disgruntled flower girl. At home he takes his boots off and wipes his hands on his dressing gown. In creating Higgins, Shaw was assuredly driving at something more than a definition of true gentility.

Before we consider what it is, however, we may pause for a moment to look at the part Eliza's father, Alfred Doolittle, plays in the comedy. Here Shaw turns from the question of social manners to the deeper question of social morality. The farce of the dustman turned moral preacher has always delighted Shaw's audiences. But just as they have rested content with the Cinderella aspect of the main story, so the ironic intention in this second transformation has been missed. One critic has even held that since Doolittle is less happy after coming into his fortune than he was before, Shaw's aim was to demonstrate the "vanities of philanthropy." This is not so much to miss Shaw's point as to turn it completely upside down. What Shaw is saying is that Doolittle after his escape from Lisson Grove is a much better social being, albeit a less comfortable one, than he was before. Critics have simply overlooked the ironic amusement with which Shaw views the dustman's discomfiture, which he regards as pure gain from the point of view of society.

Shaw seems to have been inspired to create the fable of Doolittle's sudden wealth by Dickens' use of a similar story in one of his novels. In *Our Mutual Friend*, Dickens contrasts two poor men, one a Thames-side water rat named "Rogue" Riderhood, and the other an honest garbage collector, Mr. Boffin, who unexpectedly comes into a large inheritance. Each is treated as an all-black or all-white figure in a popular melodrama. Riderhood, whom Dickens describes bluntly as a piece of "moral sewage," remains unrelievedly villainous throughout, while Boffin, a kind of illiterate Pickwick, is a paragon of benevolence both before he becomes wealthy and after. Shaw's approach is to roll Dickens' pair of poor men into one, and then to show how the man's behavior is a consequence not of his character, but of his situation.

Alfred Doolittle first appears in Wimpole Street in the hypocritical role of virtuous father, rather after the fashion of Engstrand in Ibsen's *Ghosts,* his intention being to blackmail the two men who have taken up Eliza. When Higgins bullies him out of this scheme, he changes his tack and becomes the ingratiating pimp: "Well, the truth is, Ive taken a sort of fancy to you, Governor; and if you want the girl, I'm not so set on having her back home again but that I might be open to an arrangement." This approach fails too. But Doolittle is nothing if not a resourceful rhetorician. He forthwith throws morality to the winds and argues for consideration, in an eloquent flight of philosophical oratory, as an undeserving poor man done out of his natural right to happiness by the narrow-minded prejudices of middle-class morality. Higgins and Pickering, enchanted, now offer him five pounds, which he accepts after rejecting ten as too likely to entail sobering responsibilities. But alas, the man who shrinks from ten pounds comes into several thousand a year before the play is over and finds his free and easy life at an end. What, then, is the meaning of this fable?

First of all, Doolittle's moral and social attitudes contrast

Advertising poster.

strongly with Eliza's. Eliza yearns above all things to join the respectable lower middle class. Doolittle, finding that his job as garbage collector is too low on the social scale to have any moral standards attached to it, realizes that he already has, in a sense, the prerogatives of a duke, and is loath to rise. He protests that he likes a little "ginger" in his life, "ginger" to his mind being the privilege of beating his female paramours, changing them at will, indulging in periodic drinking bouts, and pursuing life, liberty, and happiness on his own terms. But Shaw, like Carlyle, did not consider personal happiness the end of human existence. Hollow as three-quarters of middle-class morality may be, and damaging to the race on its higher levels, the imposition of minimum standards of decency on Doolittle is clear gain, any standards being better than the impunity he enjoys as a result of his poverty. If we leave his engaging impudence aside, it is a difficult thing to admire a man who wants to sell his daughter, and it is impossible to like a blackmailer. Shaw's aim as a socialist was to abolish the poor as a class on the grounds that such people were dangerous and contemptible. Shaw held it against poverty that it made Doolittle's kind of happiness all too easy. In a Shavian Utopia the Industrial Police would no doubt have bundled Doolittle off to a labor camp with as little compunction as they would a rent-collecting millionaire who took a similar view as to the world's owing him a living. Doolittle's character does not change, but he is as effectively moralized by coming into money as any hooligan athlete who has ever won a world's championship or any hillbilly moonshiner whose land has brought him a fortune in oil royalties. When Higgins, on the occasion of his marriage, asks if he is an honest man or a rogue, his answer is "A little of both, Henry, like the rest of us." Doolittle is, in short, whatever society wants to make of him.

Conventional farce would have ended with Eliza's fiasco at Mrs. Higgins' at-home, conventional romance with her triumph at the ambassador's reception and a love match between her and Higgins. [The critic adds in a footnote that: "It is worth noting that when Shaw subtitled his play 'A Romance in Five Acts,' he was using the word to refer to the transformation of Eliza into a lady, not in the sentimental-erotic sense."] But Shaw contended that most ordinary plays became interesting just when the curtain fell. What, he wants to know, will be Galatea's relation to her creator after the transformation has taken place? It was one of his favorite theories that people of high culture appear to savages or even to the average man as cold, selfish, and unfeeling simply because of their inaccessibility to the common emotions and their freedom from ordinary affectionateness or jealousy. The development of Eliza's relation to the professor in the last two acts is meant to illustrate this perception.

Higgins is in many ways a paradoxical being. He is at once a tyrannical bully and a charmer, an impish schoolboy and a flamboyant wooer of souls, a scientist with a wildly extravagant imagination and a man so blind to the nature of his own personality that he thinks of himself as timid, modest, and diffident. Like Caesar in **Caesar and Cleopatra,** he is part god and part brute; but unlike Caesar, he cannot boast that he has "nothing of man" in him. It is this manliness, which takes the form of obtuseness to the feelings of others, that leads to his first comeuppance. He and Pickering alike have both failed to grasp the fact that Eliza's heroic efforts to improve herself have not been based merely on a desire to rise in the world, and still less on any desire for perfection for its own sake, but are first of all the result of a doglike devotion to two masters who have taken trouble over her. When the men fail to pet and admire her after her triumph, her thwarted feelings turn to rage, and, desperate to provoke an emotional response from Higgins, she needles him so she may enjoy the spectacle of a god in a vulgar human fury.

Yet however much her spitfire vehemence may put us in mind of the street girl, the Eliza of this scene is far from the original Eliza of Covent Garden. There is a new dignity and even calculation in her emotional outburst. She has now mastered more than the pronunciation of the educated classes. When she meets Higgins at his mother's the next morning she is a model of poised reserve, even cuttingly cold in manner. Obviously her old commonness has forsaken her at the very moment that the experiment has ended and she must find her way independently in life. Nevertheless, Eliza's development, marked though it is, is limited in one important respect. She never gets past the stage of judging the world wholly in relation to herself. In this respect she remains a typical petite bourgeoise, who, as Higgins puts it, sees life and personal relations in commercial terms. She has nothing of the impersonality of the world-betterer, nothing of Higgins's scientific passion for reform. Once again, as with Caesar and Cleopatra, it is a case of the superhuman face to face with the all-too-human. Higgins tells Eliza he cares "for life, for humanity," and her objection is that he does not care personally for *her*. On hearing that she is going to marry Freddy, Clara's amiable but brainless brother, Higgins objects— "Can he make anything of you?" He is chagrined at seeing his duchess, so to speak, thrown away. Eliza in her turn finds such a question unintelligible: "I never thought of us making anything of one another; and you never think of anything else. I only want to be natural."

To all but the most inveterate sentimentalist the relation between Eliza and her mentor does not appear to have the makings of a marriage. Higgins lacks not only the personal tenderness Eliza craves but even the tact necessary to avoid hurting her repeatedly. Not that he wants cunning in his treatment of women. He knows, Eliza tells him, "how to twist the heart in a girl." But in the end, Higgins, who has devoted his life "to the regeneration of the human race through the most difficult science in the world," does not need a wife any more than Plato, or Swift, or Nietzsche, or Tolstoy did. Indeed, Tolstoy's marriage, a real-life instance of the world-betterer married to a flesh-and-blood woman, had a good deal of the same tragicomic conflict in it. Higgins explains to Eliza that he has grown accustomed to her face and voice and that he likes them as he likes his furniture, but he makes it brutally clear that he can also get on without them and that he does not really need her. Knowledge of these facts does not endear him to Eliza, who infinitely prefers Freddy's simple-hearted homage. As Shaw tells us in his prose sequel to the play, "Galatea never does quite like Pygmalion: his relation to

her is too godlike to be altogether agreeable." Eliza is not yearning after godhead; she likes Freddy Eynsford Hill.

The central theme of *Pygmalion* is the contrast between the Promethean passion for improving the race and the ordinary human desire for the comforts and consolations of the domestic hearth. The history of Shaw's struggle to keep this dramatic conception from being travestied in productions is in itself a long-drawn-out comedy. The first published text of the play ended with Higgins giving Eliza a string of items to shop for, including a ham and some ties; when she retorts, "Buy them yourself," he merely jingles his change in his pocket, "highly self-satisfied" at the new independent spirit she is showing. Beerbohm Tree, the original English Higgins, neatly subverted this Miller-of-Dee ending in the 1914 production:

> I had particularly coached him at the last rehearsal in the concluding lines, making him occupy himself affectionately with his mother, & throw Eliza the commission to buy the ham &c, over his shoulder. The last thing I saw as I left the house was Higgins shoving his mother rudely out of his way and wooing Eliza with appeals to buy a ham for his lonely home like a bereaved Romeo.

When Gabriel Pascal undertook to make a movie of the play in 1938, Shaw once more found he had a problem on his hands. To begin with, Pascal, in casting the part of Higgins, chose not the kind of crusty character actor Shaw wanted, but the dashingly handsome and debonair matinee idol, Leslie Howard, which led Shaw to protest, "It is amazing how hopelessly wrong Leslie is," and to add that the audience would all want him to marry Eliza, "which is just what I don't want." Shaw's own personal suggestion for the movie ending was a shot of Freddy and Eliza in their new flower and fruit shop, selling grapes. This is not, of course, the way the film actually ends. In the movie, Eliza creeps back to the laboratory after her spat with Higgins, finds him alone, and hears him ask for his slippers.

Critics who argue for a romantic reading of the play, and who dismiss Eliza's marriage to Freddy in the prose sequel as a mere piece of perversity on Shaw's part, have used what they have considered to be Shaw's condoning of this conclusion to bolster their interpretations. Donald Costello, in his meticulous comparison of the play and the film, wonders what kind of "hypnotic powers" Pascal and Howard used over Shaw to get him to accept it in lieu of his own proposal. But it is clear from Mrs. Pascal's account of the matter that Pascal did not get Shaw's approval at all:

> Pascal's answer to the additional scene in the flower shop with Freddy as Eliza's husband was silence.

> But at the sneak preview of *Pygmalion* a very nervous Pascal was tightly holding Mrs. Charlotte Shaw's hand. Mrs. Shaw and Pascal were great friends. Beside them, the white beard of Bernard Shaw seemed to be fluorescent in the darkness. Pascal was sure enough that the white beard would soon be ruffled with anger. Eliza was *not* going to marry Freddy, and there was

not going to be a flower shop. Instead the rebellious Galatea-Eliza would return to her maker, Pygmalion, with the soft and humble words:

"I washed my face and hands before I came, I did."

And the love-stricken Higgins, finding his old upper hand fast, instead of running to her would turn his chair with his back toward Eliza and, leaning back, he would push his hat up as if it were the crown of a newly anointed king, and say:

"Confound it, Eliza—where the devil are my slippers?"

When the lights went on, Shaw didn't say a word. But there was a faint smile above the white beard.

Evidently Pascal presented Shaw with a *fait accompli* he was powerless to undo. What did he think of Pascal's intimation that Eliza would devote herself happily to a lifetime of slipper fetching? The best answer to this question is the speech on the subject (omitted in the movie) which Shaw gives Higgins in the play:

> I dont and wont trade in affection. You can call me a brute because you couldnt buy a claim on me by fetching my slippers and finding my spectacles. You were a fool: I think a woman fetching a man's slippers is a disgusting sight: did I ever fetch your slippers? I think a good deal more of you for throwing them in my face. No use slaving for me and then saying you want to be cared for: who cares for a slave? . . . If you dare to set up your little dog's tricks of fetching and carrying slippers against my creation of a Duchess Eliza, I'll slam the door in your silly face.

With these sentiments ringing in his ear, anyone contemplating Pascal's ending is bound to find it amusingly bathetic.

In the screen version of the play published in 1941, Shaw added a number of scenes he had written for the movie, including the scene at the ambassador's party, but, far from following Pascal, he took pains to reword the final speeches of the play to make it clear that Eliza would marry Freddy. The well-established tradition of improving on Shaw, however, still continues. Tree and Pascal have now been succeeded by Alan Jay Lerner. In adapting **Pygmalion** to the musical stage, Mr. Lerner has retained the dialogue and business of the movie ending. In the published libretto of *My Fair Lady* he has gone a step further and added some stage directions of his own to Pascal's ending. When Higgins hears Eliza returning to the laboratory, Mr. Lerner comments, *"If he could but let himself, his face would radiate unmistakable relief and joy. If he could but let himself, he would run to her."* When Eliza reappears, he tells us that there are tears in her eyes: *"She understands."* How Shaw's ghost would chuckle over this, if he could read it.

Of course such a sentimental curtain ignores the whole meaning of the encounter between the professor and the former flower girl in the final act. When Eliza, piqued at Higgins's brusque treatment, proclaims defiantly, "I can do without you," Higgins, far from being hurt or disappointed, congratulates her quite sincerely and tells her, "I know you can. I told you you could." Her emotional independence he takes as a sign of growing self-respect. He is equally candid in his counterboast about himself, "I can do without anybody. I have my own soul: my own spark of divine fire." For Eliza, the very essence of human relations is mutual caring, for Higgins it is mutual improvement. True enough, the rage the professor rouses in her is the rage of thwarted affection, but her affection is that of an emotionally sensitive pupil, not of an amorous woman. Freddy appeals to her because he is "weak and poor" and considerate, but also because he is young and handsome and sexually to her taste. But above all, she knows Freddy wants and needs her, while Higgins doesn't. Eliza's life is the warm, passionate life of embraces, mutual recriminations, even violence, and her temperament is the volcanic temperament that makes scenes when her feelings are wounded. Higgins can be equally volcanic, but only when professional matters are concerned. His is the cold, superhuman passion for changing the world. Eliza's code is "I'll be nice to you if you'll be nice to me," Higgins's that of the artist-creator to whom human material is raw material only. The insistence that they end as lovebirds shows how popular sentiment will ignore any degree of incompatibility between a man and a woman once it has entertained the pleasant fancy of mating them. (pp. 141-51)

Louis Crompton, in his Shaw the Dramatist, *University of Nebraska Press, 1969, 261 p.*

Shaw on rehearsing the slipper incident in *Pygmalion*:

In *Pygmalion* the heroine, in a rage, throws the hero's slippers in his face. When we rehearsed this for the first time, I had taken care to have a very soft pair of velvet slippers provided; for I knew that Mrs Patrick Campbell was very dexterous, very strong, and a dead shot.

And, sure enough, when we reached this passage, Tree got the slippers well and truly delivered with unerring aim bang in his face. The effect was appalling. He had totally forgotten that there was any such incident in the play; and it seemed to him that Mrs Campbell, suddenly giving way to an impulse of diabolical wrath and hatred, had committed an unprovoked and brutal assault on him. The physical impact was nothing; but the wound to his feelings was terrible. He collapsed on the nearest chair, and left me staring in amazement, whilst the entire personnel of the theatre crowded solicitously round him, explaining that the incident was part of the play, and even exhibiting the promptbook to prove their words. But his *moral* was so shattered that it took quite a long time, and a good deal of skilful rallying and coaxing from Mrs Campbell, before he was in a condition to resume the rehearsal. The worst of it was that as it was quite evident that he would be just as surprised and wounded next time, Mrs Campbell took care that the slippers should never hit him again, and the incident was consequently one of the least convincing in the performance.

Shaw, in his Pen Portraits and Reviews by Bernard Shaw, *Constable and Co., 1931.*

Margery M. Morgan   (essay date 1972)

[*In the following excerpt, Morgan assesses* Pygmalion *as a problem play concerned with social issues.*]

The classical legend of Pygmalion supplies an image of the artist, or dreamer, that challenges too ready an acceptance of Shaw's play as a version of *Cinderella.* The title insists on recognition that the thematic importance of Higgins at least equals that of Eliza: the experimenter is a vital part of the experiment.

Like *The Doctor's Dilemma, Pygmalion* has been designed strictly on Problem Play lines. The social question it sets out to examine can be formulated in Higgins's terms: What creates 'the deepest gulf that separates class from class and soul from soul?' Taking more than a hint from Dickens's late novel on the class system and the cash nexus in Victorian society, *Our Mutual Friend,* Shaw has worked out two hypotheses: in the fantasy of the girl taken from the gutter and given a superficial education—a veneer of culture and fashionable manners—and the second fantasy of her father, the dustman, suddenly endowed with wealth. In Doolittle he presented a conflation of two Dickensian characters: Boffin, the honest serving man who inherits a vast fortune made out of dust (the dustheaps which neighbour his house being at least as symbolic as they are actual), and the villainous Silas Wegg, parasite and self-styled philosopher; the expansive humour which makes Doolittle finally an attractive character is Shaw's own contribution, and the value it represents in the play can hardly be overestimated. In *Our Mutual Friend,* Boffin himself plays Pygmalion's part in the ingeniously contrived education of Bella Wilfer into a true lady, on the principle of 'gentle is as gentle does'. It is an education of the heart which the more humbly born Lizzie Hexam, in the same novel, does not need; and the seal is set on Lizzie's natural virtue by her ultimate marriage, across all class barriers, with the regenerated Eugene, formerly a wealthy idler.

The natural virtue of Eliza Doolittle is of another kind from Lizzie Hexam's: it is the spirit that makes her commandeer a taxi, when she has been thrown a handful of money, the spirit that takes her to Higgins to ask for lessons and to purpose to pay for them an amount that fires his interest in her case:

> She offers me two-fifths of her day's income for a lesson. Two-fifths of a millionaire's income for a day would be somewhere about £60. It's handsome. By George, it's enormous! it's the biggest offer I ever had.

Boffin is designated the Golden Dustman; the gold dust from which Higgins's Galatea is made is a natural inheritance from her original and only parent. (The point that Eliza has no mother is made three times over in the play.) Neither simple acquisitiveness nor vulgar ambition to rise in society inheres in its substance. Eliza is in quest of some more real value, a richer and finer quality of life.

The way in which Doolittle's two appearances intersect the chronological development of Eliza's story is reminiscent of the Ulrich Brendel episodes in *Rosmersholm* and the way they function dramatically. True, there is a precedent in Shaw's own drama in the appearance of Lickcheese, first as poor man, then as plutocrat, in **Widowers' Houses;** but Lickcheese's part in the main plot, which keeps him on stage nearly to the end of the play, robs his entrances of the special significance that Brendel's and Doolittle's have: checking the main plot, and distancing us from it while we consider its meaning in the light of this new, compelling figure that has usurped the centre of the stage. Doolittle's appearances first as poor man, then as rich man, mark the beginning and the zenith of Eliza's social ascent. The paradox of Brendel's more prosperous, if grotesque, outer appearance, signifying his spiritual bankruptcy, is reflected in the top-hatted misery and defeat of Doolittle, which underlines the emptiness of Eliza's social success, and the irrelevance (as it then appears) of Higgins's experiment with her.

What has happened, so far, is a mere selling-out to social convention. The Professor in the haven of his laboratory, absorbed in the fascination of his special study and careless of any other concerns, appears to his own mother as a baby playing with its toys, with the peculiar irresponsibility of the baby, not realizing that its 'doll' is a human being with human feelings who has to go on living in a bigger, more complicated world outside the laboratory. The imperative implied is that every man *ought* to see what he is doing in relation to the whole society in which he lives, in the context of its values and his own. (Bringing most of his characters together, at the start, under the portico of Inigo Jones's church in Covent Garden—'the handsomest barn in England', according to its creator's description—was Shaw's visual statement of the interrelatedness of these souls, implying such an ideal of society as Peter Keegan had expressed: 'a country where the State is the Church and the Church the people . . . in which all life is human and all humanity divine'.)

But what Higgins learns from his experiment outruns what he foresaw. The discovery that teaching Eliza is not just a matter of phonetics comes first in the realization that she has to be taught grammar as well. The meeting with the Eynsford Hill family, at Mrs Higgins's At-Home, demonstrates plainly that 'you have to consider not only how a girl pronounces, but what she pronounces'; and Eliza's conversation at this stage is nothing but the utterance of an automaton that betrays its lack of individuality, first in the scientific precision of the weather report ('The shallow depression in the west of these islands . . . '), and then, with more semblance of life, in its voicing of the ignorance and melodramatic imagination of the slums:

> What call would a woman with that strength in her have to die of influenza? What become of her new straw hat that should have come to me? Somebody pinched it; and what I say is, them as pinched it done her in.

At last comes the individuality of Eliza speaking out:

> Walk! Not bloody likely . . . I am going in a taxi.

The revelation corresponds to her teacher's latest conception of his task: 'watching her lips and her teeth and her tongue, *not to mention her soul, which is the quaintest of the lot.*'

Higgins's role as *raisonneur,* in addition to principal actor, is clear in this scene. His understanding of the vulnerability of conventions to honest naturalness ('what they really think would break up the whole show') leads on to reflections on the superficiality of the culture that passes in polite (conventional) society. These undercut his insistence on the 'advantages' he has given Eliza and prepare for Mrs Higgins's summing up:

> The advantages of that poor woman who was here just now! The manners and habits that disqualify a fine lady from earning her own living without giving her a fine lady's income! Is that what you mean?

The identification of 'that poor woman' hangs in the air: it is Mrs Eynsford Hill, her daughter, and Eliza herself in so far as her part in this act has been to present a travesty of the 'lady' in this pejorative sense, the individual intimidated by the pressures of society.

The experiment with Doolittle demonstrates that money without manners is sufficient to elevate a man in the social scale, especially if he is naturally endowed with self-confidence. Higgins, even better able to elucidate the implications of what has happened in the last act, makes this point:

> Eliza, it's quite true that your father is not a snob, and that he will be quite at home in any station of life to which his eccentric destiny may call him.

The similarity between Doolittle and Higgins himself is established. Money and genius allow Higgins, also, to infringe protocol and keep to his natural manners. But Higgins is protected from 'intimidation', as Doolittle is not, by his attachment to a wise, benevolent mother.

An inveterate bachelordom characterizes Pygmalion in Ovid's version of the legend: the sculptor's disgust with women as they are is the ground of his love for the ideal woman he models. Shaw accepted the motif, and his resistance of all persuasion to end his play with Eliza's marriage to her teacher testifies to the importance he gave it. Higgins is not one of the more obvious Shavian philanderers, but he does belong in the general category, among the theoreticians. His bias is presented in realistic psychological terms admitted in a conversation with his mother:

> MRS HIGGINS. Well, you never fall in love with anyone under forty-five. When will you discover that there are some rather nice-looking young women about?
>
> HIGGINS. Oh, I cant be bothered with young women. My idea of a lovable woman is something as like you as possible. I shall never get into the way of seriously liking young women: some habits lie too deep to be changed.

He has, in fact, a second mother in his bachelor establishment in the person of the housekeeper, Mrs Pearce (comparable in her role with Emmy in **The Doctor's Dilemma**). It is she who takes him rigorously to task for his swearing, his slovenliness, his bad table manners, leaving Mrs Higgins, however aware she may be of such things, without direct responsibility for checking him, without cause for exasperation, free to give accepting affection and detached advice: to be, as perhaps no other mother is, throughout Shaw's plays, the embodiment of benevolent wisdom, a personification of the good society. Higgins's bullying manner may be symptomatic of his childish dependence:

> HIGGINS. You know, Pickering, that woman has the most extraordinary ideas about me. Here I am, a shy, diffident sort of man. Ive never been able to feel really grown-up and tremendous, like other chaps. And yet shes firmly persuaded that I'm an arbitrary overbearing bossing kind of person.

This play is not concerned with Higgins's weakness, however, but more with the way good mothering licenses irresponsible childishness and the creativity inherent in it. Higgins plays with his doll, but reacts as the good teacher and good parent, when by throwing the slippers at him she violently rejects the Cinderella part and her place in the Doll's House:

> LIZA . . . I can do without you: dont think I cant.
>
> HIGGINS. I know you can. I told you you could.

His work is successfully done only when his charge is self-reliant and independent of him. Society and marriage being what they were, and to some extent still are, Eliza's self-liberation could hardly be shown in marriage to Higgins, but only in good fellowship with him. The umbilical cord has to be cut between the artist and his work of art; the dream is idle until the dreamer abandons his special attachment to it and lets it work itself out in the world as it can, and be changed and modified as it must. This is the moral that the play *as fable* drives home in ending as it does.

Though Higgins has seemed to demonstrate the usual way of a man with a woman in this society, educating Eliza to suit his own convenience, camouflaging the fact by training her in a few useless accomplishments, and treating her as an unpaid servant, he is quite free of the motivation Doolittle betrays in his comment to Higgins and Pickering:

> I been the victim of one woman after another all my life; and I dont grudge you two getting the better of Eliza.

For the Professor's indulgence by women has not really spoiled him. He is the lucky exception that illuminates Shaw's theme of what men have made of women by the discipline of the strap, by keeping them economically dependent and subjugated, and what such women in instinctive revenge have made of men, through the discipline of the chain. Doolittle's proposal to sell his daughter to Higgins matches the latter's initial assumptions that the girl has no feelings and no power of understanding. Playing with his doll educates Higgins to the stage where he can say:

I think a woman fetching a man's slippers is a disgusting sight . . . I think a good deal more of you for throwing them in my face. No use slaving for me and then saying you want to be cared for: who cares for a slave? If you come back, come back for the sake of good fellowship . . .

The logic of *his* way of treating women catches out Doolittle and makes him a sadder man, enslaved to the task of providing for others, bound for his wedding in Hanover Square, 'tied . . . up and delivered . . . into the hands of middleclass morality', which is the morality of the drawingroom where women make the laws. He ends up as nothing else than an older Jack Tanner, Member of the Idle Rich Class.

To use Shaw's own terms, the judgements of this play are not, finally, moral judgements but vital judgements. It moves (as *Our Mutual Friend* does, in its much greater complexity and subtlety) beyond a view of democracy that depends on equalizing the advantages of wealth and education, to one that recognizes self-respect and independence of spirit (to which money and education can contribute) as the only reliable bases for an egalitarian society; it is again Higgins who sees:

> The great secret . . . is . . . having the same manner for all human souls . . . behaving as if you were in Heaven, where there are no third-class carriages, and one soul is as good as another.

But saying this is not enough: the play's vital judgements are distinctly not puritanical judgements. The validity of the unregenerate Doolittle's criticism of women is implied in his statement, 'she's only a woman and dont know how to be happy anyhow'. He recognizes women as the devotees of the official Victorian virtues of prudence and thrift, and his praise of 'Undeserving Poverty' is a plea for happiness and fullness of life as against prudence and thrift and security:

> Dont you be afraid that I'll save it and spare it and live idle on it. There wont be a penny of it left by Monday . . . Just one good spree for myself and the missus, giving pleasure to ourselves and employment to others, and satisfaction to you to think it's not been thrown away. You couldnt spend it better;
>
> . . . Undeserving poverty is my line. Taking one station in society with another, it's—it's—well, it's the only one that has any ginger in it, to my taste.

Tastes differ, but Eliza likes a little ginger, too, and can recognize from her experience the need all human beings have of it and the extent to which 'respectable' morality denies it:

> . . . my mother used to give him fourpence and tell him to go out and not come back until he'd drunk himself cheerful and loving-like. Theres lots of women has to make their husbands drunk to make them fit to live with . . . If a man has a bit of a conscience, it always takes him when he's sober; and then it makes him low-spirited.

A drop of booze just takes that off and makes him happy.

Finally, what saves Higgins himself from social intimidation is the genuine, human security, for which money is a substitute, that lets him spend his time in work that, to his taste, is 'fun'. (It is not the barbarian's taste.) He insists that his freedom is creative freedom and appeals to Eliza to join him in it:

> LIZA. What am I to come back for?
>
> HIGGINS (*bouncing up on his knees on the ottoman and leaning over it to her*). For the fun of it. Thats why I took you on.

Becoming a real woman, instead of a conventional woman, seems to involve abandoning prudence and security and the bonds of morality, and learning the value of fun and the enjoyment of freedom. It makes possible, in turn, a new, unconstrained, affectionate relation between the sexes:

> HIGGINS . . . By George, Eliza, I said I'd make a woman of you; and I have. I like you like this.
>
> LIZA. Yes: you turn round and make up to me now that I'm not afraid of you, and can do without you.
>
> HIGGINS. Of course I do, you little fool. Five minutes ago you were like a millstone round my neck. Now youre a tower of strength: a consort battleship. You and I and Pickering will be three old bachelors together instead of only two men and a silly girl.

In fact, he has made Eliza the first young woman of his acquaintance who is like his mother:

> MRS HIGGINS . . . you were surprised because she threw your slippers at you! *I* should have thrown the fire-irons at you.

As for the prognostication, in Shaw's Afterword, that Eliza will marry Freddy, it can be accepted as a device to avoid the suggestion that she (like Vivie Warren) is destined for a confined and sterile existence, after all. [The critic adds in a footnote that: "The Afterword was a final attempt to combat the Cinderella interpretation of the play. But Gabriel Pascal resisted this proposal and ended his film with an indication that Eliza would become Higgins's slipper-bringing wife. In fact, marriage to Freddy, like the suggestion that Eliza might make her living by teaching phonetics, implies taking over the role of the stronger, or the teacher, that was Higgins's with her. There is, of course, something less than satisfactory in the prospect of a marriage on these terms, especially as Freddy has shown little sign of equalling Eliza's natural genius and ability to learn."] In fact, the possibilities of life are open to the New Woman at the end of the play. (pp. 169-75)

Margery M. Morgan, in her The Shavian Playground: An Exploration of the Art of George Bernard Shaw, *Methuen & Co. Ltd., 1972, 366 p.*

Charles A. Berst   (essay date 1973)

[*Berst is an American educator and critic. In the following excerpt, he examines aesthetic, comic, mythic, and didactic elements that contribute to the success of* Pygmalion.]

Shaw called *Pygmalion* a potboiler, and subtitled it "A Romance." As such, he might well have predicted its popularity. But so many qualities of *Pygmalion* so far transcend such disparagement that the play has special interest as Shavian art at its unpretentious best. The central theme is indeed romantic; but as it evolves, its romance is more social than sexual, and fully as spiritual as social. With unselfconscious ease Shaw has combined pure fancy with a kaleidoscope of mythical associations, and, even more, with a keen social and spiritual sensibility which transmutes a romantic story into a modern myth and touching spiritual parable. Critics have overlooked most of these elements because they tend to approach the play piecemeal, isolating themselves on one strand of argument. Except for a nod in the direction of Cinderella and the mythical Pygmalion, along with a brief concern regarding Eliza's transformation, they have largely failed to come to terms with the real aesthetics of the play, the varied inner tensions which account for its special effects and its artistic success.

Pygmalion unfolds on numerous evocative levels. Most obvious is the imaginative, romantic, dramatic situation, with its lively characters and dialogue, a situation which becomes particularly keen and contentious in the brilliant portrayal of the two principals. Impressed upon this surface action are relatively clear poetic and romantic echoes of the Cinderella fairy tale and the Pygmalion legend. Somewhat more complex, but still immediately intelligible, a social lesson and conscience are projected into the comedy, first revealing the importance of phonetics in the social structure, and, more profoundly, examining the structure itself in relation to individual worth. Beyond this, Shaw becomes far more poetic and suggestive. He takes the elements of his romantic story, his myths, and his social didacticism, and he subjects them to stress in terms of poetic ambiguities and a spiritual parable. The fairy tale of Cinderella does not in fact complement the classical tale of Pygmalion; rather, one plays against the other most ironically. Further, both are counterpointed by minor but poignant themes of medieval morality and modern melodrama. Concurrently, these myths are subject to vigorous social tests. And finally, most powerfully, the action, settings, lighting, story, comedy, myths, and social commentary all aim at the expression of an archetypal pattern in which a soul awakens to true self-realization. Through successive stages of inspiration, purgation, illumination, despair, and final, brilliant personal fulfillment, Eliza progresses toward self-awareness as a human being. Most simply, hers is a movement from illusion to reality; most grandly, she undergoes a spiritual voyage from darkness to light. Thus romance, social didacticism, myth, and spiritual parable converge upon the play from their different spheres, their tension providing a mutual enrichment. And all the while the dramatic scene, vital in itself, maintains a story light enough to be widely popular.

With typical assertiveness Shaw claims in his preface a didactic purpose of making the public aware of the importance of phoneticians. He gloats over the play's success and leaps to a remarkable, thoroughly Shavian conclusion: "It is so intensely and deliberately didactic, and its subject is esteemed so dry, that I delight in throwing it at the heads of the wiseacres who repeat the parrot cry that art should never be didactic. It goes to prove my contention that art should never be anything else." To make his point Shaw is obviously turning the artistic and entertaining substance of the play topsy-turvy, since phonetics are only incidentally its subject. Clearly, great art *can* be intensely didactic, and didacticism need not imply pedantry. The play does bring phonetics into public view, but more imaginatively than dialectically. The importance of language and its use emerges as a cumulative awareness, arising more from the action than as a net result of Higgins's or Shaw's comments. Our primary attention focuses on the human ramifications of Higgins's experiment rather than on the mechanics themselves, but the phonetician and his work are always on stage, impressing their importance on the action. They convey a "message" in the best sense: to the extent that the audience is convinced by the transformation of Eliza, it may carry away some conviction of the importance of phonetics in society, and of language's essential role in revealing and even in forming character.

But the phonetic lesson, alive as it may be, is merely a stepping-stone to a more fundamental message beneath the action. The major didactic achievement of the play is its pointed objectification of the hollowness of social distinctions, and its assertion of the importance of the individual personality which such distinctions obscure. If a flower girl can to all appearances be made into a duchess in six months, the only things which distinguish a duchess are inherited social prestige and money, neither of which she has earned. The message is projected with unique clarity, confronting the perennial fairy-tale mentality which attaches some esoteric nobility or virtue to social eminence. Eliza's individual assertiveness is unquenchable, and the play gives insight into social generalities by reflecting a vitalist philosophy more than a socialist one. Not any flower girl can become a lady—only one with the appropriate drive and talents. As Candida was not held down by Burgess, Eliza is not held down by Doolittle. Clara, conversely, is scarcely a lady, but she is limited less by a lack of money than by a lack of intelligence. True gentility ultimately rests upon properly channeled personal genius, and the barriers between classes, though they provide protection for vested social interests, are vulnerable to the assault of hard work, common sense, and ability.

The didacticism of *Pygmalion* is thus important primarily as it informs the action, providing a ballast of social observation and giving further dimension to the characters. By themselves, the didactic message regarding phonetics may be interesting and the social didacticism may be true, but the phonetic lesson is scarcely world-shaking and the social implications are rather obvious. More influential in the total effect of the play are levels of myth which counterbalance and enhance its prosaic concerns. Shaw uses these imaginative levels richly and suggestively. In contrast to the coherent bones of the plot, which bear a striking resemblance in detail, arrangement, and social application to the sketch of the poor girl in Chapter 87 of Smollett's *Peregrine Pickle,* the play's mythical overtones are impressionistic and are evoked by association and selection keyed to suit the dramatic context, not by any strict ordering.

Ever present is the classical myth of Pygmalion, with its idealism, magic, and sense of vital fulfillment. In Ovid's version Pygmalion, repelled by the faults of mortal women, resolves to live single. Yet he so desires a feminine ideal that he sculptures an incomparably beautiful maiden in ivory, whereupon he attires the statue in gay garments and adorns it with jewelry. Without breath, however, the beauty is incomplete and the ideal not fully realized; so he prays to the gods, and Venus instills life into his creation. The ivory maiden suddenly gains vision, and she sees the daylight and Pygmalion at once. Pygmalion's desires are thus fulfilled, and he is united in marriage with his living ideal. A spiritual substratum beneath this tale is not difficult to discern. It appeals to the most basic yearnings of all who are to some degree disillusioned by the grossness of humanity and seek an ideal, one which might be simulated in earthly terms but which ultimately may be found only through the breath of spirit, the gift of deity.

The play offers a close parallel to this appealing level, and the associations of the myth instill a sense of magic into the play's action. But just as interesting are the points at which the two deviate. Like Pygmalion, Higgins harbors a degree of misogyny and seeks to create an ideal in Eliza. Though he is an artist in his sense of dedication, he is a cerebral one, quite Shavian, and his final proposed union is intellectual, not physical. Parallel to the legend, he creates his ivory statue by Act III, decking it in fashionable clothes and jewels, and the god of Eliza's psyche (urged, in part, by Venus) breathes life into it by Act IV, giving her sudden, clear vision of her Pygmalion. However, the creator and the created are out of tune, one existing in a world of intellectual austerity, the other inhaling a vibrant sense of being and seeking emotional fulfillment. The attraction of opposites is held in suspension by the stubborn independence of each, and the play ends in tension, not in resolution.

Contrapuntal to the classical, mythical, and spiritual tones of the Pygmalion legend are the folk-tale, fairy-tale, fanciful associations of Cinderella. The ragged, dirty, mistreated but beautiful waif who is suddenly, magically elevated to high society is common to both the play and the story. A cruel stepmother, a coach, a midnight hour of reckoning, slippers, and a desperate deserted gentleman are integral details of both plots and provide both with the exuberance of romance. There is even a doubling of the "test" in the play, as in Perrault's original version of the tale.

But again, although *Pygmalion* absorbs much of the romantic nimbus, it converts the legend to its own artistic ends. The incidents are jumbled chronologically, reapportioned, changed in context, and they involve variant emotions and significance. The golden coach is the taxi of Act I which Eliza hires in personal defiance of poverty and in assertion of her rights as a human being. The cruel step-

mother is both Doolittle's mistress and, as suggested by Higgins, a monsterized Mrs. Pearce. The slippers are Higgins's, and as Cinderella's fortunes turn upon hers, these become the symbol of Eliza's break with the past, objectifying her rejection of Cinderella notions. The magic of the fairy godmother in *Pygmalion* is social and psychological, having little to do with dress and fine jewels, and the mystery of the fairy godmother is not that of a magic wand but of her collective nature: she is something of Higgins, something of Mrs. Pearce, and a great deal of Pickering and Mrs. Higgins. Most important, the key "ball" scene is omitted from the play, because the emphasis here is not on the fairy-tale climax of the triumphant "test"—this has been rendered anticlimactic by Act III—but on the social and personal ramifications of the real world to which Eliza must adjust after the test, not the least troublesome of which is a recalcitrant prince charming.

Thus the "reality" of the play is reflected against the romance of legend and fairy tale, and the ramifications are subtle and telling. But even further, one myth is played off against the other. If we see Eliza as Galatea, we see her much as Higgins does in the first three acts—as a statue, a doll, a creature of his own making. Conversely, viewed as Cinderella (which is her own point of view), she is vitally, personally motivated from the very beginning, and Higgins's conceit and blindness as Pygmalion become obvious. The interplay of these variants, of myth against the story and of myth against myth, redounds subtly to the complexity of the ironies and to the delight of the play.

Less obvious than the classical Pygmalion legend and the Cinderella fairy tale, but nearly as pervasive, is a medieval morality element. Eliza in Act I is breaking that little Chain of Being which assumes that flower girls do not hire taxis, and the presence of an Old Testament God may be implied in the lightning that flashes as she bumps into Freddy, as well as in the church bells which remind Higgins of charity. The profound morality test comes in Act II. Here Eliza is The Tempted, most notably in terms of innocent Eve—"I'm a good girl, I am"—suffering from the sins of curiosity and ambition, lured on by Satan Higgins. The symbol of the temptation is a chocolate, taken from a bowl of fruit, the implications of which are nearly biblical: here is a sweet from the tree of the knowledge of good and evil, a psychedelic goody leading to semi-divine worlds beyond the imagination, offered by a diabolically clever and seductive tempter whose intentions are entirely selfish. The combination of hesitancy and desire in Eliza suggests the contention of the good and evil angels in her simple soul, spirits like those of the moralities, one urging the salvation of retreat, the other urging the damnation of acceptance.

The temptation is also evocative of the Faust legend, first in the medieval sense of Marlowe's *Doctor Faustus,* which is correlative to the moral context of Eve's downfall. In desiring language lessons Eliza seeks the knowledge and power of the upper classes, a presumptuous aim reminiscent of Faustus's similar but more ambitious goal. Eliza's inclination to cross a socially ordained barrier is a winsome parody of Faustus's unholy inclination to cross a divinely ordained barrier. Higgins becomes the artful spirit, the Mephistopheles who has the power to make this possible and who maneuvers through his own self-interest to render the prospect enticing. Eliza forfeits her flower-girl's soul to visions of climbing beyond her station, visions which are fully as profound to her as Faustus's are to him. And her reward is the damnation of Acts IV and V, when she comes into an awareness that her former values were unreal, that heaven has eluded her, and she cries, "Whats to become of me?" Faustus's final despair is scarcely more poignant.

But once again there is a typically Shavian twist in *Pygmalion.* The fear of Old Testament damnation in Act II and the despair of the last two acts are overcome by the enlightenment at the end. As opposed to Eve's, Eliza's soul is saved. It is at this point that the context is shifted toward Goethe's Age of Reason *Faust:* there is a salvation in the very search for transcendence above human limitations. The status quo grows brittle as it crystallizes, it does not fulfill the human spirit, and medieval patterns and inhibitions are shattered as Eliza breaks free in an assertion of individual genius and independence. As with Goethe's *Faust,* truth may be elusive, but the individual who seeks it is ennobled by his search, and it would have been true damnation for Eliza never to have tried. Mephistopheles Higgins may taunt her and work on her emotions in Act V, but she properly recognizes the devil for what he is—"Oh, you *are* a devil"—and in this she reveals her true state of grace.

The play alludes to a form of contemporary mythology as well. From sentimental fiction comes the melodramatic consciousness which Eliza and her father reflect in Act II. From Eliza's point of view, as a poor good girl she is in dire danger of being compromised by a rich, unscrupulous gentleman, a vile seducer. She is a Pamela, upholding her virtue against Squire B; a Pauline, confronted by an ultimate peril. Thus she remarks to Higgins, "I've heard of girls being drugged by the like of you," and she refuses the unreal lure of gold and diamonds—though perhaps chocolates and taxis are a different matter. Similarly, Doolittle enters as the melodramatic father of a ruined daughter, demanding satisfaction, anticipating the worst, and, in an ironic turn, deflated and disappointed that it has not occurred. In the very presentation of this consciousness Shaw laughs it away, but he makes a point in the process which is integral to his drama. If the audience can laugh at the melodrama of Eliza and at melodrama comically inverted in Doolittle, no doubt it should chuckle at the romance of Cinderella. The exposure of one should illumine the fantasy of the other. Eliza's fears are a reflection of the ignorance of the melodramatic state of mind which treats life in terms of absolutes and reality in terms of fiction.

As the mythology and didacticism provide an imaginative, provocative reference behind the scenes, there is an even deeper level which emerges from the action—that of Eliza's evolving consciousness. Commentators have observed that Eliza gains a soul in Acts IV and V, but they have failed to delineate adequately the aesthetic and dramatic terms in which it develops. Eliza's soul grows by degrees, not just at the end. Ostensibly, the lessons and example of her numerous mentors provide the basis for

growth. These Eliza absorbs in terms of her vitality and talent, her own essential qualities without which the lessons would prove futile and the transformation hopeless. She emerges as a synthesis of her education, her environment, and her special abilities, her incipient genius flowering in the broader horizons which are offered her by the relative sophistication and freedom of the upper classes. But this explanation only partially captures the poignant sense of real evolution which the play conveys. While the Cinderella and Pygmalion stories are tied irrevocably to myth by the magic of their heroines' abrupt transformation, the Eliza story evokes the overtones of a magic metamorphosis but also maintains a sense of reality through closely tracing a pilgrim's progress of the soul. Poetic realism results from the artistic and spiritual integrity with which Eliza follows an archetypal pattern. Shaw presents her spiritual growth act by act in carefully plotted, psychologically sensitive, progressive stages, and he complements these stages with special effects of setting, lighting, and timing. Thus Eliza evolves according to a soundly forceful archetypal poetry, augmented by the graphic powers of a theatrical dimension.

In Act I the darkness of the night, the rain, and the confusion of the scene reflect the darkness and confusion which envelop Eliza on multiple levels—physical, social, intellectual, and spiritual. Hers is a world of chaos, and she is swept along by it, oblivious to the suggestive portents of the lightning and the church bells. Eliza's ties to her class are apparent in her confrontation with Higgins, and the scene would be spiritually static but for the sudden inspiration of her soul by a few coins. This inspiration is pathetic and partial, but is as much as her consciousness is capable of at the moment. She howls with delight as she examines Higgins's money, which is incidental to him but the door to grand things for her; and with great exuberance and flair she indulges in the extravagance of a taxi, the symbol of a higher order of existence which is suddenly within her grasp.

Eliza enters Act II voluntarily, her ambition fired by the feeble spark of trivial good fortune. With flower-girl naïveté, she is seeking economic security and social respectability. What she scarcely realizes is that this deliberate step toward such goals sharply objectifies her initial impulse and constitutes a key second stage in a much grander quest, one leading toward spiritual emancipation. Although she is myopic as to ends, her goals seem most glorious to her, and her instincts as to the means are instinctively correct—she must have knowledge. Her immediate fate is appropriately purgatorial. The dimness and strangeness of Higgins's drawingroom laboratory offer a fit otherworldly background, an apt purgatory for a flower girl. The social battering Eliza goes through, the burning of her clothes, and the curious, hot, exotic bath amount to purifying rigors quite necessary to cleanse both soul and body: the soul, of childish notions and conceit; the body, of lice.

By Act III the body is clean but the soul still has more pretensions than depth. The light and airiness of the setting reflect the minor spiritual illumination of Eliza, which consists of a more sensitive perception of a higher state and some involvement in it. But she has adopted a new mask more than a new character, a mask which only imperfectly conceals lower-class values. In attempting to live up to the mask and in carrying it off her soul has grown, but in not reconciling the show with reality she is amusingly imperfect.

Act IV, significantly, starts at midnight. In the deflation after the party, beset by surrounding gloom, Eliza experiences the dark night of her soul, the despair of isolation and absence of meaning. But in her despair lies self-realization, since it involves an awakening to the disparity between her ambitions and her means. The values of society seem fragile when compared to her affection for Higgins, but both are frustrations when Eliza can see no hope of expressing herself through either. In this awareness her sophistication at last transcends her façade, and the soul which lays bare its realities to Higgins, causing him to lose his temper, is a soul sufficiently integrated with personality to be able to face social realities. Finally, in Act V, the daylight and the gentility of Mrs. Higgins's drawing room appropriately complement Eliza's union with the social order, now on a sophisticated plane of spiritual identification and self-knowledge. Her powers are certainly enhanced, and her sense of reality has so far advanced that now she is a match for the professor.

Thus Eliza evolves from confusion, ignorance, and illusion to coherence, knowledge, and reality. The inspiration in Act I, the quest and purgation in Act II, the minor illumination in Act III, and the purgation of the falseness in this illumination in Act IV all lead progressively toward the sophisticated unifying of spirit with personality and society in Act V. By tracing an archetypal pattern in these steps, and by richly complementing the pattern with dramatic effects, the play transcends fable on a plane of poetically endowed socio-spiritual parable. The profoundest aesthetic level of *Pygmalion* exists in this parable, which qualifies the play's less serious aspects and serves as a substratum underlying the disparities, conflicts, and incompleteness of the didacticism and the myths.

Important as they may be, the evolution of Eliza's consciousness, the didacticism, and the myths all are made an integral part of the immediate vivacity of the dramatic scene, serving primarily to give it significance, richness, and depth. Act I, for example, is no doubt the most openly didactic part of the play in terms of Shaw's avowed intention. Yet it is managed with skillful dramaturgy, and the focus soon falls more upon Eliza than upon phonetics. The setting and the action, the darkness, the after-theater confusion, and Eliza's pathetic scramble for pennies are dramatically essential to provide a brief glimpse of the flowergirl's world so that her later transformation will be the more graphic. When Higgins is brought to Eliza's attention and she wails in fear of arrest, the crowd's observation, sympathetic to the girl, falls upon the professor. Shaw thus adroitly sets up his platform, and Higgins's performance is not unlike that of a sideshow artist, or, as Pickering suggests, a music-hall performer. The audience, along with the crowd, is given a brief illustrated lesson in the skills of a phonetician and in the remarkable role phonetics can play in society. But at the same time a lively

human dimension is maintained through Eliza. As Higgins plays at his profession, Eliza is in agony, concerned about arrest, her rights, and her virtue. Thus the plight of the poor is contrasted with the privileges of gentility, gutter slang is contrasted with the king's English, ignorance with knowledge, humanity with science. As the phonetic message is exemplified, the social message is implicit, but both add to rather than diminish the essential human dynamics of the scene. With her cleverness in extracting the maximum return from her violets, her insistence on her virtue, her assertion of the sacredness of her character, and her laughter at being mimicked by Higgins, Shaw reveals in Eliza an ambition, self-respect, pride, and sense of humor which are bound to triumph dramatically over the soapbox he has provided for the phonetician.

Numerous background elements are subliminally suggestive. The churchfront setting, the lightning and thunder at Eliza's collision with Freddy, Higgins's insistence on the divinity of speech, and the bells which remind Higgins of the voice of God all introduce a quizzical suggestion of divine presence, a morality note. But the real light of the scene comes as Eliza, amazed and thrilled with the relative fortune the gentleman has thrown her, audaciously takes her coach toward the strange glories of genteel life in Act II. This action is singularly vital on many levels, since this is Eliza's first minute step toward self-realization. The spontaneity of the moment, while seemingly trivial, reverberates romantically, socially, and spiritually, all at the same time. The structure of the act is so complete that it could stand by itself. The didactic point has been made, climaxed by a Cinderella triumph. However, the momentary triumph will obviously be squashed in terms of a grander pattern, because the life of *Pygmalion* and the ultimate significance of Eliza lie in anticlimax, and that soon follows.

Act II provides a lively exposition of character which is in itself an expression of the social problem. At the same time it maintains a tension between ignorance and knowledge, illusion and reality, fairyland and fact, which renders the scene a fanciful, whimsical one, wavering between humor and pathos. These incongruous elements are manifest in the different perspectives regarding Eliza. To herself Eliza is a virtuous young woman with worldly intelligence, dignity, and great expectations. To Higgins she is personally "baggage" and professionally a phonetic experiment. To Pickering she is a naïve young woman with feelings, and due the courtesy one displays toward anything feminine; to Mrs. Pearce she is poor, underprivileged, ignorant, and common, yet a human being; to her father she is little more than the present opportunity for a good time which some quick extortion money will buy. As such views are in constant counterpoint, they provide a vibrant energy to Eliza's portrayal.

Eliza arrives in a Cinderella illusion, a taxi serving as her golden coach, an ostrich-feather hat and a shoddy coat serving as the garb of a fine lady. Her concepts of gentility are founded in the ignorance of her class, and they cling to easily observable surface elements—manners, money, and speech. With these preconceptions and a lower-class shrewdness as to the power of money, she confronts Hig-

(Top left) *Mrs. Patrick Campbell as Eliza before and after her transformation;* (top right) *scenes from* Pygmalion *in the periodical the* By-stander, *1914;* (bottom left) *a marked page from Shaw's rehearsal copy of the play;* (bottom right) *Lilli Marberg as the first Eliza Doolittle, Hofburg Theatre, Vienna, 1913.*

gins, obviously to be confounded when he does not fit her stereotype of a gentleman. As he does with her father later, Higgins completely disorients Eliza because she has no realistic context in which to judge him; the scene becomes purgatorial for her as she is reduced from haughtiness to a confusion of terror, weeping, bewilderment, and helplessness. The profane novice is scarcely prepared for *this* sort of initiation into the higher mysteries. She is only equipped to change illusions, from Cinderella to melodrama—she the poor innocent, Higgins the foul villain. It is not until Pickering suggests that she has feelings that Eliza takes up this refrain. She is manifestly incapable of expressing herself or of conceptualizing her state other than in simplistic alternatives, and, in turn, her feelings have shallow definition because she has neither the language in which to express them nor the perspective or experience to objectify them. Thus terror, rebelliousness, dismay, and indignation are all vented by a howl, through which she may reflect different emotions by intonation, but which obscures the expression of her emotion and probably obscures the emotion itself. Eliza is clearly not just a problem of phonetics, but of an entire orientation, and the humor of the scene, resulting from the wide gap in understanding between classes, is also its didactic message.

As Eliza misconstrues her predicament as a seduction peril, Higgins oversimplifies the situation as a fascinating experiment. The Cinderella dreams and Pamela fears have their counterpart in the Pygmalion obsession. By categorizing Eliza as a draggletailed guttersnipe and scarcely allowing that she has feelings, Higgins is dehumanizing her, viewing her with drastically less consideration than Pygmalion granted his ivory. He is indulging in a level of illusion as misguided and potentially more pernicious than hers. He abstracts her humanity in terms of inhuman generalizations. So Higgins becomes a devil in blindness and in method, and the action develops both as an interplay of ignorance with knowledge and of illusion with reality, and as a revelation of two kinds of oversimplification. One involves loss of individuality in dreams and ignorance; the other involves a loss of humanity in taking that ignorance for the person behind it. Eliza ironically lends herself to stereotyping, but Higgins violates his own assumed sophistication in accepting the abstraction. The courteous, considerate voice of Pickering and the prudent voice of Mrs. Pearce, much like the voices of good angels in a morality play, form a counterrefrain to Higgins's demonic, symphonic gust of enthusiasm. But, like the words of most good angels, their admonitions go unheeded.

The grand flourish with which Pygmalion Higgins ends his persuasion is typical of the vibrant associations which echo throughout the act, rendering the complex counterpoint of character, myth, and ideas so effervescent: Higgins begins as Mephistopheles, tempting Eliza with the comforts, riches, and prestige of the world—"If youre good and do whatever youre told, you shall sleep in a proper bedroom, and have lots to eat, and money to buy chocolates and take rides in taxis." He then threatens her with the plight of Cinderella—"If youre naughty and idle you will sleep in the back kitchen among the black beetles, and be walloped by Mrs Pearce with a broomstick"; he suggests the glory of Cinderella and a Happy Ending—

"At the end of six months you shall go to Buckingham Palace in a carriage, beautifully dressed"; he evokes shades of Henry VIII, Bluebeard, and melodrama—"If the King finds out youre not a lady, you will be taken by the police to the Tower of London, where your head will be cut off as a warning to other presumptuous flower girls"; he then comes to earth on a pragmatic social level, appealing to Eliza's ambition—"If you are not found out, you shall have a present of seven-and-sixpence to start life with as a lady in a shop"; and at last he concludes with an imposition of personal obligation, plus an implication of spiritual import—"If you refuse this offer you will be a most ungrateful and wicked girl; and the angels will weep for you." The temptation is overwhelming. What chance has a guttersnipe against a professor, the ivory against Pygmalion, Cinderella against her prince, Pamela against Squire B., Eve against Satan, Faust against Mephistopheles, the initiate against the high priest? The devil—paradoxically, a savior—will have her soul.

In the character of Alfred Doolittle, Shaw offers a roguish counterstatement to Eliza's aspirations and reaffirms the potential of a vital personality, even one which has compromised with the status quo. Doolittle has considerable self-knowledge without the sophistication of social advantages. The melodrama which is real to Eliza is meaningless to him, except as he tries to use it for extortion. He is too busy living in the present to lose himself to such middle-class myths as Cinderella. To rise in society is to be trapped by society's inhibitions, and he exudes a preference for the freedom of poverty over the prudence of wealth. Without hypocrisy, Doolittle is willing to face the reality of his sloth and to appreciate the value of money not saved. Yet beneath his frank philosophy there is an element of making a virtue of necessity, and the humor of his candid complacency conceals the pathos of a man who can scarcely afford morals. Everyone may have a price, but the price of the destitute must by necessity be low; refined morality is an upper-class luxury, sustained by adequate bank accounts. Thus Doolittle's rights as a father are worth about five pounds, and the prospect of Eliza entering a "career" as a kept woman is not unpleasing to him—especially when considered in the light of her earlier query: "Whood marry me?" Doolittle has dramatic appeal in his refusal to romanticize his life, and he has comic and thematic soundness in his conscious violation of the bourgeois notions of success which Eliza holds dear. His precipitant rise to the middle classes later in the play offers a comic parallel to Eliza's plight and provides delight as it tests his philosophy, revealing in the same man opposite sides of the problem of charity. As the dependent man turns independent, the social drag becomes society's crutch and develops a new compassion for the middle classes. He becomes trapped, besieged by hungry relatives, and intimidated by money, morality, and prudence. Eliza's success is the sensible man's doom. And ironically Doolittle, so aptly named, is more truly a Cinderella than Eliza, since his rise, unlike hers, comes suddenly, completely, and through no direct effort of his own. The true Cinderella is a freeloader whose success is a fairy-tale perversion of the Horatio Alger ideal. Through Doolittle, the motivation for Eliza's dreams becomes clearer, but the dreams themselves take on an additional tincture of the absurd.

In Act III myth is tested against reality, with Cinderella acting the part of a lady and Galatea submitting to critical scrutiny. Eliza has survived her preliminary purgation—the flower girl is at least superficially buried—and the bright, genteel, "at-home" setting serves to complement her budding spiritual illumination. But Eliza is thinking more in terms of Cinderella than of soul, and as Galatea she is a social success less in terms of her mythical perfection than because of her critics' stupidity. The disparity between the magic of the myth and the pretensions of the reality, added to the incongruity between the automatism of the mechanical lady-doll and her ill-concealed flower-girl psyche, account for both the humor and the meaning of the scene. Galatea, Cinderella, and Eliza do not mix. The fancily garbed, phonetically molded Galatea is an attempt to freeze Cinderella into an image of beauty and gentility, but the earthiness of Eliza's curbstone background and the vigor of her spirit are not to be confined. Consequently both myths fall apart, cracked by reality. But in her flower-girl ignorance and conceit Eliza does not see this, and in his enthusiasm Pygmalion is blind.

The only clear head in the scene is that of Mrs. Higgins, whose motherly candor and frankness toward her son cut sharply through his bluff and bluster, quietly yet clearly placing him in perspective. Mrs. Higgins quickly grasps the intrinsic reality of Eliza and sees the concomitant "problem," yet in so doing she is as gentle and kindly toward the girl as she is explicit and stern toward Higgins and Pickering. She is as capable of decorously handling the awkward experiment her son has foisted into her drawing room as she is sympathetic and delicate regarding the predicament of Mrs. Eynsford Hill. Personally, Mrs. Higgins is the ideal of candor, good manners, sophistication, and kindliness which are at the heart of true gentility, and, as such, she provides the standard against which Eliza's growth throughout the play may reasonably be measured. Parabolically, she is symbolic of the ultimate toward which Eliza strives, an all-knowing social goddess (or fairy godmother) who puts the large-talking, unmannerly devil in his place as though he were a small boy, and who reveals compassion toward a presumptuous, trespassing sinner.

The problem which Mrs. Higgins senses regarding Eliza is personified by the Eynsford Hills. Mrs. Eynsford Hill is plagued with manners and social pretensions beyond her means. She is a misfit, a social orphan, and her misfortune breeds misfortune, notably in her children. Freddy's good-hearted simplicity might be sustained by a sizeable bank account, but without financial backing he is adrift, socially above entering trade and economically below obtaining the gentleman's education which would qualify him for something better. Clara attempts to become fashionable by adopting the fads and small talk of sophisticated society, but like Eliza, whose colorful talk indicates the wretchedness of a flower-girl's existence, tinting comedy with pathos, Clara reveals through her uncouthness and abruptness the frustration of living impecuniously on the fringes of a moneyed class. Lacking Eliza's natural talents,

she is involved in a life of social tag-ends, pathetic in the disparity between her means and her ambitions, and comic in her ignorance of the disparity.

The didacticism regarding phonetics reaches its peak at this point, with Higgins claiming the alteration of a soul through his science. He is only partially correct, and the limitations of phonetics are apparent in his success. Whereas Mrs. Higgins is limited only by her inability to read Henry's patent shorthand postcards, Eliza is limited by her inability to grasp the genteel mode which enables one to walk home instead of taking a taxi and which inhibits one from using such terms as "bloody." As Mrs. Higgins observes, Eliza is a triumph of the art of phonetics and of the dressmaker, but she is *not* a lady. Her acquirements are superficial, and what she has in natural vigor and genius she lacks in restraint, sophistication, and true spiritual coherence. Thus the play pivots on this central act: the phonetic point has been made, and social implications take over; the myths tend to destroy each other, and Eliza's humanity becomes a problem. She has the manners but not the soul.

Act IV provides the greatest moment of truth for Eliza, revealing her transcendence beyond myth—myth which would, if this were a fairy tale, have rendered the party scene imperative. But any party scene could only display again the illusions of Act III, along with those gains in Eliza's social sophistication which can be better revealed in deeper personal terms here. Shaw delves beyond the point at which most plays would prepare for a rapid conclusion. Prior to this act the primary attention of the characters is on Eliza, her training and her performance. Now that the test is over, the "play" finished, the time comes for plaudits and bows, and while Pickering is generous, Eliza is shoved into the wings by Higgins. The dream has been fulfilled, midnight has tolled for Cinderella, and morning reality is at hand. Eliza's efforts and her importance are denigrated, her ego is shaken, and she awakens to the facts behind her Cinderella illusion. Her despairing cry—"Whats to become of me?"—comes as a true climax to a crescendo of serious concern which has accompanied the comedy through Acts II and III, first voiced fretfully by Mrs. Pearce, then more positively by Mrs. Higgins. The cry is reminiscent of Major Barbara's and Saint Joan's, being that of a soul suddenly jolted by an awareness of its abandonment and isolation. Eliza has compensation in her despair, but it is bitter—in the very fact that she awakens to her predicament, she reveals that she has grown up. Her painful self-awareness, the agony of this dark night of her soul, moves the play toward a realization of its deeper social and spiritual implications, elevating Eliza toward the insight of Mrs. Higgins.

Through having Eliza turn this new insight on the professor, Shaw effects a remarkable tour de force which inverts their roles. In Act II Mrs. Pearce admonished her, "You dont understand the gentleman." Now it is Higgins who does not understand, and Eliza who finally gains control of the scene with her clear appraisal of the facts. As Higgins managed Act II on a satanic cerebral plane, Eliza turns Act IV into an emotional purgation, startlingly, though covertly, like a lovers' quarrel, punctuated by the return of a ring. She rejects her flower-girl's myth and her past by throwing the slippers (which in this case the *prince* has lost) at Higgins. To Cinderella the slippers were the means to the happy ending; to Eliza these are symbolic of her social subservience and the falseness of happy endings. Ironically, when this Galatea comes to life, this Pygmalion cannot handle her. Eve foils Satan by recapturing her soul, and while it was Eve who gulped the chocolate in Act II, now it is Satan who literally munches the apple (from the same dessert dish), and there is some indication that he gains new knowledge thereby. Eliza, not having received true feeling or compassion from Higgins, at last eggs him into a rage and basks delighted both by his emotional genuineness and by her control. There is an element of love in her delight at upsetting him, as there is an implied fondness motivating his violent reaction. And finally, though Eliza has rejected the myth, she retains the romance, going down on her knees to search for the ring Higgins has flung into the fireplace, a defunct Cinderella symbolically back among the cinders. But the social barrier has been crossed on a vital level; Eliza has met Higgins on a plane of deeply wounded affection which has strong undertones of the love it overtly denies. Her accomplishment most poignantly reveals her growth.

The soul which buds in Acts III and IV comes into full flower in Act V. Eliza has developed from spiritual infancy toward the subtle maturity of Mrs. Higgins, and her gentility is almost an integral part of her personality. She has achieved a true sense of union with society and, in the process, has found considerable spiritual freedom. Eliza's development is manifested in large measure by her coherent ability to realize and express her feelings. The refinements of language and manners and the dignity of being treated as a lady have provided a means through which her intellectual and emotional being can put its discordant jumble of half-thoughts, half-ambitions, and half-feelings into an order that has not only exterior polish but interior subtlety. Her sophistication is evident in her sense of humor, which was so notably lacking in her Cinderella guise: she asks after Higgins's health, and comments on the weather in a sly, cuttingly ironic reflection of her only two subjects in Act III. She is, to all appearances, thoroughly on top of the situation, carrying off her role with a *savoir faire* cunningly designed to twist Higgins into knots. In the manner of his mother, she now treats the professor as an equal or slightly less than an equal, extolling the value of manners, likening his behavior to hers as a flower girl, and discounting her debt to his science.

Eliza's depth of social perception here effects finely honed didacticism. She is only partly right in observing that "the difference between a lady and a flower girl is not how she behaves, but how she's treated," for clearly the difference between Eliza and her former self has very much to do with how she behaves. But she is now rightly sensitive that it was Pickering and his manners more than Higgins and his phonetics that made a true lady of her. Eliza is riding too high, however, and Shaw, carefully avoiding a fairy tale, undercuts the suave lady with her howl of surprise at Doolittle. From this point on she slips occasionally into solecisms which tie her to her past and make her present personality more whole and convincing. Her snobbery to-

ward her stepmother further reveals that she is not yet fully a Mrs. Higgins. She is too close to her squalid roots to easily adopt the kindness, understanding, and integrity which transcend class distinctions.

Fairy-tale patterns are further violated when the talk turns to love and marriage, with Higgins avoiding direct personal confrontation of the issue by shifting it toward Pickering. Obliquely, the professor dodges. Less obliquely, the woman pursues (though denying it) under the guise of desiring kindness (which Pickering has amply given her), unsure of her feelings and, in striking contrast to her earlier poise, even more unsure of how to express herself. However, such comments as "You can twist the heart in a girl," "What did you do it for if you didnt care for me?" and "Every girl has a right to be loved", are strong hints as to where her disposition lies. Eliza's snobbery and attitudes now being middle class, it seems likely that her affection toward Higgins would seek the middle-class goal of marriage. When she deals in genuine personal terms with him, as opposed to maintaining her social façade, she tends to slip into flower-girl vernacular which suggests the depth of her emotions. Her final declaration of independence would be more convincing were she not to gain such pleasure in provoking Higgins to wrath. She produces Freddy as Higgins's rival in love (Freddy is significant in this context as a vapid, middle-class, surrogate prince charming, primarily useful as a foil); then, vastly more infuriating for a person of Higgins's temperament, she promotes Professor Nepommuck as Higgins's professional rival. Eliza triumphs in the notion of Higgins striking her. In this outburst he reveals emotional involvement, and even hostile involvement implies a warmth of feeling, a sense of equality, and perhaps jealousy—a reaction which is not scientific, a reality which is not mental. The emphasis of the closing dialogue thus suggests that Eliza may have found financial freedom but not emotional freedom, and Higgins's final request that she order ham and cheese for him takes this into account. Notably, his request involves a contradiction of that independence he has just extolled in her.

Higgins seems to be motivated by a desire for Eliza's companionship, not marriage. He admires her new strength of character as he admires his mother's strength of character, but he values her primarily as she serves his ego and convenience. At the beginning of the act Higgins may have been searching for Eliza with all the desperation of Cinderella's prince, but certainly not with the same disposition. His distraction is scarcely that of Romeo: "But I cant find anything. I dont know what appointments Ive got." Through discovering the unique value of Eliza's soul and feelings, he has progressed beyond the shallowness of his early callous, categorical estimates of her, but he has not learned emotional maturity. Now, devil-like, he tries to keep her for her soul and for his self-satisfaction, little else. Thus Eliza's "Oh, you *are* a devil."

A close examination of Higgins's character and comments cannot support a romantic conclusion. He is by nature celibate and self-centered, slightly perverse in both respects. His reference to sensual love in terms of thick lips and thick boots reveals a confusion and revulsion which considers marital sensualism gross. And his justification of his social egalitarianism is equally distorted. His statement that he treats all people the same, as in heaven, where there are no third-class carriages, sounds impressive at first. But it seems less noble on the second thought that it provides him with a convenient excuse both for his callousness toward Eliza and for his self-indulgence in a lack of manners. He treats everyone the same, but this is hardly admirable when he behaves as though he were the aristocrat and they all flower girls. Pickering also treats all women the same, but he is more inclined to treat them as duchesses, since he has a sensitive respect for human dignity and feelings. As Higgins's vitality tends to run at right angles to society, Pickering's vitality runs parallel. One is consequently more startling, but the other is no less real. Pickering's charity and kindliness give society a moral meaning which Higgins, with inborn egocentricity, ignores.

Higgins, finally, is a motor bus temperamentally, a Milton mentally, and a confirmed bachelor emotionally—a well-drawn composite which is, all told, a rather formidable nut to crack. He is much like a precocious, headstrong young boy. He requires a mother more than a wife and relishes the idea of an emancipated Eliza being not a woman but a bachelor buddy. In avoiding social trivia he is missing many of the details which, when considered cumulatively, make life endurable and worthwhile; in pursuing scientific truth he is pursuing obscurity, substituting mechanics for intrinsic humanity. His science is tied to the expression of life, but he is inclined to negate life for the expression. Insofar as Eliza brings him to an awareness of his dependency as a human being on other human beings, and to a perception of the limitations of his science, Galatea transforms Pygmalion, and the myth undergoes an ironic extension. But Eliza's success is a limited one, and the chance of a marriage between the two is, for anyone who closely observes Act V, highly improbable. This bachelor is truly confirmed, emotionally unsophisticated, hostile to sentiment. The myths, of course, suggest an opposite conclusion: Pygmalion marries his Galatea, Cinderella marries her prince. Higgins's Oedipus complex might even logically be channeled toward Eliza, since by Act V she so closely resembles his mother in insight and sophistication. Socially she is now a lady and eligible. But through Higgins's character Shaw counters the romantic expectations of the final act, and he does so with psychological consistency, creating a perverse tension between the anticipated and the actual. Ultimately, only the fairy-tale preconceptions of a sentimental audience can comfortably turn *Pygmalion* into *My Fair Lady*.

The play is thus comprised of divergent elements of character, myth, didacticism, and parable which are mutually enriching. Their interrelationship is in flux, but it is carefully worked to move the drama forward in terms of a metamorphosis founded in reality. Following variant patterns, the play progresses from ignorance to knowledge: the myths fade into the reality, the didacticism turns from phonetics to life, Eliza's spirit evolves from darkness to light. Even the comedy complements a rising sense of temporal and spiritual awareness, moving generally from a humor of confusion toward a humor which seeks order

and understanding. Act I thrives in chaos, the delight of the sideshow. Act II plays levels of comprehension against each other, provoking a humor of misunderstanding, of fact versus fairy tale, of science versus melodrama. Act III is Bergsonian, Eliza being comic as she is mechanical, the decorous manner of her presence being sharply incongruous with the earthy matter of her speech. Act IV involves the humor of a lovers' quarrel, with a comic peripety occurring when the underdog triumphs and the master loses all dignity. And Act V carries this to greater personal depths through a humor of inversion, involving a psychological and spiritual search in which the total complex is sensitively analyzed. With humor, myth, didacticism, and spiritual evolution thus reflecting dynamically upon one another and incorporated vitally into the vigorous story, *Pygmalion* emerges as an effective synthesis of Shaw's careful dramaturgy, intrinsic fun, and thoughtful aesthetics. (pp. 196-220)

> *Charles A. Berst, in his* Bernard Shaw and the Art of Drama, *University of Illinois Press, 1973, 343 p.*

Bernard F. Dukore   (essay date 1973)

[*Dukore is an American educator, editor, and critic. In the following excerpt, he examines thematic and structural resemblances between* Pygmalion *and Henrik Ibsen's play* A Doll's House *(1879).*]

In theme and form, *Pygmalion* resembles *Candida* and therefore *A Doll's House* as well, though in *Pygmalion* the thematic and formal parallels to Ibsen's seminal work are less pronounced than in Shaw's earlier play. Like Nora and Morell, Liza Doolittle is a doll in Henry Higgins's doll house. Shaw himself hints at the resemblance when he has Mrs. Higgins accuse her son and Pickering of being "a pretty pair of babies, playing with your live doll." Like Nora, but unlike Morell, she becomes self-reliant. Like Nora, and like Marchbanks too, she leaves the doll house, an independent human being.

In respect to the doll house metaphor, *Pygmalion* is more complex than its predecessors, for Higgins is at the same time Helmer and Morell, doll keeper and doll, and Liza both Nora and Candida. But this Morell understands how his Candida arranges his life for him: "She's useful. She knows where my things are, and remembers my appointments and so forth." When he finds that Liza has bolted, he complains of the disruption of the comfortable life she has maintained for him: "What am I to do? . . . I cant find anything. I dont know what appointments Ive got." He is his doll's doll. His servant who, because of his dependence on her is his master, plays the ultimate trump card of the servant against the master: nonexistence. She departs.

Structurally, *Pygmalion* employs the *Doll's House—Candida* pattern of exposition (Act I)—situation (II, III, IV)—discussion (IV, V). In this play of social classes, dependence and independence, phonetics, and identity, which are the subjects of the play's discussion, the expository first act sketches these themes and introduces all of the important characters but Mrs. Higgins and Doolittle.

The group under the sheltering portico of St. James's Church represents a panorama of social classes. Its conversation reflects social differences. When Pickering tries to soothe Liza by telling her, "You have a right to live where you please," a bystander sarcastically comments, "Park Lane, for instance." The scene dramatizes Liza's and Clara's concern about money, Higgins's and Pickering's lack of concern, Mrs. Eynsford Hill's attempted unconcern. Phonetics is revealed as Pickering's hobby and as Higgins's vocation as well as avocation. In *Pygmalion,* the exposition is dynamic—the antithesis of expository practice in the well-made play. It emerges through a plot with a beginning, middle, and end. Suspected of being a police informer or a plainclothesman snooping on a poor flower girl, a note-taking gentleman proves he is a phonetician by impressing the flower girl and the other bystanders with his abilities. When one of the bystanders reveals that he too is a phonetician, they exchange names, realize they had been trying to find each other, and after giving some money to the flower girl, whom they had neglected because of professional interests, go off together. The situation of this little story, reflecting the play as a whole, revolves around questions of social role, identity, and profession; in it, two phoneticians, taken up with professional matters, ignore the feelings of a human being.

The story that is the play's basic situation concerns Higgins's bet with Pickering that at an ambassadorial party he can palm off the flower girl as an aristocrat. This situation, which begins in Act II, derives from Higgins's boast in the first act: "You see this creature with her kerbstone English: the English that will keep her in the gutter to the end of her days. Well, sir, in three months I could pass that girl off as a duchess at an ambassador's garden party. I could even get her a place as a lady's maid or shop assistant, which requires better English." Liza, impressed by the last sentence and wanting "to be a lady in a flower shop stead of selling at the corner of Tottenham Court Road," comes to Higgins to learn "to talk more genteel." Pickering, whose social class has attuned him to higher aspirations, remembers the second sentence and bets Higgins he cannot make good his brag. Innocent Liza finds herself the center and object of a phonetic and social experiment, for it is both and is recognized by Higgins as both. As he later explains to his mother, he aims "to take a human being and change her into a quite different human being by creating a new speech for her. It's filling up the deepest gulf that separates class from class and soul from soul." Significantly, the first thing Liza learns is not speech but social attitude, and the first thing Higgins tries to teach her is not speech but social behavior. Higgins thunders at her to be seated and Mrs. Pearce severely orders her to sit down, but only when Pickering courteously invites her to do so and considerately places the chair in a convenient position does she sit. Shortly thereafter, Higgins gives her a handkerchief, whose function, he bullyingly insists, differs from that of a sleeve (but he does not explain in what way). In the third act the situation intensifies as Liza, with only partial success, undergoes her first test. The Eynsford Hills had seen her as a flower girl, but nothing in her present diction or conduct reminds them of it. Although Liza impresses them, she does not pass muster with Higgins's more perceptive mother, who calls her a

triumph of her son's art and of Liza's dressmaker. Act IV resolves the situation: Higgins wins the bet.

As in *A Doll's House* and *Candida,* the answer to the dramatic question (will Higgins win the bet?) resolves only the plot. The human problems—of character and conduct—are totally unresolved. What is more, the resolution of the situation intensifies these problems to the point where Higgins can no longer ignore them, as he had ignored them when Mrs. Pearce and his mother mentioned them. Now Liza confronts him with the same questions: "What am I fit for? What have you left me fit for? Where am I to go? What am I to do? What's to become of me?" As in *A Doll's House* and *Candida,* the resolution of the plot might signal the end of a conventional play. Like *A Doll's House* and *Candida,* the resolution of the plot resolves only the situation. More is necessary. Now that Liza's social alienation is critical, the principal characters must talk over what has happened and decide what is to be done. In Acts IV and V the dilemma is discussed.

The final act, which contains the bulk of the discussion and the crux of the problem, returns—like the discussions of *A Doll's House* and *Candida*—to the subjects of the exposition: social class, dependence and independence, phonetics, and identity. In *A Doll's House,* Nora enunciates a position already reached (when she invites Helmer to talk over the situation, she has already changed into day clothes). Though Candida keeps the two men (and the audience) on tenterhooks, the contest as far as she herself is concerned is really no contest. In *Pygmalion,* Higgins's position is clear from the start. Liza, however, works out her position and decides upon a course of action during the discussion, which is a new action: an attempt to solve the problem of what is to become of her. Her decision—to leave Higgins, marry Freddy, and support him by teaching phonetics—is reached during an argument that is virtually a battle. Liza's efforts to understand herself and her new relationship with society, and her decision based on that understanding, are not explanations but achievements forged before our eyes. During the discussion, Liza becomes an independent woman, capable of functioning in the new class into which she has been thrust, sure of her new identity.

An independent woman? What of the view that Liza will return to Higgins? What of the play's subtitle, "A Romance in Five Acts"? According to Shaw, there is no romantic attachment between "the middle-aged bully and the girl of eighteen." He calls the play a romance "because it is the story of a poor girl who meets a gentleman at a church door and is transformed by him, like Cinderella, into a beautiful lady." In his Preface to *Saint Joan,* Shaw uses the term in a similar sense when he mentions "the romance of [Joan's] rise." Although the question of romantic love between Higgins and Liza is raised twice, what is stressed on both occasions is its irrelevance. As far as women are concerned, says Higgins in Act II, he "might as well be a block of wood." He frankly admits to a mother fixation, and he insists that he is "a confirmed old bachelor." Liza feels no more passion toward him than he does toward her. "In short," asks Higgins during the important discussion scene in Act V, "you want me to be infatuated about you as Freddy? Is that it?" "No I dont," replies Liza. "Thats not the sort of feeling I want from you. . . . I want a little kindness." As important as the characters' discussion is what they do, or in this case what they do not do. The play dramatizes no scenes of wooing between Liza and Higgins, none of flirtation, and the only possible hint of romantic interest on his part is that he is "disagreeably surprised" upon learning that Freddy has been writing to Liza. But is this not more easily understandable as the response of a Pygmalion whose masterpiece is to be thrown away on a man he regards as a fool? On the matter of a "sentimental-erotic" ending, the play seems clear. Following the final discussion scene, Higgins asks Liza to shop for him, whereupon she exclaims, "What you are to do without me I cannot imagine" and "sweeps out"—*not* "What you *would* do without me . . . ," which might signal her return or her desire to return. According to Liza's manner and words, she will marry Freddy, and in the play's final line Higgins himself acknowledges this forthcoming event. (pp. 60-4)

> *Bernard F. Dukore, in his* Bernard Shaw, Playwright: Aspects of Shavian Drama, *University of Missouri Press, 1973, 311 p.*

Maurice Valency   (essay date 1973)

[*Valency is an American editor, dramatist, novelist, and critic. In the following excerpt, he focuses on the theme of social displacement in* Pygmalion *and examines Shaw's epilogue in relation to the play.*]

In a letter to Ellen Terry, written in 1897, Shaw had expressed his desire to cast Forbes Robertson and Mrs. Patrick Campbell in a future play: "*Caesar and Cleopatra* has been driven clean out of my head by a play I want to write for them in which he shall be a West End gentleman and she an East End dona in an apron and three orange and red ostrich feathers." It was sixteen years before Shaw could realize this ambition. The result was *Pygmalion.* He called it the last of his potboilers.

Pygmalion was finished in 1913. In order to forestall the bad notices that Shaw's plays usually elicited in London, it was first produced in German at the Hofburg Theater in Vienna in October of that year, and its success impelled Herbert Beerbohm Tree to produce it in London the following year at His Majesty's. Tree took the part of Higgins; Mrs. Patrick Campbell, who was now under contract to him, played Eliza; and Philip Merivale played Colonel Pickering. The play opened in London on 11 April 1914 and was hugely successful. It is said that in London alone, under Tree's management, it earned £13,000 in three months. It was soon performed everywhere in Europe in a variety of languages, and by the end of its run Shaw was established as the foremost living dramatist, as well as the richest.

The magnitude of this success must have astonished Shaw as much as anyone. He took it in his stride. The short preface he added when the play was published is largely a description of Henry Sweet, the phonetician, with whom he vaguely connects his hero. In this preface, Shaw wrote:

> I wish to boast that *Pygmalion* has been an extremely successful play all over Europe and North America as well as at home. It is so intensely and deliberately didactic, and its subject is esteemed so dry, that I delight in throwing it at the heads of the wiseacres who repeat the parrot cry that art should never be didactic. It goes to prove my contention that art should never be anything else.

This impressive declaration is not altogether cogent. *Pygmalion* has to do, of course, with the relation of speech to class status, but it is not a play about linguistics, any more than *The Wild Duck* is a play about photography. It is a love story. It is also a play of *déclassement,* a theme which had already generated excitement when Augier popularized it, three-quarters of a century before, with *Le Gendre de M. Poirier.*

For the nineteenth century the classic prototype of the hero tragically displaced by a superior education was, without doubt, Julien Sorel in Stendhal's *Le Rouge et le noir* (1831). That too is a love story. In the interval, the topic of *déclassement* had been exhaustively developed in the French theater in every possible genre from the melodrama of Sandeau's *Mademoiselle de Serglière,* Curel's *Les Fossiles,* and Bernstein's *Le Detour* to the grim naturalism of Brieux's *Blanchette* (1892). In England, which had to some extent been spared the social upheavals of the Great Revolution, the theme was less seriously exploited, but there were a good many plays of the order of Robertson's *Caste* which were occupied in one way or another with the problem of class. By the time of *Blanchette,* the problem was of urgent importance on both sides of the Channel, but it was now no longer principally a question of domestic relations. What troubled Brieux was the upper-class monopoly of social opportunities.

Blanchette centers on the predicament of a highly educated girl, the daughter of a village innkeeper, who because of her low birth is unable to secure the academic position for which she is qualified and is therefore condemned to choose between an unworthy marriage and a life of sin. The situation was by no means funny, and the state of affairs which it uncovered provoked much discussion, and even some measure of reform.

Like *Blanchette,* *Pygmalion* touches upon the vexing problem of finding a place in the social structure for exceptional individuals of lower-class origin emancipated by the widening trends of popular instruction, and educated beyond the capacity of society to absorb their services. In the time of *Pygmalion* this question was still under much discussion in France, and it had recently been the subject of several influential novels, among them Edouard Estannié's *Le Ferment* (1899), and Paul Bourget's *L'Etape* (1901). (pp. 312-14)

The problem was grave, but Shaw's evident awareness of its gravity did not incline him to give the subject serious treatment. *Pygmalion* is certainly among the most engaging of Shaw's plays. It is also among the lightest and most carefree. As the action is arranged, the question of the ultimate disposition of the displaced Eliza looms more and more insistently on the horizon, but from beginning to end

Higgins remains blissfully indifferent to the predicament into which his ministrations have placed his protégé and to his own responsibility for her future. This is the joke upon which the action turns.

As the play progresses, Mrs. Higgins tries to make her son aware of the seriousness of the situation he is creating, and Mrs. Pearce, his housekeeper, constantly admonishes him of the need to think what he is about. Higgins refuses to look beyond his nose. At the end of the third act, the curtain speech brings the problem sharply into focus. The expectation is, therefore, that the situation will be dramatically detonated in the last act, and this is the principal source of suspense in the latter part of the play. In fact nothing of the sort happens. Instead of staging a luxuriously explosive scene ending in a reversal, *Pygmalion* fizzles out in a *Doll's House* type of discussion which is never resolved. The play ends, indeed, with the heroine slamming the door on the hero, as in Ibsen's play, but in so deliberate a manner as to warrant the suspicion that the scene is a parody of the celebrated Ibsenist ending.

Doubtless Shaw considered that in deferring the resolution of his plot indefinitely he was following in the footsteps of the master, who also had left the *Doll's House* plot unresolved at the final curtain. But the difference between the two plays is obvious. Ibsen framed his play along the lines of conventional domestic drama, so that his final situation seemed both unusual and shocking. *Pygmalion*, on the other hand, was based on a fairy tale. It is, of course, possible to accord the patterns of myth with the facts of life through the normal methods of symbolism. This is done, for example, in Giraudoux's *Ondine*, where the realistic and the mythical are consciously related within a single statement. Naturalism is another matter. It is difficult to imagine anything artistically more inept than a rationalistic conclusion of the Cinderella story. This is, however, precisely what Shaw had in mind in the last act of *Pygmalion.*

By the time *Pygmalion* was written there were in existence innumerable stage versions of Cinderella. The fable offered an excellent basis for plays of *déclassement.* In all likelihood the direct ancestor of *Pygmalion* was Boucicault's melodrama, *Grimaldi, or the Life of an Actress* (1862), in which a Covent Garden flower-girl is educated, brought to fame, and finally adopted by a broken-down actor, who turns out to be a duke in disguise. Many other analogies have been collected. It seems clear that Shaw intended to follow in *Pygmalion* the traditional formula of such plays—the discovery, the education, the preliminary test, the crucial scene, and so on—up to the point at which the prince and the beggar maid are finally united. Shaw said of the traditional scene of the ball, which *Pygmalion* omits:

> The obligatory scene, the scene in which Eliza makes her successful début at the Ambassador's party, was the root of the play at its inception. But when I got to work I left it to the imagination of the audience, as the theatre could not afford the expense, and it made the play too long. Sir James Barrie spotted this at once and remonstrated. So when the play was screened, I added the omitted scene.

The scene of the ball which Shaw added to the screen version of the play was not, however, obligatory. It was merely decorative. A love scene at the end of the play was really obligatory. It was therefore regularly supplied by the actors from the time of Beerbohm Tree, in the teeth of the author's peremptory instructions to the contrary. The discussion which, in the fifth act, serves the purpose of a denouement therefore constitutes a serious embarrassment in the development of the action. This scene, which is actually the *scène à faire,* advances the plot not a jot further than the fourth-act curtain and is therefore both superfluous and repetitious. It is in any case quite irrelevant to an anecdote which admits of only one acceptable solution.

A myth is ordinarily an organism of very precise form. Such durable fantasies come into being as the result of a subtle interplay of psychic forces and are in every case living things carefully designed to subserve a necessary function. For this reason, myths, like trees, are constructs of limited elasticity, and any serious attempt to distort their structure will encounter resistance. No application of logic will serve to transform the myth of Cinderella into anything other than what it is. Once the fairy godmother has waved her wand and the girl's magical transformation has been effected, it is absolutely indispensable that the Prince should seek out the resulting Princess, marry her, and live happily with her forever after.

In fact, Shaw was too canny a writer to spoil his play by tampering with the vital elements of the fairy tale. It is reasonably clear in the third act that Higgins, for all his protestations, is in the toils of the Life Force, very much as Tanner is in *Man and Superman,* that he would rather die than part with Eliza, and that she is destined to live with him, more or less happily, all the rest of his life in the flat in Wimpole Street. In this regard the play is neither perverse nor inept. The epilogue is another matter.

The epilogue is a prose narrative, offered provisionally for the edification of those who insist on having the story resolved. From every point of view the proposed resolution is unsatisfactory; nevertheless it indicates a good deal about Shaw's attitude toward his characters and his play and thus affords some insight into the influences which gave the play its shape. In the epilogue it is demonstrated that Higgins belongs to the category of the unmarriageable, along with such characters as Marchbanks, Tavy, and those others whose destiny it is to produce ideas, but not children. The demonstration depends, of course, on the depiction of Higgins as a cranky and egotistical genius, whose good qualities do not include a capacity for sympathy. As Shaw portrays him, Higgins is not lovable; he is overwhelming. His single-mindedness is impressive, and it is amusing, but it is not an endearing trait. The normal expectation is that the author will manage his redemption through love. He does not. From beginning to end, his hero is as hard as nails, a sacrificial offering to the cause of realism.

Like *Caesar and Cleopatra, Pygmalion* is a play about education, a subject with which Shaw was more than ordinarily concerned, and in both plays the problem includes the precarious business of managing the transference when the pedagogical relation is at an end. After her period of schooling under Caesar's tutelage, Cleopatra has learned, presumably, how to be a queen. In *Pygmalion* Eliza learns not only how to produce upper-class sounds, but also, as a necessary by-product, how to be a self-sufficient and self-reliant person, traits for which she has already shown extraordinary native aptitude. But while Cleopatra never becomes worthy of Caesar, Eliza is in the end pre-eminently worthy of Higgins. His rejection of her in the circumstances is, from the point of view of drama, hardly acceptable.

In both these plays the comedy is predicated on the mutual relations of an unemotional man and an emotional woman. The difference in their temperature is the consequence in each case of the hero's intense preoccupation with his work, to which the heroine's emotional needs have no relevance. Thus the difference in sexual response boils down to the disparity between the biological functions of men and woman according to the doctrine of Shaw. This is also the theme of *Man and Superman.* Don Juan wants to think; Doña Ana, to breed. When they are thrown together, their relationship is not necessarily comic, but Shaw makes it a source of comedy.

In *Man and Superman* Tanner is forced by Ann into the normal domestic compromise of familial life; but neither Caesar nor Higgins is willing to relinquish any part of his psychic autonomy in this manner. Both are indifferent to the blandishments of the flesh. For this reason these plays, while provocative of reflection, seem somewhat lacking in human values, that is to say, in realism. In the abstract, Don Juan makes a good case for the intellectual life; but nobody—so long as he remains in the flesh—is wholly indifferent to the demands of the flesh, least of all Don Juan.

Pygmalion does not make a clear statement as to Higgins's sexual interests. They would seem to be nonexistent. The implication is that it would be indecent of an upper-class Englishman of the period to take any special notice of women save as domestic conveniences. Such is the suggestion also in plays of the order of Barker's *The Madras House* (1910), and it is perhaps in the light of these Islamic attitudes that *Pygmalion* should be interpreted. In our enlightened age it would be tempting to direct the play with some intimation of the homosexuality latent in these social arrangements, and this might result in a very interesting performance. It would have nothing to do with Shaw's intentions, of course; but it is only in the epilogue that we discover what these are, and there the disparity between Shaw as a dramatist and Shaw as a novelist becomes painfully apparent. If the epilogue were dramatized as a sixth act, it would doubtless be intolerable on the stage.

On the question of caste the play is clearer in its doctrine. Shaw assigns to each individual his exact specific gravity in the social order. In the epilogue to *Pygmalion* the Eynsford Hills, who cling desperately to their upper-class status in spite of their poverty, are brought down to the level of small shopkeepers. In the play itself Eliza is accepted by Mrs. Higgins as a social equal; but Higgins is willing to accept her as such only when she indicates her potentialities as a professional competitor. The astonishing rise of Mr. Doolittle is, like the elevation of Mr. Lickcheese in *Widowers' Houses,* somewhat more improbable than the

other improbabilities of the play: it is this sort of imaginative leap that causes so much of Shaw's comedy to approximate extravaganza. But, however unrealistic they may be, these unexpected reversals are refreshing, and certainly they serve a useful function. For Shaw caste is essentially a matter of character and ability, not of birth, so that once the individual is cut free of the restrictions of class, he tends to find his own level in the human hierarchy. Social mobility is indispensable to the evolutionary process.

While such is, beyond doubt, the conclusion to be drawn from the play, the epilogue suggests a contrary inference. Here Shaw declined to imagine the easy rise of his gifted heroine, even as the owner of a flower shop. On the contrary, he found it necessary, in the name of realism, to punish Eliza and her hapless spouse, Freddy Hill, by putting them through an obstacle course of economic vicissitudes as arduous as his own had been before fortune favored him.

The proposed solution of Eliza's economic problem therefore seems dismally novelistic. Experience indicates that in reality beautiful girls of exceptional ability do not marry impecunious Freddies. They marry industrial magnates of a certain age and are eventually widowed or divorced with stupendous financial settlements. The meager destiny which Shaw metes out to his Galatea in the name of realism must therefore be accounted an unpardonable intrusion of common sense not only upon the myth but also upon that aspect of the myth which is normally thought of as reality.

In fact, the mythological pattern which includes such stories as *The Ugly Duckling, Cinderella, Beauty and the Beast, King Cophetua and the Beggar Maid,* and *The Patient Griselda*—all of which depend on the ultimate recognition of the superior merits of a disprized individual—is a compensatory mechanism of the greatest efficacy in the management of feelings of inferiority. For this reason, if no other, it is indispensable that Cinderella have her prince at the end of her story, and any other culmination is in the nature of a betrayal. Happily, Shaw had the good sense to leave the way open in his play for an inference of fulfillment according to the rules of romance, and *Pygmalion* has always been played in this manner. In the end, in spite of the author, Jack has his Jill. The epilogue may therefore be dismissed as an unfortunate irrelevancy, interesting chiefly because of the insight it affords into the mentality of the author.

The myth upon which *Pygmalion* is based has, of course, nothing to do with the legend of Pygmalion and Galatea. The Pygmalion story was treated most perceptively by Pirandello in *Diana e la Tuda* (1927) fourteen years after Shaw's play was written, and it had already furnished the basis for Ibsen's *When We Dead Awaken* (1899) fourteen years before. It is possible that Shaw had Ibsen's play in mind in devising *Pygmalion,* but the relation is not very close. Higgins does not create Eliza. He merely revises her. His relation to her is not artistic, but surgical. In *When We Dead Awaken,* the sculptor Rubek is destroyed because he has preferred his creation to the living woman who informed it, and toward the end of his life he realizes with regret that in his eagerness to work he has forgotten to live. Higgins has no such difficulty. For him work and life are synonymous. He has no need of love and is quite willing to sacrifice Eliza to his career, though he obviously finds her presence more convenient than her absence.

The final scene of **Pygmalion** is in some sense a realization of the scene—which in *When We Dead Awaken* Ibsen forbore to write—in which Rubek lets Irene go after he has finished with her as a model. For Irene the epilogue is prostitution and afterwards madness. For Rubek it is disillusion, regret, and eventually death. But in **Pygmalion** Eliza parts company with Higgins long before any of these operatic developments take place. Eliza may or may not look after Higgins's shopping list after the final curtain. It is no great matter: the sequel is not likely to be tragic. From the time of Brand, Ibsen's heroes invariably live to regret their single-minded dedication to their vocation. Shaw's heroes revel in it.

Ibsen came to the conclusion relatively early in his career that the sense of vocation is a special form of madness, and that life is justified mainly by love. Shaw thought of love as a physical urge which must at all costs be prevented from interfering with a creative man's work, in which chiefly his salvation lies. The two viewpoints are diametrically opposed and reflect the profound difference in temperament between the master and his foremost disciple in the drama. In Ibsen's plays, characters like Higgins are monomaniacs who come invariably to a tragic end. Shaw, however, found his professor singularly congenial, and he gave him a distinctly comic turn.

In Higgins we are invited to see more of Henry Sweet than of Shaw, but he has a good deal of Shaw's shamelessness, his impudence, and his gift of blarney. There is, moreover, something ungainly in Higgins's insistence on the virtues of the intellectual life. He tells Eliza:

> If you cant stand the coldness of my sort of life, and the strain of it, go back to the gutter. Work til you are more a brute than a human being; and then cuddle and squabble and drink til you fall asleep. Oh, it's a fine life the life of the gutter. It's real: it's warm: it's violent: you can feel it through the thickest skin: you can taste it and smell it without any training or any work. Not like Science and Literature and Classical Music and Philosophy and Art. You find me cold, unfeeling, selfish, dont you? Very well: be off with you to the sort of people you like. Marry some sentimental hog or other with lots of money, and a thick pair of lips to kiss you with and a thick pair of boots to kick you with. If you cant appreciate what youve got, youd better get what you can appreciate.

In such passages one uncomfortably senses the intellectual snob. It would be charitable to suppose that Shaw expressed through Higgins not his own intellectual smugness, but what he imagined a character like Higgins might feel, but there are too many echoes of this attitude in Shaw's personal correspondence to make the supposition likely. In any case the passage is unfortunate, and confirms one's opinion that Higgins is not a particularly pleasant man. Even for a stage professor, he seems relatively bloodless, and there is little indication that he feels any

premonition of that sudden craving for warmth that overwhelms Brand in the precincts of the Ice Church. Nevertheless Higgins's desperate search for Eliza in the last act, his manifest jealousy of Freddy, and his exaggerated posturings in the final scene suggest that he feels some emotional need for the girl he so scornfully rejected, and that ultimately he means to get her, like an astute man of business, on his own terms.

As Shaw describes him, Higgins comically suggests madness. He considers himself to be a modest, diffident, shy, and soft-spoken man of irreproachable manners. He is in fact a brash and tyrannical egotist, generous, but rude and totally inconsiderate of others. Evidently Shaw found this type of superman a little awesome. In his epilogue he says of Eliza that she may sometimes imagine

> Higgins making love like any common man. . . . But when it comes to business, to the life that she really leads as distinguished from the life of dreams and fancies, she likes Freddy and she likes the Colonel; and she does not like Higgins and Mr Doolittle. Galatea never does quite like Pygmalion: his relation to her is too godlike to be altogether agreeable.

This observation, though witty, belies the play. If Eliza did not find Higgins likeable she could have no real emotional involvement with him, and the contrast which Shaw meant to dramatize between her romantic illusions and his cold realism could not be demonstrated. One may wonder why Shaw found it so necessary to stress Higgins's aversion from sexual involvements with so attractive a girl as Eliza. His reasons are interesting:

> When Higgins excused his indifference to young women on the ground that they had an irresistible rival in his mother, he gave the clue to his inveterate old-bachelordom. The case is uncommon only to the extent that remarkable mothers are uncommon. If an imaginative boy has a sufficiently rich mother who has intelligence, personal grace, dignity of character without harshness, and a cultivated sense of the best art of her time to enable her to make her house beautiful, she sets a standard for him against which very few women can struggle, besides effecting for him a disengagement of his affections, his sense of beauty, and his idealism from his specifically sexual impulses. This makes him a standing puzzle to the huge number of uncultivated people who have been brought up in tasteless homes by commonplace or disagreeable parents, and to whom, consequently, literature, painting, sculpture, music and affectionate personal relations come as modes of sex if they come at all. . . .

Shaw thus introduced into the Higgins-Eliza discussion what appears to be a deeply personal note. Mrs. Higgins is a personification of the ideal mother according to Shaw—a beautiful woman, charming, intelligent, and rich. She is a person of impeccable taste. Her apartment is described in detail. It is spacious, uncluttered, and decorated in accordance with the best Pre-Raphaelite standards. They contrast sharply with the Victorian jumble to which her son is committed. Mrs. Higgins wisely keeps him at some distance, but there is no doubt that she finds him amusing as well as exasperating, and she manages him adroitly like a willful child. There is no suggestion in the play of any sort of rivalry between Mrs. Higgins and Eliza. It is suggested, on the contrary, that she would make the most desirable of mothers-in-law.

The rationalization of Higgins's sexlessness in the epilogue was in all likelihood an afterthought, but it has the advantage of affording us another glimpse of the motives which underlie the play. Shaw's dependence on his mother during the early part of his life, and her habitual indifference to his concerns, were, as we have seen, amply reflected in his early novels. It is easy to discern in these fantasies the injury to his ego which her indifference caused him, and it is even possible to perceive, if we wish, something of the sort in several of the early plays, particularly in *Mrs Warren's Profession.*

The need to idealize the imaginary mother, in contrast to the real one, on the other hand, may well have influenced the characterization of the Virgin Mother in *Candida,* who rejects the young poet in terms acceptable to his narcissism, and to have led, by way of Lady Britomart in *Major Barbara* to the genial matriarch of *Pygmalion,* who unwittingly inhibits her son's sexual activity. "We cannot help suspecting," Shaw concluded, "that the disentanglement of sex from the associations with which it is so commonly confused, a disentanglement which persons of genius achieve by sheer intellectual analysis, is sometimes produced or aided by parental fascination."

The extent to which Shaw himself was subject to parental fascination must remain, in the circumstances, a matter of conjecture. What we know is that in the fullness of time this resolute bachelor married a lady who answered, in some respects, the description he gives of Mrs. Higgins, and who mothered Shaw, sometimes to his annoyance, as long as she lived. There is no special need, nor beyond a certain point is it desirable, to connect the intimate circumstances of Shaw's life with the works of his imagination. Art is a sublimation, not a reproduction of life. But there is certainly reason to suppose, if we wish, that Shaw's special brand of Don Juanism, along with the metaphysical basis assigned to it in *Man and Superman,* in short, Shaw's entire philosophic structure, was an elaborate rationalization of his own psychic situation.

The idea that class-distinctions are primarily a matter of linguistics seems fantastic at first blush, but such a notion might have made sense at a time when upper-class speech was still a monopoly of the upper classes. It is conceivable that in a classless society everyone will speak the same language. Shaw apparently took this idea with some seriousness, since in his will he left a sizeable bequest to further a system of phonetic spelling. He wrote in the preface to *Pygmalion:*

> The English have no respect for their language, and will not teach their children to speak it. They spell it so abominably that no man can teach himself what it sounds like. It is impossible for an Englishman to open his mouth without making some other Englishman hate or despise him. . . . The reformer England needs today is

an energetic phonetic enthusiast: that is why I have made such a one the hero of a popular play.

In *Pygmalion* there is nothing to suggest that Higgins is a socialist, and he has apparently no idea of leveling the classes under a common phonetic system. But the implication is that what could be done with Eliza Doolittle can be done, more or less successfully, with anyone who shows the necessary aptitude. Shaw himself had learned upper-class English ways in somewhat the same manner as Eliza, and he evidently liked the idea that in order to transform a clever garbageman into a prime minister all that is necessary is a course in speech. Such ideas were certainly current in the early decades of this century, and the vast proliferation of speech courses in those years attests to the influence of the theory.

Eliza observes very justly that what makes a lady is the manner in which she is treated. The idea that all those who make estimable sounds will be treated as ladies and gentlemen, so that socialism will spring up by itself in the wake of Wyld's *Pronouncing Dictionary,* depends, however, upon a strictly Victorian concept of the hierarchy of classes. In the 1870's, possibly, Higgins might feel some sense of the futility of his profession; but in 1913 he has the professional ardor of a true revolutionist. He tells his mother: "you have no idea how frightfully interesting it is to take a human being and change her into a quite different human being by creating a new speech for her. It's filling up the deepest gulf that separates class from class and soul from soul."

The suggestion that, if Eliza behaves like a duchess, she may well become a duchess is—however one calculates the probabilities—immediately acceptable in the theater. Consequently the intermediate stages in the assumption of Eliza are fascinating. The incongruity between what Eliza says at Mrs. Higgins's at-home, and the manner in which she says it, provided Mrs. Pat Campbell with an incomparable opportunity to display her comic talents, and the effect of Eliza's elegant rendition of "Not bloody likely" is said to have been the talk of London all during the first run of the play. Clara Hill, on the other hand, illustrates a tendency contrary to that which motivates Eliza's rise in the world. She is quite ready to affect lower-class speech patterns if they are considered fashionable. In Shaw's day the attrition of the King's English was evidently already a cause for concern:

> PICKERING: . . . Ive been away in India for several years, and manners have changed so much that I sometimes dont know whether I'm at a respectable dinnertable or in a ship's forecastle.
>
> CLARA. It's all a matter of habit. Theres no right or wrong in it. Nobody means anything by it and it's *s o* quaint, and gives such a smart emphasis to things that are not in themselves very witty. I find the new small talk delightful and quite innocent.

Possibly for Shaw these indications of the tendency to obliterate class distinctions presaged the classless society of the future, but it is more likely that he saw in this process a salutary movement of individuals to take their proper places in the social hierarchy regardless of the class into which they were born. *Pygmalion* is a play of exceptional people. Eliza, like her father, is a highly evolved individual whose potentialities would normally be stifled by the limitations of a rigidly stratified social environment. But even when she is artificially freed from the restrictions of her social class, her economic possibilities are a matter of chance and, in her time, she is in a predicament much the same as that of the general's daughter in *Hedda Gabler* or the general's daughters in *The Three Sisters.* Mr. Doolittle, on the other hand, is emancipated not by education but by money, with the result that he joins the middle class and is cursed with the need for respectability all the rest of his life.

The intimation is that social displacement is both perilous and uncomfortable no matter how it is brought about: nevertheless it is indispensable to the evolution of society. In *Pygmalion* it is accident that determines the extraordinary rise of Eliza and her father; but the rapid development of mass education in England in this period was already making it possible for the under privileged to become privileged as a matter of course. What *Pygmalion* describes is the process by which exceptional people find their way into the upper reaches of society, and from this point of view it is perhaps a satire. But its satirical intention does not obscure the underlying idea. The evolutionary principle involves a constant displacement of individuals within the class structure. The result is doubtless of benefit to the species, but it is not uniformly pleasant for the individual. Chekhov had dwelt more or less humorously on the tragic aspects of this process in *The Three Sisters,* a very sad sort of comedy. *Pygmalion,* on the contrary, is very funny; but it too has its pathetic side. Nature is insensible to suffering. Its obtuseness is mirrored in the insensitivity of Higgins, who identifies with nobody and is therefore inhuman to a degree that is not altogether agreeable. But the fact is that Eliza, as she repeatedly points out, has her feelings like anyone else; and it is in keeping this poignant consideration constantly before his audience that Shaw, for all his realism, shows his worth as a dramatist. (pp. 314-24)

> *Maurice Valency, in his* The Cart and the Trumpet: The Plays of George Bernard Shaw, *Oxford University Press, Inc., 1973, 467 p.*

J. L. Wisenthal   (essay date 1974)

[*Wisenthal is an American educator and critic. In the following excerpt he discusses the contrast in* Pygmalion *of two incompatible sets of human characteristics: the warmly human responsiveness of Eliza Doolittle and the cold professionalism of Henry Higgins.*]

The first point to be grasped about Henry Higgins in *Pygmalion* is that he is, like Dubedat [in *The Doctor's Dilemma*], an artist—as the title of the play implies. He makes a graceless flower girl into a graceful lady, as the sculptor Pygmalion created a beautiful statue out of shapeless stone. Higgins does this by teaching her how to speak correctly and beautifully; phonetics is to be regarded in this play as an artistic as well as scientific pursuit, and elegant speech is to be seen as a valuable accomplishment. Eliza

as a lady in Act IV is perhaps less happy than she was as a flower girl—people who are transformed into a higher state usually are not happy in Shaw's plays—but she is superior. (This is perhaps clearer on the stage, where one actually hears the improvement in speech and sees the corresponding improvement in appearance.) The importance and value of the training that Higgins gives to Eliza is stated explicitly in the play in his reply to his mother's charge that he and Pickering are a pair of babies playing with their live doll: "Playing!" he exclaims, "The hardest job I ever tackled: make no mistake about that, mother. But you have no idea how frightfully interesting it is to take a human being and change her into a quite different human being by creating a new speech for her. It's filling up the deepest gulf that separates class from class and soul from soul." Similarly, Shaw in the Preface stresses the crucial role which the phonetician ought to play in society. "The reformer we need most today," he writes, "is an energetic phonetic enthusiast: that is why I have made such a one the hero of a popular play." And later: "If the play makes the public aware that there are such people as phoneticians, and that they are among the most important people in England at present, it will serve its turn."

Shaw's Pygmalion regards other people not in human terms, but as so much stone to be used for his higher purposes. Therefore he simply cannot understand the concern expressed by Mrs. Pearce and his mother over Eliza's personal future. Mrs. Pearce, on the other hand, understands his lack of concern very well: "Of course I know you dont mean her any harm," she says to him; "but when you get what you call interested in people's accents, you never think or care what may happen to them or you." His behavior to Eliza all through the play is never unkind, but it is always unfeeling. He never tries to hurt her feelings; it is just that he cannot conceive of her (or anyone else) as having any feelings to be hurt.

> PICKERING. [*In good-humored remonstrance*] Does it occur to you, Higgins, that the girl has some feelings?
>
> HIGGINS. [*Looking critically at her*] Oh no, I dont think so. Not any feelings that we need bother about. [*Cheerily*] Have you, Eliza?
>
> LIZA. I got my feelings same as anyone else.
>
> HIGGINS. [*To Pickering, reflectively*] You see the difficulty?
>
> PICKERING. Eh? What difficulty?
>
> HIGGINS. To get her to talk grammar. The mere pronunciation is easy enough.

To Higgins, Eliza is merely a thing to be taught (in Acts II and III); then a thing which has been taught (in Act IV); and finally a thing which it would be agreeable and useful to have around the house (in Act V). A human being is not an end in himself with an individual personality that ought to be respected, but the raw material out of which something higher can be made. In Act II Higgins justifies the proposed experiment with Eliza on the ground that "the girl doesnt belong to anybody—is no use to anybody but me," and when in Act V Eliza tells him that

Freddy loves her and would make her happy, he replies, "Can he make anything of you? Thats the point."

For Eliza this is not the point at all; she wants a husband who will love and respect her as she is, not one who will make something of her. The fact that Higgins puts forward this particular objection to Freddy reflects his lack of understanding of Eliza. In this lack of human understanding Higgins is like Tanner [in **Man and Superman**]: he is a master only in his own higher intellectual pursuit, while in dealing with other people (especially women) he is frequently a blunderer. All through the final act Higgins reveals how little he has learned about Eliza during his months of close association with her. When she finally demonstrates that she has become independent of him, he still thinks that she will return to Wimpole Street as a companion: "Now youre a tower of strength: a consort battleship," he says to her. "You and I and Pickering will be three old bachelors together instead of only two men and a silly girl." It would be difficult to imagine terms more ludicrously inappropriate to Eliza, or less likely to appeal to her, than "consort battleship" and "old bachelor."

The key words in **Pygmalion** are gentleman and lady: they are used over and over again, with different meanings. In the first act, for example, the Bystander says of Higgins, "E's a gentleman: look at his be-oots," while Eliza says of him, "He's no gentleman, he aint, to interfere with a poor girl." In Act II she says to him, "Well, if you was a gentleman, you might ask me to sit down, I think," and she objects to being called a baggage when she has "offered to pay like any lady" for Higgins to enable her to become a "lady in a flower shop." Later she tells Higgins that she wouldn't have eaten his chocolate, "only I'm too ladylike to take it out of my mouth." In Act V the entrance of the newly enriched, formally attired Doolittle is preceded by this dialogue:

> THE PARLORMAID. Mr Henry: a gentleman wants to see you very particular. He's been sent on from Wimpole Street.
>
> HIGGINS. . . . Who is it?
>
> THE PARLORMAID. A Mr Doolittle, sir.
>
> PICKERING. Doolittle! Do you mean the dustman?
>
> THE PARLORMAID. Dustman! Oh no, sir: a gentleman.

Doolittle is identified as a gentleman by his dress, as Higgins was at the start of the play. All of these references (and others) to ladies and gentlemen provide a background to Eliza's well-known speeches to Pickering in Act V about what constitutes ladies and gentlemen: "It was from you that I learnt really nice manners; and that is what makes one a lady, isnt it? You see it was so very difficult for me with the example of Professor Higgins always before me. I was brought up to be just like him, unable to control myself, and using bad language on the slightest provocation. And I should never have known that ladies and gentlemen didnt behave like that if you hadnt been there . . . You see, really and truly, apart from the things

anyone can pick up (the dressing and the proper way of speaking, and so on), the difference between a lady and a flower girl is not how she behaves, but how she's treated. I shall always be a flower girl to Professor Higgins, because he always treats me as a flower girl, and always will; but I know I can be a lady to you, because you always treat me as a lady, and always will." Ladies and gentlemen, according to Eliza, are people with "really nice manners" (which include proper speech) and the self-respect that comes from being treated respectfully by others.

In the final act Eliza wishes to humiliate Higgins, and therefore she dismisses his role in her education as trivial and says that it was Pickering who really taught her to be a lady. This is unfair to Higgins, without whom she would still be a flower girl. It is true that Pickering has the good manners that Higgins so conspicuously lacks, and it is also true that he was necessary (although not sufficient) for her transformation. But it was Higgins who conceived the bold idea of transforming Eliza in the first place, and it was his professional skill and perseverance which enabled her to learn to speak—a vital accomplishment for her which she treats too lightly in Act V. Higgins and Pickering are, like Dubedat and Blenkinsop in **The Doctor's Dilemma,** complementary characters, each of them possessing the opposite of the other's qualities and defects. Whereas Dubedat and Blenkinsop force us to consider the relative value of creative genius and moral virtue, Higgins and Pickering force us to consider the relative value of cre-

Shaw in 1914, the year Pygmalion *opened in London.*

ative genius and good manners. Pickering's manners are as good as Higgins' are bad: Pickering is the perfect gentleman. But Higgins, though no more a real gentleman than Doolittle the dustman is, possesses qualities of a very different kind, which Pickering lacks: like Dubedat, he is the true professional and (as I have noted) artist. The difference between the two characters is brought out in the printed version of the play in the first act, where Pickering is designated "the Gentleman" and Higgins "the Note Taker" (and it is significant in this act that Higgins, who treats Eliza without any consideration, is nevertheless the one who gives her the "large" sum of money). At the beginning of Act II Higgins' professional nature is emphasized by contrast with Pickering; the act begins as Higgins' demonstration of his art ends.

> HIGGINS. [*As he shuts the last drawer*] Well, I think thats the whole show.
>
> PICKERING. It's really amazing. I havnt taken half of it in, you know.
>
> HIGGINS. Would you like to go over any of it again?
>
> PICKERING . . . No, thank you: not now. I'm quite done up for this morning.
>
> HIGGINS . . . Tired of listening to sounds?
>
> PICKERING. Yes. It's a fearful strain. I rather fancied myself because I can pronounce twenty-four distinct vowel sounds; but your hundred and thirty beat me. I cant hear a bit of difference between most of them.

It is this professional quality of Higgins to which Eliza principally owes her transformation. We can be certain that Pickering by himself would not have undertaken the experiment, and, as he tells Eliza in Act V, "He [Higgins] taught you to speak; and I couldnt have done that, you know." To this she replies merely, "Of course: that is his profession." For her the only significant acts are those which are done from human, personal motives; she cannot see anything noble or praiseworthy in what a man does as his work. (She tells Higgins that she does not want Freddy to have to work when he is her husband.) We, however, are in a position to see the value in both Pickering's human gentlemanliness and Higgins' zeal and ability, and there is no easy choice to be made between them.

Although Higgins and Pickering are deliberately contrasted characters whose qualities we are to judge in relation to each other, the two of them do not come into conflict at any point in the play; the conflict is between Higgins and Eliza, and it is out of this relationship that the play grows. Eliza is of course a much more complex character than Pickering: whereas the description *"an elderly gentleman of the amiable military type"* leaves little more to be said about him, she cannot be described so easily. For *Pygmalion* is concerned not simply with ladies and gentlemen, but with the relationship between this type and women and men (a higher type) and girls and boys (a lower type); and Eliza passes through all three of these stages. She begins in Acts I and II as a flower *girl;* in Acts III and IV she is a lady; and by the end of the play she has become a woman. We have here an ingenious version of the Pygmalion myth: Pygmalion/Higgins makes the stone/girl into a statue/lady, which Venus/the Life Force causes to come alive as a woman.

The interesting part of this development, both in the original myth and in Shaw's handling of it, is the transformation of the statue into a woman. A valuable commentary on this process in *Pygmalion* is provided by a letter that Shaw wrote to the actress Florence Farr in 1891—twenty-one years before he wrote the play—while he was giving her elocution and voice lessons:

> Prithee persevere with the speaking: I found with unspeakable delight last time that you were beginning to do it quite beautifully. There is much more to be done, of course, much ill usage in store for you, but success is now certain. You have reached the stage of the Idiotically Beautiful. There remain the stages of the Intelligently Beautiful & finally of the Powerfully Beautiful; & until you have attained the last you will never be able to compel me to recognize the substance of that soul of which I was shown a brief image by Nature for her own purposes.

This letter is indeed remarkable as an anticipation of *Pygmalion*—even its final sentence is echoed in Higgins' references to Eliza in Act V as a soul and as a part of humanity "that has come my way and been built into my house." And the progression that Shaw sets out in the letter corresponds exactly to Eliza's development in the last three acts of the play. In Act III, at Mrs. Higgins' At Home, she is Idiotically Beautiful; she is an artificial duchess, a live doll, a statue. The fact that she is now fit for the Eynsford Hills's society implies that many of the middle class never evolve beyond the statue stage, that they never become human. In Act IV she has reached the level of the Intelligently Beautiful; she is a lady not only in her accent and dress, but also in her possession of a new sensitivity, a delicacy of feeling that has hitherto been lacking. With this sensitivity she becomes aware that Higgins has no human feeling for her and regards her as a mere thing, and she therefore determines to be independent of him. This she achieves in a limited way in Act IV, when she reviles him bitterly and leaves Wimpole Street, and in a final, thorough way in Act V, when she repudiates his dominance exultantly, announcing that she will marry Freddy and support him by teaching phonetics as an assistant to Higgins' rival. The exchange that follows this declaration is the climax of the play:

> HIGGINS. [*Rising in a fury*]. What! That imposter! that humbug! that toadying ignoramus! Teach him my methods! my discoveries! You take one step in his direction and I'll wring your neck. [*He lays hands on her.*] Do you hear?
>
> LIZA. [*Defiantly non-resistant*]. Wring away. What do I care? I knew youd strike me some day. [*He lets her go, stamping with rage at having forgotten himself, and recoils so hastily that he stumbles back into his seat on the ottoman.*] Aha! Now I know how to deal with you. What a fool I was not to think of it before! You cant take away the knowledge you gave me. You said I had a finer ear than you. And I can be civil and kind to people, which is more than you can.

Aha! [*Purposely dropping her aitches to annoy him*] Thats done you, Enry Iggins, it az. Now I dont care that [*Snapping her fingers*] for your bullying and your big talk. I'll advertize it in the papers that your duchess is only a flower girl that you taught, and that she'll teach anybody to be a duchess just the same in six months for a thousand guineas. Oh, when I think of myself crawling under your feet and being trampled on and called names, when all the time I had only to lift up my finger to be as good as you, I could just kick myself.

HIGGINS. [*Wondering at her*]. You damned impudent slut, you! But it's better than snivelling; better than fetching slippers and finding spectacles, isnt it? [*Rising*] By George, Eliza, I said I'd make a woman of you; and I have. I like you like this.

This is the moment at which the sculptor sees with delighted amazement that his statue has come to life. Eliza is now Powerfully Beautiful: no longer a flower girl, more than a mere lady—a woman, who has sufficient vitality and strength of will to face life with courage and self-reliance.

Where does this leave Higgins? One point to be noted is that his statement "I said I'd make a woman of you; and I have" is not quite correct. He said he would make a lady, "a duchess," of her; it is the Life Force inherent in Eliza herself that has enabled her to become a woman (although Higgins has helped by bullying and offending her to the point where she revolts against him). And if she is a woman, what is he? According to the concept of "woman" which is implicit in his speech to her, he is a man; he has already boasted of his own self-reliance. But in other senses he is not a man: he is inhuman and immature, which is to say that he is a brute rather than a man and a boy rather than a man. (Dubedat, in *The Doctor's Dilemma,* is called a brute by Ridgeon and a child by his wife.) Higgins is described in the stage direction that introduces him as "*rather like a very impetuous baby,*" and is treated as such by his mother, for whom he feels a child's affection; and he himself says to Pickering in Act II that he has "never been able to feel really grown-up and tremendous, like other chaps." Whereas Eliza has become by the end of the play both a lady and a woman, Higgins is neither a gentleman nor (in important senses of the term) a man.

This does not mean, however, that Eliza is the outright victor. She does, it is true, humiliate Higgins in the final act, particularly in the last part. (It is interesting that both *Pygmalion* and *The Doctor's Dilemma* end with the humiliation of a man by a much younger woman.) But Higgins, though humiliated by Eliza, is still superior to her in significant ways. He is the creator of Eliza the lady, and only as a lady could she have become a woman—or so the play implies. He propounds an ideal, by which his own life is governed, which Eliza can neither understand nor live by: the ideal of a cold life of impersonal striving. Eliza, on the other hand, propounds *her* ideal: a warm life of personal friendship and love. During the discussion between Higgins and Eliza in Act V, these two ideals, and the characters who embody them, are beautifully balanced; only

at the end does Eliza seem to emerge triumphant—and even then one feels that the issue has not been finally decided. During the discussion, we have the impression that Higgins is utterly vanquished, then Eliza, then Higgins, and so on. With each speech an unexpected other side to the question springs into view. On the day on which *Pygmalion* opened in London, Shaw sent Mrs. Patrick Campbell a letter headed "FINAL ORDERS," which included the following:

> If you have ever said to Stella [Mrs. Patrick Campbell's daughter] in her childhood "I'll let you see whether you will. . . . obey me or not," and then inverted her infant shape and smacked her until the Square (not to mention the round) rang with her screams, you will . . . know how to speak the line "I'll let you see whether I'm dependent on you." There is a certain dragging intensity, also used in Act IV in "YOU thank God etc," which is wanted here to re-establish your lead after Higgins' long speech about science and classical music and so on. The author took care to re-establish it by giving Eliza a long and energetic speech in reply to him; but the ignorant slave entrusted with the part thought she knew better than the author, and cut out the speech as useless. Now she has got to do it the other way.

The line "I'll let you see whether I'm dependent on you," which Shaw removed from the play when revising the scene for the film version, occurred shortly after Eliza's reply to Higgins' "science and classical music" speech. What Shaw is saying to Mrs. Patrick Campbell in the letter is that since she has dropped the "long and energetic speech" that he had provided to re-establish Eliza's lead (that is, the one beginning "Oh, you are a cruel tyrant,"), she would have to re-establish it by giving special emphasis to the later speech. The phrase "re-establish your lead" neatly sums up Shaw's "tennis" technique in the last scene of *Pygmalion,* and in the debates which provide the climaxes of many of his other plays. (*John Bull's Other Island* offers a particularly good example.) Eliza and Hig-

---

Tree and Shaw dispute *Pygmalion's* ending:

Tree, who loved romantic endings, had hit on the idea of throwing flowers to Eliza in the brief interval between the end of the play and the fall of the curtain, thus letting the audience know that a marriage would shortly take place between the professor and the flower-girl, which was in flagrant opposition to the author's conception of their characters and relationship.

In several letters that passed between them Shaw tried to make Tree aware of the error, and Tree tried to make Shaw aware of the box-office. 'My ending makes money; you ought to be grateful,' said Tree. 'Your ending is damnable: you ought to be shot,' replied Shaw.

Hesketh Pearson, in his Beerbohm Tree: His Life and Laughter, *Methuen, 1956.*

gins keep re-establishing their respective leads, until the play ends with no clear victory for either of them. The play does not take one side or the other; it leaves us valuing both Eliza's warm human qualities and Higgins' cold professional qualities, and it leaves us faced with the dilemma that arises from the incompatibility of these two sets of virtues, perfection of the life and of the work. (pp. 118-26)

J. L. Wisenthal, in his The Marriage of Contraries: Bernard Shaw's Middle Plays, *Cambridge, Mass.: Harvard University Press, 1974, 259 p.*

Arthur Ganz   (essay date 1983)

[*Ganz is an American educator, editor, and critic. In the following excerpt, he discusses the function of the denouement in resolving the ambiguous relationship of Henry Higgins and Eliza Doolittle in* Pygmalion.]

That [*Pygmalion*] should conclude with the happy union of Higgins and Eliza would seem to be implied by its subtitle, *A Romance in Five Acts,* but at the beginning of the Postscript Shaw ignores the love-story element and announces that it is 'called a romance because the transfiguration it records seems exceedingly improbable'. However, Shaw could hardly have assumed that readers of the play, who come to the subtitle well before they come to the Postscript, would take the term 'romance' in this sense till he told them to do so. And in fact Shaw continues to send contradictory signals in the Postscript itself. He first says that Higgins remains 'one of the strongest personal interests' in Eliza's life, particularly as she is sure that no other woman is 'likely to supplant her with him'; later Shaw observes that Eliza is characteristically ill-tempered with Higgins and 'snaps his head off on the faintest provocation, or on none', telling us a moment after that 'She knows that Higgins does not need her, just as her father did not need her' but that 'his indifference is deeper than the infatuation of commoner souls'. Finally, Shaw claims that though in her fantasy life Eliza would like to drag Higgins 'off his pedestal and see him making love like any common man', she does not like him (or Mr Doolittle): 'Galatea never does quite like Pygmalion: his relation to her is too godlike to be altogether agreeable'.

But what has become an impossible tangle of ambiguous hints and contradictions in the discourse of the Postscript is held in perfect artistic stasis at the end of the play as Shaw wrote it. When Eliza, after asserting her independence, announces that she will not see Higgins again, he carelessly tells her to order a ham and Stilton cheese for the household and to buy him ties and gloves. Eliza's reply is intriguing, for she does not reject these tasks: she has already tended to some of them and evades, without refusing, the others. Her final line, 'What you are to do without me I cannot imagine', verges on being a confession that she is obliged to stay, just as Higgins' laughter at the prospect of her marrying Freddy may be either amusement at what he considers a ludicrous misalliance or a hilarious and disdainful rejection of the notion that it will actually occur. It is essential that these dubieties remain unresolved, for they are the dramatic analogues to the unre-

solvable Shavian conflicts that resonate through the play. That these conflicts have to do with familial and sexual matters is obvious enough from the passages quoted above, but they extend beyond these to social concerns as well. Like all of Shaw's great plays, *Pygmalion* deals with both social and personal affairs (granted that the emphasis here is on the latter), and as always the boundary between these areas is less clearly marked than one might expect.

Pygmalion does not at first glance seem like a socialist, much less a Fabian play, but it is. Higgins, who appears to notice little beyond his professional concerns, has noticed—no doubt in deference to the social interests of his author—with regard to flower girls and their like that 'a woman of that class looks like a worn out drudge of fifty a year after she's married'. Later Higgins explains to his mother that changing Eliza into a different being by 'creating a new speech for her' is 'filling up the deepest gulf that separates class from class and soul from soul'. These remarks, and especially the latter, cast a suggestive light on Act I, which is more than a charmingly imaginative prologue to the story of the 'squashed cabbage leaf' passed off as 'the Queen of Sheba'; it is a survey of the social, as well as linguistic distance Eliza must traverse from 'the gutter' with its 'kerbstone English' to the lower classes with their shrewd recognitions of marks of distinctions ('e's a genleman: look at his ba-oots') and latent hostility to the gentry ('You take us for dirt under your feet, dont you?'), to the shabby genteel (Shaw's own class) represented by the Eynsford-Hills, to the comfortable assurance of money and position embodied in Pickering. It is reasonable to suppose that the elimination of such nefarious social distinctions and the gradual—that is, Fabian—evolution of a classless society in which speech patterns are not a barrier is the ultimate aim of Higgins's Universal Alphabet, at least in Shaw's view (after all, the creation of a similar alphabet was the cause to which Shaw left his substantial estate). But the matter, being Shavian, does not end there. Egalitarianism is desirable not only to achieve social justice but for an even higher purpose: so that all shall be intermarriageable, that is, so that the Life Force can select couples from the total gene-pool of the population and thus have the widest latitude in breeding the Superman.

This consideration returns us again to the play's romantic, or in the full Shavian sense, sexual concerns. Eliza's demands, after she has by Higgins' efforts and her will been raised to a higher level of being, may have a metaphorical aspect, but that does not make them any less urgent. And from the point of view of the Life Force, Higgins would seem to be more suitable breeding material than Freddy. However, Higgins is not only a prospective father for Eliza's children, as her 'creator', he stands to some extent in a paternal relation to her already. Since Doolittle is her biological progenitor, Eliza has two fathers in the play, neither of whom, Shaw claims at the end of the Postscript, she likes. In actuality, Eliza addresses her father cosily as 'dad' in the last act and seems quaintly snobbish and jealous of his marrying her stepmother, 'that low common woman'. Nevertheless, she is glad enough to see the last of him in Act II, for she understands that he has come only to get money out of her new protectors and does not seem to understand, or sympathise with, his originality of character.

Since he has come to sell her for five pounds we pardon Eliza's insensitivity on this point even as we delight in the ingenuity with which Doolittle, one of Shaw's supreme comic creations, manipulates bourgeois sentimentality ('a father's heart, as it were') while seeing through the hypocrisies of 'middle-class morality', as in this proto-Brechtian exchange with Pickering, who is shocked at Doolittle's view of his daughter as a commercial property:

> PICKERING. Have you no morals, man?
>
> DOOLITTLE. [*Unabashed*] Cant afford them, Governor. Neither could you if you was as poor as me.

(Doolittle should not be granted too much charm, however; compare the amiability of Stanley Holloway's performance as perpetuated in the film of *My Fair Lady* with the extra acerbity of Wilfred Lawson's characterisation, hinting at genuine coarseness and brutality, in the Pascal film of the play.) But despite his lack of 'morals' and his characterisation of himself as 'one of the undeserving poor', Doolittle seems cheerfully committed to the work ethic, assuring Higgins that he will spend the five pounds on a spree and will not 'live idle' on it (idleness, we recall, is Shaw's bête noire): 'I'll have to go to work same as if I'd never had it. It wont pauperize me, you bet'.

Perhaps it is this latent respectability, as well as his fear of the workhouse (his assurance that he already has to dye his hair to keep his job evokes Peter Shirley in *Major Barbara*), that makes him vulnerable to the bequest that Higgins partially thrusts upon him. For just as Higgins raises Eliza from the gutter to win a bet, so he elevates her father to make a joke. Not only are the actions parallel but they are neither of them motivated by a personal concern for the recipient. In both cases the results of this 'godlike' intervention are difficult to assess. Doolittle is saved from the workhouse, but he has lost his capacity for self-gratification, his 'happiness' as he repeatedly says (evidently without having learnt, like Marchbanks, to live without it). Moreover he must now marry his 'missus', who—in a delicious comic reversal of conventional romantic suppositions—has, he tells us, 'been very low, thinking of the happy days that are no more'. For the climax of Doolittle's story, as he goes off resplendently dressed to be married at St George's Hanover Square, is what many audiences have hoped would be the climax of his daughter's. Quite in the manner of an Elizabethan dramatist, Shaw makes the subplot of *Pygmalion* a darkly comic parody of the romantic element latent in the main plot.

In so doing, he achieves at least two artistic aims: he fulfils romantic expectations even as he teases them through the comic transmutation of the 'happy' ending, and by having Eliza's fleshly father marry, Shaw—through some magical process of compensation—relieves her spiritual father of the necessity of doing the same. . . . That this relief should be granted is absolutely crucial to Shaw's instinctive strategy as he reworks the material of the Cinderella myth. Having been a rejected child who grew up to be one of the great public performers of the age, Shaw was deeply attracted to the story of the poor drudge who demonstrated her worthiness by dancing beautifully at the ball. But as the material of the play presented itself to his imagination, a considerable difficulty arose if the Fairy Godfather was to be identical with the Handsome Prince. The fantasy of parental beneficence associated with the former figure was hardly to be casually equated with the dream of erotic fulfilment embodied in the latter. Paradoxically, it is Shaw's sensitivity to these emotional resonances that leads him to modify the 'romantic' ending and thus open himself to the accusation of 'coldness'. A lesser writer would have had no hesitation in blurring these two figures and thus purveying a peculiar, though profoundly desired gratification to his audience.

The attraction between Higgins and Eliza is, nonetheless, very real, the more so, in fact, for being a dangerous one, and Shaw must try to find some dramatically viable reason for thwarting it. He offers a hint in the play, which he later expands. When Mrs Higgins complains that her son never falls in love with anyone under forty-five, he replies, 'My idea of a lovable woman is somebody as like you as possible'. Shaw explicates this suggestion in the Postscript, arguing that for an imaginative boy a mother with wealth, intelligence, grace, dignity, and artistic taste can effect 'a disengagement of his affections, his sense of beauty, and his idealism from his specifically sexual impulses'. In a post-Freudian age this notion seems somewhat naïve (though perhaps not Shaw's contention a moment later that for many people less fortunate in their upbringing 'literature, painting, sculpture, music, and affectionate personal relations come as modes of sex if they come at all') and apparently came to appear so to Shaw, who in 1939 described Higgins as 'a confirmed old bachelor with a mother-fixation', the latter term suggesting the recognition of a sexual element here. At least as much to the point are Shaw's hints to the readers and performers in the stage directions near the beginning of the play describing Higgins as '*rather like a very impetuous baby*' and noting that '*he coaxes women as a child coaxes its nurse*', hints that are born out by Higgins' boyish impetuosity, his self-absorption, and his lack of adult social control. Higgins himself confesses to Pickering, 'Ive never been able to feel really grown-up and tremendous, like other chaps', 'You can adopt her, Mrs Pearce: I'm sure a daughter would be a great amusement to you'.

But Eliza's childlike request for 'a little kindness' and her assurance that she is not making sexual demands ('Thats not the sort of feeling I want from you') are compromised by her insistence to Higgins a moment earlier that 'every girl has a right to be loved' and her boast that girls like her 'can drag gentlemen down to make love to them easy enough'. At the same time Higgins' exalted assurance that he has higher aims than personal affection ('I care for life, for humanity') and his denigration of the fleshly world, or as he calls it 'the life of the gutter' ('Work til youre more a brute than a human being; and then cuddle and squabble and drink til you fall asleep') are made doubtful by his obvious jealousy when Eliza discloses Freddy's infatuation with her: 'You have no right to encourage him'. Shaw deeply sympathises with Eliza as a rejected child even as he is both disquieted and allured by her as a woman. Higgins may be excused from being Eliza's lover on the grounds that he too is a child, but he is also a parent-figure ('Ah-ah-ah-ow-o-o! One would think you was my father'), a 'higher' father who rescues his downtrodden child but a dangerously possessive one. Wimpole Street, specified several times during the play as the location of Higgins' establishment, is, for persons with literary interests, best known as the address of another household with a gifted daughter named Elizabeth, who was held in thrall by a perversely jealous father. But Freddy is not adequate in the role of Robert Browning, and in any case Shaw's identification is with both father and daughter in all their tangled relationships. The ending of *Pygmalion* is remarkable not because it is elusive—it could hardly be otherwise—but because it holds in complex balance so much of the richness of the play. (pp. 177-86)

Arthur Ganz, in his George Bernard Shaw, *Grove Press, Inc., 1983, 227 p.*

Michael Holroyd   (essay date 1989)

[*Holroyd is a Swedish-Irish biographer whose three-volume examination of the life of Bernard Shaw is considered one of the finest literary biographies of the twentieth century. In the following excerpt from that work, he discusses* Pygmalion *in the context of Shaw's career and analyzes its plot, principal themes, and possible autobiographical basis.*]

> Ibsen was compelled to acquiesce in a happy ending for *A Doll's House* in Berlin, because he could not help himself, just as I have never been able to stop the silly and vulgar gag with which Eliza in *Pygmalion,* both here and abroad, gets the last word and implies that she is going to marry Pygmalion. [Shaw in a letter to William Archer, 19 April 1919]

Pygmalion marks the climax of Shaw's career as a writer of comedies. Fifteen years in gestation, and a return in feeling and form to the period of his *Plays Pleasant,* it emerged as an ingeniously constructed work of art, integrating Faustian legend with Cinderella fairy tale, a comedy of manners with a parable of socialism. Written in his mid-fifties, so near to his mother's death and to the flowering of his romance with Stella Campbell, the play weaves together a variety of Shavian themes, sources and obsessions, imaginatively rephrasing the relationship between his mother and Vandeleur Lee [her vocal music coach], and casting Mrs Pat as the emotional replacement for Mrs Shaw. Its vitality and charm endeared *Pygmalion* to audiences, with whom it has remained Shaw's most popular 'romance'. 'There must be something radically wrong with the play if it pleases everybody," he protested, 'but at the moment I cannot find what it is.'

He enjoyed describing *Pygmalion* as a dry didactic experiment to demonstrate how the science of phonetics could pull apart an antiquated British class system now tied together by little more than a string of impressions and appearances. 'The reformer we need most today is an energetic phonetic enthusiast,' he was to write in his Preface. Such a laboratory method of cutting down social barriers

was Shaw's gesture towards removing the power for change from fighting men who were threatening to alter the world by indiscriminate warfare, and handing it to men of words whom he promoted as 'among the most important people in England at present'. In this context, the character of Henry Higgins (who appears as a comic version of Sherlock Holmes in Act I) takes his life from the revolutionary phonetician and philologist Henry Sweet, who had died while the play was being written. Shaw (later to be appointed chairman of the British Broadcasting Corporation's Advisory Committee on Spoken English) had been introduced to Sweet in the early 1880s by his friend James Lecky. In any other country in the world, he declared, Sweet would have been 'better known than I am myself'. Writing to Robert Bridges in 1910 about the need for a phonetic institute, he had described Sweet as the man 'I had most hopes of'. It was Bridges who, the following year, retained Shaw to speak at the Phonetic Conference on spelling reform at University College, London, where he had loudly blown Sweet's trumpet. After the debate he sent a letter to Sweet explaining what he had said. 'There is no such thing as a standard pronunciation. There is no such thing as an ideal pronunciation,' he wrote.

> Nevertheless . . . it is perfectly easy to find a speaker whose speech will be accepted in every part of the English speaking world as valid 18-carat oral currency . . . all you have to do is to write down the best practicable phonetic representation of the part of Hamlet as spoken by Forbes Robertson, and publish it with a certificate signed by half a dozen persons of satisfactory social standing, NOT that the pronunciation represented is the standard pronunciation or ideal pronunciation, or correct pronunciation, or in any way binding on any human being or morally superior to Hackney cockney or Idaho american, but solely that if a man pronounces in that way he will be eligible as far as speech is concerned for the post of Lord Chief Justice, Chancellor at Oxford, Archbishop of Canterbury, Emperor, President, or Toast Master at the Mansion House.

It was this experiment, in a more sophisticated format, that Shaw transferred to Higgins's laboratory in Wimpole Street, with its phonograph, laryngoscope, tuning-forks, wax cylinders and organ pipes—'I have long given up the idea of inducing you to do anything,' he told Sweet. This is a live experiment we are shown on stage, and as with all such laboratory work it is necessary for the Frankenstein doctor to behave as if his creation were insentient. 'She's incapable of understanding anything,' Higgins assures his fellow-scientist Colonel Pickering. 'Besides, do any of us understand what we are doing? If we did, would we ever do it?' When Pickering asks: 'Does it occur to you, Higgins, that the girl has some feelings?', Higgins cheerily replies: 'Oh no, I dont think so. Not any feelings that we need bother about. Have you, Eliza?'

Shaw conducts a second social experiment through Eliza's father, Alfred Doolittle, an elderly dustman of Dickensian vitality who partly owes his existence to Boffin, the character who in *Our Mutual Friend* inherits a fortune out of dust. Doolittle is any one of us. When asked by Higgins whether he is an honest man or rogue, he answers: 'A little of both, Henry, like the rest of us.' But he is more rogue than honest man in the dusty moral climate of pre-war London. Being his name, he does as little as possible—some bribery here or there, a little blackmail, more drinking, an occasional change of mistress: and he provides positively no education at all for his illegitimate daughter 'except to give her a lick of the strap now and again'. Yet he has all the quick wits and superficial charm of the capitalist entrepreneur. He is society's free man—free of responsibilities and conscience. 'Have you no morals, man?' demands Pickering. 'Cant afford them, Governor,' Doolittle answers. Undeserving poverty is his line: 'and I mean to go on being undeserving. I like it,' he adds. His disquisition on middle-class morality is intended by Shaw to have the same subversive effect as Falstaff's discourse on honour.

Yet this is the man whom Shaw chooses as the first recipient of what he calculates to be a reasonable income-for-all. As the result of Higgins's joking reference to Doolittle as the most original moralist in England in a letter to an American philanthropist, the undeserving dustman is left £3,000 a year on behalf of the Wannafeller Moral Reform World League. In Act II he had made his entrance with 'a professional flavour of dust about him'. In Act V when his name is announced and Pickering queries, 'Do you mean the dustman?', the parlourmaid answers: 'Dustman! Oh no, sir: a gentleman.' He is splendidly dressed as if for a fashionable wedding, with dazzling silk hat, patent leather shoes and buttonhole. Shaw's point is not that a gentleman is merely a dustman with money in the same way as a flower girl with phonetic training can be passed off as a duchess: it is that moral reformation depends upon the reform of our economic system. As Eric Bentley writes: 'He was giving the idea of the gentleman an economic basis.' At a speech to the National Liberal Club in 1913, Shaw called for a constructive social scheme for the creation of gentlemen—not the sham gentlemen of hereditary qualifications who lived in idleness, but a new breed of moral gentlemen who claimed a handsome dignified existence and subsistence from their country, who gave in return the best service of which they were capable and whose ideal was to give their country more than they received from it. It is this that Doolittle dreaded and derided, and now finds himself dragged into. 'It's making a gentleman of me that I object to,' he protests. 'Who asked him to make a gentleman of me? . . . I have to live for others and not for myself: thats middle class morality.'

Shaw is at the same time conducting an experiment with the Pygmalion legend by making Higgins create a petrified social statue of Eliza. Under his tutelage she becomes a doll of 'remarkable distinction and beauty . . . speaking with pedantic correctness of pronunciation and great beauty of tone', which Mrs Higgins tells her son is 'a triumph of your art and of her dressmaker's'. This dummy figure replaces the 'draggle tailed guttersnipe . . . more brute than being' whose life Higgins acknowledges to have been real, warm and violent—'you can feel it through the thickest skin: you can taste it and smell it without any training or any work'. The classical Pygmalion, believing all women to be prostitutes, had prayed to Aphrodite to

make his ideal statue come alive so that he could marry her—which may mean, as Arnold Silver has argued, that he 'would be committing incest in marrying the woman he had fathered parthenogenetically'. Shaw's flower girl, whom Higgins has manufactured into a replica duchess by the beginning of Act IV, is then transformed by the action of the Life Force into an independent living woman—whom Higgins refuses to marry. However, the transformation scheme, in which Higgins lays his hands on Eliza like a sculptor's creative act, is a struggle the implications of which are sexual.

> *Eliza tries to control herself . . . she is on the point of screaming . . . He comes to her . . . He pulls her up . . .* LIZA [*Breathless*] *. . . She crisps her fingers frantically.* HIGGINS [*Looking at her in cool wonder*] *. . .* LIZA [*Gives a suffocated scream of fury, and instinctively darts her nails at his face*]!! HIGGINS [*Catching her wrists . . . He throws her roughly into the easy chair*] LIZA [*Crushed by superior strength and weight*]. HIGGINS [*Thundering*] Those slippers LIZA [*With bitter submission*] Those slippers

This sexual sub-text provided by the stage directions contains many sado-masochistic undertones, and is voiced as a suspicion by the other characters in the play. Pickering puts the question to Higgins simply: 'Are you a man of good character where women are concerned?' and adds 'I hope it's understood that no advantage is to be taken of her position.' Eliza herself who repeatedly insists that she's 'a good girl' is prudishly shocked by the mirror in Higgins's bathroom and tells him 'I've heard of girls being drugged by the likes of you.' Doolittle arriving to rescue his daughter from 'worse than death', then selling her to Higgins for five pounds, assures him that she will 'soon pick up your free and easy ways' and advises him to 'marry Eliza while she's young and dont know no better'. Higgins's housekeeper, Mrs Pearce, seeing him tempt Eliza with chocolates and promises of taxi-rides, bursts out: 'Stop, Mr Higgins. I wont allow it. It's you that are wicked. Go home to your parents, girl; and tell them to take better care of you.' The police inspector too, whom Higgins and Pickering call in when Eliza disappears, 'suspected us of some improper purpose', Pickering reveals. Even Higgins's mother believes that her son 'must be perfectly cracked' about his flower girl. But Higgins himself resists every innuendo.

This was important to Shaw. When he had been coaching Florence Farr he suggested that she 'should learn the science of phonetics for dramatic purposes' and be appointed Beerbohm Tree's resident professor of phonetics at His Majesty's Theatre. Sweet, of course, had been the man to teach her. 'He will probably say that two years residence at Oxford is indispensable, as he has a genius for making everything impossible both for himself and everybody else,' he had written to Florence. 'He is the most savagely Oxonian and donnish animal that ever devoted his life to abusing all the other dons . . . See him and try what you can make out of him.'

Nothing had come of Shaw's phonetic plan for Florence, and when he tried to revive it in ***Pygmalion*** Sweet's genius for 'making everything impossible' again seemed to obstruct him, and he turned his mind to another 'genius' as a model for Higgins, the author of *The Voice,* Vandeleur Lee. Higgins's asexual association with Eliza is consequently authorized by Shaw's faith in his mother's 'innocence', and written as an endorsement of his own legitimacy. The platonic arrangement depends not only on Higgins's statement that he is 'a confirmed old bachelor, and likely to remain so', as Lee had done (though not Sweet who was married), but more importantly on the professional circumstances of their relationship. 'You see, she'll be a pupil,' Higgins explains to Pickering, 'and teaching would be impossible unless pupils were sacred.' Higgins's voice tuition of Eliza takes the place of the singing lessons Lee had given Bessie (Lucinda Elizabeth Shaw) and to reinforce this substitution Shaw provides Higgins's pupil with the same name as Lee's pupil.

> HIGGINS. Whats your name?
>
> THE FLOWER GIRL. Liza Doolittle.
>
> HIGGINS. [*Declaiming gravely*] Eliza, Elizabeth, Betsy and Bess, They went to the wood to get a bird's nes':

Near the beginning of Act II Eliza complains to Higgins, 'One would think you were my father', and he replies: 'If I decide to teach you, I'll be worse than two fathers to you.' Near the end of the play he suggests to her, 'I'll adopt you as my daughter and settle money on you if you like. Or would you rather marry Pickering?' What seems clear is that Higgins can assume almost any family relationship with Eliza except that of husband. 'I've never been able to feel really grown-up and tremendous, like other chaps,' he tells Pickering. He explains the reason to his mother who has regretted his inability to fall in love with any woman under forty-five. 'My idea of a lovable woman is somebody as like you as possible,' he tells her. 'I shall never get into the way of seriously liking young women: some habits lie too deep to be changed.'

While she lives in Higgins's house, Eliza remains a bought woman and simply his creation as Galatea had been Pygmalion's. But the transformation scene, which is a deflowering of Eliza, leads to her rebirth and, with the handing over of her necklace, a severing of the umbilical cord. The scene ends with the same implicit sexuality as it began. Higgins eats his Adam-and-Eve apple, and the divorce of his previous partnership with Eliza, dramatized by the throwing-away of the ring, is complete. In the middle of this scene Higgins tells Eliza: 'Now you are free and can do what you like.' What she does is to escape to his mother's house where, the stage directions inform us, 'she is very much at home'. Finding her there in the last act, Higgins exclaims: 'Five minutes ago you were like a millstone round my neck. Now youre a tower of strength: a consort battleship.' What has apparently impressed Higgins is Eliza's statement that she will teach others 'what you taught me. I'll teach phonetics'—in much the same way as Bessie had taught 'the Method' in London independently of Lee.

In this final act, Shaw was rewriting the legend of Svengali and his pupil Trilby. When Svengali dies of a heart attack, Trilby's voice is silenced, she cannot sing at her concert,

and she follows Svengali into death. In Shaw's version Eliza's voice speaks truly once she emerges from Higgins's bullying presence and walks out to a separate life. But other forces were at work in the final act obliging Higgins himself to speak increasingly with the voice of G. B. S., the public figure that had developed from Vandeleur Lee; while Eliza comes to represent the emotions that Stella Campbell was introducing into his life. Higgins's description of Eliza as a 'consort battleship' has something of the armoured impregnability Shaw attributed to his mother ('one of those women who could act as matron of a cavalry barracks from eighteen to forty and emerge without a stain on her character'). But no one else in the play regards Eliza in this light. Mrs Higgins calls her 'naturally rather affectionate'; Doolittle admits she is 'very tender-hearted'; and Eliza herself demands: 'Every girl has a right to be loved.' She also tells Higgins that she had 'come to care for you', and though she adds that she does not 'want you to make love to me', this is clearly a tactical statement added so as not to alarm Higgins at the start of their new relationship: for love is what she does want. She wants to be valued.

What Higgins wants is less clear. He claims he has created an ideal wife—'a consort for a king'—yet, since she represents his mother, he must resist her emotional appeal with supermaniac brutality: 'I wont stop for you . . . I can do without anybody. I have . . . my own spark of divine fire . . . I care for life, for humanity; and you are a part of it that has come my way and been built into my house. What more can you or anyone ask? . . . If you cant stand the coldness of my sort of life, and the strain of it, go back to the gutter.'

The purpose of Higgins's experiment has been 'filling up the deepest gulf that separates class from class and soul from soul'. It is half successful, half a failure. The class gulf is filled at the garden party, dinner party and reception: the gulf between Eliza and Higgins remains. Eliza has changed, but Higgins admits 'I cant change my nature.' He is, as Eliza says, 'a born preacher' and that seems to be the only role he can sustain. Lacking the intimate voice, he seems 'cold, unfeeling, selfish' to Eliza. 'I only want to be natural,' she says. But can Higgins be natural? There seems a chance when, with '*sudden humility*', he confesses to her that 'I have learnt something from your idiotic notions: I confess that humbly and gratefully. And I have grown accustomed to your voice and appearance. I like them, rather.' Where will these feelings lead to if she accepts his invitation to go back to him 'for the fun of it'? There is no mention of sex: but Higgins is enticing her into the beginnings of a Shavian open marriage. The original ending of the play is carefully ambiguous, reflecting Shaw's uncertainties over his romance with Stella. He could not marry her: she could not remain for ever his pupil as an actress learning from his theatrical direction. But might they become lovers? The question is left open to our imagination:

> MRS HIGGINS. I'm afraid youve spoilt that girl, Henry. But never mind, dear: I'll buy you the tie and gloves.
>
> HIGGINS. [*Sunnily*] Oh, dont bother. She'll buy

em all right enough. Good-bye. *They kiss. Mrs Higgins runs out. Higgins, left alone, rattles his cash in his pocket; chuckles; and disports himself in a highly self-satisfied manner.*

Critics of the play have agreed with Eric Bentley that 'this is the true naturalistic ending' and that Shaw's subsequent series of attempts to clear up its ambiguity, stimulated by the actors' and public's response to the sub-text, have blurred the outline of its elegant structure. The faint poignancy of the ending lies in the half-emergent realization that there is to be no satisfactory marriage for this Cinderella; while a feminist reading tells us that Higgins cannot be approved of as a husband. Popular opinion wanted Shaw not to shatter the fairy tale—which he would do by going further. 'I call it a romance,' he told a reporter, 'because it is the story of a poor girl who meets a gentleman at a church door and is transformed by him into a beautiful lady. That is what I call romance. It is also what everybody else calls a romance, so for once we are all agreed.' But the public wanted his Miltonic bachelor to be transformed into the beautiful lady's lover. 'This is unbearable,' Shaw cried out. Once his love affair with Stella had ended, he could not bear to speculate on what might have happened that time when 'I almost condescended to romance'. He instructed his translators, therefore, that there was to be 'no sentimental nonsense' about Higgins and Eliza being lovers. 'Eliza married Freddy [Eynsford-Hill]' he told Trebitsch; 'and the notion of her marrying Higgins is disgusting.' In other words Eliza married a double-barrelled nonentity like George Cornwallis-West, and Higgins's agonizing boredom with the Eynsford-Hill family reflects Shaw's own impatience with the smart visitors who sometimes crowded him out of Stella's house.

The history of *Pygmalion* was to develop into a struggle over this ending. For the play's first publication in book form in 1916, Shaw added a sequel, like the last chapter in a novel, recounting 'what Eliza did'. Her decision not to marry Higgins, he explained, was well-considered and guided by instinct. The differences between them of age and income, when added to Higgins's mother-fixation and exclusive passion for phonetics, was too wide a gulf to bridge. He told the story of Eliza and Freddy, Mr and Mrs Eynsford-Hill, as invitingly as he could: but the public went on preferring its own version. By the 1920s he had begun advising his translators to add lines in their own languages for Higgins to end the play on. 'It is important that the actor who plays Higgins should thoroughly understand that he is not Eliza's lover,' he instructed Julio Brouta, his Spanish translator. '. . . When he is left alone on the stage at the end he should just go out on the balcony and look down making it clear that he is watching Eliza's departure in the carriage. He then comes back into the room, excited and triumphant & exclaims "Finished, and come to life! Bravo, Pygmalion!"'

After much tampering Shaw made his final version of the end on 19 August 1939.

> MRS HIGGINS. I'm afraid youve spoilt that girl, Henry. I should be uneasy about you and her if she were less fond of Colonel Pickering.
>
> HIGGINS. Pickering! Nonsense: she's going to

marry Freddy. Ha ha! Freddy! Freddy! Ha ha ha ha ha!!!!! [*He roars with laughter as the play ends.*]

But by now this laughter sounded as hollow as Higgins's prediction—and even Shaw's printers had begun to query his intentions. 'I assure you that Liza *did* marry Freddy,' he again insisted, 'and that Higgins never married anybody . . . their marriage would have been a revolting tragedy.'

The English-language film of *Pygmalion,* written and made between 1936 and 1938, gave Shaw an extra opportunity to remove 'virtually every suggestion of Higgins's possible romantic interest in Liza'. He was particularly anxious to achieve this having loathed the sentimental German and Dutch film adaptations. His screenplay even omits the word 'consort' and leaves Higgins calling Eliza a 'battleship'. But the producer of the film hired other screenwriters who added a 'sugar-sweet ending' which Shaw found out for the first time at a press show two days before its première. 'Nothing of the kind was emphasised in my scenario,' he wrote. Nevertheless it was widely reported that G. B. S. had approved the romantic reconciliation.

But one battle he apparently did win. 'Hamon, my French translator, says that it is announced that Lehar is making an operetta of *Pygmalion,*' he notified [the translator Siegfried] Trebitsch in the summer of 1921. '. . . Can you warn him that he cannot touch *Pygmalion* without infringing my copyright, and that I have no intention of allowing the history of *The Chocolate Soldier* to be repeated.' For almost thirty more years he made the same reply to all composers and resisted every pressure to 'degrade' his play into a musical. 'I absolutely forbid any such outrage,' he wrote when in his ninety-second year. *Pygmalion* was good enough 'with its own verbal music'. (pp. 325-33)

> *Michael Holroyd, in his* Bernard Shaw: The Pursuit of Power, 1898-1918, Vol. II, *Chatto & Windus, 1989, 422 p.*

David J. Gordon   (essay date 1990)

[*In the following excerpt, Gordon maintains that the problematic denouement of* Pygmalion *represents an unresolvable impasse that is the inevitable result of the conflicts established in the first three acts.*]

Pygmalion is Shaw's major achievement in the mode of the anti-sublime.

It is subtitled 'A Romance,' and certainly it generates thoroughly romantic expectations up to a point. Few literary fantasies are as irresistible as this Cinderellan metamorphosis of the cockney flower girl into the supposed princess at an ambassador's party. It is sometimes said that the momentum of this romance plot is so strong that the romantic dénouements perpetrated by Sir Beerbohm Tree and Mrs Patrick Campbell (to Shaw's disgust) and later by others, including Messrs Lerner and Loewe, are justified. But Shaw was nowhere more faithful to his own distinctive sensibility than in those potent structures of disappointment, acts 4 and 5. The Miltonic mind of Higgins and the eloquent humanity of Eliza are opposed in an absolute stalemate. There can be no compromise between the expectations of acts 1-3 and the disappointment of 4-5, as Shaw himself managed to prove by trying unsuccessfully to write a narrative continuation about Eliza's moderately happy future with Freddy, pages described accurately by Valency (1973) as 'dismally novelistic.' Shaw was, at one and the same time, romantic and anti-romantic, and this ambivalence is especially firm in **Pygmalion.** It is right that Higgins is alone at the end, laughing in denial of his failure to hold Eliza. And Eliza must be disappointed too, for the man she cannot help loving is incorrigible. Her whole story—the fantastic rise and its unexpectedly bitter end—is replayed in a farcical key by the story of Doolittle, her father.

Shaw knew that, at the peril of sentimentality, Higgins must be harsh as well as attractive. It is no accident that **Pygmalion** is the most candid of his works on the subject of incest. Higgins's incapacity for sexual love despite his unconscious seductiveness is explicitly traced to his idealisation of a superior mother. Shaw does not resort here to either of his two favourite explanations for the prevailing taboo on incest. One, drily rationalistic, is that early familiarity kills romance. The other comes closer to the truth by being its exact opposite: a mother's love is too much for a child and overwhelms him. **Pygmalion** is unique among his plays in encouraging us to make a connection between a character's early, excessive admiration of a mother and his later resistance to a woman he could otherwise love.

To suggest that Higgins represents Shaw's most direct effort of dramatic self-confrontation is not to say naïvely that he is a proxy for the author, much less a puppet, for we are dealing with an imaginative configuration, 'the dancing of an attitude' in Kenneth Burke's nice phrase, not with mere personal characteristics. The preface adverts us to a brilliant, arrogant phonetician named Henry Sweet as the original for Higgins, a proud and impatient man who did not suffer fools gladly. (Milton, Ibsen and Samuel Butler are also drawn into this portrait by association.) The arrogance of Higgins is mainly expressed as an amiable bullying, aggressive enough yet peculiarly innocent in its unguarded directness. The most important device for distancing him is to make his aggressive abruptness look comical by virtue of his lack of self-consciousness. Probably the most effective of a dozen such passages occurs in act 4, after the party:

> LIZA. . . . Whats to become of me?
>
> HIGGINS. [*Enlightened, but not at all impressed*] Oh,*thats* whats worrying you, is it? [*He thrusts his hands into his pockets, and walks about in his usual manner, rattling the contents of his pockets, as if condescending to a trivial subject out of pure kindness.*] I shouldnt bother about it if I were you. I should imagine you wont have much difficulty in settling yourself somewhere or other, though I hadnt quite realized that you were going away. [*She looks quickly at him: he does not look at her, but examines the dessert stand on the piano and decides that he will eat an apple.*]

> You might marry, you know. [*He bites a large piece out of the apple and munches it noisily.*]

Higgins's speech is a masterly, half-unconscious effort both to attract and repel. The final stage direction caps his character beautifully. Shaw's turn of phrase ('*he eats his apple with a dreamy expression of happiness, as it is quite a good one*') so neatly justifies Higgins from his own point of view and condemns him from ours.

But though we may laugh at him, Shaw insisted that he must be heroic. One of the play's insights is that intellectual or creative achievement may be significantly related to the continued presence of early idealisations. But heroic need not mean likeable, and indeed usually does not. The mother's exasperation with her son and Pickering who are playing like boys with a live doll and Eliza's anguished slipper-throwing are human protests, forcefully expressed, against the inhumanity of an heroic stance.

The romance of Eliza's rise is given considerable space before the shadows fall. Her naïveté in the early acts is extremely charming, and her father's comparable casuistry is unusually disarming. But sorrow is drawn *from* the romance. Eliza owes her transformation to a Pygmalion who must, we can see from the first, fail to live quite up to his mythic role at the last. And Doolittle's 'fall' into middle-class morality has, in a sense, been his own doing. We may regret the forlorness, but anti-climax is a central feature of Shaw's sensibility and I can readily understand his impatience with the softened ending. Higgins is so fully and honestly imagined that he really must not be allowed to toss Eliza a kiss or a rose. And bringing Freddy forward as a companion for Eliza has really nothing to do with the story of her romance. Of course, it is reasonable to assume that a young woman, romantically disappointed, will eventually make a new, more prosaic life for herself, but this makes another story.

The strength of **Pygmalion** has much to do with the unresolved tension between the 'higher' consciousness of Higgins and the 'lower' consciousness of Eliza. It is a sexually charged tension that insists on both eternal separateness and eternal reciprocity. Not every viewer or reader finds aesthetic satisfaction in that. But it may help to show how the impasse of acts 4 and 5 is prepared by the romance of the first three acts.

Each of the early acts gracefully develops a romantic situation and at the curtain gracefully turns it away. We start with a wonderful whirl of contrasting voices—the fretful Eynsford-Hills sending off their Freddy to look for a cab in the rain, the broad cockney whine of the flower girl, the nonchalant echoing of the Notetaker punctuated by the remarks of suspicious bystanders—and gradually rising from the mêlée, as the rain unnoticeably stops, the educated exchange of Pickering and Higgins playing out an irresistibly improbable recognition scene. They joke amiably about what Eliza could be and, with godlike condescension, shower her with coins. She goes off self-importantly but alone in the cab that Freddy finally obtained for his family, who have already left.

The second and third acts are constructed similarly, a movement of building up and dashing romance that is half-concealed by the charm of the humour and the expectation of later fulfilment. In the first part of act 2, Eliza arrives at Wimpole Street with her new wealth to hire Higgins as a teacher, and amid a good deal of bullying and scorn, the romantic wager is made. Enter thereupon a sordid complication, the blackmailing dustman. But he so beguiles the gentlemen and us with his casuistic defence of the undeserving poor that we do not realise, until his charismatic presence fades, that the boy-gentlemen have taken on a 'stiff job' of a less technical and more complexly human kind than they are prepared to acknowledge.

Mrs Higgins serves much the same deflationary function in the third act that Doolittle does in the second. Higgins and then Pickering enter her drawing room excitedly, arousing our expectation of a transformed Eliza performing successfully before an audience of Eynsford-Hills. We are struck for a moment by the element of truth in Higgins's statement that a change of class is like a change of soul. Then our Galatea regresses to street talk, charming Freddy and delighting Clara. But Mrs Higgins soberly and forcefully points out to us that the two 'infinitely stupid male creatures' are toying with a human life. The picture of her at the curtain (scorning men! men!! men!!!) registers one of his strongest judgements against his own kind of inhumanity, drawing its strength from his investment in the image of the judging mother.

With the structure of these acts in mind, we see more clearly that, despite further comic moments (notably the tophatted Doolittle complaining about Ezra D. Wannafeller's Moral Reform Society and Pre-Digested Cheese Trust), the fourth and fifth acts dramatise a sustained impasse. Love is in the air but checked, stifled. The fourth act plays off Higgins's triumphant egotism against Eliza's human anguish. Baffled, she throws his gift ring into the fireplace, picks it out again and flings it once more on to a dessert stand.

The fifth act sustains this mood with the addition of other voices—Mrs Higgins', Pickering's, Doolittle's. Mrs Higgins's role is to explain to the men the full humanity of Eliza. Pickering is now differentiated more clearly from Higgins, as adumbrated by his earlier politeness. Higgins naturally remains incorrigible: 'Get up and come home; and dont be a fool.' 'Very nicely put', replies his mother, 'No woman could resist such an invitation.'

He is, in fact, throughout the play, much like the incorrigible Doolittle, both in his chief virtues—utter frankness and freedom from snobbery—and in his chief vice—thinking of Eliza as a thing to manipulate. The difference is that Doolittle blandly resorts to blackmail whereas the heroically minded Higgins wants to make something of her, and scorns Freddy as a suitor because he cannot, in his terms, do so. Higgins is sincere in contrasting his own offer of a life devoted to Science and Literature with marriage to a man who can only offer money, kisses and kicks. But Eliza, though pained by the knowledge that she must give up much of higher value in making a decent, common life for herself, is resolved to do so and to do so with a measure of dignity. A harshly comic mutual rejection stamps the final moment of action. She sweeps out with mock in-

difference of his need for her; he laughs excessively at the idea of her marrying Freddy.

Shaw makes it clear that heartbreak is inevitable in either the lofty or the common life yet that each is to be respected. He checks his two most characteristic impulses—to transcend and to ridicule—and thus in effect renders judgement on his own vision. (pp. 147-51)

> *David J. Gordon, in his* Bernard Shaw and the Comic Sublime, *The Macmillan Press Ltd., 1990, 218 p.*

John A. Bertolini   (essay date 1991)

[*In the following excerpt, Bertolini applies psychological interpretations to action and characterization in* Pygmalion.]

Higgins as Pygmalion

In Susan Gubar's essay " 'The Blank Page' and the Issues of Female Creativity" [in *Writing and Sexual Difference*, ed. Elizabeth Abel], the author interprets Ovid's treatment of the Pygmalion myth as follows: "Not only has he [Pygmalion] created life, he has created female life as he would like it to be—pliable, responsive, purely physical. More important, he has evaded the humiliation, shared by many men, of acknowledging that it is *he* who is really created out of and from the *female* body."

Ms. Gubar's reading of Ovid seems to me pertinent to an understanding of Shaw's characterization of Higgins. In the epilogue, Shaw states explicitly what problem Higgins has in his romantic relationship with Eliza: he has a mother-fixation. Therefore, his adventure with Eliza, his desire "to make a woman" of her enacts his unconscious desire to deny his own creation by his mother. Higgins seems to have no father in the play (just as Eliza has no mother); Mrs. Higgins' husband is never alluded to, though Shaw does give Higgins a mysterious clergyman brother, who is alluded to, though never seen (rather like Mycroft Holmes in his elusiveness). In the stage directions, Shaw describes Higgins as *"but for his years and size, rather like an impetuous baby."* And so he is; and therefore Higgins has little insight into himself, but he does have a rare moment of self-understanding when he points out that he has "never been able to feel grown up and tremendous like other chaps." His insight makes clear his vague sense of inadequacy or helplessness that results from his tie to his mother and explains why the adventure with Eliza attracts him: in trying to create a woman, he attempts to realize a fantasy of omnipotence, to play the role of the creator. That is also why Shaw insistently connects Higgins with Milton, the rewriter of Genesis: "Would the world ever have been made if its maker had been afraid of making trouble? Making life means making trouble," Higgins asserts organ-voiced to Eliza.

Higgins attempts to deny his own derivativeness, his lack of originality, by becoming the creator of life instead of being the created of his mother, and, as I see it, thereby reflects or objectifies Shaw's own anxiety about his own derivativeness as a playwright, particularly from Shakespeare. At the same time, Shaw creates in Higgins an exemplary warning to himself of the danger for the writer of habitually recreating the real world as a world of fiction, and thinking the artificial world a fair representation of the other one. Hence, Shaw first presents Higgins to the audience as an anonymous notetaker.

Higgins the Writer, and His Mother

The image of Higgins taking notes under the portico of St. Paul's church, Covent Garden, figures him by metonymy as a playwright—note-taking being part of the playwright's practice, at least as practiced by Shaw, and by Shaw's Shakespear in ***The Dark Lady of the Sonnets,*** who walks around with his "tablets" in hand, at the ready to steal any felicitous uses of the English language that he overhears. Higgins takes his notes in shorthand, unreadable except to the tutored: "That's not proper writing, I can't read it," observes Eliza. Like Prospero with his magic books, Higgins has knowledge of strange symbols; his expertise in phonetics gives him power over others. His powers also have a theatrical aspect: he creates a performance by seeming magically to identify the places of origin of various bystanders:

> THE NOTE TAKER. [*Turning on him* (THE BY-STANDER) *genially*] And how are all your people down in Selsey?
>
> THE BYSTANDER. [*Suspiciously*] Who told you my people come from Selsey?
>
> THE NOTE TAKER. Never you mind. They did. [*To the girl*] How do you come to be up so far east? You were born in Lisson Grove.

Pickering wonders, "Do you do this for a living at a music hall?"—a question that links Higgins with Shaw as a public entertainer. Also, at the beginning of Act II, after Higgins has demonstrated his phonetic equipment to Pickering, Higgins remarks, "Well, I think thats the whole show." More significant though for Higgins' personal psychology is his ability to tell people where they come from. When challenged by the onlookers for his seeming espionage against Eliza, Higgins disarms them by retorting with what part of London bore them; he shows that he has made himself a master of origins. They cannot hide their original identities from Higgins.

I read the demonstration of his power as Higgins' desire to master his own origins, namely his derivativeness from his mother. Because the mother figure is the giver of language and speech, Higgins turns himself into a parent to Eliza. He becomes an expert in the mother tongue and does for others what he unconsciously wants to do for himself, to help them forget their origins, to escape the dependency on mother, which he both needs and needs to abjure. Another way of putting that is to say Higgins, like Milton's Satan, wants to be the author of himself.

Once Higgins' psyche is understood in such a way, then his anger at Eliza's self-emancipation from his domination can be seen as more than frustrated romantic impulses toward her, or even just possessiveness; his anger then duplicates his own ambivalence toward his own emancipation from his mother. My language here, perhaps, suggests a rather heavy-handed psychological drama, but nothing

Shaw in 1948.

could be lighter than Shaw's touch in manipulating the psychic material from which he makes the play. For one thing, Shaw takes such tangled psychological relationships as that between Higgins and his mother in stride; they are for Shaw a subject for comedy, and therefore unthreatening. Moreover, they are figurative, as Shaw employs them, of Shaw's own psychological relationship to writing, and in that way he maintains a proper perspective on the story he represents to the audience.

Higgins does not understand that his need for Eliza derives partly from his psychic investment in his mother. For example, he chooses his mother's at-home day on which to try Eliza out on society, to demonstrate that he has taught Eliza to speak the mother tongue properly, "the language of Shakespeare, Milton and the Bible." He enlists his mother's aid in Eliza's tryout by telling her he has "a phonetic job" for her. But Higgins has failed with his mother as he has not with Eliza. The phonetic job Higgins gives Eliza, Eliza successfully accomplishes; Mrs. Higgins, on the other hand, has not been able to master phonetics in spite of her son's efforts: she "cant get round his vowels," and although she likes getting Henry's postcards in his "patent shorthand," she is also grateful that he "thoughtfully" provides her with "copies in ordinary writing," which she always reads. The shorthand symbols, which are practically hieroglyphs to Mrs. Higgins, function as emblems of mysterious communications from son to mother, unconscious love messages, for Mrs. Higgins condescends to admire them but does not take the trouble to learn their meaning. Since Higgins writes his own transliteration, and Mrs. Higgins cannot decipher the original, Higgins can write to her whatever he wishes without fear of discovery. The shorthand letters nimbly encapsulate the difficulty of the child who achieves in order to win the parent's appreciation only to have the effort go begging for attention.

Moreover, since "original" and "copy" are antithetical terms, Higgins' rewriting of the original shorthand notes constitutes a metaphoric revision of origins, which is another way he has of asserting his mastery of originality. The same antithetical configuration comes into play later when Higgins angrily asserts Eliza to be a mere copy of his original self. In order to goad him in their last confrontation in Act V, Eliza claims that she will "teach phonetics," offer herself as an assistant to the ex-student of Higgins, the Hungarian, Nepommuck. Higgins responds as if his originality is being violated: "my methods! my discoveries!" A little earlier in the scene, Higgins says about Eliza, "Let her speak for herself. You will jolly well see whether she has an idea that I havnt put into her head or a word that I havnt put into her mouth. I tell you I have created this thing out of the squashed cabbage leaves of Covent Garden." It is crucial to Higgins that he be the original and she the copy. His obsession with being the author of both Eliza and himself flows from his desire to escape dependency: "I can do without anybody," he asserts to Eliza. That is his sustaining myth: complete self-sufficiency and self-authoring. Again, his need for autonomy and authority focuses on his relationship with his mother. It is not enough that he claims he created Eliza, he even offers to adopt her as his daughter and to settle money on her. In offering to become Eliza's parent, Higgins replaces his mother with himself as the original.

That is one of the reasons why he cannot marry Eliza; another is that in making her over he has made her too much like his mother and the incest taboo intervenes. The prohibition can be seen operating to produce an intense ambivalence when Higgins threatens to "wring" Eliza's neck, after she has threatened to attach herself to Nepommuck as an assistant in phonetics teaching. The word "wring," insofar as it is a homonym for "ring," recalls the ring that figured so prominently in the physical action of Act IV, where Eliza, as a sign of her utter rejection of Higgins, gave back the ring he had bought for her in Brighton, thus provoking him to dash *"the ring violently into the fireplace."* At the end of the act, Eliza retrieves the ring from the fireplace, and after considering *"for a moment what to do with it. . . . flings it down on the dessert stand,"* where she is certain that he will find it, because she knows his fondness for sweets. In doing so, Eliza points her revenge on Higgins for his original "seduction" of her into participating in the experiment, which was accomplished with the aid of a chocolate taken by Higgins from the same dessert stand. By leaving the ring there, Eliza undoes their "marriage." Behind the word "wring," therefore, lies a history of Higgins' and Eliza's romantic involvement. Now, when Higgins uses the word in that last confronta-

tion of theirs, he enacts his own ambivalence: he will choke her, he will marry her; he will make her aphonic, he will embrace her.

The ostensible subject of ***Pygmalion*** is the science of phonetics as that science affects the lives and destinies of two characters of opposite class. That subject compels Shaw for several reasons: it allows him to claim that the play is intensely "didactic," and to hurl its success with the public in the face of the "wiseacres" who discount his plays because of their didacticism; it allows him to make language, speech, and writing both the substance and the allegory of the play; and it allows him to represent his own anxiety about his own originality in complex and subtle ways.

The figurativeness of the material amounts to this: like ***The Doctor's Dilemma, Pygmalion*** enacts Shaw's own ambivalence to the profession of writing as a form of artistic creation. Only in ***Pygmalion,*** Shaw focuses his ambivalence more on his anxieties of derivativeness. Higgins, the notetaker, is the son of Mrs. Higgins the "writer."

Mrs. Higgins, the Writer

Shaw describes the tasteful decor and furnishings of Mrs. Higgins' drawing room in explicit detail, not for the sake of any putative realism, but as a way of characterizing Mrs. Higgins for the knowledgeable reader and playgoer who can recognize Morris decor, or an Elizabethan chair, or a Cecil Lawson landscape. Since she *"was brought up on Morris and Burne Jones"* and her drawing room shows it, Mrs. Higgins represents artistic antecedence for her son, a troublesome case for a son who wants to be the author of himself.

Higgins' entry into his mother's drawing room has the force of a violation; one might call it, taking the cue from Eliza's characterization of him, his "motorbus" effect: *"The door is opened violently; and Higgins enters with his hat on."* A motorbus does not have time for amenities such as hat removals; it just presses in. Mrs. Higgins meets him with a *"dismayed"* tone and demeanor; she scolds him, gently reminds him of his lack of manners by taking his hat off and presenting it to him, and tells him to "Go home at once." The comicality of her parental peremptoriness emphasizes that he has his own home to go back to, that he should not treat her home as his. The subtext is that of the parent shooing away the returning offspring from the nest. Mrs. Higgins does not want her son at her at-home because he offends all her friends: "They stop coming whenever they meet you." Henry's apparently unconscious rudeness has the unconsciously desired effect of keeping mother to himself by keeping others away. He views his difficulty as merely having "no small talk," but Mrs. Higgins sees it rather as offensiveness, not simply a lack of conversational ability: "What about your large talk?"

Her characterization of his conversation recalls Higgins' burst of laughter at Mrs. Eynsford-Hill in Act I, when she names her birthplace as "Largelady Park." Shaw designs the verbal coincidence between "large talk" and "Largelady Park" as surely as he designs the coincidence of the Eynsford Hills' being the visitors who will hear Higgins' "large talk" and the same people who heard his large talk in Act I. The image of Largelady Park (a real place, but not therefore an indication of realism in Shaw's style) suggests maternal space—like the park Venus invites Adonis into in Shakespeare's epyllion—the space Higgins would like both to escape from and to possess; hence his laughter at the naming of maternal space. There are several instances in the play of Higgins' laughing at something he alone finds funny. Indeed the play ends with him laughing at the idea of Eliza marrying Freddy. That is why I give the incident of Higgins' laughter at "Largelady Park" so much weight. Mrs. Higgins finds her son's "large talk" worrisome because of the unconscious preoccupations it indicates. (The unconscious later becomes part of the conversation when Higgins suggests that people are all more or less savages underneath.) Shaw uses the coincidence of the Eynsford Hills' visit to Mrs. Higgins' at-home as a kind of echo of Higgins' relationship with his mother, for Mrs. Eynsford Hill is the dominant mother to her son Freddy, and thus parodies Mrs. Higgins.

Before Higgins meets Eliza in Act I, Shaw spends a good deal of time drawing the configuration of the Eynsford Hill family. In the downpour of rain, Freddy is sent to find a cab. Clara complains of his lack of gumption in failing to obtain one; his mother at first defends him, but then, when he fails a second time, she scolds him, "You really are very helpless, Freddy." Then comes Freddy's collision with Eliza and her coincidentally calling him by his right name, though she does not know him at all. Mrs. Eynsford Hill's maternal radar has noted carefully the terms of her son's encounter with the street girl, and she cunningly questions Eliza as to her relationship with Freddy. That Shaw means us to take the mother's behavior as more than curiosity, but rather as maternal jealousy and dominance, can be seen from Clara's skeptical reaction to her mother's suspicion of some improper alliance between her son and the flower girl: "You might have spared Freddy *that.*" Clara sees her mother's nosy suspiciousness about Freddy's love life as ridiculous.

The downpour of rain, the allusions to wetness (Freddy is *"very wet round the ankles,"* Eliza's hair *"needs washing very badly"*), the concealed suggestions of a sea voyage (Eliza's *"little sailor hat"*), the emphasis on Freddy's childlike incompetence and his being dominated by his mother (Clara complains of his lack of gumption in failing to procure a cab, and his mother comments exasperatedly on his helplessness)—all these elements in the scene suggest that Shaw is re-creating the providential storms of Shakespeare's romances and comedies. And when these elements are combined with the various coincidences that occur in the scene, coincidences such as Higgins and Pickering happening to meet while waiting for the *"Torrents of heavy summer rain"* to stop (PICKERING: "I came from India to meet you." HIGGINS: "I was going to India to meet you."), the combination seems especially to allude to the storms of *The Comedy of Errors* and *The Tempest,* the plays of Shakespeare which most clearly connect storm and sea voyage with birthing and the psychic ties between parents and children. Shaw's dual purpose here is to make the connection with Shakespeare as a challenge (Shaw rewrites Shakespearean romance); and he establishes his

preoccupation with the psychic domination of children by parents. Insofar as Shakespeare is Shaw's parent in writing, the two purposes are closely related.

The storm is not the only way Shaw makes his play the inheritor of Shakespeare's plays. I have already mentioned Higgins' Prospero-like magic powers, his ability to reveal the hidden origins of people through his mastery of the science of phonetics (which Higgins treats more like an art); there is also Higgins' promise to transform Eliza from a "draggletailed guttersnipe" into a "duchess," and more pertinently, Nepommuck's proclamation of his discovery that she is "Hungarian," "of royal blood," "a princess" (in the Embassy ball scene Shaw wrote for the screenplay). The plots of romance usually turn upon the revelation of a daughter's being a princess (Perdita, Miranda, Elizabeth in *Henry VIII,* Una), and Shaw meets the generic test cleverly with Eliza's alleged royal descent, its fictiveness indicating Shaw's self-conscious playing with the conventions of the genre.

Like other works of romance, **Pygmalion** gives the sense of the full cycle of life from birth to death to rebirth. That is one of Shaw's purposes in patterning the five acts into night, morning, afternoon, night, morning. And like many a princess of Romance, Eliza undergoes a symbolic death when she disappears between Acts IV and V and Higgins must search for his "lost property."

Higgins' realization that Eliza has "bolted" puts him into "a state" out of proportion to the inconveniences caused by her departure—at least to the ones he lists, such as not knowing what appointments he has. His "state" points to a less-apparent cause. Higgins' involvement of Eliza in his phonetic experiment seems to have awakened otherwise repressed feelings in him that he cannot quite articulate. When he wants to test Eliza at his mother's at-home, he thinks that he merely has a "phonetic job" for his mother. Actually, he makes her part of the experiment with Eliza because on one level he is making Eliza over into his mother. His involvement with phonetics as I read it stems from his relationship with his mother. Mastery of his mother tongue by synechdoche stands for mastery of his feelings of inferiority at originating from his mother. The mother gives the son the gift of speech and the son cannot bear the burden of the debt, "the divine gift of articulate speech," as Higgins explains to Eliza. Thus, Shaw revises Racine's "A son has nothing which does not belong to his father" (*Athaliah*), to mean a son has no language except from the mother.

Shaw slyly dramatizes Mrs. Higgins' role as mother giving speech to the son in the last act, when Higgins has come to his mother's house in search of Eliza. Miss Doolittle is about to make her appearance, and Mrs. Higgins in characteristic reproving maternal tones warns her son to behave himself:

> MRS HIGGINS. Now, Henry: be good.
>
> HIGGINS. I am behaving myself perfectly.
>
> PICKERING. He is doing his best, Mrs Higgins.
>
> *A pause. Higgins throws back his head; stretches out his legs; and begins to whistle.*

MRS HIGGINS. Henry, dearest, you dont look at all nice in that attitude.

HIGGINS. [*Pulling himself together*] I was not trying to look nice, mother.

MRS HIGGINS. It doesnt matter, dear. I only wanted to make you speak.

HIGGINS. Why?

MRS HIGGINS. Because you cant speak and whistle at the same time.

Their apparently insignificant exchange here replays the mother's civilizing the child into speech: making it move from mere sound making to articulate speech.

Higgins' relationship to Eliza, therefore, must make her indebted to him in order to cancel the debt to his mother. Before Eliza leaves Wimpole Street, she is most insistent on returning to Higgins whatever does not belong to her. That is, she feels burdened with debt to him because he has made her feel that way without his ever having said so (though later he will urge the debt upon her vehemently). To become a creator, Pygmalion must deny his having been created.

Let me now put the psychological reading of Higgins' character and behavior in another context. One of Shaw's apparently most flippant (or outrageous) comments about Shakespeare, and one that has puzzled me for many years, comes in the Epistle Dedicatory to **Man and Superman,** where Shaw says of *Coriolanus* that it "is the greatest of Shakespear's comedies." I think that Shaw means a man with a mother fixation is a subject for comedy, not tragedy, that such a character resembles the great humor characters (like Argan) with their fixed ideas. To Shaw, as he is nearly always bent on underplaying the tragic view of life, that resemblance reconstitutes *Coriolanus* as a comedy. And Henry Higgins derives in part from that way of looking at Coriolanus. *Pygmalion* can be read as the tragedy of *Coriolanus* reconstituted as a comedy: both plays end with the defeat of the central character resulting from a fixation on the mother. Shaw deliberately misreads *Coriolanus* as a comedy because he must do so in order to write **Pygmalion** as a "romance." Shaw must also deal with the figure of Shakespeare the writer in the play, and he does so by means of Mrs. Higgins, who is not only the maternal transmitter of language, but is also a figure of the writer, the most original writer that could be, in that she is the mother who gives birth to the child.

Besides the little exchange where Mrs. Higgins makes her son speak in order to stop him from whistling in the last act, Shaw has various ways of defining speech as learnt from the mother. For example, he has Mrs. Pearce say of Eliza's foul language (by which she means Eliza's use of the word "bloody"), "She knows no better: she learnt it at her mother's knee. But she must not hear it from your lips." And Shaw figures Mrs. Higgins as a writer from the audience's first sight of her *"writing at an elegantly simple writing table."* He does so, because Higgins' ambivalence to his mother's dominant originality figures Shaw's own ambivalence to Shakespeare's original dominance, whose influence Shaw wishes to master and escape. I do not mean

that the play then is really "about" Shaw's struggle with Shakespeare's influence or competition, but that Shaw dramatizes Higgins the way he does because of his feelings toward the Shakespeare exemplar: to use Bloom's terminology, Shaw feels his "belatedness" in regard to Shakespeare.

Higgins communicates with his mother by writing, but he has evaded clear communication with her in writing by using his own shorthand, that is, a set of symbols different from the alphabet. His dual system of writing to his mother figures the dual set of impulses toward the mother, the conscious and the unconscious. His "patent shorthand" communications to her assert himself as the originator of language (after all he has invented a private alphabet—Shaw himself would sponsor the invention of a new alphabet in his will), but Higgins can only do so in a disguised way.

The conversation between Higgins and his mother in Act III about young women articulates the subtext of their relationship, insofar as it can be articulated. Higgins tells her he has "picked up a girl." His mother is skeptical, and asks if he does not mean "that some girl has picked *you* up?" (Even Higgins' spoken language has to be translated.) She knows him well enough to know that he would be incapable of initiating a love affair. Higgins hastily denies that he is involved in anything like that. Similarly, when Pickering wants to be assured that Eliza will be safe from any male importuning on Higgins' part, Higgins explains that although he "has taught scores of American millionairesses how to speak English: the best looking women in the world," "they might as well be blocks of wood" to him for they do not attract him. He further explains to his mother after she observes that he never falls "in love with anyone under forty-five," that he "cant be bothered with young women. My idea of a lovable woman is somebody as like you as possible. I shall never get into the way of seriously liking young women: some habits lie too deep to be changed. . . . Besides, theyre all idiots."

The emblem of Higgins' fixation on his mother is the painting of herself when young that hangs in her drawing room: *"There is a portrait of Mrs Higgins as she was when she defied fashion in her youth in one of the beautiful Rossettian costumes which, when caricatured by people who did not understand, led to the absurdities of popular aestheticism in the eighteen seventies."* Shaw uses Rossetti for two reasons here: one is that Rossetti painted "The Blessed Damozel," with the Woman, sexual and maternal, looking out from above, as the man-boy reclines, far below her, gazing up at her or dreaming of her; the other reason is that Higgins is only impressed by Eliza's looks at one point in the play, when she reappears after her first bath in a costume, *"a simple blue cotton kimono printed cunningly with small white jasmine blossoms."*

Freud published his essay *Leonardo da Vinci: A Study in Psychosexuality* in 1910; Brill's translation came in 1916, too late for Shaw to have drawn on it, and yet Higgins with his "mother fixation" and his complete absorption in his profession almost seems modeled on Freud's Leonardo, if one considers the following passages: "Leonardo was able to lead a life of abstinence and thus gave the impression of an asexual person. . . . the greater part of his sexual needs could be sublimated into a general thirst for knowledge . . . "; "The fixation on the mother, as well as the happy reminiscences of his relations with her were preserved in his unconscious but remained for the time in an inactive state. In this manner were repression, fixation and sublimation distributed in the disposal of the contributions which the sexual impulse furnished to Leonardo's psychic life." The points of intersection between Freud's Leonardo and Shaw's Higgins are the mother fixation, the impression of asexuality, and above all the sublimation of sexuality into the single-minded pursuit of activities that combine the artistic with the scientific. Higgins, in his passionate defense of the life of the intellect to Eliza (Act V), shows clearly how aware he is of the role of sublimation in his life:

> If you cant stand the coldness of my sort of life, and the strain of it, go back to the gutter. . . . Oh, it's a fine life, the life of the gutter. It's real: it's warm: it's violent: you can feel it through the thickest skin: you can taste it and smell it without any training or any work. Not like Science and Literature and Classical Music and Philosophy and Art. You find me cold, unfeeling, selfish, dont you? Very well: be off with you to the sort of people you like. Marry some sentimental hog or other with lots of money, and a thick pair of lips to kiss you with and a thick pair of boots to kick you with.

Higgins can only allow Eliza to get close to him on his own terms, that is, if she adapts to his way of life, which keeps sensuality (and violence) at a distance. His apparent asexuality is really a sublimation requiring intense concentration on himself as a professional. He focuses all his energies on his professional self in order not to think about his sexual self. Hence, his narcissism. Higgins seems hardly to notice other people, and when he does pay attention to others he seems to be interrupting his contemplation of himself and his concerns. The particular story of Higgins' narcissism that Shaw dramatizes consists in Higgins' seeing a reality, Eliza, and his mistaking her for a mere reflection of himself. He would have her be Echo to his Narcissus, (as in the Poussin painting) not even noticed by him.

In creating Higgins as a narcissistic artist figure, Shaw seems to have conflated several Ovidian characters, in addition to remaking Pygmalion into Narcissus. Higgins falls in love with Eliza as the product of his labor, just as Pygmalion and Narcissus fall in love with projections of themselves. In Ovid, Orpheus tells the story of Pygmalion, and Orpheus as a poet provides a pattern for Shaw's characterization of Higgins. Like Pygmalion, Orpheus begins by rejecting women, as does Higgins ("Besides, theyre all idiots"). As Orpheus loses Euridice twice, so does Higgins lose Eliza twice, the first time when she "bolts" from his house and he must go in search of her, and the second time, at the end of the play, when she tells him she will not see him again. In addition, Higgins as Orpheus suits Shaw's purpose insofar as Orpheus is a figure for the poet and Shaw uses Higgins as a figure for the playwright. Narcissus binds all the figures together because in him Shaw finds the model of the maker's contemplating his own work, which for Shaw means his work in competition with

Shakespeare's, and because Narcissus is the basis of Higgins' character as the self-absorbed artist.

To return to the ways in which Shaw realizes the mythic figures underlying Higgins in the action of the play: Higgins' forgetfulness, his general air of being mentally absent from the scene, or preoccupied with his own thoughts, has its counterpart in his slowness to recognize the Eynsford Hills when he meets them at his mother's house (Act III). He only remembers their original meeting when the relationship of mother and son is pressed upon him, when Freddy sits in the *Elizabethan chair:* Mrs. Eynsford Hill introduces her son Freddy to Eliza, and the son sits in a chair, the style of which copies Eliza's name (*Pygmalion* is the only play in which Shaw uses an Elizabethan chair). Moreover, earlier in the play, Shaw takes care to remind us that Eliza is a form of Elizabeth, for he makes Higgins declaim *"gravely"*, upon Eliza's telling him her name, "Eliza, Elizabeth, Betsy and Bess, / They went to the woods to steal a bird's nes'."

Higgins regresses to the pleasure of childish rhymes at the naming of Eliza because Elizabethan English was, Shaw claimed, his "mother tongue" (in the Preface to *The Admirable Bashville* . . .). Pickering completes the rhyme, and *"They laugh heartily at their own fun."* Eliza promptly tells them not to "be silly," and wishes that Higgins would "speak sensible" to her. Also, Higgins' impromptu falling into the recitation of verse puts him into a kind of competition with the Elizabethan predecessor, whom Shaw nearly always characterized by his talent for mere word-music, which did not necessarily have to make sense. Let me also note here that Higgins' rhyme points to the issue of stealing, and hence to anxieties about originality.

Shaw's self-consciousness in this scene extends to giving Higgins the tag line "By George." When Higgins' uses it to signal his sudden awareness of having met the Eynsford Hills before, his exclamation "By George" slyly reveals the origin both of the duplicated meetings and their coincidentalness. Coincidences in dramatic plots are like rhymes in poetry, they point to the dyer's hand. Like Higgins, Shaw here recalls an original, himself, by his first name George (which he disliked, always signing himself G. Bernard Shaw, or GBS, or just Bernard Shaw). And by means of the Elizabethan chair, Shaw recalls his own original (in the sense that Milton confessed to Dryden that Spenser was his original), Shakespeare. That is why Shaw next has Higgins try to replicate Freddy's movement. But instead of sitting down in the Elizabethan chair, Higgins goes to sit on the edge of his mother's writing table. Before he can do so, his mother stops him by urging that he would break it by sitting on it. The danger of breaking his mother's writing table condenses two figurative relationships: breaking his tie with his mother (the experiment with Eliza being an attempt to break that tie); and Shaw's sense of competition with his Elizabethan predecessor, displaced onto Higgins, the Miltonic professor.

The condensation that takes place here can be understood most readily if we recall Shaw's claim, expressed in the Preface to *The Admirable Bashville,* that "Elizabethan English became my mother tongue." After Eliza's exit,

Higgins drags his mother to the ottoman where Eliza had been sitting, and Shaw directs that *"she sits down in Eliza's place with her son on her left."* Higgins has unconsciously invited his mother to take Eliza's place, an action that reverses in dream-work fashion what Higgins really wants to do, to replace his mother with Eliza. (pp. 100-14)

Higgins and Eliza

Higgins never quite understands why Eliza does not just fall into line with his plans. He takes his domination of her as a matter of course. And when she leaves him the morning after the embassy ball, he reports her to the police as if her action were a crime against him. Mrs. Higgins points out to him that he cannot treat Eliza "as if she were a thief, or a lost umbrella, or something." Eliza's running away feels to Higgins as if she has stolen his originality.

In Act III, Mrs. Higgins urges her son and Pickering to consider that once they have finished their experiment with Eliza, they will not have created Eliza, they will have decreated her, for she will have no way of fitting into the world: "The manners and habits that disqualify a fine lady from earning her own living without giving her a fine lady's income." In other words, they will have declassed her upward with the same effect as if they had declassed her downward. Eliza herself comes to this same conclusion on her own after the ball, as if she shared an identity of thought with the mother of Higgins.

Eliza's whole account of her aunt's death to the company of Mrs. Higgins' at-home day parodically allegorizes Higgins' own (and Shaw's) psychic anxieties. According to Eliza people said that her aunt died of influenza, but she does not believe it. Can a writer die of "influence"? Yes, if the influence drowns the writer's originality; that is, if originality lies with the Other and not with the Self. Pygmalion's secret is also Higgins': the desire to cancel one's origin and become self-begotten. Higgins' surface anxiety in the scene, that Eliza will be guilty of some solipsism or verbal gaffe that would give her origin away as that of a presumptuous flower girl, has its counterpart in his figurative anxiety that he cannot escape his own origin. The way in which Higgins covers for Eliza in the account of her aunt's death recalls his mother's anxiety about *his* "large talk": when Eliza expresses her belief that her aunt was "done in," Higgins *"hastily"* adds, "Oh, thats the new small talk. To do a person in means to kill them." If it were not "small talk," it would be "large talk," and Higgins' secret would be out.

The idea of death by influenza and gin that is "mother's milk" figures Higgins' whole ambivalence towards his origin because it successively excites anxiety (as in the company's reaction to Eliza's account) and then restores the audience to a state of relaxation through the liberation of laughter. Eliza's denial that her aunt died of influenza leads to her own theory of her aunt's death. She believes that they who lived with her "done her in." When the company balks at such a suggestion, Eliza explains that her aunt lived amidst an unsavory crew: "They would have killed her for a hat pin, let alone a hat." Throughout Eliza's discourse, one is humorously aware that her keenness on revealing the true facts in the case (as she has de-

duced them) has most to do with her not having inherited her aunt's hat. Again, the abstract of her account, a suspicion of theft and stolen inheritances, parodies both Higgins' anxieties about his derivativeness and Shaw's fears for his own originality.

Eliza further shocks her auditors when she informs them that while her aunt was "fairly blue with" influenza, her father "kept ladling gin down her throat." Her auditors once again balk at her account, at the medical unsoundness of treating the aunt with gin, but Eliza assures them that "gin was mother's milk to her." The appearance of the image of mother's milk here condenses and renders comic the complex of Higgins' and Shaw's anxieties. For the gin-mother's milk is that which is longed after, yet that which hastens death. The aunt suddenly comes to, and then bites the bowl off the spoon—as comical and fearsome a death as one could wish to represent ambivalence. (pp. 117-19)

Higgins' ambivalence about his origin in his mother finds its most dramatic representation in the last act during Higgins' confrontation with Eliza while his mother and Pickering are present. Eliza boasts that because of what Higgins has taught her, she has irreversibly escaped her origins in Lisson Grove: "I have forgotten my own language, and can speak nothing but yours. I dont believe I could utter one of the old sounds if I tried." But, since the law of comedy is no boast without deflation, her father enters at that moment dressed for his wedding, and "her father's splendor" makes her lose "her self-possession," whereupon she lets out "one of the old sounds" of her "own language" without trying: "A-a-a-a-a-ah-ow-ooh!" Higgins exults at the revelation of her origins, the reversion to her original tongue, which is an ideational rhyme to her father's reappearance in the play. She can no more escape her origins than Higgins can his. In his mind, Eliza's slip here marks his reascent to dominance over her.

Besides having her regress to her old language, Shaw has Eliza drop the needlework she has been doing. In dropping the needlework, Eliza unwittingly contributes to Higgins' sense of *"triumph."* For Eliza answers Higgins' peremptory addresses to her by working deliberately at her embroidery, as a way of asserting her autonomy and her own mastery of an art. After Higgins thinks to settle their differences by telling her, "Get up and come home; and dont be a fool," Shaw directs: *"Eliza then takes a piece of needlework from her basket and begins to stitch at it, without taking the least notice of this outburst."*

In addition to her needlework, Eliza has two last concealed weapons to use on Higgins in their climactic struggle: one is the threat to become a teacher of phonetics; the other is the threat that she will marry Freddy. The latter wounds Higgins sorely because the creation must belong to no one but the creator. And Shaw deftly shows the unconscious sexual nature of Higgins' desire to possess his creation by the concealed double entendre in Eliza's articulation of how much Freddy wants her. Higgins, planning Eliza's future as usual, reflects that Pickering probably would not marry her because "He's as confirmed an old bachelor as I am." Eliza quickly sets him straight: "Thats not what I want; and dont you think it. Ive always had chaps enough wanting me that way. Freddy Hill writes to me twice and three times a day, sheets and sheets." She is so anxious to deny her interest in marriage or sex, that the word she uses for writing-paper brings out what is repressed by both of them, the prospect of being between the sheets. Shaw says that Higgins is *"disagreeably surprised,"* as he damns Freddy's impudence. Seeing the effect of her information, Eliza proclaims that she will marry Freddy. Then Eliza renders the coup de grace when she declares that she will become Nepommuck's assistant. Not only will the creation marry herself off to someone else, but she will also allow copying of the creator's "methods" and "discoveries." The threat to Higgins' originality is too great, and after resorting to violence (*"He lays hands on her"*), Higgins can only take refuge in pretending that Eliza will never do any such thing, and will instead come home to look after his needs.

Three gestures make up the final moments of the play: one of physical movement—Eliza *"sweeps out";* the second a verbal gesture—Mrs. Higgins reclaims her son ("I should be uneasy about you and her if she were less fond of Colonel Pickering"); the third and last a phonetic gesture—Higgins *"laughs uproariously,"* at the idea that Eliza "is going to marry Freddy." The first time Higgins laughed in the play was in Act I at the naming of Largelady Park as the birthplace of Mrs. Eynsford Hill, the domineering mother. The last time Higgins laughs, here, signifies his failure to escape the original large lady, Mrs. Higgins.

The Rest of the Story

Shaw does not designate as an epilogue his continuation of the story after the play has ended. He regards the continuation as only necessary for those who cannot see how the story should end. Shaw asserts that Eliza has instinct enough to realize that because of his "idealization" of his mother, Higgins "had not the makings of a married man in him," and therefore she marries Freddy. However, her relationship with Higgins continues. And the form of that relationship confirms for me that in retelling the story of Pygmalion the artist, Shaw figured his own relationship to writing as one of anxiety about originality.

As Shaw tells the story, Eliza and Freddy set up in a florist shop, but the business does not go very well, and the pair are compelled to go to school to learn business methods, just as Eliza had to learn phonetics. Shaw continues:

> But the effort that cost her the deepest humiliation was a request to Higgins, whose pet artistic fancy, next to Milton's verse, was calligraphy, and who himself wrote a most beautiful Italian hand, that he would teach her to write. He declared that she was congenitally incapable of forming a single letter worthy of the least of Milton's words; but she persisted; and again he suddenly threw himself into the task of teaching her with a combination of stormy intensity, concentrated patience, and occasional bursts of interesting disquisition on the beauty and nobility, the august mission and destiny, of human handwriting. Eliza ended by acquiring an extremely uncommercial script which was a positive extension of her personal beauty, and spending three times as much on stationery as anyone else be-

cause certain qualities and shapes of paper became indispensable to her.

I see here first the conjunction between Milton's poetry and handwriting as artistic concerns, which if condensed in the fashion of dreamwork or metaphor, becomes a figure for writing. Higgins' successful imparting of the art of handwriting to Eliza, I read as Shaw's resolution of his ambivalence to writing and toward his own originality. For Higgins at first declares Eliza "congenitally incapable of forming a single letter worthy of the least of Milton's words." Surely that is the writer's *first* burden: the immensity and impossibility of writing anything worthy of comparison with the achievements of the great writers. No writer can be original in that sense; every writer is at birth ("congenitally")—at the time of origin—derived and therefore unworthy. But Eliza does succeed in mastering writing—writing which is uncommercial and beautiful, and in doing so she overcomes her congenital incapacity, her original unworthiness, to become a writer, her writing being in its aesthetic dimension identical with herself, for it is both continuous with her "personal" (not physical) "beauty," and "indispensable" to her.

Shaw pays for the resolution of his ambivalence by projecting success onto the creation, Eliza, in her achievement of autonomy, rather than realizing it in Higgins. For, although Higgins never succeeds in growing up, of transcending his lack of originality, Eliza does. And it is utterly characteristic of Shaw, given that he made no distinction between the sexes, except for the anatomical one "that only matters on special occasions," that he should project his successful writing self onto a woman character, his own creation. (pp. 119-22)

> *John A. Bertolini, in his* The Playwrighting Self of Bernard Shaw, *Southern Illinois University Press, 1991, 206 p.*

FURTHER READING

Bibliography

Laurence, Dan H. *Bernard Shaw: A Bibliography.* 2 vols. Oxford: Clarendon Press, 1983.
    Inclusive primary bibliography.

Phillips, Jill M. *George Bernard Shaw: A Review of the Literature.* New York: Gordon Press, 1976, 176 p.
    Annotated bibliography of sixty works of Shavian biography and scholarship.

Wearing, J. P.; Adams, Elsie B.; and Haberman, Donald C., eds. *G. B. Shaw: An Annotated Bibliography of Writings about Him.* 3 vols. Dekalb: Northern Illinois University Press, 1986-87.
    Annotated secondary bibliography. Volume I covers commentary from 1871-1930; Volume II, 1931-1956; and Volume III, 1957-1978.

Biography

Ervine, St. John. *Bernard Shaw: His Life, Work and Friends.* New York: William Morrow & Co., 1956, 628 p.

    Detailed biography by a close friend that was begun during Shaw's lifetime.

Henderson, Archibald. *George Bernard Shaw: Man of the Century.* New York: Appleton-Century-Crofts, 1956, 969 p.

    Authorized biography regarded as the standard source for information about Shaw's life.

Holroyd, Michael. *Bernard Shaw, Volume I—1856-1898: The Search for Love.* London: Chatto & Windus, 1988, 486 p.

    Extensively researched account of the first forty-two years of Shaw's life.

————. *Bernard Shaw, Volume II—1898-1918: The Pursuit of Power.* London: Chatto & Windus, 1989, 422 p.

    Includes an account of the inception, writing, casting, and initial English production of *Pygmalion* and of Shaw's relationships with the principal actors of the first English performance, in particular with Mrs. Patrick Campbell.

————. *Bernard Shaw, Volume III—1918-1950: The Lure of Fantasy.* London: Chatto & Windus, 1991, 544 p.

    Treats the last thirty-two years of Shaw's life.

Irvine, William. *The Universe of G. B. S.* 1949. Reprint. New York: Russell & Russell, 1968, 439 p.

    Provides a vivid presentation of Shaw's social milieu and an account of Shaw's relation to and impact on his own and subsequent epochs.

Criticism

Allsop, Kenneth. "What a Corner for Shaw to Be In. . . ." *The Shavian* 1, No. 12 (May 1958): 19-20.

    Notes the popularity of the musical *My Fair Lady* and finds it "preposterous and abject that the reputation of one of the historically great artists of the Western World should depend upon his work being titivated up with music and some frou-frou from a chorus."

Bentley, Eric. *"My Fair Lady." Modern Drama* 1, No. 2 (September 1958): 135-36.

    Characterizes *My Fair Lady* as "un-Shavian in spirit" and contrary to Shaw's intent in *Pygmalion.*

Bloom, Harold, ed. *George Bernard Shaw's "Pygmalion."* New York: Chelsea House, 1988, 144 p.

    Collects previously printed essays on *Pygmalion* by Nigel Alexander, Eric Bentley, Charles A. Berst, Louis Crompton, Errol Durbach, Arthur Ganz, Lisë Pedersen, and Arnold Silver, and provides a critical introduction by the editor.

Brooks, Harold F. *"Pygmalion* and *When We Dead Awaken." Notes and Queries* 7, No. 12 (December 1960): 469-71.

    Suggests that Henrik Ibsen's play *When We Dead Awaken* was a source of inspiration for Shaw's work.

Costello, Donald P. *"Pygmalion."* In his *The Serpent's Eye: Shaw and the Cinema,* pp. 50-82. Notre Dame: University of Notre Dame Press, 1965.

    Lively, anecdotal account of writing, casting, and filming the 1938 Pascal Films version of *Pygmalion.* Costello includes numerous photographs and selections from Shaw's screenplay.

Dukore, Bernard F. " 'How Much?'—Money, Survival, and Independence." In his *Money & Politics in Ibsen, Shaw, and Brecht,* pp. 1-26. Columbia: University of Missouri Press, 1980.

    Examines the relationship between money and independence in *Pygmalion* and considers the play as Shaw's demonstration of how to eradicate class distinctions.

————, ed. *The Collected Screenplays of Bernard Shaw.* Athens: University of Georgia Press, 1980, 487 p.

    Includes sections devoted to German, Dutch, and British film versions of *Pygmalion* and the text of Shaw's screenplay for the 1938 movie directed by Gabriel Pascal. The volume includes movie stills and photographs of Shaw with various performers, on movie sets, and in Hollywood.

Evans, T. F., ed. *Shaw: The Critical Heritage.* London: Routledge & Kegan Paul, 1976, 422 p.

    Includes a selection of early reviews of *Pygmalion.* Evans also provides a biographical and critical introduction.

Fuller, Edmund. "The Plays: Second Period." In his *George Bernard Shaw: Critic of Western Morale,* pp. 38-96. New York: Charles Scribner's Sons, 1950.

    Identifies *Pygmalion* as a theatrical masterpiece elucidating one of Shaw's "specialized lesser themes": spelling reform and a new, phonetic alphabet.

Gibbs, A. M. "The End of *Pygmalion.*" In his *The Art and Mind of Shaw: Essays in Criticism,* pp. 168-76. New York: St. Martin's Press, 1983.

    Suggests that the original ending of *Pygmalion* was intended to underscore Higgins's failures and inadequacies in relationships with women.

————. *"Pygmalion."* In *Shaw: Interviews and Recollections,* edited by A. M. Gibbs. London: Macmillan, 1990, 560 p.

    Reprints reminiscences from actors Peggy Wood and Mrs. Patrick Campbell, journalist Emil Davies, and translator Alexandra Kropotkin regarding performances of *Pygmalion.*

Goodman, Randolph. *"Pygmalion."* In his *From Script to Stage: Eight Modern Plays,* pp. 291-410. New York: Rinehart Press, 1971.

    Includes biographical, critical, and anecdotal essays about Shaw; information about the principal sources of *Pygmalion,* about Shaw's 1938 screenplay, and about Alan Jay Lerner's musical comedy *My Fair Lady;* gives the play's production history; and provides interviews with people involved in stage and screen productions of the play and the musical. Goodman also supplies excerpted criticism, numerous photographs, and the text of *Pygmalion.*

Hill, Eldon C. "A Miscellany of Prewar Plays." In his *George Bernard Shaw,* pp. 100-21. Boston: Twayne, 184 p.

    Mentions the plot and central themes of *Pygmalion* in a chronological discussion of Shaw's plays in biographical and historical context.

Huggett, Richard. *The First Night of "Pygmalion": A Comedy for Two People.* London: Faber and Faber, 1969, 71 p.

    Play in which two performers undertake some forty roles to re-create the tempestuous weeks of rehearsal preceding the English premier of *Pygmalion.* Huggett drew from contemporary periodicals, biographies, memoirs, and the correspondence between Shaw and Mrs. Patrick Campbell.

———. *The Truth about "Pygmalion."* London: William Heinemann, 1969, 195 p.
Prose account of the period imaginatively re-created in *The First Night of "Pygmalion."*

Hugo, Leon. "1904-1912: Wot Price Salvation?" In his *Bernard Shaw: Playwright and Preacher,* pp. 146-71. London: Methuen & Co., 1971.
Considers the nature and function of comic elements in the scene depicting Eliza Doolittle's social debut.

Hummert, Paul A. "Shaw's Indictment of Capitalism." In his *Bernard Shaw's Marxian Romance,* pp. 91-130. Lincoln: University of Nebraska Press, 1973.
Maintains that a Marxian indictment of bourgeois marriage and a denunciation of the class differences promulgated by a capitalist society are skillfully embedded in the comedic action of *Pygmalion.*

Lauter, Paul. "*Candida* and *Pygmalion:* Shaw's Subversion of Stereotypes." *The Shaw Review* 111, No. 3 (September 1960): 14-19.
Suggests that the subtlety and skill with which Shaw exploits a stereotypical romantic plot tricks audiences into assuming that *Pygmalion* will end with the romantic pairing of its protagonist and antagonist.

Lerner, Alan Jay. "*Pygmalion* and *My Fair Lady.*" *The Shaw Bulletin* 1, No. 10 (November 1956): 4-7.
Discusses his adaptation of Shaw's play as a musical comedy.

Lorichs, Sonja. "Eliza and Clara in *Pygmalion: A Romance in Five Acts:* Phonetics, Class Discrimination and Education of Women." In her *The Unwomanly Woman in Bernard Shaw's Drama and Her Social and Political Background,* pp. 132-53. Stockholm: Uppsala, 1973.
Considers social, political, economic, and educational issues affecting women during the early twentieth century by examining the characters and fates of Eliza Doolittle and Clara Eynsford Hill.

MacCarthy, Desmond. "Play v. Film." In his *Shaw,* pp. 111-13. London: MacGibbon & Kee, 1951.
Compares the 1938 film version of *Pygmalion* with the stage play.

Morgan, Margery. "*Pygmalion.*" In *File on Shaw,* edited by Margery Morgan, pp. 68-73. London: Methuen Drama, 1989.
Notes dates of composition; gives facts of first German and English productions, including theater, cast, and director; lists principal revivals and filmed versions; quotes from salient criticism.

O'Donnell, Norbert F. "On the 'Unpleasantness' of *Pygmalion.*" *The Shaw Bulletin* I, No. 8 (May 1955): 7-10.
Asserts that the social criticism implicit in Alfred Doolittle's comic denunciation of middle-class morality is central to understanding the logic of Shaw's conclusion, in which Eliza Doolittle leaves Professor Higgins.

Pearson, Hesketh. "A Shavian Musical." *The Shavian* 1, No. 13 (September 1958): 4-6.
Recounts Shaw's negative assessments of musicals based

on his works and speculates that he would not have approved of *My Fair Lady.*

Pedersen, Lisë. "Shakespeare's *The Taming of the Shrew* vs. Shaw's *Pygmalion:* Male Chauvinism vs. Women's Lib?" In *Fabian Feminist: Bernard Shaw and Woman,* edited by Rodelle Weintraub, pp. 14-22. University Park: Pennsylvania State University Press, 1977.
Contends that *Pygmalion* was deliberately designed to challenge the central situation depicted in *Shrew:* a man's successful attempt to remake a woman's essential character.

Roy, Emil. "Pygmalion Revisited." *Ball State University Forum* XI, No. 2 (Spring 1970): 38-46.
Suggests that the conflicts between the central characters in *Pygmalion* reflect Shaw's own inner struggles between such opposing viewpoints as Platonism and Aristotelianism; revolutionary idealism and pragmatic realism; socialism and vitalism; Romanticism and Classicism.

Silver, Arnold. "*Pygmalion:* The Two Gifts of Love." In his *Bernard Shaw: The Darker Side,* pp. 177-250. Stanford: Stanford University Press, 1982.
Detailed critical study of *Pygmalion* followed by a psychobiographical interpretation.

Solomon, Stanley J. "The Ending of *Pygmalion:* A Structural View." *Educational Theatre Journal* XVI, No. 1 (March 1964): 59-63.
Analyzes the structure of the play's dramatic movement in order to evaluate problematic aspects of its denouement.

Vesonder, Timothy G. "Eliza's Choice: Transformation Myth and the Ending of *Pygmalion.*" In *Fabian Feminist: Bernard Shaw and Woman,* edited by Rodelle Weintraub, pp. 39-45. University Park: Pennsylvania State University Press, 1977.
Considers *Pygmalion* a retelling of an archetypal transformation myth in which Eliza Doolittle's acquisition of strength and independence precludes her return to Professor Higgins.

Wainger, Bertrand M. "Henry Sweet—Shaw's *Pygmalion.*" *Studies in Philosophy* XXVII, No. 4 (October 1930): 558-72.
Outlines the life and career of the scholar and phoneticist on whom Shaw partially based the character of Henry Higgins.

Ward, A. C. "*Misalliance* to *Pygmalion:* 1909-1913." In his *Bernard Shaw,* pp. 117-33. London: Longmans, Green & Co., 1951.
Outlines the plot of *Pygmalion* and suggests that Shaw's anti-romanticism led him to avoid the "dramatic imperative" of concluding with a marriage between the protagonist and antagonist—a conclusion that Ward calls conventional, probable, and in conformity with "the imponderable demands of poetic justice."

———. "Introduction to *Pygmalion.*" In *Pygmalion: A Romance in Five Acts,* by Bernard Shaw, pp. 128-32. London: Longmans, Green and Co., 1957.
Considers *Pygmalion* a problem play concerned with the social consequences of education.

Weissman, Philip. "Shaw's Childhood and *Pygmalion.*" In

his *Creativity in the Theater: A Psychoanalytic Study,* pp. 146-70. New York: Basic Books, Inc., 1965.

Suggests that Shaw unconsciously drew from childhood memories of his mother, her vocal music teacher, and his maternal grandfather in creating the characters of Eliza Doolittle, Henry Higgins, and Alfred Doolittle and the relationships between the three.

Woodbridge, Homer E. "Imagination in Control Again." In his *George Bernard Shaw: Creative Artist,* pp. 80-9. Carbondale: Southern Illinois University Press, 1963.

Considers dialect and phonetics the focus of *Pygmalion* and suggests that the play is concerned with establishing speech as a class determinant.

Additional coverage of Shaw's life and career is contained in the following sources published by Gale Research: *Contemporary Authors,* **Vols. 104, 128;** *Dictionary of Literary Biography,* **Vols. 10, 57;** *Major 20th-Century Writers;* **and** *Twentieth-Century Literary Criticism,* **Vols. 3, 9, 21.**

Wallace Stevens

1879-1955

American poet, essayist, and dramatist.

For further information on Stevens's career, see *TCLC,* Volumes 3 and 12.

INTRODUCTION

Stevens is one of the most important poets of the twentieth century. Integrating such European influences as Symbolism, Imagism, and Romanticism into his distinctly American idiom, he created a poetic language that has been praised for its originality, intricacy, and vibrancy. Throughout his works, Stevens sought to discover the interconnectedness of life and art, and in such poems as "Sunday Morning," *Notes toward a Supreme Fiction,* and "An Ordinary Evening in New Haven," he succeeded, seamlessly combining comic irony and epistemological skepticism with traditional forms and meters to reflect the complex concerns of modernity.

Stevens was born in Reading, Pennsylvania, to an upper-middle-class family of Dutch origins. His father, a prominent attorney, and his mother, a schoolteacher by training, encouraged their son's early interest in literature. As a student in the classical curriculum at Reading Boys High School, Stevens studied several languages and national literatures. In 1897 he enrolled as a special student at Harvard University, where he attended the lectures of the philosopher George Santayana and began writing lyric poetry in the style of the English Romantics. These early poems, which critics generally perceive as formally advanced and thematically derivative, were published in the *Harvard Advocate,* a student magazine that numbered Stevens as a staff member. In 1900 Stevens left Cambridge for New York City, where he pursued a career in journalism, eventually writing for the New York *Tribune.* The urging of his father persuaded Stevens to enroll at the New York Law School in 1901. He was admitted to the New York bar in 1904 and practiced law with several firms in New York City until 1908, when he accepted a position as an attorney with an insurance company. The following year Stevens married, wrote poetry and dramas when time permitted, and was in contact with the literary and artistic milieu of Greenwich Village. His New York poems were published in Harriet Monroe's *Poetry* magazine and in *Trend* in 1914. The next two years were a particularly fecund period of Stevens's poetic career; he published several poems in "little magazines," including "Sunday Morning," which appeared in *Poetry* in 1915.

Stevens moved to Hartford, Connecticut, in 1916, having accepted a position with the Hartford Accident and Indemnity Company. Although puzzling to some commentators, Stevens's career in business not only ensured him

the comfortable life-style that he desired but, as he once stated, gave "a man character as a poet to have this daily contact with a job." Writing in the evenings, on weekends, and while traveling on business in Florida and throughout the southern United States, Stevens published his New York poems, along with several more recent endeavors, as *Harmonium* in 1923. The imagistic and sensuous descriptions, orientalism, and exotic language of the volume were perceived by most reviewers as the work of a literary hedonist who ignored the "wasteland crisis" of modern society. After the publication of *Harmonium* and the birth of his daughter Holly in 1924, Stevens ceased writing poetry for the next six years. His next book, *Ideas of Order,* was not published until 1935 and was followed by *Owl's Clover,* which appeared in 1936. Stevens received some critical and popular recognition for the poems collected in *Ideas of Order* although he noted that "*Harmonium* was a better book than *Ideas of Order* notwithstanding the fact that *Ideas of Order* probably contains a small group of poems better than anything in *Harmonium.*" *Owl's Clover* departed more radically from Stevens's earlier poetry and he called the unstructured and prosaic work a complete failure. In *The Man with the Blue Guitar, and Other Poems,* published in 1937, Stevens reexamined his poetic style and returned to thematic and formal unity and a metered verse structure, traits that he had modified in *Owl's Clover*. In 1942 he published *Parts of a World* and, what many consider his greatest poetic and theoretical statement, *Notes toward a Supreme Fiction*. The late 1940s and early 1950s brought further recognition of Stevens's poetic achievements and the continued success of his career in business. The recipient of many awards and honorary degrees, he delivered several lectures on poetic theory and aesthetics, which were collected in *The Necessary Angel: Essays on Reality and the Imagination*. His *Collected Poems* were published in 1954 and he was offered the Charles Eliot Norton chair of poetry at Harvard University in 1955, which he refused, remaining with the Hartford Indemnity Company until his death that same year.

As a poet, Stevens sought to bridge the distance between consciousness and the physical world—that is, between imagination and reality—in order to regain a sense of human necessity in an apparently meaningless universe. Influenced by the secular humanism of Ralph Waldo Emerson and the aesthetic philosophy of Santayana, Stevens sought to counter the godlessness and skepticism of the modern age with a faith in art. In such early poems as "Sunday Morning," Stevens illustrated his proposition that "after one has abandoned a belief in god, poetry is that essence which takes its place as life's redemption." The stylized and evocative language of "Sunday Morning" describes the withering away of accepted religious rituals and icons—the Sabbath, the crown of thorns, the cross—and proposes new symbols and metaphors, which are now derived from secular artistic creations, as replacements for the old myths. Stevens further explores the role of art in the modern age in "Anecdote of the Jar in Tennessee," which Helen Vendler has deemed as important to the structuring of the American poetic imagination as John Keats's "Ode on a Grecian Urn" was to the English Romantic tradition. The speaker in "Anecdote of the Jar in Tennessee" discovers that order and meaning in nature must be derived from aesthetic form. Throughout Stevens's poetry his theoretical interests are balanced by a fascination with language. His interest in the sound, appearance, and etymologies of words is particularly evident in such poems as "The Comedian as the Letter C" and "Le Monocle de Mon Oncle."

Throughout the 1940s Stevens's theoretical and poetic investigations are centered on what he termed the "Supreme Fiction." Stevens introduced the phrase in his 1942 poem *Notes toward a Supreme Fiction*. That work comprises thirty short poems, a prologue, and coda, and is considered by many to encapsulate the traits of Stevens's strongest poetry: colorful concrete images, a range of poetic diction, thematic unity, and playful language. According to Stevens, the "Supreme Fiction" or "Grand Poem" is an ideal fusion of reality and the imagination. In *Notes toward a Supreme Fiction*, which was written during World War II, Stevens illustrates this fusion by conflating the terms of war and artistic creation: "Soldier, there is a war between the mind / And sky, between thought and day and night. It is / For that the poet is always in the sun, / Patches the moon together in his room / To his Virgilian cadences, up down, / Up down. It is a war that never ends."

Stevens's mature works, such as *Esthétique du Mal* and *The Auroras of Autumn*, reiterate and refine the aesthetic philosophies that he had evolved in his earlier works. In the mature poem "An Ordinary Evening in New Haven," Stevens outlines his understanding of the relationship between art, life, and language: "the theory / Of poetry is the theory of life, / As it is, in the intricate evasions of as, / In things seen and unseen, created from nothingness, / The heavens, the hells, the worlds, the longed-for lands."

Some critics have found Stevens's solution to twentieth-century metaphysical uncertainties to be rarefied and impersonal, frequently derogating his poetry for its abstraction and paucity of recognizably human characters and situations. However, Stevens insisted that his interest was not in individual personalities or social issues, but in humanism, art, and epistemology. Believing that his poetry addressed the general human condition by asking that "men turn to a fundamental glory of their own and from that create a style of bearing themselves in reality," Stevens never perceived his poetry as existing simply in the realm of aesthetics. His theoretical acumen and poetic skill have appealed to a wide range of critical schools. Harold Bloom has called Stevens the heir to the Romantic tradition in America, while poststructuralist and deconstructivist critics have praised Stevens's investigations of pure poetry and language. The diverse influences in Stevens's work are united by his unique style and his ambition to define the role of art in an age of anxiety and skepticism. The poetry that grew out of this quest represents one of the major accomplishments in modern literature.

PRINCIPAL WORKS

Harmonium (poetry) 1923
Ideas of Order (poetry) 1935
Owl's Clover (poetry) 1936
The Man with the Blue Guitar, and Other Poems (poetry) 1937
Notes toward a Supreme Fiction (poetry) 1942
Parts of a World (poetry) 1942
Esthétique du Mal (poetry) 1945
Transport to Summer (poetry) 1947
The Auroras of Autumn (poetry) 1950
The Necessary Angel: Essays on Reality and the Imagination (essays) 1951
Collected Poems (poetry) 1954
Opus Posthumous (poetry, dramas, and essays) 1957
Letters (letters) 1966
The Palm at the End of the Mind (poetry and drama) 1971

Stanley Burnshaw   (essay date 1935)

[*Burnshaw is an American poet, novelist, and critic. In response to his sharply critical review of* Ideas of Order *in the Marxist magazine the* New Masses, *Stevens composed the poem "Owl's Clover," of which "Mr. Burnshaw and the Statue" is the second section. In the follow-*

ing excerpt from that 1935 review, Burnshaw disparages what he perceives as the philosophical confusion of Ideas of Order, *contrasting the weakness in the volume to the strengths of the* Harmonium *poems.*]

Among the handful of clichés which have crept into left-wing criticism is the notion that contemporary poets—except those on the left and extreme right—have all tramped off to some escapist limbo where they are joyously gathering moonshine. That such an idiot's paradise has existed no one can deny; but today the significant middle-ground poets are laboring elsewhere. And the significant trend is being marked by such writers as Wallace Stevens and Haniel Long: poets whose artistic statures have long been recognized, whose latest books (issued in middle age) form a considered record of agitated attitudes toward the present social order. Like all impressive phenomena of the middle ground, *Pittsburgh Memoranda* and **Ideas of Order** show troubled, searching minds.

As a matter of record Haniel Long has been struggling for a "solution" ever since his singular stories and poems appeared in the liberal magazines a dozen years ago. (pp. 363-64)

Confused as it is, *Pittsburgh Memoranda* is a marvel of order alongside Wallace Stevens' volume; and yet to many readers it is something of a miracle that Stevens has at all bothered to give us his **Ideas of Order.** When **Harmonium** appeared a dozen years ago Stevens was at once set down as an incomparable verbal musician. But nobody stopped to ask if he had any ideas. It was tacitly assumed that one read him for pure poetic sensation; if he had "a message" it was carefully buried and would take no end of labor to exhume. Yet he often comes out with flat judgments and certain ideas weave through the book consistently:

> The magnificent cause of being,
> The imagination, the one reality
> In this imagined world

underlies a number of poems. Realists have been bitter at the inanity of Pope's "Whatever is is right," but Stevens plunges ahead to the final insolence: "For realists, what is is what should be." And yet it is hard to know if such a line is not Stevens posing in self-mockery. One can rarely speak surely of Stevens' ideas.

But certain general convictions he admits in such a poem as **"To One of Fictive Music."** Bound up with the sovereignty of the imagination is his belief in an interfusion of music among the elements and man. And "music is feeling . . . not sound." This trinity of principles makes the business of living to him a matter of searching out the specific harmonies.

Harmonium, then, is mainly sense poetry, but not as Keats's is sense poetry, because this serener poet is not driven to suffuse sensuous imagery with powerful subjective emotions. This is "scientific," objectified sensuousness separated from its kernel of fire and allowed to settle, cool off, and harden in the poet's mind until it emerges a strange amazing crystal. Reading this poetry becomes a venture in crystallography. It is remembered for its curious humor, its brightness, its words and phrases that one rolls on the tongue. It is the kind of verse that people con-cerned with the murderous world collapse can hardly swallow today except in tiny doses.

And it is verse that Stevens can no longer write. His harmonious cosmos is suddenly screeching with confusion. **Ideas of Order** is the record of a man who, having lost his footing, now scrambles to stand up and keep his balance. The opening poem observes

> . . . This heavy historical sail
> Through the mustiest blue of the lake
> In a wholly vertiginous boat
> Is wholly the vapidest fake. . . .

And the rest follows with all the ironical logic of such a premise. The "sudden mobs of men" may have the answer;

> But what are radiant reason and radiant will
> To warblings early in the hilarious trees . . .

Sceptical of man's desire in general, there is still much to be said for the ordering power of the imagination. But there remains a yearning—and escape is itself an irony. "Marx has ruined Nature, for the moment," he observes in self-mockery; but he can speculate on the wisdom of turning inward, and a moment later look upon collective mankind as the guilty bungler of harmonious life, in "a peanut parody for a peanut people." What answer is there in the cosmic law—"everything falls back to coldness"? With apparent earnestness he goes a step beyond his former nature-man interfusing harmony:

> Only we two are one, not you and night,
> Nor night and I, but you and I, alone,
> So much alone, so deeply by ourselves,
> So far beyond the casual solitudes,
> That night is only the background of our
>   selves . . .

And in a long poem he pours out in strange confusion his ideas of order, among them:

> If ever the search for a tranquil belief should
>   end,
> The future might stop emerging out of the past,
> Out of what is full of us; yet the search
> And the future emerging out of us seem to be
>   one.

Paraphrase, always a treacherous tool, is especially dangerous when used on so *raffiné* a poet as Stevens. Does he talk of himself when he explains that "the purple bird must have notes for his comfort that he may repeat through the gross tedium of being rare"? Does he make political reference in declaring "the union of the weakest develops strength, not wisdom"?

Asking questions may not be a reviewer's function, but uncertainties are unavoidable when reading such poets as the two under review; for the texture of their thought is made of speculations, questionings, contradictions. Acutely conscious members of a class menaced by the clashes between capital and labor, these writers are in the throes of struggle for philosophical adjustment. And their words have intense value and meaning to the sectors within the class whose confusions they articulate. Their books have deep importance for us as well.

Of course, objectively, neither poet is weakening the class in power—as yet they are potential allies as well as potential enemies—but one of them looks for a new set of values and the other earnestly propagates (however vaguely) some form of collectivism. Will Long emancipate himself from his paralyzing faith in inner perfection? Will Stevens sweep his contradictory notions into a valid Idea of Order? The answers depend not only on the personal predispositions of these poets but on their full realization of the alternatives facing them as artists. (pp. 364-66)

> Stanley Burnshaw, "Wallace Stevens and the Statue," in The Sewanee Review, *Vol. LXVIX, No. 3, Summer, 1961, pp. 355-66.*

Hi Simons   (essay date 1945)

[*Simons is an American critic and personal acquaintance of Stevens. In the following excerpt, he compares the symbiotic relationship between philosophy and poetics in Stevens's poetry to similar characteristics in the verse of the seventeenth-century English Metaphysical poets.*]

Reviewing **Parts of a World** by Wallace Stevens in the Autumn 1942 issue of *Accent,* Mr. Horace Gregory raised the question: "Is Mr. Stevens a philosopher? Can we hook ladders to his Prester John's balloon with the hope of landing safely on a terrain peopled by Zeno, Plotinus, Socrates, George Santayana, William James, John Dewey and Professor Whitehead?" Gregory thought not. "I would go further," he wrote, "and insist that Mr. Stevens is not an intellectual, and that the value of his poetry cannot be measured in intellectual terms . . . "

The same week when that criticism appeared, Mrs. Mary Colum reviewed the same volume in *The New York Times Book Review.* "The mind that the author projects into such careful and measured language," she complained, "is the philosophic speculative mind where the passions are of the intellectual rather than the sensuous order." She quoted as representative a short passage which she doubted had in it "enough sensuous delight to be poetry," and said: "It reads a little like a piece of Thomas Aquinas."

It goes of itself, as the French say, that Gregory and Mrs. Colum cannot both have understood their subject-matter correctly and yet have construed it so differently. It is irresistible to try to set one or another, possibly both, of them right. Presumptuous as it will seem, the effort is worth making because it offers an opportunity to define the genre of Stevens's poems, something that has long needed doing.

We cannot argue Mrs. Colum's strictures profitably because she did not give us their basis in reason. Gregory's premises, however, are clear enough. For him, "intellectual poetry" and "philosophical poetry" are interchangeable terms, and he uses "philosophy" in "the sense which implies the creation or the furtherance of a philosophic system." He grants Stevens's poems intelligence and evidences of "a finely tempered and inquiring mind." But he seems not quite to have exhausted those evidences; for the only philosophic substance in Stevens which he discusses is the tendency toward skepticism which he finds in **"Sad**

Strains of a Gay Waltz" and **"Examination of the Hero in a Time of War"**—this latter, a poem of affirmation if any such has been written in our distraught times.

Even on his own grounds, we must dispute Gregory's position. Stevens's six books present consistently developing attitudes toward at least four distinctively philosophic subjects; and for those to whom his poetry is worth the effort to comprehend it I list the four themes and, after each one, a few poems that mark the stages of its evolution:

> 1. The socio-esthetic problem of the relation of the artist to his environment. **"The Comedian as the Letter C"** (*Harmonium*); **"Academic Discourse at Havana"** and, by strong implication, **"Farewell to Florida"** and **"Sailing after Lunch"** (*Ideas of Order*); **"The Man with the Blue Guitar,"** XII, XV, XVII and XXVIII; **"Of Modern Poetry"** (*Parts of a World*), and the fourth poem and the epilogue of **Notes toward a Supreme Fiction.**

> 2. The esthetic-epistemological problem of the relation of imagination to reality. **"Colloquy with a Polish Aunt"** and **"Another Weeping Woman"** (*Harmonium*); **"The Idea of Order at Key West"** (*Ideas of Order*); parts v and vi of **"A Duck for Dinner"** (*Owl's Clover*); **"The Man with the Blue Guitar,"** I-IV, XXII, XXIX and XXXI; **"Connoisseur of Chaos"** and **"Poem with Rhythms"** (*Parts of a World*); and the poems on pages 12, 25, 29, 31 and 38-39 of **Notes toward a Supreme Fiction.**

> 3. The problem of belief, in both its metaphysical and theological aspects. **"Sunday Morning"** (*Harmonium*); **"Sad Strains of a Gay Waltz,"** **"Lions in Sweden"** and **"Evening without Angels"** (*Ideas of Order*); parts ii and v of **"The Greenest Continent"** (*Owl's Clover*); **"The Man with the Blue Guitar,"** V, XVIII-XXI and XXIV; **"On the Road Home,"** **"The Latest Freed Man"** and **"Asides on the Oboe"** (*Parts of a World*); in general, all of **Notes toward a Supreme Fiction.**

> 4. In connection with the preceding, a peculiar humanism most recently personified in "the hero" and "the major man." First clearly adumbrated in **"A Duck for Dinner"** (*Owl's Clover*) and **"A Thought Revolved"** (*The Man With the Blue Guitar*); the principal subject of **"Montrachet-le-Jardin"** and **"Examination of the Hero in a Time of War"** (*Parts of a World*). . . .

Any reader who will follow that outline as a guide for his own analysis of Stevens's characteristic preoccupations will conclude, I believe, that he is reading a poet quite as philosophical, in Gregory's sense, as any in our language.

Is it necessary to add that one need not "approve of" Stevens's ideas to recognize them as ideas? One need no more share all his thoughts in order to evaluate justly the independence, constancy and intensity of ratiocination embodied in his poems, than one must believe in John Donne's theology, ethics or astronomy to regard him as the classic type of the intellectual poet.

Yet if Gregory should ask me pointblank, "Is Stevens,

then, a philosopher?" I would answer: "Certainly not—Mrs. Colum to the contrary. He doesn't purport to be one. He is a poet." Of course, he doesn't transport his readers to a terrain peopled by Zeno, or Santayana, or Thomas Aquinas. He keeps them always in the realm of poetry.

This whole question of intellection and poetry was set in an illuminating frame of reference twenty years ago in connection with the revival of interest in Donne. A more realistic conception of the intellectual poet than Gregory's was worked out by Mr. T. S. Eliot in his essay on "The Metaphysical Poets." "In Chapman especially," he found, "there is a direct sensuous apprehension of thought, or a recreation of thought into feeling, which is exactly what we find in Donne." Then, on the contrast between a passage by the elder Herbert and one by Tennyson, he remarked:

> The difference is not a simple difference of degree between poets. It is something which had happened to the mind of England between the time of Donne or Lord Herbert of Cherbury and the time of Tennyson and Browning; it is the difference between the intellectual poet and the reflective poet. Tennyson and Browning are poets, and they think; but they do not feel their thought as immediately as the odour of a rose. A thought to Donne was an experience; it modified his sensibility.

Those phrases so full of insight, "a direct sensuous apprehension of thought, or a recreation of thought into feeling," precisely define the quality of Stevens's poetry that has confused readers like Mrs. Colum and Gregory. According to Eliot's definition, Stevens is an intellectual poet. For that reason, though "the value of his poetry cannot be measured in intellectual terms" *alone,* neither can it be appreciated without an equal understanding of both its intellectual component and its element of sheer sensibility. Most of those who have written about his work have assumed that he was a lyricist in the nineteenth-century tradition. To the contrary, not the least of his distinctions is that he created for himself a genre that was new in its time, except insofar as Ezra Pound and Eliot did likewise: a type of poem that may be called a lyric of ideas, an intellectual lyric. Stevens is one of the originators of the metaphysical trend in the poetry of our time.

To illustrate that view of his work I should prefer to use his latest book, the *Notes toward a Supreme Fiction.* Instead, I restrict myself to one of the shorter pieces in the volume Gregory and Mrs. Colum reviewed. Any of fifty poems might be chosen: **"Asides on the Oboe"** is sufficiently representative.

In our outline, this piece was listed as important in the development of Stevens's attitude toward the problem of belief. Its thesis is stated in a short prologue:

> It is a question, now,
> Of final belief. So, say that final belief
> Must be in a fiction.

If men's ultimate beliefs have always been in some fiction or another, the crisis of faith today may be due to the fact that our traditional myths have ceased to be credible. Thus, the

fiction of the wide river in
An empty land; the gods that Boucher killed;
And the metal heroes that time granulates—

are all "obsolete." "The wide river in / An empty land" evokes vague religious associations—the Jordan, the river of light in Dante's paradise, a stream of spirit fructifying an otherwise desert world. Following the principle of reading each poem as in the context of its author's work as a whole, we may recall here "the struggle of the idea of god / And the idea of man," in **"Mystic Garden & Middling Beast."** The present poem assumes a need to substitute some "idea of man" for "the idea of god." So there is presumptive warrant for taking the first of the obsolete fictions as the common current acceptation of religion. "The gods that Boucher killed" may be considered to refer to all anthropomorphic mythologies so familiarized and rationalized since the eighteenth century as to lose their force as objects of veneration. And I imagine that "the metal heroes that time granulates" are such ethical absolutes as Stevens satirized in **"Lions in Sweden,"**

> those sovereigns of the soul
> And savings banks, Fides, the sculptor's prize,
> All eyes and size, and galled Justitia,
> Trained to poise the tables of the law,
> Patientia forever soothing wounds
> And mighty Fortitudo, frantic bass.

In contrast with those, or whatever other doctrines and deities the reader may regard as no longer efficacious for belief,

> The philosophers' man still walks in dew,
> Still by the sea-side mutters milky lines
> Concerning an immaculate imagery.

This "philosophers' man" is a personification of "the idea of man," a prototype of Stevens's humanism. The three images by which he is presented—"walks in dew," "milky lines," and "immaculate imagery"—suggest pristine purity and thus emphasize the antithesis that, whereas other fictions of faith are obsolete, this concept is new and unblemished. To say he "still walks in dew" implies that he is in the morning of his career. "The sea-side" may be accepted as mere setting; but the sea as a metaphor for life is one of Stevens's oldest symbols, and the impression we get here is that of a contemplative person dwelling close to the common life of his time yet not engaged in the thick of it. He "mutters milky [sweet and sustaining, as well as fresh] lines / Concerning an immaculate imagery," that is, concerning an inviolate, vital conception of life.

Is the humanistic ideal, then, simply an apotheosis of the poet? Stevens is too realistic to think that. Ever since the winter of 1936-37 when he wrote **"The Man with the Blue Guitar,"** he has held to the idea of total reality as a combination of the reality of things-as-they-are and the reality of imagination. Here, the poet is not to take precedence of ordinary men, but all of us are to live ever more and more by the imagination: as in every humanism, the ideal is not humanity as is, but a regenerated humanity. So,

> If you say on the hautboy man is not enough,
> Can never stand as god, is ever wrong
> In the end, however naked, tall, there is still
> The impossible possible philosophers' man . . .

You may argue skeptically that man as god still remains man, yet there is an *ideal* of humanity to believe in and aspire to. "If you say on the hautboy" means "If you write in your verses" or "If you imagine"; for the oboe is one of many instruments—guitar, harmonium, piano, banjo, an old horn, and so on—in which Stevens has likened poetry and its source, the imagination, to music. "Naked" stands for stripped of superficial falsities; and "tall" is another metaphor, for moral stature or loftiness.

Now, the gist of the concept having been given, further predicates are added. "The impossible possible philosophers' man" is

> The central man, the human globe, responsive
> As a mirror with a voice, the man of glass,
> Who in a million diamonds sums us up.

"Central" as a metaphor for the essence, as distinguished from irrelevant superficialities, of humanity offers no difficulty. The next four images—"globe" (probably light-globe primarily, though spherical map, also, by second intention), "mirror," "glass" and "diamonds"—all suggest bright light, emitted, reflected or transmitted. Their meaning is summarized in the next line, "He is the transparence of the place in which / He is"; and, lest there be any doubt that the substance of the thought is spiritual insight, we may refer back to **"The Greenest Continent,"** where it is said that, although "The heaven of Europe is empty" now, there was a heaven once

> in which the mind
> Acquired transparence and beheld itself
> And beheld the source from which transparence
> came . . .

So the ideal man, embodying the essence of the finest in humanity, possessing especially a capacity for living by the imagination, would be a source of illumination for the rest of us. He would not live aloof, but would be "responsive / As a mirror with a voice." Responsive to our common impulses and aspirations. Like a mirror in reflecting them back, sharpened and clarified. Using his voice to keep before us the "immaculate imagery" of life at its best. In that complex sense, he would be an effulgent "man of glass, / Who in a million diamonds sums us up."

The short second section of the poem, that expresses the satisfaction inspired by belief in this humanistic fiction, scarcely needs such close analysis as what has preceded. Part III applies the conception to events current in the world of things-as-they-are, for **"Asides on the Oboe"** was written in the summer following the outbreak of the second World War.

> One year, death and war prevented the jasmine
> scent
> And the jasmine islands were bloody martyr-
> doms.

"Jasmine" was chosen, I think, because of its sweetness: death and war expunged the sweetness of life, and the good lands of the earth were turned into places of slaughter.

> How was it then with the central man? Did we

> Find peace? We found the sum of men. We
> found,
> If we found the central evil, the central good.

We have not *over*-idealized man—we recognize the inexpugnable evil—yet we insist no less on the inherent good.

> We buried the fallen without jasmine crowns.
> There was nothing he did not suffer, no; nor
> we. . . .

But wherein is the efficacy of a belief so qualified by acknowledgment of its antithesis? Merely in a hope that the good will some day return? No,

> But we and the diamond globe at last were one.
> We had always been partly one. It was as we
> came
> To see him, that we were wholly one, as we
> heard
> Him chanting for those buried in their blood,
> In the jasmine haunted forests, that we knew
> The glass man, without external reference.

More clearly than ever before, we see the ideal in its failure. We know it now, not as a figment of speculation, but immediately, as a vital part of ourselves, that has failed through our failure, that must be restored through our reconsecrated belief.

Thus, **"Asides on the Oboe"** yields to (not exorbitantly difficult) analysis a meaning for which "intellectual" is the precise adjective. But the poem is not truly understood when those ideas have been abstracted from it: they must not only be known as ideas but also felt in the terms, the imagery, the *poetry,* in which they are given. Therein are both Gregory and Mrs. Colum confounded. For if ever a piece of writing fulfilled the description, "a direct sensuous apprehension of thought, or a recreation of thought into feeling," this one does.

Intellectual intensity or, as Professor H. J. C. Grierson put it, a "strain of passionate paradoxical reasoning" is the quality which Donne introduced into English verse; and a similar "blend of argument and imagination" appears in some of the poetry of our time, that of Stevens included. Intensity of thought is evident in **"Asides on the Oboe"** from two different but, as the poem proves, not incompatible signs. The first is the directness and vigor of the rhetorical movement, and the "simple, sensuous, masculine" diction, especially noticeable in the three-line prologue and in the concluding section:

> How was it then with the central man? Did we
> Find peace? We found the sum of men. We
> found,
> If we found the central evil, the central good.

No less indicative of passion in reasoning are the richness and deep feeling of the imagery, particularly that in which the idea of "the philosophers' man" is developed and that of "the jasmine haunted forests" of war and death. Passages like those are the expression, not of a mind in which rhetorical figures blur and dispel or replace ideas, but of one to which ideas come in such figures, so that to think them is also to feel them. In *The Donne Tradition,* a brilliant elaboration upon Eliot's essay on the Metaphysicals, Mr. George Williamson says: "This intellectual intensity derives its peculiar power from the unified sensibility which makes it impossible to isolate the faculties of Donne. . . . His unified sensibility makes his images the very body of his thought, not something added to it . . . " Had Williamson been describing Stevens instead of Donne, he could not have chosen better terms.

A good many people think that I am didactic. My own idea about it is that my real danger is not didacticism, but abstraction, and abstraction looks very much like didacticism.

—*Wallace Stevens, in his* Letters of Wallace Stevens, *1967.*

Gregory feared for Stevens the danger of "the *reductio ad whimsy* of his totally serious and critical consideration of the relationship between two aspects of reality." I imagine such a line as "But we and the diamond globe at last were one" fairly represents what Gregory objected to as "stating an intellectual problem in terms of fancy." If so, he would probably find much of Donne and Vaughan, to say nothing of Crashaw, George Herbert and Cowley, equally frivolous. For the central images of **"Asides on the Oboe"** and of countless others of Stevens's compositions are conceits quite of the Metaphysical order.

A useful definition of the conceit is, a figure in which two terms of a comparison meet on limited ground but are otherwise incongruous. The Metaphysicals used this device functionally, not decoratively. To quote Williamson again: "The conceit is one of the principal means by which Donne chained analysis to ecstasy." Exactly so, the figure of "the philosophers' man" and the others connected with it are not whimsies added to the rational structure of the poem, but the means, and the only means, of defining and conveying the essential conception. So far as this one poem is concerned, all we know of "the idea of man" is what that series of images tells us—and how adequate that is we have seen. Not only does this conceit serve the author as an instrument of analysis, but we have been able to analyze its evolution from the simple personification, "the philosophers' man," to the paradox, "The impossible possible philosophers' man," on through the complex of "central man," "human globe," "mirror with a voice" and "man of glass / Who in a million diamonds sums us up," to the final symbolic paradox, "We and the diamond globe at last were one." Thus, the conceit is intellectual in intention and intellectual-imaginative in genesis and development. In addition, it performs the important function of investing the poet's thought with that "sensuous delight" which Mrs. Colum properly demands of poetry yet apparently fails to recognize sometimes when she has it before her.

Much has been written of Stevens's wit. Too often the word has been used derogatorily, as if in total ignorance of the great tradition established by poets who were celebrated in their own day, though subsequently chided, as wits. At other times the intention behind the term is equivocal, as when Gregory refers to Stevens's "comic genius," yet leaves the net impression that he may amuse us as a funny-man but not seriously interest us as a "philosopher" who might "occupy Bishop Manning's pulpit or write a supplementary volume to Professor Whitehead's *Reality and Process.*" (*sic!*)

Stevens *is* a wit (as well as, occasionally, a humorist), and this would suggest that we might understand him the better by studying his work in relation to our leading tradition of poetic wit. In discussing Andrew Marvell, Eliot defined Metaphysical wit as "a tough reasonableness beneath the slight lyric grace." Expanding that idea, Williamson demonstrated the part of reason, first in the evolution of Donne's conceits, then in the construction of his poems: "Nothing is more characteristic of Donne than the way in which thought gives a mathematical basis to the music of his emotions." Hence, the ruggedness of his verse; hence also, in part, the difficulty, the occasional obscurity, of his poems: "It is a result of the reassertion of subject-matter in poetry." If our abstract of the meaning of **"Asides on the Oboe"** proves anything, it is that intellection provides the whole basis and form for its structure. Similarly, we traced the element of reason in the elaboration of one of its principal conceits. And if this poem is typical of its author's work in confronting the reader with seemingly cryptic obscurities, that is in consequence of what Williamson designates "the astringent effect of intellect on the facility of verse." Stevens's wit, like his rhetoric, is of the same general nature as that of the Metaphysicals. And thus it helps to define his genre: it is the factor of reasonableness underlying the lyric graces of his peculiarly characteristic poem of ideas.

Every poem Stevens has written, not only in his latest period, but since about 1919 when his experimental phase finally issued in the first pieces definitely in his own kind and manner, is susceptible of the same sort of analysis we have applied to **"Asides on the Oboe."** Most of them disclose a similar content of ideas. The exceptions are pieces like **"Variations on a Summer Day"** and **"The News and the Weather,"** in which the lyrical component takes precedence of the component of thought. Yet in these as well as the intellectual lyric, the same sensibility is at work, though upon a different kind of subject-matter: Stevens's unified sensibility accounts for the singular uniformity of tone that, as many critics have observed, prevails throughout his writing.

All Stevens's poems do not equally exemplify all of Williamson's criteria of Metaphysical poetry. But neither do all those, for example, in Grierson's collection of *Metaphysical Lyrics & Poems of the Seventeenth Century.* As Eliot himself acknowledged, "Not only is it extremely difficult to define metaphysical poetry, but difficult to decide what poets practise it and in which of their verses"—the more one reads of recent criticism of the school of Donne, the more one feels that it applies to Donne but not to any school. Yet we can say of Stevens that each of his mature poems exhibits at least one Metaphysical trait and all

Metaphysical characteristics are present somewhere in his work.

I know of no evidence, however, that Stevens has been influenced by Donne and his successors. In associating him with their tradition in order to emphasize his specifically intellectual quality, we should not minimize the differences between him and his distant predecessors in the line. There is, to begin with, a vast divergency of subject-matter and of psychology, grounded in all the differences between the epoch that was nearing its end when Donne wrote and the civilization that is committing suicide now. Scarcely less important are the dissimilarities of diction and prosody produced by the social and literary vicissitudes of two centuries. Also, there is a fundamental rhetorical difference, and, since its rhetoric is one of the prime features of the Metaphysical mode, this must be defined.

Contemporary criticism has not yet agreed on a suitable name for the distinctive rhetorical device of contemporary poetry. It is the metaphor rather than the simile, but a peculiar usage of metaphor. The figure is employed not as an embellishment but as the means of discourse, and its communicative possibilities are stretched to the utmost—often, in fact, to the point of obscurity. Sometimes the emotive force of the vehicle, the written word, is stressed; again, the tenor, the idea to be conveyed. In either case, the latter is left to implication, and the distinction between traditional practice and the modern technic lies in the strictness with which that is done.

Stevens was not a master of the rhetoric of implication from the beginning of his career as a publishing poet, but the style by which he is now known was not mature until he had mastered it. **"Asides on the Oboe"** is as good an example as any of both the technic and the style resultant from it. The metaphor, "the diamond globe," is logically engendered, and explained, by the associated figures that precede it. But "the wide river in / An empty land," "the transparence of the place" and "the jasmine islands" stand as pure metaphors, affording a minimum of support to inference. For the clues to precise interpretation, we must resort to earlier poems treating analogous subject-matter. Implication could scarcely be carried further than it is in these figures; and this method of making ideas into images is a basic characteristic of Stevens's art.

I doubt that there is any parallel to that in the practice of Donne and his followers; in the half-dozen volumes of their verse through which I have pursued the question I have not found a single instance of the extreme form of implication peculiar to the more advanced poetry of our time. If we consider the simile broadly, as a comparison in which both terms are given, no matter in what grammatical relationship, that and not the metaphor is the chief rhetorical resource of the Metaphysicals, as of most English poets.

It is generally accepted that what I would call "the radical metaphor" came into American poetry from French Symbolism, partly by direct influence, partly *via* the Imagists. Stevens is one of those who introduced and naturalized it. The combination, an intellectual lyric framed on the Symbolist principle of implication, is a twentieth-century ex-

tension of the Metaphysical tradition. No one did more than Wallace Stevens to create it; and no one has done more to manifest its potentialities as an expression of intensely felt thought and a medium of formal elegance. It is his genre. (pp. 566-79)

Hi Simons, "The Genre of Wallace Stevens," in The Sewanee Review, *Vol. LIII, No. 4, Autumn, 1945, pp. 566-79.*

Louis Martz   (essay date 1958)

[*Martz is an American educator and prominent critic of English and American poetry. In the following excerpt, which originally appeared in* Literature and Belief *(1958), he chronicles Stevens's poetic development and discusses his understanding of meditation as a means of aligning reality and consciousness.*]

"In an age of disbelief," says Wallace Stevens in a late essay, "it is for the poet to supply the satisfactions of belief, in his measure and in his style." It is my purpose here to explore the nature of those satisfactions, to examine the measure and the style that Stevens achieved in his later poetry, and in this way to suggest the answer that Stevens found to his own blunt question: "What, then, is the nature of poetry in a time of disbelief?" [**"Two or Three Ideas"**].

The answer is implicit in the late poem that provides my theme and title here: **"The World as Meditation"** (1952) seems to sum up the poetical discoveries of Stevens since that time, some thirty years earlier, when his Paltry Nude started on her Spring Voyage through the world of *Harmonium,* to become at the close of that volume a complete Nomad Exquisite, fully attuned to the harmonies of nature, creating as nature herself creates:

> As the immense dew of Florida
> Brings forth
> The big-finned palm
> And green vine angering for life,
>
>   . . . .
>
> So, in me, come flinging
> Forms, flames, and the flakes of flames.

"The World as Meditation," on the other hand, finds its central proposition, not in any text from the surface of things, but in certain words of a human composer, Georges Enesco: "J'ai passé trop de temps à travailler mon violon, à voyager. Mais l'exercice essentiel du compositeur—la méditation—rien ne l'a jamais suspendu en moi. . . . Je vis un rêve permanent, qui ne s'arrête ni nuit ni jour." With those words as epigraph, the poem presents as its symbol of human achievement the figure of Penelope, awaiting the return of Ulysses. As the sun rises she awakens to the meditation that has composed her life:

> A form of fire approaches the cretonnes of Penelope,
> Whose mere savage presence awakens the world in which she dwells.
>
> She has composed, so long, a self with which to welcome him,

Companion to his self for her, which she imag-
    ined,
Two in a deep-founded sheltering, friend and
    dear friend

. . . .

But was it Ulysses? Or was it only the warmth
    of the sun
On her pillow? The thought kept beating in her
    like her heart.
The two kept beating together. It was only day.

It was Ulysses and it was not. Yet they had met,
Friend and dear friend and a planet's encourage-
    ment.
The barbarous strength within her would never
    fail.

There is, we see, a "savage presence" outside her, the primitive force of the sun, which arouses within her a "barbarous strength," some primitive human power that makes it possible for her to compose a self, with the sun's encouragement; and so she dwells in a world of belief created by her will. This sounds like the conception found at the close of Stevens' essay **"The Noble Rider"** (1942), where he mentions a certain nobility of mind that constitutes "a violence from within that protects us from a violence without. It is the imagination pressing back against the pressure of reality." Thus the violence of the sun might have aroused Penelope to the violent, ugly pressure of those outward suitors; but her imagination of Ulysses, her constant meditation of reunion with the man she constantly creates in her mind, this power presses back, composes within herself a world of value and order. Thus, as Stevens concludes in that essay, imagination "seems, in the last analysis, to have something to do with our self-preservation."

I have used two terms, both prominent in Stevens' writings: *imagination, meditation;* they are not synonymous. Meditation is the essential exercise which, constantly practiced, brings the imagination into play, releases creative power, enables the human being to compose a sensitive, intelligent, and generous self. It is the sort of self that Stevens has found fully represented in the person of George Santayana, as he points out in an essay of 1948. "Most men's lives," he regretfully concedes, "are thrust upon them" by the outward violence; but he insists:

> There can be lives, nevertheless, which exist by the deliberate choice of those that live them. To use a single illustration: it may be assumed that the life of Professor Santayana is a life in which the function of the imagination has had a function similar to its function in any deliberate work of art or letters. We have only to think of this present phase of it, in which, in his old age, he dwells in the head of the world, in the company of devoted women, in their convent, and in the company of familiar saints, whose presence does so much to make any convent an appropriate refuge for a generous and human philosopher.

And so in his late poem **"To an Old Philosopher in Rome"** (1952) he finds the fulfillment of human existence in Santayana's reconciliation of flesh and spirit on the threshold of death:

The sounds drift in. The buildings are remem-
    bered.
The life of the city never lets go, nor do you
Ever want it to. It is part of the life in your room.
Its domes are the architecture of your bed.

. . . . .

It is a kind of total grandeur at the end,
With every visible thing enlarged and yet
No more than a bed, a chair and moving nuns,
The immensest theatre, the pillared porch,
The book and candle in your ambered room,

Total grandeur of a total edifice,
Chosen by an inquisitor of structures
For himself. He stops upon this threshold,
As if the design of all his words takes form
And frame from thinking and is realized.

Such admiration for the power of *thinking,* for the constructive power of deliberate choice—this is not the sort of values that were being attributed to Stevens fifteen or twenty years ago. The central impact of Stevens' poetry up to about 1940 has been, I think, admirably summed up by Yvor Winters in his famous essay "Wallace Stevens or the Hedonist's Progress" [included in *The Anatomy of Nonsense*]. There Winters, basing his thesis primarily on **Harmonium,** saw in Stevens the cultivation of "the realm of emotion divorced from understanding," the commendation of "the emotions as a good in themselves." It was, he felt, a point of view that had led Stevens from the great poetry of **Harmonium** into a "rapid and tragic decay" of style, the sad, inevitable progress of the hedonist, "unable to think himself out of the situation into which he has wandered."

Winters has made a brilliant diagnosis of the malady; but he underestimated the patient's will to live. Looking back now, with the immense advantage of all that Stevens has published since Winters wrote, and with the equally great advantage of the recent **Opus Posthumous**—looking back now, we can see that something quite different happened. We can see something analogous to the course of Yeats's poetry. We can see a poet, by a deliberate process of self-knowledge, rebuilding himself and his poetry, rebuilding himself through his poetry, and achieving, in **Transport to Summer** (1947), a volume of meditative poetry that is in every way the equal of his great, first volume of hedonist poetry. It is not a question of setting up divisions, but of watching recessive elements in the early poetry develop into dominance.

Let us try to sketch, now, this different progress. Stevens' second volume, **Ideas of Order,** appeared in 1935; its slimness, its dominant tone, and its title are all significant of a change in the poet's outlook. The buoyancy that gave forth the bounty of **Harmonium** is gone; that force within, like "the immense dew of Florida," that had brought forth "Forms, flames, and the flakes of flames" is subsiding, although here and there it reappears, the old gay defiance of Winters:

But what are radiant reason and radiant will
To warblings early in the hilarious trees
Of summer, the drunken mother?

Or:

> What is there here but weather, what spirit
> Have I except it comes from the sun?

The trouble is that the younger Nomad Exquisite had lived by a view that the poet of the 1930's could no longer accept, for reasons he suggests in the late essay cited at the outset of this discussion: "If in the minds of men creativeness was the same thing as creation in the natural world, if a spiritual planet matched the sun, or if without any question of a spiritual planet, the light and warmth of spring revitalized all our faculties, as in a measure they do, all the bearings one takes, all the propositions one formulates would be within the scope of that particular domination"—as they were, for the most part, in *Harmonium.* "The trouble is, however, that men in general do not create in light and warmth alone," he continues. "They create in darkness and coldness. They create when they are hopeless, in the midst of antagonisms, when they are wrong, when their powers are no longer subject to their control. They create as the ministers of evil." *Ideas of Order* moves in this different world; it is filled with the tones of evening: **"A Fading of the Sun," "Gray Stones and Gray Pigeons," "Autumn Refrain," "Winter Bells," "Sad Strains of a Gay Waltz."**

> There is order in neither sea nor sun.
> The shapes have lost their glistening.
> There are these sudden mobs of men.

In this new atmosphere one poem stands out to control the chaos: the famous **"Idea of Order at Key West."** Here the speaker, significantly, stands at the far edge of Florida, his back upon that world of flame and green. The physical world now offers none of its old "comforts of the sun," but exists here as

> The meaningless plungings of water and the
>   wind,
> Theatrical distances, bronze shadows heaped
> On high horizons, mountainous atmospheres
> Of sky and sea.

The object of wonder and admiration is now a human figure, that singer by the shore whose voice made

> The sky acutest at its vanishing.
> She measured to the hour its solitude.
> She was the single artificer of the world
> In which she sang.

This is more than the Palace of Hoon, the solipsist of *Harmonium;* for the idea of order here resides in more than mental landscapes, in "More even than her voice, and ours": the idea of order is found in a unique conjunction of landscape, singer, and listener, a situation in which the listener's mind, exulting in the full strength of its powers, is able to assert the controlling force of consciousness, "Fixing emblazoned zones and fiery poles" upon the outer atmosphere, "Arranging, deepening, enchanting night"— while realizing fully that the outer universe goes its inhuman way.

The fierce strength of mind in that poem, its clipped and muted language before the final exultation, prepares the way for a striking addition to the volume *Ideas of Order,*

Wallace Stevens in Hartford, circa 1922.

when it appeared in a trade edition in the next year, 1936. The volume no longer opens with the curiously fatigued poem, **"Sailing after Lunch,"** where Stevens truly says, "My old boat goes round on a crutch / And doesn't get under way," and where he ends with the sentimental desire:

> To expunge all people and be a pupil
> Of the gorgeous wheel and so to give
> That slight transcendence to the dirty sail.

No, the volume now opens with the stirring **"Farewell to Florida,"** in which Stevens renounces all that "Florida" has symbolized in his earlier poetry: that world of vivid physical apprehension, where man created within the bounds of the natural order. "Her mind had bound me round," he says, but now he cries:

> Go on, high ship, since now, upon the shore,
> The snake has left its skin upon the floor.
> Key West sank downward under massive clouds
> And silvers and greens spread over the sea. The
>   moon
> Is at the mast-head and the past is dead.
> Her mind will never speak to me again.

And he looks forward to his engagement with a new, a tough, bitter, and turbulent subject:

> My North is leafless and lies in a wintry slime
> Both of men and clouds, a slime of men in
>   crowds.
> The men are moving as the water moves,
> This darkened water cloven by sullen swells
> Against your sides, then shoving and slithering,
> The darkness shattered, turbulent with foam.
> To be free again, to return to the violent mind
> That is their mind, these men, and that will bind
> Me round, carry me, misty deck, carry me
> To the cold, go on, high ship, go on, plunge on.

Stevens, it is clear, has determined to take his old boat out of The Pleasures of Merely Circulating, to plunge into the turmoil of the mid-thirties, to engage it somehow in his poetry. In fact, he had already begun the effort. The year before **"Farewell to Florida"** appeared he had already published the first part of what was to become his longest poetical effort, *Owl's Clover,* which appeared in 1936 in its original version of 861 lines. It is a poem that caused Stevens immense labor and, finally, intense dissatisfaction. In 1937 it reappeared with nearly 200 lines cut out; and in 1954 Stevens omitted it entirely from his *Collected Poems,* on the grounds that it was "rhetorical," Mr. Morse tells us. As a result of this drastic omission, the reader of the *Collected Poems* may emerge with a sense of the poet's steady self-possession, an ideal progress from the old gaudy style toward a sober, muted, thoughtful, pruned, and thoroughly remade poetry: for we move from *Ideas of Order* directly into **"The Man with the Blue Guitar,"** where

> The man bent over his guitar,
> A shearsman of sorts.

A shearsman indeed, a sort of tailor, cutting his cloth anew and shearing away the excess. But the effect is too neat. We need *Owl's Clover,* preferably in its first version, to tell us all the trouble of the change; and fortunately we have it all now before us once again, in the new posthumous volume. It is not a successful poem, though it contains great passages and opens remarkably well, with the firmly controlled symbols of **"The Old Woman and the Statue."** There the magnificent statue in the park represents the soaring, noble imagination of the past, "leaping in the storms of light": the statue is a work of art subtly and powerfully arranged for the human mind to grasp and be exalted. One thing, one thing only, the sculptor "had not foreseen": the old woman, "the bitter mind / In a flapping cloak," a woman so depressed that she cannot apprehend the statue's action:

> A woman walking in the autumn leaves,
> Thinking of heaven and earth and of herself
> And looking at the place in which she walked,
> As a place in which each thing was motionless
> Except the thing she felt but did not know.

That thing is the "harridan self," "Crying against a need that pressed like cold, / Deadly and deep." It is not simply physical poverty that tortures this suffering self: it is that she lives, as the second part tells us, amid "the immense detritus of a world"

> That is completely waste, that moves from waste
> To waste, out of the hopeless waste of the past
> Into a hopeful waste to come.

The hopeful waste of the future, I think, alludes to the sort of world proffered by Mr. Burnshaw, whose name adorns the original title of the second part: **"Mr. Burnshaw and the Statue"** (later altered to **"The Statue at the World's End"**). Stanley Burnshaw was the Marxist critic who in 1935 had reviewed *Ideas of Order* with considerable acuteness, though with a condescending tone: he had seen it as a book of "speculations, questionings, contradictions"—"the record of a man who, having lost his footing, now scrambles to stand up and keep his balance" [*New Masses,* 1935]. The critique, being so largely true, left its mark, as *Owl's Clover* shows in its derisive rejection of all mass-solutions that offer only "an age of concentric mobs." But what can be offered instead to the suffering self? The offering in this long second section turns out, in spite of its high rhetoric, to be surprisingly meager: it is simply the old pleasures of Florida, chanted in a weak imitation of the old hieratic style of **"Sunday Morning,"** as this passage (later removed) indicates:

> Dance, now, and with sharp voices cry, but cry
> Like damsels daubed and let your feet be bare
> To touch the grass and, as you circle, turn
> Your backs upon the vivid statue. Then,
> Weaving ring in radiant ring and quickly, fling
> Yourselves away and at a distance join
> Your hands held high and cry again, but cry,
> This time, like damsels captured by the sky,
> Seized by that possible blue.

But those waltzes had ended, long since. Clearly, the poet must try another way, and so, in his third section, Stevens turns to develop a contrast between two ways of life. One is the old way of religious meditation, where "each man,"

> Through long cloud-cloister-porches, walked
>   alone,
> Noble within perfecting solitude,
> Like a solitude of the sun, in which the mind
> Acquired tranparence and beheld itself
> And beheld the source from which transparence
>   came.

And the other is something that seems to have arisen or to be arising in place of the old religious way, something he calls Africa, a world of dense, savage, mindless animality, where

> Death, only, sits upon the serpent throne:
> Death, the herdsman of elephants,
> To whom the jaguars cry and lions roar
> Their petty dirges of fallen forest-men,
> Forever hunting or hunted, rushing through
> Endless pursuit or endlessly pursued,
> Until each tree, each evil-blossomed vine,
> Each fretful fern drops down a fear like dew.

From here on, in the middle of the poem, *Owl's Clover* provides less and less sustenance for the troubled mind trying to feed in the dark. It becomes increasingly turgid and incoherent. The old religion cannot cope with "Africa," nor can the old art of the statue; nor can the problems be met by the believers in necessity, the nostalgic admirers of the old pioneer spirit, or the worshippers of the "newest Soviet reclame." "How shall we face the edge of time?"

> Where shall we find more than derisive words?
> When shall lush chorals spiral through our fire
> And daunt that old assassin, heart's desire?

"Lush chorals"—the backward glance toward the days of *Harmonium*—is ominous, and we are not surprised to find the poem ending with a Sombre Figuration in which the poet attempts to find refuge in a vague, semi-Jungian concept of the "subman." This subman is some inner man of imagination, who lies below the torments of thought: "The man below the man below the man, / Steeped in night's opium, evading day." But the subman has a precarious tenure, for he seems to reside only in a rhetoric of empty assertion:

> And memory's lord is the lord of prophecy
> And steps forth, priestly in severity,
> Yet lord, a mask of flame, the sprawling form
> A wandering orb upon a path grown clear.

It is a relief to turn from this evasive subman to the daylight figure who shears away this outworn pomp. The sounds made by **"The Man with the Blue Guitar"** (1937) show that Stevens, within a year's hard thought, has taken quick, firm strides toward the position thoroughly established in his prose essays and his late poetry: that "the poet must get rid of the hieratic in everything that concerns him," that he must abolish "the false conception of the imagination as some incalculable *vates* within us, unhappy Rodomontade"—i.e. the opium-drugged subman must be erased, along with the style in which he had been expressed. In his place we will have something like Picasso's clear, clean image of the old Guitar Player, a product of his "blue period" (though the guitar itself happens to be tan), which was, incidentally, exhibited in Hartford in 1934. We will have an image of life explored, discovered, and developed through a language made out of "things exactly as they are," a language moving now with a tough intent toward the discovery of a self:

> Ah, but to play man number one,
> To drive the dagger in his heart,
>
> To lay his brain upon the board
> And pick the acrid colors out,
>
> To nail his thought across the door,
> Its wings spread wide to rain and snow,
>
> To strike his living hi and ho,
> To tick it, tock it, turn it true,
>
> To bang it from a savage blue,
> Jangling the metal of the strings.

This is as far as we can get from the puzzled, ruminative ebb and flow of *Owl's Clover*, with its dissolving, eddying, and often turbid blank verse: note here the crisp common diction, the strict driving rhythm of the short couplets, subtly bound together by irregular rhymes and half-rhymes, all focused on one aim: a definition of the *self* as the only province of poetry:

> Ourselves in the tune as if in space,
> Yet nothing changed, except the place

> Of things as they are and only the place
> As you play them, on the blue guitar,
>
> Placed, so, beyond the compass of change,
> Perceived in a final atmosphere;
>
> For a moment final.

We have returned to the central position of the **"Idea of Order at Key West"**: man's inner rage for order as the ultimate constructive force in man's universe, and hence the never-ending effort of the mind to control, within the mind, that outer monster, the inhuman universe:

> That I may reduce the monster to
> Myself, and then may be myself
>
> In face of the monster, be more than part
> Of it, more than the monstrous player of
>
> One of its monstrous lutes, not be
> Alone, but reduce the monster and be,
>
> Two things, the two together as one.

From this effort, he says, "I shall evolve a man."

This sequence of thirty-three tightly argued, tightly ordered meditations on a theme establishes the altered style of the later Stevens. He has here, in a deliberate act of choice, sheared away the kind of writing that he later calls "The romantic intoning, the declaimed clairvoyance," since this, he says, is the "appropriate idiom" of apotheosis; and this is not at all his subject now. Apotheosis elevates the mortal to the stature of divinity; it glorifies; and the appropriate poetry of apotheosis is therefore the hymn, the ode, the celebration, the chant. In a peculiar sense, this had been the appropriate idiom of his earlier poetry, since he was there attempting to show, as he tells the lady in **"Sunday Morning,"** that "Divinity must live within" the human realm: "Passions of rain, or moods in falling snow." Hence he uses the idiom of romantic intoning to glorify the satisfactions of this earth, often with deliberate irony: the Comedian speaks of his "first central hymns, the celebrants / Of rankest trivia"; and indeed the whole mock-heroic effect of the Comedian arises from the application of such grand intoning to the achievements of this "merest minuscule."

But in his new effort to evolve a man, a new idiom must be invented, since "apotheosis is not / The origin of the major man" for whom the poet is now searching. "He comes," says Stevens, "from reason, / Lighted at midnight by the studious eye, / Swaddled in revery." He is the meditative man, master of the essential exercise, student, scholar, rabbi of a new idiom, which Stevens in **"Of Modern Poetry"** (1940) calls "The poem of the mind in the act of finding / What will suffice." There has never been a better definition of what might be called the genre of meditative poetry. It is not, we note, a poem celebrating what suffices; nor is it any lamentation for the lack of what suffices. The difference between the true meditative poem and other poetic genres seems to be exactly this: that it alone represents "the poem of the act of the mind," the poem of the mind, in the very act of finding. One thinks of Emily Dickinson, of Hopkins, of George Herbert, and especially of Donne, in his *Divine Meditations* (*Holy Sonnets*).

But further definition of the genre, if there is really such a genre, is necessary, and Stevens suggests it all in **"Of Modern Poetry"**:

> It has to be living, to learn the speech of the
>   place.
> It has to face the men of the time and to meet
> The women of the time. It has to think about
>   war
> And it has to find what will suffice. It has
> To construct a new stage. It has to be on that
>   stage
> And, like an insatiable actor, slowly and
> With meditation, speak words that in the ear,
> In the delicatest ear of the mind, repeat,
> Exactly, that which it wants to hear, at the
>   sound
> Of which, an invisible audience listens,
> Not to the play, but to itself, expressed
> In an emotion as of two people, as of two
> Emotions becoming one.

Let me expand, with only a little liberty, the possible implications of that text. This kind of poetry must know the common speech; it must make contact with men in their normal existence, through its language, its images, and its consideration of urgent problems, such as war, of whatever kind, whether between man and man, or between body and soul, good and evil, man and his environment—the "war between the mind and sky" that Stevens describes at the end of his *Notes toward a Supreme Fiction.* It has to find what will suffice, but in order to do this, it must construct a stage on which an actor may enact the process of this finding. And as this actor speaks his meditated words, they find a growing response in a certain invisible audience, which is not simply us, the readers or listeners, but is first of all the larger, total mind of the poet himself, controlling the actor, who is some projected aspect of himself. Then, in the close, that actor and that audience, projected self and larger self, come together in a moment of emotional resolution—for a moment final. It is a process that Stevens describes thus in his **"Adagia"**: "When the mind is like a hall in which thought is like a voice speaking, the voice is always that of someone else." The voice is that of some projected self: the audience is the whole self. "It is necessary to propose an enigma to the mind," he says in another adage. "The mind always proposes a solution." All this seems to describe something very like the action in **"The Idea of Order at Key West"**: the landscape is the stage, the singer by the shore is the actor, and the poet's larger mind is the audience. It is also very like the action that one finds in Donne's *Holy Sonnets,* which we may take as a prime example of pure meditative poetry, since they seem to arise directly from the rigorous meditative exercises commonly practiced by religious men of the seventeenth century. Recall how Donne projects some aspect of himself upon a stage: the deathbed, the round earth's imagined corners, the Cross; how he then allows that self to ponder the given situation; and how, at the close, the projected self makes a subtle union with the whole mind of the poet, concluding all in the finding of what will suffice.

One can only ponder the possibilities here, and pause to stress one point. In formal religious meditation, as developed during Donne's time and later practiced (certainly) by Hopkins and (presumably) by Eliot, the process of meditation consists of something akin to that just described by Stevens. It begins with the deliberate creation of a setting and the placing of an actor there: some aspect of the self; this is the famous composition of place recommended by the Jesuit exercises. This is followed by predominantly intellectual analysis of some crucial problem pertaining to that self; and it all ends in a highly emotional resolution where the projected self and the whole mind of the meditator come together in a spirit of devotion. This threefold process is related to the old division of the soul into memory, understanding, and will; the exercise of meditation integrates these faculties.

How is it that a modern poet such as Wallace Stevens, so vastly different from the seventeenth century in the objects of his belief, should come to describe the need for a kind of poetry to which Donne's *Holy Sonnets* seem to belong: a kind that we might call the genre of meditative poetry? Donne's strenuous cultivation of this kind of poetry seems to be part of his lifelong effort to transcend and resolve his grievous sense of the fickleness, the dissolution, the transiency and fragility of all physical things. In Stevens, I think, an analogous situation called forth the analogous discipline. Stevens, in mid-career, recognized the dissolution, or the inadequacy, of his old poetic self—a recognition recorded with a wry gaiety in **"The Comedian as the Letter C."** His later poems represent a rigorous search for ways and means of evolving another kind of poetic self, in accord with the outlook expressed in the late essay dealing with the "time of disbelief": "There was always in every man the increasingly human self, which instead of remaining the observer, the non-participant, the delinquent, became constantly more and more all there was or so it seemed; and whether it was so or merely seemed so still left it for him to resolve life and the world in his own terms" [*Opus Posthumous*].

Allusions in his prose essays indicate that in this effort Stevens engaged in broad reading among tough thinkers, while all his later poetry displays a new respect for the "radiant idea" and the "radiant will." This is clear in the first part of *Notes toward a Supreme Fiction* (1942), which insists that the fiction must be, in some sense, "abstract." Not, I think, abstract in the usual sense of a philosophical abstraction; Stevens has told us plainly what he thinks of this in his **"Landscape with Boat,"** where he decries the man who "wanted imperceptible air," who "wanted the eye to see"

> And not be touched by blue. He wanted to
>   know,
> A naked man who regarded himself in the glass
> Of air, who looked for the world beneath the
>   blue,
> Without blue, without any turquoise tint or
>   phase,
> Any azure under-side or after-color.

By "abstract" Stevens seems rather to imply a quality of being taken out, abstracted in the root sense, from that world we call the outer universe: something concrete taken out of this and taken into the mind through a process of full, exact realization. From that "local abstraction" the turquoise tints and azure undersides can then radiate in all directions. This is the process that Stevens vividly describes in section VII of **"Credences of Summer,"** where he begins by scorning those who have found it too hard "to sing in face / Of the object," and have therefore fled to the woods, where they could sing "their unreal songs / Secure." In a violent reversal of mood, he advocates a fiercely opposite process:

> Three times the concentred self takes hold, three
>   times
> The thrice concentred self, having possessed
> The object, grips it in savage scrutiny,
> Once to make captive, once to subjugate
> Or yield to subjugation, once to proclaim
> The meaning of the capture, this hard prize,
> Fully made, fully apparent, fully found.

If this bears some resemblance to the old threefold process of formal meditation, it is only because Stevens has discovered for himself the same faculties, and has taught himself a way of using them for his own meditative ends. He has, in an essay of 1943, come to define the imagination as "the sum of our faculties," and has gone on to speak of "The acute intelligence of the imagination, the illimitable resources of its memory, its power to possess the moment it perceives" [*The Necessary Angel: Essays on Reality and the Imagination*].

Indeed, it appears that Stevens has been thoroughly aware of the analogy I am suggesting, for in a newly published essay, written about 1937, we find him declaring: "The poet who wishes to contemplate the good in the midst of confusion is like the mystic who wishes to contemplate God in the midst of evil . . . Resistance to the pressure of ominous and destructive circumstance consists of its conversion, so far as possible, into a different, an explicable, an amenable circumstance." And in this search, he adds, the poets "purge themselves before reality . . . in what they intend to be saintly exercises" [*Opus Posthumous*].

But if we accept Stevens' use of the term *meditation* as a proper description of his own secular exercises, we may appear to be stretching the word beyond any useful signification. Cannot any poem that contains any degree of hard thinking be thus called meditative? I do not think so, if we keep in mind the careful distinctions made by the old spiritual writer, Francois de Sales [in his *A Treatise on the Love of God* (1616)]. "Every meditation is a thought," he says, "but every thought is not a meditation; for we have thoughts, to which our mind is carried without aim or design at all, by way of a simple musing . . . And be this kind of thought as attentive as it may be, it can never bear the name of meditation." On the other hand, he says, "Sometimes we consider a thing attentively to learn its causes, effects, qualities; and this thought is named study." But "when we think of heavenly things, not to learn, but to delight in them, that is called to meditate; and the exercise thereof meditation." "So that meditation," he concludes, "is an attentive thought repeated or voluntarily maintained in the mind, to arouse the will to holy and wholesome affections and resolutions."

It seems valid to adapt this definition to the meditation of earthly things, since meditation is a process, not a subject. If we do this, then Stevensian meditation becomes: attentive thinking about concrete things with the aim of developing an affectionate understanding of how good it is to be alive. We can see the process working everywhere in his later poetry, but nowhere better than in **"The World as Meditation,"** which now needs to be read entire as an example of the full development of Stevens' meditative style. Note first how far the poem's range extends beyond the "comforts of the sun": the verbal beauty of Enesco's French draws in the cosmopolitan world of the musician, as the figure of Penelope draws in the ancient world of legend. Yet the sun exists as first cause; without it there would be nothing. Thus the poem is phrased to allow a double reference: the sun is Penelope's companion, along with Ulysses. Note too how the poem fulfills all of Stevens' requirements for this modern poetry: common speech, common images, common problems; the establishment of a stage, the placing of Penelope as actor on that stage, the imputed working of her meditative thoughts, along with the constant presence of the poet's larger mind, controlling all, and concluding all with an affectionate understanding of what will suffice.

> Is it Ulysses that approaches from the east,
> The interminable adventurer? The trees are
>   mended.
> That winter is washed away. Someone is moving
>
> On the horizon and lifting himself up above it.
> A form of fire approaches the cretonnes of Penelope,
> Whose mere savage presence awakens the world
>   in which she dwells.
>
> She has composed, so long, a self with which to
>   welcome him,
> Companion to his self for her, which she imagined,
> Two in a deep-founded sheltering, friend and
>   dear friend.
>
> The trees had been mended, as an essential exercise
> In an inhuman meditation, larger than her own.
> No winds like dogs watched over her at night.
>
> She wanted nothing he could not bring her by
>   coming alone.
> She wanted no fetchings. His arms would be her
>   necklace
> And her belt, the final fortune of their desire.
>
> But was it Ulysses? Or was it only the warmth
>   of the sun
> On her pillow? The thought kept beating in her
>   like her heart.
> The two kept beating together. It was only day.
>
> It was Ulysses and it was not. Yet they had met,
> Friend and dear friend and a planet's encouragement.
> The barbarous strength within her would never
>   fail.
>
> She would talk a little to herself as she combed
>   her hair,
> Repeating his name with its patient syllables,

Never forgetting him that kept coming constantly so near.

The world of **Harmonium** has not been discarded here, but
its reliance on the natural force of "sensibility" has been
modified, and the pleasures of that world have been included within a larger structure of existence. By 1951 Stevens could strongly question "the dogma that the origins
of poetry are to be found in the sensibility," and could suggest "if one says that a fortunate poem or a fortunate
painting is a synthesis of exceptional concentration . . .
we find that the operative force within us does not, in fact,
seem to be the sensibility, that is to say, the feelings. It
seems to be a constructive faculty, that derives its energy
more from the imagination than from the sensibility"—
imagination being, as we have seen, the "sum of our faculties" [**The Necessary Angel**]. But he adds, in his cautious
way, "I have spoken of questioning, not of denying." That
is because the old dews of Florida have never ceased to affect him. One of his very last poems, **"Prologues to What
Is Possible,"** suggests that the value of existence may have
resided in

> A flick which added to what was real and its vo-
>   cabulary,
> The way some first thing coming into Northern
>   trees
> Adds to them the whole vocabulary of the
>   South,
> The way the earliest single light in the evening
>   sky, in spring,
> Creates a fresh universe out of nothingness by
>   adding itself,
> The way a look or a touch reveals its unexpected
>   magnitudes.

There is no inconsistency here. The look, the touch, the
flick of feeling, the "times of inherent excellence," "incalculable balances," "not balances / That we achieve but
balances that happen"—these are things worth recognizing, and Stevens never ceases to celebrate them as part of
the wonder of human consciousness. But he is quick to
recognize that "the casual is not / Enough": it does not
attain the full "freshness of ourselves"; it does not satisfy
the "will to make iris frettings on the blank." Beyond the
casual apprehensions there lie the willed and reasoned
structures of the mind, which Stevens presents in two
forms. One structure occurs when the mind thoroughly
and fully concentrates upon the realization of some composition that appears to be inherent in the external scene,
as in **"Credences of Summer."**

> Let's see the very thing and nothing else.
> Let's see it with the hottest fire of sight.
> Burn everything not part of it to ash.
> Trace the gold sun about the whitened sky
> Without evasion by a single metaphor.

Thus:

> One of the limits of reality
> Presents itself in Oley when the hay,
> Baked through long days, is piled in mows. It is
> A land too ripe for enigmas, too serene.

This seems to be what Stevens means by seeing things in
their "first idea," their "every-early candor"; this is the

adequacy of landscape—for a moment final. It exists beyond us, it is no metaphor, and yet, Stevens insists, "the
first idea is an imagined thing," since it is achieved by a
calculated effort of the mind. It is part, then, "of the never-
ending meditation," a poem of the mind in the act of finding what will suffice. It may be, he says, "of a man skating,
a woman dancing, a woman / Combing," a Woman Looking at a Vase of Flowers, a Dish of Peaches in Russia, or
a Large Red Man Reading: it may be found "in the crackling summer night,"

> In the *Duft* of towns, beside a window, beside
> A lamp, in a day of the week, the time before
>   spring,
> A manner of walking, yellow fruit, a house,
> A street.

They are acts available to any man, a sort of poetry, "an
imaginative activity that diffuses itself throughout our
lives" [**The Necessary Angel**]. You return, say, from a
long vacation with your family in the mountains, dog-
tired, addle-brained, and feeling the whole expedition was
a huge mistake. Two weeks later, the snapshots return, developed in full color: you are amazed at the beauty, the
order, the focus; the trip is a success, after all. Such a realization would be, in Stevens' terms, a poetic action.

And finally, beyond such compositions, there lies the inex-
haustible "realm of resemblance," in which the faculties
of the imagination, using all their powers, "extend the object" by analogy, by metaphor. It is a realm in which the
whole mind, like Stevens' Penelope, uses the world of sensory experience as a base upon which to construct a total
edifice involving and demanding the whole stretch of
human experience. By the use of such analogies man connects the external and the internal; the action of analogy
is the mind's ultimate way of establishing its dominant,
controlling position amid the "moving chaos that never
ends." And this, too, is an activity that Stevens sees as
available to everyone.

You sit in a chair, say, admiring the beauty of your four-
year-old daughter: you call to mind certain resemblances
between her and her absent mother, between her and your
imagined image of yourself, between her and your memories and pictures of grandparents. You think, too, of certain painted images of children by Renoir or Romney; you
think of Andrew Marvell's *Picture of Little T. C. in a Prospect of Flowers;* you think of the dogwood that bloomed
last spring and of the zinnias now blooming outside. And
for a moment the object toward which all these resemblances converge, or from which they infinitely extend—
for a moment the object becomes a vital center through
which the sense of life is composed, final: "completed in
a completed scene," as Stevens says. Such is Wallace Stevens' **"World as Meditation,"** a world where the poet may
adopt the words of Valery's Architect and say, "By dint
of constructing, . . . I truly believe that I have constructed myself." (pp. 37-57)

*Louis Martz, "Wallace Stevens: The World as
Meditation," in* Modern American Poetry:
Essays in Criticism, *edited by Guy Owen, Ev-
erett/Edwards, Inc., 1972, pp. 37-57.*

Samuel French Morse (essay date 1970)

[*Morse is an American poet and critic. A noted Stevens scholar, he edited Stevens's* Opus Posthumous *and has written several studies of Stevens's life and works, including* Wallace Stevens: Poetry as Life *(1970). In the following excerpt from that work, Morse compares the early poetry of* Harmonium *with Stevens's later volume* Ideas of Order.]

The pure poetry of **Harmonium** insofar as it relates to the later poetry is not limited to the "casual" aspects of earth, "light or color, images," nor to the "poetry of words" and the "gaiety of language." But these qualities dominate the book and give it its special, even unique character. Of the poems in which light and color play the most important role, **"Sea Surface Full of Clouds"** is the most brilliant. The cumulative effect of its repetitions and rhythms, and its beautifully controlled rhymes, although they may be no more than "mechanisms," as Stevens told John Pauker, does produce a detachment in the reader: one becomes entranced with the play of water and cloud, the "resemblances" between them, in such a way that the poem becomes momentarily at least "a revelation of nature." As the moving light in each of the five cantos touches the desk of the ship to illumine sea and sky in a repetition that is more than a repetition and never the same twice—diffusing, massing, unfolding, loosening, tossing—playing upon the constantly changing and ever-present clouds and water, the mind is touched to a kind of wakefulness and responsiveness. Who, then, the mind asks, catches this superb panorama, the "strange relations" it evokes of colors and chocolate and umbrellas? Who gives the "machine" of ocean its meaning? Not, Stevens seems to imply, the "soul" or the ego; and although imagination might very well designate the force or spirit he means, imagination is too abstract a word to describe so powerful, mysterious, and pervasive a force. It cannot easily be denominated in language, because in his most profound experience of its power, it evades definition. And so he uses French, varying the phrases to describe its effect on each of the five mornings, the sound of which is as essential to its "meaning" as any literal English equivalent—indeed, any translation impoverishes the poem by robbing it of part of its mystery. So it is that the imagination transforms the world, "refreshes life" and reality, and allows one to see ocean and sky as "the veritable thing" in all their glistening, crystalline clarity.

Beyond this it was impossible to go in this direction, although he wrote other poems with the same intention off and on for the rest of his life: **"The Dwarf," "Of Hartford in a Purple Light," "Variations on a Summer Day," "The News and the Weather,"** the **"Six Discordant Songs"** (**"Metamorphosis"** and the five poems that follow it), and **"Things of August"**; but only once or twice, in **"Some Friends from Pascagoula"** and **"Autumn Refrain,"** with the same breathtaking skill and success. An alternative suggested itself in the poems which sought to define the relationship between "what we see" and "what we think," and in the poems delineating the mind's struggle to discover "what will suffice" to make life "complete in itself," an effort which provided its own satisfactions and all the drama he required. In one of the least pretentious but most perceptive essays on Stevens, Louis Martz has called attention to Stevens's "admiration for the power of thinking, for the constructive power of deliberate choice," which meant perception and perceiving even more than feeling or conception and conceptualizing, but always, in the finest poems, a single activity involving all three: in the final analysis, what has always been meant by "making." This unified activity is evident in many of the "anecdotal" poems of **Harmonium,** but the oddness of its results was perplexing, compared with most Imagist poetry and much of the traditional verse of the time, or with the poetry which found its raw material in the city, or small town life, machinery and technology, and the political and artistic ideologies competing for the allegiance of the reader as well as of the poet. In a time when *mere* oddness was often confused with originality, it was not implausible for **Harmonium** to be admired for qualities Stevens neither aimed at nor valued. The vocabulary which Marianne Moore has characterized as "benign," the fastidiousness and delight in elegance and color, and the preoccupation with "the right sensation," lent themselves to an easy identification with hedonism and dandyism; the concern with the self made it easy to think of the poetry as private and against the democratic grain. Such qualities do appear in his work; and readers who have found them unacceptable cannot be regarded as altogether insensitive to its virtues, or vulgarly wrong-headed. On the other hand, the attempts of a good many of his recent critics to see the poetry as the embodiment or statement of a self-contained philosophic order in which the poems themselves are of little intrinsic interest, represent an even more gross misunderstanding of his achievement—and, one can say, of poetry itself. Yet here, too, the very fabric of the verse can tempt one into such an error. That the voice in which the poem speaks is seldom the voice of a character whom one can recognize, or with whom one can readily identify—a Bottom or a Prospero, a Prufrock or an Eben Flood, or even a Ulysses as Tennyson saw him—is one source of difficulty. The self that speaks in his poems, although sure of its identity, uses a language that is both unmistakable and unfamiliar; and sometimes the poetry is so much a poetry of things that do not exist without the words which give them being, that it seems to lack a recognizable human voice at all. Yet these "things" do not really exist in a vacuum: more often than not, they belong to the world of commonplace reality, but they are viewed from an odd angle and in a light that makes them look unfamiliar, as in the paintings of Paul Klee. Nature dominates his world: sun, moon, stars, flowers, birds, "the junipers shagged with ice," "a Schuylkill in mid-earth," "the large-leaved day," Vesuvius, the "dust that traverses a shade"; but it also contains a good many of man's artifacts: "socks of lace / And beaded ceintures," tin cans and lard pails, "the down-town frieze," "Marianna's cart," "the window that makes it difficult / To say good-by to the past," statuary and music; and, at the beginning and the end of his life as a poet, the woman of **"Sunday Morning,"** the "you" of **"Peter Quince at the Clavier"** and the "we" of **"Le Monocle de Mon Oncle,"** the "old philosopher," "a man / Come back to see a certain house," and the aged Ariel of **"The Planet on the Table."** Even in the poems in which no speaker or thinker is identified, or in which he exists as some otherwise anonymous "one," it is usually possible to catch a glimpse of "the artist, the presence of the determining personality," the "reality" without which "no amount of other things matters much."

"**Academic Discourse at Havana**" had put the question of the "function" of the poet to the maker who had exhausted the possibilities of a world in which order seemed fixed and unchanging, even before the final apotheosis of that world had been realized in "**Sea Surface Full of Clouds.**" Although its answer suggested that the self comprised several selves, which the poet had to "reconcile" to each other in "dark, pacific words," and to nature, of which he and they were all "a part," the order of the world had altered by the time Stevens returned to poetry. The "world in flux" which had sustained him still followed its cyclic changes of season, but Miami had become a "jamboree of hoodlums" and Key West had grown "literary." This was a change he had foreseen, but it still had to be reckoned with. "**Academic Discourse at Havana,**" although it strove to compose a "benediction, sepulcher, / And epitaph" for the world of *Harmonium,* had ended with the possibility that the poet's speech might be no more than

> An incantation that the moon defines
> By mere example, opulently clear.

Life itself, "an old casino in a wood," might do no more than "define"

> An infinite incantation of our selves
> In the grand decadence of the perished swans

which were the symbol of the vanished flights of his imagination.

As early as 1926, he told Harriet Monroe,

> Perhaps, when the boom is over . . . something of [Miami's] colonial period of five or ten years ago will re-emerge and it will be possible to be at one's ease again. The little town of Everglades is as yet unaffected by the excitement, although the railroad from Fort Myers is slowly creeping downward. It may be, after all, that in a few years the only true temples will have to be found in Tobago or in the mountains of Venezuela.

He returned to Florida so long as it provided a retreat for the mind; but most of the Florida poems in *Ideas of Order* reflected unease, not the "mere being" he had once enjoyed there. The most famous of them, "**The Idea of Order at Key West,**" echoes the beautiful lines of "**Academic Discourse at Havana**":

> How pale and how possessed a night it is,
> How full of exhalations of the sea . . .

in its own conclusion, but in an exhortation that modifies and deepens the tone; for in the later poem, it is the "maker's" "rage for order" which asserts itself with such urgency, rather than the comic resignation of "the grand decadence of the perished swans":

> Ramon Fernandez, tell me, if you know,
> Why, when the singing ended and we turned
> Toward the town, tell why the glassy lights,
> The lights in the fishing boats at anchor there,
> As the night descended, tilting in the air,

> Mastered the night and portioned out the sea,
> Fixing emblazoned zones and fiery poles,
> Arranging, deepening, enchanting night.

> Oh! Blessed rage for order, pale Ramon,
> The maker's rage to order words of the sea,
> Words of the fragrant portals, dimly-starred,
> And of ourselves and of our origins,
> In ghostlier demarcations, keener sounds.

The exhortation of "**Some Friends from Pascagoula**" (not Florida, but still the "far South" that he loved) moves with astonishing vitality; and the quick, controlled energy of the rhymes is unlike anything else in the book—or in the whole body of the poetry, although it is almost a complement to "**Ploughing on Sunday.**" So, too, the witty self-scrutiny of "**Sailing after Lunch**" seems to be sustained by its unexpected and unexceptionable formality. But it was no accident, when the trade edition of *Ideas of Order* was issued, that "**Farewell to Florida,**" begun before he left Pirate's Cove in 1936, stood at the beginning of the book. So placed, it redefined the tone of all that followed, pointing up the change of scene, the change of season, the new sense of the poet's relation to himself and his world. And as our own perspective on these "Northern" and often autumnal poems lengthens, the more poignant, the more personal and moving they become, although that was hardly their intention. Though many of them lack the certitude and finesse of the best poems of *Harmonium,* they define very well the sense of what it meant to be a poet in a difficult time for poetry, much as *Responsibilities* defined in 1914 a similar sense, albeit more directly and with greater emotion, for Yeats. The blemishes of indulgence in mannerism, the strain of pumping up floods of color, only faintly disfigure "**A Postcard from the Volcano,**" "**Evening without Angels,**" "**Lions in Sweden,**" and "**Anglais Mort à Florence**"; and they disappear entirely in "**The Brave Man**" and "**Autumn Refrain,**" which was written no later than 1931:

> The skreak and skritter of evening gone
> And grackles gone and sorrows of the sun,
> The sorrows of sun, too, gone . . . the moon and moon,
> The yellow moon of words about the nightingale
> In measureless measures, not a bird for me
> But the name of a bird and the name of a nameless air
> I have never—shall never hear. And yet beneath
> The stillness of everything gone, and being still,
> Being and sitting still, something resides,
> Some skreaking and skrittering residuum,
> And grates these evasions of the nightingale
> Though I never—shall never hear that bird.
> And the stillness is in the key, all of it is,
> The stillness is all in the key of that desolate sound.

Both "**Owl's Clover**" and "**The Man with the Blue Guitar**" served the useful purpose of helping him redefine his subject, but neither was a success. "**Owl's Clover,**" with the possible exception of "**The Old Woman and the Statue,**" suffered from a weakness he put his finger on in "**The Irrational Element in Poetry,**" in which he described, in part, the concept behind it—a concept not so different from the concept behind his other work, but somehow viewed from the wrong end of the telescope:

> . . . I wanted to apply my own sensibility to something perfectly matter-of-fact [*i.e.,* the Depression, the "anxieties and tensions" of 1935-36]. The result would be a disclosure of my own sensibility or individuality . . . certainly to myself.

And he went on to say,

> While there is nothing automatic about the poem, nevertheless it has an automatic aspect in the sense that it is what I wanted it to be without knowing before it was written what I wanted it to be, even though I knew before it was written what I wanted to do. If each of us is a biological mechanism, each poet is a poetic mechanism. To the extent that what he produces is mechanical: that is to say, beyond his power to change, it is irrational. Perhaps I do not mean wholly beyond his power to change, for he might, by an effort of the will, change it. With that in mind, I mean beyond likelihood of change so long as he is being himself. This happens in the case of every poet.

He had, as he suspected, mistaken what he called the "true subject" for "the poetry of the subject"; torn between a desire for a "constant" and "orderly" development in his own work and the feeling that he was perhaps a poet "brought up in an artificial school," he had, like "the Mallarmiste," become "a proletarian novelist." He had fallen prey to the pressures of fashion. Tired of his old poems, he was casting about for a means of renewal—but his error in the long run was no greater than similar errors made by other poets of even greater scope. Moreover, he was able to learn something from his attempt, as **"The Noble Rider and the Sound of Words"** and *Notes toward a Supreme Fiction* well prove.

The antitheses of **"The Man with the Blue Guitar,"** at least in the first few sections of the poem, are evidence of an attempt to develop his subject in the orderly fashion he thought he had glimpsed in **"Owl's Clover,"** but the seesawing back and forth between what the man with the blue guitar said and what "they" said very soon becomes monotonous, and the figures intended to bear the weight of the argument of the poem remain either bleakly two-dimensional or so elliptical, like many of the "aphorisms" in **"Like Decorations in a Nigger Cemetery,"** that the effort to untangle their "meaning" seems to be more than it is worth. "The amorist / Adjective aflame," or "the lion in the lute / Before the lion locked in stone" is only a little less irritating than the jargon of nineteenth-century aesthetics, and the equivalent of its "golden oblong." The three rejected sections of the poem (printed in *Opus Posthumous*), which may have been written in the "most slapdash way," are as good as anything in the finished poem; and they have the added virtue of "seeming but a moment's thought," improvisations as natural to their author as one has a right to expect. Their holiday brightness, however, would have clashed with the tone of the rest.

What he once called "the difficult thinking" of these two long poems freed him for the short pieces that followed.

They began with the **"Canonica,"** the twelve poems in the opening pages of *Parts of a World,* including **"Poetry Is a Destructive Force," "The Poems of Our Climate," "Prelude to Objects," "Study of Two Pears," "The Glass of Water,"** and **"Add This to Rhetoric,"** all of which concerned the "problems of realization"; and **"Parochial Theme," "Dry Loaf," "Idiom of the Hero"** and **"On the Road Home,"** in which the poet's relation to a world menaced by an uncertain future was reexamined. In two of the poems, **"The Man on the Dump"** and **"The Latest Freed Man,"** the sense of momentary fulfillment, "when change composes, too," and life seems "complete in itself," reasserted itself: between one "disgust" and another—between winter and summer—"One feels the purifying change. One rejects / The trash" of a stale past and an undefined future; but whether it is "peace" or a "philosopher's honeymoon" that "one finds / On the dump," the poem does not say:

> Is it to sit among mattresses of the dead,
> Bottles, pots, shoes and grass and murmur *aptest eve:*
> Is it to hear the blatter of grackles and say
> *Invisible priest;* is it to eject, to pull
> The day to pieces and cry *stanza my stone?*
> Where was it one first heard of the truth? The the.

He had asked a similar question twenty years earlier, in **"The Indigo Glass in the Grass,"** a "trifle" he had wanted to substitute for one of the poems in **"Pecksniffiana,"** but there he had been looking for something to "contain the world," something "real," and had been more certain of the answer:

> Which is real—
> This bottle of indigo glass in the grass,
> Or the bench with the pot of geraniums, the stained
> mattress and the washed overalls drying in the sun?
> Which of these truly contains the world?
> Neither one, nor the two together.

Though he already knew that "nothing exists by itself," he had not had to face up to a world which seemed steadily growing shabbier and more uncertain; and the possibility of containment still seemed possible. What he had grown to see was the possibility of a force to sustain and to bring into a vital relationship both the poet and the external world around him, not only as a means of self-preservation but also as a means of preserving and giving value to that external world. One could not, from his point of view, have a nobler task; and for him the moments when "everything" was "bulging and blazing and big in itself," when "the pensive man," who was also the "connoisseur of chaos" could see "that eagle float / For which the intricate Alps are a single nest," were what gave life its sanction. At the end of **"The Noble Rider and the Sound of Words,"** he said:

> Late last year Epstein exhibited some of his flower paintings at the Leicester Galleries in London. A commentator in *Apollo* said: "*How with this rage can beauty hold a plea . . .* The quotation from Shakespeare's 65th sonnet pref-

aces the catalogue. . . . It would be apropos to any other flower paintings than Mr. Epstein's. His make no pretence to fragility. They shout, explode all over the picture space and generally oppose the rage of the world with such a rage of form and colour as no flower in nature or pigment has done since Van Gogh."

What ferocious beauty the line from Shakespeare puts on when used under such circumstances! While it has its modulation of despair, it holds its plea and its plea is noble. There is no element more conspicuously absent from contemporary poetry than nobility. There is no element that poets have sought after, more curiously and more piously, certain of its obscure existence. Its voice is one of the inarticulate voices which it is their business to overhear and to record. The nobility of rhetoric is, of course, a lifeless nobility. Pareto's epigram that history is a cemetery of aristocracies easily becomes another: that poetry is a cemetery of nobilities. For the sensitive poet, conscious of negations, nothing is more difficult than the affirmations of nobility and yet there is nothing that he requires of himself more persistently, since in them and in their kind alone, are to be found those sanctions that are the reasons for his being and for that occasional ecstacy, or ecstatic freedom of the mind, which is his special privilege.

It is hard to think of a thing more out of time than nobility. Looked at plainly it seems false and dead and ugly. To look at it at all makes us realize sharply that in our present, in the presence of our reality, the past looks false and is, therefore, dead and is, therefore, ugly; and we turn away from it as from something repulsive and particularly from the characteristic that it has a way of assuming: something that was noble in its day, grandeur that was, the rhetorical once. But as a wave is a force and not the water of which it is composed, which is never the same, so nobility is a force and not the manifestations of which it is composed, which are never the same. Possibly this description of it as a force will do more than anything else I can have said about it to reconcile you to it. It is not an artifice that the mind has added to human nature. The mind has added nothing to human nature. It is a violence from within that protects us from a violence without. It is the imagination pressing back against the pressure of reality. It seems, in the last analysis, to have something to do with our self-preservation; and that, no doubt, is why the expression of it, the sound of its words, helps us to live our lives.

This is as eloquent a testimony to the belief in poetry as one of the great humanities as any we are likely to have in our time, generous and free of self-seeking and self-aggrandizement. Whether it had its roots in Santayana, or Charles Mauron, or Kierkegaard, what it may owe to the "two or three dozen books" on his table that he "had never looked at before," and that in any case cannot be identified, would seem to be beside the point. The real test of its worth—of what it means—would seem to be its power to persuade one as much of its profound humane-

ness as well as of its rightness. After reading the books on his table, Stevens said, "I have concluded to say my say on my own account, with the least possible reference to others. One must stand by one's own ideas, or not at all."

The same must be said of the poems which fulfill even more precisely than *Notes toward a Supreme Fiction* the conditions by which the fiction itself, whether it be poetry or the poetry of life, is to be recognized: it must be abstract—that is, it must be limited and one's own, for it cannot be otherwise; it must change—if only in the repetitions and recurrences that give the world and the human mind identity and also threaten it with extinction; and it must give pleasure—whether it is no more than the sense of well-being that, in taking account of the "modulation of despair" common to all experience, nevertheless is its own justification or is one of the momentary "secretions of insight" in which, without egotism or vanity, we seem to be at the center of the sphere. Eliot called it "the still point of the turning world"; but Eliot's world is vain and deceiving. And although Stevens's sphere is an illusion, too, a metaphor, finally,

> It is
> As if the central poem became the world,
> And the world the central poem, each one the
> mate
> Of the other, as if summer was a spouse,
> Espoused each morning, each long afternoon,
> And the mate of summer: her mirror and her
> look,
> Her only place and person, a self of her
> That speaks, denouncing separate selves, both
> one.
> The essential poem begets the others. The light
> Of it is not a light apart, up-hill.
>
> The central poem is the poem of the whole,
> The poem of the composition of the whole,
> The composition of blue sea and of green,
> Of blue light and of green, as lesser poems,
> And the miraculous multiplex of lesser poems,
> Not merely into a whole, but a poem of
> The whole, the essential compact of the parts,
> The roundness that pulls tight the final ring . . .

In the beginning the *Notes* were to have "developed" the intuition of the supreme fiction in an orderly fashion; but they ended by "playing" with the idea, as he told Henry Church. They "are a miscellany in which it would be difficult to collect the theory latent in them," "illustrations," or, more simply, poems. The reader for whom unity is of the essence of poetry will find the *Notes* deficient; but the reader willing to take any one of the thirty sections and the epilogue, at least to begin with, on its own terms— which means that each poem must be regarded as a whole rather than as a counter fixed in a clearly articulate sequence or discourse—is likely to be better rewarded. Their "order," or the order they propose, is organic, but not to be grasped by the kind of Procrustean exegesis which has been imposed upon them. The poem iterates and reiterates again and again its own way of "delineating" its subject, to use Stevens's own word:

> It is he. The man
> In that old coat, those sagging pantaloons,

It is of him, ephebe, to make, to confect
The final elegance, not to console
Nor sanctify, but plainly to propound.

. . . . .

The poem goes from the poet's gibberish to
The gibberish of the vulgate and back again.
Does it move to and fro or is it of both

At once? Is it a luminous flittering
Or the concentration of a cloudy day?

. . . . .

He imposes orders as he thinks of them,
As the fox and snake do. It is a brave affair.
Next he builds capitols and in their corridors,

Whiter than wax, sonorous, fame as it is,
He establishes statues of reasonable men,
Who surpassed the most literate owl, the most
    erudite

Of elephants. But to impose is not
To discover. To discover an order as of
A season, to discover summer and know it,

To discover winter and know it well, to find,
Not to impose, not to have reasoned at all,
Out of nothing to have come on major weather,

It is possible, possible, possible. It must
Be possible. It must be that in time
The real will from its crude compoundings
    come . . .

Whatever the *Notes* owe to Hegel or Henri Focillon's *Life of Forms in Art,* they are first and last an attempt by the poet to "say his say on his own account, with the least possible reference to others"; their final authority and center of reference are the "commonplaces" of experience, not an order imposed upon them. The eight lines that precede **"It Must Be Abstract"** make this clear:

And for what, except for you, do I feel love?
Do I press the extremest book of the wisest man
Close to me, hidden in me day and night?
In the uncertain light of single, certain truth,
Equal in living changingness to the light
In which I meet you, in which we sit at rest,
For a moment in the central of our being,
The vivid transparence that you bring is peace.

The "you" is the supreme fiction itself—the "enigma," as he called it, as well as poetry and the world. (pp. 181-95)

> *Samuel French Morse, in his* Wallace Stevens: Poetry as Life, *Pegasus, 1970, 229 p.*

Northrop Frye   (essay date 1973)

[*A Canadian educator and critic, Frye was the author of the highly influential and controversial* Anatomy of Criticism *(1957), in which he argued that literary criticism can be scientific in its method and results. Believing that literature is wholly structured by myth and symbol, Frye views the critic's task as the explication of a work's archetypal characteristics. In the following essay, he discusses Steven's use of variation, a form he borrowed from musical composition, as a method of reconciling the conflict between reality and imagination.*]

We cannot read far in Wallace Stevens's poetry without

finding examples of a form that reminds us of the variation form in music, in which a theme is presented in a sequence of analogous but differing settings. Thus in **"Sea Surface Full of Clouds"** the same type of stanza is repeated five times, each with just enough variation to indicate that the same landscape is being seen through five different emotional moods. Another type of variation form appears in **"Thirteen Ways of Looking at a Blackbird,"** where a series of thirteen little imagist poems are related by the common theme of the blackbird, and which, to pursue the musical analogy perhaps further than it will go, gives more the effect of a chaconne or passacaglia. Sometimes the explicit theme is missing and only the variations appear, as in **"Like Decorations in a Nigger Cemetery."**

We notice also that in the titles of Stevens's poems the image of variation frequently turns up, either literally, as in **"Variations on a Summer Day,"** or metaphorically, as in **"Nuances of a Theme by Williams," "Analysis of a Theme,"** and, perhaps, **"Repetitions of a Young Captain." "The Man with the Blue Guitar"** also gives us a strong sense of reading through a set of thirty-three variations, or related imaginative presentations, of a single theme. Then again, the long meditative theoretical poems written in a blank tercet form, *Notes toward a Supreme Fiction,* **"The Auroras of Autumn," "An Ordinary Evening in New Haven," "The Pure Good of Theory,"** are all divided into sections of the same length. **"An Ordinary Evening"** has thirty-one sections of six tercets each; the *Supreme Fiction,* three parts of ten sections each, thirty sections in all, each of seven tercets; and similarly with the others. This curious formal symmetry, which cannot be an accident, also reminds us of the classical variation form in which each variation has the same periodic structure and harmonic sequence. Even the numbers that often turn up remind us of the thirty Goldberg variations, the thirty-three Diabelli waltz variations, and so on.

The variation form in Stevens is a generic application of the principle that every image in a poem is a variation of the theme or subject of that poem. This principle is the first of three "effects of analogy" mentioned in Stevens's essay of that title. There are two other "effects." One is that "every image is a restatement of the subject of the image in the terms of an attitude" [*The Necessary Angel: Essays on Reality and the Imagination*]. This is practically the same thing as Eliot's objective correlative, and is illustrated in **"Sea Surface Full of Clouds,"** where five different moods are unified by the fact that they all have the same correlative. Stevens also says, "In order to avoid abstractness, in writing, I search out instinctively things that express the abstract and yet are not in themselves abstractions" [*Letters of Wallace Stevens*]. His example is the statue in **"Owl's Clover,"** which he also calls a "variable" symbol. The implication is that such images are variations on the idea of the poem which is within the poem of words, the true as distinct from the nominal subject or theme. We note that the correlative in Stevens may pair with a concept as well as with an emotion, which helps to explain why his commentaries on his own poems in the letters are so often woodenly allegorical.

The third "effect of analogy" is that "every image is an intervention on the part of the image-maker" [*The Necessary Angel*]. This principle takes us deep into Stevens's central notion of poetry as the result of a struggle, or balance, or compromise, or tension, between the two forces that he calls imagination and reality. We notice that in the musical theme with variations, the theme is frequently a composition by someone else or comes from a different musical context. Similarly the poet works with imagination, which is what he has, and reality, which is given him. So, from Stevens's point of view, poems could be described as the variations that imagination makes on the theme of reality. In **"Sea Surface Full of Clouds"** a question is asked in each variation about who or what created the picture in front of us, and the answer, given each time in French, defines a distinctive mood of the imagination.

In a letter Stevens says, "Sometimes I believe most in the imagination for a long time, and then, without reasoning about it, turn to reality and believe in that and that alone. But both of these things project themselves endlessly and I want them to do just that." This somewhat helpless remark indicates the strength of the sense of polarity in his poetic world. Stevens often speaks of the intense pressure that the sense of external reality exerts on the modern mind. One of the **"Adagia"** says, "In the presence of extraordinary actuality, consciousness takes the place of imagination." Consciousness, by itself, is simple awareness of the external world. It sees; it may even select what it sees, but it does not fight back. The consciousness fighting back, with a subjective violence corresponding to the objective violence of external pressure, is the consciousness rising to imagination.

The imagination confronts a reality which reflects itself but is not itself. If it is weak, it may either surrender to reality or run away from it. If it surrenders, we have what is usually called realism, which, as Stevens often makes clear, is almost the opposite of what he means by reality. He says, for instance, in connection with the painting of Jack Yeats, that "the purely realistic mind never experiences any passion for reality" [*Letters of Wallace Stevens*]. This maxim would also apply to the "social realism" demanded in Marxist countries, for which Stevens never expresses anything but contempt. The imagination that runs away retreats from the genuinely imaginative world into a merely imaginary one, for, Stevens says [in a letter], "If poetry is limited to the vaticinations of the imagination, it soon becomes worthless." Certain recurring symbols in Stevens represent the kind of facile pseudoconquest of reality which the imagination pretends to make whenever reality is not there: one of them is the moon. Such imaginary triumphs take place in a self-contained world of words which is one of the things that Stevens means by false rhetoric, or **"Rodomontade."** The world of false rhetoric is a world where the imagination encounters no resistance from anything material, where the loneliness and alienation of the mind, about which Stevens speaks so eloquently, has consoled itself with pure solipsism.

Stevens says that it is a fundamental principle about the imagination that "it does not create except as it transforms" [*Letters of Wallace Stevens*]. It is the function of reality to set free the imagination and not to inhibit it. Reality is at its most inhibiting when it is most externalized, as it is in our own time. In **"Two or Three Ideas"** Stevens speaks of the way in which the pressure of externality today has created a culture of what he calls "detached styles," and which he characterizes as "the unsuccessful, the ineffective, the arbitrary, the literary, the nonumbilical, that which in its highest degree would still be words" [*Opus Posthumous*]. In one prophetic flash, which sums up the essence of the world we have been living through for the past few years, he speaks of this world of false imagination as the product of "irrationality provoked by prayer, whiskey, fasting, opium, or the hope of publicity." It follows that Stevens does not accept the mystique of the unconscious and has nothing of Yeats's or Joyce's feeling for the dreamworld as having a peculiarly close relation to the creative process. He always associates creativity with cognition, with consciousness, even with calculation. "Writing poetry is a conscious activity. While poems may very well occur, they had very much better be caused" [*Letters of Wallace Stevens*].

Stevens associates his word "reality" with the phrase "things as they are," which implies that for him reality has a close relation to the external physical world as we perceive it. The imagination contemplates "things as they are," seeing its own unreality mirrored in them, and its principle of contemplation Stevens calls resemblance or analogy. He also calls it, quite logically, **"Narcissism."** This word points to the danger of uncontrolled imagination and the ease with which it can assume that there is another reality on the other side of things as they are. Traditional religious poetry, for instance, projects heavens and hells as objective and hidden realities, though it can construct them only out of the material of things as they are. Crispin, the hero of one of Stevens's most elaborate variation poems, soon comes to a point at which he can say, "Here was the veritable ding an sich, at last." But this is a Kantian phrase, and Stevens is not Kantian: reality for him is always phenomenal, something that "seems" as well as is, and there is no alternative version of it that the poet should be trying to reach. Hidden realities always turn out to be unreal, and therefore simply mirrors of the imagination itself. Similarly, "poetry will always be a phenomenal thing" [*Letters of Wallace Stevens*].

Stevens's arguments are poetic and not philosophical, and like many poetic arguments they turn on a verbal trick. The trick in this case consists in using the special-pleading term "reality" for the external physical world, which means that conceptions set over against this "reality" have to be called, or associated with, the unreal. Stevens is not unaware of this by any means, but his use of the word "reality," which becomes almost obsessive in the letters, indicates that, like his spiritual sister Emily Dickinson, he has a Puritanic distrust of all self-transcending mental efforts, especially mysticism. More particularly, he feels that, as the poet's language is the language of sense experience and concrete imagery, any poet who bypasses things as they are, however subtly, is dodging the central difficulty of poetry. Such poets, who look for some shortcut or secret passage through reality to something else, and regard poetry as a kind of verbal magic, have what Stevens calls a "marginal" imagination, and he associates this marginal imagination, which explores itself to find its own analogue in reality, with, among others, Valéry, Eliot, and Mallarmé.

Stevens goes even further in suggesting that the conquest of reality made by the reason is also somewhat facile compared to that of the imagination, because it is possible for reason, in some degree, to live in a self-contained world and shut its gates in the face of reality. One of the products of reason is the theological belief in reality as a creation, a product of the infinite imagination of God. Such a belief is repugnant to Stevens: this would mean that reality is analogous to the imagination. The poet is a Jacob who has to wrestle with the necessary angel of reality, and if reality is itself ultimately a "supreme fiction," or something made out of nothing, then all his agonized efforts and struggles are a put-up job, something fixed or rigged, as so many wrestling matches are. Stevens says:

> The arrangement contains the desire of
> The artist. But one confides in what has no
> Concealed creator. One walks easily
>
> The unpainted shore, accepts the world
> As anything but sculpture.

So whatever the imagination may do to reality, reality continues to present something residually external, some donkey's carrot pulling us on, something sticking through everything we construct within it. Even in the moment of death (or what appears to be death, on the last page of the **Collected Poems**), we confront something "outside" giving us the sense of "a new knowledge of reality." Or, as Stevens says in prose, "Poetry has to do with reality in that concrete and individual aspect of it which the mind can never tackle altogether on its own terms, with matter that is foreign and alien in a way in which abstract systems, ideas in which we detect an inherent pattern, a structure that belongs to the ideas themselves, can never be" [**Opus Posthumous**]. The imagination is driven by a "rage for order," but it works toward, not the complete ordering of existence, but rather a sense of equipoise or balance between itself and what is not itself.

We soon come to understand that for Stevens there are different levels or degrees of reality, arranged in a ladder or mountain or winding stair in which the poet has to undertake what he calls an "ascent through illusion." In his essay **"A Collect of Philosophy"** Stevens attempts to list a few philosophical conceptions which seem to him to be inherently poetic, meaning by that, presumably, conceptions that particularly appeal to him as a poet. Among these, the theme of anabasis or ascent, the theme of Dante, looms up prominently. At the bottom of the ladder is the sense of reality as an undifferentiated external world, or what Stevens calls a *Lumpenwelt*. Such a world, Stevens says, is "all one color," a "basic slate", a sinister or scowling "pediment of appearance." As such, it forces the imagination to define itself as its opposite, or nothingness. At this point a construct emerges which is rather similar to the construct of being and nothingness in Sartre. The *Lumpenwelt* is reality on the minimum imaginative basis; the imagination on the same basis is merely the unreal: reality is everything; the imagination is nothing. The imagination never brings anything into the world, Stevens says

in an unconscious echo of the burial service, though it is not quite so true for him that it can take nothing out. This confrontation of being and nothingness, the starting point of imaginative energy, is the vision of the listener in **"The Snow Man,"** who,

> nothing himself, beholds
> Nothing that is not there and the nothing that
>   is.

Traditionally, the world of becoming has always been regarded as the product of being and nothingness. For Stevens there is no reality of being in the traditional sense of something that does not change. Whenever we try to imagine an unchanging ideal, we get involved in the hopeless paradox of Keats's Grecian urn, where the little town on the hidden side of the urn will never be inhabited to all eternity. The woman in **"Sunday Morning"** asks resentfully, "Why should she give her bounty to the dead?" but soon comes to realize that she cannot have any alternative without change, and therefore death, at the heart of it. Reality is phenomenal and belongs to the world of becoming. In the very late poem **"Of Mere Being"** the only unchanging thing about being is that it remains external, "at the end of the mind," "beyond the last thought."

Two of the requirements of the "supreme fiction" are that it must change and that it must give pleasure, and it is clear that for Stevens these two things are much the same thing, change being the only real source of pleasure. Over and over Stevens returns to what he calls "the motive for metaphor," the fact that what is change in reality is also pleasure in the imagination. The imagination, the principle of the unreal, breaks up and breaks down the tyranny of what is there by unifying itself with what is not there, and so suggesting the principle of variety in its existence. This is the point of identity on which all art is founded: in the imaginations of Cézanne and Klee, Stevens says, reality is transmuted from substance into subtlety. We get the idea of unchanging being from the thereness of the physical world, the fact that it doesn't go away. What does go away, and is to that extent unreal, is what the unreality of the imagination builds on. The imagination, in short, "skims the real for its unreal."

This kind of activity gives us a relatively simple type of variation form, the kind represented by the **"Blackbird"** poem. Here the variations are what Stevens calls the "casual exfoliations" of an imagination contemplating a real thing. The recipe for this type of variation form is given in the poem **"Someone Puts a Pineapple Together,"** one of **"Three Academic Pieces"** in *The Necessary Angel:*

> Divest reality
> Of its propriety. Admit the shaft
> Of that third planet to the table and then:

The third planet, he has explained, is the imagination, and there follow a series of twelve numbered variations on the pineapple. It is clear that such a conception of imagination and reality has much to do with the affinity to the pictorial in Stevens, with his fondness for subjects analogous to still life or landscape painting, where the real object and the imaginative variation of it are most dramatically exhibited. Such variation poems are fanciful in Coleridge's sense of the term: Stevens was familiar with Coleridge's distinction, which he acquired through his reading of I. A. Richards. They are, so to speak, cyclical poems, where the variations simply surround the theme. As such, they are not the most serious kind of writing. Stevens speaks of the almost total exclusion of "thinking" from such a poem as **"Variations on a Summer Day"** and says also, "I have no doubt that supreme poetry can be produced only on the highest possible level of the cognitive" [*Letters of Wallace Stevens*]. Again one thinks of the musical parallel. The greatest examples of the variation form, such as the last movement of Beethoven's Opus 111, do not merely diversify the theme: they are sequential and progressive forms as well, and we feel at the end that they have, so to speak, exhausted the theme, done what there is to be done with it. We have now to see if we can discover a sequential and progressive aspect to Steven's variation form also.

We began with a confrontation between imagination and reality, in which the former is a negation, the opposite of reality. Then we found that the imagination can intensify reality by seizing on the "unreal" aspect of it, the aspect that changes and therefore gives pleasure. Stevens says [in *The Necessary Angel*], "A sense of reality keen enough to be in excess of the normal sense of reality creates a reality of its own." As he goes on to say, this is a somewhat circular statement, and one would expect it to lead to some such principle as Blake's "As the Eye, such the Object," the principle that the degree of reality depends on the energy of the imagination. Stevens resists this implication, because of his constant fear that the imagination will simply replace reality and thereby deprive itself of its own material cause. For him the imagination is rather an informing principle of reality, transmuting its uniformity into variety, its "heavy scowl" into lightness and pleasure. Still, it seems clear that we cannot go on indefinitely thinking of the imagination merely as a negation or nothingness.

The fact that the imagination seizes on the changing aspect of reality means that it lives in a continuous present. This means not only that "the imperfect is our paradise," but that the imagination is always beginning. The only reason for finishing anything is that we can then be rid of it and can come around to the point at which we can begin again. The shoddiness of being fixated on the past, of refusing to discard what he calls the "hieratic" meets us everywhere in Stevens. The imagination in the sunlit world of reality is like food in hot weather: whatever is kept spoils. Hence "one of the motives in writing is renewal" [*The Necessary Angel*]. This emphasis on constant fresh beginnings is connected, naturally, with the steadfast resistance to anything resembling an echo or an influence from other poets in Stevens, in striking contrast to the absorption of echoes and influences that we find in, for instance, Eliot.

What is true of the past is also true of the future, the desire to use the imagination to make over reality that we find in so many romantics, revolutionaries, and spokesmen of the irrational. Stevens speaks of this desire with a good deal of sympathy and understanding, for instance, in his essay on the irrational in poetry, where he links the irrational, once again, with the pressure of external fact on the

Elsie Stevens in Elizabeth Park, Hartford, about 1916.

modern poet and his consequent sense of claustrophobia and desire for freedom. **"Owl's Clover"** is a carefully considered effort to come to terms with the revolutionary desire for freedom and equality on a vast social scale. But when the imagination is used as part of an attempt to make over reality, it imposes its own unreality on it. The result is that perversion of belief which we see in all religions, including the contemporary atheistic ones. Belief derives from the imaginative unreal: what we really believe in is a fiction, something we have made up ourselves. But all beliefs, when they become institutionalized, tend to ascribe some hidden reality to themselves, a projection of the imagination which can end only in disillusionment or self-hypnotism. The "romantic" of this type (Stevens uses the word romantic in several senses, but this one is pejorative) is "incapable of abstraction," abstraction being among other things the ability to hold a belief as a "supreme fiction" without projecting it to the other side of reality.

At the same time Stevens holds to an intensely social conception of poetry and its function, though a deeply conservative one. The poet, he says, should try to reach the "centre," and by this he means first of all a social center. The poet expresses among other things "that ultimate good sense which we term civilization" [*The Necessary Angel*].

For him reality includes human society as well. As such, the imagination defines the style of a culture or civilization: it is whatever it is that makes everything in Spain look Spanish, and makes every cultural product of Spain a variation on a Spanish theme. Stevens uses the phrase "variations on a theme" in connection with a closely related aspect of culture: the predominance and persistence of a convention, as in medieval or Chinese painting.

If we ask what the characteristics of such imaginative penetration of reality are in human life, the words "nobility" and "elegance" come fairly close, though Stevens admits that they are dangerous words. The quality in literature that we recognize as heroic, the power of the imagination to make things look more intensely real, is a quality of illusion in reality that is at the same time a growth in reality. The imagination is thus socially aristocratic, though not necessarily in a class sense. The more power it gains, the more freedom and privilege it enjoys, and the more confident society becomes about its culture. In a time like ours the imagination is more preoccupied in fighting its environment, which presses in on it much harder. In the poem **"Mrs. Alfred Uruguay,"** Mrs. Uruguay herself rides up a mountain in the state of the snow man, looking at her world honestly but reductively, as totally without illusion. She meets going down the mountain a "capable man" who recalls the noble rider of Stevens's earliest prose essay, whose imagination is of the same kind as her own, but is more emancipated, and hence to some extent its fulfillment. It is he who creates

> out of the martyrs' bones,
> The ultimate elegance: the imagined land.

So our confrontation between a negative imagination and a positive reality has reached the point where this negation has informed human civilization and produced a style of living. This process, considered in an individual context, is the theme of the sequential variation form **"The Comedian as the Letter C."** Crispin, the hero of the poem, begins with the principle: "Nota: Man is the intelligence of his soil," a strictly Cartesian principle in which man is the "sovereign ghost." This first variation is headed "The World without Imagination." The fourth variation brings us to "The Idea of a Colony," which begins:

> Nota: his soil is man's intelligence.
> That's better. That's worth crossing seas to find.

Stevens calls Crispin a "profitless philosopher," says that he never discovers the meaning of life, that social contact would have been a catastrophe for him, that he is an everyday man whose life has not the slightest adventure, and symbolizes him by the one letter of the alphabet which has no distinctive sound of its own. Nevertheless, Crispin works very hard to achieve his own kind of reality, and if he is not a poet he is at least a colonizer, someone who achieves a life-style out of a pilgrimage and a settlement in new surroundings. The poem as a whole goes around in an ironic circle, and Crispin ends much where he began, using his imagination as so many people do, to select and exclude rather than create, a realist who rejects reality. Hence the final line of the poem, "So may the relation of each man be clipped." Stevens may also have Crispin partly in mind when he says, "The man who has been brought

up in an artificial school becomes intemperately real. The Mallarmiste becomes the proletarian novelist" [*Opus Posthumous*]. Still, Crispin represents something of the historical process that produced the culture and the tradition out of which Stevens himself developed, moving from baroque Europe to realistic New England.

We have next to see how a negation can be an informing principle in reality. This brings us to the Stevens's conception of the "supreme fiction." The imagination informs reality through fictions or myths (the word "fictive" in Stevens means mythical), which are the elements of a model world. This model world is not "reality," because it does not exist, it is not "there"; but it is an unborn or, perhaps, potential reality which becomes a growth out of reality itself. Stevens quotes Simone Weil, obviously with approval, on the subject of "decreation," a moving from the created to the uncreated, going in the opposite direction from destruction, which moves from the created to nothingness." The conception is Stevens's, though the terms are not. The first law of the supreme fiction is that it must be abstract. It is abstract for the same reason that a god is not reducible to his image. The supreme fiction is not a thing, something to be pointed to or contemplated or thought of as achieved. In its totality, the supreme fiction is poetry or the work of the imagination as a whole, but this totality never separates from the perceiving subject or becomes external. Stevens says, "The abstract does not exist, but . . . the fictive abstract is as immanent in the mind of the poet, as the idea of God is immanent in the mind of the theologian" [*Letters of Wallace Stevens*]. This last indicates that God is one of the supreme fictions. God for Stevens, whatever he may be in himself, must be for man an unreality of the imagination, not a reality, and his creative power can manifest itself only in the creations of man. The explicit statement that God and the imagination are one is made by the "interior paramour," an anima-figure working under the direction of the imagination.

According to Stevens, "The wonder and mystery of art, as indeed of religion in the last resort, is the revelation of something 'wholly other' by which the inexpressible loneliness of thinking is broken and enriched" [*Opus Posthumous*]. The phrase "wholly other," which is in quotation marks, suggests the existential theology of Karl Barth, as relayed through a poet who calls himself a "dried-up Presbyterian." In Barth, of course, the otherness of God and the alienation of man are conditions of man's unregenerate state. God does not remain wholly other for two reasons: first, he has created and redeemed man; and second, he has revealed himself. Let us see what reality in Stevens can do along parallel lines.

When Crispin discovers that the Cartesian principle "Man is the intelligence of his soil" is less true than its reverse, that "his soil is man's intelligence," Stevens is saying that the antithesis of imagination and reality did not begin as such. Man grew out of "reality," and the consciousness which enables him also to draw away from it is a recent development. The human is "alien," but it is also "the non-human making choice of a human self" [*The Necessary Angel*]. The imagination is a product of reality, its Adam, so to speak, or exiled son. Just as, in Dante's *Pur-*

gatorio, the poet makes his way back to the Eden which is his own original home, so the imagination contemplates the "rock," the dead inert reality before it, and realizes that it is itself the rock come to life. "I am what is around me," the poet says, and he continually returns to the sense of the "wholly other" as not only the object but the origin of the sense of identity.

The rock is not dead, because it has never died; death is a process, not a condition. It represents rather the unconscious and undifferentiated external world at the bottom of the imaginative ladder, where the sense of thereness is overpowering and the imagination is simply its negation. In the course of time leaves cover the rock: life emerges from the inanimate, breaks up and diversifies the heavy *Lumpenwelt.* Life, then, if Stevens's general argument still applies, is the negation of the inanimate, the unreal at work in the real. The imagination does with "things as they are" what life does with the rock, and the poet's imagination is inseparably attached to the articulating of life in the rest of the world. The "howl" of the doves, the "cry" of the leaves, the sea in **"The Idea of Order at Key West,"** the **"Bantams in Pine-Woods,"** who are praising themselves and not a divine bantam in the rising sun, are all part of the symphony of life in which the poet has his own voice. We speak of a will to live, and similarly "imagination is the will of things."

The poem **"Oak Leaves Are Hands"** describes a "Lady Lowzen," who is also the goddess Flora, and who continues to "skim the real for its unreal" in human imagination as formerly in the vegetable world. Lady Lowzen is "chromatic," and the delight of vegetable nature in color supplies Stevens with his chief image for the imagination, which he thinks of as, so to speak, the coloring principle of reality. The basis of nature is metamorphosis, the basis of poetry is metaphor, and metaphor and metamorphosis are for Stevens interchangeable terms. Stevens completes the identification by saying "in metaphor the imagination is life" [*The Necessary Angel*]. In this context the variations which the imagination makes on reality join the Darwinian theme with variations in which every variety is a mutation thrown out toward the environment, the "reality" it has to struggle with, until a successful mutation blends and identifies with that reality.

The limit of poetry, as Stevens himself frequently remarks, has always been the imaginatively conceivable, not what is or "things as they are," and any poet deeply impressed by things as they are is apt to suffer from imaginative claustrophobia. Stevens has relegated God to the imaginative unreal, a fiction the human mind creates. He has made an uncompromising bourgeois rejection of all politically revolutionary values. He dismisses Nietzsche and his doctrine of the self-transcendence of man as being "as perfect a means of getting out of focus as a little bit too much to drink" [*Letters of Wallace Stevens*]. What is left? How much further can a "harmonious skeptic" carry his rage for order? Even things as they are present themes which the poet cannot avoid and yet can hardly deal with on their terms. For instance, a surprising number of Stevens's poems are about death, and death is one subject where the imagination, like Good Deeds in *Everyman,* may be pre-

vailed on to accompany the poet as his guide, while "reality," in whatever form or disguise, will always mutter some excuse and slope off. When Stevens gets to the point of saying that "Life and Nature are one," he has left very little room for any reality which he has not in some other context called unreal.

In Stevens's cultural situation about the only consistent "position" left is that of a secular humanism. But, he says, the more he sees of humanism the less he likes it, and, more briefly and explicitly, "humanism is not enough." He also says, "Between humanism and something else, it might be possible to create an acceptable fiction" and that "there are fictions that are extensions of reality." This last concession means that Stevens is capable, at least in his poetry, of sweeping "reality" out of the way as a superego symbol and of reducing it to its proper role as the material cause of poetry.

In reality, man is a social being, and society is partly an aggregate, a mass of men, often dominated by, and expressing their will through, some kind of hero or leader. The hero in this sense is a fiction which has been, like so many other fictions, misapplied and misunderstood by society. In two poems particularly, **"Examination of the Hero in a Time of War"** and **"Life on a Battleship,"** Stevens shows us how the dictatorial hero or charismatic leader is a false projection of the imagination, like the heavens and hells that are created by the imagination and are then asserted to be actual places in the world which is there. The genuine form of this fiction is the conception of all men as a single man, where the difference between the individual and the mass has ceased to exist. Or, as Stevens puts it, in commenting on a passage in *Notes toward a Supreme Fiction* which contains the phrase "leaner being," "The trouble with humanism is that man as God remains man, but there is an extension of man, the leaner being, in fiction, a possibly more than human human, a composite human. The act of recognizing him is the act of this leaner being moving in on us" [*Letters of Wallace Stevens*]. This "leaner being" is the "central man" or "man of glass" who is all men, and whom Stevens portrays as a titanic being striding the skies. Even Crispin reaches an apotheosis of identity with this being.

In this conception of a "general being or human universe," we are still in the area of fictions, but by now we understand that the poet "gives to life the supreme fictions without which we are unable to conceive of it" [*The Necessary Angel*]. Whatever unreal grows out of reality becomes real, like the graft of art on nature which Polixenes urges on Perdita in *The Winter's Tale.* The human universe is still a fiction and to that extent is not strictly true, but, as Abraham Cowley said of the philosophy of Thomas Hobbes, " 'Tis so like Truth 'twill serve our turn as well." In any case, on this level of fiction we can understand how poetry can be called "a transcendent analogue composed of the particulars of reality," the word "transcendent" here being used, I think, quite carefully in its philosophical sense as going beyond sense experience but not beyond the mental organization of that experience. Certain sentences in *The Necessary Angel* which Stevens mutters out of the corner of his mouth when he thinks his censor is not listening take on a new and illuminating significance. One such sentence is this one from **"Imagination as Value":** "The imagination that is satisfied by politics, whatever the nature of the politics, has not the same value as the imagination that seeks to satisfy, say, the universal mind, which, in the case of a poet, would be the imagination that tries to penetrate to basic images, basic emotions, and so to compose a fundamental poetry even older than the ancient world." This universal mind is the mind that has produced "the essential poem at the centre of things," which is *the* supreme fiction as such. In this perspective, "reality" becomes the stabilizing principle which enables us, even as we outgrow our gods, to recognize, even in the act of coming around to the beginning again, that the creative faculties are always the same faculties and that "the things created are always the same things" [*Opus Posthumous*]. In all the variations of what might be we can still hear the theme of what is there.

The supreme fiction of the "central," which is the total form of both man and the human imagination, takes us into a very different context of variability, a context less Darwinian than Thomist. It would be easy, but simplistic, to say that ultimately what is real in Stevens is the universal, the universal being the theme of which the individual is the variation. Easy, because one could quote a good many passages from the later poems, at least, in support of it; but simplistic, because the traditional context of the real universal is a kind of essential world that Stevens never at any point accepts. "Logically," says Stevens, "I ought to believe in essential imagination, but that has its difficulties" [*Letters of Wallace Stevens*]. In the early **"Peter Quince at the Clavier"** we have the line "The body dies; the body's beauty lives." Considering the number of poets, in English literature and elsewhere, who would have drawn a Platonic inference from that statement, it comes as a deliberate and calculated shock for Stevens to say:

> Beauty is momentary in the mind,
> The fitful tracing of a portal,
> But in the flesh it is immortal.

"A Collect of Philosophy" has nothing of medieval realism, though it reflects Stevens's fascination with Plato, but it does express a keen interest in such conceptions as Alexander's "compresence" of mind and existence, and, more particularly, in the great passage in Whitehead's *Science and the Modern World* in which Whitehead rejects the conception of "simple location" in space and announces the doctrine of interpenetration, the doctrine that everything is everywhere at once. Stevens's comment on this passage is, "These words are pretty obviously words from a level where everything is poetic, as if the statement that every location involves an aspect of itself in every other location produced in the imagination a universal irridescence, a dithering of presences and, say, a complex of differences" [*Opus Posthumous*]. This last phrase shows that Stevens is still thinking within the metaphor of a theme and variations.

Stevens often refers to Eliot as a poet who represents the exact opposite of everything he stood for himself, and perhaps we are now beginning to understand why. The fifth

way of looking at a blackbird, for example, is a way that Eliot constantly refuses to look at it:

> I do not know which to prefer,
> The beauty of inflections
> Or the beauty of innuendoes,
> The blackbird whistling
> Or just after.

"A Collect for Philosophy" assumes in passing that all knowledge is knowledge after the experience of the knowledge. For Eliot, the fact that there is a split second between an experience and the awareness of having had the experience is a memento of the Fall of Man. All three dimensions of time for Eliot are categories of unreality: the no longer, the not yet, and the never quite. Our ordinary existence in this time is the fallen shadow of the life we might have lived if there has been no Fall, in which experience and consciousness would be the same thing, and in which the present moment would be a real moment, an eternal now. Eliot's imagination revolves around the figure of Percival in the Grail castle, who, in the words of "The Dry Salvages," "had the experience but missed the meaning," because he was afraid to put the question that would have unified experience and meaning. In this sense we are all Prufrocks, vaguely aware that there is an "overwhelming question" to be asked, and wasting our lives in various devices for not asking it.

Stevens has nothing of Eliot's sense of the phenomenal world as a riddle, to be solved by some kind of conscious experience that annihilates it. When we start climbing the Ash-Wednesday staircase, we have to regard such things as "a slotted window bellied like the fig's fruit" as a distraction. This is because at the top of Eliot's staircase is a total unification and an absorption of reality into the infinite being of God. Like Dante whom he is following, Eliot wants his pilgrimage to pass beyond the categories of time and space and the cycle of nature that revolves within these categories. The slotted window is an image of that cycle, the vegetable cycle of flower and fruit, the cycle of human life that begins with birth from a womb. Stevens does not resemble Yeats any more closely than he resembles Eliot, but, like Yeats, he sides with the "self" in the **"Dialogue of Self and Soul."** For his Mrs. Uruguay, as for Yeats, the top of the mountain or staircase or whatever has to be climbed is the top of the natural cycle, and the fulfillment of climbing it is in coming down again. In Stevens, the imagination is life, and the only way to kill it is to take it outside nature, into a world where it has swallowed nature and become a total periphery or circumference, instead of remaining "central." So for Stevens, as in a very different way for Joyce in *Finnegans Wake,* the cycle of nature is the only possible image of whatever is beyond the cycle, "the same anew."

There is an elaborate imagery of the seasons of the year in Stevens, where summer represents the expanded and fulfilled imagination, autumn the more restricted and realistic imagination, and winter the reduction to a black-and-white world where reality is "there" and the imagination set over against it is simply unreal. The emotional focus of this imagery comes at the moment in spring when the first blush of color enters the world with "an access of color, a new and unobserved, slight dithering" (the last word echoes the comment on Whitehead already quoted), or when a bird's cry "at the earliest ending of winter" signals "a new knowledge of reality," or at Easter. "On Easter," says Stevens, "the great ghost of what we call the next world invades and vivifies this present world, so that Easter seems like a day of two lights, one the sunlight of the bare and physical end of winter, the other the double light" [*Opus Posthumous*]. What Easter symbolizes to Stevens is that we are constantly trying to close up our world on the model of our own death, to become an "owl in the sarcophagus." As long as some reality is still outside us we are still alive, and what is still external in that reality is what has a renewing power for us. This vision is the point at which "dazzle yields to a clarity and we observe," when we see the world as total process, extending over both death and life, always new, always just beginning, always full of hope, and possessed by the innocence of an uncreated world which is unreal only because it has never been fixed in death. This is also the point at which the paradox of reality and imagination comes into focus for the poet and he understands that

> We make, although inside an egg,
> Variations on the words spread sail.

(pp. 395-414)

Northrop Frye, "Wallace Stevens and the Variation Form," in Literary Theory and Structure: Essays in Honor of William K. Wimsatt, *Frank Brady, John Palmer, Martin Price, eds., Yale University Press, 1973, pp. 395-414.*

J. Hillis Miller   (essay date 1980)

[*Miller is considered an important contemporary American critic. Associated with the "Yale Critics" in the 1960s and 1970s, Miller has questioned the methods of traditional literary scholarship throughout his career and has successfully applied several critical methods to literature, most recently, deconstructionism. Based on the thought of French critic and philosopher Jacques Derrida, deconstructionism asserts the philosophical and poly-referential nature of language and literature. Applied to literary study, deconstructionism opposes the traditional view that literary criticism is the search for stable meaning, ideas, and truths in a text. Rather, deconstructionism concentrates on the linguistic elements of a text, questioning the representational function of words and delineating the way in which a work is constructed of verbal forms. In the following excerpt, Miller examines three theories of poetic representation that are operative in Stevens's poetry in order to define the relationship between signifier and signified in Stevens's verse.*]

In an essay describing the changes in occidental thought associated with the names of Marx, Freud, and Nietzsche, Michel Foucault has said [in his essay "Nietzsche, Freud, Marx"]: "l'interprétation est enfin devenue une tâche infinie. . . . A partir du XIX siècle, les signes s'enchaînent en un réseau inépuisable, lui aussi infini, non parce qu'il reposent sur une ressemblance sans bordure, mais parce qu'il y a béance et ouverture irréductibles." Foucault re-

lates this opening of an abyss of interpretation to the "refus du commencement" in Freud, Marx, and Nietzsche. The work of all three suggests that in the activity of interpretation it is impossible to go back to an unequivocal beginning that serves as the foundation of everything that follows. Whenever the interpreter reaches something apparently original, a genetic source behind which it is impossible to go, he finds himself, on the contrary, encountering something that is itself already an interpretation. The apparent source itself refers to something still farther back, and that to something behind it, ad infinitum. "Il n'y à rien d'absolument premier à interpréter, car au fond, tout est déjà interprétation, chaque signe est en lui-même non pas la chose qui s'offre à l'interprétation, mais interprétation d'autres signes."

One example at this abyss of interpretation is the way many modern poems are poems about poetry. They contain within themselves discussions of what they are and of what they mean. They enact or embody in themselves that function of poetry about which they explicitly talk. Moreover, a poem like Wallace Stevens' **"The Man with the Blue Guitar"** or **"A Primitive Like an Orb"** does not express a single unequivocal theory of poetry. For Stevens, as for so many other modern writers, the theory of poetry is the life of poetry, and nothing is more problematical or equivocal than the theory of poetry. Stevens' poetry is therefore not merely poetry about poetry. It is a poetry that is the battleground among conflicting theories of poetry, as the poet tries first one way and then another way in an endlessly renewed, endlessly frustrated attempt to "get it right," to formulate once and for all an unequivocal definition of what poetry is and to provide an illustration of this definition.

The various theories of poetry that generate in their conflict the vitality of Stevens' poetic language are not, however, modern inventions. They are not tied to a particular time in history. Nor is it an accident that just those theories are present and that the poet cannot choose among them. The conflict among three theories of poetry is as old as our Western tradition. It goes back to Plato and Aristotle, and behind them to their precursors. It may be followed through all the languages and cultures that inherit the Greek tradition, the tradition, as it has been called, of Occidental metaphysics. Moreover, the conflict among these three theories of poetry is woven into the fabric of our language. It is present in the fundamental metaphors and concepts of our speech. To use that language is to be caught in a weblike interplay among terms that makes it impossible to adopt one theory of poetry without being led, willy-nilly, to encounter the ambiguous inherence within it of the other two. The three theories are not, then, alternatives among which one may choose. Their contradictory inherence in one another generates the meditative search for "what will suffice" in Stevens' poetry.

One theory of poetry operative in Stevens' work is the idea that poetry is imitation, mimesis, analogy, copy. Truth is measured by the *adequatio* between the structure of words and the structure of nonlinguistic reality. Poetry is mirroring or matching at a distance, by analogy. The structure of the poem should correspond to the structure of reality.

Things as they are on the blue guitar must match things as they are in nature. This "Aristotelean" theory of poetry as imitation has been dominant down through all the centuries since Aristotle, for example, in nineteenth- and twentieth-century theories of realism in narrative fiction.

Already in Aristotle, however, the notion that poetry is imitation was inextricably involved with the theory of poetry as unveiling, as uncovering, as revelation, as *alētheia.* Poetry is not a mirror but a lamp. The words of poetry are that within which the truth comes to light. This assumes that reality, things as they are, is initially hidden. Language is what discovers things, that is to say, reveals them as what they are, in their being. Martin Heidegger's "Der Ursprung des Kunstwerkes" is a distinguished modern essay exploring the definition of art as *alētheia,* but a key passage of Aristotle's *On the Art of Poetry* already turns on the conflict between poetry as imitation and poetry as revelation. "As to its general origin," says Aristotle,

> we may say that Poetry has sprung from two causes, each of them a thing inherent in human nature. The first is the habit of imitation; for to imitate is instinctive with mankind; and man is superior to the other animals, for one thing, in that he is the most imitative of creatures, and learns at first by imitation. Secondly, all men take a natural pleasure in the products of imitation. . . . The explanation of this delight lies in a further characteristic of our species, the appetite for learning; for among human pleasures that of learning is the keenest. . . .

Imitation, argues Aristotle, is natural to man, part of man's nature, therefore part of nature, not opposed to it as the lie is to the truth. Imitation is not only natural to man. It is also natural for him to take pleasure in it. He takes pleasure in it because he learns by it. He learns by it the nature of things as they are, which without this imitation in words would be invisible. The *logos* as being comes into the open by way of the *logos* as words. The *logos* as the one is caught and expressed in the *logos* as the many, as differentiated, as dramatic action, as metaphor.

Poetry, according to this second theory, is an act. It is the act of the mind seeking a revelation through the words and in the words. Poetry is a revelation in the visible and reasonable of that which as the base of reason cannot be faced directly or said directly. Aristotle's example of that which cannot be shown directly on the stage because it is irrational is Oedipus' murder of Laius, the son's murder of the father. In the same way the poetry of imitation, the *logos* captured in language, is the annihilation of the *logos* as the hidden one. This annihilation cannot be shown directly, though it is the source of all poetry, for the moment of the origin of language cannot be shown in language: "in the events of the drama itself there should be nothing that does not square with our reason; but if an irrational element cannot be avoided, it must like outside of the tragedy proper, as in the case of Sophocles' *Oedipus the King.*" In the same way, in stanza XXVI of **"The Man with the Blue Guitar,"** Stevens speaks of "the murderous alphabet." Poetry is the filial inheritor of the paternal energy or will in nature that will subjugate that father. As for Aristotle the murder of Laius cannot be shown directly, so for Stevens

the "nothing that is" stands between the poet and the subject of his poetry. Both imagination and reality are liable at any moment to turn into this nothing, the "blank at the base." "Reality is a vacuum" in one of the **"Adagia."** In stanza XII of **"The Man with the Blue Guitar"** the poet in his strumming picks up "That which momentously declares / Itself not to be I and yet / Must be. It could be nothing else." In **"The Snow Man"** Stevens speaks of "Nothing that is not there and the nothing that is." A movement of thought parallel to that of Aristotle in *On the Art of Poetry* may be found in stanza XIX of Stevens' **"The Man with the Blue Guitar":**

> That I may reduce the monster to
> Myself, and then may be myself
>
> In face of the monster, be more than part
> Of it, more than the monstrous player of
>
> One of its monstrous lutes, not be
> Alone, but reduce the monster and be,
>
> Two things, the two together as one,
> And play of the monster and of myself,
>
> Or better not of myself at all,
> But of that as its intelligence,
>
> Being the lion in the lute
> Before the lion locked in stone.

For Stevens, as for Aristotle, imitation is natural to man; therefore the imagination is part of nature or one of the forces of nature. In imitation, nature comes into language so that language is part of nature too. In poetry the *logos* or "being" comes to be in language. Poetry is the "intelligence" of nature. Stevens is not satisfied to produce poetry that is adjacent to nature or merely part of it. He must "reduce the monster," engulf him, appropriate the monster entirely to himself. When the two have become one, then poetry will not be "about" nature but will be the "intelligence" of nature speaking directly. Only then can the poet "be himself " in the face of the monster. Poetry is the destruction of things as they are when the are played on the blue guitar. It is the defeat of the lion in the stone by the lion in the lute.

In one of his letters to Renato Poggioli Stevens provides a commentary on stanza XIX of **"The Man with the Blue Guitar":**

> Monster
> =nature, which I desire to reduce: master, subjugate, acquire complete control over and use freely for my own purpose, as poet. I want, as poet, to be that in nature, which constitutes nature's very self. I want to be nature in the form of a man, with all the resources of nature = I want to be the lion in the lute; and then, when I am, I want to face my parent and be his true part. I want to face nature the way two lions face one another—the lion in the lute facing the lion locked in stone. I want, as a man of the imagination, to write poetry with all the power of a monster equal in strength to that of the monster about whom I write. I want man's imagination to be completely adequate in the face of reality.

The Oedipal drama, the son's mortal battle with his father, is muted in stanza XIX itself, but emerges openly in the commentary in the letter. The poet must face his "parent" nature and appropriate his sexual power, "be his true part." Only in this way can man's imagination be completely adequate in the face of reality.

There is, however, still a third theory of poetry present in Stevens' poems. This is the notion that poetry is creation, not discovery. In this theory, there is nothing outside the text. All meaning comes into existence with language and in the interplay of language. Meaning exists only in the poem. **"The Man with the Blue Guitar"** is poetry about poetry. It is meta-poetry, a poetry of grammar in which what counts is the play of words among themselves. Words are repeated, grammatical forms change and alter, and the same word is verb, adjective, noun, in turn. **"The Man with the Blue Guitar"** is poetry about poery also in the sense that the poem itself is the action about which it talks. The pervasive metaphor of a man playing the guitar is the action of the poem itself as it takes shape. The true subject is the poem as an activity. The words about guitars and tunes are the construction blocks of a poem that accomplishes what the metaphor only talks about. Language is always referential. There must be real guitars in order for there to be a word "guitar." Nevertheless, the word "guitar" in the poem, in its interplay with all the other words, effaces any real guitar in its poetic operation. As the word "guitar" is absorbed into its interaction with other words and comes to draw its meaning from that interaction, any referential base gradually disappears and is finally abolished. Even the guitar of Picasso, which seems as if it might be referred to by the central image, is irrelevant. This may explain why Stevens in a letter told Poggioli, gently but firmly, that he did not want Picasso's *Man with a Guitar* on the cover of Poggioli's Italian translation of a group of Stevens' poems.

An interplay between metaphor and reality in which the two change places, like the hermetic egg mentioned by William Butler Yeats, which turns inside out constantly without breaking its shell, is characteristic of the structure of thought I am trying to identify. Plato, for example, must use the "metaphor" of "inscription" to describe the good kind of writing in the soul, though writing is for him secondary and derived. In the same way, Yeats must use sexual metaphors to describe the intradivine life: "God-head on Godhead in sexual spasm begot / Godhead" ["Ribh in Ecstasy"]. Things below are copies, but that which is copied can come into language only by way of the transfers of metaphor. In that sense, things above are copies of what is below. Aristotle describes metaphor—"the application to one thing of the name that belongs to another"—as the fundamental instrument of poetry: "But most important by far is it to have a command of metaphor. This is the one thing the poet cannot learn from others. It is the mark of genius; for to coin good metaphors involves an insight into the resemblances between objects that are superficially unlike" [*On the Art of Poetry*]. The difficulty, however, is to decide in the labyrinth of interchanges which is the metaphor, which the literal origin. In **"The Man with the Blue Guitar,"** the "realistic level," that is, the words describing a man with a guitar, turns out to be the derived, metaphorical level. The words and images of the poem describe the activity of the poem itself. Moreover, the language of the poem is made up of the interplay between language about reality and language about the mind in which the two change places continuously. An example is all the terms for air, weather, or atmosphere, which describe not only the external weather but "air" as melody or as behavior. Words describing the world must be used to describe the mind, for there are no literal words for subjective events. Nevertheless, the things of the external world accede to language only through words. Words are products of the imagination, so that things as they are are things as they are said on the blue guitar, according to this third of the three theories of poetry that are woven inextricably together in the text of **"The Man with the Blue Guitar."**

My explanation of Stevens by way of the presence in his work of three traditional theories of poetry is, the reader will have noticed, an example of that interpretation by way of origins that I began by challenging, with the help of Foucault. Multiple origins are still origins and imply a causal accounting, however contradictory. The power of Stevens, the power in fact of any great writer, cannot be explained by any of its sources. Holly Stevens' recent *Souvenirs and Prophesies* is a presentation, with commentary, of her father's early journals and poems. It is a good place to investigate further this question of origins.

The interest of *Souvenirs and Prophecies* is partly anecdotal. If one admires (that is hardly the word) Wallace Stevens' poetry, one is interested in every scrap of information about Stevens the man. It is nice to know that the author of **Notes toward a Supreme Fiction** was once a somewhat mawkish, sentimental, moody, shy, socially awkward young man. This young man wrote indubitably bad verses ("Some of one's early things give one the creeps," he wrote in 1950). He earnestly exhorted himself to work hard and to rise in the world. He sometimes smoked too many cigars and drank too much, made resolutions about not drinking and smoking, and then broke them, recording the breakings with defiant verve in his journal, as in the entry for July 26, 1903, written soon after Stevens graduated from New York Law School and took up his clerkship in W. G. Peckham's office:

> I've just been reading my journal. A month or two ago I was looking forward to a cigarless, punchless weary life. *En effet,* since then I have smoked Villar y Villars & Cazadores, dine at Mouquin's on French artichokes & new corn etc. with a flood of drinks from crême de cassis melée, through Burgundy, Chablis etc. to sloe gin with Mexican cigars & French cigaroots. I have lunched daily on—Heaven's knows what not (I recall a delicious calf's heart cooked whole & served with peas—pig that I am). . . .

The Stevens who emerges from these early journals is on the whole an engaging youth. He is calculated to encourage later youths to write more bad verses in the hope that these may be, as Stevens' were, the prelude to greatness. But "hang it," as Stevens says of the Frenchman who called the Canadian Rockies low, "one wants more." Most readers will search out *Souvenirs and Prophecies* for clues to the meanings and sources of Stevens' mature poetry. We want to know where that poetry comes from and how to read it. Even in the light of the best secondary studies the major poems remain to a considerable degree opaque. They speak with indubitable authority and power. They have the accent of greatness. Nevertheless, they resist analysis. The most powerful attraction of *Souvenirs and Prophecies* is the reader's hope that he may find some help in dissolving this opacity. This is the lure of explanation by origins, the *post hoc ergo propter hoc*. Somehow, where Stevens began must be capable of explaining where he went.

To a considerable degree the reader's hunger for help is satisfied. *Souvenirs and Prophecies* shows that the young Stevens was already absorbed by the turn of the seasons; the circuits of the sun and moon fascinated him. Already he saw the sun as a king: "The day of the sun is like the day of a king. It is a promenade in the morning, a sitting on the throne at noon, a pageant in the evening" (April 20, 1904). Clouds, stars, flowers, birds, the whole panoply of colors ("God! What a thing blue is!" he wrote on April 18, 1904), that abiding double fantasy of a green mountain range on the one hand and "a warm sea booming on a tropical coast", on the other—all these are already present in the early journals. There also are the vague outlines of Stevens' particular version of the ancient Occidental metaphysical system of concepts involving the presence of the present and the fleeting revelation of being in the vanishing of the instant. This conceptual system is associated always in Stevens, as in the Western tradition generally, with the rising and setting of the sun. The reader will find evidence in Stevens' journals of his early interest in the tradition of the maxim: La Rochefoucauld, Pascal, Leopardi, "Schopenhauer's psychological observations," etc. This interest flowered in the **"Adagia"** and in the aphoristic discontinuities so important in the poetry. Support would also be found in *Souvenirs and Prophecies* for a demonstration of Stevens' complex relation to the romantic tradition. He read Wordsworth, Shelley, Keats, Emerson, Whitman, and Santayana, but also Nerval, Schopenhauer, Nietzsche, and Leopardi. (This relation has been explored in Harold Bloom's distinguished book on Stevens, *Wallace Stevens: The Poems of Our Climate.*) The reader will find, finally, in what he learns in *Souvenirs and Prophecies* of Stevens' relations to his parents and of his courtship of Elsie Moll, the outlines of his version of the "family romance," a romance dramatized continuously in the later poetry.

All these relations between the Stevens of the early journals and poems and the Stevens of the great later poetry would support explanations by genetic cause. Nevertheless, the authentic voice of Stevens as a poet is not touched by such explanations. That voice is something unpredictable, savage, violent, without cause or explanation, irrational—as he always knew genuine poetry must be. It is both a voice and a way of writing. It is something continuous, a murmuring or muttering, sometimes a sing-song rhyme or a stammering alliteration. Continuously present, it is nevertheless a principle of discontinuity. It forbids explication by sources. It breaks both into the formal order of

thought and into the formal order of shapely poetry. This voice appears intermittently and faintly even in these early journals and poems, as in the passage about the calf's heart quoted above. Of course it is much more evident in the poetry beginning with **Harmonium** and after, as in **"Bantams in Pine-Woods"** ("Chieftain Iffucan of Azcan in caftan / Of tan with henna hackles, halt!"), or in **"The Man with the Blue Guitar"** ("To strike his living hi and ho, / To tick it, tock it, turn it true, / To bang it from a savage blue, / Jangling the metal of the strings . . . "), or in **"Montrachet-le-Jardin"** ("O bright, / The chick, the chidder-barn and grassy chives / And great moon, cricket-impresario, / And, hoy, the impopulous purple-plated past, / Hoy, hoy, the blue bulls kneeling down to rest. / Chome! clicks the clock . . . "), or in **"The Owl in the Sarcophagus"** ("she that in the syllable between life / And death cries quickly, in a flash of voice, / Keep you, keep you, I am gone, oh keep you as / My memory, is the mother of us all . . . ").

The intrusion of this doubling voice is figured in Stevens, among other ways, by the constant presence, just below the level of rational thinking, of the guitarist with his interminable strumming ("Nothing about him ever stayed the same, / Except this hidalgo and his eye and tune . . . "), or it is figured in that other sail of Ulysses, doubling the first one and "Alive with an enigma's flittering." The presence of this "enigma"—in the words and yet not directly named by the words—forbids any understanding of Stevens' poetry by way of origins in his family, in his reading, in the "Western tradition," in "Occidental metaphysics," in the landscapes of Pennsylvania, New Jersey, and Connecticut, or even in some intrinsic irrational property of language. In the end, the greatest value of *Souvenirs and Prophecies* is that now and then the early writing shows the first flitterings of this groundless enigma. Occasionally a strange voice appears between or behind the young Stevens' words. This is that austere and impersonal "Chome!" without which Stevens would not be the great poet he is.

To identify this disrupting element in Stevens' poetry, if it is neither imitation, nor "Being," nor merely the play of language, would require a full reading of his work. Even then, it may be that the identification would be a discovery of what cannot be named or identified in so many words, even figurative ones. In **"A Primitive Like an Orb"** the sun, "at the centre on the horizon," the presumed literal object for which the rest of the poem is a series of figurative displacements strung in appositive chains, cannot be named directly, just as the sun cannot be looked at directly. To name the sun "literally" would falsify the perpetual movement of the "as" structure of the poem. According to this structure, whatever may be named or seen is "an illusion, as it was, / Oh as, always too heavy for the sense / To seize, the obscurest as, the distant was . . . ". The title of the poem, **"A Primitive Like an Orb,"** exemplifies a linguistic structure in which the word "sun," if it were to be cited, would become in its turn only another figure for the "essential poem at the centre of things." Only as not cited literally, as effaced, absent can the word "sun" retain its status as the literal name for something that can be perceived, viewed with the naked eye, "theoretically," taking "perceived" in both the etymological sense of "seen" and in the conceptual sense of "logically understood." If the theory of poetry is the life of poetry, it is also the case that "Poetry must resist the intelligence almost successfully." The moment when the poem ceases to resist the intelligence and can be "seen through" theoretically may be the moment when the poem fails. It then fails any longer to bear a relation, even figurative, to that "Chome!" the essential poem at the center of things, which may be neither named, nor seen, nor possessed theoretically. (pp. 274-85)

> *J. Hillis Miller, "Theoretical and Atheoretical in Stevens," in* Wallace Stevens: A Celebration, *edited by Frank Doggett and Robert Buttel, Princeton University Press, 1980, pp. 274-85.*

Roy Harvey Pearce   (essay date 1980)

[*Pearce is an American educator and critic who has written extensively on nineteenth- and twentieth-century American literature. His works on Stevens include* The Act of the Mind: Essays on the Poetry of Wallace Stevens *(1965), which he edited with J. Hillis Miller, and* The Continuity of American Poetry *(1961). In the following excerpt, he examines the concept of decreation, which Stevens adopted from the philosophy of Simone Weil, in Stevens's theory of poetry and in several poems.*]

Coming upon the word "decreation," Stevens of course came upon just that—a word, not a concept. For the concept had been almost from the outset integral to what he came compulsively to call the theory of poetry. Compulsively, because that theory, could he perfect it, would support his need to solve in poems the romanticist subject-object problem, which was set for him by his understanding of the role of the poet in the modern world. Granting the presence, however varying, of the *concept* of decreation in Stevens' oeuvre, we must observe that the word "modern" is the operative term in the last sentence of this, the well-known passage in **"The Relations between Poetry and Painting"** (1951):

> This [new] reality is, also, the momentous world of poetry. Its instantaneities are the familiar intelligence of poets, although it has been the intelligence of another ambiance. Simone Weil in *La

Pesanteur et La Grâce has a chapter on what she calls decreation. She says that decreation is making pass from the created to the uncreated, but that destruction is making pass from the created to nothingness. Modern reality is a reality of decreation, in which our revelations are not the revelations of belief, but the precious portents of our own powers.

Now, treating of the reality/imagination problem, as is well known, is Stevens' central concern at the level of theory in the essays he collected in *The Necessary Angel* (1951). But it had, at least immanently, been his central concern in the practice of poetry almost from the beginning. By 1947, setting himself straight in the first of his **"Three Academic Pieces,"** he is at once bold and succinct:

> We have been trying to get at a truth about poetry, to get at one of the principles that compose the theory of poetry. It comes to this, that poetry is a part of the structure of reality. If this has been demonstrated, it pretty much amounts to saying that the structure of poetry and the structure of reality are one or, in effect, that poetry and reality are one, or should be. This may be less thesis than hypothesis.

One way of looking at the development of Stevens' poetry, then, would be to trace the development of hypothesis into thesis. And here decreation—first as a condition of the working of the imagination, then as a process, and finally as an integral component of poetic realization—is primary in Stevens' theory of poetry and in the working of the poems themselves.

I have said that the operative word in the passage I have quoted from **"The Relations between Poetry and Painting"** is "modern." Stevens himself in this essay prepares us for his emphasis on the word as he earlier sketches a brief history of French classicism, in whose period reality was not that of decreation, precisely because "revelations" could in fact be those of "belief." So too in a passage in **"The Noble Rider and the Sound of Words"** (1942). So too in a number of poems—**"Sad Strains of a Gay Waltz"** (1935), **"Mozart, 1935"** (1935), the two parts of **"Botanist on Alp"** (1934, 1935), **"Asides on the Oboe"** (1940), and **"Of Modern Poetry"** (1940). The last named begins

> The poem of the mind in the act of finding
> What will suffice. It has not always had
> To find: the scene was set; it repeated what
> Was in the script.
>   Then the theatre was changed
> To something else. Its past was a souvenir.
> It has to be living, to learn the speech of the place.
> It has to face the men of the time and to meet
> The women of the time. It has to think about war
> And it has to find what will suffice. It has
> To construct a new stage.

First Stevens defines the nature of poetry in the modern world, with its need to realize its special reality principle. Then he indicates that in the past, reality had somehow been different, during periods, to glance back at the passage I have quoted from **"The Relations between Poetry and Painting,"** in which "revelations" of reality were indeed "revelations" of belief. What formerly sufficed no longer does, since finding is no longer repetition but rather what Stevens would come to call decreation—living by learning the speech of the place, itself uncreated, just perdurably there. The poems I have named were collected in *Ideas of Order* (1935) and *Parts of a World* (1942), a period during which intellectual historians were discovering a series of past *Weltanschauungen* in which cultures were understood to be integrated to the degree that men's imaginings of reality—because it was made out to be "created"—were virtually guaranteed to be accurate. For those realities, specifically because they were under the aegis of a single unifying power, were tightly and coherently ordered to the degree that there had to be a consonance of the imagination and reality, of (to use the Emersonian terms) the Me and the Not-Me. In a letter of December 10, 1935, Stevens—as so often, in accord with the scholarship of the period—finds the right technical word for this situation: "myth." And in a letter of June 3, 1953, thinking about **"The Comedian as the Letter C"** (1923) in long perspective, he concludes that it is after all an "anti-mythological poem." That poem of course was first published in *Harmonium*. Stevens' comment on it indicates, as I have noted, that early on he viewed modern reality not as something so ordered as to lead to mythic understanding—this via the consonance of imagination and reality—but as indeed a reality of decreation.

In the poems of *Harmonium* (1923) and of *The Man with the Blue Guitar* (1937), decreation is a condition of the imagination as it is operative on reality. The imagination must be brought to grant that reality, given, in and of itself exists prior to and independent of such transformations that the imagination may and in fact does work on it. The imagination cannot absorb reality, yet it cannot do what it must do unless in so doing it acknowledges the absolute and separate existence of reality. The alternative at this stage is production or reduction—seeing the world, and thus transforming it, or thinking about it, and thus decreating it. Stevens' method here, when decreation is involved, is quite simply the method of reduction—or negation—as a way of thinking about the world. But what is reduced/negated is not the world, reality (for that is by definition impossible), but rather the imagination itself. Such a reduction/negation is, however, only temporary, a way on to a further stage; for as I have said, quoting Stevens, in the course of projecting the decreative process, the imagination discovers "the precious portents of its own powers." The intention—it is as simple as this—is to bring oneself to admit that there *is* a "reality," and so to conceive of the imagination in all its potential freedom. Thus **"Negations"** (1918), which was originally the seventh in the **"Lettres d'un Soldat"** sequence:

> Hi! The creator too is blind,
> Struggling toward his harmonious whole,
> Rejecting intermediate parts,
> Horrors and falsities and wrongs;
> Incapable master of all force,
> Too vague idealist, overwhelmed
> By an afflatus that persists.
> For this, then, we endure brief lives,
> The evanescent symmetries
> From that meticulous potter's thumb.

Here the myth of the creator is rejected, proven wrong, negated, since no one can be "master of all force." What is left is ourselves, facing up to the facts and conditions of our "brief lives," which, in the necessarily short run, even if we live beyond seventy, are our realities. The symmetries are "evanescent," not, as Blake would have it, "fearful," precisely because they are what Stevens, other poets, and writers about poetry have come to call "myths."

In this stage of Stevens' "theory," then, decreation as a condition of making poems marks a beginning, the acceptance of the limits of the imagination that is the necessary condition of its exercise. At the end of **"The Snow Man"** (1921) we are told what it would be like, not what it is, to move all the way through the decreative process:

> the listener, who listens in the snow,
> And, nothing himself, beholds
> Nothing that is not there and the nothing that
>   is.

At the end of **"Anecdote of the Jar"** (1919) we are again told, still analogically:

> It took dominion everywhere.
> The jar was gray and bare.
> It did not give of bird or bush,
> Like nothing else in Tennessee.

And Stevens in the last section of **"Nuances of a Theme by Williams"** (1918) addresses Williams' "ancient star" thus:

> Lend no part to any humanity that suffuses
>   you in its own light.

(It will be recalled that later, in 1934 and 1946, Stevens, for all his fondness for Williams' verse, found him somewhat too given to the "anti-poetic," and thus for a poet—for any man of imagination, as he was fond of saying—somewhat subservient to "reality.")

A concern with decreation, and thus with the role of reduction and negation, is, to be sure, not the primary theme of the *Harmonium* poems. (In general, they portray and celebrate the imagination's productive transformations of reality.) But it is there often enough to let us see it as immanent even in Stevens' earliest work. I would cite as further examples **"The Paltry Nude Starts on a Spring Voyage"** (1919), **"Fabliau of Florida"** (1919), **"Of the Surface of Things"** (1919), **"The Wind Shifts"** (1917), and **"The Indigo Glass in the Grass"** (1919). And it is set forth with firmness and certitude in stanza V of **"The Man with the Blue Guitar,"** as though the poet had once and for all, in his search for a theory of poetry, established for himself what is no less than a reciprocal relationship between decreation and creation:

> Do not speak to us of the greatness of poetry,
> Of the torches wisping in the underground,
>
> Of the structure of vaults upon a point of light.
> There are no shadows in our sun,
>
> Day is desire and night is sleep.
> There are no shadows anywhere.
>
> The earth, for us, is flat and bare,
> There are no shadows. Poetry

Exceeding music must take the place
Of empty heaven and its hymns,

Ourselves in poetry must take their place,
Even in the chattering of your guitar.

The motif here—the capacity to face the sun-as-reality
and its decreated earth ("flat and bare")—registers the full
acceptance of man's (the imagination's, the mind's) condition vis-à-vis modern reality, a reality of decreation.

Since what is at issue in the **Harmonium** poems—and
what is affirmed in **"The Man with the Blue Guitar"**—is
acceptance, an affirmation of decreative condition, one
could say that all this was Stevens' discovery, in his own
"modern" terms, of Keats' "negative capability"—this as
a condition of final "recreation." If so, it is appropriate to
term Stevens' later emphasis on decreation as process and
realization as moving, out of some historical necessity,
into a "negating capability." That is, decreation is no longer just a stage or a state to be, however unflinchingly,
taken into account. Now it has become a stage or a state
to be worked through. On the way to what end? To authentic creation as in fact realization, recreation.

This is the end repeatedly emphasized in the essays collected in *The Necessary Angel:*

> The mind has added nothing to human nature.
> It is a violence from within that protects us from
> a violence without. It is the imagination pressing
> back against the pressure of reality. It seems, in
> the last analysis, to have something to do with
> our self-preservation; and that, no doubt, is why
> the expression of it, the sound of its words, helps
> us to live our lives.

> Summed up, our position at the moment is that
> the poet must get rid of the hieratic in everything
> that concerns him and must move constantly in
> the direction of the credible. He must create his
> unreal out of what is real.

> The accuracy of accurate letters is an accuracy
> with respect to the structure of reality.

> Thus, if we desire to formulate an accurate theo-
> ry of poetry, we find it necessary to examine the
> structure of reality, because reality is the central
> reference for poetry.

> My final point, then, is that the imagination is
> the power that enables us to perceive the normal
> in the abnormal, the opposite of chaos in chaos.

To create the unreal out of the real one must somehow
come directly to know the real, not just accept and affirm
its existence. This, I take it, is in general the end aspired
to in the poems collected in *Transport to Summer* (1947).
The central poem of those collected in that volume is of
course *Notes toward a Supreme Fiction.* Its centrality derives from the fact that, being one of the earliest published
poems (1942) in the volume, it at once exemplifies and
comprehends the place of decreation in the originative,
initiating act out of which proceed virtually all the poems
collected along with it. (I continue to think that **"Esthétique du Mal"** [1944] should be considered integral to the
Notes. Hence the titles of the sequence should read: **"It
Must Be Abstract," "It Must Change," "It Must Give**

Pleasure," and "It Must Give Pain.") If the intention of
the **Notes** is to move us toward proposition-by-proposition
understanding, then decreation is a necessary, mediating
phase in the process. The first section of **"It Must Be Abstract"** commands:

> Begin, ephebe, by perceiving the idea
> Of this invention, this invented world,
> The inconceivable idea of the sun.

> You must become an ignorant man again
> And see the sun again with an ignorant eye
> And see it clearly in the idea of it.

The young poet is instructed that he must grasp absolutely
(per-ceive) the hard fact that reality (the "world") for him,
even at its very source ("the sun"), can be known only as
something discovered (in-vented, come upon), that for
him it cannot be known as something created (conceived).
What is at stake is accepting an even larger and harder
fact, that of the nature of "invention" itself vis-à-vis what
Stevens would come, in **"The Relations between Poetry
and Painting,"** to term "modern reality," that is, "invention" as in-vention, discovery, in no way as creation. And
the necessary condition of such acceptance is a willingness
to acknowledge that ignorance—the ignorance deriving
from decreation—is a condition of whatever knowledge,
whatever *kind* of knowledge, that poetry might in the long
run generate. This granted, this affirmed, Stevens in the
rest of the section can calmly and grandly proclaim that
there is no "source" for reality, "modern reality": "Phoebus is dead. . . ." For us there can be no myths, chthonic
or otherwise. And in what follows in **Notes toward a Supreme Fiction,** Stevens, reminding us from time to time
that decreation is a condition of the working of his poem,
can as calmly and grandly maneuver his and our way toward that series of propositions that emerges from the
parts of the **Notes** as their absolutely inevitable titles. Reality is "abstract," since to know it under the condition of
decreation we must abstract from it the idea of a creator.
"Change," "pleasure," and also "pain" are its attributes,
since, once it is decreated, those are the affects of our "perceiving" it. Sponsored by no one, existing as nothing but
uncreated *Ding an Sich,* reality necessarily yields to perception that at long last conceivable idea of a Supreme Fiction. (pp. 286-94)

I am now ready to consider some poems in which decreation as process is explicitly the concern. For decreation as
process is but implicitly the concern of the **Notes.** Meditating on the real, Stevens is able to characterize its nature
as the imagination (a violence within protecting us from
the violence without, the agent whereby we may perceive
the normal in the abnormal, the opposite of chaos in
chaos), which lets us know and learn to live with it. Our
God truly, in the words of one of the **"Adagia,"** turns out
to be a postulate of the ego; yet reality—to look ahead—
cannot in the **Notes** quite be conceived (discovered, decreated, and re-created) as the ground of our being, our
Rock. **Notes toward a Supreme Fiction** is a powerful
poem, perhaps a great poem. But it does not, as a poem,
establish the conditions whereby a satisfactory (by Stevens' measure) theory of poetry could be generated. Indeed, I now see the poems collected in *Transport to Sum-*

mer (my notion of an extended *Notes* among them) as being preparatory for the transcending efforts of the poems collected in *The Auroras of Autumn* (1950) and the transcendent effort of the *Rock* sequence in the *Collected Poems* (1954).

Decreation as process is explicitly the concern of many of the post-*Notes* poems collected in *Transport to Summer*. (One should read "transport" in reference to both its old and new meanings.) In **"The Motive for Metaphor"** (1943) we (the poet addresses us as "you") are told why we shrink from decreative process; for would we/could we carry it through, we would have to bear "The weight of primary noon, / The A B C of being . . . ". In **"No Possum, No Sop, No Taters"** (1943) we are told that in this decreated scene, "It is here, in this bad, that we reach / The last purity of the knowledge of good." In stanzas XX-XXII of **"Chocorua to Its Neighbor"** (1943), the mountain, decreating itself, addresses its shadow and discovers the source of its own being:

> Now, I, Chocorua, speak of this shadow as
> A human thing. It is an eminence,
> But of nothing, trash of sleep that will disappear
> With the special things of night, little by little,
> In day's constellation, and yet remain, yet be,
>
> Not father, but bare brother, megalfrere,
> Or by whatever boorish name a man
> Might call the common self, interior fons.
> And fond, the total man of glubbal glub,
> Political tramp with an heraldic air,
>
> Cloud-casual, metaphysical neighbor,
> But resting on me, thinking in my snow,
> Physical if the eye is quick enough,
> So that, where he was, there is an enkindling,
>   where
> He is, the air changes and grows fresh to
>   breathe.

In **"Crude Foyer"** (1947), we are told

> That there lies at the end of thought
> A foyer of the spirit in a landscape
> Of the mind, in which we sit
> And wear humanity's bleak crown. . . .

The motifs in these and other poems of their order in *Transport to Summer* are summed up in these lines from stanza V of **"Repetitions of a Young Captain"** (1944):

> On a few words of what is real in the world
> I nourish myself. I defend myself against
> Whatever remains.

Not: I am master of all I survey. Rather: I can become master of all that surveys me.

What is at issue here is not only the decreative process insofar as the imagination is capable of it or can bear it, but also the role of that process in the imagination's lifelong project of carrying out its task, at once realizing its own violence and somehow protecting itself against the realization:

> It is time that beats in the breast and it is time
> That batters against the mind, silent and proud,
> The mind that knows it is destroyed by time.
>
> **("The Pure Good of Theory,"** 1945)

In **"Credences of Summer"** (1947), particularly in its seventh section (which, so he wrote in a letter of June 18, 1953, was one of his favorite parts of the poem), Stevens is quite explicit as regards the role of the decreative process:

> Far in the woods they sang their unreal songs,
> Secure. It was difficult to sing in face
> Of the object. The singers had to avert them-
>   selves
> Or else avert the object. Deep in the woods
> They sang of summer in the common fields.
>
> They sang desiring an object that was near,
> In face of which desire no longer moved,
> Nor made of itself that which it could not
>   find . . .
> Three times the concentred self takes hold, three
>   times
> The thrice concentred self, having possessed
>
> The object, grips it in savage scrutiny,
> Once to make captive, once to subjugate
> Or yield to subjugation, once to proclaim
> The meaning of the capture, this hard prize,
> Fully made, fully apparent, fully found.

The singers have faced reality (the "object") and have retreated "far in the woods" to sing songs unreal because conceived in the face of the real—in which, as they faced it, they came to understand that they could not find themselves. The dialectic (for that is what it is) of the making of their songs is now understood to be of three stages: first, discovery of the object as reality; second and alternatively, either subjugating reality or being subjugated by it, that is, transformation or decreation; third, realization and celebration of the meaning that man, having confronted reality either as transformed or decreated, can give to his world. This last stage, as it derives from the first alternative of the second stage (transformation) yields poems of a dramatic or narrative or purely lyrical nature, such as **"Sunday Morning," "Le Monocle de Mon Oncle," "The Emperor of Ice-Cream," "Bantams in Pine-Woods,"** and all the *Harmonium* poems that are so easily available to us—easily, because as readers we find it easier to work through the transformative than the decreative mode. This last stage, then, as it derives from the second alternative of the second stage (decreation), yields meditative poems, ranging from cautious poems like **"The Snow Man"** and **"Anecdote of the Jar"** to bold poems like *Notes toward a Supreme Fiction,* **"Credences of Summer"** itself, and the great work of *The Auroras of Autumn* and the *Rock* sequence—poems not easily available to us because, reading them, we must work through that decreative mode that requires denial and doubt as a condition of achievement and certitude.

Surely, by now we easily grant that Stevens is at his greatest as a meditative poet. Integral to the meditative mode, I suggest, is decreation. What makes Stevens' meditative poems so assuredly "modern" is precisely their attending to "modern reality" as a "reality of decreation." In them Stevens realizes the Carlylean proposition with which he had begun **"The Well Dressed Man with a Beard"** (1941):

After the final no there comes a yes
And on that yes the future world depends.

Whereas this poem ends with the statement that "It can never be satisfied, the mind, never," in the great later meditative poems the mind—working through the decreative process—can indeed find its satisfactions.

Increasingly, a criterion of formal excellence, of artistic achievement in Stevens' later poems becomes the *quality* of their dialectic, as much the analytic precision of their movement as the synthesizing capacity of their tropes, their language as *topoi*. Here, above all, the act of the mind is central. Stevens himself was, however uneasily, quite conscious of this fact. In a letter of May 3, 1949, he claimed that he had "never" had "any serious contact with philosophy," yet he went on to write:

> It may be that the title of my next book will be *The Auroras of Autumn* [the poem had been published about a year before], but this is some little distance ahead and I may not like that title by-and-by as much as I like it now. Nor is there anything autobiographical about it. What underlies this sort of thing is the drift of one's ideas. From the imaginative period of the *Notes* I turned to the ideas of "Credences of Summer." At the moment I am at work on a thing called "An Ordinary Evening in New Haven." . . . But here my interest is to try to get as close to the ordinary, the commonplace and the ugly as it is possible for a poet to get. It is not a question of grim reality but of plain reality. The object is of course to purge oneself of anything false. I have been doing this since the beginning of March and intend to keep studying the subject and working on it until I am quite through with it. This is not in any sense a turning away from the ideas of "Credences of Summer": it is a development of those ideas. That sort of thing . . . would have to do with the drift of one's ideas.

From this point on, what is paramount in Steven's poems, the meditative poems, is precisely "the drift of [his] ideas," the "development of [his] ideas," variously moving through the three-stage dialectic of "Credences of Summer." If in decreation he can "purge [himself] of anything false," then, and only then, will he be able

> to proclaim
> The meaning of the capture, this hard prize,
> Fully made, fully apparent, fully found.

I cannot understand the resistance of some of Stevens' exegetes to the fact of this dialectic and to the demands it put upon him, not to say them, to take with all seriousness poetry as "the act of the mind."

If we are to understand the poems collected in *The Auroras of Autumn* and the *Rock* sequence, we must above all attend to "drift" as it is transformed into dialectic, so as to achieve to the utmost possible limit a certain apodictic quality. "The Auroras of Autumn" (1948) succeeds marvelously in this mode. We are given successively, dialectically, a meditative lyric on evil itself figured as a serpent who is that Satan of "Esthétique du Mal" whom "a capital negation" (Satan: satan) had "destroyed," so that he must now be known as "uncreated," a fact of that reality which is life itself. Now, his true power and its locus admitted, he is truly *redivivus,* a violence among other violences. Then Stevens works through negations/decreations of a place and a situation, both of them warmly domestic, then a negation/decreation of what has just been negated/decreated:

> The cancellings,
> The negations are never final. The father sits
> In space, wherever he sits, of bleak regard,
>
> As one that is strong in the bushes of his eyes.
> He says no to no and yes to yes. He says yes
> To no; and in saying yes he says farewell.

After the first four sections there follows a sequence in which there is announced that which is "fully made, fully apparent, fully found." In the last part of the final section Stevens writes:

> Turn back to where we were when we began:
> An unhappy people in a happy world.
> Now, solemnize the secretive syllables.
>
> Read to the congregation, for today
> And for tomorrow, this extremity,
> This contrivance of the spectre of the spheres,
>
> Contriving balance to contrive a whole,
> The vital, the never-failing genius,
> Fulfilling his meditations, great and small.
>
> In these unhappy he meditates a whole,
> The full of fortune and the full of fate,
> As if he lived all lives, that he might know,
>
> In hall harridan, not hushful paradise,
> To a haggling of wind and weather, by these
>   lights
> Like a blaze of summer straw, in winter's nick.

"[W]here we were when we began"—modern reality is a reality of decreation.

Stevens' control of the drift of his ideas is surest, I think, in "The Auroras of Autumn." There are of course other powerful poems in the volume named after that one, in particular "Large Red Man Reading," "The Ultimate Poem Is Abstract," "The Owl in the Sarcophagus," "A Primitive Like an Orb," "What We See Is What We Think," and, of course, "An Ordinary Evening in New Haven." And I would add to this list "The Course of a Particular" (1951). None of these, however, achieves, as regards the dialectical, meditative mode, the absolute precision and control of "The Auroras of Autumn." Suffice it to say nevertheless that they all quite systematically project that mode, again and again reaching triumphant and transcending conclusions, like the one from "A Primitive Like an Orb":

> That's it. The lover writes, the believer hears,
> The poet mumbles and the painter sees,
> Each one, his fated eccentricity,
> As a part, but part, but tenacious particle,
> Of the skeleton of the ether, the total
> Of letters, prophecies, perceptions, clods
> Of color, the giant of nothingness, each one
> And the giant ever changing, living in change.

The "giant of nothingness" is at once lover, believer, poet, painter, altogether decreated, but by virtue of being de-created each is capable, should he work his fate all the way through, of being recreated and recreating.

Himself recreated and recreating, Stevens was able in the *Rock* sequence of the **Collected Poems** to achieve what I can only call transcendence. (We can count it among our worldly blessings that he lived long enough to bring the drift of his ideas to something of a stasis.) That sequence might well be called "Beyond Decreation." Although in the May 3, 1949, letter quoted above, Stevens denied that there was anything "autobiographical" about the drift of his ideas, the poems in the *Rock* sequence are autobiographical in a specifically American fashion, in which the poet, having moved all the way through the stages of discovery, decreation, and recreation, is now sure enough of himself, his role, and his powers to discover himself for us as central, archetypal, fully realizing "the precious portents of our own powers," because they are the precious portents of *his* own powers. In **"The Plain Sense of Things"** (1952), which is marked by a mood of calmness and certitude (transcendent as opposed to transcending), he reviews the matter of the seventh section of **"Credences of Summer"**:

> After the leaves have fallen, we return
> To a plain sense of things. It is as if
> We had come to an end of the imagination,
> Inanimate in an inert savoir.
>
> It is difficult even to choose the adjective
> For this blank cold, this sadness without cause.
> The great structure has become a minor house.
> No turban walks across the lessened floors.
>
> The greenhouse never so badly needed paint.
> The chimney is fifty years old and slants to one
>   side.
> A fantastic effort has failed, a repetition
> In a repetitiousness of men and flies.
>
> Yet the absence of the imagination had
> Itself to be imagined. The great pond,
> The plain sense of it, without reflections, leaves,
> Mud, water like dirty glass, expressing silence
>
> Of a sort, silence of a rat come out to see,
> The great pond and its waste of the lilies, all this
> Had to be imagined as an inevitable knowledge,
> Required, as a necessity requires.

The requirements of necessity, which derive from the requirements of decreation, are now known, if acknowledged and lived through, to constitute the requirements, in the face of modern reality, of life itself: thus the component of autobiography in these last poems.

Thus too, the actualizing of the ultimate poet, the hero, that possible, impossible philosopher's man. The Santayana of **"To an Old Philosopher in Rome"** (1952) is one such, because he knows and lives in the knowledge of

> The human end in the spirit's greatest reach,
> The extreme of the known in the presence of the
>   extreme
> Of the unknown.

Accordingly,

> It is a kind of total grandeur at the end,
> With every visible thing enlarged and yet
> No more than a bed, a chair and moving nuns,
> The immensest theatre, the pillared porch,
> The book and candle in your ambered room,
>
> Total grandeur of a total edifice,
> Chosen by an inquisitor of structures
> For himself. He stops upon this threshold,
> As if the design of all his words takes form
> And frame from thinking and is realized.

Stevens' own transcendent certitude, the certitude of a man "seventy years later" reviewing his life—and in reviewing it first decreating and then recreating it—is fully made, fully apparent, fully found in **"The Rock"** (1954):

> It is not enough to cover the rock with leaves.
> We must be cured of it by a cure of the ground
> Or a cure of ourselves, that is equal to a cure
>
> Of the ground, a cure beyond forgetfulness.
> And yet the leaves, if they broke into bud,
> If they broke into bloom, if they bore fruit,
>
> And if we ate the incipient colorings
> Of their fresh culls might be a cure of the
>   ground.
> The fiction of the leaves is the icon
>
> Of the poem, the figuration of blessedness,
> And the icon is the man.

Modern reality, decreated, is no longer known just in terms of its attributes (as in **Notes toward a Supreme Fiction**). Recreated, it is known directly, as man is at once integral to and transcendent of it.

> It is the rock where tranquil must adduce
> Its tranquil self, the main of things, the mind,
>
> The starting point of the human and the end,
> That in which space itself is contained, the gate
> To the enclosure, day, the things illumined
>
> By day, night and that which night illumines,
> Night and its midnight-minting fragrances,
> Night's hymn of the rock, as in a vivid sleep.

But at the very end, surely, there is a cautionary note, a suggestion of even the all-too-human limits of the poet as hero. It is given only to old—and wise—men to integrate, and thus to assuage, the violence within and the violence without, to know modern reality directly, and that only momentarily. In **"The Bed of Old John Zeller"** (1944; Zeller was his grandfather, long since dead) Stevens had written:

> It is more difficult to evade
> That habit of wishing and to accept the structure
> Of things as the structure of ideas. It was the
>   structure
> Of things at least that was thought of in the old
>   peak of night.

In a poem on "the mythology of modern death," **"The Owl in the Sarcophagus"** (1947), he had concluded of him who would see deepest into reality:

> It is a child that sings itself to sleep,
> The mind, among the creatures that it makes,

The people, those by which it lives and dies.

In **"Questions Are Remarks"** (1949) he had written of one who does not ask fundamental questions about reality:

> He does not say, "Mother, my mother, who are
>   you,"
> The way the drowsy, infant, old men do.

In **"Angel Surrounded by Paysans"** (1950), the "angel of reality," "the necessary angel of earth" in whose sight we "see the earth again," tells us that he is "A figure half seen, or seen for a moment . . . ". In **"An Old Man Asleep"** (1947), the first poem in the *Rock* sequence, we are instructed that only in sleep can the old man who is addressed know "The self and the earth—your thoughts, your feelings, / Your beliefs and disbeliefs, your whole peculiar plot . . . ".

Thus the passage from the last section of **"The Rock,"** which I have quoted above, figures critically in the dialectical drift of Stevens' ideas. In fact, the *Rock* sequence concludes with **"Not Ideas about the Thing but the Thing Itself "** (1954), the most direct of all of Stevens' accounts of the immediate (as opposed to ultimate) result of the decreative process. The "new knowledge of reality"—or something "like it"—that the poet so sharply celebrates comes to him "At the earliest ending of winter":

> He knew that he heard it,
> A bird's cry, at daylight or before,
> In the early March wind.
>
> The sun was rising at six,
> No longer a battered panache above snow . . .
> It would have been outside.
>
> It was not from the vast ventriloquism
> Of sleep's faded papier-mâché . . .
> The sun was coming from outside.

It is perhaps a direct vision, then, of reality, but in any case, only for an instant, and assuredly of something coming from outside, not a product of sleep, yet possible only immediately after sleep, as if it were the aftermath of a dream-vision. Decreation, in the end, does not yield a final yes. But it is not altogether a matter of the final no. It is rather a mode for him who would yield to his own capacity for a wise passivity—he who can, in his old man's wisdom, if only for a sleepy instant, achieve at least something "like" that "new knowledge of reality" whereby he may, waking, transcend himself. A "new knowledge of reality," achieved through decreation, is now understood to be penultimate to a new knowledge of self, as before it had been understood to be penultimate to the new knowledge that is poetry.

Thus, as it must now seem after the fact of Stevens' own life, the inevitability of **"A Child Asleep in Its Own Life"** (1954):

> Among the old men that you know,
> There is one, unnamed, that broods
> On all the rest, in heavy thought.
>
> They are nothing, except in the universe
> Of that single mind. He regards them
> Outwardly and knows them inwardly,

> The sole emperor of what they are,
> Distant, yet close enough to wake
> The chords above your bed to-night.

The **"Adagia"** entry immediately following the one I have quoted as the epigraph reads: "Reality is the object seen in its greatest common sense." Common sense: decreation: reality: the theory of poetry: the theory of life. From "a child asleep in its own life" toward the "ultimate poem." From "the final no" to "a yes" on which "the future world depends." As Stevens wrote Richard Eberhart (January 20, 1954), "poetry is not a literary activity: it is a vital activity. . . . The good writers are the good thinkers." (pp. 294-307)

> *Roy Harvey Pearce, "Toward Decreation: Stevens and the 'Theory of Poetry',"* in Wallace Stevens: A Celebration, *edited by Frank Doggett and Robert Buttel, Princeton University Press, 1980, pp. 286-307.*

Joseph N. Riddel (essay date 1980)

[*Riddel is an American educator and critic who has written extensively on American poetry in the twentieth century. Although his early formalist analyses of Stevens's poetry, which are collected in his* The Clairvoyant Eye: The Poetry and Poetics of Wallace Stevens *(1965), remain influential, he has been criticized for his recent post-structuralist and deconstructivist interpretations of Stevens's verse. In the following excerpt, Riddel examines identity, language, and meaning in "Esthétique du Mal," contending that the poem ruptures accepted forms of modernist representation and introduces a new relationship between text and world.*]

At the very beginning (albeit pseudo beginning) of **"Esthétique du Mal,"** a scene of writing: someone (a poet?) "writing letters home / And, between his letters, reading paragraphs / On the sublime." A double scene; a re-staging, as in the metaphors of another poem, **"Of Modern Poetry"**: one scene/stage displacing/repeating another; a rupture in the scene of writing; a "modern" scene, as it were, reduplicating an ancient "catastrophe." The writer/reader sitting at his cafe table in Naples is one of the expeditionary forces of modern poetry, always in-between, homeless, the impoverished heir of Wordsworth and Mallarmé, sufferer of a "mal" that he can understand only in the mediations of a venerable "book." The "book" he reads, book of the "sublime" (Longinus' if you will, but in a sense, simply *the* book), arranges a world in its totality and accounts for nature and history as a fallenness, as "the most correct catastrophe." The book "made sure" of catastrophe, gives it place in the order of things. But the writer can no longer read its "correct" modulations. "He could describe / The terror of the sound because the sound / Was ancient," because Vesuvius resounds (always already) in a Book of Nature that accounts for its sublimity, its significance. But the book cannot satisfy the "hunger" of a desire that has no object, an *angst*—the dis-ease that is marked by the exile of writing. The scene of writing that marks the beginning-again of **"Esthétique du Mal"** signifies a problematics of "modernism." It is not simply, as in **"Of Modern Poetry,"** that an old "theatre" has ceased to be and a new one has come to replace it—a scene of representation in which a proper script is repeated, being replaced by a scene that composes its own stage in an "act of the mind." For the old scene (book of the sublime or theater of representation) was already itself a fiction of fiction, an aesthetic of some proper fall or "mal," and the new stage can only repeat the necessity of representation. The modern scene of writing represents, as it were, the problematic scenario of representation. In a world from which the old gods have disappeared—or have, as Stevens says elsewhere and everywhere, become fictions—"The gaiety of language is our seigneur," we who are "Natives of poverty, children of malheur."

The writer/reader of **"Esthétique du Mal"** confronts the problematical rupture that Stevens inscribed in another titular metaphor, in **"Description without Place,"** of a writing without reference, of a "book" that organizes the world according to the "nostalgias." The book of the sublime may very well "describe / The terror of the sound because the sound / Was ancient," but it now accounts for a "total past" from which the writer is exiled. If the book makes "sure" of the "most correct catastrophe," of a nature and a history made orderly in the pattern of tragic fall, the book no longer feeds the hunger for such totalizations. Ex-centric, displaced, homeless, the modern writer signifies the exile of all writing. All the old books—the Book of Nature, the book of nostalgias, the truth of all "true sympathizers"—are displaced in the beginning-again of writing that is posed in **"Esthétique du Mal."** In the very first canto of the poem, the "self," that modern figuration of the logocentric idea of the author or authorizing presence, is suspended in the very gesture by which it displaces the old gods, the "over-human god." With the end of the book of the sublime, the order of displacements, the hierarchy of signifieds, is radically disrupted. And, as in poem II, the writer's "pain" marks an unbridgeable abyss between himself and the "supremacy" of the "moon," between the self and its figural source.

It is just this self, this substitution of the modern (romantic) center for the ancient soul, this displacement of an "over-human god," "oldest parent" and "reddest lord," by the "wholly human," that is in question. The excentricity of the writer in **"Esthétique du Mal"** produces an instability; it disrupts our thinking of the chain of substitutions or orderly movement of centers that has allowed poetry to reimagine the unity of theology, history, and aesthetics. The third stanza of **"Sunday Morning"** traces the displacement of gods or centers from Jove to Christ to man and prefigures the ex-centric violence of **"Esthétique du Mal."** Every polarity—sun/moon; heaven/hell; God/Satan; metaphysical/physical—is reversed. But beyond the reversal, the notion of a stable polarity, of orderly reversal, of hierarchy succeeding hierarchy, is put into play and made to tremble. The master term, that which might govern or center all the others, is brought into question, decentered—placed "sous rature," under erasure, as we might now say. **"Esthétique du Mal"** begins to plot a condition in which the self—that homeless and provisional center of the modern scene—becomes only another name of a center now lost or dispersed in a world without center. The question of the writer, how to begin to organize my world, to re-member it, to contain it in a "book," is doubled by the impossibility of asking the question. With the end of the "book" nothing commands the play between sun and moon except a certain "freedom." The "self" no longer mediates between heaven and earth, metaphysical and physical.

The self no longer governs language, but is governed by it. Language is no longer mediation but the law of the game: "Natives of poverty, children of malheur, / The gaiety of language is our seigneur." The self is no longer at "the center of a diamond." The old mythology of moon/sun, of subject/object or inside/outside, no longer accounts for a language through which man, substituting for his "over-human god," regulates the world. No "Livre de Toutes Sortes de Fleurs d'après Nature" forms a "transparence" between two poles of reality. The "sentimentalist" fiction (the fiction of the transcendental subject) is undone (poem IV). The "inventions of sorrow" and the old "nostalgias" cannot be recuperated (poems V and X). "Panic in the face of the moon" (poem IX) ensues, an emptying out of all those follies of a "paradise of meaning" or transcendental signifieds that have accounted for the place of a self between sun and moon, as in a theater of proper images. Thus in poem VI, the spheric repetitions of the sun's day and the lunar month mark a "transmutation which, when seen, appears / To be askew." They mark, that is, a temporal play that refuses the thinking, the notion of "perfection" and produces "desire." The sun "dwells" in a "consummate prime, yet still desires / A further consummation"; and the "big bird" (is it not the figure of the self as desire?) "pecks" at the sun as if to fulfill itself, to satisfy its "appetite." In this play of desires or appetites—a play, that is, of metaphor without correction—everything revolves by "curious lapses" or ellipses. Everything moves in relation, asymptotically, desiring that "perfection" that it resists, postpones, refusing satisfaction, producing signs that are always beyond the pleasure principle.

The most famous canto (poem VIII) of **"Esthétique du Mal"** turns upon this double negation or eccentricity: "negation was eccentric." The Satanic tragedy, the denial of Satan, the denial of the negative, is modern tragedy or doubling, since it is the denial of proper displacement, the circular fiction of decentering/recentering that leads from God to man and back again. The structure of "tragedy" is an orderly fall, and its disruption is a "capital / Negation" in the most precise sense, because the structure of the fall guarantees the proper displacement of fathers by sons, a displacement repeated and formalized in the history of "filial / Revenges." Tragedy, after all, is the stage of (Hegelian) history, of necessary "negation." But the negation of Satan is a double negation, the negation of negation, a disruption of the dialectic of history, and thus a negation of the "underground," where "phantoms" (fallen images) reside until they are returned to their origin or are reerected as capital figures once again.

Stevens meditates this myth of the restoration of "tragedy," which is to say, the epoch of man, as a remythologizing of the old, deconstructed fiction of proper negation or dialectic. Thus his "passion for yes," which overthrows the "mortal no," restores the play or scene of "tragedy." This "yes of the realist" is a "must," a necessity doubled in the awareness that it is a fiction. The "passion" for "yes" reveals the movement of writing as a death. The restoration of Satan in the "yes of the realist" is a "passion" of writing that fills in the old "vacancy" or absence and begins again the assassin's movement of a language of substitutions, displacements, or temporal movement.

In **"Esthétique du Mal"** Stevens most vividly unveils the classical notion that affiliates writing and tragedy as a conundrum, or what Hart Crane called a "livid hieroglyph." The tragic structure is one of the old nostalgias, and sentimentalism is nothing more than its reversal. For example, the metaphors of poem XIII: the modern tragedy, in which the "son's life" is a "punishment" for the "father's," is only a "fragmentary tragedy"; the modern poem no matter how it is condemned not simply to repeat or overcome by a kind of doubling the condition of classical tragedy, is an economy of delay that reassures its own self-overcoming, an ease of "desire." The negations of imagination have undercut the nostalgic and sentimental, caused "panic" in the "face of the moon" (poem IX) and undone the Book of Nature (poem IV). The imagination has divested itself, turning the structure of tragedy into the play of comedy (poems V and IX). The romantic displacement of the classical, the subject's ("in-bar") undermining of the object ("ex-bar"), as in poem V, has only produced the Nietzschean emptying out of the subject. Thus the figure of in-bar's poverty (poem V), of insatiable appetite (poem VI), of the irremediable wound of time (poem VII)—in short, the entire figuration of a system that is impoverished because its transcendental origin has been toppled like a "sky divested of its fountains" (poem IX)—signifies a displacement of the "book" by the "passion" of writing, by a dissemination of productive negations. As Michel Foucault might say, men's death has accompanied God's. Writing has replaced the "book," and writing is the "assassin's scene": "The assassin discloses himself, / The force that destroys us is disclosed . . . ".

"Esthétique du Mal" limns the margins of what poem XIV calls the "extreme of logic," the "illogical" that inhabits dialectical, historical, or tragical systems. An aesthetics of "mal" is a restaging of the "lunacy" of representation that underlies the historico-metaphysical stage. In this poem all logicians are "in their graves," entombed in their systems, which are, in their turn, systems inscribing and concealing a fictitious *logos*. To question these systems is to open the tombs, to expose the missing center. Or in the figuration of poem XIV, if a poem exceeds the "reasonableness" of lakes, which one can walk around (totalize), and if lakes are like minds or minds like lakes "with clouds like lights among great tombs," then the poetic lunatic would double the logical lunatic in negating his one idea. This doubling exposes the simulacrum of the center. It remarks insistently the tombs of logic, not simply the absence of the center but its doubleness, its lunacy, as a play of lights without origin.

"Esthétique du Mal" disrupts, both in its pseudo beginning and its pseudo end, the orderly movement of an aesthetics of representation or a poetics grounded in a "reali-ty" or "physical world" and not in the "metaphysicals." The dispersed, illogical "physical" can never be totalized by the "book" but is marked by "life" as "desire." Desire and writing are a "living" that incorporates negation, death. They undo the "metaphysicals," the "book." (pp. 308-14)

Joseph N. Riddel, "Metaphoric Staging: Stevens' Beginning Again of the 'End of the Book'," in Wallace Stevens: A Celebration, *edited by Frank Doggett and Robert Buttel, Princeton University Press, 1980, pp. 308-38.*

Helen Vendler   (lecture date 1982)

[*Vendler is an American educator and critic who is universally praised as an outstanding critic of poetry. Her meticulous and rigorous studies of W. B. Yeats, John Keats, George Herbert, and Stevens influenced critical perceptions of each poet's works and development. Her writings on Wallace Stevens include* On Extended Wings: Wallace Stevens' Longer Poems *(1969) and* Wallace Stevens: Words Chosen Out of Desire *(1984). In the following excerpt from the latter work, originally delivered as a lecture in 1982, she interprets the function of symbol, allusion, and image in Stevens's poetry.*]

There are four simple recommendations for a neophyte deciphering Stevens. The first is to substitute "I" whenever Stevens says "he" or "she": for "Divinity must live within herself," read "Divinity must live within myself," and so on. Second, never trust beginnings in Stevens; the emotional heart of a lyric by Stevens is likely to be found in the middle of the poem: "Complacencies of the peignoir" is less the emotional heart of the matter (though it is close to the linguistic center) than "Death is the mother of beauty." Third, look for the context of the poem, both in Stevens' whole canon and in his poetic predecessors. Fourth, mistrust titles: **"Anecdotes of Canna"** is not about flowers and **"The Snow Man"** is not about a snow man; the bird with the coppery, keen claws is not to be found in any aviary. Not many poets would call a poem about their middle age and romantic disillusion **"Le Monocle de Mon Oncle."** These four recommendations are all pedagogical and provisional ones. They need to be followed by a fifth: When you have seen the heart of the emotional drama, reconstituted the lyric "I," gotten past the obliquity of the opening lines, and translated the odd title, then you must *undo* all you have done, and read the poem afresh, relishing the oddness of the title, reading without irritability the quirky beginning, resting in the fiction of "the anecdote of " or "two tales of " or "the sense of " or "credences of " or "notes toward," savoring the reticence of the poem's allusiveness. In short, you must repossess the poem as it exists on the page in all its originality and strangeness.

These recommendations are only indicative; in fact, Stevens' secrecies are many and various, and are always a source of aesthetic delight to him—and, eventually, to us. I want to consider here four of Stevens' characteristic secrecies: the secrecy of allusion (for which my examples will be **"Anecdote of the Jar"** and **"The Snow Man"**); the secrecy of narrative (for which my example will be **"The**

Esthétique du Mal

I

He was at Naples writing letters home
And, between his letters, reading paragraphs
On the sublime. Vesuvius had groaned
For a month. It was pleasant to be sitting there,
While the sultriest fulgurations, flickerings,
Cast corners in the glass. He could describe
The terror of the sound because the sound
Was ancient. He tried to remember the phrases: pain
Audible at noon, pain torturing itself,
Pain killing pain on the very point of pain
The volcano trembled in another ether,
As the body trembles at the end of life.

It was almost time for lunch. Pain is human.
There were roses in the cool café. His book
Made sure of the most correct catastrophe.
Except for us, Vesuvius might consume
In solid fire the utmost earth and know
No pain (ignoring the cocks that crow us up
To die) This is part of the sublimity
From which we shrink. Because we seem involved.
But the total past felt nothing when destroyed.

Page from Stevens's manuscript copy of "Esthétique du Mal."

305

Emperor of Ice Cream"); the secrecy of symbol (for which I will take up **"The Dove in the Belly"**); and the secrecy of metaphysics (for which I use **"The Hermitage at the Center"**). These secrecies are all strategies of implication. Though Stevens enjoyed being a discursive poet, and expatiating grandly on great questions (as he does in the early sequences and in **"The Idea of Order at Key West,"** for instance) his greatest originality, I believe, always lay in his more hidden forms of utterance, where his eccentricity (the base of his design) is more strongly felt than in the poems of pronouncement, even such noble ones as the poem on Santayana.

"Anecdote of the Jar," as various critics have seen, is a commentary on Keats's "Ode on a Grecian Urn." Though this is nowhere said by Stevens, the poem is not comprehensible, in matter or manner, unless it is taken to be centrally about Keats's poem. Or rather, it alludes to Keats's poem as a way of discussing the predicament of the American artist, who cannot feel confidently the possessor, as Keats felt, of the Western cultural tradition. Where Keats had London, the British Museum, and an Hellenic urn, the American poet has Tennessee, a slovenly wilderness, and a gray stoneware jar. Where Keats had cultural and legendary ornamentation, the American poet has a bare surface:

> I placed a jar in Tennessee,
> And round it was, upon a hill.
> It made the slovenly wilderness
> Surround that hill.
>
> The wilderness rose up to it,
> And sprawled around, no longer wild.
> The jar was round upon the ground
> And tall and of a port in air.
>
> It took dominion everywhere.
> The jar was gray and bare.
> It did not give of bird or bush,
> Like nothing else in Tennessee.

The poem is a revoicing of the complaint of James (one of the chief influences on Stevens) about the poverty of the American scene, and the consequent danger of thinness in American art. The language of the poem deliberately reflects the absurdity of the American artist's attempt to write a lyric: shall he use language imported from Europe ("of a port in air," "to give of ") or "plain American that cats and dogs can read" (as Marianne Moore put it) like "The jar was round upon the ground"? The poem keeps trying to write itself in inherited stanzas and showing us that it cannot, wrecking each proposed stanza form as it goes along, not only destroying its tetrameters with trimeters and pentameters, but failing to find any rhyme for "hill" except itself, abandoning its first notion of alternate rhymes for no rhyme at all, then deciding to rhyme three lines in a row ("air," "everywhere," "bare"). The American poet cannot, Stevens implies, adopt Keats's serenely purposive use of matching stanzas drawn from sonnet practice. Stevens was entirely capable, as we know from **"Sunday Morning,"** of writing memorable Keatsian lines and stanzas; so we must read the **"Anecdote of the Jar"** as a palinode—a vow to stop imitating Keats and seek a native American language that will not take the wild out

of the wilderness. The humor of the ridiculous stanzas and the equally ridiculous scenario of the **"Anecdote"** does not eliminate an awkward sublimity in the jar; nor does it eliminate the rueful pathos of the closing lines.

Unlike **"Anecdote of the Jar," "The Snow Man"** is comprehensible in itself, and does not betray, by outrageous peculiarities of language of the sort found in **"The Jar,"** an internal struggle for an appropriate language (though its French "to regard" is a minor instance of the same struggle). But we understand **"The Snow Man"** better, I think, when we see it as Stevens' answer to Keats's challenge voiced in the small impersonal poem, "In Drear-Nighted December":

> In drear-nighted December,
>   Too happy, happy tree,
> Thy branches ne'er remember
>   Their green felicity—
> The north cannot undo them
> With a sleety whistle through them,
> Nor frozen thawings glue them
>   From budding at the prime.

Keats then considers the brook which with a sweet forgetting never "pets" about the frozen time; finally, he concludes with the wish that we could imitate the forgetting of nature and live in the present, not feeling the pang of past joy:

> Ah! would 'twere so with many
>   A gentle girl and boy—
> But were there ever any
>   Writh'd not of passèd joy?
> The feel of not to feel it,
> When there is none to heal it,
> Nor numbèd sense to steel it,
>   Was never said in rhyme.

Writhing, or not writhing, over passed joy is what **"The Snow Man"** is about. Stevens here attempts the amnesia of nature, an impossible task. Borrowing Keats's phrase "not to feel," Stevens changes it into "not to think"; and he decides to accept Keats's challenge and try to say "in rhyme" "the feel of not to feel it." The attempt to numb, while not annihilating, the senses—to continue to see and hear without admitting misery and loss—creates the structure of Stevens' poem:

> One must have a mind of winter
> To regard the frost and the boughs
> Of the pinetrees crusted with snow;
>
> And have been cold a long time
> To behold the junipers shagged with ice,
> The spruces rough in the distant glitter
>
> Of the January sun; and not to think
> Of any misery in the sound of the wind,
> In the sound of a few leaves,
>
> Which is the sound of the land
> Full of the same wind
> That is blowing in the same bare place
>
> For the listener, who listens in the snow,
> And, nothing himself, beholds
> Nothing that is not there and the nothing that
>   is.

Stevens' turn from regarding to listening, from the visual to the aural, is borrowed from Keats as well, from the ode "To Autumn"; Stevens' continuation of the figure, as he executes a counterturn from listening back to beholding, "corrects" Keats's assumption that the essence of poetry is the utterance of a stream of sound, and suggests that for Stevens looking and hearing, imagery and musicality, occupy equal ground in the conception of lyric.

We can see one reason for Stevens' liking for the impersonal as a strategy in lyric (or as a secrecy of lyric) by reflecting on the impossibility of rewriting "In Drear-Nighted December" in the first-person singular; Keats too knew the advantage here (and in his autumn ode) of suppressing the lyric "I." Stevens "corrects" Keats again here by making the trees in his own poem evergreens, not deciduous trees—trees that have the same plenitude in winter as in summer. Stevens gives his pines and junipers in fact a double foliage in winter, as snow and ice encrust and shag their full branches; and he "corrects" Keats once more by placing his trees not in a dreary night in the closing month of the year but in the glitter of the sun in the month beginning the new year. "Thou hast thy beauty too," says the poet to winter, thereby going the ode "To Autumn" one better. Stevens' title tells us, on the other hand, that we would have to cease to be flesh and blood and become men of snow in order to contemplate passed joy without writhing. Here, too, he writes to correct Keats, who had written of the four seasons in the mind of man, adding, "He hath his winter too of pale misfeature, / Or else he would forget his mortal nature." Stevens suggests, correctively, that if we adopt the mind of winter we must indeed forget our mortal nature and numb our senses to the zero degree of the snow man. Stevens had so absorbed Keats that Keats acted in his mind as a perpendicular from which he constructed his own oblique poems: what we see as a secrecy of allusion was for Stevens no secrecy but rather an exfoliation of a continuing inner dialogue with Keats. Stevens' allusions, in his briefer poems, are more often to content than to language. If Keats says "tree," Stevens will say "pinetrees," "junipers," "spruces." If Keats says "the north . . . with a sleety whistle," Stevens will say "the sound of the wind." And if Keats says "crystal fretting" and "frozen time," of ice, Stevens will say "frost," "snow," "ice." If Keats says "not to feel," Stevens says "not to think."

There is yet another secrecy in **"The Snow Man,"** its concealing of progress in its series of self-embedding clauses. This special form, which we encounter also in **"Domination of Black,"** offers a syntactic version of the series of receding planes with which we are familiar in painting. We are not to think of any misery "in the sound of the wind, in the sound of a few leaves, which is the sound of the land full of the same wind that is blowing in the same bare place for the listener." The brilliantly visualized ice-shagged and snow-covered trees of the poem occupy a glittering foreground—almost an obstacle—through which we are made to pass, via the etherealizing and impalpable sound of the wind, to the fallen leaves, thence to the land, thence to the wind in a bare place, and only ultimately to the listener who is almost lost in the snow where he is said to listen. The effectual abolition of that listener to a van-

ishing-point ("nothing himself") makes the poem approach the hiding-places of unintelligibility. But this very hermeticism enables the listener to become, in a Moebius-like turning inside-out, a beholder again (as he had been a regarder and beholder at the beginning). He becomes the Emersonian transparent eyeball not on a bare common but in the midst of an unfamiliar plenitude (snow and ice for the eye, wind for the ear) that he does not want. "Exile desire for what is not," he says in effect to himself: and the receding planes suddenly become entirely frontal again, as he beholds, squarely in front of him, "nothing that is not there and the nothing that is." Without the receding into inaccessibility and remoteness that it manifests, Stevens' diction could not recover itself in such a magisterial reversal of perception. We are drawn by all of Stevens' syntactic involutions into the vertiginous abyss of things thought too long; when they can be no longer thought, then the mind collapses on itself, turns inside-out, and hears the cricket of summer forming itself out of ice. Stevens' bold stroke of the three "nothing's" closing **"The Snow Man"** announces, as with a closing of one door and the opening of another, the discovery of the abolition of one old self by a new one, which necessitates at first the contemplation of an absolute void. From this discovery comes, eventually, Stevens' great poem of the void, **"The Auroras of Autumn."** But we see in **"The Snow Man,"** through its vertigo of receding planes, the very moment in which Stevens first discovered that the self, pursued to invisibility, makes itself metaphysically visible again, if only in the form of a terrifying blank.

In alluding to a predecessor, Stevens follows the modernist strategy we are familiar with in painting—to take a known content (let us say the *Demoiselles d'Avignon*) and re-do it with violently altered lines and colors. Stevens in fact explicitly takes up the painters' strategy in **"The Paltry Nude Starts on a Spring Voyage,"** where Botticelli's *Birth of Venus* is the point of reference by which we define our own modern American Venus, born of a culture lacking mythology:

> But not on a shell, she starts,
> Archaic, for the sea.
> But on the first-found weed
> She scuds the glitters. . . .
>
> She too is discontent
> And would have purple stuff upon her arms.

Stevens' secrecies of allusion were learned perhaps from Keats; one reason that Keats's allusions are by no means fully annotated even yet, is that he rarely announces them; rather, he casually models his own writing on what he has read, in a form of what Marianne Moore would call "emotional shorthand." As we learn more about Stevens' reading, and recognize more of his allusions, many poems will be clarified, if not necessarily in their substance (we all have read **"The Snow Man"** without thinking of Keats) yet certainly in their manner of becoming, their conduct of themselves.

The next form of secrecy I want to consider is the secrecy of the implied narrative, and here I turn to another great poem, **"The Emperor of Ice Cream."** For purposes of experiment, I have put the details the poem gives us into the form of a first-person narrative; I see the poem as a rewritten form of this *ur*-narrative, in which the narrative has been changed into an impersonal form, and the linear temporal structure of narrative form has been replaced by a strict geometric spatial construction—two rooms juxtaposed. Here (with apologies) is my conjectural narrative *ur*-form of the poem, constructed purely as an explanatory device:

> I went, as a neighbor, to a house to help to lay out the corpse of an old woman who had died alone; I was helping to prepare for the home wake. I entered, familiarly, not by the front door but by the kitchen door. I was shocked and repelled as I went into the kitchen by the disorderly festival going on inside: a big muscular neighbor who worked at the cigar-factory had been called in to crank the ice-cream machine, various neighbors had sent over their scullery-girls to help out and their yard-boys bearing newspaper-wrapped flowers from their yards to decorate the house and the bier: the scullery-girls were taking advantage of the occasion to dawdle around the kitchen and flirt with the yard-boys, and they were all waiting around to have a taste of the ice-cream when it was finished. It all seemed to me crude and boisterous and squalid and unfeeling in the house of the dead—all that appetite, all that concupiscence.

> Then I left the sexuality and gluttony of the kitchen and went in to the death in the bedroom. The corpse of the old woman was lying exposed on the bed. My first impulse was to find a sheet to cover the corpse; I went to the cheap old pine dresser, but it was hard to get the sheet out of it because each of the three drawers was lacking a drawer-pull; she must have been too infirm to get to the store to get new glass knobs. But I got a sheet out, noticing that she had hand-embroidered a fantail border on it; she wanted to make it beautiful, even though she was so poor that she made her own sheets, and cut them as minimally as she could so as to get as many as possible out of a length of cloth. She cut them so short, in fact, that when I pulled the sheet up far enough to cover her face, it was too short to cover her feet. It was almost worse to have to look at her old calloused feet than to look at her face; somehow her feet were more dead, more mute, than her face had been.

> She is dead, and the fact cannot be hidden by any sheet. What remains after death, in the cold light of reality, is life—all of that life, with its coarse muscularity and crude hunger and greedy concupiscence, that is going on in the kitchen. The only god of this world is the cold god of persistent life and appetite; and I must look steadily at this repellent but true tableau—the animal life in the kitchen, the corpse in the back bedroom. Life offers no other tableau of reality, once we pierce beneath appearances.

Stevens' secrecy here, as elsewhere, is the secrecy of impersonal address. When he writes the poem, it is as though the voice of Necessity itself is speaking an immortal theater-direction, a naturalistic "Fiat": "Call the roller of big cigars, let the wenches dawdle, let the boys bring flowers,

take a sheet, spread it, let the lamp shine." And this is followed by an equally impersonal commentary: "The only emperor is the emperor of ice-cream." Here is the poem:

> Call the roller of big cigars,
> The muscular one, and bid him whip
> In kitchen cups concupiscent curds.
> Let the wenches dawdle in such dress
> As they are used to wear, and let the boys
> Bring flowers in last month's newspapers.
> Let be be finale of seem.
> The only emperor is the emperor of ice-cream.

> Take from the dresser of deal,
> Lacking the three glass knobs, that sheet
> On which she embroidered fantails once
> And spread it so as to cover her face.
> If her horny feet protrude, they come
> To show how cold she is, and dumb.
> Let the lamp affix its beam.
> The only emperor is the emperor of ice-cream.

To my mind, this has something of Joyce's "scrupulous meanness." The chill conveyed by the impersonal account conveys, better than any first-person expression of shock and pity and acknowledgment, the absolute necessity of the shock, and the pity, and the final unwilling acknowledgment of a harsh truth. We have, says Stevens' two-stanza spatial structure, no choice in the matter: death and life coexist, side by side. We are shocked by the coarseness of this, and repelled by both the gross physicality of death and the animal greed of life. But in view of the inflexible order of this coexistence, mere "personal reaction" is not an adequate vehicle. The anguish of the poem is the anguish before the absolute predictability of emotion as well as the predictability of situation. The pitiless lamp affixing its beam, the finale of "seem" in "be," the single emperor—everything here is determined, without an inch of personal leeway. The deliberate materiality of the poem, extending equally to concupiscent curds and horny feet, denies the very spontaneity—of personal desire, imagination, romantic love, and poetic vision—which any first-person account of either desire or mourning, by its very nature, implies, and which conventional elegy invokes. Stevens preserves in this poem the conventions of elegy: the corpse, the shroud, the flowers, the mourners, the ceremony of the feast, the mention of inexorable fate, the supreme Minos or Rhadamanthus, the persistence of life in the face of death. But the singing "I" of elegy is ruthlessly suppressed, and with him go at once both the dirge and the apotheosis proper to classical elegy. We may see in this poem a savage refutation of Poe's claim that the death of a beautiful woman is the proper subject for poetry: once again, a classical topic is scrawled violently over with the graffiti of modernism.

Form in Stevens, including the secrecies of form, is always a carrier of meaning. Stevens' obliquities and silent juxtapositions are neither capricious nor dispensable. But until we see what they hide (in the case of the **"Emperor,"** the prior narrative), we cannot see what they illuminate. In this case, the geometric form illustrates the absolute necessity of choosing between the two rooms. There is no place else to go; you can either be cold and dumb, or you have to join the low concupiscence in the kitchen—and such a "choice" is really no choice at all, so the only emperor is the emperor of ice cream.

Stevens' poetry is a poetry of feeling pressed to an extreme; the pressure itself produces the compression and condensation of the work. The pressure of the imagination pressing back against reality, as Stevens called it, is very great: If you confine Greece, Keats, and Tennessee in the same chamber of your mind for a time, the amalgam solidifies into the famous stoneware jar and its preposterous sulky stanzas—"Tell me, what form can possibly suit the slovenly wilderness?" Or if you confine in your mind Keats, the English winter, the New England winter, Shelley's *terza rima* in the "West Wind," and a wish to reproduce the paradox of beholding a void replete with unintelligible meaning, the elements freeze into an unrhymed *terza rima* poem surrounding the absent figure of the New England Snow Man, our false Florimel unable to conceive of melting, he has been cold for such a long time. And if you confine all those elements from life and literature in a single mind for seventy-five years, the amalgam becomes more and more reduced to those elements, those "few things / For which a fresh name always occurred" (**"Local Objects"**).

It is to the secrecies of those powerful single images that I now turn, Stevens' secrecy of symbol. Stevens is often called a symbolist poet, and the difficulty of reading him is consequently ascribed to his use of "symbols." The "decoding" of these "symbols" was the first task undertaken by the early critics of Stevens, a decoding in the easy form of equivalence: the sun "was" reality, the moon "was" imagination, green "was" the fertile earth, blue "was" the azure of the creating mind. This decoding produced some commentary of extraordinary banality, in which poem after poem was said to be "about" the encounter between "the imagination" and "reality." Commentary which impoverishes poems is a disservice to them. I think we can see now that for Stevens there was no reality except as we imagine it afresh each day. We see the *Ding-an-sich* every day; it is not hidden from us; but we can only see it *as* we locally see it, in the manner in which we see it today. Appearance, for Stevens, *is* reality. Therefore there is no encounter between "Appearance" and "Reality"—there are only the fresh "realities"—which we may equally call "appearances"—of every day. The expression of newness requires, each day, a new description, which will draw its terms from something in the world. After a while, one has used a number of terms for one's descriptions, and one begins to notice that the terms have established a network among themselves, a referentiality that does not so much extend outward to some putative "real world" as horizontally to the inwardly-extensive world of terms or images. **"Thinking of a Relation between the Images of Metaphors"** (as Stevens called it) is what all of Stevens' poems do. To see the rich nature of these poems, one must not monotonously refer them to some single external theme, whether physical or metaphysical; rather one must reveal their depth and breadth of internal reference—a reference so full in the last poems as to make them readable only in the light of the earlier poetic illusions to which they allude. To illustrate Stevens' chief form of symbolic secrecy—his self-reference—I want to look at a poem called **"The Dove in the Belly"**—one of a series of poems about doves (and pigeons, their domestic counterpart) in Stevens. (pp. 44-54)

Stevens' secrecy here is both a secrecy of reference and a secrecy of reduction—both techniques are common in his poems. The dove is Venus' dove, though not called here by its mythological name; instead, it is biologically identified as "the dove in the belly." Stevens first alluded to this dove in **"Depression before Spring,"** when the dawn announced by the crowing of the cock brings no green queen for the abandoned poet: "Ki-ki-ri-ki / Brings no rou-cou, / No rou-cou-cou." The dove appears again in Stevens' violent prayer, in **"Ghosts as Cocoons,"** to be born again into love; he asks that the ghost of an old murdered love become the cocoon of a new love, a new Psyche to his Cupid; he talks of the dove-winged blendings of the moon, hoping they will bring him a bride and blot out the "mangled smutted semi-world hacked out of dirt." Stevens' bitterest comments on change arise from these disappointments in romantic love, which remained for him the type of all illusion:

> Like a rose rabbi, later, I pursued,
> And still pursue, the origin and course
> Of love.
>   (**"Le Monocle de Mon Oncle,"** XII)

Love (as we know from the early poems) promised so much, made the world so fair with its dove-winged blendings; it combined tempestuous feeling with paradisal peace ("the incredible calm in ecstasy"), and it built a nest of solacing music in the heart. Even (as in **"The Dove in Spring"**) when its cooing turns in old age to a small howling of loss, Stevens is unwilling to let the dove die. And just as sexual love brings out his most violent language of disillusion, so, in **"The Dove in the Belly,"** when he recalls its transcendent power to transform the world, it evokes from him his most heartfelt language of praise. Under the aegis of Venus' dove, he says, the whole world takes on a glow, an excellence, a beauty, a magical brilliance, and a fruitfulness that he can never forget; and we ourselves, he continues, poor and ruined as we are, put on, under the enchantment of the tempestuous dove hidden in the belly, costumes that make us regal and ceremonious, like nobles disposed on terraces. Stevens cannot forbear to hail this miraculous radiance of love, itself a health and a salvation, inspiring as the dove of the spirit.

The poem begins by seeing all appearance as a constantly-changing play—as if appearance were a toy for us, to distract and amuse us. But we cannot be worldly and skeptical too long in the presence of love; we become instead its celebrators, glad when the dove who has built his nest in the belly is placated at last. And yet we recognize here Stevens' characteristic refusal of the first-person, whether singular or plural, his wish for an impersonal lyric voice:

The Dove in the Belly

> The whole of appearance is a toy. For this,
> The dove in the belly builds his nest and coos,
>
> Selah, tempestuous bird. How is it that
> The rivers shine and hold their mirrors up,

Like excellence collecting excellence?
How is it that the wooden trees stand up

And live and heap their panniers of green
And hold them round the sultry day? Why
    should

These mountains being high be, also, bright,
Fetched up with snow that never falls to earth?

And this great esplanade of corn, miles wide,
Is something wished for made effectual

And something more. And the people in cos-
    tumes,
Though poor, though raggeder than ruin, have
    that

Within them right for terraces—oh, brave salut!
Deep dove, placate you in your hiddenness.

Stevens' sketch of the world in this poem is done with his customary primitive simplicity: there are rivers mirroring the sky, wooden trees that come alive and turn green, bright snow-topped mountains that in summer see no snow fall, and an esplanade of ripened corn: sky, water, vegetation, mountains, and the fruits of the earth. And, inhabiting all this, people, poor and ragged, but for a moment costumed and inwardly made grand. And Stevens' celebratory rhetoric could not be simpler either; "How is it that this can happen to me; Why should the mountains be beautiful with snow as well as high?" It is the rhetoric of hyperbole—this great esplanade, the brave salut of the people. Like most devotees, Stevens fears the god he worships: "Deep dove," he prays, "placate you in your hiddenness." The dove is here a masculine dove, the Holy Spirit of transcendent inspiration confined, "in the belly," with erotic desire: if unplaced he will rage in that destructive chaos described in **"Chaos in Motion and Not in Motion,"** Stevens' account of a desire that can no longer imagine any possible mate, "Desire without an object of desire, / All mind and violence and nothing felt." Stevens alternates between the happiness I have just been describing in **"The Dove in the Belly,"** the pain of **"The Dove in Spring,"** and the absence of the dove in **"Chaos in Motion and Not in Motion."** He wishes, as he often does, that change would stop, that for once he could be "the single man / In whose breast, the dove, alighting, would grow still" (**"Thinking of a Relation between the Images of Metaphors"**). But each time the dove alights he sings a slightly different song; and though each variation comes close to the unstated theme, the dove can never resemble the dove in perfect Platonic indistinguishability. No appearance is identical to an earlier appearance; no feeling is identical to an earlier feeling; and so the task of poetry for Stevens, never ceases. As he explained in a letter, the necessary angel is reality; reality offers us, over and over, different facets of itself, soliciting our adjustments to it in those re-shiftings of perception and thought and desire that for Stevens define poesis, imagination, the construction of meaning and value. It cannot be said too often that this is an activity that every human being engages in at every moment. How is it, Stevens asks, that we do not stay the same, that we do not keep our first beliefs and our first self-constructs and our first loves? What makes us change?

And what makes the last state of affairs better (or worse) than the first? Or are they all equal?

In one sense, of course, these questions are banalities, at least in the abstract (though in the concrete they are painful enough for each one of us). Stevens' tribute to their banality and commonness appears in the simplicity of his reductions, as in **"The Dove in the Belly."** But his tribute to the unique import of the questions as they are lived by each of us appears in his devising of a unique situation and form for each poem. Like life, the poem, he said, must resist the intelligence almost successfully. It must present itself as an enigma, just as life does. We live out each poem as we live inside it. The poem-as-passage, not the poem-as-discourse, is Stevens' model, even when he appears most discursive. Consequently, each of his embodiments of the predicament of illusion or loss or reinstated belief or love is stylized into a nonce event in the shorter poems; and Stevens' commitment to the secrecy of intertextual symbols like the dove, as well as to the secrecies of an impersonal presentation and a resolutely elliptical discourse, makes him a poet knowable in the instance only when he is known in the whole.

We have seen a group of Stevens' secrecies; but I want to close with Stevens' late disavowing of secrecy—or his exploding or implosion of it. All the appeal of secrecy for Stevens arises from the wish not to betray, in both senses of the word, the contrary oscillations of his spirit. He wanted, in **"The Snow Man,"** to show that he both agreed, and did not agree, with Keats's point about the amnesia of nature, taking Keats as a point of departure and yet departing from him; he wanted, in **"The Emperor of Ice Cream,"** to acknowledge intellectually the simultaneous cohabiting of concupiscence and corpses without assenting, tonally, to their appalling co-presence; he wanted **"The Dove in the Belly"** to proclaim the hybridizing of the Holy Spirit with the visceral dove of Venus without appearing either blasphemous or ridiculous; and he wanted, in **"Anecdote of the Jar,"** to position an American jar on a new continent without forgetting the urns of Greece or the stanzas of England. Finally, however, in each of these endeavors, "a complex of emotions falls apart" (**"Credences of Summer"**). The sheer effort of finding a medium of verbal solubility for the vocabularies of Romanticism and modernism (as in the meditations on Keats) or for concupiscence and corporeal mortality (as in the **"Emperor"**), or for the Holy Spirit and Venus (as in **"The Dove in the Belly"**) seems not only impossible but perhaps deceptive. If there is no medium of verbal solubility, perhaps one can only imagine two immiscible liquids with a metonymic impermeability. Stevens writes, in this mood of wanting to assert immiscibility, a poem almost unreadable, **"The Hermitage at the Center."** It is a double-column poem, but written out with the right-hand elements (which describe the eternal fiction of desire achieved in words—Venus surrounded by her doves which make an intelligible twittering) following the left-hand elements (which describe the collapse of freshness of utterance into the twice-told, the incoherent, and the meaningless—falling leaves, a tottering wind, and unintelligible thought). It is only by a great effort of will that Stevens can resume the two columns into one at the end, by reciting one of the oldest of religious gnomic utterances, one he had used earlier in **"An Ordinary Evening in New Haven":** "And yet this end and this beginning are one." This fiction of the circular, of a primitive like an orb, informs Stevens' use of Alpha and Omega. He could not see any way that freshness could be purchased except by dissolution; nor could he see any freshness remaining unravaged by skeptical thought and emotional attrition. Here is his dilemma, as he visits his hermitage, his place of central recourse:

> The leaves on the macadam make a noise—
> How soft the grass on which the desired
> Reclines in the temperature of heaven—
>
> Like tales that were told the day before yesterday—
> Sleek in a natural nakedness,
> She attends the tintinnabula—
>
> And the wind sways like a great thing tottering—
> Of birds called up by more than the sun,
> Birds of more wit, that substitute—
>
> Which suddenly is all dissolved and gone—
> Their intelligible twittering
> For unintelligible thought.
>
> And yet this end and this beginning are one,
> And one last look at the ducks is a look
> At lucent children round her in a ring.

Stevens wrote this poem about the Elizabeth Park in Hartford, where he took frequent walks. It had a duck pond; and one of his looks at the ducks would be, he knew, his last. It is impossible to count the number of times he had looked at the ducks—each time he looked, he saw them in a new relation. The daily impersonal newness of the visible world was at first a disturbing thought to Stevens, as we know from the phenomenology, both visual and affective, of **"Sea-Surface Full of Clouds"**; it made for a troubling relativity of value (any scene is as valuable as any other scene, any mood is as true as any other mood). But now, at the end of his life, that aesthetic inexhaustibility of the world and the emotions is Stevens' only principle of faith: after every Omega an Alpha is sure to follow, and one last look at the ducks is a look at lucent children, making one more perfect orb, phrased in the childishness of a budding aesthetic—the children are "round her in a ring."

This last Venus is not only erotic but maternal (stripped of her maternal sinister possibilities exposed in **"Madame La Fleurie;"**) the intelligible twittering of her birds stands in the aesthetic order for what her children stand for in the order of nature—a harmonious replication of self guaranteeing the persistence of identity. In the hermitage at the center lives the poet, scholar-hermit, snow man, in his desolate landscape of leaves and miserable wind; but in the center there also lives the interior paramour, the fictive reclining nude amid her doves (here turned to ducks) and children. Being there together, as the Muse says in the **"Final Soliloquy,"** is "enough." But this last poem cannot patch the world quite round, even with its closing fiction of the merging of the left-hand and right-hand columns of the poem into one. It abandons the secrecy of concealed tensions for an open revelation of the chasm between the world of misery and the world of desire. It exposes secrecy for what it is—another fiction.

Stevens' secrecies have claims on us only because they are, in the end, not mystifications; and because he knew their living components and their veiled hostilities; and because the fiction they represent, that of a verbal medium in which all oppositions could coexist, is one without which poetry could not be written. (pp. 54-60)

> *Helen Vendler, in her* Wallace Stevens: Words Chosen Out of Desire, *The University of Tennessee Press, Knoxville, 1984, 86 p.*

David M. La Guardia   (essay date 1983)

[*In the following excerpt, La Guardia characterizes Stevens's last poems, which comprise* The Rock *section of his* Collected Poems, *and discusses formal and thematic variations between his early and mature verse.*]

Stevens' last poems enact a fulfillment of the earlier explorations of poetry as a process of evolving fictive certainties. The final and shortest section of ***The Collected Poems,*** *The Rock* manifests a poet able to affirm in the shadow of personal annihilation the continuing vitality of the imagination. The imminence of physical return to the earth-mother and to the rock as generative source of both physical and imaginative life prompts Stevens to adjust his late style from the impersonal tone of the meditations in **"The Auroras of Autumn"** to poems asserting the primacy of personal and individual experience. "The section, seen as a unit," [Joseph] Riddel writes, "is a carefully planned farewell" [*The Clairvoyant Eye: The Poetry and Poetics of Wallace Stevens*]. Preparing to leave the world, Stevens returns wholeheartedly to its particulars and fashions a farewell consistent to his lifelong commitment to the actual and to the sacred power of the imagination to supply meaning to an otherwise meaningless void. While it represents a visionary and metaphysical distillation, Stevens' rock issues directly from the physical, for reality is the secular temple of the imagination's redeeming power.

Acting as poet-priest of the earth's holiness, in *The Rock* Stevens advances the lineaments of the Emersonian scholar-self toward apotheosis. His pervasive interest in the central-perceiving self and its derivation intensifies, a fascination he showed in a practical way by hiring a genealogist in the early forties to trace his ancestry. Holly Stevens reports that, during a ten year period ending in 1952, over four hundred letters were written to various professional people—including several pastors of country churches in eastern Pennsylvania—concerning genealogical matters. To Hi Simons, Stevens exclaimed that "the whole thing has been an extraordinary experience: finding out about my family, etc. It is extraordinary how little seems to have survived when you first begin to study this sort of thing and then later on, when you have learned how to go about it, what an immense amount has survived and how much you can make of it." Another letter discloses that "the family picture is like a good many other pictures of a different sort. There seems to be a tremendous thickness of varnish of a more or less romantic sort all over the thing,

and I want to take that all off and get down to the real people." Enacting his familiar pattern of decreating to get to
the real, Stevens' intent is to "try to let a little daylight into
the attic of the past" and more specifically to analyze ancestral branches in order to "determine whether I fit into
the line, and how."

More than idle historical curiosity, Stevens' foray into the
roots of his heritage indicates a concern for the origins and
sources of the self. He wishes to construe the poetic self
in the facticity of its proper milieu and to transfer the fertile particulars of his origins into the imagination's life.
Having arrived in **"Final Soliloquy of the Interior Paramour"** at what Riddel calls "the ultimate discovery of his
aesthetic"—the realization that "God and the imagination
are one," Stevens seeks a finite and empirical source for
the God-encompassing self to replace the hollow heaven
occupied by the impersonal God of myth. If God and
mind are one and the mind's proper place is within a physical world, then reality constitutes the only possible heav-
en. The poet's genealogical chart therefore begins at reality's generative center. Stevens clarifies this heritage in
"The Irish Cliffs of Moher":

> Who is my father in this world, in this house,
> At the spirit's base?
>
> My father's father, his father's father, his—
> Shadows like winds
>
> Go back to a parent before thought, before
>   speech,
> At the head of the past.
>
> They go to the cliffs of Moher rising out of the
>   mist,
> Above the real,
>
> Rising out of present time and place, . . .
>   . . . . .
>
> . . . This is my father, or, maybe,
> It is as he was,
>
> A likeness, one of the race of fathers: earth
> And sea and air.

Another variation on the rock, the cliffs of Moher represent the core of all creation. They derive from the same
figure Stevens had used in **"Credences of Summer"** to denote the essential barrenness—"the natural tower of all
the world" and the "mountain on which the tower
stands." What in **"Credences"** was the "final mountain"
and "point of survey" now stands as a point of nascency
and a wellspring of poetic activity. The old man on the
tower who in the earlier poem represented regeneration
evolves into the more specific figure of the primitive earth
as "parent before thought," the vital father progenitor of
all imaginative power.

As an aging man tracing his lineage both literally and poetically, Stevens' concern is to conceive the self in its
wholeness within a concrete and sacred physical universe.
He once wrote to his niece concerning his father that "seeing him as a whole, I understand him better perhaps than
he understood himself. . . . I can really look into his
heart in which he must have concealed so many things."
All of Stevens' fathers, figurative and real, contribute to

the whole self his poems strive to define. In **"Prologues to
What Is Possible,"** he provides a fuller explanation of the
relationship between heredity, self-definition and poetry:

> What self, for example, did he contain that had
>   not yet been loosed,
> Snarling in him for discovery as his attentions
>   spread,
> As if all his hereditary lights were suddenly in-
>   creased.

By spreading his attention toward more and more particulars within life's flux, including the particulars of his own
heritage, Stevens releases newer selves snarling for discovery in the form of poems as acts of self-creation. His "hereditary" lights consist of individual "smallest lamp[s]" of
imaginative insight. Each adds "its puissant flick" as the
poet's mind supplies "A name and privilege over the ordinary of his commonplace." Meditating upon the world,
the mind creates a fresh version of the self and adds another branch to the familial tree. Nearing the end of life, Stevens desires that no selves be trapped by a failure of vision.
Instead, his mind continues its ceaseless activity as each
"flick" contributes to what is real and "Creates a fresh
universe out of nothingness by adding itself." This process
insures the continuing freshness of self and world alike.

Not surprisingly, since Stevens' investigations of self-
origin repeat the emphases of "The American Scholar"
and "Self-Reliance," he finally confronts squarely his ancestral lines to Emerson. **"Looking Across the Fields and
Watching the Birds Fly"** discusses the fundamental differences between the scholar's guise of Emerson (spoken of
as a clownish "Mr. Homburg") and a similar role for the
contemporary poet. Stevens opens the poem in a tone of
unmistakable mockery of his literary forefather:

> Among the more irritating minor ideas
> Of Mr. Homburg during his visits home
> To Concord, at the edge of things, was this:
>
> To think away the grass, the trees, the clouds,
> Not to transform them into other things,
> Is only what the sun does every day.

At the edge and not at the center, Mr. Homburg's quest
for the first idea is not "flicked by feeling." He becomes
all mind and devises a "slightly detestable *operandum*," by
which Stevens implies transcendentalism: "No doubt we
live beyond ourselves in air." Reflecting upon Emerson's
philosophy, Stevens christens himself "A new scholar replacing an older one." His office is to seek "For a human
that can be accounted for" to replace "the masculine
myths we used to make." Very subtly, the tone of mockery
switches to a tone of high seriousness as Stevens realizes
that if Emerson's transcendental, philosophical base
missed the proper mode for the man of imagination, it
caught nevertheless the essential spirit that issues from
processive living:

> What we know in what we see, what we feel in
>   what
> We hear, what we are, beyond mystic disputa-
>   tion,
> In the tumult of integrations out of the sky,
>
> And what we think, a breathing like the wind,

A moving part of a motion, a discovery
Part of a discovery, a change part of a change,

　　. . . . .

A daily majesty of meditation.

Through willing acceptance of the mantle of the modern "American Scholar," Stevens declares his affinity to the heritage of the American self extending directly from Emerson through Thoreau and Whitman to himself. Rejecting Mr. Homburg's intellective pomposity, Stevens accepts his imaginative vision. The new scholar must replace the central self as hero with the central self as human and must assume a greater responsibility of self-reliance than Emerson embraced in an era still protected by "masculine myths." Stevens indicates his acceptance of Emerson's concept of the relationship between mind and nature. The imagination responds to the "blunt laws" of the natural world and forms itself as a contrary power issuing from the same source:

The spirit comes from the body of the world,
Or so Mr. Homburg thought: the body of a
　　world
Whose blunt laws make an affectation of mind,

The mannerism of nature caught in a glass
And there become a spirit's mannerism,
A glass aswarm with things going as far as they
　　can.

Meditating the world, the glass or mirror of imagination reflects the world's mannerism, which in the process of creative transposition becomes its own. Another richly multifarious image, Stevens' "glass" is the last of several direct allusions occurring throughout *The Collected Poems* to Emerson's "transparent eyeball." For Emerson, the eye was "the best of artists" as well as the "best composer" because "by the mutual action of its structure" it could integrate dissimilar objects of whatever kind "into a well-colored and shaded globe" and produce symmetry and perspective. Aswarm with reality, Stevens' eye of imagination reconstitutes what it perceives within the form of its own container—the poem itself, the final variation on the image of the glass. Perspective comes then from the glass of imagination—the perceiving eye— filtering reality through its colors and shades and producing the glass as poem—container for the richness of the world.

Stevens consummates his investigation into the sources of the self in **"The Sail of Ulysses,"** a poem written less than two years before his death. In this piece his allusions to Emerson are less overt than in **"Looking Across the Fields and Watching the Birds Fly"** but the delineations of an Emersonian scholar-self in modern posture are unmistakable. Where Emerson had described the scholar as "Man Thinking," Stevens defines the "true creator" or poet as "the thinker / Thinking gold thoughts in a golden mind." Where Emerson's scholar plied "the slow, unhonored, and unpaid task of observation," Stevens' thinker partakes of

　　　a human loneliness,
A part of space and solitude,

　　　. . . . .

In which nothing of knowledge fails.

Finally, where the office of Emerson's scholar was "to

cheer, to raise, and to guide men by showing them facts amidst appearances," Stevens' true creator, "creating from nothingness" in a world without teleology, discovers "The joy of meaning in design / Wrenched out of chaos." In each case, Stevens' scholar continues the tradition Emerson established of a thinking man, unhonored in his genius, who discovers the world for mankind.

Ulysses becomes for Stevens a figure for the self en route. In separate places he refers to him as "The interminable adventurer" and "Symbol of the seeker." Ever so carefully in **"The Sail of Ulysses"** Stevens elaborates a justification of the ways not of God but of self to man. In a pluralism "There is no map of paradise" and "the genealogy / Of gods and men" are rightfully destroyed as man approaches generative vision:

The ancient symbols will be nothing then.
We shall have gone behind the symbols
To that which they symbolized.

Stevens repeats a lifelong emphasis that the awesome burden weighing upon the central self in a universe devoid of symbols is to be "Master of the world and of himself ":

　　　His mind presents the world
And in his mind the world revolves.

　　　. . . . .

Like things produced by a climate, the world
Goes round in the climates of the mind
And bears its floraisons of imagery.

Here Stevens makes his clearest statement concerning the imagination's metaphorical counterpart to the temporal flow of the seasons discovered in **"Credences of Summer."** As each alteration of climate produces the characteristic changes that define spring, summer, autumn, and winter, so in the seasons of the mind, parallel to but separate from literal time, the world changes according to the imagination's perception of it within the "floraisons of imagery." The infinite variety of the self specifies the infinite variety of the world. Since "the world goes round and round / In the crystal atmospheres of the mind," reality unfolds only within the scope of each individual's experience of it. This is what Emerson realized when he wrote that "to believe your own thought . . . is genius" and insisted that man must learn to detect "that gleam of light which flashes across his mind from within." For Stevens and Emerson both, freedom consists in the release of man from the intimidation of other minds and in the cultivation of the powers of his own. "How then shall the mind be less than free," Stevens asks, "Since only to know is to be free."

Once the self attains the freedom of self-knowledge, Stevens predicts a culmination, within process, of Emerson's thinking man:

The center of the self, the self
Of the future, of future man
And future place, when these are known,
A freedom at last from the mystical,
The beginning of a final order,
The order of man's right to be
As he is, the discipline of his scope
Observed as an absolute, himself.

The "final order" achieved by the central self has nothing

to do with fixity or system but involves simply the free activity of a regenerative imagination within the flux of space and solitude. In the twilight of his own selfhood, this is the order Stevens hopes to have achieved. His quest for a genealogy of the self ends in the realization that

> In the generations of thought, man's sons
> And heirs are powers of the mind,
> His only testament and estate.

Knowing he will soon die, his search constitutes an effort to solidify before his departure the consummate relevance of the creative self in the nonteleological world. He expresses this effort clearly in **"Note on Moonlight"**:

> The one moonlight, the various universe, intend-
> ed
> So much just to be seen—a purpose, empty
> Perhaps, absurd perhaps, but at least a purpose,
> Certain and ever more fresh. Ah! Certain, for
> sure . . .

Here Stevens reflects upon the glory of certitude in a universe of uncertainty. The single imagination ("one moonlight") perceives the many ("various universe") and in that act fulfills itself. That a mind standing on the edge of nothingness continues to discover fresh visions of the world, as Stevens does in his final poems, attests to the ultimate peace and freedom the self can achieve amid chaos.

Frank Doggett notices that in **"The Sail of Ulysses"** Stevens "presents all the infinite abstraction of time and space, all of reality, as depending upon the most particular form of being, the 'moment of light,' the instant of experience in one individual mind" [*Stevens' Poetry of Thought*]. (pp. 156-64)

Stevens elaborates in **"The Sail of Ulysses"** a self whose present moment in the actual world defines both self and world. As he wrote in the **"Adagia,"** "The world is myself. Life is myself." In his late poetry, he affirms that life's fullness does not wane in life's passing and that the mind's freedom is not diminished by death's presence.

Other than the title poem itself, Stevens' highest poetic achievement in *The Rock* is **"To an Old Philosopher in Rome,"** written on the occasion of George Santayana's death in 1952. The life and person of Santayana provided Stevens an emblem of the emancipated self in the modern world and an appropriately solemn twentieth-century substitute for "Mr. Homburg." While a Harvard student, Stevens had been invited to Santayana's home in Cambridge to read poems to him. Forty years later, he recalls that "I always came away from my visits to him feeling that he made up in the most genuine way for many things that I needed." When Santayana died in a Roman Catholic convent, Stevens recorded his grief in a letter to Barbara Church referring to him as "a man whose whole life is thought." Facing his own death, Stevens strongly identifies with one who lived the life of the mind and who found, like himself, abiding consolation in a materialistic and nonteleological universe. "It is one of the great human paradoxes," Riddel proposes, "that the masses of our contemporary world refuse to be lonely and are, while Santayana chose to be lonely and was not" [*The Clairvoyant Eye*]. (pp. 165-66)

Stevens reemphasizes in the poem that the "celestial possible" exists in the actual, in the "last drop of the deepest blood." "On the threshold of heaven," Santayana lies on his deathbed and catches within glimpses of flickering consciousness the spectacle of a religious street procession. The meditation assumes the perspective of the dying man's imagination. On the point of death, Santayana's life of the mind does not falter. He transmutes the figures in the street parade into a vision of heavenly movement—"the majestic movement / Of men growing small in the distances of space." Himself growing smaller and smaller in the vicissitudes of living, the old philosopher has regressed to a mere "shadow of a shape / In a confusion on bed." He is a pitiable remnant of man who for consolation must "speak to [his] pillow as if it was [himself]" and who can locate the grandeur he deserves only "In so much misery."

Nowhere else in his poetry does Stevens portray the heroic self in such absolutely diminutive circumstance. Santayana's predicament becomes a metaphor for the point Stevens has reached in his own imaginative situation when the imminence of death renders life "A light on the candle tearing against the wick." The poem celebrates, however, not the defeat but the apotheosis of the dying self. Externally miserable and pathetic, Santayana maintains the internal vitality that characterized his entire life. From the particulars of the holy city of Rome he fashions in the imagination a portrait of that "merciful Rome / Beyond, the two alike in the make of the mind." The process of the mind's uninterrupted *making* converts the human city into an otherwise unachievable heavenly city:

> It is as if in a human dignity
> Two parallels become one, a perspective, of
> which
> Men are part both in the inch and in the mile.

As [Ashley] Brown notes, parallels cannot touch except in the "miracle of old age on the verge of death that is the basis of the whole poem" [*The Achievement of Wallace Stevens*, ed. Ashley Brown]. The perspective Santayana achieves emanates from the conjuncture of "The extreme of the known in the presence of the extreme / Of the unknown." The "extreme of the known" is the dying man's experience of its own death-moment—the final knowing at the end of knowing. The "extreme of the unknown" suggests man's maximum ignorance of the state he inherits once death's moment has passed. The peace of perspective issues then from the expiring philosopher's ability to fuse the parallels of two extremes—represented by actual Rome and the Rome beyond—within the act of the mind. Since the mind's activity forms both the real world and the world of heavenly vision, man can partake of the centrality of existence—"both in the inch and in the mile"—up to his final breath.

Part of the greatness of **"To an Old Philosopher in Rome"** derives from Stevens' unrelenting attention to the concrete detail of the death-scene. If it constitutes a poverty for man not to *live* in a physical world, as Stevens previously established, he indicates here as great a poverty not to *die* in one. As Santayana lies "dozing in the depths of wakefulness," the particulars of his immediate surroundings feed and shape his celestial vision. The banners in the religious procession convert to angels' wings, the medicinal smells of the sickroom become "A fragrantness not to be spoiled" and the "newsboys" muttering" outside the window transforms into a spiritual "murmuring" within the mind. . . .

> The sounds drift in. The buildings are remembered.
> The life of the city never lets go, nor do you
> Ever want it to. It is part of the life in your room.
> It domes are the architecture of your bed.
> . . . . .
> It is a kind of total grandeur at the end,
> With every visible thing enlarged and yet
> No more than a bed, a chair and moving nuns,
> The immensest theatre, the pillared porch,
> The book and candle in your ambered room.

On his deathbed, Santayana experiences the heaven-in-earth that constitutes the only possible paradise. His "total grandeur" remains inseparable from the poverty of his end because while the imagination enlarges upon reality it does not eliminate any of its particulars. It raises them, however, to the level of the sacred and locates the seat of holiness in the minutiae of daily living. By elevating the details of the city that never lets go to the level of a spiritual vision, Santayana's secular imagination redeems itself in the precise instant of its demise. Stevens cannot help but identify and admire:

> So that we feel, in this illumined large,
> The veritable small, so that each of us
> Beholds himself in you, and hears his voice
> In yours, master and commiserable man,
> Intent on your particles of nether-do.

Stevens realizes that each man's life dissolves to the same lonely room. He clarifies in **"Lebensweisheitspielerei"** that the only persons left in "the poverty / Of autumnal space" are:

> The finally human,
> Natives of a dwindled sphere.
> . . . . .
> Each person completely touches us
> With what he is and as he is,
> In the stale grandeur of annihilation.

(pp. 166-69)

Stevens saw in George Santayana an emblem of human nature in extremis, a man whose life of the mind in "the afflatus of ruin" was so fully lived it made him "The one invulnerable man among / Crude captains, the naked majesty, if you like." Santayana knows that the heaven is actually the ground of earth: "He stops upon this threshold." There is no need to go on. After all, every heavenly city the mind has fashioned traces its genesis to the particulars of the here and now. The pluralistic universe therefore is sufficient to sustain the imagination's final puissant flick.

Like Santayana, Stevens confronts his end without remorse. Withering into winter, he accepts the final season when "It is as if / We had come to an end of the imagination." Even in this awareness, when the "great structure" of the mind "has become a minor house" and it seems "A

fantastic effort has failed," mere consciousness implies life's vibrancy:

> Yet the absence of the imagination had
> Itself to be imagined. The great pond,
> The plain sense of it, without reflections, leaves,
>
> . . . . .
> . . . all this
> Had to be imagined as an inevitable knowledge,
> Required, as a necessity requires.

Because it is an imaginative act, the mind's contemplation of its own annihilation and the scenery of its own nothingness carries forward the secular redemption implicit in the power of poetry.

In these late poems, Stevens no longer questions as he had done earlier the suitability of language to express the mind's visions. Where the man with his blue guitar complained at the inefficiency of his instrument to "play things as they are" and concluded "I cannot bring a world quite round, / Although I patch it as I can," the older Stevens discovers words are not semantic structures that impede the work of the imagination; they *do* bring the world round and fully participate in the process of mind confronting reality. In **"Prologues to What Is Possible,"** he dramatizes the resilience of the mind-language relationship. The poem opens with a simple simile: "There was an ease of mind that was like being alone in a boat at sea." In its quest to define its own well-being, the imagination elaborates a complex fiction involving ocean waves, the bright backs of rowers, the gripping of oars. During the process of pursuing words to express itself, the mind goes beyond the scope of its original intent and arrives at the point of the first idea almost in spite of itself:

> As he traveled alone, like a man lured on by a
> syllable without any meaning,
> A syllable of which he felt, with an appointed
> sureness,
> That it contained the meaning into which he
> wanted to enter,
> A meaning which, as he entered it, would shatter
> the boat and leave the oarsmen quiet
> As at a point of central arrival, an instant moment, much or little,
> Removed from any shore, from any man or
> woman, and needing none.

Like all processes, the activity of generating fictive structures leads the mind in unpredictable directions. The very effort of writing the poem, of pursuing syllables to describe the "ease of mind," leads to a central vision, the highest accomplishment of the poetic act. By joining perception to vocabulary, the poet achieves more than he bargained for: "The metaphor stirred his fear. The object with which he was compared / Was beyond his recognizing." The certainty of his fiction unsettles him because he realizes he has uncovered a new aspect of the self that he did not know was there, and that the lure of syllables will result in other metaphors equally profound and unsettling. Stevens indicates that the poet's approximations do more than "patch" reality. They uncover and reveal it. The imagination's realm involves "The loftiest syllables among loftiest things." The poet's words among the world's particulars constitute an earthly spirituality to replace what used to be "loftiest" heaven.

That which is revealed, always, is the holiness of the rock. In the title piece of his final collection, Stevens culminates his lifelong assertion of the sacred foundation of empirical living and the spiritual office of the poet's role as secular priest. . . . Stevens enacts in this holiest of poems a major assimilation and revaluation of his theory in order to discover what he refers to as the "cure" and "ground" of self and world. As Ronald Sukenick suggests, the rock represents "that base of man's life out of which he grows and from which he descends in death" [*Wallace Stevens: Musing the Obscure*]. At once birthstone and gravestone, Stevens' "synthetic" rock embodies a merging of all contraries—beginning and end, imagination and reality, permanence and impermanence. All become one in the "ground" of the mind of man.

Yet, if Stevens' poem attempts an assimilation, this does not imply a sterile reiteration of earlier premises. In the first canto of **"The Rock,"** subtitled "Seventy Years Later," Stevens expunges all of the old fictive houses in which the imagination sheltered itself:

> It is an illusion that we were ever alive,
> Lived in the houses of mothers, arranged ourselves
> By our own motions in a freedom of air.
>
> Regard the freedom of seventy years ago.
> It is no longer air. The houses still stand,
> Though they are rigid in rigid emptiness.
>
> Even our shadows, their shadows, no longer remain.
> The lives these lived in the mind are at an end.
> They never were . . .

An aspect of process, freedom cannot be defined in past moments of vitality. Stevens restates the Emersonian premise that "your action is good only whilst it is alive,— whilst it is in you." The freedom of seventy years ago is an illusion because it no longer lives but comprises the stale fixity of the remembered past. Stevens refuses to lapse into the now hollow comforts of a vibrant yesterday. He rejects the postulates of old poems such as those in **"The Man with the Blue Guitar":** "The sounds of the guitar / Were not and are not. Absurd." Seventy years later, the poet's freedom issues as always from a heroic response to present particulars.

If Stevens rejects the mind's old forms, he does not disparage them, for they were original acts of perception as much as this present poem and emanated from the same decreation-creation process. Each past poem embodied

> an illusion so desired
> That the green leaves came and covered the high rock,
> That the lilacs came and bloomed, like a blindness cleaned.

The mind's desire to cover the rock with the leaves and lilacs of its fictions must never be quenched because the poet's "vital assumption" of the nature of existence is that it consists of "an impermanence / In its permanent cold."

Himself about to become the victim of impermanence, Stevens' last poetic acts continue to affirm the fundamental pragmatic contention that change vitalizes life:

> The blooming and the musk
> Were being alive, an incessant being alive,
> A particular of being, that gross universe.

The poet fixes the rock in foliage. The leaves wither to illusion. The poet returns to the "particular," fecund, and voluptuous ("gross") universe and repeats the same process endlessly.

But the mere repetition of the process seems not enough. In the second canto, **"The Poem as Icon,"** Stevens raises the poet's poems or "leaves" to the level of sacramental objects:

> It is not enough to cover the rock with leaves.
> We must be cured of it by a cure of the ground
> Or a cure of ourselves, that is equal to a cure
>
> Of the ground, a cure beyond forgetfulness.

If the imagination simply covers the rock with leaves and imitates nature's birth-death cyclicity, it cannot escape nature's violence. The poem saves or "cures" man of the rock's violence by metaphorically redeeming him in the imagination's time scheme. The poet discovers a "cure of ourselves . . . equal to a cure / Of the ground" within the energy of each fictive act. The "ground" is the empirical world. In this poem, Stevens brings the ground of reality totally within the landscape of the imagination. External and internal grounds become one in the central mind.

As an image of sacred reality, the poem as icon participates in a secular spirituality parallel to the Christian myth of the Eucharist, in which a blessed host (the icon of Christ) is consumed and a worshiper is temporarily redeemed or cured. Stevens' imagery invokes a similar ritual:

> And yet the leaves, if they broke into bud,
> If they broke into bloom, if they bore fruit,
>
> And if we ate the incipient colorings
> Of their fresh culls might be a cure of the ground.
> The fiction of the leaves is the icon
>
> Of the poem, the figuration of blessedness,
> And the icon is the man.

Stevens carefully constructs his religious parallel around "if." In fact, the poet does not consume his own sanctifying fictions, but since his poems unite him with nature's vitality (as the communion host unites the Christian with the vital Christ) and redeem him from insignificance, fixity, and cyclical death, they constitute "figuration[s] of blessedness" in a secular universe. Through his fictions, the poet adds "New senses in the engenderings of sense" by specifying reality's rich core—"The honey in its pulp, the final found, / The plenty of the year and of the world." Most important, in covering the barren rock with leaves, the priest-poet supplies meaning to a meaningless void and eliminates the barrenness within each creative act:

> In this plenty, the poem makes meanings of the rock,

Of such mixed motion and such imagery
That its barrenness becomes a thousand things

And so exists no more. This is the cure
Of leaves and of the ground and of ourselves.
His words are both the icon and the man.

Poem, poet and world participate equally in the secular holiness. **"The Rock"** substantiates what Stevens meant when he wrote in the **"Adagia":** "After one has abandoned a belief in god, poetry is that essence which takes its place as life's redemption."

The ultimate statement of poetry's redemptive power comes in the final canto, **"Forms of the Rock in a Night-Hymn."** Stevens examines the rock's essential barrenness from the point of view of one about to die, and still finds it man's rightful home, the only paradise to which he should aspire. He avoids sentimentalizing the rock's awesome significance:

> The rock is the gray particular of man's life,
> The stone from which he rises, up—and—ho,
> The step to the bleaker depths of his
> descents . . .
>
> The rock is the stern particular of the air.

Stern and inescapable, the rock proclaims man's birth and man's doom. Infinitely larger than man, it is a "mirror of the planets," the "habitation of the whole." Yet the poet renders the rock man's own through his ability to compose night hymns, such as this one, that imbue reality with the only meaning it can possess. In Riddel's words, "the rock as both origin and end of self is discovered to have its own origin and end in the self" [*The Clairvoyant Eye*]. Subsuming the world into the horizons of the eye of imagination (the "silent rhapsodist"), the poet celebrates the rock instead of fearing it and discovers peace within the holiness of his fictions:

> It is the rock where tranquil must adduce
> Its tranquil self, the main of things, the mind,
>
> The starting point of the human and the end,
> That in which space itself is contained.

Stevens ends his poetic quest at the beginning, with the mind's eye as the first circle in a universe of flowing particulars. There is nothing surprising or contradictory in Stevens' high religious sentiment at the conclusion of his life. . . . Stevens writes poetry as a religious act and proposes his poems as sacred replacements for sterile doctrinal creeds and theories. The poet's function, revealed in **"The Rock,"** is to illumine reality within fictive hymns that vitalize the self by renewing the world. The poet's imaginative visions forever return him to the "starting point," the point of "Naked Alpha" where self and world are incessantly renewed.

Stevens closes his collection on the threshold of new life. The final poem, **"Not Ideas About the Thing But the Thing Itself,"** takes the imagination out of winter and away from death into still another spring:

> At the earliest ending of winter,
> In March, a scrawny cry from outside
> Seemed like a sound in his mind.

[Helen] Vendler errs in finding this a poem of death in which "old age . . . is in fact inhabiting a pre-history, as the soul, not yet born, waits to be reincarnated" [*On Extended Wings: Wallace Stevens' Longer Poems*]. Life, not death, reincarnates Stevens' imagination. This is a poem of beginnings, not ends. The "scrawny cry" is a bird's song "In the early March wind" announcing the advent of another cyclical phase: "He knew that he heard it, / A bird's cry, at daylight or before." Hardly a "November voice" that "cannot even articulate itself into verse," Stevens' voice of old age is clear and celebrational. A new season for the imagination's life has begun, and the mind leaps at the faraway sound that hints it is time to discard winter's fictions and dress itself anew in reality's forms. "The sun was coming from outside"—not the mind's inside idea of sun, but a new sun, a spring reality, leafless, which the imagination again must fix in foliage. Stevens' last piece indicates the imagination redeemed once more and poised in splendid anticipation:

> That scrawny cry—it was
> A chorister whose c preceded the choir.
> It was part of the colossal sun,
>
> Surrounded by its choral rings,
> Still far away. It was like
> A new knowledge of reality.

(pp. 169-76)

The growth of Stevens' poetry from *Harmonium* to *The Rock* follows the Emersonian lines of a poetic self, initially tentative and inconsistent in its creative voice, advancing with increasing confidence into the center of the life of the mind. In a world without gods and lacking any teleological base, Stevens' challenge to himself was "to find the spiritual in reality" and to "establish aesthetics in the individual mind as immeasurably a greater thing than religion." The foundation of this aesthetic is that "the mind is the most powerful thing in the world" and that it creates from the energy of original insight the necessary and exquisite fictions on which modern man, if he is to survive the death of the gods, must sustain himself. With heaven and hell destroyed, Stevens focuses the attention of his imagination on the ground of earth, the particulars of a world caught in the permanence of ceaseless change. He realizes evil as inseparable from process; by assimilating evil into his aesthetic, he frees himself from transempirical dependence and arrives at a point where the imagination begins redeeming itself by its own generative visions. Hence, the imagination recovers in the rock of an empirical world the heaven it thought it had lost. Stevens learns that "the mind that in heaven created the earth and the mind that on earth created heaven were, as it happened, one" [*Opus Posthumous*]. Both, that is, were the mind of man. In the secular and vibrant temple of his present reality, Stevens creates redeeming songs that "renew the world in a verse" and delight in the facticity of mere being. (pp. 177-78)

David M. La Guardia, in his Advance on Chaos: The Sanctifying Imagination of Wallace Stevens, *University Press of New England, 1983, 192 p.*

Fredric Jameson   (essay date 1984)

[*A leading American Marxist critic and literary theorist, Jameson has written extensively on nineteenth- and twentieth-century literature, philosophy, and culture. Jameson's self-defined "dialectical criticism" is derived from the writings of G. W. F. Hegel, the dialectical materialism of Theodore W. Adorno and Herbert Marcuse, the existentialism of Jean-Paul Sartre, and the communication theory of Jurgen Habermas. Seeking to exhibit the sociopolitical relevance of literature and culture, Jameson has applied his critical methodology to literature, criticism, and society in such influential works as* Marxism and Form: Twentieth-Century Dialectical Theories of Literature *(1971) and* The Political Unconscious: Narrative as a Socially Symbolic Act *(1981). In the following excerpt, Jameson analyzes the implicit and explicit relationships between poetry and theory, reality and symbol, and modernism and capitalism in Stevens's poetry.*]

Any evaluation of Stevens' work must start from an initial axiological paradox, which is surely more intense with Stevens than with any other major modernist figure. It must somehow be able to accommodate the seeming irreconcilable impressions of an astonishing linguistic richness on the one hand and an impoverishment or hollowness of content on the other, each of these in constant tension with one another and on various readings each seeming to draw the other into its force field and transfigure it. On the one hand, a familiar modernist practice of the unique personal or private style in these poems opens up into a wealth of vocabulary and syntactical fluidity that seems both absolute (no stammering, the voice never ends, is never reduced to silence or to awkwardness) and somehow impersonal again, as though this style were in reality something like an older rhetoric, with its collective, prepersonal capacities, its preexisting of the individual speaker who only needs to move in it as in an element. Therewith, however, one of the key features of the modernist will to style is lost: the necessity for its violent birth, for a painful conquest of the private voice over against the universal alienation of public speech: that 'initial ugliness,' as Gertrude Stein liked to say, 'which it is our business as critics to recapture [even when standing in front of the insipid canonical loveliness of the Sistine Madonna] and which is that new style's struggle to be born.' Nothing of a kind in Stevens: which is to say that in him, or for his discourse, it is for whatever reason no longer necessary to posit a whole universe of degraded speech, a whole world of prose, of the world of alienation and work, of universal instrumentalization and commodification, out of which and against which a specifically disalienating poetic language will emerge.

This extraordinarily supple and resourceful speech will then often seem to express its objects in some remarkably apt and unmediated way: more often, however, what I have called the inner hollowness of this verse will tend to return upon its language to cast some doubt upon the latter's density and authenticity. This steals upon one in those moments in which it becomes (momentarily) clear that Stevens' *only* content, from the earliest masterpieces of **Harmonium** all the way to the posthumous **Rock,** is

landscape: and that not even in the visionary sense of many of the great nature poets, for whom the momentary epiphanies of place and object world are rare events, to be preserved over against the encroaching destruction of Nature as well as the alienating features of city or man-made environment. In Stevens, nature is, however, nothing but a given, a ready-made occasion for speech—birds, wind, mountains, the sun, always ready to hand whenever poetic speech needs some kind of objective content for its own production.

This is not to say that such content in Stevens is not also historically specific, as it necessarily always must be: there must be a historical precondition even for this seemingly ahistorical availability of abstract landscape for whatever poetic ends. In fact, landscape in Stevens has a two-fold historical specificity, as a certain type of culturally marked geography, as well as a certain 'vocabulary field' of specific and culturally marked place-names. But I will argue in this first moment that Stevens must repress this specificity, whose recognition would at once deflect his work into directions like those of Williams and Olson and raise social and historical issues that would at once undermine his remarkably self-contained or autonomous aesthetic vision.

The repression of the social origins of this neutralized landscape, henceforth given as a kind of abstract 'vocabulary,' a set of neutral counters for the exercise of poetic speech (not unlike those formal, geometrical vocabulary units of the great architectural modernists such as Le Corbusier), is determined by the subject-object framework of Stevens' poetic practice which we will characterize as rigorously epistemological in all the worst senses of this word. In Stevens we never have anything but an abstract subject contemplating an object world which is thereby construed as being equally abstract. As with the great 'illustrations' of classical epistemology (in professional philosophy), where impoverished tokens from the external world (a desk, say) are drawn in as sheer indifferent 'examples,' the items of the external world must in Stevens equally be laundered of their cultural and social semantics, just as the social world and the existence of other people must equally be bracketed. But this observation is not a solution but a problem in its own right: it should logically lead to the attempt to establish the historical preconditions of even this peculiarly abstract possibility.

Indeed, the preliminary remarks on Stevens should not overhastily, in our present *historicist* and historicizing context, be taken as criticisms, not even yet as an ideological critique, of Stevens' work (we do not even yet, for one thing, know exactly what it is or does). At best, these must be seen as contradictions that will set ultimate limits for Stevens' 'achievement,' and these will be indicated in time: what is historically significant, however, is the work that is done within those limits. That it is avant-garde or elitist poetry goes without saying: but such extreme language experiments have themselves much to tell us about historical possibilities that one would not have been able to read off of other kinds of texts (the latter may well be revealing in quite different ways, for which Stevens or vanguard modernism would be quite useless). In particular, however, as damaging as the restriction to an epistemological frame-

work may be, we must here too immediately add the quali-
fication that somehow, again in ways that remain to be determined, Stevens' poetry manages to transcend the limits
of traditional epistemology: here, as in the gradual fore-
grounding of the theme of language in his work, he may
best be read as registering a process analogous to that we
will observe in French 'structuralism,' namely a dissolution of the older epistemological subject-object framework, which is bought at the cost of a certain reification
of 'Language.'

The well-known problem of beginnings or of the starting
point: we will begin with the phenomenon of the ease of
speech that has already been mentioned. It is not a particularly unusual starting point: Wordsworth critics, for example, find their privileged points of departure in the distinction of moments in which poetic speech can flow from
others which somehow block the latter and cause poetic
language to return upon itself and interrogate its own conditions of productivity. Meanwhile, in other kinds of
poets, the arbitrariness of certain poetic stances (the personal voice, say, or the prophetic mode, or the dramatic
monologue) at once by their very artificiality designate the
central problem of a more general blockage of other forms
of poetic language. What we have to do with Stevens is artificially to reconstruct a certain stance or mental element
that, once determined, accounts for this seemingly effortless coming of sentences and of their content.

This may perhaps best be evoked by a contrast with the
(contemporaneous) speech source of surrealist poetry,
which laid claim to an equally effortless flow, although one
of a clearly very different type. The problem is essentially
one of distracting oneself from everything which intimi-
dates or blocks speech: the surrealists found such an ideal
locus of spontaneity through the systematic blocking off
of conscious, rational, calculating mental and institutionalized thinking—in other words, by systematically sus-
pending the 'reality and performance principle' on the
order of free association in Freudian analysis. But this
very complex mental operation required them in effect, by
their very effort and attention to that reality principle that
has to be repressed, to preserve what they cancelled: so
that the latter (or better still the inaugural opposition between common sense prose reality and poetic language)
returns on the poetic language, which, effortless in principle at least for the poetic producer, is then wildly disso-
nant for the reader and bears all the marks of the bracketing of reality that instituted it.

Nothing of the sort, as we have said, for Stevens' form of
what may still in some way be characterized as free association. If so, then we would have to speak of something like
a free association of *preconscious* material in Stevens, to
distinguish him sharply and radically from the surrealists.
The more appropriate point of reference, as we shall see,
and one that anchors Stevens more firmly in our period
than has hitherto been done, is with Lévi-Strauss' 'discovery' of *pensée sauvage,* of the operation of great preconscious grids and associative systems, which, like a language or like several linguistic systems, subtend the
thoughts of 'primitive' peoples, that is, of tribal people
who have not yet known abstraction in the modern or 'sci-

entific' sense (who precede the emergence of 'philosophy'
in ancient Greece). The ambiguity in Levi-Strauss,
marked by our designation of such systems as being 'like'
languages, is not merely present in Stevens also: it marks
out an ambiguous space that is the precondition of the
'ease' of his discourse: namely a kind of no-man's-land in
which words and images are not yet radically distinguished from one another. In any case, as has been widely
observed, this ambiguity is at the very heart of the pseudo-
concept of the 'image' as well, about which it is never clear
whether this word designates the thing of which the image
is a representation, or the representation itself. The moment of 'structuralist' reflexivity, in which language itself
as a separate system is disengaged from *all* of its contents—whether images or things, signifieds or referents—
is a later moment, which will in fact cancel this initial moment of possibility.

The latter is thus available only on condition the systemic
levels and their dynamics are not yet differentiated: a sense
of the systemic relationship of words, which is not yet distinguished from a system of images, itself still naively able
to be assumed to be a system of the objects themselves, the
sub-systems of the natural world, or what we have called
Stevens' landscapes:

> Morning and afternoon are clasped together
>
> And North and South are an intrinsic couple
> And sun and rain a plural, like two lovers
> That walk away as one in the greenest body.
>   ***Notes toward a Supreme Fiction***

These differential relationships have not yet been dogmati-
cally codified in terms of the binary opposition of structural linguistics: if 'North' and 'South' offer such a binary opposition in its pure state, the same cannot be said for
'morning' and 'afternoon'—elements of a larger system ultimately organized around 'morning' and 'evening' but eccentric to that opposition—and even more so for 'sun' and
'rain,' in which these secondary or marginal or asymmetri-
cal oppositions have been widened to include quite different semes, before being returned to the more conventional
sexual opposition ('the lovers') and revealed to be the
unity of growth by means of the adjective 'greenest.' No
yoking of widely disparate contents in a jarring surrealist
image here: there seems to be little enough resistance to
the play of the mind across these signifying fields, and
their reunification is a victory that is not bought at any
particularly exorbitant or even visible cost.

The 'still point' from which this kind of systemic exploration, this free association of the preconscious, is possible
will then be initially one of cultural systems and collective
associations (socially institutionalized in the collective
pensée sauvage) as in Lévi-Strauss. It may be useful to
mark the cross-reference to another significant 'modernist'
literary discovery, namely Flaubert's sudden awareness of
the operation of bits of material language in consciousness, the not yet completely determinant yet ominous organization of the 'mind' by clichés, commonplaces, forms
of *'bêtise'* which are active in crystallized or reified phrases
and bits of material speech. Only where in Flaubert these
foreign bodies are immediately felt to be degraded speech
(and through *bovarysme* already prophetically linked to

the nascent media, the vehicles of propagation of these 'pseudo-thoughts'), in Stevens there is no particular sense that these associative paths are in any way inauthentic (the same is true for Lévi-Strauss, but for a different reason, namely the restriction of his work to tribal peoples 'before the fall,' objects, in his Rousseau revival, of the celebration of something like 'natural man'). Yet this is what accounts for the peculiar impersonality of Stevens' poetry and imagination: no sense of the urgent need to forge a private and uniquely personal style, to wrest one's individual *pensée sauvage* as an act of revolt from the standardized culture surrounding those last places of the authentic. Stevens' imagination situates itself at once in the universal, thereby forfeiting the peculiar glamour of the modernist poet as *poète maudit*, genius and unique stylist: *style* being above all the ambiguous and historical category in which, in high modernism, the specificity of the individual subject is expressed, manifested and preserved. This peculiarly unmodern commitment to collective association, to an already systemic cultural storehouse—a commitment that does not in Stevens involve the renunciation of the personal and the private, either, since in a sense it precedes the very emergence of the individual subject and of the latter's oppositions—accounts in another way for what we have called the hollowness or impoverishment of his content: Utopian in that it implicitly insists on the undegradedness of the cultural stereotypes, on their freshness and perhaps indeed their immediate or unmediated relationship to Nature itself, the reliance on collective automatisms, in a fallen society, cannot but be somehow, at some ultimate level, the zero degree or average common denominator of a fragmented and atomized *Gesellschaft;* hence the strategic limitation of this material to landscape, where those features may be expected to be least obvious and intrusive.

Still, there is much properly cultural material in Stevens, material that dates him oddly far more than the other great modernists of his generation, and read in a certain fashion obsessively evokes the glossy ads, the art deco, the fashions and interior design of the 20s or the more elegant productions of the silent movie era:

> When the elephant's-ear in the park
> Shrivelled in frost,
> And the leaves on the paths
> Ran like rats,
> Your lamp-light fell
> On shining pillows,
> Of sea-shades and sky-shades
> Like umbrellas in Java.
>
> "Tea"

Yet the high luxury of these characteristic interiors is a significant mechanism in the dynamics of Stevens' associative systems: these materials are allowed entrance to the verse, not because Stevens is particularly aware of their social and class character, as rather because—for obvious class reasons—they are felt in their elegance to be something like a subset of the natural. As in contemporary photorealism, the people (debutantes, jazz-age rakes, Newport aristocracy, and the like) are excluded, and only the Utopian *locus* of a peculiarly refined space for life remains behind (as also in some advertising). In fact, of course, such images are not natural, but form a specific 'signifying field'

among others in Stevens' imagination (others, related in different ways, would include the 'popular American' field of associations, Whitman, 'the emperor of ice cream,' American birds, Indian imagery, a whole marked 'American' vocabulary that intersects with various other specific vocabulary fields such as the 'French,' and so forth).

But what is important to us at present is the return of this seemingly alien content to the base-line natural system: this is achieved by means of a slippage from image to language. The glossy ad for an elegant boudoir, the luxurious empty place of reclining bodies, negligees, intimate receptions, now without any apparent discontinuity or shifting of gears now finds fulfillment in an unexpected way, by the emergence of a place-name: Java. Indeed, place-names in Stevens (he who travelled so little in his life, and was proud of the fact) play a key role in the articulation of systems of natural or landscape *images* to the operation of more properly linguistic systems: the mystery of place-names, like those of proper names generally, lies in their coordination of a general cultural system (see Lévi-Strauss on the naming system for dogs, cats, birds and horses in our culture) with the unique deictic of the here-and-now, the named individual who is incomparable and presumably not systematizable. In Stevens, the place-name will be at one and the same time the very locus and occasion for a production of images: quasi-Flaubertian *bovarysme*, the daydream about the exotic place, the free association on Java, Tehentepec, Key West, Oklahoma, Tennessee, Yucatan, Carolina, and so forth—and the emergence of another level of systematicity in language itself (the generation of place-names out of each other, their association now as a proper vocabulary field), behind which yet a deeper system is concealed and active.

That deeper system, as the majority of place-names in Stevens can testify, centers on the exoticism of the South and most notably of the whole Caribbean area (Stevens was also proud, in particular, of never having been to Europe, a set of place-names that would have been peculiarly intrusive here as we shall see in a moment). We may thus generally characterize this new and very instinct 'signifying field' as corresponding generally to what would today be called the material of the Third World (yet another reason why there is some deeper logic in including Stevens in the movement of the early 60's: only Crane of the great American modernists was also sensitive to the specificity of this material—Royal Palm or the seascapes—but Crane's aesthetics are very different from this and the resonance of his Caribbean has nothing in common with Stevens' assimilation of Third World realities to a place-name system and an occasion for infinite imagining reverie).

Yet it is clearly a peculiar view of the Third World, which one might seek to concretize by the experience of the world tour, the liner cruise through the islands, a peculiarly disengaged luxury tourist's contemplative contact with ports and maps (a specific moment, one would think, of aristocratic or moneyed tourism in the 1920s, which has little socially in common with the more universal tourism of the present day). This impoverished experience reconfirms our notion of the underlying purely epistemological stance of Stevens' work—a detached subject contemplating a static object in a suspension of praxis or even rootedness—and is documented in Stevens' one autobiographical 'novel' or narrative, **"The Comedian as the Letter C."** Yet if this is the phenomenological experience, the 'social equivalent' of Stevens' fascination with place-names, it also betrays a far deeper social and economic source which is that of the consumption of luxury products and objects at a particular moment in the development of modern capitalism, and reflects, one might say, a kind of luxury-mercantilist *Weltanschauung,* a view of the 'world system' as so many sources for expensive imported goods. There is, in other words, a subterranean relationship between the 'umbrella in Java'—the fantasy of the exotic holiday—and the 'umbrella *from* Java,' the luxury item whose own capacity to generate images, daydreams and semic associations lies in its origins in a distant place and culture, and in the momentary function of a Third World handicraft industry to produce just such objects of consumption for the First World.

What we have called the Third World material in Stevens is thus not some mere private aberration in his work, not some mere adjunct due to the accidents of his personal history, his means, travel, and the culture of the age; but is rather a fundamental piece in the overall system, the way by which the latter comes to know a global closure and thus a universality (both Hartford *and* Yucatan, both First and Third Worlds) on which its other procedures depend. At the same time, by means of this crucial mediation of Third World material, a bridge is made between image and word (by means of place-names), and a transformation of purely social and cultural objects (the interiors, the furnishings, the jazz-age luxury items) back into Nature and virtual landscape, since they all come to be associated with exotic *places.*

With the completion of his 'world' by such Third World material, then, it would seem that an autonomous or semi-autonomous space has been achieved that can now be felt to 'represent' the real world in its fundamental oppositions (nature versus culture, or in other words, landscape versus luxury consumption objects; and First World versus Third World). The next step in our inquiry is to investigate the process of autonomization by which this new 'ideal' world of 'representation' is felt to separate itself from the empirical one.

But we must first dispel the impression that this ideal sphere of images and words is some Parmenidean place of changelessness or of static being: our characterization of the content of Stevens' world as hollow or impoverished designated the nature of the link between the 'ideal' and the 'empirical' in Stevens. On the other hand, once we enter completely the realm of the 'poem,' it is clear that there is a great fluidity, a wealth of movement and micro-event that must now be accounted for in some more adequate fashion. We have suggested that the space of possibility onto which Stevens' imagination for whatever accidents of personal history or inclination happened—that space which unexpectedly opens up a seemingly limitless movement of poetic discourse, without barriers, in all directions—this space is essentially that designated by 'structuralism', or by Theory as the Symbolic Order, or in

a different way by Hegel as 'objective spirit,' or by Durkheim as 'collective consciousness': that is, the ensemble of representations, representational systems, and their various levels (concepts, images, words), in which the individual consciousness or subject must dwell, and about which the thinkers of this period increasingly suspect that, more than a mere element for thought, or even constellations floating in the mind, this whole system may in fact determine and program individual consciousness to a far greater degree than had hitherto been imagined. This 'discovery,' if it can really be called that, is significantly contemporaneous with the emergence of media society (or of the *société de consommation*), and may thus be expected at least in part to register this tremendous quantitative increase in material images and representations of all kinds in the new cultural space in question. Always accepting the conception of a Symbolic Order as a kind of space and dynamic beyond the individual subject, we do not, however, necessarily need to endorse the various models and hypotheses devised by high structuralism to describe this new space, and essentially extrapolated from linguistic systems (binary oppositions, the Greimas semantic rectangle, even the more multidimensional projections of a Lévi-Strauss or a Foucault of immense systemic relations in constant transformation).

Stevens' freedom to move within the Symbolic Order is at least in part ensured by the absence of such codified models, which often restrict inquiry or exploration in advance. Now that Stevens' work is over and 'complete,' it would certainly seem possible to imagine an enlarged and complex structural analysis capable of mapping it out after the fact: here we will essentially be content to stress the multiplicity of sub-systems in this ideal space, which is closed, if at all, only in the sense that the Einsteinian universe is closed, by folding back on itself, such that one never meets anything but contents of the same order, rather than, as in traditional closure, by the arrival at limits beyond which some radical otherness or difference from the system is felt to exist.

These 'sub-systems,' or 'fields' as I prefer to call them, are thus in themselves capable of infinite expansion and combination: the dominant one, what in another kind of writer one would have been tempted to call that of the pastiche of Elizabethan language (what I have earlier characterized as the rediscovery, in a modernizing world of *styles,* of an essentially rhetorical practice in Stevens)—this field is capable of as much formal variety, of as unlimited a mutability, as clouds themselves (to use a characteristic Stevens image), and one could, in a pinch, dwell in it forever, were it not for the perpetually nagging sense that it is not itself really a world but merely a specific language. Each of these fields is thus essentially complete, with its own oppositions and its own rich possibilities of dissonance and contradiction: in such a field, for example, 'grammarians' can be 'gloomy' and still wear 'golden gowns.' Such eventful tensions are felt to be an interesting heterogeneity only *within* the limits of the field itself: when, as we are admonished to do by the letter 'G,' we step outside that particular stylistic field, such variety once again falls back into a kind of homogeneity.

What has to be added, however, is the observation that there is also a play of eventfulness, of dissonance, of contradiction and variety or heterogeneity at the *intersections* between the various fields: as when a pseudo-Elizabethan vocabulary, for instance, like two galaxies colliding and interpenetrating on their distinct paths through space, momentarily knows interference with a pseudo-American, Whitmanesque, folkloric vocabulary field, all shot through with hoots and 'barbaric' sounds and yawps. . . . These intersystemic combinations ought clearly to produce an even richer sense of eventfulness than those that take place within any given system (all the more so since, as I have suggested, the systems involved are themselves disparate—some being systems of images, some of concepts, and some, simply, of vocabularies and 'style').

Yet this is not necessarily the case either: in fact, what tends to happen when a single sub-system or field intersects with another is rather a bracketing or a distantiation in which each is precisely grasped as a 'field,' seen now for what is an ideal system of representations rather than a 'world.' Here, too, a certain movement of structuralism, or rather its immediate prehistory, coming upon an analogous phenomenon, has proposed a concept for this process which is relevant: this is Barthes' early notion of 'connotation,' derived from Hjemslev and later repudiated in Barthes' middle or 'mature' structuralist period. Connotation designated a set of messages given off, not by the 'things themselves' but by the modes of representation of those things; a moment, in other words, in which (to use another characteristic formulation of the period) the medium turns into its own message, or rather begins to emit its own messages; in which the former 'message' or denotation is henceforth only the occasion or pretext for new second-degree messages couched in the language of signs or styles or representational systems themselves. But Barthes' account, at least in relation to Stevens' poetry, needs to be elaborated and refined: for here it is clear that we have to do, not merely with isolated connotations, but with a play between whole 'systems' of connotation among each other, systems in which the reference withdraws in order the more surely to foreground style or representation as its new object (in that sense, the concept of connotation would offer yet an alternate model for theorizing the gradual autonomization of Stevens' systems, their reorganization into some ideal sphere beyond the empirical world itself). Thus, even this form of intersystemic play (as open-ended, clearly, as is each of the systems itself) ultimately undergoes an autoreferential momentum in which its very content, at the latter's strongest, ends up rather designating a play of forms.

With this, we may begin to observe the dynamics of autonomization proper as they can be viewed within the small-scale model or experimental laboratory situation of this poetic language:

> Just as my fingers on these keys
> Make music, so the selfsame sounds
> On my spirit make a music, too.
> **"Peter Quince at the Clavier"**

It is the quintessential Kantian moment in which, as con-

temporary middle-class subjectivity is forced back inside its own head, the idea of the thing peels off the 'thing itself,' now forever out of reach—less, to be sure, as a Kantian noumenon than as an infinitely receding 'referent,' image separating from the thing, idea from image, word from idea, so that as the poem systematically drives itself deeper and deeper into the Symbolic Order, the 'absent cause' of its content appears at ever greater distance in the imagined cosmos, its final symbolic form that 'absolute referent,' as Derrida has called it, the sun, in which, in some ultimate quintessence, all reference becomes itself concentrated and reduced to a point, a pure locus without dimension:

> The sun no longer shares our works . . .
> Not to be part of the sun? To stand
>
> Remote and call it merciful?
> The strings are cold on the blue guitar.
> **"The Man with the Blue Guitar"**

But this absolute referent was already present in various guises in the earlier poems, most strikingly perhaps in that remarkable exercise **"Thirteen Ways of Looking at a Blackbird,"** in a form Stevens virtually invented for modern poetry, the theme and variations, where the referent is first the intense black point of the 'eye of the blackbird,' only to return in various forms of punctuation and interference within consciousness as the shadow cast by the real.

This is the most crucial moment in Stevens' poetic operation, the unresolvable contradiction on which the whole system turns and depends absolutely: reference must be preserved at the same time that it is bracketed, and that it is affirmed of it that it can never be known, that it stands outside the system. The system autonomizes itself as a microcosm, a self-contained faithful Utopian reflexion and representation of 'things as they are': but in order to assure its continuing autonomy it must retain the link with the real of which it is the Hegelian 'inverted world' or the complete mirror reflexion. This link with the real—what we will shortly characterize as the link between the autonomized *sign* (signifier/signified) and the referent—cannot within this system be theorized. We are therefore given two absolute and incommensurable, self-contradictory formulations: on the one hand, 'nothing changed by the blue guitar.' Since the space of the Symbolic Order is the space of the images, ideas and names of 'things as they are,' the latter persevere serenely in their being, unmodified by their symbolic representation,

> nothing changed, except the place
>
> Of things as they are and only the place
> As you play them, on the blue guitar,
>
> Placed so, beyond the compass of change;
> Perceived in a final atmosphere. . . .

Yet the opposite is also true, and its affirmation is equally necessary to the poetic system—namely, that in some Utopian sense, everything is changed by the 'supreme fiction' of the Symbolic Order. Here is then once again the great paradox of the Symbolic Order thus conceived: it is both ideological and Utopian, both a simple reflexion or projection of the real with all its contradictions, and a small-scale model or Utopian microcosm of the real in which the latter can be changed or modified—one is reminded of Burke's characterization of the ambiguity of the 'symbolic act' and the cultural generally, on the one hand, a merely *symbolic* act which is not praxis and which changes nothing, yet on the other a genuine symbolic *act* which has at least the symbolic value of genuine praxis.

My point is that both of these contradictory formulations serve a non-theoretical function, namely to preserve the parallelism between a semi-autonomous symbolic space and the space of reality: this is a functional necessity for Stevens' system, since, as we shall see shortly, when in post-modernism the referent vanishes altogether, with it go the properly symbolic possibilities of Stevens' own specific subject-object relationship. Yet from this necessity (which Stevens must hold in being, which he must not allow to proceed further along the momentum of a properly post-modernist disintegration) a certain number of consequences flow—some of them ideologies, or strategies of ideological containment (in order to keep this contradictory system control) in and some of them inevitable structural results and limits of the system itself, among these that very quality of Stevens' poetry which we posed as an initial problem, namely the ambiguous sense of richness and impoverishment. We will formulate these structural consequences under three headings, with the preliminary reminder that the dialectic outlined up to this point is not ideological and does not yet imply the ideological critique of Stevens' work about to be summarized. Up till now, what we have described is an objective experience of a certain capacity of language or the Symbolic, which for whatever personal accidents Stevens felt himself impelled to explore, of which he made himself the objective vehicle or recording apparatus. The symbolic space opened up by Stevens' work, the autonomization of image from thing, idea from image, name from idea, is in itself neither true nor false, neither scientific nor ideological: it is an experience, and a historical experience, and not a theory about language or a choice susceptible of ethical or political judgement. But given the instability of this experience, which needs to be safeguarded and perpetuated by various strategies, the ideological now makes its appearance as what the Formalists would have called 'the motivation of the device.'

The strong form of ideology taken in Stevens' work is what we have since come to identify in the most general sense as existentialism (including within it that 'fiction-making' thematics of Nietzsche's work which is its initial moment). Here the familiar and banal motifs of *Geworfenheit* and absurdity make their predictable appearance: the death of God, the disappearance of religion, now determine a radically meaningless world in which alone poetry or fiction can restore at least an appearance of meaning, assuming for the moderns the function that religion used to secure in more traditional social systems:

> The earth, for us, is flat and bare.
> There are no shadows. Poetry
>
> Exceeding music must take the place
> Of empty heaven and its hymns,

> Ourselves in poetry must take their place,
> Even in the chattering of your guitar.

This ideology is then systematically elaborated and produced in the poems on death and the religion of art, from the early *Sunday Morning* on, in what are surely for us today the least interesting parts of the Stevens canon.

Yet what must be insisted on is the innate instability of existentialism (understood here as an ideology rather than as a technical and rigorous form of philosophical discourse). For as soon as we come to be convinced of the fictionality of meaning, the whole operation loses its interest: philosophies of 'as if' are notoriously unsatisfying and self-unravelling. Yet when such an ideology unravels, then the very conception of fiction disappears along with it. In order to prevent this dissolution of the poetic system, something like an Absolute Fiction must be desperately maintained:

> But to impose is not
> To discover. To discover an order as of
> A season, to discover summer and know it,
>
> To discover winter and know it well, to find,
> Not to impose, not to have reasoned at all,
> Out of nothing to have come on major weather,
>
> It is possible, possible, possible. It must
> Be possible. It must be that in time
> The real will from its crude compoundings
>   come,
>
> Seeming at first a beast disgorged, unlike,
> Warmed by a desperate milk. To find the real,
> To be stripped of every fiction except one,
>
> The fiction of an absolute—Angel,
> Be silent in your luminous cloud and hear
> The luminous melody of proper sound.
>   ***Notes toward a Supreme Fiction***

Here then the ultimate 'referent' is affirmed by the very movement that denies it, and what is less an ideology than a desperate conceptual prestidigitation reaffirms the impossible, the Angel, the absent cause, the Absolute or necessary fiction.

Yet in a final moment this desperate systemic readjustment has practical consequences which are like the price to be paid for its continuing existence. This is the great lateral movement of autoreferentiality referred to in the beginning, in which the act of designating the absent referent (blackbird's eye or the sun itself, the impossible Angel) turns out at one and the same time to be a process of designating the Symbolic or poetic space in question as symbolic or poetic, as fictional, such that the poetry will now come to turn on itself and in all of its rotations continue to designate nothing but itself. Hence the richness and impoverishment we spoke of: infinitely rich as the projection of a whole world, a whole geography, this language at once empties itself by calling attention to its own hollowness as that which is merely the image of the thing, and not the thing itself. Yet at this point, at which Stevens would be indistinguishable from the autoreferentiality of high modernism generally, an unusual permutation takes place, and a new thing—theory itself—emerges. What before was merely 'poetic' discourse, with its traditional and banal problems of the nature of specifically poetic discourse and of the aesthetic as nonpractical and noncognitive, suddenly opens up into a new form of discourse which is theoretical and poetic all at once, in which 'the theory of poetry' becomes at one with 'the life of poetry.' (pp. 11-19)

Fredric Jameson, "Wallace Stevens," in New Orleans Review, *Vol. 11, No. 1, Spring, 1984, pp. 10-19.*

Richard Gray   (essay date 1984)

[*In the following excerpt, Gray discusses Stevens's "kinship" with English Romanticism, French Symbolism, and American literature and philosophy in an examination of the general characteristics of Stevens's poetry.*]

'Poetry is the subject of the poem', wrote Wallace Stevens in **'The Man with the Blue Guitar'**. 'From this the poem issues and / To this returns.' Characteristically, Stevens meant a number of things by this, if only because as he saw it and expressed it in his **'Adagia'**, 'Poetry and materia poetica are interchangeable terms.' 'Poetry' for him included 'that / Irrational moment' when the mind feels reconciled, at one with its surroundings as well as 'the gaiety . . . of language' or indeed any other means the mind might employ to achieve this feeling. On a more elementary level, however, by 'poetry' Stevens also meant the poetry of other people, or statements made about poetry by other people with whom, perhaps, he felt he had some kind of intellectual *rapport.* For like many artists in different fields during this century—like Joyce, for instance, or Picasso or Stravinsky—Stevens was fascinated by the nature of his own art, and felt compelled to explore its possibilities and limitations. His work is nothing if not self-conscious. It almost asks us to look for contents and antecedents; it virtually obliges us to see it, and its creator, in terms of a particular time and place. In seeing things in this way, of course, there is the danger of becoming the kind of reader that Stevens deplored in one of his letters, 'who spends his time dissecting what he reads for echoes, imitations, influences, as if no one was ever simply himself but is always compounded of a lot of other people'. Not to do so, though, or rather not to look for signs of *kinship,* of spiritual resemblance rather than influence, would be to ignore Stevens's centrality and, quite possibly, underestimate his importance. Stevens was a great original, certainly: as indeed anyone who believes that 'All poetry is experimental poetry' must be. But he was a great original precisely because he could absorb and cope with so much pressure—because he could gather up so many different threads and out of them weave something entirely personal, coherent and new.

The first and probably most obvious sign of kinship is to be found in Stevens's 'final belief', the impulse that shapes and gives life to all of his work, and which marks him as a true heir of the Romantics. 'I do very much have a dislike of disorder', he admitted once, 'One of the first things I do when I get home at night is to make people take things off radiator tops'. Put in a characteristically self-mocking way, this sums up the nature of the impulse: a 'rage for

order', for form and a sense of meaning recovered, however temporarily, from the essential chaos of life. For Stevens, in fact, as for most of the great Romantic poets and philosophers, reality is not something given to us, which our minds receive passively, but is on the contrary something made, the product of an interchange, an interplay or dialectic between our minds and our given circumstances. We, or more accurately our consciousnesses, are not simply blank pieces of paper, Stevens felt, on which the world writes its messages, not just mirrors that reflect our environment; rather, they are lamps, active, creative things which illuminate that environment, helping to give it shape and perspective and so making it adequate, even if only momentarily, to ordinary human desires. 'The imagination', declared Stevens echoing Blake and Coleridge, 'is the power of the mind over the possibilities of things'; 'like light, it adds nothing, except itself'.

Stevens was sometimes irritated by references to the Romantics. 'The past is my own', he insisted in one of his letters, 'not something marked Coleridge, Wordsworth etc. I know of no one who has been particularly important to me'. Nevertheless, when one looks in detail at what Stevens terms his 'reality-imagination complex', it is not difficult to see several correspondences. 'Conceptions are artificial', Stevens argued; our world is always, in a sense, an imagined one, because as soon as we begin to think about it we begin to structure it according to some law—such as the scientific law of cause and effect. We begin, in effect, to 'read' and interpret it in the same way that, instinctively, we read and interpret a written text. On this level, the mind or imagination, as Stevens described it, broadly corresponds to what Coleridge, in *Biographia Literaria* called the primary imagination: 'the living power and prime agent of all human perception, and . . . a repetition in the finite mind of the eternal act of creation in the infinite I AM'. Much more important for Stevens, though, were those acts of the mind which made it correspond with what Coleridge termed the secondary imagination; that is to say, those acts whereby man attempts quite consciously to give significance to his life—to devise some moral or aesthetic order, however fragile or provisional, which can give coherence and a sense of purpose to things. This kind of order was what Stevens called a 'supreme fiction'; and for him, as for Coleridge, the prime creator of such fictions was the poet. The poet, according to Stevens, strives for a 'precise equilibrium' between the mind and its environment at any given moment in time; and then creates a fiction which is at once true to our experience of the world and true to his and our need for value and meaning.

It is worth emphasizing that Stevens was no different from Coleridge and other Romantics, either, in insisting on the fact of change. We are always altering, Stevens believed, our given circumstances alter too, and the fictive world created out of the synthesis or union of the two must invariably respond to this. We must be reassessing our personal needs and given circumstances continually so as to devise new ideas which do full justice to the dynamic nature of both mind and world; and the poet, in turn, must be writing new poems, new fictions all the time so as to pay his tribute to the metamorphic nature of things. Stevens's favourite metaphor for this was the seasons, with winter seen as the bare, icy reality void of all fictive covering; spring as the moment when the imagination and the world come together and embrace; summer as the period of fruition, when the marriage between the desires of the mind and the things of the world is complete and harmonious; and autumn as the moment when the fiction no longer suffices because the imagination that created it, and the world it was created for, have altered, requiring new fictions, fresh identities and relationships. As this rather bare outline indicates, perhaps, the imagery of sexual congress and conflict mingles with that of natural growth and decay to describe what Stevens, in one of his poems, termed the imagination's 'ancient cycle'; and in this respect, again, he was not so very different from a writer like Coleridge. Consider, for example, these two brief passages, one from 'Dejection: An Ode' and the other from *Notes toward a Supreme Fiction:*

> O Lady! we receive but what we give
> And in our life alone does Nature live. . . .
>
> Joy, Lady! is the spirit and the power
> Which wedding Nature to us gives in dower
> A new Earth and a new Heaven. . . .
>   . . . . .
> Two things of opposite natures seem to depend
> On one another, as a man depends
> On a woman, day on night, the imagined
>
> On the real. This is the origin of change.
> Winter and spring, cold copulars, embrace
> And forth the particulars of rapture come.

Mind and world, night and day, male and female: both writers see life here as a marriage of opposites. Joy, or a sense of meaning, is the offspring of this marriage. And what Coleridge called dejection, a sense of melancholy and futility, comes when the marriage fails; when, for example, the world is too much with us and the mind becomes a passive instrument—or, alternatively, when the mind escapes from the pressures of the world completely and withdraws into solipsism and day-dreaming.

'A poet looks at the world as a man looks at a woman.' This, from the **'Adagia',** offers a variation on the sexual metaphor: and it is also a reminder of just how seductive, for Stevens, was the figure of the poet. For Stevens was no less of a Romantic in this, his tendency to see the fabulator, the maker of poems, as a latter-day prophet: someone who creates the myths that give meaning to people's lives and so enables them to survive—and who also offers an example to his audience, by showing them how to devise their own myths as well as listen to his. Stevens was quite categorical about this. For, whenever he discussed the task or function of the poet, the thrust of his argument was invariably the same. 'I think', he would say,

> . . . that he fulfills himself only as he sees his imagination become the light in the minds of others. His rôle, in short, is to help people to live their lives. [**'Noble Rider and the Sound of Words'**]

In effect, Stevens returned the poet to his ancient rôle of bard or myth-maker, offering purpose and a sense of meaning to his tribe. And to this he added another, more peculiarly Romantic and American, dimension: which

was that of hero. For the poet, Stevens suggested, is his own hero because his mind, his representative imagination, is the catalyst of events. Instead of a third person protagonist, the poet, the 'I' of the poem, occupies the centre of the stage; there, 'like an insatiable actor, slowly and / with meditation', he speaks words and acts out a drama to which

> an invisible audience listens,
> Not to the play, but to itself, expressed
> In an emotion as of two people, as of two
> Emotions becoming one.
>   **['Of Modern Poetry']**

To the extent that Stevens did attribute such an extraordinarily powerful and central rôle to the poet, he was of course revealing a kinship with some of the later poets and philosophers in the Romantic tradition, like Matthew Arnold, Henri Bergson—and, above all, George Santayana. While he was still a student at Harvard, Stevens became acquainted with Santayana and was often invited to visit him; he read the older man some of his early poetry and then, much later, addressed one of his finest poems, **'To an Old Philosopher in Rome',** to him. In a way, Stevens seems to have regarded Santayana as a saint—a type, anyway, of the imaginative man, who can use his mind to redeem the essential poverty of life—and Santayana's ideas served as a lamp and guide to the poet throughout his career, illuminating his way, his various poetic voyages, and giving him some hazy sense of a possible destination. This famous passage from the **'Adagia',** for example, recalls Santayana's suggestion that 'religion and poetry are identical in essence', since both, ignoring 'matters of fact', 'repair to the material of existence . . . and then out of that . . . material . . . build new structures, richer, finer, fitted to the primary tendencies of our nature':

> The final belief is to believe in a fiction, which you know to be a fiction, there being nothing else. The exquisite truth is to know that it is a fiction and that you believe in it willingly.

'Poetry', said Stevens elsewhere, in **'The Man with the Blue Guitar',** ' . . . must take the place / Of empty heaven and its hymns.' For him, as for Santayana, the old religious myths had crumbled and poetry had now to act as a means of redemption. The poet had to replace the priest (or, alternatively, the priest had to accept the rôle of poet). Art had to replace the liturgy of the church. Imaginative belief, or what Coleridge called 'a willing suspension of disbelief', had to replace religious faith. And a possible earthly paradise, created here and now out of the marriage between mind and world, had to replace the vision of a heavenly paradise situated in some great hereafter. Beginning with an essentially Romantic belief in 'The imagination, the one reality / In this imagined world', and building slowly and meditatively on this, Stevens ended in fact with another centrally Romantic notion—that (to quote from the **'Adagia'** again)

> in the absence of a belief in God, the mind turns to its own creations and examines them, not alone from the aesthetic point of view, but for what they reveal, for what they validate and invalidate, for the support they give.

To dwell on Stevens's Romanticism, however, to the exclusion of other aspects of his poetic character would be to forget how very important to him both the French poets—and, in particular, the Symbolistes, their immediate precursors and successors—and his own American background were. The kinship with the French was undoubtedly less crucial than is often supposed; many commentators have exaggerated it, perhaps because it is fairly obvious—a matter, more often than not, of vocabulary and idiom. Nevertheless, it proved useful to Stevens in several respects, and not least in his efforts to distinguish himself from the English tradition. 'Nothing could be more inappropriate to American literature than its English source', he . . . declared [in the **'Adagia'**], 'since the Americans are not British in sensibility'. And one way he chose to underline this in his early work was by adopting, on occasion, a self-consciously Gallic tone, with phrases from the French, a smattering of French words—or that demureness of statement combined with elegance of manner and the kind of sonorous, precious and witty language that is often associated with such poets of the late nineteenth century as Verlaine and Laforgue. In turn, the later work often recalls more recent French poets like Valéry, in its openly philosophical approach, its confident use of large abstractions, and its extraordinarily complex network of figurative reference.

Perhaps the French poet with whom Stevens shared most, however, was not Verlaine, Laforgue, or even Valéry, but Baudelaire because, in this case at least, the sense of kinship operated on a rather deeper level. Certainly, the parallels in technique are evident here as well. Both Baudelaire and Stevens manage, for instance, to combine rule and misrule in their poems. Their rhythms are elegantly exact; the movement of each line is measured and poised; and the structure of each of their longer pieces seems to be premeditated, precise, a matter of inherited rather than imitative form. And yet, on the other hand, their language can be bizarre; their imagery gaudy, intentionally startling; and, on closer inspection, it seems that their longer poems do not so much progress as stand still or go round in a circle—existing in space, really, rather than time. As several critics have observed, Baudelaire was at once a Romantic writer and a Classical one, which is perhaps one of the reasons why he described the right to be inconsistent as 'a right in which everyone is interested'. Exactly the same could be said of Stevens, who openly admitted to a correspondent that he liked to move 'in many directions at once'. 'No man of imagination is prim', he added defiantly, 'the thing is a contradiction in terms.'

'May it be', asked Stevens half-seriously when he was just 26, 'that I am only a New Jersey Epicurean?' That question leads indirectly to the other, deeper level on which Baudelaire and Stevens meet: which is their shared insistence on the artificial, figurative nature of their poetic worlds. Very often, this insistence led them to play the literary dandy. Even if it did not, however, even when the tone was more agonized or philosophical, there was invariably this emphasis on the poet as maker, inventing a world rather than simply reporting one—and, in doing so, uncovering a possibility available to everyone. One of the most vivid and memorable descriptions of this activity—

of the mind giving life whatever savour or meaning it possesses—occurs in **'The Idea of Order at Key West'**. In it, the poet describes a woman whom he once heard singing by the sea (a traditional figure for raw experience), who becomes identified for him with the 'blessed rage for order', the need that singer, poet, and all of us must feel to discover form and significance in our lives. 'When she sang', the poet declares,

> the sea
> Whatever self it had, became the self
> That was her song, for she was the maker. Then
> we,
> As we beheld her striding there alone,
> Knew that there never was a world for her
> Except the one she sang and, singing, made.

The stress on that final 'made' is enormous, reminding us of the infinite series of makings that add up to the experience of the poem: the woman 'makes' or interprets the scene, and in turn each reader, each time he reads the piece, 'makes' or interprets what he sees and hears.

It may be worth pointing out that, in reminding us constantly of the figurative nature of poetic truth and the fictive nature of poetry, Stevens is (as so often) poised between paradoxes. The world the poem creates is real, Stevens seems to be saying, because the material for it is discovered *in* reality; and yet it is unreal, a fiction in a way, because it depends on the mind then reshaping that material. It is true in the sense that it reproduces a true—that is to say, a true Romantic-Symboliste—version of things; but it is untrue in that it does not reflect 'the first idea', pure, unadorned fact. Above all, it is perfect and complete in so far as it represents a perfect marriage, a complete synthesis of mind and circumstance; and yet it is imperfect, incomplete to the extent that, as mind and circumstance change, the poet must go on to devise new marriages, new syntheses, and so in effect new poems. Of course, Stevens never tried to achieve a logical reconciliation of these opposites because, like so many writers since the Romantic revolution, he realized that his beliefs stemmed from a profound illogic, a deep unreason. 'The poem', Stevens suggested [in the **"Adagia'**], 'reveals itself only to the ignorant man' for the simple reason that it depends on contradictions which can never be explained or argued away—but which can perhaps be reconciled with the help, and under the 'miraculous influence', of the imagination.

'Do I contradict myself? / Very well then I contradict myself, / (I am large, I contain multitudes)' [Walt Whitman, 'Song of Myself']. That would be one way of dismissing any objections Stevens's paradoxes might raise: the lofty gesture of a poet like Walt Whitman who insists that his self-contradictions are part of his representative nature, his attempt to register the variety of his homeplace. Which leads me, inevitably, to the native context; for all his kinship with the English Romantics and poets like Baudelaire, Stevens was nothing if not an American writer—and someone who believed that (to quote one of his very last poems) 'a mythology reflects its region'. 'The gods of China', Stevens declared, 'are always Chinese' [**'Two or Three Ideas'**]; that is, the world the imagination embraces is always a specific, local one and the fictions created out of that embrace must bear the stamp of their locality. 'One turns with something like ferocity toward a land that one loves', he said elsewhere, in a revealing discussion of another poet, John Crowe Ransom, ' . . . to demand that it surrender, reveal, that in itself which one loves' ['**John Crowe Ransom: Tennessean**']. As Stevens saw it, this consummation devoutly to be wished, this marriage between a particular person and place, was 'a vital affair, not an affair of the heart . . . , but an affair of the whole being, a fundamental affair of life'. It was not simply a matter of idiom and gesture, in other words, but of identity and vision. Of course, the paraphernalia of American culture is there in Stevens's poems—things like coffee, saxophones and large sombreros—and, like Whitman, Stevens shows that he has fallen in love with American names. But these things matter less, as a mark of origin, than the fact that Stevens chose as his starting-point what he called 'human loneliness / A part of space and solitude' ['**The Sail of Ulysses**']; like every great American poet, in fact, he began with the isolated consciousness—Whitman's 'essential Me'—and then progressed from there to the new dimensions, the moments of self-assertion or communion, which that consciousness struggles gamely to create.

Here, however, we are confronted with another paradox in Stevens's work. Like so many American writers, Stevens began with the isolated self, the separate mind and its world; unlike most of them, though, he then moved in two quite different directions, which could perhaps be termed *centripetal* and *centrifugal*. The centripetal movement recalls that arch-egotist and solipsist, Edgar Allan Poe; and, to some extent, Stevens does sound very much like Poe. The self, he insists, creates its own world, and the poem presents us with a supreme version of that world—which is self-contained, fixed and (in a sense, as I have already suggested) perfect. The centrifugal movement, in turn, recalls Emily Dickinson. For Stevens can be quite as insistent as Dickinson was that the self is fragile, evanescent, dwarfed by its surroundings, and that the world it creates must—due to the limitations of its creator—be provisional and incomplete. In some respects, Stevens's poems resemble Poe's in that they drive inwards upon what Poe, in one of his reviews, called 'the circumscribed Eden' of the poet's dream. 'Pure' or 'closed' poems in a way, they are as autonomous and intangible as the worlds they describe; they exist in their own special dimension, or, as Stevens himself put it once, 'beyond the compass of change / Perceived in a final atmosphere' ['**The Man with the Blue Guitar**']. In other respects, though, Stevens's poems seem far more like Dickinson's, edging out tentatively as they do towards the boundaries of perception. 'Open' poems of a kind, they tend to emphasize their arbitrariness, to offer themselves up to reinterpretation and reinvention—and so to remind us that they are (to quote Stevens [in *Notes toward a Supreme Fiction*]) 'inconstant objects of inconstant cause / In a universe of inconstancy'.

Just how Stevens manages to walk this tightrope between 'open' and 'closed' structures is beautifully illustrated by one of his most famous earlier pieces, '**Anecdote of the Jar**'. The animating conception in this poem is very simple: the jar serves as a point which orders all that surrounds it. It performs the function of the imagination just as its surroundings, organized for a moment into a series of significant relationships, perform the function of reality. What complicates things, however, and gives an additional dimension to the poem is its form, the way in which Stevens chooses to flesh out this conception. '**Anecdote of the Jar**' begins with a series of unrhymed couplets, continues with them until the eighth line, and then suddenly presents the reader with two end-stopped lines, set off for the first time by rhyme:

> It took dominion everywhere.
> The jar was gray and bare.

It sounds for a moment as if the argument is completed, the poem rounded off. But then, it turns out, it is not; and the premature finality of the lines I have quoted gives an air of *un*finality to the two lines which follow, and which form yet another unrhymed couplet. Even this, the feeling that things have not quite been rounded off, is not left unqualified, however, because the last line returns us to a word used in the first line: 'Tennessee'. Joining the end to the beginning, the poet still seems to be trying to round the poem off, to seal it; and we, the readers, cannot really be sure that he has failed. So we are made to feel that the work is at once complete *and* incomplete, that the argument has been concluded and yet that something has been missed out, left hanging loose. '**Anecdote of the Jar**' is, in effect, made to imitate in its form (as well as describe in its content) the continuing act of the imagination, by which worlds are created that are complete in themselves and yet subject to alteration. The mind behind the poem has apparently composed things for a moment, achieved an order 'beyond the compass of change'; and yet it intimates that it must give that order up soon and—casting aside 'the rotted names', obsolete forms and vocabulary—submit itself to 'a universe of inconstancy'.

'**Anecdote of the Jar**' is exemplary in several ways. The same essential structure, for instance, is used with a difference in '**Thirteen Ways of Looking at a Blackbird**'. Here, a blackbird serves as a focal point, a means of bringing out the significance of the context in which it is involved. The meaning of the bird depends on each context, just as the meaning of the context depends on it, with the result that there is exactly the same condition of interdependence between the bird and each of its settings as there is between the jar and its surroundings: a condition which (it need hardly be added) Stevens felt to be characteristic of the relationship between the imagination and its surroundings. In the first section of the poem, for example, the blackbird provides a focal point for the landscape it composes in the same way that a compositional centre composes a landscape painting; and, in doing so, it provides a paradigm of the way the mind orders reality by discovering significant relations in it.

> Among twenty snowy mountains,
> The only moving thing
> Was the eye of the blackbird.

In this case, the snowy surroundings are static, and the eye/I of the blackbird offers the only motion. By contrast, in the final section the terms are reversed:

It was evening all afternoon.
It was snowing
And it was going to snow.
The blackbird sat
In the cedar-limbs.

Now the blackbird is motionless in a world of swirling, snowy movement. The bird has become a still point; the imagination is, apparently, at rest; and the poet, making the last lines echo the first, seems to be bringing things full circle, rounding them off. Everything appears to be completed; that is, until we are reminded that, for Stevens, winter was a beginning as well as an end. This section concludes **'Thirteen Ways'**, certainly; but by reminding us of the process of decreation—what Stevens called [in a letter] 'getting rid of the paint to get at the world itself'—it also acts as a prelude to further imaginative activity, an opening to poems as yet to be written. Once again, things are complete and yet somehow incomplete, closed and at the same time open.

Quite apart from the structure, the tone and idiom of **'Anecdote of the Jar'** are also characteristic. The tone is serio-comic as with so many of Stevens's poems, especially the earlier ones; here as in, say, **'Bantams in Pinewoods'** or **'Le Monocle de Mon Oncle'** the poet uses wit and irony to qualify and complicate matters further, and so prevent the reader from coming to too simple or final a conclusion. And the idiom, in turn, is characterized by repetition and echo ('round . . . Surround . . . around . . . round . . . ground'), a series of significant if often subterranean connections. This repetitive pattern becomes far more elaborate in some of the longer pieces, with the result that poems like (for example) **'Sunday Morning'** or **'The Idea of Order at Key West'** resemble mosaics, in which the poet seems to be trying to construct his own personal version of the imaginative fictions he celebrates. Complex designs of word, sound and image, they offer the reader a special world, in this case a verbal one, which may be abstracted from and so depend upon our given surroundings—but which has its own innate structure and system of cross-reference.

It would be wrong, however, to dwell on **'Anecdote of the Jar'** as if it summed up the whole of Stevens's work, even in its paradoxes and ambiguities. No one poem can do that; and not merely because the later poetry is, on the whole, less spry and balletic than the earlier—more meditative and austere, more discursive and openly philosophical. It is also because Stevens rarely allowed himself to be contained by a particular idiom even within the space of one poem. Each of his pieces is complexly layered, moving almost casually and quite unpredictably between high rhetoric and the colloquial, book-words, foreign borrowings, and native slang. As a result, each seems unique in a way, with its own particular rhythms and adjustments—its own special way of turning the world into words. Of modern poetry, Stevens once said,

> It is like the voice of . . . some . . . figure concealed. . . . There is no accompaniment. If occasionally the poet touches the triangle or one of the cymbals, he does it only because he feels like doing it. Instead of a musician we have an orator

Stevens, his daughter Holly (center), an unidentified child, and "The Snow Man" (1929).

whose speech sometimes resembles music. [**'Effects of Analogy'**]

This passage, from the poem that concludes the third section of *Notes toward a Supreme Fiction,* suggests something of what he meant. The poem is a hymn to the earth, which Stevens describes as a 'fat girl' and addresses in exactly the same way that earlier poets addressed God or their mistress. Like God, the poet suggests, the earth is mysterious, hidden, infinite in its surprises; like the tradiional notion of the mistress she is also enticing but elusive, given to radically varying changes of mood. More important, perhaps: like both, she can only be understood through an act of the imagination, a poem or fiction of some kind—something in which her changeableness, her extraordinary vitality and variety, can be caught for a moment in a single, crystalline image.

> Fat girl, terrestrial, my summer, my night
> How is it I find you in difference, see you there
> In a moving contour, a change not quite completed?
> . . . . .
> Even so when I think of you as strong or tired.
>
> Bent over work, anxious, content, alone,

You remain the more than natural figure. You
Become the soft-footed phantom, the irrational

Distortion, however fragrant, however dear.
That's it: the more than rational distortion,
The fiction that results from feeling. Yes, that.

They will get it straight one day at the Sorbonne.
We shall return at twilight from the lecture
Pleased that the irrational is rational.

Until flicked by feeling, in a gildered street,
I call you by name, my green, my fluent mundo.
You will have stopped revolving except in crys-
tal.

The image of the revolving crystal is, of course, an image
of an image: a fictional embodiment of the kind of imaginative fiction that can at once recover the world about us,
in all its brightness, plenitude, and vitality, and raise it to
a higher power, a superior dimension of reality. And with
this image we are back, really, where we began, at the centre of the Romantic-Symbolist tradition, which is the great
tradition in modern poetry; since the forms of knowledge
and vision that Stevens celebrates here are no different
from those celebrated by the great Romantic poets and
their successors when they have talked, for example, about
the truth of the imagination, the power and suggestiveness
of the deep image, or described the world as a forest of
symbols. In its own way, the crystal corresponds to—
which is to say, has the same basic significance and performs the same symbolic function as—Coleridge's moon
imagery, Keats's nightingale and urn, or the memorable
allusion to the dancer that concludes Yeats's 'Among
School Children'. For it summarizes in the only way possible for Stevens (that is, in an imaginative way) what was
for him the central fact of life: the ability of the mind to
achieve a kind of redemption—by working *with* the world
to abstract something of value out of that world, and so
(as Stevens himself put it once) build a bridge between fact
and miracle.

'Why do poets in particular resent the attribution of the
influence of other poets?' asked Stevens in a letter to Richard Eberhart. 'It seems to me that the true answer is that
with a true poet his poetry is the same thing as his vital
self. It is not possible for anyone else to touch it'. This necessarily brief essay has been in no sense an attempt to deny
the simple fact that Stevens states here; like every 'true
poet', Stevens declared his own unique being in his work—
developed his own personal sense of things, and of himself,
using his own characteristic voice. Despite what some critics may assert, however, Stevens was not a solipsist, any
more than he was an aesthete or a hedonist; he was 'a man
speaking to men' (to borrow a familiar but nevertheless
useful phrase from Wordsworth) preoccupied with 'what
will suffice' and enable us all to live our lives. 'We can
never have great poetry', Stevens insisted in one of his very
last speeches, 'unless we believe that poetry serves great
ends'; and, in pursuit of those ends, he willingly absorbed
the best that had been thought and said by other writers—
other people who had tried to make their imagination the
light in the minds of their readers—to absorb it and then
make it a part of his own meditations. He was a solitary
poet, of course, and something of an eccentric visionary—

aware, even while he sought knowledge, that 'always there
is another life / A life beyond this present knowing' [**'The
Sail of Ulysses'**]. But his very solitude made him an heir
of the Romantics, as well as a kinsman of Poe, Dickinson
and Whitman; while his visions were shared ones, their eccentricity deriving not from any personal idiosyncrasies
but from the fact that, in an age of disbelief, the truth can
only be arrived at, he felt, by the most circuitous and stony
of routes. The figure of Santayana perhaps best sums up
this central paradox, of being apart from and yet a part
of things. For in describing his former mentor, in **'To an
Old Philosopher in Rome'**, Stevens seems to be describing
himself—or, to be more accurate, his own particular
choices and best possibilities. 'Be orator', he implores Santayana,

> but with an accurate tongue
> And without eloquence . . .
>
> So that we feel, in this illumined large,
> The veritable small, so that each of us
> Beholds himself in you, and hears his voice
> In yours, master and commiserable man. . . . .

Throughout his life, Stevens sought exactly the kind of
dual rôle, of 'master and commiserable man', that he asks
Santayana to assume here: which is why, in the end, his
poetry bears so many signs of kinship with others, living
and dead, while remaining utterly and unmistakably his
own. (pp. 41-56)

> *Richard Gray, "Poetry and the Subject of the
> Poem: Wallace Stevens," in* Modern Ameri-
> can Poetry, *edited by R. W. (Herbie) Butter-
> field, London: Vision Press, 1984, pp. 41-57.*

Bonnie Costello   (essay date 1985)

[*Costello is an American educator and critic. In the following excerpt, she analyzes the influence of the visual
arts on Stevens's poetry and revises many of the conclusions drawn by Michel Benamou in his essay "Poetry
and Painting," excerpted in* TCLC, *Vol. 3, p. 457.*]

Writers have habitually directed their nostalgia for presence onto the visual arts. While painting is a kind of language, its sensuous immediacy helps it to overcome the
distance inherent in representation in a way that the arbitrary signing of words cannot. Stevens frequently compared the enterprise of painting with his own of poetry,
and often expressed a yearning for the condition of the visual arts. The many references Stevens makes to painting
and to artists in poems, prose, and correspondence demonstrate the central place it held in his reflective life. "On
my death there will be found carved on my heart . . . the
name of Aix-en-Provence," he wrote in a letter to Thomas
McGreevy. It is significant that we should find the name,
not the image of Cézanne's home carved there. For Stevens expressed his admiration for the visual arts not in imitation, but rather in allusion.

[In his *Wallace Stevens and the Symbolist Imagination*]
Michel Benamou surveyed the intricate subject of Stevens
and painting . . . and offered some valuable direction for
appreciating Stevens' pictorial qualities and conceptual af-

finities to the visual arts. But we need a more precise view of what may have attracted Stevens to the visual arts and what poetic use he made of his experience of painting.

One can say clearly what approaches Stevens did not take. He seldom used painting as a focusing device (as did Auden), a formal model (as did Williams), an image of the still moment (as did Keats and Eliot), or a source of emblemata (as Moore so often did). Stevens' poems do not, for the most part, visualize their subjects, making the reader a beholder of an imagined pictorial space. In fact, Stevens' poetry hardly resembles painting at all. He did not need to copy the effects of painting because he had available to him a whole array of *literary* devices and effects by which absent qualities are imported into a work. It is a mistake, I think, to match Stevens to this or that movement in painting, to this or that artist, for he suggests the entire enterprise of painting through naming, allusion, metaphor, narration, argument, and other literary means. Hals, Poussin, Claude, Constable, Corot, Dufy, Picasso are invoked, not imitated. The elements and techniques of painting—light, color, shape, line, plane, space, grisaille, chiaroscuro, etching—are not approximated in language but brought to mind. Stevens does not abandon poetic genres for painterly ones—portrait, still life, landscape— but borrows their associations. These subtle differences distinguish Stevens from other moderns—Williams, Stein, Apollinaire—who responded to other possibilities in the visual arts.

Williams, for instance, thought of words as "pigments put on." In an interview with Walter Sutton he remarked: "I've attempted to fuse the poetry and the painting, to make it the same thing" [*Interviews with William Carlos Williams,* ed. Linda Wagner]. Several books have been dedicated to exploring what Williams meant by this and similar comments. Bram Djikstra's ground-breaking study, *Hieroglyphics of a New Speech,* studied Williams' attraction to the special kinds of seeing claimed by Modernist art: analytic cubism and its methods of fragmentation and multiple perspective; the assemblages of collage; the isolation and intensification of objects by American painters like Charles Demuth and Marsden Hartley. Most recently, Henry Sayre's *The Visual Text of William Carlos Williams* argues that Williams' response to painting is based on form rather than image, and examines the tension between the experience of the page and of visual rhyme and representational and aural structures.

All the studies of Williams agree that he takes the analogy with painting literally and strives for an equivalency of effect in words. Stevens' relation to painting is a far more figurative and conceptual one. He is less interested in the practice of painting than in its theory, quoting Picasso's notion of art as a "horde of destructions" and Klee's notion of "the organic center of all movement in time and place." He was less interested in the particulars of technique (the building up of surface against illusion in Cézanne, or the breaking and reassembling in Gris) than in the condition of visual art and the special experience of beauty suggested within that condition (Cézanne's struggle for realization, or Gris' freeing of the imagination from the tyranny of the eye). Visual art aimed at a continuity

between sensuous apprehension of surface and reference to a sensuous world. Its bodiliness, its immanence, its spatial presence, attracted Stevens as a cure for rhetoric. Of course no work of visual art achieves what it projects as its essence. The pure condition Stevens invokes belongs to the idea of painting rather than to its technique. What drew him to the theory of painting most of all, however, was its struggle to define the essence of its medium and its special relation to reality. The habit of broadly applying categories like "Cubism" or "Impressionism" (as Benamou does) proves particularly faulty with respect to Stevens' poetry. My argument falls between those who use the references to painting as an invitation to apply painterly categories to the poems, and those who read the references to painting as transparent metaphors for art, especially poetic art. They *are* metaphors, but as such they cannot be taken for granted.

Each reference to painting may have a local expedience. The "album of Corot" in **"Like Decorations in a Nigger Cemetery,"** for instance, may suggest the special quality of nostalgia captured in Corot's "Souvenir de Montefontaine" or any other of his "souvenir" paintings. The reference to "the world seen through arches" in **"Botanist on Alp (No. 1)"** recalls the rock arches that appear repeatedly in Claude's paintings and suggests the entire concept of framed and idealized vision in Claude. But taken together, these allusions indicate a significant impulse in Stevens to associate his art with that of painting, and often suggest an ideal of realization appropriate to the sister art. Although Stevens' poems abound in references to particular artists and their works, it is finally the idea or ideal of painting, its struggle to define an imaginative space with a presence to rival natural experience, that attracts him; and in the transfer to his own verbal medium, the idea of painting becomes a poetic one, "not to be realized" but always imagined.

Fred Miller Robinson's essay, "Poems that Took the Place of Mountains: Realization in Stevens and Cézanne" [*The Centennial Review,* 1970], is particularly helpful in understanding the distinction between an artist's ideals and his methods. The struggle for realization that motivated Cézanne was by definition never satisfied, just as Stevens' "supreme fiction" remains an imaginative goal. But more than a parallel is involved here. Stevens often thought of the struggle for realization in terms of the enterprise of painting, even though he never attempted to imitate the methods of painting.

Stevens' essay, **"The Relations between Poetry and Painting,"** provides little help on this subject; any art could fit the loose terms of his comparison. Stevens identifies no techniques of painting that poets might employ, no influence of one artist on another. The essay moves toward erasing difference by invoking the larger category "art," which he renames "poetry." But this renaming does matter, for it preserves the sense of difference that he cannot erase. The essay, written from the point of view of poetry, defines a certain attitude toward the visual arts. Indeed, he nearly sidesteps painting as such by claiming that poets find the "sayings" about painting useful. The essay at first might seem better named "The Relations between Poetry and Art Theory," or as Stevens says, "the relations between poetry in paint and poetry in words." Criticism and theory are inherently closer to poetry than to painting, since in the first case the medium of language is shared. Indeed, the very analogy between the arts is, in a sense, a literary trope. But Stevens cannot assimilate painting into poetry. Its point of view lingers to change the atmosphere of the poetic by associating it with "composition," as opposed to "sensibility." Even the sayings of painters do not escape the conditions from which they arise, but bring them along when they are associated with poetry. This contagion—the contagion of analogy, not of imitation—is my subject.

A better preface to this subject than Stevens' own is Walter Pater's "The School of Giorgione," which Stevens probably read. Pater begins with a primary differentiation among the arts in terms of media: "That the sensuous material of each art brings with it a special phase or quality of beauty, untranslatable into the forms of any other, an order of impressions distinct in kind—is the beginning of all aesthetic criticism." The goal of each art is to purify itself in order to achieve this "special phase or quality of beauty." Painting, for instance, should rid itself of literature, which for Pater means discursiveness and rhetoricity, and aim at pictoriality. Yet, paradoxically, "in its special mode of handling its given material, each art may be observed to pass into the condition of some other art." Pater maintains a distinction between the medium and the condition of each art, a distinction Stevens adapts. By "medium" Pater means, for example, the material of paint and the techniques developed for handling that material. By "condition" he means each art's special mode of reaching the imagination, its representational structure and its "special mode or quality of beauty." These are inseparable but not identical for Pater, as for Stevens; but that does not prevent a given art from invoking the condition of another through its own particular medium. The Paterian crossing of the arts involves a "partial alienation [of an art] from its own limitations, through which the arts are able, not indeed to supply the place of each other but reciprocally to lend each other new forces." In this view the purity of the arts and the exchange between the arts are not at odds. Indeed, in praising Giorgione's school for realizing its goals within pictorial form, Pater calls their work "pictorial poetry." "They belong to a sort of poetry which tells itself without an articulated story." It is in this spirit, perhaps, that Stevens speaks of the poetry of impressionism.

And it is in this spirit that Stevens speaks, conversely, in **"Effects of Analogy,"** of pictorialization as the essential aim of poetry. Although describing a distinctly rhetorical device—analogy—he expresses his frustration with the limitations of language, which he, following Pater, identifies with discursiveness and rhetoricity. Allegory, in particular, is the enemy. True analogy promises a "consummation" of terms—not the pictorialization of descriptions or emblemata, but an objectification of imagination. Stevens writes, "The effect of analogy is the effect of the degree of appositeness . . . the imaginative projection, the imaginative deviation, raises the question of rightness, as if in the vast association of ideas there existed for every object its appointed objectification. In such a case, the object

and its image become inseparable" [*The Necessary Angel: Essays on Reality and the Imagination*]. At the end of the essay Stevens explicitly calls the structure of analogy itself a "pictorialization"—though he means the word figuratively, as restatement or illustration. It is clear nonetheless that the visual remains the touchstone of figuration for him. In this way the analogy between poetry and painting becomes for Stevens a meta-analogy. In seeking for the essence of poetry Stevens distances himself from its limitations, and by invoking painting in various ways he borrows new forces. The limitations inherent in literature—its inescapable discursiveness and rhetoricity, what Paul de Man would call its inescapably allegorical nature—make a place in Stevens' imagination for painting. Stevens identifies analogy as emotional in origin: "The nature of the image is analogous with the emotion from which it springs." If we take painting itself (as opposed to this painting or that) as a major analogy, we may identify it with an emotion everywhere in Stevens—a yearning for the conditions of immanence, unity, presentness, and the incarnation of imagination in materiality.

Anterior to the metaphor of painting in Stevens is the very privileged metaphor of the eye, which is more than a substitute term for consciousness of reality. Stevens' development reflects his ambivalence about the eye's domination of consciousness, but it remains a determinant and touchstone. The figure—the agent of the eye—haunts all conceptualization. He tells us in **"Crude Foyer"** that "the eye is the mind," and in **"Fishscale Sunrise"** that "the mind is smaller than the eye." And yet the imagination must experience some freedom from the eye to validate itself. In addressing this central problem, painting offered a direction—a liberation from visual reality that nevertheless made a truce with the eye. Stevens' attraction to painting is based, in part, on his alienation from the very rhetoricity and discursiveness so dominant in his own poetry. The visual thinking of painters suggested direct access to a space in which the world might find its imaginative apposite. The language of poetry, at least as Stevens employed it, might gesture toward that space, but could not create it. On the other hand, Stevens saw the figurative as the root of all thought, and embodiment as its irreducible condition. The reimagined first idea, then, must be a figure, not its dependent theory or thought. Painting not only suggested a path to immanence not available in poetry (at least in the highly discursive and rhetorical poetry of Wallace Stevens), it also seemed truer as an imitation of thought.

In arguing that Stevens' poetry expresses a yearning for the condition of the visual arts I must acknowledge that he occasionally links painting and poetry as two different forms of rhetoric, opposing them to nature. But the distinction between reality and its representations in Stevens is far less significant than the distinction between what he calls "evading metaphor" and "figure," the latter somehow achieving immanence where the former only removes the beholder from the presence of nature. In **"Add This to Rhetoric"** Stevens begins by distinguishing between being in nature—simple growth—and the arrangement of being through language. He treats painting and speech together here as forms of rhetoric, using painting as an analogy for the "posed" and "framed" aspect of speech:

> The buildings pose in the sky
> and, as you paint, the clouds,
> Grisaille, impearled, profound,
> Pfft. . . . In the way you speak
> You arrange, the thing is posed,
> What in nature merely grows.

Here Stevens suggests that the intervention of "rhetoric" determines the structure of perception itself, so that the "thing" in its natural state of growth remains elusive. Even "stones pose in the falling night." As he so often does, Stevens divides the worlds of imagination and reality, of rhetoric and nature, into moonlight and sunlight. As the sun comes up in the second stanza, a new authenticity of being promises to rise with it:

> To-morrow when the sun,
> For all your images,
> Comes up as the sun, bull fire,
> Your images will have left
> No shadow of themselves.
> The poses of speech, of paint,
> Of music—Her body lies
> Worn out, her arm falls down,
> Her fingers touch the ground.
> Above her, to the left,
> A brush of white, the obscure,
> The moon without a shape,
> A fringed eye in a crypt.
> The sense creates the pose.
> In this it moves and speaks.
> This is the figure and not
> An evading metaphor.
>
> Add this. It is to add.

The second stanza seems to contrast with the first by suggesting a refreshed vision of reality against the decay of old images. But the image that lies suspended in the poem no longer contrasts nature and its poses. The distinction is now rather between figure and evading metaphor. Stevens does not spell out the difference between these terms, but together they suggest his desire to reserve a region of immanence within representation. The "figure" is clearly a visual concept, for the corresponding image is a tableau ("Above her, to the left,"). Within that tableau, however, we see the erasure of the figure—the "fringed eye in a crypt" and "the moon without a shape." Stevens here approaches the nexus between sense and transcendence within a visual vocabulary.

Stevens' poems constantly search for a reimagining, a representation that will be free of the touch of rhetoric or will achieve "the pure rhetoric of a language without words." Metaphor, as a substitute, removes the imaginer from the immediate experience. The figure promises something less shadowy, more substantial, and thus more immediate. Thus to add the figure to rhetoric would be to make rhetoric more real. But the final line of the poem reinstates Stevens' ambivalence about all representation. "It is to add" might as easily be taken as an expression of disappointment, for an addition is not a transformation. Stevens remains insecure in his belief in the power of the figure, his "supreme fiction." But the poem indicates at least his need

to define the space of authenticity not outside or beyond but within representation. Stevens' allusions to painting helped him develop this special place for the figure in opposition to evading metaphor—helped him sustain, that is, an idealized project for art.

In *Harmonium,* as many have noted, Stevens expresses his visual intensity through images. Michel Benamou has suggested that **"Sunday Morning"** evokes Matisse; Helen Vendler finds a source in Manet's "Woman with a Parrot," acquired by the Metropolitan Museum of Art in New York in 1866. In **"Sunday Morning"** we enter an interior life through a contrast of surface intensity and blur, just as in Manet areas of detail work against rough, impressionistic ones. Poem and painting share the woman in peignoir, the orange, and the overall suggestion of sensuous pleasure recently enjoyed against a somber, meditative background. If the painting is a source of the poem, the parrot has been transplanted to the rug and given the more poetic name "cockatoo," as if to create a verbal equivalent to Manet's visual exoticism. But **"Sunday Morning"** does not dwell on this initial image or on any other; it veers off into interior dialogue, into areas to which poetry has privileged access. We are quickly thwarted if we try to match Stevens' poems to particular visual sources. While **"Sea Surface Full of Clouds"** is also strikingly imagistic, its transformations, suggesting one of Monet's series, are driven as much by linguistic as by visual elements. The poem never truly depicts anything. Stevens seemed to discover in this early book that poetry could never aim at the quality of painting through pictoriality, and the image recedes in later volumes. Yet the metaphors of painting (of which there are few in *Harmonium*) increase dramatically in *Parts of a World.*

In **"Poem Written at Morning,"** for instance, Stevens insistently identifies the enterprises of poetry and painting:

> A sunny day's complete Poussiniana
> Divide it from itself. It is this or that
> And it is not.
>   By metaphor you paint
> A thing.

But as the poem goes on, a certain differentiation emerges between the terms metaphor and paint, and with that difference a sense of lack in each, a vacillating preference. The identification raises problems in the later repetition of "The senses paint by metaphor." This phrasing still sets painting as the end or desired condition, metaphor as the means, making the poem tautological. Painting is never aimed at metaphor. We do not, that is, have a corollary concept by which transcendence is achieved through a visual immediacy. Yet to paint, in this poem, means not only to render visible but to give the world a certain aspect, a certain emotional cast or conceptual character. Paint, then, becomes an end rather than a means, while metaphor remains a means. The poem begins with a condition of painting ("by metaphor you paint a thing"). One would expect this poem to begin with the "thing" itself, but the thing is already represented in the first line, so that the accomplishment of painting is given originating power. "A sunny day's complete Poussiniana" describes less the rhetoricity of a day which is completely Poussin-like than the completeness of effect, the immanence and autonomy achieved by Poussin, so that nature and Poussin are the same, as nature and Homer were to Pope.

But perhaps uncomfortable with the priority of painting, the poem moves away from its initial subject to analyze a thing, a pineapple. As the poem continues, that full presence earlier described as "a sunny day's complete Poussiniana" gives way to something more elusive:

> Thus, the pineapple was a leather fruit,
> A fruit for pewter, thorned and palmed and blue,
> To be served by men of ice.
>   The senses paint
> By metaphor. The juice was fragranter
> Than wettest cinnamon.

The metaphors are not pictorial, but engage all the senses toward a conceptualization of the object. Poetry, it seems to suggest, is not bound to one sensuous aspect and is thus "truer" because it can conceptualize by a chorus of all:

> The truth must be
> That you do not see, you experience, you feel,
> That the buxom eye brings merely its element
> To the total thing.

Yet the "total thing" is lost, indeed chased away by metaphor, to become "a shapeless giant forced upward." We no longer have the timeless or at least tenseless (the first line having no temporal designation) completeness of the sunny day's Poussiniana, but a mere epitaph: The poem ends, "Green were the curls upon that head." It is hard to find the balance in adding the debits and credits of each art.

If we take the poem's argument as a narrative, the introduction of metaphor into the poem is connected with the advent of time and loss. Painting, then, is identified with a tenseless spatiality; but this is a poem, marked in its title as temporally burdened. The end of the poem denies the privilege of the eye as access to completeness. But painting of course involves more than the eye, is itself metaphoric, just as metaphor is figurative. The final effect is both a merging and an ambivalence. Perhaps Stevens is deconstructing Poussin's illusion of completeness. Or perhaps he is trying to have it both ways by his surface identification. But internally the poem expresses nostalgia for the figurative power of painting even while it deconstructs that power.

Of course in reading the poem in this way I place extra weight on the word "paint" and on the fact of Poussin's medium. One could try to ignore these details and read the poem as a contrast between classical illusionism and modern conceptualization, between Poussin and Juan Gris, or equivalently between Racine and Stevens. The pineapple was a favorite Cubist motif, and the attempt of some Cubists was to liberate painting from the tyranny of the eye. Stevens quotes Juan Gris in **"The Relations between Poetry and Painting"** as giving the imagination priority over the visual, and quotes Braque's aphorism, "The senses deform, the mind forms." Conversely, in the same essay, he identifies Poussin with Racine. But "a sunny day's complete Raciniana" or even "Virgiliana" would have a very different effect in the poem. It is the pictoriality of Poussin

that matters here, a condition for which literature has no substitute, but from which it is always borrowing.

The poem's structure, from completeness to division, from painting to metaphor, from presence to absence, suggests a concept of the Fall for which the poem may have an iconographic source. The iconographic reading of the poem, that is, reinforces its aesthetic argument. Stevens may have been thinking of Poussin's "Spring," which depicts Eden's completeness of ripe fruit before its harvest. Iconography provides the most literal kind of association with literature, but in its sensuous immediacy and incarnation of meaning maintains a difference from language that might have appealed to Stevens. Iconography helps define the difference between figure and evading metaphor. Like Keats, his major precursor, Stevens recognizes the special power of the visual arts to preserve ephemeral subjects. The sunny day is complete in Poussin even if in nature or narration it must decline.

"The Common Life" offers another example of how poetry borrows rather than copies the pictoriality of the visual arts. The poem seems to be describing something visual (perhaps a work by Klee, who often plays with verbal and visual signs on a single surface), but no distinct pictorial image emerges:

> That's the down-town frieze,
> Principally the church steeple,
> A black line beside a white line;
> And the stack of the electric plant,
> A black line drawn on flat air.

Instead of organizing one visual focus, the image, as we shall see, undergoes a metamorphosis, from landscape to geometric drawing to text. The subject holding these images together is "the common life": the dreariness of the common, but perhaps also the abstractness of the common. (In that second sense the term "common" is no longer pejorative.) On a primary level all the images serve to reinforce this subject, suggesting absence of color, third dimension, movement, particularity, vitality. But the two metaphors also modify each other so that the qualities of drawing (spatiality, line, background) combine with qualities of textuality (print, page, volume). Toward the end of the poem we begin to imagine the graphic aspects of a book through a subtle punning on the words "volume" and "outline" that conflates visual and textual categories:

> The paper is whiter
> For these black lines.
> It glares beneath the webs
> Of wire, the designs of ink,
> The planes that ought to have genius,
> The volumes like marble ruins
> Outlined and having alphabetical
> Notations and footnotes.

Textual abstraction takes on a kind of materiality by its identification with visual abstraction. And the discursive and rhetorical aspect of the poem yields to the immediacy of the figure. By the end of the poem the referential subject has disappeared almost completely, supplanted by the figure of the text.

I have been discussing examples that invoke the visual arts

for their privileged *figurative* power. The poems do not attempt to simulate the graphic presence of visual art, but import it into the poem by association. This loyalty to literary method is most apparent in the many poems which tell the story of a beholder. The reader does not share in the act of beholding, but rather in its interpretation, in the story of the beholder's consciousness. Stevens thus utilizes poetry's privileged *interpretive* power, its temporal dimension and its special access to mental conditions. But the terms of the interpretation often suggest the motivations and feelings appropriate to the enterprise of painting. (Only in this sense does the Picasso connection in **"The Man with the Blue Guitar"** make sense.) That is, an objectification (as opposed to interpretation) of such experience would be visual rather than verbal.

This highly speculative claim is supported by the titles of these poems about beholders, which often imitate the titles of paintings: **"Landscape with Boat," "Botanist on Alp (No. 1)," "Botanist on Alp (No. 2)," "Woman Looking at a Vase of Flowers," "Bouquet of Roses in Sunlight."** While titles are the most literary component of painting, these in particular suggest distinctly painterly subjects and approaches. Since they have little narrative or conceptual implication—as opposed to, say, **"Anecdote of the Jar"** or **"The Idea of Order at Key West"**—they put the poems in a painter's space. Such titles provide visual foci to counterbalance the interiority of the subsequent discourse. But they are not iconographic, as are such titles as **"Angel Surrounded by Paysans"** (based on a painting Stevens owned) or **"The Virgin Carrying a Lantern,"** which invite narrative and interpretation. Landscape and still life are the genres of those who place visual *above* literary values. Williams, again wishing to identify the effects of painting and poetry, argued in "Still Life" that the poised object bears within it a Homeric narrative. But we do not "read" landscape or still life in any usual narrative sense. They declare a primary visual experience to which the poem will address itself. Stevens in this sense plants the enterprise of painting in the reader's mind when he describes the predicaments, successes, and failures of his beholders. The condition these poems either gesture toward or yearn for is the condition of visual epiphany, a wordless condition defined in opposition to discursiveness and rhetoricity. Their titles ask us to think of these poems in terms of design rather than statement, as ways of seeing rather than of saying. Such titles help to loose poetry from its dependence on statement. And yet that freedom remains, in Stevens, largely *hypothetical*. Discursiveness remains a dominant element in his compositions, an ordering principle.

"Botanist on Alp (No. 1)" clearly asks us to consider the place of painting in culture, indeed measures other ways of ordering (the botanists' taxonomic realism, Marxist historicism and materialism) against the achievement of painting. Of course it is not painting in general, but Claude's painting, especially his integrations of nature and architectural ruin, that offered an ideal. Still, Claude's precedent and the title together suggest that Modernism might seek its appropriate order in this medium. Against the incursions of materialism and historicism any art promises a sustaining, timeless, and elevating vision, but perhaps visual art best of all because it combines materiali-

ty and imagination. The "poem" in **"Botanist on Alp (No. 2)"** does not offer an order but a compensatory or consolatory accompaniment to the vision of the "crosses glittering." This is a search for sustaining vision, not sustaining utterance. Virgil could not easily substitute for Claude in **"Botanist on Alp (No. 1)."**

> But in Claude how near one was
> (In a world that was resting on pillars,
> That was seen through arches)
> To the central composition,
> The essential theme.

But the painting prescribed by the title is, of course, an impossible one, or at least a ridiculous one. The botanist is incapable of the sublime, incapable of composition: "Corridors of cloudy thoughts, / Seem pretty much one: / I don't know what." Still, the modern problem as it is posed here seems more than metaphorically a problem of seeing, which suggests that solutions might be sought on a visual plane.

"Landscape with Boat" similarly uses a title to mark the absence of a successful act of beholding. Stevens' negations are the negations of painting. In place of the old master is the antimaster (as Marx replaced Claude), who refuses "any turquoise tint or phase, / Any azure under-side or after-color." Instead of brushing on, he brushes away the thunder, undoing illusion. We have only the hint of an image at the end, as the northern abstractive mentality yields to the Mediterranean sensory allure. Of course painting is a metaphor here; but it is precisely my point that metaphors cannot be taken for granted, that they change our attitude toward a subject. The failure of the ascetic's vision is a failure of the eye.

The problem of Modernism's negations (especially Cubist negations) is again the subject of **"Study of Two Pears,"** whose title clearly invokes visual art. The concerns of the body of the poem—shape, color, outline, resemblance—also derive from painting. As does Cubist painting, the poem suggests both a struggle to see reality as it is and to create an imaginative reality. The poem ends ironically, for while the pears are not seen as the observer wills (not as viols, nudes, or bottles), it is only these willed images that *are* seen. The poem seems to move in this direction toward the last two stanzas where the reality of the pears is entirely elusive—a glistening at best. Even their shadows are only defined as "blobs on the green cloth." The dull, flat language of **"Study of Two Pears"** may reflect the dullness of bondage to visual fact. Such objectivism is only an "opusculum paedagogum." But the poem also perhaps testifies to the failure of language to represent adequately the allure of visual fact (it "glistens"). Without metaphor (without viols, nudes, or bottles) language is nothing, and yet metaphor implies an evasion, a removal from positive direct experience. Stevens' ambivalence about the eye centers, then, on his allusions to painting. Here his own stance as observer/describer seems inadequate to capture observation. The poem does not offer an equivalence in language to Cubist concerns and techniques, but rather a description of those concerns and techniques, a substitution rather than an apposition.

In bringing together poetry and painting as he does, Stevens attempts to fuse the visible and the invisible in a most uncompromising fashion. His name for that fusion is the figure. **"Woman Looking at a Vase of Flowers"** and **"Bouquet of Roses in Sunlight"** tell the story of successful vision, in which the senses take their place in cooperation with imagination, figuration is achieved, and rhetoricity is escaped without cost to subjectivity. In both these poems Stevens associates the focal moment of beholding with painting; but he uses the body of each poem to narrate and interpret rather than to duplicate this moment.

"Woman Looking at a Vase of Flowers" is a lyric accompaniment to a visual event. The poet narrates the interior space of the beholder, a space taken up with the act of seeing. The little owl within her may hoot, but she herself is silent. The title directs our attention to the mute picture, but the devices of the poem are conspicuously literary. "It was as if" generates the poem. The terms of comparison are entirely relational rather than substantive, so they can shift position in the rhetorical structure of analogy: "The wind dissolving into birds . . . / . . . the sea poured out again / In east wind beating the shutters at night." The duality of approach, the combinatory nature of analogy, is emphasized repeatedly against the *unity* of the act of looking. And the narrative tells of something in the past, an event that once occurred—"it *was*," as against the continuous present of the "woman looking." While the narrative is anticipatory and recollective, the woman's experience fills the moment. Without consciousness of time, "without clairvoyance," she is caught up in the gaze. The metaphors introduce an analogy with painting, with the movement from palette to canvas to illusion:

> High blue became particular
> In leaf and bud and how the red,
> Flicked into pieces, points of air,
> Became—how the central, essential red
> Escaped its large abstraction

Even without a concept of the divine, the concept of sensous reality remains intentional, the incarnation of idea into visual medium:

> the inhuman colors fell
> Into place beside her, where she was,
> Like human conciliations, more like
> A profounder reconciling, an act,
> An affirmation free from doubt.

The artist is not present here, but in a sense the beholder embodies the artist while she distances the act of creation. One almost feels that in conceiving this poem Stevens circled back into a pictorial process, inferring from an image an original formless condition of color-idea from which the image was generated or "flicked" like a brush. The argument by design without a concept of God invites the idea of the beholder as painter. While the "vase of flowers" is the object beheld, it is also, perhaps, the counterpart of the woman's imagination, which gathers and arranges the scattered particulars of nature into a visual order.

"Bouquet of Roses in Sunlight" again uses literary means to express a condition of beholding that only painting can approach. Again there is little here that can be called pictorial—the discursiveness of the poem advertises itself in syllogistic rhetoric ("say that," "and yet," "so"), presenting and redefining oppositions. Yet the condition it describes is one of apparent freedom from rhetoricity. The very directive voice of the poem stands in opposition to the condition of freedom it dictates. That is, while the poem's method of understanding is literary, the mode of understanding it wishes us to conceive is more atuned to the visual arts—color as feeling; presymbolic sensation rooted in unconscious emotion; direct unity of sensation and imagination. Stevens emphasizes that this experience is still a reimagining—a seeming, not an objectification—but it has a quality of immanence, of meaning inherent in an act of looking. The suggestion of painting begins at the outset, not only with the title, but with the notion of visual "effect"—black reds, pink yellows, orange whites, and so forth: a reality of color. Further, the experience here is of "meaning with no speech," transformation through sense and not through metaphor that seems "beyond the rhetorician's touch." The objectification of a reimagining without the evasions of metaphor, without rhetoric, is *the figure,* the primary condition of painting.

The seeing of reality as artistic creation is one subject of **"Holiday in Reality,"** in which Stevens begins as a beholder in a gallery, finds it stifling, and then enters an imagined garden, a "green world." In the gallery Stevens meditates on the work of a northern consciousness, on paintings such as the snowman, not Cézanne, might likely produce:

> It was something to see that their white was different
> Sharp as white paint in the January sun;
>
> Something to feel that they needed another yellow,
> Less Aix than Stockholm, hardly a yellow at all,
>
> A vibrancy not to be taken for granted, from
> A sun in an almost colorless, cold heaven.

Stevens pretends at first to reserve judgment on these artists ("It was something to see"), but then goes on to identify their conceptual failings:

> Why should they not know they had everything
> of their own
> As each had a particular woman and her touch?

Their desire to depersonalize vision is, for Stevens, at odds with the drama of beholding. Although attracted to the ambition of this art, he finds its results stifling: "It is impossible to breathe at Durand-Ruel's." Like the gloriously subjective figure in **"Tea at the Palaz of Hoon,"** Stevens declares in the second half of the poem that the objects of nature "are real only if I make them so"; yet as the imagination dictates reality, the objects it creates take on the quality of otherness and unreality and are seen "more truly and more strange":

> Whistle
> For me, grow green for me and, as you whistle
> and grow green,
>
> Intangible arrows quiver and stick in the skin
> And I taste at the root of the tongue the unreal
> of what is real.

It should be observed that this taste of reality is not entirely pleasant ("Intangible arrows quiver and stick in the skin"). The garden is clearly an Eden that can fall, not an immortal world of white paint. The structure of the poem superficially suggests a division between art and reality, but the sense of reality itself emerges as the moment of strangeness in the imagination's conjuring (like Marianne Moore's real toad in the imaginary garden). Reality is, in a sense, a product of creative imagination. Thus it is a "holiday" rather than a norm. The division is rather between two types of art—the snowman's art of pristine, ascetic vision and the southerly art (of Cézanne?) that welcomes the spirit's participation in perception.

The poems I have been discussing all demonstrate the Paterian condition of alienation from the limitations of one's art form. Like Pater, Stevens invokes the sister art in such a way as to maintain the integrity of his fostering art. The moments of visual epiphany indeed seem to pass into the condition of painting: exceeding verbality, filled with colors and shapes not reducible to symbolic counterwords. It is not surprising that when the hero of **"The Latest Freed Man"** escapes "doctrine" or feels that he has, he approaches visual epiphany; his eye lights on objects with little narrative or interpretive potential—a rug, a chair, a picture. Indeed, he sees a "portrait of Vidal"; the *art* dealer, Vidal, "qui fait fi des jolliesses banales," who said "fi" to pretty banalities, becomes for a moment the figure of major man.

Thus far the conditions of painting that I have mentioned are located in illusionistic representation; but Stevens also greatly admired the achievements of several abstract artists, particularly Klee, Mondrian, and Brancusi. These artists escaped derivativeness and displayed an ideal commitment to abstraction. To Barbara Church, Stevens wrote that Arp lacks "integrity as an abstractionist" but that "for Mondrian the abstract was the abstract." And two days later, to Thomas McGreevy: "Arp is fastidious not forceful. His forms will never constitute a 'visionary language.' Unlike Brancusi they never intimidate one with their possibilities." Intimidation before the possibilities of a "visionary language" suggested in certain works of art is exactly the theme of *Notes toward a Supreme Fiction* with its challenging dictum, "It must be abstract." In rejecting naïve anthropomorphic and organic values (such as he finds in Arp and complains about in *Notes*) Stevens evokes painting once again: "The air is not a mirror but bare board, / Coulisse bright-dark, tragic chiaroscuro." Since the world is not a reflection of ourselves, since we "live in a world that is not our own," we must invent one, the poem insists. That "invented world" is nonobjective, but still, in a sense, visually representable. Although he declares it is "Not to be realized because not to / Be seen," it is nevertheless through a visual artist that Stevens gains access to his subject. "Weather by Franz Hals" is, for Stevens, abstract, "brushed up by brushy winds in brushy clouds, / Wetted by blue, colder for white." The supreme fiction

> must be visible or invisible,
> Invisible or visible or both:
> A seeing and unseeing in the eye.

Hals represents clouds that "preceded us." (They stand in the background of his portraits, and Stevens seems to read them as a kind of first condition out of which human identity, the being of the portrait, emerges.) But this "weather," this "mere air" is "an abstraction blooded, as a man by thought." Abstraction remains "in the eye" even if invisible, an ideal of embodiment without loss of sublimity. Abstraction is not itself a "thought" separable from image. One would expect thought to be aligned with abstraction, but Stevens' syntax identifies thought with blood, with something embodied and concrete. If thought is blood, if the first idea is not a mere abstraction, then perhaps the hermit in the poet's metaphors, the first idea or first condition of things, is, after all, the irreducible figurative aspect of thought, which painting, especially abstract painting, addresses. The figuration of abstract painting seems to do without the "as if," without the structure of substitution on which rhetoric relies. It brings the alien, abstract first idea, the condition of the clouds, into the realm of the intelligible without anthropomorphism.

Stevens everywhere explores the idea that the sister arts are pulled together by the ambitions and latent tendencies of each. Just as a latent textuality haunts all visual images, so a latent figurativeness haunts all discourse. Stevens inherited from Pater (and later from Valéry) a desire for purity in the arts, but also a sense of their deep reciprocity. We have been exploring the associations of painting imported into Stevens' poetry by literary means. His writing on art completes this reciprocity. Just as Pater wrote of the "poetry" of the School of Giorgione, so Stevens writes of a work by Raoul Dufy that "it is an exploitation of fact by a man of elevation. It is a surface of prose changeable with the luster of poetry and thought" [*Opus Posthumous*]. Yet these are artists who, for Stevens, achieve their "poetic" quality in pursuit of, not in betrayal of, the essence of their medium, recalling the Paterian paradox. It is in pursuit of that essence that Stevens' poetry passes into the condition of the visual arts. (pp. 65-85)

> Bonnie Costello, "Effects of an Analogy: Wallace Stevens and Painting," in Wallace Stevens: The Poetics of Modernism, *edited by Albert Gelpi, Cambridge University Press, 1985, pp. 65-85.*

Michael Davidson   (essay date 1985)

[*Davidson is an American educator and critic whose works include several studies of contemporary poetry and poetics. In the following excerpt, he characterizes the formal and thematic concerns of Stevens's poetry and traces the influence of Stevens's poetics on modern American poetry.*]

In one of his first letters to Charles Olson, Robert Creeley quotes with approval a definition of poetry given by Wallace Stevens: "Poetic form in its proper sense is a question of what appears within the poem itself . . . By appearance within the poem itself one means the things created and existing there. . . ." Creeley adds: "Basic. Yet they won't see it, that it cannot be a box or a bag or what you will." Stevens' definition stayed with Creeley, and appeared in a later letter as part of a harangue against the technical skills of W. H. Auden: "Anyhow, form has now become so useless a term that I blush to use it. I wd imply a little of Stevens' use (the things created *in* a poem and existing there . . .) & too, go over into: the possible casts or methods for a way into a 'subject'." Creeley then adds his own version of Stevens' definition in terms that have become somewhat more familiar: "To make it clear: that form is never more than an *extension* of content." The rest is literary history. Creeley's remarks found their way into Olson's "Projective Verse" essay, in which Olson proposes a physiological, oral poetry that would have made Wallace Stevens wince. And although we tend to read that essay in terms of Pound and Williams, it is interesting to note the important role that Stevens played in the formation of what has become one of the canonical texts of Postmodernist poetics.

Creeley's remarks, of course, are hardly original; they are basic to any organicist theory and can be found in variant forms throughout Romantic literature. What Stevens offered Creeley and his generation of poets was a particular version of romantic organicism in which poetry evolves according to laws discovered in the act of composition. The validity of these laws does not end with the poem in some kind of Kantian disinterestedness. These laws replicate mental orders that cannot, because of the constraints of ordinary discourse, be articulated. The poet uses the poem to discover aspects of psychological and natural life that, while near to hand, are nevertheless mediated by alien rhetorics. Coleridge's definition of poetry as that which contains "in itself the reason why it is so, and not otherwise" [*Biographia Literaria*] had been hardened into New Critical versions of autotelic form. Stevens reintroduced into theories of Romanticism what Coleridge elsewhere calls "form as proceeding," that might serve as a paradigm for more recent open-ended and processual modes. And although Stevens was not, himself, a prosodic innovator, he awakened poets to the sheer combustive potential of language pushed to its maximum semantic and acoustic potential. More important, Stevens explored as thoroughly as any poet of his generation the vital contingencies between poetic language and what he called "the exquisite environment of fact" [**"Adagia"**]. If Coleridge, Emerson, Dickinson, and Whitman are Stevens' most obvious forebears in this poetics, he is the poet who most significantly translates this heritage into the present day.

Wallace Stevens' influence on contemporary poets is so pervasive, in fact, that discussion is almost superfluous beyond the most generalized level. In a recent issue of *The Wallace Stevens Journal,* a number of poets were asked to comment on Stevens' impact on their writing, and the opinions expressed are as varied as the poets themselves. Robert Creeley admires the "teasing clarity of his propositions, . . . the fact that words [become] such substance of a world 'out of whole cloth,' so to speak." David Ignatow respects Stevens' Whitmanian defiance of "this greyness that his eyes met everywhere." W. S. Merwin is intrigued by Stevens' landscapes, "at once familiar, a revelation, and a composition of unimaginable depths and richnesses." Richard Wilbur rejoices "in the versatile energy with which he faced the aesthetic challenge of every mood, place, and weather." Richard Hugo is even inspired by the photos of Stevens that appear on the dust jackets

of his books. How is the genealogist of influence to reconcile the variety of such tributes into a common set of concerns?

We should know better, however, than to trust the overt testimony found in *festschriften.* The theory of influence is tainted, we have come to understand, by false notions of continuity and causality. We must look at the poems themselves—in the interstices of their rhetoric—for evidence not only of what they say *about* Stevens but what they forget to say, what they cannot, in order to be the poems they are, admit to themselves. The most famous version of this theory claims that "strong poets" willfully misread their predecessors in a kind of Oedipal rejection of authority and power. In order for the new poet to write, he must systematically destroy his precursors and create a place for himself. (I use the masculine pronoun to indicate that this battle seems so far to have been fought only among males.) The value of this act lies not in the poems thus created but in the dialogue established between and among poems. Influence, as Harold Bloom conceives it, "means that there are *no* tests, but only relationships *between* tests" [*A Map of Misreading*]. What is generated out of this antigenealogical genealogy is less literary history than a kind of gnostic eschatology by which the death of poetry is forestalled and the life of sublimation maintained for another generation. The bounty of misprision, according to Bloom, is anxiety; and among strong poets there is much anxiety, particularly among belated modern American poets who must compensate all the more forcefully for their felt distance from an established tradition.

Bloom's theory is particularly important for our subject since it offers a salutary critique of formalist as well as literary historical definitions of tradition, and because it emphasizes Stevens' central influence upon more recent poets like John Ashbery and A. R. Ammons. But according to Bloom, such "ephebes" are produced, as it were, by artificial insemination, so that even the most Stevensian of contemporary poets must deny his literary parent:

> I don't consider myself any avatar of Wallace Stevens. It's true that some of my earlier work sounds very much like Wallace Stevens, but I certainly don't think it does throughout, certainly not to the extent [Bloom] says it does, and I don't think Stevens would have thought so either. ["An Interview with John Ashbery," *San Francisco Review of Books,* 1977]

Ashbery would seem to be executing his own poetic clinamen in relation to Bloom, overcompensating for a reading that has locked him into one tradition at the expense of others. The poet who wrote the very Stevensian "Clypsydra" or "Fragment," so the reading has it, could not be the same who wrote "Europe" or the poems in *The Tennis Court Oath* (a fearful disaster, says Bloom). And the poet who in *Three Poems* and "Self-Portrait in a Convex Mirror" seems a logical heir to **"An Ordinary Evening in New Haven"** or **"The Auroras of Autumn"** could not, at the same time, be the heir to *Impressions d'Afrique, The Large Glass,* or *Tender Buttons.* Little wonder, then, that Ashbery should swerve so violently.

For all Bloom's virtues in reminding us of the problematic

nature of influence as conceived along traditional histori-cist lines, he has severely limited the contextual field in which we may read literary history. A poet's development, according to his theory, may occur solely along psycho-pathological lines; there is no room for a history other than literary history and no room for value outside aes-thetics. Whatever temporality may have been opened in the poem or evoked beyond the page is spatialized by "re-visionary ratios" or tropes by which the poet swerves, empties out, purges, and reappropriates the tradition. These ratios are rhetorical stations of the cross in a psy-chological quest romance that the poet cannot recognize for himself. Thus, only the critic may complete the her-meneutic circle begun by the poet, closing off the poem and the history in which it is produced. Finally, the very democratic ethos that lies within Bloom's exemplars (Whitman, Emerson, Stevens, Crane) is violated by the notion of the "strong poet," one who turns self-reliance into willful misappropriation.

It is important to our current understanding of Stevens that this Oedipalized version of influence be qualified, be-cause it fails to address some of the important ways in which the poet has been read in the postwar period. It lim-its the kind and scope of influence to those poets who most resemble him at the level of rhetorical surface. Ashbery obviously "looks like" Stevens; but one could also say that the nature of the younger poet's verbal play—the indeter-minacy of his pronouns in *Three Poems,* for example—serves a very different purpose than that of the older poet. Stevens seldom reflects the kind of personal insecurity and crisis that one finds in Ashbery, even though both share a tendency toward a discursive, wandering style. At the same time, a poet like Louis Zukofsky, usually thought to extend directly from the Poundian tradition, is most like Stevens in his concern for the moral worth of poetic lan-guage, "an instant certainty of the words of a poem bring-ing at least two persons and then maybe many persons, even peoples together" ["For Wallace Stevens," in *Prepo-sitions*]. This is much like the Stevens who feels that the poet's role is "to help people to live their lives" [*The Nec-essary Angel: Essays on Reality and the Imagination*].

Having argued the inadequacies of Bloom's theory of in-fluence, I would like to suggest an alternative reading of Stevens in the light of certain contemporary poets, using *Notes toward a Supreme Fiction* as a touchstone. Neces-sarily, my coverage of this large topic must remain some-what schematic and my selection of poets limited. I am not proposing a theory of influence, but rather a study of ele-ments in Stevens' poetics that have helped generate at least one tradition in postwar poetry. I would see his influence, in this regard, as occupying three general areas: the use of the long poem in producing a destructive or decreative po-etics; the operational or performative use of language to create a philosophical poetry; and the transformation, by these means, of a poetry of "place" into a poetry of "occa-sions."

Notes toward a Supreme Fiction is a particularly appro-priate poem with which to examine Stevens' influence since one of its primary concerns is pedagogy:

   Begin, ephebe, by perceiving the idea

   Of this invention, this invented world,
   The inconceivable idea of the sun.

Yet Stevens' is a pedagogy without texts or instructions, without cultural markers or "luminous moments"—without, we might say, method. The young poet must "be-come an ignorant man again / And see the sun again with an ignorant eye." In a paradox that haunts all of American literature, from Emerson to the present, the new poet must read so that he shall no longer have to read again. His po-etic act shall not be the artisanal fabrication of a self-sufficient world; rather, his task is a violent one, to "press / A bitter utterance from [his] writhing, dumb, // Yet vol-uble dumb violence." We recognize this poetic violence as that described in **"The Noble Rider and the Sound of Words,"** "a violence from within that protects us from a violence without."

If poetry is a destructive as well as instructive force, it is all the more so in Stevens' later work, where the pursuit of a supreme fiction is merged with an increasingly inter-rogative and discursive style. Whereas in the lyrics and ex-ercises of **Harmonium** the poet wrote brilliant, often witty variations on philosophical matters, from the mid-1930s on his method was to dramatize the mind in its speculative acts. As Roy Harvey Pearce points out, the change in Ste-vens' later style is not a radical departure but represents a logical evolution from the problems advanced in his early lyrics. In perspectivist exercises like **"Thirteen Ways of Looking at a Blackbird"** or **"Sea Surface Full of Clouds,"** the thing itself—whether a jar, a landscape, or a flock of pigeons—constellates senses of order for the per-ceiver. Each poem illustrates the poet discovering, as does the avuncular figure in **"Le Monocle de Mon Oncle,"** "That fluttering things have so distinct a shade." It was perhaps inevitable that this discovery should incur the consequences of its own relativism. No longer could Ste-vens continue to illustrate the "maker's rage to order words of the sea" out of a barren reality. He had to "be / In the difficulty of what it is to be."

Louis Zukofsky on Stevens's poetics:

Along with all the elegance of intellect a grass roots or local, often barbaric voice in Stevens' poems makes him in their pored-over image of American landscape the genius of its soil: at one with the eccentric native genius of *the Arkansaw* in his poem "The Jack Rabbit." Shunning doctrine, dogma, the shows that teach ignorance, it has somehow suffered the history of the Americas—the continuing portions of all his-tory whatever the scholarly gaps. Reading him I am led to hope that my own poems, tho different, sound that native and kind. If it's Florida, if it's the Caribbean, Uruguay, or wherever Stevens' landscapes exist without imposed shout-ing and spouting: indigenous like Winslow Homer's palm tree in a Florida wind, tho Stevens is never after describing a painting. In sound—words or waves—whatever takes place exists. As he said, along about the '50ies, *poetry is the subject of the poem.*

Louis Zukofsky, in his Prepositions: The Collected Essays of Louis Zukofsky, *University of California Press, 1981.*

It may seem superfluous to point out that this destructive poetics of Stevens' later style increasingly manifests itself in long poems. Their length is no small factor in their method, providing the imagination with a capacious field for exercising its faculties. We tend to think of the Modernist long poem in terms of its formal strategies of collage and pastiche, its generic preference for epic or dramatic modes, its thematic concerns with historical and cultural renewal. Stevens offers a distinct alternative to this paradigm by offering a version of the Romantic crisis poem in which the modulations of the poet's attentions become the poem's subject and ultimate verification. Unlike their Romantic precursors ("Dejection, An Ode," "Alastor," "Tintern Abbey"), Stevens' long poems do not appeal to some ultimate value (Joy, Truth, Beauty) to resolve the contrarieties introduced, even though they may utilize such abstractions as polemical centers for meditation. This form of long, exploratory poem has become one of the primary models for contemporary poets in their attempt to move beyond the single, self-sufficient lyric to the "poem of a life." Works such as A. R. Ammons' *Sphere,* Robert Duncan's *Passages,* Robert Kelly's *The Loom,* John Berryman's *Dream Songs,* John Ashbery's *Three Poems,* and James Merrill's *The Changing Light at Sandover* could be seen as variations on this mode.

Hermeneutic criticism has seized upon such poems as central to its discussion of a distinctly Postmodern poetics. Using Heidegger's analysis of Dasein in *Being and Time,* this criticism sees the open-ended, processual style of Stevens' long poems as destructive, both in literary and philosophical terms. As a text, ***Notes toward a Supreme Fiction*** (so the reading might go) proposes no strategies of closure, no consistent pattern of rhetorical figures, no mythological centers of sustaining narratives. In fact, as the opening cantos indicate, the very lack of such formal cultural signs inaugurates the poem: "Phoebus is dead, ephebe. But Phoebus was / A name for something that never could be named." The poet is thus able to step beyond the closed, spatial text of high Modernism into a more speculative, temporarily generative text whose end is not literary history but existential disclosure. As a philosophical project, the authentically Postmodern poem dis-covers (*aletheia*) or uncovers the temporal nature of Being, not by reference to some cultural cyclicity on the order of Yeats or Pound, but through its momentary, wandering interrogation. This "endlessly elaborating poem," as Stevens calls it, is able to work out the fullest implications of its subject by constantly exposing itself to change.

I have presented this brief overview of the hermeneutic position because it has become, for better or worse, one of the major forums for examining the Postmodern long poem. . . . I would like to suggest here that while such interpretation says much about the temporality of texts, it suggests even more about the temporality of their reception—the way in which the reader, lacking any stable interpretive counters, must engage directly the poet's explorations. Stevens was acutely conscious of this dimension, in theory and in practice:

> Anyone who has read a long poem day after day, as for example *The Faerie Queene,* knows how the poem comes to possess the reader and how it naturalizes him in its own imagination and liberates him there. [*The Necessary Angel*]

The complexity of *Notes,* its syntactic and linguistic play, its endless rearrangement of point of view, are all part of this naturalization process by which the poem "refreshes life so that we share, / For a moment, the first idea."

Notes is no *Faerie Queene,* however potent its personifications and fables. As its title implies, the poem does not propose completion or closure. It is tentative, accumulative, speculative. The preposition in its title stresses the series' projective stance. Where in an earlier period Stevens might have made notes "on" the theme of a supreme fiction, this poem may only point "toward." Both subject and method are concisely embodied in the opening lines of Canto VII of the opening section:

> It feels good as it is without the giant,
> A thinker of the first idea. Perhaps
> The truth depends on a walk around a lake,
>
> A composing as the body tires, a stop
> To see hepatica, a stop to watch
> A definition growing certain and
>
> A wait within that certainty

This passage described what Heidegger might call the "forestructure" *(Vorhabe)* of Stevens' metaphysics. The truth may no longer be grounded in a first cause, a "thinker of the first idea." In the desultory way of the poem itself, the truth "depends on a walk around a lake." Stevens resists analogy; the truth is not "like" a walk but depends upon the natural circumstance—the weather, water, hepatica to be viewed—as well as upon those acts of pausing, observing, and meandering by which the natural is absorbed. The definition of a supreme fiction never becomes certain; it grows toward certainty.

The occasion for this passage is similar to that in John Ashbery's "The Skaters." There the image of skaters gliding in random trajectories over a frozen surface serves as a model for the composing process as well as for cognitive acts. Ashbery does not represent skaters in his poem; rather, he "skates" himself, pausing to "watch / A definition growing certain" in random observations:

> A great wind lifted these cardboard panels
> Horizontal in the air. At once the perspective
>   with the horse
> Disappeared in a bigarrure of squiggly lines. The
>   image with the crocodile in it became no longer apparent.
> Thus a great wind cleanses, as a new ruler
> Edits new laws, sweeping the very breath of the
>   streets
> Into posterior trash.

Ashbery's use of definite article and demonstrative pronoun presumes an intimacy with the reader, even though the scene being described has no contextual referent. We are asked to witness the poet's witness, not to verify the accuracy of his perceptions against the proof of the world. Like Stevens, Ashbery is "not ready / To line phrases with the costly stuff of explanation," because this can only supplement a paraphrase for that which exists as sheer potential. Both poets realize that in the long poem, as Ashbery puts it,

> the carnivorous
> Way of these lines is to devour their own nature,
> leaving
> Nothing but a bitter impression of absence,
>   which as we know involves presence, but still.
> Nevertheless these are fundamental absences,
>   struggling to get up and be off themselves.

As Ashbery's oxymoron indicates, the absences created by poetry are "fundamental," as basic to creation as the ice upon which the skaters skate and yet as ephemeral as the pattern of the skaters' tracks. To create an "absence in reality" is not to add to or subtract from the world but to circulate within it, as Stevens says, "Until merely going round is a final good."

Ashbery's casual, discursive tone is essential to the process, a way of negotiating between poles of presence and absence without assuming a fixed perspective. What may appear as a dandyish mode of diffidence actually represents a more complex response to the difficulties of positing a self-sufficient subject that orders the perceived world by means of some comprehensive rhetoric. Neither of the Modernist poles—Imagist directness nor New Critical irony and impersonality—offers a sufficient alternative to the crisis of self-presence that has emerged in the recent period. One offers an ideal of limitation, the other of mediation; both imply a degree of authorial control and detachment whose boundaries contemporary poets are eager to efface. And while Stevens' tone is not that of Ashbery, he offers an analogously problematic perspective in which no one voice in the poem is constitutive, in which the speaking subject becomes one of the many fictions on the way to what he calls the "monster Myself."

Stevens' bounty to Ashbery and other ephebes would seem to be "intricate evasions of as." His favorite position, as a philosophical poet, is to be moving between the poles of oppositions, attempting to "compound the imagination's Latin with / The lingua franca et jocundissima." Commentators have amply considered his debts in this relativism to Nietzsche, Bergson, Whitehead, James, Husserl, and others. It seems pointless to argue against Stevens as a philosophical poet, as does Helen Vendler, in favor of some inner narrative among the poems. More pertinent for our concern with contemporary poetics is the way in which those ideas are made manifest in particular formal strategies.

As a philosophical poet Stevens is not a particularly profound thinker; he tends throughout his work to reframe a rather elementary conflict between the imagination and reality. But few poets have ever embodied—"blooded"—abstractions in sensuous language more effectively than Stevens. (His titles alone would seem to have generated a subgenre of philosophical epigram among recent poets.) In the early poetry, this sensuous rendering of ideas manifests itself in the brilliant colorations of **"Sunday Morning"** or **"Sea Surface Full of Clouds,"** in which "pungent oranges and bright, green wings" or "chop-house choco-

late / And sham umbrellas" provide an almost expressionist surface for the poet's interrogations. His images are seldom tied to single objects or landscapes but tend to fracture, exfoliate, reform like the clouds that endlessly populate his poems. There is no easy tenor—vehicle relationship to his metaphors; they refer less to things or concepts than to themselves as material objects. As J. Hillis Miller observes [in *Poets of Reality: Six Twentieth-Century Writers*], "[they] entirely contain their own reality" to the extent that a blackbird, a pineapple, or a sea surface must be perpetually "put together" in order to "be" at all.

What is more pertinent to our concern with the later poems is Stevens' treatment of language as a system—its acoustics, its syntax, its pragmatics—in dramatizing ideas. When, at the end of **"The Snow Man,"** Stevens invokes the "Nothing that is not there and the nothing that is," he provides a linguistic equivalent to a paradox for which images are entirely inadequate. His double negatives literally produce a "nothing" that is both full and empty at the same time. When he titles a poem, **"Le Monocle de Mon Oncle,"** as Geoffrey Hartman points out, he captures in the minute phonemic difference between two words something of the larger semantic resonance of the poem—the ironic portrayal of the uncle, metonymically figured in his eyepiece. This kind of operative or performative use of language has had an increasingly important function for contemporary poets as a way of writing a poetry of ideas within the very terms that those ideas present. Two examples from *Notes* and one from a contemporary poet will serve as illustration.

In the famous fourth section of **"It Must be Abstract,"** Stevens mocks mimesis by providing a series of modifiers that refuse to modify:

> We are the mimics. Clouds are pedagogues
> The air is not a mirror but bare board,
> Coulisse bright-dark, tragic chiaroscuro
>
> And comic color of the rose, in which
> Abysmal instruments make sounds like pips
> Of the sweeping meanings that we add to them.

The general theme of this section is the impossibility of arriving at a truly objective perception of reality: "Adam in Eden was the father of Descartes / And Eve made air the mirror of herself." But air is not a mirror; it is an emptiness that we must fill, even though we are taught by clouds ("pedagogues") how solid that air can be. To dramatize the fact that in order to learn, we must already have projected human qualities and meanings onto nature, Stevens creates a series of phrases that are quite literally "fictions of air." The theatrical implications of "bare board" lead to "Coulisse bright-dark," which is then supplemented by "tragic chiaroscuro" and "comic color of the rose," each modifier giving a slightly different substance to air, dramatizing it by oxymoron. In two lines we have both tragedy and comedy, air and substance, stage and reality, light and dark, barrenness and flower, monochrome and color. Stevens' point in this elegant subordination is that we live in a "Theater / Of Trope," a world that must be framed as fiction in order to know it as fact. Stevens' phrases occupy the appropriate syntactical positions to modify "air," but instead of giving it form they only provide shadings and contrasts, abstract color and nuance. By means of this chiaroscuro Stevens is able to use language to mirror without relying on an object to be reflected, thus extending and elaborating his postlapsarian theme.

My second example of Stevens' performative use of language could be viewed as an outgrowth of the first. In Canto III of **"It Must Give Pleasure"** he again addressed repetition and mimicry, this time with regard to the problem of incarnation:

> A lasting visage in a lasting bush,
> A face of stone in an unending red,
> Red-emerald, red-slitted-blue, a face of slate,
>
> An ancient forehead hung with heavy hair,
> The channel slots of rain, the red-rose-red
> And weathered and the ruby-water-worn,
>
> The vines around the throat, the shapeless lips,
> The frown like serpents basking on the brow,
> The spent feeling leaving nothing of itself,
>
> Red-in-red repetitions never going
> Away, a little rusty, a little rouged,
> A little roughened and ruder, a crown
>
> The eye could not escape, a red renown
> Blowing itself upon the tedious ear.
> An effulgence faded, dull cornelian
>
> Too venerably used. That might have been.
> It might and might have been. But as it was,
> A dead shepherd brought tremendous chords
> from hell
>
> And bade the sheep carouse. Or so they said.
> Children in love with them brought early flow-
> ers
> And scattered them about, no two alike.

Stevens' comments on this poem indicate that, at one level, the problem is less the nature of deity, that "lasting visage in a lasting bush," than the conditions of its worship:

> The first thing one sees of any deity is the face, so that the elementary idea of God is a face: a lasting visage in a lasting bush. Adoration is a form of face to face. When the compulsion to adoration grows less, or merely changes, unless the change is complete, the face changes and, in the case of a face at which one has looked for a long time, changes that are slight may appear to the observer to be melodramatic. We struggle with the face, see it everywhere & try to express the changes. [*Letters of Wallace Stevens*]

This last sentence could serve as a description of Stevens' method in the canto itself: a struggle to see the face of an incomprehensible idea in its changeability and to "express the changes" in our perception of it. In order to focus his own perception, he describes a colossus, a "face of stone" reminiscent of Ozymandias, not standing mute and abandoned. This statue is a variation on others in Stevens' writing, from the equestrian statues in **"The Noble Rider and the Sound of Words"** to that of General Du Pay in *Notes.* As with these others, the ideals which the statue represents have lost their relationship to the reality from which

they sprang. The face no longer inspires; it is "An effulgence faded."

Stevens' secular task is to resurrect from this shell of deity the possibility of change. He does so thematically by introducing the image of a "dead shepherd" who combines both Christ and Orpheus, Word and speaker of the Word. Helen Vendler worries that this image, so briefly introduced, is "a much less successful invention than the colossal head" [*On Extended Wings: Wallace Stevens's Longer Poems*]. This might be so, were it not for the qualifying phrase, "Or so they said," that so severely brackets the authority of this apotheosis, drawing attention to the essentially fictional nature of the new Logos. Stevens provides his own transformative act, linguistically, by decreasing the "face of stone" by a series of variations on the word "red." He first describes the head in minute detail, cataloging its "ancient forehead," its "shapeless lips," but quickly turns from description to evocation. The "unending red" background in which the head exists—the red of barren reality—soon becomes "Red-emerald, red-slitted blue." Finally, Stevens rings changes on the word itself, providing "Red-in-red repetitions" in the subtle modulations of "rusty," "roughed," "roughened," "ruder," "red renown," "cornelian." Stevens is able both to sustain the endurance of reality (an unending red) in the creation of supreme fictions and, at the same time, to suggest the variability of that fiction as the perspectives from which it is viewed change. Within his Nietzschean allegory, Stevens is able to release the Logos as origin, source, first idea to its function as language, play, Orphic transformation. Like the words themselves, variations on a single term, the flowers brought by "Children in love with them" are "no two alike."

My third example, from a contemporary poet, Michael Palmer, deals with certain fallacies in what Palmer calls in his title, "The Project of Linear Inquiry." His concern is to present a series of postulates that seem to fall into a logical sequence but which are diverted by other associations. The poem opens as follows:

> [Let *a* be taken as . . .]
> a liquid line beneath the skin
> and *b* where the blue tiles meet
> body and the body's bridge
> a seeming road here, endless
>
> rain pearling light
> chamber after chamber
> of dust-weighted air
> the project of seeing things
> so to speak, or things seen
>
> namely a hand, namely
> the logic of the hand
> holding a bell or clouded lens
> the vase perched impossibly near the edge
> obscuring the metal tines.

We are first introduced to an incomplete postulate in brackets—"Let *a* be taken as . . . "—that, although fragmentary, is nonetheless partially continued in the next line by means of the indefinite article: "a liquid line beneath the skin." We then encounter a second postulate, this time without brackets: "and *b* where the blue tiles meet." Instead of terminating, however, this phrase continues into other words beginning with "b" ("body" and "body's bridge"). This progress from a to b, from liquid line to the meeting point of blue tiles (another kind of line), then leads to other linear forms, a "bridge" and a "road." Contextual frames established in one line are dismantled in the next; and semantic elements from one line create new referential frames in subsequent lines. Whatever proof had been intended by the sequence of postulation has been overtaken by a series of imagistic and linguistic substitutions that, in a sense, obey one kind of logic by means of another. Lines nine and ten, the most Stevensian lines of the example, could serve as a definition of Palmer's problem, "the project of seeing things / so to speak," which I would paraphrase as the problem of reconciling phenomena, received experientially or sensually, with a logical grammar. Each image is given precise definition ("the vase perched impossibly near the edge / obscuring the metal tines"), yet images do not combine to complete a single picture. Instead, signification occurs, despite the failure of "linear inquiry" to account for all aspects of the production of meaning. Palmer shows us not the *results* of inquiry but the *processes,* not the proof but the project.

Part of the difficulty in reading both this and the Stevens examples is that their words function more as instances than as signs. We must learn to read diacritically as well as semantically. When Stevens says of the poem, "It must be abstract," he means abstraction not as generalization but, paradoxically, as the intensification of particularity to the point where a word no longer exists within any conventional context. In order to see a thing we must "unsee" it, abstract it and defamiliarize it, create a language with the same freshness and poignancy as the thing itself. And unlike the Symbolist attempt to create, through unexpected conjunction and association, a world quite apart from the one we inhabit, Stevens invites closer and closer participation with a world we have forgotten how to see.

What I have described as Stevens' linguistic abstraction accompanies a central romantic theme of personal and spiritual alienation. The fall of man, so the familiar version goes, is a fall into a demythologized world, a world of neutral signs, in which an Adamic language of unmediated presence has been lost. To paraphrase one of Stevens' titles, man lives in a "description without a place." **Notes toward a Supreme Fiction** takes as one of its premises that man is estranged from what is most familiar:

> From this the poem springs: that we live in a
>   place
> That is not our own and, much more, not our-
>   selves

This alienation is both destructive and creative: In order to conceive of a place as "ours," we must destroy it as "other" and naturalize it in our own terms. This act of transformation generates another kind of reality, "the supreme fictions without which we are unable to conceive of [the world]." The sense of alienation that Stevens feels is a prerequisite to any metaphysics whatever and serves as an important corrective to the idealizing tendencies to which he was always subject. My earlier reference to Heraclitus (man's estrangement from what is familiar) should

also be read as a reference to the many contemporary poets who have used this fragment to describe the same sense of disparity between place and imagination, thing and word, precept and concept.

At first glance, contemporary poetry might seem to reflect quite the opposite sense of place. Gary Snyder's identification with the Pacific Northwest; Charles Olson's dedication to Gloucester; Robert Bly's association with the northern Midwest; and Frank O'Hara's passion for New York would suggest a regionalist ethos entirely inhospitable to Stevens' propositional landscapes. We are used to thinking of contemporary poets' strong identification with locale in terms of their desire to establish contact with atavistic, aboriginal forces latent in specific places. We are told that, reacting against the Modernist fetish of European high culture, contemporary poets have taken up Whitman's and Emerson's call for an American epic based on American soil and have approved Williams' struggle to maintain "contact" with local, indigenous subjects. But this "immanentist" position, as Charles Altieri characterizes it, with its precedents in Wordsworthian pantheism and Emersonian idealism, is the second part of a two-stage process. Preceding it is the recognition of essential solitude and a sense of disparity between the world of intransigent glyphs and one's own language. A few quotations will illustrate the variety of ways in which this rift is expressed:

> we want to go home and exist in a quietude like merriment but we can't go home as ourselves but wearing the faces of many answering things until, faceless, we can't tell we're home because we are. (A. R. Ammons)

> Words are what sticks to the real. We use them to push the real, to drag the real into the poem. They are what we hold on with, nothing else. They are as valuable in themselves as rope with nothing to be tied to. (Jack Spicer)

> I am certain, without ever having been there, I would be bored to sickness walking through Gloucester. Buildings as such are not important. The wash of the sea is not interesting in itself, that is luxuria, a degrading thing, people as they stand, must be created. (Edward Dorn)

> What [Poe] wanted was connected with no particular place; therefore it *must* be where he *was.* (William Carlos Williams)

> and I have lost what is always and everywhere present, the scene of my selves, the occasion of these ruses, which I myself and singly must now kill and save the serpent in their midst. (Frank O'Hara)

Each quotation could be read as a variation on the Stevens lines quoted earlier. Place offers no solace by itself; the wash of the sea, the buildings of the town, are entirely separate from the poem. Words, by themselves, are similarly inadequate; as Spicer says, they are "what sticks to the real . . . as valuable in themselves as rope with nothing to be tied to." Ammons' "home" and O'Hara's "scene" may be attained only by effacing the ideal of a central self "until, faceless, we can't tell we're / / home because we are." The disparity felt is not the existential agony of a

Sartre or a Kafka; it is rather the necessary occasion by which the familiar may be recognized as such. In numerous contemporary poems, from Adrienne Rich's "Diving into the Wreck," to Sylvia Plath's "The Colossus," to Charles Olson's "The Librarian," the poet encounters an alien landscape whose outlines are familiar but whose terms of order and coherence remain obscure. The poet uses the poem to investigate this area, whether based on fragments from a dream, a series of field notes, a day's random occasions, or lines from a poem. The transition from this "not-at-homeness" to "home" is described vividly by Robert Duncan:

> Often I am Permitted to Return to a Meadow
>
> as if it were a scene made-up by the mind,
> that is not mine, but is a made place,
>
> that is mine, it is so near to the heart

Duncan describes a place that could be the poem itself—"mine" because "near to the heart," yet "not mine" because received from without. Access to this meadow is gained by "permission," not by demand. The poet experiences the same uncanny visitation as the dreamer who receives the dream both as a foreign text and as a story in which he is the central character.

The allegory of man's alienation from reality and his subsequent marriage *to* reality is present in all of Stevens' poems, from Crispin attempting to "stem verboseness in the sea" to the Interior Paramour, who makes a "dwelling in the evening air." In ***Notes toward a Supreme Fiction,*** it takes the form of a "mystic marriage in Catawba" between a "great captain and the maiden Bawda." The bride, as her name implies, is part of the place itself and not about it:

> They married well because the marriage place
> Was what they loved. It was neither heaven nor
>   hell.
> They were love's characters come face to face.

The place in which (to which) they are married is not a symbolic place, guaranteed by biblical decree, but a place made of themselves in the same way that Williams feels Poe created his poetry. Stevens' Catawba, like his New Haven, Key West, or Tennessee, is a wilderness from which springs desire:

> And not to have is the beginning of desire.
> To have what is not is its ancient cycle.
> It is desire at the end of winter, when
>
> It observes the effortless weather turning blue
> And sees the myosotis on its bush
> Being virile, it hears the calendar hymn.
>
> It knows that what it has is what is not
> And throws it away like a thing of another time,
> As morning throws off stale moonlight and
>   shabby sleep.

Out of this dialectic of desire comes the openness to change that Stevens feels is necessary to the poem, a condition that Robert Duncan calls "permission" to enter the field of creative life. Thus a "place of first permission" exists not as part of some archetypal ahistorical principle but

as that which projects a possible future, "As morning throws off stale moonlight and shabby sleep." Place is the becoming conscious of more than place, transforming spatial reality into occasion. As Charles Olson says of geography [in his *Maximus Poems*],

> It is the imposing
> of all those antecedent predecessions, the preces-
>   sions
>
> of me, the generation of those facts
> which are my words, it is coming
>
> from all that I no longer am, yet am,
> the slow westward motion of
>
> more than I am

In this essay I have resisted the term "Postmodernism" almost successfully—"resisted" because the term now serves too many masters, and "almost" because, like any fiction, supreme or critical, it must be continually reinvented. As a literary historical term, Postmodernism serves the relatively simple purpose of differentiating between one generation and another. As a critical term, it implies a constellation of responses to the Kantian aesthetic revolution as formulated by the Symbolist poetics of the New Critics. Stevens, along with Gertrude Stein, Beckett, and Williams, occupies a central position in the transition between Modernism and Postmodernism. He inherits an ideal of pure poetry—even a theory of correspondences—from Symbolism, but the direction of his linguistic experimentation is toward something quite different from Mallarmé's mystical nether realm or Baudelaire's forest of symbols. And although he states that "Poetry / Exceeding music must take the place / Of empty heaven and its hymns," his is no Paterian religion of art. Stevens' linguistic indeterminacy is directed toward a determinate world, a fact that links him more to Williams than to his other contemporaries. But where Williams focuses on the thing, Stevens focuses on the apprehension of the thing. Both believe in the essential worth of red wheelbarrows and jars, but they find themselves looking at these objects from entirely different perspectives. As a Modernist, Stevens occupies a position somewhere between Henry James and Charles Ives—between an artist who made the house of fiction out of fluctuating moods and subtle inflections, and an artist for whom the criteria of performability and realization seemed an unnecessary bother. Finally, Stevens' is a critical poetry, as I believe contemporary poetry, in its best estate, can be: critical of its own ability to achieve a supreme fiction at the expense of the world, critical of language in service to a transcendental ideal.

But Stevens' critical function stops here, at the border of institutions and ideologies. His well-known difficulties in responding to the specific conditions of historical change reflect a willingness to uphold the barrier between aesthetic and material production. If "Life consists / Of propositions about life," as he says in **"Men Made Out of Words,"** there is the danger that all such propositions are equally valuable and that their origin is entirely monologic rather than part of human dialogue. It has been for later poets to take up the kind of propositional, philosophical poetry that Stevens began and direct it toward particular social and ideological forms. Works like Ed Dorn's *Slinger,* David Antin's talk pieces, and the work of the language poets seem to extend Stevens' propositional logic into investigations of discursive and pragmatic communicational models. *Notes toward a Supreme Fiction* may now have become "Notes toward the Ideologies of Supreme Fictions."

I do not mean to imply that the single achievement of Postmodernist poetry, with or without Stevens, has been its politicization of poetry, but rather that in undermining certain formalist models of high Modernism, it has attempted to enlarge the dialogic and discursive possibilities of poetry. It has called into question the nature of the single, self-sufficient subject, while opening a dialogue with the reader as coproducer of the text. It has brought the material nature of its own creation into sharp focus, treating poetic language not as a separate, sacrosanct domain (the poetic function) but as a dimension of sign and thus a social product. If Wallace Stevens seems an unlikely benefactor of these events, it is because he so successfully provided us with the means to interrogate and refashion his pedagogy in our own terms. "We reason of these things with later reason," the poet reasons, "And we make of what we see, what we see clearly / And have seen, a place dependent on ourselves." We might add: a place dependent on ourselves in Wallace Stevens. (pp. 141-58)

> *Michael Davidson, "Notes Beyond the 'Notes':
> Wallace Stevens and Contemporary Poetics,"
> in* Wallace Stevens: The Poetics of Modernism, *edited by Albert Gelpi, Cambridge University Press, 1985, pp. 141-60.*

Jacqueline Vaught Brogan   (essay date 1988)

[*Brogan is an American poet, educator, and critic. Her work on Stevens includes several essays as well as her* Stevens and Simile: A Theory of Language *(1986). In the following excerpt, she examines the treatment and characterization of women in Stevens's poetry.*]

It would be easy to oversimplify the subject of sexism and Stevens as sexism *in* Stevens. The various biographies devoted to Wallace Stevens . . . have all, individually and collectively, given us information about his private life, especially in relation to his wife, that make it increasingly difficult to think of Stevens as that innocent, cherub-like person that Randall Jarrell once described him as being. I have in mind, for example, Stevens' effective silencing of Elsie (as described by the family chauffeur to Peter Brazeau), or the disturbing way in which he "scripted" her—literally made her an object of his pen, renaming her according to his needs—as seen in the previously unpublished letters to his wife included in Joan Richardson's biography. In light of these new facts about Stevens' personal life, it is perhaps not surprising to find a recent and almost scathing indictment of Stevens' irresponsibility, if not moral failure, in his relationship with and to women. Yet my subject here is not sexism *in* Stevens, in the sense of Stevens' being a sexist individual, nor is it trying to psychoanalyze what in Stevens' life might or might not have led to a troubled psyche, particularly concerning women.

It seems almost too easy to point to Stevens' mother as a figure for the imagination, in continual conflict with his father as a figure for pragmatic action and reason. I think, too, that one could exploit the fact that Elsie Moll Stevens, who was so clearly perceived by Stevens in the early years as his muse, should be at once the girl from the wrong side of the tracks, possibly illegitimate, and the model for the goddess on the liberty coin, the two archetypal—and equally dehumanizing—ways of viewing women in our culture thus both being accidentally inscribed in Elsie's life. Although these various facts may suggest, once again, that the personal *is* political, I want to distinguish as much as possible the subject of sexism *in* Stevens from sexism *and* Stevens, even if finally the two topics prove inseparable. What interests me here, therefore, is what happens to Stevens' poetry as he engages in the (perhaps conscious) suppression of what *he* perceives to be his feminine voice or, more accurately, that part of his poetic voice which is feminine metaphorically in the way that the idea of "feminine" itself is metaphorical. My conclusion is that while Stevens would always suffer from a schism within himself, one which was ultimately derived from cultural biases against women (and which would affect his poetry in a number of important ways), he would also come as close as it was possible for a person in his time and circumstance to "curing" himself of the "infection in the sentence" that the dominant, phallocentric structures in our culture inevitably breed.

The distinction I am making between sexism *in* Stevens and sexism *and* Stevens is not meant to deny the fact that there are sexist innuendoes in Stevens' poetry. Certain sexist assumptions, including the one that denigrating women is humorous, account for a number of his poems, including **"To a High-Toned Old Christian Woman."** It is not merely institutionalized religion which Stevens is mocking there. "To a High-Toned Old Christian Man" does not seem nearly as funny, and I speculate that trying to make *"widowers* wince" would not be perceived as being especially witty either. Similar attitudes also inform **"Lulu Gay"** and **"Lulu Morose,"** although the first of these, in which Lulu tells the eunuchs what the barbarians have done to her, is immediately more problematic. It is probably right to the point that the males who have been castrated have lost their "voice" as well—they cannot talk (but only ululate). Certainly, we find an archetypal expression of sexism in that poem with the wonderful title, **"Good Man, Bad Woman."** In fact, such basic sexist attitudes—even if we are charitable and conclude that Stevens intends to poke fun at such attitudes—govern a variety of poems. There is no character in all of Stevens' poetry, for example, with quite the same sense of grotesque humor as the woman of **"The Emperor of Ice-Cream"**—dead, lying on a deal dresser with her "horned feet" protruding—unless it is the "lady dying of diabetes" in **"A Thought Revolved."**

When we find instances of such blatant sexism *in* Stevens, it is useful to remember the cultural context within which he produced his work. When Stevens began publishing in earnest, the women's suffrage movement was well under way and frequently was the subject of essays in the magazines in which Stevens was publishing (and which he was presumably reading himself). Many of these essays are surprisingly sophisticated. As early as 1914 Edna Kenton was distinguishing between different *kinds* of feminisms— i.e., the largely Anglo-American drive for identical rights vs. the German feminists' fight for "different" but equal rights for women. Yet even in such magazines as *The Trend,* which seems far more sympathetic to the women's movement than most since it kept a running tally on which states were supporting women's suffrage, we find some rather appallingly sexist essays, among them "The Land of the Hen-Pecked" or "Rule the Women or They'll Rule You." The title of this last one sounds much like Stevens in **"Good Man, Bad Woman"** when he says, "She can corrode your world, if never you."

In fact, as Joan Kelly and Sandra Gilbert (among others) have pointed out, what strides women have made in gaining civic and political rights have also historically been accompanied by periods of increased hostility toward women. This conflict—i.e., the liberation of woman politically and the increased resentment toward, if not repression of, her personally—accounts for the overwhelming number of poems written during Stevens' early period that expose women's status (or lack of status) in the early part of this century. For example, we find in magazines to which Stevens himself was contributing H. D.'s "Priapus" and "Acon," Alice Groff's "Herm-Aphrodite-Us," the five poems about women that Pound published in a 1915 issue of *Others,* Skipwith Cannell's "Ikons," published the following year, or Kenneth Burke's "Adam's Song, and Mine." The overt tension in this phase of the battle of the sexes toward which all of these poems point is made explicit in Helen Hoyt's "Homage," cited in part below:

> Not as a man I felt you in my brooding,
> But merely a babe. . . .
> . . . . .
> Sometimes I wished to feed you at my breast.
>
> Not to myself, I knew, belonged your homage;
> I but the vessel of your holy drinking,
> The channel to you of that olden wonder
> Of love and womanhood,—I, but a woman.
> . . . . .
> Do you think I did not kneel when you were
>   kneeling?
> Even lowlier bowed my head, and bowed my
>   heart.

What makes this poem particularly interesting is the difficulty in assessing how much irony may or may not have been intended here, although it is important to note, both for her own work and for a sense of the times in which Stevens first began publishing, that Helen Hoyt would edit a special issue of women poets for *Others* one year after publishing this poem. Nevertheless, when we do find sexist assumptions or innuendoes in Stevens' work, we face a similar dilemma in frequently being unable to determine precisely how much Stevens is reflecting cultural biases or just how much he is "revising" such biases through ironic reflections.

Yet despite this very complicated context, it is possible to see the ways in which Stevens' perhaps conscious, perhaps unconscious "phallocentric" perspective manifests itself

in the dynamics, even the problematics of his poetry. That problematic may not be the conflict between imagination and reality (as has been traditionally assumed), nor even the battle between competing theories of language, but rather a problematic between feminine and masculine expression—i.e., between the male authorial voice that strives to achieve significance and the culturally delineated suppression or silencing of feminine voice that struggles, nonetheless, precisely for expression in Stevens' works. Put differently, in Stevens' work we can see the ways in which our culturally inscribed notions of male/author/authority and our culturally inscribed repression of the rest of our human voice (even within ourselves, and within Stevens as well) frustrate the attempt at poetic expression itself, while informing what expressions are achieved in the individual poems.

To understand this critical facet of Stevens' work, it is important first to stress the fact that from the rejection of the feminine figure in **"Farewell to Florida"** to her reception in **"Final Soliloquy of the Interior Paramour,"** Stevens' poetry remains highly self-conscious about the fact that it *is* wrestling with the feminine figure and, usually in a rather Jungian fashion, specifically with the feminine figure within. I offer four texts, taken variously from his essays, letters, **Collected Poems** and **Opus Posthumous** over the course of his career as a mere sampling of this self-conscious struggle.

First, from **"Farewell without a Guitar,"** written in 1954, just one year before he died:

> Spring's bright paradise has come to this.
> Now the thousand-leaved green falls to the
>   ground.
> Farewell, my days.
>   . . . . .
>
>   The reflections and repetitions,
> The blows and buffets of fresh senses
> Of the rider that was,
>
> Are a final construction,
> Like glass and sun, of male reality
> And of that other and her desire.

While the rather poignantly glossed "rider that was" refers to the failure of Stevens' attempt to create—and to become—the "Noble Rider" of 1942, it is possible to say that from **"To the One of Fictive Music"** (1922) to the end of his life, much of Stevens' corpus is written in response to that significant "other." Yet *this* female figure, so nebulously and delicately evoked, is not the Elsie he largely dominated in his personal life, nor his mother—nor a high-toned old Christian woman for that matter—but precisely a part of himself that he could never fully come to know except as "she" was traced in his poetry.

Significantly, in the second of these texts (section ten of **"Esthétique du Mal"**), Stevens distinguishes between two sets of female figures in his poetry, implicitly suggesting an awareness of a problem in his figurations of women and, even more implicitly, suggesting the possibility of resolution in an androgynous figure:

> He had studied the nostalgias. In these

> He sought the most grossly maternal, the crea-
>   ture
> Who most fecundly assuaged him, the softest
> Woman with a vague moustache and not the
>   mauve
> *Maman.* His anima liked its animal
> And liked it unsubjugated, so that home
> Was a return to birth. . . .
>   . . . . .
> It is true there were other mothers, singular
> In form, lovers of heaven and earth, she-wolves
> And forest tigresses and women mixed
> With the sea. These were fantastic.

These "other mothers," immediately troped in the text to the monstrous "she-wolves" and "tigresses"—are the "fantastic" manifestations of his own feminine voice, or anima, repressed throughout most of his poetic career. Thus, one effect of his conscious repression of the feminine principle in **"Farewell to Florida"** (though there is ample evidence of unconscious repression before that poem appeared in 1936) manifests itself in the extreme attention to "man number one" in **"The Man with the Blue Guitar"** (1937) with, however, a concurrent monstrous version of his poetic self which he has largely tried to subjugate. It is both culturally and poetically predictable that whereas this "monster" in **"The Man with the Blue Guitar"** (the "lion in the lute / Before the lion locked in stone") *may* be male, in general the uncomposed and, therefore, potentially destructive aspect of his creative energy is perceived by—or figured by—Stevens as a (threatening) woman.

This fact leads to a third text, a passage from **"The Figure of the Youth as Virile Poet."** After making the rather remarkable statement that "The centuries have a way of being male," and before insisting that the "character of [the] poet" must be seen as *"virile"*—otherwise "the masculine nature that we propose for one that must be the master of our lives will be lost" (italics mine)—Stevens says:

> When we look back at the face of the seven-
> teenth century, it is at the rigorous face of the
> rigorous thinker and, say, the Miltonic image of
> a poet, severe and determined. In effect, what we
> are remembering is the rather haggard back-
> ground of the incredible, the imagination with-
> out intelligence, from which a younger figure is
> emerging, stepping forward in the company of
> a muse of its own, *still half-beast and somehow
> more than human, a kind of sister of the Mino-
> taur.* The younger figure is the intelligence that
> endures. It is the imagination of the son still
> bearing the antique imagination of the father.
> (italics mine)

The essentially androgynous character of this figure (since the "sister" is also the "son"), together with the one cited above, bears further study—particularly in the context of the often frustrated quest for androgynous union traced in much of the romantic poetry preceding (and anticipating) Jungian theory. Nevertheless, as I read this particular essay, Stevens is seriously engaged here in a deliberate battle to overcome the kind of schism within himself that would give rise precisely to this kind of distortion, in which the feminine aspect is marked and perpetually

marred by "monstrous" displacement. Yet at least in 1942 when this essay was written, Stevens' own language gets in the way of such a cure. Not only does he still think of the poet as someone who must *master* our lives (and who must be male), he also writes these ironically self-defeating words at the very point the "figure of the youth as virile poet" supposedly speaks or finds his *own* voice:

> No longer do I believe that there is a mystic
> muse, sister of the Minotaur. This is another of
> the monsters I had for nurse, whom I have wast-
> ed. I am myself a part of what is real, and it is
> my own speech and the strength of it, this only,
> that I hear or ever shall.

What is the most provocative about this passage, especially since it is in such conflict with the semantic intent, is that even as he rejects the "sister of the Minotaur" at the supposed moment of self-identification, he reinstates the *figure of the monster* as a (presumably female) nurse.

The last text is simply the letter which followed Howard Baker's analysis of Wallace Stevens in *Southern Review* ("Wallace Stevens and Other Poets") in which Baker describes Stevens' poetry in Jungian terms. In a letter to Ronald Latimer in 1935, Stevens writes:

> There is in the last number of the *Southern Re-
> view,* or *Quarterly,* an extremely intelligent anal-
> ysis of my work by Howard Baker. No one be-
> fore has ever come as close to me as Mr. Baker
> does in that article.

This letter is important to the subject because it clarifies that Stevens thought of his own poetry, even at an early point, in somewhat Jungian terms and that, therefore, attention to the male and female figures (and hence to their voices or lack of voices) in Stevens' work is central to our understanding of it.

Clearly, Stevens does engage in the repression of the "feminine" aspect of his own creativity or creative voice in a variety of ways. It may well be that the culturally-encouraged suppression of women—specifically the silencing of women—is internalized in Stevens, so that his psyche feels at once a longing for this displaced self (hence, the omnipresent "she," the "other and her desire") and, simultaneously, feels threatened by what might be chaos, uncontrollable, if he abandons his "rage for order" by allowing her to speak. But, whatever the reasons, "a kind of sister of the Minotaur" is the uncanny, and uncomfortable, figure repressed—ambivalently and ambiguously held—in the white space of Stevens' texts.

This repression manifests itself ironically, if not subversively, in Stevens' work throughout his poetic career. Most obviously, Stevens rejects the feminine figures of ***Harmonium,*** especially the figures of female, fecund nature in the 1936 **"Farewell to Florida"** (the poem, notably, with which he opened the *second* version of ***Ideas of Order***). There he accuses "her" of having bound "[him] round" and says that he will return to the land of the "violent mind," which is equivalent to the land of the violent men. Yet repression of the feminine figure occurs in Stevens in more subtle and ultimately more significant ways, although the particular, conscious rejection of the feminine seen in **"Farewell to Florida"** encouraged the more ab-stract, philosophical poetry of the next many years to come.

Ironically, one of the most "telling" marks of Stevens' re-pression of the feminine is that in his poetry female figures almost never speak. If any voice is heard at all (and that itself is a subject to take up below), it is that of a male, as in **"Two Figures in Dense Violet Night"**:

> Be the voice of night and Florida in my ear.
> Use dusky words and dusky images.
> Darken your speech.
>
> Speak, even, as if I did not hear you speaking,
> But spoke for you perfectly in my thoughts,
> Conceiving words,
>
> As the night conceives the sea-sounds in silence,
> And out of their droning sibilants makes
> A serenade.

One exception to this generalization is the woman in **"Metropolitan Melancholy,"** the "purple woman" with the "lavender tongue" who "Said hic, said hac / Said ha." Another is the quoted *Encore un instant de bonheur,* words that Stevens immediately dismisses: "The words / Are a woman's words, unlikely to satisfy / The taste of even a country connoisseur." Here, it is admittedly diffi-cult to distinguish the repression of the feminine voice from basic sexism. Nevertheless, a glance at the *Concor-dance* to Stevens' poetry reveals that, surprisingly, "words" are not Stevens' most popular theme, but "man" or "men" (appearing 507 times) and, especially, man speaking. Women appear in Stevens' poetry about one fifth as frequently—a total of 106 times in comparison to the 507 for men. But in contrast to the men, they almost never have a voice. From the early **"All Over Minnesota,"** where the "voice of the wind is male," through **"A Thought Revolved,"** to *The Necessary Angel,* the idea of "voice" itself is perceived by Stevens as exclusively mascu-line. But then, I think we can say, he protests too much.

One extension of this verbal "repression" is the fact that not only do the female figures in Stevens' poetry rarely speak, they rarely move. Consider the difference between his earliest and most famous male and female characters, **"The Comedian as the Letter C"** and the complacent woman of **"Sunday Morning."** In a very disturbing way, women in his poetry remain too obviously figures—empty ciphers for masculine rumination and scripting, even de-scription. The woman of **"Sunday Morning"** has several sisters, among them **"So-and-So Reclining on Her Couch"** and **"Romance for a Demoiselle Lying in the Grass,"** in which Stevens writes that

> The monotony
> Is like your port which conceals
> All your characters
> And their desires.

In the course of the poem this female figure is either troped to or revealed to be a guitar—Stevens closes the poem with "Clasp me, / Delicatest machine." But this revelation, if we can call it that, further "objectifies" the feminine, even if metaphorically, "concealing" her behind a phallocentric and concomitantly erotic perspective that is reminiscent

Eduard Manet, "Woman with a Parrot," which Helen Vendler has cited as a source for Steven's poem "Sunday Morning" (1915).

of the elders' view of Susanna in **"Peter Quince at the Cla-vier."**

Nonetheless, precisely because he still retains the idea of a feminine muse (even if she may be figured as a "kind of sister of the Minotaur"), Stevens' attempts to repress or silence the feminine leaves *him* in the position of never being able to speak. Almost without exception, Stevens' greatest attempts at poetic expression, the words of that "virile poet," are instances of failures of speech—words about the words he *would* say, if he could—signs, shall we say, of the failure of both logocentric and phallocentric or-dering. For example, Stevens says in *Notes toward a Su-preme Fiction* that it is

> As if the waves at last were never broken,
> As if the language suddenly, with ease,
> Said things it had laboriously spoken.

Again in **"A Primitive Like an Orb,"** Stevens writes with an implicit pathos that "It is / As if the central poem be-came the world, / And the world the central poem, each one the mate / Of the other, as if summer was a spouse, / Espoused each morning." Thus, despite his sustained at-tempt to evoke—or to become—the "virile" poet, one whose words both "master" and are "a part" of what is real, that which he cannot order or "master" insists upon being heard, however ironically, in the very silence of the gap between "as" and "if," that is, between "order" and the "abyss," as these terms are metaphorically and sexually conceived. The white writing of such texts is perversely and subversively the trace of the repressed voice that refuses to (or cannot) coincide with the phallic and verbal structures Stevens professes to order in his words. Hence Stevens' lifelong frustration about his inability to get "straight to the word, / Straight to the transfixing object"—and hence, also, his desire.

From this perspective, **"The Idea of Order at Key West"** can be seen to reiterate this basic problematic in Stevens' verse, rather than embodying one of his more successful figurations of women, as many critics have assumed. In contrast to the other women figures mentioned so far, the celebrated female figure of this poem is, superficially, neither mocked or denigrated; she is also supposedly vocal and dynamic, walking and singing by the shore:

> And when she sang, the sea,
> Whatever self it had, became the self
> That was her song, for she was the maker. Then we,
> As we beheld her striding there alone,
> Knew that there never was a world for her
> Except the one she sang and, singing, made.

However alluring this poem may be, we run the risk of being ruled by rhetoric if we fail to note that ultimately—and even in the narrative development of the text itself—this "woman" is simply a figure for (and thus a sign or empty cipher for) Stevens himself and the way *he* sings. The clearest sign of this fact is found in the very next line, where he abruptly breaks in with, "Ramon Fernandez, tell me, if you know . . ." This rupture is the most overt sign in the poem of the nature of the poetic "order" (even "rage for order") that Stevens has in mind. This thematic is inscribed throughout the poem: lights "master" the night, "portion" out the sea, "arrange" and "deepen" night, so that the words, in a kind of phallic "mastering," ironically create the "fragrant portals," essentially create the feminine. But what do we hear from this feminine voice which is simultaneously created, disclosed in the portals, and repressed, silenced by the "mastering" and by the actual appropriation of the unheard feminine voice to Stevens' own? From the opening stanza, that other voice remains literally "beyond" us and ourselves:

> She sang beyond the genius of the sea.
> The water never formed to mind or voice,
> Like a body wholly body, fluttering
> Its empty sleeves; and yet its mimic motion
> Made constant cry, caused constantly a cry,
> That was not ours although we understood,
> Inhuman, of the veritable ocean.

The need for this control—the imperative to create and to control a world in words—can in part be explained historically and culturally. The Great Depression, the Great War, the felt menace of a second world war to come would easily give rise to the need to defend oneself against looming chaos, a fact which is amply demonstrated by the poems of Stevens' middle period. But I think at least part of the explanation for Stevens' apparent need to break into the text—to silence this feminine figure, however lovely

we may feel she may be—lies in her uncanny reflection, that "sister of the Minotaur." The lovely, virtually "inhuman" woman by the sea and the somewhat unsettling "half-beast" who is "yet more than human" are two faces, as it were, of the same *figure* which, as figure, also means absence and repression. Instead of the madwoman in the attic, this is a (potentially) mad woman in a maze, specifically a linguistic maze.

The idealized version of the figure, the one who remains beyond speech, desired but controlled, together with her monstrous counterpart account for many of Stevens' more "fantastic" female characters. The idealized figure is found in **"To the One of Fictive Music,"** where, for example, Stevens creates a feminine trilogy of sister, mother, and diviner love, in **"Infanta Marina,"** where "She" can make "of the motions of her wrist / The grandiose gestures / Of her thought," as well as in **"Apostrophe to Vincentine"** and **"Bouquet of Belle Scavoir."** Yet her monstrous counterpart is found in **"The Woman Who Blamed Life on a Spaniard,"** where "she never clears / But spreads an evil lustre whose increase / Is evil," in the fifth of **"Five Grotesque Pieces"** (entitled **"Outside of Wedlock"**), where she is figured as "an old bitch, an old drunk, / That has been yelling in the dark," even in **"The Common Life,"** where quite significantly, given the title, "The women have only one side." In **"The Old Woman and the Statue,"** she has all the attributes of a witch:

> But her he had not foreseen: the bitter mind
> In a flapping cloak. She walked along the paths
> Of the park with chalky brow scratched over black
> And black by thought that could not understand
> Or, if it understood, repressed itself
> Without any pity in a somnolent dream.

Still, it would not be accurate to reduce Stevens' poetry to reiterating endlessly this conflict within himself. If Stevens suffered (and I think he did suffer) from a schism within himself, he also seems not only to have been aware of that but to have tried to "cure" himself. Even as early as **"Last Look at the Lilacs,"** he is contemptuous of that rational "caliper," that "arrogantly male, / Patron and imager." And he also condemns, albeit playfully, that "Damned universal cock" in **"Bantams in Pine-Woods"** who, in a quintessentially phallocentric way, thinks that he is the center of the universe. To this end I see an important development between **"The Idea of Order at Key West"** and his well-known **"Final Soliloquy of the Interior Paramour."**

In contrast to the earlier poem of 1934, in Stevens' 1950 lyric divisiveness in voice and in self is recognized rather than being "written over" or suppressed. The divisiveness is even explicitly held within the interior (rather than being fallaciously described as a split between a dominating male poet/author/authority and a submitting, potentially chaotic feminine world). As the word "paramour" suggests, there is a romance, even an intimacy/communion/communication in this poem that is dependent upon "dif-ference" (to use Heidegger's term). The most telling sign of this is the plural pronoun "we" and that most feminine of articles, the "shawl," wrapped tightly round them since they "are poor":

> Light the first light of evening, as in a room
> In which we rest and, for small reason, think
> The world imagined is the ultimate good.
> This is, therefore, the intensest rendezvous.
> It is in that thought that we collect ourselves,
> Out of all the indifferences, into one thing:
>
> Within a single thing, a single shawl
> Wrapped tightly round us, since we are
>   poor . . .

Even though Stevens' characteristic tone of dominance is absent in this poem, the recognition and recovery of the feminine voice does not undermine the poetic authorship as Stevens obviously feared it would in **"Farewell to Florida."** Instead, the recovery of this voice gives expression to what is beyond control, beyond order, beyond dominance in our actual lives and *thereby endows with significance* that little which we can order in words:

> Out of this same light, out of the central mind,
> We make a dwelling in the evening air,
> In which being there together is enough.

In this poem the phallocentric "central mind" is consciously exposed *as a fiction*—not in any way heralded as the "ideal realm" where the "new bourgeois man feels historically untouchable," as Frank Lentricchia has recently argued. From the opening stanza, there is only "small reason" to "think / The world imagined is the ultimate good," a delicate disclaimer which quietly but continually dismantles the covert assumptions about and equations of reason, thinking, imagination, and essentially all Western (or at least Platonic) idealizations. But in submitting to the realization of the fictionality of our orderings—including the largely phallocentric privileging of the idea of order itself—*this* poem manages finally to be heard as fully human and humane. In essence, the recovery here of the feminine voice, which is so silenced in his early poems, especially after *Harmonium,* opens up the space in Stevens for the magnificent voice of his later years, one heard, for example, in **"The Planet on the Table"** and **"Lebensweisheitspielerei,"** where he admits, in opposition to the "portentous enunciation" of his earlier work, that

>   The proud and the strong
> Have departed.
>
> Those that are left are the unaccomplished,
> The finally human,
> Natives of a dwindled sphere

—but a sphere in which "Each person completely touches *us*" (italics mine).

We should note that such a development as I have sketched here is itself reductive in a way. Certainly in **"Madame La Fleurie,"** also a very late poem, we see the monstrous and bearded inversion of mother earth in the "bearded queen" who is devouring him. Similarly, the mother in **"World Without Peculiarity"** becomes a hating "thing upon his breast." Yet, in general, the development I have described is accurate. As he says in **"Artificial Populations,"** a poem written the year he died, "This artificial population [rosy men and women of the rose] is like / A healing-point in the sickness of the mind."

How this "cure" was accomplished is itself a topic for an-

other lengthy study, but I would like to offer a brief summary of certain touchstones in this process. After his obvious attempt to gain total voice in **"The Figure of the Youth as Virile Poet,"** Stevens becomes increasingly obsessed with "the sound / Of right joining," "The final relation, the marriage of the rest." We see this desire thematized in his letters when he, perhaps surprisingly given his personal life, uses the pleasure that "a man and woman find in each other's company" as an illustration of the "pleasure" of "Cross-reflections, modifications, counterbalances, . . . giving and taking" of the "various faculties of the mind"; and it is repeated two years later in the seventh section of *Notes toward a Supreme Fiction:*

> Perhaps there are times of inherent excellence,
>
> As when the cock crows on the left and all
> Is well, incalculable balances . . .
>   . . . . .
>   not balances
> That we achieve but balances that happen,
>
> As a man and woman meet and love forthwith.

Yet despite his efforts to achieve this balance in *Notes toward a Supreme Fiction,* Nanzia Nunzio, for example, fails to achieve this promise, her erotic power being so contingent upon her willingness to be scripted or subjugated:

> Speak to me that, which spoken, will array me
> In its own only precious ornament.
>   . . . . .
> Clothe me entire in the final filament,
> So that I tremble with such love so known
> And myself am precious for your perfecting.

The maiden Bawda and her captain perhaps fare better: at least they are both "love's characters come face to face." Yet the last numbered section of the poem names the "Fat girl" as the "irrational . . . the more than rational distortion," phrases reminiscent of those used in the same year to describe the "sister of the Minotaur." Certainly Stevens has not achieved communion with his interior paramour at this point, despite his desire to do so.

But in **"Of Modern Poetry,"** written two years before, and later in **"Burghers of Petty Death,"** we find men and women together, more successfully figured as equal representatives of humanity. "Modern Poetry," Stevens says, "has to be living, to learn the speech of the place. / It has to face the men of the time and to meet / The women of the time." In the second poem, written in 1946, Stevens says:

> These are the small townsmen of death,
> A man and a woman, like two leaves
> That keep clinging to a tree,
> Before winter freezes and grows black—

This "woman," equal in her humanness to the "man," marks a new moment in Stevens in which "she" is not only validated but recognized both as a presence and as a human being rather than tracing, in either idealized or "monstrous" discourse, the path of failed signification and signifiers. If I were to indulge in psychological explanations, I would consider the possibility that the sheer, overwhelming and uncontrollable violence of the Second World War reduced all human beings in Stevens' eyes to the position of "women" in the ironically-realized, metaphorical sense of the word. We are all without power, not just women, in this modern world, unable to control the world and possibly our own lives.

Between **"Of Modern Poetry"** and **"Burghers of Petty Death,"** we see Stevens dismiss a figure of a "bright red woman" for (presumably) a real one in a poem intriguingly called **"Debris of Life and Mind"**:

> She will think about them not quite able to sing.
> Besides, when the sky is so blue, things sing
> themselves,
>
> Even for her, already for her. She will listen
> And feel that her color is a meditation,
>
> The most gay and yet not so gay as it was.
> Stay here. Speak of familiar things a while.

The unexpected turn in the last line toward domestic intimacy, especially for such a previously "exotic" poet, enacts what is both a personal and poetic passage, a "fall," we might say, into the more fully human. Certainly his request, open to rejection, vulnerable, and wistful, is quite different in tone from the whole panoply of "hero" poems that preceded this poem and the earlier "rage for order."

In **"Auroras of Autumn,"** published in 1947, Stevens implies, at least, that he meets his anima in an intense "rendezvous" that prepares the way for **"Final Soliloquy"**:

> This sense of the activity of fate—
> The rendezvous, when she came alone,
> By her coming became a freedom of the two,
> An isolation which only the two could share.

As Frank Doggett and Dorothy Emerson have rightly suggested, this "isolation" is an isolation because it is a rendezvous within himself, between his masculine and feminine selves. What is most revealing about this description, however, is that it is specifically a "freedom of the two," a phrase which claims at least to have finally achieved what Stevens desired as early as **"The Man with the Blue Guitar"**: reduction of the "monster to / Myself" so that he can "be, / Two things, the two together as one." It is also much to the point here that the "mother" who "invites humanity to her house" in this poem "has grown old." Ultimately, she too is more vulnerable (and, therefore, human) than mythic—as is the woman in **"Things of August"** (1949), where "She is exhausted and a little old." In addition, as Milton J. Bates has already pointed out [in his *Wallace Stevens: A Mythology of Self*], it is at this moment in his career that Stevens begins so frequently to characterize himself as a child, but, I would add, usually as a child of both parents, or both sexes, rather than being strictly the son "only of man" as in the earlier **"A Thought Revolved."**

Finally, in **"Angel Surrounded by Paysans"** (1949), we come across a supposedly masculine character, "a man / Of the mind," who finally *speaks* with what I see as Stevens' previously repressed feminine voice. There is no control, no mastering, no portioning of the night:

> Am I not,
> Myself, only half of a figure of a sort,
>
> A figure half seen, or seen for a moment, a man
> Of the mind, an apparition apparelled in
> Apparels of such lightest look that a turn
> Of my shoulder and quickly, too quickly, I am
> gone?

The angel is, in fact, a "necessary angel," but one who is questioning rather than "ordering," one who is, admittedly, too easily gone, subject to change—a sign of the mutability of our best linguistic orderings. But he—she—is also finally heard *through* the door (instead of being held off beyond the portals), heard, even if only whispering. This poem, which ends the last volume of poetry that Stevens wrote before *The Rock,* achieves something of a resolution (emphasizing far more the "solution" or mixing than the earlier tone of "resolve") that finds a final plenitude in the great lyrics of his last volume, including **"Final Soliloquy of the Interior Paramour."** (pp. 102-15)

Jacqueline Vaught Brogan, " 'Sister of the Minotaur': Sexism and Stevens," in The Wallace Stevens Journal, *Vol. XII, No. 2, Fall, 1988, pp. 102-18.*

Frank Lentricchia   (essay date 1988)

[*An American educator and critic, Lentricchia emphasizes the social aspect of literature and language in all of his writings. While Lentricchia's criticism has focused on the relationship between poetry and identity, as in* The Gaiety of Language: An Essay on the Radical Poetics of W. B. Yeats and Wallace Stevens *(1968), his more recent work has addressed the social responsibility of literature, theory, and criticism. His* Criticism and Social Change *(1984) addresses the responsibilities of the critic in society and further defines his understanding of the relationship between culture and society. In the following excerpt, Lentricchia examines the dual identities of Stevens as both businessman and poet, discusses the treatment of class concerns in his poetry, and places Stevens's work in the context of high modernist poetry.*]

The standard generalization about Wallace Stevens' poetic development is that as he grew older he put on the vocal weight which enabled him to transcend the mere aesthetic perfections of his earlier poems—so sensuously full, so exquisitely achieved, so intellectually empty. Aside from Yvor Winters and his few (and ever fewer) devotees it is hard to find serious readers of Stevens who don't believe that he actually grew up as he grew older and that the proof of his maturity lies in his later long poems where (so it goes) he at last achieved the requisite (churchly) tone of high seriousness and important human reference. That old contention of Stevens' critics is strongly echoed in a wider cultural dimension in the self-reflexive song of canonical modernism, in the full terror that modernists feel for their own social relevance. Beginning with aestheticist principles, modernists ask, with an art that presumably turns its back on the world, refuses representation, turns inward to sensation and impression, as Pater urged, how can we put art back in—give it connection, power, or, in Stevens' words, "a ministry in the world"? Whether they write poems, narratives of character, or narratives of ideas called critical theory, that's long been a panicky question of literary modernism. And the story I am telling about Stevens and his culture is maybe the most vivid example that I can give of an anxiety framed by this classic contradiction of the middle-class world: on the one hand, our retreat to the interior, whether of our homes, our families, or our writing—wherein we indulge the sentiment that our private life is our authentic life—and our concurrent disavowal of all possibility for happiness in the public sphere, or in relationships not sanctioned by the public sphere; a retreat, a disavowal, on the other hand, incessantly accompanied by an incipiently explosive dissatisfaction with all private (and aestheticizing) solutions to pains whose sources are not personal and which require keen attention to history's plots. Georg Lukács's excoriation of the subjective and plotless qualities of high-modernist literature is perfectly just as far as it goes. But what it leaves out is one of the most interesting things about high modernists—their pre-Lukácian discomfort with what they suspect as their own self-trivializing ahistoricism.

Reviewers of Stevens' first volume said over and again, in so many words, that he was a precious little aesthete—that he had nothing to say and, even worse, that his poems were on principle mindless: maybe gemlike, but also without point. These negative assessments bothered Stevens but not for the usual egoistic reasons. The fact is that he had heard it all before. His reviewers had only uttered publicly what he was telling his friends in letters in the months when he was deciding on the contents of *Harmonium,* reading over all he had written in the previous decade, thinking about what to keep in and what to keep out. He was saying in those painfully self-conscious days that his poems were "horrid cocoons from which later abortive insects had sprung"; they were "witherlings"; "debilitated." At best, "preliminary minutiae"; at worst, "garbage" from which no "crisp salad" could be picked. Stevens, at forty-four, would not be one of those writers who could by reading his old things over gather sustenance. He was one of those modernists who suffered from a severe originality neurosis whose sources were equally literary and economic, whose obsessive force was determined by equally decisive experiences of the literary avant-garde and the decadent edge of consumer capitalism. As his master category of value, originality simply makes nonsense of the conventional modernist opposition of aesthetics and economics because it not only prized the new as the different, the rare, and the strange, but could and did find triggering releases of pleasure equally in original poems and in exotic fruits bought at a specialty market for gourmet shoppers. He was one of those writers who find their old things just old—and psychically unprofitable to reencounter. And given the significant social role he had imagined and would imagine for poetry from his Harvard years on to the end of his life, his judgment upon what he had actually managed to produce from his late twenties through his early forties must have felt bitterly ironic. Yet, I think, not really despairing. For even as he condemned himself in self-disgust, he was allowing himself the hopeful fiction of organic growth. He might be looking at abortions but he could imagine and believe in the possibility of full-term

birth and teleological perfection both for himself and for his poetic project—a distinction which became harder and harder to make as he absorbed the full failure of his marriage to Elsie Moll.

His project was not wrong from the start. The origin was in fact good. His beginning as an aesthete, if only a beginning, in the delights of pure perception and linguistic riot, was yet the right sort of beginning. For him the aesthetic was an isolated moment, withdrawn from the social mess and forever free from didactic and political translation. As he grew older and more critical of the canonical modernism he partly endorsed, he began to believe that if the autonomous aesthetic moment was to become the urgent and compelling moment he always felt it inherently to be, then it would somehow have to carry its purity beyond itself, back into the social mess, to his rhetorical target: the culturally and economically privileged readers who, like himself, needed to transform the basic joyless conditions of their existence. **"It Must Give Pleasure"** is the title of the final section of *Notes toward a Supreme Fiction. It* must give pleasure because little else does. He declared in a characteristic moment in the essays he wrote in the later years of his career that poetry helps us to live our lives, and lucky for us that it does—we get so little help from anyplace else. He once told his wife that the nine-to-five working-day Wallace was nothing—the sources of his authentic selfhood were at home, quite literally: the site of his marriage and (for this aesthetic burgher) the site of poetic activity. But when love and marriage parted, making his marriage an empty form, his writing became the final source of selfhood: his last resort. The fate of his poetic project turned out to be indistinguishable from the fate of pleasure. The most poignant and definitive image I've ever seen drawn of what Stevens became as a man, after his marriage collapsed, was drawn by Stevens himself in a letter written in his seventieth year: "We have a very good time here. We go upstairs at night long before dark. Nothing could be more exciting than to sit in the quiet of one's room watching the fireflies." The "we" referred to, Elsie and himself, is a "we" long limited to pronominal designation. In fact, "we" are not having a good time. As "we" fades to the impersonal "one," Stevens is relieved of the embarrassment of openly saying to his correspondent "my room." They go upstairs long before dark to separate bedrooms they'd chosen many years before—Elsie to do God knows what, he never tells us, he to watch the flashing of fireflies in their mating game, to feel excitement that he can't share except with his interior lover, his own creative impulse, whose power to bring him "vivid transparence" he defines as the power of peace itself: poetry, Stevens' ultimate mating game, a game best played with only one player in the game, a last resort but also a best resort because in this game reliance on another is not a possibility.

The idea of the long poem became attractive to Stevens in the prepublication period of *Harmonium* because it promised to resolve the painful and difficult-to-disentangle questions of his literary stature and his marriage (hard to call it his love life), neither of which he could separate from his economic role as a male, from the social disease that I have called econo-machismo. The long poem, not the small pleasures of minority—those little things he had praised of Dr. Campion and Verlaine—could be the signature at once of his maleness and of his cultural relevance, a figure of his emerging social prowess at a time when he began to have doubts about his sexual prowess.

"Witherlings," that coinage for his early poems was just right: a live thing too soon dead, dried up because unnourished by what it most needed but could not from itself generate—a sustaining environment of thought. "Witherlings": literary modernism's great ideal, autonomous life, as aborted life. And "witherlings" in another sense, a thing withered in the human sense of the metaphor: the thing in question, now, not a tender shoot of plant life but an intention to speak and to act—*the aesthete as minister*—stunned into silence and paralysis (as in: he was withered by her scorching tone). The long poem, which would speak discursively as well as be, could never be figured by a decoration on a trivial thing (like a fan) in the hand of a leisured woman—the decoration, like useless autonomous art, a signifier of leisured life; the fan, an indulgent necessity (like autonomous art) for those unused to and unwilling to sweat and whose cultural advantages (like the experience of autonomous art) presuppose economic advantages. Real men, like Gainsborough, paint landscapes and portraits, not decorations on fans; real men, if they write poetry, go for the long poem of public (epic) import, not the small lyric of bourgeois delight. The poet who in his thirties felt himself marginalized by his social context as a ladylike dabbler in after-hours verse writing would become in his imaginative life at least (or is it at most?) a Latin lover courting what has to seem for the male modernist a forbidden woman, the epic muse who not only inspired but also had been possessed by a special sort of man, the sort embodied by Homer, Virgil, Dante, Milton. With those types she was obviously well bedded; could she be persuaded to try somebody new and so apparently ill-endowed for the task of epic loving? Could ladylike Stevens become one of those he had once called "your man-poets"? He wasn't sure and he marked his doubts with a humor which is always the sign (if we can trust Robert Frost's surmise about this) of virtually unbearable and unshareable inner seriousness: "I find this prolonged attention to a single subject has the same result that prolonged attention to a senora has according to the authorities. All manner of favors drop from it. Only it requires a skill in the varying of the serenade that occasionally makes one feel like a Guatemalan when one particularly wants to feel like an Italian" [*Letters of Wallace Stevens*].

In the time between the publication of *Harmonium* (1923) and his second volume, *Ideas of Order* (1935), specifically in the period between 1923 and 1930 or so, or for about seven years, Stevens wrote hardly anything. His literary sterility in those years can't be explained by the largely indifferent and hostile reception of *Harmonium;* bad reviews didn't silence him because he was their virtual author. In **"The Comedian as the Letter C,"** his first attempt at a long poem, Stevens was a previewer of *Harmonium*'s reception, more harsh than any of his actual reviewers. The **"Comedian"** is a severe and hilarious reflection on a poet, like himself, who seemed to him to deserve the deflating mockery of epithets like "lutanist of fleas" and "Socrates of snails," as well as sexually caustic allegorization as a skin-

ny sailor trying to conduct the sublimely frightening music of a sea storm with a pathetically inadequate little baton: as if poetic and sexual inadequacy were somehow each other's proper sign.

Self-disappointment and the need to think through self-revision are better but not sufficient explanations of his literary silence: if he was experimenting with new longer forms and new ambition, he was doing it in his head, or in drafts which no one will ever see. He certainly wasn't trying out his new self in the little magazine scene whose editors constantly requested his work and likely would have published pretty much anything he might have given them. By 1923 he was a respected avant-garde writer whose attractiveness was enhanced by his privacy and mysteriousness. He turned down many requests for poems; he had nothing to give. And while he was imagining but doing very little about earning his poetic manhood he was living out and doing a great deal about earning the sort of manhood that his American middle-class superego taught him to desire or pay the price in guilt.

From 1924 to 1932 he lived in a noisy two-family house, on a busy street in Hartford. In 1932, having saved up enough, he bought his first and only house (for $20,000, in cash). In this period he became a father who did what typical working fathers do—exercise their fatherhood after supper and on weekends, or precisely during those times when this father, unlike most working fathers, wanted to but couldn't do the reading and writing which were the basis for his other career. One of the few poetic exhibits we have from this period is an occasional verse, done for Valentine's Day 1925. It is an offhanded, sweet little thing, as its genre demanded, but nevertheless an elegy for his recent poetic death dipped in bitters, in which he tries to rationalize his quotidian obligations as a new kind of poetry, expressed in doggerel, the perfect representation of the well-grooved routine his everyday life had become. Not the poetry of everyday life, but everyday life as poetry:

> Though Valentine brings love
> And Spring brings beauty
> They do not make me rise
> To my poetic duty
> But Elsie and Holly do
> And do it daily—
> Much more than Valentine or Spring
> And very much more gaily.

In this post-*Harmonium* period he seems to have made his greatest effort—in which he succeeded—to rise to the corporate top of his business world: the right sort of thing to do for a man with family responsibilities, who was sole source of the family's income, who wanted his own home, and who liked really nice things, like oriental rugs. But poetry was power and freedom over circumstances—Stevens, like most writers since the late eighteenth century, needed to believe that—and the more financially unstable the writer, the more he believes that proposition of aesthetic idealism, the promise that there will be refuge even in the filthy prison house of capitalism. Stevens undefensively knew and admitted and even celebrated another, more commonly held proposition: that money was power and freedom, too. Cultural capital, money of the mind, is good, even if it is the opium of the intellectuals: it is a *kind* of money. But money itself, ah! money itself, whatever it is, it certainly is not a *kind* of money. The logic, which Stevens never resisted, is that money is a kind of poetry. In 1935, the middle of the Depression, when he was earning $25,000 a year (roughly the equivalent of $200,000 a year in our terms), when, in other words, he'd made it financially—after 1935 his poetic production simply mushroomed—he wrote this to a business associate:

> Our house has been a great delight to us, but it is still quite incomplete inside. . . . It has cost a great deal of money to get it where it is and, while it is pleasant to buy all these things, and no one likes to do it more than I do, still it is equally pleasant to feel that you are not the creature of circumstances, but are (at least to a certain degree) the master of the situation, which can only be if you have the savings banks sagging with your money and the presidents of the insurance companies stopping their cars to ask the privilege of taking you to the office. For my part, I never really lived until I had a home, say, with a package of books from Paris or London. [*Letters*]

Unlike most writers in his romantic tradition he knew that feelings of power and freedom in imagination were precisely the sorts of effects produced by a capitalist economic context in those (writers and intellectuals) who hate capitalist economic contexts; he seemed to know that aesthetic purity was economically encased; that imaginative power was good, to be sure, but that economic power was a more basic good because it enables (as it makes us desire) both the aesthetic good and the aesthetic goods (books from Paris and London) that he required. Can cultural power, however acquired and whatever its origin, turn on its economic base, become a liberating and constructive force in its own right? Believing in that proposition is not the opium of intellectuals, it's our LSD. Yet it may not be completely naive to think that art and intellect are forces of social change. Marxists, of course, think so; on the other hand, the textbook critics on the Christian New Right, who practice a different sort of hermeneutics of suspicion, also think so; even T. S. Eliot thought so. It is possible that the addition I allude to is a necessary addiction, a need of literary types to "turn on" politically because all the while we fear our political irrelevance. Stevens himself constantly chewed over the idea, and though he tended to reject the notion that literary force is also political force—the artist has no social role, he said more than once in his letters of the thirties and in his essays—it may be that the deep intellectual unity of his later career was produced by his encounter with radical thought in the thirties. Stevens emerged from that encounter thinking that Stanley Burnshaw's Marxist critique of his work was intelligent and probing—a fact contemptuously buried by [Harold] Bloom and [Joseph] Riddel, among other champions of the poet; he emerged believing in the social responsibility of his poetry, everything he says to the contrary notwithstanding. How more responsible (and guilty) can you get than, on the one hand, to write the rarefied lyric that Stevens writes, and, on the other, to assert that poets help people to live their lives?

What Burnshaw's critique of *Ideas of Order* did was to crystallize for Stevens his own class position and at the same time that of his ideal and (as it would seem to him) inevitable audience. Stevens found Burnshaw's review "most interesting" because it "placed" him in a "new setting." That new setting, the "middle ground" of the middle class, is the socio-economic space of those who are both potential allies and potential enemies of class struggle. Burnshaw's insight into this "contradiction," as he called it, of the middle class—into, really, the undemarcated and therefore (at best) confused quality of class struggle in the United States—is matched and one-upped by Stevens in a letter written shortly after he read Burnshaw in *The New Masses:*

> I hope I am headed left, but there are lefts and lefts, and certainly I am not headed for the ghastly left of *Masses*. The rich man and the comfortable man of imagination are not nearly so rich nor nearly so comfortable as he believes them to be. And, what is more, his poor men are not nearly so poor.

In the United States, the middle ground is vaster than Burnshaw thinks and the high and low grounds are narrower and not as melodramatically in opposition as the Manichean metaphors of Communist party rhetoric would make them out to be. As the poet of the middle ground, of those not subject to revolutionary hunger (we need the pun), whose basic sustenance was more or less assured (the "more or less" assuring also a conservative anxiety, a willingness to rock the boat ever so gently), it was Stevens' "role to help people"—people: the middle class is easily universalized in American discourse—"to help people live their lives. [The poet] has had immensely to do with giving life whatever savor it possesses" [*The Necessary Angel: Essays on Reality and the Imagination*]. To supply savor is to supply aesthetic, not biological, necessity: to supply what Marx in *The German Ideology* called the "new needs" (or felt lacks) of women and men after their life-sustaining necessities have been met and they begin to produce not only their sustenance but also the means of reproducing their sustenance. At the point at which leisure becomes real and, in the same moment, really problematic, "we" need a civilized poet. Stevens believed it to be a need of cultural life and death whose satisfaction would determine our "happiness," or lack thereof, outside and irrespective of our political state (which for the middle class rhymes with fate).

It was also in this period of his economic growth and literary self-critique that one of the crueler jokes of literary history that I know was played out. Stevens, a major figure in the insurance business, according to those who know, the best in the field of surety bonds in the country, developed a serious case of rising-executive sickness: high blood pressure bad enough that he was advised not only to lose a great deal of weight but also to get to bed as early as possible on the faultless medical theory that a sleeping man's pressure can't help but be good. Stevens assented to the advice: so after supper there was the noise of a two-family house (the landlord had young children), there was the new baby, there were the domestic chores he regularly pitched in on, then lights out at nine. The joke is that the blood pressure problem was so serious that this well-connected insurance executive could not buy life insurance, not then, not ever—and the "then" I refer to was 1929, 1930, 1931, etc. One reason he worked well past retirement age, practically to the day he died, is that he liked his work (there can be no question about this). Another reason was that he had to because there was one part of his material context—the physiological part—over which he could not become master. Add to that his unquestioned and perhaps unquestionable feeling, which was something like an unavoidable affective accompaniment of his patriarchal formation, that it was his duty to take care of Elsie and Holly. And given the situation of those three, it could not have been otherwise. At these levels his brute material situation was not subject to his personal manipulation: his literary power could not touch it. (pp. 206-16)

> Frank Lentricchia, "Writing after Hours: Penelope's Poetry—The Later Wallace Stevens," in his Ariel and the Police, *The University of Wisconsin Press, 1988, pp. 196-244.*

FURTHER READING

Bibliography

Edelstein, J. M. *Wallace Stevens: A Descriptive Bibliography.* Pittsburgh: University of Pittsburgh Press, 1973, 429 p.
Includes both primary and secondary sources.

Biography

Brazeau, Peter. *Parts of a World: Wallace Stevens Remembered.* Berkeley: North Point Press, 1983, 330 p.
"Oral portrait" of Stevens compiled through interviews with his contemporaries.

Richardson, Joan. *Wallace Stevens: A Biography, The Early Years, 1879-1923.* New York: William Morrow, 1986, 591 p.
Studies Stevens's life from birth to the publication of *Harmonium.*

————. *Wallace Stevens: The Later Years 1923-1955.* New York: William Morrow, 1988, 462 p.
Documents the life and career of Stevens from the publication of *Harmonium* until his death.

Weiss, Theodore. "Wallace Stevens: Lunching with Hoon." In his *The Man from Porlock: Engagements 1944-1981,* pp. 58-98. Princeton: Princeton University Press, 1982.
Recounts the circumstances of Weiss's visit with Stevens and reflects on the diverse components of Stevens's life.

Criticism

Alter, Robert. "Borges, Stevens, and Post-Symbolist Writing." In his *Motives for Fiction,* pp. 134-43. Cambridge: Harvard University Press, 1984.
Compares the works of the Argentinean author Jorge Luis Borges and Stevens, noting the paradoxical and unstable meanings of symbols in the writings of both authors.

Arensberg, Mary. "White Mythology and the American Sublime: Stevens' Auroral Fantasy." In *The American Sublime,* edited by Mary Arensberg, pp. 153-72. Albany: State University of New York Press, 1986.
Freudian reading of Stevens's early poems.

Axelrod, Steven Gould, and Deese, Helen, eds. *Critical Essays on Wallace Stevens.* Boston: G. K. Hall, 1988, 265 p.
Collects representative criticism on Stevens's poetry and poetic theory.

Bahti, Timothy. "End and Ending: On the Lyric Technique of Some Wallace Stevens Poems." *Modern Language Notes* 105, No. 5 (December 1990): 1046-62.
Examines the semantic and rhetorical qualities of Stevens's poems in a discussion that stresses the importance of linguistic construction over thematic content.

Baker, Carlos. "Wallace Stevens: *La vie antérieure* and *Le bel aujourd'hui.*" In his *The Echoing Green: Romanticism, Modernism, and the Phenomena of Transference in Poetry,* pp. 277-309. Princeton: Princeton University Press, 1984.
Traces the influence of the English Romantics in Stevens's work.

Bates, Milton J. *Wallace Stevens: A Mythology of Self.* Berkeley: University of California Press, 1985, 319 p.
Historical study of Stevens's life and works.

Beehler, Michael. *T. S. Eliot, Wallace Stevens, and the Discourses of Difference.* Baton Rouge: Louisiana State University Press, 1987, 182 p.
Compares the strategies of representation used by Stevens and Eliot in order to clarify the differences between their poetry and poetics.

Benamou, Michel. *Wallace Stevens and the Symbolist Imagination.* Princeton: Princeton University Press, 1972, 154 p.
Discusses the influence of the French Symbolist poets Jules Laforgue, Charles Baudelaire, and Stephane Mallarmé and analyzes the importance of pictorial language in Stevens's poetry.

Berger, Charles. *Forms of Farewell: The Late Poetry of Wallace Stevens.* Madison: University of Wisconsin Press, 1985, 198 p.
Offers a reading of the major poems of Wallace Stevens's last decade and "provides a shape, or a plot, to the final movement of his career."

Bevis, William W. *Mind of Winter: Wallace Stevens, Meditation, and Literature.* Pittsburgh: University of Pittsburgh Press, 1988, 343 p.
Examines meditative moments in Stevens's poetry.

Blackmur, R. P. "The Substance That Prevails." In *Outsider at the Heart of Things,* edited by James T. Jones, pp. 148-60. Urbana: University of Illinois Press, 1989.
Examines the complementary relationship between lyricism and theory in Stevens's poetry.

Blasing, Mutlu Konuk. "Wallace Stevens: The Exquisite Errors of Time." In his *American Poetry: The Rhetoric of Its Forms,* pp. 84-100. New Haven, Conn.: Yale University Press, 1987.
Reconsiders the influence of English and American Romanticism on Stevens's poetry.

Blessington, Francis C., and Rotella, Guy, eds. *The Motive for Metaphor: Essays on Modern Poetry.* Boston: Northeastern University Press, 1983, 171 p.

Collection of biographical and critical essays that includes Samuel French Morse's essay on Stevens's descriptions of landscape and his years in Hartford; Frank Doggett and Dorothy Emerson's analysis of Stevens's poetic theory; Peter Brazeau's discussion of Stevens's relationship to his extended family; and Robert Buttel's comparison of the treatment of old age in the poetry of W. B. Yeats and Stevens.

Bloom, Harold. *Wallace Stevens: The Poems of Our Climate.* Ithaca, N.Y.: Cornell University Press, 1977, 413 p.
Overview of Stevens's poetry and poetics and interpretation of Stevens's place within the American literary canon.

Bové, Paul A. "Fiction, Risk, and Deconstruction: The Poetry of Wallace Stevens." In his *Destructive Poetics: Heidegger and Modern American Poetry,* pp. 181-97. New York: Columbia University Press, 1980.
Analyzes identity, language, and the role of the imagination in Stevens's poetry.

Brogan, Jacqueline Vaught. *Stevens and Simile: A Theory of Language.* Princeton: Princeton University Press, 1986, 214 p.
Discusses word-play, paranomasia, and figurative language in Stevens's poetry.

Bromwich, David. "Stevens and the Idea of the Hero." *Raritan* VII, No. 1 (Summer 1987): 1-27.
Analyzes the hero of several poems in light of Stevens's interest in the pragmatist philosophy of William James and the nihilistic philosophy of Friedrich Nietzsche.

Carroll, Joseph. *Wallace Stevens' Supreme Fiction: A New Romanticism.* Baton Rouge: Louisiana State University Press, 1987, 361 p.
Traces the influence of the English Romantics in Stevens's poetry by analyzing his treatment of such Romantic topics as the imagination, nature, and identity.

Cook, Eleanor. "Directions in Reading Wallace Stevens: Up, Down, Across." In *Lyric Poetry: Beyond New Criticism,* edited by Chaviva Hosek and Patricia Parker, pp. 298-309. Ithaca, N.Y.: Cornell University Press, 1985.
Exegesis of the themes and images in the poem "An Ordinary Evening in New Haven."

——. *Poetry, Word-Play, and Word-War in Wallace Stevens.* Princeton: Princeton University Press, 1988, 325 p.
Relates Stevens's word-play to theme, image, and plot in his poems.

Daiches, David. "The American Experience, From Puritanism through Post-Puritanism to Agnosticism: Edward Taylor, Emily Dickinson, Wallace Stevens." In his *God and the Poets: The Gifford Lectures, 1983,* pp. 153-75. Oxford: Oxford University Press, 1984.
Places Stevens's poetry in the context of the agnostic tradition in America.

Doggett, Frank. *Wallace Stevens: The Making of the Poem.* Baltimore: Johns Hopkins University Press, 1980, 160 p.
Discusses Stevens's poetry with respect to the poetic theory outlined in his letters.

Donoghue, Denis. "Stevens's Gibberish." In his *Reading America: Essays on American Literature,* pp. 158-74. New York: Alfred A. Knopf, 1987.

Assesses to what degree Stevens is a philosophical poet by analyzing the relationship between rationality and the imagination in several poems.

Dotterer, Ronald L. "The Fictive and the Real: Myth and Form in the Poetry of Wallace Stevens and William Carlos Williams." In *The Binding of Proteus: Perspectives on Myth and the Literary Process,* edited by Marjorie W. McCune, Tucker Orbison, and Philip M. Withim, pp. 221-48. Lewisburg, Pa.: Bucknell University Press, 1980.
Formalist analysis that compares Williams's *Paterson* and Stevens's *Notes toward a Supreme Fiction,* concentrating on the relationship between reality and fictionality in each work.

Dougherty, Jay. " 'Sunday Morning' and 'Sunday Morning'." *English Language Notes* XXVII, No. 1 (September 1989): 61-8.
Compares the two published versions of "Sunday Morning," which vary in length and in the sequence of the stanzas.

Doyle, Charles, ed. *Wallace Stevens: The Critical Heritage.* London: Routledge & Kegan Paul, 1985, 503 p.
Collects essays and reviews on Stevens's work written by his contemporaries.

Ehrenpreis, Irvin. "Stevens." In *Poetries of America: Essays on the Relation of Character to Style by Irvin Ehrenpreis,* edited by Daniel Albright, pp. 26-41. Charlottesville: University Press of Virginia, 1989.
Analyzes word-play, punning, and humor in Stevens's poetry.

Estrin, Barbara L. "Seeing through the Woman in Wallace Stevens's *Notes toward a Supreme Fiction.*" *Contemporary Literature* 31, No. 2 (Summer 1990): 208-26.
Examines the interplay of genus, gender, and nature in *Notes toward a Supreme Fiction.*

Fisher, Barbara M. *Wallace Stevens: The Intensest Rendezvous.* Charlottesville: University Press of Virginia, 1990, 185 p.
Proposes that "erotic energy is the key to Stevens's work and, further, that it is these dynamics—that is, the presence of eros and the transformations of eros—that determine the vital structures and the configuration of the entire [Stevens] canon."

Gelpi, Albert, ed. *Wallace Stevens: The Poetics of Modernism.* Cambridge: Cambridge University Press, 1985, 165 p.
Collects essays that address Stevens's relationship to modernism.

Halliday, Mark. "Stevens and Solitude." *Essays in Literature* 16, No. 1 (Spring 1989): 85-111.
Examines Stevens's treatment of solipsism and community.

Jarraway, David R. "Crispin's Dependent 'Airs': Psychic Crisis in Early Stevens." *Wallace Stevens Journal* 14, No. 1 (Spring 1990): 21-32.
Traces the "active-passive" dynamic of Freud's Oedipal triangle in the poem "The Comedian as the Letter C."

Keller, Lynn. " 'Thinkers without Final Thoughts': The Continuity between Stevens and Ashbery." In her *Re-making It New: Contemporary American Poetry and the Modernist*

Tradition, pp. 15-41. Cambridge: Cambridge University Press, 1987.

Discusses Stevens's influence on American poet John Ashbery and the latter poet's divergence from the modernist and surrealist strains in Stevens's verse.

Kermode, Frank. *Wallace Stevens.* 1960. Reprint. New York: Chip's Bookshop, 1979, 135 p.

Overview of the stylistic, thematic, and philosophical characteristics of Stevens's poetry.

Leggett, B. J. *Wallace Stevens and Poetic Theory: Conceiving the Supreme Fiction.* Chapel Hill: University of North Carolina Press, 1987, 224 p.

Analyzes critical interpretations of the relationship between poetic theory and practice in Stevens's poetry.

Leonard, J. S., and Wharton, C. E. *The Fluent Mundo: Wallace Stevens and the Structure of Reality.* Athens: University of Georgia Press, 1988, 208 p.

Examines the relationship between imagination and reality in Stevens's poetry.

MacLeod, Glen. "Surrealism and the Supreme Fiction: 'It Must Give Pleasure'." *Wallace Stevens Journal* 14, No. 1 (Spring 1990): 33-8.

Examines Stevens's treatment of the irrational in the last section of *Notes toward a Supreme Fiction* and in the essay "The Irrational Element in Poetry" in order to trace the influence of Surrealism in his poetry.

Mariani, Paul. "Williams and Stevens: Storming the Edifice." In his *A Usable Past: Essays on Modern & Contemporary Poetry,* pp. 95-104. Amherst: University of Massachusetts Press, 1984.

Discusses the relationship between William Carlos Williams and Stevens, the terms of their friendship, and the ways in which the poetry of each responds to the work of the other.

Mollinger, Robert N. "The Literary Symbol: Wallace Stevens's Archetypal Hero" and "The Literary Oeuvre—Levels of Meaning: Wallace Stevens's Poetry." In his *Psychoanalysis and Literature: An Introduction,* pp. 61-72, 121-34. Chicago: Nelson-Hall, 1981.

Jungian analyses of the hero and literary symbol in Stevens's poetry.

Nyquist, Mary. "Musing on Susanna's Music." In *Lyric Poetry: Beyond New Criticism,* pp. 310-27, edited by Chaviva Hosek and Patricia Parker. Ithaca, N.Y.: Cornell University Press, 1985.

Discusses Stevens's poetic technique and his understanding of his poetic vocation.

Parkinson, Thomas. "Wallace Stevens on Sunday Morning." In his *Poets, Poems, Movements,* pp. 107-16. Ann Arbor, Mich.: UMI Research Press, 1987.

Reflects on the images, style, themes, and import of "Sunday Morning."

Patke, Rajeev S. *The Long Poems of Wallace Stevens: An Interpretative Study.* Cambridge: Cambridge University Press, 1985, 263 p.

Contends that Stevens's long poems bring "to focus in a single, extended and homogeneous form the problems he encountered and the strategies he evolved in using poetry as a means of making sense of his experience of living."

Pearce, Roy Harvey. "The Cry and the Occasion: Rereading Stevens." In his *Gesta Humanorum: Studies in the Historicist Mode,* pp. 121-55. Columbia: University of Missouri Press, 1987.

Discusses what Pearce calls the dialectical process of "Invention, Decreation, and Re-creation" in Stevens's poetry.

————, and Miller, J. Hillis, eds. *The Act of the Mind: Essays on the Poetry of Wallace Stevens.* Baltimore: Johns Hopkins University Press, 1965, 287 p.

Collects essays that address thematic, structural, and theoretical aspects of Stevens's work.

Perloff, Marjorie. "Pound/Stevens: Whose Era?" In her *The Dance of the Intellect: Studies in the Poetry of the Pound Tradition,* pp. 1-32. Cambridge: Cambridge University Press, 1985.

Contrasts the poetry of Stevens and Ezra Pound. Perloff contends that the discord that exists between their two styles and aesthetic theories evidences the existence of various strands of modernism.

Quinn, Sister Bernetta. "Wallace Stevens: 'The Peace of the Last Intelligence'." *Renascence* XLI, No. 4 (Summer 1989): 191-208.

Rebukes critics who have dismissed the relevance of Stevens's death-bed conversion to Catholicism and stresses the importance of the event to an overall interpretation of Stevens's life and works.

Riddel, Joseph N. *The Clairvoyant Eye: The Poetry and Poetics of Wallace Stevens.* Baton Rouge: Louisiana State University Press, 1965, 308 p.

Considers each period of Stevens's poetic development in a discussion of general characteristics of his poetry and poetics.

Robinson, Fred Miller. "Wallace Stevens: The Poet as Comedian." In his *The Comedy of Language: Studies in Modern Comic Literature,* pp. 89-126. Amherst: University of Massachusetts Press, 1980.

Examines comic elements in relation to plot, drama, and character in Stevens's poetry.

Schaum, Melita. *Wallace Stevens and the Critical Schools.* Tuscaloosa: University of Alabama Press, 1988, 199 p.

Explores vicissitudes in the critical reception of Stevens's poetry, perceiving Stevens's poems as a "literary *arena* . . . in which major critical assumptions continue to be determined and debated."

Scott, Nathan A., Jr. "Steven's Route—Transcendence Downward." In his *The Poetics of Belief: Studies in Coleridge, Arnold, Pater, Santayana, Stevens, and Heidegger,* pp. 115-45. Chapel Hill: University of North Carolina Press, 1985.

Discusses Stevens as a religious poet, who, in seeking to replace a faith in transcendence with an understanding of reality, creates a spiritual humanism.

Smith, Lyle H., Jr. "The Argument of 'Sunday Morning'." *College Literature* XIII, No. 3 (Fall 1986): 254-65.

Contrasts the weak formal structure of "Sunday Morning" with the poem's imagistic strengths and explicates the secular humanist argument thematized in the poem.

Steinman, Lisa M. "Wallace Stevens: Getting the World Right." In her *Made in America: Science, Technology, and*

American Modernist Poets, pp. 133-68. New Haven, Conn.: Yale University Press, 1987.

> Compares Stevens's relationship to American culture with those attitudes held by other American Modernist writers and investigates the influence of scientific theories on Stevens's poetry.

Vendler, Helen. *On Extended Wings: Wallace Stevens' Longer Poems.* Cambridge: Harvard University Press, 1969, 334 p.

> Interprets the long poems in relation to literary and theoretical concerns evident throughout Stevens's oeuvre.

Wagner, C. Roland. "Wallace Stevens: The Concealed Self." *Wallace Stevens Journal* XII, No. 2 (Fall 1988): 83-101.

> Reevaluates Stevens's mature poetry with reference to his "susceptivity to the nurturing female others of his mind—his wife, his mother, his secret childhood divinities," and discusses his alleged death-bed conversion to Catholicism.

Walker, David. *The Transparent Lyric: Reading and Meaning in the Poetry of Stevens and Williams.* Princeton: Princeton University Press, 1984, 203 p.

> Examines several poems by Stevens and William Carlos Williams and compares their styles "within the broader context of an investigation of a modern lyric genre."

Wallace, Ronald. "Wallace Stevens: The Revenge of Music on Bassoons." In his *God Be with the Clown: Humor in American Poetry,* pp. 141-168. Columbia: University of Missouri Press, 1984.

> Discusses humorous interludes in Stevens's poetry and stresses the importance of comedy throughout Stevens's oeuvre.

Woodman, Leonora. *Stanza My Stone: Wallace Stevens and the Hermetic Tradition.* West Lafayette, Ind.: Purdue University Press, 1983, 193 p.

> Analyzes the concordance of Stevens's concepts of self, imagination, and nature with the religious philosophy of Hermeticism.

Woodward, Kathleen. "Wallace Stevens and *The Rock:* Not Ideas about Nobility but the Thing Itself." In her *At Last, The Real Distinguished Thing: The Late Poems of Eliot, Pound, Stevens, and Williams,* pp. 99-131. Columbus: Ohio State University Press, 1980.

> Examines the manner in which changes in Stevens's attitudes toward religion, aging, and aesthetics are reflected in his mature poetry.

Zukofsky, Louis. "For Wallace Stevens." *Prepositions: The Collected Critical Essays of Louis Zukofsky,* rev. ed., pp. 24-38. Berkeley: University of California Press, 1981.

> Reflections on Stevens's poetry and life.

Additional coverage of Stevens's life and career is contained in the following sources published by Gale Research: *Concise Dictionary of American Literary Biography 1929-1941; Contemporary Authors,* Vols. 104, 124; *Dictionary of Literary Biography,* Vol. 54; *Major 20th-Century Writers;* and *Twentieth-Century Literary Criticism,* Vols. 3, 12.

Dylan Thomas

1914-1953

(Full name Dylan Marlais Thomas) Welsh poet, short story writer, dramatist, screenplay writer, essayist, and novelist.

For further information on Thomas's life and career, see *TCLC,* Volumes 1 and 8.

INTRODUCTION

Thomas is remembered as much for his bohemian lifestyle as he is for his subjective and frequently abstruse poetry. In the 1930s, when a trend toward social and political commentary dominated the arts, Thomas began pursuing more personal themes that originated in his own experiences. The worlds of childhood, dream, and nature are favorite aspects of existence which he celebrated in one of the richest poetic and prose styles in modern literature.

Thomas was born and raised in Swansea, South Wales. His interest in literature was encouraged by his father, a grammar school English teacher, and Thomas's earliest poems were printed in small literary journals. He published his first volume of poetry, *18 Poems,* when he was nineteen. Beginning in 1934 Thomas established a pattern of moving between London, where he indulged in alcohol and epitomized the raucous image of the artist, and various rural communities, where he actually wrote his poems. After World War II, financial need prompted him to devote more energy to his lucrative short stories and screenplays rather than to poetry. Later Thomas gained public attention as a touring poet who captivated audiences with readings of his obscure poetry and highly sonorous prose. At the height of his popularity in the early 1950s, Thomas began a series of public readings in America, bringing about a revival of the oral presentation of poetry. Though well-received on tour, Thomas was ill equipped to handle the constant pressure to perform. Biographers report that he drank prodigiously and behaved outrageously. In late 1953, Thomas fell unconscious after one of his poetry readings and died of alcohol poisoning.

Thomas's first work, *18 Poems,* is largely based on his childhood and adolescent experiences. Often described as incantatory, *18 Poems* records Thomas's experimentation with vibrant imagery and with sound as "verbal music," initiating a poetic style that has been admired for its evocative mingling of sound and sense by some critics and dismissed as gratuitously obscure by others. Thomas's second book of poetry, *Twenty-Five Poems,* was published in 1936 and concerns many of the same themes as his first work. In these poems, Thomas questions or comments upon religion, using images and terminology from Christian mythology, history, and doctrine. Because so much of Thomas's early work focuses on the polarity of birth

and death, the critic William York Tindall referred to this phase as the poet's "womb-tomb" period. In "And Death Shall Have No Dominion," which is considered a breakthrough work in his career, Thomas addressed Christian ideas of life and death, ultimately defying death and celebrating the possibility of eternal life. Another acclaimed work, "Altarwise by Owl-Light," is a sequence of ten sonnets discussing the crucifixion of Christ. Both poignant and comic, the sequence is generally regarded as one of Thomas's best works, and Thomas himself viewed it as the most mature poetry of his first major period of creativity. A slightly later work of this phase, *The Map of Love,* a collection of poetry and short stories, shows signs of his dabbling in Surrealist technique.

The physical and psychic havoc of World War II deeply affected Thomas and shaped the major work of his middle period, which began with the publication of *Deaths and Entrances* in 1946. In this volume Thomas employed simpler, more intelligible language and imagery. His final volume of poems, *In Country Sleep,* demonstrates, according to critics, his confrontation with the inevitability of his own death. These poems exude beauty and confidence, while affirming an eternal cycle of life, death, and rebirth.

Thomas wrote mostly prose and screenplays during the last years of his life. Previous to this period, his best-known prose work was *Portrait of the Artist as a Young Dog,* a collection of semiautobiographical short stories that stylistically bear comparison to James Joyce's *Dubliners* (1914) and *Portrait of the Artist as a Young Man* (1916). Both Joyce's and Thomas's works offer negative views of their respective homelands—Ireland and Wales—each depicting what "for artists," as Kenneth Seib has observed, "is a world of death, sterility, and spiritual debasement." The most significant prose piece to issue from Thomas's later period is the "play for voices," *Under Milk Wood.* Again critics have noted similarities between Thomas and Joyce. In *Under Milk Wood* and *Ulysses* (1922), each author captures the life of a whole society as it is reflected in a single day; for Joyce it is the urban life in Dublin, while for Thomas it is the Welsh village community of Llareggub. David Holbrook, one of Thomas's harshest critics, has found *Under Milk Wood* unenlightening and sexually perverse, reflecting an unfeeling and diseased view of life. Other critics praise the work for its life-affirming, universal significance.

From the outset of Thomas's career, critical disagreement has existed regarding his poetic stature and importance. Many commentators disparage Thomas's work as too narrow and unvarying; he essentially confined himself to the lyric expression of what Stephen Spender has called "certain primary, dithyrambic occasions," chiefly birth, love, and death. Edith Sitwell spoke for many critics in her early assessment of Thomas's works as she puzzled over the poet's distorted syntax and religious symbolism. The influence of the seventeenth-century metaphysical poets is often cited in connection with Thomas's unorthodox religious imagery, while the influence of the Romantic poets is seen in his recurrent vision of pristine beauty in childhood and nature. Nearly all critics praise the intricate craftsmanship of Thomas's works, noting his vivid imagery, involved word play, fractured syntax, and personal symbology as carefully wrought stylizations that have changed the course of modern poetry.

PRINCIPAL WORKS

18 Poems (poetry) 1934
Twenty-Five Poems (poetry) 1936
The Map of Love (poetry and short stories) 1939
The World I Breathe (poetry and sketches) 1939
Portrait of the Artist as a Young Dog (short stories) 1940
New Poems (poetry) 1943
Deaths and Entrances (poetry) 1946
Twenty-Six Poems (poetry) 1950
Collected Poems, 1934-1952 (poetry) 1952
In Country Sleep (poetry) 1952
The Doctor and the Devils (drama) 1953
Quite Early One Morning (sketches and essays) 1954
Under Milk Wood (drama) 1954
Adventures in the Skin Trade, and Other Stories (unfinished novel and short stories) 1955
A Prospect of the Sea, and Other Stories and Prose (short stories and sketches) 1955

Dylan Thomas: Letters to Vernon Watkins (letters) 1957
Selected Letters (letters) 1966
The Notebooks of Dylan Thomas (poetry) 1967; also published as *Poet in the Making: The Notebooks of Dylan Thomas,* 1968
Dylan Thomas: Early Prose Writings (short stories and essays) 1971
The Death of the King's Canary [with John Davenport] (novel) 1976
The Collected Stories (short stories) 1983
Dylan Thomas: The Collected Letters (letters) 1985
Dlyan Thomas: Collected Poems, 1934-1953 (poetry) 1988

Edith Sitwell   (essay date 1947)

[*An English poet, biographer, and critic, Sitwell experimented widely with sound and rhythmic structure in her poetry. Colored with idiosyncratic imagery and highly personal allusions, her works reflect her belief that sound and rhythm should take precedence over meaning in poetry. Accordingly, she composed her poetry to be spoken aloud and often gave flamboyant recitals of her works. Throughout her career, Sitwell also used her influence to draw attention to younger writers, including Thomas, Wilfred Owen, and Allen Ginsberg. In the following essay, she extols Thomas's poetry.*]

'Sir George Beaumont' said Coleridge, in *Anima Poetae,* 'found great advantage in learning to draw through gauze spectacles.'

I do not know if Coleridge was intending a gibe. But in any case, no better portrait could be given of a dilettante. The amateur almost invariably softens and blurs.

A great deal of the verse that is published to-day is hopelessly amateurish and the authors seem to have *tried* to learn to see (they rarely succeed in doing so), through gauze spectacles.

It is very natural that people so occupied, people who spend their lives in 'measuring the irregularities of Michael Angelo and Socrates by village scales'—in short, *les apôtres du petit bonheur,* should be scared by—should distrust—Dylan Thomas.

In my *A Poet's Notebook* I have a quotation about the painter who paints a tree becoming a tree.

This condensation of essence, this power of 'becoming the Tree', is one of the powers that makes Mr. Thomas the great poet he is. His poems appear, at first sight, strange. But if you heard a tree speak to you in its own language, its own voice, would not that, too, appear strange to you?

In the essay *Nature* (Tiefurt Journal 1782) Goethe wrote: 'She' (Nature) 'has thought and she broods unceasingly, not as a man but as Nature. . . . She has neither language nor speech, but she creates tongues and hearts through which she speaks and feels. . . . It was not I who spoke of her. Nay, it was she who spoke it all, true and false. Hers is the blame for all things, hers the credit.'

Mr. Thomas, also, is a poet through whom Nature speaks.

The *apôtres du petit bonheur* regard the mind as a little machine confined in a box, which will tell the time to the minute, and which will tick at certain reactions.

Mr. Thomas's mind is not a clock. It does not tell the fleeting minute.

In William James' *Principles of Psychology,* he quotes Condillac as saying 'The first time we see light, we *are* it rather than *see* it.' It is this becoming that the poet needs.

Sometimes, as with certain other great poets, a phrase, with him, will mean two things, both equally true. When Shakespeare wrote:

'Men have died and worms have eaten them, but not for love' did he not mean 'men have died, but not for love', *and* 'worms have eaten them, but not for love'? I think so.

In each poem by Mr. Thomas, there is an infinite power of germination.

Take the beautiful Fourth Poem from **The Map of Love.** This, like many another poem by a great poet, is all things to all men. It is not the poet's possession only, it is also ours. The poem moves on two levels, that of the day, and that of eternity.

The two lovers lie, in a silence of love, between the image of Life—the wandering, ever-changing sea—and the image of Death, 'the strata of the shore' (the lives, perhaps, that have gone before)—'the red rock'—and Time, that is identified with the sand:

> the grains as they hurry
> Hiding the golden mountains and mansions
> Of the grave, gay, seaside land.

These lovely lines have, I think, two significances—the grave one, of the actual mountains and mansions made golden to the young people by the light of the sun and of their love, and soon to be overwhelmed by the sands of Time—and the gay one, that of the mountains and castles made by the children at the edge of the sea, and soon to be covered over by the other sands blown by the wind.

Over the young people, 'the heavenly music over the sand' sighs to them of those yellow grains and of the wandering faithless sea—but Time is no longer terrible to them in their silence of love.

The poem is of the greatest beauty, both visually and orally.

The phrase 'the lunar silences' holds the actual light of the sea in it. The sound is like that of the heavenly music over the sand, like the sea-airs. Sometimes it changes like the wind, moves with the beauty of waves. It is of an unsurpassable technical achievement.

In that great poem **'A Refusal to Mourn the Death, by Fire, of a Child in London',** with its dark and magnificent, proud movement, we see Death in its reality, as a return to the beginning of all things—as only a robing, a sacred

investiture, in those who have been our friends since the begining of time—

> the grains beyond age, the dark veins of her
> mother,

—(Earth, her mother). Bird, beast and flower have their part in the making of mankind, and in its root. The water drop is holy, the ear of corn a place of prayer. The all-humbling Darkness itself is a begetting force. Even grief, even tears, are a begetting . . . though here this life must not come into being—(as a rival, perhaps, to the dead child). The stations of the breath are the stations of the Cross.

I do not know any short poem of our time which has more greatness. (pp. 17-18)

> *Edith Sitwell, "Comment on Dylan Thomas,"
> in* The Critic: A Quarterly Review of Criticism, *Vol. 1, No. 2, Autumn, 1947, pp. 17-18.*

W. S. Merwin   (essay date 1953)

[*Merwin is an American poet, short story writer, and critic whose poetry frequently displays a moral concern for the state of contemporary society. In the following essay originally published in* Adam International Review *in 1953, he focuses on Thomas's role as a religious poet.*]

Apart from the verse prologue to his **Collected Poems, 1934-1952,** and the poem **'In My Craft or Sullen Art',** both of which I mean to discuss later, the two salient remarks that I have known Dylan Thomas to make about his own poetry were one in a letter to Henry Treece where he described the manner in which he wrote poetry, and the prose statement at the beginning of the **Collected Poems** concerning the purpose of his poetry: 'These poems', he says, 'are written for the love of Man and in praise of God.' It is not because I am taking Dylan Thomas at his prose—a poet may be the last person to be able to speak accurately, in prose, about his own poetry—but because I am trying to take his poems at their word, that I wish to consider Dylan Thomas as a religious poet, and notice some of the means, the craft and language with which he has made his themes.

I think it is safer at this point not to set up a pair of artificial antinomies: as it were, the religious artist and whatever we may call his opposite, but to start by saying that the religious artist is primarily a celebrator. A celebrator in the ritual sense: a maker and performer of a rite. And also a celebrator in the sense of one who participates in the rite, and whom the rite makes joyful. That which he celebrates is Creation, and more particularly the human condition. For he will see himself, man, as a metaphor or analogy of the world. The human imagination will be for him the image of the divine imagination; the work of art and the artist will be analogous with the world and its Creator. In both man and the world he will perceive a force of love or creation which is more divine than either man or the world, and a force of death or destruction which is more terrible than man or the world. Although his ultimate vision is the tragic one of creation through suffering, his ultimate sense will be of joy. For in the act of love, the central act of Creation, he will see the force of love, in man and the world, merge inextricably and mysteriously with the force of death, and yet from this union new creation born through suffering. And his vocation as an individual artist will be to remake in terms of celebration the details of life, to save that which is individual and thereby mortal, by imagining it, making it, in terms of what he conceives to be the eternal. The emotion which drives him to this making will be compassion, or better, love of Life and the particulars of life.

The poems of Dylan Thomas are peculiarly consistent: as I understand them, they are the work of a religious poet trying, at times desperately, to find and come to grips with his subject, finding it, and making it into a poetry of celebration—into some of the greatest poetry that has been written in our time. How much of this was consciously aimed at, and how much was at least half-dark necessity, I suspect but do not know; but I think the religious theme as I have described it is the main vein of Dylan Thomas's poetry. He has written a number of genuine personal poems in which the 'I' is overtly the individual poet, but these for the most part are well along in his work, and many of them deal with the religious theme from their particular vantage. In most of the earlier poems the 'I' is 'man' trying to find a means of imagining and thereby redeeming his condition; much of the seemingly baroque and motiveless 'agony' of the earlier poems stems from the desperateness of this need.

The brilliant and powerful first poem in the book, **'I see the boys of summer',** presents doom as the final reality in the very moments of man's euphory, and insofar as man ignores or is truly ignorant of this fact about his condition, the poet describes him with contempt. He recommends that the passage of time, and death, be challenged and embraced, but he can give no reason why they should be—birth and death are an endless loveless dull round—and the poem ends in ironic despair. But by the third poem, **'A process in the weather of the heart',** which describes the growing of death in life, the natural world and the human body are consistently metaphoric of each other; the heart at the end of the poem is the sea, which 'gives up its dead', though it does so through its own death. In the fourth poem, **'Before I knocked',** man is seen as Christ his divine image, and there is an attempt at presenting human life as a continuity by describing the prenatal growth of the consciousness of death, and in the fifth, **'The force that through the green fuse drives the flower',** the doom within life is described again, but described because of compassion for things mortal, and the compassion makes the poet at once wish to be able to communicate with all other things that are doomed, to tell them he understands their plight because his own is similar, and makes him feel the depth to which he is inarticulate and painfully unable to do so.

But dumb compassion for mortality, though relieved by this remarkable poem and by the beautiful but hardly more than putative sea-faiths of **'Where once the waters of your face',** could not rest content. In the poem, **'If I were tickled by the rub of love',** the poet states that if love

were real to him he would have the means of facing the fear of death; the poem's remarkable and hopeful conclusion, since the reality of love does not seem attainable, is 'I would be tickled by the rub that is: / Man by my metaphor'. And in the next poem, **'Our Eunuch Dreams',** he examines 'reality' and its simulacra in terms of each other, concluding that the world is real, and is an image of man, and the poem ends in faith and joy. The poem, **'Especially when the October wind',** takes this development a stage further: here the poet first fully assumes his Orphic role, celebrating a particular day, a particular place, in autumn, offering to make it, or aspects of it, and as he names and celebrates them, doing so.

This is moving forward a bit too fast and smooth; (if the poems are not arranged chronologically, then as far as I can see Dylan Thomas has put them in an order admirably suited to present his theme). For a day in autumn, or even man's condition may to some extent be named and remade and redeemed without love, but personal particular death remains real to the poet. And without the reality of love, the 'Have faith . . . And who remain shall flower as they love', of **'Our Eunuch Dreams',** comes to ring hollow to him. The perception of death as the very urge and joy in the act of love, in the poem, **'When like a running grave',** makes both sexual love and the love of the world impossible: the poet advocates despair of either and, instead, love of death himself for his devilish iniquity. And in **'From love's first fever to her plague'** Dylan Thomas vainly tried, as a way out, to make a myth of his own physical growth, but concludes that even the creations of the imagination are futile: 'The root of tongues ends in a spent-out cancer'. This poem, reasonably enough if what I am saying makes sense, is one of the few poems of Dylan Thomas's which seems uncompleted, less as if he had not bothered to write it out to an end than as if he had known no end to write it out to.

In the next poem, **'In the beginning',** he found what he needed: the poem is about creation, and sees the creation of the world as the metaphor of the creation of man. It sees the individual man through his divine image Christ; (it is worth comparing this poem with **'Before I knocked'** to see how much more sure of his subject Dylan Thomas has become); and it sees imaginative creation and natural creation as one: 'In the beginning was the word, the word / That from the solid bases of the light / Abstracted all the letters of the void'. **'Light breaks where no sun shines'** is a further elaboration of the vision of man as a metaphor of the world.

I can see several reasons why the next two poems, **'I fellowed sleep',** and **'I dreamed my genesis'** should have been written as about dreams. **'I fellowed sleep'** is a visionary poem about uncreated ghosts, the dreams of the world which the world climbs always to create. A dream can be a kind of metaphor—as in **'Our Eunuch Dreams'**—once the imagination has harnessed it; but the *sense* of the subject is not always certain in this poem, which I take to mean that it would have been almost impossible for Dylan Thomas to have approached it more directly—and even St. Augustine admitted that our responsibility to dreams is different from our responsibility to the rest of Creation.

(What it comes down to, of course, is that Dylan Thomas wrote his poems as he could, and the use of dream-subjects helped him to get a step *closer* to what he was trying to say.) **'I dreamed my genesis'** describes man's birth through his death, his knowledge of death in his birth, and his passage into the world.

In these earlier poems, as in Dylan Thomas's poetry generally, the language is what is most immediately striking. A language for a poet is always raw even if vitiated; Dylan Thomas's most characteristic twistings of the expected idiom have been mentioned often enough; the puns, the using of one part of speech for another, the manipulation of colloquialisms. He has done violence to the language when it was necessary to his theme—and at times when it was not: even in his later poems he can be vulgar, precious, meretriciously clever. And the style of these earlier poems is often egregious and turgid—a thing is said with devious novelty merely to avoid saying it any other way; as though the words came first and the subject as it could. (And the kind of poetry which he once described himself as writing in a letter to Henry Treece sounded as though it might very well be more a poetry of warring conclusions than of imaginative wholes.) But I think all this is a further indication of the intensity with which Dylan Thomas, with all the means at his disposal, was trying to find and make his subject—but the fact that a poet however gifted may find his subject only with difficulty does not necessarily indicate that he has no subject: it may merely indicate that he has a subject which is difficult to find. It is interesting how many of Dylan Thomas's 'private' recurring words, many of which he uses already in these poems, bear directly on the theme I have been talking about: the constant use of the word 'die' in the sense both of physical death and of sexual climax; 'grain' which is also the dust of the dead; 'grief' to designate the experience of 'death' in the sexual act; 'lock' and 'key' as sexual symbols. Also in these poems one finds already Dylan Thomas's characteristic development of a poem by repetition. There is peculiar to this manner of a live poem's progression of a kind of chaste passion and anonymity whatever the subject; at the same time it gives the language and/or emotion of the subject an exceptional range for improvization. And it presents strikingly, as might a ritual, the difference between the movement of the subject and the movement of the poem.

I have tried to indicate the direction which I think Dylan Thomas's earlier poetry was following, the theme it was trying to make and serve. It would be possible to follow the uses and developments of this theme through many of the succeeding poems, but often less directly, for as his knowledge of the theme deepened and became more comprehensive, the range of experience he was able to handle increased; his skill in his craft at the same time was growing more varied; and in particular he began writing more overtly occasional and personal poems; **'Out of the sighs'** is to my reading the first genuinely personal poem in the *Collected Poems.* After **'I dreamed my genesis'**, there are a group of poems which explore the relationship of love and death, the world as duality, the subject of the continual creation of the world and of the individual. I think the culmination of these particular poems, though it is not the

last in the group, is **'I in my intricate image'** where the exultant conclusion already has the ring and vision of much of Dylan Thomas's later poetry: 'This was the god of beginning in the intricate seawhirl, / And my images roared and rose on heaven's hill.'

Such a poem as **'Do you not father me'** carries both the subject of the individual's continuity in man's continuing creation, which Dylan Thomas had first developed in **'Before I Knocked'**, and the subject of **'The force that through the green fuse drives the flower'** a stage further by identifying man the creator-creature with all other mortal creatures. **'A grief ago'** explores the theme in terms of the act of love itself, and for the sake of the loved one. The sonnet sequence, **'Altar-wise by owl-light'** is a glorification of the act of creation, identifying man with that which he conceives as divine. The power and compassion of the personal poems increase; the occasions become more genuinely intense as they become more direct: **'I have longed to move away'**, **'I make this in a warring absence'**, **'After the funeral'**, especially the deeply moving **'A Refusal to Mourn the Death, by Fire, of a Child in London'**.

True personal poetry, where the poet speaks in his own voice directly about his particular experience, is rarer than might seem, particularly among modern poets, and, of course, especially so if it be personal poetry of any stature. Some of Dylan Thomas's personal poems are among the most moving and powerful he has written. And in these poems as well, both the fear, and still more important, the joy, have as their reference the religious artist's vision of the world. The theme of **'Hold hard, these ancient minutes in the cuckoo's mouth'** (where we already have the hawk and birds of **'Over Sir John's Hill'**) becomes more intimate in **'When all my five and country senses see'**, in **'We lying by seasand'**, and **'Twenty-four years'**; enormously amplified, it is still the background, with the personal fate foremost, in the poem which for me is, until now, the culmination of Dylan Thomas's personal poetry: **'In the White Giant's Thigh'**. In this poem it is ancient, desperate barren love which haunts the speaker and lures his creative powers themselves down to death. The poems which bid that death be defied become more actual, more direct with mastery: in the earliest poems the motive for defiance seemed no better than desperation, but in the recent villanelle, **'Do not go gentle into that good night'** (which, with Empson's 'Missing Dates' seems to me one of the great poems in this form in English) it is quite clearly love—love at such a pass as to be otherwise helpless against death. And the exultation of such marvellous poems as **'Poem in October'**, **'Fern Hill'**, **'Poem on his Birthday'**, and **'Author's Prologue'** is not an exultation proper to the liberal humanist: it is the exuberance of a man drunk with the holiness and wonder of creation, with the reality and terror and ubiquity of death, but with love as God, as more powerful than death.

I think that in general it is the later poems of Dylan Thomas which represent his most important achievement. As love and compassion both have become more sure and comprehensive, so his poetry has become, among other things, increasingly dramatic. I do not find this surprising; I think the work of a religious artist, as his scope and mastery increased, would naturally tend to become more dramatic. For an art which is dramatic cannot burgeon if existence is seen as pointless and fragmentary; but a sense of the reality of love and a sense of the reality of the imagination would seem to me to be two of the most potent means of seeing creation as capable of order (the imagination makes order) and as significantly varied (love embraces details rather than generalities). And as the act of celebration—the metaphor—became more real it would tend to gain a dimension, gain independence of the individual 'lyric' moment (become less 'subjective') and become ritual or dramatic. One can see how a love poem would probably be more dramatic than a generalized statement of private anguish: a case in point, I think, is **'Especially when the October wind'** where the *audience,* more explicit than in the earlier poems, may be the reader, but might very well be the beloved; and where the works of the imagination are mentioned 'made' as things with a 'life of their own'. (I should have thought, nevertheless, that his peculiar pitch of language would have precluded his writing poetry that was explicitly dramatic. It would be of immense interest to see what he has done with his hitherto unpublished choral fragment 'The Town That Was Mad' [an early version of *Under Milk Wood*].) As his poetry has grown more dramatic, Dylan Thomas's tragic vision of Creation has deepened and grown richer, and with it his power of joy. The faith, sure of itself but not sure why, of **'A grief ago'**, is a tragic faith; the sense of death is more real and terrible in so magnificent and tender a recent poem as **'In Country Sleep'**, but the faith is the same, and certain why it is there, and joyful.

'A Winter's Tale' is one of the few narrative poems Dylan Thomas has attempted, and I think it is one of the great poems he has written. Its achievement is if anything still more remarkable: for in **'A Winter's Tale'** the fact has made myth. I say this without knowing whether or not Dylan Thomas used a known legend for the 'story' of his poem—for several reasons I suspect that he did. It might have run something like this: "Once in the dead of winter, in the middle of the night, a man who lived alone in a house in the woods saw outside a beautiful she-bird, and all around her it was spring. He ran from the house to find her; she flew ahead of him, and all night he ran and at last she came down and he came to where she was; she put her wings over him and the spring faded back to winter; then she rose and vanished, and when spring came and the snow melted they found his body lying on a hill-top". (I know of a similar legend among the American Indians.) The main reasons why I suspect that the poem comes from some such legend is that it contains most of the essential elements of a mid-winter ceremony of the re-birth of the year (of the earth, of man). In Wales until the Christian era, and among parts of the population for a long time afterwards, the presiding deity was a goddess; the midwinter rite was in her praise; she was often represented as a bird; the all-night running of the bride-groom corresponds with the marriage labours in many legends. Also the illusory vision of spring, coming from the land of the dead in Dylan Thomas's poem, and then the reality of winter coming back, might very possibly have come from a confusion of time-sequence such as often happens in legends when their ritual decays—that is, if the poem was

based on some such legend, then we might suppose that in the original ritual the real spring came, and that the one-night version was later. But my point is that what I have persistently called Dylan Thomas's 'religious' vision of Creation is completely congruous with the vision of life which made the re-birth ritual in the first place. And as poetry comes to be in a manner similar to that in which legend does, Dylan Thomas might very possibly have invented a story whose mythical ramifications were thus comprehensive and deep. He has 'made' the myth whether or not he invented the skeletal story, for it is his own imagination which has given it its immediacy and power, which has seen love-in-death, the 'she-bird', with such certainty as heavenly and all-powerful, which has made articulate within the metaphor itself the triumph of the rite which is life.

In two other major later poems, **'Vision and Prayer'** and **'Over Sir John's Hill'** the mythology and vision are developed in a different, and dramatic, direction. In these poems the poet, while presenting the condition of Creation, intercedes on behalf of mortality. This is a different kind of standing-apart from that of the earlier poems, for there it was the failure to conceive of Creation as ordered, and at the same time the overweening preoccupation with personal doom (however generalized) which kept the poet separate. In these poems he bespeaks the tragic order as he sees it, and it is in his very capacity of witness and tongue and celebrator that he stands-without as intercessor. In **'Vision and Prayer'**, because of the vision of man as divine, as love (Christ), of Creation as divine and therefore of resurrection as real, he prays that death may die indeed. In **'Over Sir John's Hill'** he would redeem mortality itself:

> . . . and I who hear the tune of the slow,
> Wear-willow river, grave,
> Before the lunge of the night, the notes on this
>   time-shaken
> Stone for the sake of the souls of the slain birds
>   sailing.

Dylan Thomas's own sense of his poetic vocation has been stated more clearly than anywhere else in two poems, **'In My Craft or Sullen Art'** and the **'Author's Prologue'** to the *Collected Poems.* In the former he states that he writes his poems 'Not for ambition or bread', nor for public acclaim nor for the edification of the self-righteous, nor for the dead, but for the lovers 'With all their griefs in their arms'. If the act of love is conceived as the central holy act of Creation, where love, in joy and then in pain and then in joy, overcomes death, it is clear why he should have felt that his poems were so directed. In **'Author's Prologue'** as in **'In My Craft or Sullen Art'**, where he has written 'I labour by singing light', the creative act, in this case the creation of the imagination, is seen as holy:

> . . . song
> Is a burning and crested act,
> The fire of birds in
> The world's turning wood. . . .

It is seen as triumphant over death:

> I build my bellowing ark
> To the best of my love

As the flood begins. . . .

and moreover as perpetual, present always, making anew, now: 'And the flood flowers now'. This is the office of celebration, it is the reason for the faith and the joy, it is the statement of vocation of a great religious poet. As for the 'craft', Dylan Thomas remains the most skillful maker of verse writing English; the stanzaic forms which he often fashioned for his rhythms are as complex and, for him, un-hampering and informative as they seem to have been among the Welsh ollaves. He has 'made' what seems to me to be the major theme to a point of masterful authority, and in the range and intensity of passion which he controlled he surpassed any of his contemporaries. He seems to have assimilated most of his primary influences (though the 'debt' to Joyce in particular was more than verbal—Joyce was prodigiously an artist of celebration—and the 'debt' to Hopkin's 'The Windhover' bore recent fruit in **'Over Sir John's Hill'**). He has survived the fads of the thirties, the first wave of fashion and notoriety. He has 'arrived'. How the future will judge him, we cannot tell. We only know that Thomas is a major poet of our century and nobody will be able to ignore him. (pp. 59-67)

> *W. S. Merwin, "The Religious Poet," in* A Casebook on Dylan Thomas, *edited by John Malcolm Brinnin, Thomas Y. Crowell Company, 1960, pp. 59-67.*

Elder Olson   (essay date 1954)

[*An American poet and critic, Olson is a founding member of the Chicago, or neo-Aristotelian, critics. While adhering to the group's belief in a pluralistic approach to criticism, he emphasizes an Aristotelian synthesis of plot, character, theme, and form in his interpretations of contemporary literature. In the following essay, first published in 1954 in the periodical* Poetry, *Olson discusses Thomas's treatment of theme and use of language to illumine what many consider the obscure aspect of Thomas's poems.*]

There is some evidence that even well-equipped readers have found the poetry of Dylan Thomas difficult; and one would be surprised, considering the nature of his work, if the case were otherwise. It is, in the first place, work characterized by unusually powerful and original conceptions, formulated in symbols difficult in themselves and complex in their interrelations. Secondly, what we may call the "dramatic presentation" of his poetry—roughly, the whole body of clues by which a reader determines who is speaking in the poem, to whom, of what, in what circumstances—is full of deliberate, even studied, ambiguity. Again, an even greater ambiguity, and even more studied, pervades his language, to a degree where it—the first thing we have to go by, in any literary composition—seems to exploit all the possibilities of the formal enigma. Finally—although this is not a matter of poetic structure but of historical accident—Thomas is working in a tradition not likely to be familiar to his readers.

Much has been said, by Miss Sitwell and others, about the grandeur of Thomas's "themes"; however, since no artistic work was ever good or bad simply by virtue of its dealing with a certain theme, I presume that what these critics have in mind is the *constituted* theme—what the poet has made of it, not what the theme in itself is—or, in a word, the conception governing the work. The artistic excellence of a work is dependent upon whether the conception itself is of value, and upon whether it has so dominated the whole construction of the piece as to be fully realized in it and enhanced by it. When Thomas's power of conception is at its height, when it masters all the elements of the poem, something like sublimity results; when the conception is merely odd, fanciful, or otherwise trivial, or when his handling of it obscures, distorts, or otherwise fails to manifest itself, he fails.

"The Ballad of the Long-Legged Bait," to take one of his best poems as an example, has as its bare theme the notion that salvation must be won through mortification of the flesh. A common enough notion; but in the fiery imagination of Thomas the process of purification becomes the strange voyage of a lone fisherman; the bait is "A girl alive with his hooks through her lips"; she is "all the wanting flesh his enemy," "Sin who had a woman's shape"; and the quarry sought is no less than all that Time and Death have taken, for since Sin brought Time and Death into the world, the abolition of Sin will restore all that has been lost. With the death of the girl, the sea gives up its dead, as foretold in Revelation 20:13; Eden returns, "A garden holding to her hand / With birds and animals"; and the sea disappears, accomplishing the prophecy of Revelation 21:1 ("and there was no more sea"). In the terrible actuality of the voyage we never guess its essential fantasy; "the whole / Of the sea is hilly with whales," "All the fishes were rayed in blood," and most beautifully:

> He saw the storm smoke out to kill
> With fuming bows and ram of ice,
> Fire on starlight, rake Jesu's stream;
> And nothing shone on the water's face
> But the oil and bubble of the moon . . .

As in these last lines the storm is given the menace, the fury and power of a kind of supernatural warship, firing "on starlight" until nothing shines but "the oil and bubble of the moon," so the theme of the whole poem is given the emotional power of its legend: the subduing of sensual desire becomes mysterious and cruel as the immolation of the girl, the salvation takes on the beauty and mystery of the resurrection of the dead and the past from the sea.

Similarly, **"Fern Hill"** and **"Poem in October,"** luminous with all the weathers of childhood; **"A Refusal to Mourn the Death, by Fire, of a Child in London,"** apprehending the child's death in its relation to the whole universe (all creation is spanned, awesomely, from beginning to end, in the first stanza, and the last carries us back to the "first dead"); the **"Altarwise by Owl-light"** sonnet-sequence (surely among the greater poems of our century): all these are founded upon conceptions possible, we feel, only to a man of great imagination and feeling. On the other hand, such pieces as **"Shall Gods Be Said to Thump the Clouds,"** **"Why East Wind Chills,"** and **"Ears in the Turrets"** rest upon trivialities; their themes are conceived with too little imagination, and with too little relation to humanity, to leave us anything but indifferent.

Thomas the poet has much less range than Thomas the prose-writer. The poet is the greater, but the prose-writer assumes far more characters and enters into far more moods and shades of moods. The poet is a single character, and he is a poet only of the most exalted states of mind—the most exalted grief, joy, tenderness, or terror. Such lofty art demands great energy of thought and feeling, and all the accoutrements of lofty style; but when the lofty conception is lacking, energy becomes violence or plain noisiness, the tragic passions become melodramatic or morbid, ecstasy becomes hysteria, and the high style becomes obscure bombast. When the bard is not the bard, the bardic robes may easily be put off; not so the habitual paraphernalia of his art. When Thomas is not master of his tricks, his tricks master him; he is then capable, quite without any artistic point so far as I can see, of calling the dead Christ a "stiff," of having Jesus say, "I smelt the maggot in my stool," or of devising such fake nightmares as "'His mother's womb had a tongue that lapped up mud.'" In his good work or his bad, his devices remain the same; it is their employment that differs.

The point in employing any literary device is that in the circumstances it discharges its function better than any other. Metaphor and simile, for instance (if we leave aside their instructive function of making the unfamiliar known in terms of the familiar), have two principal functions in poetry: either they isolate a quality or qualities by indicating something else which has them, or they serve as an indication of thought, feeling, or character; and it is thus that poet controls the feelings and ideas of his reader. When Enobarbus says that Cleopatra's barge "burnt" on the water, its fire-like brilliance is singled out; when Hamlet calls the world "a rank, unweeded garden" he manifests his state of mind. Both kinds fail, of course, if no real or fancied resemblance can be found to justify the analogy; but the former kind fails in its special function when the qualities isolated are, either in kind or degree, insufficient to produce the idea which must be grasped or the emotion which must be felt; and the latter kind fails in its special function when it fails to identify thought, feeling, or character.

When, in the passage cited earlier, Thomas gives us the storm conceived in all its power, presented in metaphor which discloses fully that conception, he succeeds wonderfully in the first kind; when he makes rain into milk from "an old god's dugs . . . pressed and pricked," he fails miserably in it. "In the groin of the natural doorway I crouched like a tailor / Sewing a shroud for a journey" is an excellent simile of the second kind, for it is a sharp index of the frame of mind of one who sees the womb itself as preparation for the grave; but "my love pulls the pale, nippled air / Prides of tomorrow suckling in her eyes" can hardly be said to identify the state of mind of the lover, or to offer any vision of his beloved with which we might reasonably be expected to be sympathetic.

I have already mentioned Thomas's dramatic and linguistic obscurity. The former is usually a relatively simple matter; for instance, appropriate titles would have made clear that **"Where Once the Waters of Your Face"** treats of a sea-channel gone dry, that **"When Once the Twilight Locks No Longer"** is the Spirit talking of man's death-dream, that **"Light Breaks Where No Sun Shines," "Foster the Light,"** and **"The Force That through the Green Fuse Drives the Flower"** are all variations on the macrocosm-microcosm theme, and that **"If My Head Hurt a Hair's Foot"** is a dialogue between an unborn child and its mother. There is no more point in such concealment, I think, than there would be in a dramatist's concealing the characters and the assignment of speeches in a play. Similarly with "the white giant's thigh"; if, as Thomas is alleged to have said, all is clear to one who knows that the "thigh" is a landmark on a Welsh hill, the reader should have been informed in a note; any effect which depends upon accidental ignorance can never be permanent, and is not worth trying for.

Yet if these obscurities are faults, those who damn Thomas's and much other contemporary poetry simply on the ground of its obscurity are badly mistaken. This amounts to legislation; whereas the artist is properly bound by no law but the dictates of the individual work. Moreover, it is always necessary for the literary artist, in the simplest lyric or the most extended narrative or play, at times to conceal and at times to disclose, in order to effect surprise and suspense, the subtlest shading of emotion into emotion, and the most delicate or vehement degree of emotion. It is precisely in the manipulation of language to these ends that Thomas, at his best, shows himself a master; consciously or unconsciously, he is in the tradition of the great Welsh enigmatic poets of the fourteenth century, and he seems to have learned or inherited all their art. He is particularly master of the sentence artfully delayed and suspended, through many surprising turns, until its unexpected accomplishment, and also of the mysterious paraphrase which, resolved at its conclusion, illuminates the whole poem. He is at his best in the latter in the magnificent **"Sonnets"**; at his worst, perhaps, in **"Because the Pleasure-Bird Whistles,"** but the latter illustrates his procedure more clearly. "Because the pleasure-bird whistles after the hot wires" means "Because the song-bird sings more sweetly after being blinded (with red-hot needles or wires)"; "drug-white shower of nerves and food" means "snow," snow being seen both as the "snow" of cocaine-addicts and as manna from heaven; "a wind that plucked a goose" means "a wind full of feathery snow"; "the wild tongue breaks its tombs" and the "red, wagged root" refer to fire; "bum city" refers to Sodom, "bum" meaning simultaneously "bad" and "given to sodomy"; the "frozen wife" and "the salt person" are of course Lot's wife; and so on.

He becomes easier to read if one is aware of his linguistic devices. He is fond of ambiguous syntax, and achieves it sometimes by punctuation, as in **"O miracle of fishes! The long dead bite!"** which leads us to think both expressions are phrases, whereas the last is a sentence; sometimes by lack of punctuation, as in the first three lines of **"A Refusal to Mourn,"** where hyphenation would have clarified everything, thus: "Never until the mankind-making / Bird-beast- and flower- / Fathering and all-humbling darkness"; sometimes by delaying the complement in phrase or clause, as in the first stanza of **"Poem in October,"** where many words intervene between "hearing" and its infinitive object "beckon," and many again between "beckon" and its object "myself"; sometimes by setting up apparent grammatical parallelism where none in fact exists, as in "talloweyed," which is a compound adjective, and "tallow I," which is adjective modifying personal pronoun. He is not merely fond of puns, but of using them to effect transition; thus in the "Sonnets" a pun on "poker" makes the transition from sonnet 4 to the imagery of sonnet 5.

Thomas exhibits astonishing variety in his statement of similitudes. Most commonly he uses compound expressions with metaphorical implications, as in "lamb white days" (days innocent as a lamb is white) or in "And a black cap of jack- / Daws Sir John's just hill dons," where the hill capped with jack-daws is seen as a judge donning the black cap for the pronouncement of the death-sentence. He is fond, too, of confusing the reader as to what is metaphorical and what is literal; for example, "Where once the waters of your face" leads the reader to suppose "waters" metaphorical and "face" literal, whereas the reverse is the case. He sometimes offers an apparently impossible statement, whether taken metaphorically or literally, and then indicates its metaphorical meaning much later; for exam-

ple, in **"Our Eunuch Dreams"** "one-dimensioned ghosts" seems impossible, even though he is talking of images on a movie screen; it is only when he speaks of the photograph's "one-sided skins" that we understand "one-dimensioned" to mean a facade merely, something having no farther side. He is much given to various kinds of implied but unstated metaphor; for example, the storm-warship metaphor, where the warship is given only by implication, and again in "the stations of the breath" where he effects metaphor by substituting "breath" where we expect "cross."

It is difficult to say whether he has progressed much or not. There are extraordinarily fine poems in all his phases; but as he eliminates the faults of one period, he acquires new ones in another. His first poems are sometimes unnecessarily obscure through terseness; his later, sometimes obvious and verbose. In his earlier work the thoughts and emotions are sometimes too complex for lyric treatment; in his later, too simple for the elaboration he gives them. It is difficult, too, to say how he may develop; we must be grateful for the genius already manifest, and for the rest, have faith in the poet, a faith by no means without firm foundation. (pp. 65-70)

Elder Olson, "The Poetry of Dylan Thomas," in his On Value Judgements in the Arts and Other Essays, *The University of Chicago Press, 1976, pp. 65-70.*

Raymond Williams (essay date 1959)

[*Williams was an English educator, author, and critic whose interest in the relationship between literature and society informed his literary theory. In the following essay originally published in* Critical Quarterly *in 1959, Williams studies themes and techniques in* Under Milk Wood.]

Under Milk Wood, in approximately its published form, was first played in New York only a few weeks before Dylan Thomas died there. His work on it, during the last months of his life, was work against time and breakdown, yet in essence we can regard it as complete. The marks of the history of the play are, nevertheless, quite evident, and in particular the many revisions which the plan of the play underwent remain as separable layers, if not in the total effect of the work, at least in its formal construction. The play grew from a broadcast talk, **"Quite Early One Morning,"** which described the dreams and waking of a small Welsh seaside town. Daniel Jones, in his preface to **Under Milk Wood,** describes the stages through which this developed towards the work as we now have it. There was the insertion, and subsequent abandonment, of a plot, in which the town was to be declared an insane area, and the blind Captain Cat, at a trial of sanity, was to call the inhabitants in their own defence. The defence was to be abandoned, finally, after the prosecution's description of a sane town, the inhabitants of Llaregyb at once petitioning to be cordoned off from such sanity. Thomas worked on this scheme, under the title "The Town was Mad," but later changed the action back to a simple time-sequence description of Llaregyb itself. This was published, as far

---

Thomas on his poetry (1934 letter to Pamela Hansford Johnson):

The old, fertile days are gone, and now a poem is the hardest and most thankless act of creation. I have written a poem since my last letter, but it is so entirely obscure that I dare not let it out even unto the eyes of such a kind and commiserating world as yours. I am getting more obscure day by day. It gives me now a *physical* pain to write poetry. I feel all my muscles contract as I try to drag out, from the whirlpooling words around my everlasting ideas of the importance of death on the living, some connected words that will explain how the starry system of the dead is seen, ordered as in the grave's sky, along the orbit of a foot or a flower. But when the words do come, I pick them so thoroughly of their *live* associations that only the *death* in the words remains. And I could scream, with real, physical pain, when a line of mine is seen naked on paper and seen to be as meaningless as a Sanskrit limerick. I shall never be understood. I think I shall send no more poetry away, but write stories alone. All day yesterday I was working, as hard as a navvy, on six lines of a poem. I finished them, but had, in the labour of them, picked and cleaned them so much that nothing but their barbaric sounds remained. Or if I did write a line, "My dead upon the orbit of a rose," I saw that "dead" did not mean "dead," "orbit" not "orbit" and "rose" most certainly not "rose." Even "upon" was a syllable too many, lengthened for the inhibited reason of rhythm. My lines, *all* my lines, are of the tenth intensity. They are not the words that express what I want to express; they are the only words I can find that come near to expressing a half. And that's no good. I'm a freak user of words, not a poet. That's really the truth. No self-pity there. A freak *user* of words, not a poet. That's terribly true.

Thomas, in Constantine FitzGibbon's The Life of Dylan Thomas, *Little, Brown and Co., 1965.*

as it had been written—up to the delivery of letters by the postman Willy Nilly—as *Llaregyb, a Piece for Radio Perhaps,* in 1952. Then this was again revised, the title changed to "Under Milk Wood," and performed, again incomplete, in May 1953. John Malcolm Brinnin has described the last-minute writing and revision for this performance, which was part of Thomas's American reading tour. By the following October, having left aside certain things he had planned to include, Thomas had finished the play as we now have it.

This confused and racing history seems not to have affected the spirit of *Under Milk Wood,* though the loss of "The Town was Mad" is a thing to regret. It is in construction that the different intentions are evident, and in particular in the multiplication of narrators. The original narrator, the blind Captain Cat, was an obvious device for radio. Then, in the scheme of "The Town was Mad," Captain Cat became a central character, so that eventually another narrator was necessary. With his public readings in mind, and following also the habits of this kind of radio play, Thomas moved steadily back towards emphasis on the narrative voice. In the final version there are two narrators, First Voice and Second Voice, and there is also narration by Captain Cat and the Voice of a Guidebook. Formally, this is confusing, though part of the difficulty lies in the whole concept of a play for voices.

A primary complaint against the majority drama of this century has been the thinness, the single dimension, of its language. The development of domestic drama, and the emergence of the theory of naturalism, had brought themes and situations nearer to ordinary everyday life at the sacrifice of the older intensity of dramatic language. The words to be spoken by ordinary people in ordinary situations must be a facsimile of their ordinary conversation, rather than a literary expression of their whole experience. But then the paradox is that the very method chosen to authenticate the reality of the experience—that the play sounds like actual people talking—turns, in its overall effect, to a deep conviction that, after all, important elements of reality have been excluded. And this is, indeed, not difficult to understand, when we consider the nature of speech and experience, and ask ourselves to what extent our own sense of personal reality, the full actuality of our experience, can in fact be adequately communicated in the terms of ordinary conversation. Many of our deepest and richest experiences are unlikely to be reducible to conversational terms, and it is precisely the faculty we honour in poets that, by means of art, such experiences can find public expression.

However, in the case of drama, it is not easy to accommodate this kind of communication within the framework of an action limited to observed external probability. The revolt against naturalism, which has distinguished the drama of this century, is a many-sided attempt to get beyond the limitations imposed by a criterion of reality which is essentially external. The difficulty has been, throughout, that in certain respects drama is inescapably explicit, has inescapably to be shown. The idea of the play for voices, primarily developed in terms of sound broadcasting, is one of many attempts to make a new convention in which the necessary explicitness is preserved, yet without limitation to a single dimension of reality. It is a very difficult undertaking, and it is not surprising that the device of narration should have gained such a crucial importance. In terms of recent stage drama, narrative can be called undramatic, but in fact, on a longer view, it can be seen that in some of the most satisfactory dramatic forms ever achieved—in Athenian tragic drama in particular—narrative has had an important place. The rehabilitation of narrative, in broadcast drama, was a sound instinct, and *Under Milk Wood,* in spite of the crudity of its narrative structure, is the most successful example we have of its dramatic usefulness.

There is another reason for the emphasis on narrative. The craft of dialogue, in modern drama, has been ordinarily so much practised in terms of naturalism, that to a poet, or a writer with similar intentions, it has come to seem the hardest and most baffling part of drama: not only because it is in any case difficult, but because to lapse into the dialogue of a single dimension is so easy and so frustrating. Narrative, in comparison, is free, and in a way is turned to in relief. There is a similar turning, wherever possible, to such devices as chorus and song, because these again follow relatively directly from kinds of writing practised elsewhere. In the case of *Under Milk Wood,* the narrative structure must be seen, finally, as in part a successful convention for a particular kind of play, in part a residue of weakness following from both general and personal inexperience in this kind of dramatic attempt.

I have distinguished three elements—three kinds of writing—in *Under Milk Wood:* narrative, dialogue, song. If we look at examples of each, we can make certain important judgments of value. The narrative of the first and second voices is, in my opinion, relatively unsuccessful—perhaps, indeed, because it was too well-known, too easy a manner. This sinuous, decorated, atmospheric writing has become commonplace in broadcast drama, and I think it is ordinarily unsatisfactory, and particularly so in Dylan Thomas, where it opens the gate to certain observable weaknesses of his poetry. Near the beginning, for instance, we find

> the hunched, courters'-and-rabbits' wood limping invisible down to the sloeblack, slow, black, crowblack, fishingboat-bobbing sea.

The "sloeblack, slow, black, crowblack" device seems a nervous habit rather than actual description; a facile assonance rather than a true dramatic rhythm. This can be seen more clearly by contrast with a piece of successful narration, where significantly Thomas is involved with action and character rather than with suggestion of an atmosphere:

> The Reverend Eli Jenkins, in Bethesda House, gropes out of bed into his preacher's black, combs back his bard's white hair, forgets to wash, pads barefoot downstairs, opens the front door, stands in the doorway and, looking out at the day and up at the eternal hill, and hearing the sea break and the gab of birds, remembers his own verses . . .

The suggestiveness of the former piece is strictly casual,

a simply verbal device, whereas in the latter piece the rhythms point and make the action, and the verbal order plays its part in character. "His bard's white hair" is not merely decorative, like "sloe-black"; it contains both relevant meanings, the man's appearance and the sense, in the word order, of the bard's part he is acting. The rhythmic stop and surprise, so casually placed, of "forgets to wash," is again serving the whole situation being presented. It is the difference between dramatic writing and unattached tremolo.

There is some significance in this distinction, when extended to Thomas's work as a whole. *Under Milk Wood* is important because it seems to break a personal deadlock, a long imprisonment in a particular kind of practised effect, in much the same way that Yeats's plays mark the development from the imprisoning "wan, pale, languishing" world of his early poetry to the fine hardness and clarity of his later work. It is a movement out of a self-regarding personal rhythm into a more mature and more varied world. Whenever Thomas touches the action of his town and its people, there is a sudden sharpening and deepening, very different in effect from the posing rhythms of the anxious, word-locked, suggestive observer.

The actual voices are very different from the atmospheric voices of the narrators:

> 2W. And look at Ocky Milkman's wife that nobody's ever seen
>
> 1W. he keeps her in the cupboard with the empties
>
> 3W. and think of Dai Bread with two wives
>
> 2W. one for the daytime one for the night.
>
> 4W. Men are brutes on the quiet.

It is ordinarily this one sharp comic lilt, but it is markedly better than

> The lust and lilt and lather and emerald breeze
> and crackle of the bird-praise and body of
> Spring. . . .

The imprisoning rhythm is broken whenever the drama is actual, and it is interesting to notice that it is also broken for the songs, which are not set romantic pieces, but ballads in the mood of the successful dialogue:

> In Pembroke City when I was young
> I lived by the Castle Keep
> Sixpence a week was my wages
> For working for the chimbley sweep.

Those of us who were most critical of Dylan Thomas's earlier method, though recognizing that it had produced three of four remarkable poems, welcomed *Under Milk Wood* because it was the beginning of a break-out from a fixed, affected manner, which he seems to have recognized, in his last years, as increasingly unable to express all the varied life that was actually his experience, and that at last broke through in this play.

The main literary source of *Under Milk Wood* is the similar "play for voices" in the Circe episode (Part Two, section twelve) of Joyce's *Ulysses*. The parallels are remarkable, and some of them should be cited. I will put what in *Ulysses* is printed as stage-direction (though of course it is not this) into the narrative-voice form which Thomas adopted:

> N. Ellen Bloom, in pantomime dame's stringed mobcap, crinoline and bustle, widow Twankey's blouse with muttonleg sleeves buttoned behind, grey mittens and cameo broach, her hair plaited in a crispine net, appears over the staircase banisters, a slanted candlestick in her hand and cries out in shrill alarm
>
> EB. O blessed Redeemer, what have they done to him! My smelling salts!
>
> N. She hauls up a reef of skirt and ransacks the pouch of her striped blay petticoat. A phial, an Agnus Dei, a shrivelled potato and a celluloid doll fall out.
>
> EB. Sacred Heart of Mary, where were you at all, at all?
>
> N. Bloom, mumbling, his eyes downcast, begins to bestow his parcels in his filled pockets but desists, muttering. A voice, sharply
>
> V. Poldy!
>
> B. Who?
>
> N. He ducks and wards off a blow clumsily.
>
> B. At your service.
>
> N. He looks up. Beside her mirage of datepalms a handsome woman in Turkish costume stands before him . . .

If we compare this with the ordinary method of *Under Milk Wood*, the technical continuity is obvious:

> N. Mr. Pugh reads, as he forks the shroud meat in, from *Lives of the Great Poisoners*. He has bound a plain brown-paper cover round the book. Slyly, between slow mouthfuls, he sidespies up at Mrs. Pugh, poisons her with his eye, then goes on reading. He underlines certain passages and smiles in secret.
>
> MRS. P. Persons with manners do not read at table,
>
> N. says Mrs. Pugh. She swallows a digestive tablet as big as a horsepill, washing it down with clouded peasoup water.
>
> MRS. P. Some persons were brought up in pigsties.
>
> P. Pigs don't read at table, dear.
>
> N. Bitterly she flicks dust from the broken cruet. It settles on the pie in a thin gnat-rain.

The continuity, moreover, is in more than technique. Compare:

> Mr. Pugh minces among bad vats and jeroboams, tiptoes through spinneys of murdering herbs, agony dancing in his crucibles, and mixes especially for Mrs. Pugh a venomous porridge unknown to toxicologists which will scald and

viper through her until her ears fall off like figs. (Thomas)

I shall have you slaughtered and skewered in my stables and enjoy a slice of you with crisp crackling from the baking tin basted and baked like sucking pig with rice and lemon or currant sauce. It will hurt you. (Joyce)

Soon it will be time to get up.
Tell me your tasks, in order.
I must put my pyjamas in the drawer marked pyjamas.
I must take my cold bath which is good for me. (Thomas)

You will make the beds, get my tub ready, empty the pisspots in the
different rooms. You'll be taught the error of your ways. (Joyce)

There is an evident similarity between **Under Milk Wood** and *Ulysses* (each covering the life of an ordinary day), not only in kinds of imagination, but also in certain marked rhythms. I do not make the comparison to show Thomas unoriginal, though that he learned from Joyce is obvious. The interest is rather in the kinds of speech both are able to develop, as alternatives to one-dimensional "public" conversation. Thomas is writing for speaking, rather than writing speech (conversation) in the ordinary sense. The ordinary poetic alternative to conversation has been rhetoric, but this is by no means the only variant. There is the chorus of cries:

Try your luck on spinning Jenny! Ten to one bar one!

Sell the monkey, boys! Sell the monkey! I'll give ten to one! Ten to one bar one! (Joyce)

How's it above? Is there rum and laverbread? Bosoms and robins?

Concertinas? Ebenezer's bell? Fighting and onions? (Thomas)

Or the simple, hard chanting:

I gave it to Molly
Because she was jolly
The leg of the duck
The leg of the duck. (Joyce)

Boys boys boys
Kiss Gwennie where she says
Or give her a penny.
Go on, Gwennie. (Thomas)

By weaving a pattern of voices, rather than an ordinary conversational sequence, the reach of the drama is significantly enlarged. It can include not only things said, but things left unsaid, the interpenetration of things seen and imagined, the images of memory and dream, the sharp rhythmic contrasts of this voice and that, this tone and that, this convention and others. When we first read *Ulysses*, it seems that we are reading actual conversation, hearing our own full voices, spoken and unspoken, for the first time. The ordinary dialogue of a naturalist play seems, by comparison, artificial and theatrical. **Under Milk Wood** is slighter than *Ulysses*, but there is the same achievement of

a living convention: the voices, in their strange patterns, are among the most real we have heard. This success raises interesting possibilities for the drama as a whole, when we remember that, in England at any rate, the ordinary modern alternative to naturalism has been, not a pattern of voices, but the single general-purpose poetic rhythm of Eliot or Fry. It is significant that the varied pattern of voices has been achieved only in the context of an abandonment of ordinary naturalistic action. The Circe scene in *Ulysses*, and **Under Milk Wood**, follow the methods of expressionist drama, which similarly aims not at representation but at a pattern of experience. Yet it is not only in modern expressionism that we find this intention; we find it also in Ibsen's *Peer Gynt*, in the *Walpurgisnacht* scene of Goethe's *Faust*, and, interestingly, in the storm-scenes in *Lear*. The pattern of voices of Lear, the Fool, and Edgar as Poor Tom seems to me basically similar, in method and intention, to this writing by Joyce and Thomas. *Lear* is an obviously greater work, and the storm-writing is only one element in it, but the resemblance matters, and the authority of *Lear* is important, if we are not to confine our conception of drama to a single-level, tidy, public representation.

I have emphasized technical points, in the foregoing analysis, because we are still searching for a satisfactory contemporary dramatic form, and the partial success of **Under Milk Wood** is particularly instructive. It was not written for the stage, yet in fact, after some rearrangement, it was staged very successfully. It remains true, in the drama and the theatre, that we do not know what we can do until we have tried; our ordinary conceptions of what is theatrically possible, what is properly dramatic, remain timid and custom-bound, though constant experiment is essential. **Under Milk Wood** justifies itself, if only as this.

Yet in substance, also, it is not inconsiderable. It is true that it is very much a boy's-eye view, like most of Thomas's writing of this kind. Yet there is a warmth of acceptance in the experience, a willing return to the absorbed absolutes of boyhood, which deserve recognition in a period soured by a continual, prematurely-aged rejection. It is not a mature work, but the retained extravagance of an adolescent's imaginings. Yet it moves, at its best, into a genuine involvement, an actual sharing of experience, which is not the least of the dramatic virtues.

Is it an expressionist play, dramatising a mind, or a poetic documentary, dramatising a way of life? In the main, of course, it is the latter, but through the medley of voices, through the diverse experiences, a single voice and a recognisable experience emerge. The play can be seen in three parts:

(a) *Night and Dreams:* "you can hear their dreams"

(b) *Waking and Morning:* "rising and raising . . . the shops squeak open"

(c) *Afternoon, Dusk and Night:* "the sunny slow lolling afternoon . . . down in the dusking town . . . dusk is drowning for ever. It is all at once night now"

The distribution of interest is characteristic. The strong feelings are of dream, hiding, the effort of waking to the pretences of the day. Single feeling, in these modes, flows through the many voices. At near the beginning and near the end are the drowning memories of the blind Captain Cat—the private poetry; and again, by contrast, the morning and evening verses of Eli Jenkins—the public poetry of woken self-conscious sentiment. The neighbours' chorus clacks through the day with its hard, waking judgments. The three fullest portraits—of Mog Edwards and his Myfanwy, of Mrs. Ogmore-Pritchard and her dead husbands, of Pugh obsequiously hiding his hatreds—have a clear family likeness: the rejection of love, in whatever terms—money, house-pride, cold self-sufficiency. These are the hated, woken world, set in relief by the exceptions—the loving, fighting Cherry Owens; the dreamers of love—Lily, Gossamer, Bessie, Waldo and Sinbad; Dai Bread and his two wives; Polly Garter. The town is mad because the exceptions are so many, but only because we hear their dreams. Only, at the climax of the day, another world breaks through, and "the morning is all singing"— the three songs, two of the children, one by Polly Garter, between morning and night.

It is not a formal structure, but the shape of the experience is clear. The little town is observed, but in a curve of feeling familiar from Thomas's poems: a short curve from darkness to darkness, with the songs and dreams of the day cut through by the hard, mask-ridden, uproariously laughed-at world. This, in the end, is the experience, in a single voice, and the chosen technique, which we have discussed formally, must now be seen as necessary to the experience. The language of dream, of song, of unexpressed feeling is the primary experience, and counter-pointed with it is the public language of chorus and rhetoric. The people, in the end, hardly talk *to* each other; each is locked in a world of dream or a convention of public behaviour. In the storm-scenes in *Lear*, Edgar and Lear are like this; the technique follows from the kind of experience. The play for voices has many uses, but for experience of this kind it is the only adequate form. In at last bringing these feelings through to his triumphantly actual dramatic world, Dylan Thomas wrote his adequate epilogue, his uproarious and singing lament. (pp. 89-98)

> *Raymond Williams, "Dylan Thomas's Play for Voices," in* Dylan Thomas: A Collection of Critical Essays, *edited by C. B. Cox, Prentice-Hall, Inc., 1966, pp. 89-98.*

William York Tindall   (essay date 1962)

[*Tindall was a noted American scholar and literary critic who wrote extensively on twentieth-century literature. He is best known for his writings on James Joyce, particularly his* A Reader's Guide to James Joyce *(1959), a concise but thorough introduction to Joyce's works. In the following excerpt from his* A Reader's Guide to Dylan Thomas, *Tindall surveys the reception of Thomas's poetry and prose and analyzes the major characteristics of his works.*]

In 1933, when Thomas burst upon London with his marvels, readers were dazzled. Here, the better sort felt, were things beyond them yet their own, things from the madhouse or the analyst's couch, craftily rearranged. Here, dense to the point of clotting, was something rich and strange. As if Victoria had never laid her hand on Britain, here was something of more than Elizabethan abundance—deeper than the roots of aspidistras. Nothing in these extravagant riddles like the sociable verses of Auden or the austerities of Eliot, who had just proclaimed himself royalist, classicist, and Anglo-Catholic. When, in 1950, Thomas burst upon New York, he proclaimed his individuality: "First, I am a Welshman. Second, I am a drunkard. Third, I am a heterosexual."

To proclaim this suddenly at a party on West 11th Street was to disconcert decorum. Part of Thomas' impact was personal. He displayed his person everywhere: in bars, in parlors, on platforms, and on campuses, where he would have chased the girls had he been able to run. Almost everyone in London, New York, and Oklahoma saw, heard, or met him. Since I was around at the time, I knew him a little, too. Sometimes a little seemed enough; but sentiment always broke through. In my closet, held in trust for posterity, is an empty Dylan Thomas beer bottle (Budweiser) which I mean someday to present to a museum.

More of us loved than hated the irresponsible, charming, outrageous man; for he was our bourgeois idea of what a poet should be. Wallace Stevens looked and acted like an insurance man. Thomas looked and acted like a poet. There he was, prancing, eloquently declaiming, lying in his puke, puzzling us. Enchanting us, too. Little wonder that he became a popular poet, as popular as any in our time—be the rival Eliot or Frost.

Thomas was our Bunthorne. The analogy, however, is inexact; for although Thomas talked about the daisies in deep, transcendental phrases and although heavy dragoons hooted their displeasure as lovesick ladies followed the "greenery-yallery" young man about, he was not an "aesthetic sham." As he talked, what his followers like most about him was his voice—not what he said (which, after all, they could not understand) but how he said it. No triumph here of sense but of tone. Whether on academic stages, on phonograph records, or broadcast

Thomas, circa 1938.

through the air, this voice, we knew, was the true voice of feeling. Whether he read the poems of others or his own, this voice, delivering words from the printed page and bringing them to the ear, seemed poetry's proper vehicle or poetry itself. A poem, we found, is something to be read aloud by Thomas; and even as we accosted his poems silently, we could hear him read. Lacking experience or memory, we could put another record on the gramophone. The personality of the poet may still get between us and the poems, but not this voice.

Inevitably, a great poet with this voice and that presence displeased as well as pleased. England was crowded with heavy dragoons, for whom the trouble with Thomas was that he came from the lower middle class. His father was a schoolteacher. Thomas wore no old school tie, his upper lip was far from stiff, and everything about him seemed too much. In short, he was a slob. It may be that he was not born in Dublin, but Swansea is almost as outlandish. The shouts of the uniformed establishment—or its remnant, flying high above the aspidistra but sure Victoria is still around—made the higher praise of Dame Edith all but inaudible. Hers was not alone, of course. Many Englishmen were generous and perceptive from the start; but the opposition, always louder, has been growing, despite the death of *Scrutiny,* since Thomas' death. What the unfortunate outsider left us offers nothing to survivors of F. R. Leavis in the age of C. P. Snow. Without earnestness or any sense of its importance, Thomas would have seemed uncommitted in the committee room, where his poems would seem irreverent. He has an idiom of his own—and style. Incapable of understatement, dullness, or discourse in the manner of George Eliot, he has joined Joyce among established villains. Neither is like Anthony Powell, still less like John Betjeman.

The opposition, more amusing than the loyal support, demands more notice here. It is likely that T. S. Eliot's disapproval, in the third of his *Four Quartets,* of those who explore womb, tomb, and dream by "recurrent" images of "pre-conscious terrors" means disapproval of Thomas. But Sweeney's approval of birth, copulation, and death, Thomas' area, proves that Eliot's disapproval of these precedes his acquaintance with Thomas. Eliot's objections to what Thomas stood for are as impersonal as the objective correlative. Not so the more recent objections of Kingsley Amis, who, in "A Poet's Epitaph" (1957), says that "drunk with words," this poet "should have stuck to spewing beer, not ink." Thomas is even more plainly suggested by the satiric portrait of Probert, the ignominious Welsh poet, in *That Uncertain Feeling* (1955), Amis' second novel. From Probert's middle-class mouth, which has "all the mobility of a partly-collapsed inner-tube," come repulsive sounds, "woaded with pit-dirt and sheep-shit." Turning bits of the Bible back to front ("In the word was the beginning," for example) and slapping "Dai Christ" on the back, this outsider fills his poetic play with lines like these: "But, Bowen *bach,* they buried you at batlight . . . under the woman's hair of grass, you and your wound." Buried Bowen replies: "I was Bowen Thomas, tailor of Llados"—or Sodall backwards, a witty variant upon Thomas' Llareggub, which, in the interests of delicacy

perhaps, the English publisher of *Under Milk Wood* has changed to Llaregyb.

New Lines (1956), an anthology of poems to which Amis contributed, summarizes the recent reaction. Although unnamed in the introductory manifesto, Thomas is plainly there, supporting "the debilitating theory that poetry *must* be metaphorical." In place of his "diffuse and sentimental verbiage or hollow technical pirouettes," his "arrangement of images of sex and violence tapped straight from the unconscious," and his "*naïvetés* and nostalgias of childhood," let us, the editor implores, have decent, rational verse, something like that of John Betjeman or like the prose of George Orwell. Plainly, Thomas is out of fashion. Amis' "Against Romanticism," a poem exemplifying the ideal of this fashionable group, calls for pedestrian decency, "pallid" and "plain." Let no spellbinding complexities or swooning images divert us from our road to a temperate zone. Amis likes it there.

Robert Graves, late of the Royal Welch Fusiliers, lent his voice to the decent chorus. What the manifestoes of Sir Charles (better known as Sir C. P.) say about Joyce could be applied to Thomas—though Lady Snow found him congenial. Many of his friends, Geoffrey Grigson among them, joined his enemies, who forgot that, whatever their distaste, Thomas remains a great poet. Look down your nose at him and you look up.

American taste, commonly lagging ten or twenty years behind British, still finds Thomas all right. Students in school and college adore him, convinced that "if this young man expresses himself in terms too deep for *me,* / Why, what a very singularly deep young man this deep young man must be!" Deep critics, still under Empson's spell, rush to the *Explicator* with explications, and rush back to quarrel with rivals. Incorrigibly analytic, we welcome all complexities. Joyce and Thomas are still our darlings, whatever their status in Britain. Whatever the British reaction against symbol, image, and all romantic trickery, we are still romantics, and who more romantic than Thomas? That he was lower-middle-class or indecorous means little here, where Llareggub is still Llareggub. He died, we think, a poet's death as he had lived the life of a poet; and his death was suitably here. Maybe Thomas was not at home with "strangers" of our sort, but we are at home with him.

My survey of the British and American criticism of Thomas, both favorable and unfavorable, has uncovered several widely-held notions about him: that, a sport among the poets of the Auden generation, Thomas had no interest in politics and society; that he was a religious poet, a surrealist, a disciple of Freud, a composer of nonsense verse, and a student of Welsh "cynghanedd"—that he was deeply learned or incredibly ignorant. Though each of these notions has something to commend it, none fits Thomas exactly.

Concerning his political innocence: it is plain that obscure poems about womb, tomb, and childhood seem beside the concern and manner of the Party. Thomas sounds nothing like Stephen Spender or Hugh MacDiarmid. Yet, when asked whether he took his stand with "any political or politico-economic party or creed," Thomas replied (in **"Replies to an Enquiry"**) that he took his stand "with any revolutionary body" that asserts man's right to share in the fruits of production. "Only through such an essentially revolutionary body can there be the possibility of a communal art." But it is up to a revolutionary poet to declare himself as unmistakably in poetry as in prose. Thomas' poetic method, surely not that of "communal art," hid the pinkness of his heart. **"Our eunuch dreams"** and **"All all and all,"** despite unsocialistic obscurities, are as socialistic in theme as most poems of the period. My reading of **"Our eunuch dreams"** affords textual evidence and circumstance. For such discoveries you need nothing but a clue, close reading, and the liberal imagination.

Religion is more of a problem. Thomas called himself a "holy maker," whose poems are written "in praise of God." Indeed, God and Christ are rarely absent from his service; and the later poems, abounding in bells, books, and candles, are as ritualistic as anything by Hopkins or Eliot. Like Bunyan, Thomas was always asking what he could do to be saved. What, if not religious, would he want to ask for that for? Clearly there is something so holy about some of his poems that critics cannot be blamed for detecting it. But holiness of what kind? That of the church of St. Sulpice or that of the Muir Woods?

Father was a skeptic, but grandfather was a preacher. As a boy, Thomas attended Sunday school and chapel—Presbyterian, he told me—where he got "tipsy on salvation's bottle." His familiarity with the Bible, which remained a principal source of his imagery, and with *Pilgrim's Progress* dates from this time. "The black spit of the chapel fold" left it, never to return; but it had done its work on him, as on Lawrence. Both remained essentially Protestant without being Christian, and both remained Puritans. Anti-Catholicism is the chapel's heritage. Though Thomas loved the poetry of Hopkins, he loathed him as a Papist. One evening at dinner in my house, Thomas violently rebuked my wife for being a Catholic. Why, then, if he left the chapel and hated the church, did he fill **"Altarwise"** and **"Vision and Prayer"** with Christian imagery? Why and to whom was he always praying, and in what interests always exhorting?

Some of his prayers are to the devil, who, in **"Incarnate devil"** is God's creative colleague. In **"Poem in October"** God is mythical. **"Death shall have no dominion,"** whatever its ritualistic manner, is far from orthodox. The Saviour who figures in **"Altarwise"** is dismissed in **"There was a saviour."** But, whether praised or dismissed, God and Christ are always around in Thomas' poetry—not in their proper capacities, however, but as metaphors for nature, poet, and their creative powers. "He did not believe in God, but God had made this summer full of blue winds."

Like any vegetable-loving romantic, singing "the green fuse" as transcendental Bunthorne once sang "an attachment *à la* Plato for a bashful young potato," Thomas found nature holy. "The country is holy," he says in the prayer for his daughter. A statement of this kind is extraordinary; for he preferred images. Those he had acquired from the chapel and from Hopkins or Joyce were handy and suitable for expressing natural holiness—and

so were sermon, prayer, and ritual. God creates by the Word, and Jesus suffers for mankind. So too the poet. What better images for himself could he find? Both Lawrence and Joyce, who were always confusing themselves with God, Christ, or Lucifer, had anticipated Thomas. When, therefore, he talks about God or Christ, he has nature in mind or himself, as creator and sufferer. Creating by the word, he became the Word. The holiness of Thomas is a romantic holiness, at once diffused and concentrated, that finds its expression in the images and rituals of chapel and church. His churches have weathercocks, not crosses, on the steeples.

Some think Thomas a follower of Freud. The Biblical images of the early poems—water, towers, snakes, and ladders—must owe something to *The Interpretation of Dreams.* Indeed, behind these poems, in the capacity of patrons, Freud and monotheistic Moses appear to walk hand in hand. Many of Thomas' poems are dreams, and many seem constructed according to Freud's dreamwork: by condensation, displacement, and symbolizing. Delighting in the interpretation of his friends' dreams, according to elementary Freud, Thomas spent a happy half hour on one of my wife's dreams after he had forgiven or forgotten her religion—or else, keeping it wickedly in mind. Like Thomas himself, the hero of **"The Mouse and the Woman,"** a manifestly Freudian story, "could translate every symbol of his dreams," and, when writing, "let the dream dictate its rhythm." When asked by the editor of *New Verse* (see **"Replies to an Enquiry"**) if he had been influenced by Freud, Thomas said, "Yes." Like Freud, he continued, he brings the hidden to light; but, exceeding the master, he proposes to "drag further into the clean nakedness of light more even of the hidden causes than Freud could realize." Persuaded by such evidence, I used to think Thomas more of a Freudian than he was. It is true that, like most of us, he had a smattering of Freud, picked up maybe from glancing through the book of dreams; and what he found he found use for in his poems and stories. But now I think Freud one of their lesser elements, useful for adding a dimension to the Bible, a greater element. That Jacob's ladder and Eve's snake were also Freud's seemed pleasing and instructive.

Surrealism, which diverted some poets from the Party in the middle 'thirties and brought others to it, is an application of Freud. That Thomas was a surrealist is another widely-received notion—and not without reason; for there is madness in his method. Open his stories at random and you find images like these: "four-breasted stems at the poles of the summer sea-ends, eyes in the sea-shells." Here surely is more than customary of the "irrational element" that Yeats thought a distinguishing mark of great poetry, and here are words for what Dali was doing in paint. The poems of Thomas also abound in strangely juxtaposed images of the same sort. Several of his poems and stories proved suitable for publication by *Contemporary Poetry and Prose,* the surrealist magazine. Roger Roughton, its editor, was a friend of Thomas, and David Gascoyne, the principal surrealist of England, was an acquaintance. At the Surrealist Exhibition of 1936, crowded with friends and acquaintances, Thomas carried a cup of boiled string around. "Weak or strong?" he asked, offering it to André

Breton, Sir Herbert Read, and the buffoons of the unconscious. Reviewing *The Map of Love,* Thomas' third book, Sir Herbert, the patron of British surrealism, found it "necessary to introduce the spectre of surrealism here"; for "here, if anywhere we find that transcendence of reality through the paranoic faculty of the poetic imagination which is the avowed aim of the surrealist. . . . There is no evidence to suggest that Mr. Thomas has ever read Lautréamont, but the similarity is occasionally striking." It is, indeed, but with a difference. The ideal of surrealism was "psychic automatism" or writing without conscious control. Always deliberate, Thomas consciously controlled matters from the unconscious, or matters like them, for planned effects. Like Freud's dreamwork, surrealism offered another dimension—another method to complicate that of the Sunday school. Any good artist finds use for what he finds around him.

Surrealism, which he found there, is nonsense by definition. Even a marginal and artificial surrealist like Thomas, a fellow traveler at a distance and with maps of love, invites the displeasure of the rational and the polite. Distracted by surfaces, Robert Graves thought Thomas beyond rhyme or reason. Vernon Watkins, a sympathetic friend, threw up his hands at some of the poems, which, in his opinion, make no sense at all. Some readers are like Peter De Vries, who, when asked what he thought of the work of Thomas, replied: "It's nice work if you can get it. I don't get it." Other readers, taking the poems as Rorschach tests, find what they like in Thomas' meaningless blots and squiggles. Unable to follow the more formidable poems, one critic wrote a book to express his inability. But a semi-surrealist surface, complicated by Freud and the Bible, does not guarantee nonsense. Close reading and comparison of texts prove Thomas as rational and orderly as any poet this side of Alexander Pope. Thomas is merely difficult. If his complex of methods sometimes resulted in clotting, we must remember that nobody is successful all of the time.

Thomas was a Welshman. Therefore, it is tempting to think him a student of Celtic lore and an adept at "cynghanedd" or the harmonious and complicated interweaving of sounds that the bards of Wales have always been adept at. Thomas the bard or wizard, casting dark-vowelled spells, was one of his masks. But ignorance of Welsh kept him from bardic poetry and its system. "Cynghanedd," he admitted in a letter, "is a foreign, and closed form to me." The occasional and unsystematic interweaving of sounds in his poems shows a likelier debt to Hopkins, who was a student of Welsh. Yet, second-hand though Thomas' trickery with vowels and consonants may be, it is more or less Welsh in character and feeling—almost as Welsh in respect of these as the poetry of Hopkins. Thomas once told me that he was content to hint the Welsh techniques he lacked. As for "the deep Celtic significance" detected by critics in image and theme, Thomas cheerfully disclaimed it. A poet of Swansea, after all, is Anglo-Welsh, and, unless a learned man, closer to the traditions of England than of Wales.

Some critics think Thomas a second Eliot, deeply learned. John L. Sweeney in his introduction to *Selected Writings*

finds Thomas all but Grierson's rival in knowledge of seventeenth-century metaphysical poetry. Though flattered, Thomas modestly admitted in a letter to Donald A. Roberts that Sweeney "pays tribute to an erudition I do not possess." Elder Olson finds Thomas a profound student of astrology, plotting amid astrolabes and symboled charts the zodiacal career of Hercules. Others, noting Thomas' references to pryamids and the "third eye," have found the poet an Egyptologist and an occultist. Nothing is unlikelier. All that Thomas knew of zodiac, pyramid, and the occult eye could have come—and probably did—from ten minutes at a friend's bookcase with some work by Mme. Blavatsky, A. E. Waite, or J. H. Breasted, opened at random. Never one to rummage public libraries and lacking a library of his own, Thomas, the graduate of Swansea Grammar School, was not the deeply learned man some think.

Others, going to the opposite extreme, think him deeply ignorant. His reading, they say, consisted of thrillers, detective stories, horror stories, and science fiction, the area he chose when book reviewing. It is certain that *Dracula,* with its red-eyed "undead" emerging by batlight from their sheets and tombs, was one of his favorite books. Its influence may be detected throughout his poems and stories. But that Thomas, ignorant as the dawn, warbled wood-notes wild is no less unlikely. Neither deeply learned nor deeply ignorant, he was, like most of us, somewhere betwixt and between. He differs from most of us in being able to use what he picked up here and there, unsystematically. It may be that he knew no book well, but he leafed through many. His poems, stories, letters, essays, and recitations make it easy to list the books he had a nodding acquaintance with and put to excellent use.

Yeats, said Thomas, was his favorite poet. Yet he did not own a copy of his favorite, and, when called upon by the B.B.C. to read some poems of Yeats, Thomas had to ask Vernon Watkins what to read. From him Thomas first heard about "Lapis Lazuli," which he recited at every college in America. We do not always know what we love. This seems the case with Joyce, another favorite. The effect of *Dubliners* and *A Portrait of the Artist* is evident in Thomas' stories, especially those of Swansea or "little Dublin." His obsession with portraits of the artist and with young dog-gods may owe something to Joyce, whose portrait he sketched—or so I like to think—in **"The Mouse and the Woman."** The Thomistic hero of this story asks aid of a Joycean "wise old man," with whom he has read the "classic books": "On an Irish harp you would pluck tunes until the geese, like the seven geese of the Wandering Jew, rose squawking into the air. Father, speak to me, your only son." Our hero asks in vain; for the godlike old man has "a nest of mice in the tangle of the frozen beard." Thomas must have glanced *Ulysses* through without getting much help, except for that Wandering Jew; but *Finnegans Wake,* which he proclaimed the greatest book of our times and his favorite above all others, is another matter. Certainly Joyce's verbal play and his vision of cyclical process had an effect on Thomas; yet when I spent an hour or so with him over a copy of *Finnegan,* everything we came across seemed news to him. It is likely that Thomas had read a few pages of *Work in Prog-*

ress as it appeared in *transition,* a magazine he was familiar with. A few pages—and why turn more?—were all he needed to reveal the method and to establish love. Nobody has found better use for fewer pages of *Finnegan* than he.

The poems of Thomas suggest his acquaintance with Hopkins, not only with "The Windhover" and "The Wreck of the Deutschland," but with poems that few know, "Penmaen Pool" and "The Half-way House," for example. Hopkins, whose "womb-of-all, home-of-all, hearse-of-all" and "warm-laid grave of a womb-life grey" state Thomas' early theme, presides over his later rhythms as well as his approaches to cynghannedd and his customary confusion of sun and Son. Embarrassed by this heavy debt and uneasy with a Jesuit, Thomas spoke of him reluctantly, and, when he did, claimed independence. My poems, said Thomas, "came out of the blue of my head. . . . The only truth about my poems, is that I make them up."

Both firmly established in his head, Eliot and Auden helped make the poems up. Since, however, Thomas was busy declaring his independence of both, his references to them are not always cordial. "Pope Eliot" sometimes declined to publish Thomas' poems in the *Criterion;* and Faber and Faber, which published most good poets of the 'thirties, did not publish Thomas. In 1937 Thomas congratulated Auden on his "seventieth birthday." Wilfred Owen, more congenial than these, was a Welshman, skilled at dissonance. Thomas liked him as much as he liked Thomas Hardy, Walter de la Mare, and Wm. Empson. Of American poets, Thomas singled Stevens out for dispraise and Hart Crane, some of whose lines (those of "Recitative," for example) seemed agreeable, for praise. Francis Thompson's "Hound of Heaven" and "Ode to the Setting Sun" were pleasing, especially the latter, which proclaims "Birth and Death inseparable on earth: / For they are twain yet one, and Death is Birth." What *Adventures in the Skin Trade,* the story of Samuel Bennet, does not owe to Dickens, it appears to owe to the images of enclosure in Samuel Beckett's *Murphy,* which, unaccountably abandoning thrillers, Thomas reviewed in the *New English Weekly* in 1938.

The debt to D. H. Lawrence is no less than that to Joyce, who rules Thomas' words as Lawrence his themes: rebirth, for example, and the world of bird, beast, and flower. Thomas, who read Lawrence's poems from beginning to end, must have come upon some of the novels on the shelves of friends or on their parlor tables.

Among estimable older writers, aside from Dickens, Whitman, Melville, Beddoes, and Tennyson, were Wordsworth and Blake, from whose *Book of Thel* Thomas quotes in **"The Visitor."** Worms, sick roses, and heaven and hell fascinated him.

T. S. Eliot had taught poets to esteem the seventeenth century. Thomas esteemed it. Surprising juxtapositions, elaborate metaphors, puns and paradoxes, discordant concords of above and below, of macrocosm and microcosm, of the secular and the divine—all the armory of wit—were what he needed to supplement Joyce, Hopkins, and Lawrence. Not a deep student of that century, however, Thomas seems commonly to have confined his reading to Grierson's anthology of metaphysical lyrics; for all but two or three of the poems he refers to are there, where, no doubt, he first came upon them. Of Donne, Thomas knew the more familiar poems, the most famous of the Devotions, and the equally famous, and even more suitably charnal, last sermon, "Death's Duell," with its wombs and tombs, winding sheets and worms, deaths and entrances: "Wee have a winding sheete in our Mothers wombe . . . for we come to seeke a grave." Donne left young Thomas little to say. Vaughan was a Welshman; and Grierson's Vaughan, who says "Others, whose birth is in the tomb, / And cannot quit the womb," proceeded to the glories of recaptured childhood, leaving riper Thomas little to say. He read Marvell on worms and graves, Herbert on Easter wings, and Milton on Christ's Nativity, all in Grierson. Though sometimes as extravagant as Crashaw or as juicy as Cleveland, with his "jelly in a glove," Thomas passed both by.

Of the King James Bible, Thomas knew Genesis, the Gospels, some of the Epistles, and the Apocalypse. So much for Sunday school; but he had read some plays of Shakespeare in Swansea Grammar School. Such, then, is the extent of Thomas' effectual learning—so far as I see it now, though for all I know he may have dipped into a summary of Hegel, a pamphlet on agronomy, *The Undertaker's Manual,* or a treatise on Bartók, who, Thomas told me, was the composer for him.

So equipped, he began to write poems, at once physical and metaphysical, about womb and tomb, life and death, or the natural and supernatural process of creation and destruction. Creation, which includes world, child, and poem, may be cosmic, sexual, or aesthetic. The creator may be poet or God or both together with their common tool, the word—or any man, for whose tool Thomas found many words. In the process of creation and destruction he found what Baudelaire calls "the horror and ecstasy of life." When horror won life's duel, womb and tomb, indistinguishably one, seem a hole Thomas was trying to crawl back into. More cheerful than poems on this, his many poems on poems and his many portraits of the artist show the better side of creation and creator although these portraits are not without intimation of mortality and, whatever the implication of divinity, not without self-criticism. Even self-mockery may be solipsistic, but sometimes Thomas on Thomas is more devastating than his severest critic.

Take the picture of Samuel Bennet with a bottle on his finger in *Adventures in the Skin Trade.* A symbolic concentrate, this bottled boy suggests all we know about Thomas and all we need to know. According to Freud, a bottle is female; yet, a translucent shape and the product of a craftsman's breath, a bottle is an image of poetry. Stuck with both, the frustrated, helpless, and happy poet is also stuck with the bottle's contents; for once it was full of beer. Something to attract notice—a kind of passport to society, the bottle gets him into trouble in bars and bathrooms. Stuck in the bottle, a finger, more than phallic, is what a poet writes with. That this finger is his little finger adds to the fun. Nobody more pathetic, significant, and absurd than this oracle of the bottle.

No matter what the ostensible subject of his prose or verse, Thomas always wrote about himself. A poem by Thomas about Jesus, the zodiac, or a worm is about Thomas. What but Joyce did Joyce write about? And yet he wrote about the world, entirely.

Among Thomas' solipsistic poems some concern his dreams and some his fears, horrors, and anxieties. His myths and archetypal voyages reveal himself as hero or captain. Some poems, of the graveyard school, look through another's grave at his own or at himself as elegist. Some celebrate his wife, his troubles around the house, and his children; some his childhood, and some, the places he loved or loves: the park, the farm, and Laugharne with its cobbles and cockles. Some blast his enemies; and some, in the service of a Puritan conscience, denounce the wicked city, Bunyan's Vanity Fair. Some concern his fear of war and some the war itself. Some are the poems of a naughty boy; for naughtiness, another of his masks, was also the most natural thing in the world. In mood and tone the poems range from the meditative and resigned to the mantic and exuberant, from the merry to the severe and hortatory. The sadness of a man aware of time and death underlies them all. Of whatever kind and whatever the mood, these poems record his struggles from darkness to the light, or, since he never quite got there, toward it. Beer is dark and light, mild and bitter, and the light is bitter. "My poetry," he says in **"Replies to an Enquiry,"** "is . . . the record of my individual struggle from darkness to some measure of light."

Though important, these themes are less important than his genius and his craft with words. Like Joyce, Yeats, and Hopkins, but like few Englishmen since Hopkins, Thomas was in love with words. "The word is too much with us," says the hero of **"The Orchards,"** creating a "world of words." Marlais, this hero, is Dylan Marlais Thomas, whose most lovable book—neither *Finnegan* nor the poems of Hopkins—was the dictionary. Nobody since Joyce has put that handbook for wizards to better use. Among the spelling words of Thomas, which range in kind from slang to the jargon of disciplines, are obsessive favorites, which ran all but autonomously away with him: "weathers," for example, or "forked"; for every virtue carries its own excess. Excessive too, maybe, his verbal play, the derangements that renew the language of the tribe, reveal a craftsman's delight, and, by their gaiety, relieve black humor—and his was almost as black as Beckett's. Words were Thomas' matter, his tool, and his refuge; but so great his delight in them and in what Rimbaud called their "alchemy" that, as Thomas complains, they sometimes got between him and the object. Sometimes they became the object. It may be, as logical positivists affirm, that the trouble with words is their ambiguity; but for Thomas this was their glory. As he forked his meanings out, they forked, miraculously. Double talk became triple under his bottled finger, and often quadruple. Nobody's ambiguities are more accurate.

More than meanings working together or at war, words are also the sounds of meanings. "Poetry is sound," said Thomas, aware, however, that "to articulate sweet sounds together," as Yeats puts it, is to order agreeable meanings.

Conspiracies of sound and sense, Thomas' poems are "many sounding minded." More than the shapes of sound, they are the sounds and meanings of shape. Nobody a more musical shaper since God and Satan "fiddled" in the garden time.

So fiddled, the fiddling shapes of words are pictures, too. Those who compare Thomas with Bartók must also compare him with Dali. "Image, all image," says Marlais, the wordy boy of **"The Orchards."** As the words of Marlais Thomas multiply, the images quarrel. So he says in a frequently-quoted letter to Henry Treece:

> A poem by myself needs a host of images, because its centre is a host of images. I make one image . . . let it breed another, let that image contradict the first, make of the third image bred out of the other two together, a fourth contradictory image, and let them all, within my imposed formal limits, conflict. Each image holds within it the seed of its own destruction, and my dialectical method, as I understand it, is a constant building up and breaking down of the images that come out of the central seed, which is itself destructive and constructive at the same time.

We may be sure that the juxtaposition of incompatibles, whether of sound or pictures, is Thomas' method; but that the process is systematically "dialectical" I cannot be sure. It is clear, however, that his poems, not only shapes of sound and meaning, are shapes of quarrels among them. Sometimes the relationships among these contenders are troubled by uncertainty of syntax, a further and no less calculated ambiguity that allows the mind to go off in several directions within what we trust are "imposed formal limits."

Ambiguities of syntax and words, concordant discords of word and image are the cause of his effects and a cause of his obscurity. Privacy was another. Not even their Biblical or Freudian possibilities make his images altogether public. His trees have more branches than those of Genesis or the Gospels. His towers and seas are taller or wider than Freud's. Such privacies could be protective: to conceal what he had to reveal. Maybe, agreeing with the magazine *transition* and damning the plain reader, Thomas thought poetry expression rather than communication. In any case, he did his best—or so it looks—to make his readers his "strangers."

Yet, somewhere below these manifest confusions lies that "central seed," the latent sense from which the surface sprouted and flowered. Deeply planted, to be sure, the sense is always there. Never only things in themselves or autonomous shapes, his poems are also about things. In the beginning of each poem was the word; but words embody image and idea, and to know one you must find the other. Disappointed when readers made no sense of his images, Thomas liked to translate them into ideas. He rebuked Dame Edith for mistranslation. To him the poems were simple transactions between plain sense and a dialectical process of image, acting as sense's surrogate. His approach was easier than ours. Knowing what he had in mind, he worked from idea to limited images. We must work from unlimited images to hidden idea and back to images, where we linger; for a system of images is more than its translation, and what the poet makes may be more than what he makes of it and more or less than what he intends. Striding on two levels, his intricate images interact with one another and with their common origin. Striding on the double, the poem consists of these interactions. No matter what the critics say, density and obscurity are no sure signs of value; but maybe such interactions are. (pp. 4-19)

> *William York Tindall, in his* A Reader's Guide to Dylan Thomas, *The Noonday Press, 1962, 305 p.*

Ralph Maud   (essay date 1963)

[*Maud is an English-born American educator and critic who has written and edited numerous studies on Thomas, including* The Notebooks of Dylan Thomas *(1967),* Dylan Thomas in Print: A Bibliographical Story *(1970), and* Entrances to Dylan Thomas's Poetry. *In the following excerpt from the last-named work, Maud examines what he considers Thomas's oblique approach to such intimate subjects as sex, death, and religion.*]

To express the important and intimate facts of experience without seeming to blurt them out—this is the task the poet sets himself. Thomas in his youth made several important poems from the personal, and dangerously bathetic, subject of onanism. He did so by stating sexual waste not in terms unbearably close to the subject but in remoter images such as nightmare and graveyard figures. In his marriage poems, where the secrets of the marriage bed—so to speak—are in jeopardy, much of the energy generated is in the holding back, in the forging of configurations that let out the secrets with sufficient caution, turning into fine poetry what would otherwise be mere salacious information. That these controls are esthetic rather than prudish is clear from the shamelessly sexual subject that the words do, finally, communicate. Take, for instance, the vigorous representation of sexual union in the first two stanzas of **"A grief ago"**:

> A grief ago,
> She who was who I hold, the fats and flower,
> Or, water-lammed, from the scythe-sided thorn,
> Hell wind and sea,
> A stem cementing, wrestled up the tower,
> Rose maid and male,
> Or, masted venus, through the paddler's bowl
> Sailed up the sun;
>
> Who is my grief,
> A chrysalis unwrinkling on the iron,
> Wrenched by my fingerman, the leaden bud
> Shot through the leaf,
> Was who was folded on the rod the aaron
> Rose cast to plague,
> The horn and ball of water on the frog
> Housed in the side.

Our grammar books won't let Thomas get away with "She who was who I hold." Actually few people have qualms about using "who" for "whom" where it feels natural to do so. But we might challenge the second "who" on other

grounds. Is it really needed at all? Is there a significant change if we recast the lines?

> A grief ago
> She who I hold [did such and such].

Two things are lost by dropping the "She who was who I hold." First, the idea that the "she" now being held is a somewhat different person from the "she" who *was* being held a grief before; second, the universalizing that comes with this kind of "who," which has something of the sense of "whoever at all." The "she I hold" is a far too familiar body of bones. "She who was who I hold" is the mysteriously estranged loved one. We are made more remote from the particular intimate act of love, but perhaps all the closer to the essential nature of it. The distancing is achieved here and elsewhere by using syntax as though it were a lock-gate, allowing meaning to come slowly through regulated compartments. This delay in completing the sense is important in dealing with intimate things; it avoids the danger of flippancy. Moreover, to disturb customary syntax is to affect normal space and time relationships. **"A grief ago"** takes place all within the few moments after sexual union, but by means of the syntax we are flashed back to genesis and forward to the day of judgment; the history of the world is concentrated into the moment.

Thomas' abnormal syntax may occasionally be confusing; but it is rare that grammatical requirements are not rigorously met. The first stanza of **"A grief ago"** is a good test case. If we italicize the three main verbs, the actions of the subject "she," and enclose in brackets appositional descriptive material (adverbs being put into parentheses), the stanza becomes:

> (A grief ago,)
> She [who was who I hold,] [the fats and flower,]
> [Or, water-lammed, (from the scythe-sided
>   thorn,)
> Hell wind and sea,]
> [A stem cementing,] *wrestled* (up the tower),
> *Rose* [maid and male],
> Or [, masted venus,] (through the paddler's
>   bowl)
> *Sailed* (up the sun).

The stanza is clearly a "she did something" sentence. That "something" is one action; but Thomas uses syntax that will allow for three very active verbs, each with graphic adverbial adjuncts, while adding several appositional descriptions of the "she," all this with correct, though difficult, grammar.

Literary craftsmanship has traditionally met the challenge of blank paper by such devices of amplification and compression. **"A Refusal to Mourn the Death, by Fire, of a Child in London"** is in the same tradition as, though a good deal more serious than, Chaucer's *occupatio*, the rhetorical technique of confessing it to be beyond his skill to describe what he then goes on to describe. The "I am dumb to tell" of **"The force that through the green fuse drives the flower"** is the same device of volubly protesting a lack of words. And there are many other techniques. The rhetorical question, which goes at least part of the way to answering itself, is common in Thomas:

What shall it tell me if a timeless insect
Says the world wears away?
                          ("Here in this spring").

It structures the first two stanzas of **"How shall my animal"** and the opening lines of **"Vision and Prayer."** Thomas has messengers within his poems. "I tell her this" in **"A grief ago"** is a good example. Quaintly, in **"A Winter's Tale,"** the tale itself is brought into the poem like a boat, "pale breath of cattle at the stealthy sail." **"Poem in October"** opens with the morning beckoning the poet with its harbor noises. In **"Over Sir John's hill"** the poet reads psalms in "the leaves of the water" and hears "death" in a shell. The first half of the **"Ballad of the Long-legged Bait"** is mainly made up of running commentary from a number of incidental personae such as "the dwindling ships" and "the laughing fish." One happy form of amplification is to express the negative of what *doesn't* happen in order to communicate what *does:*

> . . . the lover's rub
> That wipes away not crow's-foot nor the lock
> Of sick old manhood on the fallen jaws
>   ("If I were tickled by the rub of love");

or to pretend ignorance of which of two possibilities pertains, where both (or neither, as in the case of dreams and movies in **"Our eunuch dreams"**) apply:

> I know not whether
> Adam or Eve, the adorned holy bullock
> Or the white ewe lamb
> Or the chosen virgin
> Laid in her snow
> On the altar of London,
> Was the first to die
>   ("Ceremony After a Fire Raid").

An extreme example of this use of the rhetorical negative is in the Prayer part of **"Vision and Prayer,"** where the poet prays in the name of the wrong people:

> In the name of the lost who glory in
>   The swinish plains of carrion
>   · · · · ·
>   In the name of the wanton
> Lost on the unchristened mountain
>
>   · · · · ·
>
>   O in the name
>   Of no one
>   Now or
>
>   No
>   One to
>   Be . . .

But he is praying, in their unholy or nonexistent names, for the *opposite* of what he wants. He prays

> That he [Christ] let the dead lie though they
>   moan
> For his briared hands to hoist them
> To the shrine of his world's wound
>
>   · · · · ·
>
>   May the crimson
> Sun spin a grave grey
> And the color of clay

Stream upon his martyrdom.

All this could have been done much more easily with a single positive statement; but two wrongs make a right—and also a poem.

The choice of metaphor, as well as the syntactical arrangement, is an important factor in distancing. The man in the street is often an expert at handling sexual matters with images that utilize metaphoric wordplay. Few would be unwilling to concede Thomas supremacy in this area, however. See him at work in the first stanza of **"A grief ago,"** where the girl's motions are the focus of attention. Cementing a stem, she wrestles up the tower; rises maid and male; as a masted venus, she sails up the sun through the paddler's bowl. These are images for the welcoming of penetration, a highly erotic subject; but Thomas has managed to find words that communicate the event without eroticism. "Masted venus"—why doesn't this image, a most dynamic way of saying that the female is completely possessed ("masted") by the male, strike us as prurient? One reason is the sharpness of the wording, the opposite of slyness. Further, the image, as well as being sexually symbolic, has to take its place in the literal image-narrative. The venus is masted *like a boat* and, in the next line, *sails.* The sailing image is remote from any pictorial representation of joined parts of the body.

Another description of complete penetration, in **"The tombstone told when she died,"** is a contrast:

> I died before bedtime came
> But my womb was bellowing
> And I felt with my bare fall
> A blazing red harsh head tear up
> And the dear floods of his hair.

Thomas himself was troubled by this warmer, closer imagery:

> The word "dear" fits in, I think, with "though
> her eyes smiled," which comes earlier. I wanted
> the girl's *terrible* reaction to orgastic [sic] death
> to be suddenly altered into a kind of despairing
> love. As I see it now, it strikes me as very moving, but it may be too much of a shock, a bathetic
> shock perhaps.

Yes, the passage *is* moving and vivid (the "hair" is pubic hair), which is just what the imagery of **"A grief ago"** isn't. To be moved one must be struck by a familiar chord. Perhaps the most immediately moving lines in **"A grief ago"** are:

> Tugged through the days
> Her ropes of heritage.

They draw on a fairly conventional image of struggle and oppression. But in these lines—and those from **"The tombstone told when she died"**—Thomas is least himself. He is most himself when he has forced us to take a new view of something (a "masted venus" for instance) by putting us at a distance from the intimate.

Freud discovered that the unconscious or sleeping mind is a great coiner of euphemistic metaphors, and that the coinage shows certain consistencies. To know about the specific figures that the unconscious mind repeatedly uses as metaphors should, on the face of it, be useful in studying poetry. After all, poetry is at one stage or another a heeding of the sights and sounds from the muse in the unconscious. But, strictly speaking, Freudian symbols arise from the need of our minds "to give a *disguised* representation to their latent thoughts" [Sigmund Freud in *The Interpretation of Dreams,* 1937]. Freud is really dealing with what happens when the mind works against itself. Only when we find an author *unwittingly* producing symbols we recognize as Freudian can we apply Freud's theory—though one might challenge the value of reading into a work levels of meaning of which the author was not himself aware. Thomas was very clear on this point. His answer to the *New Verse* question on Freudian influence shows him to be well aware of the significance of repression and actively interested in combatting it. He wanted to go further than Freud:

> Poetry must drag further into the clean nakedness of light more even of the hidden causes than Freud could realize.

Thus the applicability of Freud to Thomas seems severely limited. The symbolism behind which a repressed mind hides itself should be approached differently from the symbolism by means of which the poet consciously desires to reveal.

At the same time, the well-known Freudian symbols constitute a shared sexual language. Everything today is either concave or convex. Such a word as "crocodile" (used twice by Thomas) can gain a simple denotative meaning from being in the Freudian bestiary. Thomas must have known he was being Freudian in certain places—the dream sequences at the beginning of *Under Milk Wood,* for instance. Another case, perhaps, is in **"Into her Lying Down Head."** A room generally represents a woman, and the snake is the most important symbol of the male member. So we can decode the sexual event behind the words:

> There where a numberless tongue
> Wound their room with a male moan,
> His faith around her flew undone
> And darkness hung the walls with baskets of snakes.

As Thomas puts it: "Man is denying his partner man or woman and whores with the whole night." The question, however, is whether or not we really need recourse to Freud. The associational logic that our dreaming mind is said to exhibit in its symbol-making is equally available to our waking mind. If the sleeping mind "deceives" itself with a dream of Aaron's rod, for instance, the poet should be able to use the same analogizing process in order to communicate deliberately the sexual significance. We simply do not need Freud to tell us that scythe, thorn, stem, tower, mast, paddle, and sun are male symbols, and fats, flower, and bowl are female; nor to divulge the secret of the water imagery in the mythology of **"A grief ago":** "The people's sea drives on her"; "The dens of shape / Shape all her whelps with the long voice of water"; "Let her inhale her dead, through seed and solid / Draw in their seas." Water and the sea are naturally associated with conception and birth; the physical processes involve

fluids at every stage, seminal to amniotic. And one does not feel especially relieved to find this association confirmed by Freud. What Freud contributes to an understanding of sexual imagery is just what we can now (post-Freudians that we are) most take for granted, i.e. that sexual matters will generally be imaged by some physically similar counterpart. One tussles with the intricacy of Thomas' imagery in somewhat the same manner as Freud tackled dreams, but trusting that the poet's creating, censoring, and selecting mind has a responsibility and skill that the dreaming mind does not; in short, that the distancing is esthetic rather than psychotic, conscious rather than the result of repression in the unconscious.

Let us see, then, with or without Freud, what we can make of perhaps the most obscure and involved sexual imagery in **"A grief ago":**

> [She] Was who was folded on the rod the aaron
> Rose cast to plague,
> The horn and ball of water on the frog
> Housed in the side.

The context indicates that the girl is folded on (wrapped around) a male rod. This rod is described as the one which "the aaron rose cast to plague." In the Biblical story, "Aaron stretched out his hand with his rod, and smote the dust of the earth, and it became lice." For the second applicable meaning of "plague" we turn back to **"From love's first fever to her plague"** where the word means "production of offspring." Plague breeds, and children are a pestilence. So that when the "aaron rose" (i.e. herself acting like Aaron) casts the rod to plague, she can be said to be creating children by means of it, "cast" recalling the fishing image for sexual reproduction in **"Ballad of the Long-legged Bait."** The masculinity of "aaron" is softened by an echo of the feminine "sharon rose." "Rose" itself is a common symbol for the female. No one can doubt what is going on when we have rod and rose together. But no more than in previous instances is the imagery erotic. The complexity makes its own demands on our attention, and thus keeps us at a distance from the sexual event.

"Horn and ball of water on the frog" is perhaps even more difficult. Grammar indicates that the phrase is equivalent to the "rod" above. "Horn," at least, has well-established phallic connotations. "Ball" added to "horn" is, one presumes, completing a stylized representation. "Of water" makes a connection with "water-lammed" in the first stanza and the other water imagery generally symbolic of insemination and gestation. The horn and ball of water are "housed in the side"—the Miltonic sense of "side" as the womb. "On the frog" is not only grotesque but unclear. "Frog" probably has its root meaning of "jump." Brought into the poem because of the Egyptian plague of frogs—another of Thomas' superficial associations—the image evokes the sufficiently suggestive physical action, leapfrog. The wording "on the frog" denotes a continuous action, like "on the hop" or "on the make." One has no need to investigate what the phrase might mean to a patient of Freud's, but rather what possible ways there are of playing on the normal meaning of "frog" and "leap-frog." One enters Thomas' sexual imagery, like his other imagery, through the dictionary meanings and the verbal turns he seems likely to be making.

Provided there is an essential connectedness between the thing and the distancing image, the remoter the image the more esthetically effective it is. Hence the telling use of death imagery for sexual matters. Love and death are, paradoxically, both far apart and very close. This paradox, which gives the title of **"A grief ago"** its significance, is at the core of the conception stanzas of the poem:

> And she who lies,
> Like exodus a chapter from the garden,
> Brand of the lily's anger on her ring,
> Tugged through the days
> Her ropes of heritage, the wars of pardon,
> On field and sand
> The twelve triangles of the cherub wind
> Engraving going.

> Who then is she,
> She holding me? The people's sea drives on her,
> Drives out the father from the caesared camp;
> The dens of shape
> Shape all her whelps with the long voice of
>   water,
> That she I have,
> The country-handed grave boxed into love,
> Rise before dark.

> The night is near,
> A nitric shape that leaps her, time and acid;
> I tell her this: before the suncock cast
> Her bone to fire,
> Let her inhale her dead, through seed and solid
> Draw in their seas,
> So cross her hand with their grave gipsy eyes,
> And close her fist.

Behind the wit of "And she who lies, / Like exodus a chapter from the garden," which uses Old Testament imagery to denote the resting of the withdrawn couple, is the serious identification of the girl with Eve and of the sexual act with the first sin against purity in Eden. God's command to go out and multiply was coincident with His imposing the penalty of mortality. It is as though death forces one to love. Thomas gives us the image of the grave "boxing" the girl into love. The grave has "countries" for hands, countries a symbol of national and personal history and endurance—as in the lines:

> [She] Tugged through the days
> Her ropes of heritage, the wars of pardon,
> On field and sand
> The twelve triangles of the cherub wind
> Engraving going.

The tug-of-war image represents the burden that the Fall has imposed. The wind is the agent of death, not only wearing the girl down, but engraving, bringing her to her grave. Death is the lover who leaps her—and then we have the lover as the herald of doomsday and also, with the apocalyptic "suncock" and its connotations of male potency, of birth. There is a long literary tradition for lovers dying in sex, but Thomas' is a far more serious use of the conceit than probably any since the seventeenth century. The dead hover over the conception; they are in a mystical way the ingredients of life: "Let her inhale her dead."

Thomas often expresses the sexual in religious terms. With characteristic frankness and sacrilegiousness—frank and sacrilegious because the cross, as something that has to be borne, cannot escape phallic connotations in this poem—the "old ram rod" of **"Lament"** sighs:

> When I was a man you could call a man
> And the black cross of the holy house.

Thomas can say with truth, "I know the legend / Of Adam and Eve is never for a second / Silent in my service" (**"Ceremony After a Fire Raid"**). In a sense, the religious merely serves for esthetic purposes. The range of basically non-sacred religious imagery runs from the casual

> And the sabbath rang slowly
> In the pebbles of the holy streams
>   (**"Fern Hill"**)

to the emphatic

> No. Not for Christ's dazzling bed
>   (**"If my head hurt a hair's foot"**).

At times Christ is used as a simile:

> The young stars told me,
> Hurling into beginning like Christ the child
>   (**"Unluckily for a Death"**).

But then we have the reverse situation. Christ appears as Himself in some poems, and metaphors are then found for Him. And just as Christ is used rather cavalierly in figures of speech, so are rather cavalier figures of speech found for Christ. There is sometimes real doubt whether Christ is being praised or defamed. In the Buffalo notebooks, an undated epigram reads, in part:

> If God is praised in poem one
> Show no surprise when in the next
> I worship wood or sun or none.

One of Thomas' first published poems, in *Adelphi* (September 1933), has the same duality:

> No man believes who cries not, God is not,
>
>   . . . . .
>
> Believe and be saved. No man believes
> Who curses not what makes and saves.
>
>   . . . . .
>
> And this is true, no man can live
> Who does not bury God in a deep grave
> And then raise up the skeleton again.

The same scorn seems to appear in such poems as **"Incarnate devil"** and **"Shall gods be said to thump the clouds"** to say nothing of more juvenile poems left in manuscript. But **"Before I knocked"** is a different matter; it is a harsh, sincere reaction to the idea of Christ's mortality:

> You who bow down at cross and altar,
> Remember me and pity Him
> Who took my flesh and bone for armour
> And doublecrossed my mother's womb.

This harshness, and the "Jack of Christ" in other poems, is a deliberate distancing device, whose effect lies in the commitment to a deity that one dares disparage. Thomas talked of his father's atheism, an atheism which

> had nothing to do with whether there was a god or not, but was a violent and personal dislike for God. He would glare out of the window and growl: "It's raining, blast Him!" or, "The sun is shining—Lord, what foolishness!"

Thomas' own attitude to Christ is probably closer to his father's than to that of Hopkins or Francis Thompson, say. Even in his most devotional poem, **"Vision and Prayer,"** Thomas has achieved distancing (paradoxically) by getting so close to the birth of Christ that it ceases to be a sentimental nativity and becomes the birth of the poet's own child in the next room.

To avoid identifying the chief character, certainly one way of distancing, is one of the several means used in Thomas' other main Christian document, the sonnet sequence **"Altarwise by owl-light."** In the first sonnet he is "the gentleman," and "that gentleman of wounds" (which helps); but he is other things as well:

> Altarwise by owl-light in the half-way house
> The gentleman lay graveward with his furies;
> Abaddon in the hangnail cracked from Adam,
> And, from his fork, a dog among the fairies,
> The atlas-eater with a jaw for news,
> Bit out the mandrake with to-morrow's scream.
> Then, penny-eyed, that gentleman of wounds,
> Old cock from nowheres and the heaven's egg,
> With bones unbuttoned to the half-way winds,
> Hatched from the windy salvage on one leg,
> Scraped at my cradle in a walking word
> That night of time under the Christward shelter:
> I am the long world's gentleman, he said,
> And share my bed with Capricorn and Cancer. . . .

Thomas gave the "literal" reading [of the "atlas-eater" lines]:

> a world-devouring ghost creature bit out the horror of to-morrow from a gentleman's loins.

In other words, this is a form of castration. One thinks immediately of sonnet VIII:

> I by the tree of thieves, all glory's sawbones,
> Unsex the skeleton this mountain minute.

Again, the religious is expressed in sexual terms, the violence of the crucifixion being like a castration, the sacrifice a self-castration. Gods of other cultures have performed this act; but the whole problem is made more difficult in sonnet I by the castration's being performed by a strange creature described first as a dog and then an atlas-eater. And Thomas doesn't clarify too much in his further "literal" interpretation of the lines. There is no hint of the Christian key:

> A "jaw for news" is an obvious variation of a "nose for news", and means that the mouth of the creature can taste already the horror that has not yet come, or can sense its coming, can thrust its tongue into the news that has not yet been made, can savour the enormity of the progeny before the seed stirs, can realise the crumbling

of dead flesh before the opening of the womb that delivers that flesh to to-morrow. What is this creature? It's the dog among the fairies, the rip and cur among the myths, the snapper at demons, the scarer of ghosts, the wizard's heel-chaser.

Trying to make the creature seem a literal atlas-eater with a jaw for news, he keeps re-phrasing the image. He tries to find synonyms for the dog among the fairies. But, imagination having got the better of analysis, he is in effect writing a continuation of the poem. We are left to do the analyzing. The creature that bites out the mandrake is, in its simplest terms, biting out a symbol of mortality; the creature senses the "crumbling of dead flesh" and bites it out. The event just before this in the poem is syntactically an exact parallel: "Abaddon in the hangnail" cracks off from Adam. "Adam" is Christ the Man, the second Adam, in this crucifixion scene. "Abaddon in the hangnail" is the devil, the devil in the flesh, another symbol for sin and mortality. The event is the Redemption. Man is being released from sin and death through the physical violence done to Christ's body. Who performs this physical violence? In the first image, the Abaddon cracks off without an agent being present. In the castration image proper, the agent is the "atlas-eater," whom Thomas describes as a "world-devouring ghost creature." Let us take him up on that word *ghost,* and postulate the Holy Ghost, who certainly is a "wizard's heel-chaser" (i.e. "a dog among the fairies") in the sense brought out in Milton's "Nativity Ode," one of Thomas' favorite poems, the pagan gods fleeing before Him. It is perhaps better not to stick to the conventional Trinity. Rather let us put it that the spiritual element in the Christ figure is working the miracle of Redemption on the physical Christ, the "sawbones" (doctor, who heals, saves) aspect of Christ operating on the "skeleton" Christ, as sonnet VIII has it. After all, it is none other than Christ himself who gave himself up to torture and death. This is a one-man drama, which Thomas splits into multiple roles.

It is basic to Thomas' idiom that a person should divide and walk on two levels, and see himself walking there. The Godhead does this in **"Before I knocked"**:

> I, born of flesh and ghost, was neither
> A ghost nor man, but mortal ghost.
> And I was struck down by death's feather.
> I was mortal to the last
> Long breath that carried to my father
> The message of his dying christ.

The ordinary individual can be a trinity in himself:

> My hero bares my side and sees his heart
> Tread, like a naked Venus,
> The beach of flesh, and wind her bloodred plait
>   (**"My hero bares his nerves"**);
>
> I sent my creature scouting on the globe,
> That, globe itself of hair and bone
> That, sewn to me by nerve and brain,
> Had stringed my flask of matter to his rib
>   (**"When once the twilight locks no longer"**).

We have to be sure of this ingrained notion of split-identity in Thomas, because it is the only reasonable key to the first sonnet. For Christ is not only on the Cross (and, as we have seen, the Redemption involves more than one aspect of His personality), but He is also the Christ child in the cradle:

> [The gentleman of wounds]
> Scraped at my cradle in a walking word
> That night of time under the Christward shelter.

The "Christward shelter" gives us the nativity scene; there is no point in trying to imagine the poet in a Swansea cradle. The use of "my" is just another example of the "me-Him" split that we come across so often in Thomas. Here Christ just off the Cross comes to visit the newly-born Christ. The Nativity is put against the backdrop of Calvary. It is as though the Babe were being told the significance of His incarnation "in a walking word" by the Christ who has just "Hatched from the windy salvage on one leg." "Hatched" is the key word in the sonnet. It refers to the crucifixion: "on one leg" is a grotesquely simple way of speaking of the upright of the Cross, and "the windy salvage" is this world of mortality, a "salvage" because it is the thing saved by Christ. Though used to indicate death, "hatched" has at the same time all the connotations of birth, birth into everlasting life, Christ's second nativity. Thomas' sonnet sequence on the significance of Christ, then, begins appropriately with the Nativity as the subject of the first sonnet—but the Nativity approached so obliquely that we have to shed all conventional sentiments by the time we arrive at it. This is the final aim of distancing: not to obscure, but to prevent us from rushing in with the hackneyed, with our own notions rather than the poet's. (pp. 81-101)

> *Ralph Maud, in his* Entrances to Dylan Thomas's Poetry, *University of Pittsburgh Press, 1963, 175 p.*

Thomas and his wife Caitlin, circa 1938.

Don McKay   (essay date 1986)

> [*In the following essay, McKay analyzes Thomas's poetic craftsmanship in the sonnet sequence "Altarwise by Owl-Light."*]

One interesting entrance to the question of Dylan Thomas's craftsmanship is offered by the place he tends to assume, or be assigned, among modern poets. Donald Davie, in *Thomas Hardy and British Poetry*, finds 'tragic significance to the fact that Hardy is said to have been Dylan Thomas' favourite poet, whereas Yeats was his chosen master.' This tragedy evidently lies in what Davie perceives to be the abandonment of temporality by poets like Thomas and his friend Vernon Watkins for the eternal, atemporal, and mythic. Davie is referring to Vernon Watkins's comment, in his introduction to Thomas's letters to him, that Dylan 'understood . . . why I could never write a poem dominated by time, as Hardy could.' This, Watkins goes on, 'was also true of Dylan, though some critics have mistakenly thought to find such poems in his work. It illustrates our affinity on a deeper level: his poems spoke to me with the voice of metaphysical truth. . . .'

But we might do well to ask again whether the time-bound poems of Hardy are not a stronger conditioner than most

have supposed. What is often seen in Thomas as an address to a timeless world of mythic pattern is more appropriately construed as the reverse: a pulling of such still structures into the flux of temporality. Thomas's work resembles Hardy's in that it frequently brings the mechanism of the poems to the fore, using fixed stanzas with intricate rhyme and metrical schemes. He experiments with elaborate forms like the sonnet and the villanelle and does not, even in the leisurely later poems, accept the option of free verse from Lawrence and Whitman, with whom he seems to be philosophically in sympathy. Still less can one discover the influence of the vers librists or their descendants, Pound, Eliot, and the imagists. *Madeness* is an essential part of the character of Thomas's poems, a constant reminder of the poet's presence in the work. The comparison with Hardy is instructive: in the structures of both poets we feel an obvious arbitrariness, revealing a human craftsman using available materials, rather than the inspired recipient of ineluctable design. One thinks of '**Author's Prologue**' with the mirror-image rhyme scheme and Thomas's comment to his publisher: 'Why I acrosticked myself like this, don't ask me.' Whatever the reason, one effect of the exercise is to impress readers by flourishing his credentials as a virtuoso technician. One also thinks of the seventy-two lines in **'I, in my intricate image'** ending with some variation of the 'L' sound, and the difficulty of reconciling this monotone with the intricacy mentioned in the title. Reading Thomas, as with Hardy, we are generally aware of a craftsman making the poem in time, rather than flying on viewless wings.

But it is quite apparent that there is a fundamental dissimilarity between Thomas's craft and Hardy's. Whereas Hardy is always *homo faber,* Thomas is more often *homo ludens.* Thomas's formal play, his willingness to wear rhetoric as a costume, distinguishes him from Hardy, the 'humbler' craftsman. Donald Davie's image of Hardy as a nineteenth-century engineer constructing a complex, open-faced mechanism holds true in a general way. Thomas is 'crafty' rather than humble in the control and manipulation of his craft, and the complementary image for him, which I wish to elaborate in the pages which follow, is the trickster. Let me begin by quoting the well-known, flamboyant response Thomas made to a student inquiring about his use of technical devices.

> I am a painstaking, conscientious, involved, and devious craftsman in words, however unsuccessful the result so often appears, and to whatever wrong uses I may apply my technical paraphernalia. I use everything and anything to make my poems work and move in the direction I want them to: old tricks, new tricks, puns, portmanteau-words, paradox, allusion, paronomasia, paragram, catachresis, slang, assonantal rhymes, vowel rhymes, sprung rhythm. Every device there is in language is there to be used if you will. Poets have got to enjoy themselves sometimes, and the twisting and convolutions of words, the inventions and contrivances, are all part of the joy that is part of the painful, voluntary work.

No doubt more than a little of the trickster's invention and contrivance has gone into the invention of this response of the poet's. One imagines Thomas leafing through a literary handbook to pick plums. In fact, the style of Thomas's response reflects this element in his 'devious' craftsmanship—the hoopla of a showman showing off, rather than concealing, his artfulness.

It is not difficult to discern the sly presence of the trickster everywhere in Thomas's work infecting all the other roles and voices he takes up: child, father, lover, bard, mystic, elegist. Any tendency to pomp, to institutionalized rhetoric, or indeed to any static form or concept, is undone by his saving presence. Thomas can afford to be as rhetorical and even pompously oracular as he sometimes is, because the trickster's tongue is in the poet's cheek. We might think of the narrator's ironical exposure of himself as the 'bard on a raised hearth' in **'After the funeral'** and the consequent doubleness we experience in reading. A tension is created between the voices of the serious mourner and the ironical observer, two dialects within the poem. Such doubleness, *duplicity,* is an important ingredient in any Thomas poem, managed by such tactics as polysemous references, bravura allusiveness, intricacy of form, and the teasing interplay of transparence and opacity.

Among particular figures of speech available to devious craftsmen, Thomas revels in puns and displaced clichés. Included in the list of rhetorical techniques he credits to himself in the letter quoted above are two subspecies of the pun, paronomasia and paragram, besides the pun itself. Thomas's word-play is sometimes simple ('once below a time,' 'capsized field'), sometimes complex ('Shall you turn cockwise on a tufted axle'), sometimes esoteric (*Aaron's rod* combining with *Arianrod,* mother of the mythological Dylan, in **'A grief ago'**). While we may admire and enjoy these so-called lower forms of wit, most readers have difficulty reconciling such verbal play with profound meanings. In puns, meaning is made to abandon the safe route from signifier to signified, and to reside, or more accurately to occur, in the play of signifiers, exploiting the accidental phonic coincidences between them. There is no semantic relation between Aaron's rod and Arianrod, cock and clock, cap sized and capsized, until the poet draws them together. A related trick is the transferred epithet, a fairly simple device whereby the modifiers of adjacent nouns exchange places, as in the phrase 'sharp, enamelled eyes and spectacled claws.' There is a similar impression of linguistic deformation created by Thomas's use of catachresis, that is, metaphor or implied metaphor which is abnormally stretched. We might well nominate catachresis as the paradigm figure of speech for all Thomas's obscure poems, and especially the sonnets. A catachretic metaphor registers the poet's acrobatic skill and daring along with (and sometimes to the exclusion of) the analogy proposed by the figure.

> And from the windy West came two-gunned Gabriel

> When the worm builds with the gold straws of venom
> My nest of mercies in the rude, red tree.

Such metaphors are performances, tricks which appear as tricks, rather than secret, subtle mechanisms. In his use of such devices as puns, displaced clichés, transferred epithets, and catachresis, we can sense a willed grotesquerie in Thomas's craft, a deliberate violation of decorum. Hardy's elaborate mechanisms are compatible with the voice he develops: ruminative, rooted, honest, having a folk artist's due regard for the complicated turn or embellishment. Thomas's most extreme fancy-work seems extra to the text, like a game going on apart from the poem's sense. But, as often in recent criticism, it appears that what is from one perspective marginal, merely ornamental, or superfluous turns out, once we have shifted to a less centralist mode of reading, to function as the unsung matrix or ground-work for the whole. In general, we may say, Thomas's technical perversity is a sure sign of the trickster, the presiding deity of his work.

The element of the trickster in Thomas's writing gives him a special, privileged relationship to the mythic structures his work everywhere invokes. Within a mythological structure, the trickster is the maverick, the mischievous, unpredictable, sometimes anarchic member of the pantheon, the seed of disorder within the system, the ambassador from chaos. But he may also serve as the link between transcendent gods and mortals, between the synchronic world of myth and the historical world of events. Sometimes the trickster confers such great gifts as medicine or fire, as Nanabozho does in Ojibway myths, functioning as the medium by which power devolves from gods to men. But more often his schemes backfire, with disastrous results for himself and for mankind.

In Thomas's revision of biblical myth, it is the devil who performs the trickster's linking and transmitting function. In **'Incarnate devil'** Satan is the initiator (or perpetrator) of time itself, stinging the static circle into wakefulness—a dubious gift, perhaps, but an essential one if man is to be independent from God, the 'warden' who 'played down pardon from the heavens' hill.' Emphasizing the trickster's role in cosmogony itself (rather than introducing him as a belated intruder in the creation story) can be a symbolic way to stress certain features of creation: the flawed nature of existence is acknowledged as part of its essence rather than an aberration later perpetrated by man; diachronic energy is given a place at least equal to synchronic design; and creative activity is seen as primarily a subversive exercise. These are consequences evident throughout Thomas's imagery, but especially in his use of the serpent or worm as the double agent of creation and destruction. The worm is the eater of our flesh in poems such as **'The force that through the green fuse drives the flower'** and **'If I were tickled by the rub of love,'** and it is the creative instrument in others like **'Before I knocked'** (the 'fathering worm,'), **'When once the twilight,'** and sonnet three of the Altarwise sequence. In that third sonnet the image of 'the tree-tailed worm that mounted Eve' aggresively conflates Eden's two subversive elements and combines them with the phallus. The worm's role in the sonnets extends, as we shall see, to the redemptive function foreseen at the end of the sequence. Something of this infringement on Christ's role by the trickster worm is implied in the idea of 'mounting' Eve. Besides crude sexual congress, this suggests the common metaphysical conceit of Christ's tree on Mount Calvary overcoming Eden's tree of knowledge, a redemptive function which here seems to belong to the worm.

But it is the role of Thomas as a poet, rather than the implications of his imagery, that I particularly wish to stress, for Thomas inhabits his mythic contexts in the same way the trickster lives in his—subversively. Embraced and even sustained by the structure, he dwells within it in a constant state of opposition, continually testing and interrogating its conventions, and attempting to steal power from the authorities, with consequences that are ambiguously creative/destructive for the sense of his poems. Shortly after the publication of the Altarwise sonnets in 1936, Thomas made some comments on a 'misreading' which Edith Sitwell had perpetrated in the *Sunday Times.* Sitwell had somewhat breezily declared that the 'atlas-eater with a jaw for news' from sonnet one referred to 'the violent speed and sensation-loving, horror-loving craze of modern life.' Writing to Henry Treece, Thomas took her to task for failing to take 'the literal meaning,' as though that were self-evident, and went on to provide his own gloss on the phrase: 'What is this creature? It's the dog among the fairies, *the rip and cur among the myths,* the snapper at demons, the scarer of ghosts, the wizard's heel-chaser.' This creature within the poem is behaving as

Thomas does in the exercise of his craft. Especially in the phrase I have italicized, we can hear the echo of the poet's own attitude to his mythic inheritance. For Thomas in the sonnets is himself a dog among the fairies, a rip and cur among the myths, a saboteur of inherited systems.

Critics of the Altarwise sonnets have sometimes tended to rationalize their extravagances and explain away their obliquity, as Elder Olson [in his *The Poetry of Dylan Thomas*] and H. H. Kleinman [in his *The Religious Sonnets of Dylan Thomas*] do in their virtuoso exegeses. These interpretations concentrate upon some 'metaphysical truth' such as Vernon Watkins affirmed to be the basis of Thomas's poetry and his own. In terms of the model offered by **'To-day, this insect,'** they give privileged status to the ageless voice's mythopoeic utterances over the voice of the temporally located, destructive artist. Interestingly, Vernon Watkins himself can take such a view of Thomas's poetics only by ignoring the thrust of some comments he made on one of Watkins's poems, 'Call It All Names, But Do Not Call It Rest.' Thomas wrote Watkins in March, 1938, recommending that he include a 'destructive' element in the poem. 'A motive has been rarefied, it should be made common. I don't ask you for vulgarity, though I miss it; I think I ask you for a little creative destruction, destructive creation: "I build a flying tower, and I pull it down." ' Such an inclusion of the trickster's demolition work within Watkins's mythopoeic would, for Thomas, have the effect of bringing the poem out of timelessness into time, making it a 'vulgar' event and not just a structure: 'I can see the sensitive picking of words, but none of the strong inevitable pulling that makes a poem an event, a happening, an action perhaps, not a still life or an experience put down, placed, regulated. . . .' Now that some recent critical theory has accustomed us to the phenomenon of conceptual systems which hold the seeds of their destruction, we should be able to read poems like the sonnets in a style which agrees more closely with the poet's. Because it is usual for critics to assume that Thomas is the celebrator of organically integrated existence, awareness of the trickster's perversity causes some interpretive difficulties. Critics lacking the faith of Olson, Kleinman, or Watkins often conclude that Thomas unfortunately suffered some serious lapses and wrote failures like the Altarwise sonnets. John Bayley approaches this problem when he expresses dissatisfaction with some poems which 'seem to have no owner,' using the figure of ventriloquism to illustrate how his ear picks up a vacuum in the rhetoric ["Chains and the Poet," *Dylan Thomas: New Critical Essays,* ed. Walford Davies]. The trickster's duplicity reduces the reader's experience of a reliable voice or presence within language, and creates reflective surfaces which defer meanings without the assurance of a point of semantic closure. Bayley, in another essay on Thomas, pauses in the middle of an ingenious exegesis of **'Out of the sighs,'** considers his position, then gives up the exercise altogether, declaring: 'But I have no confidence that the reader is intended to pursue these crossword clues of association: they may be simply misleading, and my tentative exegesis of the poem may bear no relation to the impression other readers may get from it' ["Dylan Thomas," *Dylan Thomas: A Collection of Critical Essays,* ed. C. B. Cox].

But let us acknowledge that readers who have sought systems and codes within Thomas's work, including myself, have done so with some justification. In fact, we have been virtually propelled on this quest by the poet, who was fond of making broad universalizing gestures which hint, when they don't actually declare, that he possesses a symbolic system. To Pamela Hansford Johnson (for whom he acted many roles in the broad spectrum between Antichrist and the dying Keats) he intoned: 'All around us, now and forever, a spirit is bearing and killing and resurrecting a body.' To Glyn Jones he declared that 'My own obscurity is quite an unfashionable one derived . . . from the cosmic significance of the human anatomy.' Both these statements, made in 1933 and 1934 about the time the Altarwise sonnets were being composed, are somewhat qualified by the many voices which cohabit in the letters, each straining against, and undermining, its neighbours. But they are representative of the mythic and symbolic tone struck in many early poems, and particularly in the sonnets. The effect is produced, in part, by using the embracing first person, or 'everyman' narrator, and writing of personal existence as though it were an exemplary tale, told against a cosmic backdrop and populated with familiar names: Adam, Abaddon, Christ, Mary. These gestures serve the same function as symbol of the cross of tales at the end of **'To-day, this insect'**: they are the symbols of symbolization, indicating that a synchronic structure lies behind the many misdirections of time. We are encouraged to read Thomas's work as we might read Blake, in whose path, he told Pamela Hansford Johnson, he followed, or Yeats, whom he idolized.

To do so would of course be to push the trickster firmly into the background. But let us also acknowledge that we might read the sonnets under the trickster's banner, or under that of Rimbaud, his representative in Thomas's experience, and conduct a counter-interpretation stressing, at every juncture, our uncertainty among polysemous interactive images, our mounting vertigo as diverse symbolic systems are activated and released, our chronic inability to domesticate passages of non-directive syntax. Such an exercise might have the value of rectifying a critical imbalance by throwing emphasis upon the other extreme, the flying tower as raw, fragmented material rather than an erect structure. But my aim is neither to deconstruct the sonnets nor to construct another wholly integrated interpretation. Rather I wish to establish a style of reading which agrees with the poet's style of composition, using the trickster as the model of their creator, and perceiving the creation and destruction of meaning as simultaneous cognate functions. Consequently, what follows is an approach rather than a thorough treatment of the sonnets, an attempt to establish linguistic and poetic principles by pursuing hypotheses and investigating representative passages. I am after their thrust and spirit, and hope to capture some of those Barthesian pleasures we may experience if we can survive those moments of interpretive nausea when other readers like John Bayley have given up. There are, I am suggesting, embracing principles which make indeterminacy necessary; I am hopeful that an understanding of these will make it possible for us to reach and enjoy the sonnets' particular style of mischief.

It is useful to remind ourselves that Thomas was, during the thirties, a self-conscious radical who adopted a subversive stance towards all inherited structures of belief. Inspired variously by the examples of Lawrence, Blake, and Joyce, he adopts, in his letters of the period, the role of the revolutionary outsider. But since the strategy of subversion in religion, politics, social decorum, and sex extends also to his own postures, we find his most extreme theoretical statements undercut with irony or self-ridicule. After a brief polemical outburst to Pamela Hansford Johnson ending with 'The state of the future is not to be an economic despotism or a Christian Utopia. It is the state of Functional Anarchy,' he begins the next paragraph with 'And a fol fol dol and a reel of cotton. So much for that.' Thomas cannot be fixed to doctrine, not even to the revolutionary systems like Marxism and Lawrentian sexual consciousness which he sometimes arrogated. He inhabits systems, both conventional and revisionist, in a provisional way; but he does not, like Rimbaud or Artaud, place himself nakedly outside all structures as their exemplary inquisitor.

One instance from his letters may serve to illustrate the general tendency in Thomas's thinking within systems. Defending his anatomical imagery to Pamela Hansford Johnson, he calls upon an image from Donne:

> But I fail to see how the emphasizing of the body can, in any way, be regarded as hideous. The body, its appearance, death, and disease, is a fact sure as the fact of a tree. It has its roots in the same earth as the tree. The greatest description of our own "earthiness" is to be found in John Donne's Devotions, where he describes man as earth of the earth, his body earth, his hair a wild shrub growing out of the land. All thoughts and actions emanate from the body. Therefore the description of thought or action—however abstruse it may be—can be beaten home by bringing it onto a physical level.

Thomas has emptied the symbol of Donne's intention to dissuade men from carnal pursuits and to foster spirituality, and infused it with his own line of thought, oriented in the direction of D. H. Lawrence. It is typical of Thomas to use traditional sources in myth and literature wrenched from context in such an aggressive way that the aggression—the *kidnapping*—is itself a telling feature of the symbol in its new Thomas-controlled situation. That is, the act of allusion is itself part of the symbol's signification, registering the poet's bold determination to dislodge the symbol from its embracing structure and bend to his own will a former member of an authoritative system. Whether Thomas invents his own system or not, his style of allusion serves notice that he will be no slave to another man's, even when he has stolen pieces of it.

This aggressive orientation towards precursors may be contrasted to Eliot's restraint in *The Waste Land*. Quotations from other authors are guests in that poem, and are generally allowed to retain the voices in which they spoke originally. Although they function within *The Waste Land* under Eliot's ultimate control, their original senses are not violated, and they are permitted to resonate fully within themselves. They often appear with enough of their original contexts ('You! hypocrite lecteur!—mon sembla-ble,—mon frère!') that their spirit as literary languages is retained and they can function as dialects within the multi-lingual poem. By such gestures Eliot adds to his local and intertextual meanings the signals of homage to the original text and reverence to tradition itself. Thomas, as trickster, does not wish to inherit anything: he wants to lay claims, to seize, steal, to establish the rule of his individual talent over all constituents of his poetry, even, one senses, over language itself. His allusive strategy denies his sources the ability to ring the clear note of themselves or establish firm links with tradition. Instead they are swallowed by the teeming imagery, gathered quickly into the syntactical flow and forbidden any nostalgia for the lost context. There is a general process of vulgarizing the traditional source, the element Thomas missed in Vernon Watkins's poetry. The expression 'a dog among the fairies' sums up the poet's relationship to the élite. And in its context in sonnet one the phrase is itself a dog among fairies, in the sense that it is an uncouth, mundane expression (a slur on homosexuals is suggested) mingling familiarly with such dignitaries as Abaddon, Adam, and Christ.

Thomas inherits the sonnet with a typical gesture of independence, imposing his personal stamp on the old form by placing the sestet first in each poem. One might wish to argue that choosing the sonnet sequence in the first place was a rather conventional decision. However, something of Thomas's technical perversity emerges when we consider the anomaly that Thomas is handling materials of an apparently epic scale within this condensed mode, where the poet is generally free to write lyrically and subjectively with few of the epic writer's responsibilities to narrative coherence or established tradition. The choice of form, then, is a first step in the subjectification of myth, and necessitates such compacting and combining of its mythological constituents that the private integrity of each is seriously compromised, as in Tokyo subway cars during rush hour. The very virtuosity of Thomas's allusiveness within these close quarters guarantees that no one mythic system—Christianity, the Heracles cycle, astrology, the Freudian family romance—can achieve dominion as the organizing strain: in a film crowded with famous actors there is no star, and more power is reserved by the director for himself. When such nominees as Christ or Heracles are proposed for hero, the interpreter is forced to postulate such modifications, inversions, and hybridizations of his persona that his self-identity becomes most problematic. My father-in-law had the same watch for forty years, during which time, as he was fond of pointing out, he replaced the crystal, the face, the strap and the escapement several times each.

Quite apart from Thomas's characteristic style of allusion to external sources, the home-grown symbols in the sonnets generally wear the stamp of their manufacture, that quality of *madeness* discussed earlier: 'My camel's eyes will needle through the shroud,' 'Adam, time's joker, on a witch of cardboard,' 'Pin-legged on pole-hills with a black medusa.' Much of the aesthetic interest in lines like these lies in watching a virtuoso *bricoleur* or handyman making a rickety structure out of scraps. Even when the materials derive from mythic contexts, he treats them *as*

though they were scraps: Adam can enter the deck of cards as the joker, the trickster of that context; Medusa as goddess or jelly-fish shows up on some pole-hills suggestive of Calvary. Christ and Egyptian funerary rites (sonnet nine) exist democratically in the same milieu with a hellfire preacher, pirates, Rip Van Winkle, references to novels by Henry Miller, card tricks, and sexual puns. One of the chief effects of this medley-making for the extensive biblical imagery is the neutralization of the moral imperatives of religion. Even Rushworth Kidder, who sees Thomas as a religious poet, considers that the sonnets, although packed with biblical imagery, exclude 'religious commitment' [in his *Dylan Thomas: The Country of the Spirit*], There is in fact a carnival atmosphere in the sonnets, a sense of illusion and flamboyance, as each item declares itself, like an item in a Mardi Gras parade, momentous and momentary. Since the syntax here, as in **'To-day, this insect'** is generally permissive and sometimes quite dissolute, there is little to check or organize the tumble and flow. As we read, the unregulated phrases tend to rub and mingle promiscuously, creating a reading experience that is both exciting and disturbing.

A test run through a particular passage in sonnet two will provide examples of this behaviour.

> The horizontal cross-bones of Abaddon,
> You by the cavern over the black stairs,
> Rung bone and blade, the verticals of Adam,
> And, manned by midnight, Jacob to the stars.

In this passage it is difficult to settle on a subject (cross-bones? You? verticals? Rung, bone and blade?) or an active verb (Rung as ungrammatical for 'rang,' and deformed, as it is in sonnet three, to fit on Jacob's ladder? Jacob meaning 'to climb spiritually'?). There is a good deal of local and immediate excitement generated by the obvious associations and the potential relationships an indeterminate syntax allows: the destroying angel, pirate's flag and cave, swordfighting, Adam's aspirations, and Jacob's ladder. These are further riches to be experienced as we play the ladder against the 'black stairs,' and discover them both to be composed of vertical and horizontals, which react with images in other sonnets. Aren't these the elements of the cross from sonnet eight, and of the globe itself, seen as a ladder of latitude and longitude in sonnet three?

> We rung our weathering changes on the ladder,
> Said the antipodes, and twice spring chimed.

Global verticals and horizontals may also throw us back to the closing lines of the first sonnet, where the two tropics are presented as bed-mates of the long world's gentleman.

> I am the long world's gentleman, he said,
> And share my bed with Capricorn and Cancer.

Our minds can range freely amid such associations (other readers will have their own sets, and mine may have shifted next week) because they are not directed by the syntax, and the corresponding thematic phenomena—narrative and argument—do not speak compellingly. To put this in linguistic terms: the syntagmatic function of words-in-sequence, their local usage (which we may imagine as a horizontal axis), does not place the normal regulatory stress on their vertical paradigmatic functions, their universalizing associations. As a reading proceeds, assuming that we allow the seductions of this craft to occur, these associations may tend to converge towards synthesis. We may, for example, begin to see a unified symbol in the images of the figure on the ladder, the long world's gentleman stretched on the globe, and Christ on the cross. We may move further to intellectualize this as a common theme of aspiration and ascent, figured in the ladder/cross/latitudes and longitudes, all of them made by combining Adam's verticals with Abaddon's rungs of suffering, a paradigmatic emblem of the human struggle uniting Genesis and Revelation. But the strong centralizing symbol which would support this hypothesis (the way the cross of tales/trees of stories supplies assurance of mythic integrity in **'To-day, this insect'**) is not provided, and we are left instead with an elegant and witty possibility, uncertain as to whether the wit and elegance are the poet's or our own. It is at this point in the interpretive process that roads diverge. Do we remain with the play of imagery or move to a hypothetical bounding structure? It is very tempting to read beyond the poem, supplying such connections as syntax, argument, and dominant symbol as though the poet had absent-mindedly omitted them. In fact, it seems to be a general rule in reading that our desire for integration increases in proportion to the poet's refusal to satisfy it, a phenomenon which can lead to such brilliant fantasies as the star chart which Elder Olson proposes as a key to the sonnets.

In the sonnets, all integrating forces are weakened, and we are thrown back into a play of images. Even with the trope of metaphor itself, conventions are missing which would have assisted us towards an integrated reading. Thomas seldom uses similes or metaphors in their basic rhetorical formulations, which would indicate clearly that phrase B is a trope for phrase A, and so may be taken for it. Without such indications, we often find ourselves uncertain whether phrase B is an extension of phrase A, or whether a wholly new character or function has entered the fray. A typically ambiguous apposition might work like this: 'The bald queen of dream, the knave of knives, oiling the bloody oyster.' Are there two creatures oiling the oyster, one bald and one knavish, or do we have a single, bisexual, regal, knife-wielding oiler of oysters to contend with? This is a simplified rendition of the problem in sonnet one, where the reader is bound to be unsure whether phrases introducing Abaddon, the dog among the fairies, and the atlas-eater should function as tropes for one another, as tropes for the gentleman, or as separate characters.

> Altarwise by owl-light in the half-way house
> The gentleman lay graveward with his furies;
> Abaddon in the hangnail cracked from Adam,
> And, from his fork, a dog among the fairies,
> The atlas-eater with a jaw for news,
> Bit out the mandrake with to-morrow's scream.

Are all of these new faces on the quasi-mythic scene or, perhaps, all phrases we may substitute for the gentleman? Are Abaddon, the dog, and the atlas-eater all epithets for one unnamed character? Whose fork is it? And so on.

Corresponding to the relational difficulties encountered in the sonnets, there is an insistence upon substantiveness, upon each thing being established in itself. Without relational guideposts (syntax, theme, narrative, metaphorical relationship) each item in sonnet one's sestet proposes itself to be independent, symbolic, and important. This effect is increased by the ubiquity of the definite article, which turns images into identifying epithets or titles. In the first sonnet alone we have the half-way house, the gentleman, the atlas-eater, the mandrake, the heaven's egg, the half-way winds, the windy salvage, and the long world's gentleman. If we experimentally replace all those definite articles with indefinite ones (or, where appropriate, omit the article altogether) then read through the sonnet, the mythic portentousness, the conspicuous symbolhood of its constituents is greatly reduced. To call Babe Ruth 'a sultan of swat' or Lana Turner 'a sweater girl' would be to reduce them to the rest of us, to suggest that any of us could, with luck and practice, achieve those levels of competence. Identifying epithets are linguistic institutions, and do not need to participate in ordinary, accidental time, accumulating significance diachronically; they are already archetypes, packed with the protein of meaning, full of their own essences. Consequently, even when the reference is obscure, such items claim the stature of myth; we feel that the fake gentleman, the bagpipe-breasted ladies, the tall fish, the ladder, and the lamped calligrapher are important, but we're not sure why, and this places additional stress on the reading. In general, the emphatic nominative values in the poem encourage us to look for a stable structure, while the weak relational values frustrate that pursuit, suggesting that the flying tower exists only in fragmentary form.

One way we might perceive pattern in the sonnets without risking over-reading is to displace emphasis from narrative to style and observe that their real hero is the poet's craft itself. This, however, would not acknowledge those unmistakable signals of mythic narration, signals that the sonnets are either telling, or pretending to tell, a story of universal application. An hypothesis closer to the spirit of the poem is that the hero is in some way an incarnation of that craft—a trickster. But this, too, has its problems. How would a trickster be likely to appear? To ask this question is to probe a paradox. 'The trickster' is itself an identifying epithet which I have been quietly using as a convenient means of surrounding a set of deconstructive phenomena; it is a personification of elusiveness which gives it misleading substance. The interpretive problem which confronts us now is, I think, parallel to the problem Thomas faced while composing the sonnets. In order to delineate his protagonist accurately he had to avoid delineating him too boldly; an obvious trickster, like a conspicuous spy, would be a contradiction in terms.

One way Thomas handles this difficulty is to problematize the idea of character itself. We have already observed how Thomas's strategy of ambiguous apposition leaves us uncertain as to whether we are dealing with one character or several. A related, more dynamic, strategy is the crossing of opposed characters, an effect which is created by making them share attributes or functions. In **'To-day, this insect'** and **'I see the boys of summer'** we can observe struggles between figures of authority and subversive youth. The ageless voice and the destructive artist fill these roles in the former poem, the old men and the boys of summer in the latter. Both these poems reach a form of synthesis between the destruction that breeds obscurity and time-honoured values of tradition. The synthesis is implied in the cross of tales behind the fabulous curtain, and overtly stated in the closing section of **'I see the boys of summer,'** which acts openly as the third stage of a dialectical triad.

> I am the man your father was.
> We are the sons of flint and pitch.
> O see the poles are kissing as they cross.

The simultaneity that is described by these figures of synthesis, 'the cross,' is acted out in the Altarwise sonnets. In the first sonnet we meet the antagonists—the narrator's 'I' and the long world's gentleman—and immediately discover that their beings and functions are intertwined by linguistic action. The long world's gentleman, who proclaims himself boldly to the narrator in the last lines, is also known as 'the gentleman,' and as 'that gentleman of wounds' in the first sonnet, and as 'the wounded whisper,' 'the fake gentleman,' 'the long wound,' 'my gentle wound,' and 'my long gentleman' in those which follow. To construe a single being in that string of aliases (he is also known by the synecdoche 'old cock from nowhere' in sonnets one and six, and may be 'the black ram' of sonnet three) is of course to brook a considerable attenuation of the idea of character. We are persuaded to accept some latitude in the notion of persons, running through linguistic permutations of the words 'long,' 'gentleman,' and 'wound,' in order to achieve a measure of coherence.

As these antagonists are introduced they are already crossing. In the difficult opening lines, two contrary narratives compete for dominance in the same syntactical structure: the gentleman creates the child/narrator, while he is simultaneously destroyed by his creation. In the act of reading, this ambiguity functions like those figure-ground puzzles in which one sees either a vase or two faces, depending on one's point of view. As noted above, this ambiguity is due in part to the open relation of phrases in apposition. Here are the lines again.

> Altarwise by owl-light in the half-way house
> The gentleman lay graveward with his furies;
> Abaddon in the hangnail cracked from Adam,
> And, from his fork, a dog among the fairies,
> The atlas-eater with a jaw for news,
> Bit out the mandrake with to-morrow's scream.

It is crucial to this crossing that 'his fork' can be read as the gentleman's loins or as the child's birth as a divided being, the sense in which Thomas uses the word 'fork' in **'In the beginning.'** It is also crucial that the mandrake serve not only as a symbol of the gentleman's phallus but also as an *homunculus* representing the body of the child. Hence the gentlemen 'bites out' the child's body in procreation; the child being created bites out the gentleman's phallus: the two acts are simultaneous both imagistically and syntactically. Abaddon, the destroying angel, and Adam, infant man and the father of mankind, may then be seen to represent functions filled simultaneously by the

gentleman and the child/narrator, and not as the fixed symbolic identities of either one.

When we read this way, remaining open to possibility, exploring illicit syntactical and narrative deformations without relinquishing our native desire for overall sense, we may come to view characters as moments in the ongoing process, beings upon which the actions of the poem work to wean them away from substance into energy. Characters become events; the balance shifts from nouns performing actions to actions using nouns as their agents. In a simple poem like **'The force that through the green fuse drives the flower,'** Thomas can lay out modes of simultaneity in a form that is syntactically rigorous: there is a natural force which is at once creative and destructive; and this force affects the narrator equally with the physical world.

> The force that through the green fuse drives the
>   flower
> Drives my green age; that blasts the roots of
>   trees
> Is my destroyer.
> And I am dumb to tell the crooked rose
> My youth is bent by the same wintry fever.

The syntactical formula established by this stanza is used, with only slight variation, in all four. This regular, explanatory syntax carries its own signal. The force is tamed by language which seems to hold and dispense it in perfectly cadenced, uniform structures. There are few such formal or syntactical checks in the sonnets, where the energies native to language, amplified by the associative relations, often seem to propagate without natural enemies.

The antagonists who cross in the opening sestet of sonnet one are permitted by the octave's regular syntax to emerge as relatively distinct and independent figures. It is as though there were an absolute simultaneity of being during the creative act, a moment of pure energy which sweeps away stable identity. In the aftermath the narrative 'I' is clearly seen to be a child in his cradle, and the long world's gentleman is developed in a series of epithets culminating in his self-declaration in the last two lines.

> Then, penny-eyed, that gentleman of wounds,
> Old cock from nowheres and the heaven's egg,
> With bones unbuttoned to the half-way winds,
> Hatched from the windy salvage on one leg,
> Scraped at my cradle in a walking word
> That night of time under the Christward shelter:
> I am the long world's gentleman, he said,
> And share my bed with Capricorn and Cancer.

Distinctive attributes are suggested here: the long world's gentleman is a creator; he is wounded, in all likelihood by the child who 'bit out the mandrake'; and he seems to be a cosmological man, something akin to the sun-hero Elder Olson sees voyaging between the tropics. On the one hand, these epithets drawn from various symbolic systems substantiate the figure; but on the other they create new problems because the attributes are contradictory. He is both a Christ-like figure, as reinforced in the crucifixion which occurs in sonnet eight, and a much lustier fertility figure, an 'Old cock' who shares his bed with two cosmic figures. The phrase 'Old cock from nowheres and the heaven's egg' dramatizes the problem, since it blatantly contradicts itself: wandering bum from a negative matrix like a character by Samuel Beckett, or legatee of the gods, hatched from the heaven's egg like Castor and Pollux? Two alien philosophies, two attitudes to structure, two relationships to tradition, are implied. Adding to the sense of the old cock as sexual athlete working against his Christ-like qualities is the implicit reference to the work of Henry Miller, whose notorious tropics novels were favourites of Thomas's. (**'Lament,'** the poetic biography of an 'old ram rod' who is gradually reduced from virility to domesticated entropy, was originally dedicated to Miller.) By having his figure 'hatched from the windy salvage on one leg,' Thomas wittily plays the Christ-like and reprobate elements at once: a crucified man is one-legged (cf 'pinlegged on pole-hills' in sonnet five); but so also is a pirate like Long John Silver, the fictional trickster who hatches from several windy salvages, and whose name may be echoed by the long world's gentleman. Perhaps the method of characterization, the *bricolage,* and the diversity of attributes are of greatest significance here. By creating such strains, Thomas insists on the supremacy of his intention over those encoded in the source materials. We can, I think, see in the combination of saviour and reprobate, of victim and aggressor, outsider from nowheres and insider from the heaven's egg, Thomas's own version of the trickster inhabiting his own myth with subversive élan.

Before the long world's gentleman crosses with the narrator again in sonnet eight, we may (again assuming some elasticity in 'character') identify him as an active agent in sonnets four and five. As everywhere in the sonnets, these contexts are capable of provoking whole cabbalas of speculative explication. I will attempt to confine mine to the appearance of the gentleman in relation to the narrator. In sonnet four there is a 'wounded whisper' who is nagged by the narrator's sharp, unanswerable questions. We might see these as indications that the narrator is probing the conditions of life, interrogating existence in a way which fits the trickster's methods and will be recognized by anyone who has survived a five-year-old.

> What is the metre of the dictionary?
> The size of genesis? the short spark's gender?
> Shade without shape? the shape of Pharaoh's
>   echo?
> (My shape of age nagging the wounded whisper).
> Which sixth of wind blew out the burning gentry?
> (Questions are hunchbacks to the poker marrow).

These questions have the enigmatic bite of cosmic riddles or koans, answerable, if at all, only in metaphors which extend conventional notions of reality. Such riddling is a linguistic probing for loopholes, an undoing of the ordinary by the poetic consciousness. It is aimed at the parent representing the established order—the long world's gentleman now recast as gentry, or Pharaoh—and seems to contribute to his decline.

When the gentleman appears in sonnet five we may well ask whether Thomas has moved from composite portraiture to the splitting of characters. Is the 'fake gentleman in suit of spades' another version of the figure, or his inauthentic surrogate, an impostor?

> And from the Windy West came two-gunned
>   Gabriel,
> From Jesu's sleeve trumped up the king of spots,
> The sheath-decked jacks, queen with a shuffled
>   heart;
> Said the fake gentleman in suit of spades,
> Black-tongued and tipsy from salvation's bottle.

The passage speaks about, and demonstrates, the craft of illusions—sleight of hand in poker, tall tales in religion and the Wild West. Thomas displaces the biblical characters to the saloon where they lose their traditional attributes and play dubious poker. What's the king of spots doing up Jesu's sleeve, in either a card-playing or a theological context? But beyond the usual image-play and mythic dislocation there is a duplicity to the narrative structure. Thomas withholds the important news that the first three lines are spoken by the fake gentleman, surely no reliable source, until the fourth line, with the result that we are likely to read them first as 'gospel,' then as 'pseudo-gospel' or windy religiosity. Analysed synchronically, the passage seems to be a tale within a tale within a tale. The fake gentleman, himself drunk on religion, told a story about two-gunned Gabriel, who was involved in a card game in which the cards played mysteriously allegorical roles. There is no firm ground in these lines; nothing is what it seems; no one is bona fide. The narrator, having identified the gentleman as a fake, turns away from his religiosity to embark on a sea voyage which is filled with surreal adventures strongly suggestive of sexuality.

Interaction between the protagonists reaches a climax in sonnet eight, where there is a crucifixion, and a subsequent spreading of blessings of mankind. But more importantly for those interested in the subversions of craft, there is an interpretative problem arising out of mythological anomaly. The sonnet clearly contains a narrator and a crucified victim, who is addressed by the narrator as 'Jack Christ,' and whom we may identify as the long world's gentleman because the Mary figure is called the 'long wound's woman.' But this sorting of personae leaves the narrator, and not the crucified Christ-figure, making the large gestures which embrace humanity. It is the narrator who suffers the heaven's children through his heartbeat; and it is from his nipples that the rainbow which surrounds the globe originates.

> This was the sky, Jack Christ, each minstrel
>   angle
> Drove in the heaven-driven of the nails
> Till the three-coloured rainbow from my nipples
> From pole to pole leapt round the snail-waked
>   world.
> I by the tree of thieves, all glory's sawbones,
> Unsex the skeleton this mountain minute,
> And by this blowclock witness of the sun
> Suffer the heaven's children through my heartbeat.

A consistent religious interpretation cannot tolerate the usurpation of Christ's role by the narrator. H. H. Kleinman admits the difficulty with the speakers, then presents a reading which preserves the integrity of the mythic paradigm by splitting the narrative voice and assuming the narrator's identification with Christ.

> It is difficult at times to determine who the speaker is in the sonnet. The 'Jack Christ,' for example, is confusing because it sounds like direct address. But Thomas has mixed pronouns and shifted tenses before; and the only conclusion I can draw is that his identification with Christ in this sonnet is complete. . . . In the seventh line [the first in the octave, quoted above] it is Thomas who speaks for a moment, in the role of guide, to point out the place of the Crucifixion; but, before the line is ended, Christ speaks again.

This is one way out of the difficulty, although the strain of the interpretive doctrine on the poetic action is intense. Kleinman, and most other critics, are skirting an outrage which is, if we read along the lines we've been following, close to the heart of Thomas's poetics: the narrator, 'all glory's sawbones,' unsexes the skeleton, and, with this symbol of potency in hand, is able to spread divine power to humanity. 'This blowclock,' following hard upon the unsexing, may surely be read as the gentleman's genitalia; this form of apotheosis was prefigured by the action of biting out the mandrake during the creative act. The word brings with it an association which reinforces the idea of a fertility symbol: a blowclock is a dandelion head gone to seed, and 'blowing the clock' means dispersing the seeds with a puff of breath. Thomas is violating the integrity of the Christian myth by moving the redemptive function from the Christ-figure to the narrator and by superimposing a fertility rite on the crucifixion. His actions as a poet are equivalent to the actions of the narrator: both are stealing power from the authorities, and both insist that it be disseminated within the temporal sphere.

It is frequently observed that the later Thomas envisioned a more harmonious universe, while he modified the furious dialectics of these early poems towards the relaxed and easy lyrics of the forties. In sonnet ten, such a vision is projected as a final resolution to his strategies of creative destruction and destructive creation. Significantly enough, Thomas presents an image of two 'bark towers' in a flying garden, an edenic context which will come about when the creative and destructive forces unite, and the poet is, presumably, not perpetually dismantling his flying towers.

> Green as beginning, let the garden diving
> Soar, with its two bark towers, to that Day
> When the worm builds with the gold straws of
>   venom
> My nest of mercies in the rude, red tree.

The trickster worm, ubiquitous in Thomas's imagery and craft, is to be the active agent in bringing about this marvellous upper-case Day, making a nest in the cross out of venom. Providing the vehicle for the worm's activities is, as we've observed, one motive of Thomas's poetics. We should also note, in this sonnet, that the narrator is keeping this climactic vision suspended while continuing to practise an art which subverts and recreates inherited materials, essentially the same suspension of closure as the bardic poet maintains in **'After the funeral.'** The 'shipracked' gospel and the 'blown word' indicate that he is

dealing with the scraps and salvaged fragments rather than whole doctrines. And he throws the flying garden up out of a very obscure context which (whatever else it does) reforms biblical materials in an aggressively irreverent manner.

> Let the first Peter from a rainbow's quayrail
> Ask the tall fish swept from the bible east,
> What rhubarb man peeled in her foam-blue
>   channel
> Has sown a flying garden round that sea-ghost?

Is Peter asking impertinent questions of Christ? Is the flying garden created by the mating of Mary and a rhubarb man? That the last, apocalyptic images should owe their being to this obscure context (the garden is sown here) is entirely appropriate. For these are still the tactics of the trickster, the tactics of the worm, that architect of human paradise. (pp. 375-93)

> *Don McKay, "Crafty Dylan and the Altarwise Sonnets: 'I Build a Flying Tower and I Pull It Down'," in* University of Toronto Quarterly, *Vol. LV, No. 4, Summer, 1986, pp. 375-94.*

Linden Peach   (essay date 1988)

[*In the following excerpt from his* The Prose Writing of Dylan Thomas, *Peach studies Thomas's delineation of the individual within a community, noting similarities between James Joyce's* Dubliners *(1914) and* A Portrait of the Artist as a Young Man *(1916) and Thomas's later prose.*]

While [Thomas's] early work was written under the shadow of Caradoc Evans's influence, [his] later work was written under the influence of James Joyce. The latter has been noted but never really explored. Yet it was crucial to Thomas's developing concern with the relationship between the community and the individual.

There is, of course, no single explanation for why the period 1938-40 was such an important period of transition as far as Thomas's prose style was concerned. It would be short-sighted not to take into account the poor reception which the collections of short stories and poetry received in 1937. Indeed, if the poor reception were not enough Thomas's attempts to get them published in the first place had been fraught with difficulty. *The Burning Baby* which Thomas had contracted with the Europa Press had run into difficulties at the eleventh hour when the printers refused to go ahead because the work was believed to be obscene.

There is no gainsaying, though, the influence of Joyce's *A Portrait of the Artist as a Young Man* and of the *Dubliners.* Without embarking upon a copious exploration of the significance, Tindall, for example, attaches great importance to both of them [*A Reader's Guide to Dylan Thomas*]. Certainly the similarities between the scheme of James Joyce's collection, *Dubliners,* and of **Portrait of the Artist as a Young Dog** are too obvious to be overlooked: each is a series of stories grouped according to different phases of growing up even though Thomas, unlike Joyce, does not include the emergence from adolescence.

It would be inconceivable, however, to attribute the transition to a realistic prose style to Thomas's reading of Joyce's work as if it were comparable to Paul's experience upon the road to Damascus. The transition to a realistic style was undoubtedly a gradual process over a number of years. In 1936 Thomas was bent on developing the surrealistic aspect of his work. He attended the surrealistic exhibition in London and was working on **'The Mouse and the Woman'**. But in writing **'A Prospect of the Sea'** Thomas was beginning to insert into the larger surrealistic framework more authentic accounts of the gradual awakening of sexual awareness in an adolescent than he had attempted to date. Although Thomas fudges the demarcation between dream and reality, young girl and princess, and in surrealistic vein gives expression to deep subconscious fears of sexuality, there are aspects which suggest that the seeds for this episode may have been sown by an incident in James Joyce's *A Portrait of the Artist as a Young Man*. In Joyce's work, Stephen Dedalus sees a young girl wading in a stream:

> She seemed like one whom magic had changed into the likeness of a strange and beautiful seabird. Her long slender bare legs were delicate as a crane's and pure save where an emerald trail of seaweed had fashioned itself as a sign upon the flesh. Her thighs, fuller and soft-hued as ivory, were bared almost to the hips, where the white fringes of her drawers were like feathering of soft white down. Her slate-blue skirts were kilted boldly about her waist and dove-tailed behind her.

There are, of course, important differences between this passage and the one in Thomas's story which we are arguing was inspired by it. Joyce's passage seems more obviously rooted in the author's personal experience; Thomas's smacks overtly of fantasy. But in both stories the girl's skirt is lifted to the waist and the boy is disarmed by the girl's boldness. The girl in Thomas's piece is more audacious and inviting. She has dispensed with drawers and the boy can see she is well sun-tanned:

> All of it happened in half a second. The girl in the torn cotton frock sat down on the grass and crossed her legs; a real wind from nowhere lifted her frock, and up to her waist she was brown as an acorn.

The disappearances of the girls are not without similarity. In Joyce's book:

> Long, long she suffered his gaze and then quietly withdrew her eyes from his and bent them towards the stream, gently stirring the water with her foot hither and thither. The first faint noise of gently moving water broke the silence, low and faint, and whispering, faint as the bells of sleep. . . . He turned away from her suddenly and set off across the strand. His cheeks were aflame; his body was aglow; his limbs were trembling. On and on and on and on he strode, far out over the sands, singing wildly to the sea, crying to greet the advent of the life that had cried to him.

In Thomas's story the stress is on fear, disappointment

and loss. Like the girl in Joyce's story, the girl in Thomas's story leaves very suddenly and inexplicably:

> Now her face was a white drop of water in the horizontal rainfall. . . . Now the heart in her breast was a small red bell that rang in a wave. . . . He cried again, but she had mingled with the people moving in and out. Their tides were drawn by a grave moon that never lost an arc. . . . The bell in her breast was ringing over the sand. . . . He ran to the yellow foot of the dunes, calling over his shoulder. 'Run out of the sea'. . . . He stumbled on over sand and sandflowers like a blind boy in the sun.

The bell image is taken up and developed by Thomas, but the young man while running frantically as in Joyce's work is chasing after the girl not running as an expression of his uplifted spirits.

There are several examples in the prose written in the late 1930s and early 1940s of Thomas's expansion of ideas from Joyce's work. There can be little doubt that Mrs. Dacey in *Adventures in the Skin Trade* is based upon Mrs. Mooney in 'The Boarding House' in the *Dubliners* and that Polly in Thomas's story is based upon Polly in Joyce's story. Joyce says of Mrs. Mooney that 'she governed the house cunningly and firmly, knew when to give credit, when to be stern and when to let things pass'. When Mrs. Dacey first appears in *Adventures in the Skin Trade* she has the steely, self-sufficiency of Mrs. Mooney. The first words she utters are germane with her appearance:

> A tall, thin, dignified woman came through the private door at the back of the shop, her hands clasped in front of her. She was dressed in black almost down to the ankles, with a severe white collar, and she held her head primly as though it might spill. God help the other nine hundred and ninety-nine. But she smiled then, and her eyes were sharp and light; the dullness raced from her mouth, leaving it cruel and happy.
>
> 'Take your trotter off the door', she said.

This impression of her as candid and outspoken is confirmed by the description of her spectacles with 'steel rims and a hanging chain'. The fact that she hides her private self behind her public face is reinforced by the way in which when she first enters the story it is through a private door and she wears a dress down to the ankles. (In *Under Milk Wood* . . . Jack Black has a nightshirt down to and tied at the ankles).

While no more a clone of Joyce's Polly than Mrs. Dacey is of Mrs. Mooney, Thomas's character is clearly indebted to her Irish namesake. Joyce describes an aspect of Polly which once again Thomas picks up and develops:

> As Polly was very lively, the intention was to give her the run of the young men. Besides, young men like to feel that there is a young woman not very far away. Polly, of course, flirted with the young men, but Mrs. Mooney, who was a shrewd judge, knew that the young men were only passing the time away; none of them meant business.

Thomas's Polly, too, is a flirt; and Dylan Thomas takes up

and develops the mischevious aspect, the obvious enjoyment in teasing men and leading them on. Both characters display a stubborn, rebellious kind of sexuality. Polly Mooney sings to herself:

> I'm a . . . naughty girl
> You needn't sham:
> You know I am.

As Joyce says of her: 'Her eyes, which were grey with a shade of green through them, had a habit of glancing upwards when she spoke with anyone, which made her look like a little perverse madonna.' It is this aspect of Polly Mooney that Thomas stresses in the first meeting between his character and Samuel Bennet where Polly's habit of 'glancing upwards' is transformed into a disarming 'upward stare':

> Polly bent over Samuel's hand and he saw down
> her dress. She knew that he was looking, but she
> did not start back or spread her hand across the
> neck of her dress; she raised her head and stared
> at his eyes. I shall always remember this, he said
> to himself.

Joyce encouraged Thomas to think about his own sexual awakening. In many ways this was compatible with the concern in the early stories with sexuality and a repressive environment. Under Joyce's influence, Thomas began to think about the role of repression in his own life and, as we shall see, fear, shame and guilt enter into several of the stories about his adolescence. But Joyce also encouraged Thomas to think about the community in which he grew up and the way in which this could become a major force in his writing. Thomas's early stories concern people who live outside the main community, in isolated rural areas. Often they involve people travelling considerable distances, as in **'The Holy Six'** and **'The School for Witches'**, which only serve to underline the isolation of the localities in which they are set and the limited possibilities of fulfilment for the people who live in them.

In most of the stories in *A Portrait of the Artist as a Young Dog,* however, the focus of interest has shifted from isolated rural communities to urban South Wales and at the same time Thomas seems to have managed to get himself out from under Caradoc Evans's influence. Hence, the stories have a kind of double perspective: looking inward and back to his own development while at the same time also looking outward to the community.

In writing *Under Milk Wood,* Thomas admittedly returns to the rural community of Llareggub. Yet here, unlike in the early stories, there is a sense of a close community which we do not have in the pre 1937 work and the realisation of which could only have followed the delineation of community in *A Portrait of the Artist as a Young Dog.* As Lawrence Lerner has said: the 'really urban thing about it is the closeness and curiosity of the neighbours' [in his *The Uses of Nostalgia: Studies in Pastoral Poetry*].

There are several ways in which the delineation of community in *A Portrait of the Artist as a Young Dog* owes much to Joyce's *Dubliners.* Thomas's post 1938 prose writing is distinguished from the early work by the precision of the description. How much Thomas's new realism

Thomas reading poetry.

owes to Joyce is obvious by placing an extract from the two authors side by side. Joyce's precise mode of description is well-illustrated in this piece from 'A Painful Case':

> When he gained the crest of the Magazine Hill
> he halted and looked along the river towards
> Dublin, the lights of which burned redly and
> hospitably in the cold night. . . . Beyond the
> river he saw a goods train winding out of the
> Knightsbridge Station, like a worm with a fiery
> head winding through the darkness, obstinately
> and laboriously It passed slowly out of sight; but
> still he heard in his ears the laborious drone of
> the engine reiterating the syllables of her name.

The extent to which Thomas followed Joyce is evident in this passage. There is the same attention to detail and the same sense of recreating a particular community. But Thomas combines precision with more elaborate imagery:

> The strangers, huddled against the wall, their
> hands deep in their pockets, their cigarettes
> sparkling, stared, I thought, at the thickening of
> the dark over the empty sands, but their eyes
> may have been closed. A train raced over us, and
> the arch shook. Over the shore, behind the vanishing train, smoke clouds flew together, rags of

wings and hollow bodies of great birds black as tunnels, and broke up lazily; cinders fell through a sieve in the air, and the sparks were put out by the wet dark before they reached the sand.

The above passage demonstrates how Thomas developed under Joyce's influence not only a new-found precision in his writing but a deep-rooted melancholy. At the end of *Portrait of the Artist as a Young Dog* Jack finds himself alone as 'all round him the disturbed inhabitants of the house were falling back into sleep'. This type of scene occurs again in **'Just Like Little Dogs'** and the melancholy is enhanced by the contrast between the warmth of family and community, on the one hand, and the individual's solitariness, on the other:

> Families sat down to supper in rows of short houses, the wireless sets on, the daughters' young men sat in front rooms. In neighbouring houses they read the news off the table-cloth, and the potatoes from dinner were fried up.

Solitariness enhances Thomas's sense of his own individual being: 'I was a lonely nightwalker and a steady stander-at-corners. I liked to walk through the wet town after midnight when the streets were deserted and the window lights out, alone and alive . . . '. While he is detached from the community in a physical sense as an onlooker he also establishes a vicarious, albeit melancholic, sympathy with it:

> I never felt more a part of the remote and over-pressing world, or more full of love and arrogance and pity and humility, not for myself alone, but for the living earth I suffered on . . .

Here Thomas was undoubtedly influenced by passages from stories such as Joyce's 'Two Gallants' where, Lenehan compares his loneliness on the street with the sense of belonging he still hopes to find:

> How pleasant it would be to have a warm fire to sit by and a good dinner to sit down to. He had walked the streets long enough with friends and with girls. . . . All hope had not left him . . . he might yet be able to settle down in some snug corner and live happily if he could only come across some good simpleminded girl with a little of the ready.

All this is not to say that the melancholy was actually implanted by Joyce. But the way in which Thomas appropriated and developed the contrast between the melancholic individual and the community enables us to see how Joyce helped Thomas to realise and articulate an important aspect of his experience of the Welsh urban community in which he grew up.

The characters in *Portrait of the Artist as a Young Dog* belong to the Welsh working-class of surburban Swansea whereas the early stories contain characters who belong to a rural and more puritanical Wales. The stories lift these people out of the anonymity of working-class city life but always with an awareness that they belong to a community and way of life that is disappearing as the final scene of *Portrait of the Artist as a Young Dog* forcefully suggests:

> Then he walked out of the house on to the waste space and under the leaning cranes and ladders. The light of the one weak lamp in a rusty circle fell across the brick heaps and the broken wood and the dust that had been houses once, where the small and hardly known and never-to-be-forgotten people of the dirty town had lived and loved and died and, always, lost.

Here the pathos is heightened, as in Gray's 'Elegy in a Country Churchyard', by the sense of 'for them nomore' and by the way the people are distanced so as to exclude any grossness in their actual existence, and by the sense of futility with which the passage closes 'and, always, lost'.

Despite his claim in 1946 that all writing coming out of Wales is simply English, Thomas, in his own work, tried to reproduce the rhythms and idiosyncracies that distinguish Anglo-Welsh from simply English speech. Here Thomas was following a lead set by Carodoc Evans even though Thomas reproduces the English speech of people whose first language is English, albeit influenced by certain characteristics of the Welsh tongue, while Evans tried to reproduce the speech of a people whose first language was Welsh or translated Welsh speech into English while trying to retain the flavour of the original. Thomas follows Evans also in trying to relate speech closely to character and in exploiting the contrast between people's styles of speech for comic and/or dramatic effect.

Contrast is an important part of the following exchange between Rachel and Ianto from Evans's 'An Offender in Siôn', although it is undermined somewhat by over-reliance upon the inversion of the subject-verb-object pattern. Rachel's greater clarity of speech reflects the greater acuity of mind, while Ianto's less agile speech prepares us for his sudden violent outburst:

> In the morning Ianto [sic] went to Coed. Rachel saw him when he was afar off, and she put on her a white apron and she puffed up her hair.
>
> 'How you was, female?' asked Ianto.
>
> Rachel feigned pleasure. 'Put yourself in a chair', she said.
>
> 'Here am I on small business'.
>
> 'Certain sure me', replied Rachel. 'Close the door will I'.
>
> 'No-no, Rachel Enoch Coed. Heap of dung you are to flaunt your body before me'.
>
> 'Deal you evenly now with your maid', Rachel pleaded. 'Sorry am I to know your message'.

The contrast between English speech rhythms and Welsh speech rhythms is a critical part of Evans's 'The Pretender' where the English speaking Maria returns home to her Welsh village:

> A tall girl stepped out of a third-class compartment.
>
> 'Maria', exclaimed Twmi, 'How you are?'
>
> 'How are you, dad?' she returned, in English, taking the tips of his fingers in her gloved hands,

and kissing him on the brim of his hat. 'And ma, is she well?'

The English that Maria speaks is colder and more formal than her father's Welsh as are her mannerisms. She can only take the tips of his fingers and kiss the brim of his hat. Only at the end of the story when she rediscovers her Welsh is Maria able to communicate fully.

In Thomas's **'The Peaches'** the absence of a Welsh idiom is associated, as in 'The Pretender', with distance and formality, with a sense of superiority, extreme forwardness and a lack of caring. It is a crucial part of the tension in Mrs. Williams's visit between herself, the Welsh boys and Annie:

> 'Don't bother about me, there's a dear', said Mrs. Williams. 'There's a lovely fox!' she flashed finger of rings at the glass case.
>
> 'It's real blood', I told Jack, and we climbed over the sofa to the table.
>
> 'No, it isn't', he cried, 'it's red ink'.
>
> 'Oh, your shoes!' said Annie.
>
> 'Don't tread on the sofa, Jack, there's a dear'.
>
> 'If it isn't ink it's paint then'.
>
> Gwilym said: 'Shall I get you a bit of cake, Mrs. Williams?'
>
> Annie rattled the tea-cups. 'There isn't a single bit of cake in the house', she cried, 'we forgot to order it from the shop; not a single bit. Oh, Mrs. Williams!'
>
> Mrs. Williams said: 'Just a cup of tea thanks'. She was still sweating because she had walked all the way from the car. It spoiled her powder. She sparkled her rings and dabbed at her face.

There are several techniques here. The natural warmth of Dylan and Gwilym contrasts with Annie's unease and anxiety to impress and Mrs. Williams's stiff-backed reticence and uncomfortableness. The pertinent association of a character with an object such as jewellery or clothes—in the case of Mrs. Williams with rings and also in this story of Annie with her scruffy gym shoes—is a long established technique of description which Thomas both employs and regularly parodies. But neither of these techniques is more important than the effective contrast between the genteel and the ordinary working-class idiom.

Although Evans was an early influence upon Thomas's use of dialogue, the greater subtlety and precision of the dialogue in *Portrait of the Artist as a Young Dog* compared with the early prose undoubtedly owed much to Joyce's *Dubliners*. In particular Joyce, like Thomas and Evans, but with a more sophisticated ear than the latter, matches dialogue with character; as for example in the way Corley speaks roughly to belie his air of gentility:

> 'One night, man', he said, 'I was going along Dame Street and I spotted a fine tart under Waterhouse's clock, and said good night, you know. . . . The next Sunday, man, I met her by appointment. We went out to Donnybrook and

I brought her into a field there. She told me she used to go with a dairyman. . . . It was fine, man. Cigarettes every night she'd bring me, and paying the tram out and back. And one night she brought me two bloody fine cigars—O, the real cheese you know, that the old fellow used to smoke. . . . I was afraid, man, she'd get in the family way. But she's up to the dodge . . . ' She doesn't know my name. I was too hairy to tell her that man. But she thinks I'm a bit of class, you know.

Joyce encouraged Thomas to turn his ear to the popular usages of Anglo-Welsh speech as he had turned his ear to the Anglo-Irish tongue. Thus in **'Old Garbo'** we have a recreation of popular idiom which is far more precise than anything attempted by Evans:

> 'They look all right in their working clothes', he said. 'You catch them when they're all dolled up, they're awful. I knew a little nurse once, she looked a peach in her uniform, really refined; no, really, I mean. I picked her up on the prom one night, she was in her Sunday best. There's a difference; she looked like a bit of Marks and Spencer's'.

As in Joyce's case, the effect is achieved by a combination of popular usage and rhythm. But Thomas followed Joyce in the way snippets of dialogue are used to convey a sense of excitement or humour, as in the following sequence from Joyce's 'Araby':

> At the door of the stall a young lady was talking and laughing with two young gentlemen. I remarked their English accents and listened vaguely to their conversation:
>
> 'O, I never said such a thing!'
>
> 'O, but you did!'
>
> 'O, but you didn't'
>
> 'Didn't she say that?'
>
> 'Yes, I heard her'
>
> 'O, there's a . . . fib!'

So accurate is the ear for the rhythm that in Thomas's case, too, the reader feels as if he is eavesdropping as in this example from **'Old Garbo'**:

> The bar was empty. An old man whose hands trembled but behind the counter, staring at his turnip watch.
>
> 'Merry Christmas, Pa.'
>
> 'Good evening, Mr. F.'
>
> 'Drop of rum, Pa.'
>
> A red bottle shook over two glasses.
>
> 'Very special poison, son.'
>
> 'This'll make your eyes bulge', said Mr. Farr.

The contrast between Polly's voice and Samuel's is an essential part of the exchange in which Polly tries to persuade Samuel who has his finger stuck in a bottle to take a bath with her. Samuel's Anglo-Welsh lilt is an appropriate medium for his mounting terror. Polly's precise, accurate grammar aptly conveys her command and self-confidence quite apart from the way in which she, like Polly Mooney, enjoys teasing men:

> 'You do being quiet. Do being a quiet lady sitting on a bath, Polly'.
>
> 'I will if you'll come and have a swim with me. You promised'. She patted her hair into place.
>
> 'Where?'
>
> 'In the bath. You get in first, go on. You can't break your promise'.
>
> George Ring, he whispered, gallop upstairs now and bite your way through the door. She wants me to sit with my overcoat on and my bottle on my finger in the cold, greasy bath, in the half-dark bathroom, under the sneering birds.
>
> 'I've got a new suit', he said.
>
> 'Take it off, silly. I don't want you to go in the bath with your clothes on. Look, I'll put something over the window so you can undress in the dark. Then I'll undress, too. I'll come in the bath with you. Sam, are you frightened?'
>
> 'I don't know. Couldn't we take our clothes off and not go in the bath? I mean, if we want to take them off at all. Someone might come in. It's terribly cold, Polly. Terribly cold'.
>
> 'You're frightened. You're frightened to lie in the water with me. You won't be cold for long'.
>
> 'But there's no sense in it. I don't want to go in the bath. Let's sit here and you do being glad, Polly'.

In **'Where Tawe Flows'** Thomas uses the contrast between the different ways of speaking to help convey the tension between Mrs. Evans and the others:

> When sober, Mr. Roberts addressed Mrs. Evans [sic] as 'Ma'am' and kept the talk to weather and colds. He sprang to his feet and offered her his chair.
>
> 'No, thank you, Mr. Roberts', she said in a clear, hard voice, 'I'm going to bed at once. The cold disagrees with me'.
>
> Go to bed plain Maud, thought young Mr. Thomas, 'Will you have a little warm, Mrs. Evans, before you retire?' he said.
>
> She shook her head, gave the friends a thin smile, and said to Mr. Evans: 'Put the world right before you come to bed'.

Where characters are less individualistic than Mrs. Evans and the others in **'Where Tawe Flows'**, Thomas, like Evans, exaggerates the Anglo-Welsh speech rhythms. In **'Old Garbo'** the women who gossip are not intended as individuals but vehicles for unsympathetic malice:

> 'Mrs. Harris's little girl got the message wrong. Old Garbo's daughter's right as rain, the baby was born dead. Now the old girls want their

money back, but they can't find Garbo anywhere'. He licked his hand. I know where she's gone.

> His friend said: 'To a boozer over the bridge'.
>
> In low voices the women reviled Mrs. Prothero, liar, adulteress, mother of bastards, thief.
>
> 'She got you know what'.
>
> 'Never cured it'.
>
> 'Got Charlie tattooed on her'.
>
> 'Three and eight she owes me'.
>
> 'Two and ten'.
>
> 'Money for my teeth'.
>
> 'One and a tanner out of my Old Age'.

The speed of the exchange here, and the faithful, although slightly caricatured, reproduction of the Anglo-Welsh idiom, anticipates the exchange between voices in *Under Milk Wood:*

> First Neighbour
> Poor Mrs. Waldo
> Second Neighbour
> What she puts up with
> First Neighbour
> Never should of married
> Second Neighbour
> If she didn't have to

As in **'Old Garbo'** the snippets are able to convey not just the malice but the claustrophobic pressure a small-knit community can exert on its members.

Raymond Williams [in his "Dylan Thomas's Play for Voices," *The Critical Quarterly,* 1959] has already adequately demonstrated that the weaving of a pattern of voices, rather than an ordinary conversational sequence, which we have in *Under Milk Wood* is indebted to the 'play for voices' in the Circe episode in Joyce's *Ulysses.* He identifies several specific techniques which Thomas undoubtedly borrowed from Joyce. Both employ simple, hard chanting:

> I gave it to Molly
> Because she was jolly
> The leg of the duck
> The leg of the duck
>
> (Joyce)
>
> Boys boys boys
> Kiss Gwennie where she says
> Or give her a penny.
> Go, on Gwennie.
>
> (Thomas)

Both employ a chorus of cries:

> Try your luck on Spinning Jenny! Ten to one bar one! Sell the monkey, boys! Sell the monkey! I'll give ten to one! Ten to one bar one! (Joyce)
>
> How's it above? Is there rum and laverbread? Bosoms and robins: Concertinas? Ebenezer's bell? Fighting and onions? (Thomas)

The examples cited by Williams are repeated here because they demonstrate Williams's thesis, but also they illustrate a difference between Thomas's use of a pattern of voices and Joyce's which Williams does not point out. Thomas makes more extensive *dramatic* use of these techniques than Joyce. The chorus of voices contains not only inquisitiveness but a deep-rooted anxiety and in the chanting there is a sense of menace which gradually builds up into the pressure put upon Dicky who will not go along with the game. This difference between Joyce and Thomas is evident in some of the other examples that Williams cites. Mr. Pugh's scheme for his wife is fanciful and melodramatic but not without a strain of plausibility. We feel that in the midst of all his scheming there could be a real threat:

> Mr. Pugh minces among bad vats and jeroboams, tiptoes through spinneys of murdering herbs, agony dancing in his crucibles, and mixes especially for Mrs. Pugh a venemous porridge unknown to toxicologists which will scald and viper through her until her ears fall off like figs.

This is not the case in *Ulysses:*

> I shall have you slaughtered and skewered in my stables and enjoy a slice of you with crisp crackling from the baking tin basted and baked like suckling pig with rice and lemon or currant sauce. It will hurt you.

Understanding the dramatic use Thomas made of what he borrowed from *Ulysses* undermines [David] Holbrook's charge [in his *Dylan Thomas and Poetic Dissociation*] that realising the indebtedness only shows Thomas's prose as derivative and inferior. Holbrook finds in the account of Mog Edwards and Miss Price a number of borrowings from Joyce. Mog is described as

> her lover, tall as the town clock tower, Samson-syrup-gold-maned, whacking thighed and piping hot, thunderbolt-bass'd and barnacle-breasted, flailing up the cockles with his eyes like blow lamps and scooping low over lonely loving hotwater bottled body.

Holbrook draws attention to the parallel passage from Joyce:

> Bronze by gold, Miss Douce's head . . . sauntering gold hair. . . . She bronze, dealing from her jar thick syrup liquor for his lips . . . and syrupped with her voice. . . . Neatly she poured slowsyrupy sloe. . . . Smack. She let free sudden in rebound her nipped elastic garter smack-warm against her smackable woman's warm-hosed thigh . . .

Yet drawing attention to the parallel is of little use without considering the way in which the gold maned syrup and the smack image is used to suggest the idealised image she has of him and the confident swagger the way in which he imagines himself going to her. These images and self-images are undermined by the realisation in the work that neither of these dreams will be realised. Thus it does not say much to say as Holbrook does that Miss Price's 'yes, Mog, yes, Mog, yes, yes, yes' is an importation of Joyce's line from the end of *Ulysses:* 'Yes and his heart was going

like mad and yes I said yes I will yes'. Thomas may well intend us to remember Joyce's line but his is more desperate, more breathless, germane with the intensity of her unfulfilled passion and exacerbating the irony that she and her lover do not meet.

Joyce's work had a far-reaching, almost revolutionary effect on Thomas's style of prose writing because of a profound similarity between the two of them as writers. Thomas's work betrays several preoccupations that he has in common with Joyce which are developed in *Portrait of the Artist as a Young Dog* and subsequent writing. The most important of these is Thomas's interest in characters who are emotionally imprisoned, themselves manifesting a larger, cultural strait-jacket. Joyce's famous comment to Stanislaus about his own countrymen—'what's the matter with you is that you're afraid to live. You and people like you. The city is suffering from hemiplegia of the will'— virtually summarises Thomas's view of his own countrymen. According to Joyce it was his main reason for writing the *Dubliners:* 'I call the series *Dubliners* to betray the soul of that hemiplegia or paralysis which many consider a city'. All the stories present variations on the theme of paralysis: sexual, moral, political, intellectual, religious.

The idea of being trapped is a recurring theme in Thomas's prose. In **'Who Do you Wish Was With Us'** Ray carries with him the imprisonment of his home. His impressions of the towns he passes through with his friend, the young Dylan, betrays his deep-rooted unhappiness:

> Wasn't it gay in town this morning. Everybody laughing and smiling in their summer outfits. The kids were playing and everybody was happy

These images of freedom and fulfilment are what Ray otherwise spends his life dreaming of. But here they only serve to remind him of the prison from which he has only won a reprieve. It is not long before Ray's mind returns to his domestic nightmare:

> I used to hold my father down on the bed when he had fits. I had to change the sheets twice a day for my brother, there was blood on everything.

Dylan tries to counter his friend's depression with suggestions that become increasingly desperate: to explore, climb down to the sea, write an article and make a fortune. But taking hold of an opportunity to confide in another and unburden himself, Ray slips further and further into his own particular family prison knowing that 'once his joy in the wild, warm water was over he would return to the painful house'. In **'The Fight'**, reminding us that the way that the old have often been victims of abuse and violence is not a product of our own mass media age, Mr. Samuels, trapped by his age, and the misfortune to live beside the school railings, has to endure apples, stones and balls through his bedroom window. The story opens with an account of how Mr. Samuels has to endure Dylan staring at him, hiding uncomfortably behind his paper while the young boy waits for the old man to lose his temper.

The notion of endurance is part of Thomas's interest in the idea of being trapped in *Adventures in the Skin Trade* and elsewhere. Once Samuel in the first story in *Adventures in the Skin Trade* has vandalised his parents' living room he has to wait in his own bedroom for the time of the train so that he can leave, listening to his family bustling and making preparations for his departure while all the time worrying that they will discover what he has done, believing that eventually he would have to cut his own throat on a piece of broken china. In **'The Fight'** old Mr. Samuels has to try and sit-out the young Dylan's staring at him. In **'Where Tawe Flows'** Mary has to pull her boyfriend under the table in order to avoid her drunken father. Then she has to crouch painfully while her father finishes off the lovers' supper and licks both plates clean, all the while swearing and grumbling to himself.

In *Adventures in the Skin Trade* the concept of being trapped assumes a larger significance as part of a general failure of communication between people. Thomas becomes preoccupied with the idea of people living, as it were, on separate islands, unable to indulge in spontaneous, genuine communication. So many of the characters are cut off from one another and never become anything more than strangers to everyone else and even to themselves. Here, of course, Thomas is making explicit a motif implicit in the marriage between Uncle Jim and Aunt Annie, in *Portrait of the Artist as a Young Dog* and entering also into stories such as **'Patricia, Edith and Arnold'**, **'Where the Tawe Flows'** and **'Old Garbo'**. As Samuel Bennet leaves home for London through the back window of the cab he sees 'three strangers waving'. His moment of leaving is one of awkward reticence and embarrassment: 'His father shook him by the hand. His mother kissed him on the mouth'. The muddle on the landing that morning epitomises the way members of the family have lived as a group under the same roof but have not really communicated with each other:

> The family rushed in and out of the bathroom, never stopping to wash, and collided on the narrow top of the stairs as they nagged and bustled to get him ready.

Thomas's interest in the failure of people to communicate, in the way people remained locked within themselves, is betrayed also in his description of the travellers in the station restaurant: 'cold, stiff people with time to kill sat staring at their tea and the clock, inventing replies to questions that would never be asked'. The words 'stiff' and 'cold' remind us of corpses and later in the description of the station Thomas again evokes this sense of 'living death': 'the lonely crowd went out in a funeral procession, leaving ash and tea-leaves and newspapers'. It is evoked also in *Adventures in the Skin Trade* in the account of Rose who disappears out of sight of the others behind all the furniture heaped into Allingham's room: 'Now she was dead still on a sunk bed between the column of chairs, buried alive, soft and fat and lost in a grave in a house.' Not only are the ash, tea-leaves and newspapers evoked in the account of the station items intended for immediate consumption that soon become redundant, hence suggesting a sense of waste, but they are props which enable people to endure the isolation. Although the characters of the later stories are more fully realised than those of the early stories, Thomas carries over from the early prose, albeit in a less sensational way, an interest in how a repressive religious culture remains as a lingering influence upon the individu-

al. **'One Warm Saturday'** describes especially vividly the fears experienced by a young man, Jack, approaching a young girl, Lou, about whom he fantasises:

> He thought to run out of the room and through the miracle-making Gardens, to rush into his house and hide his head in the bed-clothes and lie all night there, dressed and trembling, her voice in his ears, his green eyes wide awake under his closed eyelids.

In this particular story it is not just the anxiety but the struggle of the adolescent to overcome the fear of rejection and the idea of sex as shameful that Thomas is exploring. Jack tries telling himself: 'But only a sick boy with tossed blood would run from his proper love into a dream, lie down in a bedroom that was full of shame.' It is too simple to suggest, as many critics have, that the stories delineate only a gradual loss of courage and boldness. The early-teenage Dylan is more full of confidence than the boy in his late teens for adolescence brings problems and fears unknown to the younger boy.

No other word recurs with as potent a puritan connotation as 'shame'. In **'One Warm Saturday'** the shame is explicitly sexual but in other stories it is also linked with the Welsh Nonconformist insistence upon respectability and the sense of somehow having failed against this yardstick. In **'Where Tawe Flows'** Mary, having been forced by the early return of her drunken father to hide under a table with her lover, finds it hard to get over her shame. The outmoded notions of puritanism are said to be responsible for her burden even though one character tries to argue that 'puritanism is a spent force'. As Mr. Evans in the story tellingly points out it is the most sensitive people who are most susceptible to its influence: 'the fact remains that an incident like that has a lasting effect on a proud, sensitive girl like Mary'. Later Mary's marriage to a respectable young man is called off because her uncle, who was to give her away, misses the wedding because he is in bed with a prostitute and 'the William Hugheses wouldn't have the niece of a man who died in those circumstances'.

The effect of shame—a sense of failure or worthlessness induced by an oppressive close-knit community—is one of the subjects of **'Old Garbo'**, a story to which we referred earlier. Mrs. Prothero, having spent most of the collection made for her by friends and neighbours in the belief that her daughter is dead, is unable to face them again when it transpires that her daughter is not dead though her grandchild is still-born. This is an especially invidious rendering of the subject because Mrs. Prothero, through no fault of her own, has been led to believe that her daughter is dead. She takes what is left of the money and spends it on drink, and eventually commits suicide rather than endure the disgrace and the hostility of the wagging tongues. While it is hinted that there might be other skeletons in Mrs. Prothero's past magnified by gossip to which this would be added, it is difficult to see that Mrs. Prothero on this occasion has done much of which to be ashamed. But the reader is able to appreciate the pressure of living inside a small-knit community and how vicious tongues can soon isolate and condemn the victim of their malice. Thomas observes, in commenting upon the empty pub, how Old

Garbo's death causes the gossips to regret their vindictiveness: 'none of Old Garbo's friends came in that night'.

The story, **'The Peaches'**, is so titled because the exotic fruit, reserved for a special visitor, signifies the aspect of Welsh chapel-going culture around which the narrative is woven. Annie's concern to set a good table to impress Mrs. Williams is part and parcel of the chapel subculture's preoccupation with respectability. As the references to the Bible carried by Mrs. Williams and to the Bible in the house indicate, we are confronted here with more than simply working-class respectability which prided itself in being superior to the criminal and brutish. Around the Welsh chapel, more so than around churches, a subculture evolved with an ethic of respectability, responsibility and often sobriety (hence, Annie's unhappiness with Jim's drinking and gambling). The values of this chapel subculture filtered through to many Welsh people who were not themselves regular chapel-goers. Thomas himself was not influenced extensively by the chapel in a direct way, like some of the characters in the early stories, but rather the values of the subculture reached him through this two-step process. Indeed an appreciation of this chapel subculture is vital to understanding Mrs. Williams's visit in the first place. The chapel subculture's members, often active in local government, administration, trade unions and friendly societies, were in many ways the ideal social inferiors of the middle-classes. **'The Peaches'** focusses upon the dichotomy between the upper-class aspirations of the subculture's members, the high esteem in which they held the upper-classes, and the less than enthusiastic upper or middle-class acknowledgement of their pretensions.

For Annie upper-class respectability is defined by a number of recognisable codes of behaviour: laying a good table, getting out the best table cloth, receiving visitors in one's best clothes. These are not the codes which the upper-classes might see as defining themselves. They define the chapel subculture's perceptions of what it means to be upper-class.

The way in which the codes are undermined in turn epitomises the way in which the narrative as a whole subverts the upper-class pretentions of the working-class. The peaches are themselves an old tin of fruit which has been in storage for some time; the best table cloth has a stain in it; Annie's best dress smells of moth balls and is worn, unintentionally, with torn gym-shoes. What it means to be of a higher-class is exposed in the narrative as not worthy of being placed on a pedestal by the insufferable behaviour of Mrs. Williams: she is small-minded, intolerant, rude, and predacious. The story presents us, though, with the upper-class as seen through working-class eyes. Thus, there is a rather simple dichotomy between the working-class characters—who are warm, spontaneous, considerate—and the upper-class characters who are cold, stiff-backed and unable to communicate with those outside their own class. But codes such as the stained cloth, the Sunday best out of mothballs and Annie's excessive fawning—'trying to smile and curtsy, tidying her hair, wiping her hands on her pinafore'—undermine the aspirations reflected by them.

Most of the characters from Thomas's urban, chapel sub-

culture aspire, nevertheless, to respectability. Unfortunately, to be seen to be respectable is sometimes more important than actually being respectable. In **'One Warm Saturday'**, Mrs. Franklin complaining about the lovers who take advantage of Swansea's dunes, maintains 'if you go for a constitutional after stop-tap along the sands you might as well be in Sodom and Gomorrah'. She is tripped up smartly by one of her young friends: 'Hark to Mrs. Grundy! I see her with a blackman last Wednesday, round by the museum.' Not to be shamed, Mrs. Franklin pleads for the respectability of her lover: 'He was an Indian from the University College' she cleverly changes the issue to one of racial prejudice: 'Everyone's brothers under the skin.' Yet she sidesteps into touch for in her eyes to be black is not as respectable as to be white so she has to insist 'there is no tar brush in my family', to dispell doubt among her friends.

The censorious nature of a close-knit puritan community, shame and respectability are important motifs in *Under Milk Wood* epitomised in the way in which Waldo recalls both his mother's and his wife's fear of what the neighbours will say. The sing-song rhythms of the Anglo-Welsh lilt render gossip a fast-flowing stream of invective which Captain Cat parodies:

> Who's having a baby, who blacked whose eye,
> seen Polly Garter giving her belly an airing,
> there should be a law, seen Mrs. Beynon's new
> mauve jumper, it's her old grey jumper dyed,
> who's dead, who's dying, there's a lovely day, oh
> the cost of soapflakes!

His mocking imitation brings out the vicious way in which the community insists upon thinking the worst of everybody. He exposes the envy—the new mauve jumper must be the old grey one dyed—and also the inconsistency. Almost in the same breath that they condemn Polly for her promiscuity they jeer at Mae—'seventeen and never been kissed ho, ho'—for her chastity and reticence. Through gossip and harsh condemnation, the community imposes its own kind of discipline on those who do not conform, parodied in the way the girls taunt the boy, Dicky:

> Put him in the river
> Up to his liver
> Quick Quick Dirty Dick
> Beat him on the bum
> With a rhubarb stick

In the account of the treatment handed out to Dicky the girls are described as birds of prey and the viciousness of the close-knit community further emphasised by the way the sins of the parents are visited on the children:

> And the shrill girls giggle and master around
> him and squeal as they clutch and thrash, and
> he blubbers away downhill with his patched
> pants falling, and his tear-splashed blush burns
> all the way as the triumphant bird-like sisters
> scream with buttons in their claws and the bully
> brothers hoot after him his little nickname and
> his mother's shame and his father's wickedness
> with the loose wild barefoot women of the hovels
> of the hills.

Once again it is both ironical and hypocritical that the

children who condemn his parents for their impropriety turn on Dicky because he refuses to kiss Gwennie or pay a forfeit of a penny because his mother had forbidden him.

Caradoc Evans had no time for small communities especially small Welsh communities, remembering in *Ideas* (1916) 'little villages hidden in valleys and reeking with malice'. The sentiment pervades his short stories and seems to have rubbed off on Thomas. In **'The Orchards'** Llareggub—bugger all backwards—is the telling name of a village and is, of course, also the name of the community in *Under Milk Wood* (though the name for the sake of, supposedly, propriety was spelt Llaregyb in the 1954 edition of the play). In **'The Burning Baby'** Llareggub is the name of a 'sow-faced woman' who first taught Rhys Rhys the 'terrors' of the flesh.

However, Evans was not the only influence on Thomas in this respect. Once again we have to return to James Joyce for there are enough parallels between the work of the Irish and Anglo-Welsh writer to suggest that the former awakened Thomas to the significance of the concepts of respectability and shame in a puritan community. They enter into several of the stories within *Dubliners*. Like Thomas in **'Old Garbo'**, Joyce is particularly interested in the sense of isolation concomitant with the ignominy as is evident in the case of Duffy:

> He gnawed the rectitude of his life; he felt that he had been outcast from life's feast. One human being had seemed to love him and he had denied her life and happiness: he had sentenced her to ignominy, a death of shame.

In particular, both Thomas and Joyce shared a concern with the way in which an inherited sense of guilt straitjackets human behaviour. Thus, in 'The Boarding House' the pressure upon Doran to do the 'correct thing' by Polly is as much internal as external:

> It was not altogether his fault that it had happened. He remembered well, with the curious patient memory of the celibate, the first casual caresses of her dress, her breath, her fingers had given him. . . . But delirium passes. He echoed her phrase, applying it to himself: "what am I to do?" The instinct of the celibate warned him to hold back. But the sin was there; even his sense of honour told him that reparation must be made for such a sin.

As in Thomas's work, there is no gainsaying the censorious nature of community and the influence of communal judgements. Thus Doran struggles not only with conscience and his own misgivings but the opinion of his friends:

> First of all there was her disreputable father, and then her mother's boarding house was beginning to get a certain fame. He had a notion that he was being had. He could imagine his friends talking of the affair and laughing. She *was* a little vulgar; sometimes she said 'I seen' and 'If I had've known'.

On a first reading of the prose pieces written after *Portrait of the Artist as a Young Dog*, it might appear that the realism of that autobiographical work has finally come into its own. There is more indulgence in description and a greater enthusiasm for vividly recreating on the page every last detail that storms the eyes of an attentive and sensitive observer. The inventiveness that inspired all kinds of surrealistic twists and turns in the early prose, now reveals itself in fresh and appropriate images:

> Our snow was not only shaken from whitewish buckets down the sky, it came shawling out of the ground and swam and drifted out of the arms and hands and bodies of the trees; snow grew overnight on the roofs of the houses like a pure and grandfather moss, minutely white-ivied the walls and settled on the postman, opening the gate, like a dumb thunderstorm of white, torn Christmas cards.

But the main subjects of the prose pieces written between *Portrait of the Artist as Young Dog* and *Under Milk Wood* are the creative capacities and potential of memory. Hence one moment we are in a real, wintry Swansea and the next moment in a more fantastic kind of Wales. But this is not the same kind of sudden shifting and turning which pervades the early prose. Like Coleridge in his lime-tree bower, Thomas escapes through imagination to the 'undecaying wonder of the world' which he believed he had experienced as a child:

> Years and years and years ago, when I was a boy, when there were wolves in Wales, and birds the colour of red-flannel petticoats whisked past the harp-shaped hills, when we sang and wallowed all night and day in caves that smelt like Sunday afternoons in damp front farmhouse parlours, and we chased, with the jawbones of deacons, the English and the bears, before the motor-car, before the wheel, before the duchess-faced horse, when we rode the daft and happy hills bareback it snowed and it snowed.

Apart from joking about his age, Thomas is anxious to suggest how in those days colours did seem more intense, definitions did seem sharper and life did seem more carefree. Parts of this description—'wallowed all night and day' and 'we rode the daft and happy hills'—are redolent of **'Fern Hill'** where he remembered he was 'green and carefree' and ran 'his heedless ways'. But whereas **'Fern Hill'** is based upon a rather solitary pursuit of happiness, the piece from which this description is taken, **'A Child's Christmas in Wales'**, celebrates community, friendship and family. The passage combines three sets of myths associated with childhood (the myth of a lost innocence), Christmas (the myths of community and family spirit) and Wales (the myth of a distinct and intact cultural heritage focussed upon singing, the harp and women in shawls and red petticoats). As in **'Fern Hill'** where hay fields are as high as houses, the child's sense of exaggeration, lack of proportion and imagination are stressed. The exaggeration in this piece, however, is an acknowledgement of the capacity of memory to distort. He admits that he is recreating the kind of childhood a middleaged writer would like to believe existed: 'In goes my hand into that wool-white, bell-tongued ball of holidays resting at the rim of the carol-singing sea'. In other words, it is nearly all fantasy.

The radio talks, broadcast between 1943 and 1946 betray a serious concern to understand the processes of memory and its place as a resource of the writer and the relationship between what is remembered and what is written up as literature. The preoccupation with memory is evident even from the titles of the talks: **'Reminiscences of Childhood'**, **'Memories of Christmas'**, **'Holiday Memory'**, **'The Crumb of One Man's Year'**. It is a preoccupation that developed throughout the 1940s as shown by the changes made in 1953 to the 1943 version of **'Reminiscences of Childhood'**. Whereas the 1943 version closes with a eulogy to 'the fine, live people, the spirit of Wales itself', the 1953 version keeps more closely to the subject of recalling memories and the way a writer imposes a meaning and order on memories that they do not have. In the last third of the description of his native Swansea he admits: 'Never was there such a town.' The talk closes by reaffirming a point that emerged earlier in the description: 'The memories of childhood have no order, and no end.' It is a subject he returns to in **'The Crumbs of One Man's Year'**. The talk was written as he says while he was 'slung as though in a hammock, or a lull, between one Christmas for ever over and a New Year nearing full of relentless surprises' and the imagery with which he writes about the problem of recall is appropriate to the time of year. He is particularly fascinated with the haphazard nature of recall: 'of what has gone I know only shilly-shally snatches and freckled plaids, flecks and dabs, dazzle and froth.' But linked with this is a profounder concern with the way in which the individual seems rushed along by time, only occasionally achieving an intense awareness: 'a simple second caught in coursing snow-light, an instant, gay or sorry, struck motionless in the curve of flight like a bird or a scythe'. Here Thomas may be remembering the Preface to D. H. Lawrence's *New Poems;* 'One great mystery of time is terra incognita to us: the instant. The most superb mystery we have hardly recognised: the immediate, instant self. The quick of all time is the instant.' However, Thomas, introduces a melancholic note through the image of loss and waste: 'the spindrift leaf and stray-paper whirl, canter quarrel, and people-chase of everybody's street'. (pp. 61-86)

> *Linden Peach, in his* The Prose Writing of Dylan Thomas, *The Macmillan Press Ltd., 1988, 144 p.*

Oh, & I forgot. I'm not influenced by Welsh bardic poetry. I can't read Welsh.

—*Thomas, 1952*

Sheila Deane   (essay date 1989)

[*In the following excerpt from her* Bardic Style in the Poetry of Gerard Manley Hopkins, W. B. Yeats & Dylan Thomas, *Deane examines Thomas's affinities with Welsh bardic techniques.*]

In a review of the English Festival of Spoken Poetry, Dylan Thomas describes the effect and importance of reading aloud. He notices that when the speakers

> put that noise on paper, which is a poem, into their chests and throats, and let it out. . . . Known words grow wings, print springs and shoots; the voice discovers the poet's ear; it's found that a poem on a page is only half a poem.

This appreciation for the life that the voice can give a poem is apparent in all of his own work, from the first early poems, which he jokingly claimed the next door neighbors knew by heart, to the last poems, so often recited and performed for his audiences. Even though a concern for the sound of a poem, and especially for the way that a poem can present itself as a product of the breath, is found in all of Thomas's work, it is still possible to see that the later poetry is more influenced by vocal textures and values than the earlier. Vernon Watkins, who in some ways took Pamela Hansford Johnson's place as a test audience for Thomas after 1937, noticed that after the completion of *Twenty-Five Poems,* Thomas's style, in both poetry and prose, underwent a gradual change,

> not exactly of language, but of approach. The change was, I think, heralded by the little poem which begins: "Once it was the colour of saying. . . ." This, and the other poems of *The Map of Love,* showed that, while he had now resolved to write only stories about real people, his poetry had also moved in the direction of the living voice. (Quoted by Gwen Watkins, *Portrait of a Friend*)

The argument against such a development has, of course, been thoroughly elaborated by [Ralph] Maud and others on the basis of Thomas's notebooks, which clearly demonstrate that he took the material for later poems from some of his earliest drafts. Therefore, the poems published in *The Map of Love* actually precede the poems published in *Twenty-Five Poems,* which again precede *Eighteen Poems.* However, such a scheme applies only to the content of the poems and indicates that Thomas had imagined the settings and problems of certain works many years before he finished writing them; in terms of their style the later poems are an advance on the earlier, and Thomas's meticulous revisions were an attempt to transform the early notebook drafts into works more consistent with his developing interests and skills. And, as Watkins observes, the poems were altered in a way that brought them closer to the properties and energies of voice. Even a quick glance through *Collected Poems* illustrates this: the poems that follow **"Altarwise by owl-light"** seem less carved and more spoken for the most part; the line lengths become more flexible and irregular in appearance; the stanzas become longer, more intricate as a rule; and, generally, the phrasing and expression in poems such as **"I make this in a warring absence," "How shall my animal," "A saint about to fall," "Poem in October," "Unluckily for a Death,"** and **"The hunchback in the park"** are more sonorous, demonstrative, and oratorical than in most of the earlier poems.

This very gradual stylistic development gives the impression of a poet coming to accept a certain idiom at the same time as he is creating it. Previously, Thomas had wanted to be considered among the *avant-garde* writers; now he began to allow the traditional elements in his poetry to play a more central role. Before, he had wanted to be thought of as an international writer; now he allowed some local and regional concerns to enter the poetry, and he turned his attention to certain memories and scenes of Wales. Before, he recorded his sympathy with the "dark" forces in nature, the rebellious and destructive forces; but now his poetry moves "towards some measure of light," and its stance seems to change from a rebellious one to a celebratory one. Previously, his poetry traced the adventure of the body; now it turned to the energy of the voice. Of course, Thomas would always want to have it both ways. The later concerns exist in the early poems, as the early concerns exist in the later poems, but they exist more as influences than controlling factors. Moreover, the development is natural and organic, in that the later concerns arise out of an investigation of the earlier ones, are, in a sense, *won* from the disturbing and relentless enquiry of the early poems. Thomas becomes a bardic poet because his poetic enquiry leads him towards a bardic idiom, not because he has decided to imitate the ancient Welsh bards, or reintroduce ancient bardic techniques.

Properly then, the bardic voice in Thomas's poetry begins at this point, for, although he was familiar with, and friends with, other Anglo-Welsh artists, some of whom were interested in bardism (Vernon Watkins, for instance, was never reluctant to let his poetry record his fascination with Celtic mythology and Welsh traditions), and although he had used his poetry to respond to, and elaborate upon, Celtic mythological tales, he had been unwilling to foreground such Welsh material or to experiment very thoroughly with the techniques of bardic poetry. The poem that is sometimes thought of as the turning point is **"After the funeral,"** since comparison between the first version that Thomas wrote in 1933 when his aunt died and the final version completed in 1938 indicates a basic reorientation on the poet's part which significantly alters the tone and shape of the poem, the position of the speaker within the poem, and, most important, the purpose for writing the poem. The first version is impersonal and dispassionate, a cold commentary on the hypocrisy of the churchgoers (reminiscent of Caradoc Evans), and a focus upon the dead body that is intentionally disrespectful and disconcerting:

> Another gossip's toy has lost its use,
> Broken lies buried amid broken toys,
> Of flesh and bone lies hungry for the flies,
> Waits for the natron and the mummy paint.
> With dead lips pursed and dry bright eyes,
> Another well of rumours and cold lies
> Has dried, and one more joke has lost its point.

Maud notes the "satiric world-weariness" of this poem, and links it with another that Thomas wrote only a month later, **"O make me a mask."** In many of the drafts in the notebook, Maud says, "his poems are, in a sense, the mask he was making; he looks out from them with a cold, often satirical stare." It is perhaps a poetic stance that is kin to Yeats's in the conclusion to "Under Ben Bulben": "Cast a cold eye / On life, on death." But ironically, in 1938,

when Yeats is writing "Under Ben Bulben," Thomas is writing the final version of **"After the funeral,"** a version which attempts to move from a cold impersonality to a warm and affectionate intimacy.

In the final version, Thomas self-consciously tries out the bardic stance. He writes a traditional poem, an elegy, and he uses the form to praise and celebrate the worth of his aunt and his aunt's world. He locates the poem in the homely context of the funeral and relaxes his universalizing and generalizing tendencies in order to evoke this particular woman and this particular event. He moves through all the details of an actual situation so that the reader feels himself to be among the mourners:

> After the funeral, mule praises, brays,
> Windshake of sailshaped ears, muffle-toed tap
> Tap happily of one peg in the thick
> Grave's foot, blinds down the lids, the teeth in
>   black,
> The spittled eyes, the salt ponds in the sleeves.
>
>   . . . . .
>
> I stand, for this memorial's sake, alone
> In the snivelling hours with dead, humped Ann
> Whose hooded, fountain heart once fell in pud-
>   dles
> Round the parched worlds of Wales and
>   drowned each sun
> (Though this for her is a monstrous image blind-
>   ly
> Magnified out of praise; her death was a still
>   drop;
> She would not have me sinking in the holy
> Flood of her heart's fame; she would lie dumb
>   and deep
> And need no druid of her broken body).
> But I, Ann's bard on a raised hearth, call all
> The seas to service that her wood-tongued virtue
> Babble like a bellbuoy over the hymning heads,
> Bow down the walls of the ferned and foxy
>   woods
> That her love sing and swing through a brown
>   chapel,
>
>   . . . . .
>
> I know her scrubbed and sour humble hands
> Lie with religion in their cramp, her threadbare
> Whisper in a damp word, her wits drilled hol-
>   low,
> Her fist of a face died clenched on a round pain;
> And sculptured Ann is seventy years of stone.
> These cloud-sopped, marble hands, this monu-
>   mental
> Argument of the hewn voice, gesture and psalm,
> Storm me forever over her grave until
> The stuffed lung of the fox twitch and cry Love
> And the strutting fern lay seeds on the black sill.

This is obviously a different business from **"Incarnate devil"** or **"Altarwise by owl-light."** The poem is shaped like an immediate, spontaneous experience, whereas earlier works advertise their fictional and mythic nature. There is, also, in this work a sustained sense that the poet is speaking out loud, whereas earlier poems could be read more as acts of the mind. In general, it is a full, noisy poem, an enactment of all the different forms of praise that could take place in such a setting. And the poet's dilemma is how to fit his own voice to the occasion. He was not satisfied with his earlier response, but neither is he entirely comfortable with his new approach. The poem that results from these dissatisfactions becomes a remarkable example of vocal vacillation. In some lines he tries the satiric tones that characterized the earlier attempt: "the snivelling hours with dead, humped Ann," "her scrubbed and sour humble hands," "her wits drilled hollow." In other lines he pushes the occasion to its rhetorical heights: "the holy flood of her heart's fame," "her wood-tongued virtue," "her love sing and swing through a brown chapel." It is as if he felt the need for both approaches—the satiric diminishment *and* the bardic magnification—in order to properly surround the event, in order to really enclose what he felt about Ann and her death in a poem. The satiric, or realistic, approach is not sufficient, because it cannot see through this ordinary, sad, funeral to a larger, more loving context. But the bardic approach, with its grand gestures and its determination to see through the ordinary into the magnificent, is out of touch with the simplicity of the event, and constitutes, as the poet realizes, a gross distortion of his aunt's death, a "monstrous image." The combined efforts of both approaches, however, can suggest that Ann's death, perhaps all deaths, lie somewhere between "a still drop" and "all the seas," and the customary response of the mourner may be somewhere between the cold mask of the satirist and the warm praise of the bard. So **"After the funeral"** moves self-consciously from one voice to the other, perhaps finishing in the bardic voice, but with such an odd pair of images' that the reader is made to question the sincerity (or even sanity) of that last voice.

The creation of a voice that could have something to say **"After the funeral"** is, however, only one of the poem's projects. A voice disappears after it has spoken, a poem does not. A voice exists only in time, a poem must exist in space as well. It is this second project of **"After the funeral"** Thomas draws attention to when he says, at the conclusion of the poem, that "this monumental / Argument of the hewn voice, gesture and psalm, / Storm me forever over her grave . . ." He claims that what gives the poem the immortality all elegists crave is the fact that it is a blend of temporal and spatial elements, a voice and a shape. Each of his descriptions of the poem is another configuration of that blend: the nouns, "voice" and "argument," refer to human sounds that exist in time, while their adjectives, "hewn" and "monumental," refer to entities that take up space. The last configuration is perhaps the most perfect blend, for, while a psalm is human music that exists in time, it has been preserved in the Bible, whereas a gesture is an action that occupies space but is generally thought of as more fleeting. At any rate, what Thomas wants to achieve in **"After the funeral"** is what he longingly describes as "the sound of shape" in sonnet 7 of the "Altarwise" sequence, or more drolly as a "noise on paper" in the review of the English Festival of Spoken Poetry. The long impassioned flow of the poem (it is the longest stichic work in *Collected Poems* aside from the **"Author's Prologue"**) is balanced, therefore, by an extremely stringent system of corresponding images, linked phrases, and rhymed words. The poem presents itself as

a spontaneous utterance, but this is offset by the carefully worked conceits, such as the one that parallels the whole affair with forms of water, from the tears of the mourners to the fountain of Ann's love, and finally to the "storm" of the poem. The analogy is always there, offering the reader, at each point, a more poetic and elemental way of seeing the funeral. But all these natural and elemental metaphors in the poem—rain, wood, and stone—do not have a distancing effect, do not cover the dead body of the woman with comforting or sentimental parallels; rather, they make the experience more intimate and disturbing, as for instance, when Ann is described as "seventy years of stone," and the image conveys all the cold, unmoving weight of the dead woman. A good example of the way the language works to promote not just the voice but the artifice of the poem can be found in the poet's parenthetical disclaimer. The passage is given all the markings of an impulsive aside, but it is perhaps the most carefully constructed section of the poem: "She would not have me sinking in the holy / Flood of her heart's fame; she would lie dumb and deep / And need no druid of her broken body." Notice that these three lines each have their own alliterative pattern ("flood," "fame;" "dumb," "deep;" "broken," "body"), but they also, like the lines in stanza 34 of *The Wreck of the Deutschland,* have an alliterative link to the next line ("holy," "heart;" "dumb," "druid"). There is a rhyme scheme for the beginning of each line ("would," "Flood," "need") and a rhyme scheme for the end of each line ("holy," "body"). There are rhymes within lines ("fame," "dumb;" "need," "druid"), and a rhyme that encloses the whole passage, pulling together two disparate words for Ann ("She" and "body").

Clearly, Thomas intended the "storm" of **"After the funeral"** to be a very "watertight" one. It may be that in order to incorporate the energy of the voice and the rhythm of the breath in his works he found he had to use a longer, more flexible line than he was accustomed to, but such a line can easily sound Whitmanesque, an uncontrolled or shapeless flow of words, so Thomas may have felt the need for something to brace the line and found it in an intensified system of rhymes. Yeats also rejected free verse for the very reason that he considered it to be too close to the way he felt and thought; free verse could not therefore offer him a stylistic check or balance. "Because I need a passionate syntax for passionate subject-matter I compel myself to accept those traditional metres that have developed with the language." Hopkins also felt that the most vigorous language required the greatest restraint. When his friend Robert Bridges suggests that Whitman was an influence on his poetry, Hopkins carefully delineates all the ways that his poetry is more "highly wrought" than that of Whitman. He writes: "The long lines are not rhythm run to seed: everything is weighed and timed in them." The decision to weigh, time, and thoroughly regulate the vitality of his verse may, however, have developed from his recognition of an affinity with writers like Whitman: "I always knew in my heart Walt Whitman's mind to be more like my own than any other man's living. As he is a very great scoundrel that is not a pleasant confession." Each of these poets—Thomas, Yeats, Hopkins—seems to have chosen certain verse structures and formal controls partly *because* they went against what he felt was natural to him. For each of them, writing was not just an expression of the self, but an exercise for the self; the poem was not just a text, but also a test. I think it is that sensibility in particular that makes their work bardic.

Thomas himself regarded **"After the funeral"** as a sort of turning point, and claimed that it occupied a unique place in his poetic canon. He said that it was

> the only one I have written that is, directly, about the life and death of any one particular human being I knew—and not about the very many lives and deaths whether seen, as in my first poems, in the tumultuous world of my own being or, as in the later poems, in war, grief, and the great holes and corners of the universal love.

This statement shows **"After the funeral"** to be a sort of channel through which the poet passed on his way from poems about himself to poems about others, as if the elegy for his aunt was the first reach outwards, the first widening of the poetic sphere. It is, therefore, the first poem to offer his new vision of poetry and the role of the poet. In it, Thomas begins to propose a vision of poetry as something for use, and a vision of the poet as someone who operates on behalf of others. His early poems have "first-line" titles that refuse to designate or categorize the poem, that stress the fact that the poem is a verbal construction that does not require an external reference point, but his later poems use titles in order to direct the reader's attention to the function and location of the poem in the ordinary world: **"Poem on his birthday," "On the Marriage of a Virgin," "On a Wedding Anniversary," "After the funeral."** The titles of the later poems reveal their purpose, showing the poem to be a **"Lament,"** or a **"Ceremony After a Fire Raid,"** or a **"Vision and Prayer."** The later poems all seem to be such *used* things: they are curses and blessings, lullabies, prayers, elegies and commemorations. In fact, the word "prayer," which is so common in the later poems as an alias for poetry, appears for the first time in **"Altarwise by owl-light"**: "Now stamp the Lord's Prayer on a grain of rice." It is possible that Thomas, in an effort to deal with the difficulties of linguistic mediacy that he explored in the "Altarwise" sonnets, chose to fashion his poems into tools, to close the gap between language and the world by putting language at the service of the world. It is somewhat similar to the tactics of William Morris, who sought to reconcile art and life through craft, who, in effect, put art out to work. Morris, painting on his furniture, transforms both the painting and the furniture, just as Thomas, "Ann's bard on a raised hearth," makes poetic language more functional and domestic, while at the same time elevating and exalting Ann. He treats poetry as a craft and a service, and he realizes that this treatment places him squarely in the path of the bardic tradition.

Compare, for instance, the way that Idris Bell describes the bardic profession in his study, *The Nature of Poetry as Conceived by the Welsh Bards* with Thomas's statements about poetry in the **"Poetic Manifesto."** There would have been no direct borrowing between the **"Manifesto"** (1951) and Beil's work (1955), but they are roughly contemporary and demonstrate how close Thomas's poetic

was to the sort of poetic that scholars were attributing to the ancient Welsh bards. Bell writes that the bard

> was a professional craftsman. . . . Since the poet's was a social function, his calling a whole-time profession, emphasis was naturally laid on the *art* of poetry. Poetry was a craft, which, like any other craft, had to be learned; the words "carpenter" and "carpentry" are frequently applied to poets and poetry.

Thomas writes in the **"Manifesto"**:

> What I like to do is to treat words as a craftsman does his wood or stone or what-have-you, to hew, carve, mould, coil, polish and plane them into patterns, sequences, sculptures, fugures of sound expressing some lyrical impulse, some spiritual doubt or conviction, some dimly-realised truth I must try to reach and realise.

The business of the poem, as Thomas sees it, is to solidify some "impulse" or idea of the poet's, to be a practical and coherent manifestation of his private, chaotic world. This understanding coincides with the way the bard views his work; he thinks of his poem as the script and record of a performance, and his poetic devices serve to make that performance more effective and memorable. For both Thomas and the bard, a poem is the shape of the voice. And it is this shape, this craftsmanship, in the poem that renders it useful to others, that enables it to speak on behalf of others. The first satiric poem on the occasion of Ann's death was simply an "argument," speaking for the poet, but the second poem is a "hewn argument," speaking for all people who are trying to come to terms with death. Thomas's statement on the place of **"After the funeral"** in his canon is, in a way, an acknowledgment that whatever happened between the first and second version of the poem happened to all his work, and the language with which he discusses his poetry bears this out. He thought of his early poems as "intricate images," "fibs of vision," but the later poetry is more simply described as "labour" or "the work of words." Poetry changes from being a war, a rebellion, an ambush, to being a contribution, a dedication, even a job. It is so, Thomas feels, even if no one is paying him (as was often the case) and even if no one is paying attention:

> Not for the proud man apart
> From the raging moon I write
>
> . . . . .
>
> But for the lovers, their arms
> Round the griefs of the ages,
> Who pay no praise or wages
> Nor heed my craft or art.

It may be possible to attribute some of this change to incidents in Thomas's life. In 1937 he married Caitlin Macnamara and they had their first son, Llewelyn, in 1939 (born, coincidentally, only two days after the death of Yeats). These experiences provided him with new insights into relationships, a new sense of belonging, but they may also have brought a disconcerting sense of greater responsibility. Yeats's death, for instance, partly deprives him of that literary "old guard" against which he had constructed his poetic, while the birth of his son makes him, metaphorically, into the "womb" around the "war" of the new generation. He discovers that the standard he rebelled against has been replaced by himself, and that he is the new order against which another youth will rebel. The situation may not have been entirely satisfying to Thomas, but gradually, it seems to have inclined him towards the creation of a more traditional and generous poetry. Thomas was also beginning to miss Wales at this time. He had had his fill of London and other large cities and was becoming nostalgic for the small Welsh towns and villages of his youth. Thomas even began to imagine, as Hopkins had before him, that such places were essentially still unfallen, little Edens that had managed to elude the fate of the ruined and ruinous cities. When Llewelyn was six weeks old, Thomas wrote to his friend Bert Trick, saying:

> Though I'm set in a life now, two stone heavier but not a feather steadier, though never again will I fit into Swansea quite so happily and comfortably as I did . . . I'm strong and sentimental for the town and the people. . . . But one small close society is closed to me, and the social grief is natural. We're all moving away; and every single decisive action happens in a blaze of disappointment.

Thomas and his new family were never financially stable enough to completely eliminate the transient life, but after 1940 their principal residences, their *homes,* were in small seaside towns in the west of Wales, either in New Quay or Laugharne.

Several factors, therefore, come together to influence the development of Thomas's later style: his interest in the agency of the voice and the effectiveness of reading aloud; his decision to intensify formal control through elaborate rhyme schemes and other kinds of verbal craftsmanship; his tendency to see poetry as more functional and serviceable than before; his relationship with his family that gave him opportunities for more occasional and commemorative verse; and his gradual movement back to the villages and country places of Wales. These factors, one might say, provide a fertile soil for the bardic style, make the development of such a style easier. This is something that most of Thomas's critics could agree on. What those critics are really interested in, however, is the extent to which Thomas consciously fostered such a style. The following discussion will attempt to clarify the matter by concentrating on Thomas's experiments with the principles of bardic versification.

In 1941, Thomas sold his notebooks, ending his use of those drafts of poems he had written in his early youth. Ackerman notes that this "decisive break with his poetry of adolescence" occurred when he was twenty-six, the age at which Keats died (*Welsh Dylan*). It was as if Thomas was forcing himself to set off in a new poetic direction, to write about his new interests and convictions and surroundings. This new direction is reflected in the poems he wrote after selling the notebooks, which were published, appropriately, as **Deaths and Entrances** in 1946. More than any other work in his canon, these poems seem to be consciously experimenting with unusual and difficult formal strategies, and the inspiration for some of these strategies seems to have come from Welsh bardic practice.

One of the aims of bardic poetry was to give the poem aural charm, an aim that Thomas naturally had sympathy

The Boat House in Laugharne, Wales, where Thomas lived from 1949 until his death.

with, since even as early as 1934 he had described poetry as "an art that is primarily dependent upon the musical mingling of vowels and consonants," which is also a reasonable definition of *cynghanedd.* But even before the bard had attended to the network of verbal harmony that he could achieve with vowels and consonants, he created a musical pattern in his verse based on syllabic measurement. The classical meters for Welsh poetry were all syllabic, and it is the syllabic line that forms the basis of Thomas's poetic rhythm in *Deaths and Entrances.* For instance, the third poem in that volume, **"Poem in October,"** composed in 1944, was written to celebrate Thomas's thirtieth birthday. In letters to Vernon Watkins, Thomas said it was the first "place poem" he had ever written, and that it was necessary to read it aloud in order to hear its "lovely slow lyrical movement." That movement is the consequence of the poem's syllabic meter and variable line lengths. Each stanza in the poem follows the same pattern: it has ten lines, and the syllabic count for each line is 9, 12, 9, 3, 5, 12, 12, 5, 3, 9. The regularity of the system is countered by the variability of the line lengths, so the reader experiences the poem partly as a vacillating action, an ebb and flow, but also as an unchanging, almost stately procession.

> Pale rain over the dwindling harbour
> And over the sea wet church the size of a snail
> With its horns through the mist and the cas-
> tle
> Brown as owls
> But all the gardens
> Of spring and summer were blooming in the tall
> tales
> Beyond the border and under the lark full cloud.
> There I could marvel
> My birthday
> Away but the weather turned around.
>
> It turned away from the blithe country
> And down the other air and the blue altered sky
> Streamed again with a wonder of summer
> With apples
> Pears and red currants
> And I saw in the turning so clearly a child's
> Forgotten mornings when he walked with his
> mother
> Through the parables
> Of sunlight
> And the legends of the green chapels. . . .

In *The Dragon Has Two Tongues,* Glyn Jones notices the intricate syllabic patterning of Thomas's later poetry, and he also notes the similarity between Thomas's practices and the principles of Welsh prosody. He suggests that Thomas may have learned about Welsh prosody through an article of his. He explains:

> In 1939 I wrote an article in *Life and Letters Today* on "Hopkins and Welsh Prosody," in which I mentioned this fact about *cerdd dafod.* I sometimes wonder if Dylan got his idea of basing his lines on a count of syllables, rather than a count of feet, from it. I know he was a reader of and a contributor to the magazine at the time. Counting syllables was in itself nothing new to him; he had been doing it pretty strictly in **Eighteen Poems.** But there the iambic foot was near-

ly always the rhythmic basis of his line in a way it was not when in his later work a count of syllables replaced a count of accents.

In some of the poems in **Deaths and Entrances,** then, Thomas may have been consciously following a bardic example, or he may have developed a more intricate and flexible syllabic line after reading Jones's article on Hopkins, but whatever the case, it is clear that a syllabic pattern was an extra discipline attached to the composition of the poem, another way to make the "living stream" more "watertight." And his increased use of such measures shows that he was always moving towards a more exacting and difficult artifice, towards a heightening of the tension between the inner agility of the poem and the rigidity of the poem's container.

In bardic poetry the syllabic count is only the beginning of the difficulties. Eurys Rowlands writes in an essay on "*Cynghanedd,* Metre, Prosody" that

> if anything is generally recognised about medieval Welsh poetry it is the fact that it was designed to produce aural interest. The reason for this is that on the basis of syllabic metres was superimposed *cynghanedd,* a word meaning "harmony" used as a technical term for the complex and intricate system of sound correspondences which became an integral part of Welsh prosody from the late thirteenth century onwards.

There has been much speculation among Thomas's critics concerning his knowledge of *cynghanedd.* [In a footnote Deane cites John Ackerman in *Dylan Thomas: His Life and Work,* Walford Davies in *Dylan Thomas,* R. B. Kershner in *Dylan Thomas: The Poet and His Critics,* and William Moynihan in *The Craft and Art of Dylan Thomas.*] The general consensus seems to be that Thomas knew a little bit about the practice, probably learned, for the most part, from articles that discussed Hopkins's use of *cynghanedd.* It is often pointed out that Thomas could have read Wyn Griffith's article "The Welsh Influence in Hopkins's Poetry" in the Hopkins number of *New Verse* in 1935, or Glyn Jones's article "Hopkins and Welsh Prosody" in *Life and Letters Today* in 1939, or even Gweneth Lilly's more comprehensive study "The Welsh Influence in the Poetry of Gerard Manley Hopkins" in *The Modern Language Review* of 1943. But it seems unlikely that a poet, living in Wales, and with several friends who were studying or writing Welsh poetry, would be unacquainted with the very basic information about *cynghanedd* contained in those articles. A. Talfan Davies, although he supports the view that Thomas was greatly influenced by Hopkins, says that on many occasions he discussed with Thomas "in fair detail the intricacies of *cynghanedd*" ("Influence of Welsh Prosody on Modern English Poetry"). And yet, if Thomas knew all about this form of poetic "harmony," why are there not more perfect examples of it in his poems?

The problem is that the rules of *cynghanedd* are very strict and specific, and therefore, Thomas believed, unsuitable for the English language. In his 1946 broadcast on Welsh poets, Thomas talks about Glyn Jones's use of these practices in a way that is not wholly complimentary:

He has tried, in several English poems, to use the very difficult ancient bardic forms. These forms rely on a great deal of assonance and alliteration and most complicated internal rhyming; and these effects in English have, in the hands of the few who have attempted to use them, succeeded only in warping, crabbing, and obscuring the natural genius of the English language.

And if Thomas's earliest assessment of Hopkins is recalled, his sense that "the language was violated and estranged by the efforts of compressing the already unfamiliar imagery," it would suggest that Thomas found the strict application of *cynghanedd* unnatural, and felt that it did not draw upon, or enhance, any of the strengths of the English language. Consequently, he did not force his own poems to comply with the "ancient bardic forms," but rather invented new rules and forms to shape his poetic discourse, rules just as intricate and exacting as the traditional ones, but, he hoped, more responsive to the English tongue, and more expressive of it. And the new rules he invented were based on the way he understood the traditional rules to work; in other words, he extracted from *cynghanedd* its characteristic principles and central purpose, and used those principles and purpose for the creation of his own forms. His aim was to achieve a compromise, a form that would reconcile both the demand for rigor made by Welsh poetry and the demand for flexibility made by the English language. For instance, the foundation of *cynghanedd* is multiple rhyming; almost every important word in the poem is linked to others through alliteration or consonantal rhyme. Thomas essentially adapted this system for his own purposes. On the one hand he set up elaborate and constricting rhyme schemes, but on the other hand, he used partial and slant rhymes, as if he felt that the euphony of partial rhyme allowed for greater musicality than the monotonous repetition of full rhymes. Watkins explains Thomas's practice:

> He certainly did not like writing in unrhymed form. He welcomed obstacles and difficulties. But he also did not like, as he once told me, finding his rhymes labelled for him like the stations on railway-tickets. He wanted to preserve a strictness of choice in language with which direct rhyme sometimes interfered. So he resorted to assonance and dissonance and built his stanzas on a fabric of exact language in which the line endings were musically and mathematically balanced, and enhanced, rather than reproduced, the sound that had gone before. (Quoted by Gwen Watkins, *Portrait of a Friend*)

Thomas, then, constructs his poetry as the ancient bards did, on a mathematical and musical basis, attentive to the count of syllables and the texture of sounds in the poem, and aware that these sounds and numbers serve the energy of the poem, in an important way. They are like the bloodstream of the poem, channelling, intensifying, or disrupting if need be, the momentum of the poem. Two lines from **"Poem in October"** will illustrate the process: "And I saw in the turning so clearly a child's / Forgotten mornings when he walked with his mother." These lines certainly do not parade their verbal harmony as overtly as many of Thomas's other lines do; nonetheless, they have an intri-

cate system of links and rhymes that serve as the vehicle of the poet's vision. To begin with, although one line articulates the poet's present and the following line his past, both lines are given equal mathematical weight; each line has twelve syllables and four primary stresses. The consonance is quiet, but pervasive, in "saw," "so;" "clearly," "child's;" and "when," "walked," "with." And the assonantal links reinforce the poet's consideration of himself as an "I" to a vision of himself as a "child," from what he "saw" to where he once "walked." The closest rhyme between the two lines informs the reader that the poet's "turning" is towards earlier "mornings," and the strongest alliteration completes those "mornings" with his "mother." In effect, then, the poet is following his memories into the past, becoming for a moment the child he was, and this metamorphosis is carried out not only by the meanings of the words and the syntax of the lines, but also by the music of the words and the mathematics of the lines.

But *cynghanedd* is more than an aural harmony; it also presents a visual pattern. In bardic verse, the dense rhymes and correspondences may have been intended as formulaic elements, poetic devices to foreground the shape of the work that was being recited. Consonantal coloring and intricate repetition would give listeners a sense of the form of the poem even as it was passing in time. And much of Thomas's artifice has this effect; it seems intended to present a shape in time, to show what crafted thing has come from the sounds that the poet uttered. Sometimes Thomas went to great lengths to make this pattern in the poem. In **"I make this in a warring absence"** he ended nearly all the lines with one of three sounds, *n, d,* and *s.* In stanzas 1, 2, and 5 most lines end with *n,* in stanzas 3, 4, and 9 most lines end with *s,* in stanzas 6 and 7 most lines end with *d,* and stanza 8 has a combination of all three endings. An even more impressive display of the same technique is found in **"I, in my intricate image,"** where 101 of the 108 lines end in a word with an upright letter, an ascender, and in eighty-one lines that letter is *l.* This format could be thought of as a reversal of the bardic technique *cymeriad llythrennol,* which means "letter embellishment" and refers to the practice of repeating the same letter at the beginning of each poetic line. A notorious example is a work by the fifteenth-century poet, Dafydd ap Edmund. Since he wrote at a time when bardic practices had been thoroughly institutionalized, he seems to have taken it upon himself to make those practices more difficult and elaborate than they had been before, and therefore, he tends to be known primarily for his preoccupation with form and his self-conscious artistry. He uses *cymeriad llythrennol,* for instance, in an impassioned serenade of forty-two lines, an attempt at seduction in which, nonetheless, every line begins with the letter *d.* Thomas is definitely playing this sort of game in his poems, but he makes it less obtrusive by transferring it to the end of his lines, where English readers expect some link or embellishment, rather than placing it at the beginning of the line, where they do not. Even his rhyme schemes have something of this game to them. The most fascinating rhyme scheme is the "mirror-image" scheme of the **"Author's Prologue"** to *Collected Poems,* in which the second verse rhymes backwards with the first, so that the last line of the poem rhymes with the first line of the poem. Since each verse is fifty-one lines, the rhymes cannot actually be heard, and Thomas wrote, "Why I acrosticked myself like this, don't ask me." The poem is, in effect, using rhyme not as an aural device but as a visual device, as a way of making the poem's flow into a crafted design, the poet's speech into the poet's handiwork.

The poem that begins the volume *Deaths and Entrances* is another good example of Thomas's dexterity. A. Talfan Davies, in fact, points to **"The Conversation of Prayer"** as coming closest to the artistry of the Welsh *awdlau*, and sees, in Thomas's poem and the bardic odes, an intricate formality that could be compared to a Celtic knot ("Influence of Welsh Prosody on Modern English Poetry"):

> The conversation of *prayers* about to be *said*
> By the child going to *bed* and the man on the
>   *stairs*
> Who climbs to his dying *love* in her high *room*,
> The one not caring to *whom* in his sleep he will
>   *move*
> And the other full of *tears* that she will be
>   *dead*, . . .

The rhymes are braided in this way throughout the entire poem, providing a phonetic parallel to the image of the stairs, and also to the way that the poet has entwined the lives of the child and the man, the experience of sleep and the experience of death. Moreover, Thomas has created a border of consonance in the first part of every line ("conversation," "child," "climbs," "caring") to stand against the braided rhymes of the second part of every line. Such complexity is a product of Thomas's own intentions and regulations, but his apparent need for a visual design that is woven into the words of the poem is something he has in common with the bards, and various techniques that the bards used to enhance the complexity of their verse may well have intrigued and inspired Thomas.

The poem that most clearly calls attention to itself as both a sight and a sound is **"Vision and Prayer."** It does so with the title, of course, and also with its strong, singing lines and unusual stanzaic forms. The poem is a chant and a hieroglyph; on the one hand the words beat out an insistent, almost wailing rhythm, which the stops and starts of the varied line lengths make even more frenetic and urgent, while on the other hand the words take their place in the stilled pattern of the poem, contribute to the substance and outline of a *carmen figuratum*, the shape and mute gesture of song. What the pattern does is allow Thomas to illustrate . . . how a person's experience seems to be composed of two conflicting and complementary forces. The first part of the poem, the six diamond-shaped stanzas, describes the poet's vision of someone being born in the next room—God, or his son, or himself—while he is dying. The second part of the poem, the six wing-shaped stanzas, is his prayer (or the prayer of the one in the next room) for the coming of God; that is, either the coming of God as a child to earth, or the coming of God on the last day to awaken the dead. One wonders whether the fact that Thomas's son, Llewelyn, was being born as Yeats was dying served as an inspiration for this poem. But Thomas has always been fascinated by the doubleness of vision that certain Christian paradoxes offered and he en-

ergetically conflates two situations in this poem in order to make the paradox more exciting. Even in an early poem, **"Before I knocked,"** Thomas creates grammatical and visual enigmas to correspond to the paradox that Christ is both father and son:

> I was a mortal to the last
> Long breath that carried to my father
> The message of his dying christ.
>
> You who bow down at cross and altar
> Remember me and pity Him
> Who took my flesh and bone for armour
> And double-crossed my mother's womb.

Mary's womb is "double-crossed" because it is the place where the father becomes the son, mortal and dying, but the son will later die into eternal life and become the father. A similar "double-cross" is acted out in **"Vision and Prayer,"** and made even more conspicuous by the ebb and flow, inhaling and exhaling of the verses: the way that each first half of a stanza mirrors its second half, and the shape of the first half of the poem, the vision, fulfills the shape of the second half, the prayer. If **"Vision and Prayer"** were composed of ordinary stanzas, the second part of the poem would seem to be a sequel to the first, rather than being a version of the first and occurring at the same time. It is the visual design of the poem that allows Thomas to put the two experiences in the same room, or womb.

"Vision and Prayer" is, in a way, one of Thomas's answers to **"Altarwise by owl-light."** The religious sentiments are more excited and convinced than they are in the earlier sequence, and the imagery drawn from Christian mythology is not as challenged by other contrasting or unrelated images. In its treatment of language **"Vision and Prayer"** is also a response to the problems raised by the "Altarwise" sonnets. If the "wound" in discourse can be healed with craftsmanship and use, then the poet has reason to foreground the design and physicality of his poem. The stanzaic shapes display the poem as a verbal object, words that have been treated "as a craftsman does his wood or stone or what-have-you." And this attentiveness to the materiality of his medium, to the pattern-making potential of language, does not diminish the poem's ability to communicate its ideas, since it is the complementary stanzaic shapes that enforce the simultaneity of the poem's two halves, the reciprocity of the poem's two events. As with the works of Hopkins and Yeats, the most intricate pattern or rigid frame only intensifies the ability of the poem to say itself.

One of Thomas's favorite biblical passages was John 1.1: "In the beginning was the Word, and the Word was with God, and the Word was God." This passage had special significance for him because it accorded with his own experience. For him, in the beginning, there had been simply words:

> The first poems I knew were nursery rhymes,
> and before I could read them for myself I had
> come to love just the words of them, the words
> alone. What the words stood for, symbolised, or
> meant, was of very secondary importance. . . .
> And these words were, to me, as the notes of
> bells, the sounds of musical instruments, the

noises of wind, sea, and rain, the rattle of milk-carts, the clopping of hooves on cobbles, the fingering of branches on a window pane, might be to someone, deaf from birth, who has miraculously found his hearing. I did not care what the words said, overmuch, nor what happened to Jack & Jill & the Mother Goose rest of them; I cared for the shapes of sound that their names, and the words describing their actions, made in my ears; I cared for the colours the words cast on my eyes.

What Thomas does with this primary experience is to use it as a touchstone for all his adult poetic craft. He felt that to treat the word as the beginning and its meaning as secondary was a way to make the language of one's time a personal possession again, to cancel out the deadening and conventional associations of the past and bring the word to the reader reborn. The point is to ensure that when he uses a word, such as "clopping" or "fingering" he is, first, sensitive to how it works, as a sound, as a shape, and this sensitivity to what the word *does* provides the foundation for his experiments with what the word conventionally means. Thomas clarifies these priorities in a review of John Clare's poetry, in which he criticizes Clare for accepting the language of his time without question:

> Though words were his active medium, Clare worked towards them, not out of them, describing and cataloguing the objects that met his eyes. In the beginning was the object, not the word. He could not realise, and consequently his expression suffered, that the word is the object. . . . Language to him was rarely more than a vehicle, often somebody else's, to carry along an individual body of feeling and incident.

For Thomas, the word is an object in itself, and the stuff of his art. Its meaning is not unimportant, but it is important not to think of it only as a transmitter of meaning. In order for language to be new and fully operative in the poem, the poet must be aware of all it is doing to the reader above and beyond the transmission of meaning, and for that the poet has to remember the effect language had on him when he was a child, before he understood meanings. This necessity is what makes the remembered child within Thomas a co-composer in so many of his works. For a child's apprehension of language as meaningless "shapes of sound" is a selfish joy, while an adult's attention to the meanings of words is a social business, but in poetry the two work together, the child's unspoilt perceptions lightening the load of adult communication.

Ironically, then, bardic craftsmanship and discipline may have been a way for Thomas to get back to an experience of language that he associated with childhood and freedom. It is an irony that is played out, semantically and musically, in the last verse of **"Fern Hill"**:

> Nothing I cared, in the lamb white days, that
>   time would take me
> Up to the swallow thronged loft by the shadow
>   of my hand,
>   In the moon that is always rising,
>   Nor that riding to sleep
>   I should hear him fly with the high fields

> And wake to the farm forever fled from the
>   childless land.
> Oh as I was young and easy in the mercy of his
>   means,
>   Time held me green and dying
>   Though I sang in my chains like the sea.

There is a partial rhyme scheme controlling the last word of each line, but the rhymes between lines are often more insistent. "Means," the last word in line 7, is only mildly rhymed with "sleep" in line 4 or "fields" in line 5, but more emphatically linked with "green" in line 8 and "chains" in line 9. "Sleep," in fact, is linked assonantally with "hear" and this is then counterpointed by the assonantal link between "riding" and "fly." Close rhymes occur within lines ("lamb," "time;" "swallow," "shadow;" "fly," "high;" "easy," "mercy"), and perhaps the most overt relationships between words are forged with alliteration ("time," "take;" "rising," "riding;" "farm," "forever," "fled;" "mercy," "means;" "sang," "sea"). There are also three modified instances of *cynghanedd sain*, in lines 5 ("hear," "fly," "high," "fields"), 7 ("young," "easy," "mercy," "means"), and 9 ("I," "sang," "chains," "sea"). In short, Thomas has made the principle of rhyme and harmony operative in the entire stanza, rather than just at the end of each line. The result, as Louise Murdy has observed in *Sound and Sense in Dylan Thomas's Poetry,* is a form of "phonetic symbolism." Like Hopkins, Thomas wanted his poems to be a network of interconnected words; each word contributes its sound, shape, and meaning to the design of the stanza, but each word also receives something from the stanza, is "charged" with extra significance by its position and relations. The stanza becomes a web of words that the poet can use, like a spider, to catch a particularly elusive meaning. In this last stanza of **"Fern Hill,"** for instance, the web serves to catch and clarify that last line. In the first place, the phonetic tension that is built up in the stanza is between fricatives, *s* and *f*, usually combined with open vowels, and dentals, *t* and *d*, usually combined with closed vowels. A phrase like "fly with the high fields" uses breathy consonants and open vowels to suggest great freedom, while, in contrast, the phrases "time would take me" or "time held me" suggest constraint. It is as if there are two phonetic "camps" in the stanza, one representing the forces of childhood, innocence, and freedom, while the other represents the forces of time, experience, and limitation. And yet this last verse of the poem is the "momentary peace" in that war, because although both the poet and the child he remembers himself to be are "dying," neither one cares. The child does not care because he does not know; his peace is the peace that precedes the battle. The poet does not care because he has learned to use the tension in his art; his peace is the peace that follows the battle. Consequently, in this last verse, the limitations of time and the energy of the individual come together in one experience, just as "solid and fluid," "flesh and blood" make one body in Thomas's early poems. Notice, for instance, how at the beginning of the stanza there is a euphony between the words of darkness—"time," "thronged," "moon"—but by the end of the stanza this same euphony is associated with the words of childhood—"farm," "young," "green," and "sang." The most important word in the stanza, "chains," partially rhymes with "sang" and therefore leads back to the "young" words, but it also rhymes with time's "means," and its only alliterative link is with the "childless" land. The last word, "sea," alliterates with "sang" and also encloses the stanza with a rhyme to "me" in the first line. These interconnections clarify the matter of the verse, which is that both the memory of his young energy and the experience of time's limitations are necessary for his work, that his "song" is the conciliation and consequence of "chains" and "sea." The stanza is itself an illustration of this thought, for its energy is embodied in time and channelled in chains of rhyming words. A final grammatical note, just to complicate the issue, is that the last line appears to suggest that the sea is representative of unbridled freedom, and that the poet, in singing "like the sea," demonstrates his ability to overcome limitations. But in fact, the sea in **"Refusal to Mourn"** is "tumbling in harness," and what the sea is harnessed to, of course, is the moon. In this last verse of **"Fern Hill"** the moon is an agent of experience and a forerunner of death, so in singing "like the sea" the poet has not overcome limitation, but rather accepted it, and allowed it to shape his art. (pp. 197-215)

> *Sheila Deane, "Kinship and Craftsmanship,"*
> *in her* Bardic Style in the Poetry of Gerard
> Manley Hopkins, W. B. Yeats & Dylan
> Thomas, *UMI Research Press, 1989, pp. 197-*
> *215.*

John Ackerman   (essay date 1991)

[*In the following excerpt from his* A Dylan Thomas Companion: Life, Poetry and Prose, *Ackerman discusses Thomas's early short stories, emphasizing the similarities in technique and theme between these works and his poems.*]

Though he thought it less important than his poetry, throughout his career Dylan Thomas's prose composition was linked with his development as a poet, but this is particularly so in the early stories, which are close in theme and language to the early verse. These stories are strong in style and atmosphere and sensuous power but weak in narrative, being introspective and subjective to an unusual degree. Certainly the stories are close to the universe of the early poems, being richly charged in their language, almost surreal in the worlds they create, and owing much to a fertile imagination and an adolescent's obsessional, introspective concerns with religion, sex and death. 'Naturally, my early poems and stories, two sides of an unresolved argument, came out of a person who came willy-nilly out of one particular atmosphere and environment' Dylan Thomas declared in 1952, turning our attention to the personality and Welsh background that produced them. The prose is essentially a poet's prose, being sensuous, strongly rhythmic, and rich in metaphor; and like Thomas's own poetry at this time it is impassioned, apocalyptic, and the magic of the word and the emotions of the author direct the narrative.

Apart from four experimental prose pieces, including three stories-in-progress published in the *Swansea Gram-*

mar School Magazine, Thomas's first actual story was the bizarre but compelling **'After the Fair'**, written soon after his nineteenth birthday. It is a haunting tale that shows already his gift for dialogue. It also has an element of realism that was to take a lesser role in the early stories but anticipates his later comic, sharply focused prose style. Such early stories as **'The Tree'** are rich in biblical rhythms and echoes, while the satiric tone of **'The Burning Baby'**, a notable tale based on the episode of Dr William Price's cremation of his son, in its grotesque portraiture of lecherous and incestuous ministers clearly shows the influence of the Anglo-Welsh writer Caradoc Evans, whom Dylan Thomas greatly admired. It is in this story, written in December 1934, that the palingram 'Llareggub' first appears. Regrettably publishers were too squeamish to publish a collection of these stories in the thirties; and apart from the six included in *The Map of Love,* though published in America in 1955 several remained unavailable in book form in this country until 1971. Contrasting these stories with his later broadcast reminiscences when writing to his publishers in 1953 Dylan Thomas aptly described them as 'very young and violent and romantic' and as 'the death and blood . . . group typified by **"The Burning Baby"** ', a characteristically succinct and balanced judgement.

'After the Fair' has an unusually clear narrative outline and precise yet poetic evocation of scene and atmosphere that anticipates his later broadcasts:

> The fair was over, the lights in the coco-nut stalls were put out, and the wooden horses stood still in the darkness, waiting for the music and the hum of the machines that would set them trotting forward. One by one, in every booth, the naptha jets were turned down and the canvases pulled over the little gaming tables. The crowd went home, and there were lights in the windows of the caravans.

The central character is a young girl who has left home, and she walks through the deserted fair, her loneliness and the strangely magical setting poignantly conveyed:

> Nobody had noticed the girl. In her black clothes she stood against the side of the round-abouts, hearing the last feet tread upon the sawdust and the last voices die in the distance. Then, all alone on the deserted ground, surrounded by the shapes of wooden horses and cheap fairy boats, she looked for a place to sleep. Now here and now there, she raised the canvas that shrouded the coco-nut stalls and peered into the warm darkness. . . . Once she stepped on the boards; the bells round a horse's throat jingled and were still; she did not dare breathe again until all was quiet and the darkness had forgotten the noise of the bells. . . . But there was nowhere, nowhere in all the fair for her to sleep.

In this clear, musical prose, sensitively conveying sound and touch and sight, we see the girl arrive at the Fat Man's caravan, their beautifully controlled conversation edged with that humour Thomas was to develop in the *Portrait of the Artist as a Young Dog* stories. The tale closes with the arresting, fantastic, and compellingly surreal image of the girl, holding a baby she tries to comfort, and the Fat

Man riding the speeding roundabout in the dark, wind-swept night:

> As the roundabout started, slowly at first and slowly gaining speed, the child at the girl's breast stopped crying and clapped its hands. The night wind tore through its hair, the music jangled in its ears. Round and round the wooden horses sped, drowning the cries of the wind with the beating of their hooves.
>
> And so the men from the caravans found them, the Fat Man and the girl in black with a baby in her arms, racing round and round on their mechanical steeds to the ever-increasing music of the organ.

Regrettably perhaps Thomas moved from this more objective and realistic handling of experience, albeit occasionally touched by fantasy, to obsessively introspective solipsistic, often morbid, preoccupations in his prose: more original in style and theme but more limited in appeal. These tales depict a phantasmagoric world, usually of dark, perverse passions, though sometimes attractively and sensuously lyrical as in '**A Prospect of the Sea**', and, though they are separate stories, Thomas was probably speaking of them in his references to 'the linking together of several short story sequences' for they often read more like sequences than plotted narratives. Discussing in 1953 a collection that would include some of these early tales and the later broadcast reminiscences of childhood, Thomas suggests an interesting autobiographical unity such 'a hotchpotch of a book' would nevertheless possess, throwing valuable light on his conception of these early stories: 'a kind of oblique autobiography: *a growing-up told (a) in stories written while growing up, and (b) in memories of childhood written when grown up*'. The two very different accounts of growing up were of course published posthumously and separately as *A Prospect of the Sea* and *Quite Early One Morning.*

In 1934 Thomas wrote of 'My novel of the Jarvis Valley . . . with a chorus of deadly sins, anagrammatised as old gentlemen, with the incarnated figures of Love and Death . . . an Immaculate Conception . . . a mock Christ, and the Holy Ghost'. As we shall see a mock Christ is the naif hero/victim of '**The Tree**', while the anagrammatised old gentlemen appear in '**The Holy Six**'. In '**The Holy Six**' Thomas conveys an atmosphere of primitive, sensual, mephitic, phantasmagoria, and the six clerical gentlemen are also symbols, as in a progress of the mediaeval Seven Deadly Sins. From the beginning Thomas delighted in such devices as anagram, and clearly Stul is an anagram of 'lust', Edger of 'greed', Vyne of 'envy', and Rafe of 'fear'; so that to Mr Rafe the women represent a 'Massacre of the flesh', 'the shaping wombs' meant 'the death of the flesh' and 'the male nerve was pulled alone'. Other characters include Mr Luctyre (cruelty) and Mr Stipe (spite), and the story is again set in the Jarvis valley. We learn of such familiar figures as Mr and Mrs Owen, the Reverend Mr Davies of Llareggub, and even the 'bald girls from [distant] Merthyr'! The story opens in poetically apocalyptic vein, and the Holy Six make their bizarre entrance:

The Holy Six of Wales sat in silence. The day was drawing to a close, and the heat of the first discussion grew cooler with the falling sun. All through the afternoon they had talked of nothing but the disappearance of the rector of Llareggub, and now, as the first lack of light moved in a visible shape and colour through the room, and their tongues were tired, and they heard the voices in their nerves, they waited only for the first darkness to set in. At the first signs of night they would step from the table, adjust their hats and smiles, and walk into the wicked streets. Where the women smiled under the lamps, and the promise of the old sickness stirred in the fingertips of the girls in the dark doorways, the Six would pass dreaming, to the scrape of their boots on the pavement, of the women throughout the town smiling and doctoring love. To Mr Stul the women drifted in a maze of hair, and touched him in a raw place. The women drifted around Mr Edger. He caught them close to him, holding their misty limbs to his with no love or fire. The women moved again, with the grace of cats, edging down the darker alleys where Mr Vyne, envious of their slant-eyed beauty, would scrape and bow. To Mr Rafe, their beauties, washed in blood, were enemies of the fluttering eyes.

An earlier story, '**The Enemies**', had told of the Reverend Mr Davies's misadventure, losing his way in the Jarvis hills and arriving at the home of Mr and Mrs Owen. Interestingly, this tale reveals the closeness of the themes of these narratives to Thomas's early poetry, for the poet's pantheistic vision, pagan in its atavistic overtones, is vividly registered. Thus the lost clergyman 'is frightened of the worm in the earth, of the copulation in the tree, of the living grease in the soil'. Threatened by these dark pantheistic forces he 'felt desolation in his vein', a phrase used in the poem '**This bread I break**' written six weeks earlier. An eerily anthropomorphic world of nature besets the frightened clergyman: 'Outside the window was the brown body of the earth, the green skin of the grass, and the breasts of the Jarvis hills; there was a wind that chilled the animal earth, and a sun that had drunk up the dews of the fields; there was creation sweating out of the pores of the trees.' Christian conflicts are imaged at the story's end, when confronted by the 'dark mind . . . and dark body' of Mr and Mrs Owen, he 'stared and prayed, like an old god beset by his enemies'. Likewise in '**The Visitor**' in dying Peter's vision when 'the dead, picked to the symmetrical bones, were huddled in under the soil by the wind . . . the worm and the death-beetle undid the fibres of the animal bones . . . and the weeds through the sockets and the flowers on the vanished breasts sprouted up with the colours of the dead life fresh on their leaves' we are moving in the world of the poetry of this period. Such poems as '**The force that through the green fuse drives the flower**' and '**And death shall have no dominion**' are echoed in the imaging of death, a visitor like the thief in the later verse of '**In Country Sleep**' though at this stage more violent than benign, but in Dylan's phrase about these stories 'the incarnated figure . . . of death':

> And the blood that had flowed, flowed over the ground, strengthening the blades of the grass, fulfilling the wind-planted seeds in its course,

into the mouth of the spring. Suddenly all the streams were red with blood, a score of winding veins. . . . He saw the streams and the beating water, how the flowers shot out of the death.

Notably, the somewhat morbid poetic fantasy reaches an unusually arresting narrative climax to close this significantly titled tale **'The Visitor'**:

Rhiannon, he said, hold my hand, Rhiannon.

She did not hear him, but stood over his bed and fixed him with an unbreakable sorrow.

Hold my hand, he said. And then: Why are you putting the sheet over my face?

Here Dylan Thomas's notion of the mysterious and inarticulate unity of man and nature in death is disturbingly and dramatically conveyed.

'The Tree', the second story Thomas wrote and the first in his poetic, apocalyptic and biblical vein, is darkly, even savagely, lyrical, though it benefits from a clearer narrative progression. Here the poet has a tale to tell; and he tells it with apt dialogue and dramatic effect. Set in the Jarvis hills, again the natural world is more threatening than benign, and Bible-reading, as in Caradoc Evans's stories, is a rather sinister pastime. Even the child, a constant figure in Thomas's prose writing, is more malevolent than innocent as he listens to the gardener:

'In the beginning', he would say 'there was a tree.'

'What kind of tree?'

'The tree where the blackbird's whistling.'

'A hawk, a hawk', cried the child . . .

The gardener would look up at the tree, seeing a monstrous hawk perched on a bough or an eagle swinging in the wind.

We learn that 'the gardener loved the Bible . . . reading of the first love and the legend of apples and serpents. But the death of Christ on the tree he loved most'. While moving in primitive, Old Testament landscapes the inner lives of these larger-than-life figures follow pagan nature-worship and beliefs:

His [the gardener] world moved and changed as spring moved along the branches, changing their nakedness; his God grew up like a Tree from the apple-shaped earth, giving bud to His children and letting His children be blown from their places by the breezes of winter; winter and death moved in one wind.

Such writing recalls the creative-destructive unity of man and nature perceived in poems such as **'The force that through the green fuse drives the flower'**, also written towards the end of 1933.

In the strange countryside of the Jarvis hills, with its primitive intensities and simplicities, rural Carmarthenshire transformed by biblical atmospherics clearly neighbours the stark world of Caradoc Evans's rural Cardiganshire, as in the idiot's entry to the tale:

There was an idiot to the east of the country who walked the land like a beggar. Now at a farmhouse and now at a widow's cottage he begged for his bread. A parson gave him a suit, and it lapped round his hungry ribs and shoulders and waved in the wind as he shambled over the fields.

But unlike Caradoc's suffering troglodytes, Dylan Thomas's idiot is nourished by his mysterious and lyrical bond with the natural world, an empathy Keatsian in its sensitivity and sensuousness but more metaphysical in its implications:

He had known of the Jarvis Hills; their shapes rose over the slopes of the county to be seen for miles around, but no one had told him of the valley lying under the hills. Bethlehem, said the idiot to the valley, turning over the sounds of the word and giving it all the glory of the Welsh morning. He brothered the world around him, sipped at the air, as a child newly born sips and brothers the light. The life of the Jarvis valley, steaming up from the body of the grass and the trees and the long hand of the stream, lent him a new blood. Night had emptied the idiot's veins, and dawn in the valley filled them again.

'Bethlehem', said the idiot to the valley.

On Christmas morning the child discovers the idiot, observes his Christ-like patience:

So the child found him under the shelter of the tree, bearing the torture of the weather with a divine patience, letting his long hair flow where it would, with his mouth set in a sad smile.

As in his early poetry Dylan Thomas seems to be exploring the relationship between biblical story and contemporary reality as the crucifixion in the garden proceeds swiftly, dramatically, yet with an ironically casual, almost homely touch: 'Stand up against the tree.' The idiot, still smiling, stood up with his back to the elder. 'Put out your arms like this.' The idiot put out his arms.

The child ran as fast as he could to the gardener's shed, and, returning over the sodden lawns, saw that the idiot had not moved but stood, straight and smiling, with his back to the tree and his arms stretched out.

'Let me tie your hands.'

The idiot felt the wire that had not mended the rake close round his wrists. It cut into the flesh, and the blood from the cuts fell shining on to the tree.

'Brother', he said. He saw that the child held silver nails in the palm of his hand.

Wittily, in this snowy Christmas setting, and aptly relating biblical and present time, the reference to Bethlehem clearly echoes the Carmarthenshire village of that name, a hamlet near Llangadog. Thereby, too, the idiot's innocence and holiness in this Welsh Bethlehem setting is identified with that of Christ's childhood, and we may aptly recall Dylan Thomas's reference to 'a mock Christ' in 'my novel of the Jarvis Valley'. In this story biblical narrative has been interpreted in modern and personal terms, as in Thomas's early verse, for evidently poet and prose writer run together here. *The Map of Love* contains both prose and verse, a rare form of publication in a major poet, yet so shared are the themes and language that the resulting whole is one of perfect harmony.

Undoubtedly the most striking of Dylan Thomas's early stories is **'The Burning Baby'**, its title the provisional one for the hoped-for publication of these stories in the thirties. In addition to the poetic power of the language it sustains the dramatic progress of its emotions and plot. Thomas's fellow Anglo-Welsh writer and friend at this time, Mr Glyn Jones, has valuably suggested the source of this compelling tale. Visiting Aberystwyth with Dylan Thomas in 1934 to meet Caradoc Evans, Glyn Jones told him the story of Dr William Price of Llantrisant, the Welsh doctor and druidic figure who chanted pagan addresses to the moon, boasted of supernatural powers, named his much-loved illegitimate son Iesu Grist (Jesus Christ) and cremated him on a hilltop when he died at five years of age, chanting wild laments over the body. Incidentally, Dr Price's successful defence of himself at a subsequent trial made cremation legal in this country. Glyn Jones recalls that Dylan listened to this story while smoking and lounging on his bed at their Aberystwyth hotel, so engrossed that he afterwards discovered the bedsheet to be riddled with cigarette burns! Clearly the incident of the child's cremation fired the poet's imagination; and indeed the death by fire of a child he was later to commemorate memorably in his poetry, and similar themes of nature's role are explored in both, although a subsidiary element in this satiric but elemental tale.

Evidently influenced by Caradoc Evans's stories, religious hypocrisy is mocked, for the central character is the vicar Rhys Rhys and the child he burns is the baby his daughter conceives by him. This event opens the tale:

> They said that Rhys was burning his baby when a gorse bush broke into fire on the summit of the hill. The bush, burning merrily, assumed to them the sad white features and the rickety limbs of the vicar's burning baby. What the wind had not blown away of the baby's ashes, Rhys Rhys had sealed in a stone jar.

Soon we meet the vicar's eldest son, a changeling, an idiot, with long green hair, who has had strange sexual adventures, for his sister 'was to him as ugly as the sowfaced woman of Llareggub who had taught him the terrors of the flesh. He remembered the advances of that unlovely woman'. Interestingly, this is the first appearance of the word 'Llareggub', its coining a device employed also in Samuel Butler's title *Erewhon*. The son enters the scene vividly in this primeval world, Thomas delighting in the evocation of Gothic horror:

> They heard his son howl in the wind. They saw him walking over the hill, holding a dead animal up to the light of the stars. They saw him in the valley shadows as he moved, with the motion of a man cutting wheat, over the brows of the fields. In a sanatorium he coughed his lungs into a basin, stirring his fingers delightedly in the blood. What moved with invisible scythe

through the valley was a shadow and a handful of shadows cast by the grave sun.

Such writing not only brings to mind Thomas's own tubercular symptoms as an adolescent and his preoccupation with this, but the rural farm landscapes near Blaen Cwm and Fern Hill farm, albeit here imaginatively re-created in somewhat sinister colours. The morbid description of the boy's discovery of a dead rabbit is used to release feelings of horror and cruelty:

> The rabbit's head was riddled with pellets, the dogs had torn open its belly, and the marks of a ferret's teeth were upon its throat. He lifted it gently up, tickling it behind the ears. The blood from its head dropped on his hand. Through the rip in the belly, its intestines had dropped out and coiled on the stone.

This shares something with Thomas's description, though presented with grim humour, of a not dissimilar incident in a letter written from Blaen Cwm in 1933.

> Some hours ago a man came into the kitchen, opened the bag he was carrying, and dropped the riddled bodies of eight rabbits onto the floor. He said it was a good sport, showed me their torn bellies and opened heads, brought out the ferret from his pocket for me to see. The ferret might have been his own child, he fondled it so. . . . He called it Billy Fach.

Interestingly, too, the same paragraph in the letter relates that 'There are a few books on the floor beside me—an anthology of poetry from Jonson to Dryden, the prose of Donne, a Psychology of Insanity.' He also lists a Bible.

But to return to the unfolding narrative of **'The Burning Baby'** we read that 'It was, they said, on a fine sabbath morning in the middle of summer that Rhys Rhys fell in love with his daughter.' Clearly the adolescent poet is morbidly obsessed with the corruption of the flesh:

> He [Rhys Rhys] moved his hand up and down her arm. Only the awkward and the ugly, only the barren bring forth fruit. The flesh of her arm was red with the smoothing of his hand. He touched her breast. From the touch of her breast he knew each inch of flesh upon her. Why do you touch me there? she said.

Rhys Rhys's immolation of the child his daughter conceives by him is described in the light of the minister's religious guilt and horror at the corruption of the flesh, albeit his own. It is an eloquent and dramatic scene:

> Surrounded by shadows, he prayed before the flaming stack, and the sparks of the heather blew past his smile. Burn, child, poor flesh, mean flesh, flesh, flesh, sick sorry flesh, flesh of the foul womb, burn back to dust, he prayed.

Undoubtedly hypocrisy is the chief target of Thomas's ferocious satire, and like Caradoc Evans his rooted instinct is to mock and wound the Nonconformist clergy, depicted in their chapel setting and ethos:

> That night he preached of the sins of the flesh. O God in the image of our flesh, he prayed.

His daughter sat in the front pew, and stroked
her arm. She would have touched her breast
where he had touched it, but the eyes of the congregation were upon her.

Flesh, flesh, flesh, said the vicar.

Dylan Thomas's mockery turns to a sardonic, biting comedy as he attributes perverse desires to the religious and
'respectable' in his satiric attack, exploiting its possibilities
on a wider, but less realistic canvas than Caradoc Evans:

> Rhys Rhys sat in his study, the stem of his pipe
> stuck between his flybuttons, the bible unopened
> on his knees. The day of God was over, and the
> sun, like another sabbath, went down behind the
> hills. . . . Merry with desire, Rhys Rhys cast
> the bible on the floor. He reached for another
> book, and read, in the lamplit darkness, of the
> old woman who had deceived the devil. The
> devil is poor flesh, said Rhys Rhys.

Characteristically, too, Dylan Thomas sets the burning of
the child's body in the familiar pattern and symmetry of
nature's and man's dissolution; such words as 'worm' and
'star' derived from the language of his early poetry:

> The fruit of the flesh falls with the worm from
> the tree. Conceiving the worm, the bark crum-
> bles. There lay the poor star of flesh that had
> dropped, like the bead of a woman's milk,
> through the nipples of the wormy tree.

Written shortly before his twentieth birthday 'The Burning Baby' both dramatically and poetically notably embodies his emotional, intellectual and instinctual preoccupations at this point.

Perhaps the most charming and pleasing of these early
tales are the lyrical effusions such as 'A Prospect of the
Sea', a beautiful evocation of high summer in Carmarthenshire countryside as experienced by a boy already a
precocious pantheist. Is not this a picture of those green
and golden summers of 'Fern Hill', in prose, but a powerfully sensuous and rhapsodic one?

> It was high summer, and the boy was lying in the
> corn. He was happy because he had no work to
> do and the weather was hot. He heard the corn
> sway from side to side above him, and the noise
> of birds who whistled from the branches of the
> trees that hid the house. Lying flat on his back,
> he stared up into the unbrokenly blue sky falling
> over the edge of the corn. The wind, after the
> warm rain before noon, smelt of rabbits and cat-
> tle. . . . Now he was riding on the sea, swim-
> ming through the golden corn waves, gliding
> along the heavens like a bird. . . . This was the
> best summer since the first seasons of the world.
> He did not believe in God, but God had made
> this summer full of blue winds and heat and pi-
> geons in the house wood.

A dream-like country girl, half princess, half temptress,
appears and kisses him, exciting his desires and fears, but
'if he cried aloud to his uncle in the hidden house, she
would make new animals, beckon Carmarthen tigers out
of the mile-away wood'. The afternoon moves to evening
in a richly poetic prose, both precise and evocative in its

effect, that demonstrates Thomas's early mastery of image
and rhythm, particularly in the creation of a haunting, ho-
listic pastoralism:

> The afternoon was dying; lazily, namelessly
> drifting westward through the insects in the
> shade, over hill and tree and river and corn and
> grass to the evening shaping in the sea; blowing
> away; being blown away from Wales in a wind,
> in the slow, blue grains, like a wind full of
> dreams and medicines; down the tide of the sun
> on to the grey and chanting shore where the
> birds from Noah's ark glide by with bushes in
> their mouths, and tomorrow and tomorrow
> tower over the cracked sand-castles.

Such writing anticipates the visionary and healing pantheism of the last poems. But now, racing the boy to the sea,
Venus-like the girl disappears in the 'flesh and bone water'
and waves. 'Come back! Come back!' cries the boy, his
words, like Captain Cat's later in *Under Milk Wood,*
chiming the theme that was to shape Thomas's development as a prose writer. That development was an ever
more poignant search for *temps perdu,* a quest later enriched by humorous and exact recollection. The story ends
on a note of bucolic romanticism and pastoral healing that
is sustained by biblical myth and language, not unlike the
later poem 'Prologue':

> On a hill to the horizon stood an old man build-
> ing a boat . . . And through the sky, out of the
> beds and gardens, down the white precipice built
> of feathers, the loud combs and mounds, from
> the caves in the hill, the cloudy shapes of birds
> and beasts and insects drifted into the hewn
> door. A dove with a green petal followed in the
> raven's flight. Cool rain began to fall.

This story was first published in 1937, shortly before 'Prologue to an Adventure', which appeared in the first number of Keidrych Rhys's magazine *Wales* and which it
seems was to be part of a 'reversed version of *Pilgrim's
Progress*' and 'tells of the adventures of Anti-Christian in
his travels from the city of Zion to the City of Destruction'
as Dylan wrote. This prose piece whose opening sentence
'As I walked through the wilderness of this world, as I
walked through the wilderness, as I walked through the
city with the loud electric faces' graced the front cover of
Wales, told of the wanderings of Daniel Dom and his visit
to the pub/club called Seven Sins. But Dylan Thomas
turned from the style and preoccupations of the early stories to the very different prose of the *Portrait* stories when
just over a year later he published 'A Visit to Grandpa's',
the first of these autobiographical, humorous and nostalgi-
cally recollected stories of childhood and adolescence. It
was a fruitful and maturing change of direction. Clearly
the early fiction, influenced by the climate of Freudian
psychology, its expression echoing biblical language and
rhythms, is dominated by the sexual and death-haunted
preoccupations of an inwardly turned and highly poetic
imagination. It explores rites whereby the natural world
unites the living and the dead, and registers the passing
from innocence to experience, particularly in the sexual
terms. That passage is marked by considerable guilt and
morbidity. I think such factors as Thomas's work as a
journalist in Swansea, his marriage to Caitlin in 1937 and

their settling in Laugharne in 1938, turned Thomas's eye away from his introspective intensities and outward to the world around him, both realistically observed and exactly recollected. Once he had discovered this new direction in **'A Visit to Grandpa's'** he followed it with sureness and vigour, perhaps prompted, too, by the refusal of several publishers to publish the proposed collection of sixteen stories titled 'The Burning Baby' fearing they might offend public taste at that time. Dylan Thomas spoke of **'A Prospect of the Sea'** as 'one of my own favourites' when his editor at Dent, Richard Church, excluded it from *The Map of Love,* complaining that it had 'moments of sensuality without purpose [and it] brings us near the danger zone'. Even as late as 1955 when Dent posthumously published *A Prospect of the Sea,* the phrase 'the death from playing with yourself' was excluded from this title story. However, Richard Church had perceptively urged Dylan, as he records in 1936, 'to write a story about my earlier world' in contrast to what the poet referred to as the 'twenty difficult and violent tales' in his letter of reply to him. But whatever the motives and inner compulsions, in two years the highly charged prose of the tales in *The Map of Love,* of which Thomas's description of himself in 1934 as 'I am a Symbol Simon' is an apt description, had given way to that rich and authentic blend of the pathos and comedy of compassionately observed Welsh life. It became Thomas's *forte* as a prose writer. (pp. 166-79)

> *John Ackerman, in his* A Dylan Thomas
> Companion: Life, Poetry and Prose, *The
> Macmillan Press Ltd., 1991, 309 p.*

FURTHER READING

Bibliography

Gaston, Georg. *Dylan Thomas: A Reference Guide.* Boston: G. K. Hall, 1987, 213 p.
    Comprehensive listing of secondary sources.

Maud, Ralph. *Dylan Thomas in Print: A Bibliographical History.* Pittsburgh: University of Pittsburgh Press, 1970, 261 p.
    Intended as a "readable and lively" bibliography. Maud presents a thorough listing of primary and secondary sources.

Rolph, J. Alexander. *Dylan Thomas: A Bibliography.* London: J. M. Dent & Sons, 1956, 108 p.
    First full-length bibliography of works by and about Thomas, including a foreword by Edith Sitwell as well as illustrations.

Biography

Ackerman, John. *Dylan Thomas: His Life and Work.* London: Oxford University Press, 1964, 201 p.
    Critical biography highlighting the influence of Thomas's Welsh background on his works.

Brinnin, John Malcolm. *Dylan Thomas in America: An Inti-*

mate Journal. 1955. Reprint. London: Arlington Books, 1988, 313 p.
    Chronicle of Thomas's four reading tours in America from 1950 to 1953.

Davies, Walford. *Dylan Thomas.* Rev. ed. New York: St. Martin's Press, 1990, 68 p.
    Biographical study stressing the importance of Welsh culture and landscape in Thomas's works.

Ferris, Paul. *Dylan Thomas.* London: Hodder and Stoughton, 1977, 309 p.
    Comprehensive biography incorporating previously unused or unpublished archive material as well as interviews with numerous friends and acquaintances of Thomas.

FitzGibbon, Constantine. *The Life of Dylan Thomas.* Boston: Little, Brown and Co., 1965, 370 p.
    Authorized critical biography.

Korg, Jacob. *Dylan Thomas.* New York: Twayne Publishers, 1965, 205 p.
    General biographical and critical survey.

Read, Bill. *The Days of Dylan Thomas.* New York: McGraw-Hill, 1964, 189 p.
    Biography featuring diverse photographs by Rollie McKenna and others.

Criticism

Bold, Alan, ed. *Dylan Thomas: Craft or Sullen Art.* London: Vision Press, 1990, 181 p.
    Essays stressing Thomas's works rather than his public image. Bold states: "This book aims to shift the emphasis from the wild Welshman to the serious man of letters."

Brinnin, John Malcolm, ed. *A Casebook on Dylan Thomas.* New York: Thomas Y. Crowell Co., 1960, 322 p.
    Collects reviews, essays, and appreciations by such noted critics and contemporaries of Thomas as Elder Olson, Henry Treece, and Geoffrey Grigson, as well as a selection of Thomas's most noted poems.

Cleverdon, Douglas. *The Growth of Milk Wood.* London: J. M. Dent & Sons, 1969, 124 p.
    Examines the eleven versions of *Under Milk Wood,* discussing Thomas's composition of the work and offering a textual analysis of its variations.

Cox, C. B., ed. *Dylan Thomas: A Collection of Critical Essays.* Englewood Cliffs, N.J.: Prentice-Hall, 1966, 186 p.
    Includes essays written in the decade following Thomas's death by David Daiches, Ralph Maud, Elder Olson, and others.

Daiches, David. "Contemporary Poetry in Britain." *Poetry* LXII, No. 3 (June 1943): 150-64.
    Discusses Thomas's influence on his contemporaries. Daiches states that Thomas "has restored violence and passion to English poetic imagery, and in his search for myths and symbols he had discovered (or rediscovered) that intensity of utterance can enrich meaning as well as analytic precision."

Davies, Walford, ed. *Dylan Thomas: New Critical Essays.* London: J. M. Dent & Sons, 1972, 282 p.
    Includes contributions by such critics as John Wain,

John Bayley, and David Holbrook, offering a "critical climate in which Thomas is seen variously as consummate artist, crippled genius, erudite metaphysical or psychological curiosity."

Gaston, Georg, ed. *Critical Essays on Dylan Thomas.* Boston: G. K. Hall, 1989, 197 p.

Contains essays written since Thomas's death that focus on "three major areas: his craft, his religion, and his influential reputation."

Greenway, William. "Dylan Thomas and 'The Flesh's Vision'." *College Literature* XVI, No. 3 (Fall 1989): 274-80.

Studies Thomas's use of multiple perspectives in his poetry.

Holbrook, David. *Dylan Thomas: The Code of Night.* London: Athlone Press, 1972, 271 p.

Psychoanalytic examination of Thomas's poetry, maintaining that Thomas "suffered a profound confusion of identity."

Kertzer, Jonathan. "Dylan Thomas." In his *Poetic Argument: Studies in Modern Poetry.* Kingston, Ontario: McGill-Queen's University Press, 1988, 201 p.

Analyzes Thomas's attempt to reconcile the intellect and emotion in his poetry. Kertzer asserts: "I wish to show how he devised an equivocal system with which to argue against death, a system that is challenged by its own claims about unreason, since it frustrates the poet even as it liberates him."

Kleinman, H. H. *The Religious Sonnets of Dylan Thomas: A Study in Imagery and Meaning.* Berkeley: University of California Press, 1963, 153 p.

In-depth analysis of the "Altarwise" sonnet sequence. Kleinman asserts: "I believe the sonnets are a deeply moving statement of religious perplexity concluding in spiritual certainty. They reflect the wonder, awe, doubt, and faith of a young poet who could not reconcile the capacity of divine pity with the necessity of human sacrifice."

Olson, Elder. *The Poetry of Dylan Thomas.* Chicago: University of Chicago Press, 1954, 164 p.

Important early study of Thomas's poetry with an extensive analysis of the "Altarwise" sonnet sequence.

Pratt, Annis. *Dylan Thomas's Early Prose: A Study in Creative Mythology.* Pittsburgh: University of Pittsburgh Press, 1970, 226 p.

Study of Thomas's "early prose and its effects upon the early and later poetry."

Tedlock, E. W., ed. *Dylan Thomas: The Legend and the Poet: A Collection of Biographical and Critical Essays.* Westport, Conn.: Greenwood Press, 1960, 283 p.

Collects essays highlighting aspects of Thomas's life and poetry.

Volsik, Paul. "Neo-Romanticism and the Poetry of Dylan Thomas." *Etudes Anglaises* XLII, No. 1 (January-March 1989): 39-54.

Places Thomas among neo-Romantic artists and writers whose influence was felt from the 1930s to the 1950s in England.

Additional coverage of Thomas's life and career is contained in the following sources published by Gale Research: *Contemporary Authors,* **Vols. 104, 120;** *Dictionary of Literary Biography,* **Vols. 13, 20;** *Major 20th-Century Writers; Poetry Criticism,* **Vol. 2;** *Short Story Criticism,* **Vol. 3;** *Something about the Author,* **Vol. 60; and** *Twentieth-Century Literary Criticism,* **Vols. 1, 8.**

Price Warung

1855-1911

(Pseudonym of William Astley) English-born Australian short story writer, essayist, and journalist.

INTRODUCTION

Warung was the author of regional and historical fiction chiefly about the Australian convict system. His short stories first appeared in the Sydney *Bulletin* during the 1890s, when that journal provided the principal forum for a developing national literature, and are considered representative of the attitudes and ambitions of a generation of young Australian writers seeking to establish a national identity.

Warung was born in Liverpool, England, and raised in Melbourne, Australia. After working in bookstores during his youth, in 1876 he and a friend founded a newspaper, the Richmond *Guardian,* which soon failed. Later that year he found work with the Riverine *Herald* in Echuca, north of Melbourne. Warung was disabled for several years during this time with a degenerative nerve disease; on his recovery in 1880 he worked as a journalist in Victoria and Tasmania. After his marriage in 1884 he settled in New South Wales, working chiefly as a free-lance writer and editor and becoming active in Labour and nationalistic Federation politics thereafter. During the 1890s he became one of the most prolific contributors of fiction and essays to the *Bulletin* and other periodicals. His five volumes of short stories appeared between 1892 and 1898. Throughout his life Warung suffered recurrences of the nerve disorder that had afflicted him in his twenties, and commentators believe that for much of his life Warung was addicted to drugs that may have been prescribed initially for this condition. For several years he was confined intermittently to an asylum in Lidcombe, New South Wales, before his death in 1911.

Most of Warung's short stories deal with the more brutal aspects of the convict system, such as the practice of assignment, whereby the colonial government leased convict labor to private employers under often harsh conditions. Warung's antipathy for the British administration of Australia's penal institutions has been cited as the salient characteristic of his fiction and the source of some stylistic and thematic weaknesses. For example, H. M. Green has described Warung's convict characters as "little more than figures representative of wronged humanity," and other critics have noted that Warung invariably depicted officials as one-dimensional caricatures of unalloyed evil. Further, some critics have noted that Warung often seems to dwell with grim satisfaction on the more grisly details of the violence that is a staple feature of his stories. In "The Pegging-Out of Overseer Franke," for example, he is unsparing in his detailed account of a convict who, after

being unjustly beaten, overpowers an overseer, flogs and shoots the man, and then stakes him out on an anthill to await an agonizing death. Cecil Hadgraft has commented that "this appalling recital Warung offers almost with relish."

Critics familiar with Warung's journalistic background initially assumed that his short stories were largely reportorial transcriptions of actual events as recalled by participants. Indeed, Warung claimed to have devoted years to gathering oral accounts from former officials and convicts, although his claim remains unsubstantiated. Most commentators conclude that Warung may have drawn on factual reports or on popularized accounts of the exploits of figures from Australia's past, but that his stories are substantially fictional. Critics acknowledge that far from providing an impartial historical interpretation, Warung created fiction that was biased in its portrayal of British administration of the penal system and instrumental in codifying a body of popular myth about Australia's convict past. A less accomplished writer than his contemporaries and fellow *Bulletin* contributors Henry Lawson and A. B. Paterson, Warung has never been widely known outside of Australia. He retains a measure of renown within his adopted country, however, for his chronicles of a distinctive chapter from Australia's past.

PRINCIPAL WORKS

Tales of the Convict System (short stories) 1892
Tales of the Early Days (short stories) 1894; also published as *Tales of Australian Early Days,* 1894
Tales of the Old Regime and The Bullet of the Fated Ten (short stories) 1897
Half-Crown Bob and Tales of the Riverine (short stories) 1898
Tales of the Isle of Death (Norfolk Island) (short stories) 1898

The Athenaeum (essay date 1894)

[*In the following review of* Tales of Australian Early Days, *the critic condemns Warung's brutal subject matter and empathy with the convicts about whom he writes.*]

Tales of Australian Early Days, by Price Warung, should never have been written; but as it has been published our advice is that it should not be read. Of what possible use can it be to rake up again the unspeakable horrors of Norfolk Island or of Port Arthur? If any reader, from a love of the horrible, wishes to gloat over the miseries of criminals, he can do so in Marcus Clarke's *His Natural Life;* or if he is desirous to study the question of "Prison Discipline," he will find it ably discussed in the *Secrets of the Prison House,* by Major Arthur Griffiths, where every phase of it is explained, from the extreme indulgence at Elmira to the savage severities of Siberian gaols. Mr. Price Warung's book, however, possesses this feature of interest, that it is written entirely from the prisoners' point of view. Every provocation, every mitigating circumstance, is put forward, and their atrocities are never mentioned with censure; but even a cursory perusal of these pages will cause the reflecting reader to pause before he condemns a discipline which had to deal with doubly and trebly convicted criminals, debased to a degree which can scarcely be conceived. If the punishment was brutal, the recipients were lower than brutes. The following outrage, we are told, occurred at Sydney, where prisoners were worked before second and third convictions consigned the worst of that unhappy class to Norfolk Island. It was the work of a "gentleman" convict, who, like all other prisoners, was, we imagine, innocent of the crime for which he was "sent out," and whose subsequent conduct is extolled as that of a hero. His "gentlemanlike" feelings led to the following act of revenge for a flogging:—"Blast you—yes. You cut the gentleman out of me with the cat—you die." Having

stunned the overseer with a blow of a pickaxe, and fired a bullet through the palm of his hand,—

In the afternoon they pegged out overseer Franke. On an ant-hill, on a wooded gully rise, they fastened him down with tent lines. His right hand was stretched out with tightened cord again—this time to a special peg. A track of sugar was made from the orifice of the ant-bed to the hole in the hand, in case the industrious little creatures should not otherwise perceive so appetizing a banquet as that shattered fragment of official humanity. Before they pegged him out they flogged overseer Franke. After they pegged him out they placed some victuals and water—just outside his reach. It was Mann who suggested that last refinement. In fact it was the gentleman whom the cat had robbed of his gentlehood that devised the means for keeping the latter-day Tantalus busy while he lived. . . . Absalom West found Franke's skeleton in 1824.

> *"Stories of Life Abroad," in* The Athenaeum, *No. 3473, May 19, 1894, p. 842.*

Vance Palmer (essay date 1954)

[*Palmer was a novelist, editor, critic, and literary historian of his native Australia. In the following excerpt, he provides a brief biographical sketch of Warung and discusses Warung's contributions of convict fiction to the* Bulletin.]

[The periodical the Sydney *Bulletin*], under J. F. Archibald, is associated in the popular mind with the Nineties, and with the dream of establishing a self-contained and self-sufficient democracy. . . . The *Bulletin*'s pages reflected all that was vague and all that was positive in the life of the time, and the literature it helped to bring into being remains as the most definite proof that, during the period, a creative spirit, inspired by a new outlook on the Australian world, was actually at work in the country.

In the beginning, J. F. Archibald, its chief begetter, had conceived the paper as a sharpshooter, dancing about on the fringes of society and firing squibs with gay malice at the kind of cruelty and hypocrisy he personally detested. Its weapons were to be the pointed paragraph and the satirical drawing: the republican flag it sported was to be used as a provocative piece of drapery to wave before the bull.

But the needs of the day and its own chequered experience had brought a sense of responsibility. (p. 88)

In the bleak atmosphere of the early nineties, with banks and financial institutions still coming to earth with a dull thud and the drought searing the Western plains, the time had come to turn aside from Utopian schemes and concentrate on a practical programme. The *Bulletin* announced that it stood for a republican form of government; payment of members; one person, one vote; state revenue derived directly from the land; complete secularization of education; reform of the criminal code and the prison system; a united Australia and protection against the world. It denounced religious interference with politics, foreign titles, the Chinese, and imperial federation.

This was its final formulation of the Australian Dream. All the original elements were there, though reduced to political jargon and placed, apparently, in the *Bulletin's* order of importance. (pp. 89-90)

One of the chief things the *Bulletin* had set out to destroy was the tradition of the convict system that still, in its view, cast an ugly shadow over the life of the country. Archibald saw traces of it in the heavy sentences judges occasionally dealt out for minor crimes, in the pretensions of some of the leading families, in the spirit of flunkeyism that prevailed in official and social life. No romantic aura, the paper insisted, should be allowed to surround the early days. (p. 95)

Archibald's instrument for revealing this sordid past was Price Warung (William Astley), a writer of original power, who concentrated on the period with a passionate intensity and made it the basis of his work. To an extent, Price Warung was a man of mystery. He had few friends and was never one of the gay and not-so-gay bohemians who hovered around the *Bulletin* office on pay-day, inventing pathetic stories that might touch the heart of the accountant. Price Warung had come to Melbourne in the late fifties as a child of four, his father being one of a small group who tried to run the *Age* on co-operative lines before it was taken over by David Syme and his brother. He was brought up in Richmond, and in one of his stories speaks of having his interest in the transportation-system aroused by an old convict there who had told him tales of it when he was a boy. Slipping easily into journalism, he founded the *Richmond Guardian* with a partner at the age of twenty-one and then, when it died, moved about the country to serve on various papers. With his fierce, democratic convictions and his passionate belief in a future that would wipe out the stains of the convict past, he was so typical a figure of the time that it is worth while trying to penetrate the fog that still hangs about his memory.

'I knew William Astley as well as he was known to most people,' says Fred Broomfield, 'and that was never much, for he was suspicious and secretive, and his temperament, as the phrenologists say, was "saturnine". At all events I knew him long before he was "Price Warung," when he was editing an illustrated weekly in Sydney. It was called the *Australian Graphic,* and its specialism was the printing of pictures from etched glass. The black-and-white artist, Tom Durkin, had charge of the process, but the journal was short-lived. Astley was a young man when I first met him, about twenty-five, a year older than myself . . .He was a man of middle height, broad-shouldered and deep-chested. His skin was not exactly olive, rather it resembled smoky ivory—dark but clear. His eyes were very bright, beady, brilliant. He had a trick of putting his head on one side and glimpsing up at you meditatively, as if you were a mouse being fascinated to an early death by a highly-intelligent and calculating owl. He was always well-dressed, natty but unobtrusive; his suit dark, his tie dark, no jewellery. He gave you by his manner the impression that he was the confidential agent of a mysterious and hidden personality of consummate power and resource—the keeper of dark and deadly secrets it would be death to reveal.'

At the many meetings of the early nineties when various schemes were being discussed—the project of a workers' daily, the Paraguay expedition, nationalization of land—Astley was a conspicuous figure. Sir George Beeby speaks of how, when he himself was a youth, freshly come to Sydney with a mind wide-open for ideas, he fell completely under Astley's spell, and trailed from one meeting to another in the hope of seeing and hearing him.

'I didn't know anything about him as a writer—probably he had not written any of his convict stories then—but he used to appear at political meetings as if he'd stepped down from some other world and was ready to give us the benefit of his wisdom. Well-dressed, good-looking, and in some queer way "distinguished". Yet no suggestion of the charlatan about him. I used to follow him about: I'd never met a man who filled me with such admiration and positive awe.'

In his stories, this strange being moved over a narrow field, but his penetration of convict life was deeper than Marcus Clarke's and showed a warmer human feeling. Many of the stories collected in such volumes as ***Tales of the Convict System, Tales of the Early Days,*** and ***Tales of the Old Regime,*** are merely fragments, based on incidents the author had dug up from the records and only welded into unity by the application of violence. But in his longer story, **"The Ring,"** Price Warung showed what he could do when not confined to a narrow space. It tells of Captain Maconochie and his attempt, when made Governor of Norfolk Island, to institute a more humane system among the 'lifers' immured there. Maconochie was a sensitive, idealistic man who had been one of the pioneers of prison reform in England. He believed that the worst convicts could be redeemed: now had come his chance to put his ideas into practice among some of the most brutalized human beings ever gathered together. Inevitably, in the story, he fails. These doomed men have worked out a philosophy and a ritual that give their imaginations some release and act as a shield against authority. All the accepted values are reversed: 'Evil be thou my Good' is the note of it, and an anonymous hooded figure acts as Satan, the Lord. If any of the convicts showed signs of weakening or responding in any way to Christian treatment he would immediately be put to death. What can the simple Maconochie do in the face of such diabolism? The only success he has is that one of the toughest convicts does so respond, and goes with open eyes to meet his fate. The subtlety, power, and conviction with which Price Warung describes this kindling of a faint light in the dark raises the little novel almost to the plane of Tolstoy's *Master and Man.*

What Price Warung brought to the *Bulletin,* apart from his convict stories, was a set of sincere beliefs and a capacity for sustained writing. He was never a member of the staff, but he could be counted upon to sum up a public man's achievements in a masterly way, as in his articles on Parkes and Higinbotham when they died, or to guide the footsteps of a wandering politician into the right path by austere though friendly criticism, as in his long open letter to Edmund Barton after the first Federal Convention. (pp. 96-9)

Vance Palmer, "The Bushman's Bible," in his The Legend of the Nineties, *Melbourne University Press*, 1954, pp. 88-108.

Frederick T. Macartney   (essay date 1957)

[*In the following excerpt, the critic maintains that Warung's stories of convict life are characterized chiefly by a florid style, sensationalism of already lurid fact, and acrimony toward the convict system.*]

The general impression created by published appraisals of William Astley's stories, which he wrote under the pen-name of "Price Warung", is singularly misleading. The most outright example is Dr E. Morris Miller's remark in *Australian Literature* (1940) that "After the manner of a scientist, he was subservient to the facts and presented them with an impartiality that at times almost defeated the role of *raconteur.*"

Astley is known mainly for his tales of convict life, and like other writers of fiction dealing with the penal system, he selects the more sensational happenings, which are necessarily the most grim. They are accordingly so appalling that they need no emphasis, but he habitually adds a tone of almost personal acrimony. It is as remote from the scientific spirit (ascribed to him in the above quotation) as anything could be, and it is just as far from impartial historical interpretation. We are concerned with it here as the fault which, with some accompanying floridities of style, cheapens his writing. Persistent denunciation on the level of his generalization of the penal official as "that lesser man" illustrates it. Even when mentioning instances of humane feeling he cannot resist the opportunity for peevish gibes. Writing of Captain Maconochie's attempt to improve conditions on Norfolk Island he remarks that "to the undisguised delight of the Colonial Secretary's Office, Sydney, and the Deputy Commissariat-General's Department of Sydney and Norfolk Island, it failed", though his own version of Maconochie's efforts in the series, "Secret Society of the Ring" shows them frustrated by the ingrained criminality of the convicts themselves. Moreover, Gipps, Governor of New South Wales at the time, though he had little faith in Maconochie's ideas, gave him such aid as was practicable, and after a visit of inspection wrote a favourable report on some aspects of Maconochie's scheme, which was terminated by the English authorities, who considered it defeated the deterrent purpose of transportation and who substituted another plan. Astley's imaginative reconstruction of **"A Day with Governor Arthur"**, picturing that personage "with steely-grey eyes that look with critical disbelief in everything except the system", is a very glib hyperbole of even his rigid rule. The story **"In the Granary"** contains the typical puerile sarcasm: "Not being an officer and gentleman, and not, therefore wholly intoxicated with the absolutism of power, Overseer Cook shuddered." This vilification of officialdom is carried to the point of ascribing to the horses bred by a military captain the viciousness attributed to their master, by whom they were "invariably guaranteed as of no vice, and they inevitably killed a man when rising three years". Astley's aspersion of authority even spills over to the legal profession of his own day, whose occupation of

a building in which convicts were formerly confined is to him appropriate for "their polished blackguardism", and he also describes one of his contemporaneous characters who has stood for parliament unsuccessfully as "still, therefore, an honoured member of the community and unqualified for gaol". The feeble reliance on mechanical generalizations which these extracts typify is shown also in his description of convicts who in the privations of escape have eaten human flesh as thereafter distinguished by a "slavering mouth", and, at the other extreme, by the reference to a gentleman convict whose "delicate nostrils of the long nose, the sweep of the eyelashes, and the chiselling of the mouth, indicated blood and gentle nurture"

Far from being subservient to facts, he interprets them freely to suit his purpose. Amid the typical overloading of **"The Pegging-Out of Overseer Franke"**, a laboured periphrasis suggests that the freeing of convicts was a rarity, though figures for the time of the story, the régime of the humane Macquarie with his policy of convict rehabilitation, indicate the release of about one in every five or six. The incredibility of many episodes embroidering the facts is illustrated by the main incident of **"In the Granary"**. A convict confined in a covered pit ten feet deep leaps to the trapdoor above him, dragging down the attendant who lowers food through it, despite the fact that the convict is of short stature, undernourished, has a seven-pound weight attached to each foot, and that the take-off for the leap is a floor space of eight feet by six. An unlikely situation of another sort is that of **"Captain Maconochie's 'Bounty for Crime' "**, in which Maconochie leaves his wife alone with a brutalized criminal to show belief in the latter's possibility of regeneration, which ensues, though with his precipitate relapse into crime when later told that Maconochie had taken precautions for his wife's protection. No less contrived is the readiness of the ladies in **"Parson Ford's Confessional"** to believe the result of the humorous trick played on the clergyman. Likewise, in **"The Amour of Constable Crake"** a girl's impersonation of her brother to save him from transportation is even less believable in convict circumstances than in the old-fashioned romances in which the device abounds.

In **"The *Henry Porcher* Bolter"** Astley states that his interest in convict themes began through boyhood acquaintance with the absconder of that story. In **"The Initiation of Pine Tree Jack"** he speaks of having perused "hundreds of thousands of pages, printed and in manuscript", relating to the Norfolk Island settlement; one series of tales, when first printed in the *Bulletin* in 1892, was preceded by a statement that the author had "devoted twenty years to the study of early Australia, and had formed in that period a unique collection of manuscript with an index of nearly 300,000 entries"; and in a note in a copy of *Tales of the Isle of Death* in the Mitchell Library he refers to "viva voce testimony" given to him by "former officials and convicts", their total number "exceeding 800". Allowing for the statistical exuberance of all this, that he did engage in considerable research is made plain by his writings, as well as by the fact that he was accommodated with a table at the Sydney Public Library in a room ordinarily reserved for the staff, one of whom described him, in a sense not confined to his work as a writer of fiction, as "something of a romancer", boasting of his library of "thirty thousand volumes", of which, with his equally wonderful collection of manuscripts, nothing has apparently ever been seen by anybody else. (pp. 105-07)

He published four books of convict stories: *Tales of the Convict System* (1892), *Tales of the Early Days* (1894), *Tales of the Old Regime* (1897), and *Tales of the Isle of Death* (1898). Another volume, *Half-Crown Bob and Tales of the Riverine* (1898) consists of stories derived from experience at Echuca, bringing in the old Murray River steamer trade. There are additionally a good many stories of various kinds, not included in the books, in the columns of the *Bulletin* from 1890 to 1897, and in that same journal (August to September 1892) appeared three instalments of **"Bushranging and Outlawry in Australasia"**, a project never completed, also five **"Sketches of a Life of Action"**, referring to Sir George Grey (January to March 1891), an appreciation of George Higinbotham as **"The Greatest of Australia's Dead"** (7th January 1893), and another obituary article, **"Within an Ace of Greatness"** (9th May 1896), on Sir Henry Parkes.

The "Riverine" stories take little categorical advantage of the Murray transport life then so important and now a fascinating memory, but use it as not much more than a drop-scene, with figures moving in front of it rather than in more real distance. A posturing of the characters and facile situations have not here, as in the convict tales, the excuse of a restricted set of conditions. A counterpart of the contrivances there is some sentimentality here, worst in **"The Idyl of Melool Woodpile"**, which also repeats the conventionalized picture of a man "of far from rude parentage, whose delicacy of breeding was apparent in the nostrils and the angle of the face, and in the long wiry fingers that played with the Collins axe which he held in his grasp". The title-story, **"Half-Crown Bob"**, the longest in the collection, is among the best, though it follows an old sentimental pattern. **"Dictionary Ned"** is another, but it sags in the middle with the evangelical heaviness of the repentance of an educated derelict known as College Bill, entailing a not very convincing legacy. The main characters in both live up to their labels rather too obviously. A waggish flavour mitigates such faults in **"The Incineration of Dictionary Ned"**. It tells of a race between two steamboats, in which the winner overcomes a shortage of fuel by using a coffin and its contents which it is conveying for burial ashore.

We must dismiss the notion that Astley's convict tales, his main output, are strictly faithful to facts or impartial in the use of them. Had they been written while the convict system existed their exaggerations might have the excuse of serviceability, though this does not make bad artistry good; but they are the product of an era relieved of transportation and rightly regarding it as an abomination, engendered by social circumstances that permitted flogging in the army and navy, whence our early administrators were derived. A wise representation of any period tries to understand it according to its view of things and its difficulties, as an alternative to sweeping condemnation of any class or rank of men as monsters. "It is worth noting"— using words in *The Foundation of Australia* by Eris

O'Brien regarding the cruellest penal practices, which were not part of the original sentence but applied for offences while serving it—"that the secondary punishments inflicted on convicts in Australia from 1788 to 1821, in their worst excesses were modelled on the régime that existed in England, and generally speaking, were far less severe and more cognizant of human rights than those sanctioned and approved by certain Englishmen whom history and *belles-lettres* would incline us to regard in a far different light".

Obviously, when fiction draws upon particular facts a presentation or interpretation of them purporting to be true is undesirable if it is misleading. The story-writer can use facts without being enslaved by them, and it is only fair to Astley to say that all he claims outright is that, as he wrote concerning "Tales of the Isle of Death," "an episode of fact underlies each story in this book", however he may overlay it. His ability to tell a plain story is evident enough to cause regret that he was not more moderate, yet the garish highlighting of his convict tales is what makes the best of them effective, as in the sinister tension of the "Secret Society of the Ring" series and another, **"The Bullet of the Fated Ten"**. The two "Liberation" stories in *Tales of the Old Regime* turn this power to account with a gruesomeness that almost seems to revel in the repellent details. Serle in his *Dictionary of Australian Biography* refers to "a certain starkness" in Astley's work. The comment is apt at any rate in the sense that the interest is immediate, not subtle or deeply meditated; but for that reason, along with others indicated here, Serle's additional statement that Astley "must be ranked among the best writers of Australian short stories" might be hard to sustain. (pp. 109-11)

> *Frederick T. Macartney, "Sidelights on Price Warung," in his* Australian Literary Essays, *Angus and Robertson, 1957, pp. 105-11.*

Cecil Hadgraft   (essay date 1960)

[*Hadgraft is an Australian educator and critic. In the following excerpt, he identifies Warung's antipathy for the Australian penal system and bias against its administrators as the principal attributes of his fiction.*]

The rich field of horror and injustice during the convict system serves as material for the short stories of Price Warung. This is the pen-name adopted by William Astley (1855-1911). He was a journalist and freelance writer all his life and knew conditions in Victoria, Tasmania, and New South Wales. His strong democratic sympathies were shown in his activities in the Labour cause. Like Marcus Clarke he studied the old penal system and made use of this knowledge in his short stories.

Warung's work lies half-way between pure fiction and documentary writing: he makes up dialogue and names and modifies events; but the names of real persons occur as well, and many of the events have a basis in fact. His sympathies become a bias. Hating the cruelties he recounts, he extends the hatred to officials, to the System and even, one sometimes feels, to the mere exercise of official authority. He is on the side of the underdog; but the underdog under the System was, as Warung well knew, not invariably a deserving case. So he is obliged to pick and choose—many of his convict heroes or chief characters are educated men of good birth. He is not under the same restriction when dealing with officials, since he considers that all of them, with hardly any exceptions, have been indelibly tainted by the prevalent brutality. A striking example of this attitude appears in **"The Pegging-Out of Overseer Franke"** in the volume, *Tales of the Early Days* (1894). The wretched victim is stunned; then on regaining consciousness he has his hand used as a target, is flogged, and then is pegged out beside an anthill. This appalling recital Warung offers almost with relish. Nothing, it seems, is too bad for an official. The point made, however, is that brutality brutalises. The ring-leader in the affair is a gentleman convict named Edgar Allison Mann, who is himself aware of this:

> . . . when the back of a gently-born transport had once been stained with the infamous stigma of the lash-point, only two things, if he were not to become utterly bestial, remained for him to do: to kill his tyrant, and—to die . . .

> "Flog me, and by God who looks from the heaven above, you're a dead man, Mr. Franke."

But Mann is flogged, and what he dreads comes to pass—he becomes a beast:

> After they pegged him out, they placed some victuals and water—just outside his reach. It was Mann who suggested that last refinement.

Warung's stories, then, are strong meat, and his method of narration corresponds. He has a capacity to hold interest, to awaken and sustain suspense—to tell, that is, an exciting tale. (pp. 93-4)

> Cecil Hadgraft, "Turn of the Century: Fiction," in his Australian Literature: A Critical Account to 1955, *William Heinemann Ltd., 1960, pp. 84-104.*

H. M. Green   (essay date 1961)

[*Green is an Australian literary historian and critic. In the following excerpt, he evaluates Warung's convict fiction, noting in particular his journalistic style.*]

["Price Warung" (William Astley, Liverpool, England, 1854-1911)] was a writer of gloomy power, but his nightmares are, in essence at least, a part of history, his horrors are purely physical, and his style is journalistic rather than literary, and as rough and hard as the life that he describes. Astley made his pen-name out of his mother's maiden name and the aboriginal name for Sydney. He was brought to Melbourne as a child of four, became a journalist and is said to have spent nearly twenty years investigating the facts of convictism before he published his first book [*Tales of the Convict System*]; its contents had appeared already in the *Bulletin*. Astley probably knew as much about "the System" as anybody has done. His talent was smaller, his craftsmanship inferior, and his literary personality much less marked than Marcus Clarke's; his men and women are mere sketches of types, and his work does not possess Clarke's all-pervading romantic appeal; but talent he has, and it is marked, though of a quite differ-

ent kind: he was not a romantic but an uncompromising realist, and he lacks Clarke's characteristic tendency to the sentimental and melodramatic, though he can be both at times. Astley's is a documentary style, simple, direct, and circumstantial, concerned not with comment but only with a re-creation of the facts; he reproduces rather than creates, and is by comparison with Clarke a reporter rather than a literary artist; nevertheless he is by no means without imagination, particularly in his account of the secret society of the Ring, and his stories in general gain by their restraint, even if they lack something that Clarke might have given them. And Astley is democratic as Clarke is not: in reading *His Natural Life* our sympathies are with a romantic, sensitive, and educated hero and his undeserved cumulation of misfortunes, though we feel also for ordinary sufferers as they come into the story; in reading Astley we sympathize with the convicts generally, as human beings, and with particular individuals mainly as exemplifying what as a body they all have to suffer. Astley's loathing and horror of the System and its evils are deep and sincere, and he knows how to convey them to his readers; he can be extremely vivid, and, partly because in reading him we are not preoccupied with a particular individual but with the horrors and brutalities themselves, as experienced by men, and occasionally women, who are little more than figures representative of wronged humanity, he is able to make us feel a part of the System in a way that Clarke does not, still less other writers of convict stories, Hay for instance. Yet, like Clarke, and like Hay also, Astley's style is sometimes strained in the attempt to heighten an effect, as when, telling of the blasphemous travesty of a prayer that formed part of the Ring's ceremonial, he says that "The infamous parody of that pathetic appeal as recited by the 'One' dare not be quoted"; and, of the initiation ceremony, "What completed it may not be described, not even hinted". His work is very uneven, the stories in the first book being comparatively commonplace; the Ring stories are far superior, and so, in another way, are the two stories of the liberation of the six prisoners who have been working in "Murderers' Pit" in the Port Arthur coal mines; here is an extract from the second of these stories, **"The Liberation of the Other Three"**. The opening of the pit is blocked by an iron grating and the prisoners' rations are lowered to them daily; they have contrived to cut through the grating and are saving half their rations in order to provide food for their escape. Three of the older hands have murdered the other three and propped them up in order that they may be seen at the daily inspection and their rations lowered as before; but Jones, the leader, has decided to murder the remaining two also, so that he may have plenty of food for himself:

> With a bag of provisions round each of their necks, they began the ascent.
>
> . . . . .
>
> Half-way up Jones stopped. "Plenty o' time, boys. No hurry. An' yer'd better 'and me yer bag, 'Ardy; I'm stronger'n you. 'Old tight ter me w'iles yer looses it." Hardy—fool!—obeyed.
>
> Ten feet higher Jones paused again.
>
> "Toothy, 'and yer bag to 'Ardy. W'iles yer does

it, I'll climb an' jest put my grub outside; I'll be freer to 'elp yer."

They trusted him still, and while he clambered up, Tooth passed his bag to Hardy. Jones went back to where he had left them.

"Steady, lads, for the last tussle! Don't lose 'art now, pals! an' keep a clear 'ead."

. . . . .

A few feet higher. . . .

"Now, 'Ardy, stash 'im with yer foot! we want orl th' grub for oursel's!"

The devilish hint spoke Hardy's own mind. He thrust one of his feet downwards, and with a horrid yell Tooth was—liberated. The light went out.

"Well done, 'Ardy. An' now it's me an' you."

The accent of approbation changed in its breathing into one of menace. And with the change fell, on Hardy's head, a blow with a cut bar. At least, it had been intended for his head, but, through the going out of the light, the blow was misdirected, and slipped on his shoulder.

Hardy shrieked, "God! That's your playin' fair, is it! But if I go, ye'll go too."

He sprang upwards. . . . One awful struggle in mid-air, and—

The rest of the Other Three were liberated.

The non-convict sketches in Astley's last book are unimportant. He wished to write a novel and histories of convictism and bushranging, but was unable to finish any of them; his health was poor and during his last years he was an invalid. (pp. 564-66)

> H. M. Green, "Third Period, 1890-1923: Self-Conscious Nationalism—The Short Story," in his A History of Australian Literature, Pure and Applied: Vol. I, 1789-1923, Angus and Robertson, 1961, pp. 555-83.

Laurie Hergenhan (essay date 1983)

[*Hergenhan is an Australian educator and critic. In the following excerpt from a discussion of Warung in his critical survey of Australian convict fiction, Hergenhan examines ways that three characteristic stories—"Secret Society of the Ring," "The Henry Porcher Bolter," and "How Muster-Master Stoneman Earned His Breakfast"—convey Warung's concern with the relationship between Australia's historical past and its political development beyond colonialism.*]

For a brief period in the early 1890s, Price Warung (William Astley) was the most prolific contributor of short stories to the *Bulletin* and, as with it, his literary reputation has been bound up with a message of democratic nationalism. After some initial success, aided by *Bulletin* promotion, his stories, mostly about the convict system, were soon forgotten, surviving (in any popular sense) mainly in a trickle of representation in the occasional anthologies. . . . (p. 62)

Reviewing in 1892 Henry Parkes's history of Australia, Warung commented: "If the book is not all that one could wish, it is still a work that must be consulted by the publicists of the present as well as by the historical writers of a future time." Warung was himself writing, in the 1890s, of the past as a guide to the present, and viewing both as the inheritance of the future. His success as story writer and political journalist depends largely on such connections, for this was the way he could make the past reverberate for later times, the mark of any good historical writer.

To explore the nature of the values Warung purveyed and his efforts "to connect" eras, it is helpful to look closely at three stories: the **"Secret Society of the Ring"** . . . ; **"The *Henry Porcher* Bolter"** (about a convict escapee); and **"How Muster-Master Stoneman Earned His Breakfast"**.

The **"Secret Society of the Ring"** (hereafter referred to as **"The Ring"**) is basically a story about the possible reform and redemption of convicts, with the conflicting hope and pessimism, and the constraining pressures, both individual and social. Maconochie, the reformer of convict history, is used as an idealist with a scheme for helping hardened convicts. Unlike most of his other plans, this one combines "heart and head", sympathy and a "hard logical apprehension of the facts". His appeal is to "the sense of fraternity which seldom died out": convicts are divided into farming groups, and good or bad behaviour is to affect the "group mates" not just the individual. The main obstacles are the divided loyalties of the convicts and the brutalizing effects of the system. The convicts have reacted against this by substituting a counter-authority, "the Ring", which inverts the basic values on which the system is supposedly based: justice and improvement. This inversion takes the form of an anti-Christian demonism, in the spirit of "Evil be thou my Good". The convicts fear the Ring's despotism (which equals if not surpasses that of the system), but it provides a sustaining group pride because of its traditions and its power—two pillars of the system.

In **"The Ring"**, then, Warung has set up a play of forces with implications reaching beyond its setting to the battle of the non-privileged against the "powers that be"—society. The battle of the two main convict characters, Reynell and Felix, is to fight free of the two coercive authorities of the Ring and the system to embrace a "higher" and a truly communal one. This involves fighting to believe that "it's never too late to repair the past" (as Maconochie advises).

Maconochie as idealist-reformer also has his ordeal: to see his scheme founder. This is presaged in one of the most dramatic moments of the story when he realizes the truth of the taunt of one of the Ring leaders: the system is not founded on justice—British law provides for "just punishment" but "not to give over the offenders to 'unusual punishment' and utter corruption". It is a strength of this story that Warung (untypically) reveals the mixed nature of his characters. Maconochie's reaction shows his human clay: "But what could Maconochie do? Argument imperilled his authority, and after all *he* did not invent the System. So—." This points to the predicament of idealists faced with practicalities: how can they hope to succeed if they inherit a defective social system? Should they not start anew and at the grass roots? But how can one person or group hope to succeed in this?

These lurking questions involve the possibilities of change as developed through the fates of the two convicts, Reynell and Felix. Reynell is won over by Maconochie's scheme but the Ring in retaliation, condemns him to death, ordering the simple ex-farm labourer, Felix, who is bound to him by gratitude and affection, to murder him. After a battle of loyalties, Felix decides to sacrifice himself for Reynell by getting himself shot, though he is in an "agony of doubt" when this happens, thinking (rightly) that his sacrifice may be in vain because his death will seem merely an accident. The ironic conclusion, with its author's comment, would appear to resolve this doubt: Reynell has already committed suicide so "Bill Felix's sacrifice was in vain, after all". Whereas one convict has despaired, the other has displayed "more heart than head" in his bungling behaviour. Felix, though sympathetic and under terrible pressures, is incapable of thinking the issues through, and his devotion is neither recognized by others for what it is, nor has it any practical result. Vance Palmer . . . rightly points to the "kindling of a faint light in the darkness", but any glint of the heroic is engulfed in the ironic (even bitter) blackness of the ending.

"The Ring", as well as being a story of suspense and gothic horrors, is also a moral fable. It suggests that the good impulses of brotherhood can only be destroyed by the system and that, by implication, this loss can be altered only by radical change, not philanthropy—past wrongs cannot be remedied by reform within a flawed social system. The awareness of readers, "outside" the story, that the system had long been abolished, does not lessen its pessimism at its deepest level. Basic problems of social change which the story raises still remain. In the 1890s, as later, hopes of aware reformers like Warung were offset by doubts and remained largely unfulfilled. In this sense **"The Ring"** can be read as a parable for all times.

The pessimism of **"The Ring"** is typical of Warung's stories. Only one or two convicts are redeemed, in death, and even the possibility of winning freedom is mentioned only once (except for the small group of emancipist tales where those emancipists who are not downtrodden join in the corrupt economic competitiveness of the "Pure Merinoes"). The stories about the Riverine are just as "black" as the convict ones, for in this world, too, hopes and ideals are blighted by human flaws, by harsh circumstance or tragic accident.

Warung's pessimism can seem too often an imposed habit or affliction of mind, stretched to the point of unconscious self-parody and not (as in **"The Ring"**) as vision, growing out of insight and out of a situation, and tested against alternatives. **"The *Henry Porcher* Bolter"** (hereafter **"The Bolter"**) is useful in pursuing further questions of the social content of Warung's fiction—idealism and pessimism, connections between past and present, and solidarity—because it raises these questions in a more personal context, supposedly showing how the system came to interest, indeed to obsess, him. It seems unlikely that the subject

was introduced to him by an old lag in the way this story suggests. (pp. 62-4)

"The Bolter" concerns an old convict, Shovey, an escapee, living in suburban Melbourne (Richmond) in the late 1860s and early 1870s. The story divides into two parts: firstly, Shovey's relationship with a young boy (Warung himself, we are told) in the "present" of the tale; and, secondly, Shovey's guilty past. Shovey is a bibliomaniac, and his book-littered retreat shows him entombed in the past: "he lived in his books and died among them", his isolation broken only by visits from the boy. Shovey's recalled history is marked by betrayal and revenge among convicts. He steals the pardon of one of a group (Dillon), as deputed by his mates, then betrays them by fleeing to Hobart where the pattern is repeated.

In contrast to **"The Ring"** and most Warung stories, the betrayals in **"The Bolter"** are so presented as to be more condemned than condoned. The main offender is Shovey who makes only gestures towards gaining Dillon his freedom, even into the 1870s.

Another difference from the typical Warung story is that in **"The Bolter"** a part of the legacy of the system is shown through a *freed* convict, not through the handed-down corruption of officials which becomes lodged in the bureaucracy itself. (This was Warung's major moral about the system, just as it was in the *Bulletin's History of Botany Bay,* appearing shortly before his tales began to be published in that paper.) What was kept alive by the ex-convict (and perhaps handed on to the boy, as we shall see) is guilt, along with a suspiciousness and anger. Warung must have often met such attitudes in gathering the oral testimony (from the 1870s to the 1890s) that was an important part of his source material, but it did not suit his political beliefs and purpose to include these feelings as part of the system's destructive legacy (as Brian Penton was to do in *Landtakers*).

The little that is directly told in **"The Bolter"** about what made Warung into a chronicler of the system is perfunctorily (and evasively) cleared out of the way near the beginning. We are told that "How the writer [as a boy] came to know him need not here be related". Shovey did two "services" for the boy: introducing him to the system, a service of "very questionable value", and making him "free of a marvellous collection of books . . . to which privilege also the [present] writer has his doubts". He is doubtful because otherwise he "might have developed into a portly and wealthy banker, instead of a hard-up journalist". This remark, Warung says, is "not altogether by the way" because "but for the 'bolter' and his books these 'Tales of the Old Regime' [collected in *Tales of the Old Regime and The Bullet of the Fated Ten*] would never have been written". Thus, the tone of apparently flippant self-deprecation is replaced by a more serious one.

Offsetting any reservations about the bolter's influence are indirect suggestions of its mainly positive value. The two opening paragraphs (placed in the 1890s) set a symbolic atmosphere. Shovey's old house, "dilapidated" inside, "weather-stained" externally, has been mainly untenanted. It is not too fanciful to see the house as suggesting the past of Australia. It is as "ancient a building as you will find in the suburbs of young Melbourne". It would have had even fewer tenants if the landlord's agent had informed intending lessees of its "eerie legend": that here a "bolter", advertised for in the *Sydney Gazette* of 1827, was found "stark-stiff dead" in the early 1870s.

The house is "within a stone's throw" of the one where Peter Lalor died. Here Warung links the convict past and the era of the gold discoveries with its Eureka protest against injustice. This bridging of 1827, the 1850s, the 1870s, and even the 1890s (the present from which the story departs) is to be reinforced by the introduction of other historical figures, Fawkner (whom Shovey knew) and Redmond Barry.

This assembling of historical figures is not unusual in Warung's stories, but here the emphasis is more than usual on them as "folk" figures. This is emphasized rather than undercut by the fact that Warung leaves it to us to fill in their historical significance. If time has proved that many Australians do not know and value their past enough to keep this significance alive, so that Warung's symbolic figures do not "work" for many readers, then this is not only a judgment on the risk he took but an expression of one of the underlying themes of this story and of all his fiction: the past should be kept alive. This need is implied not only in the symbolism of the untenanted house, and the folk figures, but also (presumably) in what the boy has grown up to do as the author, Warung, as the exposer of the wrongs of the past—in contrast to Shovey's concealment, and also to the suppression of the convict past practised by society in Warung's day, and later. The final words of **"The Bolter"**—"And we know how magistrates were not unbribable in those days"—challenge, by their irony, the divorcing of the past from the present. Whereas Shovey's books represent an attempt to ease his guilt by wallowing in the past, Warung, as he reminds us in the story, has chosen an active role as author as well as user of books—as worker for the present who draws on the past.

The view of Shovey as a positive influence would appear, however, to be only "part of the story", as is suggested by some of the boy's responses and by the doubts of the grown man, Warung, about "the questionable value" of the influence. The story is evasive about any permanently harmful effects on the boy, and one has to listen carefully to hints and overtones which heighten the symbolic nature of **"The Bolter"**. We are told little of the relationship of old man and boy. There was an "intimacy of a kind" between one who was "not a lovable character" and the boy who regarded him with "something of respect and more of fear" (the attitude of convicts to the tyrannical Ring). What were the effects, we may wonder, of Shovey's hectoring suspiciousness and anger (which alternate with his need for sympathy), his forcing of his guilty secret on the boy, and the latter's readiness to accept it, however reluctant and unlikely a confidant he might seem? The boy flees from Shovey in one of his wild moods, never to see him again (for he dies soon afterwards). The boy deserts him feeling *"angered as well as alarmed"* (my italics) at his domineering manner, climaxing in his paranoid aligning

of the boy with "all the rest, traitors and spies". The boy also perhaps recoils from the burden of guilt. He may be frightened by intimations of how much he already understands (not altogether consciously), a knowledge arising not only from his having been tutored in the system and from Shovey but also from his own (unstated) experience. The story invites one to such speculation by its tantalizing suggestions. What is clear is that out of his knowledge the boy partly anticipates Shovey's disclosure. In a "flash" the boy realizes Shovey's "personal interest in the system" and, significantly, at this point he picks up the book recording Shovey's past, to the latter's consternation. And it is the boy who "guesses" a little later, "not altogether at random", the basis of the secret.

The attraction-repulsion the boy feels towards Shovey is intimated but not explored in the story, and we are left wondering what exactly was the nature of the boy's attraction to him and to the system and how this influenced him as the adult writer, Price Warung. Was the adult expiating Shovey's guilt which he had made his own or otherwise taken to heart? A guilt demanding the relief of "objective" externalization and documentation, both available through Warung's use of the system? Was Warung himself afraid of becoming a prisoner of the past?

Such speculations arise from hints and suggestions only, but it is worth stepping outside the story, even if this involves more speculation, and applying them more widely to Warung himself, as the story half invites us to do. Warung may have embodied more of himself than he realized, not in the slight "author" role, but in Shovey and his relationship with the boy.

A tone of vindictiveness can enter into Warung's stories, particularly when injustice is raised and when this involves British imperialism and its officials (including politicians). Sometimes accompanying this is what might appear to be an inconsistent "relish" for the horrors he is condemning. A story called **"The Felicitious Reminiscences of Scourger James"** illustrates both feelings. Here Warung, drawing on experience, makes a rare appearance as interviewer-historian visiting an old men's home in Launceston. He insinuatingly encourages the simple James with jujubes and other rewards to relate his gory experiences in a gloating way, even to mime them, and when the demonstration "cat" [cat-o'-nine-tails; a kind of whip] is "thoughtlessly" left behind, James's fellow invalids revenge themselves "with what considering their age and debility, was an astonishing and commendable strength of flagellation". It is an unpleasant (verging on "sick") story of a kind Warung could write. He would seem to be having it both ways, relishing horrors that appal him, somewhat in the manner of Shovey, with his defensive anger freely projected and his wallowing in the records of the past he has so unsuccessfully escaped. [In a review in *Australian Literary Studies,* 1976] Brian Elliott sees Warung's anger in political terms, as "an aggressive assertion of a certain kind of class-conscious belligerency, enunciated in the name of socialism", but granted that Warung's radicalism may be involved it is possible to see his politics and his stories as a channel more than a source of his angry crusading role.

A morbid and obsessive preoccupation with the convict past was a criticism Warung had to face early and to which he was particularly sensitive. He defended himself to Sir Henry Parkes by arguing that the system, did have its "infamy" ("I did not make my subject") but added that he aimed to "cover with successive series of stories the whole field of Australian life—political, mining, pastoral, etc". But he never went on to do this, though he made plans. His defensiveness towards criticism of the "blackness" of his convict pictures led him to emphasize and exaggerate the huge amount of historical research he actually did (as part of a busy life), for he was in his day a respected bibliographer, book collector and historian. . . . If he encouraged the exaggeration of himself as an authority on the system, the tendency to regard him as such among contemporary and later critics arose mainly from his success as a fiction writer in being able to give his stories such an air of historical truth.

His research into the system had, however, a mixed result, as he states (and implies) in **"The Bolter"**. So far as his personal life was concerned, his book collecting led him not only into debt, but apparently into questionable dealings. In his literary work, the historical detail can be excessive, a vice of an antiquarian. And, in this case, his antiquarianism became crucially linked with his reputation. (Shovey apparently lived for his book collecting.)

It is possible, then, to see parallels to Shovey's aggressive (and defensive) anger, and his morbid preoccupation with the past in Warung's life and in the stories, but the question remains whether there are any parallels to the underlying guilt of **"The Bolter"**. We have seen how betrayal is a recurrent theme of the fiction, but it rarely involves guilt because it is seen as forced on victims or practised by hardened officials. To turn to Warung's life presents problems because so little is known of it. If, for instance, **"The Bolter"** suggests the possibility of the schoolboy/Warung expiating the guilt of a father or surrogate father, speculation must stop here, for virtually nothing is recorded of Warung's father (or mother, or wife, for that matter). Warung was "a second son" (nothing is known of siblings) and was aged four when his family emigrated from Liverpool to Australia in 1859, "*probably* in search of gold" (my italics). The most interesting speculation about the immigration is that Warung may have seen himself as a scapegoat of English society, for according to family tradition the Astleys had "come down in the world" [Barry Andrews, *Price Warung*].

It is impossible, then, to hope to relate **"The Bolter"** to Warung's life in any close or definite way, but selected aspects of the life should be mentioned. He had a history of unspecified nervous breakdowns, apparently beginning early in his life (when he was twenty-three) at Echuca, the setting of some of his black tales of the Riverine. He also suffered from a degenerative and painful disease of the spinal column, *tabes dorsalis,* a form of tertiary syphilis (in his case probably not congenital) which "increasingly hampered him after 1891 [when he was probably first aware of it is not known] and eventually caused his death in 1911". Associated with this illness was an addiction to morphine, though here again details (including origins) remain vague. Perhaps as a result of his illnesses, his life shows alternating patterns, on the one hand of inactivity and strenuous work, on the other of solitariness and social involvement. Both patterns, perhaps associated, could have been established by the Echuca breakdown, though the regularity of the pattern is unclear. In 1903 chronic illness forced Warung's resignation from his last job, as first editor of the *Bathurst Argus,* and from then on he dropped out of public life, living in obscurity and poverty, and presumably alone, having had to sell his library years before (unlike Shovey). (His wife had returned home to Launceston in the 1890s and had also suffered severe illness.) The picture of the hard-up journalist in **"The Bolter"** is a gross understatement of what overtook Warung and what he must have seen looming. He was found wandering and with amnesia in Sydney in December 1910, and was sent to Rookwood Benevolent Asylum. Though rescued by friends he returned there shortly before he died the next year.

A sketch of aspects of Warung's life is enough to show, then, that his mental and physical disabilities could help to explain his preoccupation with suffering and his dark vision. Whether he felt to blame for his trials or that they were foisted on him we do not know—he could have felt both. Either way we have in his illnesses, which he must have kept secret for as long as he could, and possibly in attitudes illness may have bred or exacerbated, a possible source for "a personal interest in the System" and something of a counterpart to Shovey's situation. Here, too, perhaps may lie some of the origins of his themes of social involvement and the relationship of past and present.

Just as it would be misleading to paint Warung's personal life as all black (he did have his time of fruitful literary and political work, and he could be sociable), it would be distorting to omit the positive beliefs he not only held but clung to in his political and journalistic work. A good introduction to this positive side is provided by an early review of selections of Marcus Clarke. Here Warung saw *His Natural Life* as the "joint symbol of both the strengths and weakness of [Clarke's] *character*" (my italics). In fact Warung pays as much attention to Clarke's character as to the virtues of the novel. The weaknesses of character are raised apropos of a much exaggerated story of Clarke's editor (Mackinnon), about his having to be locked up by his publisher and the novel dragged out of him sheet by sheet. Swallowing this story as gospel, Warung finds a moral in it—as much for himself as for others. For all his genius, Clarke supposedly lacked "that practical perception of duty, and of the obligations of man to man, which is the essential bond of social unity. . . . The ballast which gives stability to the craft of the average individual . . . cannot be dispensed with by the genius without the risk of shipwreck". A "similar disaster overwhelmed Gordon and Kendall" who formed with Clarke "a sad trilogy" amongst literature's most "mournful records".

The moral for Warung seems clear: to avoid shipwreck himself he must not isolate himself from society, seeking to evade either personal responsibilities or life's "slings and arrows"; rather, he must seek and promote solidarity with his fellows, for his own sake as well as theirs. This is what Warung attempted through his political activities (for example, as a member of the Labor and National Federation movements), and in his journalistic work as well as his fiction, both being inseparable from his politics. In both he purveyed a message, anti-imperialist and pro-democratic. In his best journalism and stories he saw difficulties in the achieving of "social unity" and full democracy, though he could write with passionate fluency about these ideals. He wrote less well in both genres when laying about him with the righteous sword of blame, or less commonly when raising up heroes. Political commitment can be a strength in the tales contributing to the sincerity of feeling which Palmer and others have admired, but it could lead to strident attacks on pet hates. [In his *Price Warung*, Barry] Andrews argues that Warung needed little encouragement from the *Bulletin* in politicizing the convict myth but that, nevertheless, he was indulged by [the editor] Archibald who could be rabidly anti-British himself.

Warung's journalism (which can only be briefly glanced at here) is necessary to a full view of the man and his work. At its best it expressed an intelligent and sincere idealism not found in the fiction. In distinguishing the success and failure of Parkes as fighter for democracy, Warung's understanding showed an unusual complexity, for Warung rarely saw character or achievement as mixed. The familiar theme of past and present underlies the Parkes piece in the praise of his early achievements, in the lament for his later betrayal of his ideals, and in the relating of the two. Warung saw Parkes's strengths and weaknesses as interlinked:

> Parkes the opportunist and the historian; Parkes who looked upon life as a fiction, humanity as a puppet, politics as a farce, patriotism and public spirit and freedom as terms to juggle away the senses of the people as conjurors juggle away the vision of their patrons; Parkes the charlatan—was born [within a year or two of responsible government] . . . Parkes a martyr! [as he claimed in his history] A fine joke truly! . . . [yet] in the mighty struggle to keep the *Empire* alive, to pay his way, to feed his family, to fight public foes and private antagonism, and to resolutely pursue his ideal to make the paper the trusted organ of an educated democracy, he mounted to heights of self-abnegation. . . . Egotist always in the first period as in the second Parkes was [until the end of his *Empire* writings] filled with the superb egotism of the martyr heart, between which and selfishness there is little distinction. . . . But once occasion had passed, Parkes faltered, craved for less ethereal air, lost faith in the ideals and purposes of humanity, furled the wings of his soul.

This is Warung at his best as political journalist, and may express something of his own struggle, political and personal.

A sense of the historian of vision (a forerunner of Manning Clark?) in Warung who is lost to us, except for pieces such as the Parkes, because he undertook no sustained work of history, is suggested by his lament for the failure of Sir Redmond Barry's idea for a six-volume political history of Victoria:

> To gain them [the projected six volumes] replete with the symbols of the time; eloquent of its passions, its enmities, and its aspirations; and significant—in their reports, their caricatures, their satires, their *ana,* their *mots,* their imprecations—of the agony of national travail, Australia would sacrifice every other page of locally-recorded speech she possesses. For those six volumes would have told the mighty dramatic story of the birth epoch of Australian democracy.

This passage can be applied to Warung's convict stories, suggesting that his capacities and passion as historian found an outlet in them, for they give us something of all he suggests, though not so much "the agony of national travail" as the agony of the preceding sterility (as Warung saw it).

Before this survey of Warung's tales is concluded, some brief comments on some aspects not yet touched upon are necessary to give an idea of how they can vary in nature though remaining similar, even insistent in theme. **"The Bolter"** and **"The Ring"** (Warung's longest story) are in some ways untypical in their approaches. The latter is more of a moral fable (as well as a gothic tale of suspense), the former more of a symbolic tale, than is usual. He could also write good social comedy. But it is an insistent grounding in factuality, suggesting historical realism, that is the hallmark of Warung's method. As Brian Elliott hazards, he may be the first Australian "realist" writer, both in method and in the championing of the underdog which accompanies it.

A good example of this style is **"How Muster-Master Stoneman Earned His Breakfast"** (hereafter **"Stoneman"**). Here Warung's realist technique excellently serves one of his main effects or themes: the irrationality of the system as embodied in regulations and their administration, the absurdity and pettiness of officialdom and officials. For the system can be petty as well as perverse, absurd as well as evil, and its absurdity and pettiness can be as horrifying a cruelty as any. The epigraph Warung chose for his first collection viewed the system as a monument of "combined absurdity and wickedness". The combination adds force to many of his stories, with irony often pointing up the absurdity. The way convicts are trapped by the "facts" of the overall environment (not simply the physical), imposed by regulations, contributes to the absurdity of this environment, the facts being sometimes stubbornly immovable, sometimes malleable to suit corrupt officials. (Of the convict writers, only Keneally is as concerned with the inescapability of authority, and in him too this evokes the absurd and the "black".) Unlike other fiction writers of the system, Clarke, Porter, Keneally and White, Warung uses facts as his memorable images as well as for his settings, for they carry the charges of meaning found in the *imagery* as well as the situations in the other writers. Warung is not noted for his imagery, nor for natural landscape (largely ignored), but rather for his environmental landscape in the widest sense—working and living conditions determined by regulations. This bent is probably a reflection of Warung's politics and of his times. No convict writer has been as thoroughgoing in his treatment of environment, and the similarity (amounting almost to repetition) of his themes is offset by an accompanying variety of scene, for the convict environment (including the mentality of officials and enslaved) is manifested in a wide range of detailed samples, if mainly within conditions of secondary punishment. This variety, embracing ninety-four stories, is an extraordinary feat of imagination and research and deserves more recognition and use by historians and literary critics.

The ironic title **"How Muster-Master Stoneman Earned His Breakfast"** suggests the underlying patterns of officialdom and the "natural" human, one at odds with the other (cf. **"The *Henry Porcher* Bolter"**). The enmeshing detail of regulations, the system's machinery, is unremittingly evoked as the action unfolds. For instance, the third paragraph gives us the "cage" (a local term for gaol); the muster-station established by Governor Davey; the time in year, month, hour; the convict's number; the ship on which he was transported; his sentence; the road-gang overseer; the paysheets of His Britannic Majesty's Colonial Penal Establishment; and "H.B.M.'s Colonial representatives, police, judicial and gubernatorial". All these things are there as part of the mental and physical scene but also as part of the machinery or network. The story mounts to a cluster of crowning absurdities: a convict is flogged for a new offence before he is hanged, and he is tried for yet another offence, a "second murder", after his hanging, so that it can be held "punctually" at 9.05 a.m.

A story such as this does not seem sealed off from the present by its historical realism. Its very specificity contributes not only to the vivid, dramatic impact, a strength of Warung's, but also functions as a set of images connecting the story to later times by implications of "applicability". The story is about bureaucracy and its petty power, not only about sickening cruelty, and so the visceral impact is part of the effect.

Stories such as **"Stoneman"** survive through what they tell us of deeper structures of society rather than the psychological complexities of individuals (whereas Clarke had combined both). Although **"Stoneman"** contains individual figures (rather than individualized characters) it conveys a sense of a social group and of a "group fate", for what happens to convict Glancy suggests that similar coercive forces can work through a variety of guises. This group sense is typical of many of the stories (e.g., **"The Ring"**), and again it is something Warung conveyed to a greater degree than previous convict writers, looking forward to Keneally's use of history as "a parable for the present". When Warung does use heroes and villains, such as Maconochie and John Price, they have a symbolic function, not individuality.

As a final comment on Warung's approach, mention should be made of what may be an innovation, making him an early explorer of a kind of discontinuous narrative (as Lawson can be seen). By arranging for a number of figures, both historic and fictional (though the latter are often based on real personages or "cases"), to reappear in his stories, sometimes in a major, sometimes in a minor, role (even a mere mention, or a footnote), Warung built up a special sense of a *world* of convictism. It is a closed world with an apparent rather than a real mobility for, as officials or convicts move from place to place or change places in the hierarchy, neither they nor the basic situations really change. All stories were part of one or other of five series but all were also part of a series. At its best, this world which he made into *the* world becomes an intense and revealing one, gaining from its exclusive concentration; at its worst, it becomes predictable, suggestive of a rigid, perhaps (unconsciously) baffled, mind.

Very few of Warung's tales lack obvious literary flaws, yet he remains important for his stories and for his attempts to come to terms with Australian history. His most evident contribution was to confirm the convict legend but he added something of his own. He could use the past as a way of understanding himself and his own times, and of going beyond both. He was the first fiction writer to connect the system with Australia's specific development beyond colonial status. In connecting past and present, and at the same time bringing into relation corresponding parts of himself (including political interests), he could sometimes unify his talents. He wrote best when least self-conscious and moralistic, for the dramatic force of his tales can extend below the surface. But he could retreat into the past, carrying grievances and problems for would-be burial there. He was driven to embrace social change . . . , and his being driven involved rigidities and obsessions as well as creative complexities of doubts and pessimism. (pp. 65-74)

> *Laurie Hergenhan, "Price Warung and the Convicts: A View from (and of) the Nineties,"* in his Unnatural Lives: Studies in Australian Fiction about the Convicts, from James Tucker to Patrick White, *University of Queensland Press, 1983, pp. 62-74.*

FURTHER READING

Bibliography

Andrews, Barry. "Price Warung: Some Bibliographical Details and a Checklist of the Stories." *Australian Literary Studies* 3, No. 4 (October 1968): 290-304.
  Discusses sources for and publishing histories of Warung's short stories. The critic includes a chronologically arranged checklist of 111 stories, supplying detailed publication information for each.

————. "Price Warung: Some Corrections and Additions." *Australian Literary Studies* 7, No. 1 (May 1975): 95-8.
  Emends and updates the bibliographic information provided in *Australian Literary Studies,* October 1968 (cited above).

Andrews, Barry G., and Wilde, William H. "William Astley (1855-1911)." In their *Australian Literature to 1900: A Guide to Information Sources,* pp. 107-09. Detroit: Gale Research Co., 1980.

Provides biographical information, a selected list of Warung's works, and a brief annotated list of criticism. Additional works that include references to Warung are cited in sections devoted to bibliographies and to literary history and criticism.

Miller, E. Morris, and Macartney, Frederick T. "Warung, Price." In their *Australian Literature: A Bibliography to 1938, Extended to 1950*, pp. 482-83. Rev. ed. Sydney: Angus and Robertson, 1956.

Lists Warung's principal short story collections and provides a biographical and critical sketch.

Criticism

Andrews, Barry. *Price Warung (William Astley)*. Boston: Twayne, 1976, 197 p.

Biographical and critical overview. Andrews includes a chronology and a bibliography of primary and secondary sources.

Hergenhan, Laurie. "Convict Legends, Australian Legends: Price Warung, the Palmers and Others, 1927-1970." In his *Unnatural Lives: Studies in Australian Fiction about the Con-victs, from James Tucker to Patrick White*, pp. 122-29. St. Lucia: University of Queensland Press, 1983.

Notes the importance of Australian critics Nettie Palmer and Vance Palmer in assessments of Warung and of the significance of convict fiction within a national literary tradition.

Murray-Smith, S. Review of *Convict Days*, by Price Warung. *Overland*, No. 18 (August 1960): 56-7.

Identifies Warung as one of Australia's best short story writers of the 1890s and discusses principal themes of his convict fiction.

Poole, Joan E. "A Source for 'John Price's Bar of Steel'." *Southerly* 27, No. 4 (1967): 300-01.

Summarizes the plot of Warung's story and notes the record of a criminal case which may have been his source.

Ward, Russel. "The Founding Fathers." In his *The Australian Legend*, pp. 36-66. Melbourne: Oxford University Press, 1958.

Asserts that primary research among ex-convicts informs much of Warung's short fiction.

Twentieth-Century Literary Criticism

Cumulative Indexes
Volumes 1-45

This Index Includes References to Entries in These Gale Series

Black Literature Criticism provides excerpts from criticism of the most significant works of black authors of all nationalities over the past 200 years. Complete in three volumes.

Children's Literature Review includes excerpts from reviews, criticism, and commentary on works of authors and illustrators who create books for children.

Classical and Medieval Literature Criticism offers excerpts of criticism on the works of world authors from classical antiquity through the fourteenth century.

Contemporary Authors series encompasses five related series. *Contemporary Authors* provides biographical and bibliographical information on more than 99,000 writers of fiction, nonfiction, poetry, journalism, drama, and film. *Contemporary Authors New Revision Series* provides completely updated information on active authors covered in previously published volumes of *CA. Contemporary Authors Permanent Series* consists of updated listings for deceased and inactive authors removed from the original volumes 9-36 when those volumes were revised. *Contemporary Authors Autobiography Series* presents specially commissioned autobiographies by leading contemporary writers. *Contemporary Authors Bibliographical Series* contains primary and secondary bibliographies as well as analytical bibliographical essays by authorities on major modern authors.

Contemporary Literary Criticism presents excerpts of criticism on the works of novelists, poets, dramatists, short story writers, scriptwriters, and other creative writers who are now living or who have died since 1960.

Dictionary of Literary Biography comprises four related series. *Dictionary of Literary Biography* furnishes illustrated overviews of authors' lives and works and places them in the larger perspective of literary history. *Dictionary of Literary Biography Documentary Series* illuminates the careers of major figures through a selection of literary documents, including letters, interviews, and photographs. *Dictionary of Literary Biography Yearbook* summarizes the past year's literary activity and includes updated and new entries on individual au-

thors. A cumulative index to authors and articles is included in each new volume. *Concise Dictionary of American Literary Biography*, a six-volume series, collects revised and updated sketches on major American authors that were originally presented in *Dictionary of Literary Biography*.

Drama Criticism provides excerpts of criticism on the works of playwrights of all nationalities and periods of literary history.

Literature Criticism from 1400 to 1800 compiles significant passages from the most noteworthy criticism on authors of the fifteenth through the eighteenth centuries.

Nineteenth-Century Literature Criticism offers significant passages from criticism on authors who died between 1800 and 1899.

Poetry Criticism presents excerpts of criticism on the works of poets from all eras, movements, and nationalities.

Short Story Criticism combines excerpts of criticism on short fiction by writers of all eras and nationalities.

Something about the Author series encompasses three related series. *Something about the Author* contains well-illustrated biographical sketches on authors and illustrators of juvenile and young adult literature from all eras. *Something about the Author Autobiography Series* presents specially commissioned autobiographies by prominent authors and illustrators of books for children and young adults. *Authors & Artists for Young Adults* provides high school and junior high school students with profiles of their favorite creative artists.

Twentieth-Century Literary Criticism contains critical excerpts by the most significant commentators on poets, novelists, short story writers, dramatists, and philosophers who died between 1900 and 1960.

Yesterday's Authors of Books for Children contains heavily illustrated entries on children's writers who died before 1961. Complete in two volumes.

Literary Criticism Series
Cumulative Author Index

This index lists all author entries in the Gale Literary Criticism Series and includes cross-references to other Gale sources. References in the index are identified as follows:

AAYA: *Authors & Artists for Young Adults,* Volumes 1-7
BLC: *Black Literature Criticism,* Volumes 1-3
CA: *Contemporary Authors* (original series), Volumes 1-136
CAAS: *Contemporary Authors Autobiography Series,* Volumes 1-15
CABS: *Contemporary Authors Bibliographical Series,* Volumes 1-3
CANR: *Contemporary Authors New Revision Series,* Volumes 1-35
CAP: *Contemporary Authors Permanent Series,* Volumes 1-2
CA-R: *Contemporary Authors* (first revision), Volumes 1-44
CDALB: *Concise Dictionary of American Literary Biography,* Volumes 1-6
CLC: *Contemporary Literary Criticism,* Volumes 1-70
CLR: *Children's Literature Review,* Volumes 1-25
CMLC: *Classical and Medieval Literature Criticism,* Volumes 1-8
DC: *Drama Criticism,* Volumes 1-2
DLB: *Dictionary of Literary Biography,* Volumes 1-114
DLB-DS: *Dictionary of Literary Biography Documentary Series,* Volumes 1-9
DLB-Y: *Dictionary of Literary Biography Yearbook,* Volumes 1980-1990
LC: *Literature Criticism from 1400 to 1800,* Volumes 1-19
NCLC: *Nineteenth-Century Literature Criticism,* Volumes 1-35
PC: *Poetry Criticism,* Volumes 1-4
SAAS: *Something about the Author Autobiography Series,* Volumes 1-14
SATA: *Something about the Author,* Volumes 1-68
SSC: *Short Story Criticism,* Volumes 1-9
TCLC: *Twentieth-Century Literary Criticism,* Volumes 1-45
YABC: *Yesterday's Authors of Books for Children,* Volumes 1-2

A. E. 1867-1935 . . . . TCLC 3, 10
See also Russell, George William
See also DLB 19

Abbey, Edward 1927-1989 . . . . . . CLC 36, 59
See also CANR 2; CA 45-48;
obituary CA 128

Abbott, Lee K., Jr. 19??- . . . . CLC 48

Abe, Kobo 1924- . . . . CLC 8, 22, 53
See also CANR 24; CA 65-68

Abell, Kjeld 1901-1961 . . . . CLC 15
See also obituary CA 111

Abish, Walter 1931- . . . . CLC 22
See also CA 101

Abrahams, Peter (Henry) 1919- . . . . . CLC 4
See also CA 57-60

Abrams, M(eyer) H(oward) 1912- . . . CLC 24
See also CANR 13; CA 57-60; DLB 67

Abse, Dannie 1923- . . . . CLC 7, 29
See also CAAS 1; CANR 4; CA 53-56;
DLB 27

Achebe, (Albert) Chinua(lumogu)
1930- . . . . CLC 1, 3, 5, 7, 11, 26, 51
See also BLC 1; CLR 20; CANR 6, 26;
CA 1-4R; SATA 38, 40

Acker, Kathy 1948- . . . . CLC 45
See also CA 117, 122

Ackroyd, Peter 1949- . . . . CLC 34, 52
See also CA 123, 127

Acorn, Milton 1923- . . . . CLC 15
See also CA 103; DLB 53

Adamov, Arthur 1908-1970 . . . . . . CLC 4, 25
See also CAP 2; CA 17-18;
obituary CA 25-28R

Adams, Alice (Boyd) 1926- . . . CLC 6, 13, 46
See also CANR 26; CA 81-84; DLB-Y 86

Adams, Douglas (Noel) 1952- . . . CLC 27, 60
See also CA 106; DLB-Y 83

Adams, Francis 1862-1893 . . . . NCLC 33

Adams, Henry (Brooks)
1838-1918 . . . . TCLC 4
See also CA 104; DLB 12, 47

Adams, Richard (George)
1920- . . . . CLC 4, 5, 18
See also CLR 20; CANR 3; CA 49-52;
SATA 7

Adamson, Joy(-Friederike Victoria)
1910-1980 . . . . CLC 17
See also CANR 22; CA 69-72;
obituary CA 93-96; SATA 11;
obituary SATA 22

Adcock, (Kareen) Fleur 1934- . . . . . . CLC 41
See also CANR 11; CA 25-28R; DLB 40

Addams, Charles (Samuel)
1912-1988 . . . . CLC 30
See also CANR 12; CA 61-64;
obituary CA 126

Addison, Joseph 1672-1719 . . . . LC 18
See also DLB 101

Adler, C(arole) S(chwerdtfeger)
1932- . . . . CLC 35
See also CANR 19; CA 89-92; SATA 26

Adler, Renata 1938- . . . . CLC 8, 31
See also CANR 5, 22; CA 49-52

Ady, Endre 1877-1919 . . . . TCLC 11
See also CA 107

Afton, Effie 1825-1911
See Harper, Francis Ellen Watkins

Agee, James 1909-1955 . . . . TCLC 1, 19
See also CA 108; DLB 2, 26;
CDALB 1941-1968

Andric, Ivo 1892-1975 . . . . **CLC 8**
See also CA 81-84; obituary CA 57-60

Angelique, Pierre 1897-1962
See Bataille, Georges

Angell, Roger 1920- . . . . **CLC 26**
See also CANR 13; CA 57-60

Angelou, Maya 1928- . . . . **CLC 12, 35, 64**
See also BLC 1; CANR 19; CA 65-68;
SATA 49; DLB 38

Annensky, Innokenty 1856-1909 . . . **TCLC 14**
See also CA 110

Anouilh, Jean (Marie Lucien Pierre)
1910-1987 . . . . . . **CLC 1, 3, 8, 13, 40, 50**
See also CA 17-20R; obituary CA 123

Anthony, Florence 1947-
See Ai

Anthony (Jacob), Piers 1934- . . . . . . **CLC 35**
See also Jacob, Piers A(nthony)
D(illingham)
See also DLB 8

Antoninus, Brother 1912-
See Everson, William (Oliver)

Antonioni, Michelangelo 1912- . . . . . **CLC 20**
See also CA 73-76

Antschel, Paul 1920-1970 . . . . . . **CLC 10, 19**
See also Celan, Paul
See also CA 85-88

Anwar, Chairil 1922-1949 . . . . **TCLC 22**
See also CA 121

Apollinaire, Guillaume
1880-1918 . . . . **TCLC 3, 8**
See also Kostrowitzki, Wilhelm Apollinaris
de

Appelfeld, Aharon 1932- . . . . **CLC 23, 47**
See also CA 112

Apple, Max (Isaac) 1941- . . . . **CLC 9, 33**
See also CANR 19; CA 81-84

Appleman, Philip (Dean) 1926- . . . . . **CLC 51**
See also CANR 6; CA 13-16R

Apuleius, (Lucius) (Madaurensis)
125?-175? . . . . **CMLC 1**

Aquin, Hubert 1929-1977 . . . . **CLC 15**
See also CA 105; DLB 53

Aragon, Louis 1897-1982 . . . . **CLC 3, 22**
See also CA 69-72; obituary CA 108;
DLB 72

Arany, Janos 1817-1882 . . . . **NCLC 34**

Arbuthnot, John 1667-1735 . . . . **LC 1**

Archer, Jeffrey (Howard) 1940- . . . . **CLC 28**
See also CANR 22; CA 77-80

Archer, Jules 1915- . . . . **CLC 12**
See also CANR 6; CA 9-12R; SAAS 5;
SATA 4

Arden, John 1930- . . . . **CLC 6, 13, 15**
See also CAAS 4; CA 13-16R; DLB 13

Arenas, Reinaldo 1943- . . . . **CLC 41**
See also CA 124, 128

Arendt, Hannah 1906-1975 . . . . **CLC 66**
See also CA 19-20R; obituary CA 61-64

Aretino, Pietro 1492-1556 . . . . **LC 12**

Arguedas, Jose Maria
1911-1969 . . . . **CLC 10, 18**
See also CA 89-92

Argueta, Manlio 1936- . . . . **CLC 31**

Ariosto, Ludovico 1474-1533 . . . . **LC 6**

Aristophanes
c. 450 B. C.-c. 385 B. C. . . . . . **CMLC 4;
DC 2**

Arlt, Roberto 1900-1942 . . . . **TCLC 29**
See also CA 123

Armah, Ayi Kwei 1939- . . . . **CLC 5, 33**
See also BLC 1; CANR 21; CA 61-64

Armatrading, Joan 1950- . . . . **CLC 17**
See also CA 114

Arnim, Achim von (Ludwig Joachim von
Arnim) 1781-1831 . . . . **NCLC 5**
See also DLB 90

Arnold, Matthew 1822-1888 . . . **NCLC 6, 29**
See also DLB 32, 57

Arnold, Thomas 1795-1842 . . . . . . **NCLC 18**
See also DLB 55

Arnow, Harriette (Louisa Simpson)
1908-1986 . . . . **CLC 2, 7, 18**
See also CANR 14; CA 9-12R;
obituary CA 118; SATA 42, 47; DLB 6

Arp, Jean 1887-1966 . . . . **CLC 5**
See also CA 81-84; obituary CA 25-28R

Arquette, Lois S(teinmetz) 1934-
See Duncan (Steinmetz Arquette), Lois
See also SATA 1

Arrabal, Fernando 1932- . . . **CLC 2, 9, 18, 58**
See also CANR 15; CA 9-12R

Arrick, Fran 19??- . . . . **CLC 30**

Artaud, Antonin 1896-1948 . . . . . **TCLC 3, 36**
See also CA 104

Arthur, Ruth M(abel) 1905-1979 . . . . **CLC 12**
See also CANR 4; CA 9-12R;
obituary CA 85-88; SATA 7;
obituary SATA 26

Artsybashev, Mikhail Petrarch
1878-1927 . . . . **TCLC 31**

Arundel, Honor (Morfydd)
1919-1973 . . . . **CLC 17**
See also CAP 2; CA 21-22;
obituary CA 41-44R; SATA 4;
obituary SATA 24

Asch, Sholem 1880-1957 . . . . **TCLC 3**
See also CA 105

Ashbery, John (Lawrence)
1927- . . . **CLC 2, 3, 4, 6, 9, 13, 15, 25, 41**
See also CANR 9; CA 5-8R; DLB 5;
DLB-Y 81

Ashton-Warner, Sylvia (Constance)
1908-1984 . . . . **CLC 19**
See also CA 69-72; obituary CA 112

Asimov, Isaac 1920- . . . . **CLC 1, 3, 9, 19, 26**
See also CLR 12; CANR 2, 19; CA 1-4R;
SATA 1, 26; DLB 8

Astley, Thea (Beatrice May)
1925- . . . . **CLC 41**
See also CANR 11; CA 65-68

Astley, William 1855-1911
See Warung, Price

Aston, James 1906-1964
See White, T(erence) H(anbury)

Asturias, Miguel Angel
1899-1974 . . . . **CLC 3, 8, 13**
See also CAP 2; CA 25-28;
obituary CA 49-52

Atheling, William, Jr. 1921-1975
See Blish, James (Benjamin)

Atherton, Gertrude (Franklin Horn)
1857-1948 . . . . **TCLC 2**
See also CA 104; DLB 9, 78

Attaway, William 1911?-1986
See also BLC 1; DLB 76

Atwood, Margaret (Eleanor)
1939- . . . . **CLC 2, 3, 4, 8, 13, 15, 25, 44;
SSC 2**
See also CANR 3, 24; CA 49-52; SATA 50;
DLB 53

Aubin, Penelope 1685-1731? . . . . **LC 9**
See also DLB 39

Auchincloss, Louis (Stanton)
1917- . . . . **CLC 4, 6, 9, 18, 45**
See also CANR 6; CA 1-4R; DLB 2;
DLB-Y 80

Auden, W(ystan) H(ugh)
1907-1973 . . . . . **CLC 1, 2, 3, 4, 6, 9, 11,
14, 43; PC 1**
See also CANR 5; CA 9-12R;
obituary CA 45-48; DLB 10, 20

Audiberti, Jacques 1899-1965 . . . . . . **CLC 38**
See also obituary CA 25-28R

Auel, Jean M(arie) 1936- . . . . **CLC 31**
See also CANR 21; CA 103

Auerbach, Erich 1892-1957 . . . . **TCLC 43**
See also CA 118

Augier, Emile 1820-1889 . . . . **NCLC 31**

Augustine, St. 354-430 . . . . **CMLC 6**

Austen, Jane
1775-1817 . . . . **NCLC 1, 13, 19, 33**

Auster, Paul 1947- . . . . **CLC 47**
See also CANR 23; CA 69-72

Austin, Mary (Hunter)
1868-1934 . . . . **TCLC 25**
See also CA 109; DLB 9

Averroes 1126-1198 . . . . **CMLC 7**

Avison, Margaret 1918- . . . . **CLC 2, 4**
See also CA 17-20R; DLB 53

Ayckbourn, Alan 1939- . . . . **CLC 5, 8, 18, 33**
See also CA 21-24R; DLB 13

Aydy, Catherine 1937-
See Tennant, Emma

Ayme, Marcel (Andre) 1902-1967 . . . **CLC 11**
See also CA 89-92; DLB 72

Ayrton, Michael 1921-1975 . . . . **CLC 7**
See also CANR 9, 21; CA 5-8R;
obituary CA 61-64

Azorin 1874-1967 . . . . **CLC 11**
See also Martinez Ruiz, Jose

Azuela, Mariano 1873-1952 . . . . **TCLC 3**
See also CA 104

"Bab" 1836-1911
See Gilbert, (Sir) W(illiam) S(chwenck)

Babel, Isaak (Emmanuilovich)
1894-1941 . . . . **TCLC 2, 13**
See also CA 104

Besant, Annie (Wood) 1847-1933 . . . **TCLC 9**
See also CA 105

Bessie, Alvah 1904-1985. . . . . **CLC 23**
See also CANR 2; CA 5-8R;
obituary CA 116; DLB 26

Beti, Mongo 1932- . . . . **CLC 27**
See also Beyidi, Alexandre
See also BLC 1

Betjeman, (Sir) John
1906-1984 . . . . **CLC 2, 6, 10, 34, 43**
See also CA 9-12R; obituary CA 112;
DLB 20; DLB-Y 84

Betti, Ugo 1892-1953 . . . . **TCLC 5**
See also CA 104

Betts, Doris (Waugh) 1932- . . . . **CLC 3, 6, 28**
See also CANR 9; CA 13-16R; DLB-Y 82

Bialik, Chaim Nachman
1873-1934 . . . . **TCLC 25**

Bidart, Frank 19??- . . . . **CLC 33**

Bienek, Horst 1930- . . . . **CLC 7, 11**
See also CA 73-76; DLB 75

Bierce, Ambrose (Gwinett)
1842-1914? . . . . . . **TCLC 1, 7, 44; SSC 9**
See also CA 104; DLB 11, 12, 23, 71, 74;
CDALB 1865-1917

Billington, Rachel 1942- . . . . **CLC 43**
See also CA 33-36R

Binyon, T(imothy) J(ohn) 1936- . . . . **CLC 34**
See also CA 111

Bioy Casares, Adolfo 1914- . . . . **CLC 4, 8, 13**
See also CANR 19; CA 29-32R

Birch, Allison 1974?- . . . . **CLC 65**

Bird, Robert Montgomery
1806-1854 . . . . **NCLC 1**

Birdwell, Cleo 1936-
See DeLillo, Don

Birney (Alfred) Earle
1904- . . . . **CLC 1, 4, 6, 11**
See also CANR 5, 20; CA 1-4R

Bishop, Elizabeth
1911-1979 . . . . . **CLC 1, 4, 9, 13, 15, 32;**
PC 3
See also CANR 26; CA 7-8R;
obituary CA 89-92; CABS 2;
obituary SATA 24; DLB 5

Bishop, John 1935- . . . . **CLC 10**
See also CA 105

Bissett, Bill 1939- . . . . **CLC 18**
See also CANR 15; CA 69-72; DLB 53

Bitov, Andrei (Georgievich) 1937- . . . **CLC 57**

Biyidi, Alexandre 1932-
See Beti, Mongo
See also CA 114, 124

Bjornson, Bjornstjerne (Martinius)
1832-1910 . . . . **TCLC 7, 37**
See also CA 104

Blackburn, Paul 1926-1971 . . . . . . **CLC 9, 43**
See also CA 81-84; obituary CA 33-36R;
DLB 16; DLB-Y 81

Black Elk 1863-1950 . . . . **TCLC 33**

Blackmore, R(ichard) D(oddridge)
1825-1900 . . . . **TCLC 27**
See also CA 120; DLB 18

Blackmur, R(ichard) P(almer)
1904-1965 . . . . **CLC 2, 24**
See also CAP 1; CA 11-12;
obituary CA 25-28R; DLB 63

Blackwood, Algernon (Henry)
1869-1951 . . . . **TCLC 5**
See also CA 105

Blackwood, Caroline 1931- . . . . **CLC 6, 9**
See also CA 85-88; DLB 14

Blair, Eric Arthur 1903-1950
See Orwell, George
See also CA 104; SATA 29

Blais, Marie-Claire
1939- . . . . **CLC 2, 4, 6, 13, 22**
See also CAAS 4; CA 21-24R; DLB 53

Blaise, Clark 1940- . . . . **CLC 29**
See also CAAS 3; CANR 5; CA 53-56R;
DLB 53

Blake, Nicholas 1904-1972
See Day Lewis, C(ecil)

Blake, William 1757-1827 . . . . **NCLC 13**
See also SATA 30

Blasco Ibanez, Vicente
1867-1928 . . . . **TCLC 12**
See also CA 110

Blatty, William Peter 1928- . . . . **CLC 2**
See also CANR 9; CA 5-8R

Blessing, Lee 1949- . . . . **CLC 54**

Blish, James (Benjamin)
1921-1975 . . . . **CLC 14**
See also CANR 3; CA 1-4R;
obituary CA 57-60; DLB 8

Blixen, Karen (Christentze Dinesen)
1885-1962
See Dinesen, Isak
See also CAP 2; CA 25-28; SATA 44

Bloch, Robert (Albert) 1917- . . . . **CLC 33**
See also CANR 5; CA 5-8R; SATA 12;
DLB 44

Blok, Aleksandr (Aleksandrovich)
1880-1921 . . . . **TCLC 5**
See also CA 104

Bloom, Harold 1930- . . . . **CLC 24, 65**
See also CA 13-16R; DLB 67

Blount, Roy (Alton), Jr. 1941- . . . . . **CLC 38**
See also CANR 10; CA 53-56

Bloy, Leon 1846-1917. . . . . **TCLC 22**
See also CA 121

Blume, Judy (Sussman Kitchens)
1938- . . . . **CLC 12, 30**
See also CLR 2, 15; CANR 13; CA 29-32R;
SATA 2, 31; DLB 52

Blunden, Edmund (Charles)
1896-1974 . . . . **CLC 2, 56**
See also CAP 2; CA 17-18;
obituary CA 45-48; DLB 20

Bly, Robert (Elwood)
1926- . . . . **CLC 1, 2, 5, 10, 15, 38**
See also CA 5-8R; DLB 5

Bochco, Steven 1944?- . . . . **CLC 35**

Bodenheim, Maxwell 1892-1954 . . . **TCLC 44**
See also CA 110; DLB 9, 45

Bodker, Cecil 1927- . . . . **CLC 21**
See also CLR 23; CANR 13; CA 73-76;
SATA 14

Boell, Heinrich (Theodor) 1917-1985
See Boll, Heinrich
See also CANR 24; CA 21-24R;
obituary CA 116

Bogan, Louise 1897-1970 . . . . . **CLC 4, 39, 46**
See also CA 73-76; obituary CA 25-28R;
DLB 45

Bogarde, Dirk 1921- . . . . **CLC 19**
See also Van Den Bogarde, Derek (Jules
Gaspard Ulric) Niven
See also DLB 14

Bogosian, Eric 1953- . . . . **CLC 45**

Bograd, Larry 1953- . . . . **CLC 35**
See also CA 93-96; SATA 33

Bohl de Faber, Cecilia 1796-1877
See Caballero, Fernan

Boiardo, Matteo Maria 1441-1494 . . . . **LC 6**

Boileau-Despreaux, Nicolas
1636-1711 . . . . **LC 3**

Boland, Eavan (Aisling) 1944- . . . **CLC 40, 67**
See also DLB 40

Boll, Heinrich (Theodor)
1917-1985 . . . **CLC 2, 3, 6, 9, 11, 15, 27,**
39
See also Boell, Heinrich (Theodor)
See also DLB 69; DLB-Y 85

Bolt, Robert (Oxton) 1924- . . . . **CLC 14**
See also CA 17-20R; DLB 13

Bonaventura . . . . **NCLC 35**
See also DLB 90

Bond, Edward 1934- . . . . **CLC 4, 6, 13, 23**
See also CA 25-28R; DLB 13

Bonham, Frank 1914- . . . . **CLC 12**
See also CANR 4; CA 9-12R; SAAS 3;
SATA 1, 49

Bonnefoy, Yves 1923- . . . . **CLC 9, 15, 58**
See also CA 85-88

Bontemps, Arna (Wendell)
1902-1973 . . . . **CLC 1, 18**
See also BLC 1; CLR 6; CANR 4;
CA 1-4R; obituary CA 41-44R; SATA 2,
44; obituary SATA 24; DLB 48, 51

Booth, Martin 1944- . . . . **CLC 13**
See also CAAS 2; CA 93-96

Booth, Philip 1925- . . . . **CLC 23**
See also CANR 5; CA 5-8R; DLB-Y 82

Booth, Wayne C(layson) 1921- . . . . . **CLC 24**
See also CAAS 5; CANR 3; CA 1-4R;
DLB 67

Borchert, Wolfgang 1921-1947 . . . . . **TCLC 5**
See also CA 104; DLB 69

Borges, Jorge Luis
1899-1986 . . . **CLC 1, 2, 3, 4, 6, 8, 9, 10,**
13, 19, 44, 48; SSC 4
See also CANR 19; CA 21-24R; DLB-Y 86

Borowski, Tadeusz 1922-1951 . . . . . . **TCLC 9**
See also CA 106

Borrow, George (Henry)
1803-1881 . . . . **NCLC 9**
See also DLB 21, 55

Bosschere, Jean de 1878-1953 . . . . . **TCLC 19**
See also CA 115

Boswell, James 1740-1795 . . . . **LC 4**

Brooke, Rupert (Chawner)
1887-1915 . . . . TCLC 2, 7
See also CA 104; DLB 19

Brooke-Rose, Christine 1926- . . . . . . CLC 40
See also CA 13-16R; DLB 14

Brookner, Anita 1928- . . . . . . CLC 32, 34, 51
See also CA 114, 120; DLB-Y 87

Brooks, Cleanth 1906- . . . . CLC 24
See also CA 17-20R; DLB 63

Brooks, Gwendolyn
1917- . . . . CLC 1, 2, 4, 5, 15, 49
See also BLC 1; CANR 1, 27; CA 1-4R;
SATA 6; DLB 5, 76; CDALB 1941-1968

Brooks, Mel 1926- . . . . CLC 12
See also Kaminsky, Melvin
See also CA 65-68; DLB 26

Brooks, Peter 1938- . . . . CLC 34
See also CANR 1; CA 45-48

Brooks, Van Wyck 1886-1963 . . . . . . CLC 29
See also CANR 6; CA 1-4R; DLB 45, 63

Brophy, Brigid (Antonia)
1929- . . . . CLC 6, 11, 29
See also CAAS 4; CANR 25; CA 5-8R;
DLB 14

Brosman, Catharine Savage 1934- . . . . CLC 9
See also CANR 21; CA 61-64

Broughton, T(homas) Alan 1936- . . . CLC 19
See also CANR 2, 23; CA 45-48

Broumas, Olga 1949- . . . . CLC 10
See also CANR 20; CA 85-88

Brown, Charles Brockden
1771-1810 . . . . NCLC 22
See also DLB 37, 59, 73;
CDALB 1640-1865

Brown, Christy 1932-1981 . . . . CLC 63
See also CA 105; obituary CA 104

Brown, Claude 1937- . . . . CLC 30
See also BLC 1; CA 73-76

Brown, Dee (Alexander) 1908- . . CLC 18, 47
See also CAAS 6; CANR 11; CA 13-16R;
SATA 5; DLB-Y 80

Brown, George Douglas 1869-1902
See Douglas, George

Brown, George Mackay 1921- . . . . CLC 5, 28
See also CAAS 6; CANR 12; CA 21-24R;
SATA 35; DLB 14, 27

Brown, H. Rap 1943-
See Al-Amin, Jamil Abdullah

Brown, Hubert Gerold 1943-
See Al-Amin, Jamil Abdullah

Brown, Rita Mae 1944- . . . . CLC 18, 43
See also CANR 2, 11; CA 45-48

Brown, Rosellen 1939- . . . . CLC 32
See also CANR 14; CA 77-80

Brown, Sterling A(llen)
1901-1989 . . . . CLC 1, 23, 59
See also BLC 1; CANR 26; CA 85-88;
obituary CA 127; DLB 48, 51, 63

Brown, William Wells
1816?-1884 . . . . NCLC 2; DC 1
See also BLC 1; DLB 3, 50

Browne, Jackson 1950- . . . . CLC 21
See also CA 120

Browning, Elizabeth Barrett
1806-1861 . . . . NCLC 1, 16
See also DLB 32

Browning, Robert
1812-1889 . . . . NCLC 19; PC 2
See also YABC 1; DLB 32

Browning, Tod 1882-1962 . . . . CLC 16
See also obituary CA 117

Bruccoli, Matthew J(oseph) 1931- . . CLC 34
See also CANR 7; CA 9-12R

Bruce, Lenny 1925-1966 . . . . CLC 21
See also Schneider, Leonard Alfred

Bruin, John 1924-
See Brutus, Dennis

Brunner, John (Kilian Houston)
1934- . . . . CLC 8, 10
See also CAAS 8; CANR 2; CA 1-4R

Brutus, Dennis 1924- . . . . CLC 43
See also BLC 1; CANR 2, 27; CA 49-52

Bryan, C(ourtlandt) D(ixon) B(arnes)
1936- . . . . CLC 29
See also CANR 13; CA 73-76

Bryant, William Cullen
1794-1878 . . . . NCLC 6
See also DLB 3, 43, 59; CDALB 1640-1865

Bryusov, Valery (Yakovlevich)
1873-1924 . . . . TCLC 10
See also CA 107

Buchan, John 1875-1940 . . . . TCLC 41
See also YABC 2; brief entry CA 108;
DLB 34, 70

Buchanan, George 1506-1582 . . . . LC 4

Buchheim, Lothar-Gunther 1918- . . . . CLC 6
See also CA 85-88

Buchner, (Karl) Georg
1813-1837 . . . . NCLC 26

Buchwald, Art(hur) 1925- . . . . CLC 33
See also CANR 21; CA 5-8R; SATA 10

Buck, Pearl S(ydenstricker)
1892-1973 . . . . CLC 7, 11, 18
See also CANR 1; CA 1-4R;
obituary CA 41-44R; SATA 1, 25; DLB 9

Buckler, Ernest 1908-1984 . . . . CLC 13
See also CAP 1; CA 11-12;
obituary CA 114; SATA 47

Buckley, Vincent (Thomas)
1925-1988 . . . . CLC 57
See also CA 101

Buckley, William F(rank), Jr.
1925- . . . . CLC 7, 18, 37
See also CANR 1, 24; CA 1-4R; DLB-Y 80

Buechner, (Carl) Frederick
1926- . . . . CLC 2, 4, 6, 9
See also CANR 11; CA 13-16R; DLB-Y 80

Buell, John (Edward) 1927- . . . . CLC 10
See also CA 1-4R; DLB 53

Buero Vallejo, Antonio 1916- . . . CLC 15, 46
See also CANR 24; CA 106

Bukowski, Charles 1920- . . . . CLC 2, 5, 9, 41
See also CA 17-20R; DLB 5

Bulgakov, Mikhail (Afanas'evich)
1891-1940 . . . . TCLC 2, 16
See also CA 105

Bullins, Ed 1935- . . . . CLC 1, 5, 7
See also BLC 1; CANR 24; CA 49-52;
DLB 7, 38

**Bulwer-Lytton, (Lord) Edward (George Earle
Lytton)** 1803-1873 . . . . NCLC 1
See also Lytton, Edward Bulwer
See also DLB 21

Bunin, Ivan (Alexeyevich)
1870-1953 . . . . TCLC 6; SSC 5
See also CA 104

Bunting, Basil 1900-1985 . . . . CLC 10, 39, 47
See also CANR 7; CA 53-56;
obituary CA 115; DLB 20

Bunuel, Luis 1900-1983 . . . . CLC 16
See also CA 101; obituary CA 110

Bunyan, John 1628-1688 . . . . LC 4
See also DLB 39

Burgess (Wilson, John) Anthony
1917- . . . . . CLC 1, 2, 4, 5, 8, 10, 13, 15,
22, 40, 62
See also Wilson, John (Anthony) Burgess
See also DLB 14

Burke, Edmund 1729-1797 . . . . LC 7

Burke, Kenneth (Duva) 1897- . . . . CLC 2, 24
See also CA 5-8R; DLB 45, 63

Burney, Fanny 1752-1840 . . . . NCLC 12
See also DLB 39

Burns, Robert 1759-1796 . . . . LC 3

Burns, Tex 1908?-
See L'Amour, Louis (Dearborn)

Burnshaw, Stanley 1906- . . . . . . CLC 3, 13, 44
See also CA 9-12R; DLB 48

Burr, Anne 1937- . . . . CLC 6
See also CA 25-28R

Burroughs, Edgar Rice
1875-1950 . . . . TCLC 2, 32
See also CA 104; SATA 41; DLB 8

Burroughs, William S(eward)
1914- . . . . CLC 1, 2, 5, 15, 22, 42
See also CANR 20; CA 9-12R; DLB 2, 8,
16; DLB-Y 81

Busch, Frederick 1941- . . . CLC 7, 10, 18, 47
See also CAAS 1; CA 33-36R; DLB 6

Bush, Ronald 19??- . . . . CLC 34

Butler, Octavia E(stelle) 1947- . . . . . CLC 38
See also CANR 12, 24; CA 73-76; DLB 33

Butler, Samuel 1612-1680 . . . . LC 16
See also DLB 101

Butler, Samuel 1835-1902 . . . . . . TCLC 1, 33
See also CA 104; DLB 18, 57

Butor, Michel (Marie Francois)
1926- . . . . CLC 1, 3, 8, 11, 15
See also CA 9-12R

Buzo, Alexander 1944- . . . . CLC 61
See also CANR 17; CA 97-100

Buzzati, Dino 1906-1972 . . . . CLC 36
See also obituary CA 33-36R

Byars, Betsy 1928- . . . . CLC 35
See also CLR 1, 16; CANR 18; CA 33-36R;
SAAS 1; SATA 4, 46; DLB 52

Byatt, A(ntonia) S(usan Drabble)
1936- . . . . CLC 19, 65
See also CANR 13, 33; CA 13-16R;
DLB 14

Ende, Michael 1930-.............. **CLC 31**
See also CLR 14; CA 118, 124; SATA 42;
DLB 75

Endo, Shusaku 1923- ..... **CLC 7, 14, 19, 54**
See also CANR 21; CA 29-32R

Engel, Marian 1933-1985......... **CLC 36**
See also CANR 12; CA 25-28R; DLB 53

Engelhardt, Frederick 1911-1986
See Hubbard, L(afayette) Ron(ald)

Enright, D(ennis) J(oseph)
1920- .... **CLC 4, 8, 31**
See also CANR 1; CA 1-4R; SATA 25;
DLB 27

Enzensberger, Hans Magnus
1929- .... **CLC 43**
See also CA 116, 119

Ephron, Nora 1941-........... **CLC 17, 31**
See also CANR 12; CA 65-68

Epstein, Daniel Mark 1948- .... **CLC 7**
See also CANR 2; CA 49-52

Epstein, Jacob 1956- .... **CLC 19**
See also CA 114

Epstein, Joseph 1937-............. **CLC 39**
See also CA 112, 119

Epstein, Leslie 1938- .... **CLC 27**
See also CANR 23; CA 73-76

Equiano, Olaudah 1745?-1797....... **LC 16**
See also BLC 2; DLB 37, 50

Erasmus, Desiderius 1469?-1536..... **LC 16**

Erdman, Paul E(mil) 1932- .... **CLC 25**
See also CANR 13; CA 61-64

Erdrich, Louise 1954-......... **CLC 39, 54**
See also CA 114

Erenburg, Ilya (Grigoryevich) 1891-1967
See Ehrenburg, Ilya (Grigoryevich)

Erickson, Steve 1950-............. **CLC 64**
See also CA 129

Eseki, Bruno 1919-
See Mphahlele, Ezekiel

Esenin, Sergei (Aleksandrovich)
1895-1925 .... **TCLC 4**
See also CA 104

Eshleman, Clayton 1935-........... **CLC 7**
See also CAAS 6; CA 33-36R; DLB 5

Espriu, Salvador 1913-1985......... **CLC 9**
See also obituary CA 115

Estleman, Loren D. 1952- .... **CLC 48**
See also CA 85-88

Evans, Marian 1819-1880
See Eliot, George

Evans, Mary Ann 1819-1880
See Eliot, George

Evarts, Esther 1900-1972
See Benson, Sally

Everett, Percival L. 1957?- .... **CLC 57**
See also CA 129

Everson, Ronald G(ilmour) 1903- ... **CLC 27**
See also CA 17-20R; DLB 88

Everson, William (Oliver)
1912- .... **CLC 1, 5, 14**
See also CANR 20; CA 9-12R; DLB 5, 16

Everyman 1495- .... **DC 2**

Evtushenko, Evgenii (Aleksandrovich) 1933-
See Yevtushenko, Yevgeny

Ewart, Gavin (Buchanan)
1916-.................... **CLC 13, 46**
See also CANR 17; CA 89-92; DLB 40

Ewers, Hanns Heinz 1871-1943 ... **TCLC 12**
See also CA 109

Ewing, Frederick R. 1918-
See Sturgeon, Theodore (Hamilton)

Exley, Frederick (Earl) 1929-.... **CLC 6, 11**
See also CA 81-84; DLB-Y 81

Ezekiel, Nissim 1924-............. **CLC 61**
See also CA 61-64

Ezekiel, Tish O'Dowd 1943-....... **CLC 34**

Fagen, Donald 1948-.............. **CLC 26**

Fair, Ronald L. 1932-............. **CLC 18**
See also CANR 25; CA 69-72; DLB 33

Fairbairns, Zoe (Ann) 1948- .... **CLC 32**
See also CANR 21; CA 103

Fairfield, Cicily Isabel 1892-1983
See West, Rebecca

Fallaci, Oriana 1930-............. **CLC 11**
See also CANR 15; CA 77-80

Faludy, George 1913-............. **CLC 42**
See also CA 21-24R

Fanon, Frantz 1925-1961
See also BLC 2; CA 116; obituary CA 89-92

Fante, John 1909-1983............ **CLC 60**
See also CANR 23; CA 69-72;
obituary CA 109; DLB-Y 83

Farah, Nuruddin 1945-............ **CLC 53**
See also BLC 2; CA 106

Fargue, Leon-Paul 1876-1947 ..... **TCLC 11**
See also CA 109

Farigoule, Louis 1885-1972
See Romains, Jules

Farina, Richard 1937?-1966........ **CLC 9**
See also CA 81-84; obituary CA 25-28R

Farley, Walter 1920- .... **CLC 17**
See also CANR 8; CA 17-20R; SATA 2, 43;
DLB 22

Farmer, Philip Jose 1918-....... **CLC 1, 19**
See also CANR 4; CA 1-4R; DLB 8

Farrell, J(ames) G(ordon)
1935-1979 .... **CLC 6**
See also CA 73-76; obituary CA 89-92;
DLB 14

Farrell, James T(homas)
1904-1979 .... **CLC 1, 4, 8, 11, 66**
See also CANR 9; CA 5-8R;
obituary CA 89-92; DLB 4, 9, 86;
DLB-DS 2

Farrell, M. J. 1904-
See Keane, Molly

Fassbinder, Rainer Werner
1946-1982 .... **CLC 20**
See also CA 93-96; obituary CA 106

Fast, Howard (Melvin) 1914- ...... **CLC 23**
See also CANR 1; CA 1-4R; SATA 7;
DLB 9

Faulkner, William (Cuthbert)
1897-1962 .... **CLC 1, 3, 6, 8, 9, 11, 14,
18, 28, 52, 68; SSC 1**
See also CANR 33; CA 81-84; DLB 9, 11,
44, 102; DLB-Y 86; DLB-DS 2;
CDALB 1929-1941

Fauset, Jessie Redmon
1882-1961 .... **CLC 19, 54**
See also BLC 2; CA 109; DLB 51

Faust, Irvin 1924-................. **CLC 8**
See also CA 33-36R; DLB 2, 28; DLB-Y 80

Fearing, Kenneth (Flexner)
1902-1961 .... **CLC 51**
See also CA 93-96; DLB 9

Federman, Raymond 1928- ...... **CLC 6, 47**
See also CANR 10; CA 17-20R; DLB-Y 80

Federspiel, J(urg) F. 1931-........ **CLC 42**

Feiffer, Jules 1929-.......... **CLC 2, 8, 64**
See also CANR 30; CA 17-20R; SATA 8,
61; DLB 7, 44; AAYA 3

Feinberg, David B. 1956-.......... **CLC 59**

Feinstein, Elaine 1930-............ **CLC 36**
See also CAAS 1; CA 69-72; DLB 14, 40

Feke, Gilbert David 1976?-......... **CLC 65**

Feldman, Irving (Mordecai) 1928-.... **CLC 7**
See also CANR 1; CA 1-4R

Fellini, Federico 1920-............. **CLC 16**
See also CA 65-68

Felsen, Gregor 1916-
See Felsen, Henry Gregor

Felsen, Henry Gregor 1916- .... **CLC 17**
See also CANR 1; CA 1-4R; SAAS 2;
SATA 1

Fenton, James (Martin) 1949-...... **CLC 32**
See also CA 102; DLB 40

Ferber, Edna 1887-1968........... **CLC 18**
See also CA 5-8R; obituary CA 25-28R;
SATA 7; DLB 9, 28, 86

Ferguson, Samuel 1810-1886..... **NCLC 33**
See also DLB 32

Ferlinghetti, Lawrence (Monsanto)
1919?- .... **CLC 2, 6, 10, 27; PC 1**
See also CANR 3; CA 5-8R; DLB 5, 16;
CDALB 1941-1968

Ferrier, Susan (Edmonstone)
1782-1854 .... **NCLC 8**

Ferrigno, Robert 19??-............. **CLC 65**

Feuchtwanger, Lion 1884-1958 ..... **TCLC 3**
See also CA 104; DLB 66

Feydeau, Georges 1862-1921...... **TCLC 22**
See also CA 113

Ficino, Marsilio 1433-1499 .... **LC 12**

Fiedler, Leslie A(aron)
1917- .... **CLC 4, 13, 24**
See also CANR 7; CA 9-12R; DLB 28, 67

Field, Andrew 1938-............... **CLC 44**
See also CANR 25; CA 97-100

Field, Eugene 1850-1895 .... **NCLC 3**
See also SATA 16; DLB 21, 23, 42

Field, Michael .... **TCLC 43**

Fielding, Henry 1707-1754 .... **LC 1**
See also DLB 39, 84

Guiney, Louise Imogen
　　1861-1920 . . . . TCLC **41**
　　See also DLB 54

Guiraldes, Ricardo　1886-1927 . . . . . TCLC **39**

Gunn, Bill　1934-1989 . . . . CLC **5**
　　See also Gunn, William Harrison
　　See also DLB 38

Gunn, Thom(son William)
　　1929- . . . . CLC **3, 6, 18, 32**
　　See also CANR 9; CA 17-20R; DLB 27

Gunn, William Harrison　1934-1989
　　See Gunn, Bill
　　See also CANR 12, 25; CA 13-16R;
　　　obituary CA 128

Gunnars, Kristjana　1948- . . . . CLC **69**
　　See also CA 113; DLB 60

Gurganus, Allan　1947- . . . . CLC **70**

Gurney, A(lbert) R(amsdell), Jr.
　　1930- . . . . CLC **32, 50, 54**
　　See also CA 77-80

Gurney, Ivor (Bertie)　1890-1937 . . . TCLC **33**

Gustafson, Ralph (Barker)　1909- . . . . CLC **36**
　　See also CANR 8; CA 21-24R; DLB 88

Guthrie, A(lfred) B(ertram), Jr.
　　1901- . . . . CLC **23**
　　See also CA 57-60; DLB 6

Guthrie, Woodrow Wilson　1912-1967
　　See Guthrie, Woody
　　See also CA 113; obituary CA 93-96

Guthrie, Woody　1912-1967 . . . . CLC **35**
　　See also Guthrie, Woodrow Wilson

Guy, Rosa (Cuthbert)　1928- . . . . CLC **26**
　　See also CLR 13; CANR 14; CA 17-20R;
　　　SATA 14; DLB 33

Haavikko, Paavo (Juhani)
　　1931- . . . . CLC **18, 34**
　　See also CA 106

Hacker, Marilyn　1942- . . . . CLC **5, 9, 23**
　　See also CA 77-80

Haggard, (Sir) H(enry) Rider
　　1856-1925 . . . . TCLC **11**
　　See also CA 108; SATA 16; DLB 70

Haig-Brown, Roderick L(angmere)
　　1908-1976 . . . . CLC **21**
　　See also CANR 4; CA 5-8R;
　　　obituary CA 69-72; SATA 12; DLB 88

Hailey, Arthur　1920- . . . . CLC **5**
　　See also CANR 2; CA 1-4R; DLB-Y 82

Hailey, Elizabeth Forsythe　1938- . . . CLC **40**
　　See also CAAS 1; CANR 15; CA 93-96

Haines, John　1924- . . . . CLC **58**
　　See also CANR 13; CA 19-20R; DLB 5

Haldeman, Joe　1943- . . . . CLC **61**
　　See also CA 53-56; DLB 8

Haley, Alex (Palmer)　1921- . . . . . . CLC **8, 12**
　　See also BLC 2; CA 77-80; DLB 38

Haliburton, Thomas Chandler
　　1796-1865 . . . . NCLC **15**
　　See also DLB 11

Hall, Donald (Andrew, Jr.)
　　1928- . . . . CLC **1, 13, 37, 59**
　　See also CAAS 7; CANR 2; CA 5-8R;
　　　SATA 23; DLB 5

Hall, James Norman　1887-1951 . . . TCLC **23**
　　See also CA 123; SATA 21

Hall, (Marguerite) Radclyffe
　　1886-1943 . . . . TCLC **12**
　　See also CA 110

Hall, Rodney　1935- . . . . CLC **51**
　　See also CA 109

Halpern, Daniel　1945- . . . . CLC **14**
　　See also CA 33-36R

Hamburger, Michael (Peter Leopold)
　　1924- . . . . CLC **5, 14**
　　See also CAAS 4; CANR 2; CA 5-8R;
　　　DLB 27

Hamill, Pete　1935- . . . . CLC **10**
　　See also CANR 18; CA 25-28R

Hamilton, Edmond　1904-1977 . . . . CLC **1**
　　See also CANR 3; CA 1-4R; DLB 8

Hamilton, Gail　1911-
　　See Corcoran, Barbara

Hamilton, Ian　1938- . . . . CLC **55**
　　See also CA 106; DLB 40

Hamilton, Mollie　1909?-
　　See Kaye, M(ary) M(argaret)

Hamilton, (Anthony Walter) Patrick
　　1904-1962 . . . . CLC **51**
　　See also obituary CA 113; DLB 10

Hamilton, Virginia (Esther)　1936- . . . CLC **26**
　　See also CLR 1, 11; CANR 20; CA 25-28R;
　　　SATA 4; DLB 33, 52

Hammett, (Samuel) Dashiell
　　1894-1961 . . . . CLC **3, 5, 10, 19, 47**
　　See also CA 81-84; DLB-DS 6

Hammon, Jupiter　1711?-1800? . . . . NCLC **5**
　　See also BLC 2; DLB 31, 50, 31, 50

Hamner, Earl (Henry), Jr.　1923- . . . CLC **12**
　　See also CA 73-76; DLB 6

Hampton, Christopher (James)
　　1946- . . . . CLC **4**
　　See also CA 25-28R; DLB 13

Hamsun, Knut　1859-1952 . . . . . . TCLC **2, 14**
　　See also Pedersen, Knut

Handke, Peter　1942- . . CLC **5, 8, 10, 15, 38**
　　See also CA 77-80; DLB 85

Hanley, James　1901-1985 . . . CLC **3, 5, 8, 13**
　　See also CA 73-76; obituary CA 117

Hannah, Barry　1942- . . . . CLC **23, 38**
　　See also CA 108, 110; DLB 6

Hansberry, Lorraine (Vivian)
　　1930-1965 . . . . CLC **17, 62; DC 2**
　　See also BLC 2; CA 109;
　　　obituary CA 25-28R; CABS 3; DLB 7, 38;
　　　CDALB 1941-1968

Hansen, Joseph　1923- . . . . CLC **38**
　　See also CANR 16; CA 29-32R

Hansen, Martin　1909-1955 . . . . TCLC **32**

Hanson, Kenneth O(stlin)　1922- . . . . CLC **13**
　　See also CANR 7; CA 53-56

Hardenberg, Friedrich (Leopold Freiherr) von
　　1772-1801
　　See Novalis

Hardwick, Elizabeth　1916- . . . . CLC **13**
　　See also CANR 3; CA 5-8R; DLB 6

Hardy, Thomas
　　1840-1928 . . . TCLC **4, 10, 18, 32; SSC 2**
　　See also CA 104, 123; SATA 25; DLB 18,
　　　19

Hare, David　1947- . . . . CLC **29, 58**
　　See also CA 97-100; DLB 13

Harlan, Louis R(udolph)　1922- . . . . . CLC **34**
　　See also CANR 25; CA 21-24R

Harling, Robert　1951?- . . . . CLC **53**

Harmon, William (Ruth)　1938- . . . . . CLC **38**
　　See also CANR 14; CA 33-36R

Harper, Frances Ellen Watkins
　　1825-1911 . . . . TCLC **14**
　　See also BLC 2; CA 125;
　　　brief entry CA 111; DLB 50

Harper, Michael S(teven)　1938- . . CLC **7, 22**
　　See also CANR 24; CA 33-36R; DLB 41

Harris, Christie (Lucy Irwin)
　　1907- . . . . CLC **12**
　　See also CANR 6; CA 5-8R; SATA 6;
　　　DLB 88

Harris, Frank　1856-1931 . . . . TCLC **24**
　　See also CAAS 1; CA 109

Harris, George Washington
　　1814-1869 . . . . NCLC **23**
　　See also DLB 3, 11

Harris, Joel Chandler　1848-1908 . . . TCLC **2**
　　See also YABC 1; CA 104; DLB 11, 23, 42,
　　　78, 91

Harris, John (Wyndham Parkes Lucas)
　　Beynon　1903-1969 . . . . CLC **19**
　　See also Wyndham, John
　　See also CA 102; obituary CA 89-92

Harris, MacDonald　1921- . . . . CLC **9**
　　See also Heiney, Donald (William)

Harris, Mark　1922- . . . . CLC **19**
　　See also CAAS 3; CANR 2; CA 5-8R;
　　　DLB 2; DLB-Y 80

Harris, (Theodore) Wilson　1921- . . . . CLC **25**
　　See also CANR 11, 27; CA 65-68

Harrison, Harry (Max)　1925- . . . . . . CLC **42**
　　See also CANR 5, 21; CA 1-4R; SATA 4;
　　　DLB 8

Harrison, James (Thomas)　1937- . . . CLC **66**
　　See also Harrison, Jim
　　See also CANR 8; CA 13-16R

Harrison, Jim　1937- . . . . CLC **6, 14, 33**
　　See also Harrison, James (Thomas)
　　See also DLB-Y 82

Harrison, Kathryn　1961- . . . . CLC **70**

Harrison, Tony　1937- . . . . CLC **43**
　　See also CA 65-68; DLB 40

Harriss, Will(ard Irvin)　1922- . . . . . . CLC **34**
　　See also CA 111

Hart, Josephine　1942?- . . . . CLC **70**

Hart, Moss　1904-1961 . . . . CLC **66**
　　See also Conrad, Robert Arnold
　　See also obituary CA 89-92; DLB 7

Harte, (Francis) Bret(t)
　　1836?-1902 . . . . TCLC **1, 25; SSC 8**
　　See also brief entry CA 104; SATA 26;
　　　DLB 12, 64, 74, 79; CDALB 1865-1917

Hesse, Hermann
  1877-1962 ... CLC **1, 2, 3, 6, 11, 17, 25, 69; SSC 9**
    See also CAP 2; CA 17-18; SATA 50; DLB 66

Heyen, William 1940- .... CLC **13, 18**
    See also CAAS 9; CA 33-36R; DLB 5

Heyerdahl, Thor 1914-............ CLC **26**
    See also CANR 5, 22; CA 5-8R; SATA 2, 52

Heym, Georg (Theodor Franz Arthur)
  1887-1912 .... TCLC **9**
    See also CA 106

Heym, Stefan 1913-.............. CLC **41**
    See also CANR 4; CA 9-12R; DLB 69

Heyse, Paul (Johann Ludwig von)
  1830-1914 .... TCLC **8**
    See also CA 104

Hibbert, Eleanor (Burford) 1906-.... CLC **7**
    See also CANR 9, 28; CA 17-20R; SATA 2

Higgins, George V(incent)
  1939- .... CLC **4, 7, 10, 18**
    See also CAAS 5; CANR 17; CA 77-80; DLB 2; DLB-Y 81

Higginson, Thomas Wentworth
  1823-1911 .... TCLC **36**
    See also DLB 1, 64

Highsmith, (Mary) Patricia
  1921- .... CLC **2, 4, 14, 42**
    See also CANR 1, 20; CA 1-4R

Highwater, Jamake 1942- .... CLC **12**
    See also CLR 17; CAAS 7; CANR 10; CA 65-68; SATA 30, 32; DLB 52; DLB-Y 85

Hijuelos, Oscar 1951- .... CLC **65**
    See also CA 123

Hikmet (Ran), Nazim 1902-1963.... CLC **40**
    See also obituary CA 93-96

Hildesheimer, Wolfgang 1916- ..... CLC **49**
    See also CA 101; DLB 69

Hill, Geoffrey (William)
  1932- .... CLC **5, 8, 18, 45**
    See also CANR 21; CA 81-84; DLB 40

Hill, George Roy 1922- .... CLC **26**
    See also CA 110, 122

Hill, Susan B. 1942-.............. CLC **4**
    See also CANR 29; CA 33-36R; DLB 14

Hillerman, Tony 1925-............ CLC **62**
    See also CANR 21; CA 29-32R; SATA 6

Hilliard, Noel (Harvey) 1929-...... CLC **15**
    See also CANR 7; CA 9-12R

Hillis, Richard Lyle 1956-
    See Hillis, Rick

Hillis, Rick 1956-................ CLC **66**
    See also Hillis, Richard Lyle

Hilton, James 1900-1954......... TCLC **21**
    See also CA 108; SATA 34; DLB 34, 77

Himes, Chester (Bomar)
  1909-1984 .... CLC **2, 4, 7, 18, 58**
    See also BLC 2; CANR 22; CA 25-28R; obituary CA 114; DLB 2, 76

Hinde, Thomas 1926-.......... CLC **6, 11**
    See also Chitty, (Sir) Thomas Willes

Hine, (William) Daryl 1936-....... CLC **15**
    See also CANR 1, 20; CA 1-4R; DLB 60

Hinton, S(usan) E(loise) 1950- ..... CLC **30**
    See also CLR 3, 23; CA 81-84; SATA 19, 58; AAYA 2

Hippius (Merezhkovsky), Zinaida (Nikolayevna) 1869-1945...... TCLC **9**
    See also Gippius, Zinaida (Nikolayevna)

Hiraoka, Kimitake 1925-1970
    See Mishima, Yukio
    See also CA 97-100; obituary CA 29-32R

Hirsch, Edward (Mark) 1950-... CLC **31, 50**
    See also CANR 20; CA 104

Hitchcock, (Sir) Alfred (Joseph)
  1899-1980 .... CLC **16**
    See also obituary CA 97-100; SATA 27; obituary SATA 24

Hoagland, Edward 1932- .... CLC **28**
    See also CANR 2; CA 1-4R; SATA 51; DLB 6

Hoban, Russell C(onwell) 1925- .. CLC **7, 25**
    See also CLR 3; CANR 23; CA 5-8R; SATA 1, 40; DLB 52

Hobson, Laura Z(ametkin)
  1900-1986 .... CLC **7, 25**
    See also CA 17-20R; obituary CA 118; SATA 52; DLB 28

Hochhuth, Rolf 1931-........ CLC **4, 11, 18**
    See also CA 5-8R

Hochman, Sandra 1936-.......... CLC **3, 8**
    See also CA 5-8R; DLB 5

Hochwalder, Fritz 1911-1986 ...... CLC **36**
    See also CA 29-32R; obituary CA 120

Hocking, Mary (Eunice) 1921- ..... CLC **13**
    See also CANR 18; CA 101

Hodgins, Jack 1938-.............. CLC **23**
    See also CA 93-96; DLB 60

Hodgson, William Hope
  1877-1918 .... TCLC **13**
    See also CA 111; DLB 70

Hoffman, Alice 1952-............. CLC **51**
    See also CA 77-80

Hoffman, Daniel (Gerard)
  1923- .... CLC **6, 13, 23**
    See also CANR 4; CA 1-4R; DLB 5

Hoffman, Stanley 1944-............ CLC **5**
    See also CA 77-80

Hoffman, William M(oses) 1939- ... CLC **40**
    See also CANR 11; CA 57-60

Hoffmann, E(rnst) T(heodor) A(madeus)
  1776-1822 .... NCLC **2**
    See also SATA 27; DLB 90

Hoffmann, Gert 1932- .... CLC **54**

Hofmannsthal, Hugo (Laurenz August Hofmann Edler) von
  1874-1929 .... TCLC **11**
    See also CA 106; DLB 81

Hogg, James 1770-1835.......... NCLC **4**

Holbach, Paul Henri Thiry, Baron d'
  1723-1789 .... LC **14**

Holberg, Ludvig 1684-1754 .... LC **6**

Holden, Ursula 1921-............. CLC **18**
    See also CAAS 8; CANR 22; CA 101

Holderlin, (Johann Christian) Friedrich
  1770-1843 .... NCLC **16; PC 4**

Holdstock, Robert (P.) 1948-....... CLC **39**

Holland, Isabelle 1920- .... CLC **21**
    See also CANR 10, 25; CA 21-24R; SATA 8

Holland, Marcus 1900-1985
    See Caldwell, (Janet Miriam) Taylor (Holland)

Hollander, John 1929-...... CLC **2, 5, 8, 14**
    See also CANR 1; CA 1-4R; SATA 13; DLB 5

Holleran, Andrew 1943?-.......... CLC **38**

Hollinghurst, Alan 1954-.......... CLC **55**
    See also CA 114

Hollis, Jim 1916-
    See Summers, Hollis (Spurgeon, Jr.)

Holmes, John Clellon 1926-1988.... CLC **56**
    See also CANR 4; CA 9-10R; obituary CA 125; DLB 16

Holmes, Oliver Wendell
  1809-1894 .... NCLC **14**
    See also SATA 34; DLB 1; CDALB 1640-1865

Holt, Victoria 1906-
    See Hibbert, Eleanor (Burford)

Holub, Miroslav 1923-............. CLC **4**
    See also CANR 10; CA 21-24R

Homer c. 8th century B.C.-........ CMLC **1**

Honig, Edwin 1919-............... CLC **33**
    See also CAAS 8; CANR 4; CA 5-8R; DLB 5

Hood, Hugh (John Blagdon)
  1928- .... CLC **15, 28**
    See also CANR 1; CA 49-52; DLB 53

Hood, Thomas 1799-1845........ NCLC **16**

Hooker, (Peter) Jeremy 1941-...... CLC **43**
    See also CANR 22; CA 77-80; DLB 40

Hope, A(lec) D(erwent) 1907-.... CLC **3, 51**
    See also CA 21-24R

Hope, Christopher (David Tully)
  1944- .... CLC **52**
    See also CA 106

Hopkins, Gerard Manley
  1844-1889 .... NCLC **17**
    See also DLB 35, 57

Hopkins, John (Richard) 1931-...... CLC **4**
    See also CA 85-88

Hopkins, Pauline Elizabeth
  1859-1930 .... TCLC **28**
    See also BLC 2; DLB 50

Horgan, Paul 1903- .... CLC **9, 53**
    See also CANR 9; CA 13-16R; SATA 13; DLB-Y 85

Horovitz, Israel 1939- .... CLC **56**
    See also CA 33-36R; DLB 7

Horvath, Odon von 1901-1938 .... TCLC **45**
    See also brief entry CA 118; DLB 85

Horwitz, Julius 1920-1986......... CLC **14**
    See also CANR 12; CA 9-12R; obituary CA 119

Hospital, Janette Turner 1942-..... CLC **42**
    See also CA 108

Ivanov, Vyacheslav (Ivanovich)
1866-1949 .... TCLC 33
See also CA 122

Ivask, Ivar (Vidrik) 1927- .... CLC 14
See also CANR 24; CA 37-40R

Jackson, Jesse 1908-1983 .... CLC 12
See also CANR 27; CA 25-28R;
obituary CA 109; SATA 2, 29, 48

Jackson, Laura (Riding) 1901- ...... CLC 7
See also Riding, Laura
See also CANR 28; CA 65-68; DLB 48

Jackson, Shirley
1919-1965 .... CLC 11, 60; SSC 9
See also CANR 4; CA 1-4R;
obituary CA 25-28R; SATA 2; DLB 6;
CDALB 1941-1968

Jacob, (Cyprien) Max 1876-1944 ... TCLC 6
See also CA 104

Jacob, Piers A(nthony) D(illingham) 1934-
See Anthony (Jacob), Piers
See also CA 21-24R

Jacobs, Jim 1942- and **Casey, Warren**
1942- .... CLC 12
See also CA 97-100

Jacobs, Jim 1942-
See Jacobs, Jim and Casey, Warren
See also CA 97-100

Jacobs, W(illiam) W(ymark)
1863-1943 .... TCLC 22
See also CA 121

Jacobsen, Jens Peter 1847-1885 .. NCLC 34

Jacobsen, Josephine 1908- .... CLC 48
See also CANR 23; CA 33-36R

Jacobson, Dan 1929- .... CLC 4, 14
See also CANR 2, 25; CA 1-4R; DLB 14

Jagger, Mick 1944-............... CLC 17

Jakes, John (William) 1932- .... CLC 29
See also CANR 10; CA 57-60; DLB-Y 83

James, C(yril) L(ionel) R(obert)
1901-1989 .... CLC 33
See also CA 117, 125; obituary CA 128

James, Daniel 1911-1988
See Santiago, Danny
See also obituary CA 125

James, Henry (Jr.)
1843-1916 ... TCLC 2, 11, 24, 40; SSC 8
See also CA 132; brief entry CA 104;
DLB 12, 71, 74; CDALB 1865-1917

James, M(ontague) R(hodes)
1862-1936 .... TCLC 6
See also CA 104

James, P(hyllis) D(orothy)
1920- .... CLC 18, 46
See also CANR 17; CA 21-24R

James, William 1842-1910 ..... TCLC 15, 32
See also CA 109

Jami, Nur al-Din 'Abd al-Rahman
1414-1492 .... LC 9

Jandl, Ernst 1925- .... CLC 34

Janowitz, Tama 1957- .... CLC 43
See also CA 106

Jarrell, Randall
1914-1965 ...... CLC 1, 2, 6, 9, 13, 49
See also CLR 6; CANR 6; CA 5-8R;
obituary CA 25-28R; CABS 2; SATA 7;
DLB 48, 52; CDALB 1941-1968

Jarry, Alfred 1873-1907....... TCLC 2, 14
See also CA 104

Jeake, Samuel, Jr. 1889-1973
See Aiken, Conrad

Jean Paul 1763-1825 .... NCLC 7

Jeffers, (John) Robinson
1887-1962 .... CLC 2, 3, 11, 15, 54
See also CA 85-88; DLB 45;
CDALB 1917-1929

Jefferson, Thomas 1743-1826 .... NCLC 11
See also DLB 31; CDALB 1640-1865

Jeffrey, Francis 1773-1850....... NCLC 33

Jellicoe, (Patricia) Ann 1927- ...... CLC 27
See also CA 85-88; DLB 13

Jen, Gish 1955-................. CLC 70

Jenkins, (John) Robin 1912- .... CLC 52
See also CANR 1; CA 4R; DLB 14

Jennings, Elizabeth (Joan)
1926- .... CLC 5, 14
See also CAAS 5; CANR 8; CA 61-64;
DLB 27

Jennings, Waylon 1937-.......... CLC 21

Jensen, Johannes V. 1873-1950.... TCLC 41

Jensen, Laura (Linnea) 1948- ...... CLC 37
See also CA 103

Jerome, Jerome K. 1859-1927..... TCLC 23
See also CA 119; DLB 10, 34

Jerrold, Douglas William
1803-1857 .... NCLC 2

Jewett, (Theodora) Sarah Orne
1849-1909 .... TCLC 1, 22; SSC 6
See also CA 108, 127; SATA 15; DLB 12,
74

Jewsbury, Geraldine (Endsor)
1812-1880 .... NCLC 22
See also DLB 21

Jhabvala, Ruth Prawer
1927- .... CLC 4, 8, 29
See also CANR 2, 29; CA 1-4R

Jiles, Paulette 1943-.......... CLC 13, 58
See also CA 101

Jimenez (Mantecon), Juan Ramon
1881-1958 .... TCLC 4
See also CA 104

Joel, Billy 1949-................ CLC 26
See also Joel, William Martin

Joel, William Martin 1949-
See Joel, Billy
See also CA 108

John of the Cross, St. 1542-1591 .... LC 18

Johnson, B(ryan) S(tanley William)
1933-1973 .... CLC 6, 9
See also CANR 9; CA 9-12R;
obituary CA 53-56; DLB 14, 40

Johnson, Charles (Richard)
1948- .... CLC 7, 51, 65
See also BLC 2; CA 116; DLB 33

Johnson, Denis 1949-............. CLC 52
See also CA 117, 121

Johnson, Diane 1934-........ CLC 5, 13, 48
See also CANR 17; CA 41-44R; DLB-Y 80

Johnson, Eyvind (Olof Verner)
1900-1976 .... CLC 14
See also CA 73-76; obituary CA 69-72

Johnson, Fenton 1888-1958
See also BLC 2; CA 124;
brief entry CA 118; DLB 45, 50

Johnson, James Weldon
1871-1938 .... TCLC 3, 19
See also Johnson, James William
See also BLC 2; CA 125;
brief entry CA 104; SATA 31; DLB 51;
CDALB 1917-1929

Johnson, James William 1871-1938
See Johnson, James Weldon
See also SATA 31

Johnson, Joyce 1935-............. CLC 58
See also CA 125, 129

Johnson, Lionel (Pigot)
1867-1902 .... TCLC 19
See also CA 117; DLB 19

Johnson, Marguerita 1928-
See Angelou, Maya

Johnson, Pamela Hansford
1912-1981 .... CLC 1, 7, 27
See also CANR 2, 28; CA 1-4R;
obituary CA 104; DLB 15

Johnson, Samuel 1709-1784........ LC 15
See also DLB 39, 95

Johnson, Uwe
1934-1984 .... CLC 5, 10, 15, 40
See also CANR 1; CA 1-4R;
obituary CA 112; DLB 75

Johnston, George (Benson) 1913- ... CLC 51
See also CANR 5, 20; CA 1-4R; DLB 88

Johnston, Jennifer 1930-........... CLC 7
See also CA 85-88; DLB 14

Jolley, Elizabeth 1923-............ CLC 46
See also CA 127

Jones, D(ouglas) G(ordon) 1929-.... CLC 10
See also CANR 13; CA 29-32R, 113;
DLB 53

Jones, David
1895-1974 .... CLC 2, 4, 7, 13, 42
See also CANR 28; CA 9-12R;
obituary CA 53-56; DLB 20

Jones, David Robert 1947-
See Bowie, David
See also CA 103

Jones, Diana Wynne 1934- .... CLC 26
See also CLR 23; CANR 4, 26; CA 49-52;
SAAS 7; SATA 9

Jones, Gayl 1949-............... CLC 6, 9
See also BLC 2; CANR 27; CA 77-80;
DLB 33

Jones, James 1921-1977.... CLC 1, 3, 10, 39
See also CANR 6; CA 1-4R;
obituary CA 69-72; DLB 2

Jones, (Everett) LeRoi
1934- .... CLC 1, 2, 3, 5, 10, 14, 33
See also Baraka, Amiri; Baraka, Imamu
Amiri
See also CA 21-24R

Jones, Louis B. 19??-............. CLC 65

Jones, Madison (Percy, Jr.)   1925- ... **CLC 4**
See also CAAS 11; CANR 7; CA 13-16R

Jones, Mervyn   1922- .... **CLC 10, 52**
See also CAAS 5; CANR 1; CA 45-48

Jones, Mick   1956?- .... **CLC 30**
See also The Clash

Jones, Nettie   19??- .... **CLC 34**

Jones, Preston   1936-1979 .... **CLC 10**
See also CA 73-76; obituary CA 89-92;
DLB 7

Jones, Robert F(rancis)   1934- .... **CLC 7**
See also CANR 2; CA 49-52

Jones, Rod   1953- .... **CLC 50**
See also CA 128

Jones, Terry   1942?- .... **CLC 21**
See also Monty Python
See also CA 112, 116; SATA 51

Jong, Erica   1942- .... **CLC 4, 6, 8, 18**
See also CANR 26; CA 73-76; DLB 2, 5, 28

Jonson, Ben(jamin)   1572(?)-1637...... **LC 6**
See also DLB 62

Jordan, June   1936- .... **CLC 5, 11, 23**
See also CLR 10; CANR 25; CA 33-36R;
SATA 4; DLB 38; AAYA 2

Jordan, Pat(rick M.)   1941- .... **CLC 37**
See also CANR 25; CA 33-36R

Josipovici, Gabriel (David)
1940- .... **CLC 6, 43**
See also CAAS 8; CA 37-40R; DLB 14

Joubert, Joseph   1754-1824 .... **NCLC 9**

Jouve, Pierre Jean   1887-1976...... **CLC 47**
See also obituary CA 65-68

Joyce, James (Augustine Aloysius)
1882-1941 ...... **TCLC 3, 8, 16, 26, 35;
SSC 3**
See also CA 104, 126; DLB 10, 19, 36

Jozsef, Attila   1905-1937......... **TCLC 22**
See also CA 116

Juana Ines de la Cruz   1651?-1695 .... **LC 5**

Julian of Norwich   1342?-1416? .... **LC 6**

Just, Ward S(wift)   1935- .... **CLC 4, 27**
See also CA 25-28R

Justice, Donald (Rodney)   1925- .. **CLC 6, 19**
See also CANR 26; CA 5-8R; DLB-Y 83

Juvenal   c. 55-c. 127 .... **CMLC 8**

Kacew, Romain   1914-1980
See Gary, Romain
See also CA 108; obituary CA 102

Kacewgary, Romain   1914-1980
See Gary, Romain

Kadare, Ismail   1936- .... **CLC 52**

Kadohata, Cynthia   19??- .... **CLC 59**

Kafka, Franz
1883-1924 .... **TCLC 2, 6, 13, 29; SSC 5**
See also CA 105, 126; DLB 81

Kahn, Roger   1927- .... **CLC 30**
See also CA 25-28R; SATA 37

Kaiser, (Friedrich Karl) Georg
1878-1945 .... **TCLC 9**
See also CA 106

Kaletski, Alexander   1946- .... **CLC 39**
See also CA 118

Kallman, Chester (Simon)
1921-1975 .... **CLC 2**
See also CANR 3; CA 45-48;
obituary CA 53-56

Kaminsky, Melvin   1926-
See Brooks, Mel
See also CANR 16; CA 65-68

Kaminsky, Stuart   1934- .... **CLC 59**
See also CANR 29; CA 73-76

Kane, Paul   1941-
See Simon, Paul

Kanin, Garson   1912- .... **CLC 22**
See also CANR 7; CA 5-8R; DLB 7

Kaniuk, Yoram   1930- .... **CLC 19**

Kant, Immanuel   1724-1804 ...... **NCLC 27**

Kantor, MacKinlay   1904-1977 ...... **CLC 7**
See also CA 61-64; obituary CA 73-76;
DLB 9

Kaplan, David Michael   1946- ...... **CLC 50**

Kaplan, James   19??- .... **CLC 59**

Karamzin, Nikolai Mikhailovich
1766-1826 .... **NCLC 3**

Karapanou, Margarita   1946- .... **CLC 13**
See also CA 101

Karl, Frederick R(obert)   1927- ..... **CLC 34**
See also CANR 3; CA 5-8R

Kassef, Romain   1914-1980
See Gary, Romain

Katz, Steve   1935- .... **CLC 47**
See also CANR 12; CA 25-28R; DLB-Y 83

Kauffman, Janet   1945- .... **CLC 42**
See also CA 117; DLB-Y 86

Kaufman, Bob (Garnell)
1925-1986 .... **CLC 49**
See also CANR 22; CA 41-44R;
obituary CA 118; DLB 16, 41

Kaufman, George S(imon)
1889-1961 .... **CLC 38**
See also CA 108; obituary CA 93-96; DLB 7

Kaufman, Sue   1926-1977 .... **CLC 3, 8**
See also Barondess, Sue K(aufman)

Kavan, Anna   1904-1968 .... **CLC 5, 13**
See also Edmonds, Helen (Woods)
See also CANR 6; CA 5-8R

Kavanagh, Patrick (Joseph Gregory)
1905-1967 .... **CLC 22**
See also CA 123; obituary CA 25-28R;
DLB 15, 20

Kawabata, Yasunari
1899-1972 .... **CLC 2, 5, 9, 18**
See also CA 93-96; obituary CA 33-36R

Kaye, M(ary) M(argaret)   1909?- .... **CLC 28**
See also CANR 24; CA 89-92

Kaye, Mollie   1909?-
See Kaye, M(ary) M(argaret)

Kaye-Smith, Sheila   1887-1956..... **TCLC 20**
See also CA 118; DLB 36

Kaymor, Patrice Maguilene   1906-
See Senghor, Leopold Sedar

Kazan, Elia   1909- .... **CLC 6, 16, 63**
See also CA 21-24R

Kazantzakis, Nikos
1885?-1957............. **TCLC 2, 5, 33**
See also CA 105

Kazin, Alfred   1915- .... **CLC 34, 38**
See also CAAS 7; CANR 1; CA 1-4R;
DLB 67

Keane, Mary Nesta (Skrine)   1904-
See Keane, Molly
See also CA 108, 114

Keane, Molly   1904- .... **CLC 31**
See also Keane, Mary Nesta (Skrine)

Keates, Jonathan   19??- .... **CLC 34**

Keaton, Buster   1895-1966 .... **CLC 20**

Keaton, Joseph Francis   1895-1966
See Keaton, Buster

Keats, John   1795-1821...... **NCLC 8; PC 1**

Keene, Donald   1922- .... **CLC 34**
See also CANR 5; CA 1-4R

Keillor, Garrison   1942- .... **CLC 40**
See also Keillor, Gary (Edward)
See also CA 111; SATA 58; DLB-Y 87;
AAYA 2

Keillor, Gary (Edward)
See Keillor, Garrison
See also CA 111, 117

Kell, Joseph   1917-
See Burgess (Wilson, John) Anthony

Keller, Gottfried   1819-1890....... **NCLC 2**

Kellerman, Jonathan (S.)   1949- ..... **CLC 44**
See also CANR 29; CA 106

Kelley, William Melvin   1937- ...... **CLC 22**
See also CANR 27; CA 77-80; DLB 33

Kellogg, Marjorie   1922- .... **CLC 2**
See also CA 81-84

Kelly, M. T.   1947- .... **CLC 55**
See also CANR 19; CA 97-100

Kelman, James   1946- .... **CLC 58**

Kemal, Yashar   1922- .... **CLC 14, 29**
See also CA 89-92

Kemble, Fanny   1809-1893 .... **NCLC 18**
See also DLB 32

Kemelman, Harry   1908- .... **CLC 2**
See also CANR 6; CA 9-12R; DLB 28

Kempe, Margery   1373?-1440? .... **LC 6**

Kempis, Thomas á   1380-1471 .... **LC 11**

Kendall, Henry   1839-1882....... **NCLC 12**

Keneally, Thomas (Michael)
1935- ...... **CLC 5, 8, 10, 14, 19, 27, 43**
See also CANR 10; CA 85-88

Kennedy, Adrienne   1931-
See also BLC 2; CANR 26; CA 103;
CABS 3; DLB 38

Kennedy, Adrienne (Lita)   1931- .... **CLC 66**
See also CANR 26; CA 103; CABS 3;
DLB 38

Kennedy, John Pendleton
1795-1870 .... **NCLC 2**
See also DLB 3

Kennedy, Joseph Charles   1929- ...... **CLC 8**
See also Kennedy, X. J.
See also CANR 4, 30; CA 1-4R; SATA 14

Author Index

Lewis, (Percy) Wyndham
1882?-1957................TCLC **2, 9**
See also CA 104; DLB 15

Lewisohn, Ludwig 1883-1955..... TCLC **19**
See also CA 73-76, 107;
obituary CA 29-32R; DLB 4, 9, 28

L'Heureux, John (Clarke) 1934-.... CLC **52**
See also CANR 23; CA 15-16R

Lieber, Stanley Martin 1922-
See Lee, Stan

Lieberman, Laurence (James)
1935-..................... CLC **4, 36**
See also CANR 8; CA 17-20R

Li Fei-kan 1904-............... CLC **18**
See also Pa Chin
See also CA 105

Lifton, Robert Jay 1926-......... CLC **67**
See also CANR 27; CA 17-18R

Lightfoot, Gordon (Meredith)
1938-....................... CLC **26**
See also CA 109

Ligotti, Thomas 1953- .... CLC **44**
See also CA 123

Liliencron, Detlev von
1844-1909 .... TCLC **18**
See also CA 117

Lima, Jose Lezama 1910-1976
See Lezama Lima, Jose

Lima Barreto, (Alfonso Henriques de)
1881-1922 .... TCLC **23**
See also CA 117

Limonov, Eduard 1943-.......... CLC **67**

Lincoln, Abraham 1809-1865..... NCLC **18**

Lind, Jakov 1927-......... CLC **1, 2, 4, 27**
See also Landwirth, Heinz
See also CAAS 4; CA 9-12R

Lindsay, David 1876-1945........ TCLC **15**
See also CA 113

Lindsay, (Nicholas) Vachel
1879-1931 .... TCLC **17**
See also CA 114; SATA 40; DLB 54;
CDALB 1865-1917

Linney, Romulus 1930- .... CLC **51**
See also CA 1-4R

Li Po 701-763 .... CMLC **2**

Lipsius, Justus 1547-1606 .... LC **16**

Lipsyte, Robert (Michael) 1938-.... CLC **21**
See also CLR 23; CANR 8; CA 17-20R;
SATA 5

Lish, Gordon (Jay) 1934-......... CLC **45**
See also CA 113, 117

Lispector, Clarice 1925-1977....... CLC **43**
See also obituary CA 116

Littell, Robert 1935?-............. CLC **42**
See also CA 109, 112

Little, Malcolm 1925-1965
See also BLC 2; CA 125; obituary CA 111

Liu E 1857-1909............... TCLC **15**
See also CA 115

Lively, Penelope 1933-......... CLC **32, 50**
See also CLR 7; CANR 29; CA 41-44R;
SATA 7; DLB 14

Livesay, Dorothy 1909-......... CLC **4, 15**
See also CAAS 8; CA 25-28R; DLB 68

Lizardi, Jose Joaquin Fernandez de
1776-1827 .... NCLC **30**

Llewellyn, Richard 1906-1983....... CLC **7**
See also Llewellyn Lloyd, Richard (Dafydd
Vyvyan)
See also DLB 15

Llewellyn Lloyd, Richard (Dafydd Vyvyan)
1906-1983
See Llewellyn, Richard
See also CANR 7; CA 53-56;
obituary CA 111; SATA 11, 37

Llosa, Mario Vargas 1936-
See Vargas Llosa, Mario

Lloyd, Richard Llewellyn 1906-
See Llewellyn, Richard

Locke, Alain 1886-1954......... TCLC **43**
See also CA 124, 106; DLB 51

Locke, John 1632-1704 .... LC **7**
See also DLB 31

Lockhart, John Gibson
1794-1854 .... NCLC **6**

Lodge, David (John) 1935-....... CLC **36**
See also CANR 19; CA 17-20R; DLB 14

Loewinsohn, Ron(ald William)
1937-....................... CLC **52**
See also CA 25-28R

Logan, John 1923-............... CLC **5**
See also CA 77-80; obituary CA 124; DLB 5

Lo Kuan-chung 1330?-1400? .... LC **12**

Lombino, S. A. 1926-
See Hunter, Evan

London, Jack
1876-1916 ...... TCLC **9, 15, 39**; SSC **4**
See also London, John Griffith
See also SATA 18; DLB 8, 12, 78;
CDALB 1865-1917

London, John Griffith 1876-1916
See London, Jack
See also CA 110, 119

Long, Emmett 1925-
See Leonard, Elmore

Longbaugh, Harry 1931-
See Goldman, William (W.)

Longfellow, Henry Wadsworth
1807-1882 .... NCLC **2**
See also SATA 19; DLB 1, 59;
CDALB 1640-1865

Longley, Michael 1939-........... CLC **29**
See also CA 102; DLB 40

Longus fl. c. 2nd century- .... CMLC **7**

Lopate, Phillip 1943- .... CLC **29**
See also CA 97-100; DLB-Y 80

Lopez Portillo (y Pacheco), Jose
1920-....................... CLC **46**
See also CA 129

Lopez y Fuentes, Gregorio
1897-1966 .... CLC **32**

Lord, Bette Bao 1938- .... CLC **23**
See also CA 107; SATA 58

Lorde, Audre (Geraldine) 1934-..... CLC **18**
See also BLC 2; CANR 16, 26; CA 25-28R;
DLB 41

Loti, Pierre 1850-1923........... TCLC **11**
See also Viaud, (Louis Marie) Julien

Louie, David Wong 1954- .... CLC **70**

Lovecraft, H(oward) P(hillips)
1890-1937 .... TCLC **4, 22**; SSC **3**
See also CA 104

Lovelace, Earl 1935-.............. CLC **51**
See also CA 77-80

Lowell, Amy 1874-1925........ TCLC **1, 8**
See also CA 104; DLB 54

Lowell, James Russell 1819-1891 .. NCLC **2**
See also DLB 1, 11, 64, 79;
CDALB 1640-1865

Lowell, Robert (Traill Spence, Jr.)
1917-1977 ... CLC **1, 2, 3, 4, 5, 8, 9, 11,
15, 37**; PC **3**
See also CANR 26; CA 9-10R;
obituary CA 73-76; CABS 2; DLB 5

Lowndes, Marie (Adelaide) Belloc
1868-1947 .... TCLC **12**
See also CA 107; DLB 70

Lowry, (Clarence) Malcolm
1909-1957 .... TCLC **6, 40**
See also CA 105, 131; DLB 15

Loy, Mina 1882-1966............. CLC **28**
See also CA 113; DLB 4, 54

Lucas, Craig.................... CLC **64**

Lucas, George 1944-.............. CLC **16**
See also CANR 30; CA 77-80; SATA 56;
AAYA 1

Lucas, Victoria 1932-1963
See Plath, Sylvia

Ludlam, Charles 1943-1987..... CLC **46, 50**
See also CA 85-88; obituary CA 122

Ludlum, Robert 1927- .... CLC **22, 43**
See also CANR 25; CA 33-36R; DLB-Y 82

Ludwig, Ken 19??- .... CLC **60**

Ludwig, Otto 1813-1865.......... NCLC **4**

Lugones, Leopoldo 1874-1938..... TCLC **15**
See also CA 116

Lu Hsun 1881-1936 .... TCLC **3**

Lukacs, Georg 1885-1971.......... CLC **24**
See also Lukacs, Gyorgy

Lukacs, Gyorgy 1885-1971
See Lukacs, Georg
See also CA 101; obituary CA 29-32R

Luke, Peter (Ambrose Cyprian)
1919-....................... CLC **38**
See also CA 81-84; DLB 13

Lurie (Bishop), Alison
1926-................CLC **4, 5, 18, 39**
See also CANR 2, 17; CA 1-4R; SATA 46;
DLB 2

Lustig, Arnost 1926-.............. CLC **56**
See also CA 69-72; SATA 56; AAYA 3

Luther, Martin 1483-1546........... LC **9**

Luzi, Mario 1914-................ CLC **13**
See also CANR 9; CA 61-64

Lynch, David 1946- .... CLC **66**
See also CA 129; brief entry CA 124

Lynn, Kenneth S(chuyler) 1923-.... CLC **50**
See also CANR 3, 27; CA 1-4R

Miles, Josephine (Louise)
    1911-1985 . . . . CLC **1, 2, 14, 34, 39**
    See also CANR 2; CA 1-4R;
    obituary CA 116; DLB 48

Mill, John Stuart   1806-1873 . . . . . NCLC **11**
    See also DLB 55

Millar, Kenneth   1915-1983 . . . . CLC **14**
    See also Macdonald, Ross
    See also CANR 16; CA 9-12R;
    obituary CA 110; DLB 2; DLB-Y 83;
    DLB-DS 6

Millay, Edna St. Vincent
    1892-1950 . . . . TCLC **4**
    See also CA 103; DLB 45;
    CDALB 1917-1929

Miller, Arthur
    1915- . . . . . . CLC **1, 2, 6, 10, 15, 26, 47;**
                         DC 1
    See also CANR 2, 30; CA 1-4R; CABS 3;
    DLB 7; CDALB 1941-1968

Miller, Henry (Valentine)
    1891-1980 . . . . CLC **1, 2, 4, 9, 14, 43**
    See also CA 9-12R; obituary CA 97-100;
    DLB 4, 9; DLB-Y 80; CDALB 1929-1941

Miller, Jason   1939?- . . . . CLC **2**
    See also CA 73-76; DLB 7

Miller, Sue   19??- . . . . CLC **44**

Miller, Walter M(ichael), Jr.
    1923- . . . . CLC **4, 30**
    See also CA 85-88; DLB 8

Millett, Kate   1934- . . . . CLC **67**
    See also CANR 32; CA 73-76

Millhauser, Steven   1943- . . . . CLC **21, 54**
    See also CA 108, 110, 111; DLB 2

Millin, Sarah Gertrude   1889-1968 . . CLC **49**
    See also CA 102; obituary CA 93-96

Milne, A(lan) A(lexander)
    1882-1956 . . . . TCLC **6**
    See also CLR 1, 26; YABC 1; CA 104, 133;
    DLB 10, 77, 100

Milner, Ron(ald)   1938- . . . . CLC **56**
    See also BLC 3; CANR 24; CA 73-76;
    DLB 38

Milosz Czeslaw
    1911- . . . . CLC **5, 11, 22, 31, 56**
    See also CANR 23; CA 81-84

Milton, John   1608-1674 . . . . LC **9**

Miner, Valerie (Jane)   1947- . . . . CLC **40**
    See also CA 97-100

Minot, Susan   1956- . . . . CLC **44**

Minus, Ed   1938- . . . . CLC **39**

Miro (Ferrer), Gabriel (Francisco Victor)
    1879-1930 . . . . TCLC **5**
    See also CA 104

Mishima, Yukio
    1925-1970 . . . . CLC **2, 4, 6, 9, 27; DC 1;**
                          SSC 4
    See also Hiraoka, Kimitake

Mistral, Gabriela   1889-1957 . . . . TCLC **2**
    See also CA 104

Mitchell, James Leslie   1901-1935
    See Gibbon, Lewis Grassic
    See also CA 104; DLB 15

Mitchell, Joni   1943- . . . . CLC **12**
    See also CA 112

Mitchell (Marsh), Margaret (Munnerlyn)
    1900-1949 . . . . TCLC **11**
    See also CA 109, 125; DLB 9

Mitchell, S. Weir   1829-1914 . . . . . TCLC **36**

Mitchell, W(illiam) O(rmond)
    1914- . . . . CLC **25**
    See also CANR 15; CA 77-80; DLB 88

Mitford, Mary Russell   1787-1855. . NCLC **4**

Mitford, Nancy   1904-1973 . . . . CLC **44**
    See also CA 9-12R

Miyamoto Yuriko   1899-1951 . . . . . TCLC **37**

Mo, Timothy   1950- . . . . CLC **46**
    See also CA 117

Modarressi, Taghi   1931- . . . . CLC **44**
    See also CA 121

Modiano, Patrick (Jean)   1945- . . . . . CLC **18**
    See also CANR 17; CA 85-88; DLB 83

Mofolo, Thomas (Mokopu)
    1876-1948 . . . . TCLC **22**
    See also BLC 3; brief entry CA 121

Mohr, Nicholasa   1935- . . . . CLC **12**
    See also CLR 22; CANR 1; CA 49-52;
    SAAS 8; SATA 8

Mojtabai, A(nn) G(race)
    1938- . . . . CLC **5, 9, 15, 29**
    See also CA 85-88

Moliere   1622-1673 . . . . LC **10**

Molnar, Ferenc   1878-1952 . . . . TCLC **20**
    See also CA 109

Momaday, N(avarre) Scott
    1934- . . . . CLC **2, 19**
    See also CANR 14; CA 25-28R; SATA 30,
    48

Monroe, Harriet   1860-1936 . . . . . . TCLC **12**
    See also CA 109; DLB 54, 91

Montagu, Elizabeth   1720-1800 . . . . NCLC **7**

Montagu, Lady Mary (Pierrepont) Wortley
    1689-1762 . . . . LC **9**

Montague, John (Patrick)
    1929- . . . . CLC **13, 46**
    See also CANR 9; CA 9-12R; DLB 40

Montaigne, Michel (Eyquem) de
    1533-1592 . . . . LC **8**

Montale, Eugenio   1896-1981 . . . CLC **7, 9, 18**
    See also CANR 30; CA 17-20R;
    obituary CA 104

Montesquieu, Charles-Louis de Secondat
    1689-1755 . . . . LC **7**

Montgomery, Marion (H., Jr.)
    1925- . . . . CLC **7**
    See also CANR 3; CA 1-4R; DLB 6

Montgomery, Robert Bruce   1921-1978
    See Crispin, Edmund
    See also CA 104

Montherlant, Henri (Milon) de
    1896-1972 . . . . CLC **8, 19**
    See also CA 85-88; obituary CA 37-40R;
    DLB 72

Monty Python . . . . CLC **21**

Moodie, Susanna (Strickland)
    1803-1885 . . . . NCLC **14**

Mooney, Ted   1951- . . . . CLC **25**

Moorcock, Michael (John)
    1939- . . . . CLC **5, 27, 58**
    See also CAAS 5; CANR 2, 17; CA 45-48;
    DLB 14

Moore, Brian
    1921- . . . . CLC **1, 3, 5, 7, 8, 19, 32**
    See also CANR 1, 25; CA 1-4R

Moore, George (Augustus)
    1852-1933 . . . . TCLC **7**
    See also CA 104; DLB 10, 18, 57

Moore, Lorrie   1957- . . . . CLC **39, 45, 68**
    See also Moore, Marie Lorena

Moore, Marianne (Craig)
    1887-1972 . . . CLC **1, 2, 4, 8, 10, 13, 19,**
                           47; PC 4
    See also CANR 3; CA 1-4R;
    obituary CA 33-36R; SATA 20; DLB 45;
    DLB-DS 7; CDALB 1929-1941

Moore, Marie Lorena   1957-
    See Moore, Lorrie
    See also CA 116

Moore, Thomas   1779-1852 . . . . NCLC **6**

Morand, Paul   1888-1976 . . . . CLC **41**
    See also obituary CA 69-72; DLB 65

Morante, Elsa   1918-1985 . . . . CLC **8, 47**
    See also CA 85-88; obituary CA 117

Moravia, Alberto
    1907- . . . . CLC **2, 7, 11, 18, 27, 46**
    See also Pincherle, Alberto

More, Hannah   1745-1833 . . . . NCLC **27**

More, Henry   1614-1687 . . . . LC **9**

More, Sir Thomas   1478-1535 . . . . LC **10**

Moreas, Jean   1856-1910 . . . . TCLC **18**

Morgan, Berry   1919- . . . . CLC **6**
    See also CA 49-52; DLB 6

Morgan, Edwin (George)   1920- . . . . . CLC **31**
    See also CANR 3; CA 7-8R; DLB 27

Morgan, (George) Frederick
    1922- . . . . CLC **23**
    See also CANR 21; CA 17-20R

Morgan, Janet   1945- . . . . CLC **39**
    See also CA 65-68

Morgan, Lady   1776?-1859 . . . . NCLC **29**

Morgan, Robin   1941- . . . . CLC **2**
    See also CA 69-72

Morgan, Seth   1949-1990 . . . . CLC **65**
    See also CA 132

Morgenstern, Christian (Otto Josef Wolfgang)
    1871-1914 . . . . TCLC **8**
    See also CA 105

Moricz, Zsigmond   1879-1942 . . . . . TCLC **33**

Morike, Eduard (Friedrich)
    1804-1875 . . . . NCLC **10**

Mori Ogai   1862-1922 . . . . TCLC **14**
    See also Mori Rintaro

Mori Rintaro   1862-1922
    See Mori Ogai
    See also CA 110

Moritz, Karl Philipp   1756-1793 . . . . . . LC **2**

Morris, Julian   1916-
    See West, Morris L.

Morris, Steveland Judkins 1950-
See Wonder, Stevie
See also CA 111

Morris, William 1834-1896 .... NCLC 4
See also DLB 18, 35, 57

Morris, Wright (Marion)
1910- .... CLC 1, 3, 7, 18, 37
See also CANR 21; CA 9-12R; DLB 2;
DLB-Y 81

Morrison, James Douglas 1943-1971
See Morrison, Jim
See also CA 73-76

Morrison, Jim 1943-1971......... CLC 17
See also Morrison, James Douglas

Morrison, Toni 1931-..... CLC 4, 10, 22, 55
See also BLC 3; CANR 27; CA 29-32R;
SATA 57; DLB 6, 33; DLB-Y 81;
CDALB 1968-1987; AAYA 1

Morrison, Van 1945- .... CLC 21
See also CA 116

Mortimer, John (Clifford)
1923- .... CLC 28, 43
See also CANR 21; CA 13-16R; DLB 13

Mortimer, Penelope (Ruth) 1918-.... CLC 5
See also CA 57-60

Mosher, Howard Frank 19??- ...... CLC 62

Mosley, Nicholas 1923-........ CLC 43, 70
See also CA 69-72; DLB 14

Moss, Howard
1922-1987 .... CLC 7, 14, 45, 50
See also CANR 1; CA 1-4R;
obituary CA 123; DLB 5

Motion, Andrew (Peter) 1952-...... CLC 47
See also DLB 40

Motley, Willard (Francis)
1912-1965 .... CLC 18
See also CA 117; obituary CA 106; DLB 76

Mott, Michael (Charles Alston)
1930- .... CLC 15, 34
See also CAAS 7; CANR 7, 29; CA 5-8R

Mowat, Farley (McGill) 1921- ..... CLC 26
See also CLR 20; CANR 4, 24; CA 1-4R;
SATA 3, 55; DLB 68; AAYA 1

Mphahlele, Es'kia 1919-
See Mphahlele, Ezekiel

Mphahlele, Ezekiel 1919-......... CLC 25
See also BLC 3; CANR 26; CA 81-84

Mqhayi, S(amuel) E(dward) K(rune Loliwe)
1875-1945 .... TCLC 25
See also BLC 3

Mrozek, Slawomir 1930-........ CLC 3, 13
See also CAAS 10; CANR 29; CA 13-16R

Mtwa, Percy 19??-................ CLC 47

Mueller, Lisel 1924-.......... CLC 13, 51
See also CA 93-96

Muir, Edwin 1887-1959 .... TCLC 2
See also CA 104; DLB 20

Muir, John 1838-1914 .... TCLC 28

Mujica Lainez, Manuel
1910-1984 .... CLC 31
See also CA 81-84; obituary CA 112

Mukherjee, Bharati 1940-........ CLC 53
See also CA 107; DLB 60

Muldoon, Paul 1951- .... CLC 32
See also CA 113, 129; DLB 40

Mulisch, Harry (Kurt Victor)
1927-....................... CLC 42
See also CANR 6, 26; CA 9-12R

Mull, Martin 1943-.............. CLC 17
See also CA 105

Munford, Robert 1737?-1783......... LC 5
See also DLB 31

Munro, Alice (Laidlaw)
1931- .... CLC 6, 10, 19, 50; SSC 3
See also CA 33-36R; SATA 29; DLB 53

Munro, H(ector) H(ugh) 1870-1916
See Saki
See also CA 104; DLB 34

Murasaki, Lady c. 11th century-... CMLC 1

Murdoch, (Jean) Iris
1919- ...... CLC 1, 2, 3, 4, 6, 8, 11, 15,
22, 31, 51
See also CANR 8; CA 13-16R; DLB 14

Murphy, Richard 1927- .... CLC 41
See also CA 29-32R; DLB 40

Murphy, Sylvia 19??-............. CLC 34

Murphy, Thomas (Bernard) 1935-... CLC 51
See also CA 101

Murray, Les(lie) A(llan) 1938- ..... CLC 40
See also CANR 11, 27; CA 21-24R

Murry, John Middleton
1889-1957 .... TCLC 16
See also CA 118

Musgrave, Susan 1951- .... CLC 13, 54
See also CA 69-72

Musil, Robert (Edler von)
1880-1942 .... TCLC 12
See also CA 109; DLB 81

Musset, (Louis Charles) Alfred de
1810-1857 .... NCLC 7

Myers, Walter Dean 1937- .... CLC 35
See also BLC 3; CLR 4, 16; CANR 20;
CA 33-36R; SAAS 2; SATA 27, 41;
DLB 33; AAYA 4

Myers, Walter M. 1937-
See Myers, Walter Dean

Nabokov, Vladimir (Vladimirovich)
1899-1977 .... CLC 1, 2, 3, 6, 8, 11, 15,
23, 44, 46, 64
See also CANR 20; CA 5-8R;
obituary CA 69-72; DLB 2; DLB-Y 80;
DLB-DS 3; CDALB 1941-1968

Nagy, Laszlo 1925-1978........... CLC 7
See also CA 129; obituary CA 112

Naipaul, Shiva(dhar Srinivasa)
1945-1985 .... CLC 32, 39
See also CA 110, 112; obituary CA 116;
DLB-Y 85

Naipaul, V(idiadhar) S(urajprasad)
1932-.......... CLC 4, 7, 9, 13, 18, 37
See also CANR 1; CA 1-4R; DLB-Y 85

Nakos, Ioulia 1899?-
See Nakos, Lilika

Nakos, Lilika 1899?- .... CLC 29

Nakou, Lilika 1899?-
See Nakos, Lilika

Narayan, R(asipuram) K(rishnaswami)
1906-.................. CLC 7, 28, 47
See also CA 81-84

Nash, (Fredric) Ogden 1902-1971 .. CLC 23
See also CAP 1; CA 13-14;
obituary CA 29-32R; SATA 2, 46;
DLB 11

Nathan, George Jean 1882-1958 ... TCLC 18
See also CA 114

Natsume, Kinnosuke 1867-1916
See Natsume, Soseki
See also CA 104

Natsume, Soseki 1867-1916..... TCLC 2, 10
See also Natsume, Kinnosuke

Natti, (Mary) Lee 1919-
See Kingman, (Mary) Lee
See also CANR 2; CA 7-8R

Naylor, Gloria 1950- .... CLC 28, 52
See also BLC 3; CANR 27; CA 107;
AAYA 6

Neff, Debra 1972-................ CLC 59

Neihardt, John G(neisenau)
1881-1973 .... CLC 32
See also CAP 1; CA 13-14; DLB 9, 54

Nekrasov, Nikolai Alekseevich
1821-1878 .... NCLC 11

Nelligan, Emile 1879-1941....... TCLC 14
See also CA 114; DLB 92

Nelson, Willie 1933-.............. CLC 17
See also CA 107

Nemerov, Howard 1920- .... CLC 2, 6, 9, 36
See also CANR 1, 27; CA 1-4R; CABS 2;
DLB 5, 6; DLB-Y 83

Neruda, Pablo
1904-1973 .... CLC 1, 2, 5, 7, 9, 28, 62;
PC 4
See also CAP 2; CA 19-20;
obituary CA 45-48

Nerval, Gerard de 1808-1855...... NCLC 1

Nervo, (Jose) Amado (Ruiz de)
1870-1919 .... TCLC 11
See also CA 109

Neufeld, John (Arthur) 1938- ...... CLC 17
See also CANR 11; CA 25-28R; SAAS 3;
SATA 6

Neville, Emily Cheney 1919-....... CLC 12
See also CANR 3; CA 5-8R; SAAS 2;
SATA 1

Newbound, Bernard Slade 1930-
See Slade, Bernard
See also CA 81-84

Newby, P(ercy) H(oward)
1918-.................... CLC 2, 13
See also CA 5-8R; DLB 15

Newlove, Donald 1928- .... CLC 6
See also CANR 25; CA 29-32R

Newlove, John (Herbert) 1938-..... CLC 14
See also CANR 9, 25; CA 21-24R

Newman, Charles 1938-.......... CLC 2, 8
See also CA 21-24R

Newman, Edwin (Harold) 1919- .... CLC 14
See also CANR 5; CA 69-72

Newton, Suzanne 1936-........... CLC 35
See also CANR 14; CA 41-44R; SATA 5

Pollitt, Katha 1949-............. CLC 28
See also CA 120, 122

Pollock, Sharon 19??-............. CLC 50
See also DLB 60

Pomerance, Bernard 1940-........ CLC 13
See also CA 101

Ponge, Francis (Jean Gaston Alfred)
1899-.................... CLC 6, 18
See also CA 85-88; obituary CA 126

Pontoppidan, Henrik 1857-1943 ... TCLC 29
See also obituary CA 126

Poole, Josephine 1933-............ CLC 17
See also CANR 10; CA 21-24R; SAAS 2;
SATA 5

Popa, Vasko 1922-.............. CLC 19
See also CA 112

Pope, Alexander 1688-1744......... LC 3

Porter, Connie 1960- .... CLC 70

Porter, Gene Stratton 1863-1924 .. TCLC 21
See also CA 112

Porter, Katherine Anne
1890-1980 ..... CLC 1, 3, 7, 10, 13, 15,
27; SSC 4
See also CANR 1; CA 1-4R;
obituary CA 101; obituary SATA 23, 39;
DLB 4, 9; DLB-Y 80

Porter, Peter (Neville Frederick)
1929-................. CLC 5, 13, 33
See also CA 85-88; DLB 40

Porter, William Sydney 1862-1910
See Henry, O.
See also YABC 2; CA 104; DLB 12, 78, 79;
CDALB 1865-1917

Post, Melville D. 1871-1930 ...... TCLC 39
See also brief entry CA 110

Potok, Chaim 1929- .... CLC 2, 7, 14, 26
See also CANR 19; CA 17-20R; SATA 33;
DLB 28

Potter, Dennis (Christopher George)
1935-.................... CLC 58
See also CA 107

Pound, Ezra (Loomis)
1885-1972 ..... CLC 1, 2, 3, 4, 5, 7, 10,
13, 18, 34, 48, 50; PC 4
See also CA 5-8R; obituary CA 37-40R;
DLB 4, 45, 63; CDALB 1917-1929

Povod, Reinaldo 1959-............ CLC 44

Powell, Adam Clayton, Jr. 1908-1972
See also BLC 3; CA 102;
obituary CA 33-36R

Powell, Anthony (Dymoke)
1905-.......... CLC 1, 3, 7, 9, 10, 31
See also CANR 1; CA 1-4R; DLB 15

Powell, Dawn 1897-1965 .... CLC 66
See also CA 5-8R

Powell, Padgett 1952-............. CLC 34
See also CA 126

Powers, J(ames) F(arl)
1917-.......... CLC 1, 4, 8, 57; SSC 4
See also CANR 2; CA 1-4R

Powers, John J(ames) 1945-
See Powers, John R.

Powers, John R. 1945-............ CLC 66
See also Powers, John J(ames)
See also CA 69-72

Pownall, David 1938-............. CLC 10
See also CA 89-92; DLB 14

Powys, John Cowper
1872-1963 .... CLC 7, 9, 15, 46
See also CA 85-88; DLB 15

Powys, T(heodore) F(rancis)
1875-1953 .... TCLC 9
See also CA 106; DLB 36

Prager, Emily 1952-.............. CLC 56

Pratt, E(dwin) J(ohn) 1883-1964.... CLC 19
See also obituary CA 93-96; DLB 92

Premchand 1880-1936 .... TCLC 21

Preussler, Otfried 1923-.......... CLC 17
See also CA 77-80; SATA 24

Prevert, Jacques (Henri Marie)
1900-1977 .... CLC 15
See also CANR 29; CA 77-80;
obituary CA 69-72; obituary SATA 30

Prevost, Abbe (Antoine Francois)
1697-1763 .... LC 1

Price, (Edward) Reynolds
1933-......... CLC 3, 6, 13, 43, 50, 63
See also CANR 1; CA 1-4R; DLB 2

Price, Richard 1949- .... CLC 6, 12
See also CANR 3; CA 49-52; DLB-Y 81

Prichard, Katharine Susannah
1883-1969 .... CLC 46
See also CAP 1; CA 11-12

Priestley, J(ohn) B(oynton)
1894-1984 .... CLC 2, 5, 9, 34
See also CA 9-12R; obituary CA 113;
DLB 10, 34, 77; DLB-Y 84

Prince (Rogers Nelson) 1958?- ..... CLC 35

Prince, F(rank) T(empleton) 1912- .. CLC 22
See also CA 101; DLB 20

Prior, Matthew 1664-1721........... LC 4

Pritchard, William H(arrison)
1932-..................... CLC 34
See also CANR 23; CA 65-68

Pritchett, V(ictor) S(awdon)
1900-............... CLC 5, 13, 15, 41
See also CA 61-64; DLB 15

Probst, Mark 1925- .... CLC 59
See also CA 130

Procaccino, Michael 1946-
See Cristofer, Michael

Prokosch, Frederic 1908-1989.... CLC 4, 48
See also CA 73-76; obituary CA 128;
DLB 48

Prose, Francine 1947-............. CLC 45
See also CA 109, 112

Proust, Marcel 1871-1922 .. TCLC 7, 13, 33
See also CA 104, 120; DLB 65

Pryor, Richard 1940-............. CLC 26
See also CA 122

Przybyszewski, Stanislaw
1868-1927 .... TCLC 36
See also DLB 66

Puig, Manuel
1932-1990 .... CLC 3, 5, 10, 28, 65
See also CANR 2, 32; CA 45-48

Purdy, A(lfred) W(ellington)
1918-................ CLC 3, 6, 14, 50
See also CA 81-84

Purdy, James (Amos)
1923-............ CLC 2, 4, 10, 28, 52
See also CAAS 1; CANR 19; CA 33-36R;
DLB 2

Pushkin, Alexander (Sergeyevich)
1799-1837 .... NCLC 3, 27

P'u Sung-ling 1640-1715 .... LC 3

Puzo, Mario 1920-......... CLC 1, 2, 6, 36
See also CANR 4; CA 65-68; DLB 6

Pym, Barbara (Mary Crampton)
1913-1980 .... CLC 13, 19, 37
See also CANR 13; CAP 1; CA 13-14;
obituary CA 97-100; DLB 14; DLB-Y 87

Pynchon, Thomas (Ruggles, Jr.)
1937-..... CLC 2, 3, 6, 9, 11, 18, 33, 62
See also CANR 22; CA 17-20R; DLB 2

Quarrington, Paul 1954?-.......... CLC 65
See also CA 129

Quasimodo, Salvatore 1901-1968 ... CLC 10
See also CAP 1; CA 15-16;
obituary CA 25-28R

Queen, Ellery 1905-1982 .... CLC 3, 11
See also Dannay, Frederic; Lee, Manfred
B(ennington)

Queneau, Raymond
1903-1976 .... CLC 2, 5, 10, 42
See also CA 77-80; obituary CA 69-72;
DLB 72

Quin, Ann (Marie) 1936-1973 .... CLC 6
See also CA 9-12R; obituary CA 45-48;
DLB 14

Quinn, Simon 1942-
See Smith, Martin Cruz
See also CANR 6, 23; CA 85-88

Quiroga, Horacio (Sylvestre)
1878-1937 .... TCLC 20
See also CA 117

Quoirez, Francoise 1935-
See Sagan, Francoise
See also CANR 6; CA 49-52

Raabe, Wilhelm 1831-1910 .... TCLC 45

Rabe, David (William) 1940-... CLC 4, 8, 33
See also CA 85-88; CABS 3; DLB 7

Rabelais, Francois 1494?-1553........ LC 5

Rabinovitch, Sholem 1859-1916
See Aleichem, Sholom
See also CA 104

Rachen, Kurt von 1911-1986
See Hubbard, L(afayette) Ron(ald)

Radcliffe, Ann (Ward) 1764-1823 .. NCLC 6
See also DLB 39

Radiguet, Raymond 1903-1923 .... TCLC 29
See also DLB 65

Radnoti, Miklos 1909-1944 .... TCLC 16
See also CA 118

Rado, James 1939-.............. CLC 17
See also CA 105

Radomski, James 1932-
See Rado, James

Author Index

Sophocles
c. 496? B.C.-c. 406? B.C. . . . . . **CMLC 2;
DC 1**

Sorrentino, Gilbert
1929- . . . . **CLC 3, 7, 14, 22, 40**
See also CANR 14; CA 77-80; DLB 5;
DLB-Y 80

Soto, Gary 1952- . . . . **CLC 32**
See also CA 119, 125; DLB 82

Soupault, Philippe 1897-1990 . . . . . . **CLC 68**
See also CA 116; obituary CA 131

Souster, (Holmes) Raymond
1921- . . . . **CLC 5, 14**
See also CANR 13; CA 13-16R; DLB 88

Southern, Terry 1926- . . . . **CLC 7**
See also CANR 1; CA 1-4R; DLB 2

Southey, Robert 1774-1843 . . . . **NCLC 8**
See also SATA 54

Southworth, Emma Dorothy Eliza Nevitte
1819-1899 . . . . **NCLC 26**

Soyinka, Wole
1934- . . . . **CLC 3, 5, 14, 36, 44; DC 2**
See also BLC 3; CANR 27; CA 13-16R;
DLB-Y 86

Spackman, W(illiam) M(ode)
1905- . . . . **CLC 46**
See also CA 81-84

Spacks, Barry 1931- . . . . **CLC 14**
See also CA 29-32R

Spanidou, Irini 1946- . . . . **CLC 44**

Spark, Muriel (Sarah)
1918- . . . . **CLC 2, 3, 5, 8, 13, 18, 40**
See also CANR 12; CA 5-8R; DLB 15

Spencer, Elizabeth 1921- . . . . **CLC 22**
See also CA 13-16R; SATA 14; DLB 6

Spencer, Scott 1945- . . . . **CLC 30**
See also CA 113; DLB-Y 86

Spender, Stephen (Harold)
1909- . . . . **CLC 1, 2, 5, 10, 41**
See also CA 9-12R; DLB 20

Spengler, Oswald 1880-1936 . . . . . . **TCLC 25**
See also CA 118

Spenser, Edmund 1552?-1599 . . . . **LC 5**

Spicer, Jack 1925-1965 . . . . **CLC 8, 18**
See also CA 85-88; DLB 5, 16

Spielberg, Peter 1929- . . . . **CLC 6**
See also CANR 4; CA 5-8R; DLB-Y 81

Spielberg, Steven 1947- . . . . **CLC 20**
See also CA 77-80; SATA 32

Spillane, Frank Morrison 1918-
See Spillane, Mickey
See also CA 25-28R

Spillane, Mickey 1918- . . . . **CLC 3, 13**
See also Spillane, Frank Morrison

Spinoza, Benedictus de 1632-1677 . . . . **LC 9**

Spinrad, Norman (Richard) 1940- . . . **CLC 46**
See also CANR 20; CA 37-40R; DLB 8

Spitteler, Carl (Friedrich Georg)
1845-1924 . . . . **TCLC 12**
See also CA 109

Spivack, Kathleen (Romola Drucker)
1938- . . . . **CLC 6**
See also CA 49-52

Spoto, Donald 1941- . . . . **CLC 39**
See also CANR 11; CA 65-68

Springsteen, Bruce 1949- . . . . **CLC 17**
See also CA 111

Spurling, Hilary 1940- . . . . **CLC 34**
See also CANR 25; CA 104

Squires, (James) Radcliffe 1917- . . . . **CLC 51**
See also CANR 6, 21; CA 1-4R

**Stael-Holstein, Anne Louise Germaine Necker,
Baronne de** 1766-1817 . . . . **NCLC 3**

Stafford, Jean 1915-1979 . . . **CLC 4, 7, 19, 68**
See also CANR 3; CA 1-4R;
obituary CA 85-88; obituary SATA 22;
DLB 2

Stafford, William (Edgar)
1914- . . . . **CLC 4, 7, 29**
See also CAAS 3; CANR 5, 22; CA 5-8R;
DLB 5

Stannard, Martin 1947- . . . . **CLC 44**

Stanton, Maura 1946- . . . . **CLC 9**
See also CANR 15; CA 89-92

Stapledon, (William) Olaf
1886-1950 . . . . **TCLC 22**
See also CA 111; DLB 15

Starbuck, George (Edwin) 1931- . . . . **CLC 53**
See also CANR 23; CA 21-22R

Stark, Richard 1933-
See Westlake, Donald E(dwin)

Stead, Christina (Ellen)
1902-1983 . . . . **CLC 2, 5, 8, 32**
See also CA 13-16R; obituary CA 109

Steele, Sir Richard 1672-1729 . . . . . . **LC 18**
See also DLB 84, 101

Steele, Timothy (Reid) 1948- . . . . **CLC 45**
See also CANR 16; CA 93-96

Steffens, (Joseph) Lincoln
1866-1936 . . . . **TCLC 20**
See also CA 117; SAAS 1

Stegner, Wallace (Earle) 1909- . . . **CLC 9, 49**
See also CANR 1, 21; CA 1-4R; DLB 9

Stein, Gertrude 1874-1946 . . . **TCLC 1, 6, 28**
See also CA 104; DLB 4, 54, 86;
CDALB 1917-1929

Steinbeck, John (Ernst)
1902-1968 . . . . . **CLC 1, 5, 9, 13, 21, 34,
45, 59**
See also CANR 1; CA 1-4R;
obituary CA 25-28R; SATA 9; DLB 7, 9;
DLB-DS 2; CDALB 1929-1941

Steinem, Gloria 1934- . . . . **CLC 63**
See also CANR 28; CA 53-56

Steiner, George 1929- . . . . **CLC 24**
See also CA 73-76; DLB 67

Steiner, Rudolf(us Josephus Laurentius)
1861-1925 . . . . **TCLC 13**
See also CA 107

Stendhal 1783-1842 . . . . **NCLC 23**

Stephen, Leslie 1832-1904 . . . . **TCLC 23**
See also CANR 9; CA 21-24R, 123;
DLB 57

Stephens, James 1882?-1950 . . . . **TCLC 4**
See also CA 104; DLB 19

Stephens, Reed
See Donaldson, Stephen R.

Steptoe, Lydia 1892-1982
See Barnes, Djuna

Sterchi, Beat 1949- . . . . **CLC 65**

Sterling, George 1869-1926 . . . . **TCLC 20**
See also CA 117; DLB 54

Stern, Gerald 1925- . . . . **CLC 40**
See also CA 81-84

Stern, Richard G(ustave) 1928- . . . **CLC 4, 39**
See also CANR 1, 25; CA 1-4R; DLB 87

Sternberg, Jonas 1894-1969
See Sternberg, Josef von

Sternberg, Josef von 1894-1969 . . . . . **CLC 20**
See also CA 81-84

Sterne, Laurence 1713-1768 . . . . **LC 2**
See also DLB 39

Sternheim, (William Adolf) Carl
1878-1942 . . . . **TCLC 8**
See also CA 105

Stevens, Mark 19??- . . . . **CLC 34**

Stevens, Wallace
1879-1955 . . . . **TCLC 3, 12, 45**
See also CA 124; brief entry CA 104;
DLB 54; CDALB 1929-1941

Stevenson, Anne (Katharine)
1933- . . . . **CLC 7, 33**
See also Elvin, Anne Katharine Stevenson
See also CANR 9; CA 17-18R; DLB 40

Stevenson, Robert Louis
1850-1894 . . . . **NCLC 5, 14**
See also CLR 10, 11; YABC 2; DLB 18, 57

Stewart, J(ohn) I(nnes) M(ackintosh)
1906- . . . . **CLC 7, 14, 32**
See also CAAS 3; CA 85-88

Stewart, Mary (Florence Elinor)
1916- . . . . **CLC 7, 35**
See also CANR 1; CA 1-4R; SATA 12

Stewart, Will 1908-
See Williamson, Jack
See also CANR 23; CA 17-18R

Still, James 1906- . . . . **CLC 49**
See also CANR 10, 26; CA 65-68;
SATA 29; DLB 9

Sting 1951-
See The Police

Stitt, Milan 1941- . . . . **CLC 29**
See also CA 69-72

Stoker, Abraham
See Stoker, Bram
See also CA 105; SATA 29

Stoker, Bram 1847-1912 . . . . **TCLC 8**
See also Stoker, Abraham
See also SATA 29; DLB 36, 70

Stolz, Mary (Slattery) 1920- . . . . **CLC 12**
See also CANR 13; CA 5-8R; SAAS 3;
SATA 10

Stone, Irving 1903-1989 . . . . **CLC 7**
See also CAAS 3; CANR 1; CA 1-4R, 129;
SATA 3

Stone, Robert (Anthony)
1937?- . . . . **CLC 5, 23, 42**
See also CANR 23; CA 85-88

Stoppard, Tom
1937- . . . **CLC 1, 3, 4, 5, 8, 15, 29, 34, 63**
See also CA 81-84; DLB 13; DLB-Y 85

Tremain, Rose 1943-............ **CLC 42**
See also CA 97-100; DLB 14

Tremblay, Michel 1942-.......... **CLC 29**
See also CA 116; DLB 60

Trevanian 1925- .... **CLC 29**
See also CA 108

Trevor, William 1928- ..... **CLC 7, 9, 14, 25**
See also Cox, William Trevor
See also DLB 14

Trifonov, Yuri (Valentinovich)
1925-1981 .... **CLC 45**
See also obituary CA 103, 126

Trilling, Lionel 1905-1975 .... **CLC 9, 11, 24**
See also CANR 10; CA 9-12R;
obituary CA 61-64; DLB 28, 63

Trogdon, William 1939-
See Heat Moon, William Least
See also CA 115, 119

Trollope, Anthony 1815-1882 .. **NCLC 6, 33**
See also SATA 22; DLB 21, 57

Trollope, Frances 1780-1863 ..... **NCLC 30**
See also DLB 21

Trotsky, Leon (Davidovich)
1879-1940 ....**TCLC 22**
See also CA 118

Trotter (Cockburn), Catharine
1679-1749 .... **LC 8**
See also DLB 84

Trow, George W. S. 1943-........ **CLC 52**
See also CA 126

Troyat, Henri 1911-.............. **CLC 23**
See also CANR 2; CA 45-48

Trudeau, G(arretson) B(eekman) 1948-
See Trudeau, Garry
See also CA 81-84; SATA 35

Trudeau, Garry 1948-............. **CLC 12**
See also Trudeau, G(arretson) B(eekman)

Truffaut, Francois 1932-1984....... **CLC 20**
See also CA 81-84; obituary CA 113

Trumbo, Dalton 1905-1976 .... **CLC 19**
See also CANR 10; CA 21-24R;
obituary CA 69-72; DLB 26

Trumbull, John 1750-1831....... **NCLC 30**
See also DLB 31

Tryon, Thomas 1926-........... **CLC 3, 11**
See also CA 29-32R

Ts'ao Hsueh-ch'in 1715?-1763........ **LC 1**

Tse, Isaac 1904-1991
See Singer, Isaac Bashevis

Tsushima Shuji 1909-1948
See Dazai Osamu
See also CA 107

Tsvetaeva (Efron), Marina (Ivanovna)
1892-1941 .... **TCLC 7, 35**
See also CA 104, 128

Tuck, Lily 1938-................. **CLC 70**

Tunis, John R(oberts) 1889-1975 ... **CLC 12**
See also CA 61-64; SATA 30, 37; DLB 22

Tuohy, Frank 1925- .... **CLC 37**
See also DLB 14

Tuohy, John Francis 1925-
See Tuohy, Frank
See also CANR 3; CA 5-8R

Turco, Lewis (Putnam) 1934- ... **CLC 11, 63**
See also CANR 24; CA 13-16R; DLB-Y 84

Turgenev, Ivan
1818-1883 .... **NCLC 21; SSC 7**

Turner, Frederick 1943-........... **CLC 48**
See also CANR 12; CA 73-76; DLB 40

Tutu, Desmond 1931-
See also BLC 3; CA 125

Tutuola, Amos 1920- .... **CLC 5, 14, 29**
See also BLC 3; CANR 27; CA 9-12R

Twain, Mark
1835-1910 ... **TCLC 6, 12, 19, 36; SSC 6**
See also Clemens, Samuel Langhorne
See also YABC 2; DLB 11, 12, 23, 64, 74

Tyler, Anne
1941- .... **CLC 7, 11, 18, 28, 44, 59**
See also CANR 11; CA 9-12R; SATA 7;
DLB 6; DLB-Y 82

Tyler, Royall 1757-1826.......... **NCLC 3**
See also DLB 37

Tynan (Hinkson), Katharine
1861-1931 .... **TCLC 3**
See also CA 104

Tytell, John 1939- .... **CLC 50**
See also CA 29-32R

Tyutchev, Fyodor 1803-1873..... **NCLC 34**

Tzara, Tristan 1896-1963.......... **CLC 47**
See also Rosenfeld, Samuel

Uhry, Alfred 1947?-.............. **CLC 55**
See also CA 127

Unamuno (y Jugo), Miguel de
1864-1936 .... **TCLC 2, 9**
See also CA 104

Underwood, Miles 1909-1981
See Glassco, John

Undset, Sigrid 1882-1949.......... **TCLC 3**
See also CA 104

Ungaretti, Giuseppe
1888-1970 .... **CLC 7, 11, 15**
See also CAP 2; CA 19-20;
obituary CA 25-28R

Unger, Douglas 1952-............. **CLC 34**
See also CA 130

Unger, Eva 1932-
See Figes, Eva

Updike, John (Hoyer)
1932- ...... **CLC 1, 2, 3, 5, 7, 9, 13, 15,
23, 34, 43, 70**
See also CANR 4, 33; CA 1-4R; CABS 1;
DLB 2, 5; DLB-Y 80, 82; DLB-DS 3;
CDALB 1968-1988

Urdang, Constance (Henriette)
1922- .... **CLC 47**
See also CANR 9, 24; CA 21-24R

Uris, Leon (Marcus) 1924-....... **CLC 7, 32**
See also CANR 1; CA 1-4R; SATA 49

Ustinov, Peter (Alexander) 1921-.... **CLC 1**
See also CANR 25; CA 13-16R; DLB 13

Vaculik, Ludvik 1926-............. **CLC 7**
See also CA 53-56

Valenzuela, Luisa 1938-........... **CLC 31**
See also CA 101

Valera (y Acala-Galiano), Juan
1824-1905 .... **TCLC 10**
See also CA 106

Valery, Paul (Ambroise Toussaint Jules)
1871-1945 .... **TCLC 4, 15**
See also CA 104, 122

Valle-Inclan (y Montenegro), Ramon (Maria)
del 1866-1936............... **TCLC 5**
See also CA 106

Vallejo, Cesar (Abraham)
1892-1938 .... **TCLC 3**
See also CA 105

Van Ash, Cay 1918-.............. **CLC 34**

Vance, Jack 1916?-................ **CLC 35**
See also DLB 8

Vance, John Holbrook 1916?-
See Vance, Jack
See also CANR 17; CA 29-32R

Van Den Bogarde, Derek (Jules Gaspard
Ulric) Niven 1921-
See Bogarde, Dirk
See also CA 77-80

Vandenburgh, Jane 19??-.......... **CLC 59**

Vanderhaeghe, Guy 1951- .... **CLC 41**
See also CA 113

Van der Post, Laurens (Jan) 1906-... **CLC 5**
See also CA 5-8R

Van de Wetering, Janwillem
1931- .... **CLC 47**
See also CANR 4; CA 49-52

Van Dine, S. S. 1888-1939....... **TCLC 23**

Van Doren, Carl (Clinton)
1885-1950 .... **TCLC 18**
See also CA 111

Van Doren, Mark 1894-1972..... **CLC 6, 10**
See also CANR 3; CA 1-4R;
obituary CA 37-40R; DLB 45

Van Druten, John (William)
1901-1957 .... **TCLC 2**
See also CA 104; DLB 10

Van Duyn, Mona 1921-....... **CLC 3, 7, 63**
See also CANR 7; CA 9-12R; DLB 5

Van Itallie, Jean-Claude 1936- ...... **CLC 3**
See also CAAS 2; CANR 1; CA 45-48;
DLB 7

Van Ostaijen, Paul 1896-1928..... **TCLC 33**

Van Peebles, Melvin 1932- ...... **CLC 2, 20**
See also CA 85-88

Vansittart, Peter 1920-............. **CLC 42**
See also CANR 3; CA 1-4R

Van Vechten, Carl 1880-1964 ...... **CLC 33**
See also obituary CA 89-92; DLB 4, 9, 51

Van Vogt, A(lfred) E(lton) 1912-..... **CLC 1**
See also CANR 28; CA 21-24R; SATA 14;
DLB 8

Varda, Agnes 1928- .... **CLC 16**
See also CA 116, 122

Vargas Llosa, (Jorge) Mario (Pedro)
1936- .... **CLC 3, 6, 9, 10, 15, 31, 42**
See also CANR 18; CA 73-76

Vassa, Gustavus 1745?-1797
See Equiano, Olaudah

Vassilikos, Vassilis 1933-......... **CLC 4, 8**
See also CA 81-84

Warren, Robert Penn
1905-1989 ... **CLC 1, 4, 6, 8, 10, 13, 18, 39, 53, 59; SSC 4**
See also CANR 10; CA 13-16R. 129. 130; SATA 46; DLB 2, 48; DLB-Y 80; CDALB 1968-1987

Warshofsky, Isaac 1904-1991
See Singer, Isaac Bashevis

Warton, Thomas 1728-1790........ **LC 15**

Warung, Price 1855-1911........ **TCLC 45**

Washington, Booker T(aliaferro)
1856-1915 .... **TCLC 10**
See also BLC 3; CA 114, 125; SATA 28

Wassermann, Jakob 1873-1934..... **TCLC 6**
See also CA 104; DLB 66

Wasserstein, Wendy 1950-...... **CLC 32, 59**
See also CA 121; CABS 3

Waterhouse, Keith (Spencer)
1929-........................ **CLC 47**
See also CA 5-8R; DLB 13, 15

Waters, Roger 1944-
See Pink Floyd

Wa Thiong'o, Ngugi
1938-................ **CLC 3, 7, 13, 36**
See also Ngugi, James (Thiong'o); Ngugi wa Thiong'o

Watkins, Paul 1964-............. **CLC 55**

Watkins, Vernon (Phillips)
1906-1967 .... **CLC 43**
See also CAP 1; CA 9-10; obituary CA 25-28R; DLB 20

Waugh, Auberon (Alexander) 1939-.. **CLC 7**
See also CANR 6, 22; CA 45-48; DLB 14

Waugh, Evelyn (Arthur St. John)
1903-1966 ... **CLC 1, 3, 8, 13, 19, 27, 44**
See also CANR 22; CA 85-88; obituary CA 25-28R; DLB 15

Waugh, Harriet 1944- .... **CLC 6**
See also CANR 22; CA 85-88

Webb, Beatrice (Potter)
1858-1943 .... **TCLC 22**
See also CA 117

Webb, Charles (Richard) 1939-...... **CLC 7**
See also CA 25-28R

Webb, James H(enry), Jr. 1946-.... **CLC 22**
See also CA 81-84

Webb, Mary (Gladys Meredith)
1881-1927 .... **TCLC 24**
See also CA 123; DLB 34

Webb, Phyllis 1927-.............. **CLC 18**
See also CANR 23; CA 104; DLB 53

Webb, Sidney (James)
1859-1947 .... **TCLC 22**
See also CA 117

Webber, Andrew Lloyd 1948-...... **CLC 21**

Weber, Lenora Mattingly
1895-1971 .... **CLC 12**
See also CAP 1; CA 19-20; obituary CA 29-32R; SATA 2; obituary SATA 26

Webster, John 1580?-1634?......... **DC 2**
See also DLB 58

Webster, Noah 1758-1843 .... **NCLC 30**
See also DLB 1, 37, 42, 43, 73

Wedekind, (Benjamin) Frank(lin)
1864-1918 .... **TCLC 7**
See also CA 104

Weidman, Jerome 1913-............ **CLC 7**
See also CANR 1; CA 1-4R; DLB 28

Weil, Simone 1909-1943......... **TCLC 23**
See also CA 117

Weinstein, Nathan Wallenstein 1903-1940
See West, Nathanael

Weir, Peter 1944-................ **CLC 20**
See also CA 113, 123

Weiss, Peter (Ulrich)
1916-1982 .... **CLC 3, 15, 51**
See also CANR 3; CA 45-48; obituary CA 106; DLB 69

Weiss, Theodore (Russell)
1916-................... **CLC 3, 8, 14**
See also CAAS 2; CA 9-12R; DLB 5

Welch, (Maurice) Denton
1915-1948 .... **TCLC 22**
See also CA 121

Welch, James 1940-........ **CLC 6, 14, 52**
See also CA 85-88

Weldon, Fay
1933-........ **CLC 6, 9, 11, 19, 36, 59**
See also CANR 16; CA 21-24R; DLB 14

Wellek, Rene 1903- .... **CLC 28**
See also CAAS 7; CANR 8; CA 5-8R; DLB 63

Weller, Michael 1942-......... **CLC 10, 53**
See also CA 85-88

Weller, Paul 1958-.............. **CLC 26**

Wellershoff, Dieter 1925-.......... **CLC 46**
See also CANR 16; CA 89-92

Welles, (George) Orson
1915-1985 .... **CLC 20**
See also CA 93-96; obituary CA 117

Wellman, Mac 1945- .... **CLC 65**

Wellman, Manly Wade 1903-1986 .. **CLC 49**
See also CANR 6, 16; CA 1-4R; obituary CA 118; SATA 6, 47

Wells, Carolyn 1862-1942 .... **TCLC 35**
See also CA 113; DLB 11

Wells, H(erbert) G(eorge)
1866-1946 ...... **TCLC 6, 12, 19; SSC 6**
See also CA 110, 121; SATA 20; DLB 34, 70

Wells, Rosemary 1943-............ **CLC 12**
See also CLR 16; CA 85-88; SAAS 1; SATA 18

Welty, Eudora (Alice)
1909- .... **CLC 1, 2, 5, 14, 22, 33; SSC 1**
See also CA 9-12R; CABS 1; DLB 2; DLB-Y 87; CDALB 1941-1968

Wen I-to 1899-1946 .... **TCLC 28**

Werfel, Franz (V.) 1890-1945 ..... **TCLC 8**
See also CA 104; DLB 81

Wergeland, Henrik Arnold
1808-1845 .... **NCLC 5**

Wersba, Barbara 1932-............ **CLC 30**
See also CLR 3; CANR 16; CA 29-32R; SAAS 2; SATA 1, 58; DLB 52

Wertmuller, Lina 1928-........... **CLC 16**
See also CA 97-100

Wescott, Glenway 1901-1987....... **CLC 13**
See also CANR 23; CA 13-16R; obituary CA 121; DLB 4, 9

Wesker, Arnold 1932- ....**CLC 3, 5, 42**
See also CAAS 7; CANR 1; CA 1-4R; DLB 13

Wesley, Richard (Errol) 1945-....... **CLC 7**
See also CA 57-60; DLB 38

Wessel, Johan Herman 1742-1785 .... **LC 7**

West, Anthony (Panther)
1914-1987 .... **CLC 50**
See also CANR 3, 19; CA 45-48; DLB 15

West, Jessamyn 1907-1984 ...... **CLC 7, 17**
See also CA 9-12R; obituary CA 112; obituary SATA 37; DLB 6; DLB-Y 84

West, Morris L(anglo) 1916-..... **CLC 6, 33**
See also CA 5-8R; obituary CA 124

West, Nathanael
1903-1940 .... **TCLC 1, 14, 44**
See also CA 104, 125; DLB 4, 9, 28; CDALB 1929-1941

West, Paul 1930- .... **CLC 7, 14**
See also CAAS 7; CANR 22; CA 13-16R; DLB 14

West, Rebecca 1892-1983 .. **CLC 7, 9, 31, 50**
See also CANR 19; CA 5-8R; obituary CA 109; DLB 36; DLB-Y 83

Westall, Robert (Atkinson) 1929-... **CLC 17**
See also CLR 13; CANR 18; CA 69-72; SAAS 2; SATA 23

Westlake, Donald E(dwin)
1933-.................... **CLC 7, 33**
See also CANR 16; CA 17-20R

Westmacott, Mary 1890-1976
See Christie, (Dame) Agatha (Mary Clarissa)

Whalen, Philip 1923- .... **CLC 6, 29**
See also CANR 5; CA 9-12R; DLB 16

Wharton, Edith (Newbold Jones)
1862-1937 .... **TCLC 3, 9, 27; SSC 6**
See also CA 104; DLB 4, 9, 12, 78; CDALB 1865-1917

Wharton, William 1925-........ **CLC 18, 37**
See also CA 93-96; DLB-Y 80

Wheatley (Peters), Phillis
1753?-1784................ **LC 3; PC 3**
See also BLC 3; DLB 31, 50; CDALB 1640-1865

Wheelock, John Hall 1886-1978.... **CLC 14**
See also CANR 14; CA 13-16R; obituary CA 77-80; DLB 45

Whelan, John 1900-
See O'Faolain, Sean

Whitaker, Rodney 1925-
See Trevanian

White, E(lwyn) B(rooks)
1899-1985 .... **CLC 10, 34, 39**
See also CLR 1; CANR 16; CA 13-16R; obituary CA 116; SATA 2, 29, 44; obituary SATA 44; DLB 11, 22

White, Edmund III 1940-.......... **CLC 27**
See also CANR 3, 19; CA 45-48

White, Patrick (Victor Martindale)
1912-1990 .. **CLC 3, 4, 5, 7, 9, 18, 65, 69**
See also CA 81-84; obituary CA 132

Author Index

Zuckmayer, Carl 1896-1977 . . . . **CLC 18**
  See also CA 69-72; DLB 56

Zukofsky, Louis
   1904-1978 . . . . **CLC 1, 2, 4, 7, 11, 18**
  See also CA 9-12R; obituary CA 77-80;
  DLB 5

Zweig, Paul 1935-1984 . . . . **CLC 34, 42**
  See also CA 85-88; obituary CA 113

Zweig, Stefan 1881-1942 . . . . **TCLC 17**
  See also CA 112; DLB 81

Literary Criticism Series
Cumulative Topic Index

This index lists all topic entries in the Gale Literary Criticism Series *Contemporary Literary Criticism, Literature Criticism from 1400 to 1800, Nineteenth-Century Literature Criticism,* and *Twentieth-Century Literary Criticism.*

TCLC Cumulative Nationality Index

AMERICAN

Adams, Henry **4**
Agee, James **1, 19**
Anderson, Maxwell **2**
Anderson, Sherwood **1, 10, 24**
Atherton, Gertrude **2**
Austin, Mary **25**
Barry, Philip **11**
Baum, L. Frank **7**
Beard, Charles A. **15**
Belasco, David **3**
Bell, James Madison **43**
Benchley, Robert **1**
Benét, Stephen Vincent **7**
Benét, William Rose **28**
Bierce, Ambrose **1, 7, 44**
Black Elk **33**
Bodenheim, Maxwell **44**
Bourne, Randolph S. **16**
Bradford, Gamaliel **36**
Bromfield, Louis **11**
Burroughs, Edgar Rice **2, 32**
Cabell, James Branch **6**
Cable, George Washington **4**
Cather, Willa **1, 11, 31**
Chambers, Robert W. **41**
Chandler, Raymond **1, 7**
Chapman, John Jay **7**
Chesnutt, Charles Waddell **5, 39**
Chopin, Kate **5, 14**
Comstock, Anthony **13**
Cotter, Joseph Seamon, Sr. **28**
Cram, Ralph Adams **45**
Crane, Hart **2, 5**
Crane, Stephen **11, 17, 32**
Crawford, F. Marion **10**
Crothers, Rachel **19**
Cullen, Countee **4, 37**
Davis, Rebecca Harding **6**

Davis, Richard Harding **24**
Day, Clarence **25**
DeVoto, Bernard **29**
Dreiser, Theodore **10, 18, 35**
Dunbar, Paul Laurence **2, 12**
Dunne, Finley Peter **28**
Fisher, Rudolph **11**
Fitzgerald, F. Scott **1, 6, 14, 28**
Flecker, James Elroy **43**
Fletcher, John Gould **35**
Forten, Charlotte L. **16**
Freeman, Douglas Southall **11**
Freeman, Mary Wilkins **9**
Futrelle, Jacques **19**
Gale, Zona **7**
Garland, Hamlin **3**
Gilman, Charlotte Perkins **9, 37**
Glasgow, Ellen **2, 7**
Goldman, Emma **13**
Grey, Zane **6**
Guiney, Louise Imogen **41**
Hall, James Norman **23**
Harper, Frances Ellen Watkins **14**
Harris, Joel Chandler **2**
Harte, Bret **1, 25**
Hawthorne, Julian **25**
Hearn, Lafcadio **9**
Henry, O. **1, 19**
Hergesheimer, Joseph **11**
Higginson, Thomas Wentworth **36**
Hopkins, Pauline Elizabeth **28**
Howard, Robert E. **8**
Howe, Julia Ward **21**
Howells, William Dean **7, 17, 41**
James, Henry **2, 11, 24, 40**
James, William **15, 32**
Jewett, Sarah Orne **1, 22**
Johnson, James Weldon **3, 19**
Kornbluth, C. M. **8**

Kuttner, Henry **10**
Lardner, Ring **2, 14**
Lewis, Sinclair **4, 13, 23, 39**
Lewisohn, Ludwig **19**
Lindsay, Vachel **17**
Locke, Alain **43**
London, Jack **9, 15, 39**
Lovecraft, H. P. **4, 22**
Lowell, Amy **1, 8**
Marquis, Don **7**
Masters, Edgar Lee **2, 25**
McCoy, Horace **28**
McKay, Claude **7, 41**
Mencken, H. L. **13**
Millay, Edna St. Vincent **4**
Mitchell, Margaret **11**
Mitchell, S. Weir **36**
Monroe, Harriet **12**
Muir, John **28**
Nathan, George Jean **18**
Nordhoff, Charles **23**
Norris, Frank **24**
O'Neill, Eugene **1, 6, 27**
Oskison, John M. **35**
Phillips, David Graham **44**
Porter, Gene Stratton **21**
Post, Melville **39**
Rawlings, Marjorie Kinnan **4**
Reed, John **9**
Roberts, Kenneth **23**
Robinson, Edwin Arlington **5**
Rogers, Will **8**
Rölvaag, O. E. **17**
Rourke, Constance **12**
Runyon, Damon **10**
Saltus, Edgar **8**
Santayana, George **40**
Sherwood, Robert E. **3**
Slesinger, Tess **10**

Nationality Index

TCLC Title Index to Volume 45

ISBN 0-8103-2427-X